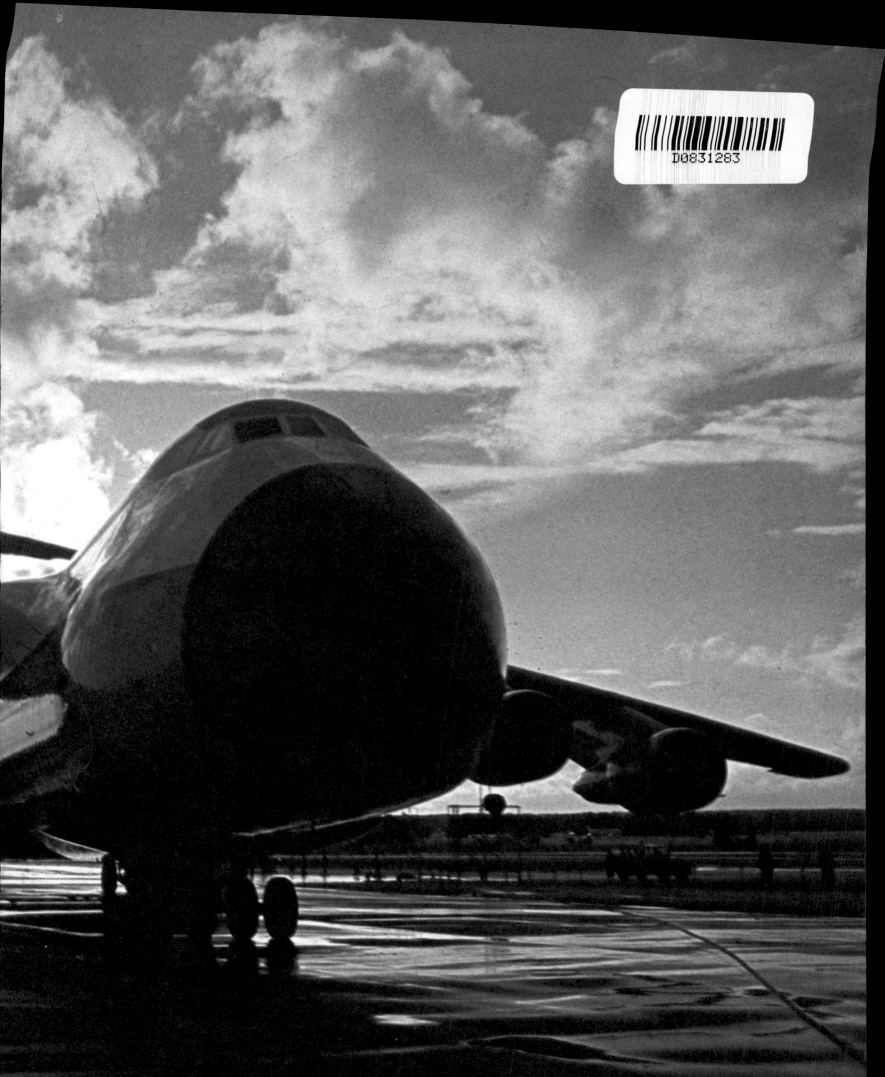

The International Encyclopedia of Aviation

The Internation1 Encyclopedia of
Aviation

General Editor
David Mondey

Assistant Compiler
Jane's All The World's Aircraft

Foreword by Juan Trippe
Founder and Honorary Chairman
Pan American World Airways

First published 1977 by
Octopus Books Limited
59 Grosvenor Street
London W1

© 1977 Octopus Books Limited

ISBN 0 7064 0603 6

Produced by Mandarin Publishers Limited
22a Westlands Road
Quarry Bay, Hong Kong

Printed in Hong Kong

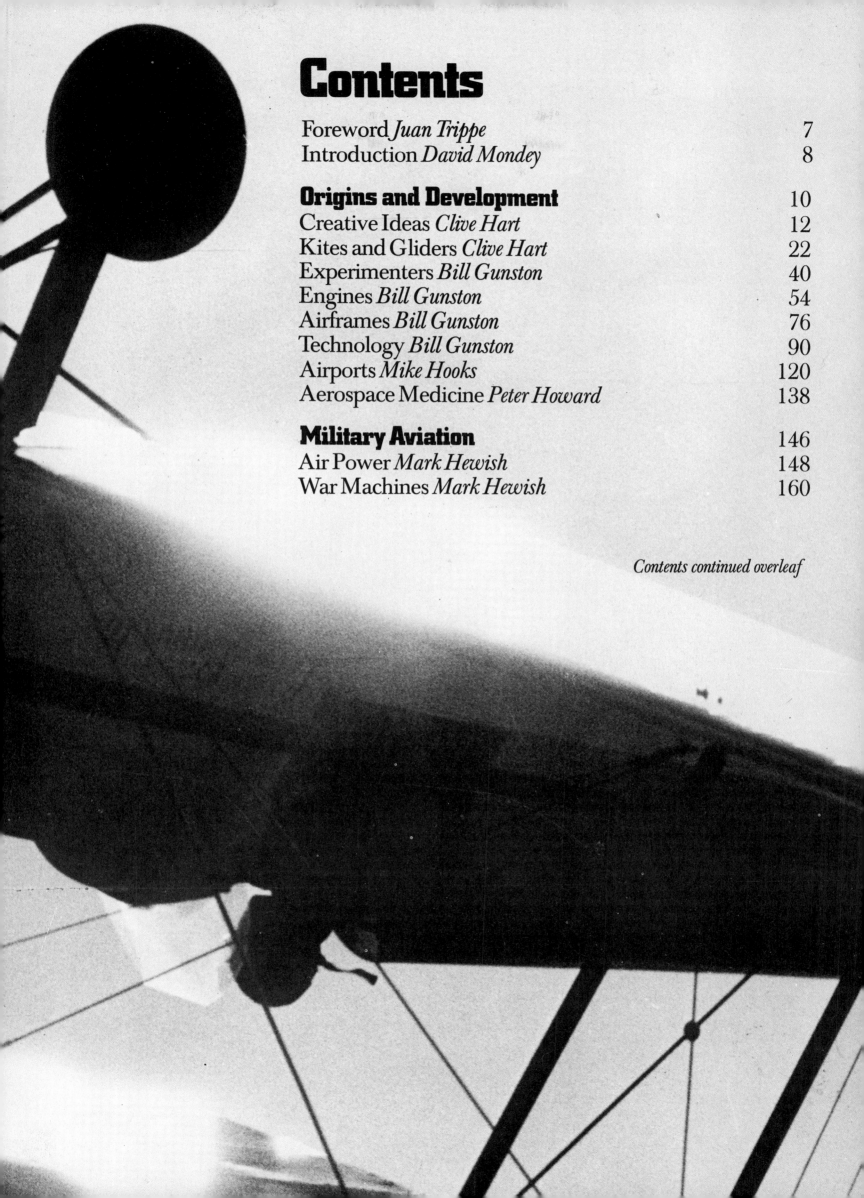

Contents

Contents continued overleaf

International Consultants

United Kingdom
Kenneth Munson
*Assistant Compiler 'Jane's All the World's
Aircraft' and author and editor 'Pocket
Encyclopedia of World Aircraft'*

United States
John W Dennison, BS, MA
*US aviation historian currently employed
by the US Department of Defense*

Australia
Henry R Rayner, MVO, BA
*Director of Public Relations, Defence
Department, Australia and author of a
history of the RAAF*

Canada
Neil A Macdougall, BSc, MA
*Contributing editor 'The Aeroplane' and
senior commercial pilot*

France
Jean Liron
*French aviation historian and contributing
editor 'Aviation Magazine International'*

Germany
Peter Pletschacher
*Co-editor 'FlugRevue', former press officer
Dornier GmbH and winner Otto
Lilienthal Award*

New Zealand
David Henderson
*Editor and contributor New Zealand
aviation publications*

South Africa
Ray L Watts
*African aviation historian and a director of
the Aviation Society of Africa*

Foreword

As this Encyclopedia goes to press, humankind has known powered flight for about three-quarters of a century. The penchant of human beings for perceiving themselves in flight goes back in time far beyond the Wright Brothers. Dreams of flight are recorded among the earliest of myths. Only in the twentieth century, however, have the dreams come true; or, to put the matter another way, we of the twentieth century are able to see and do what our predecessors could only dream about—are able to see and undertake what earlier generations could visualize but could not bring about.

And what exactly has been brought about? As the contents table of this encyclopedia shows, the seed that was with Icarus has produced a descendant plant with many branches. For example, powered flight now impartially embraces the supersonic bomber; the rotary wing flying crane; computer-brained missiles fired from submarines in the depths of the seas; privately owned business jets; moon rockets with lunar landers; and fleets of civil airliners carrying needed mail and goods to where they could not otherwise be taken, and carrying tourists in the millions from one continent to another.

Those of us who are primarily concerned with civil aviation should be among the first to pay tribute to the accomplishments of military aviation, not only for its contribution to national security but for what military aviation consistently has done to advance the state of the art. However, we still harbor the hope and the conviction, that it is the peaceful use of aviation that means the most, and will continue to mean the most, to the people of the world; that the low-fare airliner with its tourists is more significant than the bomber with its atom bombs; and that space flight, as epitomized by the American Space Shuttle program will be notable for its peaceful rather than its military application—as, for example, in capturing abundant solar energy for the use of all on earth.

The record as set forth in this book is a good one, an impressive one. But as you read, remember that you are reading about the beginning, not the end.

Introduction

Almost invariably the most difficult section to write of any book is the introduction. When the aim has been, from the onset, to create an all-embracing volume to cover the entire history of aviation, the task is even more complicated.

This is no place for me to tell you anything about the excitement that is an integral part of the aviation scene. This you can read for yourself in the pages which follow. Rather would I explain how you can use this book to find the answer to a particular question, or to expand your knowledge of some branch of aviation. This is not to suggest that you should not browse, or read through an entire section: but in so doing you may find a subject mentioned briefly and seek the short-cut to more detailed information.

In broad outlines, you can guide your reading by reference to the contents page which gives, in some detail, the various sections of the book and their contributors. You may be surprised to find that the conventional chronological format has not been followed. This was intentional from the moment that the work was planned. Because we were concerned not only to tell the tale but also to explain how and why aviation evolved in the way it did we chose a subject format rather than a strictly historical one. Thus in the chapter on War Machines the major sub-sections are Reconnaissance Aircraft, Bombers, Fighters, etc. rather than World War I, World War II, etc. The approach followed allowed for both analysis and straightforward description. An additional plus to this arrangement is that the book is easy to use as a reference source.

As you read through a particular section you will find sub-headings which will help you to follow a special interest. Invariably, brief mention of indirectly related subjects will appear in most sections, but the detailed index at the end of the volume should enable you to pinpoint the fact you are seeking. And

ENDPAPERS: *Lockheed C-5A Galaxy*
HALF-TITLE: *Focke-Wulf FW.200 Condor*
TITLE SPREAD: *AV-8A Harrier*
CONTENTS SPREAD: *Stampe aerobatic aeroplane*
FOREWORD SPREAD: *Dassault (Mystère) Falcon 20*
THIS SPREAD: *Britten-Norman Trislander*

within this work there are a number of detailed studies of such items as 'How an aeroplane is flown', and these can be found listed in the index under the heading of 'Special features'.

Of necessity, the aim to cover the history of aviation, rocketry and space flight in a single, manageable volume, has imposed the need to condense the available material – written and pictorial – to key developments. Obviously, we have been as objective as possible in our selection, but inevitably a certain amount of disagreement will arise over the omissions. This is only to be expected, and, in fact, is a sign of the dynamism of aviation.

Aviation knows no boundaries. Great contributions have come from all nations. In acknowledging the international nature of aviation we have been aided considerably by our respected international consultants who have used their specialized knowledge to help maintain an equitable balance.

One other matter relating to an international readership is the need to give specification and performance details in both Imperial and metric notations. The metric equivalents used in this work are those in general use throughout the world, and which have been accepted internationally by common usage in the world's aviation press, and by such specialized publications as *Jane's All the World's Aircraft*.

As General Editor of this encyclopedia I must thank, most sincerely, those who have contributed enthusiastically the words and pictures which are the building blocks of any book. There must also be another great thank-you to the production team and artists who have taken words and pictures to create this book.

I trust you will enjoy our combined efforts.

D.M.
Surbiton 1977

Creative Ideas

BELOW: *Leonardo da Vinci's designs for a flying machine were based on the workings of a bird's wing. This drawing shows the pulleys intended to work the joints and the movable wingtip sections.*

BELOW: *Some of Leonardo's designs pushed ingenuity far beyond practicality. These wings were intended to be flapped by turning a handle which alternately wound and unwound cords wrapped round a drum.*

RIGHT: *For this ornithopter, drawn in about 1487, the downstroke of the wings was produced by kicking the legs backwards, while the upstroke, needing less strength, was performed by the hands and arms.*

Although it is now natural to us to think of all forms of flight, except rocket propulsion, as dependent upon properties of the air, the essential role which air plays in providing a lifting force was not even vaguely understood until quite late in the history of man's attempts to fly.

Many early commentators, from at least as long ago as the days of Aristotle (4th century BC), thought it obvious that the flight of a bird, which aspiring aeronauts should attempt to imitate, was directly analogous to the action of swimming, which was in turn thought of as a process of pushing back against a resistance, as one pushes against the ground in walking. A bird, it was believed, flapped its wings downwards and backwards, pressing itself up and along against the air which lay behind.

Just as a swimmer is light in comparison with the water in which he is immersed, so it was assumed that a bird is built with sufficient inherent lightness to be able to sustain itself with little effort. In Aristotelian physics which, in a variety of forms, was generally dominant until the coming of the 'New Science' in the 17th century, both 'heaviness' and 'lightness' were believed to be positive qualities of the four 'elements' from which all things were made. The apparent density of an object was determined by the degree

PREVIOUS PAGES: *Early aviation experimenter Guillon gets ready to make an attempt on Epsom Downs on 11 April 1907 in his Guilly and Clouzy aeroplane.*

to which one or the other of these qualities dominated, and it seemed natural to early observers to think of birds as having a greater proportion of 'lightness' than man and other earthbound creatures.

The lightness, which was not just the absence of weight but a positive tendency to rise, was especially concentrated in the feathers, which explains why so many of those who, equipped with flimsy flying apparatus, threw themselves off towers and other eminences, so often chose feathers for their wings. As a bird can in fact fly neither because it is inherently light nor because it pushes down and back against the air (see p. 16), early concepts of flight suffered from a misunderstanding of two fundamental aspects of the physical laws associated with movement in a fluid medium: first, the principles of displacement and relative mass; second, the function of the flow of air over a curved surface to produce lift.

Mediaeval speculation

Although potential mediaeval fliers possessed neither an understanding of the essential principles nor the necessary technology, many thinkers engaged in active speculation about the possibility of human flight. Most famous of all, perhaps, was Friar Roger Bacon (c. 1220 to 1292), who wrote, 'It's possible to make Engines for flying, a man sitting in the midst whereof, by turning only about an Instrument, which moves artificiall Wings made to beat the Aire, much after the fashion of a Birds flight'.

More impractical, but perhaps more ingenious and imaginative, was the idea proposed by Albert of Saxony (14th century), who suggested that as the element of 'fire' is lighter than air, just as air is lighter than water, so a ship filled with 'fire' might be made to float on the upper surface of the atmosphere. As the nature of elemental fire was a matter of controversy, Albert and his contemporaries were uncertain as to how hazardous such an undertaking might be. Any such ideas were nevertheless commonly held to be spiritually as well as physically dangerous, since, although flight would bring about the fulfilment of an age-old desire, it would also place man 'out of his element', above his station, and thus make him guilty of pride. The disastrous end to many practical attempts at flying served only to reinforce this powerful prejudice and slow the progress of aviation.

Leonardo da Vinci

In the early days many people engaged in dangerous flapping or gliding experiments unsupported by rational theory. Of the few who worked with intelligence and real seriousness, Leonardo da Vinci (1452 to 1519), was undoubtedly the most impressive. His ideas about bird flight were more sophisticated than those of most, and were based on the careful observations of a man blessed with the eye of a great painter. They were nonetheless totally mistaken, including not only the almost universal assumption of downward and backward wing movements, but also a

and forth relative to the cabin; that the air inside the cabin is moving relative to the earth at speeds of hundreds of miles an hour does not affect the bird's motion relative to the air mass in which it is flying. A steady wind is moving relative to the earth in just the same way as the air inside the cabin, and affects the flight of the bird, or of any other flying object, just as little. Ground speed and airspeed are thus two very different frames of reference which need to be kept clearly distinguished. The earlier misconception about the effects of a steady wind on a flying machine or balloon was to form the basis of many futile designs from Renaissance times until almost the present day. Highly imaginative balloons and airships were often drawn with sails which, apart from the occasional effects of turbulence, would always have hung limply in the dead calm air bearing them along.

While Leonardo's hope that he might profit from the energy of the winds was totally unfounded, it resulted in some very sensitive analyses of the potentialities of gliding flight. Had he ever built a rigid glider, instead of devoting nearly all of his attention to flappers, he might well have made significant advances along the road which was later to be followed by Otto Lilienthal.

The nature of the air
The air is a mixture of gases, principally nitrogen (about 77 per cent) and oxygen (about 21 per cent). It surrounds the earth to a distance of several hundred miles, being most dense at sea level and thinning out rapidly with increase of height. At sea level the pressure which it exerts, in all directions, is sufficient to sustain a column of mercury (as used in barometers – literally 'pressure meters') to a height of about 760mm (29·92 in). Variations in climatic conditions cause this average pressure to fluctuate quite widely from day to day, and even from hour to hour, and as pressure readings are used to determine an aircraft's height above ground or sea level (on the 'altimeter'), pilots always need accurate and up to date information about variations in local barometric pressures.

Other than in special circumstances ('inversions'), there is a steady decrease in the temperature, as one rises through the lower regions of the atmosphere (the 'troposphere'), averaging about 2°C per 300m (1,000ft). After a few kilometres, the exact height varying with latitude, the temperature ceases to fall and remains fairly constant. Beyond that point, known as the tropopause, is the upper atmosphere, the stratosphere.

Apart from the effect on the altimeter of decreasing pressure, pilots need to take account of the change in performance of lifting surfaces, engine airspeed indicators and other instruments resulting from differences of both temperature and pressure. Winds at altitude are often stronger than those at sea level and may differ from them markedly in direction. Although steady winds have no effect on aircraft handling, they are of course a crucial factor in navigation, ground speed and therefore the aircraft's fuel consumption.

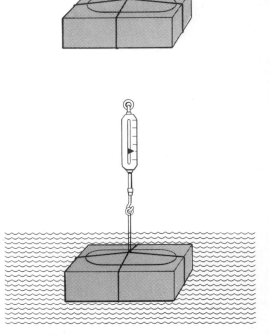

RIGHT: *This early 19th century engraving illustrates the means by which a balloon can be filled with a gas of a lower density than that of air to achieve aerostatic lift sufficient to carry passengers.*

Displacement
The ancient Greek scientist Archimedes (c. 287 to 212 BC) is credited with having been the first to understand that when an object is immersed in a fluid (e.g., water or air), its apparent weight is reduced by an amount equal to the weight of the fluid which it displaces. If a brick weighing, say, 3kg (6·6lb) occupies the same amount of space as ½kg (1·1lb) of water, it will appear to weigh only 2½kg (5·5lb) when totally immersed. The same principle applies even when the object to be immersed is initially lighter than the displaced fluid. A gas-filled balloon which weighs 200kg (441lb) and which occupies the same space as does 500kg (1,102lb) of air at sea level, will, when immersed in air, have its apparent weight reduced by 500kg (1,102lb). It will therefore weigh *minus* 300kg (661lb), which means the balloon will experience an upward lifting force of 300kg (661lb).

This kind of lift, the basic principle of aerostation (ballooning), has always been readily observable in the rising of hot air, which is lighter, as a result of expansion, than is cold air. But when smoke was seen to rise above fires, early speculators thought they were watching the effects of the inherent lightness of the 'element' of fire contained in the smoke. In the 15th century Giovanni da Fontana discussed the possibility of making a hot air balloon based on the rising of smoke, while even the Montgolfier brothers, who built the first man-carrying hot air balloon, tried to determine what kinds of smoke contained the highest concentration of 'lightness'.

ABOVE: *The story of a flying monk, Kaspar Mohr, is depicted in this 17th century scene from a monastery in Schussenried (Germany). The artist has supplemented the usual arm movements by providing the flier with cords enabling him to add leg power to the downstroke.*
RIGHT: *When a brick is immersed in water its weight, as measured by the spring balance, is reduced by an amount equal to the weight of the water it displaces. The brick in air weighs 3kg (6·6lb) (top); when immersed the brick weighs 2·5kg (5·5lb) (bottom).*

belief that the bird 'squeezes' the air by a grasping motion of the wingtips, creating a series of dense air masses on which to support itself.

Basing his work on these ideas and on repeated observations of birds in soaring flight, Leonardo, who was a professional engineer as well as a painter, spent many years designing a variety of ornithopters, or flapping machines, some of which were relatively simple sets of artificial wings while others were full scale flying chariots. The plans were often meticulously thought out and included many fine points of engineering detail.

Leonardo believed that the ability of a bird to soar without flapping was dependent on the presence of a horizontal wind. If a bird raised the leading edge of its wings while facing upwind, so creating a positive 'angle of attack', it would, he thought, be raised by the wedgelike action of the air driving underneath. The inadequacy of contemporary ideas about gravity and relative motion misled Leonardo, rendering him incapable of grasping that (ignoring gusts and other changes of velocity) the relative motion of the air over the ground has no effect on the aerodynamics of flight. Although a bird's ground speed will of course be influenced by any wind which may be blowing, giving it far greater range downwind than upwind, its airspeed will be in no way affected, whatever its direction of flight.

Imagine a bird flying inside the cabin of a jumbo jet which is travelling fast over the ground. The bird may fly as it pleases, back

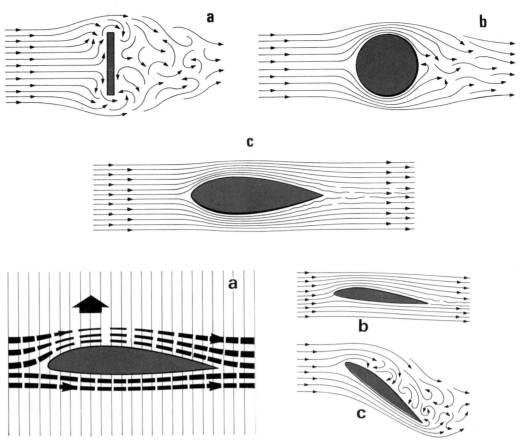

TOP: *The relative amounts of drag produced in a steady airstream by objects of the same cross-sectional area but with differing degrees of streamlining: (a) Flat plate (b) Ball (c) Streamlined shape.*

ABOVE: *(a) Cross-section of a typical aerofoil in an airstream. (b) Airflow over a wing in normal forward flight. (c) Airflow at the point of stall, where the wing is tilted at a high angle and lift rapidly decreases.*

Aerostatic lift

The same principle underlies the lift both of a hot air balloon and of a gas filled balloon. In both cases the envelope, being filled with a substance lighter than that which surrounds it, experiences an upward force equal to the difference between the weight of the displaced air and the weight of the gas or hot air in the balloon, plus the weight of the basket, etc. This difference in weight represents the maximum load which the balloon will then support in level flight.

As water is almost incompressible, its density remains virtually constant up to very considerable depths. By contrast the density of air, which is highly compressible, varies greatly with depth: at about 16km (10 miles) above the earth's surface it is only about one tenth of its value at sea level. Since a given volume of air is therefore lighter with increasing height, a point will be reached when the displaced air weighs the same as the whole balloon, after which the balloon will cease to rise. In most balloons the attainment of this height is delayed by the fact that the gas or hot air in the envelope, being subjected to less and less pressure, tends to make the envelope expand and displace more air, thus partially counteracting the effects of decreasing lift.

Aerodynamic lift

If an aerofoil such as an aircraft's wing is held at an appropriate angle of attack to an airstream, a difference is created in the total sums of the velocities of the parts of the airstream flowing over the upper and lower surfaces. This difference, known as 'circulation', is the basis of aerodynamic lift. The sum of the velocities over the top of the aerofoil is greater than that over the bottom, and one of the basic physical laws of aerodynamics, 'Bernoulli's theorem', says in effect that, other things being equal, the faster a liquid or gas flows, the lower is its static pressure. This means that the downward pressure of the air on top of the wing is less than the upward pressure on the bottom, so that the wing experiences lift.

Up to the point at which the wing stalls, an increase in the angle of attack increases the 'circulation' and thus increases the total lift. For any given airspeed a pilot may therefore vary the lift by raising or lowering the aircraft's nose.

The circulation theory of lift was first enunciated by the Englishman F. W. Lanchester, in an address given in 1894 to the Birmingham Natural History Society and later published in his book *Aerodynamics* (1907). The idea was independently developed in Germany by Ludwig Prandtl.

Drag and vortices

The movement of air over an aircraft's wings (or of the aircraft through still air, which amounts to the same thing) results not only in lift, but also in the production of a number of different kinds of 'drag'. Apart from the retarding force created by friction between the airflow and the surface area of the aeroplane ('skin friction' on the so-called 'wetted area'), the main drag elements are 'profile drag' and 'induced drag'. Profile drag is a measure of the amount of energy consumed in disturbing the uniform horizontal flow, pushing it aside and to some degree breaking it up into turbulence. With an aircraft as with a motor car, profile drag may be reduced by 'streamlining', the effectiveness of which may be judged from comparing the drag created by a flat circular plate held at right angles to the airflow, with a sphere of the same diameter, and by a fully streamlined figure of the same maximum thickness.

While profile drag wastes energy, and while, consistent with other design considerations, it must be reduced as much as possible, it is less important than induced drag. When an ordinary wing is pushed through the air, the flow over the top and bottom surfaces is not exactly parallel with the direction of motion: on the bottom it is angled slightly outwards, towards the wing tips, while on the top it is angled slightly in, towards the fuselage. This is a result of the high pressure underneath trying to 'leak' around the wing tips towards the region of low pressure. When the two airflows meet at the trailing edge they are therefore moving at a slight angle to one another and form swirling vortices in the wake of the wing ('wake turbulence'). These normally roll up together to form a single powerful vortex trailing back from each wing tip, the direction of the spiral being such that when seen from behind, the lefthand vortex turns clockwise while the righthand vortex turns anti-

BELOW LEFT: *These diagrams illustrate the wide variations possible in the aspect ratios of different aircraft. The aspect ratio is the ratio of the span to the chord of an aerofoil: (a) a sailplane has a high aspect ratio – a large span and small chord; (b) a lightplane has a low aspect ratio – a small span and large chord.*

BELOW RIGHT: *Wing tip vortices being shed from a typical aircraft in flight. Such vortices can sometimes become visible at high altitudes, owing to the condensation of water vapour. The diagrams below, based on the work of the physicist F. W. Lanchester, explain in detail how these vortices are formed.*

the theory of lift was fully investigated in the late 19th century.

A bird's wing may be considered as performing two related but separate functions: first, it provides a horizontal lifting force, or 'thrust', which pulls the bird through the air and creates a horizontal airflow over the wings; second, its cambered aerofoil shape provides a vertical lifting force which sustains the bird's weight. For centuries it seemed desirable to most experimenters to imitate nature by aiming at a single unified system of lift and thrust through the construction of artificial flapping wings. Some work on ornithopters, by no means all of it negligible, continues to be done, but successful manned flight did not become a reality until the idea of separating the systems of lift and thrust were fully conceived. In a modern aeroplane the wing, which contributes most of the lift, remains essentially rigid. The thrust is provided by an engine driving a stream of air or hot gases backwards and thereby causing the aircraft to move with equal momentum in the opposite direction (compare the recoil from a gun).

Although the creation of a lightweight engine was necessary before the separation of lift and thrust could be successfully achieved, credit for the first important insight into the matter in connection with heavier-than-air flight must go to Sir George Cayley (1773 to 1857), rightly dubbed 'the Father of Aerial Navigation'. In 1799 Cayley had a silver disc engraved with a now famous design for a man-carrying aeroplane, equipped with rigid wings and flappers for propulsion. Three centuries earlier, Leonardo da Vinci went on one occasion at least part of the way towards abandoning his usual assumptions when he sketched a design for a hang glider with flappable wing tips, the inboard sections of the wings remaining rigid. It is possible that this machine might have brought some limited success, but there is no evidence that Leonardo ever tried it in practice, and he did not proceed with the idea.

Stability and flight control

Stability may be broadly defined as the tendency of an aircraft to remain in the condition of flight selected by the pilot: straight and level, turning, climbing, or descending. The degree of stability must be carefully designed, since if the aircraft is unstable it will be difficult or impossible to control, while if it is overendowed with stability it will be difficult to manoeuvre quickly or may require excessive effort (stick forces) from the pilot.

Since an aircraft is free to move in all three dimensions of space, it needs to be both stable and controllable about three axes: (a) a vertical axis perpendicular to the surface of the wings; (b) a longitudinal axis passing through the fuselage from front to back; (c) a horizontal axis passing through the wings approximately from tip to tip. The three kinds of movement about these axes are called respectively *yaw*, *roll* and *pitch*.

Automatic stability in yaw is effected by a vertical fin at the rear. If the nose of an aircraft is gusted to the left, say, the fin will be

ABOVE: *Four diagrams from F. W. Lanchester's* Aerodynamics *(1907). ON THE LEFT: The production of trailing edge vortices and the way they gather together to form a single wingtip vortex.* CENTRE: *The components of airstream velocity which lead to the creation of the vortices.* RIGHT: *Angled airflow over the upper (above) and the lower (below) surfaces of a wing, resulting in vortices at the trailing edge.*

clockwise. The energy consumed in these vortices must of course be derived from the aircraft's engine.

The effect of speed on the two forms of drag differs. While profile drag increases with increasing speed, induced drag is greatest at low speeds and high angles of attack. The turbulence which results from induced vortices can be a serious hazard to other aircraft. Since an aeroplane flies most slowly when taking off and landing, it is then that the vortices are at their most powerful, and unless light aircraft remain several miles behind large, slow-moving jets,

there is a grave danger of their being thrown totally out of control.

Separation of lift and thrust

A bird flies by pushing its wings downward through the air so that the 'primary' or 'flight' feathers at the wing tips (or, in some birds, the wing tips as a whole) twist upwards at the trailing edge, while on the upstroke the trailing edges are twisted slightly down. Each downward movement of a wing is analogous to the movement of a propeller blade through the same arc, forward 'lift' being produced and used to pull the bird along. During the downstroke, the lift also has a vertical component which, together with the upward lift resulting from the forward motion of the whole wing, sustains the bird in the air. (The upstroke, which contributes further vertical lift, actually retards the bird's forward progress a little.) Although some aspects of these movements and forces were understood by G. A. Borelli as early as 1680, they were not properly analyzed until

ABOVE: *The separation of lift from thrust in the modern jet- or rocket-powered aeroplane was prefigured in the early 14th century by Giovanni da Fontana's drawing of a rocket bird.*
ABOVE RIGHT: *The earliest of Sir George Cayley's aeronautical sketches was also one of the most prophetic. This engraving on a small silver disc, dated 1799, shows a design for a man-powered aircraft with a boat-shaped hull, curved fixed wing of low aspect ratio, adjustable cruciform tail unit and hand-operated flappers.*

CENTRE RIGHT: *Plan view of Cayley's first proposal for an aircraft.*
RIGHT: *In 1680 G. A. Borelli understood that a bird does not push backwards against the air, but that flapping causes the primary feathers of the wings to flex up and down about a line near the leading edge. In his great work, De motu animalium, Borelli proved conclusively that man was incapable of self-powered flight and thus opened new and productive paths of thought on flight.*

placed at an angle to the airflow, producing lift on its left side which will tend to pull the aircraft back into line with the airflow. A fixed horizontal tailplane confers stability in pitch by being so rigged that in normal flight its angle of attack is less than that of the wings and may often, in fact, be zero. As a consequence, any change in pitch angle of the whole aircraft causes a change in lift on the tailplane proportionally greater than that on the wings. This additional lift acts in the direction opposite to the original pitch change and so tends to return the aircraft to its normal flight path.

Stability in roll is achieved by setting the wings at a slight upward angle (*dihedral*), or by arranging the centre of gravity to be below the level of the wings (*pendulous stability*). The operation of the stabilizing forces in roll is slightly more complex than is the case with the other kinds of stability, and depends on the tendency of the aircraft to sideslip if rolled, or banked, sideways in level flight. If dihedral is used, the lift on the downgoing wing is increased by the slip, so introducing a correcting force which rights the aircraft, while pendulous stability is based on the tendency of the centre of gravity to swing back to the vertical as if it were momentarily suspended beneath a pressure point created by the lateral airflow in the slip. It should be noted that the initial ten-

dency to sideslip is essential to the function of both kinds of lateral stability.

In a conventional aircraft, control about the three axes is achieved by the use of a rudder (behind the fin), the elevators (behind the tailplane), and the ailerons (behind the wingtips). All three 'control surfaces' function by varying the total curvature and angle of attack of the aerofoil which they comprise in conjunction with the fixed surfaces ahead of them. Thus if the pilot lowers the elevators (by pushing forward on the stick or control column), the total effective curvature of the tailplane/elevator combination is increased, and, since the trailing edge is now lower than the leading edge, the angle of attack is also increased. The combined surface then acts to produce more lift, and the tail will rise. The rudder acts similarly, to move the rear of the aircraft from side to side (yaw), while the ailerons, which act simultaneously in opposite directions (one rising while the other is lowered), decrease the lift on one wing tip while increasing it on the other, so causing the aircraft to roll as a result of the asymmetrical forces on the wings.

The forces which operate in the three axes of movement are not independent, but interact in various ways, so that harmonized and coordinated use of the control surfaces is necessary. Use of rudder alone will result in roll as well as yaw, use of aileron alone will

cause yaw as well as roll, while turns require attention to height and speed control with the elevators. In a powered aircraft changes in thrust, controlled by the engine throttle, also affect the function of the control surfaces.

Despite sporadic insights, such as the incorporation by Cayley of a combined adjustable elevator and rudder into his model glider of 1804, or the foreshadowing of modern methods in a prophetic design by Alphonse Pénaud in 1876, the coordinated use of controls was slow to emerge. A full understanding of their interrelationship began only with the successful solution by the Wright brothers of the problems of 'adverse yaw'. An increase in the curvature and angle of attack of an aerofoil, such as occurs when a control surface is depressed, results not only in increased lift but also in increased drag, and the same occurs if the change in aerofoil configuration is brought about by the bending or twisting of a wing tip, as was done by the Wrights. While this increase in drag is not of great significance in the case of elevators and rudders, it was the cause of great difficulties in the control of roll until the Wrights found a cure in the coordinated use of rudder. In many modern aircraft sophisticated modifications of design detail reduce the adverse performance effects of aileron drag.

LEFT: *The three axes about which an aircraft moves. From top: the lateral (side-to-side) axis; the vertical (through top and belly) axis; and the longitudinal (nose-to-tail) axis.*
ABOVE: *The cable-operated control system of a conventional modern aircraft. This shows the location of levers, pulleys and cable turn-buckles used to adjust the system and attain the correct tension. Some aircraft have a different system: they use a single push-pull rod or tube.*
NEAR RIGHT ABOVE: *Stability in pitch is achieved by having the horizontal tailplane set at a smaller angle of attack than that of the wings. Changes in pitch angle then have a proportionally greater effect on the lift of the tailplane, tending to return the aircraft to level flight.*

NEAR RIGHT CENTRE: *Wings set at a dihedral angle give stability in roll. If, when out of balance, the aircraft slips sideways, the down-going wing produces proportionally greater lift, which counteracts the roll, and restores the aircraft to level flight.*
NEAR RIGHT BELOW: *Pendulous stability counteracts unwanted roll when the centre of gravity of the aircraft swings back to the level position beneath a lateral pressure centre created by the airstream in the direction of the sideslip.*
CENTRE RIGHT ABOVE: *The forces acting on an aircraft in balanced level flight, where the opposing forces are in equilibrium: lift balances weight, and thrust balances drag.*

Forces in flight

In straight and level flight the total aero-dynamic reaction of the wing in response to the airflow is a force which acts both upwards and backwards, the degree of backward slope of the force being determined by the 'lift : drag ratio'. By definition, the 'lift' is that part of the total force which acts at right angles to the airflow, irrespective of the aircraft's direction of travel relative to the earth, while the 'drag' is that part of the total force which acts at right angles to the lift, parallel to the airflow. Thus, if the aircraft is in a vertical dive, the lift will be parallel to the ground and the drag will act vertically upwards. More lift is produced at some points on the aerofoil surface than at others, the amounts varying with different angles of attack and airspeeds. For any given flight condition, however, a point may be found on the curve of the aerofoil through which all of the resultant forces may be said to act. That point is known as the 'centre of pressure'.

At a constant airspeed in straight and level flight, four forces act in equilibrium: the lift exactly balances the weight (if it is greater than the weight the aircraft will rise, while if it is less the aircraft will sink); the thrust, provided by the engine, exactly balances the drag (if it is greater than the drag the air-craft will accelerate, while if it is less the aircraft will slow down). Any changes in air-speed will also affect the velocity of the air moving over the upper and lower surfaces of the wings, increasing or decreasing the static pressure, and thus affecting the lift.

Forces in a balanced turn

In a balanced turn the aircraft is banked towards the inside of the circle. If a turn is made with insufficient bank a skid away from the centre of the intended circle will result, while too much bank will cause the aircraft to slip downwards towards the centre of the turn. The correct degree of bank depends on the radius of the turn and on the speed, the situation being analogous to the motion of a car around a curved road which is banked up on the outside of the turn. For any banked curve there is one precise speed at which the car will tend neither to skid outwards nor to slip inwards.

Since the aeroplane is banked in the turn, the lift, which is by definition at right angles to the airflow, is no longer vertical but is angled towards the inside of the circle, thus providing a horizontal force which in fact keeps the aeroplane turning. The upward component of the lift, being less than in straight and level flight, no longer balances the weight, and unless the pilot takes appro-priate action (by raising the nose a little, or by applying power, or both) the aircraft will sink and will begin to describe a 'spiral dive'. In a correctly banked turn, no matter how steep, the aircraft is in perfect balance: a pendulum will remain hanging parallel to the vertical axis of the fuselage and a glass of water will not spill.

Stalling

The lift produced by wings of conventional aerofoil shape may be continuously increased by increasing the angle of attack up to about 16°. Beyond that point the airflow over the upper surfaces is subject to forces too great to allow it to flow smoothly, with the result that it separates from the surface, becomes turbulent, and causes the lift to decay. At that point the wing is said to stall. Not only does the lift decrease beyond the stalling angle, often very rapidly, but the centre of pressure, which up to the stall has been moving continuously forward towards the leading edge of the wing, rapidly retreats in the direction of the trailing edge. Beyond the stall the aircraft therefore suddenly has insufficient lift and is nose heavy. If attempts are made to keep the nose up the aircraft will sink rapidly, and since the wings are stalled there will be a loss of control.

Small departures from symmetry, together with other factors such as the spiralling slip-stream from a propeller, may cause one wing to stall before the other, so that the aircraft falls sideways out of control in a sometimes alarming fashion. In a conventional aircraft, recovery consists in lowering the elevators, keeping straight with the rudder, and apply-ing power. The angle of attack is thereby reduced and the rapid build up of lift enables control to be regained.

The speed at which the stall occurs varies with the effective weight of the aircraft and with the loading on the wings (the total forces acting in the direction opposite to the lift). The loading is markedly increased by the centrifugal force of a tight turn or a pull out from a dive, and in these manoeuvres the

ABOVE: *Forces in a balanced turn. More lift is needed than in level flight, since the lift must not only provide a vertical component to balance the weight, but must also provide the centripetal force which keeps the aircraft in the turn.*

LEFT: *Cross-section of a typical supersonic aerofoil, showing the shock waves which build up at the leading and trailing edges.*

BELOW: *One of Air France's Concordes in flight. Its thin wings, high degree of sweepback and carefully streamlined shape from the pointed nose to the tail are examples of the special features of design necessary to combat the extra drag problems caused by shock waves at supersonic speeds.*

stalling angle may be reached at a speed very much higher than usual. A stall under such conditions is known as a 'high speed stall'.

Boundary layer control

Owing to the friction which exists between the airflow and the aerofoil, the layer of air close to the surface, the boundary layer, is subject to very powerful retarding forces which slow it up. Fast flowing layers of air therefore have to pass over slower layers beneath. If this flow pattern is everywhere smooth, the boundary layer is said to be laminar, while if the air is unable to travel smoothly the flow is said to be turbulent. The usual tendency is for the flow to be laminar near the leading edge and to grow turbulent at a point further back towards the trailing edge, known as the 'transition point'.

Boundary Layer Control (BLC) has become an important branch of applied aerodynamics, especially in connection with transonic and supersonic flight. A variety of devices has been invented to ensure that the flow remains laminar, although paradoxically it is sometimes beneficial to encourage a small amount of controlled turbulence very close to the wing, since this has the effect of preventing or delaying wholesale breakdown of the flow pattern ('separation').

Slats, slots and flaps all serve to control the boundary layer, as well as to alter the geometry and surface area of a wing, while the most readily observable devices for creating a small amount of boundary layer turbulence

are the vortex generators (small plates a centimeter or two in height), which may be seen in rows on the upper surfaces of some high speed wings.

Supersonic flight

At speeds approaching the speed of sound new factors, resulting from the compressibility of air, affect the function of an aerofoil. As an aircraft passes through the air, disturbances are continually generated, and in subsonic flight these are dissipated through the surrounding air in the form of waves, which escape from the region of the aircraft at the speed of sound. As that speed is approached, however, the disturbances ahead of the aircraft are unable to escape fast enough. A piling up of such disturbances,

known as a 'shock wave', results. (A similar shock wave, at very much lower speeds, may be seen trailing back on either side of a duck swimming across a still pond.)

Shock waves are generated by various parts of an aircraft travelling near, at or beyond the speed of sound, and in the case of a wing they appear, in the fully formed condition, at the leading and trailing edges. As they are a potential source of rapid increases in drag, they require special geometrical features in the design of aircraft intended for transonic or supersonic flight. These features include the use of thin wings, symmetrically shaped aerofoil sections, pointed leading and trailing edges, high degrees of sweepback, and the careful graduation of cross-sectional area of the entire aircraft from nose to tail.

How an Aeroplane is Flown

Very early in the history of powered flight, the layout and function of the basic controls were standardized. The one significant variation among modern light aircraft is the designer's choice of either a 'stick' or a 'control column' for combined control of pitch and bank. The stick is free to move in any direction about a pivot on the floor between the pilot's legs, while the column moves only back and forth for control of pitch, control of roll being effected by turning a quadrant wheel or crossbar with handles. Many pilots, especially those who enjoy aerobatics, prefer the stick, which allows for easier harmonization of the controls. (A stick nevertheless has some minor disadvantages, such as making it harder to hold a map on one's knee.)

The primary controls consist of the stick or column, rudder pedals (or a turnable rudder bar), and the throttle, which is hand operated. As the throttle may be placed, according to the aircraft's design, on either side of the pilot, it is necessary to be able to fly ambidextrously. A light but positive grip is used on the stick, while the other hand operates the throttle, which is moved forward to increase power. Either hand may be needed, according to the particular aircraft, for flap levers, switches, and trimmers. If a variable pitch (or constant speed) propeller is fitted, its control lever is normally placed next to the throttle. Wheel brakes, which were uncommon in early aircraft, have now become standard; they are usually operated by toe (or sometimes heel) pedals associated with the rudder pedals.

The stick moves in the 'natural' sense. That is, the nose of the aircraft is lowered by pressing the stick forward, and raised by pressing it back. (Although these adjustments will often result in a descent or in a climb, respectively, they will not always do so, the relative movement in the vertical direction being dependent on other factors as well as attitude.) Movement of the stick left or right banks the aircraft left or right. Pilots sometimes disagree as to whether the rudder controls also work in a natural sense. Forward pressure with the right foot yaws the aircraft to the right, this movement being therefore opposite to the turning of a bicycle's handlebars. It may be more helpful to think of steering a skiff by hand held lines (right hand forward for a turn to the right), but in any case pilots rapidly grow accustomed to the required direction of movement.

What follows is a description of the bare essentials in the handling of a single-engined light aircraft flying one circuit at an aerodrome (i.e., take-off, return downwind, and landing). The aircraft is assumed to have a stick, left hand throttle, fixed pitch propeller rotating clockwise as seen by the pilot, and a fixed tricycle landing gear. Trimmers, flaps, brakes, and many other details are ignored. While substantial differences arise in the handling of other types, the conventional light aeroplane still provides a common basis of experience for the coordinated use of controls.

Once cleared for take-off and lined up on the runway, the pilot opens the throttle, pushing it smoothly forward, until the engine reaches take-off power (which may be the same as full power). The stick is held a little back, to relieve the pressure on the comparatively fragile nose-wheel, and as the aircraft begins to move forward the airflow over the tail surfaces rapidly establishes rudder control. Engine torque and forces associated with the slipstream create a tendency to swing to the left, and this must be counteracted by pressure on the right rudder pedal. The control surfaces grow more responsive with increasing airspeed, and finer adjustments are needed to keep the aircraft running straight. When flying speed has been reached, progressive back pressure on the stick raises the nose, increasing the angle of attack of the wings which then provide sufficient lift for take-off. The stick is used to settle the aircraft into a climb at the best climbing speed: moving the stick forward increases

LEFT: *Cherokee. The Cherokee Archer II, made by the Piper Company, is typical of modern light touring aircraft designed for safety and comfort.*

ABOVE LEFT: *A Cessna cockpit, showing dual control columns, rudder pedals on the floor, flight instruments (left), engine instruments (right), throttle in the middle.*

ABOVE RIGHT: *Rallye. The range of low wing Rallye aircraft, made in France, are especially useful for their ability to operate from very short runways.*

Flying a circuit

the speed (by reducing the angle of attack, and hence the induced drag), while back pressure reduces speed. Angle of climb and rate of climb are controlled indirectly by maintaining a predetermined airspeed.

Once past the end of the runway and at a safe height (say about 150m, or 500ft), the pilot initiates a gentle turn (usually to the left), still climbing. This he does by gentle movement of the stick to the left, applying at the same time a little left rudder, which may need no more than a relaxation of the pressure which he has been maintaining with his right foot. To maintain the appropriate angle of bank once it has been established, the stick is returned to the central position, and may even need to be pressed a little to the right, to prevent the aircraft from overbanking.

With the turn completed, the aircraft is returned to the straight climb until 'circuit height' is reached (usually 300m, or 1,000ft). In order to level out, the pilot presses the stick gently forward until the aircraft is

in level flight. It now begins to accelerate and reaches circuit cruising speed in a few seconds. As that speed is approached, the pilot eases back the throttle to cruising power. With reduction of power, the tendency to yaw to the left decreases or may vanish altogether, and the pilot adjusts his use of rudder accordingly.

A level turn to the left is now made, to head downwind, parallel to the runway. This time the aircraft is banked a little more steeply and, in view of the lower power setting, a little more left rudder may be needed than in the climbing turn. The stick is gently moved both to the left and back, a slight increase in angle of attack, and a consequent slight loss of airspeed, being necessary in order to provide additional lift in the turn. If the turn were executed without backpressure on the stick, the nose would drop and the aircraft would lose height. A third turn at the end of the 'downwind leg' of the circuit is followed by the start of the descent, the pilot easing back the throttle and

using the elevators to maintain an appropriate airspeed. Once again the rudder pressure must be adjusted since at a very low power setting there may be a tendency to yaw to the right.

A final, descending turn establishes the aircraft on the descent path in line with the runway. In a descending turn the aircraft may resist the application of bank, so that a positive pressure of the stick to the left may prove necessary. Since there is more drag in the turn than in straight flight, the stick must be used to maintain airspeed.

On the final approach the aircraft's attitude, speed and angle of descent are controlled by coordinated use of stick and throttle. Once the runway threshold is reached, and when the aircraft is some 5m (16ft) or so above the ground, the stick is used to level off, power is progressively reduced, and the aircraft is kept flying for as long as possible by continuous very slight increases in angle of attack, produced by further

back pressure. When the moment of touchdown is reached, the aircraft should ideally be flying as slowly as possible, very near the stall, and therefore in a marked nose up attitude.

During the flight the pilot has been keeping a careful lookout for other traffic; he has been monitoring the flight and engine instruments, adjusting the aircraft's attitude in relation to the horizon, allowing for the effects of wind, and trying as much as possible to be at one with the machine. Man is not properly equipped for movement in three dimensions, and there is no doubt that flying by 'feel' alone can be extremely hazardous, as anyone knows who has tried to fly (accompanied by another pilot!) with his eyes closed. Coordination and a sense of balance are nevertheless essential, since an aeroplane is not pushed around the sky like an airborne motor car; to maintain balance it must be continuously and delicately manoeuvred in relation to its three axes of freedom .

Kites and Gliders

Although kites vary widely in their characteristics and design, they may generally be defined as aerodynes (flying machines that are heavier than air) tethered to the ground by a flexible line or lines, and capable of being sustained at a positive angle to the horizon by lift resulting from airspeed in a horizontal wind. (The airspeed may be augmented by 'groundpower', e.g. by running with the line or by attaching it to a moving vehicle.)

As with any flying machine, the kite's aerofoil surfaces produce both lift and drag, and the higher the lift:drag ratio the greater is the angle of flight. A diagram of forces may be drawn for a kite in steady flight analogous to that which represents an aeroplane flying straight and level. The aeroplane's weight is exactly balanced by its lift, and its drag by its thrust. In the case of the kite, the lift is balanced by the weight plus the downward vertical component of the 'thrust' (i.e., the pull of the flying line), while the drag is balanced by the horizontal component of the thrust. For the attainment of greatest height

ABOVE, BELOW & TOP RIGHT: *Modern versions of traditional Chinese kite designs.*

BOTTOM RIGHT: *An early European kite which appeared in Kyeser's* Bellifortis *of 1405.*

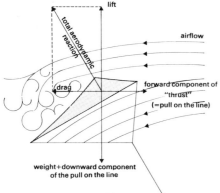

ABOVE: *Forces acting on a kite.*

and for the lifting of the heaviest loads, a kite should clearly be designed to have maximum overall lift combined with the best possible lift:drag ratio, while for towing drogues, vehicles, etc., a high ratio of drag is needed.

Although most kites consist of a symmetrical, rigid framework covered with a light fabric such as paper or cloth, several high performance kites developed in recent years have no rigid members at all, but use air pressure, controlled by shroud lines and flexible fabric keels, to maintain the correct aerodynamic shape. The absence of rigid members not only reduces the kite's weight, thereby increasing its angle of flight, but also enables the kite to assume a more aerodynamically satisfactory shape than is possible with most rigid designs.

In contrast to an aeroplane or glider in normal flight, most simple kites are usually stalled, the turbulence on the upper surface producing a great deal of drag. The best non-rigid kites are designed to fly at angles below the stall, and the cover of some simple kites, such as the Eddy bow, can be made to assume a shape approximating to a curved aerofoil, which results in efficient, unstalled flight.

The early history of kites

Where and when kites began is not entirely clear. Although they were probably known in China several centuries before Christ, the earliest firm evidence of their having been used there dates from about the 2nd or 3rd

century BC. In various parts of the Pacific, kites rather different from those flown in China have been known for many centuries, and it is possible that they were independently invented. In any case, the kite is not only the earliest recorded form of aircraft but is also among the earliest of discrete technological objects having a continuous history.

Chinese kites and their derivatives in Japan, Korea and South-East Asia, fall into two broad categories. The first is a simple, rectangular design consisting of a framework of crossed sticks covered by paper or cloth and using a multileg bridle attached to various points on the surface. Such kites were used not only for creating spectacular effects at the kite flying festivals which used to be common in the east, but also for lifting heavy weights and even men. The second is a broad category of figure kites representing men, animals, dragons, insects, and inanimate objects. Such kites are usually smaller than the rectangular ones and have always been flown entirely for recreational purposes. It was not until about 1,000 years ago, however, that kites in China began to be associated with the play of children. Before then they appear to have been used exclusively as an adult form of amusement.

It is difficult to decide what may be the earliest references to kites in China. Their use by General Han Hsin (d 196 BC) to measure the distance between his troops and an enemy stronghold may be antedated by the inventions of Mo Tsu and Kungshu Phan (both contemporaries of Confucius), who are

credited with the construction of wooden birds which flew briefly before being destroyed. In one story Kungshu Phan is also said to have designed wooden man-lifting kites which were flown over a city in a state of siege.

However they originated, kites rapidly came to be used for religious, recreational and military purposes throughout most of Asia and Oceania. Their ceremonial func-

tion is an immediate reflexion of the powerful effect on the human psyche of the concept of rising upwards to the heavens, and of the godlike associations of flight in general. The western myths of Daedalus, Pegasus and the flights of angels have their equivalents in a fund of eastern flight myths, including a great many concerning kites. Polynesian myths are especially rich in stories of the personification of kites, or of the manifestation of the gods in kite form.

Early European kites

Many of the kites which today are common in the West had their origins in Asia, but it is possible that some of the earliest European kites were largely indigenous creations. The first clear evidence of a kite in Europe appears in a 14th-century book by Walter de Milemete, *De nobilitatibus sapientiis et prudentiis regum* ('Of the Nobility, Wisdom and Prudence of Kings') completed in 1326 to 1327. It is a roundtopped, plane surface kite with a long, sinuous tail of cloth. Three soldiers are using it to drop a bomb (interestingly fitted with fins) over the walls of an enemy castle. Although this illustration is not discussed in the text of the book, a very similar kite is fully explained in a German manuscript of about 1430, the author of which was clearly a skilled and practised kite maker and flier.

While these pennon-shaped kites may be a purely European invention, they may owe a part of their origin to a similar, more complex, but nonflying object: the military used by adults rather than by children and were commonly associated with the noble art of warfare.

Later European kites
The pennon kites remained in use until late in the 16th century, when they began to be supplanted by smaller, neater and aerodynamically superior kites from the east. These were imported in increasing numbers by the sailors and merchants whose ships plied between Europe and the Indies. The ordinary lozenge, or 'kite shaped', kite reached us from Indonesia, together with the common variant which has a rounded top. Although the earliest known illustration of such kites in Europe shows it being flown by children in Middelburg, Holland (1618), the new kites, like the old ones, were commonly associated with adult activities. The first English illustration (1634), shows one being flown by a man taking part in a fireworks display. The tail of his kite is a string of 'jumping jacks', which are intended to astonish the audience by exploding noisily in the air.

By the second half of the 17th century kites had lost most of their interest for adults, but their popularity among children rapidly grew, as may be gathered from the increasing frequency with which they appear in illustrations of children at play. Not until the rapid rise of serious aerodynamic experimentation in the later 19th century did kites again catch more than the sporadic attention of European adults.

standard known as the *draco* (dragon). The *draco*, which seems to have originated in the region of what is now Iran, was a banner consisting of a carved wooden head, with open mouth, placed on the top of a pole. Behind the head a cloth tube, or windsock, was allowed to billow out when the banner was held aloft by the standard bearer, or *draconarius*. In some cases the head seems to have been provided with a burning lamp to produce smoke from the dragon's mouth. These standards, used to frighten the enemy and encourage the home troops, were adopted by the Romans early in the 2nd century AD, and were familiar in Europe until the 16th century. They certainly influenced the design of the flat, pennon kites and may even have inspired them. In any case, the kites, like the *draco* standards, were

Lawrence Hargrave, working alone in far-off Australia, experimented widely with kites in pursuit of his goal of manned flight.
TOP: *His second design, in 1896, was for this man-carrying box-kite aeroplane.*
RIGHT: *Hargrave in the field.*
ABOVE: *Hargrave's third design emerged in 1902. Made of tinplate and fitted with floats, it lacked a suitable engine.*
BELOW: *Hargrave's two-cell box kites.*

Lawrence Hargrave

Living in New South Wales, Australia, far from the main centres of aeronautical interest in Europe and America, Lawrence Hargrave (1850 to 1915) worked patiently and methodically at the problems of aeronautics during the decades just before and just after the turn of the century.

Although he was equipped with no more than a basic grounding in mathematics and the physical sciences, Hargrave was a good draftsman, a first class mechanic and a remarkably acute objective observer. In the 1880s and 1890s he undertook to explore the principles of flight by examining the behaviour of a series of small flying models powered by twisted rubber or by simple compressed air motors arranged to drive flapping wings or screw propellers. While the best of these

were capable of sustained flight over encouragingly long distances, Hargrave grew increasingly interested in how birds soar in flight without flapping their wings, a problem which he investigated by means of kites.

Hargrave's grasp of the principles of relative motion and fluid mechanics was not altogether sound. Although the theoretical arguments in his notebooks are more sophisticated than those of Leonardo da Vinci, he shared with him the mistaken belief that a body floating freely in a horizontally and uniformly flowing fluid medium can absorb energy from the flow. This error encouraged Hargrave in his work on so-called 'soaring kites', which he tried to make fly beyond the zenith (upwind of the flier). Part of the theory was sound, since Hargrave rightly believed, and was able to show, that a well made kite

may be made to absorb the energy of a gust and move momentarily upwind. His beautifully fashioned aerofoil wings gave him useful experience, but the general idea, being based on misapprehensions of physical laws, led to a dead end.

While the matter of soaring never entirely faded from Hargrave's mind, it sometimes took second place to his other main aerodynamic concern: the need for stability in the design of any practical flying machine. From this arose his invention of the now familiar box kite, which he always preferred to call a 'cellular kite'. The first of these, made early in 1893, contained a number of boxes, or cells, and thus resembled, as he said, 'two pieces of honeycomb put on the ends of a stick'. The multicellular kites soon gave way to the simpler design using only one cell, or box, at each end of the frame, and Hargrave achieved some fine results with a number of box kites whose surfaces were given the shape of curved aerofoils. In the first decade of the 20th century a great many European gliders and aeroplanes were powered derivatives of the Hargrave kite.

Among the most serious of Hargrave's mistakes was his excessive concern for stability. While he was commendably concerned to design a flying machine which would be safe to use, he developed the idea to the detriment of manoeuvrability, and it is significant that the stabilizing vertical surfaces of his box kites (sometimes called 'side curtains') disappeared from European aircraft after only a few years.

ABOVE: *Kite-flying in Japan is — even today — a very popular sport.*
LEFT: *No nation has ever been more devoted to the construction of large kites than Japan. Occasionally, rectangular, bowed models like this, ultimately of Chinese origin, were built large enough to carry a man, and there are many stories of warriors or robbers using them to soar off into the sky.*
TOP RIGHT: *Alexander Graham Bell was a prolific inventor who constructed several kites capable of lifting a person. This one, called* Siamese Twins, *was built in 1905.*
BELOW: *S. F. Cody (on the left) and his war kite of 1903.*

Alexander Graham Bell

Bell, an American, (1847–1922) took the idea of stability still further, with the result that his experimental kites, though often spectacular, were totally impractical as a basis for flying machines. Bell's enthusiasm and breadth of imagination partly compensated for a lack of serious scientific training in aeronautics. Having sufficient means to experiment on a fairly grand scale, he tried a wide variety of kites as a source of lift before deciding to set about refining the Hargrave box kite in order to make it stabler and stronger. As Bell soon found, a single Hargrave kite, which he called 'the high-water mark of progress in the nineteenth century', could not be scaled up to the size of a machine large enough to carry a man without encountering problems of weight and strength.

By early in the 20th century Bell's progressive developments of the box kite had led him to evolve an essentially new design, the tetrahedral kite. In its simplest form this consists of a regular four-sided figure, bounded on each side by an equilateral triangle and with a rigid frame member along each of the edges. By covering any two of the triangular sides, one arrives at a strong and simple structure whose large dihedral angle confers a good deal of stability. Any number of such cells may be connected together without changing the surface:weight ratio, and Bell accordingly began building multicellular kites capable of lifting a man.

The *Siamese Twins*, built in 1905, contained 1,829 cells, each about 25cm (10in)

on a side. Two years later Bell launched the *Cygnet*, consisting of 3,393 cells and provided with a central opening in which a man could lie. This was tested over Baddeck Bay, Nova Scotia, on 6 December 1907, with Lieutenant Thomas E. Selfridge of the US Army aboard. The kite rose to a height of 51m (168ft) and flew stably for 7 minutes, towed by a steamer. On landing in the water it was destroyed, but Selfridge escaped with a wetting. (Less than a year later Selfridge died in the first fatal crash in the history of powered flight.)

Although Bell experimented with the addition of engines and propellers to his kites, his unwieldy and fragile structures, dominated by an obsession with stability and safety, had already become little more than curiosities and soon faded from the scene. In recent years Bell tetrahedrals have nevertheless been enthusiastically adopted by sporting kite fliers.

The kite in war

Rectangular or round kites of enormous size, sometimes with multiple tails, were often built by the Chinese and Japanese, and very large kites, potentially capable of lifting a man, are sometimes seen in the east today. There is no doubt that the Chinese used them to carry soldiers aloft for observing enemy troops, and they may even have lifted men surreptitiously over enemy lines. In the West the kite was not seriously considered as a possible aid to warfare until the mid 19th century, when Admiral Sir Arthur Cochrane made some trials with kites about 4m (13ft)

long, to see if they might be useful in drawing torpedoes towards a target. Although Cochrane's trials were thought successful, little or nothing seems to have come of the idea. In the 1890s, however, there began an intense period of development of military kites which came to an end only with the adoption of the aeroplane as a fully practicable vehicle. Captain B. F. S. Baden-Powell, brother of the founder of the scouting movement and a keen member (later President) of the Aeronautical Society, began trials in 1894 with a view to developing a reliable system of man-

lifters. After a year of experiments, during which he discovered that his first kite, about 11m (36ft) high, was unwieldy and was best replaced by trains of smaller ones, Baden-Powell patented a design which could easily lift observers to heights of 100m (328ft) or more. Although these 'levitor' or 'war' kites were never officially adopted, they provided some of the stimulus for Samuel F. Cody's subsequent development of a much stabler and safer system. For a short period in the 1900s the Cody kites formed a part of the British Army's official equipment.

Cody's manlifters, which were tried at sea as well as on land, were highly efficient winged box kites. A train of them was raised until sufficient lift had been created, and then a further kite, from which a man was suspended in a basket, was allowed to run up the line on a trolley. The man was equipped with a camera, a telescope, a fire-arm, a telephone for contact with the ground, and a system of lines and brakes for controlling his movement. Similar manlifting apparatus was also developed in other parts of the world, including Russia and France.

Although the adoption of the aeroplane as a military weapon soon rendered the man-lifters redundant, kites continued to be used in limited ways for military purposes up to the end of World War II. During World War I the German U-boats vastly increased their observational range by sending a man up in a basket suspended beneath a box kite which could later be folded for stowage and which was controlled, when aloft, by lines and pulleys operated by the observer. This simple version of the Cody system was soon replaced by a safer design which allowed the observer, now sitting on a keel-like structure within the kite itself, to convert the kite into a glider in case of a sudden emergency requiring the U-boat to dive.

During World War II the Germans again flew observation kites, this time using apparatus of a more highly developed kind. The kite was in effect a small unpowered autogiro with three rotating blades above a tubular steel fuselage. The pilot was provided with a control column and rudder bar. With both this and the earlier designs a sufficient wind to sustain the kites could always be maintained by the U-boat's forward movement over the surface.

The US Navy made use of kites for a time to carry barrage wires over convoys, and US trainee gunners were helped by the use of kites as targets. Paul E. Garber developed an especially successful target kite, consisting of a large bow kite with a rudder and twin control lines. A silhouette of an aeroplane was painted on the surface, and the kite could be manipulated very nimbly to simulate most aerobatic manoeuvres.

Survival equipment used by airmen having to ditch in the sea during World War II sometimes included a simple collapsible box kite which was used to raise a radio aerial and distress signal.

The kite in peace
Kite fishing Kite fishing is probably the oldest known peaceful application of kites. Until recent times it was widespread in parts of Indonesia, Melanesia and Polynesia, and may have sprung up independently among a number of Oceanic peoples. The technique varied a little from place to place, and a great many different kites were used, although most of them were made of large leaves sewn together. The kite was flown to a considerable height by a fisherman standing on the shore or paddling a canoe. In addition to the flying line, a second line hung from the kite into the water, ending either in a hook or in a lure which trailed along the surface. In some parts the lure was an ingenious loop about 10cm (4in) long, fashioned from the web of a special spider which was cultivated and 'milked' for the purpose. Long-snouted garfish would attack the loop, mistaking it for prey, and would become entangled. Both kite and line would then be hauled in, and the loop reconstituted for a further catch. Up to ten fish might be caught with a single loop. Kites enabled the fisherman both to work in dangerous or otherwise inaccessible places and to conceal his presence from the fish. Although the technique has now largely died out in Oceania, a number of Western fishermen have adopted the idea.

Meteorological kites Many people have heard of how Benjamin Franklin used a kite in June 1752 to demonstrate the electrical nature of lightning. This, although one of the first uses of kites for meteorological purposes, was preceded three years earlier by the work of Alexander Wilson, a Scottish scientist who, with the help of a young man called Thomas Melvill, used a train of kites to raise thermometers to the height of the clouds. The thermometers were arranged to fall at predetermined intervals and were equipped with tassels to slow their rate of descent.

From the middle of the 18th century a number of investigators used kites to repeat Franklin's experiment or to gather other information about temperature, cloud height, etc., but it was not until the birth of meteorology as a strict science in the later part of the 19th century that kites were systematically used to study the weather. The British meteorologist E. D. Archibald used diamond-

In the 19th century kites were taken seriously as a life-saving device for shipwrecks.
TOP LEFT: *Jobert's kite, from the man who also built twisted-rubber ornithopters.*
TOP CENTRE: *An ingenious but untried design, Chatfield's Storm Kite.*
TOP RIGHT: *From World War I, a German U-Boat's man-lifting observation box kite.*
BELOW AND RIGHT: *Using kites like these, made from leaves, kite-fishing has gone on for centuries in Indonesia and the South Pacific.*

shaped kites in 1883 to measure wind velocities, and a year or two later the US Weather Bureau experimented with three-stick or 'barndoor' kites.

The invention in Australia, soon afterwards, of the Hargrave box kite provided a stronger and more reliable tool, and in the 1890s many weather stations both in America and in Europe used Hargrave kites to study conditions at heights of several kilometres. In July 1933 the last US Weather Bureau kite station was closed, after sounding balloons had rendered the kites obsolete. Not only did the launching and retrieval of trains of kites, sometimes pulling as much as 14·5km (9 miles) of wire, need much time and effort, but the growth of aviation had turned the previously harmless kites into a serious hazard.

Life saving As early as 1760 suggestions were offered for the use of kites to save lives in cases of shipwreck. As most shipwrecks occurred on a lee shore, kites flown from the ship could carry a line to potential rescuers. Many such devices, some of them steerable by multiple control lines, were patented by hopeful inventors.

Kite photography Although many aerial photographs were taken in the 19th century by balloonists, kites offered a cheaper and easier means of raising a camera. Lightweight shutter release systems were devised for taking photographs automatically from kites, often with excellent results. Kite photography is still occasionally practised.

RIGHT: *Thayer's life-saving kite system.*
BELOW: *Specially strengthened Hargrave box kites were used for two or three decades to gather weather information from heights of 8km (5 miles) or more. This one was used at the Blue Hill Observatory, Massachusetts, USA.*
BELOW RIGHT: *Many 18th and 19th century experimenters used kites to conduct electricity to the ground following Benjamin Franklin's example. The Frenchman de Romas showed that a pigeon insulated from the ground would not be hurt.*

Leaflet and supply dropping It seems that the first leaflet raid was carried out in China in the 13th century. A besieged army raised leaflets on kites which were allowed to fall by cutting the strings at the appropriate moment. During the American Civil War, presidential amnesty notes were once distributed to Confederate sympathizers in this way. In 1870, during the Franco-Prussian War, French smugglers used kites to lift contraband over the walls of Paris.

Other uses Kites have always proved surprisingly versatile. Work on the bridge across Niagara Falls was begun by commissioning a boy to fly a line across on a kite. (He was paid $10.) In 1901 Marconi used a kite to raise the aerial in Newfoundland from which the first transatlantic transmission was sent. In the 19th century hunters occasionally used kites shaped like hawks which frightened game birds into staying in the undergrowth

LEFT: *One of the more novel aeronautical vehicles, which did work after a fashion, was this* Char Volant *or kite-carriage. Its designer, an Englishman called George Pocock, had merely attached a large round-topped kite to a lightweight horseless carriage and used the one to pull the other along. Surprisingly, the kite-carriage made a successful journey along the road from Bristol to Marlborough in 1827.*
BELOW LEFT: *Pocock en route, 1827.*
BELOW: *Hang gliding has benefited from Rogallo's research into flexible wings.*
RIGHT: *A parachutist of the US Army's display team flying a Parafoil.*

until the beaters arrived to put them up. Among the most exciting of recent suggestions is the idea of developing a light wind-powered generator which might be kept permanently in the fast jet streams by a kite, whose flying line would double as an electric cable. Naturally, careful thought would need to be given to the aviation hazard.

Traction

In ancient Polynesia kites seem to have been used to pull canoes, while in 18th century America Benjamin Franklin reports having allowed himself to be pulled across a pond by a simple paper kite. In about 1825 came one of the most celebrated instances of the use of kite for traction: George Pocock's invention of the *Char Volant*. Pocock, a Bristol school teacher, used large arch-topped kites to pull a specially designed lightweight carriage at speeds of up to 32 km/h (20mph). Lacking the modern hazards

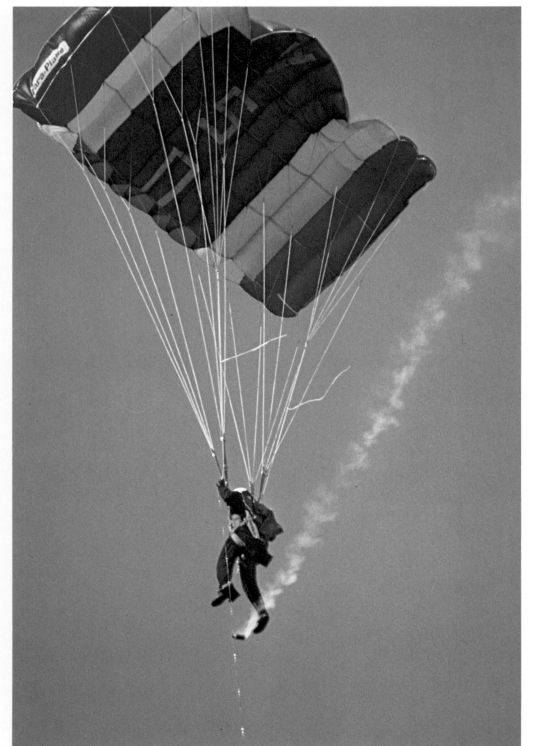

of electric cables and telegraph poles, Pocock was able to cover long distances in the west of England. Since then kite traction has been provided principally for boats. If the kites are flown, as were Pocock's, by a system of control lines enabling their heading to be altered, the carriage or vessel can readily be manoeuvred. The forces act just as they do with a fixed sail, and tacking into wind is not difficult.

The most fruitful modern uses of kites in connection with vehicles did not, however, emerge until the perfection of the non-rigid kite. Various non-rigid designs have been tried since at least as early as the late 19th century, when Baden-Powell flew one. Although this was successful, he did not proceed with it, preferring instead to develop his hexagonal manlifters. While many of the earliest non-rigid kites were little more than asymmetrically rigged circular parachutes, the line being attached where the load is

normally carried, more sophisticated and more efficient shapes have emerged in recent years, most of them ultimately owing their existence to Francis Rogallo.

Francis Rogallo's flex wings

In 1945, after the end of World War II, Rogallo began serious research on the design of flexible wings, the aim being initially to develop a kite whose lift would approximate to that of an aeroplane wing, but whose shape would be determined by a combination of wind pressure and the tension on shroud lines. A stable non-rigid kite was evolved in 1948 and a patent application filed. The early Rogallo kites needed as many as 28 shroud lines, but as these were difficult to handle he simplified the design until as few as four lines were required. Since Rogallo's early experiments were not subsidized, he had to work independently, even installing in his house a large electric fan which created a draught through a doorway and so provided him with a primitive wind tunnel.

In the 1950s and '60s, a good deal of work was carried out on the application of the Flex wing kites, as they were called. Two American aircraft companies in particular, Ryan and North American, explored their potential as the basis of gliders and dirigible parachutes. Among other results of this research was the creation of the Fleep ('flying jeep'), a new form of shorthaul vehicle which can work from difficult terrain lifting quite heavy loads. For this and other applications the delta wing shape of the true Rogallo Flex wing was modified to include rigid members at the leading edges and at the centre, though these rigid members were sometimes no more than inflated cylinders of fabric. Apart from its use in such vehicles as the Fleep, the Rogallo configuration is seen in a number of ski kites and ground-powered manlifters, and it has grown still more familiar in the '70s with the growth of interest in delta-winged hang gliders.

The Jalbert Parafoil

The greatest single advance in kite design since Rogallo was made by Domina C. Jalbert, of the Jalbert Aerology Laboratory, Inc., in Boca Raton, Florida. The Jalbert Parafoil has undergone continuous development since its invention in the early 60s. Like a Rogallo Flex wing, it is entirely nonrigid, and is therefore light, efficient and almost indestructible. The Parafoil is essentially a high-lift wing of low aspect ratio, both upper and lower surfaces being formed of cloth or sheet plastic. The surfaces are separated by vertical ribs whose shape is that of a thick aerofoil section, and the leading edge is open so that wind pressure keeps the kite inflated to aerofoil shape. Ventral fins and shroud lines are used to stabilize it and to maintain the correct angle of attack. The Parafoil, which flies at angles below the stall, has an astonishingly high lift:drag ratio and has found numerous applications for both military and meteorological work. It is perhaps most commonly seen freed of its flying line and forming the basis of a steerable parachute, which makes possible controlled glides over long distances.

Mechanics' Magazine,

MUSEUM, REGISTER, JOURNAL, AND GAZETTE.

No. 1520.]   SATURDAY, SEPTEMBER 25, 1852.   [Price 3*d*., Stamped 4*d*.

Edited by J. C. Robertson, 166, Fleet-street.

SIR GEORGE CAYLEY'S GOVERNABLE PARACHUTES.

Fig. 2.

Fig. 1.

A glider is an aerodyne (heavier than air machine) which descends continuously through the air under the influence of gravity. It has no power unit, but produces lift over its wing surfaces as a result of its forward and downward motion relative to the air. An aeroplane whose engine is stopped or is fully throttled back is functioning as a glider.

When a glider is descending at a steady speed, the total aerodynamic force on the wing acts vertically upwards, exactly balancing the weight. The lift, by definition at right angles to the relative airflow (glide path), is angled forward, providing a forward component of force which exactly balances the backward horizontal component of the drag. All the forces are thus in equilibrium, and the glider accelerates neither forwards nor

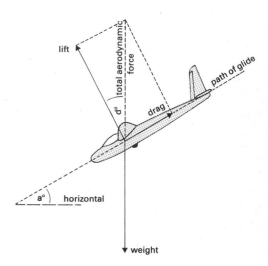

downwards. It is clear that the smaller the value of the drag, the flatter will be the angle of glide. The glide angle is, in fact, solely determined by the lift:drag ratio and, surprisingly though it may seem, is independent of the glider's weight. Other things being equal, increasing the glider's weight increases the speed of descent along the glide path but does not alter the angle of that path.

Gliders do not, of course, always descend continuously relative to the ground, but are capable of soaring to very considerable altitudes. Except occasionally when pulling up in certain manoeuvres and trading speed for height, a glider can rise only by flying in air which is rising faster than the glider's own inherent rate of sink. Glider pilots therefore seek out areas where the wind is deflected upwards by hills, or where differences of ground temperature have created *thermals* – columns of warm, rising air.

Ancestors of the glider

The first man-made gliders to have achieved

BELOW: *In 1804 Sir George Cayley made a prophetic model glider consisting of an arch-topped kite on a pole, with a cruciform tail unit the angle of which could be varied in any direction. At the front was a weight to adjust the centre of gravity.*
ABOVE: *Cayley's earlier designs were refined over the years, and by 1852 he was able to publish his outstanding design for a fixed-wing glider. He called this a 'governable parachute', and included a brilliant description of how to fly it. For this and his other wide-ranging theoretical works, Cayley is often regarded as the inventor of the aeroplane or the 'Father of Aviation'.*

ABOVE RIGHT: *A diagram to illustrate the balance of forces operating on a glider descending at the flattest glide angle and at constant speed.*
FACING PAGE
ABOVE: *Otto Lilienthal was a gifted gliding pioneer who lost his life following an uncontrolled stall in 1896. He is pictured here standing atop his artificial hill near Berlin in 1894. It is interesting to notice how 'bird-like' appeared the man whose work was based on nature's wings.*
BELOW RIGHT: *Perhaps this 2,000-year-old Egyptian wooden bird (or flying fish) is an ancient attempt to build a flying model.*

By 1809 he had built a full sized glider which was tested in short hops with a boy on board, and late in life, in 1849, he built a triplane glider which once or twice carried a boy for a few yards.

In 1852 Cayley designed an elegant and refined fixed wing monoplane, features of which may have been incorporated into a man-carrying machine (probably another triplane), built in 1853. In this glider Cayley's coachman was privileged to make the first recorded flight in an aircraft of approximately modern configuration. The coachman, doubtless unaware that he was making history, gave in his notice immediately afterwards, complaining that he was 'hired to drive and not to fly'.

Later 19th century gliding attempts

In 1804, the same year in which he made his first kite glider, Cayley built a 'whirling arm' for testing the lift on a flat surface at varying angles of attack. In 1808 he investigated the movement of the centre of pressure, and in 1809 described some of the properties of cambered aerofoils. Between that time and the end of the century the science of aerodynamics was gradually established. In 1864 Count Ferdinand d'Esterno published a book on bird flight which greatly increased the available information on soaring; the Englishman Francis Wenham, who delivered and had published, in 1866, a highly important paper on *Aerial Locomotion*, worked at the theory of aerofoils and investigated the properties of multiplane structures; in 1884 Horatio Phillips, another Englishman, published further valuable findings on aerofoils. Practical work was also continuing: Wenham tested multiplane gliders; Jean-Marie le Bris tried a bird-shaped glider in 1857, and another in 1868; in the 1880s John Montgomery made a series of rather unsuccessful trials in America. Despite the growth of theoretical knowledge, the experiments were often of a hit and miss nature, and it was not until the work of Otto Lilienthal that mature theoretical insight was combined with a high degree of practical aeronautical skill.

Otto Lilienthal

Lilienthal (1848–1896) was among the most gifted and remarkable of the pioneers immediately preceding the Wrights. A well-trained engineer, he had, from his earliest years, been devoted to the idea of manned flight, which he attempted to realize through a meticulous study of birds and through a series of controlled experiments. Like many before him, he was convinced that success could be achieved only by a close imitation of the flapping flight of birds, a belief which he

limited success may have been model birds. A number of accounts, going back 2,000 years and more, tell of the invention of ingenious flying objects, variously described as wooden birds or wooden kites. In the West the earliest mention of the construction of such a model by a real person is the story of the wooden dove said to have been made by Archytas of Tarentum, a Greek mathematician of the 4th century BC. Although this account speaks of the dove as having been propelled by the force of a spirit or gas contained within it, there seems little likelihood that any form of jet or rocket propulsion could have been devised at that time. If this story and one or two others like it have any basis in fact, the birds were probably lightweight wooden gliders carried some distance by the wind.

Tower jumpers

From the earliest times many foolish men – and also some skilled experimenters – have attempted to fly with the aid of wings strapped or tied to their arms and bodies. Although most of these attempts concern the use of unstable and totally ineffective flapping apparatus, it seems possible, even likely, that in a number of cases rigid wings were tried, and that a combination of luck and intuition led to the achievement of steep glides which usually ended in semi-controlled crashes.

Sir George Cayley

It was to need many centuries of fruitless experiment before the idea of flapping gave way to serious trials with fixed wings. Even Leonardo da Vinci rarely departed from the designs of ornithopters. The first successful full scale glider conceived and built after a rational consideration of aerodynamic problems was Cayley's man-carrying machine of 1853. As early as 1804 he had built a model glider using an arch-topped kite fixed to a pole, which served as combined wing and fuselage, with an adjustable cruciform tail unit and a sliding weight at the nose for altering the position of the centre of gravity.

expressed in a brilliant and highly influential book, *Der Vogelflug als Grundlage der Fliegekunst* ('Bird Flight as the Basis of Aviation'), published in 1889. Unlike many other ornithopterists, Lilienthal understood the general principles of flapping flight. In 1893 and 1895 he built two powered man-carrying ornithopters which, however inefficient, would have begun to provide controllable propulsion and lift. Although the first of these was tested as a glider, neither of them ever made powered flights. However misguided Lilienthal's concentration on flapping may have been, his observations of birds served him well, for he was a true airman, concerned to learn from experience in flight and not to theorize for too long before trying his ideas in practice.

Although, until his tragic and untimely death in 1896, Lilienthal saw the creation of a successful ornithopter as his ultimate aim, most of his experimenting was done with fixed-wing hang gliders from which he hoped to learn the secrets of stability and control. In the last years of his life he was moving towards the use of control surfaces, having tried wing tip steering airbrakes and a form of full-span leading edge flap, and had made notes about wing warping, rudder control and (in a limited form) elevator control. Before his death he had applied these ideas very little in practice, and all of his gliders were manoeuvred by changes of the position of the centre of gravity, brought about by swinging movements of the pilot's body.

From 1891 until his fatal crash 5 years

later, he flew a total of 18 different types, the first 12 of which were monoplanes. For a time he was attracted to the possibilities of biplanes, which he found in some respects easier to manoeuvre, and Nos. 13, 14 and 15 were of biplane configuration. For his earliest flights Lilienthal launched himself from natural heights, but in 1893, after he had had a large hangar built, he began flying from its 10m (33ft) roof. After further trials from natural heights he finally made an artificial mound 15m (50ft) high, from which he could glide in any direction, according to the direction of the wind.

Lilienthal's gliders were strongly constructed and braced, with an engineer's attention to appropriate distributions of stress and loading. He conducted many careful investigations into the properties of aerofoil shapes and drew up tables of lifting forces under various conditions. For his last flight he used one of his No. 11 gliders, his 'Normal Flying Apparatus'. The accident which caused his death was the result not of a structural failure, but of the inadequacy of Lilienthal's control system to cope with sudden changes of attitude. When he was about 15m (50ft) high, a gust pitched the nose up beyond the stalling angle. The starboard wing stalled first, dropped sharply, and caused the glider to sideslip rapidly to the ground. Lilienthal had insufficient height in which to recover, and suffered a broken spine in the crash. He died the next day, 10 August 1896 in Berlin's Bergmann Clinic. However, his work continued to inspire subsequent aviation pioneers.

MAIN PICTURE: *Otto Lilienthal airborne in 1894. In the last five years of his life Lilienthal flew 18 different types of glider, 12 of which were monoplanes. He could fly whatever the wind direction, thanks to a 15m (50ft) conical mound he constructed in 1893 close to his hangar.*

BELOW: *Lilienthal gliding from his artificial hill in June, 1895. It is interesting to notice that he has raised his knees to adjust the monoplane's centre of gravity.*
BELOW RIGHT: *Lilienthal flying another of his biplane gliders in 1895.*

Percy Pilcher

The aeronautical work of the Scot, Percy Pilcher (1866–1899), was closely related to that of Lilienthal, whom Pilcher met and many of whose ideas and techniques he adopted. Although it had been an interest of long standing, Pilcher did not begin practical work on aviation until 1895, after he had spent some time in the navy and had trained as an engineer. While inspired by the successes of Lilienthal and indebted both to him and to Octave Chanute for much essential material, he was a man of independent temperament who wished to make his own contributions to aviation. Despite having received firm contrary advice from Lilienthal, he unaccountably insisted on first trying a glider which wholly lacked a tailplane. This, of course, he found to be uncontrollable in pitch, and he soon afterwards ruefully admitted his mistake. The *Bat*, as he called it, was equipped with a vertical fin and had monoplane wings with pronounced dihedral. Even after he had diagnosed the trouble and added horizontal stabilizing surfaces at the tail, the large vertical surface area, contributed by the combination of fin and dihedral, caused stability problems in gusty conditions at low airspeed, and in his later gliders he abandoned excessive dihedral in favour of a configuration essentially similar to that of Lilienthal's monoplanes.

The fourth of Pilcher's gliders, the *Hawk*, was the one with which he had most success, although ironically it was a structural failure in the *Hawk* which was to bring about his

LEFT: *Around the turn of the century Octave Chanute built this glider which was to have a great influence on the Wright brothers.*
BOTTOM LEFT: *Three views of the influential biplane hang glider, which was flown by Chanute's young engineer-assistant A M Herring.*
BELOW: *Percy Pilcher's* Hawk, *showing the spring-loaded undercarriage and hinged tail of this successful—but fatal—hang glider.*
RIGHT: *When he died flying the* Hawk *in 1899, Pilcher left this powered glider design behind. Unfortunately, it was never tested.*
BOTTOM RIGHT: *One of Chanute's first multiplane gliders, which he began building, testing and refining in 1896.*

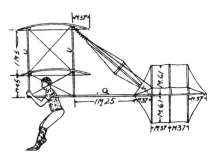

fatal accident. As with all of Lilienthal's and Pilcher's machines, the *Hawk* was a hang glider depending upon body movements to alter the position of the centre of gravity. It was equipped with a device which (with variations) he had adopted from Lilienthal: although the tail unit was not controllable by the pilot, it was hinged so that it could move freely upwards. Lilienthal's reason for incorporating this apparently odd arrangement was to ensure against a sharp pitch down of the nose (which he always feared) resulting from upward gusts at the tail. The *Hawk* was not only powerfully braced with the help of kingposts, but was also equipped with a sturdy spring loaded landing gear to absorb some of the energy of a heavy landing. When he was flying this glider in poor weather conditions on 30 September 1899, a bamboo rod snapped in the tailplane structure, causing the machine to fall out of control from a height of about 10m (33ft). Pilcher died of his injuries on 2 October 1899 without ever recovering consciousness.

Pilcher was an enthusiastic, imaginative and energetic young man, more ebullient than Lilienthal and inclined to want to proceed faster. At his death he was well advanced with the development of a powered glider, originally patented as a monoplane resembling the *Hawk*, but built as a multiplane. For this machine he even designed, built and bench-tested a lightweight motor. Unfortunately, his machine was never even tested as a glider.

Although it is just possible that Pilcher might, had he lived, have preceded the Wrights in the achievement of powered flight, he was surprisingly little interested in control surfaces, and was still a very long way from solving the problems of stability and control which the Wrights were soon to overcome. Pilcher was nevertheless outstanding in his concern to learn the feel of flying from experience in the air, and in this he showed a marked superiority to many of the enthusiastic 'powered hoppers' of the late 19th century.

Octave Chanute

The French-born American Octave Chanute (1832–1910) began practical aeronautical experiments only late in his life, but through his support and encouragement of the Wrights, the publication of his classic history *Progress in Flying Machines* (1894) and the success of some aspects of his own hang gliders, he exerted a powerful and beneficial influence on the subsequent development of aviation.

In 1896 Chanute began building and testing multiplane gliders which, because of his age, he wisely decided not to fly himself, employing instead the services of a young engineer, A. M. Herring. The successful outcome of these experiments was a biplane glider with cruciform tail unit which, while looking back to Cayley's triplane design and Lilienthal's biplanes, may also be seen as the immediate ancestor of the Wrights' machines. In 1900, the Wrights, who had already been experimenting for some time, wrote to

Chanute to seek his advice. Chanute responded by offering assistance of many kinds and soon established a close relationship with the Wrights.

There can be no doubt that the Wrights benefited a good deal from Chanute's previous work, as well as from his active encouragement, but there were fundamental differences in their approaches which make it wise to be guarded in assessing the extent of the younger men's debt. Until he observed at first hand the Wrights' work with inherently unstable configurations, Chanute, in common with many others, had given absolute priority to the idea of stability, and even after the Wrights were well advanced with the development of their biplane gliders Chanute, who in fact always favoured triplanes, was still experimenting with devices for promoting automatic stability. He nevertheless responded positively to the advice which he received from his pilot, Herring, and recognized that success could be achieved only by experience gained in the air. While the Wrights benefited greatly from their adoption of Chanute's strongly braced biplane glider structure, Chanute showed little interest in the need for controllable aerofoil surfaces, and contributed little to a solution of the problems of flight control.

The Wright brothers' patent design for a biplane kite, an original design which owed nothing to Hargrave.

ABOVE: *Unlike the Wright machines, many early European gliders and powered aircraft owed a good deal to the Hargrave box kite. This float glider, constructed by Voisin and Archdeacon in 1905, shows clearly both Wright and Hargrave features. From Wright they borrowed biplane wings and forward elevator; from Hargrave a stabilizing tail unit.*
BELOW: *The Wright biplane evolved directly from their experiments with gliders.*

OPPOSITE PAGE
TOP: *The Wright brothers' patent design for a biplane kite, an original design which owed nothing to Hargrave. The kite was their first aircraft (built in August 1899). The special feature of the kite was the warped wing-tips which enabled the kite to bank or to right itself. It was fitted with a fixed horizontal tailplane and wings which could be moved in relation to one another in order to shift the centre of gravity.*

The Wright brothers

The Wrights worked towards ultimate success by undertaking a rationally ordered sequence of experiments, beginning in 1899 with the construction and testing of a biplane kite, the wings of which could be twisted, or 'warped'. Like Lilienthal, Wilbur Wright initially found bird flight the best source of understanding, though with the significant difference that he first concentrated not on propulsion or stability, but on control: 'My observations on the flight of buzzards led me to believe that they regain their lateral balance when partly overturned by a gust of wind, by a torsion of the tips of the wings.'

The biplane kite, about 1·5m (5ft) in span, was stabilized by a fixed tailplane and was so arranged that the two 'wings' could be moved in relation to each other to introduce 'stagger' and so shift the centre of gravity. The kite, which had no side-curtains and was not (as is sometimes asserted) in any way derived from Hargrave's box kites, provided useful information and, following their correspondence with Chanute in 1900, the Wrights progressed to tests with full-scale gliders. In the autumn of that year they flew their first glider over the sand dunes of Kitty Hawk, North Carolina, making a few short manned glides but testing it as a kite for the greater part of the time. The wing warping idea was incorporated, together with a forward elevator (characteristic of Wright aeroplanes for the next decade), but there was neither a rudder nor a fixed fin, the Wrights having not yet begun the development of control surfaces for intentional manoeuvring.

It was during this series of experiments that the Wrights confirmed their suspicions about the disadvantages of excessive inherent stability. The three gliders which they flew in the later months of 1900, 1901 and 1902, were all built so as to be inherently unstable in roll. Unlike so many of the early aeroplanes and gliders which were to be flown in Europe in the first decade of the century, none of the Wright gliders was provided with dihedral or with vertical stabilizing surfaces.

The degree of camber, the wing loading and the rigging angle of the wings were all based on information which they gathered for themselves, with the aid of apparatus constructed at home, the Wrights having discovered that all previously published figures, even those of Lilienthal, were unreliable. It was with the use of these progressively developed gliders that they surmounted the basic control problems and were able to embark on the construction of a practical powered flying machine.

Their most salient success, and their greatest single contribution to the advance of aircraft control systems, was their correct diagnosis of a problem which they unexpectedly encountered when using the wing warping device. To their initial surprise, the upgoing wing, whose lift had been increased by a downward warp of the trailing edge at the tip, tended to be retarded, thus turning the glider against the bank, a condition which eventually led to the dropping of the raised wing as it slowed down and stalled in the inside of a tight circle. The trouble was caused by 'warp drag' ('aileron drag', or 'adverse yaw'), discussed in Chapter One. In an initial attempt to cure it, the Wrights equipped their gliders with a fixed fin at the rear, hoping thus to counteract the yaw, but it soon grew apparent that the adverse yaw could be avoided only by some positive use of rudder in the direction of bank. In September 1902, they modified their third glider so that the fins, now free to move as rudders, were coupled to the warping mechanism. The Wrights were then able not only to correct unintentional wing drops without sideslip, but were also able to initiate balanced turns. This glider, now fully controllable about all three axes, formed the basis of the *Flyer No. 1*, which was to make the celebrated first sustained and controlled powered flight from level ground on 17 December 1903.

The glider in war

Although their limited ability to manoeuvre makes gliders relatively defenceless, they have played a significant part in modern warfare. During World War II, in particular, large gliders were used as troop carriers. Towed by bombers or other large aircraft, they were released over suitable terrain such as open fields or beaches where they were usually abandoned.

A typical troop carrying glider, which saw much service in the allied invasion of Europe, was the Airspeed Horsa, a wooden highwing cantilever monoplane with a span of 26.84m (88ft). The Horsa, which could accommodate 15 fully armed troops and their equip-

ment, had dual controls in the extreme nose position, giving the pilot excellent visibility. As it was essential that gliders of this type could land in very short distances, the Horsa was provided with spoilers on both the upper and the lower surfaces of the wings, and had large split flaps.

A rather bigger troop carrier designed in America was the Waco YCG–13, a tailwheel type which could lift several tons of freight and supplies, or 30 fully armed troops.

The allied gliders looked small, however, in comparison with the Messerschmidt Gigant, used by the Germans. With a span of 55.2m (181ft) the Gigant could carry as many as 130 troops. Although it was used on various fronts during World War II, it was not entirely successful, being awkward to fly and needing a very powerful launching tug. The standard towing arrangement was a formation of three Me–110s, but for a time the Germans experimented with an interested compound tug aircraft, consisting of two twin engined Heinkel He–111s joined side by side with a fifth engine at the point of junction. Later the Gigant was converted into a powered transport aircraft with six engines.

Gliders were sometimes used to carry supplies over very long distances. The Germans towed them as far as the Russian front, while on 4 July 1943, the British Transport Command set up a record by using a C–47 Dakota to tow a Waco CG–4A glider across the Atlantic in a total flying time of 28 hours. The glider carried vaccines, and spares for radios, aircraft, and land vehicles.

The glider as an auxiliary war weapon came into its own during World War II. Both the Allied and the Axis powers built giant gliders to carry troops and supplies. The two most notable achievements of glider troop carriers were the invasion of Crete by German airborne troops in May 1941 and the landing of Allied troops behind the Normandy beachheads on D-Day.
BELOW: *Deutsche Lastensgler GO242.*
BOTTOM: *Deutsche Lastensgler GO244B.*

Experimenters

By 1809 Sir George Cayley's extensive experiments and writings had laid a groundwork that made the confused ignorance of 1799 seem like a prehistoric era. He had discussed the fixed wing, its aerofoil section, its centre of pressure, the need for dihedral angle, the need for a fixed fin and tailplane for stability and the use of movable control surfaces such as a rudder and elevators. He had begun to use models for his research into wing lift and the basic problem of stability and control. Later he discussed converti-planes (having a wing which doubled as a powered lifting rotor), internal-combustion engines (never considered previously), jet propulsion for aircraft (with what we today call vectored thrust) and many other far-seeing ideas which, at the time, were incapable of being realized. He built a simple device which can be described as the first aeronautical research tool, which alone called for completely new thinking. It was a whirling arm, mounted on a vertical pillar rotated by a falling weight and thus having a constant drive torque. The arm was pivoted to the pillar like a see-saw; on one end was a section of wing and on the other a weight on a sliding horizontal scale. Cayley could thus measure the lift of different wing aerofoil sections, different planforms, different wing sizes (bearing in mind the constant effective thrust), and the effect of varying the angle of incidence. All this as long ago as 1804.

Cayley never doubted the eventual success of the aeroplane, nor that its achievement rested on the perfection of a suitable engine; in his words: 'It is only necessary to have a first mover, which will generate more power in a given time, in proportion to its weight, than the animal system of muscles.' He soon decided the steam engine was unlikely to offer sufficient power: weight ratio, and in a search for a higher power: weight

ABOVE: *Sir George Cayley (1773–1857) is known as 'The Father of the Aeroplane'. He was the first person to establish aerodynamics as a science, and to break away from bird flight with flapping wings and instead use separate lift and propulsion, thus producing the aeroplane.*
BELOW: *In 1809 it was reported that Jacob Degen of Vienna had flown with this muscle-powered ornithopter. In fact it had no hope of flying; what Degen did was hang it under a balloon and then make large jumps while pumping the 'wings' up and down.*
ABOVE RIGHT: *Henson's* Ariel, *an aerial steam carriage, was a futuristic drawing published in 1843. Though never built, it was not only a bold concept but also surprisingly well schemed, like a modern aeroplane. The chief omission was any form of flight control.*
RIGHT: *This model is a copy of the world's first successful flying model aeroplane, made by Félix Du Temple about 1857. Later this courageous naval officer actually made a 'hop' in a full-size machine, but as he had no proper engine could not remain airborne.*

ratio in the field of internal combustion experimented with a small engine running on gunpowder. In 1807 he published his specification for another completely new invention, the hot-air engine, but though he saw this through to industrial use, he never succeeded in his quest for a good aero engine. He therefore had to confine his full-scale flight research to gliders. His first such machine was almost a direct enlargement of models he had flown down the Yorkshire slopes around 1800 (which were probably the first stable and steerable glider models ever to fly). His first man-carrying glider appeared in 1809, and with 27·87m² (300sq ft) of wing often flew short distances with a man or boy, but usually with ballast.

In 1809 Cayley was spurred into publishing the first of a monumental three-part treatise *On Aerial Navigation*, by the report that Jacob Degen had flown in Vienna. The truth of the matter was that the Austrian had merely become the first to play at balloon-jumping. He had fixed himself under a balloon which almost lifted him off the ground and then 'flown' by flapping left and right clack-valve wings. A clack-valve is like those in the heart, which open automatically in one direction but shut tight in the other. The valves helped Degen lift his big wings on their upward strokes, and then shut as he pulled the wings down. Though it was good fun, and Degen certainly 'flew' after a fashion, he made no contribution to either ballooning or aeroplane flight.

Cayley explored various further configurations, including an unpublished tandem-wing layout in 1815, and his final machine was a triplane with passenger car suspended underneath. He was reluctant to úse large braced surfaces, and this led him to restrict wing span and instead use more wings. His big 1849 triplane made several 'piloted'

carriages or galloping coaches, and full-scale experiments, possibly with aircraft tethered in a high wind. There were two parts to the problem: how to design and construct an aeroplane; and how to fly it. It is remarkable that hardly any of the experimenters for the next 50 years tried to solve the second part, and most of them made no methodical attack on the first. It seems incredible that many experimenters simply built an aeroplane. Some then got aboard, while the majority got others to act as the first 'test pilots' and operate the controls. They appear to have taken it for granted that, if the the machine would fly, the 'aviator' would be able to fly it.

Cayley is not known ever to have flown his own gliders, and possibly the first man to have the confidence to fly his own machine (if we discount early parachutists) was L. C. Letur. His contraption was as much a parachute as a glider, and has some affinity with the sport parachutes of today, but though never intended for sustained flight it is important because the man flew it himself. He made several apparently stable glides from balloons in 1853 to 1854 before the wind dragged him over some trees, tipping him out and probably qualifying him as the first human to be killed in serious heavier-than-air flight.

This tragedy focused more attention on the problem. Michel Loup sketched a bird-like aeroplane which attempted to reconcile nature and engineering by fitting two propellers into bird-shaped fixed wings. In 1857

flights, the longest and last in 1853, but the occupants served only as ballast; the tail controls were locked and there was no lateral control, Cayley relying on the wing dihedral and the pendulum stability of the underslung car. One of their many advanced features was the use of wheels with tensioned-wire spokes, yet another Cayley 'first' that much later became standard on bicycles and the first successful wheeled aeroplanes.

William Samuel Henson

William Samuel Henson, of Chard, Somerset, was more of a visionary, but fanciful impressions of his remarkable 'An Aerial Steam Carriage' were widely published in 1843, and firmly set people thinking for the first time of a machine along the lines of what we today recognize as an aeroplane. It had a practical wing (supposed to span 45·72m [150ft]) with sensible bracing, a cabin fuselage directly under the wing, pilot-controlled rudder and 'slab' tailplane, and twin screw propellers. Nor did Henson merely dream. He not only tried to fly at least one model, in 1847, but he built a working steam engine, and calculated that a refined version for his machine would give 30 horsepower for a weight of 272kg (600lb) with boiler and water. His friend John Stringfellow likewise consistently worked on lightweight steam engines, running excellent ones in 1844 and 1848. In the latter year he was busy trying to fly a steam-driven model even more advanced than Henson's but lacking a rear fin or rudder; it could not maintain height when flying free.

Experiments of the mid-19th century

By the mid-19th century there thus existed, thanks to Cayley, a bedrock of knowledge which took human heavier-than-air flight out of the realm of mythology (though it certainly did not make it popularly respectable, because anyone who dabbled in the subject was judged to be a crank). There were the prospects of suitable engines, and the stage was set for the experiments that would solve the basic problems of aviation, though this was to take until the next century. It is essential at this point to look afresh at the problem of flight and how it was attacked. It is probably self-evident today that flight could be achieved only after a methodical study, making the greatest possible use of models, whirling arms (such as Cayley had used), models held out of railway

Félix du Temple, a French naval officer, drew a more practical machine with single tractor propeller and simpler geometry. Probably in the following year he flew a model of this design which became the first powered heavier-than-air device ever to sustain itself in free flight. But in 1857 another French sailor, Jean-Marie Le Bris, had boldly attempted to fly a full-size glider. As a sea-captain Le Bris had intently studied the effortless flight of the albatross. When he retired he tried to build an albatross glider, with a span of 14·94m (49ft) and wing area of 20m² (215sq ft). He was one of those who thought the thing to do was simply get in and fly. His glider was potentially good, and it did make one short glide after launch downhill from a farm cart. Then it crashed, and Le Bris broke a leg. Undismayed, he even-

Experimental Aircraft, 1901-1908

TOP LEFT: *This monoplane with small upper wing just got off the ground near Amiens in December 1908. It was built by Henri Robart.*

FAR LEFT CENTRE: *Lestage's flying machine built in 1907, which had wings mounted on revolving frames.*

FAR LEFT BELOW: *Rather like a powered hang-glider, Ellehammer's first aeroplane flew in 1906 tethered to a central post.*

LEFT: *Raoul Vendome's No 2 made only a few brief hops in 1909, but had pivoted wings to give powerful lateral control.*

TOP: *Another mistake was this multiplane built by Count D'Ecquevilley in 1908. A single large wing would have been better.*

ABOVE: *Ambroise Goupy built the world's first powered triplane in 1908. It made short hops.*

RIGHT: *Close-up of the engine of Bellamy's uncompleted machine at Weybridge in 1907.*

tually built a second glider, and in 1868 this, too, crashed, but with only ballast on board. The use of ballast highlights one of the basic faults of most of the early experimenters: they did not appreciate what Cayley had emphasized about the importance of control surfaces. Le Bris may have had a controllable horizontal tail, but he had no rudder and no wing controls. He was thus in no position to 'fly' the glider at all.

At about the same time, in 1858 to 1859, Frank H. Wenham in England was flying models with multiple superimposed wings. He had been told by Cayley that the leverage on large monoplane wings was 'terrific' and should be avoided (Cayley was criticizing Henson's Aerial Steam Carriage), so Wenham adopted the multi-wing layout. He was probably the first actually to fly multi-wing gliders, and his research not only confirmed Cayley's in showing the superiority of the cambered aerofoil, but also demonstrated that the centre of pressure was quite close to the leading edge. He therefore decided that most of the rear part of the wing was not worth having, which meant in effect that he built his wings with high aspect ratio. In 1866

Wenham helped found the Aeronautical Society of Great Britain – today the Royal Aeronautical Society – and in its first Annual Report he published a drawing of a man-carrying glider with five superimposed high-aspect-ratio wings.

Two years later the infant Society held an aeronautical exhibition at London's Crystal Palace, the first such gathering of air-minded people in history. Prominent in the engraving on the front page of the *Illustrated Times* for 4 July 1868, was the triplane built by String-fellow, and this again was an attempt to follow Cayley's principles. Stringfellow used two propellers driven by an engine in the fin-like fuselage, but could not get the machine to maintain height. Like virtually all contemporary flying machines, it lacked a control system, but its world-wide publicity inspired almost every subsequent 19th-century aviator, and thus its influence was great.

Most designers of the 1860s had little idea of the kind of control system needed. Very few recognized the need for any movable surfaces other than a rudder (generally accepted, because they were needed on ships) and, less often, a movable horizontal surface, either in front or behind. In 1868 Matthew Boulton patented a highly impractical orni-

thopter in which auxiliary 'ailerons' were fitted, but these were not for lateral control and, in fact, would have constituted a serious hazard had they been used. In 1870 Richard Harte patented a true aeroplane wing with ailerons; but even he failed to appreciate the need for lateral control, though he provided the means for it. His ailerons were deflected to counteract torque from the propeller, by imparting a roll in the opposite direction. As a second possibility he thought the ailerons could be used to help steer, by increasing drag at one wing-tip. The purpose for which ailerons are vitally needed never occurred to him, or to any other experimenters of the 19th century.

Experimenters of the late 19th century
In 1870–71 Alphonse Pénaud triggered off a craze that multiplied the number of people building successful model aircraft by at least 1,000. He did it by a simple model aeroplane which he called the 'Planophore', with a pusher propeller powered by twisted rubber. His was a beautifully simple cantilever monoplane with inherent stability along the lines laid down by Cayley, and though subsequent experimenters built some large monstrosities, this little model ensured that most flying models from 1871 onwards would actually fly. Pénaud's full-size aeroplane of 1876 remained a paper project only, but though it was virtually an all-wing design it had such advanced features as a glass-domed cockpit canopy and retractable landing gear. Its main advantage was in confirming the need for a rudder and elevators, both moved by the same control column, and

tractor propellers.

Of machines actually built, that of du Temple deserves special mention, because it made the first attempted flight by a powered man-carrying aeroplane. It was identical in configuration to du Temple's model and patent of 1857, apart from replacement of the boat-like fuselage by a light framework. It is difficult to see the reason for the swept-forward wings, which must have put the centre of pressure far ahead of the centre of gravity, besides making the machine unstable in pitch. But in 1874 it was ready to be tested, and its steam power plant had been run at full power with the aircraft tethered. Du Temple actually got it airborne after a run down a sloping ramp, but it flopped to the ground almost at once. This probably saved du Temple's life, because he had no proper control system.

An even less likely machine was the 'Aerial Steamer' tested at the Crystal Palace in 1875. It was built by Thomas Moy, who was a pioneer of the hydrofoil boat by proxy, because, to see how his wings worked, he tested them in 1861 under a boat, which was lifted 'quite out of the water'. His wing-supported boat worked well, but unfortunately he had little idea how to construct an aeroplane, and when he tested it he was wise to stay on the ground and have the machine tethered on a circular track. It did manage to lift off, and was possibly the first aeroplane in history to do so entirely under its own power.

In 1879 Victor Tatin achieved complete success with a small model which again reinforced the rightness of the 'aeroplane' shape with tractor screws, fixed wing and rear tail. He cheated, because instead of an on-board power source, the cylindrical fuselage housed a store of compressed air, which quickly ran down. But his model took off smoothly at 8m/sec (about 18mph) and gained much publicity. Less well known were the tandem-wing models of D. S. Brown of the early 1870s, which are thought to have been inspired by a proposal by Thomas Walker in 1831. Brown was a painstaking and scientific worker, and his scholarly report of 1874 certainly influenced Langley, whose work is described later. Another worker who was little-known in his day was the Russian, Alexander F. Mojhaiski who – probably after building models – constructed a large monoplane which, in 1884, was launched down a sloping ramp near St Petersburg,

BELOW LEFT: *Penaud's design for a twin-propeller monoplane, patented in 1876 but never built, an extremely sophisticated concept for the 19th century.*
LEFT: *The model flown by Tatin in 1879, powered by compressed air.*
BELOW: *In 1890 Clement Ader was the first man to take off in a powered plane but his Eole could not sustain flight.*

piloted by I. N. Golubev. It had one tractor propeller and two pushers, the latter being located either in slots in the large rectangular wings, as in the model now on view in the Soviet Union, or behind the trailing edge according to a contemporary print; the latter shows a steam engine smoking furiously. This big machine took off, as did du Temple's, but sank again at once. This was fortunate, for it appears to have had no controls except small elevators.

Little appears to have happened in the 1880s, though by this time the number of experimenters was certainly above 100. Many of them found it hard to avoid thinking of birds, or even dragonflies, and one of the leading 'birdmen' was L. P. Mouillard. His book on bird flight, *L'Empire de l'Air* (1881), emphasized the importance to birds of sustained gliding. Mouillard had himself built many gliders from 1856, and he was helpful in once again ramming home the belief that, before one could hope to soar aloft in a powered aeroplane, its pilot had to learn to fly. Today we may find it difficult to comprehend that this belief was shared by few of the early experimenters. Hardly any made any attempt to 'walk before they could run' by building gliders or solving the basic problem of control. Today we can see that trying to take off in an improperly designed aeroplane, with no proper control system, would be almost suicidal; to do so without having any idea how to fly in the first place is simply nonsensical.

Yet this is just what happened at least 40 times between 1850 and 1910. Possibly the outstanding case came on 9 October 1890, at Armainvilliers, when Clément Ader tested his *Eole*. This flying machine contained a truly outstanding steam engine, which after a careful study in 1960, was calculated to have weighed only about 1·13kg (2·5lb) per horsepower (most contemporary engines weighed from 5·5 to 68kg [12 to 150lb] per horsepower). Unfortunately, almost

everything else about the *Eole* was wrong, and though it had great bat-like wings with a span of 14·94m (49ft), and a semi-enclosed cabin, the occupant had no way whatever of controlling the aircraft other than by moving a steam throttle valve. On the date above, Ader did become the first human ever to rise off level ground in a self-propelled flying machine, but he correctly called the flight 'tentative'. He was airborne for a distance estimated at 50m (164ft).

Far more significant progress was made by Horatio F. Phillips in England, but his work was less spectacular and less publicized. His outlook was the one needed; instead of rushing to build and try to fly a powered machine, he set to work with aerofoils and tested them day and night. Much of his research was done in wind tunnels, the obvious tool for an aircraft designer, although they appear never to have existed until one was built by Wenham, helped by John Browning, in 1871. This tunnel was immediately publicized through the Aeronautical Society, and Phillips used it and also built his own. He worked on wings throughout

the 1870s, and in 1884 took out his first patent. In this he described the wing section as it has existed more or less ever since. His long studies showed him that a wing for the low speeds then envisaged should have separate upper and lower surfaces, appreciable thickness, a dipping leading edge (the 'Phillips entry') and an upper surface curved much more than the underside. He found, as Cayley had reported but many found hard to believe, that most of the lift was generated by the reduced pressure over the upper surface, especially over the front upper portion. He took out many further patents, and in 1893 successfully flew a large, unmanned aeroplane which lifted off a circular track at Harrow, although tethers restrained it. Sadly, this great researcher was convinced that the answer lay in many very narrow wings. His 1893 model did lift off, but he had no success with a later machine, built in 1907, which had 200 slim wings arranged in four groups, each looking like a Venetian blind. By that time he might have been expected to realize that this conviction was the one part of his great work that was faulty.

The outstanding work of the 1890s was the fabulous research of Lilienthal, outlined in Chapter 2. When he was killed, Otto Lilienthal had far more flight-time to his credit than every other heavier-than-air pilot in history combined, but he was unlike most experimenters in that his objective was to learn how to fly. He was toying with a powered flapping wing tip machine at the time of his death in August 1896, but powered flight was not his central ambition. On the other hand his great pupil, Englishman Percy S. Pilcher, was working towards powered flight and was well advanced with a lightweight oil engine when he, too, was killed gliding in 1899. The third important glider figure of the 1890s was the American Octave Chanute (Chapter 2), but he had little direct personal interest in engines.

Hiram Maxim

The other great figure of the 1890s was wealthy American Hiram (later Sir Hiram) Maxim. Originally an electrical engineer, Maxim lived in England and invented among other things the machine gun that bears his name which led to the most famous gun of all in the history of armies and air forces, the Vickers. He had the resources to do things on the grand scale and, after spending a reputed £20,000, tested a gigantic 'flying machine' at Baldwyn's Park, Kent. He did much prior research, and in any case did not intend this machine to make a free flight. What impressed was not its design but its size: not for many years was the world to see another flying machine with a span of 31·70m (104ft), wing area of 371·6sq m (4,000sq ft) and weight of 3,629kg (8,000lb), complete with crew of 4! The two propellers, each 5·43m (17ft 10in) in diameter, were driven by a pair of amazingly advanced compound steam engines with very-high-pressure boilers and maximum output at 180 horse power each. Excluding the boilers and fuel, the specific weight was 0·67kg (1·55lb) per horsepower, which is little short of fantastic in comparison with other steam engines of 1894. Their combined power accelerated the monster biplane to an estimated 66·93km/h (42mph), at which it lifted from its rail track, broke one of the guard rails added to prevent free flight, and was safely brought to a halt. There seems every likelihood that, had full power been maintained, this vast 'flying test rig' would have climbed purposefully away.

the powered aeroplane. He, more than any other pioneer of flight, followed what might have been thought the logical and sensible path in perfecting a stable and controllable kite and then turning this into an aeroplane. Moreover, his work on engines was wholly sound and promising, concentrating on lightweight petrol engines and including the first rotary engine, with fixed crankshaft and rotating radial cylinders, ever to run (many credit Hargrave with inventing the rotary engine itself). Outstanding as was his engine

gramme of powered models which differed from most in the scale of backing available in the form of facilities and test equipment. Langley decided to use the Brown tandemwing layout, because the Englishman's experiments were so successful and documented in scholarly fashion. Langley called all his machines 'Aerodromes' and, apart from having no control system, were well designed and built. Features included highly cambered single-surface wings, usually of equal size, a fixed cruciform 'Penaud tail' and a central engine driving two pusher propellers. It took Langley ten years to produce a successful model, but in 1896 he made good flights with two models each weighing about 11·8kg (26lb) and with a span of about 1·83m (6ft). The best flights covered 914 and 1,280 m (3,000 and 4,200ft) in 45 seconds. Langley had devoted most of his time to the beautiful small steam engines that powered these models. He almost ignored the vital fact that he could not control their flight. He also chose to launch them by catapult over water at Quantico, Virginia, which with models may have been a good idea. They flew steadily, and this was an achievement in itself. Langley made no attempt to consider a machine that could be steered, and ignored any sort of landing gear.

In 1898 Langley had decided to let others carry on the good work; but war with Spain suddenly prompted the US Government to

It would almost certainly have crashed, because it had no controls other than fore and aft elevators.

In 1897 Ader began testing *Avion III* (his second machine was left unfinished), which was no advance on *Eole* apart from being even larger and having two engine/propeller units. Fortunately for Ader it never left the ground, but 9 years afterwards he claimed it had flown 300m (984ft), because by that time aeroplane flight was an accomplished fact and Ader wanted to be 'first'.

In 1899 a much more methodical experimenter visited England: Lawrence Hargrave. Working virtually isolated in Australia, he had by 1893 perfected the box kite, as related in Chapter 2, but only as a stepping-stone to

work, Hargrave's greatest contribution was the box kite configuration, which combined light weight, structural elegance and rigidity, and acceptable flight stability. In the period 1905 to 1910 it was Hargrave's work in New South Wales in 1880 to 1899 that served as the basis for most of the world's aeroplanes.

Samuel Pierpont Langley

By the beginning of the 20th century aeronautic attention began to be focused on experiments in the United States. America's most eminent scientific institution, the Smithsonian, had as its Secretary an astronomer, Professor Samuel Pierpont Langley. He had become interested in heavier-than-air flight in 1886, and embarked on a sensible pro-

ABOVE LEFT: *A model of the giant steam-driven machine of Sir Hiram Maxim, which became airborne in 1894 but accomplished little.*
CENTRE LEFT: *Ader's second machine,* Avion III *of 1897. It was even less successful than his* Eole *of 1890.*
BELOW LEFT: *Another view of Ader's* Avion III *with its bat-like wings folded.*
ABOVE: *S. P. Langley's important but wholly unsuccessful* Aerodrome *on its houseboat on the Potomac in 1903.*
RIGHT: *The Wright brothers succeeded because they were methodical. They tested aerofoils in the world's first wind tunnel, seen here.*

see if flying machines might have practical use. They asked Langley to build a full-size man-carrying Aerodrome, and contracts were signed. This was extraordinary, and far more than just the first time anyone had considered buying a flying machine. It was the first time any official body had even taken the idea of aeroplane flight seriously, which was almost universally regarded as a subject for scorn and ridicule. The reasons for official interest lay in Langley's stature and eminence; the fact that he was a scientist rather than a crazy inventor; and the success of his models for if they flew, it was reasoned, so could a man-carrying machine.

Langley collaborated with the brilliant Charles M. Manley and Stephen M. Balzer, who created what was by far the most advanced and lightest engine for its power the world had ever seen (see p. 55). In 1901 he successfully flew a quarter-scale model of his man-carrying Aerodrome, and this was the first machine ever to fly with a petrol engine. Finally, on 7 October 1903, Manley climbed aboard the full-scale machine which, like the models, was to be launched by catapult from a houseboat. It plunged into the river Potomac. On 8 December it plunged into the river again, and that was the end of the Aerodromes.

It is almost beyond our modern comprehension why Langley, with so much going for him, should have ignored the whole question of flight control, and also chosen not to use a wheeled landing gear for land take-offs. Arguments have raged over what

happened on his two launch attempts. Some say the machine suffered immediate structural failure, even before it left the catapult, and others insist it fouled the launching mechanism on each occasion. Certainly the splendid engine was not at fault, though the machine needed at least two instead of only one. In 1914, Glenn Curtiss took the same machine and made short hops with it over Lake Keika. Sensibly Curtiss fitted it with floats. For several years afterwards the Smithsonian made extravagant claims about the 1903 Aerodrome; what they did not disclose, but must have known, was that before flying it Curtiss had secretly and dishonestly altered it in major particulars, in order to try to diminish a patent claim of priority by the Wright brothers.

Somewhat similar to Langley's models, and often reported to have been based on them, the world's first flying boat was tested by Austrian Wilhelm Kress on the Tullnerbach reservoir in October 1901. It had twin waterproofed hulls, three wings in tandem

and a good tail with fin, rudder, tailplane and elevators. Two pusher propellers were driven by a heavy Daimler petrol engine said to weigh 13·61kg (30lb) per horsepower. Sadly, the machine capsized and sank when Kress swerved to avoid an obstruction, but both Chanute and Wilbur Wright thought it capable of flight. A much more dangerous European design was that of Karl Jatho of Hanover, which made short hops in 1903 – said to be of 18m (59ft) on 18 August and 60m (197ft) in November. This contrivance was just a kite with a 9hp engine and pusher propeller; Jatho had no control whatever.

The Wright Brothers
We come now to the great Wright brothers, whose extremely important research with gliders was outlined in Chapter 2. Their success where so many had failed rested upon a methodical approach, which, instead of deciding what to build and then trying to fly it, began with first principles, painstaking research with a wind tunnel and other tools,

and eventually led to the brothers learning how to fly. It is significant that, to avoid a nose dive such as that in which Lilienthal and many others since have met their deaths, they adopted a pilot-controlled forward elevator or foreplane. This enabled the pilot, lying prone on the lower wing, to keep watching the angle of the elevator and match this with the elevator's position with respect to the horizon. Today canard (tail-first) aircraft are often the best arrangement, but at the turn of the century the front-elevator layout led the Wrights into a blind alley and could have cost either his life.

In particular, the adoption of an inherently unstable configuration was an unnecessary error, because by 1910 it was appreciated that full control could be achieved whilst still having an inherently stable aeroplane that would fly 'hands off' – which would have been suicidal in a Wright Flyer. Yet another strange quirk of the Wrights was their reluctance to take off normally, with wheels (which would have made it much easier to handle their Flyers on the ground); instead they stuck to skids resting on a trolley running on a prepared track, to cumbersome handling trucks, one fixed under each lower wing and removed when the Flyer was on its runway, and to catapult take-off with a cable pulled by a falling heavy weight.

None of these criticisms in any way detracts from the Wrights' achievement, which makes theirs by a very wide margin indeed the greatest name in the entire history of flight. But it reflects the sad situation in which they found themselves after 1905, when, unable to settle agreements for the sale of their machines, beset by spies and would-be copyists and with the world generally unaware or sceptical of their achievements, they stayed on the ground for more than two and a half years. Design choices that seemed prudent in 1902 to 1903 had by 1908 become outmoded, yet the painstaking and dogged brothers were very reluctant to make major changes, which might have helped them, to a refined and proven technique.

Powered flight

By 1903 Wilbur and Orville were the only experienced pilots in the world. They knew more about flying even than Lilienthal, because unlike the German they were using a control system built into the Flyer. This system comprised warping wings, operated by a hip cradle swung to right or left by the pilot lying on it; biplane elevators in front driven by a fore/aft lever which cunningly not only rocked the surfaces bodily but changed their camber from convex to concave to give maximum up or down thrust; and twin rear rudders linked to the warp cradle to give a smoothly banked turn.

During their gliding in 1901 to 1902 the Wrights had discovered that warping could have an effect opposite to that intended, the asymmetric drag at the wing tips swinging the machine in yaw and causing the wing it was desired to raise going down still further. The fixed fin made things worse by accentuating the yaw and speeding up the high wing. Long and potentially hazardous experiments in 1902 gradually led to the linked warping and rudder control, with the aid of which the Wrights became the first aviators in history to make turns, or, indeed, to control an aeroplane in flight at all.

Most people know how, searching for wind at bleak Kitty Hawk, Wilbur won the toss and attempted to fly into a 32 to 35km/h (20 to 22mph) wind on Monday 14 December 1903. The original powered Flyer had a span of 12·29m (40ft 4in), a length of 6·43m (21ft 1in), a flying weight (i.e. fully loaded) of about 338kg (746lb), and a water-cooled engine with four cylinders lying on their side and developing about 13 horsepower. No catapult was used with this Flyer. Wilbur simply opened the throttle at about 10.35am and accelerated down the launching rail with the skids resting on a free trolley. He became airborne, the nose rose, Wilbur over-corrected and the Flyer ploughed into the sand. It was maddening, but Wilbur was completely unhurt and the somewhat bent Flyer was repaired and made airworthy in 48 hours. Some reports claim Wilbur tried to climb too

ABOVE: *Orville Wright piloting the No 3 glider in the autumn of 1902. Until 1902 the Wrights had had complete faith in existing aeronautical data, but it made their second glider a failure. With No 3 they based the design entirely on their own research, and it flew well, making more than 950 successful glides on the bleak sandhills at Kitty Hawk, North Carolina.*

BELOW: *The original powered Wright Flyer at Kill Devil Hill, Kitty Hawk, on 14 December 1903. It was on this day that the first attempt to fly under power was made. Wilbur won the toss and took off, soon after this picture was taken, but ploughed into the sand, causing slight damage. After the Flyer had been repaired it was brought out on Thursday 17 December and made four good flights, the first in the hands of Orville.*

RIGHT: *A model of an early biplane built in 1908 by Gabriel Voisin. It was based loosely on the designs of the Australian pioneer Lawrence Hargrave drawn up for his box kites, as was an early machine constructed by Santos-Dumont. The vertical surfaces between the main planes (of which there were six in the Santos-Dumont machine) were reduced to four in this design in order to increase the lateral stability.*

steeply and stalled. Whatever the cause, he was content to claim a 'flight' lasting just 3½ seconds, and this is not considered to rank as a flight at all. On the Wednesday the Wrights were confident of success on the morrow, and sent word to the staff at the weather and life-saving station four miles away. Next morning, 17 December, was blustery and bitterly cold, with a north wind gusting at about 40 km/h (25mph) and ice on the puddles from recent rains. Five men arrived from the weather and lifesaving station, and a man and a boy came from other localities. The Wrights rigged up a camera on a tripod to photograph the first take-off, and assigned one of the visitors to work it at the appropriate moment. It was Orville's turn, and at about 10.35am he accelerated along the rail. The camera was operated, and it shows not only the Flyer climbing away on man's first flight, but also the muddy footsteps left by Wilbur as he ran alongside at the start, holding the bottom wing. About 12 seconds were covered at about 13km/h (8mph) ground speed, or 48km/h (30mph) airspeed, equivalent to a ground distance of 36·58m (120ft) and an air distance of over 152·4m (500ft).

Man had flown at last! Orville had wobbled and undulated, as was to be expected in such conditions, but there was not the slightest doubt the Flyer could fly. After man-handling the machine back to the rail and making an inspection it was flown again: Wilbur covered 53·34m (175ft) ground distance (213 m [700ft] through the wind) at higher speed in 11 seconds. Then Orville flew for 15 seconds, covering 61m (200ft) (air distance 259m [850ft]). Finally, at about noon, Wilbur kept going for no less than 59 seconds, covering 259·7m (852ft) of ground (an air distance of about 792m [2,600ft]). Unfortunately the elevator was damaged in the final landing. The brothers were gaining experience, and had petrol enough for a flight of 18 minutes. They had intended after lunch to fly all the way to the weather station, and there is no reason to doubt that one of them could have done it. But with a repair needed and winter set in they went back to

Dayton, well pleased with their success.

In 1904 the brothers did all their flying at the world's first aerodrome, on Huffman Prairie, a 90-acre pasture at Simms Station about 13km (8 miles) east of Dayton. Flyer *No 2* was similar to the first, but its elevators and rudders were raised well clear of the ground and it had a new upright engine of 15–16hp. By November 1904 flights had become routine, with accelerated towed take-off to make them relatively independent of ground conditions. Durations ranged up to over five minutes, and most important of all was the ability to make sure turns and fly a circuit. Twice in 1904 the Wrights invited the Press, but the engine refused to start on both occasions; the newspapermen never came back, and completely disbelieved the tales of the few locals. However, recent investigation suggests that the 'failures' were deliberately staged to convince the Press that the Wrights were unable to fly and therefore keep the trials private. Subsequently the Wrights built Flyer *No 3*, generally regarded as the

ferably with a simple glider, and that a successful flying machine had to have some means of control. Instead, the European experimenters were satisfied to start by building their definitive powered aircraft, believing that they could be driven like a car. The only exceptions were French Captain Ferdinand Ferber who, in 1902 to 1904, flew copies of the Wright gliders, and the young French Voisin brothers Charles and, much more important, Gabriel. The latter was commissioned by Ernest Archdeacon to build a glider that could be towed by a motor boat on the Seine. Helped by another youth, Louis Blériot, Gabriel Voisin first built a Hargrave-style box kite landplane which was towed into the air by a car in March 1905, without a pilot. This brief test cannot have offered Voisin much information.

He changed the design for Archdeacon's float-glider, adding a large biplane box-kite tail which contributed to the lift. Control in pitch was provided by a foreplane, as in the Wright machines, but there were no other

world's first completely practical aeroplane. Though it flew only 49 times, compared with 105 flights by *No 2*, it logged much more flight-time – a total of 3hr 5min, with flights lasting up to 38 minutes and covering 39km (24·25 miles). Seven Flyer *No 4* models were built, one being shipped to France in 1908, where Wilbur amazed the Europeans, who were not only unable to fly under control, but had not even appreciated that control was needed. By this time passengers were being carried, flights were extending to over 2hr duration and, by the end of 1908, the brothers had logged 36hr 20min in the air, or roughly six times the total flight-time of all other aviators combined.

European experiments, 1900–1914
During the first six years of the 20th century (1901 to 1907) European experimenters made extraordinarily poor progress. With Lilienthal and Pilcher dead, there seemed to be nobody left with the basic understanding that an aviator had first to learn to fly, pre-

controls. Fortunately the glider was basically stable – possibly a matter of luck – and it flew quite well with Gabriel Voisin at the controls on 8 June 1905. A little later a slightly different float-glider, built jointly by Voisin and Blériot, showed that supposed inherent stability was no substitute for a control system. On its first take-off, on 18 July 1905, it tilted and slid stright into the Seine, Voisin narrowly escaping being drowned.

Gabriel Voisin was not deterred, but before he achieved real success the first European powered flight had been made by the glamorous little Brazilian, Alberto Santos-Dumont, who had already become the rage of Paris by his exploits in airships. In early 1906 he was building his first heavier-than-air machine. At first glance it looks quite normal, with the engine and propeller at one end, close to the biplane wings, and the biplane tail at the other; it is only when we see which way the pilot is facing that it is seen to be an odd freak, with the tail far in front and the wings right at the back.

Experimental Aircraft, 1908-1914

ABOVE LEFT: *50hp Gnome rotary engine of Spencer's biplane 1911.*
ABOVE: *This Farman III was built for Roger Sommer, who flew it at the Reims meeting.*
LEFT: *Cody seated in his much-modified biplane, at the Lanark meeting in August 1910.*
BELOW: *This Voisin was fitted with a 37mm Hotchkiss cannon as early as 1910.*
BOTTOM: *T. O. M. Sopwith flew his Howard Wright biplane from Kent to Belgium in 1910.*

TOP FAR LEFT: *After flying a Voisin-built triplane in 1908, Baron de Caters flew this Voisin biplane at Châlons in April 1909.*
TOP LEFT: *One of the last of the classic Wright flyers was this Astra biplane of 1911, with 70hp Renault engine.*
CENTRE LEFT: *German aviator Alfred Friedrich, seen in the rear cockpit of his Blériot, flew from Germany to France in 1913.*
FAR LEFT: *This trim biplane was the Harvard I, of July 1910. It was based to some degree on the Blériot monoplane.*
LEFT: *The early aviator Colliex sitting at the controls of his Voisin aeroplane. The Voisin designs, though successful, were outdated by about 1910.*

ABOVE: *Alberto Santos-Dumont standing in front of one of his popular little Demoiselle monoplanes of 1907. The pilot sat under the warping wings and controlled flight by a combined rear rudder and elevator, side rudders and forward elevator.*
RIGHT: *After Phillips the next to test a flying machine in Britain was A. V. Roe, whose biplane made short hops at Brooklands in 1908. His 1909 triplane flew better.*
BELOW: *Trajan Vuia in his Vuia I tractor monoplane. Unfortunately he had no proper system of control, so his early aircraft—though they influenced others—were in themselves failures.*

Santos-Dumont, having, like other Europeans of the day, omitted to experiment with gliders or learn how to fly, found it difficult to test his machine without getting in and flying it. He did at least try. The 14-*bis* was finished in July 1906 and it was slung on a pulley from a long overhead cable, and pulled by a trotting donkey (why the wealthy pilot did not use one of his cars is a mystery). Then it was borne aloft slung beneath his *No 1* airship, but as it was not cast off to glide to the ground it is difficult to see the reason for this curious experiment. The 14-*bis* made a short hop of 7m (23ft) on 13 September, but was damaged in a bad landing. Santos-Dumont took out the 24hp Antoinette engine and put in one of the first 50hp versions of this superb purpose-designed French aero engine, and flew 60m (197ft) on 23 October. He then made the important modification of adding ailerons, intended to be worked by a body harness as he stood up in the machine's balloon basket. On 12 November, at Bagatelle, Paris, he made six flights, on the last of which he kept going strongly for over 21 seconds, covering 220m (722ft). This ranks as the first successful powered flight by anyone other than the Wrights, though how controllable or practical the 14-*bis* was is arguable.

Nobody copied it, and Santos-Dumont later turned to tricky little monoplanes called Demoiselles, with warping wings. Blériot experimented with the same pusher canard arrangement, but with monoplanes. He had been influenced by the first man

ABOVE LEFT: *One of the most beautiful of all early aircraft, the Levavasseur Antoinette VII won the Altitude Prize at Reims. It was built for the Anglo-Frenchman Hubert Latham.*
ABOVE RIGHT: *Commander Schwann's Avro of 1911, one of the first seaplanes. The engine was a 35 hp Green, one of the few British types.*
RIGHT: *Front view of the Santos-Dumont 19-bis, an unsuccessful form of Demoiselle with the engine between the wheels, with belt drive.*
BELOW: *Henri Farman was one of the greatest early aviator-designers. Like several of his rivals, he was a Briton living in France.*

ever to try to fly an aeroplane of the kind we have today, with tractor propeller, monoplane wing and rear tail. This man was the Paris-domiciled Romanian Trajan Vuia, and though his attempts to fly in March to October 1906 never achieved hops better than 10m (33ft) his sensible design made a great impression. One of those who was impressed was Blériot, and while in 1907 Voisin and Henri Farman at last achieved real success with classic box kite biplanes, Blériot built better and better tractor monoplanes. By this time aviation was at last beginning to 'take off'. Leon Levavasseur's Antoinette met the demand for a light and reliable engine, and after 1908 another engine, the Gnome rotary, came on the scene; soon there were many possible engines, and Blériot usually chose a REP or Anzani.

Farman, an Englishman living in France, was certainly the first European to fly a practical and fully controllable machine. Built for him by Voisin in the summer of 1907, the *Voisin-Farman I* first 'hopped' on 30 September. On 26 October it flew for almost a minute, on 8 November it made a definite turn, and on 9 November Farman flew the first complete circle in Europe. A little later Farman was flying with proper ailerons, because—apparently alone among Europeans – he had grasped the underlying importance of lateral control, as explained in the original patent of the Wrights. Once he had added ailerons Farman could fly as he wished, and on 30 October 1908, he made the world's first cross-country flight, 27km (16·78 miles)

from Bouy to Reims. On the next day Blériot flew his *VIII-ter* a slightly greater distance. And on 25 July 1909, Blériot flew his *XI* from France to England, to make the first international and first overseas flight.

Floatplanes
By this time aeroplanes could be designed to order, and industries had sprung up to build aeroplanes and teach the customers how to fly. Though heavier-than-air flight had begun to have useful applications, stalling and spinning were not yet understood, and experiments were still needed – as they still are. In March 1910 Henri Fabre successfully flew a float-seaplane, and this idea was enthusiastically taken up by American Glenn Curtiss. In January 1911 Curtiss flew a much better seaplane, and the following month he flew the first amphibian, which was equipped with

both floats and wheels.

In 1912 the Royal Aircraft Factory at Farnborough flew the B.S.1 (B.S. for 'Blériot Scout', which meant it had a tractor propeller but did not indicate any other link with Blériot), which is generally regarded as the first purpose-designed military aircraft. In France the Deperdussin company built fast racers with radically different streamlined fuselages of monocoque construction. A. V. Roe in England built an enclosed cabin machine; the Short brothers built multi-engined aircraft, and experiments were made in taking off and landing on short platforms on warships. Perhaps the pinnacle of the pre-war achievements was the large, four-engined aircraft built by the young Igor Sikorsky in Russia in 1913, from which stemmed the world's first transports and strategic bombers.

Engines

All human flight depends on either buoyancy (achieved by lighter-than-air aerostats) or a source of power. With kites the source of power is the wind, reacted by a tethering line. With sailplanes it is a combination of gravity plus upcurrents of air, either in thermals or caused by wind over steep hillsides. Other aircraft need mechanical power, produced by muscles, by burning fuel or some other energy source such as stretched elastic, compressed air or electricity. Before 1895 nobody knew what was the best form of power for aviation. W. S. Henson in 1843 proposed a steam aeroplane and made a successful working model of its engine.

The first powered aircraft to fly, discounting impractical balloons supposed to be rowed by oars, was Henri Giffard's airship of 1852, which cruised at about 11km/h (7 mph) on a steam installation weighing 53kg (117lb) per horsepower. This relationship, which results in a figure called specific weight (total mass of an engine divided by its maximum power output), is an important one in comparing one aero engine with another. For long-range aircraft, an even more important variable is specific fuel consumption, which can be regarded as either the amount of fuel burned to generate unit quantity of energy (such as one horsepower-

hour; one horsepower developed for one hour) or the rate at which fuel must be burned to generate unit power (such as one horsepower).

Late 19th century

There seemed in the late 19th century to be little immediate prospect of making an aero engine light, powerful and reliable. Several experimenters tried gunpowder as a fuel for

an engine, though none tried to build a rocket aeroplane, which would have had a far greater chance of success. A major advance came in 1872 when Austrian Paul Hänlein built an airship filled with coal gas, of which part was fed to a Lenoir-type gas engine. This was the first internal-combustion engine to fly, though it weighed 93kg (205lb)/hp and of course reduced the available lift by gradually consuming the gas in the envelope.

In 1883 the Tissandier brothers made successful flights with an airship driven by a 1½-hp electric motor fed by 24 bichromate batteries. Though the specific weight was a poor 182kg (400lb)/hp, the results were satisfactory. A much better electric airship flew in 1884: La France by Renard and Krebs, with a 9-hp motor weighing 531kg (1,170lb), or 59kg (130lb)/hp. A further great advance came in 1888 when Gottlieb Daimler, pioneer of the petrol engine, saw one of his employees fly Wölfert's first powered airship, on the thrust of a propeller driven by a 2-hp single-cylinder Daimler engine.

In Australia, Lawrence Hargrave had been experimenting with rubber, clockwork and compressed-air motors since 1884, and in 1889 he built (but did not fly) a superb three-cylinder rotary engine fed from a long

BELOW: *This engine was the key to successful powered flight. It was designed by the Wright brothers with their gifted mechanic Charlie Taylor, and built mainly by the latter. It gave about 13 horsepower.*

ABOVE: *The five-cylinder radial engine used in S. P. Langley's Aerodrome. Built by Charles Manley, it was very much ahead of its time in having spark ignition and a carburetted petrol feed.*

FAR RIGHT: *When it burst on a delighted world of aviators in 1907–08 the Gnome appeared the answer to the engine problem. Designed by the French Seguin brothers, it was amazingly light and simple.*

compressed-air bottle intended to fit inside a fuselage. A rotary engine has a fixed crankshaft. Around it cylinders are arranged radially and, together with the crankcase and propeller, they rotate. One advantage was expected to be the ability of one of the cylinders to run at an acceptable temperature merely by having air-cooling fins, without heavy and troublesome water-cooling circuits (though this did not apply to a compressed-air engine, which hardly got warm). So far as is known no heavier-than-air machine ever flew with a compressed-air engine. Whether one flew on steam power is arguable. Sir Hiram Maxim's huge biplane of 1894 was powered by two compound steam engines of very advanced design, each calculated to develop 180hp at the remarkable steam pressure of 22·5kg/cm² (320lb/sq in), and with a specific weight of only 0·70kg (1·55lb)/hp exclusive of the heavy boilers and furnace. Clément Ader's *Eole* of 1890 had a much smaller steam engine, judged in 1960 to have developed 20hp for a net weight (without fuel or water) of only 23kg (51lb).

1900–1910

Undoubtedly the outstanding engine at the turn of the century was that of the American Charles Manley. Far ahead of its time, this was a five-cylinder radial, with carburetted petrol feed (the carburettor's function is to convert the bulk liquid into highly combustible petrol/air vapour) and spark ignition, and cooled by a water circuit. It developed more than 50hp and weighed

only 1·63kg (3·6lb)/hp, but achieved nothing because of the ridiculous launch system of the aircraft, S. P. Langley's *Aerodrome*, in which it was installed.

A contemporary engine was that first built by the Wright brothers. Though this was pedestrian and uninspired by comparison, it has a greater place in history because it powered the first successful aeroplane, the Wright 1903 Flyer. Features included four water-cooled cylinders in line, lying horizontally, fuel carburation by dripping on to a hot surface, and a large flywheel and two gearwheels driving the pusher propellers in opposite directions by chains. The weight was about the same as Manley's engine, 82kg (180lb); the power was said by the Wrights to be 12hp and estimated in 1961 at 'about 13hp'. Chief detail designer and constructor was the Wrights' mechanic, Charles Taylor.

A far more advanced engine was built in France. Léon Levavasseur named his engines (and subsequently his aeroplanes) after a friend's daughter, Antoinette. His first Antoinette engine dated from about 1901, most of the early ones being used in his speedboats. By 1905 a water-cooled vee-8 was in production rated at 50hp and weighing about 50kg (110lb), giving a specific weight of 1·0kg (2·2lb)/hp which was not generally to be surpassed for 25 years. Two features which were ahead of their time were evaporative (steam) cooling and direct fuel injection. These, however, harmed reliability, leaving the main commercial field to a yet more

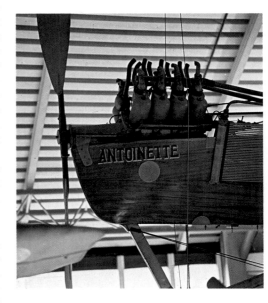

BELOW: *The vee-8 Antoinette engine, designed by Levavasseur, was in fact of more lasting importance than even the Gnome rotaries. Two new features in this engine were evaporative cooling and direct fuel injection.*

revolutionary French engine, the Gnome rotary, designed by the Séguin brothers and first marketed in 1908. This differed in almost every respect from contemporary car engines and from other aero engines either before or since, but it offered a combination of high power/weight ratio and good reliability which no other engine of the day could match.

The first Gnomes had five cylinders, were

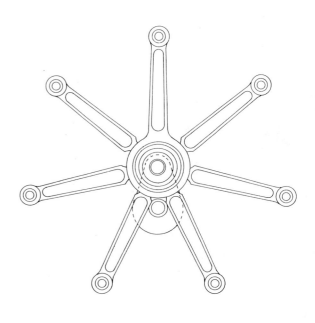

rated at 50hp and weighed 61kg (135lb), a specific weight of 1·22kg (2·7lb)/hp. Each cylinder was expensive, because it began life as a solid forging in special steel which was then machined away to leave a thin-walled cylinder with cooling fins. The carburettor fed mixture through the hollow fixed crankshaft into the crankcase. From here it escaped through spring-loaded valves in the heads of the pistons into the cylinders. After ignition,

ABOVE LEFT: *The dreaded Fokker E (Eindekker) was the first aircraft to go into production with an engine synchronized with a gun.*

ABOVE LEFT: *This Mercedes four-cylinder engine of 1909 started a classic breed.*
ABOVE: *One Mercedes offspring was the six-cylinder Benz Bz.IV, made in thousands.*

the hot gas escaped through valves in the cylinder heads (the closed ends of the cylinders) which were opened at the appropriate times by push rods driven by a fixed cam-ring in the crankcase. Though suffering from fundamental shortcomings, the Gnome rotary gave high power and, with the flywheel effect of the whirling engine, even torque. Furthermore, the rotating finned cylinders were self-cooling. Castor-oil lubricant was added to the fuel so that the combustible mixture passing through the crankcase and over the bearing surfaces obviated the need for a separate lubrication system. Burnt castor oil has a distinctive smell forever associated with these engines, which with designs derived from them made up 80 percent of the engines in World War I before 1917.

World War I

By 1910 more than 70 companies, virtually all of them in Western Europe, were making aero engines. Very few of them, however, saw war service in any numbers, for until 1916 the Gnome rotary dominated in the industry. This was made as the Bentley Rotary B.R.1 in Britain, the Thulin in Sweden and the Oberursel UR.I in Germany. The same basic engine was developed to have nine cylinders and then appeared in a two-row form, virtually two seven-cylinder engines joined together with the rear row 'staggered' by 25·7° so that its cylinders would be cooled by air passing between those of the front row. This two-row cylinder configuration was later to become the dominant form of high-power piston aero engines.

By 1911 the Séguin brothers had produced a different Gnome which attempted to overcome unreliability caused by the malfunctioning of the hot counterweight-operated valve in the head of the piston. In the Gnome Monosoupape (single-valve) the piston had no valve and the mixture escaped from the whirling crankcase into the cylinders via ports in the cylinder walls, uncovered by each piston near the bottom of its stroke. Many thousands of 'Mono' engines served the Allies throughout World War I.

Around 1911 other makers circumvented the Séguin patents by building other rotary engines. In the Le Rhône there were separate inlet and exhaust valves in each cylinder head, cunningly operated by a single rocker and rod which was pushed to open the exhaust valve and pulled to open the inlet valve, admitting mixture supplied through a pipe up the outside as in other engines. The Clerget was similar but had separate push-rods for the two valves in each cylinder head. Thousands of these engines were made between 1913 and 1918, with others by

BELOW: *This nine-cylinder Le Rhône rotary was a descendant of the Gnome.*

ABOVE: *The most powerful Mercedes offshoot was the 375hp Rolls-Royce Eagle vee-12.*

Oberursel, BMW, Goebel and Siemens u. Halske in Germany, Bentley, Allen and other companies in Britain, and ten companies in France and the United States.

One outstanding engine of 1910 was the French Renault vee-8, of 80hp, with air-cooled cylinders and geared drive. It inspired the 90hp, Royal Aircraft Factory (RAF)

engine of 1913. From these were derived vee-8 air-cooled and vee-12 air- and water-cooled engines rated up to 260hp. The Salmson (Canton-Unné) was a unique static radial with water-cooled cylinders, usually made with 9 or 14 cylinders giving from 110 to 240hp. Nearly all German-designed engines were solid, robust and reliable, with six water-cooled cylinders in line; produced with large cylinders, they gave up to 300hp. Makers included Mercedes, Maybach, BMW, Benz and Austro-Daimler. Anzani, whose three-cylinder 20hp engine had powered Blériot's early machines, developed static radial and 'fan' engines with various numbers of cylinders. These could be anything up to 20 (2 radial rows of 10).

To provide Britain with powerful engines of native design, the Admiralty towed the 1914 TT-winning Mercedes car to Rolls-Royce where its engine inspired the Hawk (used in Royal Naval Air Service (RNAS) blimps) as well as the outstanding water-cooled vee-12 Falcon of 190-260hp and Eagle of up to 360hp. Most important of all

How a Piston Engine Works

a *induction stroke* **b** *compression stroke* **c** *combustion stroke* **d** *exhaust stroke*

In about 1850, Etienne Lenoir was developing an engine in which a piston was driven along a cylinder by the pressure of a burning mixture of air and coal-gas. At that time the only engines in common use were steam-driven, where the burning took place not in the cylinder but under a separate boiler. The new gas engine burned its fuel inside the cylinder, and so was called an internal-combustion engine. Compared with steam engines, both pressure and temperature inside the cylinder during the working stroke – the down-stroke of the piston, pushed by expanding gas – were much higher. This meant that the efficiency was greater, more power being developed for a given rate of consumption of fuel. In the petrol (gasoline) engine, developed in about 1880, the pressures and temperatures could rise even higher, particularly in the diesel engine where they were highest of all. Moreover, these newer engines were more useful because, when used in a vehicle, they could carry greater amounts of their liquid fuel.

In all these engines the basic principle is that a mixture of fuel and air is burned in a closed space, generating hot gas under high pressure. The expanding gas pushes down a piston, which via a connecting rod and crank turns a shaft. As the shaft continues to rotate, the crank and connecting rod then return the piston to the top of the cylinder. In the most common type of petrol engine, the form of more than 99 per cent of all aircraft piston engines, the piston makes only one working stroke in every four strokes, two up and two down. This is therefore called the four-stroke cycle, or

Otto cycle after the engineer who originally developed it.

On the first stroke (the induction stroke) the piston is pulled down by the crank, drawing in fresh fuel/air mixture through the open inlet valve. Near the limit of the piston's travel (called bottom dead centre), the inlet valve is closed by the mechanism which links the valves to the rotating crankshaft. The rotating crank then pushes the piston back up the cylinder on the second stroke (the compression stroke), squeezing the mixture into a small space (the clearance volume) at the top of the cylinder. Here it is ignited by a sparking plug, a device supplied with pulses of high-voltage electricity to make hot sparks at the appropriate moments. The mixture instantly begins to burn at the sparking plug, and the flame expands very quickly in a spherical shape (in the way a ripple grows on a pond, but in three dimensions) until it has consumed the whole mixture. Though the combustion is fast, it is not the same as an explosion. Sometimes, because of hot spots of carbon in the cylinder or the use of inferior fuel, the whole mixture ignites more or less at once. This is called detonation, or knocking and, because it results in excessive temperatures and violent pressures, it can soon cause severe damage. With proper combustion the whole mixture burns smoothly and cleanly. The hot gas does not damage the piston or cylinder, but its very high pressure imparts a large force on the top of the piston, pushing it down on the third stroke, the working stroke. Near the bottom of this stroke, the valve gear opens the exhaust valve so that the hot gas begins to escape. On the

fourth (upward) stroke, the exhaust stroke, nearly all the gas is expelled by the rising piston.

In most engines several cylinders are used to give smoother running with more frequent working strokes. There are many ways in which the cylinders can be arranged. Today the most common engines for light aircraft are of the horizontally opposed type – the flat-twin, flat-four or flat-six – with horizontal 'pots' (cylinders) on the left and right sides of the central crankcase. The opposing cylinders are often not quite aligned, so that their connecting rods can work side-by-side on the same crankpin. If they are in line, one conrod has to have a Y-shaped end to fit on each side of its partner. In the higher power ranges, the radial is the preferred arrangement, with the cylinders disposed like spokes of a wheel around a central crankcase. There may be five, seven or nine cylinders, one of which will drive a master rod to which all the others are pivoted. For even more power, the two-row (in the pre-jet era, even the four-row) radial is necessary, with the second-row cylinders behind the gaps between the front-row cylinders. This is to improve cooling, because all modern radials have cylinders cooled by air flowing between deep, close-spaced fins which provide a large surface area over which to dissipate the excess heat. Nearly all light aircraft engines are also air-cooled, but today a few water-cooled engines, such as are fitted to most cars, are becoming popular for some small aircraft and helicopters. Water cooling can make an engine quieter, and some engineers claim that it can make it more

efficient. Conversely, such engines need a system of water pipes and a radiator which adds to bulk, weight and possibly drag, and which can leak. Air-cooled engines are generally considered to be superior when operating in conditions of extreme cold or extreme heat.

Not unnaturally, it does not suffice merely to pipe petrol or other fuel from the tank to the cylinder. For a petrol engine to run properly it must be supplied with a perfect mixture of about 15 parts of air by weight to 1 of fuel (about 9,000:1 by volume), and this needs either a carburettor or a fuel injection system. The carburettor measures a small, steady flow of fuel and allows it to mix with the flow of air entering the inlet manifold which ducts the mixture to the cylinders. A fuel-injection system measures the engine's exact needs and supplies extremely small doses of fuel to each cylinder in turn. In general, a fuel-rich mixture is used at take-off and a lean, or weak, mixture for economical running in cruising flight. The pilot can control the mixture in some engines, while in others it is adjusted automatically. As an aircraft climbs, air density decreases and so the amount of fuel supplied has to be decreased in proportion. Engines needing high power at high altitudes are supercharged by a fan which is driven by the engine at several times crankshaft speed in order to blow extra air into the cylinders. Other gears drive the valves, and in many engines the propeller is turned more slowly than the crankshaft by a reduction gear, because it may be more efficient and quieter to use a bigger propeller turning at reduced speed.

LEFT: *Pratt & Whitney built 35,000 Wasps in
35 years (1926–60). This one came off the line in
1935. Thousands are still in use.*
BELOW: *The DH Canada Otter is a utility transport
flying on Wasp power.*
BOTTOM: *Another classic US engine was the Wright
Cyclone which strove to take over from the British
Jupiter as No 1 in the world.*

Allied engines was the American Liberty, designed for the US Army by a team led by the chief engineers of Packard and Hall-Scott in the first three months of America's participation in the war. The Liberty was designed to give 400hp and to be mass-produced with interchangeable parts. A water-cooled vee-12, it had separate cylinders and direct drive, and was of extremely simple design.

Swiss Marc Birkigt, chief engineer of a Spanish car company, designed a number of Hispano-Suiza products (including a famed aircraft cannon), among them the outstanding water-cooled vee-8 and vee-12 engines made in vast numbers in France, Britain and the United States. The later geared Hispanos were troublesome, and the RAF S.E.5a scout finally did well with a British development, the direct-drive Wolseley Viper. Curtiss in the United States supplied the OX–5 water-cooled vee-8 rated at 90hp for the JN–4 trainer, and in Italy the Fiat A–20 vee-12 and Isotta-Fraschini were important water-cooled types.

The 1920s
By the 1918 Armistice, the rotary had become outmoded, and refined engines of between 300 and 400hp were in production. Geared drives were becoming common, especially for bigger aircraft, to enable large-diameter propellers to turn more slowly, while the engine speed was increased to give greater power (power is force multiplied by speed). Much more advanced carburettors, able to

maintain the correct mixture strength for all powers and altitudes were also in use. Experiments began with variable-pitch propellers and with greatly improved cooling systems, using air or water, which instead of adding to drag actually increased propulsive thrust. Early engines were started by 'swinging the propeller', a dangerous and arduous task which was especially difficult with large aircraft and seaplanes. Electric starters began to appear, as did gas starting, in which the cylinders were pumped in sequence with fuel-rich mixture from a unit installed in the aircraft; this looked like a motor-cycle engine, one half actually being an engine and the other a pump. Much greater attention was paid to reducing weight and improving reliability, with strict control of material specifications, surface finish and fatigue properties.

Few wartime engines survived the need for long and reliable use. Liberty 12 engines were an exception, and so were German BMW and Junkers water-cooled six-in-lines. The British RAF 8a turned into the Siddeley (later Armstrong Siddeley) Jaguar, a small-diameter two-row radial with 14 cylinders rated at between 400 and 450hp and soon to appear with geared drive and supercharger. The Napier Lion had three banks of four water-cooled cylinders spaced at 60° in the W or broad-arrow configuration, and served reliably at around 450hp in large aircraft. Designed at Cosmos, the Bristol Jupiter was planned as a powerful and simple nine-cylinder radial, with four valves per cylinder,

and began life in 1920 at a little over 400hp. The Aircraft Disposal Co (ADC) produced engines using up some of the thousands of surplus Renault and RAF parts, and Frank Halford split this vee-8 in half to produce the Cirrus, weighing 122kg (268lb) and rated at 80hp, to give the first reliable lightplane engine. Its four upright cylinders were air-cooled. From it was evolved a completely fresh design, produced for de Havilland and called the Gipsy. Towards the end of the 1920s this was inverted, the cylinders hanging down to give the pilot a better view, under the name Gipsy Major. Rated at 130hp, it was the pre-eminent lightplane engine of the 1930s.

Rolls-Royce gradually came back in the 1920s with the Condor, designed in 1918 as a scaled-up Eagle with four-valve cylinders. In 1922 it was redesigned and a small number, producing 650 to 670hp, was used in heavy aircraft and airships. Lorraine, Hispano-Suiza and Farman in France continued with high-power water-cooled engines; the German Junkers L.5 and BMW.VI carried on the tradition of six-in-line engines of robust and reliable type; and several makers struggled in Italy. Most American engines were air-cooled, an outstanding series being the Wright Whirlwind radials which began with seven cylinders at 220hp and soon included five- and nine-cylinder models rated at 140 and 300hp respectively. The seven-cylinder model gained fame with Lindbergh's Atlantic crossing in 1927. Two years earlier, a group of engineers had left

BELOW: *The Schneider Trophy exerted a powerful influence on engine design by making designers concentrate on sheer speed. This made a streamlined-looking nose appear all-important, leading from the Curtiss V-1500 (D-12) in the Curtiss R3C (a) via the Rolls-Royce R in the S-6B (b) to the Fiat AS.6 in the Macchi 72 (c). Yet the air-cooled radial eventually proved superior for all uses.*

BOTTOM AND RIGHT: *These drawings of a Pratt & Whitney Wasp show basic features of a simple aircooled radial. Air is drawn in through a carburettor, where petrol vapour is added, and then compressed by the super-charger before being admitted to each of the nine cylinders in sequence. Only one cylinder is shown in the side view, driving the master connecting rod to which the rods from the other cylinders are pivoted.*

Wright to found Pratt & Whitney Aircraft; their completely new design, materializing as the Wasp, ran on Christmas Eve, 1925. Its fresh and skilled design soon put this 400hp engine into the forefront of US naval and military pursuit (fighter) markets, and began the world's biggest production of aero engines. By 1930 Wright had produced the outstanding new R–1820 Cyclone (1,820 cu in displacement: the piston area multiplied by the number of pistons, multiplied by the piston stroke from bottom to top dead centre). Pratt & Whitney was meanwhile producing the R–1340 Wasp and R–1690 Hornet, available with geared drive and super-charger. These swept away the big 800hp, water-cooled Packard and 650hp Curtiss Conqueror, the last early water-cooled engines in the United States.

This was remarkable because, in 1921, the Curtiss D–12 water-cooled vee-12 had led all other American engines and won the Schneider Trophy in 1923. Rated at 440–475hp, it could be installed, unlike almost all its rivals, in a streamlined, pointed nose. Fairey used it in the Fox bomber (faster than contemporary British fighters) and made the D–12 as the Felix. For the 1925 Schneider race the Curtiss gave 600hp, but was beaten by boosted Fiat engines, which in turn were beaten by a racing version of the Napier Lion giving 875hp for a specific weight of 0·48kg (1·06lb)/hp. To beat the D–12, Rolls-Royce produced the F, later named Kestrel, as a trim water-cooled upright vee-12 giving 480 to 525hp. An important feature was that

each block of six cylinders was a single light-alloy casting, with a separate casting bolted on top containing the heads and valve gear. A larger relative was the Buzzard of 825hp. The Schneider Trophy races gave increasing impetus to the push towards higher powers and higher stresses, and led to revolutionary changes in supercharging, cooling and the type of fuel used.

ABOVE: *Typical piston arrangements. (a) Clerget nine-cylinder rotary, mass-produced in World War I, but representing a dying species. (b) DH Gipsy Major inverted four in-line aircooled, designed in the 1920s for the first private-owner light aircraft. (c) Turbo-Compound 18-cylinder two-row radial with three exhaust turbines, an extremely complex and efficient engine representing the pinnacle of the piston-engine art around 1950. (d) Rolls-Royce Merlin liquid-cooled vee-12 (front view), typical of World War II engines. (e) Continental 10-360 'flat six' aircooled, typical of the final families of aircraft piston engines still being made.*

explodes almost spontaneously throughout its whole bulk, causing excessive heat and a violent mechanical shock. Eventually, in 1930, the US Army Air Corps issued a specification for '87-octane' fuel (100-octane having anti-knock properties equal to those of a reference fuel, iso-octane), with an allowed small proportion of an anti-knock additive, Tetra-Ethyl Lead (TEL). At first TEL caused fouling of sparking plugs and corroded exhaust valves, but designers learned to make engines which could live with 'leaded' fuel. Over the remaining years of the high-power piston engine, the fuel was to be at least as important to power as was the engine itself.

Another major development concerned supercharging. Due to falling atmospheric density, engines draw progressively smaller masses of air into their cylinders as the aircraft climbs. To keep mixture strength correct, the fuel flow must therefore be reduced in proportion, thus reducing the power. A 500hp engine would give only 250hp at 6,688m (22,000ft) and less than 125hp at 12,160m (40,000ft). Various types of supercharger were experimented with in World War I to force in more air and maintain power. The favoured type was the centrifugal blower, geared up to run faster than the crankshaft. Rateau of France was the only company in production with a supercharger by 1918. Sanford Moss at General Electric (GE) in the USA tried the difficult task of driving the supercharger with a turbine spun by the white-hot exhaust gas. This increased not only power but also efficiency through the extraction of what otherwise would have been wasted energy.

Fuel and supercharger development enabled Britain in 1931 to win permanently the Schneider Trophy. From the Rolls-Royce Buzzard was developed the R racing engine, with higher compression ratio and much bigger gear-driven supercharger. Whereas the Buzzard gave about 825hp, the R gave 1,545hp on its first run in May 1929, using a fuel comprising 78 per cent benzol, 22 per cent light gasoline (petrol) plus a little TEL. By September 1929 the power was 1,900hp at 2,900rpm, at a boost pressure of 0·86kg/cm² (12·25lb/sq in) above atmospheric pressure. In this case the supercharger was being used not to maintain power at altitude but to increase it at sea level, the most severe test of any engine. For the 1931 race the power reached 2,360hp at 3,200rpm, using 30 per cent benzol, 60 per cent methanol and 10 per cent acetone, plus a little TEL. For an attack on the world speed record the sprint version gave 2,783hp, which for a weight of 740kg (1,630lb) achieved the incredible ratio of 0·266kg (0·586lb)/hp. This work facilitated the design of the Merlin, a slightly smaller engine of 1,650cu in which began life at 990hp in 1936 but gave 1,300hp with specially imported 100-octane fuel in the Battle of Britain..

During the 1930s Wright increased the power of the R-1820 Cyclone from 500 to 1,200hp by engineering refinement and by developing the ability to run on 100-octane fuel. In parallel came the R-2600 Cyclone 14-cylinder two-row engine, of 1,300-1,900

Throughout the heyday of the aircraft piston engine, from 1914 to 1950, there were heated arguments over which type was best. The broadest subdivision was into the water-cooled in-line (which included vee and other in-line arrangements) and the air-cooled radial. On balance, most of the advantages lay with the latter. It made more economical use of material, was cheaper to build, needed no heavy and complex cooling system, and for the same reason offered higher reliability. Installed in a fighter, its much shorter length improved the aircraft's power of manoeuvre. As the cooling needed no water, the air-cooled engine could work perfectly in the coldest climates; and it could also work much better in the hottest regions, because the cylinders could still dissipate their heat easily to the air, whereas the difference in temperature between the hot water and the air was much less. The installed weight was usually very much less, even though the weights of bare engines of equal power might not be very different.

The one advantage the water-cooled engine did have was that it often looked more streamlined, but even this was usually misleading because one had to take into account the drag of the cooling radiator. (Later, by about 1940, designers learned how to make both air-cooled and liquid-cooled engines have 'negative cooling drag' – in other words, to gain forward thrust from the cooling airflow.) It so happens that, during the crucial 1930s, aircraft designers achieved higher speeds with liquid-cooled

engines, but this was simply because they did not at that time know how to install the air-cooled radial engines properly. When they found out, such fighters as the Vought Corsair, the first in America to reach 645km/h (400mph), Republic Thunderbolt (the fastest piston-engined fighter, in one version), Focke-Wulf 190 and Hawker Tempest (faster with a radial) at last set the record straight. Today, the world piston-engine speed record has for many years been held by an aircraft with an air-cooled radial engine.

1930-39

Since World War I it had been recognized that the aviation piston engine, because it was run so hard, would be a leader in the fight to find fuels less prone to detonation or 'knocking'. This is a condition in which, if an engine is run at too high a compression ratio or at too high a power, the mixture in the cylinders does not burn evenly over a period of a few thousandths of a second, but hp, and the 18-cylinder R–3350 Duplex Cyclone rated at 1,750hp in 1939 and ultimately to give more than twice as much. Rival Pratt & Whitney concentrated on the R–1830 Twin Wasp, with two rows each having seven Wasp-size cylinders. Allison Division of General Motors boldly schemed a vee-12 of modern design with liquid cooling, the V–1710 (vee, 1,710cu in), which, like the Merlin, was cooled not by water but by a mixture of water and ethylene glycol, giving lower freezing point, higher boiling point and a smaller and lighter radiator and cooling system. Hispano-Suiza was pre-eminent among French liquid-cooled engine manufacturers, with the 12Y series rated at 860 to 1,000hp and made in the Soviet Union as well as other countries. German designers concentrated on inverted-vee 12-cylinder engines with direct fuel injection, a system at first regarded as complex and costly but which ultimately came to dominate over the traditional carburettor with its float chamber prohibiting inverted operation and a choke tube prone to icing. Daimler-Benz produced the DB600 of around 690hp in 1935 and the 1,000hp DB601 three years later. Junkers produced the similarly powered and timed Jumo 210 and 211 in addition to a series of economical but weighty two-stroke diesels having six double-ended cylinders fed in the centre and driving crankshafts along the top and bottom of a strangely thin and flat-sided engine. These were the only aircraft diesels made in large numbers, despite the widespread belief that the diesel's fuel economy and ability to burn cheap oil fuel would commend it for long-range use.

Among air-cooled radials the Jupiter had been dominant in the 1920s, being license-produced in every country possessing an aircraft industry and flying in 229 types of aircraft. From it were developed two even more important engines, the short-stroke Mercury of 550 to 950hp for fast aircraft and the Pegasus, which was the same size as the Jupiter, but greatly refined and ultimately giving powers in excess of 1,000hp. Roy Fedden, the Bristol chief engineer, could find no simple way to make a two-row radial with four valves per cylinder, but after many years of heartbreak perfected a new radial family with sleeve valves: the traditional poppet valve was eliminated and replaced by an oscillating thin-walled sleeve interposed between the piston and cylinder, with ports in the sleeve intermittently lining up with inlet or exhaust ports in the walls of the cylinder. The first sleeve-valve engines were the 900hp Mercury-sized Perseus, the 500hp Aquila, the 14-cylinder two-row Taurus of 1,000hp and the 14-cylinder Hercules of around 1,400hp.

By 1937 the desperate need to increase production led to the Mercury being selected for 'shadow production' by a consortium of car firms, and soon the Hercules was to follow suit. Napier made unusual air-cooled engines with four banks of cylinders in H configuration, the most powerful being the 24-cylinder Dagger of 1,000hp. In France Gnome-Rhône made Jupiters, sidestepped Bristol patents with engines having only two

BELOW: *The pre-eminent aero engine of 1920–35 was the Bristol Jupiter, which in the early 1930s developed into the Pegasus, shown here.*

BELOW LEFT: *America's last liquid-cooled engine was the Allison V-1710.*
BELOW RIGHT: *This 1,000 hp DB 600 led to many inverted vee-12 engines for the Luftwaffe.*
BOTTOM: *Over 150,000 Rolls-Royce Merlins were built in World War II.*

valves per cylinder and went into production with the 14-cylinder two-row Mistral Major of 900hp in 1931. In Germany the BMW Hornet (Pratt & Whitney) was developed into the 132 of 1,000hp, while Bramo (later merged into BMW) built the similar 323 Fafnir.

World War II

The demands of war were for ever-higher power and mass-production of established engines, two objectives in conflict. The Rolls-Royce Merlin was developed with two-stage mechanically driven supercharger and intercooler to double its power at high altitude, and both Rolls and American Packard V–1650 versions were rated at over 2,000hp on 115/145-grade fuel by 1945. The X-layout Vulture was a failure, but the Griffon of 2,239cu in went into production for fighters and remains in use to the present day in the Avro Shackleton. The Hercules likewise exceeded 2,000hp, and was joined by the 18-cylinder Centaurus of 3,270cu in Britain's most powerful piston engine. It powered many fighters and large aircraft, and also remains in use. The Hercules and Merlin were the leading British wartime engines, available in vast numbers as standard 'power eggs' needing no special installation design (for example, either could fit the Lancaster, Halifax or Beaufighter). Britain's other high-power engine was the 2,200hp Napier Sabre, which had 24 liquid-cooled sleeve-valve cylinders arranged in flat-H form.

In the United States, sleeve valves did not reach production, the effort going into gigantic output of refined but established engines. In terms of horsepower manufactured per month, the leading engine was the Pratt & Whitney R–2800 Double Wasp, a superb 18-cylinder unit of 1,800 to 2,800hp and used in large numbers for military and civil aircraft right up to the present day (Canadair CL–215 fire-patrol amphibians and de Havilland Canada Caribou transports). Even larger numbers were made of the R–1830 Twin Wasp, used in the Consolidated B–24 Liberator with turbochargers, and the Wright R–1820 Cyclone, turbocharged for the Boeing B–17. The biggest US engine was the Wright R–3350, with two turbochargers per engine in the Boeing B–29. At the end of the war came the monster Pratt & Whitney R–4360 Wasp Major, with four rows each of seven cylinders, for which 115/145-grade fuel was created; it gave more than 3,000hp from the outset.

Little of note was done by Italy, Japan or the Soviet Union, though all conducted a vast amount of development work. Germany, however, produced the outstanding BMW 801 radial of about 2,000hp; the Daimler-Benz DB603 and 605; the Junkers Jumo 211 and 213 inverted-vee-12 engines, often as power eggs interchangeable with radials; and a wealth of unsuccessful double DB engines and complex prototypes intended to give much greater power at altitude. Piston engines since World War II are discussed later. (See pp. 69–71.)

engine is a turbojet, and one eventually ran in April 1937 after Whittle had spent years trying to interest the Air Ministry and private industry. But much earlier, in 1926, A. A. Griffith had begun to study a gas turbine geared down to a propeller, forming a direct successor to the piston engine and intended to give higher power and greater aircraft performance. After even greater delays this led to the test of a compressor in 1937 at Metropolitan-Vickers Ltd. This compressor was of the axial type, in which numerous rows of radial blades rotate like multi-blade propellers between interleaved rows of fixed stator blades; as in steam turbines the air under compression flows axially parallel to the shaft. After unnecessary delays amount-

Early gas turbines

Gas turbines had been considered for aircraft propulsion since long before the Wright Brothers, but the first to propose a practical scheme was Sir Frank Whittle who, as a cadet in 1928, suggested using such an engine purely to discharge a propulsive jet. The engine he proposed comprised an air compressor delivering to a combustion chamber where fuel – usually of a kerosene type – was continuously burned at constant pressure to deliver a steady flow of hot gas to drive a turbine connected to the compressor. Except for that extracted by the turbine, all energy in the jet was used to propel the engine by direct reaction, the hot gas being accelerated through a suitably profiled nozzle. Such an

ing to more than 11 years, this work led to the Metrovick F.2 Beryl turbojet, first run in December 1941 and used to power a Gloster Meteor twin-jet in November 1943.

From the outset Whittle chose to use the centrifugal type of compressor. Such a compressor resembles a disc carrying curved radial vanes on its face (on both sides, in Whittle's engines, to handle twice the airflow), spun at very high speed. Air is ducted to the centre of the compressor, from where it is flung outwards between the vanes by centrifugal force. The air leaves the periphery of the compressor moving at extremely high speed, and this high speed is then converted into high pressure by slowing the air down in an expanding duct called a diffuser.

The centrifugal compressor, which is the usual kind of blower used in a vacuum cleaner, has the advantage of being robust, resistant to damage and relatively cheap to make.

In contrast, the axial compressor is usually made of hundreds of costly parts, and is also more likely to be damaged (for example, by the ingestion of stones or lumps of ice). At first, designers often tended to shrink from the axial compressor because it was technically more difficult, but for supersonic aircraft it was essential because the fat centrifugal type had too much frontal area for any given engine thrust.

A few early designers used radial-flow turbines, which work rather like a centri-

How a Gas Turbine Works

Section through a typical turbojet engine
(a) Front bearing (b) Inlet guide vanes
(c) Compressor blades (d) Stator blade

(e) Diffuser section (f) Centre bearing
(g) Fuel spray manifold
(h) Combustion chamber

(i) Rear bearing (j) Turbine guide
(k) Two-stage turbine blade
(l) Exhaust duct

Most heat engines work by compressing a fluid – air, steam, combustible mixture or hot gas – and heating it; then it is allowed to expand, giving up energy to do useful work. In piston aero engines, the process is conducted in a series of oscillating cycles, giving an intermittent output. The gas turbine, on the other hand, operates continuously and gives a steady output. Apart from this, it operates in principle very like the piston engine, and it runs on air heated by having fuel burned in it to produce a flow of hot gas. It is also based on a rotating shaft, but in the simplest form of gas turbine this shaft merely transmits power inside the engine, and does not directly play a part in propelling the aircraft.

In the simplest gas turbine the shaft drives a compressor, which draws in fresh air and delivers it under pressure. The compressor may be of many forms, but nearly all aircraft gas turbines use either an axial or a centrifugal type. The axial has the form of a cylindrical drum, spinning at high speed. Around it project hundreds of blades, in size perhaps comparable to a playing-card, each of which is curved like a miniature wing. The spinning rotor is encased in a tight-fitting casing, from the inside of which stationary, or stator, blades project in rows interspersed with the moving blades, on the rotor. Altogether there may be as many as 1,000 blades, arranged in radial rows which are alternately fixed and moving. Air enters at one end of the compressor and is compressed by each stage of fixed and moving blades in succession, finally being delivered at the high-pressure end at a pressure up to 20 or even 30 times that of the surrounding atmosphere. The axial is tricky to perfect, and costly to build, but it has a small frontal area and extremely high performance. The rival centrifugal is simple and cheap, and less prone to damage, but seldom can it compress the airflow more than five to nine times; it also has a large frontal area. A centrifugal compressor comprises a spinning disc with radially arranged guide-vanes which accept the airflow near the centre and fling it off at high speed around the edge. The surrounding casing and ducting, called the diffuzer, slow the air down and turn the kinetic energy of its speed into pressure. Today, centrifugal compressors are favoured for the engines of light aircraft and small helicopters, while axials are preferred for transports and military aircraft.

From the compressor, the flow of hot, compressed air enters the combustion chamber where liquid fuel or fuel vapour is sprayed in and burned. The result is a steady flow of extremely hot gas, moving at high velocity and at a white heat which would soften or melt most materials. It passes first through a ring of fixed turbine/nozzle guide-vanes, or stator blades, made of special alloy which stays strong even when white hot. These direct the gas on to a row of

curved blades (often called 'buckets' in North America) fixed around the periphery of a disc in a similar way to the radial blades of an axial compressor. The disc and blades form the turbine rotor, and the centre of the disc is fixed to a shaft coupling it to the compressor, the whole being freely running in ball bearings, which are able to resist endloads, and roller bearings. The usual form of a turbine is of the impulse/reaction type, the blades being pushed round partly by the aerodynamic force (as if they were miniature wings) and partly by the change in momentum of the high-speed gas as its direction is changed by the curved blades.

This is the sum total of basic elements needed to make a gas turbine. Of course there is a bit more to it. The bearings have to be carefully designed to stand up to extremely high speeds, high temperatures and small errors of alignment or vibration. The compressor, combustion chamber and turbine must be linked by small air-gaps or pipes to provide high-pressure cooling air to the hottest parts, especially the turbine nozzles, rotor disc and, above all, the vital rotor blades. It was the lack of a material capable of withstanding the enormous loads imposed on the rotor blades at the high temperature of the gas flow which held back the gas turbine for many years. As in all heat engines, efficiency of a gas turbine is improved by running it hotter, but in the early jet engines the blades softened and stretched under the colossal centrifugal loads, or else broke off at the roots. Gradually, special high-nickel alloys were developed which remained strong even when almost white hot – between 1950 and 1977 the gas temperature of advanced engines rose from 810°C (1,490°F) to more than 1,300°C (2,372°F), equivalent in round figures to four times the power for twice the fuel consumption. Thus, specific fuel consumption – unit weight of fuel burned per unit force of thrust per hour, the best measure of efficiency – has been halved. In recent years great advances have been made in

the development of air-cooled rotor blades, containing complex air-cooling systems which keep the metal several hundred degrees cooler than the surrounding gas. They are made of 'directionally solidified' material which, in effect, makes the 'grain' in the metal's molecular structure run along the length of the blade instead of randomly or across it. Other features of a practical gas turbine include gear-driven accessories – at the very least a fuel pump, a control system to match the fuel supply to the engine's needs, and a starter to bring the engine up to the self-sustaining speed at which, when the fuel supply is turned on and ignited, the engine will continue to run.

This basic engine can be called a gas-producer; in some engines it is called the core, because it lies in the centre. But it can propel aircraft with the addition of nothing more than a suitable jetpipe and nozzle to convert as much as possible of the energy in the gas jet into propulsive thrust. Such an engine is a turbojet, and it is the simplest useful gas turbine. In the turbojet the turbine extracts from the gas flow only enough energy to drive the compressor. Turbojets are light and relatively cheap, but at low speeds have high fuel consumption. Because their propulsive jet has a high velocity they are noisy, and they are best suited to short-duration missiles and targets, sporting aircraft and trainers. They are also suitable for supersonic aircraft, but the need for high thrust and small frontal area can be better met by adding a reheat jetpipe or afterburner behind a turbojet in order to give increased thrust. This solution, however, carries the penalty of moderate increases in weight and cost and severe increases in fuel consumption and noise.

An afterburner is a swollen jetpipe in which extra fuel is burned. As there is no turbine to worry about, the gas can be raised to extremely high temperature, so that it issues as a supersonic jet in which glowing 'shock diamonds' are visible, marking the reflections of internal shock-

waves from the junction of the jet with the surrounding air. An afterburner needs a nozzle of increased area and convergent/divergent profile. Usually the afterburner is used only at take-off and for supersonic flight, so that at other times its fuel supply is switched off and the nozzle is closed down and changed in shape to suit unaugmented operation.

For subsonic aircraft the propulsive efficiency can be increased by making the gas generator (core) accelerate a much larger airflow, but more gently. This has the added benefits of reducing specific fuel consumption and greatly abating noise. One way of achieving this is to make the compressor bigger. Some of the air it delivers is then ducted straight to a propelling nozzle, which usually surrounds the core and blankets the hot jet, reducing noise still further. In modern transport aircraft the best arrangement is to use a separate Low-Pressure (LP) compressor, as described in the text, handling five to eight times the core airflow (i.e., with a by-pass ratio of 5 to 8). Intermediate forms of engine, with a by-pass ratio of about 1, are called by-pass jets and are used in modern combat aircraft.

All these engines need extra turbine power, obtained by adding extra stages on the turbine rotor(s). Another solution is to use this extra turbine power to drive a traditional gear and propeller. In this case the engine then becomes a turboprop.

Another kind of gas turbine is the turboshaft, in which the extra turbine power is taken to a gearbox through which an output shaft drives the rotor system of a helicopter (or a heavy road vehicle, train or ship). The fuel system is arranged in all these engines so as automatically to match the flow of fuel to the load on the output shaft. To prolong blade life, the fuel flow in most gas turbines is normally governed to keep the turbine temperature at less than the permitted maximum, but to allow it to be raised to the limit in case of sudden emergency (such as failure of another engine).

engines this gave terrible problems. Nobody had ever released heat at such a rate in such a small space, and engineers found it impossible to stop the thin sheet chambers from cracking and burning up. Some engines had tubular chambers, each with its own fuel burner(s) and inner flame tube, while others adopted the annular arrangement in which combustion occupies a continuous chamber wrapped around the engine. Today the annular type is dominant.

In Germany Pabst von Ohain did not begin turbojet study until 1935, but had the good fortune to interest Ernst Heinkel, who was able both to finance an engine and fly it in an aircraft, far sooner than the bitterly divided and frustrated British. The HeS 1 (not a practical engine, fed by hydrogen gas) ran in March 1937. The wholly practical HeS 3B ran at 500kg (1,100lb) thrust in 1939, and powered the world's first turbojet aircraft, the He 178, on 27 August of that year; it weighed some 363kg (800lb). Heinkel flew a twin-jet fighter, the He 280, with two HeS 8A engines, on 5 April 1941, but this work eventually came to nothing. Of potentially greater significance were the axial turbojets developed by BMW, Bramo and Junkers from 1938. By 1944 the BMW 003A was in mass-production at 800kg (1,760lb) thrust and the Junkers Jumo 004B in mass-production at 900kg (1,980lb). Though handicapped by poor materials, these were slim, simple and extremely useful axial engines which were made at rates more than 40 times greater than any of the Allied engines.

Apart from a wealth of more advanced turbojet, fan and turboprop developments, the Germans also produced aircraft rocket engines. The Walter company flew a rocket of 500kg (1,100lb) thrust in the He 176 in June 1939 and were in production with the HWK 509 engine, running on concentrated hydrogen peroxide and a mixture of methanol and hydrazine hydrate, in 1944. Fitted to the Me 163B interceptor, this engine was rated at 200 to 1,700kg (440 to 3,750lb) thrust at all heights. In 1941 an earlier version drove a prototype Me 163 at over 1,000 km/h (620mph), a speed never before reached by man.

After intense bickering, Whittle's outstanding work eventually bore fruit in the work of three companies, Power Jets, BTH and Rover, who tried not to collaborate but were eventually goaded into getting the W.1 engine, of 386kg (850lb) thrust, into the air in the Gloster E.28/39 in May 1941. Much happier work by Halford's team at de Havilland led to the H.1 (Goblin), and two

TOP LEFT: *The Walter 109–506 series of liquid-propellent rockets of World War II were the first to power piloted aircraft.*
TOP RIGHT: *Most famous of many aircraft powered by Walter 509-series rockets was the Me 163B Schwalbe tailless interceptor.*
CENTRE: *Whittle's pioneer original engine in its final much-rebuilt form, photographed in 1944. It is today in Washington.*
ABOVE: *First aircraft to fly with the Whittle engine, the Gloster E.28/39 proved a valuable aircraft. Two were built and flew intensively for four years (one crashed, one survives).*

fugal compressor in reverse, but today the axial-flow turbine is almost universal. Most gas turbines are of the combined impulse/reaction type, the turbine rotor being spun partly by the momentum of the hot gas hitting the blades (called 'buckets' in the United States) at high speed, and partly by the pressure variation of the flow round the blades like that round a wing which gives lift. But between the compressor and turbine comes the combustion system, and in early of these, then rated at 680kg (1,500lb) each, powered the first Meteor in March 1943. But before this, in October 1942, the dynamic Americans had learned of Whittle's work, Americanized the W.2B as the GE (Schenectady) I–A of 590kg (1,300lb) thrust, and flown two in the Bell XP–59A. The Goblin powered de Havilland's own fighter, the Vampire, in September 1943, and the outstanding American Lockheed XP–80 Shooting Star in January 1944.

Gas-turbine programmes had been started in the United States before General H. H. Arnold imported the Whittle technology in May 1941. After much study in 1940, the NACA Army Air Corps and Navy set up the Durand Committee in February 1941 which recommended three engines: the Allis-Chalmers turbofan, which did not materialize, the GE (Lynn) XT31 turboprop and the Westinghouse 19A small axial turbojet, both of which were produced. Pratt & Whitney, like others in Europe, was trying to perfect a compound engine comprising a free-piston diesel feeding gas to a turboprop.

Other early gas turbines included the Japanese Ne-series axial turbojets, Swedish Lysholm turbojets and turboprops, Italian Caproni-Campini projects (the CC–1 jet aircraft was powered by a piston-engine driving a compressor) and French work which included a turbojet by Rateau, a turboprop by SOCEMA and a small turbo-shaft engine by Turboméca. The turboshaft engine is a turbojet fitted with one or more turbine stages whose function is to extract as much energy as possible from the gas flow, making it available at a high-speed drive shaft (coupled, for example, to a helicopter gearbox). The turboprop is similar but incorporates a gearbox driving a slow-speed output shaft matched to a suitable propeller which provides nearly all the propulsive thrust, especially at slow flight speeds. The turbofan is an intermediate between the turboprop and turbojet, and can have various forms. Today, virtually all have a front fan in the form of a large-diameter multi-bladed axial compressor functioning as a propeller (its inner portions also super-charging the core engine or gas generator which provides the power). Some early turbofans, often then called 'ducted fans', had the fan arranged at the rear, sometimes with double-deck blades around the original turbine and sometimes, as in the Metrovick F.3 and F.5, as a separate unit added behind a turbojet.

Turbojets of the 1950s

In October 1940, a production order was placed for 160 Power Jets W.2B engines for 80 Meteor fighters per month, but the British effort was so badly directed (despite great work by Mond Nickel on special turbine alloys and by Lucas on combustion problems) that progress was slow until the Power Jets/ BTH/Rover responsibility was passed to Rolls-Royce in December 1942. Thereafter Power Jets did research only, and Rolls-Royce at last got the British programme moving. The Meteor F.1 with Rolls-Royce Welland turbojets of 772kg (1,700lb) thrust entered service in June 1944, the F.3 with

907kg (2,000lb) Derwent Is in December 1944 and the F.4 with 1,588kg (3,500lb) Derwent 5s in 1948, three years after a Mk 4 had gained the world speed record at 975 km/h (606mph). All these were pure Whittle-formula engines, with a double-sided centri-fugal compressor, a large-diameter diffuser to convert air velocity to pressure and turn the air through 90°, a surrounding array of separate combustion chambers (cans) and a single-stage turbine. In September 1945 a Meteor flew with Derwents fitted with reduction gears driving small propellers (this first turboprop was called the Trent). Derwents rated at 1,634kg (3,600lb) thrust remained in production until 1955. An enlarged engine, the Nene of 2,270kg (5,000 lb) thrust, flew in a Lockheed XP–80 in July 1945. This powerful and reliable engine was the main base for jet technology in

France, the Soviet Union and many other countries, and was also extremely important in the United States where it was made as the Pratt & Whitney J42. The Rolls-Royce Tay, of 2,835kg (6,250lb) thrust, became the Hispano Verdon and Pratt & Whitney J48, representing the pinnacle of the Whittle centrifugal engine.

Both Verdon and J48 became the first production engines to be boosted by an afterburner (reheat jetpipe) in which, at the cost of greatly increased fuel consumption, thrust is augmented for short periods by

burning extra fuel between the turbine and nozzle. The gas temperature can be raised to more than 1,800°C (3,272°F) but the technique adds to engine bulk and mass and requires a nozzle whose area and profile can be varied. Actuation systems able to withstand the high temperature and resist the large forces were difficult to develop. A simple way of boosting thrust or shaft-power by a modest amount is water injection. Purified water, or a mixture of water and alcohol or methanol, is sprayed into the air entering the engine. The liquid quickly evaporates, cooling the air and increasing its density so that the mass flow (weight of air 'swallowed' each second by the engine) is increased. This not only raises thrust or power directly, but also allows more fuel to be burned without exceeding the permissible turbine temperature limits. In fact, in some

engines the water is injected not upstream of the compressor but into the combustion chamber, where its sole function is to cool the flow and allow more fuel to be burned. Of course, thrust or power is more or less directly proportional to the rate at which fuel is burned.

In 1943 Rolls-Royce had begun the development of axial engines, and these eventually led to the Avon which entered service at 2,950kg (6,500lb) thrust in 1951. By the time the Avon went out of production in Sweden in 1974, at an afterburning thrust rating of 7,761kg; (17,110lb), it had been produced in greater numbers than any other British gas turbine. In 1957 it had become the first engine in the world in service with turbine rotor blades cooled by multiple air holes. Early German engines had blades wrapped from sheet, but the modern forged or cast air-cooled turbine has dramatically improved engine performance by increasing the allowable difference between the metal temperature of the blade and the temperature of the gas; today, with far more refined cooling, the difference can exceed 340°C (644°F). In 1957 the Avon also became the first Vertical Take-Off and Landing (VTOL) jet engine to make a full transition, in the Ryan X–13 Vertijet. In 1958 it became the first jet in transatlantic airline service, the first in service with a noise-suppressing nozzle and the first to have a thrust-reverser to help slow the aircraft after landing. In 1959 it became the first jet in service on short airline sectors and the first to reach a time between overhauls of 1,000 hours, which was swiftly extended to 10,000.

Most Avons were of a later type, with the separate combustion chambers replaced by an annular chamber housing separate flame tubes (the so-called can-annular system) and with the superior compressor of a rival engine, the Sapphire. The Sapphire had begun life as the Metrovick F.9 and gone into production at Armstrong Siddeley (later Bristol Siddeley) and, in Americanized form, as the Wright J65. Rated at 3,266 to 4,980kg (7,200 to 11,000lb) thrust, it was an outstanding and important engine during the urgent re-armament at the time of the Korean War in 1950–53. Armstrong Siddeley had taken over Metrovick gas turbines in 1947, and via the Mamba turboprop produced the Viper as a short-life, simple turbojet for target Remotely Piloted Vehicles (RPVs) in 1951. Rated at 744kg (1,640lb) thrust, it was later turned into a very long-life engine for piloted aircraft and is still in production at ratings up to 1,814kg (4,000lb) thrust.

From 1941 the leader in the United States was GE. The Lynn (steam-turbine) plant gave up the T31 turboprop, but the Schenectady (turbosupercharger) team moved to Ohio and went from strength to strength. From the Whittle I–A came the J31 of 907kg (2,000lb) thrust and then the I–40, handed to Allison to build as the J33 at ratings up to 3,720kg (8,200lb) thrust with afterburner. In 1942 work began on a completely new engine with an axial compressor, owing only part of its combustion and turbine technology to Whittle. As the TG–180 this ran at 1,700kg (3,750lb) thrust and was built in batches as the J35 by the Chevrolet division of General Motors, powering the first North American XP–86 Sabre. Passed to Allison in 1946, the J35 was greatly developed and again made in very large numbers. Meanwhile GE refined the design into the TG–190, which as the J47 was made in larger numbers than any other gas turbine in history (36,500), more than half being installed in Boeing B–47s. Relatively small numbers were made of the Allison J71 and

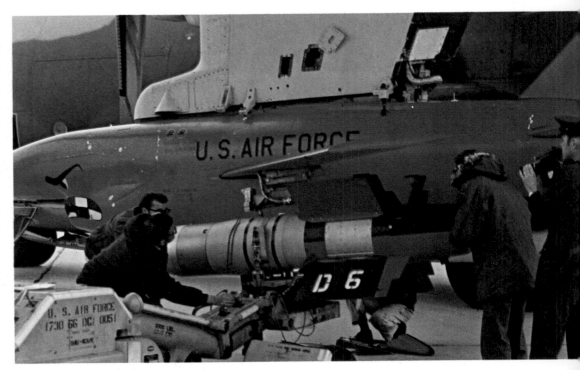

GE J73, both in the 4,536kg (10,000lb) thrust class. The big supersonic GE J53 reached 10,775kg (23,750lb) thrust on test, but was abandoned.

By 1948 the need for greater efficiency was leading to higher turbine gas temperature, made possible by improved alloys, and higher compressor pressure ratio. The centrifugal and early axial engines had been unable to compress the airflow more than about six times (a pressure ratio of six). Roughly double this figure seemed possible with new forms of compressor. Merely increasing the

ABOVE LEFT: *This sectioned Rolls-Royce Derwent of 3,500lb thrust shows a typical turbojet of 1945. A few are still flying.*

LEFT: *When the Derwent was new Rolls-Royce produced the axial-compressor Avon. This 17,000lb-thrust version is still serving.*

TOP: *Slightly larger than the Derwent, the Rolls-Royce Nene of 1945 gave 5,000lb thrust and was a world leader until about 1952.*

CENTRE: *Since 1970 the RPV has emerged as an important market for special families of small jet engines. This is a Teledyne Ryan 234.*

ABOVE: *This cutaway Rolls-Royce Viper 630 of 4,000lb thrust is today's descendant of a simple 1,640lb engine of 25 years ago.*

number of axial stages would not do; the engine became unwieldy and the compressor misbehaved and 'choked', the airflow stalling as on a wing operated at an excessive angle of attack and breaking down entirely. To make the air flow properly, existing axial engines needed spring-loaded safety valves to blow off air through the case, and pivoted inlet guide-vanes whose angle could be adjusted (especially when the engine was being started). Two new ideas were introduced: the two-spool engine and the variable stator.

GE adopted the latter, running the first J79 turbojet in 1953. Slightly larger than a J47, it had no fewer than 17 compressor stages, with the inlet vanes and next six stator stages all with variable incidence, driven by fuel-pressurized rams to maintain the correct airflow angles. Today, more than

the combustion chamber and ignited, and the gas flow then drives the LP spool. At all times the two spools run at their own best speed, called N1 and N2 and indicated to the pilot.

The first two-spool Pratt & Whitney engine ran in June 1949, and the prototype of a redesigned model, the wasp-waisted JT3, ran in January 1950. A robust and conservative engine, the JT3 received the military designation J57 and was made in large numbers at about 5,900kg (13,000lb) thrust, with water injection, for the Boeing B–52 and KC–135, the Douglas Skywarrior and many other aircraft, and at about 6,805 to 8,165kg (15,000 to 18,000lb) thrust with afterburner for many supersonic fighters. The civil JT3C was the original engine of the long-range 707 and DC–8 and, when JT3 production ceased in 1965, more than 21,200 had been delivered.

in the radical BE.53 engine with four swivelling nozzles to give lift or thrust and first run in 1959. Rolls-Royce pioneered simple, light-weight 'lift jets' for Vertical/Short Take-Off and Landing (V/STOL) aircraft.

Westinghouse developed its X19 (J30) into the 24C, which was built in numbers as the J34 of about 1,475kg (3,250lb) thrust; the bigger J40 was a dismal failure, causing Westinghouse to give up aircraft propulsion, though the J34 is still in service in booster pods on the Lockheed P–2 Neptune and Fairchild C–119. Wright likewise proved unable to compete, and this proud name faded from the scene. But in Europe a very pedestrian axial engine, based on wartime BMW designs, was taken to the production stage in 1954 by the French SNECMA company as the Atar 101C of 2,813kg (6,200lb) thrust. It was subsequently further developed

16,500 have been delivered, the engine being claimed to have logged more Mach 2 flight-time than all other engines combined, and with afterburning ratings of 6,805 to 8,120kg (15,000 to 17,900lb) thrust. Small numbers of non-afterburning commercial CJ–805 and CJ–805–23 aft-fan versions were also made.

Pratt & Whitney adopted the two-spool (also called two-shaft, dual-compressor or split-compressor) configuration. Instead of having one turbine driving one compressor, there are mechanically separate Low-Pressure (LP) and High-Pressure (HP) 'spools', the HP shaft being a tube surrounding the LP shaft, usually with a roller bearing between them. The starter drives only the HP spool, comprising the rear part of the compressor (smaller than the long-bladed LP spool), drive shaft and HP turbine. When this has reached the correct speed, fuel is supplied to

A closely similar British engine was the Bristol Olympus, run in 1949 and produced in 1954 at 4,990kg (11,000lb) thrust, developed in 1957 to 6,125kg (13,500lb) and by 1960 to 7,713kg (17,000lb) and then 9,074kg (20,000lb) thrust. Today, the same basic engine has been further developed as the power unit of the Concorde Mach 2 transport, with a rating of 17,240kg (38,000lb) thrust with afterburner. This is the largest growth in thrust of any aero engine.

Bristol later developed the very simple Orpheus single-shaft turbojet for tactical fighters. The de Havilland Engine Co continued building the Goblin, and the larger Ghost was chosen to power the Comet, the first jet civil airliner, which entered service in May 1952. There followed the Gyron Junior with an axial compressor and cast air-cooled blades, while Bristol cooled blades were used

as the Atar 9C of 6,400kg (14,110lb) thrust with afterburner and produced since 1959 for the Mirage III and 5.

In the Soviet Union, Vladimir Klimov refined the VK–1 centrifugal turbojet from the British Nene, and produced the totally new series of single-shaft axial engines designated AM–5, AM–9 and RD–9 for the Mikoyan MiG–19, Yakovlev Yak–25 and other fighters. Arkhip Lyulka produced the considerably more powerful AL–7 series, rated up to 9,980kg (22,000lb) thrust with afterburner, Alex Mikulin was responsible for the large and robust AM–3 (RD–3) single-shaft engine rated at nearly 9,525kg (21,000lb) thrust in the Tu–16 bomber and Tu–104 civil air-liner, and Sergei Tumansky produced the R–11 for the MiG–21 interceptor which entered production in 1956 rated at 5,100kg (11,240lb) thrust.

At this time the US Air Force and Navy were interested in a turbojet system drawing energy from a nuclear reactor but, though enormous funds were applied, this difficult nuclear-propulsion programme was dropped before any system had flown. Likewise, a later project to use high-energy (so-called 'zip') fuel based on boron/hydrocarbon compounds was halted in August 1959, though the zip-fuel engine, the GE J93, was continued and, using special kerosene, flew in the Mach 3 North American XB–70 in 1964.

Turboprops of the 1950s

Bristol, a late starter in gas turbines in Britain, planned a complex turboprop in 1942 which featured axial and centrifugal compressors, reverse-flow combustion (air entered near the rear and flowed forwards) and a heat exchanger to improve economy by extracting heat otherwise wasted in the efflux. This ran in 1945 as the Theseus and was developed into the 4,500hp Proteus, of which a few are still flying in Bristol Britannias – many more serve in fast naval craft and other surface applications. Armstrong Siddeley's Python of 4,000hp, which powered the Westland Wyvern strike fighter from 1953 to 1957, was the sole outcome of the axial effort begun at Farnborough by Griffith nearly 30 years earlier. In contrast, Rolls-Royce in 1945 quickly produced a simple turboprop by scaling-up the supercharger of a Griffon piston engine to make the compressor and then adding a combustion chamber, turbine and gearbox. The result was the Dart, possibly Britain's most cost-effective engine. It is still in full production after more than 30 years, with nearly 7,000 engines delivered. Conversely, Napier turboprops were abandoned after the 2,800hp Eland was already in military and airline service, though the Gazelle of around 1,650hp survived as a helicopter turboshaft supported by Rolls-Royce.

In the United States, Allison took many years to get a reliable turboprop but by 1956 the T56 (civil, Model 501) was in production for the Lockheed C–130 Hercules military transport and for the civil Electra. A single-shaft engine, it carries the propeller gearbox on long struts ahead of the power section, and the C–130, Lockheed P–3 Orion, Grumman Hawkeye and other programmes have proved so successful that this 4,900hp unit is still in production with more than 10,000 delivered. At the other end of the scale, Allison produced the Model 250 (T63) in 1959 to meet a need for a simple engine of 250hp; this has today grown to the 350 to 650hp range. The engine is still in production for helicopters and light turboprop aeroplanes, with again more than 10,000 units delivered. GE produced the T58 in 1957 as a 1,000hp helicopter engine, and it remains in production with many thousands delivered (some made by Rolls-Royce as the Gnome) rated up to 1,800hp. Garrett AiResearch made about 25,000 small, non-flying gas turbines before launching the 600hp TPE331 (T76) single-shaft turboprop, with tandem centrifugal compressors. This is still in production at up to 1,000hp. In 1959 Pratt & Whitney Canada launched the 578hp PT6 free-

LEFT: *Flame blasts from the afterburner of a General Electric J79 at full power on a testbed.*
ABOVE: *This engine for a prototype B–52 was one of the first of the classic P&W J57 two-spool turbojets.*

BELOW: *Between 1949 and 1957 the Bristol Olympus increased in thrust from 9,140lb to 21,000lb (in this Mk 301 version). Today the Olympus 593 gives 38,000lb in Concorde.*

BELOW: *Engineers work on the General Electric J93 designed for the Mach 3 six-engined B–70. Giving scale is a Mach 2 J79.*

BOTTOM LEFT: *About to take off, this Spanish Mirage III DE is typical of many Mirage types.*
BOTTOM RIGHT: *One of the world's earliest supersonic combat aircraft, the MiG–19 has been produced under licence in China.*

turbine engine (like the Bristol turboprops, it has one turbine driving the compressor and a free turbine driving just the output shaft); today there are 20 versions including turboprops rated up to 1,200hp, helicopter engines as single and twin units, models for airborne auxiliary services, trains, ships and other uses. Production for aircraft propulsion alone is running at 2,350 per year for more than 1,300 customers.

In 1946 Pratt & Whitney began development of the big single-shaft PT–2 engine which flew in the nose of a Boeing B–17 in 1950 and finally went into production for the Boeing C–133 as the T34 of 7,500hp. Rolls-Royce's two-spool RB.109 of April 1955 became the 6,100hp Tyne, still in limited production by a European consortium for the Transall and used in many other aircraft. An even more powerful unit is the Soviet NK–12M, designed mainly by Germans working under Nikolai Kuznetsov in the period 1947 to 1952. It produced around 14,800hp for the Tupolev Tu–95, Tu–114 and Tu–126. Smaller Soviet turboprops include Alex Ivchenko's 4,000hp AI–20 and 2,500hp AI–24, both simple single-shaft engines, while

turboshaft units for helicopters include the 1,500hp Isotov TV2 and the Soloviev D–25V of between 5,500 and 6,500hp. Both of the latter have a free-turbine drive at the rear.

Armstrong Siddeley developed the single-shaft Mamba into the Double Mamba, rated at up to 3,875hp and able to operate with either power section shut down and its propeller (front or rear of a double co-axial unit) feathered. But by far the most successful European producer of small gas turbines has been Turboméca, which since 1952 has sold 15,000 engines in 94 countries, with a further 12,000 built under licence, mostly by Teledyne CAE in the United States. Big-selling shaft engines include the single-shaft Artouste helicopter unit (400 to 600hp), Astazou turboshaft/turboprop (550 to 1,200hp), Bastan turboprop (1,000 to 1,400hp) and free-turbine Turmo (1,400 to 1,600hp). There are also the new 650hp Arriel and 1,800hp Makila.

Work by a German team between 1949 and 1954 led to the Avco Lycoming T53 free-turbine engine, since developed from 650hp to 1,800hp and used in numerous helicopters, fixed-wing V/STOL and turboprop aeroplanes; deliveries so far exceed 18,000 engines. The slightly larger T55 (LTC4) began life at 2,400hp and is now in production at ratings to 4,600hp. Pratt & Whitney added a free output turbine to a small turbojet, the J60 of 1,361kg (3,000lb) thrust, to produce the JFTD12 rated at 4,000 to 4,800hp. The latest shaft-drive engines are mainly for future

8. The fan seldom has more than two stages, and usually only one; in a small engine it is driven by a reduction gear. The by-pass engine has a by-pass ratio of less than 1; it is essentially a two-spool turbojet with slightly oversized blades on the LP spool, or over the first three to five stages of it. Rolls-Royce failed to select the correct by-pass ratio in the early 1950s, and launched the Conway by-pass jet with a ratio of only 0·3. This was designed at 4,990kg (11,000lb) thrust, entered production at 6,805kg (15,000lb) and saw civil and military service at 7,940 to 10,205kg (17,500 to 22,500lb) thrust, later versions having the by-pass ratio raised to 0·6. This was the first turbofan of any kind in airline service, the first cooled-blade engine in airline service (1960) and the first aero engine to reach 10,000 hours between overhauls (1966). The Conway spurred Pratt & Whitmey to produce a hasty conversion of the JT3C, the JT3D with three compressor stages replaced by two fan stages and with an extra stage on the LP turbine. By boldly choosing a by-pass ratio of 1·5, this conver-

helicopters. The GE T700, of 1,536hp, is certain of large sales for many new civil and military helicopters. Like the Rolls-Royce Gem of 900hp, it has been designed to set new standards of low-cost and trouble-free operation while causing minimal environmental pollution (which means making less noise and pumping out less heat on to which a missile could home). GE is producing a scaled-up T58, the T64 of 2,800 to 4,400hp, in both turboshaft and turboprop forms, while AiResearch has left the 240hp and 470 hp brackets in which it built prototypes. Avco Lycoming, however, has taken great care with the 600 to 650hp LTS101 (turboshaft) and LTP101 (turboprop) engines which, alongside Allison engines, appear to be Turboméca's chief rivals for future light helicopters and aeroplanes.

Modern jet engines

The term jet engine loosely includes rockets, ramjets, turbojets, turbofans and an intermediate category called by-pass jets. In most modern turbofans, especially for subsonic aircraft, the by-pass ratio (ratio of cold air by-passed around the core to the hot core flow) is seldom less than 3 and may be 5·5 or up to

BELOW: *Soviet engines have in the past been very conservative. This Kuznetsov NK 8–4 is in the class of the earlier R-R Conway.*

sion surpassed the Conway and the JT3D is still in production with more than 8,500 delivered at ratings up to 9,528kg (21,000lb). The Conway also triggered the Soviet Ivchenko AI–25, Kuznetsov NK–8 and Soloviev D–20 and D–30, all with by-pass ratios lower than would be chosen today.

The next generation after the Conway and JT3D were the smaller Rolls-Royce Spey and Pratt & Whitney JT8D, both planned as civil engines with by-pass ratios close to 1, pressure ratios around 18, and mass flows (maximum airflow at take-off) of about 93kg (205lb)/sec for the Spey and 145kg (320lb)/sec for the JT8D. Both have been built in large numbers, the US engine having gradually developed from 6,350 to 7,260kg (14,000 to 16,000lb) thrust and the Spey growing from 4,470 to 5,445kg (9,850 to 12,000lb) and with a Mach 2 military version giving over 9,300kg (20,500lb) thrust with afterburner. Refanned models of both engines are rated at around 7,713kg (17,000lb) thrust, with much larger single-stage fans (of the kind they

should have had at the outset) raising by-pass ratio to almost 2 and dramatically cutting noise and specific fuel consumption. In an age of escalating development costs, refanning old engines is becoming more attractive than designing new ones.

The first modern High By-Pass Ratio (HBPR) turbofans stemmed from the US Air Force Lockheed C–5A freighter. GE won the C–5A propulsion contract with the TF39 of 18,780kg (41,400lb) thrust. It was a bold design with a by-pass ratio of 8, reflecting the modest 815km/h (507mph) speed of the C–5A, a 1·25 stage fan with a pressure ratio of 1·55 and a single-spool variable-stator compressor reaching 16·8 in 16 stages, giving an overall pressure ratio of 26·04. From this, GE developed the CF6–6 for the civil McDonnell Douglas DC–10, with ratings near 18,145kg (40,000lb) thrust, a by-pass ratio of 5·9 and a pressure ratio of 28·1. Adding booster stages behind the fan with variable by-pass doors resulted in the CF6–50 series, used in the DC–10–30, Airbus

TOP: *Rolls-Royce Conway turbofans were among the first engines to be assembled upright. When this one has been 'dressed' with its accessories it will look quite different.*
ABOVE: *Virtually identical Pratt & Whitney F100 two-shaft turbofans power the F–15 and F–16 fighters. The nearer example of this 23,810lb-thrust engine shows the variable-profile afterburner nozzle.*
ABOVE RIGHT: *The extremely ordinary Pratt & Whitney JT8D has become the most widely used airliner engine. Rated at 14,000 to 17,000lb, it powers the Boeing 727 and 737, DC–9, Mercure and Caravelles.*
RIGHT: *Rated at 3,500 to 4,000lb thrust, the Garrett AiResearch TFE731 is a typical business jet and trainer engine. The large fan is driven by a reduction gear, so there is close affinity with turboprops.*
FAR RIGHT TOP: *Designed by Rolls-Royce and built by a partnership involving MTU of West Germany and Fiat of Italy, the Turbo-Union RB.199 is in 1977 the most modern combat engine. Its first application is to power the Tornado.*
FAR RIGHT BELOW: *General Electric CF6–50 turbofans being prepared for shipment from Cincinnati. These 49,000–54,000lb engines power the Airbus A300 and Boeing YC–14, most DC–10s and some Boeing 747s.*

Industrie A300B and some Boeing 747s. These engines have increased core airflow, giving a by-pass ratio of only 4·4 but a pressure ratio of 31·5 and thrusts of 22,680 to 24,500kg (50,000 to 54,000lb). Rival Pratt & Whitney produced the JT9D with a fan rotating on the LP shaft with three or four LP compressor stages, at a by-pass ratio close to 5, and with an 11-stage HP spool giving the more modest overall pressure ratio of 21 to 24. Thrusts of 19,504 to 24,040kg (43,000 to 53,000lb) are produced. In Britain Rolls-Royce chose three shafts in the RB.211–22 (single-stage fan, seven-stage Intermediate-Pressure, (IP), and six-stage LP) giving a pressure ratio of 25 for fewer stages and with better handling. The chosen by-pass ratio was 5 and thrust 19,050kg (42,000lb). Rolls then developed a new higher-flow core in the RB.211–524 giving better results than any rival at thrusts from 19,960 to 24,500kg (44,000 to 54,000lb), and with a large margin of extra thrust in climb and cruise. All these great engines have

been successful, and all are competing keenly for lucrative business over the next 20 years.

To meet an apparent need for smaller engines, American GE and French SNECMA are jointly producing the CFM International CFM56, which uses the core of the GE F101 supersonic bomber engine, an outstandingly advanced unit operating at high pressures and very high temperatures, matched with a new SNECMA fan giving a by-pass ratio of 6 and thrust around 9,980kg (22,000lb). Pratt & Whitney, with partners in other countries, is working on the more conservative JT10D, to be rated at 11,115 to 12,250kg (24,500 to 27,000lb) thrust and also projected with cropped fan blades to meet the needs of aircraft requiring about 8,620kg (19,000lb) thrust. In smaller categories are the Japanese FJR710 of 4,990kg (11,000lb), GE CF34 of about 3,855kg (8,500lb), Rolls-Royce M45 of about 3,402kg (7,500lb) and Avco Lycoming ALF502 of about 2,950kg (6,500lb) thrust. All have efficient cores and high by-passing ratios, but only the M45 is in commercial service, though the CF34 is a version of the TF34 military engine and the Avco unit uses the proven core of the T55. In the Soviet Union the new bureau of Vladimir Lotarev has produced an advanced HBPR engine, the D–36, in the 6,350kg (14,000lb) thrust class.

Among military engines the outstanding leader in Europe is the Turbo-Union RB.199, two of which power the multi-role Panavia Tornado. The RB.199 has three shafts, a very efficient fan, an advanced afterburner which doubles thrust from 3,402 to 6,804kg (7,500 to 15,000lb), and an extremely efficient variable nozzle. Much more conservative is the Rolls-Royce/Turboméca Adour two-shaft engine, rated at 2,359kg (5,200lb) thrust in the Hawker Siddeley Hawk and up to 3,629kg (8,000lb) thrust with afterburner for the SEPECAT Jaguar and Mitsubishi FST–2. Dominant engines in the United States are the powerful Pratt & Whitney F100 and GE F404. In the 1960s Pratt & Whitney produced the TF30 turbofan for the General Dynamics F–111, but this was not outstanding until the final version, the TF30–100 of 11,385kg (25,100lb) thrust with afterburner, became available for the last few aircraft. In contrast, the F100 is an outstanding engine in all respects, delivering about 10,890kg (24,000lb) thrust with afterburner and giving a combat thrust-to-weight ratio which substantially exceeds one-to-one in the twin-engined McDonnell Douglas F–15 and single-engined General Dynamics F–16. By-pass ratio is about 0·7, pressure ratio 23, and fuel consumption, size and weight are all less than in TF30 versions of lower thrust. The F404 is a low by-pass turbojet of some 7,258kg (16,000lb) thrust and, like the F100, has a thrust/weight ratio of about 8. Little is known of the many outstanding new Soviet engines, but technically they are catching up fast and it would be unwise to assume, as has been possible hitherto, that their design represents only a copy of the previous generation of Western engines.

Since 1959 GE has achieved considerable success with the small single-shaft J85 turbojet, of which more than 12,000 have been produced, almost all for Northrop T–38 trainers and F–5 fighters. This engine began life at 1,746kg (3,850lb) thrust with afterburner and is now usually rated at 2,268kg (5,000lb). Its success confirms the continuing appeal of old-fashioned but proven designs. The civil CJ610 has likewise proved a winner, rated at about 1,360kg (3,000lb) thrust, and with customers carefully protected by aftersales support and spares at guaranteed prices. About 2,000 of these simple engines are in use, plus 800 aft-fan CF700s rated at 1,928kg (4,250lb) in some Dassault Falcon and Rockwell Sabre business jets. But Garrett AiResearch is now taking a good slice of the business jet market with the excellent TFE731 of 1,588kg (3,500lb) thrust, in which the HP turbine drives a centrifugal compressor and the three-stage LP turbine drives a four-stage LP compressor as well as, via a 0·555 reduction gear, the single-stage fan which has a 2·66 by-pass ratio. AiResearch has also developed a radical three-shaft turbofan in the 2,268kg (5,000lb) thrust class, the ATF3, in which the entire core airflow is twice reversed. Core air passes through the fan, which has a by-pass ratio of 3, then through the five-stage IP compressor, and then curls round and inwards at the rear of the engine where it encounters the centrifugal HP compressor – this brings overall pressure ratio to about 24. It then passes forwards through the combustion chamber, HP, IP and LP turbines, and finally turns another 180° to exit into the fan (by-pass) airflow through eight sets of cascades. Though seemingly complex, the ATF3 has proved a success. After some years of military flying as the XF104 it was in 1976 launched on the civil market in a new Dassault Falcon.

Modern piston engines

Almost all piston engines since 1945 have come from the United States and eastern Europe. It is especially sad that Britain's world-renowned Gipsy series of lightplane engines should have collapsed, leaving the field today almost wholly in the excellent hands of Avco Lycoming and Teledyne Continental. During the 1930s there were many US light-engine firms, including Warner, LeBlond, Kinner, Jacobs, Ranger, Aeromarine, Menasco and Franklin. They built engines of many shapes, but since 1945 the horizontally opposed flat-four and flat-six have accounted for more than 95 per cent of all light-engine sales, and almost all come from Avco Lycoming and Teledyne Continental. Engines range from 65 to about 400 hp, with a general growth among the best-sellers over the years from around 140hp to a current rating between 250 and 350hp. Most today have fuel injection and geared drives, and turbochargers are often available. Many engines can run upright in helicopter installations, and the larger types carry a freon compressor for cabin cooling in hot weather, or a cabin pressurization supercharger.

Large piston engines died slowly, the Pratt & Whitney R–2800 and Wright R–3350 being especially successful in both military and civil aircraft. The latter was finally certificated in 1954 as the Turbo-Compound, with its exhaust discharged through three high-speed blow-down turbines disposed at 120° around its rear. This added about 1,000 hp to the propeller shaft, turning a 2,500hp engine into an economical 3,500 to 3,700hp unit which, in the Douglas DC–7C and Lockheed L–1649, at last produced true transatlantic airliners. They had but two years of glory before the turboprops and turbojets swept them away almost overnight.

Today the main repository of the piston engine is the agricultural market, which needs a robust and economical 'farm truck' engine to work all day at sea level. Another worthwhile market is the helicopter, but for lower power engines below 500hp. A rapidly increasing proportion of the world output of piston aero engines comes from Poland and Czechoslovakia. Both produce engines of their own and Soviet design, carefully refined for helicopter and agricultural use. There are strong signs that water-cooled car-type engines producing about 300 to 500hp will break into this large market. The gigantic

TOP LEFT: *Curtiss-Wright Wankel-type rotating combustion engine.*
TOP RIGHT: *The RFB/Grumman American Fanliner has Wankel-driven shrouded fan propulsion.*
CENTRE: *The Teledyne Continental 10520A is a 285hp flat-six with direct fuel injection.*

ultralight and homebuilt market should also not be overlooked, although it has still to decide whether it prefers four-stroke or two-stroke engines and is being told that air-cooling will account for a rapidly decreasing proportion of the total. This market has also shown great interest in the well known Wankel-type Rotating Combustion (RC) engine, in which the piston rotates instead of oscillating up and down. Curtiss-Wright in the USA and many firms in Japan and Germany are developing RC engines for aviation.

FAR LEFT TOP: *The McDonnell Douglas F–15 Eagle is typical of modern fighters.*
TOP CENTRE LEFT: *The Jaguar International, a version exported to Ecuador and Oman.*
ABOVE CENTRE LEFT: *Much bigger than the Jaguar, the GD F–111 flies similar missions.*
LEFT: *The Dassault Breguet Falcon 20 (Mystère 20) was the first business jet with turbofans.*
ABOVE: *The 600–650hp Avco Lycoming LTP 101 turboprop is used in many lightplanes.*

Airframes

Early aeroplanes were mainly built of traditional materials such as ash, birch, spruce and other hardwoods; bamboo, steel (almost always in thin sections such as tube, or as reinforcing plates at wood-joints) and small amounts of aluminium, which was then new and rather costly. The structure took the form of many parts joined together by glueing, pinning or bolting, to form a strong but light framework. This was then braced with numerous tensioned wires and the aerodynamic surfaces covered with good fabric such as varnished silk (the Wrights began with unbleached muslin) or rubberized waterproof linen fabric.

From the start it was realized that the main structural members were the spars which spanned the wing from tip to tip. These bear the main bending and shear loads in most wings, and for a spar to break would be catastrophic. Early spars were made of glued and pinned wood, usually ash, arranged either in the form of a box section or an 'I'. In either case the tension and compression loads are borne by the booms at top and bottom, while the vertical walls joining the booms are the webs. Along the spars were arranged ribs, lying in a fore-and-aft (chordwise) direction and usually built up from pieces of plywood, strip wood, and even aluminium strip or steel tube, to form the correct aerofoil section. Internal wires braced the wing to form a strong structure before covering. The fuselage (body) was a wire-braced girder framework, with a basis of four strong longerons of ash or spruce joined by vertical and transverse struts, though steel tubes were sometimes used as compression members.

The majority of aircraft produced up to 1935 were biplanes, although in World War I triplanes and quadruplanes were flown. The use of superimposed lifting planes enabled the classic boxkite structure to be used, with its combination of lightness and rigidity. By 1915 this structure had been refined in several ways. Interplane struts, linking the spars of upper and lower wings, were no longer of constant section but were tapered at the ends in a way forming an effective compromise between strength, weight, drag and ease of manufacture.

Round section piano wire for bracing had been replaced by the Rafwire (from the initials of the Royal Aircraft Factory) with lenticular (sharp-edged and flattened) section having much lower drag. Rafwires used to 'sing' in the air, the vibration soon leading to dangerous fatigue failure, until dampers were added, often in the form of small 'acorn' fairings where the wires crossed.

Apart from this, aerodynamic refinement was usually conspicuously lacking, and the structure was regarded as a basis on which to

BELOW LEFT: *Blériot XI with details of (a) fuselage section (b) typical frame/longeron joint and (c) wing-spar wire bracing fitting.*
RIGHT: *A Sopwith Camel with detail of wooden wing structure with internal wire bracing typical of World War I aircraft.*
BOTTOM: *The Gastambide-Mengin experimental aircraft (a type of Antoinette) was built in 1908. Here the struts are being checked.*

hang an unstreamlined engine, fuel tank, water radiator and other items. There were a few notable exceptions, such as the racing French Deperdussins of 1912 to 1913 which introduced monocoque (single-shell) structure. The classic example of monocoque construction is a lobster claw, showing how a strong skin can obviate the need for any internal skeleton or supporting framework. The Deperdussin fuselage was eventually perfected as a finely streamlined body of circular section, made from multiple veneers of tulip wood glued together over a jig or former, a shaped mould to ensure that the finished assembly had the correct shape. During World War I many aircraft moved a small way towards monocoque construction by having plywood skinning, able to bear some of the load, and dispensing with internal bracing wires (but retaining an internal skeleton framework).

This traditional form of construction, often loosely termed 'mixed' because different materials are employed, gradually underwent complete change. The eventual choice of most constructors was an all-metal 'stressed-skin' structure, and a few remarkable examples were built before 1920, but between these and the final development there were several intermediate stages. One of the major changes was the gradual adoption of an all-metal structure, often as a direct substitution for wood and with little change in the basic form and arrangement of the parts, and retaining a fabric covering. Another was the progressive reduction in the number of external bracing wires needed, and the eventual change from the braced biplane to the strut-and wire-braced monoplane and, in some cases, to the cantilever (unbraced) monoplane. A further fundamental change was the substitution of thin metal skin for fabric, though with stresses in the skin kept very low. The final change, which took 20 years to become established, was to make the metal skin bear the major part of the structural loads, and thus go most of the way towards realizing the structurally efficient monocoque form.

A major influence on aircraft structures was the accidental discovery by the German Durener Metallwerke in 1909 of the favourable properties of an aluminium alloy containing a little copper and magnesium. It was almost as light as aluminium, but much stronger, and it still had the good quality of stretching appreciably before breaking instead of snapping suddenly. The company called it Duralumin, and it was subsequently the subject of extensive research to obtain the best properties (surprisingly, it was not until 1934 that these properties were properly exploited).

One of the first to want to build an all-Dural aeroplane was Professor Hugo Junkers of Germany, and during World War I he designed several production aircraft of remarkably advanced cantilever monoplane design (plus an unusual cantilever biplane) with all-Dural structure. From then until 1933 Junkers favoured a skin stiffened by corrugations running fore-and-aft. Though the result was robust, and better able to stand up to rough usage than any rival machines, the drag was considerably higher than Junkers realized and performance was thereby held back. Several other builders used Duralumin construction, notably Short Brothers in Britain (with the Silver Streak biplane of 1920) and the German Rohrbach company (with a series of extremely clean monoplane flying boats built during 1923 to 1926, all of which featured smooth, stressed-skin construction.

Stressed-skin construction was only very slowly adopted generally, and a favoured structure for military machines in 1923 to 1925 was a framework of bolted and riveted steel strip, with wings spars of complicated built-up form achieved by riveting together a number of lengths of rolled strip to give the required cross-section with no flat areas which could buckle. Fabric covering was almost universal, though some large machines, such as the Soviet Tupolev TB–3 and French Amiot 143 bombers, had Duralumin skin to make them less prone to accidental damage.

During the late 1920s many great designers, especially the American John K. Northrop,

LEFT: *The Sopwith Schneider under construction at Kingston-upon-Thames. The Schneider was a floatplane version of the Sopwith Tabloid and was built specially for the Schneider Trophy Race of 1914. Despite the great speeds attained by the monocoque Deperdussin, the traditional biplane structure was decided upon for the Schneider. This was due to military discouragement of monoplanes in Britain. However, interplane struts and landing and flying wires were reduced to a minimum and special attention was paid to float construction. It came first in the race at an average speed of 140km/h (86·8mph).*

FAR LEFT BELOW: *The 1931 Boeing P–12C was one of the first fighters with a fuselage of bolted light alloy. It was a high-performance fighter built for both the Army and Navy. The Navy version was designated F4B–2 and was a forerunner of modern carrier fighters. Both were developed from earlier Boeing fighters with fuselages of welded steel tube. A total of 554 of the series were built, 366 as P–12s and 188 as F4Bs. The F4B had a span of 9m (30ft), a length of 6m (20ft) and was powered by one 500hp Pratt & Whitney R–1340. First deliveries were made in September 1929 and they continued to be built for several years.*

FAR LEFT BOTTOM: *The Junkers F13 was the first strut-free, all-metal civil aircraft. A low-wing cantilever monoplane, the F13 first appeared in 1919 and more than 40 were used by Lufthansa and other airlines. The F13 could operate on wheels, skis or floats.*
BELOW LEFT: *A DC–3 with details of (a) multi-spar wing section (b) outer wing bolted joint and (c) fuselage attachment. In addition to its stressed-skin monoplane structure, the DC–3 was the first aircraft to incorporate the failsafe multi-spar wing.*
BELOW: *Junkers Ju 52/3m and a detail of its structure of corrugated metal skin panels.*

refined the all-metal airframe until, by 1932, it had reached almost its present form. The advances were numerous. The cantilever monoplane could have a thick high-lift wing which could transmit all the flight loads through its skin, supported by many spanwise 'stringers', yet still have less weight and drag than a braced structure. Instead of having just two spars, such a wing could have six or more. This eventually yielded quite unexpected dividends in the Douglas DC–3 by making the wing resistant to fatigue–the progressive weakening of a structure bent back and forth, as a wing is in turbulent air. Unlike the old biplane wings, the cantilever monoplane wing could be made of graduated strength and uniform stress from tip to tip by varying the thickness of the spar booms and skin. Higher structure loading resulted from the trend towards higher wing loadings (aircraft weight divided by wing area), so the stress in the material rose and the metal was used more efficiently.

Most aircraft in World War II were of all-metal stressed-skin construction, though it was still rare to find a truly efficient structure in which the metal in the skin carried the same stress as that in the most highly stressed members, such as the spar booms. Fast aircraft had smooth exterior surfaces obtained by the use of 'flush' (countersunk) rivets, which such advanced machines as the Boeing B–29 bomber pointed the way to the future by having such large loads in the wings that the skin was no longer mere commercial thin sheet, but formed from sheet more than 15·8 mm (⅝in) thick. There were also some developments in the 1930s which were quite outside the normal mainstream of aircraft structures.

One of these unusual forms of structure was the Geodetic type, devised by Barnes (later Sir Barnes) Wallis of Vickers as a result of his long experience with airships. (See page 339.) A geodetic (strictly, a 'geodesic') is the shortest line that can be drawn between two points on a curved surface. Wallis saw that an aeroplane can be made with fairly regular surface curvature all over, and he developed a metal basketwork in which the entire airframe is assembled from quite small geodetic members pinned together at the joints (structurally called nodes, because the loads are applied only at the nodes). Each member experiences pure tension, as a tie, or pure compression, as a strut, with no bending load at all. All of the flight loads could be carried wholly within this basketwork lying in the surface (thus forming a kind of monocoque), though spars and longerons were added to take the bending loads, because the unsupported basketwork could be bent an unacceptable amount.

The first two types of completely Geodetic aircraft were the Wellesley and Wellington bombers, both of which had long range and wings of high aspect ratio. Fabric covering was no problem because they were quite slow, and the Wellington, in particular, had so much structural redundancy (a term which means there were many load-paths, so that one or more could be removed without the

LEFT AND BELOW: *The Vickers Wellington was the only British bomber to remain in production throughout World War II, a tribute to its unique, durable construction. The cutaway diagram shows a wing section revealing its geodetic construction which consisted of a basket-like light alloy framework built up of short, curved sections (detail).*
BOTTOM: *Wellingtons under construction clearly show the geodetic lattice framework of the fuselage.*

comb (a sandwich with an interior like a honeycomb) for structural purposes, had by World War II developed a completely new family of adhesives, which his company, then called Aero Research, marketed under the name of Redux. This was supplied either as a powder or in sheet form, cut to fit the joints to be bonded. The bonding was then made with both heat and pressure. With big airframe parts a large 'autoclave', a form of high-pressure oven was used. Redux made it possible to join metal parts by adhesive for the first time, and it was used in production of such successors to the Mosquito as the Vampire, Hornet and Dove. Later the successor to Aero Research, Ciba, developed a new adhesive, Araldite, which is familiar to everybody, as well as being important in aircraft construction.

One of the advantages of using adhesives is that joints are made with a continuous bond over an area, whereas rivets or bolts fasten parts only at small locations where there is a hole. Holes inevitably cause discontinuities in the material, and are likely to increase the stress in it when under load. Until after World War II this was no problem, because, provided designers and builders followed established codes of practice which had been built up over many years of often painful experience, they knew nothing would be likely to break. But from 1945 onwards aircraft, and especially civil aircraft, began to come apart in the air. Examination of the wreckage revealed the uncomfortable fact that the cause was metal fatigue. The popular way of demonstrating fatigue is to break off an open tin-can lid by bending it back and forth. Gradually the strip of metal along the bend seems to weaken, until the lid simply falls away without needing any perceptible pull. During the 1920s a few engineers admitted there might be fatigue problems in engines, but never in aircraft; as late as 1947 many loudly ridiculed Professor A. G. Pugsley when he pointed out that, even on the scanty evidence available at that time, the fatigue life of civil airliners might be similar to the planned lifetimes of such machines. In other words, just by normal flying through the turbulent sky, such aircraft might fall apart before they were retired from service.

In fact, trouble hit hard and soon. Those who lived through it will never forget the mysterious disappearance of two de Havilland Comet I jetliners, later shown in one case to have been caused by the explosive rupturing of the whole fuselage because the repeated pressurization had caused a crack to appear at a corner of a cut-out – foolishly, a square aperture instead of a round one – for an ADF loop aerial. The crack could have occurred at one of the Comet I's square windows, because when a complete airframe was tested under simulated flight conditions for the equivalent of a modest total lifetime it blew apart at one of the windows. This test was one of the first in which the whole fuselage was filled with, and immersed in, water. If air had been used the explosive failure would have badly distorted the specimen and caused havoc over a wide area, but water is almost incompressible.

Recognition that aircraft do have a fatigue

structure collapsing) that these aircraft gained a reputation for continuing to fly with airframe damage that would have caused catastrophic failure in a conventional structure.

The other unusual wartime structure was to be found in the Mosquito, an aircraft of extremely high performance built almost entirely of wood. The company responsible, Britain's de Havilland, had used wood for its Comet racer of 1934, and had subsequently experimented with a new form of construction called a 'sandwich', in which two load-bearing skins are firmly bonded to a low-density core. Each skin by itself would bend and buckle, but when the three layers are bonded together the result is thick enough to be completely stable under load. The Mos-

quito had wings with inner and outer skins of plywood bonded by strong adhesive to spanwise spruce stringers; the fuselage was made of plywood sandwich with a core of balsa wood, the very light wood often used by aeromodellers. The resulting structure was light and strong, and had the advantages of smooth inside and outside surfaces allowing the easy incorporation of cut-outs and attachment points. The main problem was that tropical environments reduced the strength of the adhesive.

Most of the adhesive bonding in the Mosquito was formaldehyde cement, a resin superior to the old casein glues used in earlier wooden aircraft. But N. A. de Bruyne, one of the pioneers of sandwich structures, and one of the first in the world to market a honey-

LEFT AND BELOW: *Besides the Wellington, the de Havilland Mosquito possessed an unusual structure. Although built almost entirely of wood, it had tremendous performance and survival capability. The airframe consisted of a unique sandwich form in which two load-bearing skins were firmly bonded to a low-density core. The details show (a) fuselage half-shell (b) wing section (c) fuselage top scarf joint and (d) end-grain balsa sandwich fuselage panel.*

problem came just in time to avoid massive trouble, because modern transports fly more hours each year than pre-1945 aircraft flew in their entire lifetime. In addition to the good practice of avoiding all 'stress-raisers' – sudden changes in section, sharp corners, scratches, roughness, etc. – modern structures are designed to fly a safe life greater than the expected aircraft lifetime, which in

ABOVE RIGHT: *The scene at Hatfield on 27 July 1949 a few minutes before the first flight of the Comet prototype. The Comet was the first jet airliner and demonstrated tragically the disastrous effects of metal fatigue.*

the case of airliners may be 40,000 to 60,000 hours. Such a life is achieved partly by attention to every detail of the structure, and limiting the maximum stresses in the most adverse conditions, partly by reducing the number of stress reversals by deliberately building in a static stress (for example, by tightening up joints so that they are under high tension even when the aircraft is not flying), and partly by using fatigue-resistant forms of structure with fewer joints and fewer discontinuities. On top of this, a form of structure called 'fail safe' has been devised in which, by use of multiple redundant load paths, the aircraft will not crash even if a

Type: de Havilland Comet 1
No of passengers: 36
Engines: Four 2,018kg (4,450lb) thrust de Havilland Ghost turbojets
Cruising speed: 789km/h (490mph)
Ceiling: 12,190m (40,000ft)
Range: 2,816km (1,750 miles)
Weight: 47,627kg (105,000lb)
Span: 35·05m (115ft)
Length: 28·35m (93ft)

major fatigue crack should break one of the members.

The number of forms of structure introduced since 1950 is greater than in the previous 50 years. Sandwiches are today common, especially for secondary structure such as the area of wing behind the main wing box, fairings, large doors and access panels, and the whole exterior skin of some supersonic aircraft. Fillings in the sandwiches are often low-density foams, but more often are honeycombs of papers, plastics or various metals bonded to the face sheets by brazing or by adhesives. This form of structure is especially resistant to the high-frequency fatigue caused by intense noise, and is commonly used for making engine pods. Honeycombs with inner cells open to the atmosphere are used as noise-absorbing materials. Other structures, including large exterior skin panels in aircraft from bombers to lightplanes, are stabilized by bonding or spot-welding an inner skin of corrugated sheet, while most all-metal

lightplanes incorporate at least some exterior skin stabilized by chordal grooves or raised corrugations reminiscent of the old Junkers skins. As they are short, these stiffeners have low drag, and they allow the interior (of the rudder or other part) to be greatly simplified at a saving in cost.

During the 1930s it was realized that modern skin panels with 3-D curvature must be stretched or stamped by large presses, and the best answer, found in the United States, was the stretch-press. The sheet is gripped at each end by jaws held on hydraulic jacks and pulled bodily around a male die having the shape of the part needed. The sheet deforms plastically and springs back only very slightly. Almost all modern skin panels are stretch-pressed, except for the thinner and smaller panels for lightplanes which are pressed on more traditional tools. Subsequently the structure is assembled by automatic or manual riveting, adhesive bonding or spot-welding. But many of the largest skin panels, and

the most vital other parts, are made without any joints.

One way of forming a complicated part in a single piece is by casting, by pouring molten metal or alloy into a mould; today this is used to make the blades for advanced turbine engines, which have to be of heat-resistant alloys very hard to shape by other means, but castings have been important in only a few types of aircraft. Another method is forging, when a rough workpiece is squeezed or thumped into shape, either at room temperature or while very hot. Forging may be done by a tremendous, slow squeeze by a gigantic press, either between a pair of shaped dies (moulds) or open; alternatively it may be done by repeated mechanical hammer blows, which in High-Energy-Rate Forming (HERF) involve catching the workpiece between two equal masses driven together by gas pressure from rapid combustion or similar high-speed impulse. Forging can even be done by explosives or suddenly applied intense magnetic fields. Virtually all the parts of aircraft bearing the highest concentrated loads are forgings; examples are landing-gear shock struts, root ribs, spar booms, tailplane attachments and fin anchorages.

Among the first large aircraft forgings were engine mountings squeezed out in magnesium alloy by huge presses in Germany before World War II. After the war the US Air Force launched a 'heavy press program' as a national effort at a cost of over $570,000,000, as a result of which the US Air Force supersonic 'Century series' fighters were designed to have complete fuselage frames and wing spars squeezed out as single pieces. With closed-die forging such parts can be forged as an almost finished item, but a little machining (cutting to shape) is still needed. With such massive workpieces, the machine-tool industry, again led by the USA, developed monster machine tools of the family known as routers or millers, able to shape workpieces of a size never before seen outside shipyards. Parts

15·24m (50ft) by 9·14m (30ft) are today not exceptional, and a few are much longer. During the 1950s the aircraft industry led the world in Numerically Controlled (NC) machining. The workpiece is today designed with the aid of a digital computer, and the same computer then guides the machine tool(s) with perfect precision to shape the actual part. Aircraft still have to be designed by humans, and drawn in detail on paper, but the drudgery of doing the stress calculations and making the drawings is now all done by digital computers. The drawings are mainly for reference, and the cutting of the metal happens without human hands being involved – except, of course, to press the 'start' button.

Though advanced aircraft incorporate complex machined forgings, most of the machining is done on skins and detail parts. Until after World War II skin was merely uniform sheet, cut to shape. With such aircraft as the North American F–86 Sabre and

TOP LEFT: *The Robin is a typical example of a modern mass-produced light aircraft. The Robin DR 400/180 (1) is built of wood and the detail (1a) shows wing profile and section. The Robin Hr 100/Tiara (2) is built of metal. The detail (2a) shows the wing profile and section.*

ABOVE LEFT: *The Rockwell B–1 (3). The diagrams illustrate (3a) a wing skin panel integrally machined from thick aluminium billet (3b) all-composite tailplane structure (built by Grumman) pivoting in a box made of titanium and (3c) a forged and machined tailplane pivot frame.*

TOP: *The North American XB–70 (4) developed new construction techniques. Details show (4a) welded stainless-steel honeycomb wing section (4b) leading-edge spar and wing skin honeycomb panel joint and (4c) wing-tip fold rotary actuator fitting.*

ABOVE: *The F–86 Sabre (5) benefited from new construction technology. The details illustrate (5a) rear fuselage, which could be removed for engine change (5b) an inboard wing section with thick skin panel and (5c) wing construction showing leading edge attached by piano hinge for quick removal and access to controls and systems.*

rear of the fixed part of the wing, was added as lighter 'secondary structure' made by traditional methods in thinner sheet, as were slats, flaps and control surfaces.

Wing boxes were the first parts to be made by some of the new methods in the 1950s. One new method was chem-milling, again pioneered in the United States. The entire skin is marked out into thinner and thicker portions, and the latter are protected by special coatings. The whole part, perhaps up to an inch thick and bigger than the floor of a living room, is put into a bath of acid or other corrosive chemical. After an exact time under controlled conditions the skin or slab is eaten away to the desired shape, usually with most of its area much reduced but the full thickness left where it was protected. Chem-milling is fast, does not distort the slab or harm its properties, and leaves no tool marks that could cause fatigue cracks.

It is very difficult to chem-mill deep grooves or complex forms, though since 1955 Britain has been in the forefront of a more versatile process called Electro-Chemical Machining (ECM), in which the acid bath is replaced by a bath of salty electrolyte, as in a battery, and the cutting is done by a soft copper tool carrying a powerful electric current. ECM can produce wonderfully detailed and exact results in the toughest and most challenging materials, and two of the ways in which it differs from ordinary machining are that the tool never touches the work and the liquid flow carries away the 'cut' material in the form of a sludge looking like fine mud. ECM is used for a high proportion of the parts of the latest engines, and is coming into use in airframe construction.

However, the bulk of modern airframe parts needing to be shaped in more than one dimension are not etched or ECM-shaped, but machined on special tools. Cutting from the solid, colloquially called 'hogging', became common in 1952, partly because avoiding joints improves fatigue life and partly because a one-piece component can be cheaper and usually lighter than one assembled from many parts. The usual name for this type of structure is integral construction. Today integral stiffening is found not only in wing boxes, where it began, but throughout advanced airframes.

During the 1950s aircraft speeds increased at a rate never equalled at any other time, and methods of construction were hard-pressed to keep pace. Aluminium alloys are adequate up to temperatures around 150°C (302°F), which can be reached after sustained flight at Mach 2 even in the −60°C (−76°F) air of the stratosphere. Acrylic plastics such as perspex become dangerously softened above this temperature. In the early 1950s there was no alternative but to make most of the exposed parts of the airframe of Mach 2-plus aircraft out of stainless steel. In America's Convair B–58 Hustler bomber, though it was not capable of exceeding Mach 2, most of the skin was made of stainless honeycomb sandwich, which called for years of intense research to perfect methods of brazing it and then inspecting to make sure the inaccessible interior was correctly bonded.

Far more useful was the North American

TOP: *The Concorde illustrates an aircraft of integral construction structure. Cutting from the solid-'hogging'-first became common in the early 1950s and was subsequently widely adopted due to its improvement of aircraft fatigue life. The cutaways show (a) a wing spar and fuselage bulkhead carved by large machines from fixed slabs of light alloy, (b) the forward wing section with flexible pin-jointed mountings and (c) droop nose and visor.*
ABOVE: *Electro-chemically machined parts with (inset) technicians inspecting the process.*

Boeing B–47 Stratojet it became worth while to use non-uniform sheet, thickest at the wing roots and tapered off towards the tips. By this time it had become universal in advanced aircraft to build the wing as an extremely strong 'box' consisting of upper and lower skins joined by front and rear spars, with many stringers and a few strong ribs, the whole assembly then being sealed by a rubbery lining to form an integral fuel tank. Sometimes this box extended to the leading edge, but usually the leading edge, like the

X–15, the fastest aircraft yet built, in which the whole airframe primary structure was welded from refractory high-nickel alloys, similar to those used for gas-turbine rotor blades, which had to be annealed at up to 1,095°C (2,003°F) and then 'aged' at 705°C (1,301°F) in furnaces big enough to swallow the whole aircraft. Almost all the 'plumbing' in this Mach 6·8 aircraft was welded or brazed, and virtually all the components and equipment had to be of unusual heat-resistant materials.

Progress with missiles and spaceflight in 1955 to 1965 led to a revolution in advanced structures, and also in fascinating methods of cooling the exterior to avoid their burning up like a meteor in the atmosphere. Manned aircraft, with 3,542km/h (2,200mph) performant but challenging metal titanium, which was so difficult to produce from its natural state it was more expensive than gold, and is still more costly than most other aircraft metals. In the early 1950s it was used only for such parts as exhaust pipes and engine nacelles, but gradually its valuable property of coming between aluminium and steel led to its widespread use, especially in supersonic machines.

Titanium's strength at temperatures of 150–250°C (302–482°F) is much greater than aluminium, and it is much lighter than steel, but it posed large problems. Among the first aircraft made chiefly of titanium were America's Lockheed Blackbird (YF–12 and SR–71) high-altitude reconnaissance aircraft, with 3,542km/h (2,200mph) performance, skin temperatures up to 320°C (608 °F) over the whole airframe and engine nozzles white hot. Lockheed vice-president 'Kelly' Johnson recorded: 'Of the first 6,000 pieces we fabricated of Beta B–120 titanium we lost 95 per cent. With the help of Titanium Metals we attacked the problem vigorously, investigating such factors as hydrogen embrittlement, heat-treatment procedures, forming methods and design for production. We solved these problems, but at considerable cost.' At first B–120 seemed impossible to cut, and drills had to be re-ground after every ten holes; but by the end of development of these aircraft the alloy was being cut ten times faster, and drills were lasting 119 holes. The aircraft got their name from their exterior coat of high-emissivity black paint, a colour previously used on the X–15. Previously, slow aircraft had been kept cool in hot sunshine by painting the upper surface white.

Since 1966 there has been one more complete revolution in aircraft structures: the increasing use of composite materials. These are materials made up of two parts, which can either be thought of as a 'matrix' reinforced by very strong and stiff splinters or threads, or else as very strong and stiff splinters or threads stuck together with the adhesive that forms the matrix.

Composites were experimented with as early as 1920, when designers tried such combinations as brown paper layers stuck on top of each other with glue whilst being bent to the shape of the aircraft, and a sort of plastic made from seaweed which again was moulded with layers of wrapping paper. By 1950 glass

RIGHT AND BELOW: Stainless steel was the answer in the 1950s to the problem of increased skin temperatures due to the faster speeds of aircraft. The Convair B–58 Hustler was one of the first aircraft to act as a 'heat-sink' allowing continuous absorption of high skin heat and avoiding dangerous variations in metal temperature. The cutaway shows a detail of a brazed stainless-steel honeycomb sandwich panel.

BELOW: Airframe technology was put to the test in the X–15, the world's fastest aircraft. At speeds approaching Mach 7 skin temperature could rise to over 650°C (1200°F). A special nickel-chromium alloy, Inconel X, was used for the skin while the primary load structures were built of stainless steel and titanium.

fibre was already in production for airframe parts, but only for items such as radomes, fairings and wing-tips that did not bear severe stress. The spun glass is moulded with resin adhesive to form a neat and light one-piece shell which stands up to the action of the weather and can be made to have considerable strength and resistance to impacts. Several designers tried to build complete 'plastic aircraft', but they were hampered by lack of prior experience (so that airworthiness authorities imposed severe factors of safety to avoid failures, making the airframe heavy) and by the fact that glass is strong but not stiff and so the structure distorted more than a metal one.

At this point it is essential briefly to mention aeroelasticity. Thousands of people spend their whole lives solving aeroelastic problems, but it is a subject too complex to go into deeply here. It is impossible to avoid in modern aircraft, because no aeroplane or helicopter is rigid, but can distort or vibrate in an almost limitless number of ways. In

B-1 MATERIALS
AV-1

% OF DCPR WT	
ALUMINUM	41.3
STEEL	6.6
TITANIUM	21.0
COMPOSITES	.3
FIBERGLASS	
POLYIMIDE QUARTZ	30.8
OTHERS	

TOP: *Diagram of the different materials and sub-assemblies of the Rockwell B-1.*
ABOVE CENTRE AND ABOVE: *Glass-fibre and glass-reinforced plastics are increasingly attractive materials for certain aircraft structures, especially gliders and sailplanes. The Gläsflugel Hornet is typical of modern sailplane construction. The cutaway shows a wing section of glass-fibre and polystyrene foam—light, flexible and very smooth.*

early aircraft speeds were low enough for this to be generally ignored.

Aeroelasticity is caused by aerodynamic forces, elastic forces in the structure, inertia forces due to the masses of material, and certain other inputs, and can result in oscillation, buffet, control reversal (the surface has an effect opposite to that intended because it distorts the part of the structure to which it is hinged), vibration and, the most serious of all, divergence, in which the distortion has the effect of increasing the load causing it, so that a complete wing or tail may be broken. Today complete aircraft are resonance-tested before or during the start of the flight-test programme, by carefully suspending them and then 'exciting' them by vibrators which can shake the whole airframe at any desired frequency.

Many of us have discovered that if we shake a seemingly strong handrail barrier (or a high balcony, for example) at its natural resonant frequency we could quickly break it, though it would be many times too strong for us to break by a steady force. Likewise many aircraft, before aeroelasticity was fully recognized, oscillated and broke before the pilot could alter the condition that was causing it. Flutter can be induced in flight-testing either by deliberately exciting the airframe, at different airspeeds, with controllable vibrators or by firing a quick-burning rocket fixed at the wing-tip or tail (called a 'bonker'), which imparts a vicious blow as if from a giant hammer. The resulting oscillations are measured both with and without such systems as autopilots and yaw-dampers in use.

In general, wooden aircraft have been less prone to aeroelastic problems than metal ones, but this is partly because they usually fly at lower speeds. Even today a significant proportion of lightplanes are built of wood, though this is influenced by the fact that some of the builders simply lack the facilities to handle modern metal construction. Where a good strength:weight ratio and a smooth streamline form are combined with low airspeeds, as in the sailplane, glass-fibre or Glass-Reinforced Plastic (GRP) is extremely attractive. A large and increasing proportion of sailplanes are 'glass', and their flexibility gives the pilot a smoother ride and results in none of the aeroelastic problems that would occur at higher speeds. GRP is also used for some parts of powered aircraft and even for modern propeller blades, fans and fan ducts.

In the early post-war era other composites were investigated for aircraft construction, notably Durestos, a resin-bonded material

Construction of the Airbus A.300B

The Airbus A300B is the most modern civil aircraft in use. Six countries have collaborated to design and build it. The main members of Airbus Industrie are Deutsche Airbus (MBB and VFW-Fokker) in Germany, Aérospatiale in France, Fokker-VFW in the Netherlands, Spain's CASA and Hawker Siddeley of Britain. Original design and testing was done by Hawker, Aérospatiale and Deutsche Airbus, and these companies employ 100,000 people in 39 factories. Of these, some 26,900 are engaged directly on the A300B programme. The largest single parts are the left and right wing boxes, and three million man-hours went into the design of the wing alone. Hawker later added a further 900,000 man-hours in refinement and improvement, though the basic design never changed. Indeed, much of the refinement was deliberately making the wing 'worse' by simplifying it, because in its original form it performed beyond all expectation, a fact first indicated during the 3,700 hours of wind-tunnel testing completed by the end of 1968 using 41 models in 6 tunnels in England, 1 in France, 2 in Germany and 1 in the Netherlands.

Aérospatiale builds the centre section, which is the same width as the fuselage and forms an integral unit with the lower centre fuselage. Hawker builds the left and right wings at Chester, and it is there that the wing

aluminium-copper alloy. Each wing has three upper and three lower skins, the joints being above and below Rib 9, where the engine pylon is hung, and inboard from there along the centre spar. This spar, which runs across the aircraft between the engine ribs (Rib 9), is fabricated, which means it is built up from many parts. The rest of the primary structure is integrally stiffened and machined from large slabs or forgings.

Upper and lower skins are held while being machined by large numbers of suction cups. When one is finished, the air supply is reversed and the table of the machine tool, 18·29m (60ft) by 3·66m (12ft), becomes an air-cushion pallet on which the skin 'floats'. This is of great value in exactly positioning the fresh billet and in taking off the finished skin. After careful inspection by eye and by NC-controlled machines, to verify exact dimensions and ensure that there are no scratches or toolmarks, the skins are squeezed in a (1,221·82-tonne) 1,200-ton press to beyond the aerofoil profile of the wing. On release from the press they spring back to the exact curvature needed.

During World War II the popular figure of the aircraft industry was Rosie the Riveter, a hastily-trained girl with a rivet gun. In building modern aircraft such as the A300B, manual riveting of this kind is still possible, though it is hard to find. In making the wing the philosophy never changes: giant machines, computer control, and precise, repeatable results. Drilling is done automatically, with a surface finish of 152·4 micro-centimetres (60 micro-

having the same coefficient of expansion as the spars and skins of the wing, otherwise a wing that fitted in winter would not fit in summer.

The wing assembly jig consists basically of seven pairs of cylindrical columns, on which are mounted the many locating points that ensure not only the wing itself will be exactly the right shape, but also that it will precisely fit the centre section made in France. Most of the joints between the heavy spars and skins are made with Hi-Lok or Taper-Lok bolts, each of which fits like part of a watch. After assembly, the wing box has its root-end profile machined, and it also has to be sealed to form an integral fuel tank. Eventually these vast tanks become quite complex, with multiple covers, baffles, pipes, booster pumps, drains (the position of which was decided after exhaustive studies with one-fifth scale model wings) and manhole covers fitted into large holes, around which the skin has its full thickness of 25·4mm (1in).

When the wing box is finished, the pair for one Airbus are loaded into an Aero Spacelines Super Guppy aircraft and flown to Bremen, Germany, where the movable surfaces are added. Most of these are made in the Netherlands by Fokker-VFW and comprise, on each left or right wing: one inboard tabbed Fowler flap; two inboard airbrake/lift dumpers, an all-speed aileron (in line with the engine), two outboard tabbed Fowler flaps; five outboard airbrake/lift dumpers; a wing tip low-speed aileron; three large sections of powered slat, and, on the B2K and B4 models, an inboard Kruger flap and fuselage-mounted retractable 'notch' to give a perfect leading edge profile without the gap seen in other aircraft. These surfaces are fabricated by riveting and incorporate bonded and honeycomb structures. It is typical of modern-aircraft design that extensive studies with computers were

the parts to the assembly hall at Toulouse, where powerful jacks and fixtures lift each into exact position for mating with its neighbour. The towering Messier-Hispano landing gears are attached, and in a few days the aircraft is standing on its own ten tyres. The General Electric engines, 61·3 per cent shipped from the United States and the rest (including some of the most advanced technology portions) made in Germany and France, are packaged inside their enormous cowling pods which are mainly made by an American company's new French factory at Toulouse. The process of turning the bare airframe into a finished Airbus then occupies several weeks and represents much more than half the total cost. Thousands of items arrive from factories in France, the United States, Britain, Germany and other European countries, and the great size of the aircraft facilitates installation by allowing many personnel to be on board at the same time.

Tons of furnishing materials, including thermal and sound insulation, are among the last parts to be added before the customer's own choice of interior begins to take shape. Before furnishing is completed the 'green aircraft' (i.e., unfurnished

ABOVE: *Final assembly line of the Airbus at Toulouse, France.*
LEFT: *One of Air France's Airbuses.*

skins, the biggest single pieces of metal in the aircraft, are NC-machined by enormous millers. The skins begin life as slabs in Davenport, Iowa, USA. Computer tape controls the cutting heads as they carve out the original thick sheet to an integrally stiffened skin weighing about 19 per cent as much, the mountain of swarf and chips, representing 18 per cent of the original slab, being returned to the light-alloy supplier.

The skin materials are not all the same: upper skins are unclad aluminium-zinc alloy for compression, while the undersurfaces are strong

inches) or better than 76·2 micro-centimetres (30 micro-inches) if the holes are then reamed. The stringers that stiffen each skin are positioned and clamped, and a Drivmatic machine then runs along each stringer cold-forming the rivets from automatically supplied headless slugs. Each is automatically shaved flush by a small milling cutter as soon as it is formed. Then the stiffened skins are held in a gigantic vertical assembly fixture where the wing box is assembled. So big and so accurate are the operations, that the entire fixture has to be linked by light-alloy beams

undertaken just to decide on the materials for the tracks along which run the slats and flaps. The answer was machined forgings in titanium for the slats, and light alloy forgings for the flaps, with the track faces made from wear-resistant steel inserts.

The same kind of attention to detail, and extreme precision even in parts as big as a house, characterize the construction of the fuselage sections and vertical tail in Germany, the nose, flight deck and engine pylons in France, and the horizontal tail and doors in Spain. Finally the Super Guppy brings all

and without avionics) may have begun acceptance flying. It will spend a day or two in the world's most modern paint shop, where weather-resistant epoxy-based paints dress the exterior in the colourful scheme of a national airline. The customer's livery is exactly recorded and marked out partly manually and partly automatically, applied with spray-guns and brushes from gondolas mounted on telescopic rams travelling on overhead gantries in the roof. A painter can zoom from the nose to the tip of the fin almost 17m (55ft) above the exactly level concrete floor.

which a 'tow' of a few thousand filaments looking like black string is wound over a former into the shape of the workpiece whilst bonded with adhesive.

Unlike many fibres, carbon or graphite can be made in lengths measured in miles. Each filament is much finer than human hair, and it will not break until the stress has reached levels 5, 10 or even 20 times the limit for metals. Compared with glass, the black fibre is much stiffer, so a CFRP structure can be made not only amazingly strong and light but also rigid. Finished CFRP items can be made most readily by buying prepreg, the standard raw-material form, and then cutting it (thin sheet can be cut with scissors) and bonding it under heat and pressure to form the desired part.

From the start it was recognized that CFRP would not be cheap, though over the years costs have fallen in a predictable way as small pilot plants have given way to bulk industrial production. Carbon fibre is inherently much cheaper than its main rival, boron, developed mainly by the US Air Force, which has to be produced by depositing the boron metal as condensed vapour, in an atmosphere of boron trichloride, on a white-hot wire of tungsten! Boron filament thus grows on the white-hot wire like the ring-growths of a tree. It can thus be made thicker than carbon fibre and is very strong and stiff, and has been vigorously promoted in the United States in matrices of epoxy resin, polyimide high-temperature resin, phenolic resin, titanium, aluminium and magnesium. With the backing of numerous military programmes boron filament, mainly used in boron-epoxy composite, has been in production for US aircraft since 1973. The first batches of boron-epoxy prepreg cost $209 per pound, but the second year's production cost $107 per pound, at which level those selling it claim that airframe component cost becomes 'comparable to titanium'. Among the earliest uses for boron-epoxy composite were reinforcement of the General Dynamics F–111F wing hinge, stiffening of the Sikorsky CH–54B tailboom, complete manufacture of 50 rudders for McDonnell Douglas F–4 Phantoms as a test programme (the aircraft all entered service in the usual way), manufacture of the tailplanes of the Grumman F–14 Tomcat, and manufacture of both vertical and horizontal tails of the McDonnell Douglas F–15 Eagle. Since 1973 boron prepreg has not fallen significantly in price, and with the benefit of more American companies interested in CFRP boron now finds the going tough.

CFRP has not had the backing of big military programmes, because there have been none in Britain, but in a quiet way it has gradually taken over a vast number of markets. To show its versatility the biggest outlet for carbon fibre is in the shafts of golf clubs, with tennis rackets and fishing rods running close behind.

Carbon-fibre prepreg has also been used to stiffen countless structures in glass fibre or aluminium, including many aircraft structures, but its real worth is best seen in components designed to be made in CFRP. The almost ideal initial application was the manu-

reinforced by short filaments of asbestos. In bulk asbestos has little strength (we think of it as flabby fire insulation), but many substances can develop fantastic strength when in the form of fine filaments. This is because a single crystal of material has perfect properties, sometimes millions of times better than bulk material in which astronomic numbers of crystals are lumped together with weak joints. Even glass, which is not a crystalline material, is far stronger weight-for-weight as a fine filament than as a solid mass. Single filaments of asbestos are even better, but are difficult to produce in long lengths. Much research was done in 1945 to 1955 on various composites to try to get good adhesion between the filament and the matrix, and to get the highest proportion of strong filament into the final composite. Obviously, 100 per cent is impossible, because there has to be a matrix to stick the filaments or short fibres together. Among the other composites on which work began at that time were filaments of stainless steel in aluminium, silica

in aluminium and boron in magnesium.

Then, in 1963 to 1965, workers at Britain's Royal Aircraft Establishment at Farnborough produced fibres of carbon or graphite which appeared to exceed all others in their combination of strength, stiffness and low density. Such fibres had been studied in Japan, though not as structural material, and it was the British team that first pushed through 'carbon fibre' as an aerospace material that could be reliably produced in quantity and used efficiently. The first production method was to heat a commercial man-made fibre, Polyacrilonitrile (PAN), in a furnace until it had turned to almost pure crystalline carbon. It then had to be heat-treated and stretched, at white heat, to develop strength which, in comparison with metals, seemed like science fiction. Selected resins were then used to stick the fibres together to make either prepreg (prefabricated strip or sheet), of solid Carbon-Fibre Reinforced Plastic (CFRP), or a finished item by a laborious but ideal process called filament winding, in

LEFT: *An early use of boron-epoxy prepreg composite was in the test manufacture of rudders for F–4 Phantoms.*
BELOW LEFT: *Boron-epoxy prepreg was also used in the manufacture of the F–15's horizontal and vertical tails.*
BELOW: *The F–14 Tomcat with details of (a) electron-beam welded titanium wing pivot box (b) boron-fibre tailplane skins and (c) machined rear fuselage spectacle frame with detachable tailplane fittings.*
RIGHT: *Assembly of the Boeing 747.*
BELOW RIGHT: *Carbon-fibre was tried for the fan blades of the Rolls-Royce RB.211 engine.*

facture of the fan blades for the Rolls-Royce RB.211 engine, where CFRP saved a remarkable amount of total engine weight and had other advantages, but this was killed by the inability of Rolls-Royce to make the blade leading edge sufficiently resistant to wear and severe impact.

In a low key several European firms eventually got into production with CFRP helicopter rotor blades, transport aircraft floors, fighter control surfaces (such as Sweden's Saab Viggen canard), rocket-motor pressure vessels and many other parts. Most customers for the Boeing 747 specify British CFRP floors because they are much lighter than the alternative aluminium/balsa sandwich and last at least seven times as long. CFRP is routinely fitted to aircraft of quite modest performance; for example, the landing-gear doors of VFW-Fokker 614 are CFRP panels bonded over Nomex honeycomb, which gives a 30 per cent saving in weight over the alternative GRP construction.

Technology

None of man's creations has spurred the development of as much new technology as the modern aircraft. Gas dynamics (the behaviour of air or gas in motion), new materials, new forms of engine, new kinds of structure, new weapons, the processing and display of information, methods of navigation, systems for moving or controlling things remotely, and perhaps above all the vast field of electronics – all have been driven on at a cracking pace by the needs of aviation, and have subsequently percolated through industry and society into the whole spectrum of modern life. Some of the advances are discussed in special chapters (notably, engines and airframes). Others are explained in chapters dealing with particular classes of aircraft, or with military and civil aviation. In this chapter a broad overview is given of the main advances made in the field of aviation, with the emphasis entirely on the aircraft itself, although it is worth mentioning that aviation has also produced advances of other kinds.

LEFT: *Levavasseur's Antoinettes established features that were to become common on later aircraft. These included a mainplane in front of the tailplane and a tractor propeller.*
BELOW: *The Rockwell International B–1 is the largest variable-wing aeroplane in flight.*

BOTTOM LEFT: *An unusually shaped aircraft is the Martin X–24B. It is a wingless aeroplane with the whole structure acting as an aerofoil.*
BOTTOM RIGHT: *The delta-shaped wing solved a number of design problems of high-speed flight. Illustrated is the Mirage 50. (See also page 461.)*

sian one, was that the main wing should be slightly higher than the rear one, to act like a slat. Miles produced Libellula (a species of dragonfly) aircraft between 1941 and 1943 which were again of the tandem-wing type. The main advantage of the tandem-wing aeroplane is that it has a much larger CG range than normal; in other words it can still fly safely with a lot of load near either the front or rear.

During World War II several canard fighters appeared, with vertical surfaces either ahead of the pusher propeller or on the wing trailing edges or tips. Conversely, the Messerschmitt Me 163 was of the so-called tailless family, with no separate horizontal surface at all. After 1945 jet fighters continued these unusual forms and the tailless delta, with more or less triangular-shaped wing, became quite common. The delta shape wing neatly solved several problems; the elevators could be far behind the CG for good control;

Shape

One of the arguments of those who attempt to scorn the work of the Wright brothers is that they settled on the wrong shape of aeroplane. They put the horizontal tail in front, the vertical tail at the back, used biplane surfaces everywhere, made the pilot lie on the wing on one side of the centreline to balance the engine on the other side, and used two sets of chains to drive two pusher propellers. This arrangement had many drawbacks, and several early aviators appreciated the simplicity of just fixing the propeller to the engine, but then they were not sure whether to make it pull or push.

One has only to study the aeroplanes of Louis Blériot to see how undecided designers were. Some Blériots were tractors (propeller in front) and some pushers, while the arrangement of tail and control surfaces varied from day to day. Many designers used tandem, or even circular, wings.

By 1910 most, but by no means all, designers had agreed that the classic aeroplane had one or more sets of wings near the Centre of Gravity (CG), and both vertical and horizontal tail surfaces. Until 1950 it was almost universal to have a fixed fin (vertical

stabilizer) carrying a hinged rudder, and a fixed tailplane (stabilizer) carrying hinged elevators. In general, the further away these surfaces are from the CG, the smaller they need to be, because the moment (turning or stabilizing effect) is roughly proportional to the surface area multiplied by the distance from the axis of rotation.

The Canard

Probably the main alternative aeroplane configuration is the 'canard' (French for duck), or tail-first, layout. It is rare to have a design with *all* the 'tail' surfaces in front; a canard usually has the horizontal tail in front and vertical tail at the rear. One reason for this configuration is that if the horizontal tail were to stall it would cause the aircraft automatically to pitch nose-down, thus unstalling and returning to controllable flight, whereas with a rear tailplane the stall of that surface would be disastrous. Professor Focke built a canard in 1909, and then exhaustively tried the *Ente* (German for duck) in 1930, finally concluding that there was no great advantage.

Many designers, including Delanne and Miles, experimented with a different shape in which there were essentially two wings. The Delanne idea, based on an earlier Rus-

the wing could have a very low thickness/chord (t/c) ratio (thickness divided by chord, i.e. the distance from leading to trailing edge); and the result came out light and with low transonic drag.

Eventually, fighter designers realized that the best wing is one of conventional form but with low aspect ratio. A fighter needs a wing of large area, for maximum power of manoeuvre, and low t/c ratio for supersonic performance. To carry a large load the wing needs high-lift devices while multi-role aircraft need a variable-sweep 'swing wing' mounted on pivots. In this arrangement, the wings can be spread out to give a long, slender surface for take-off, slow-speed loitering and landing, or folded back to give a very small span for supersonic flight.

It is especially important to have the smallest possible span and area for supersonic flight at low level, to avoid the crew having an impossibly rough ride. One large bomber, the Rockwell International B–1, even has a Low-Altitude Ride Control (LARC) system which senses atmospheric turbulence and works control surfaces on the aircraft to counter it and keep the crew compartment travelling in a smooth, straight line.

Aspect ratio

Aspect ratio is crucial to aircraft design. The slowest and most efficient aircraft need the highest possible aspect ratio; sailplanes and man-powered aircraft have extremely slender wings with a ratio of 25 to 35 in order to act on the greatest possible airflow. Most aircraft have an aspect ratio of between 5 and 11, while fighters and supersonic transports typically lie in the range 1·5 to 3·5. In the years immediately following World War II the arrow-shaped swept wing was almost universally adopted, along with the delta, to allow aircraft to reach higher transonic speeds. The first jet airliner, the de Havilland Comet, had a virtually unswept wing, but the Tupolev Tu–104, Boeing 707 and Douglas DC–8 all had wings swept back at about 35°. Later, the very fast Boeing 747 raised the angle to over 37°, but today highly swept wings are rare. The very fastest aircraft, such as the North American X–15 and Lockheed A–11/YF–12/SR–71 Blackbird family, have no sweepback at all. In general, long-range aircraft today have more sweep and short-range aircraft have less, but the trend with all subsonic transports is towards more slender wings with less sweep.

During the early 1950s a rash of problems with early transonic or supersonic wings led to a succession of 'fixes' which have in the main taken their place as permanent features of aircraft design. One is the turbulator or vortex generator, which is a small fin no bigger than a playing card, set at an angle to the airflow. Behind it streams a writhing

TOP: *In the 1950s a number of 'fixes' were devised to solve problems of high-speed wings. The two illustrated are the sawcut (left) and the dogtooth (right). The sawcut straightens the airflow and stops it slipping in a spanwise direction. The dogtooth acts as a vortex generator and fence combined.*
ABOVE RIGHT: *Another solution to the spanwise flow of air was the fence. Fences can be clearly seen on the MiG–15 shown.*

ABOVE CENTRE: *Swept wings were almost universally adopted after World War II. The DC–8 has wings swept back at 35°.*
ABOVE: *The North American X–15, the fastest aircraft that has ever flown, has no sweep-back at all. It has an aspect ratio of 2·5 and the tail and wing are of the same thickness.*
RIGHT: *The variable-incidence wing of the F–8 Crusader aids in take-off and landing.*

vortex which, though it increases drag, stirs up the air downstream and mixes the high-speed free-stream flow with the sluggish boundary layer covering the immediate proximity to the aircraft skin.

Airflow can also be improved by reducing the cross-section taper of control surfaces and terminating them with a blunt instead of a sharp trailing edge. The air is fooled into thinking the surface has a wider chord and sharp trailing edge, so drag is not significantly affected, but blunt rudders and ailerons are often the sign of a problem which might have been avoided. Another 'fix' is the flow-breaker or stall inducer, a small projection along the leading edge of a wing, which promotes breakaway of flow at high angle of attack (angle to the airflow). This ensures that the stall will start at the leading edge and not at some other portion of the wing causing possible loss of controllability.

A common fault of early swept or delta wings was sharp deflection of the airflow towards the wing tips, especially over the upper surface. This was often caused by a region of high pressure above the wing resulting from local shockwaves, the strong pressure waves formed when supersonic flow is present. The ideal wing has the airflow passing straight across from front to rear, as seen from above, and the simplest and crudest answer to the outward or spanwise flow was to add a fence, a thin wall aligned with the fore-and-aft direction round the leading edge and extending back across the upper surface. Some Soviet MiG fighters had as many as six large fences, and even today four is a common number.

Another of the 'fixes' of the early 1950s is the dogtooth. Early swept or delta wings were frequently improved by extending the chord of the outer portion, and drooping the extended leading edge slightly down to reduce the leading-edge angle of attack at high altitude.

In most aircraft the inboard end of the extra area forms a major discontinuity, called a dogtooth (because it looks like a curved canine tooth from end-on). This creates a powerful vortex which swirls back over the wing, especially at high angles of attack, and thus acts as a vortex generator and fence combined.

Yet another feature which became important in the early 1950s on fast fighters is the variable-incidence wing, which instead of being rigidly fixed to the fuselage is mounted on pivots. In fact, the attitude of the wing (its angle of attack or incidence) cannot alter for any given flight condition; the effect of the pivots is to cause the attitude of the fuselage to alter. In the Vought F–8 Crusader fighter, a variable-incidence wing enables the aircraft to land with the fuselage in a level, or even slightly nose-down, attitude, giving the pilot a good view ahead and allowing the main landing gears to be short.

Very fast aircraft

Extremely fast aircraft present their own problems. The North American XB–70 Valkyrie bomber, which happened to have a canard foreplane, was designed to make use of 'compression lift' caused by compressing the flow behind the inclined shockwaves under the wing. At supersonic speed, the air was forced to pass under the wing between the down-turned wing tips and a huge box containing the six engines. At subsonic speed, the wing tips (which were hinged) were raised to the normal position.

The XB–70 was one of the first modern aircraft to have two 'verticals' (tail fins). In the 1930s designers often gave aircraft two or more tail fins, sometimes in order to place fins and rudders in the slipstream from wing-mounted engines. Today, except for aircraft which for unrelated reasons have two tail booms (such as the Rockwell OV–10 Bronco and Israel Aircraft Industries Arava, which need two booms to carry the tail because freight must be loaded through a full-height rear door), virtually every aeroplane has a single vertical tail. Often, for structural or aerodynamic reasons, the horizontal tail is mounted on top, giving the so-called T-tail.

Most aeroplanes with two vertical tails are fighters, the first being the Mikoyan MiG–25. Two vertical tails can give better power of manoeuvre, especially at high angles of attack in a dogfight. They also give a measure of redundancy (in the McDonnell Douglas F–15 Eagle, either vertical tail could control the aircraft alone) and reduce overall height – they were needed on the Grumman F–14 Tomcat to hold height to 5·18m (17ft) to fit carrier hangars. Yet another feature of the latest dogfighters is a long forebody strake, a greatly extended wing root which has a sharp edge to create a strong vortex at high angles of attack and increase lift and improve control. A similar feature is seen on the Anglo-French Concorde supersonic transport.

More lift

The lift of a wing is proportional to its shape (the cross-section profile or aerofoil section), to its area and to the square of the airspeed. Thus the lift at 200km/h (124·2mph) will be not twice the lift at 100km/h (62·1mph) but four times as great. It is also dependent upon its setting to the airflow, or angle of attack. Most wings have to be turned to a slight negative (nose-down) angle of attack before they will not give any lift at all. At a more pronounced negative angle they will give negative lift, in other words a down-force; this is the setting when an aeroplane flies inverted.

Slats

In the early days of aviation a stall was often fatal. It could lead to a spin, a stabilized condition in which the aircraft fell to the ground in a stalled spiral, with its controls more or less ineffective. In about 1920, Frederick Handley Page perfected a device to postpone the stall; he added a small auxiliary winglet called a slat ahead of the wing leading edge. At a high angle of attack, the lift on the slat pulled it away from the main wing on pivoted links, opening a gap called the slot (other wings had fixed slots built into their structure). The air was guided by the slot to keep flowing across the top of the wing, and thus the stall was delayed to an even more extreme angle. In modern aircraft the slat is often very large and strong, and instead of being allowed to pull open automatically it is pushed open by rows of hydraulic rams.

It so happens that supersonic aircraft with wings which are very long from front to rear (large root chord) but of small span, in other words with extremely low aspect ratio, do not follow the classic behaviour as angle of attack is increased. When the angle gets to about 20°, by which time ordinary wings would have stalled, the lift reaches a maximum, but no stall is encountered. If the aircraft has sufficient power or momentum it can go on flying at angles as high as 60°, with the nose pointing skywards. Drag is then extremely high, but the lift is still equal to the weight and flight can be continued.

Early flaps

Even before the slat was invented, wings had been fitted with flaps. At first these were simple hinged surfaces. The plain flap is just a hinged part of the trailing edge which can be depressed before landing in order to increase lift and drag. The split flap is hinged to the underside of the rear part of the wing. This also increases drag but does not greatly increase lift. Both normally need considerable force to operate because they have to be pushed down against the airflow, but with small and relatively slow aircraft a pilot can normally push them down by a hand-lever driving the flap by a linkage.

By 1935 aircraft were becoming larger and faster, and since then flaps have been usually driven by power (see Systems subsection). At this time several more efficient kinds of flap came into use. The principle of the slat, in which the airflow is accelerated through a narrow slot, is used in the slotted flap, in which the leading edge of the lowered flap leaves a slot under the streamlined lower rear part of the wing. The air flowing through this slot follows the upper surface of the flap, whereas with the plain flap it just breaks away (in other words the plain flap stalls when it is lowered). The slotted flap can therefore generate much more lift.

The next stage was obvious: by 1944 the first aircraft were in use with a double-slotted flap, and in the best-selling Boeing 727 of 1962 a triple-slotted flap was used. This can give extremely high lift, and thus allows the aircraft to land relatively slowly despite having a small, highly loaded wing of thin aerofoil section. Other flaps include the Junkers double-aerofoil (virtually a narrow auxiliary wing carried behind the main wing on pivots); the Youngman (a much larger auxiliary wing which could be rotated positively to increase lift and drag for landing or negatively to act as an air brake for dive bombing); and the very important Fowler which, though usually only a single surface, marked a major breakthrough in that it was not just hinged to the wing but mounted on guide tracks projecting behind the trailing edge. The initial movement of the Fowler was rearwards, increasing wing area and greatly augmenting lift. As the flap continued to extend its angle progressively increased, so that the final part of its travel did not add much lift but added a lot of drag.

Modern flaps, which are usually double-slotted or tabbed Fowlers (Fowlers with an auxiliary split or plain trailing-edge flap on the main flap), are carried by wheeled carriages running along strong forged steel or titanium tracks. Sometimes several hundred horsepower are needed to drive large flaps, and the common actuation system is a free-running cross-shaft inside the wing driving all flap sections by bevel gearboxes and ball-bearing screwjacks.

Such powerful flaps are almost always partnered by powered leading edge systems, usually driven by similar hydraulic cross-shafts energized automatically so that leading-edge and trailing edge surfaces operate together. Sometimes the leading edge merely 'droops', by hingeing downwards when the flaps are lowered. Often large slats are used, while some aircraft have leading-edge flaps such as the Krüger type, hinged to linkages which extend them out and forwards to provide a powerful, bluff, high-lift leading edge in place of the sharp surface needed for high-speed flight. Boeing and Airbus Industrie use a further refinement: the flexible Krüger, whose profile changes as it is extended.

ABOVE: *Leading-edge devices: (a) drooped leading edge (b) slat (c) Krüger slat.*
RIGHT: *Flaps and slats on an Airbus.*

BELOW CENTRE: *The layer of air closest to the wing surface, the boundary layer, is subject to strong retarding frictional forces causing turbulence. Aerodynamicists have invented a number of methods to control the boundary layer. The MiG–21 (left) and the F–4 Phantom (right) are both fitted with the Attinello flap, a simple blown flap used to control the boundary layer and to increase the efficacy of the flap. Without blowing the flap would stall when lowered.*

BELOW: *Boundary Layer Control on the Hawker Siddeley Buccaneer multi-role aircraft, which first entered service in July 1962. The tailplane possesses a slit along the leading edge while the wing has very powerful blowing slits across the upper leading edge and over the upper surfaces of the flaps and ailerons. The blowing system has a built-in failsafe device to allow all the slits to be fully blown in the event of the failure of either of the engines.*

BELOW: *Three examples of engine-augmented lift. From top to bottom, the Buffalo jet flap, Upper Surface Blowing on the YC–14, and the Externally Blown Flap (EBF) on the YC–15. The complex flap sections of the DHC–5 Buffalo receive four sets of engine-supplied air. The YC–15 has two-segment flaps in the wake of the four engines. The YC–14 relies on the Coanda effect to make use of Upper Surface Blowing.*
BOTTOM LEFT: *The Boeing YC–14.*

Boundary layer control

During the early 1950s, fighter designers began to use high-pressure air bled from the jet engines, by fastening a valve and stainless-steel pipe to the engine compressors, to blow at high speed (often faster than sound) through narrow slits in various parts of the airframe. This was often called 'Boundary Layer Control' (BLC), but in its simplest form it was used solely to increase the effectiveness of the flaps. So-called 'blown' flaps are usually of the plain type, but of wide chord and thus very powerful. Without blowing they would stall when lowered, and be less effective, but blowing a sheet of very hot, high-pressure air from a slit or row of holes just above the leading edge of the flap forces the air flowing over the wing sharply down across the depressed flap to give a dramatic increase in lift. Named the Attinello flap after its inventor, this simple blown flap is used on such important aircraft as the Lockheed F–104 Starfighter, McDonnell Douglas F–4 Phantom and the Mikoyan MiG–21.

The Hawker Siddeley Buccaneer bomber has a much more advanced system in which the high-pressure air is blown over the flaps, along the leading-edges and along the leading-edge of the tailplane. This reconciles the need for a low-level attack aircraft to have a small wing (and, in this case, small tail) with the need to lift and control a heavy aircraft at modest speeds for carrier landing.

One shortcoming of simple flap blowing is that the need to reduce engine fuel-flow inevitably reduces the thrust available, so the

BELOW: *The Hunting H.126 was the only aircraft to use specially designed jet flaps, developed at the National Gas Turbine Establishment in the United Kingdom, to increase lift. The engine exhaust gases are conducted through pipes and ejected across the flaps from slots running the length of the wing's trailing edge. The detail (bottom) shows the ejector duct inside the wing. Reaction control nozzles are located at the wing-tips and rudder to improve control at low airspeeds.*

BELOW RIGHT: *The Br Michelin V was a WWI bomber of French design but constructed in Britain. The picture shows how everything was left out in the airstream; even the fuel tanks can be seen hung under the upper wing. It is hardly surprising that at full throttle this machine could only reach 138km/h (86mph). In those days reliability (which in the case of these aircraft was not very good) was far more important than streamlining to reduce aerodynamic drag.*

BOTTOM: *The Boeing 747 affords a staggering contrast to the Breguet Michelin. Though it weighs approximately 200 times as much, its aerodynamic drag is actually less when in cruising flight. The photograph, however, shows it on take-off, with leading-edge and trailing-edge flaps extended, landing gears down, and the auxiliary inlets around the engines opened to admit extra air. This particular aircraft is carrying a fifth engine as cargo to be taken to a distant engineering base.*

result is that the engines give less power at crucial times (landing, and possibly take-off). There are several other methods of using engine power to increase lift. One is to discharge the whole, or most, of the engine efflux through specially designed 'jet' flaps, made in the form of ejector ducts in heat-resistant material. First flown in the Hunting H.126 Jet Flap research aircraft in Britain in 1963, it is now flying in more advanced form in the National Aeronautics and Space Administration (NASA) 'augmentor wing' de Havilland Canada, DHC-5 Buffalo, with complex flap sections through which pass four sets of engine-supplied or entrained airflow. The entire fan airflow from this aircraft's Spey engines is ducted through large pipes to feed the flaps, blown ailerons and BLC on the fuselage, to reduce drag as well as increase lift. This aircraft can fly controllably at just over 75km/h (47mph).

Upper Surface Blowing

In the US Air Force Advanced Medium Short Take-Off and Landing (STOL) Transport (AMST) programme, two further ways of increasing the lift of a large transport have been investigated. The less advanced of these methods is the externally blown flap, explored on the McDonnell Douglas YC-15. In most aircraft with engine pods on the wings the flaps are deliberately omitted directly behind the engines to avoid the hot blast and buffet of the jet. In contrast, the YC-15 has extremely powerful two-segment flaps extended out and down directly in the wake of the four

engines, which are mounted close beneath the wing to blow right into the flaps.

The Boeing YC-14, on the other hand, has technically more difficult Upper-Surface Blowing (USB). This relies on the Coanda effect, i.e. the property of a fluid flow to cling to a surface even if that surface arches away. The Coanda effect can be demonstrated visibly by holding a bottle horizontally under a gently running tap; the water does not flow off the sides of the bottle but clings to the lower part and runs off at the lowest point. In the same way the YC-14 has two powerful CF6-50 turbofans mounted close above the wing roots. Their gigantic efflux, squashed against the wing by flattened nozzles and guided outwards by vortex generators, passes over inboard flap sections that can be depressed to 75°. The Coanda effect is so powerful that the engine jets likewise turn through the same angle, point almost straight down and thus give lift almost equal to the combined thrust of the engines. Special control systems automatically rearrange the flaps if either engine fails. A four-engined rebuilt de Havilland Canada Buffalo is now exploring USB for civil use.

Less drag

From early in the era of aeroplane flight, aviators have sought to reduce drag (which can loosely be translated as 'air resistance'). The fundamental method of achieving this objective is by streamlining, or making all parts of aircraft the shape of a streamline, the

path followed by smoothly flowing particles of air. In a large measure, drag reduction depended on structure, and real advances were made only with the adoption of the stressed-skin all-metal airframe. Smooth metal skin, flush rivets, carefully streamlined cockpits (preferably with canopies) and retractable landing gear all made major contributions. So did improved engine installations. Many arguments had revolved around the supposed lower drag of the water-cooled in-line engine compared with the bluff-fronted air-cooled radial, but these arguments were usually based on faulty reasoning which in turn rested on poor installations.

Retractable landing gears were sketched before 1914, but flown systems date from 1919 and production arrangements from 1931. In most cases the United States took the lead, and in early schemes the lower part of the main tyres projected to offer something on which to land in the event of failure (by the pilot or the system) to extend the gear before alighting. Early schemes were often complicated and heavy, and usually required arduous hand-cranking to operate. Not until 1935 did elegant geometries appear, the neatest fighter main gears folding inwards or outwards to be housed in the wing in front of or behind the wing front spar.

Reducing thickness/chord ratio

The coming of jets demanded a speeding-up of the process of reducing wing t/c ratio which had begun in the early 1930s. During the 1930s fighter aircraft were designed on the

LEFT: *The increase in aircraft speeds after World War II demanded a parallel reduction in wing thickness/chord (t/c) ratio. In fighters, such as the Hawker Hunter illustrated, t/c ratio fell to about 8 per cent compared with the 20 per cent common in the 1930s.*
RIGHT: *The t/c ratio fell even further in supersonic fighters. In the Dassault Mirage III it was reduced to about 3·5 per cent. Although the thin wings helped to reduce drag it correspondingly gave poor lift at low speeds, and consequently the aircraft had to take off and land at very high speeds.*
BELOW: *The first aircraft to be profiled to Richard Whitcomb's area rule was the F–102. The top picture shows the prototype YF–102; the bottom picture shows a production F–102A designed with the area rule in mind. Nose and tail were lengthened and mid-fuselage waisted.*
BELOW LEFT: *Radiator fitting on a Hurricane.*
BELOW RIGHT: *In the North American P–51 Mustang the radiator was placed under the real fuselage and the duct profiled to give positive thrust.*
BOTTOM RIGHT: *This Curtiss Cox racer of 1921 was a glaring example of clumsy engine installation with the radiators projecting on each side. Two years later Curtiss streamlined his engines but could still do little about the radiators.*

assumption that it had to have a t/c ratio of about 20 per cent (i.e., the chord was five times the maximum thickness) and a bomber one of 25 per cent. As speeds and engine powers increased these figures fell. After World War II the laminar aerofoils became universal for fast aircraft, and t/c ratio fell to about 8 per cent in aircraft such as the Lockheed Shooting Star and Hawker Hunter, to 5 per cent in supersonic fighters and to a remarkable region between 3·3 and 3·5 per cent in the Convair B–58, Lockheed F–104 and Dassault Mirage III. These extremely thin wings helped early Mach 2 aircraft to keep drag lower than available engine thrust but had the drawback of giving poor lift at low speeds, so all three aircraft took off and landed at exceptionally high speeds.

The area rule
Richard T. Whitcomb postulated in 1953 a general rule for shapes with minimum transonic drag. Called the area rule, this states that the total cross-sectional area of an aeroplane intended to fly faster than sound should increase uniformly from nose to tail. In other words, a projection such as a canopy, wing, fin, drop tank or other excrescence should be compensated for by reduction elsewhere. Some early area-ruled aircraft, such as the F–102 (which thereafter went supersonic) and Buccaneer, showed obviously waisted mid-fuselages and bulged extremities, but modern supersonic aircraft obey the rule in subtler ways. Supersonic aircraft also tend to have shallow cockpit canopies, vee windscreens and modest taper angles on noses and other portions. Their overall fineness ratio, a measure of slenderness broadly equivalent to length divided by body diameter, has to be high. It is for this reason that passengers cannot sit ten-abreast in a Concorde as they can in subsonic aircraft. Yet some aircraft intended to lead to hypersonic (many times faster than sound) aerospace aircraft, able to fly in the atmosphere or in space, are very bluff and fat. Examples are the M2–F2 and HL–10 'lifting bodies', and the Space Shuttle which is due to go into operation in 1979.

Laminar flow
All aircraft, supersonic or not, are today made as accurately as possible, with the smoothest attainable skin, to reduce the drag in the boundary layer due to skin friction. The laminar-flow wing helps because the airflow accelerates over the front part of the wing to the thickest part, and in an accelerating flow it is easier to keep the boundary layer laminar, or smooth. But over the rear part of the wing the flow slows down again, and the boundary layer then tends to break away from the surface and become turbulent, giving higher drag. This effect occurs wherever the flow slows down relative to the aircraft, and it was to avoid this that designers of early low-wing monoplanes often filled in the junction between the rear part of the wing and the fuselage with large fillets.

Propulsion

Early engine installations were crude. Petrol and water-cooling pipes had to be free from leaks, and the propeller was carved to the correct shape from multiple laminations of hardwood, but streamlining was conspicuously absent. Curtiss caused a stir with his streamlined D–12 engine installation of 1923, but even then the water radiator was merely a relative of a car radiator stuck in the airstream. By 1928 radiators were beginning to be enclosed in shaped ducts, which eventually had the form of a diffuzer – a duct fatter in the middle, to slow down the airflow – so that the air lingered as it passed the hot radiator surfaces and then accelerated back through the exit to the atmosphere. In many fighters there was no duct, but the radiator was mounted on vertical slides, with rubber water hoses, and the pilot could crank it out into the airstream just far enough to keep the temperatures within limits. But the ducted

radiator was eventually recognized to be essentially a propulsion system; by adding heat to an airflow its energy is increased, and by 1941 the radiator of the North American P–51 Mustang, under the rear fuselage, and the radiators of the de Havilland Mosquito, inside the inner wing leading edges, were giving not drag but positive thrust. By this time the coolant was not water but ethylene glycol, and the cooling circuit operated under pressure, with thermostatic control to adjust the position of the air exit flap(s).

Radial engines

Air-cooled radial engines never suffered the penalty of water circuits, but it took many years to discover how to instal one correctly. The first major step forward was the addition of the Townend ring in 1928. This American development was a circular aerofoil closely surrounding the engine and so shaped that it helped to pull the aircraft along. Throughout the 1930s, as engine designers added more

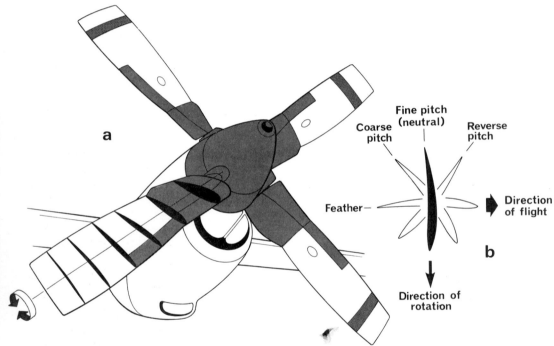

filling the gap between spinner and cowl, driven at 3·14 times crankshaft speed.

The Germans also led the field in installing all their aircraft engines in a uniform manner, with common mountings and piping suitable for either liquid-cooled inverted-vee or air-cooled radial engines.

Propellers

If anything, development of propellers exceeded that of engines in the pre-jet era. By 1930 many propellers had blades separate from the hub and individually replaceable. This made repairs easier and allowed the three-blade propeller (difficult with wood) to become common. But though these detachable blades could often be set in the hub at any of a range of angles, the far bigger advance was a propeller able to change its pitch in flight. For take-off and landing a fine pitch is needed. Like a nut on a fine-pitch screw-thread, this needs many turns and makes slow progress, so the engine can run at full throttle (or, for landing, can still run at high speed when throttled back) despite the low airspeed. In cruising flight the pitch needs to be much coarser, to allow a high airspeed to be matched with low engine speed and low fuel consumption. In a dive the pitch needs to be coarser still, while following engine failure the propeller-blades should ideally be turned edge-on so that the engine is 'feathered' and does not rotate or cause much drag.

These advances came in stages. The first mass-produced variable-pitch (v-p) propeller was the Hamilton of 1926, first sold in numbers in 1933. Later, by 1936, the Hydromatic propeller came into use, with blades positioned by bevel gears turned by a drum-cam. The cam was rotated via curved slots and rollers by a hydraulic piston in the hub. Unlike the bracket-type propeller this piston was double-acting, and the blades could be set to any chosen angle. When a Constant-Speed Unit (CSU) was added to the engine, the propeller could be automatically controlled to maintain any desired engine speed, being called a constant-speed propeller.

There were many other types of propeller, some having hubs containing electric motors and gearboxes. Blades were made of aluminium 'densified wood' (multiple veneers bonded under very high pressure, with a tough plastic casing) or welded sheets of stainless steel with a hollow interior. By the 1960s, Vertical/Short Take-Off and Landing (V/STOL) aircraft were using lightweight blades of glass-fibre, and today such blades are stiffened by carbon fibre. By 1944 propellers began to have an extra pitch setting: reverse pitch, giving backwards thrust when the throttle was opened to help slow aircraft after landing. Another feature of the modern propeller is beta control, by which the pilot can adjust pitch of each propeller directly to help in ground manoeuvring. Yet another device is a multi-engine synchronizer to cut out unpleasant aural 'beats' when several engines are running at slightly different speeds. Today the emphasis is strongly on increasing the size of propellers and reducing their rotational speed, to give a dramatic reduction in noise.

Propellers for turboprops are included in

TOP: *Three-blade propellers on the Bristol Blenheim bomber. These were primitive, with just two pitch settings: 'coarse' and 'fine'.*
ABOVE: *The propeller of the Lockheed C–130 Hercules (a) showing blade sections and twist. Schematic view of pitch change and blade rotation (b).*
TOP RIGHT: *A view of the wooden paddle propellers of a Santos Dumont aircraft of 1907.*
ABOVE RIGHT: *This Piper Navajo of the Spanish Air Force is typical of modern light planes, with constant-speed anti-iced propellers.*
RIGHT: *The inlet system of the Concorde: (a) take-off (b) noise-abatement climb (c) supersonic cruise (d) reverse thrust.*

and deeper fins to the engine cylinders, the installation designers fitted longer and closer-fitting cowlings, usually with hinged flaps or sliding shutters at the rear called gills (cowl flaps in North America) to control the cooling airflow. These gills had to be partly or wholly open for taxiing and take-off but closed or under thermostatic control in cruising flight, to reduce drag and avoid tail buffet.

Getting rid of the exhaust was accomplished in the early days by having plain stacks or a long pipe. During the 1920s, radial engines began to gather the exhaust into a manifold, either around the front crankcase or behind the cylinders. But the installation that was a major advance was that of the BMW 801 in the Focke-Wulf Fw 190, and in this the individual stacks were taken to ejector exhausts projecting through the fuselage behind the engine. This big engine was closely cowled, and to keep it cool at low speeds a fan was provided with blades the above history, but for the turbojet a new device had to be added: the thrust reverser. This matured in 1959 in two forms. One had upper and lower internal clamshells to seal off the nozzle and simultaneously open upper and lower cascade apertures (holes bridged by multiple deflector aerofoils), which ejected the jet in a diagonally forwards direction. The other had external upper and lower clamshells which either formed the skin of the engine nacelle or blocked the jet downstream of the nozzle and diverted it diagonally forwards.

Noise abatement

In recent years the increasing wish to avoid the nuisance of aircraft noise has been reflected in palliatives for existing propulsion systems and changed design features for new ones. The fundamental advance has been the high by-pass ratio fan engine, which makes today's 'Jumbo' of 362,875kg (800,000lb) gross weight many times quieter than earlier jets weighing less than one-tenth as much. Those older aircraft have been quietened by various noise-suppression methods. One is to line the walls of the inlet duct and nozzle with hollow sandwich material, one form being light-alloy honeycomb with a hole on the inner skin in the centre of each honeycomb cell; sound energy is constantly attenuated (used up) in each of the thousands of cells. Another palliative is the noise-suppressing nozzle, which typically is a multi-lobe shape rather like a flower or star with rounded rays. The long wavy boundary of the nozzle speeds mixing of the hot gas with the cool atmosphere and cuts down the violent shearing action which causes most of the noise in a high-velocity jet. Modern engines are quieter because designers select the best numbers of fan, turbine and compressor blades, adjust the axial spacings and use quiet-running gearwheels.

The variable nozzles needed for afterburners are discussed in Chapter 4. Supersonic aircraft also need variable air inlets, though sometimes, as in the General Dynamics F–16, such complication is omitted to save money. A fixed inlet begins to lose efficiency at Mach numbers beyond unity, and is seldom seen in an aircraft capable of more than Mach 1·3.

The ideal solution is to have an inlet which at take-off is opened wide, to swallow all the air it can get, but which progressively closes down as altitude and Mach number are gained, until in supersonic flight there is a large wedge protruding into, and almost closing off, the inlet duct. In addition there must be various auxiliary inlet doors, dump and spill doors and even doors through which air is sometimes sucked in and sometimes blown out. At all times there is a large airflow round the engine inside its nacelle, and in supersonic flight this flow probably becomes a kind of hurricane, passing out round the nozzle which acts as a powerful ejector, or air pump.

Propulsion control system

There are many other facets of propulsion systems. One which deserves discussion is the control system. In the earliest aero engines this comprised a single electrical switch which opened or closed the primary ignition circuit; a pilot had to adjust his landing approach by switching the engine off and then on again (it was known as 'blipping'). By 1920 virtually every engine had a throttle, like the accelerator of a car, and during the 1930s such extra features were added as automatic mix-ture control (to adjust the fuel: air ratio sup-plied to the cylinders), automatic compensa-tion for altitude and automatic boost control in supercharged engines to secure maximum power without the risk of overstressing the engine in denser air. Generally similar de-vices controlled early gas turbines, but gradu-ally the engine became more demanding, and supersonic powerplants, with variable inlets, variable nozzles, extensive air-bleed systems and other ancillary services, required a com-puter. Today, the most advanced aircraft have digital electronic control systems which constantly assess from hundreds to thousands

ABOVE: *The Rolls-Royce Avon RA.29/6 typifies the first 1,000-hour TBO civil jet engine.*

of channels of data and automatically take virtually all the work-load off the pilot.

A little should also be said about main-tenance and reliability. In the early 1930s the Bristol Jupiter gained headlines because it could be safely left to run, installed in an aero-plane, for 400 hours. By 1950 much more complex piston engines had Time Between Overhauls (TBOs) of 1,800 or 2,000 hours. By 1959 the Avon turbojet gained headlines because it was the first gas turbine to have a TBO in an aircraft of 1,000 hours, but very soon airline jet engines were achieving TBOs between 15,000 and 18,000 hours. Today the whole TBO concept has largely been replaced by on-condition maintenance, except for small piston engines, for which TBOs are mandatory in many countries. The engine is left alone, and if it works properly is not dis-turbed. Sensors built into the engine instal-lation warn of any vibration – even though too slight to be felt directly by the crew – while magnetic chip detectors constantly search for microscopic metal particles in the oil. Between long flights, or perhaps daily, a service engineer gives the engine a keen in-spection with a borescope – a thin tube con-taining a light source and optics which can be slid into the heart of the engine through various small holes – to allow the vital com-bustion liner, flame tubes, turbine rotor, sta-tor blades and other parts to be visually studied in fine detail without undoing a single bolt. Should anything need replace-ment, it can be done in the latest engines without taking the engine out of the aircraft; thanks to 'modular' construction, the rele-vant portion can be exchanged while leaving the other modules in place.

ABOVE: *Three contrasting landing gears.* ABOVE, *the four-wheel bogie of the Airbus A300B.* ABOVE RIGHT, *the Mosquito had twin shock struts sprung with rubber blocks in compression.* RIGHT, *twin oleo legs of the Wellington.*
TOP RIGHT: *The cross-Channel Blériot XI had wheels sprung by rubber belts in tension.*
CENTRE RIGHT: *The Hawker Fury fighters for Yugoslavia had Dowty internally sprung wheels.*
RIGHT: *The 28 wheels of the Lockheed C–5A are used to spread the load on unpaved airstrips.*

Landing and take-off

From the start of aeroplane flight it was clear that some form of sprung landing gear was needed. In early aircraft the springing was usually by bungee (rubber cord), but this had the drawback of bouncing badly. No proper answer was forthcoming until, around 1930, designers began to accept the cost penalty of landing-gear legs designed by engineers and made with precision. By far the most common was the oleo leg, and this is still the case for all except lightplanes. The oleo uses sliding pistons or cylinders, various fluids such as air, nitrogen, oil or special liquids with very large molecules (to make them more compressible), and valves to allow the leg to collapse readily without bouncing back.

When main gears were made retractable, most European countries chose single legs for fighters and lightplanes and twin-leg gears for bombers, the latter having one leg resting on each end of the wheel axle and folded either to the front or rear to lie in the nacelles of the engines. American aircraft, and the German Junkers Ju 88 normally had single legs, those of the Ju 88 being unusual in being sprung by stacks of chamfered rings of springy steel. Another unusual shock strut (leg) was that of the de Havilland Mosquito, which was sprung by a stack of rubber blocks. As aircraft weight grew, so did the number of tyres needed to spread the load on airfield surfaces. The Focke-Wulf Fw 200 Condor had twin

ABOVE: *From 1916 until about 1945 most aircraft had tailwheel-type landing gears, such as that of the Piper Pawnee agricultural machine (a). Today almost all have nosewheels, such as on the Grumman American Traveler (b).*

BELOW: *Lockheed F–104 Starfighter landing gears support 13,600kg (30,000lb) at over 320km/h (200mph) and occupy little space when retracted. Springing is by small 'Liquid Spring' shock struts pivoted near the tops of the hinged legs.*

RIGHT: *In the 1920s large, heavy aircraft had extremely large wheels, with vast low-pressure tyres. This Armstrong Whitworth Ensign typifies such gears. Today there would be numerous, much smaller wheels.*

BOTTOM: *In 1950 Boeing designed the B–52 heavy bomber to have unique landing gears with four two-wheel trucks, all on the fuselage, and small outrigger wheels under the outer wings. The main trucks can steer so that in cross-wind landings the B–52 can 'crab' along diagonally.*

wheels on complicated legs, the Messerschmitt Me 323 and Arado Ar 232 freighters had numerous small wheels along the fuselage, but the heaviest aircraft of World War II, the Boeing B–29, had single legs each supported by two tyres. Since 1945 there have been numerous landing-gear configurations, with an especially diverse number of schemes on V/STOL aircraft.

Wheels, tyres and brakes

In the earliest aircraft, wheels and tyres resembled those of cycles, but today the typical wheel is a squat drum of magnesium alloy, with the whole interior occupied by the brake. It is fitted with a special tyre with multiple plies of rubberized fabric inflated to a pressure which may be as high as 21·1 kg/cm² (300lb/sq in) – or ten times the pressure of most car tyres. Aircraft designed to operate from unpaved surfaces are usually light; if they are heavy they must have 'high-flotation' landing gear with multiple low-pressure tyres. Many aircraft take off and land at speeds as high as 322km/h (200mph) or more, and unless the runway surface is

RIGHT: One of the most widely used anti-skid brake systems is the Dunlop Maxaret. A small wheel spins at high speed, driven by its rubber rim in contact with the main wheel. If the latter locks, the small wheel stops rotating, and via special valves instantly eases pressure on the brakes, thus restoring rotation.
BELOW: Heaviest combat aircraft of World War II, the Boeing B–29 bomber set the fashion in having two wheels on each main and nose leg. Exactly the same arrangement is still seen on numerous aircraft. Another pioneer B–29 feature, now almost universal, was steerable nose landing gear.
BELOW RIGHT: The Soviet Sukhoi Su–7BM is one of many modern tactical aircraft designed to operate from unpaved airstrips under battle conditions. It has large low-pressure tyres, a braking-parachute installation and optional ATO (assisted take-off) rockets, which can be clipped on when needed and then jettisoned.

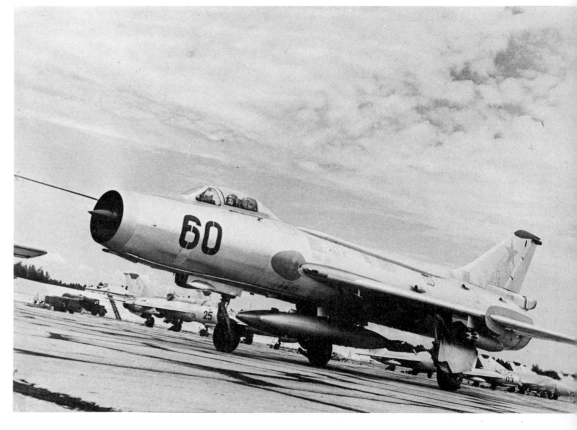

clean and dry this causes problems. Even a 13mm (0·5in) layer of water can make the aircraft 'aquaplane', skating across the water out of contact with the runway, and tyres have to be designed as high-capacity water pumps to eject water to each side. Many tyres have side ridges forming spray deflectors to prevent water in bulk from hitting the flaps or other areas at high speed. The tread may be plain, ribbed or covered with 'dimple' depressions to give an instant indication of wear.

Brakes in aircraft have to absorb hundreds to thousands of times more kinetic energy than those in cars or heavy trucks. The Rejected Take-Off (RTO), perhaps following sudden engine failure, of a Concorde involves stopping almost 203,000kg (200 tons) moving at over 322km/h (200mph), and to certificate such aircraft this must be demonstrated using wheel brakes alone.

Early aircraft brakes were simple friction bands, often pulled tight by a cockpit lever and cables rather like early car brakes. By 1940 hydraulic actuation was usual, with differential operation (more on one side of the aircraft and less on the other) to assist

turning, or to resist 'swing', the unwanted and unstable tendency to turn often experienced with tailwheel-type landing gear. If not smartly nipped in the bud, this caused a 'group loop' which could break the landing gear. Today virtually all aircraft have brakes controlled from foot pedals pressed down by the toes. Some landing gears still have pneumatic or hydraulic pressure applied to brake shoes pressed against the inside of the wheel drum, but nearly all fast or large aircraft use disc or multi-disc brakes in which the pressure pads squeeze one or more discs keyed to revolve with the wheel.

The problem of dissipating millions of foot-pounds of kinetic energy in the small space of an aircraft wheel is difficult. Brake discs can soon become bright cherry-red with heat, and fan cooling is needed. In extreme cases the high temperature could make the tyre explode, so the wheel incorporates fuzible plugs which, after a severe emergency stop, can melt and let the air out safely. All heavy or fast aircraft have anti-skid systems which allow the pilot to 'stamp on the brakes', even on an icy runway, without fear of skidding.

These systems exactly balance brake pressure against the speed of rotation of the wheel, relaxing pressure the moment the wheel tends to lock. The latest brake discs or rings are of special material able to absorb large amounts of heat and stay strong at high temperature. On the Lockheed C–5A they are of beryllium, and on the Concorde of reinforced carbon.

RATOG and JATO

Sometimes special equipment is needed to boost take-off or halt the aircraft after landing. Rocket-Assisted Take-Off Gear (RATOG) or Jet-Assisted Take-Off (JATO) was pioneered in the Soviet Union in 1934 and then taken up afresh in Germany, Britain and the USA ten years later. Solid-fuel motors (rarely, pressurized water or liquid-propellants) are either built into the aircraft or clipped on externally, with canted thrust axes passing through the aircraft centre of gravity to avoid any tendency to pitch the nose up or down. Sometimes the empty bottles are retained on board, but usually they jettison themselves as their short-time thrust decays. Extreme examples of boosted take-off were the experiments in zero-length (i.e., no run) take-off with supersonic fighters between 1956 and 1959, in which single enormous rockets thrust the aircraft diagonally off a missile-like launcher which could be inside a bombproof shelter.

Arrester systems began with various arrangements of wires on the decks of aircraft carriers; this is recorded on page 213, where the catapults used to launch aircraft from carriers and other vessels are also discussed. By 1955 arrester gear was being installed at military airfields. Alternatively, a safety net can be installed across the upwind end of the runway to arrest aircraft which for any reason overshoot. These nets usually incorporate numerous vertical strips of nylon webbing strong enough to pull the aircraft back without causing major airframe damage. Civil airports seldom use nets, but some have large overrun areas filled with particulate material such as Pulverized Fuel Ash (PFA), which is preferable to gravel because it does not dam-

increase in drag than the downgoing aileron, causing yaw opposite to that needed for a correct turn. One answer was to connect up the ailerons so that the upgoing one went up a lot while the other went down only a little, balancing out drag on each side. Another was the Frise aileron of 1926 which was hinged well back from the leading edge so that, when deflected up, the leading edge projected into the slipstream under the wing to cause more drag.

As aircraft became larger and faster, the forces on control surfaces naturally increased, until simple hinged surfaces became difficult to move. Well before World War I, designers had often eased the load by putting some of the area at the end of a surface ahead of the hinge axis. This was called a horn balance, and is still sometimes used, although a different form of aerodynamic balance is now much more common. The hinges are set back from the leading edge, as in the Frise aileron, so that the force on the leading part of the surface partly offsets that aft of the hinge.

The first tabs had actually been for trimming, the task of balancing out the masses and aerodynamic forces all over the aircraft so that the pilot could take his hands off the controls. Sometimes lengths of cord would be fixed along one side of the trailing edge of an aileron or other surface to get the trim right, while the elevators might be trimmed by an adjustable spring fixed to the bottom of the control column. Then, during World War I, it became common to fix tabs of aluminium to the trailing edge; these trim tabs were simply bent until the force of the tab on the control surface achieved the required perfectly trimmed condition.

By 1933, control surfaces were beginning to be fitted with hinged trim tabs, a much better idea because they could be driven through irreversible gears from handwheels in the cockpit. This allowed the pilot to retrim the aircraft in the air, greatly easing strain on long flights because previously he might have had to apply a large control force all the time to maintain straight and level flight.

ABOVE: *The Short Southampton flying boat had a primitive servo tab to operate the rudder.*

ABOVE AND RIGHT: *Spring tabs were fitted to the Hawker Tempest fighter of 1944. These are seen as solid black on the ailerons in the plan view.*

age the aircraft. Many aircraft also have braking parachutes, or drag chutes, which can be released from an internal box on pilot command. The parachute increases drag and thus slows down the aircraft. When the speed has been reduced sufficiently the chute(s) can be jettisoned for repacking and re-use.

Flight control

The difficulty of controlling a flying machine posed more of a barrier to early aviation than lack of an engine. After the Wrights had shown how aeroplanes could be controlled laterally, by warping the wings, the aileron was resurrected and by 1912 almost all aeroplanes used the arrangement of aerodynamic surfaces most often seen today. For stability there are fixed surfaces at the back, like the tail on a dart. For control there are movable surfaces: rudder for yaw, ailerons for roll and elevators for pitch. In modern aircraft this arrangement is often modified, as described below.

From early days until after World War II, flight-control systems were worked manually, operated by the muscles of the pilot (sometimes two strong pilots working together). Problems were simple. One was that, when the aircraft was rolling, the upgoing aileron (on the downgoing wing) suffered a larger

It was also found necessary to use mass balance. As each control surface had weight, it could be deflected by sharply moving the part of the airframe to which it was hinged. Air turbulence and other disturbances could thus cause some surfaces to flutter, oscillating so violently that they could tear off or break the aircraft. One cure was mass balance. At first, streamlined weights were fixed on diagonal arms projecting ahead of the hinge axis but today mass balance is invariably internal, either at the leading edge (well ahead of the hinge axis) or on projecting arms which are normally flush with the fixed surface. To get more mass into a small space, patented heavy alloys or depleted uranium are used to make the balance weights.

Tabs

By the 1920s the biggest aircraft were appearing with 'servo surfaces' carried on arms behind control surfaces, notably the rudder. These auxiliary surfaces were small and easily moved by the pilot. The air load acting on them then moved the main surface. By 1933 this clumsy arrangement was being replaced by neat tabs carried directly on the control-surface trailing edge. As before, the pilot merely drove the servo tab(s) which in turn did the hard work in moving the main surface(s).

Thus many aircraft in World War II had control surfaces with both servo tabs to ease manoeuvres and trim tabs to enable the aircraft to fly 'hands off'. Alternatives to the servo tab also appeared. One was the balance tab, or geared tab. Here the tab was linked by pivoted arms to the fixed surface, and the pilot drove the main control surface. When he moved the main surface, the tab was automatically deflected to help him, and the gearing of the linkage was arranged to leave a pleasant residual control load. Too powerful a tab could lead to instability and overcontrol, and in some aircraft the controls were so light that anti-balance tabs had to be added, like geared tabs but moving in the opposite direction to add to the pilot's load.

By 1942, fighters were being fitted with a further refinement, the spring tab. Here the pilot drove both a servo tab and, via a springy link (such as a torsion rod), the main surface. This had the advantage of giving progressive assistance at higher speeds, because then the main surface was more difficult to move and the greater deflection of the spring-link resulted in greater movement of the tab. Attention was also paid to the leading edge, which was precisely matched with the fixed structure and was sometimes extended in a shallow beak or hinged flap moving inside close-fitting balance chambers.

ABOVE: *Zero-length launch by rocket of an F–104G Starfighter.* RIGHT AND BELOW: *Cessna lightplane control surfaces, typical of those in most fixed-wing aircraft:* (a) aileron (b) elevator (c) rudder (d) roll to the left, prior to turning left (e) roll to the right prior to turning right (f) nose-up pitch, to climb or if sustained to loop (g) nose-down pitch, to dive (h) yaw to the left, with 'left rudder' (i) yaw to the right.

Autopilots

Back in the 1920s several pioneers had improved the automatic pilots (autopilots) which had been the subject of experiments since 1912. The objective was merely to keep aircraft on a straight and level course, irrespective of its trimming or possible upsets by air turbulence. What was needed was a gyroscope to sense rotation of the aircraft about each axis in which the autopilot exercised authority, plus a method of linking the sensed rotation to the flight-control system. Thus, should the aircraft begin to dive, the nose-down rotation would be detected and measured (almost always electrically, but sometimes pneumatically) and the resulting signal fed to a servo power unit capable of bodily moving the flying controls (in this case the elevators) to restore level flight. By 1939 autopilots were refined products available from specialist suppliers. They could command pitch, yaw and roll movements, not only to correct unwanted disturbances but also to make the aircraft do desired manoeuvres such as a correctly banked turn.

During and after World War II, autopilots acquired additional capabilities. They could be commanded to fly the aircraft to a particular compass heading, or to hold a particular airspeed or Mach number or fly to a chosen altitude and then hold it indefinitely, air turbulence notwithstanding.

Any installed autopilot system clearly had to have some carefully determined authority over the flight-control system. Its output signals were linked to a mechanical system capable of bodily moving the control surfaces, with or without causing corresponding movement of the cockpit flying controls. This mechanical system was sometimes electric, sometimes hydraulic and sometimes pneumatic, and could take the form of direct servo jacks connected either to whichever surfaces the autopilot had authority over or to the interconnecting linkage between the surfaces and the cockpit.

Establishing the authority was difficult. Suppose, for instance, that the autopilot were to encounter very turbulent air. To maintain straight and level flight at a constant altitude it clearly had to exert an immediate and powerful output, beyond the capability of a human pilot. Or suppose the autopilot were to go wrong, and issue a command to the flight controls to go 'hard over' in a way which could cause an unwanted manoeuvre violent enough to break the aircraft. The answer was to incorporate automatic protection circuits against incorrect outputs, or to enable the pilot to overcome such outputs, and to provide for almost immediate autopilot disengagement. Eventually autopilots became much more complex to enable bad-weather landing.

As the autopilot incorporated means for moving the flight-control surfaces independently of the pilot, it was a short step to adding mechanical boosters to help a pilot move the controls of extremely large aircraft. Early powered controls during World War II were cumbersome, fault-prone and needed extensive protection to limit their authority and prevent the aircraft being broken in flight or flown into the ground. Eventually, reliable

Inertial platform

Air data computer

Airspeed and altitude data

Amplifier

b

1232 Miles   278 Course

Heading   Course

Horizontal situation Display

Autopilot controller

a

Air

primary flight control surfaces

secondary flight control surfaces

double slotted flap

rudder

air brake

independent all moving taileron

intake controllers

control and stability augmentation system

spoilers

throttle and wing sweep controls

leading edge slats

air data computer   throttle controls

control transmitter

quadruplex taileron actuator

TOP: *A simplified inertial system showing a schematic air-driven gyroscope (a) with a geared synchro pick-off (electrically driven gyros are used today). In the centre (b) is the inertial platform with three gyros arranged with axes mutually perpendicular, feeding acceleration data to an air-data computer and amplifier which in turn drives the Horizontal Situation Indicator (HSI) and, via a controller, the automatic pilot. The HSI gives a readout of course, track, deviation from track and distance to destination or next waypoint. Automatic pilots have been the subject of experiments since the early days of aviation. However, the first successful system was developed by Elmer Sperry and used in a Curtiss flying boat in 1912.*

ABOVE CENTRE: *Panavia Tornado flight-control system, with dotted lines showing the position of the fully swept wing in which the trailing-edge flaps cannot be used and the spoilers are used to act as airbrakes. At all speeds the left and right tailerons (tailplanes or horizontal stabilizers) are the primary controls for pitch and roll, the spoilers being used differentially to increase roll control at low speeds. At low speeds, with wings unswept, the flaps and leading-edge slats increase wing lift greatly at high angles of attack for short-field (STOL) operation.*
ABOVE: *Tornado taileron power unit.*
RIGHT: *De Havilland Canada 'Dash 7' STOL transport, showing T-tail adopted to keep the tailplane in clear air at high attack angles.*

servo-boosters were devised with a mechanical pilot-input and a hydraulic output to the surface(s). The boosters were not irreversible, and could still be overcome by either the surface or the pilot; the latter still supplied part of the force needed, and the surface could flutter if not properly mass-balanced. But by 1955, despite such achievements as Boeing's all-manual 707 and Bristol's all-servo-tabbed Britannia, most large or fast aircraft had a completely new kind of system, the fully powered Flight-Control System (FCS).

Powered flight control system

In this the pilot's cockpit flight controls are merely input devices like the tuning knob on a radio. When the pilot moves any of them he commands a complex system to spring instantly to life and, via many limiters, checks and balances, causes Powered Flying-Control Units (PFCUs) to move the correct

need autostabilizers to damp out oscillations, caused by transonic or supersonic flight through rough air, at a frequency too rapid for an autopilot (or a human pilot) to handle. Autostabilizers usually act on the rudder and often on the horizontal tail surface, but seldom on the ailerons.

Some powered systems make provision for manual reversion in the event of failure, though the pilot has a hard task and the aircraft may be limited in permissible airspeed. Many modern systems make no such provision, so the powered system must be essentially foolproof. In a combat aircraft, the autopilot will usually be intimately linked with a radar and other sensors, weapons and their control/aiming systems, an air-data system (to measure with great accuracy the properties of the surrounding atmosphere), navigation systems, an angle-of-attack sensor and other devices, all tied into a powerful digital computer working in real time to manage the

fixed tailplane and no separate elevators. In lightplanes they are manually driven, but in supersonic aircraft they are fully powered, and in most fighters they can be driven together, to behave as elevators, or differentially (one up, the other down) to roll the aircraft. Roll is normally controlled by traditional ailerons, though some aircraft have them well inboard to avoid twisting the wing and most big airliners have 'high-speed ailerons' inboard, between sections of flap, and 'low-speed ailerons' outboard which are often locked centrally above a particular indicated airspeed or Mach number.

Combat aircraft and most airliners also have spoilers, which are flat surfaces driven by powerful rams to hinge up from the upper surface of the wing against the airstream. Used symmetrically they serve as powerful destroyers of lift and increasers of drag, for a fast let-down to a runway without increasing speed. After landing they can be flicked open

surface(s) exactly the required amount. The PFCU usually has mechanical input signalling and an output which may be a hydraulic jack, a hydraulic motor driving a ball-screwjack, or some other device.

This system has the advantage of being irreversible, so the surface cannot flutter and cannot move at all unless commanded. But the pilot, not being connected to the surface, can no longer 'feel' the things he is doing to the aircraft. The answer is an artificial-feel system, which may be a simple arrangement of springs but in any high-speed aircraft has to involve springs, bob-weights to increase the pilot load in proportion to aircraft acceleration and a hydraulic, pneumatic or electric servo-system to make the pilot load proportional to indicated airspeed and/or Mach number. In this way the aircraft is made to respond correctly in both dense air at sea level and thin air in the stratosphere.

Even this is still only the beginning of a modern FCS. Almost all high-speed aircraft

whole mission. The autopilot is often triplicated or quadruplicated in carefully planned ways, so that if any one 'channel' were to suffer a fault, the rest would outvote it. Even with faults in two channels automatic flight would be possible, but at some point it would be correct for the pilot to break into the closed loop of the control system (this is intended to occur infrequently, once in, say, 100,000 flights). The linkage between the pilot/autopilot/computer input and the PFCUs is increasingly not mechanical at all but electrical. In these Fly By Wire (FBW) systems the signals are transmitted along multi-core ribbons which are lighter than mechanical control runs, can go anywhere in the airframe and are much more accurate.

Before concluding this important section, the point must be made that the traditional arrangement of movable surfaces so carefully outlined earlier no longer applies to an increasing proportion of aircraft. Today's horizontal tails are often single surfaces, with no

to act as 'lift dumpers' to put the full weight on to the wheels to increase the power of the brakes. During the landing approach some aircraft have Direct Lift Control (DLC) in which the spoilers in effect become primary flight control surfaces to allow the pilot to adjust rate of descent instantly without altering speed or attitude. In many aircraft the spoilers can be used differentially to serve as the primary roll control, with ailerons locked inoperative (a swing-wing aircraft in the fully swept position invariably uses spoilers and/or a rolling tailplane, which is sometimes called a 'taileron').

Yet a further modern feature is subdivision of control surfaces into two to four sections, each driven by a PFCU in a different circuit to guard against failure. A visible feature of many aircraft today is the T-tail, with horizontal surfaces mounted on the vertical surface, while some supersonic machines have twin vertical surfaces which may slope outwards and often are one-piece (serving as both fin and rudder). The list of new features is endless. For example, the Grumman F–14 Tomcat has a Mach/sweep programmer so that the wings automatically pivot to the optimum sweep angle without the pilot's attention.

Safety

Before 1920 some aircraft were equipped with navigation lights (red on the left wing with 110° arc of visibility, green on the right and white at the tail), and today this unchanged system has been supplemented by powerful landing lamps (usually retractable) and multi-million-candlepower rotating or flashing beacons visible for many miles in clear night air. By 1925 the first fire extinguishers were in wide use, and today aircraft incorporate sensors to detect flame or smoke, crash systems triggered by impact or mechanical deformation, and various other triggers which can set off extinguishing systems either generally or in specific locations such as a chosen baggage hold or engine pod. Fuel tanks are made self-sealing after a puncture, crashproof by design, and filled with a very light sponge-like substance called reticulated foam (this can be inside and/or surrounding the tanks) to inhibit fire. Inert nitrogen is pumped into the space above the fuel, and not only the fuel supply receptacle but the whole aircraft is 'bonded' with electrical conductors from stem to stern and from tip to tip (and, on the ground, to an electrical earth) to prevent any spark having to jump

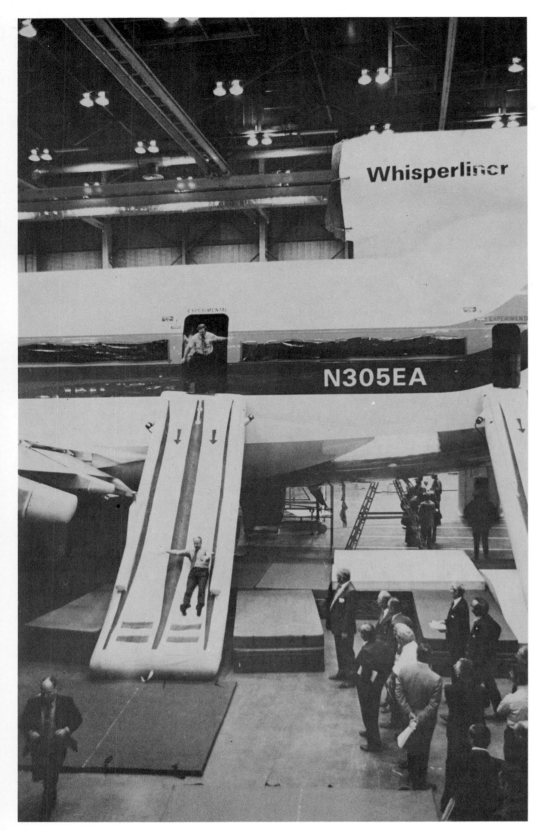

into an undulating surface which cracked ice as fast as it formed, so that it blew away in the slipstream. By 1942 many aircraft had electro-thermal ice protection, and a little later hot-air systems became common. From much earlier the extremely vulnerable choke tube of the carburettor, where the local drop in air pressure reduces temperature and promotes icing which stops the engine, was heated by circulating engine oil through its walls.

Gas-turbine engines made available ample supplies of hot air for anti-icing ('anti' prevents ice from forming; 'de' disperses it after it has formed) and today the preferred method on large aircraft is to duct extremely hot air from the engine compressors along the wing and tail leading edges and also to the engine inlets and pilot windscreens. Many areas, and a few complete aircraft, are protected by electric methods using elements embedded in rubber or sprayed on (for example, Spraymat can be sprayed on the airframe and Sierracin or Triplex methods give a transparent film on the windscreen).

Safety equipment carried by aircraft included an axe as soon as all-metal fuselages made emergency egress potentially difficult, and by the late 1930s all large aircraft included an inflatable dinghy (life raft) usually housed in the upper part of the wing or fuselage and released on a tether-link as soon as the aircraft settled in the water. Dinghies grew elaborate, with handholds, stabilizing pouches, anti-exposure screen, handcranked radio, sea-dye (fluorescein) tablet, concave-bladed knife on a tether, solar still for drinking water, rations and medical supplies. Crew flying clothing incorporated parachute harness and integral or separate parachute pack (plus dinghy for fighter pilots), whistle, marker, Mae West life jacket, torch and, by 1953, miniature radio beacon.

By 1943 certain fighters and early jet aircraft had led to the development of ejection seats fired by the occupier to make a clean emergency escape in high-speed flight. For further description see page 142. A few aircraft have complete jettisonable cockpits which, after soft landing, can be used as a radio-equipped survival shelter. It is hoped to devise crew capsules provided with rudimentary wings and propulsion so that, after separation from a crippled combat aircraft, the crew can fly perhaps 80km (50 miles) towards their base. A quite different emergency escape system is the quickly inflatable slide which extends from below the doors of airliners to allow passengers to slide perhaps 9m (30ft) to the ground.

Modern aircraft also incorporate literally hundreds of devices and subsystems to improve safety. Most are associated with particular functioning items, and serve duties similar to the fuzes that protect a domestic electrical appliance in preventing overspeed, overtemperature and similar faulty conditions. Throughout the whole aircraft a Built-In Test Equipment (BITE) installation may continuously monitor the performance and behaviour of very large numbers of devices and either give immediate warning or record any fault on a wire or tape recorder which is played back after each mission. There are

TOP LEFT: *A carrier landing by a Grumman F–14A Tomcat multi-role fighter. This versatile but costly aircraft can automatically adjust the sweep of its outer wings to suit the demands of air combat or other situations.*
CENTRE LEFT: *Anti-icing positions on the HS.748 transport: (a) pulsating pneumatic rubber de-icing boots (b) electro-thermal engine ice protection (c) electro-thermal windscreens (d) ice-detection probe.*
LEFT: *Inflatable rubber dinghies are now standard equipment on large aircraft. These are usually housed in the upper part of the wing or fuselage and released on a tether-link as soon as the aircraft is settled on the water.*
ABOVE: *Almost all large civil transports have to be equipped with inflatable escape slides so that all occupants can quickly evacuate a grounded aircraft. That shown is the one utilized on an Eastern Airlines TriStar.*

an air-gap. Static wicks in the form of billions of fine conductive filaments hang behind trailing edges to disperse into the atmosphere any electrical charge that could otherwise build up and eventually cause a potentially dangerous electrical flash.

De-icing systems

By 1932 de-icing systems were coming into use. One company supplied paste which when brushed on to external surfaces such as leading edges and control-surface hinges prevented ice from forming. Goodrich supplied tailor-made pulsating rubber de-icers in the form of flat tubes attached along the leading edges. Pneumatic pressure supplied to the centre and then the outer strips in rhythmic sequence turned the vulnerable leading edge several families of recorders, all concerned with safety. The type just mentioned is usually called a maintenance recorder. The Cockpit Voice Recorder (CVR) makes a hard-copy record of all radio or intercom traffic during each flight – this may have significance in a court of law. There is a wealth of types of Flight-Data Recorders (FDRs) and Airborne Integrated Data Systems (AIDS) which monitor everything from crew procedures to engine health, while most commercial transports have to carry a special FDR protected against extremely severe impacts. crushing loads and temperatures. This crash recorder, which remains playable after an accident, has to record at least altitude, airspeed, vertical acceleration, pitch angle (nose up or down), heading and elapsed time, at intervals of one second throughout the flight. Most record 50 parameters, including control-surface positions.

Stall warning system

One of the most vital systems in advanced aeroplanes is the stall warner. Most wings stall whenever they exceed a critical angle of attack, and this can occur at any speed, the minimum stalling speed being in unaccelerated (i.e., straight and level) flight. A stall-warning system thus has to measure angle of attack, which it may do by sensing dynamic pressure at two small holes, one pointing 45° above the horizon dead ahead and the other 45° down, or at other lesser angles. In normal flight the pressures are approximately equal, but as angle of attack increases they diverge until at a preset value the alarm is triggered. The system must actually be more complicated, because the stall danger depends on the rate of increase of angle of attack; thus, it is less dangerous to fly steadily at just below stalling angle than to pull a tight turn so violently that this same angle is exceeded at a high rate of increase.

The warning may be visual in the cockpit, or a loud horn or other aural alarm. With continued increase in angle of attack, a 'stick shaker' can come into play, banging the pilot's control column or yoke to and fro, making a loud clacking noise and taking it out of his hands. If he is determined to stall the aircraft, and keeps pulling back, a stick pusher so powerful no pilot can fight it suddenly thrusts the stick forward, changing the nose-up command to a firm nose-down one. The only way the pilot can beat this is to 'dump' the entire system by a positive action on a clearly marked control.

Most aircraft probably crash flying into the ground while fully serviceable, usually in cloud or fog. The Ground-Proximity Warning System (GPWS) is an attempt to prevent this.

Yet another and even more difficult safety system is the Collision-Avoidance System (CAS). One company has had a CAS in constant use since 1964; it is called Eros, from 'Eliminate Range-Zero System', range-zero meaning a collision.

The cockpit

Every instrument in the modern cockpit is the result of many years of invention and re-

TOP: *This sketch of a DC–9–10 illustrates the basic principle of the Ground-Proximity Warning System (GPWS), now mandatory on most large civil transport aircraft. The system senses potential collisions with the ground or other obstructions and, while issuing loud audible warnings, pulls up the nose of the aircraft.*
CENTRE: *The basic navigational vector diagram (a) which old-time navigators were continually having to plot on charts, showing the effect of particular winds. The Airspeed Indicator (ASI) pitot/static system (b), showing how dynamic pressure inflates the capsule while static pressure from the side-facing small holes is fed to the instrument case. A typical traditional ASI presentation (c) (it would be in position (a) in the panel below it).*

ABOVE: *During World War II the basic blind-flying panel in British aircraft was standardized in this form, to ease the task of pilots who flew many types of aircraft. ASI (a) as shown at (c) above, but here used for the key diagram (b) artificial horizon (c) altimeter (d) turn/slip indicator, also called turn and bank indicator or turn co-ordinator (e) gyro compass or directional gyro and (f) rate of climb indicator, also called Vertical Speed Indicator or VSI.*
ABOVE RIGHT: *The cockpit of one of the first Spitfires, which was protected by a thick, bullet-proof screen.*
RIGHT: *In 1938 this Ensign transport was the last word in airline flight decks. In the centre are the autopilot panel and the engine throttle levers.*

finement. Apart from the tachometer, which measures engine speed (today not by a mechanical spinning drive but by electrical signals transmitted by a small generator on each engine), the first instrument was the the AirSpeed Indicator (ASI). Almost all operate by differential pressure between an air pipe sensing static pressure from sideways-facing perforations in the ASI pitot/static head (an electrically de-iced tube carried somewhere on the aircraft where the air is undisturbed), and dynamic or pitot pressure, sensed by a tube with an open end facing dead ahead. Since World War II the ASI has been backed up by, or integrated with, the Machmeter which indicates Mach number. This is basically an ASI capsule working in conjunction with an altitude capsule.

Altitude capsules are connected to static pressure only, and a stack of them can drive the altimeter which tells the pilot his 'pressure height' above the Earth. It actually indicates outside air pressure, and the altimeter must be corrected or re-set to take account of the fact that atmospheric pressure varies both with time and geographical position. The radio altimeter gives true height above ground by a radar method, measuring the time taken by a signal to reach the Earth and return.

Another height instrument is the Vertical Speed Indicator (VSI) which measures rate of climb or descent by sensing expansion or contraction of a capsule fed with static pressure and also open to the instrument via a small orifice (it is like an altimeter with a capsule having a slow leak). In steady flight the pressures inside and outside the capsule balance, but climbing or descending causes imbalance which drives the indicator needle.

Gyro instruments

There are many other pressure-type instruments, some of them in complicated air-data systems, but the other large family are gyro instruments. Most modern gyros are driven electrically. Some are 'floated' on liquid or gaseous bearings, without mechanical contact anywhere, to give perfect centring and almost zero friction. Some gyros measure angular displacement of the aircraft about any or all of its three axes; rate gyros are free in only two axes and thus measure not turn but rate of turn about the third axis, at $90°$ to each of the others.

One of the simplest gyro instruments is the Direction Indicator (DI). It contains no magnet and suffers from 'wander' over a period of time, and from error caused by the Earth's rotation, so it must be reset occasionally against one of the compass systems. It contains a single gyro spinning about an axis maintained horizontal relative to the carrier aircraft, which will 'topple' the gyro if it does aerobatics, and provides an accurate heading reference for short periods and, especially, for precise turns. Another instrument, the artificial horizon, contains a gyro with axis vertical and this drives a horizon bar which moves parallel with the Earth's horizon, either above or below, with or without tilt, in relation to a fixed gull-wing shape representing the aircraft seen from behind. Yet another basic gyro instrument is the turn-a   j

b   k

c   l

d

   m

   n

e

f   o

g

h

i

and-slip indicator; in its simplest form this contains a rate gyro with axis horizontal to indicate rate of turn, and a simple pendulous display (such as a heavy ball in a liquid-filled curved tube) to indicate any inward slip or outward skid.

In principle, aircraft magnetic compasses resemble those used as toys or on ships, but the remote compass is a rather different device with a 'fluxvalve' in one wing tip which is not free to rotate and senses the aircraft heading in relation to the local Earth's magnetic field. All aircraft compasses incorporate complicated devices for correcting errors caused by aircraft magnetism, aircraft manoeuvres and several other possible sources of error. Special compasses were devized for flying near the Earth's magnetic poles.

Display systems

On the basis of new technology the flight deck has been completely altered in the past 15 years. One major change is that the most obvious instruments today are big combined displays such as a Director Horizon (DH) or Horizontal Situation Indicator (HSI). A much bigger change is the gradual move towards even more integrated displays in which moving-map projected pictures, radar pictures, television pictures, alphanumeric data and even a real or imaged view of the Earth ahead are all presented on a single screen. Many advanced aircraft have at least one Head-Down Display (HDD) of this kind on the pilot's instrument panel, plus a Head-Up Display (HUD).

TOP: *A modern fighter cockpit, the F–15 Eagle: (a) Head-Up Display (HUD) which the pilot reads while also looking through it at what lies ahead (b) Identification Friend/Foe (IFF) controller (c) vertical situation display (d) HUD controller (e) navaids selector (f) radar controller (g) Tac Electronic Warfare System (TEWS) (h) IFF controller (i) communications panel (j) Ultra Hi-Frequency (UHF) selector (k) mode selector (l) TEWS display (m) HSI (n) warnings (o) navigation panel.*
ABOVE: *Flight deck of the modern B–1 bomber.*
ABOVE RIGHT: *Three sketches of the S–3A Viking showing location of basic systems. Fuel System, Electrical System and Basic Flight Controls (top):*

1 *Wing integral fuel tanks*
2 *Auxiliary tanks*
3 *In flight refuelling probe (retractable)*
4 *Fuel dump and vent pipes*
5 *Engine driven electrical generator*
6 *Emergency generator*
7 *Electrical load distribution panels*
8 *General Electric T–34 engine*
9 *Auxiliary power plant*
10 *Ailerons*

11 *Slotted flaps*
12 *Spoilers*
13 *Rudder*
14 *All moving tailplane with flaps*
15 *Drooping leading edges*
16 *Leading edge electric actuators*
17 *Electrically heated windscreen panels*
Hydraulic System, Pneumatic System and Landing Gear (centre):
18 *Engine driven hydraulic pump*
19 *Hydraulic accumulators*
20 *Aileron flap and spoiler servo controls*
21 *Wing fold rotary actuators*
22 *Rudder actuator*
23 *Tail fold jack*
24 *Tailplane actuator*
25 *Arrestor hook jack*
26 *Main landing gear jack*
27 *Weapons bay door actuators*
28 *Nosewheel jack*
29 *Environmental control system*
30 *Avionics cooling ducts*
31 *Cabin air conditioning ducts*
32 *Wing leading edge de-icing ducts*
33 *Tailplane de-icing ducts*
34 *Rearward retracting main landing gear*
35 *Rearward retracting nosewheel leg*
36 *Catapult strop attachment*
Operational Equipment (bottom):
37   *Search radar*
38 *Pilot's seat*
39 *Co-pilot*
40 *Tactical control officer*
41 *Sensor control officer*
42 *Forward avionics bay (port and starboard)*
43 *Forward Looking Infra-Red scanner (FLIR)*
44 *Mission control avionics (port and starboard)*
45 *Univac control computer*
46 *Weapons bay (port and starboard) with two torpedoes each side*
47 *Sonobuoy launch tubes*
48 *Aft avionics bay (port and starboard)*
49 *Magnetic anomaly detector boom (MAD)*
50 *Wing tip sensors*

The modern HUD is a fantastically complex device in which, without interfering with forward view, aiming marks are projected on to the windscreen for air-to-air or air-to-ground missions, symbology and alphanumerics for navigation and, in the most recent forms, synthetic pictures of the Earth ahead obtained from target sensors.

Radar has been combined with HUD displays, but all the latest installations use Forward-Looking Infra-Red (FLIR) and Low-Light Level Television (LLLTV) to give detailed pictures of scenes that either look dark to the pilot or cannot be seen at all. Thus, today's pilot can fly major parts of the mission, including all the most difficult phases such as making an attack or making a landing in bad weather, without ever having to look 'head-down' inside the cockpit.

Systems

The earliest functioning system in aeroplanes was that supplying fuel to the engine. Tanks are either metal, sometimes forming an integral part of the airframe, or a flexible bag made of multiple layers of nylons or neoprene rubbers. Combat-aircraft tanks incorporate layers of material which swell on contact with fuel and thus seal bullet holes. All modern tanks include a form of fireproofing, often achieved by purging the space above the fuel with inert gas and using low-density foam to prevent any explosion.

Baffles stop what may be many tons of fuel from sloshing about during turbulence or manoeuvres, and one-way valves prevent fuel from running from one tank to another unless this is intended. The whole system may be gravity-filled, as in a car, but in all large or advanced aircraft one or more pressure-fuelling sockets are provided through which fuel can be pumped in at rates up to 9,143 litres (2,000 gal) per minute. Military aircraft can often be refuelled in flight through such a connection, either via a fixed, detachable or retractable probe thrust into the tanker's drogue or via a receptacle into which the tanker thrusts a rigid telescopic boom.

Special proportioners distribute the fuel accurately in multi-engined aircraft, under the impulse of electrically driven (sometimes air-turbine driven) booster pumps in the bottoms of the tanks and high-pressure pumps on the engines.

LEFT: *Flight refuelling by the probe/drogue method is simple and it enables one tanker (such as this Victor K.2) to refuel three aircraft (such as the Jaguar) simultaneously. The receiver aircraft thrusts its probe into the drogue on the end of the hose trailed by the tanker's power-driven reel unit (detail bottom left). The fuel transfer is automatic.*

ABOVE: *Flight refuelling by the Boeing Flying Boom method of a Boeing E–4B airborne command post (based on the Boeing 747). This aircraft along with the Lockheed C–5A Galaxy is the largest aircraft refuelled in the air.*

BELOW: *Sketch of a Boeing 707–3J9C of the Imperial Iranian Air Force (IIAF). Unlike American tanker versions it has two hosereel/drogue units at the wing tips as well as a Flying Boom under the rear fuselage. The two are needed to preserve compatibility with the IIAF's varied assortment of warplanes, which have several refuelling methods.*

RIGHT: *Typical multi-plunger hydraulic pump:*
1 Inlet from reservoir
2 1st stage pump
3/4 1st stage relief valve and compensator
5 Off-loading valve
6 Off-loading actuator
7 High pressure pistons
8 Cam drive
9 1st stage feed annulus
10 High pressure delivery annulus
11 High pressure outlet
12 Return to reservoir

TOP RIGHT: *A unique form of drop tank was the Two-Component Pod (TCP) carried by the 2,250km/h (1,400mph) B–58 Hustler bomber until its retirement in 1969. The crane is lowering the nuclear-weapon portion into the fuel-carrying portion.*

Extreme care is taken to eliminate water from the fuel, and prevent any that may reach the tanks from getting into the system where, at high altitude, it would freeze and cause blockages. The aircraft filters are heated to melt any ice crystals which do enter. Special valves control the flow throughout the system, to allow fuel to flow no matter what the attitude of the aircraft and also to allow air or nitrogen into or out of the system to balance out the pressure differences between sea level and high altitudes. Even at extreme altitude the fuel must not be allowed to boil and cause bubbles in the system, despite the fact that the fuel may serve as the 'heat sink' to which nearly all waste heat in the aircraft is rejected.

The whole system is designed so that, as fuel is consumed, the aircraft's CG shifts by the smallest amount; conversely, in some aircraft (notably Concorde) fuel is pumped from one part of the aircraft to another deliberately to change the CG position and

counteract trim changes between subsonic and supersonic flight. Special features in supersonic aircraft are fuel systems to supply the afterburners and either special fuel or special provisions to stop the accumulation of tarry or 'coked' residues caused by long 'soaking' at high temperature because of kinetic heating. Many aircraft carry external drop tanks, which need self-sealing connec-

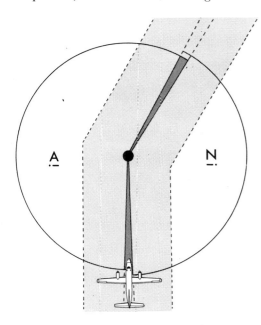

ABOVE: *The old radio range, seen from above, guided aircraft along fixed tracks by means of Morse, A and N, forming a steady central note.*

tions, valves for filling and supply through the same couplings, swivelling mounts for swing wings and, often, cartridge jettison plungers to throw an expended tank well clear of the aircraft to avoid damage.

Electrical systems

An electrical system is today carried on almost every aeroplane, though it may be no more complex than that of a car. But large and advanced aircraft often have electrical systems capable of generating current at a rate equivalent to many hundreds of horsepower, and the number of separate parts in the system may exceed 15,000. There are usually three kinds of current on board. Raw Alternating Current (AC) is like electricity in the home, and it is almost invariably three-phase at 115/200 volts generated by alternators (AC generators) on each engine. For emergency use another alternator may be driven by a Ram-Air Turbine (RAT): a windmill that can be spun by the slipstream when necessary; a Monofuel Emergency Power Unit (MEPU): a stand-by device burning special fuel; or an Auxiliary Power Unit (APU): a versatile package used either in emergency or when the main engines are not running, such as when the aircraft is in-between flights). Raw AC is used for many purposes, but by far the biggest loads are heating, for anti-icing the airframe and systems, for heating ovens in the galley and similar base loads.

The avionics (aviation electronics) need precisely controlled frequency, and this exactly controlled AC has to be generated by alternators kept running at precisely constant speed. This involves using either a Constant-Speed Drive (CSD) to turn the alternator(s) or a self-contained device called an Integrated-Drive Generator (IDG). The third kind of electricity is Direct Current (DC), used for many services and also stored in batteries, which in most advanced aircraft are of the nickel-cadmium type.

In most aircraft, all (or nearly all) the demands for mechanical power are supplied hydraulically. Typical examples are landing-gear retraction and locking, nosewheel steering, flaps, leading-edge devices, tailplanes, powered flying controls, swing-wings, cargo doors, airstairs (retractable stairways) and, in most large or fast aircraft, wheel brakes. Early systems used mineral oils at pressures up to 35·15kg/cm² (500lb/sq in), but today most use less inflammable fluids specially tailored for the job at pressures of 211 or 281 kg/cm² (3,000 or 4,000lb/sq in).

Compressed air is used in two main ways. In one there is high pressure in the order of hundreds or thousands of pounds per square inch and very little flow; in the other the pressure is in the order of tens of pounds per square inch and the flow may be enormous. The first type of pneumatic system is used either as a main power service in light aircraft, or (at lower pressure) to drive certain instruments, or to pressurize tanks, or where the environment is too hot for hydraulics (for example, to drive variable afterburning-engine nozzles), or as a local self-contained system and especially for one-shot emergency use. Often one-shot systems use gas from solid-fuel generators like completely enclosed rockets.

In large aircraft the biggest on-board system is that providing cabin pressurization and air-conditioning, and this either uses engine-driven compressors or, in jet aircraft, air 'bled' or 'tapped' from the engine compressors. Very large flows may be used, and the air passes through large duct systems where it is cooled, dried or moistened, and finally supplied to the inhabited areas and cargo holds at carefully controlled pressure and temperature.

Navigation Aids

The first airborne navaid was the Direction-Finding (D/F) loop aerial, a conductive coil which could be rotated until the received signal from a ground radio station was reduced to zero in the so-called null position, and the loop was then at 90° to the direction of the ground station. Navigators could obtain D/F bearings on two ground stations in quick succession and thus, by drawing the two lines on a map, obtain a 'fix' (a known aircraft position). Today the succeesor of the D/F loop is the Automatic Direction Finder (ADF), in which an immediate bearing to any selected ground station is indicated on an instrument.

Airways

In the late 1920s the United States began a nationwide system of 'airways' which survives today and now encompasses the globe. Each airway was at first a single invisible radio beam sent out from a ground station and pointing at the next. At the ground station were four aerials, two of which continuously transmitted the Morse letter A ($\cdot$ –) while the other two transmitted the letter N (– $\cdot$). As the dots and dashes were keyed precisely together the two signals merged along the centreline of the airway into a continuous note. If the aircraft was just off the centreline an A or N would be heard, while passing directly over the station caused the signal to disappear entirely for a short time.

This system was called Radio Range, and it was the basis for airways worldwide until after 1945. Its obvious drawback was that it provided only two, or four, routes to fly; the system was not much help to pilots who wanted to fly a different route. So the next step in this American scheme was to build a different kind of lighthouse called a Very-High-frequency Omni-directional Radio-range (VOR). This combines two sets of

BELOW: *Diagrams explaining aspects of VOR: (a) transmission pattern of a typical VOR beacon showing variation in signal in different directions (b) aircraft flying at 270° fixes position by VOR 1 at 204° and VOR 2 at 314° (c) a typical VOR compass display with needles driven by transmission from selected VOR ground stations.*

ABOVE CENTRE: *Distance-Measuring Equipment (DME) interrogates a ground station to give a distance readout, in this case 68 nautical miles.*
ABOVE: *First used by the RAF in late 1942, H₂S was the first airborne radar used for ground mapping. Modern radars can usually do the same job, though in wartime such duty is hazardous because the radar signals can attract hostile fighters. In this sketch a bomber is flying over a river estuary and picking up the water areas in very dark hues, while the land appears brighter. Cities would be brighter still.*
RIGHT: *Panavia Tornado seen from above showing the four beams from its doppler navigational radar. Measuring the frequency changes of the reflections from the Earth's surface of the four beams gives a precise measure of the speed of the aircraft along the four beam-directions, from which an airborne computer can continuously work out the true ground speed and track (and, if necessary, the current wind at the height at which the aircraft is flying).*

precisely timed radio signals in such a way that an indicator in the aircraft can immediately show the bearing from each VOR station. But again there are severe limitations: VOR gives no help in using the whole of the airspace and again restricts aircraft to congested airways (which may not be the routes each aircraft wishes to follow); and a separate device called Distance-Measuring Equipment (DME) has to be used to give range information.

Gee, Loran and Decca

In 1940 British radio engineers urgently produced a completely new navaid to help RAF bombers find their targets. Called ('Gee', it was uncanny in its accuracy; furthermore, it was able to fill the whole sky with guiding signals so that aircraft did not have to follow any prearranged route. It worked with one master ground station and two slave stations. In the original Gee system, the three stations were in different parts of England, but their signals could be used by bombers far over Germany. The master station sent out alternate single and double pulses controlled precisely by an electronic clock. These pulses were received by the aircraft and by the two slave stations, one of which automatically re-radiated the signals after each single pulse and the other re-radiated after each double pulse. In the aircraft a cathode-ray tube showed spikes of light which, by presenting a picture of the time differences of the three sets of signals, told the navigator his position.

Gee was the first R-nav (area-navigation) system, and the first hyperbolic system, so called because lines of equal time-difference from the ground stations appeared as hyperbolae on a map. Another was Loran (long-range navigation), which was developed a little later than Gee to use longer wavelengths, and thus give guidance over greater distances. Even today Loran is very important to civil and military craft flying over the oceans and more remote areas of the globe.

In the years after 1945 the British Decca company saw that the future need was for a refined R-nav system which would be usable over the whole airspace, right down to sea level, and which would have extremely high accuracy to assist in the same control of dense traffic right down to the Instrument Landing System (ILS) on the approach to the runway. The Decca navigation system was developed to meet these needs. A hyperbolic system like Gee, it differed in using continuous radio waves instead of pulses, emitted by a master and three slaves. At first, navigators had to plot their position on special hyperbolic maps, using three sets of dial instruments called Decometers. By 1951, however, the aircraft track could be automatically plotted on a moving map called a Flight Log, giving for the first time an exact picture of aircraft position at all times. Later, Decca grew into a wide family of navaids, all intrinsically more accurate than VOR/DME and far more flexible and useful.

Tragically, Decca did not happen to be American and, at the crucial meeting of the International Civil Aviation Organization (ICAO) in 1958 to decide on the standard world navaid, decisions were taken not on

LEFT: *The principle of the original Decca Navigator system is illustrated by a map of the Nova Scotia chain. Continuous radio signals emitted in synchronization by the master and slave stations are picked up and analyzed by the aircraft, which compares the time-delays from the various stations. Matching the times from any two stations fix the aircraft on a hyperbolic position-line, some of which are plotted. In the 1945 system the navigator had to read the position-lines off dial instruments called Decometers, two of which are shown. Soon the system was made automatic, one method being to make the signals drive a pen across a roller-blind moving chart to give a continuous readout of aircraft position. Today Decca is combined with other systems to give foolproof navigation over any desired track at any desired height.*
BELOW LEFT: *Predecessor of Decca was the Gee system, the first radio navaid in the world other than the very limited radio range. The range forced aircraft to fly preset paths, but Gee allowed them to fly anywhere they wished, and this was vital for the first users were RAF bombers over Germany in 1942. Gee sent out pulses of radio energy from master and slave ground stations and was a direct ancestor of Decca. Later the United States derived from Gee a long-range system called Loran, and this is still in use in both civil and military aircraft, though over the past 30 years Loran has been developed very considerably.*

red co-ordinate   green co-ordinate

the basis of merit but of political pressure. The consequence was a predictable win for VOR/DME, as a result of which the world has been covered with several thousand of these restrictive and outmoded stations which even today are the universal standard navaid. But commonsense has combined with increasing operating difficulty in the busiest airspace to force even the United States to take another look at the situation.

To take an ocean of air and carve it into narrow congested canals was not very clever, and today a wealth of R-nav systems, pioneered by Decca, are in use. Some are techniques which partly overcome the more serious shortcomings of the enforced system now in use, but most are completely new.

Two of the navaids on all large transport aircraft do not require any ground stations but are self-contained in the aircraft. Doppler radar uses the Doppler shift in the frequency of a signal caused by motion of its source relative to an observer; the classic case

to help understanding of Doppler is the way the pitch of a fast-moving noise, such as a train whistle or a low-flying aircraft, sounds higher as it approaches and lower as it departs. The aircraft transmits radio waves in a fan of four narrow beams, which strike the ground and are reflected back to the aircraft. By exactly comparing the shifts in frequency of the reflected signals, the airborne navigator can determine track and speed over the ground. Thus, no matter what the wind might be, the position of the aircraft is continuously updated.

Inertial navigation systems

The other self-contained navaid is the most valuable of all. Inertial Navigation Systems (INS) could not be made until technology existed to make gyros and accelerometers with an almost incredibly high accuracy, far more precise than the parts of the most expensive watch. Though a modern INS is too complex to attempt to describe, its principle

could hardly be simpler. Imagine that inside the aircraft was a weight hung on a fine thread. With the aircraft parked on the apron the weight would hang straight down, but when the pilot released the brakes the weight would move to the rear. As the aircraft went round bends on the airport, the weight would swing out to the side. Such a system would be very rough and ready, but if we could measure continuously the position of the weight, and relate it to the passage of time, it would tell us how fast the aircraft was moving and in which direction.

The INS uses three sets of accelerometers which are in effect much more accurate counterparts of our simple pendulum. They continuously measure and record the acceleration of the aircraft in the fore/aft, left/right and up/down directions. Super-accurate gyros are used to hold the accelerometer platform exactly level relative to the surface of the Earth below, because even a very small tilt would be interpreted by the accelerometers as a small false acceleration. A modern INS platform is held level with the same accuracy as needed to point a light-beam at a small coin 0·5km (0·31 miles) away, while the accelerometers could measure the acceleration of a car which took three hours to go from rest to a speed of 40km/h (25mph).

Doppler and INS have made the most advanced aircraft able to navigate with great precision anywhere in the world without outside help. But there are many other navaids available for all kinds of customer. Some are simple, and aimed at the private pilot. Some use satellites orbiting the Earth. Omega is the latest radio navaid, a hyperbolic system using Very-Low-Frequency (VLF) signals and able to cover the whole globe with only eight ground stations. Omega signals from the other side of the world are now guiding not only aircraft but submerged submarines.

Airports
their design and development

The first six decades of commercial aviation have seen the growth of the passenger airliner from a converted 120km/h (80mph) military biplane to the supersonic Concorde, travelling at twice the speed of sound.

Airport development has had to keep pace with new demands by the airlines, for there is little point in introducing high performance jets if time is wasted on the ground through badly designed or outdated handling facilities and procedures for both aircraft and passengers.

The first airports, in the strict sense of the

word, were commissioned in Germany in 1910 for the Zeppelin airships operated by the Delag company for passenger flights, and, by 1913, airship sheds, incorporating passenger handling facilities, existed at a number of German cities. All were served by rail links, and Delag carried almost 34,000 passengers in nearly 1,600 flights before war broke out in 1914, although it should be emphasized that these were not regular scheduled services.

A flying-boat service in 1914 heralded the dawn of passenger flying in the USA, but the first major step was the setting up, in the early 1920s, of a transcontinental air mail service which required the establishment of aerodromes across the country. Most regular aerodromes had two right-angle runways up to 762m (2,500ft) long, plus a 500,000 candle power beacon revolving on a tower, while emergency landing grounds had beacons a tenth of this power. By 1923 a lighted airway was set up, with acetylene-gas beacons at three-mile intervals along the routes.

Converted ex-military de Havilland D.H.9A and D.H.16 single-engined biplanes began the first scheduled passenger and cargo flights on 25 August 1919 from Hounslow Aerodrome, near London, to Le Bourget Airport, Paris. A reciprocal French service began the following month, using converted single-engined Breguet 14s, but these were soon followed by larger aircraft.

London's first real civil airport was opened at Croydon on 1 April 1920. It rapidly became one of the world's most famous airports until, overtaken by urban housing development and lacking space for expansion, it closed in September 1959.

As well as a rotating 'searchlight' beacon which could be seen from the air, Croydon also had wireless communication, and developed the rudimentary essentials of an air traffic control system which, in its initial form, involved a man with a red flag giving pilots the 'all clear' for take off! In spite of the spartan nature of these early operations, some 17,800 flights carrying nearly 47,000

passengers were made on cross-Channel services between August 1919 and March 1924.

As Croydon developed it was enlarged, and a new terminal came into use in January 1928. Airport boundary and obstruction lighting was installed, and a new red flashing beacon that could be seen up to 120km (80 miles) away in good weather conditions. Mobile and fixed landing floodlights and an illuminated wind direction indicator brought Croydon up to a high standard for its time, and airport development continued all over Europe in parallel with Croydon's upgrading. In many cases, hard runways were laid – Stockholm's Bromma Airport, for instance, opened in 1936 with Europe's first paved runways – but Croydon remained a grass airfield to the end of its days.

Le Bourget, the first international airport for Paris, was particularly well equipped for night-flying and in its time was one of Europe's most important airports.

Germany was well in the forefront of European airport development. Deutsche Lufthansa, the national airline, operated a large domestic network of air routes from Berlin, initially using Johannisthal Aerodrome. From the mid-1920s, the new Zentralflughafen Tempelhof, less than 3km (2 miles) from the city centre was also available.

Tempelhof, which had reached its fully developed form by 1938, was one of Europe's most advanced airports. It had a number of interesting features, not least of which was the massive terminal and hangar block, a curved structure which to this day has the distinction of being the world's third largest building. Designed to handle up to 300,000 passengers a year, Tempelhof had a unique advantage in that large aircraft could be taxied up beneath the terminal canopy for loading and unloading passengers. The inevitable necessity for longer runways led in October 1974 to the opening of the rebuilt Tegel Airport to replace urban, hemmed-in Tempelhof, although the latter will always be remembered with affection by West Berliners as the terminus for the Berlin Air Lift of 1948.

In the mid-1930s, there was a demand in certain European countries for seaplane and flying-boat operations. Some airports on the coast or near rivers were able to cater for these; Copenhagen's Kastrup, for instance, had a jetty, and Italy had a number of terminals for its considerable domestic and international flying-boat services to such cities as Rome, Venice, Genoa, Trieste, Barcelona, Lisbon, Brindisi, Palermo and Tunis. Operations of aircraft from water had certain advantages – no long runways were needed, although a buoy-marked area was necessary for take-off and landing. Flying-boat terminals could be incorporated in port areas.

New York's first airport, at Newark, was

FAR LEFT: *A Consolidated PBY at Edmonton Airport, Alberta. This is the oldest municipally-owned airport in Canada, and was opened in January 1927.*
FAR LEFT BELOW: *This photograph, which dates from the early 1930s, illustrates the rudimentary form air traffic control took at that time. A Lufthansa Junkers Ju 52/3m is being given instructions for take-off by a flag operator.*

BELOW LEFT: *An aerial view of the new ultra-modern airport Kansas City International. It was built at a cost of 250 million dollars, and has two runways each 3,200m (10,500ft) in length—the original city airport has one of 1,500m (4,900ft) and one of 2,100m (6,900ft). Its infrastructure was derived from the concept of a circular satellite space station, with a large central terminal and smaller subsidiary ones.*

BELOW LEFT: *View of Christchurch International Airport, New Zealand. This is a single runway airport handling a fairly large amount of traffic, and is now having its runway extended.*
BOTTOM: *One of the Deutsche Lufthansa buses which operated a shuttle service from Berlin city centre to Templehof Airport during the late 1920s, here seen picking up passengers from a Junkers G 24.*

opened on 1 October 1928 and boasted a 488m (1,600ft) hard-surfaced runway, claimed to be the first in the world. Combined hangars and passenger terminals were built, and the airport handled 20,000 passengers in 1930, a considerable figure for the time.

In spite of continued development at Newark, New York needed further airports for its rapidly growing airline traffic, and the New York Municipal Airport – La Guardia Field – was opened on 2 December 1939 to be followed in July 1948 by Idlewild Airport, now better known as John F. Kennedy International.

Without question, the world's busiest airport is Chicago/O'Hare, which in 1975 recorded 666,600 aircraft movements, giving an average daily total of take-offs and landings of almost 2,000! More than 37 million passengers were processed through the airport in the same period.

In Canada, airport development was slow, and by 1922 there were only 37 licensed 'air harbours' – 23 for landplanes, 12 for flying-boats and 2 which served both. Most landing grounds were very small, 6 of them being under 275m (900ft) square. By 1930, the number of licensed aerodromes had risen to 77, and a Prairie Air Mail Service had begun, linking Winnipeg with Calgary and Edmonton; the latter is Canada's oldest municipally-owned airport, licensed in June 1926 and opened the following January.

Development continued through the 1930s, the aim being to provide a lighted airport every 160km (100 miles), plus a number of emergency fields, and World War II provided a stimulus for considerable airport expansion.

Australia's two principal cities, Sydney and Melbourne, have had airports since 1921; by April 1936, 200 landing grounds had been prepared for civil aviation by the Commonwealth Government, and local authorities had established and licensed another 181 public aerodromes. An airline network was gradually built up and by 1976 there were 468 civil aerodromes, including service-owned facilities used by civil aircraft. Passenger traffic through the capital city air-

ports accounted for 78 per cent of all domestic airline passengers in 1975.

A brand-new airport, Melbourne/Tullamarine, was opened in the early 1970s, while Sydney's Kingsford Smith Airport was given new terminal facilities and runway extensions around the same time. A new international terminal was opened at Brisbane in December 1975, and other airport expansion work is being carried out.

Across the Tasman Sea, New Zealand was a slow starter in aviation; although there was some air taxi and charter work in the early 1920s, the first company was not registered until 1934. Subsequent growth in air services up to the outbreak of World War II provided a network of routes covering the North and South Islands; regular international services did not begin until October 1950, when Wellington and Sydney were linked.

Currently, New Zealand has some 80 public and 230 private aerodromes, including about 100 water landing areas. Auckland, Wellington and Christchurch are the three

main airports; runways at the first two have recently been extended and Auckland has a new terminal. A similar terminal is planned for Wellington, and Christchurch is having its runway extended.

Development and operating costs of the main airports are shared by central and local government. Management is provided by local authorities, while the Civil Aviation Division of the Ministry of Transport is responsible for aviation safety and the air navigation facilities.

South Africa's airport development was also slow, but by 1932 there were 42 licensed aerodromes, including two at Cape Town and one each at Durban, Johannesburg and Kimberley. By 1936, the total had risen to 53, and by 1939 Cape Town's Wingfield Aerodrome had the Union's first aerodrome blind approach beacon.

Johannesburg/Jan Smuts Airport, opened in 1963, is the country's main international airport, and is notable for its elevation of 1,690m (5,500ft) above sea-level. This naturally dictates a long runway (for 'hot and high' take-off conditions) with a length of 4,420m

(14,500ft). Other important airports, similarly named after South African statesmen, are Capetown/D. F. Malan, Durban/Louis Botha and Bloemfontein/J. B. M. Hertzog.

In the Soviet Union, the first regular air service began in the summer of 1922, linking Moscow with Nizhny Novgorod (now known as Gorky). Moscow was naturally the main hub for early services, but linked routes radiated from such cities as Leningrad, Kiev and Tashkent.

As in other countries, the early airports were of a makeshift character; most were grass fields, but flying-boats, operating from lakes and rivers, helped to establish air links.

In 1932, a new unit, Grazhdaviastroi, was established within the Civil Air Fleet for the planning of airports and installations; it was later renamed Aeroproyekt. After World War II considerable effort went into airport construction and Aeroproyekt planned for no less than 1,220 airports by 1990, to increase to 2,000 ten years after. Aeroflot, the Soviet state airline, carried 302 million passengers in the period 1965 to 1970, and forecast 500 million in the following five-year period. The airline now serves some 3,500 Soviet towns and cities.

Airport design

In commercial aviation's early days, the design and development of airports was less beset with problems than it is today.

Open areas on the outskirts of cities were

more numerous and land was relatively cheap. People rarely worried about aircraft noise – there were not that many aircraft anyway – and in fact, with air travel in its infancy, the opening of passenger services was welcomed as a prestige operation. A city on an air route had 'arrived'.

Because land could be acquired easily, airport developers gave little thought to planning for the future. They bought or leased the land but did not take options on adjoining areas for future extension. The predictable result was that as the airport flourished, so did the city, and buildings began to spring up around airports, gradually encroaching until, in some cases, the airport was totally surrounded. Too late, the airport developers realized that as aircraft got bigger they needed longer runways, and so the story began again.

The airlines, with new aircraft in prospect, were able to say in effect that they would be unable to serve a city because its runway was too short, so it became necessary to build a

new airport outside the city boundary. If it was too far away there were complaints that the time gained in flying was being wasted in ground transportation, but if it was built too close the urban encroachment began again, and as aircraft became noisier so complaints increased.

Nowadays, it is necessary in some cases to build airports a considerable distance from the cities they serve. Montreal's new Mirabel Airport is a good example; it is 56km (35 miles) from the city centre, but it is important to remember that the main factor is not so much distance as time. An airport only 19km (12 miles) from a city but with poor surface transport may take longer to reach than one 48km (30 miles) away that is served by an expressway or direct rail link.

Runways and terminals

Grass runways were adequate for the earlier transport aircraft, but as aircraft became heavier hard runways became necessary.

Runways were orientated depending on local conditions, such as the prevailing wind direction and size, height and position of obstructions in the area. By 1940, the US Civil Aeronautics Board was specifying 910m (3,000ft) runways for scheduled operation of small transport aircraft, and the 1,830m (6,000ft) longest runway at New York/La Guardia was exceptional. The longest runways at commercial airports are now in the region of 4,570m (15,000ft)

Multiple runway layouts are common at many civil airports, but there are some which still have a single runway – not necessarily by choice, as there may not be room for expansion, or there may be financial reasons. The single runway airport is of course at a serious disadvantage. It may be closed for a number of hours by a small incident, such as an aircraft skidding off the edge and blocking the runway, or may have to close down completely for a matter of two or three weeks for its runway to be resurfaced.

A single runway airport may be upgraded by building a second runway parallel to the first, taking less additional land than a cross runway, but doubling the airport's aircraft handling potential – assuming, of course, that the terminal capacity is sufficient for the extra passengers.

Airport runway designs are numerous – runways may be parallel and in line, parallel but staggered, or at right or acute angles to one another; runway layout must be linked with the architect's terminal plan.

At London/Heathrow, the terminal area is in the centre of the airport between the various runways, and linked to outside roads by tunnels. Heathrow has been subject to so much extension since it opened in 1946 that the central area is now too small and con-

gested, but because of its 'island' location it is incapable of enlargement.

Use of a parallel runway system with runways about 1,524m (5,000ft) apart has much to commend it. One runway can be used for landings while take-offs are made simultaneously from the other, and the aircraft have less distance to travel between terminal and runways. A number of new airport designs now use this basic concept with slight local variations.

The enormous Dallas–Fort Worth Airport, opened in 1974, has a central 'spine' road giving access to the terminal areas situated on each side. By its final stage, due for completion in 2001, DFW will have 13 semi-circular terminal units, with four north–south and two north-west/south-east runways. The first phase, now in operation, covers five terminal units, two parallel north/south runways, and one north-west/south-east. The present terminals have 65 gate positions and handled nearly 11 million passengers in 1976.

The new Paris/Charles de Gaulle Airport opened in 1974 with a single runway, but in its final form (due to be completed about 1990) two pairs of staggered parallel runways and one cross runway are planned. There will eventually be two terminals, and the first of these, Aerogare 1, is built on the satellite concept. The central circular terminal, 200m (656ft) in diameter, is linked by tunnels with moving walkways to seven satellite terminals, in effect large waiting lounges, each of which can handle up to four aircraft simultaneously, depending on size.

The Aerogare has 11 floors, the top 4 of which are car parks, and the basement contains baggage handling facilities. Passengers coming by car may use drive-in check-in desks, leaving their baggage before proceeding to the car park, from where they descend by lift to the departure floor.

The idea of a circular terminal is certainly not new – one could cite London/Gatwick's 'Beehive', opened in 1936. With a diameter of about 55m (180ft) the building looked attractive but, in the opinion of contemporary American aviation writer John Walter Wood, the rigidity of the plan caused confusion among passengers and the circular design prohibited subsequent extension. There were, he said, problems with the aircraft circulation around the terminal because of the one-way system, with manoeuvring taking place in a confined area. Gatwick did, however, have one unique feature – covered walkways which could be run out on rails from the terminal to the aircraft in inclement weather, enabling passengers to reach the aircraft and remain dry. Gatwick also claims another first – the first airport piers to be constructed in Europe, which were a feature

BOTTOM: *The terminal at Cologne/Bonn Airport has been designed to be as compact and functional as possible. There are different, separated levels for traffic from arrivals and departures, to keep all passengers moving smoothly. Note the two star-shaped satellite terminals.*

BELOW: *An Air France Boeing 747 parked at Paris/Charles de Gaulle Airport. The terminal consists of a ring-shaped central building surrounded by seven satellites. It opened in 1974 with a single runway but will eventually have two pairs of staggered parallel runways and one cross runway.*

BOTTOM: *Gatwick Airport, London, is a good example of a single runway airport. It is served by a motorway and a direct rail service to London. It is designed so that the passengers can come straight from the railway station into the terminal, thus cutting down a great deal of unnecessary delay.*

of the new post-war terminal.

Toronto Airport also liked the idea of a circular terminal, but called it the Aeroquay. It proved highly successful in use, but when it came to building a second terminal the Canadian Department of Transport opted for a less expensive linear design instead of the three Aeroquays proposed.

Washington's Dulles Airport is interesting on several counts. With two parallel and one cross-wind runway, it was the first airport designed specifically for jet aircraft, and was also the first designed from the outset to use mobile lounges to transport passengers between the terminal and the aircraft. The terminal is 183m (600ft) long and capable of extension to three times this length. Designed by architect Eero Saarinen, the building is a superb example of what can be achieved in airport architecture, and is a fitting terminal for the US end of the western world's first transatlantic supersonic passenger services operated by Concorde from London and Paris to Washington.

Airport operation

Airports may be operated by a country's airport authority, its department of transport, by local authorities, by airlines, by private owners or by contractors.

In the last category, one of the largest companies specializing in staffing and managing airports under contract to governments is International Aeradio Ltd. (IAL), based in the United Kingdom, near London/Heathrow Airport.

IAL has 24 subsidiary and associate companies in 17 overseas territories from the West Indies to Singapore. With its staff of 3,500 it can, if required, provide a complete service from airport feasibility studies to design, construction and full operation.

Airport finance

In some cases, notably the USA, funding for airports comes from the issue of bonds, particularly where a large amount of money is required for development work. The Federal Aviation Administration operates an exten-

sive Airport Development Aid Program which has enabled considerable expansion of many US airports in the last two decades.

Ideally airports should be self-supporting, or better still make a profit. An airport derives its revenue from a number of sources, which generally come under two headings – traffic operations and commercial operations. Landing fees and concessions are the airport's most lucrative sectors. Concessions cover a wide range of items including fuel and oil, various shops, restaurants, car parking and car hire services, flight insurance and advertising.

Staff costs account for a great deal of expenditure, followed by depreciation. The balance is split between rent and rates, utility and general services, equipment and supplies, maintenance and repairs and other expenses.

An analysis of operating revenues of a group of US airports, each of which handled more than two million passengers a year, showed that average percentage distribution was 37 per cent airfield area (landing fees, fuel and oil sales, airline catering, etc); 10·2 per cent hangar and building areas; 2·7 per cent systems and services; 15·8 per cent terminal areas (airline rents, boarding guards, etc), and 34·3 per cent concessions.

Moving the passenger

Many of the early airports were close to city centres, and most were served by public transport. In some cases the airlines used their own buses to bring passengers from town terminals. With few private cars, there was no parking problem. Today, as airports are built further from the cities they serve, passenger movement becomes a major factor in the consideration of an airport's design.

airbridges the passenger will walk across the apron and up a mobile staircase into the aircraft. Some aircraft, such as the BAC One-Eleven, are equipped with a built-in retractable staircase in the rear fuselage.

In this comparatively short journey, the passenger will be using quite a lot of airport equipment, and it is worth describing this and explaining how it evolved.

Check-in and baggage handling

From the very first passenger-carrying air services, it was necessary to check-in passengers and baggage and to weigh both, as weights were very critical on early aircraft which did not have the reserves of power available on today's airliners.

trollies for towing to the aircraft.

An automatic baggage sorting system was built by the French Teleflex company at Paris/Orly Airport. The bag is placed on a deposit conveyor at the check-in desk while ticket details are verified by computer; it then moves to a second position for weighing and tagging. The coded destination is marked magnetically and the bag moves to a waiting position until the computer, sensing a space on the baggage conveyor, releases the bag. As it passes down the conveyor belt, detectors sense the magnetic coding and the bag is diverted at its terminal to await transportation to the aircraft.

Another French company, Saxby Otis, has developed an electric driverless tractor

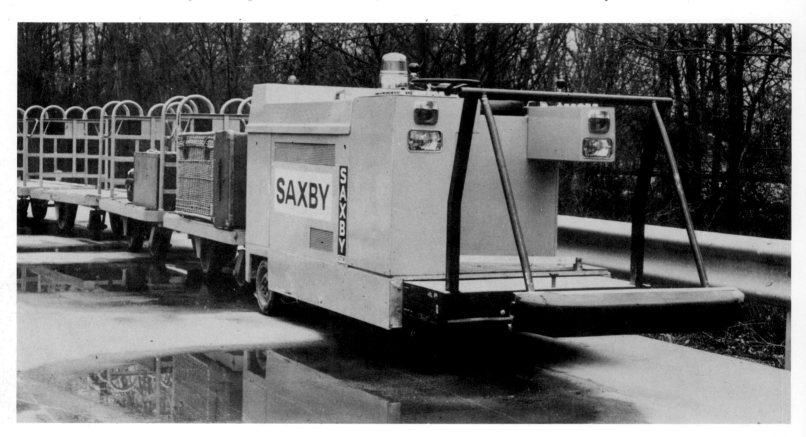

There are still very few specially built rapid transit links between airport and city, and the best-served airports are those on a railway line or with an autoroute connection.

Even so, the airport's handling responsibilities begin when the passenger arrives, either incoming by air or outgoing by surface transport. Basically, the departing passenger will move into the terminal to check-in at the appropriate airline desk, be relieved of his baggage, pass through passport and customs controls (if he is departing on an international flight), and into the departure lounge. Here he will be able to make his duty-free purchases (again, only if he is leaving the country).

When his flight is called over the public address system and shown on the information boards, the passenger will leave the lounge, pass through a security check and walk, or travel by moving walkway, to the departure gate. At this point he will either be taken by bus to the aircraft if it is parked away from the terminal, or will board the aircraft through an airbridge or air jetty connecting it to the terminal building. In the case of a smaller airport not equipped with

Passengers were issued with tickets which described the airline's liability in case of accidents. The requirements for passenger handling remain the same today, except that passengers are not weighed, an average weight being allowed by the airline. Today's big difference, however, has been brought about by the necessity of handling loads of up to 400 passengers on a single flight; the difference can be summarized in one word – computerization.

The computer age has meant a revolution in the airlines' seat reservations and check-in systems. Many of the larger international airlines now operate a push-button reservation system, by which they can feed in information at Sydney, for example, and find out within seconds if a seat is available on a specific flight from any airport in the world linked to their reservation system. The system can also make a reservation and can be further adapted to provide automatic ticketing.

Once the passenger and his baggage are checked, the baggage goes on to a moving belt behind the counter and passes onto a baggage sorting area before being loaded on

for the new Paris/Charles de Gaulle Airport. The tractor tows luggage trailers from the central luggage sorting point in the terminal building through underground tunnels to the seven satellite terminals. It is steered automatically by means of a front-mounted probe which follows cables beneath the roadway surface, the load destination being pre-programmed. About 70 such tractors are in use at the airport.

Most baggage is carried in holds beneath the aircraft's floor, and is loaded by means of an inclined conveyor belt mounted on a light truck chassis, but in recent years there has been a growing trend towards pre-packing baggage in containers which may be carried on an aircraft's main deck. These are more often used on wide-body high-capacity aircraft, when passenger loads are lower than those for which the aircraft were designed. Some Boeing 747s, for instance, have been converted to passenger/cargo combinations (combis), where the fitting of removable bulkheads in the fuselage, combined with quickly removable seats, can very easily provide the required combination of passenger and cargo load.

BELOW LEFT: *One of the electric driverless tractors developed for Paris/Charles de Gaulle Airport being tested. They are used to tow baggage trailers from the main terminal via underground tunnels to the satellite terminals. Steering is by means of cables buried in the roadway surface.*
BELOW: *The US Department of Transportation has developed a uniform system of symbols to help passengers. The symbols illustrated are a selection of the basic types which may be seen at American airports.*
LEFT FROM TOP: *Ticket purchase and baggage check-in, baggage claim, customs, immigration.* CENTRE: *Car rental, restaurant, coffee shop, bar.* RIGHT: *Lost and found, baggage lockers, elevator, men's toilets.*

RIGHT: *Most airports have now installed security systems to cope with the enormous amount of passengers' baggage to be checked. One of these is the American Scanray X-ray system; here the image it produces clearly reveals two pistols concealed among the rest of the luggage.*
BELOW: *Security systems in use at Helsinki Airport. Passengers themselves are checked by walking through a Finnish Metor metal detector, and hand baggage is inspected by an American Bendix X-ray system between the coils of the Metor. Events of the past few years have made these elaborate precautions necessary to ensure the safety of the millions of travellers using the world's airlines every year.*

So much for departing baggage; arriving baggage begins the sequence of return to its owner by a reversal of the loading process. It is delivered from the aircraft to the terminal's baggage arrivals area, where it is off-loaded from the vehicle or container and placed onto a conveyor taking it to the baggage collection point in the arrivals hall. Here it is expelled onto a conveyor belt or 'carousel' bearing the flight number from which it has just come, and is collected by its owner.

There are several types of baggage conveyor, including a French system, the Teleflex Diplodocus, which, by use of a soft pressure cushion system, can carry baggage vertically upwards for short distances. This is valuable where constraints apply in a terminal design, making it difficult to provide space for a long, inclined conveyor.

Several variations on the baggage collection conveyor may be seen, ranging from the 'carousel' which, as its name implies, is a circular roundabout, to flat endless conveyors in a racetrack pattern. Here again, the type used will depend on the amount of space available, the degree of use the system may expect, and the amount of money available.

Information systems
To find his way to a seat in the aircraft, the passenger must be guided. It must always be assumed by the terminal planner that the passenger is making his first flight, and has no knowledge of airports and their systems. Because a large number of people of many nationalities use international airports, it is desirable to express certain basic information in the form of diagrams, or pictographs as they are called, and there has been considerable work on designs over the past decade. Details of flight times, destinations, etc, are now generally displayed on large information boards in departure and arrival halls.

These boards operate on several different systems – coloured lights, flap turn-over letters and so on – but the information they give is equally comprehensive and readily understandable. They are operated from a central point, and the information fed into the main boards is repeated on smaller boards in departure lounges, and sometimes at departure gates. In some cases, repeater displays are given via a closed-circuit television system at points around the terminal.

Security
While airport owners have always been conscious of the need for security from the very earliest days of civil aviation, events of the last decade involving sabotage, hijacking and other criminal activities have necessitated considerable expenditure on security systems for checking the passenger and his baggage. Initially, simple metal detectors were used, but later it was necessary to produce screening equipment which could detect explosives in addition to firearms carried in passengers' baggage.

Many screening systems are now in use throughout the world; most consist of a metal-detection framework through which the passenger walks and which gives the operator an audible or visual signal of the presence of metal objects on the passenger, and a unit for baggage which provides an X-ray picture of the bag's contents to the operator.

The full radiation dosage of all these systems is very low, and is carefully monitored by government departments to ensure that it does not even approach the danger level.

Reaching the aircraft

The larger airport terminals are usually connected to the aircraft by a telescopic covered walkway, known as an airbridge. These come in a variety of shapes and sizes – in single or double forms, the latter for use with wide-body aircraft demanding a large passenger flow. With a double bridge, it is possible to feed passengers into two entrances in the aircraft simultaneously, the forward entrance for passengers with seats at the front of the aircraft, and the centre or rear entrance for other passengers.

One of the early pioneers of the airbridge concept was Aviobridge of the Netherlands – now part of the huge Dutch/German VFW-Fokker group. Naturally enough, Amsterdam/Schiphol, the Netherlands' premier airport, has a considerable number of Aviobridges.

Some airbridges or jetways have fixed anchorage points on the apron, the aircraft taxiing to a marked position and the end of the bridge extending out to meet its doorways, while other bridges have wheel-mounted ends and can be driven around an arc, enabling more flexibility in aircraft parking positions.

A simpler form of airbridge is the air jetty. This consists of a short, fixed tunnel connected to the terminal or passenger loading pier, and a very short telescopic front section which extends out to the aircraft's passenger door. The aircraft taxies up to the jetty, being

ABOVE: *The Boothe Plane-Mate mobile lounge is now in use at several airports to transport passengers to and from aircraft parked away from the terminal. Washington/Dulles Airport was the first one to be designed specifically for their operation.*
ABOVE RIGHT: *Guidance for pilots lining up with air jetties is here provided by lightweight striped bars which make contact with the windscreen when the aircraft is in the right position. The height of the bar is adjustable in order to fit different aircraft.*
RIGHT: *One of the satellite terminals at Brussels National Airport, Belgium. It is connected by an enclosed walkway to the main terminal building. This is the most common type of arrangement for getting passengers from one part of the terminal to another.*
FACING PAGE
ABOVE LEFT: *Telescopic covered walkways or airbridges are the usual means of connecting the terminal to the aircraft. Here Fokker-VFW Aviobridges are simultaneously serving a DC-9, three DC-10s and a Boeing 747 of KLM at Amsterdam/Schiphol Airport.*
ABOVE CENTRE: *In order to avoid an overlong chassis and steeply inclined staircase, these airliner steps made by the French company Douaisis have a 180° turn, and the height of the upper flight is adjustable to fit even the very large aircraft.*
ABOVE RIGHT: *The LTV Airtrains passenger-moving system in use at Dallas/Fort Worth Airport consists of remotely controlled vehicles which move along a specially built concrete trackway. It links not only the terminals but also outlying points such as car parks and cargo areas.*
BELOW: *New types of Aviobridges have been developed to serve special needs. Here an overwing Aviobridge is used to serve the rear door of a Boeing 747, while the front door is served by a standard type.*

aligned by the pilot by means of markings on the apron, on the terminal or, in some cases, by a coloured light system adjacent to the jetty, the correct colour sequence showing if the aircraft is properly lined up. A simple indicator is a lightweight striped bar extending from the jetty; the aircraft moves forward until the bar contacts the windscreen.

Where airbridges are not available, or where aircraft have to be parked some distance from the terminal, specially designed buses are used. In some cases, such as the German-built Neoplan vehicle, there are doors at each end to allow rapid loading and unloading of passengers.

However, the passenger still has to get into the aircraft, and while in the early days a small pair of steps sufficed, the high sill heights of the larger modern passenger aircraft necessitate wheel-mounted staircases.

These range from a simple, open staircase, with side rails which may be manually pushed into position, to sophisticated covered-in self-propelled stairways which may be adjusted hydraulically to the sill height. A French company, Douaisis, concerned by the increasing chassis length of mobile staircases as aircraft became bigger and the steps had to be made higher and therefore longer, has designed a unit which has a 180° turn in the staircase, enabling a greater height to be reached without increasing the length of the chassis.

Another way of getting passengers to their aircraft, although one which has taken much longer to establish itself, is the mobile lounge. Developed in the USA, this consists of a lounge with a capacity of about 150 passengers, mounted on a four-wheel chassis. The lounge section can be elevated from ground level to the height needed to load passengers into an aircraft and is self-propelled, operating from the terminal loading gate in much the same manner as an air jetty, with an extending connecting doorway.

Washington/Dulles was the first airport to be designed specifically for mobile lounge operation, and uses these exclusively. The lounges, built by Boothe Airside Systems and christened Plane-Mates, are considered to have several advantages over more conventional schemes for getting passengers and aircraft together. The lower cost of a smaller terminal (no in-built lounges required, as the passengers go straight from check-in to their mobile lounge) is one obvious saving, and mobile lounge makers claim that eliminating the use of airside buses makes a considerable saving.

Within the terminal, the passenger may have a fairly long walk between the terminal entrance or check-in desks and his departure gate. To alleviate this, some airports are installing moving walkways or travelators, continuous rubber belting moving at walking speed on which the passenger may stand or walk. These may be installed on a level or inclined plane, with the obvious proviso that the incline must not be too steep or the passenger would be unable to balance!

In some of the very large American air-

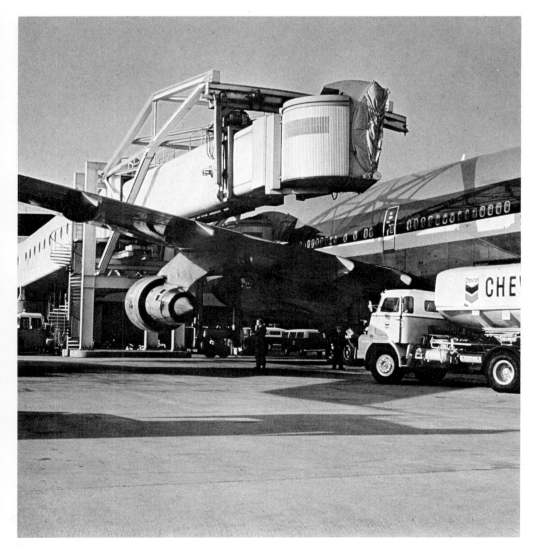

ports where there are a number of terminals, perhaps operated by different airlines, the transit vehicle has found favour. An example of this system is to be found at Tampa Airport, Florida, where the transit vehicles serve four satellite terminals, each accommodating up to seven aircraft. An elevated concrete trackway connects each satellite to the main terminal and carries electrically powered remotely controlled 125-passenger coaches locked on to a central guide beam. The trackways are duplicated, each operating two coaches moving simultaneously in opposite directions and taking 40 seconds to complete the satellite to terminal journey.

At peak periods, the eight-coach Tampa system is said to be capable of moving 3,000 passengers in 10 minutes. Operated from a sophisticated control point, the system is computer-controlled and monitored; the centre is continually manned. Similar systems with variations are in use at several US airports.

At Dallas–Fort Worth Airport, a transit system built by LTV and known as Airtrans provides a link not only within the terminals but also to outlying points around the airport such as car parks and cargo areas. With 21km (13 miles) of track in its initial form, Airtrans consists of rubber-tyred 40-passenger cars running under computer control in a reinforced concrete guideway. A maximum operating speed of 27km/h (17mph) maintains an 18-second separation between successive cars; there are almost 70 vehicles in use at the present time.

BELOW : *Mobile runway lighting systems were fairly primitive in the early days of passenger travel. This photograph shows a cart equipped with lamps which was used by Lufthansa when the airline first began its operations.*

RIGHT : *This giant snow-clearing unit used by the Russian airline Aeroflot in the severe winters of the Soviet Union has a bulldozer blade to push snow aside, a brush in the centre and a blower at the rear to blow snow clear of the swept runway.*

CENTRE RIGHT : *The French Bertin TS-2 runway ice-removal vehicle used hot air from a gas turbine.*
FAR RIGHT : *Test running the engine of a DC–9 with silencers (de-tuners) in position. In the background, de-tuners for the Boeing 747.*

Fire and rescue services

The fire and rescue service is a most important part of an airport's operation. Without a service of this type, which must reach certain defined standards, an airport will not be given a license to operate.

There has been a steady development in the field of airport fire and crash rescue vehicles. Early requirements could be met by virtually standard fire engines, but now there is a whole range of purpose-built fire-fighting equipment, from small rapid intervention vehicles (RIVs) to very large multi-wheel appliances.

The purpose of the high-speed RIV is to get to the incident in the fastest possible time, and to contain the fire until the arrival, some seconds later, of the large-capacity vehicles which use foam to smother the flames. While most fire-fighting vehicles are wheel-mounted, there are some interesting exceptions. The Canadian company Canadair Flextrac has supplied six caterpillar-tracked fire tenders to the Indian Airports Authority, while Auckland Airport, New Zealand, uses an SRN.6 Hovercraft for traversing the mud flats and shallow waters around the airport at low tide.

Some airports have foam-laying equipment for use in emergencies. For instance, if an aircraft is unable to lower its undercarriage, a carpet of foam is laid on the runway so that the aircraft may touch down smoothly on its belly on the foam, which will smother sparks caused by friction of the aircraft's surfaces on contact with the runway.

A hazard less easy to deal with causes problems at some airports. Flocks of birds rising into the air at the approach of an aircraft create considerable danger. Their ingestion by an aircraft engine can cause it to stop, while 'bird strikes' on other parts of the aircraft have been known to cause crashes.

Various methods of scaring birds have been tried by the airport authorities, ranging from a vehicle with loudspeakers driving down the runway and relaying tape recordings of bird distress calls, to the use of birds of prey, such as falcons and goshawks. But the only answer seems to be that the area must be made less attractive for birds to nest and roost. Such ornithological attractions as rubbish dumps must not be allowed in the vicinity of airports.

Snow and ice clearance are major problems at some airports; a closed runway can mean diversions to another airport or prevent aircraft from leaving, with subsequent loss of revenue. In the more temperate climates the problem is usually resolved fairly easily, except in cases of an exceptionally heavy or untypical fall, but in such countries as Canada, where high snowfalls can be expected, most airports are well equipped to deal with such a situation.

A paper by the Airport Facilities Branch of the Canadian Ministry of Transport describes the snow removal operation. A high-speed runway sweeper with a 4·27m (14ft)

wide brush clears a 3·66m (12ft) path at speeds up to 48km/h (30mph) on snow up to 7·6cm (3in) deep. Once several widths have been cleared, the ploughs are used in conjunction to pick up and cast aside the loose snow. Blowers, operating at speeds up to 40km/h (25mph), follow the plough and sweeper, blowing the snow at high speed over the runway edge, and this is finally removed at least 7·62m (25ft) beyond the edge of the runway lighting.

Too much slush or water on runways can cause an aircraft to aquaplane or skid, so a device is used to measure and record runway friction. Towed up and down a runway behind a vehicle, this device can assess whether or not the runway is safe for operations. One way to lessen the danger of water build-up on runways is to cut transverse grooves in the surface, enabling surplus water to drain away.

Runway lighting must be kept clean, particularly after snow, and specialized equipment is available for this purpose. The French Bertin company has produced a semi-automatic cleaning device named Fluxojet which, it is claimed, can clean 100 lights in an hour. The method is to place a 'head' connected to sources of air pressure over the light windows, blow a powder over the glass at high pressure to remove the dirt, and use suction to remove the residue into a waste tank.

Bertin also produces the Thermosoufflant, a large wheeled vehicle used for melting snow and ice on runways by means of heat generated by a gas turbine in the vehicle.

Fog has always been a source of concern at airports. During World War II experiments were carried out at certain RAF stations in England in an effort to clear fog sufficiently for aircraft returning from operations to land safely. The FIDO system (Fog Investigation and Dispersal Operation) consisted of petrol burners installed along the edge of runways and ignited when aircraft were approaching to land. Several thousand safe landings were made with the aid of FIDO, but it would have been prohibitively expensive in peacetime commercial operations, especially in view of the progress made in automatic landing. Another method is cloud seeding, used successfully by airlines on the US West Coast.

However, the versatile Bertin company has developed a fog dispersal system, Turboclair, which has been installed at Paris/Charles de Gaulle Airport following successful tests at Paris/Orly. This consists of gas turbines in bunkers alongside the runway, fog being dispersed by the heat from the turbines' efflux.

Moving damaged aircraft

The moving of aircraft which have suffered damage in emergency landings must be carried out carefully to avoid further damage, and must also be done as rapidly as possible, particularly if the aircraft is blocking a runway. One system, designed by a UK company, RFD Inflatables Ltd, uses pneumatic bags (elevators) which are inserted under the aircraft at certain points and then inflated to raise it. When a sufficient height has been reached, the landing gear may be lowered if it is undamaged, and the aircraft is then towed away. If the landing gear is damaged, inflatable tracks are laid and a jacking system lifts the aircraft clear of the ground, allowing it to be towed along the tracks.

Aircraft support

A wide range of equipment can be listed under this broad heading. Some of the vehicles are adapted by airports and airlines from standard vehicles, for instance the small 'follow me' cars and pick-ups used at some airports to guide aircraft to their allotted parking spaces. Others are purpose-designed.

The largest vehicles to be seen at an airport are the fuellers, of which there are two types: the standard tanker and the hydrant dispenser.

Tankers and the aircraft they serve have grown together. When commercial aviation began it was necessary to hand-pump fuel into an aircraft's tanks, often standing on the top wing of a biplane to do so, while in some more primitive areas it was necessary to strain all fuel before it went into the aircraft.

Today's large-capacity aircraft may demand more than 90,000 litres (23,775 US gallons) of fuel. This would require an exceedingly large and heavy tanker – for instance, a Gloster Saro articulated tanker fuelling Boeing 747s at Brussels National Airport in 1970 had an 82,000-litre (21,663 US gallons) capacity and was more than 21m (70ft) long. Such a vehicle needs considerable manoeuvring areas on the apron, and in these days when rapid aircraft turnrounds are demanded, very high fuel flow rates become necessary. The big Gloster Saro vehicle is capable of pumping 3,782 litres (999 US gallons) a minute.

With a hydrant system, fuel is piped from the airport's fuel farm to points on the apron area, and the hydrant dispenser, a much smaller vehicle than the tanker, is connected to the hydrant, forming the link between this and the aircraft's fuel tanks. The dispenser measures the fuel flow and quantity, and modern dispensers can achieve a flow rate of 5,550 litres/min (1,466 US gallons/min)

simultaneously through four hoses. Fuel filters ensure that the fuel is not contaminated.

Because of the necessity to provide underground piping, a hydrant system can be costly to instal, and it offers less flexibility than tankers but the disadvantages are offset by a higher flow rate. It is also cheaper to operate in terms of manpower. When an airport apron is being extended, enlarging of a hydrant system can be expensive, and for these reasons it seems likely that both tankers and hydrants will be used during the foreseeable future.

The need to move aircraft on the ground has led to a revolution in the design of very powerful towing vehicles, or tugs. When aircraft were smaller and lighter they could be towed by conventional tractors, but the advent of the large post-war airliner has demanded a radical re-think by the tractor designer. The T–800S jumbo tug built by the US International Harvester Company is typical of the large-capacity aircraft tugs; it is able to pull a Boeing 747 weighing about 362,850kg (800,000lb) and itself weighs 49,000kg (108,000lb). Powered by a pair of eight-cylinder turbocharged 300hp diesel engines, it has a driving cab at each end and can be driven from either. The cabs may be elevated or lowered flush with the body of the tractor, which is known as a 'low profile' type because it is only 1·57m (5ft 2in) high and can be driven beneath the fuselages of large aircraft.

All tugs need a towbar to tow aircraft; these are normally connected to the aircraft's nose-wheel undercarriage leg and come in a variety of sizes with varying endplate fittings which will adapt to various types of aircraft.

Air cargo is a fast-growing part of air transport operations, and special terminals with a considerable amount of computerized equipment are now in use at many airports. Much of the cargo-handling gear is computer-controlled and monitored, including cargo sorting in some cases.

When cargo is delivered to the terminal by standard road vehicles, specially designed cargo handling equipment is necessary to reach the loading doors of the aircraft. In the case of all-cargo aircraft, much of the load consists of goods ready packed in large oblong containers, the standard size being 6·1m long by 2·4m wide by 2·4m deep (20ft × 8ft × 8ft). The benefit of this type of container traffic is that it can travel equally easily by road, rail, sea or air, and there is considerable interchange traffic between these modes.

The largest cargo loaders currently in service are made in the USA; Cochran Airport Systems' Model 320 loader has a lifting capacity of 27,215kg (60,000lb), with a hydraulically powered cable-operated lift mechanism. It is a self-propelled vehicle with a six-cylinder engine. Some of the smaller loaders in use, lifting around 13,605kg (30,000lb), are raised and lowered by the scissor-lift principle – steel crossover beams which lay flat when the loading platform is at chassis level and become X-shaped as the platform is raised.

The platform decks of the loaders are fitted with a series of rollers or bearings on which containers are rolled into or from the aircraft, which have similar rollers on the floor of their cargo holds. Some of the smaller loading platforms are towed by tractors, while the smallest container trailers – 'dollies' – are tractor-towed and normally built to a fixed height. Some variants incorporate a turntable for easier movement of the containers onto the larger container loaders.

A wide variety of service vehicles may be seen clustered round an aircraft being prepared for flight; a Lufthansa description of

TOP: *Moving Sabena's Boeing 747s requires a large tug to avoid having to use the 747's own power. Here a French-built Secmafer SF700 is being used for the job. This is typical of the large capacity aircraft tugs, being very heavy itself and quite powerful enough to tow even a jumbo jet loaded with fuel and cargo.*

ABOVE: *Fire precaution is an important part of an airport's services. Here a turn-out by the Frankfurt Airport fire department shows the wide variety of vehicles available.*
TOP RIGHT: *A lorry-mounted 'cherry-picker' maintenance platform servicing the tail of a DC–10 belonging to the French airline UTA.*

CENTRE RIGHT: *Loading cargo containers on a Seaboard World Airlines Boeing 747 Freighter with a purpose-designed cargo transporter and cargo-loading elevator.*
RIGHT: *Refuelling an aircraft from a hydrant on the apron using a hydrant-dispenser vehicle as a go-between.*

'ramp lice' may sound unkind, but somehow aptly describes the scene. They include vehicles for cleaning out aircraft toilets, for replenishing water supplies, galleys and so on, and ground power units (GPU). These GPUs provide power for the aircraft's electrical systems when the engines are not running, and also for engine starting. Some aircraft are fitted with airborne power units (APUs), small engines which maintain the aircraft's electrical supply when it is on the ground, making it independent from the airport's electrical services. These are particularly useful at very busy airports, where GPUs may all be in use, or at more remote airports where they may be in short supply.

Some airports are now using electrical power systems which can supply power to the aircraft on the apron from a ring main fed into the airport's central generating plant. The Dallas–Fort Worth Braniff Airways terminal has a built-in power supply for this purpose, and there are others at London/Heathrow, Brussels National and Stockholm/Arlanda airports. While the idea has not yet gained overall acceptance, the general consensus of the airports using it is that it results in cleaner apron areas and cuts down noise and pollution caused by GPUs and APUs.

Aircraft maintenance
All the previously mentioned equipment is used when the aircraft is at the terminal apron. Another range of equipment comes into play in the airline maintenance areas.

The biggest piece of hangar equipment is undoubtedly the maintenance docking system. British Airways at London/Heathrow has a new dock for its Lockheed TriStar fleet. When a TriStar has to undergo routine maintenance, it is towed into the hangar along marked guidelines and the dock, consisting of working platforms at five levels, is moved into position around the aircraft, enabling engineers to work on all parts of the aircraft and its engines.

Some cleaning is carried out while the aircraft is docked, but when external cleaning is needed at other times it can be done on the parking apron by specially equipped vehicles which incorporate a mobile platform on an extending arm with a hose attachment. These 'cherry pickers', as they are known, can also be used for high-level maintenance, windscreen cleaning, fire-fighting and clearance of ice and snow from the aircraft's surfaces.

Airlines also need a considerable amount of test equipment, ranging from engine test cells to rigs for testing engine fuel flows. Engine testing is a necessary part of aircraft maintenance, and many airlines have built noise mufflers, or detuners, for this purpose. Swissair, at its Zurich maintenance base, has a massive installation capable of testing all four engines of a Boeing 747 simultaneously. The four large silencer tubes, each nearly 24m (78ft) long are enclosed in concrete foundations faired into a 7m (23ft) high wall which is 56m (184ft) long.

When mufflers are not available, blast deflectors are installed to enable aircraft to run up their engines to full power in the maintenance area without the jet blast affecting nearby vehicles and installations.

Monitoring and measuring

Perhaps the major complaint levelled at airports concerns noise, and unfairly so, since the airport itself does not generate the noise about which the complaints are made. This comes from its customers, the airlines, but airport authorities find themselves acting as buffers between airlines and the incensed local population, who may have legitimate cause for complaint.

The various means of quietening aircraft by the fitting of so-called 'hush kits' to their engines, changing the aircraft's angle of approach to landing, and so on, are described fully on page 101. Many airports now have noise monitoring equipment. This is set up at a number of points on and around the airport, and the noise measurements recorded are passed automatically to a central recording and control point for analysis.

As an incentive to airlines to reduce noise, Frankfurt Airport operated a scheme under which aircraft were awarded a number of points per landing, and at the end of the year the airlines with the best 'quietness' record were given a cash bonus.

Effective air traffic control at an airport demands continuous knowledge of weather conditions and visibility, and to obtain this two pieces of equipment are used. A ceilometer is an optical radar which gives the height of the cloud base above an airport, by measuring time taken for a pulse of light to travel from the transmitter to the cloud base and return to the receiver. The light source in the case of a newly developed ceilometer by the UK Plessey Company is a semiconductor laser.

To measure horizontal visibility, a system known as runway visual range (RVR) has been developed. Before this, markers were placed at fixed intervals along a runway within view of a runway control caravan. By counting the markers visible the observer could ascertain the range of visibility.

The most modern means of measurement in this field is instrumented visual range (IVR), the first fully automated system for the purpose, which has been developed by a UK company, Marconi Radar Systems. Operating from installations alongside the runway, IVR feeds range measurements automatically to a central monitoring point.

Movement of aircraft on the ground in bad visibility is helped by a radar equipment in the control tower known as ASMI – Aerodrome Surface Movement Indicator. Using a very short wavelength, this enables aircraft to be directed along taxiways.

Air Traffic Control

A description of Air Traffic Control (ATC) services on an international basis would take several books. This section therefore deals with ATC as it affects air traffic arriving at, departing from or overflying Australia.

In Australia, the National Air Traffic Control Service is a joint civil and military control service under the Departments of Transport and Defence. ATC has direct responsibility for the movement of civil and military aircraft over Australia. The Australian airspace is divided into five Flight Information Regions (FIRs) – Queensland, New South Wales, Victoria, Tasmania, South Australia, Northern Territory and Western Australia. Each region has its own ATC centre. The Sydney Area Approach Control Centre (AACC) at Sydney (Kingsford-Smith) airport, for example, covers airspace from Albury, in the south, to Coffs Harbour and Moree, in the north. Going east, it covers a large slice of the Pacific Ocean, and additionally as far north as the Equator and extending south of Tasmania. The western boundary reaches almost as far as Broken Hill. Airspace in the FIRs is divided into sectors – some for aircraft overflying en route, some scheduled into terminals, covering the principal airports of Australia.

Each sector has a Sector Controller (SECT) who manages operations and who is also responsible for the transfer of air traffic to adjoining sectors as it comes into and goes out of his sector. He has the assistance of a sector radar controller who is responsible for separation of traffic, chiefly by radar. Radar display presents a bright image on a screen, giving the aircraft's position and direction. The radar scanner linked to the centre, provides a sweep of a section of sky. A bright blip (or paint) on the controller's screen gives the aircraft's position. Radar controllers at the AACC can handle up to 12 aircraft simultaneously. At major airports in Australia radar controllers no longer work in the dark – they have been working in 'daylight' conditions for some years. Sector controllers maintain continuous contact with adjoining sectors to ensure correct separation between aircraft. A military controller at the ATC coordinates the movement of military aircraft crossing civil air routes.

The AACC Operations Room is under the supervision of a Senior Area Approach Controller (SAAC) who controls a watch of about 25 controllers and 5 flight data officers. There are 4 watch teams which provide a 24-hour service. Controllers monitor aircraft with flight progress strips which, for each aircraft, show the call sign, aircraft type, point of departure, destination, and estimated times over selected points en route. The strips are arranged in geographical order and time sequence and are prepared by the flight data officers. They are up-dated as fresh information comes in. The controller talks to aircraft by radio telephone in his particular area of responsibility. Continuous landline connections allow him to liaise with controllers in other centres. Placed above the controller's radar screen is a close-circuit TV screen. Displayed here are the locations of thunderstorms within a radius of 50 nautical miles.

Approach and landing control

Aircraft pass through various controls out of the airways system into an airport and to a selected terminal and terminal gate. Bright radar display units are provided for the approach/radar controllers in the AACC room. In the operations positions are the approach controller and three radar directors.

The approach controller accepts the aircraft which has been released and transferred by the sector controllers and takes his first radio call from the aircraft. He instructs the captain of the aircraft on landing procedures and runway use.

The radar directors, after the aircraft has been released by sector control, will sequence traffic, using surveillance radar, for bringing aircraft to the point of final approach about

Traffic at Selected World Airports

Any listing of the world's airports based on the number of aircraft movements or passengers handled and placed in order of traffic would inevitably include a large proportion of US airports in the first 20. A conservative estimate of 180,000 civil aircraft in the US indicates why this is so.

The listing below therefore gives a more balanced picture, in alphabetical order, of airport traffic throughout the world, both in terms of passengers and cargo. It is based on statistics from the Aeroport de Paris and the British Airports Authority for 1975.

Toronto Airport, Canada

Melbourne International Airport

Pretoria Airport, South Africa

JFK Airport, New York

Frankfurt Airport, West Germany

IATA code	Airport	Total aircraft movements	Total passengers	Cargo (tonnes)
ADD	Addis Ababa (Ethiopia)	29,400	178,100	6,053
ALG	Algiers/Dar el Beida (Algeria)	56,200	1,808,000	14,650
AMS	Amsterdam/Schiphol (Netherlands)	173,300	7,534,300	226,322
ATL	Atlanta/Hartsfield (USA)	469,000	25,268,900	201,942
ATH	Athens (Greece)	98,500	5,085,200	33,600
BKK	Bangkok/Don Muang (Thailand)	50,200	2,580,800	52,809
TXL/THF	Berlin/Tegel & Tempelhof (West Germany)	55,500	3,992,600	13,529
BLZ	Blantyre/Chileka (Malawi)	16,600	281,200	3,977
BOS	Boston/Logan (USA)	258,500	10,515,400	142,295
BRU	Brussels National (Belgium)	97,100	3,942,900	100,412
CCU	Calcutta (India)	30,400	1,008,600	10,682
CCS	Caracas/Maiquetia (Venezuela)	73,400	2,715,100	78,597
CHI	Chicago/O'Hare (USA)	666,600	37,123,000	544,745
CPH	Copenhagen/Kastrup (Denmark)	163,000	7,575,800	129,615
DFW	Dallas-Fort Worth (USA)	341,400	10,864,900	63,920
DEN	Denver/Stapleton (USA)	386,500	12,026,400	94,089
DLA	Douala (Cameroon)	23,200	295,800	18,010
DUB	Dublin (Irish/Republic)	79,400	2,193,600	42,300
DUS	Dusseldorf/Lohausen (West Germany)	113,100	5,124,100	27,198
FRA	Frankfurt (West Germany)	209,200	11,967,900	404,157
GUA	Guatemala/La Aurora (Guatemala)	83,400	596,700	13,765
HEL	Helsinki (Finland)	86,000	2,812,700	18,606
HKG	Hong Kong/Kai Tak (Hong Kong)	83,200	3,872,100	102,257
IST	Istanbul/Yesilkoy (Turkey)	49,800	2,807,100	16,866
JNB	Johannesburg (South Africa)	64,200	3,131,900	71,204
KUL	Kuala Lumpur (Malaysia)	42,400	1,362,600	11,239
LIS	Lisbon/Portrela (Portugal)	45,000	2,372,900	35,962
LGW	London/Gatwick (UK)	105,100	5,343,500	75,266
LHR	London/Heathrow (UK)	276,100	21,294,800	405,005
LAX	Los Angeles International (USA)	453,600	23,719,000	558,205
MAD	Madrid/Barajas (Spain)	118,700	7,966,400	108,830
MEL	Melbourne/Tullamarine (Australia)	96,000	4,536,000	67,900
MIA	Miami International (USA)	287,600	12,068,100	337,690
LIN	Milan/Linate (Italy)	89,400	4,032,700	52,043
YUL	Montreal/Dorval (Canada)	191,200	6,630,700	178,600
SVO	Moscow/Sheremetievo (USSR)	43,400	2,387,300	44,506
MUC	Munich/Riem (West Germany)	116,700	4,259,800	25,205
LGA	New York/La Guardia (USA)	299,200	13,185,500	45,862
JFK	New York/John F Kennedy (USA)	300,800	19,475,800	876,366
OSA	Osaka (Japan)	133,600	11,354,500	115,330
OSL	Oslo/Fornebu & Gardemoen (Norway)	132,400	3,037,400	23,099
PMI	Palma (Majorca)	74,500	6,802,600	22,919
PTY	Panama/Tocumen (Panama)	22,500	980,000	32,484
CDG	Paris/Charles de Gaulle (France)	85,800	6,009,800	220,244
LBG	Paris/Le Bourget (France)	84,200	1,463,600	16,315
ORY	Paris/Orly (France)	150,100	10,611,400	119,871
PHL	Philadelphia (USA)	298,100	7,515,100	109,725
PRG	Prague/Ruzyne (Czechoslovakia)	84,900	3,662,000	32,176
GIG	Rio de Janeiro/Galaeo (Brazil)	77,800	3,997,600	72,213
FCO	Rome/Fiumicino (Italy)	142,800	8,278,500	172,600
SFO	San Francisco International (USA)	326,700	17,503,800	294,432
CGH	Sao Paulo/Congonhas (Brazil)	109,300	3,609,900	33,989
SIN	Singapore/Paya Lebar (Singapore)	65,000	3,981,600	64,188
ARN	Stockholm/Arlanda (Sweden)	84,900	3,662,000	32,176
SYD	Sydney/Kingsford Smith (Australia)	156,700	6,692,500	96,900
YYZ	Toronto/Malton (Canada)	237,700	10,404,300	163,100
TUN	Tunis/Carthage (Tunisia)	27,100	1,500,600	7,642
VIE	Vienna/Schwechat (Austria)	62,800	2,022,400	23,625
DCA	Washington National (USA)	306,500	10,810,100	34,714
ZRH	Zurich/Kloten (Switzerland)	138,000	5,963,400	113,787

BELOW: *A Plessey AR–5 surveillance radar at Nairobi Airport, Kenya. This radar provides a coverage of 435km (270 miles) at heights of up to 30,500m (100,000ft),*
BOTTOM: *The VASI (Visual Approach Slope Indicator) shows the pilot when he is on the correct approach path by means of red and white lights.* TOP: *Overshooting – white on white.* CENTRE: *Correct approach – red on white.* BOTTOM: *Undershooting; red on red.*
BELOW RIGHT: *Controllers in an operations room at the London Air Traffic Control Centre. The diagonal strips in front of them are individual aircraft strips; the radar scope shows the area of the radar sweep.*

16km (10 miles) from the runway touchdown point. Radar directors have the responsibility of ensuring that correct separation between aircraft is maintained. Separation varies – it could be as much as 16km (10 miles) for smaller aircraft which may be behind wide-bodied jets like 747s, DC–10s, Tristars and others. These types produce considerable wake turbulence which could endanger smaller aircraft, unless adequate separation is maintained.

At busy periods over major airports in Australia – in much the same way as airports in other parts of the world – aircraft waiting to land may have to go into a 'stack', in a selected airspace near the airport. This could mean that an aircraft may have to circle a radio beacon some 50 nautical miles from

to Sydney, Australia's busiest domestic air route – sector control to approach control to tower control and finally to surface movement control which brings the passengers to their final debarcation.

Radar

So far as the airport is concerned, two radars are used: surveillance and precision approach.

Surveillance radar is used by the airport controller mainly to separate aircraft tracks and position the aircraft for their landing approach. Generally speaking, the controller brings in the aircraft with this radar to a point just before it is positioned on an imaginary line extended from the centre-line of the runway, and then hands over control to

the airport at a prescribed altitude until told to descend by approach control. The top of the stack could be at 6,100m (20,000ft) and aircraft are called on to descend in steps of 300m (1000ft) until they can finally leave the bottom of the stack at 900m (3,000ft) for a final approach to land. An aircraft on final approach and lined up with the runway it has been instructed to use, is then handed over, or transferred, to the airport control tower which will actually bring it in to land.

The tower controller uses a radar display calibrated in miles. The blip on the screen indicates the aircraft's movements on the approach to land. Once the aircraft has landed and turned off the runway on to one of the taxiways, tower control hands it over to the surface movement controllers. They then marshal the aircraft on the ground to the appropriate terminal and terminal gate. So that is the sequence of controls for an aircraft flying, for example, from Melbourne the pilot for either a visual or an instrument landing.

Precision approach radar (PAR) is, as its name implies, a more precise method of control, but, in its original form, is now used less frequently as 80 to 90 per cent of major international airports are equipped with instrument landing systems (ILS), which have a high degree of accuracy. When combined with surveillance radar, ILS renders PAR unnecessary.

Instrument Landing Systems (ILS)

Introduced in its basic form in 1929, an ILS now consists of a ground transmitter which projects a narrow radio beam into the air to the left and right of the runway centreline at an angle to the glide path – the path an aircraft takes on its normal landing approach in a controlled descent.

The radio beam is received by equipment in the aircraft, and displayed on cockpit instruments as vertical and horizontal lines showing the pilot his position in relation to the beam. The pilot positions the aircraft merely by keeping the lines crossed at the centre of the instrument, thereby ensuring that his approach is at the right height and angle for landing.

Microwave Landing Systems (MLS)

ILS was adopted by the International Civil Aviation Organization (ICAO) in 1949, but with constantly increasing air traffic the scientists have been looking at ways to improve the basic system. Certain drawbacks are evident with ILS – aircraft approaches are confined to a single narrow path, siting of the equipment at some airports is difficult because surrounding topography and buildings can cause reflections, and only a limited number of frequencies are available for transmission.

The planners are now looking at microwave landing systems (MLS) which would generate narrow beams more easily than ILS and would have far more channels available. A number of advantages are claimed – simple installation, none of the routine flight calibration necessary with ILS, no critical adjustments and high basic immunity from interference. Prototype equipment is currently being tested, with full production scheduled for 1978.

A Typical Flight

Air Canada Flight AC857, London to Toronto

Air Canada's Flight AC857 from London to Toronto on a day in late October 1976 is typical of many international flights.

It had featured in the airline's schedules months ahead, but this description takes up the story on the day of the flight.

The aircraft, Boeing 747 C–FTOE, the fifth of Air Canada's six 747s, arrives at London/Heathrow Airport on an inbound flight the day previous to departure, and is thoroughly checked over by Air Canada's London maintenance crew.

The first crew member to arrive at the airport is the Flight Director, 30 minutes ahead of the rest of the crew. His initial task is to check with the flight dispatch office on the forecast weather so that he can plan meal-times to avoid turbulent conditions as far as possible, and to get a list from terminal control of any VIPs, passengers who require special meals or special equipment, such as wheel-chairs. The flight meals are supplied by Air Canada's own commissary unit at the airport.

The Flight Director is in charge of a cabin crew consisting of a purser, assistant purser and 11 flight attendants; during the flight he is responsible for looking after three accounts – for the on board duty-free goods, for the bar service, and for the hire of headsets. These, used for in-flight entertainment (music or the sound track of movies) are provided free in first class but because of an IATA regulation are charged in economy seating.

The flight crew, pilot (captain), co-pilot (first officer) and flight engineer (second officer) arrive at the airport about an hour before scheduled departure time. The captain and first officer go to flight dispatch for their briefing, while the second officer goes to the aircraft to oversee the fuelling.

Briefing is routine and therefore only takes about 10 minutes instead of the usual 20 associated with Atlantic weather; flight dispatch has

already received weather actuals and other information from the destination and specified alternative airports, and has prepared a weather chart showing recommended and available routes.

On acceptance of his route, the captain is given a printout with all details of the flight, including the course, times and distances to the various waypoints along the route etc. Armed with this information, the first officer plots the course on a flight progress chart. (Unlike most other airlines, Air Canada produces all its own airways, progress and landing charts.) The flight plan is then confirmed with air traffic control and filed with the National Air Traffic Service, with copies to the ATC regions through which it will pass, the destination airport and the alternatives.

Boarding of AC857 begins at 11.20 for 12.20 departure. Passengers pass through security checks with their hand baggage, their suitcases being X-rayed after baggage and ticket check-in.

The aircraft takes on 95,000kg (209,000lb/154.5 US tons) of fuel for its flight to Toronto and is expected to use about 75,900kg (167,000lb).

Push back by tug from the air jetty at Heathrow's No. 3 terminal begins at 12.25, and following the completion of the cockpit check list, C-FTOE moves out to the runway threshold to await take-off clearance from air traffic control.

At a take-off weight of 285,300kg (642,000lb/321 US tons) with 293 passengers aboard, the jumbo is airborne at 12.42 from runway 10R after a 28-second run, and turns left to join the airway at Brookmans Park, near Hatfield, at a height of 1,500m (5,000ft). Rate of climb is 400m/min (1,300ft/min) passing through slight turbulence between 6,400–7,000m (21,000–23,000ft) on the way to cruise altitude.

As the aircraft passes through the successive height bands assigned to it by air traffic control, the co-pilot reports the height and obtains clearance to the next required height.

Because of other traffic, it is not possible to obtain the desired cruising height of 11,900m (39,000ft) until somewhat later in the flight.

Cruising at Mach 0.84 (84 per cent of the speed of sound at the appropriate altitude), the aircraft becomes lighter as it burns off its fuel, consequently the flight engineer needs to keep the captain informed of the maximum power to be achieved by the engines to maintain the normal cruising speed. This is done by using a small manual calculator.

A cockpit display shows the distance to the next VOR along the airway and the aircraft is cleared to the Stornoway VOR, reaching 9,450m (31,000ft) over Stornoway.

Over the Midlands, the aircraft's inertial navigation system (INS) is brought into operation. Built by Litton Industries in the USA as the model LTN–72, this highly sophisticated computerized equipment guides the aircraft along its route. The waypoints plotted on the flight progress chart are fed into the computer, and once the INS has been activated it controls the aircraft's autopilot, making allowances for wind, drift and so on. The aircraft is flown along the selected track by use of 2-axis gyros. The only external input required for INS is the air temperature.

As each waypoint is reached, INS, through the autopilot, automatically turns the aircraft on to the appropriate course for the next waypoint, and a cockpit display shows the distance and time to the next point, as with the VOR beacons.

A maximum of 9 waypoints may be accommodated in the INS, and since 12 are required for this flight it is necessary to re-programme the system in flight to insert the remaining waypoints. This is achieved by switching the system to 'remote' and re-programming. The INS is duplicated to provide a cross-check and a fall-back system in case of failure, although this is very infrequent.

Another 747 contrailing 610m (2,000ft) above and to the left gradually diverges from our course and

disappears to the west as the airways are left and the aircraft climbs to 10,500m (35,000ft). ATC at Gander, Newfoundland, can be heard at 14.05, forty minutes before flying over Reykjavik, Iceland.

With long flights, the necessity to maintain a continuous listening watch on radio frequencies is eliminated by Selective Calling (Selcal). With this, the aircraft has a permanent call-sign – in this case BJEF – and when the ground controller wishes to communicate he calls this on the aircraft's frequency and a visible and audible warning is given to the crew to listen for a message.

In addition to standard instruments, Air Canada's 747s are fitted with weather radar, with a small presentation screen in front and to one side of the pilot and co-pilot. The radar can be adjusted to show the weather situation at ranges of 48, 160 or 480km (30, 100 or 300 miles).

Flying from east to west following the sun, southern Greenland and northern Canada are crossed. An eventual altitude of 11,300m (37,000ft) has been granted by ATC, but at 19.36 Toronto Control Centre authorizes the 747 to begin its descent, initially down to 7,300m (24,000ft). By 19.50 the aircraft is at 3,000m (10,000ft).

The 747's huge flaps are lowered at 2,600m (8,600ft) and the aeroplane edges out over Lake Ontario to begin its descent to runway 32 at Toronto International Airport for an ILS approach in good weather. The landing gear is lowered at 580m (1,900ft) and the fence is crossed. The 747 touches down at 257km/h (160mph) and taxies to the gate at Terminal 2, reaching the stand at 20.06 London time (15.06 Toronto time), 7 hours and 40 minutes from Heathrow, about 5,200km (3,230 miles).

Around 15,000kg (33,000lb/16.5 US tons) of fuel remains in the tanks and the landing weight is 212,000kg (446,000lb/233 US tons). More fuel has been used than estimated because it had not been possible to obtain the higher cruising altitude.

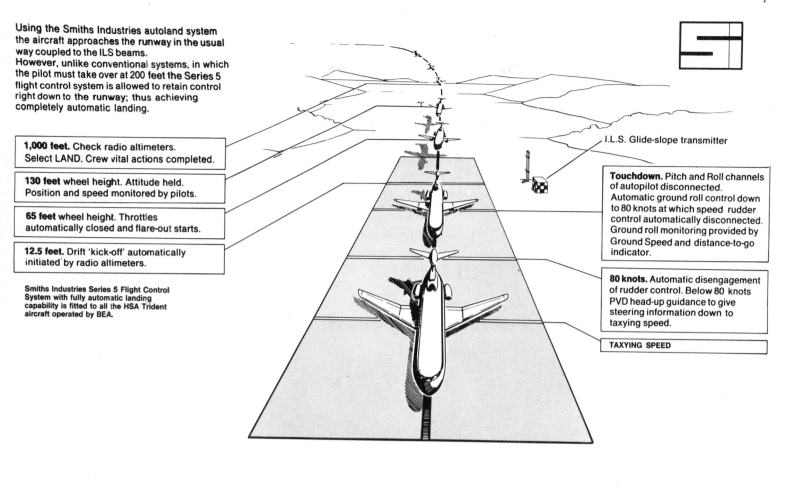

Using the Smiths Industries autoland system the aircraft approaches the runway in the usual way coupled to the ILS beams.
However, unlike conventional systems, in which the pilot must take over at 200 feet the Series 5 flight control system is allowed to retain control right down to the runway; thus achieving completely automatic landing.

1,000 feet. Check radio altimeters. Select LAND. Crew vital actions completed.

130 feet wheel height. Attitude held. Position and speed monitored by pilots.

65 feet wheel height. Throttles automatically closed and flare-out starts.

12.5 feet. Drift 'kick-off' automatically initiated by radio altimeters.

Smiths Industries Series 5 Flight Control System with fully automatic landing capability is fitted to all the HSA Trident aircraft operated by BEA.

I.L.S. Glide-slope transmitter

Touchdown. Pitch and Roll channels of autopilot disconnected. Automatic ground roll control down to 80 knots at which speed rudder control automatically disconnected. Ground roll monitoring provided by Ground Speed and distance-to-go indicator.

80 knots. Automatic disengagement of rudder control. Below 80 knots PVD head-up guidance to give steering information down to taxying speed.

TAXYING SPEED

I.L.S. localiser transmitter

Autoland

An automatic landing system is primarily designed to enable an aircraft to land in conditions of poor visibility or even nil visibility from inside the aircraft.

Smiths Industries in the UK pioneered their Autoland system in collaboration with the Royal Aircraft Establishment's Blind Landing Experimental Unit in 1947, and it was the first fully automatic landing system to enter scheduled passenger service, doing so in May 1967 aboard BEA Tridents.

The Autoland system can be used at any ILS-equipped airport where the terrain and runway lighting are acceptable to the airworthiness authority and airlines using the system. Basically, the pilot selects the required radio aids for the runway on which he will land, programmes the system and sets the required approach speed. Autoland then controls the aircraft right on to the runway, with the pilot monitoring the cockpit instruments. The descent and runway alignment are directed by the airport's ILS beam, while the aircraft's speed is controlled by an automatic throttle. At 40m (130ft) altitude, the autopilot controls the aircraft at a constant altitude down to 20m (65ft), when three highly accurate radio altimeters level it out for touchdown. Should the pilot wish to abandon the approach, he merely selects full power on the throttles and the climb away sequence is carried out automatically. After touchdown, rudder control is disengaged

automatically at 148km/h (92mph) groundspeed and the pilot controls the steering, using the runway markings and centreline lighting as guides. This has proved adequate even in very low visibility.

Airport lighting

Airport runway lighting has been developed to an extremely high degree of efficiency. Approach lighting to the runways, centreline lighting on the runway, and runway edge lights all demand careful design. They must be intense, but not dazzling; recessed centreline lighting in particular must be able to withstand heavy shocks caused by aircraft landing gear, while runway edge lighting has to stand up to jet blast from aircraft with wing-mounted engines.

Part of the approach lighting is the VASI (Visual Approach Slope Indicator), designed by scientists at the UK Royal Aircraft Establishment, Farnborough, and initially developed by Thorn Lighting Ltd. It was adopted as a world standard by ICAO, the International Civil Aviation Organization, in June 1961.

Basically, the unit consists of two parallel rows of VASI lights on each side of the runway, just beyond the threshold. As the aircraft approaches to land, the pilot sees the two sets of lights. If he is approaching correctly, he will see the near lights as white, the farther as red. If both are white he is too high, if both red, too low.

A recent Thorn development, the mini-VASI, provides a similar guidance but uses two lights instead of three and is much lower to combat jet blast. This new system was commissioned at its first airport, London/Gatwick, in October 1976.

In order to differentiate between runways, taxiways and aprons at night, ICAO has declared a standard colour coding for airport lighting. White is used for approach lights, runway centreline and runway edges; blue is used only for taxiway edge lighting; green denotes threshold lights and taxiway centreline, while red appears as obstruction lighting and as colour coding for the last 914m (3,000ft) of the runway centreline.

TOP: *Smiths Industries Ltd Autoland system as used by British Airways' Trident airliners.*
ABOVE: *The new mini-VASI lighting system compared with a standard VASI installation.*

Aerospace Medicine

Aviation medicine embraces all the factors which affect the safety, efficiency and comfort of people who fly, whether aircrew or passengers. In its widest sense it includes the medical certification of private pilots, the fitness of patients to fly, standards of hygiene in the preparation of in-flight meals, and the spread of communicable diseases such as smallpox and yellow fever.

For the present purpose aviation medicine can better be defined as the study of the stresses imposed by a strange environment upon those who choose to enter it, with the aim of establishing the bounds of safe exposure. It is not enough, however, simply to specify limits which must not be exceeded, because the ideal may be unattainable, or

RIGHT: *Diagram to illustrate respiration. As the rib muscles contract, the ribs move outwards, increasing the capacity of the chest, and at the same time the diaphragm moves downwards. The lungs expand and air is sucked into them in an effort to equalize the pressure. Air is then forced out again as the rib muscles relax, moving the ribs inwards and the diaphragm upwards and thus decreasing the space in the lungs.*
FAR RIGHT: *The structure of the ear. The outer ear is connected by the auditory meatus to the ear drum, which separates it from the middle ear. The middle ear is filled with air and communicates with the outside air by way of the eustachian tube, which opens to let in air when we sneeze or swallow, keeping the air pressure equal on both sides of the eardrum. It is only if the pressure is unequal that we become conscious of discomfort.*

uneconomic, or just unpopular. Compromises are as inevitable in aviation medicine as in technology, and secondary safeguards must be available if primary systems should fail. The specification of these is also the responsibility of the practitioner of aviation medicine.

The environmental stresses faced by astronauts and cosmonauts are, with the single exception of weightlessness, very similar to those that confront the military pilot or the Concorde passenger. The fact that 'space medicine' is an extension of the older science is acknowledged in the title of this chapter, and in its final paragraphs.

The Effects of Altitude

Pressure changes

The pressure of the atmosphere falls progressively during ascent. At 5,485m (18,000 ft) it is reduced to one-half, at 10,060m (33,000ft) to one-quarter, and at 18,290m (60,000ft) – within the operating band of supersonic transport aircraft – to only one-fourteenth of the normal atmospheric pressure at sea level.

The composition of the air, however, does not change; at all altitudes it consists of about 21 per cent oxygen, the rest being nitrogen with a smattering of other inert gases. Un-

fortunately, the workings of the human body pay little heed to the mathematical niceties of percentages and fractions. The fundamental law of altitude is that the space occupied by a quantity of gas expands when the pressure is reduced. Conversely, a given volume of gas at a low pressure contains fewer molecules than the same volume at a higher pressure. These simple rules are responsible for all the aeromedical problems of altitude.

Large amounts of gas are contained in the lungs and in various cavities such as the nasal sinuses, the ears and the gut. These compartments must be held in pressure equilibrium with the atmosphere, and all are therefore affected by changes in altitude. Breath-

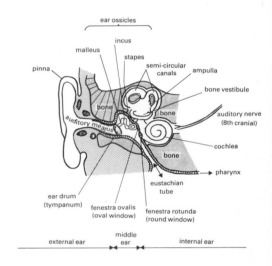

ing ensures that the balance is maintained in the lungs, but the expansion or contraction of gas in other sites can cause symptoms, embarrassment or pain. The escape of surplus gas from the cavity of the middle ear during ascent is often perceived as a 'popping', but it is rarely uncomfortable. Trouble may arise during descent, however, because the cavity of the middle ear is guarded by a flap valve, which closes as the external pressure rises and prevents easy equilibration with the atmosphere. Experienced air travellers learn to avoid the resulting deafness and pain by regularly clearing their ears – swallowing or yawning is usually enough. Babies can achieve the same end more noisily by crying during descent.

The nasal sinuses usually give no trouble during ascent, though a congested sinus may give rise to pain which is explosively relieved when the block is cleared by escaping gas. Re-inflation during descent is not easy, and sufferers from acute sinusitis who fly often have to pay for their misfortune with pain that lasts for some hours after their return to earth, as the sinuses only gradually refill with the normal volume of gas.

A feeling of fullness or distension results from the increase in the volume of intestinal gases at altitude, but speedy relief is denied only to the socially inhibited.

Decompression sickness

'Decompression sickness' is the omnibus term for a variety of symptoms caused by a reduction in the pressure surrounding the body. It was recognized long before aviation began; the older name of 'caisson disease' betokens its occurrence in tunnel workers, and the descriptive phrase 'the bends' derives from deep-sea diving. The first authentic case of decompression sickness at high altitude was described in 1930, but it was not until World War II that the need to fly prolonged missions at high altitudes resulted in an alarming incidence of 'bends' and of more serious symptoms in aircrew.

The most likely cause of decompression sickness is the release of small bubbles of gas from tissues and organs. At sea level, the gases dissolved in the body fluids are in equilibrium with those in the lungs. When the external pressure is reduced by ascent, oxygen and carbon dioxide are freely exchanged between the blood and the tissues but nitrogen, which is less soluble, cannot easily move to restore the pressure balance. As a result, some parts of the body become super-saturated with nitrogen and can be compared with a soda-water syphon which also contains dissolved gas under pressure and which, when disturbed or connected to the outside world, discharges a stream of small bubbles.

Decompression sickness rarely occurs at altitudes less than 7,620m (25,000ft) – equivalent to about one-third of an atmosphere – but it becomes increasingly common at greater heights. For this reason it is seen only in military aviators and in pioneers, such as balloonists, who ascend to high altitudes with inadequate precautions. Its commonest form (the 'bends') is characterized by pain in the joints, which is made worse by exercise. In serious cases the central nervous system may be affected, leading to 'Divers' paralysis' and sometimes to death.

The treatment of decompression sickness is to return the sufferer to a higher environmental pressure, at which the bubbles can once again enter solution. In mild cases of the bends it is often sufficient to reduce the altitude to 5,485m (18,000ft) or less, but occasionally it is necessary to expose an afflicted pilot to a pressure greater than one atmosphere before his symptoms disappear. For him, and for the stricken diver, the final return to sea level must be conducted very slowly and with great caution.

If an exposure to high altitude is known to be inevitable, the risk of decompression sickness can be reduced by breathing pure oxygen before and during ascent. This allows much of the nitrogen in the tissues to be flushed out by the more readily diffuzible gas, so that super-saturation is less severe. To remove *all* the nitrogen in this way would require at least 24 hours, but valuable insurance is given by even an hour or so of pre-oxygenation.

Oxygen lack

The body depends absolutely upon the delivery of oxygen to the tissues and organs in proportion to their need. This vital transport system can be disrupted by many factors but, to the aviator, the most critical problem is that of supply. Oxygen accounts for about one-fifth of the total barometric pressure, but within the lung, where exchange with the blood takes place, the 'pressure space' for oxygen is much less because the gas is saturated with water vapour and diluted with carbon dioxide. These two components remain almost constant irrespective of altitude, so that the oxygen pressure in the lungs falls more dramatically than does the barometer. By 3,050m (10,000ft) it has already fallen to a barely acceptable level, while at 15,140m (50,000ft) the pressures of water vapour and carbon dioxide combined are equal to the barometric pressure, leaving no 'room' for oxygen. At 19,200m (63,000ft) the pressure of the atmosphere is the same as that of water vapour, and the lungs are then filled with 'steam'.

Although the effects of such extremes will obviously be catastrophic, oxygen lack (hy-poxia) presents a serious hazard at much lower altitudes, the signs and symptoms of mild hypoxia merging almost imperceptibly with normal behaviour. There is in fact a close similarity between the early stages of intoxication and of oxygen lack. Both can produce light-headedness, irresponsibility and a lack of insight, irritability and belligerence, slurring of speech and difficulty in focusing, and both can eventually progress to stupor, unconsciousness and even death. It is a generally accepted rule that hypoxia is not significant below 3,050m (10,000ft), but night vision suffers at heights as low as 1,525m (5,000ft). There is great individual variability both in tolerance and in the nature of the symptoms.

The fact that hypoxia is a hazard of altitude and that it can be prevented or cured by breathing oxygen has been known since the earliest days of aviation. In 1875 Tissandier and two companions made an epic flight in the balloon *Zenith*, and on the advice of the first true practitioner of aviation medi-

Altitude		Relative pressure	Limits	
FT	M			
0	0	100	Sea level – normal conditions	**Air required**
4,000	1,200	86	Impairment of night vision	
8,000	2,400	74	Maximum cabin altitude for airliners	
10,000	3,000	69	Safe air-breathing limit	
18,000	5,500	50	Half sea-level pressure	**Oxygen required**
24,000	7,300	39	Lower limit for decompression sickness	
33,000	10,000	26	100 per cent oxygen equivalent to breathing air at sea level	
40,000	12,000	19	100 per cent oxygen equivalent to breathing air at 10,000 ft	**Pressure suit required**
63,000	19,000	6	Water boils at body temperature	
65,000	20,000	5	Cruising altitude, supersonic transport aircraft	

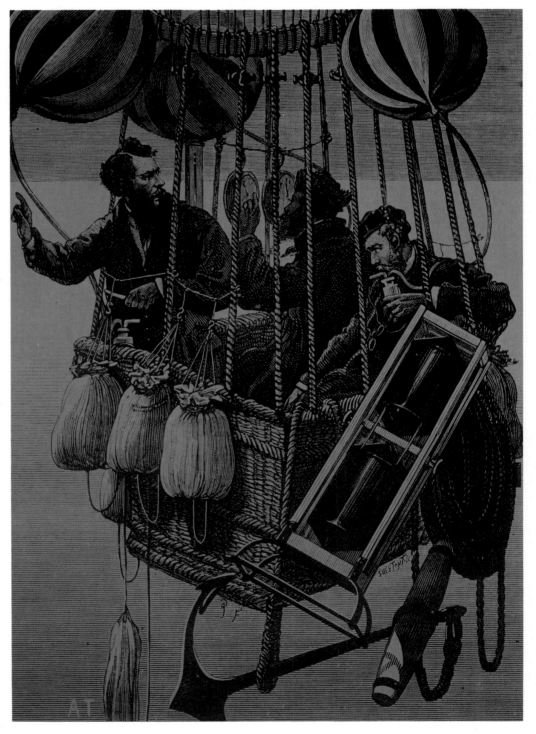

RIGHT: *The balloon* Zenith *which on 15 April 1875 carried Gaston Tissandier and two companions to a height of 7,900m (26,000ft). The three striped bags contained supplementary oxygen, but not enough of it, because Tissandier himself was the only one of the three to survive the ascent – the other two succumbed to the effects of the extremely high altitude, lost consciousness, and died.*

cine they took with them rubber bags containing oxygen. They intended to take a breath whenever they felt weak or affected by oxygen lack, but the impairment of judgment which is characteristic of hypoxia prevented them from using their supply (which was in any case woefully inadequate) when it was really needed. *Zenith* reached a height of more than 7,925m (26,000ft), and remained above 6,095m (20,000ft) for a considerable time. All its occupants lost consciousness, and when it returned to earth only Tissandier was still alive. His passengers were the first recorded victims of altitude hypoxia.

Oxygen lack can be prevented most simply by replacing *all* the inert nitrogen in the air with oxygen, but there are good physiological and economic arguments for keeping the oxygen pressure in the lungs close to its normal level. This principle of 'airmix' is adopted in most military aircraft. At 7,620m (25,000ft), for example, the required concentration of oxygen is only 50 per cent, and it is not until a height of 10,060m (33,000ft) is reached that pure oxygen is required to hold the gas mixture in the lungs in its sea-level state. However, just as an altitude of 3,050m (10,000ft) can safely be tolerated if air alone is breathed, 100 per cent oxygen can be used up to 12,190m (40,000ft).

Even this human limit for flight at great altitude is not an insurmountable one. The force of the atmosphere alone can no longer sustain the supply of oxygen to the blood, but the gas can be delivered to the lungs at a higher pressure – in engineering terms, the body can be 'super-charged'. With a well fitting mask and a simple oxygen system, the safe altitude can be extended in this way to about 13,715m (45,000ft), but higher breathing pressures lead to over-distension of the chest. This can be prevented by giving external support, and the combination of positive pressure-breathing and counterpressure was used to great effect in World War II to achieve altitudes well in excess of 15,240m (50,000ft) for short periods of time.

Still greater altitudes can be tolerated if the entire man is encased in a pressurized bag, so that he is surrounded by, and breathes from, an artificial atmosphere maintained at the required pressure. Such 'pressure suits' have a long and honourable history, from the altitude records set in the 1930s to the lunar explorations of the 1970s. However, they are hot, bulky, uncomfortable and rigid, and they cannot be regarded, either in aviation or in astronautics, as anything more than a protection against an emergency situation.

The pressure cabin is merely a sophisticated extension of the pressure suit. It consists of a sealed compartment into which air is pumped to maintain an effective internal altitude considerably lower than that at which the aircraft flies. In civil airliners the cabin environment is usually not allowed to exceed 1,830m to 2,440m (6,000 to 8,000ft), giving an ample margin of safety from the 3,050m (10,000ft) limit already mentioned. Passengers and crew alike can enjoy 'shirt-sleeve' flight in an atmosphere which is adjusted for pressure, temperature and humidity. If the pressure cabin fails, however, the occupants are suddenly exposed to the low atmospheric pressure of the outside world.

The cruising altitude of jet airliners ranges from about 6,095 to 10,670m (20,000 to 35,000ft), and their aerodynamic characteristics are such that several minutes may be occupied in a descent to below 3,050m (10,000ft). During this time oxygen must be supplied to everyone on board. Considerable effort and ingenuity has been employed in the development of a supply system which is automatic in operation and relatively foolproof; the result is the 'drop-down' mask that most air travellers have seen demonstrated but which very few have had occasion to use.

Supersonic transport aircraft pose special problems, because they cruise at altitudes much beyond the capability of simpler oxygen systems. A loss of cabin pressure at 18,290m (60,000ft) and a slow descent to a safe height would result in unconsciousness in all cases and death in some. The only solution is to ensure that the cabin altitude can never exceed that at which the standard passenger oxygen system gives full protection, and a pressure equivalent to 7,620m (25,000 ft) has been chosen as this maximum. The design of Concorde makes provision for this requirement; the windows (which are the most vulnerable parts of a cabin) are small to limit both the rate and the degree of pressure loss, and 'flood-flow' equipment is installed so that large quantities of air can be supplied to overcome the breach. With these safeguards, the risk following a decompression is no greater for supersonic passengers than for less elevated travellers.

The price of a pressure cabin offering a low-altitude environment is paid in weight and complexity, and it is not feasible to apply civil standards in high-performance military aircraft. Moreover, the very small volume of the average fighter cockpit will, in the event of a failure, equilibrate very rapidly with the atmosphere and an 'explosive decompression' from, say, 2,440m (8,000ft) to 15,240m (50,000ft) represents an extreme hazard. Military pilots can, however, wear an oxygen mask throughout flight, and the cabin pressure need therefore only be high enough to prevent the occurrence of decompression sickness; that is, an equivalent altitude of about 7,620m (25,000ft) is sufficient. From that height a sudden loss of pressure is not catastrophic, and the fact that the pilot is already connected to an oxygen system allows the concentration and pressure of the gas in the lungs to be adjusted automatically and without delay to meet the new conditions. In some cases, two levels of cabin pressurization are available; a 'cruise' setting which provides a relatively low altitude, and a 'combat' setting to be selected when the risk of pressure loss is greater.

The Force Environment

The human body does not respond to unvarying speed but is very sensitive to changes in either the rate or the direction of travel. These produce forces which can conveniently be measured in terms of the Earth's gravity, g, which gives the body its normal weight, and they are sensed as alterations in the direction or degree of 'heaviness'. The forces induced by alterations of speed are usually small; less than 1g. They may last for a relatively long time (for example, during take-off), but they have little physiological effect. Only in emergencies such as crashes, when the change of speed is abrupt, are the forces large and the results disastrous. They are depressingly familiar, and can be seen on any highway.

The accelerations produced by changes in the direction of flight act outwards from the centre of rotation, and their magnitude is determined by the square of the speed and the tightness of the turn. The agile manoeuvres of military aircraft can involve large accelerations. At 483km/h (300mph) a turn with a radius of 0·8km (0·5 miles) results in a centrifugal force of 2·5g; at 724km/h (450 mph) the stress is more than twice as great. The times for which the forces act may be long; in the two examples given, turns

through 360° would take 38 seconds and 25 seconds respectively. By contrast, an airliner adjusts its course in a wide sweep, so that its passengers may hardly be aware of the acceleration involved. At a speed of 724 km/h (450mph) the turning radius might be 4·8km (3 miles), and the time needed to complete a full circle would be 130 seconds.

The earliest sensations of sustained acceleration are those of increased weight and of being thrust into the seat. At 2g it is just possible to rise from the sitting position; at 3g the legs become almost too heavy to lift; at 6g the arms cannot be raised above the head. Tolerance for such forces is set by their effect upon the heart and circulation. The blood pressure at head level falls progressively as the g is increased, and the supply of

blood to the eye and the brain is correspondingly reduced. At first, vision becomes veiled and sight for peripheral objects is lost. As the acceleration rises, this 'grey-out' becomes more severe, passing through a stage of tunnel vision to the complete loss known as 'blackout'. (Although its existence had been known previously, blackout came into practical prominence for the first time in the Schneider Trophy race of 1931, when pilots were unable to see the pylons around which they were making their fast turns.) Still higher forces jeopardize the circulation to the brain, and cause a loss of consciousness.

Tolerance of acceleration varies between individuals and can be considerably modified by voluntary action. Tensing of the muscles, straining, shouting and crouching all raise the blood pressure and so delay the arrival of blackout. Most aircrew have learned to use one or more of these tricks; indeed, it is difficult to pull an aircraft into a tight turn without tensing the muscles. Helped only by his own efforts, an average pilot can withstand about 6g for a few seconds without loss of vision, but he must give most of his attention to 'fighting the g'.

The need to provide protection automatically is met by an anti-g suit, which essentially comprises a pair of inflatable trousers supplied with gas under the control of a g-sensitive valve, so that the pressure exerted on the abdomen and the legs is always pro-

LEFT: *The pilot of a North American F–100 Super Sabre wearing a special suit to protect him against the pressures and very large g-forces involved in flying this aircraft. The inflatable sections exert pressure on the body which helps to maintain the blood pressure. Without this aid, the pilot's vision may become distorted through lack of blood in the brain and eyes, and may possibly result in tunnel vision or complete blackout.*

BELOW: *The world is divided into several different time zones, most of which are one hour ahead or behind the next one. An imaginary line, known as the International Date Line, is drawn through the Pacific Ocean to indicate where one passes into the next day. This occurs because east of Greenwich the time is ahead, west of it the time is behind and as a result the zones would eventually coincide without the presence of this line.*

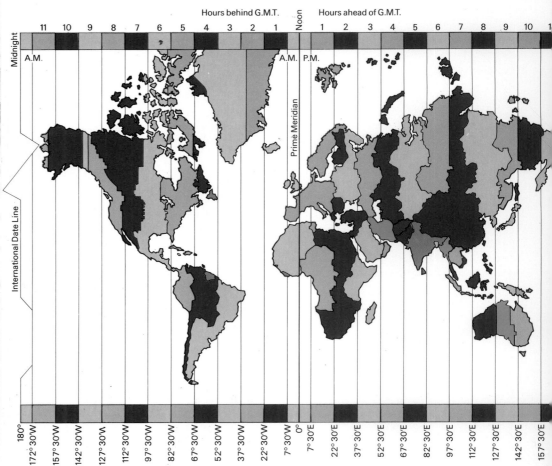

portional to the applied acceleration. An anti-g suit affords approximately 1·5g of protection and, if used in conjunction with crouching and straining, it raises the limit of tolerance to about 8g for 10 seconds or longer. Further gains can be achieved only by devices such as reclining seats, which reduce the vertical distance through which the heavy blood must be pumped from the heart to the brain. This principle is carried to its logical extreme in the almost supine posture adopted by astronauts.

Escape systems
The controlled application of high but brief accelerations in a precisely ordered sequence lies at the heart of the escape systems used in military aircraft. In the days of low-speed flight and of open cockpits it was possible for an aviator simply to climb from his seat, to jump clear of the structure and to pull the rip-cord of his parachute. But at speeds above about 322km/h (200mph) 'bailing-out' becomes impossible, because the would-be escaper does not have the strength to clamber out in the teeth of the wind. Moreover, a manually operated parachute cannot be used safely below 91 to 122m (300 to 400ft) because there is no time for it to open fully and begin to retard the descent before the man hits the ground.

Present-day automatic escape systems

have been successfully used at supersonic speed at high altitudes and at zero speed on the runway. The only action required of the pilot is to pull a handle mounted on his seat. The cockpit canopy is jettisoned to clear the path for the subsequent ejection and an explosive charge then propels the seat up guide rails attached to the aircraft structure. A rocket motor next ignites, to sustain guided thrust and so to increase the upward velocity of the seat. (It is this added velocity which makes escape possible from a stationary aircraft.) After a brief delay, the seat is stabilized by the deployment of a small drogue parachute; this in turn draws the main canopy from its container. The harness is released and the seat falls away separately, leaving the aviator to descend on his fully opened parachute.

Each phase of the escape (including the landing) involves acceleration or deceleration, but the greatest force is applied in the first tenth of a second, during which the seat reaches a vertical speed of about 24·4m (80ft)/sec. A properly restrained man can withstand an acceleration of 25g in the spinal axis, but the ejection force comes close to the limit of human tolerance. In fact, transient backache is an almost inevitable consequence of ejection and a crushed vertebra is a not uncommon complication, although it is rarely a serious injury.

The shock forces of parachute opening are normally less than the 20g or so which can be tolerated by an unsupported body, but in ejections at very high speeds deployment of the main canopy must be delayed so that the abrupt deceleration of the system does not break both the parachute and the man. A g-sensitive device therefore inhibits the sequence until most of the forward momentum has been lost. Parachute opening forces are also excessive at great altitudes, and not until the seat, stabilized by its small drogue, has descended to below 3,050m (10,000ft) is the main canopy allowed to blossom. This stratagem also ensures a rapid return to a height at which air can safely be breathed without needing extra oxygen.

Jet Lag

A business tycoon may leave London at 3PM and, after a tiring flight lasting 6 hours, arrive in Washington at 4PM local time. Two hours later, when his body clock denotes bedtime, his colleagues bid him welcome with cocktails and dinner. When he is allowed to sleep (which he probably does fitfully) he wakes at his 'normal' 7 o'clock to hear the American chimes of 2AM. After a week in which his biological pendulum, his alertness and his temper gradually adjust to match the imposed working and social schedules he

BELOW: *The sequence of events during automatic ejection. (a) the miniature detonating cord (MDC) blows open the canopy of the cockpit (b) the rocket-assisted seat leaves the aircraft (c) the seat is slowed down and steadied by the small drogue parachute (d) the pilot separates from the seat and the parachute begins to deploy (e) the aviator descends on his now fully opened parachute to make a safe, gentle landing.*

ABOVE RIGHT: *A modern ejection seat for military aircraft provides for safe escape at all speeds and all altitudes, and even from a stationary aircraft on the ground. The only action required of the pilot is to pull the firing handle – everything else is operated automatically in this remarkable 'zero-zero' system.*

returns home, only to face the whole problem again in reverse. He now finds it hard to sleep at what he has learned to regard as 6PM, or to rise before mid-day local time.

The effects of this discrepancy between internal and external clocks are known as 'jet-lag'. (They could as logically be termed 'jet-lead', but we always seem to catch up with time and never to precede it.) The condition is real enough, and it is specific to the

Head box with primary parachute

Shoulder straps

Harness with quick release fitting

Personal survival pack in seat-pan

Seat firing handle

Leg restraint lines

Drogue parachute pack

Automatic sequence mechanisms

Mounting bracket

Oxygen system and personal services

Rocket pack

rapid passage across time-zones that characterizes modern air transport. Complicating factors such as the tedium of a long air journey, exposure to noise and a 'canned' atmosphere, or the exchange of one climate for another can be ruled out because jet-lag is not induced by flights of similar length in a north–south direction, which do not involve time shifts.

The sleep clock is merely the most obvious of a number of biological rhythms having a period of around 24 hours. It is also the only one that can be manipulated to suit circumstance – the executive can force himself to stay awake when politeness or politics dictate, but he cannot control the cycles of the subtle biochemistries of mood or reasoning or creativity. The speed with which these sundry clocks can be re-set varies from person to person and within individuals; young people usually suffer less from jet-lag than do their elders, and their 'bio-rhythms' more rapidly reach a new equilibrium.

In the leisurely world of ocean travel clocks are set forward or back each night, so that passengers may gently adapt to the new time-frame that awaits them at their destination. The voyage to New York lasts about five days and traverses five time-zones. From this relationship has come the rule of thumb that one full day of recovery is needed for each hour of time-shift. It is as good a guide

as any, but few air travellers can follow it strictly. The majority must adapt as best they can, and it is fortunate that most of them are not required to take momentous decisions on the day after arrival. The best advice is to abide by 'home' time, but this is only possible/ practicable given a brief visit, an iron will and a civilization that serves breakfast at any hour. At least one airline finds it worthwhile to impose this regimen on its crews.

Claims that supersonic airliners can reduce jet-lag are false, because the problem is one of geography. A regular supersonic shuttle service between London and New York would, however, allow the city magnate to fly to America, conduct his business for 4 hours, and return home within the day. He would undoubtedly be fatigued, but he would not be de-synchronized.

Space Medicine

The twin aims of space medicine are the same as those of aviation medicine: to ensure that the environment is habitable, and to provide protection against failures in the life-support systems. Flight in a vacuum. however, sets special problems. For example, the cabin atmosphere cannot be provided by compressing the outside air, because there is none. The simplest solution is to fill the spacecraft with pure oxygen at a low pressure, to give a cabin altitude of about 7,620m (25,000ft), but one disadvantage of an oxygen atmosphere was demonstrated tragically when three astronauts were incinerated in an Apollo capsule during a pre-flight rehearsal. In contrast to American practice, the Russians have used an air-filled cabin maintained at sea-level pressure, despite the attendant penalties of greater capsule weight and the higher risk of decompression. The best com-

UPPER PORTABLE LIFE SUPPORT SYSTEM
ATTACHMENT BRACKET

HELMET ATTACHING
NECK RING

ELECTRICAL
CONNECTOR

MULTIPLE WATER CONNECTOR

TORSO TIEDOWN ADJUSTMENT
STRAP ASSEMBLY

GAS CONNECTOR
(INLET)

GAS CONNECTOR (INLET)

GAS CONNECTOR
(OUTLET)

GAS CONNECTOR (OUTLET)

PRESSURE GAGE

PRESSURE RELIEF VALVE

LOWER PORTABLE LIFE
SUPPORT SYSTEM
ATTACHMENT BRACKET

GLOVE ATTACHING
DISCONNECT

ENTRY SLIDE FASTENER

LUNAR MODULE RESTRAINT
AND TETHER ATTACHMENTS

URINE TRANSFER FITTING

BIOMEDICAL INJECTION PATCH

COMMAND MODULE
COUCH RESTRAINT

Centre Eyeshade

Hinge Assembly

Viewport

Side Eyeshade

Sun Visor
Assembly

Protective Visor
Assembly

Thermal Cover
Assembly

TOP LEFT : *Diagram of the type of space suit
used by the crew of the Apollo spacecraft for landings
on the Moon. It is really a personal pressure cabin
containing its own built-in life support system,
to meet every need of the astronaut from the moment of
take-off to the landing.*
ABOVE : *The type of helmet used on the Apollo
Moon landings. It incorporated several different pieces
of equipment to act as a protection against heat,
glare, radiation and the effects of a vacuum on the
workings of the body.*

TOP RIGHT : *The accelerations of space flight.
The upper graph shows a typical Apollo launch
profile, the middle one is the re-entry pattern of
Apollo 7 from Earth orbit, and the lower one
illustrates the successful re-entry from lunar orbit of
Apollo 10.*
OPPOSITE PAGE TOP LEFT : *Eugene A Cernan, the
commander of Apollo 17, the sixth lunar landing
mission, practising with a lunar drill during
extravehicular activity (EVA) training at the
Kennedy Space Center.*

promise probably lies between the two extremes, and consists of oxygen and helium in approximately equal parts with a cabin altitude of some 5,485m (18,000ft). Both nations have given much attention to variations of this theme.

The gas lost by leakage and the oxygen consumed in respiration must be replaced from supplies carried on-board, and exhaled carbon dioxide must be absorbed. Each man uses about 1kg (2·2lb) of oxygen a day, and produces an equivalent amount of carbon dioxide; thus, very long flights would entail the carriage of prohibitively massive stores. Electrical and chemical methods can be used to generate oxygen by the hydrolysis of water or by 'cracking' carbon dioxide, but these processes are prodigal of energy. They offer only partial relief to the problems of supply, and for inter-planetary flights the development of systems involving photosynthesis by green plants will be essential.

Space suit

The safeguard against loss of cabin pressure is a space suit, which is also required for extra-vehicular activities such as lunar exploration. It is similar to the pressure suit of the military aviator but is more complex because, like the space cabin, it must be an entirely self-contained source of all the astronaut's environmental needs.

To achieve orbital velocity (about 8km or 5 miles/sec) astronauts must be exposed to high accelerations, and the return to Earth involves forces of the same order as those applied during launch. Early space flights involved peaks of about 7g during launch and up to 12g during re-entry, both spread over several minutes. With the larger vehicles of the Apollo and Skylab missions, the forces

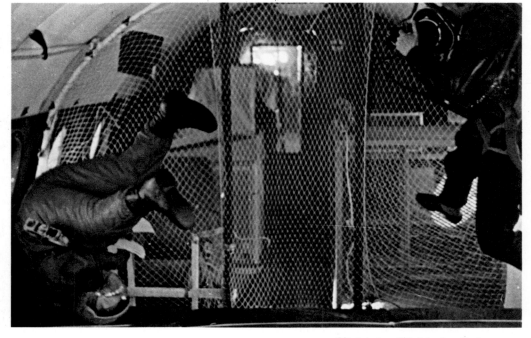

were lower and more prolonged, but even so the accelerations were well beyond the tolerance of pilots in conventional seats. For this reason, astronauts travel in a supine posture, so that the forces are applied at right angles to the long axis of the body. The Space Shuttle will carry mixed crews whose stamina may be less than that of professional astronauts, and the specification for that vehicle accordingly requires that the acceleration shall not exceed 3g. If this value were sustained throughout the launch period, orbital velocity would be reached in about $4\frac{1}{2}$ minutes.

Weightlessness

When the thrust from the launching rocket decays to zero, the spacecraft and its occupants become weightless, and remain so until external forces are again applied either for manoeuvring or for re-entry. The short-term effects of weightlessness upon the body are not serious, because all the vital functions (such as respiration, the circulation of the blood, speech, swallowing, digestion and excretion) are independent of gravity. Locomotion has its hazards, because a weightless body floats unless it is anchored, and attempts to walk may result in painful collisions with the surroundings. More seriously, the absence of a normal gravitational input produces an exaggerated response to rotational forces, and spacemen who are strongly resistant to other forms of motion sickness have suffered from nausea or even vomiting until they have found their 'space legs'.

Two other consequences of weightlessness become apparent only after the return to Earth. One is the tendency of astronauts to faint when standing, because their circulatory systems no longer compensate ade-

quately for the stress of gravity. The cause is complex, but a major factor is that weightlessness provokes a substantial reduction in the fluid content of the body regardless of the amount of liquid consumed. As a result, there is an insufficient volume of blood available to sustain the circulation at 1g. Normal tolerance for gravity returns within a few days as the fluid balance is restored.

The second hidden effect of prolonged weightlessness affects the skeleton. Weight-bearing appears to be essential to the stability of the mineral content of bones, and in the absence of gravity calcium salts are absorbed into the blood and excreted by the kidneys. The process can be partly but not entirely prevented by diet and by exercises designed to apply stress periodically to bones, and

TOP RIGHT: *The interior of Skylab. A medical inspection is being undertaken under the weightless conditions. A body will here float freely, thus helping the doctor to get at inaccessible parts of the body, such as the inside of the mouth.*
ABOVE: *Before man could travel in space, he needed to gain experience of weightlessness. In this photograph Soviet cosmonauts are seen training in a transport aircraft which is flying in a free-fall trajectory, providing a short period of zero gravity to simulate the conditions of Space.*

joints, and its implications for very long space flights remain a matter of some concern. Despite dire predictions of irreparable damage, however, there is no reason to believe that plans for interplanetary flight will be thwarted by insoluble medical or physiological problems.

Military Aviation

Air Power

Far-seeing men predicted the use of aircraft in war even before practical flying machines had been built. With the benefit of hindsight it appears obvious that the Wright Brothers' achievement radically altered the basic principles of warfare. At the time, however, this was not readily appreciated. For example, when Santos-Dumont made the first flight in Europe (in 1906) the British newspaper magnate Lord Northcliffe criticized his editors for not giving the event more prominence. 'The news is not that men can fly, but that England is no longer an island,' he said. How prophetically he spoke became evident soon enough in the conflict of World War I.

'See, not fight'

As World War I opened the major powers had done little to further the cause of military aviation.

'Aviation is good sport, but for the Army it is useless', declared the French General Foch. While in September 1914 the German General Staff reported, 'Experience has shown that a real combat in the air, such as journalists and romancers have described, should be considered a myth. The duty of the aviator is to see, not to fight.'

In short term policy the authorities were correct. The really important contributions of aircraft to the war effort were in reconnaissance and artillery spotting missions. Thus by spotting Russian troop movements before the Battle of Tannenberg the Germans were able to prepare a victorious counter-offensive. Hindenburg wrote in his memoirs that 'without airmen there would have been no Tannenberg'.

The British Army used four squadrons of aircraft to scout ahead of its advance from landings on the French coast in August 1914, and airborne reconnaissance played an extremely important part. Indeed, it was more effective in aiding strategic decisions such as where and when to take a stand rather than in day-to-day operations which required a rapid and continuous flow of information.

The German Army introduced special high-trajectory anti-aircraft guns to deter Allied reconnaissance machines, and the Allies followed suit. The resultant demand for fast, high-flying observation aircraft gave rise to some outstanding two-seaters. The obvious next step was to fight like with like.

Origins of air combat

France originated organized air combat. From January 1915 an *Escadrille de Chasse* was allocated to each field army, using types such as two-seat Morane-Saulnier Ls, in which the observer was armed with a machine-gun, and single-seat Morane-Saulnier Ns having forward-firing weapons and deflector plates on the propeller blades.

In the early summer of 1915 Major-General Sir David Henderson, commander

PREVIOUS PAGES:
The Hawker Siddeley Hawk jet trainer.

of Britain's Royal Flying Corps on the Western Front, proposed the use of fighter packs in an offensive role.

Henderson's successor, Brigadier-General Hugh Trenchard, put the plan into practice at the Somme offensive in the summer of 1916. He allocated only 6 of his 27 fighter squadrons to support the British Fourth Army, and used four squadrons as a Headquarters Wing for air superiority. The plan might have succeeded if more aircraft had been used, but Trenchard also insisted on the available forces being employed on continuous dawn-to-dusk patrols rather than intermittent missions.

Some two weeks after the opening of the Somme offensive the German Army Air Service replied by grouping fighters into specialist squadrons, first the *Jagdstaffeln* (*Jastas* for short) and then the larger *Jagdgeschwader*. The latter were sent in at critical points on the front and moved up and down the lines of their own transport units. Their garishly painted aeroplanes (leading the Allies to dub them 'flying circuses') presented a formidable aspect in the air. And for a time they gained local tactical superiority.

The practice of using aircraft largely independently of the army was employed effectively by the Americans. In 1918 General John Pershing, Commander-in-Chief of the American Expeditionary Force, appointed Major-General Mason M. Patrick as commander of his air component. In August of that year Patrick concentrated all his front-line squadrons, plus some borrowed from the French, in the sector held by the newly formed US First Army. They were placed under the tactical command of Colonel William Mitchell, and when the Americans went on the offensive in September he successfully accomplished what Trenchard had first attempted. Only a small number of aircraft were assigned to the close support of assault troops and the rest were used to bomb and strafe airfields, communications centres, targets of opportunity and other aircraft.

Strategic bombing in World War I

Even while fighters and fighter tactics showed an increasing sophistication, important developments were taking place in other areas of aerial warfare. It must be remembered that fighters were produced in the first place to provide protection for reconnaissance and bomber aircraft. We have already noted the effects and early successes of reconnaissance missions. The future of air power lay, however, in the concept of strategic bombing.

Germany planned to destroy the French Army in six weeks, and accordingly a 36-aircraft strategic-bombing force was set up near Bruges in September 1914 in preparation for attacks on Britain. Dunkirk was bombed in January 1915, but the forward air bases necessary for worthwhile operations against Britain with the primitive and unreliable aeroplanes then available failed to materialize and the force was later withdrawn.

From May 1917 the Zeppelins which had been attacking Britain were replaced by fleets of up to 40 or so heavy bombers such as the Gotha G.IV and G.V and the Staaken R.VI. Their raids caused extensive damage but they were not employed in sufficient concentrations to have a serious effect on the course of the war.

France also set up a strategic-bombing force early in the war, under the direction of Commandant Barès. The 1ère *Groupe de Bombardement,* equipped with 18 Voisins, was led by Commandant de Göys and laid the basis of long-range bombing. It was later joined by two other *Groupes* and was one reason for the German decision to take a more

ABOVE: *Pictured in July 1918, this RAF (Fighter Command) Squadron was equipped with one of the best aircraft of the time, the Royal Aircraft Factory's S.E.5a.*
LEFT: *This German Zeppelin, L.53, was shot down in August, 1918 by an RAF Sopwith Camel. Against well-armed fighters the dirigible's military days were numbered.*

obviously aggressive part in the air war.

In the spring of 1916, Britain established a strategic-bombing force in the shape of Sopwith 1½-Strutters, for day operations and Short Bombers and Caudron G.4s for night missions. From October 1917 Trenchard, commander of the Royal Flying Corps, was instructed to renew the bombing offensive, using D.H.4s, F.E.2bs and, later, Handley Page 0/100s. When Trenchard resigned from the position of Chief of Staff he was appointed to command what became, in June 1918, the Independent Force. This incorporated the earlier strategic-bombing units and was planned to be expanded into the Inter-Allied Independent Air Force, including bombers from the US, France and Italy plus at least 40 squadrons of the RAF. France – and especially Marshal Foch, who was sure that the war would be won by surface forces alone – objected to the idea of an independent group on her soil, however, and the total strength by the Armistice was fewer than a dozen squadrons. The Independent Force dropped 550 tonnes of bombs during its career, half on airfields and the other half on industrial centres in the Rhineland.

LEFT: *Arming a German Gotha heavy bomber. By early in 1917 Zeppelins had become deathtraps in the face of the new generation of Allied fighters. This signalled the dawn of the strategic bomber and among the first was this German type which could deliver up to 500kg (1,100lb) of bombs from a height of 3,650m (12,000ft).*
BELOW LEFT: *Photographed over Quetta along the North-West Frontier of British India, this is an example of the highly successful Bristol Fighter.*

military aviation recommended against the establishment of an independent air service.

The Army Air Force was reorganized as the Army Air Corps (USAAC), however, and the Navy was left free to pursue its own airborne activities. The USAAC was concerned almost exclusively with army support until the construction of long-range bombers and air-defence fighters in the 1930s. Mitchell's ideas were later embraced by the United States – after his death – and the North American B–25 bomber was named after him.

In the early 1920s Britain developed a method, known as air control of under-developed areas, for policing Iraq and Trans-jordan. The move was surprisingly successful, but the targets of reprisal raids were undefended villages attacked in good weather under the best conditions – exactly the opposite of what would be found in Europe.

After France occupied the Ruhr in 1923, Britain's Salisbury Committee recommended that the RAF should always be strong enough to defend the homeland against the strongest Continental air force within striking range. The nebulous principle of 'air parity' was therefore adopted. This worked reasonably well as long as France was seen as the potential – if unlikely – aggressor. It was later to break down, however, when parity was required to be maintained with what Hitler deliberately made an unknown quantity: the *Luftwaffe*.

Germany deliberately fostered a false impression of the size of the newly formed *Luftwaffe*, encouraging potential enemies to believe that it was larger than it really was. This played an important role at the Munich conference in 1938, when Chamberlain and other negotiators believed that refusal to acquiesce to Hitler's demands would result in massive destruction from the air.

Under the terms of the Treaty of Versailles, Germany was prohibited from having an air force, but a Defence Ministry was permitted and this contained a small air staff. German manufacturers designed a range of airliners, trainers and fast communication aircraft which laid the basis for the later bombers, fighters and attack types. The national airline, Deutsche Lufthansa, ran training courses and airmindedness was encouraged by instruction in gliding and powered flying. When Hitler came to power in 1933 he initiated massive rearmament, with the *Luftwaffe* to the fore. Its first Chief of Staff, Lieutenant-General Max Wever, was influenced by Douhet's ideas and in 1935 began the 'Ural Bomber' project for a long-range strategic weapon. Wever died in an air crash in the following year, however, and his successors saw the *Luftwaffe*'s primary role as army support.

An independent air ministry

It is difficult to overestimate the effect of establishing overall control of aircraft production and operation. General von Hoeppner, who took over command of the German Army Air Service at its lowest ebb, has been credited with having 'transformed a beaten, dispirited force into one which could claim a comparative superiority by the spring of 1917 and was still a formidable one later when outnumbered and outfought'. Yet both he and Inspector of Flying Troops Major Siegert, who had commanded the strategic-bombing force in Belgium during the autumn of 1914, despaired of matching Britain's organization. The British had established an independent Air Ministry at the end of 1917, but attempts to set up a German Air Department failed. Britain also had an Aircraft Supply Department, whereas the German Army and Navy competed for aircraft and engines. In the last ten months of the war alone, the British industry produced 27,000 aircraft.

Between the wars

In 1919 Trenchard was reappointed Chief of the Air Staff, a position which he held for a further ten years, and Mitchell became Assistant Chief of the US Army Air Force. Mitchell admitted to having been profoundly impressed by Trenchard, whom he met in 1917, and with these two men at or near the top of their professions the doctrine of strategic air power held sway. They were supported by the Italian General Giulio Douhet, who in 1921 published *The Command of the Air*, a treatise reinforcing the need for independent air action and asserting that in future wars the most effective method of winning would be to attack the enemy's homeland with a rain of bombs. Two years later Mussolini did set up the *Regia Aeronautica* as an independent force, although its actions in Abyssinia and Spain neither denied nor confirmed Douhet's predictions.

Mitchell also campaigned for an independent US Air Force. To demonstrate the power of an air arm Mitchell masterminded the bombing of three surrendered German warships in 1921 and later similar attacks on three US battleships which were due to be scrapped. These actions were carried out in optimum conditions and against no defences, but many hailed the achievements as sounding the death knell of the capital ship. In 1925 Mitchell was court-martialled for insubordination as a result of persistent criticism of his superiors; he was sentenced to be suspended from duty for five years. Subsequently, a board set up to examine the future of US

RIGHT: *This Martin MB-2 biplane bomber of 1918 was a development of the MB-1, America's first twin-engined bomber. During July 1921 – and then again in 1923 – 'Billy' Mitchell used MB-2s to demonstrate dramatically the vulnerability of warships to air power. He sank five battleships anchored for tests in Chesapeake Bay, including the 'unsinkable' captured German Ostfriesland. Meanwhile, the MB-2 became standard US Army Air Corps equipment for several years.*

Operations during the Spanish Civil War showed that aircraft could be used very effectively as a tactical weapon, and this experience helped mould the *Blitzkrieg* combination of armoured forces, rapidly moving mechanized infantry and close-support aircraft.

France was not prepared for defence against the German onslaught. Haunted by memories of World War I her planners put their faith in the Maginot Line of fixed fortifications. The fighter force was certainly more effective than the bomber arm in 1940, but not sufficiently so.

Both Russia and Japan were building up their air forces, and in particular, the Japanese Navy's air arm expanded rapidly. But in neither country was there an outstanding aerial strategist who held sway over his fellows. The Soviet Air Force was being trained by tactically-orientated German officers. Japan did carry out strategic raids on the Chinese mainland from 1937, but her bombers were outfought by packs of Russian fighters in the Nomonhan war two years later.

Blitzkrieg

Air power came of age in World War II. Strategic bombing was the key to Allied victory, although the extent of its contribution is still hotly debated. The invasion of Poland appeared to vindicate the *Luftwaffe's* concentration on army support; a combination of Stuka dive-bombers and the Panzer tank forces rapidly brought about a victory.

In the ensuing lull on the ground, RAF Bomber Command mounted daylight attacks on German peripheral targets with its force of Vickers Wellington, Armstrong Whitworth Whitley and Handley Page Hampden medium bombers. The bombers were underarmed, had no self-sealing fuel tanks and were not escorted. They were, not surprisingly, badly mauled by German fighters and had to be transferred from day to night operations. The myth that bombers offering mutual support could make effective daylight attacks was effectively destroyed.

In the spring of 1940 German forces invaded Denmark and Norway, and Allied support for the latter country had to be withdrawn as a result of failure to gain local air superiority and because of disruption of communication and supply links by enemy air attacks. Then it was the turn of Belgium, Holland and France, where *Blitzkrieg* operations quickly overcame the defences.

It was during the Battle of Britain in the summer of 1940 that the *Luftwaffe* failed seriously for the first time. Its bombers were underarmed and carried too small a bombload. After sustaining heavy losses they were given fighter escorts, but these fighters might have been more effectively employed in taking on Fighter Command directly. The overall direction of what was intended to be a strategic offensive was blurred, and German resources were diversified to attack other targets, such as shipping, rather than concentrating on the job in hand. Then Hitler, in retaliation for a small raid on Berlin, ordered his bombers to be used against cities rather than RAF airfields and similar targets. Meanwhile, bombing of the German invasion fleet being assembled in Channel ports caused considerable damage, and Hitler was forced to postpone the invasion.

BOMBER & FIGHTER RANGES FROM GREAT BRITAIN

Armstrong Whitworth Whitley V (1940) 3,000
Short Stirling I (1941) 3,500
Avro Lancaster III (1942) 7,000
Douglas A-20G Havoc (1943) 4,000
Vickers Wellington X (1943) 4,500
Supermarine Spitfire XIVE (1944)
Supermarine Spitfire HFIXE (1943)
Fairey Battle I (1939) 1,000
Avro Lancaster III (1942) 14,000
North American P-51D Mustang (1944)
North American P-51C Mustang (1943)
Short Stirling I (1941) 14,000
Martin B-26G Marauder (1944) 4,000
Avro Manchester (1941) 8,100
Boeing B-17F (1942) 4,000
Hawker Hurricane I (1940)
Hawker Tempest V (1944)
Boeing B-17G (1943) 6,000
Supermarine Spitfire VC (1942)
Consolidated B-24J Liberator (1944)
Lockheed P-38G Lightning (1943) 5,000
North American B-25J Mitchell (1940) 4,000
Handley Page Hampden (1940) 2,000
Handley Page Halifax (1941) 5,800
Republic P-47D Thunderbolt (1944)
de Havilland Mosquito BIV (1942) 2,000
Supermarine Spitfire IA (1940)
Bristol Blenheim I (1939) 1,000
de Havilland Mosquito NFII (1942)
Handley Page Hampden (1940) 4,000
de Havilland Mosquito FBVI (1943)
Hawker Typhoon (1942)

RAF Scampton
London
RAF Biggin Hill
Hamburg
Bremen
Berlin
Essen • Dortmund
Düsseldorf
Cologne
Frankfurt
Leipzig
Dresden
Stuttgart
Munich

400 miles
400 miles
600 miles
600 miles
800 miles
800 miles
1,000 miles
1,000 miles
1,200 miles
1,200 miles

Leningrad

BOMBER RANGES
BOMB LOADS IN LBS.
FIGHTER RANGES

ABOVE: *A German V-2 rocket (officially known as A-4) photographed on its mobile launch-ramp. This forerunner of the modern ballistic missile could carry a 970kg (2,000lb) high-explosive warhead for up to 320km (200 miles) and was developed by the famous Dr Wernher von Braun.*

TOP: *A flight of Curtiss-Wright SB2C Helldivers returns to its base aboard the USS Hornet after an attack on Japanese shipping in the China Sea. These two-seat dive-bombers were one of the main carrier-based aircraft types used by the Americans during the Pacific war.*

Bomber Command

In November 1940 Air Chief Marshal Dowding was succeeded as head of RAF Fighter Command by Air Marshal Sholto Douglas, a supporter of the 'big wing' theory developed by Air Vice-Marshal Leigh-Mallory. This involved assembling wings, consisting of several squadrons, to intercept attacks. But gradually the British emphasis was switched from defence to offence, with bombers replacing fighters as the priority. Taking the war back to Germany was seen as being the only way to start winning, although the tide was still running in Germany's favour. In other areas tactical operations continued. Coastal Command was helping to win the Battle of the Atlantic and some 60 per cent of U-boat losses were caused by aircraft action (including those sunk by air-sown mines). Also the Fleet Air Arm, operating from aircraft carriers, was helping to safeguard supplies of arms, raw materials, fuel and food. Bomber Command resisted moves to allocate a sizable part of its force to anti-submarine operations, preferring to gird its loins for the strategic attack on Germany. It was, however, responsible for sinking or badly damaging a number of capital ships, including the anchored battleship *Tirpitz*.

In February 1942 Air Marshal Arthur 'Bomber' Harris took charge of Bomber Command. He was convinced that strategic bombing would win the war, and at the end of May he mounted his first 1,000-bomber raid. The offensive continued unabated until March 1944, with the British night actions later being supplemented by US daylight raids. From the spring of 1943 the attackers were on top, but there were still unpleasant shocks. One of these was the mauling of an unescorted Boeing B–17 force at Schweinfurt, where the Flying Fortresses' close box formation and defensive armament of up to 13 machine-guns each failed to deter the *Luftwaffe* fighters.

It is widely accepted that D-Day would not have been possible without strategic bombing to disrupt arms production, fuel supplies and logistics. After the landings, heavy bombers were used in the close-support role as well as their major tasks, but this was only possible because Allied fighters had virtual command of the air. Retaliation by the *Luftwaffe* with V1 flying bombs and by the German Army with V2 ballistic missiles (see Chapter 19) was too late to be decisive.

Carrier power

If the strategic bomber was one of World War II's decisive weapons, the aircraft carrier was another. Swordfish torpedo bombers helped sink the *Bismarck* early in the war and virtually eliminated the Italian fleet in Taranto harbour in late 1940, but the most audacious attack by naval aircraft was the Japanese assault on the US base at Pearl Harbor, Hawaii, in December 1941. This action marked the transference of power from the battleship to the carrier, and yet the Japanese let the supreme prize – the US Navy's carrier fleet, which was not in Pearl Harbor at the time of the attack – slip from their grasp. After six months of runaway successes the Imperial Japanese Navy began to be driven back by the US Navy's carrier force. Strategic bombing of Japanese targets was the responsibility of Boeing B–29 Superfortresses, and the incendiary raids on Tokyo, largely constructed from wood, probably represented the nearest that such a policy ever came to destroying a population's will to resist. It is perhaps significant that the Pacific war was finally ended by the weapon which was to remove the last remaining doubts about the future possibilities of

TOP: *Col Paul Tibbets (right) in front of the B–29 Superfortress he piloted to drop the world's first atomic bomb on the Japanese city of Hiroshima in August 1945. B–29s of the US Strategic Air Command were replaced by eight-jet B–52 Stratofortress bombers in the mid-1950s.*
ABOVE: *A pair of Japanese Nakajima B5Ns. At the time of Pearl Harbor these were Japan's main torpedo-bombers.*

153

effective strategic bombing: the atomic bomb.

Air power is not measured just in terms of heavy bombers and fighters, however. It also includes elements such as the ability to deliver invading forces rapidly into action against surprised defenders. This was graphically illustrated by the dropping of German paratroops on Crete and the Allies' use of gliders to transport men and equipment. Massive transport fleets were required in addition to the combat air forces.

Korea and Vietnam

In the two major, sustained conflicts since 1945 – Korea and Indo-China/Vietnam – air power has played an important but not decisive role. Carpet-bombing of Korean targets by Boeing B–29s was not notably successful, and while close air support was vitally necessary it too failed to destroy the enemy's ability to keep himself supplied and armed. Many of the types thrown into action were unsuitable for the tasks which they were called upon to perform, and the basic thinking behind their employment was also awry. The troops wanted close air support against pinpoint targets between a few metres and a few kilometres in front of them. Many planners, however, were still obsessed with the idea that interdiction against rear targets was the surest way of crippling the enemy.

The United States no longer had a monopoly on atomic weapons and could not threaten their use indiscriminately. In the spring of 1951 General Douglas MacArthur, Commander-in-Chief of United Nations forces in Korea, was dismissed for persistently advocating attacks on Chinese industrial centres. Later, with General Eisenhower as US President, more or less overt threats of atomic attacks on China may have contributed to the ceasefire negotiated in 1953.

Strategic Air Command

After the end of World War II the US Air Force gained a specialist heavy-bomber wing in the form of Strategic Air Command. The Convair B–36, originally designed to bomb Germany from the US, was equally capable of deployment against the Soviet Union. This was followed by the all-jet Boeing B–47 and B–52. Russia concentrated on long-range missiles (see Chapter 19) as its strategic striking force. Britain relegated her V-bombers to other, non-strategic, roles. Both France and the US, though, retain manned bombers alongside their missile arsenals. The latest aircraft to enter the strategic arena are the Rockwell B–1 and Russia's Tupolev Backfire, although the Soviet Union maintains that Backfire is not a strategic weapon and disputes that it should be included in strategic-arms limitation agreements.

Air power in the Middle East

In the Middle East, air power proved decisive – as far as it was allowed to go – during the 1956 Suez crisis, was instrumental in bringing about Israeli victory in 1967 but played a lesser role in 1973. On the first two occasions pre-emptive strikes destroyed the Arabs' air forces but, in the October war, ground forces were able to counter air action fairly effectively. The Israelis gained temporary

air superiority, but the Arabs declined to commit their fighters when surface-to-air missiles were proving an effective substitute. The one strategic force used in 1973, the US Air Force's fleet of C–5 and C–141 transports which took part in Operation Nickel Grass to resupply Israel, performed extremely creditably and reminded the world yet again that there is more to warfare than fighting. Both superpowers also used strategic reconnaissance during the conflict, with Russian Mikoyan MiG–25s and probably US Air Force Lockheed SR–71 Blackbirds supplementing satellite coverage.

NATO and the Warsaw Pact

One role of air power in the modern world is as a straightforward extension of the foot soldier, cavalry or artillery. Supersonic intercepters and ground-attack aircraft can destroy targets quickly and accurately, help ground and sea forces in both defence and attack, and protect the homeland. The air forces of the North Atlantic Treaty Organization (NATO) and the Warsaw Pact face each other in central Europe for just this purpose. The 'tripwire' doctrine formerly adopted by NATO has been replaced by one of flexible response. An incursion into the Western alliance's territory by Soviet Bloc forces would now be countered by a spoiling action rather than the immediate use of nuclear weapons. The Warsaw Pact greatly outnumbers NATO in tanks, so air power is the major balancing factor. The Soviet Union is also superior in numbers of aircraft, but until recently the gap has been substantially narrowed by the West's more advanced airborne electronics. Now that Russian navigation and attack equipment is improving, while the numerical preponderance is being maintained, the balance of air power in Europe is subtly changing.

NATO members such as Britain and Germany maintain a mixed force of offensive and defensive aircraft, as does France, which has withdrawn from the alliance. The United States and Canada, also members, divide their forces between their own territory and bases in Europe.

The Berlin Airlift showed that the aircraft

ABOVE: *As a Dakota comes in to land, this Douglas Globemaster unloads its valuable cargo during the Berlin Airlift of 1948.*
BELOW: *US Navy strike planes lined up on the deck of USS* Kitty Hawk *during operations off the coast of North Vietnam in 1972.*

had come of age as a transport vehicle, and countries with overseas responsibilities today maintain large fleets of cargo aircraft. This is especially so in the United States, which would have to reinforce its troops in Europe if war broke out.

Off-shore patrols

Maritime aviation is also assuming ever greater importance. Specialized aircraft operating from land bases or aircraft carriers are used to track and destroy submarines and surface ships. Countries surrounded by water or with important shipping lanes passing close to their coasts, such as Australia, New Zealand and South Africa, place great emphasis on maritime patrol. As offshore resources, such as minerals and fish, are exploited they have to be defended against saboteurs and illegal fishing.

So it can be seen that aircraft are of great importance on many levels. Perhaps the most important aspects of air power, however, are the ones which are often neglected – an industry able to provide the equipment, a training organization to supply operators of all types, a political organization which defines the overall objectives and ensures that they are met, and a military command and control structure that turns an air force into an organism which can change and respond to demands.

ABOVE CENTRE: *The second Tornado MRCA prototype, fitted with two large fuel tanks and four 450kg (1,000lb) bombs during tests in 1975. By the early 1980s over 800 of these planes will be entering service with the air forces of Britain, Italy and West Germany.*

TOP RIGHT: *During a training exercise in Korea over 3,000 paratroops descend from Fairchild C–119 Flying Boxcars.*
ABOVE: *Two Dassault Mirage IIIs of the RAAF. These French fighters have been exported to many foreign air forces.*

Air Forces of the World

Abu Dhabi
Small but well equipped force in the Arabian Gulf. Jet aircraft include Mirage and Hunter fighter-bombers.

Afghanistan
Operates under military agreement with Soviet Union and all aircraft are supplied by Russia. Equipment includes MiG–21 fighters.

Albania
Uses Chinese-built versions of Russian aircraft, including MiG–21 fighters.

Algeria
Combat aircraft mostly supplied by Russia, although other types bought from the West. Fighters include MiG–21s, with MiG–17s and Su–7s for ground-attack.

Angola
Equipped by Soviet Union following independence in 1975. Modern types such as MiG–21s took part in civil war during 1976.

Argentina
Operates wide variety of Western-supplied combat aircraft, including Mirage intercepters, Canberra bombers and Skyhawks for ground-attack. Also uses Argentine-developed Pucara counter-insurgency type. Navy operates Skyhawks and Trackers from carrier *25 de Mayo*.

Australia
Powerful force with influence over large areas of ocean. Sole non-US operator of F–111 swing-wing bomber and has more than 100 Mirage intercepters. New P–3C Orion maritime-patrollers to be followed by modern fighters and attack aircraft. Navy operates Skyhawks, Trackers and helicopters from aircraft carrier HMAS *Melbourne*.

Austria
Small force with roles limited by treaty with Russia. Operates Saab 105 fighter-bombers and plans to introduce modern fighters.

Bangladesh
Uses Russian combat aircraft, including MiG–21s, since breaking away from Pakistan.

Belgium
Member of Nato and is one of four European members of the alliance to place initial export order for F–16 air-combat fighter. Collaborating with Holland, Denmark and Norway on F–16 production. Earlier types include Starfighters for interception and attack, plus Mirage 5s for the latter role.

Bolivia
Uses mainly piston-engined types and early jets in counter-insurgency roles. Sabres operated as fighters and Embraer Xavantes used for attack.

Brazil
Largest South American air force. Mirage IIIs form part of integrated air-defence system, with F–5Es for ground attack. Brazil's thriving aircraft industry supplies the air force with several types, including Xavante light strike aircraft and Bandeirante multi-purpose transports. Trackers and Navy helicopters are flown from the aircraft carrier *Minas Gerais*, and a large transport fleet is operated.

Brunei
Small helicopter force used to support the army.

Bulgaria
Member of Warsaw Pact, with all equipment supplied by Soviet Bloc. MiG–21 and MiG–19 fighters backed up by earlier MiG–17s.

Burma
Mainly counter-insurgency force operating early jet types such as Sabres, Vampires and Shooting Stars.

Cambodia
Being re-equipped with Russian types following Communist take-over in 1975.

Cameroun
Internal security force with no large combat aircraft. Receives aid and equipment from France.

Canada
Nato member, with forces based in Europe as well as in Canada. Equipment includes Starfighters and Voodoos, with Canadian designations CF–104 and CF–101 respectively, plus CF–5s. A force of Orion maritime-patrol aircraft will replace the indigenously developed Canadair Argus.

Central African Republic
Operates transport types and helicopters, but no heavy combat aircraft.

Chad
Another ex-French colony, with Sky-raiders for attack and a small fleet of transport types.

Chile
Recent acquisitions include F–5Es and additional A–37s from the US, following Britain's refusal to supply the military government with further combat aircraft to add to the substantial force of Hunters. A number of earlier types make up the second-line strength.

China (Communist)
One of the world's largest air forces. Operates mainly Russian-designed types, built under licence at first and then copied after the deterioration of relations with the Soviet Union. These include MiG–21s, MiG–19s (known as the Shenyang F–6), MiG–17s (F–4s) and MiG–15s (F–2s). The F–9 has been developed in China from the MiG–19, and Tu–16 Badgers are operated in the bombing role. Beriev Be–6s fly maritime-patrol missions and there is a large transport fleet. The Rolls-Royce Spey military turbofan is to be built under licence and may power Chinese-designed aircraft.

China (Nationalist)
Powerful air force operating US types, some of which are built in Taiwan itself. New F–5Es are joining earlier F–5A fighters and will replace nearly 300 Sabre fighter-bombers. Super Sabres and Starfighters also act as fighters, and large fleets of transports, helicopters and trainers are operated.

Colombia
A force of Mirage 5 fighter-bombers forms the front line, with older jets and piston-engined types backing them up. The air force runs its own airline, Satena, for internal services.

Congo Republic
Operates transports and helicopters of French, US and Russian origin. Provided support for Marxist forces in Angola during the civil war.

Cuba
Russian-supplied since the 1958 revolution. Types include MiG–21s, some of which are the modern MiG–21MF variant, together with MiG–19s and MiG–17s. Helicopters, transports and trainers have also been received from the Eastern Bloc.

Czechoslovakia
Member of the Warsaw Pact, operating a modern force of various marks of MiG, including about 170 MiG–21s, plus Su–7s for ground-attack. Sizable transport, training and helicopter fleets are also operated.

Dahomey
Uses the normal collection of transports and helicopters supplied as standard by France to its former colonies.

Denmark
Nato member, and one of the four European parties to the alliance to order F–16s in the 'arms deal of the century'. Denmark is one of only two export customers for the Swedish Saab Draken, which is used as a fighter-bomber and for reconnaissance. Other combat types include Super Sabres and Starfighters.

Dominica
Operates a variety of early jet and piston-engined types, such as Mustangs, Vampires, Invaders and Catalinas.

Dubai
Small but expanding force in the Arabian Gulf. The only combat aircraft are Macchi MB.326s, and the association with Italy has been continued by purchase of the G.222 transport.

Ecuador
One of the first export customers, along with Oman, for the Anglo–French Jaguar fighter-bomber. These are replacing Shooting Stars, and other equipment includes Canberras and Strikemasters.

Egypt
Since the October 1973 war with Israel, Egypt has turned towards the West rather than Russia to equip its air force. Types already supplied include helicopters and Mirage fighter-bombers, with negotiations continuing towards further purchases and agreements for licence production in Egypt. Other Arab countries – Saudi Arabia being the major contributor – will finance the operation and will receive aircraft from Egyptian production lines.

Ethiopia
Jet equipment includes F–5Es, A–37 ground-attack aircraft and Canberra bombers, plus F–5As supplied by Iran and some remaining Sabres. The combat aircraft have recently been used against forces trying to separate Eritrea from the rest of the country.

Finland
Finland receives military equipment from both Russia and the West, the former supplying MiG–21 fighters and Europe contributing Drakens from Sweden and Hawks from Britain. The Finnish aircraft company, Valmet, builds Drakens under licence and has developed its own basic trainer.

France
One of the most powerful air forces in Europe, despite the withdrawal of France from the military activities of Nato. The Mirage F.1 is replacing early jet types and the Delta Mirage 2000 is being developed to take over from Mirage IIIs. Some 200 Jaguar ground-attack aircraft are being supplied to the Armée de l'Air, as are the same number of Alpha Jet trainers. The land-based strategic force comprises ballistic missiles together with Mirage IVs and a supporting tanker force of KC–135s. The extremely successful French aerospace industry is able to supply almost all the air force's needs, including transports, trainers, helicopters and maritime-patrol aircraft, and it is a major exporter. The Navy has two aircraft carriers, *Foch* and *Clemenceau*, and the Super Etendard has been developed to extend their effectiveness into the 1980s.

Gabon
A small force of Mirage IIIs comprises the combat element, with a varied transport fleet consisting of helicopters and fixed-wing types from France, the US and Japan.

Germany (East)
A member of the Warsaw Pact, with substantial Russian forces stationed in the country as well as its own defences. Modern front-line equipment includes late-model MiG–21s and Su–7s as intercepters and fighter-bombers, backed up by MiG–17s and supported by fleets of transports, helicopters and trainers.

Germany (West)
The strongest European member of Nato, operating more than 250 Phantoms, several hundred Starfighters and Aeritalia G.91s for light attack. The last-named are being replaced by Franco–German Alpha Jets, and the Starfighters are to be superseded by the Panavia Tornado multi-role combat aircraft being developed jointly with Britain and Italy. The powerful naval air arm will receive 112 of Germany's 322 Tornados. The German Government is an enthusiastic advocate of collaborative development programmes, additional examples being the Transall transport and Atlantic maritime-patrol aircraft. Large fleets of trainers and helicopters are also operated.

Ghana
The air force's only combat aircraft are a handful of MB.326s, but these are supported by a variety of general-purpose transport, patrol and training types.

Great Britain
A major European contributor to Nato, with forces based in Germany and the Mediterranean as well as in the United Kingdom. Phantoms have largely replaced Lightnings in the interception role, and ground-attack duties have in turn been taken over by Jaguars. Buccaneers, Canberras and Vulcans are to be superseded by the tri-national Panavia Tornado, and some Victor former V-bombers have been converted into tankers. The Hawk jet trainer is joining the earlier Jet Provost, and maritime-patrol is the responsibility of Nimrods. Basic training is carried out on Bulldogs, and a wide range of helicopters, transports and subsidiary types support the main combat element. The Navy's last aircraft carrier, HMS *Ark Royal*, is being withdrawn but fixed-wing naval aviation will continue with the Sea Harrier, developed from the land-based variants operated since 1969.

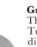

Greece
The modernization of the Greek and Turkish air forces has been spurred by differences over Cyprus, with Greece receiving Phantoms, Corsairs and Mirage F.1s, together with new transports and trainers. Older types include Starfighters and Delta Daggers, plus F–5As used for reconnaissance.

Guatemala
A small number of A–37 attack aircraft make up the combat element. Jet trainers are also operated, along with a small fleet of transports and helicopters.

Guinea
Operates Russian-supplied aircraft, including a handful of MiG–17s plus small numbers of trainers and transports.

Guyana
Has no armed types, using only light transports and helicopters.

Haiti
Operates a number of obsolescent Mustang fighter-bombers and some armed Cessna 337 light aircraft. Also trainers, transports and helicopters.

Haute-Volta
Has no combat aircraft, acting as a transport force only. The standard range of types supplied to French ex-colonies is on strength.

Honduras
Operates a rarity in the 1970s, the F4U Corsair, together with Invader bombers. Shooting Star reconnaissance/trainers are the only jet types.

Hong Kong
A policing force only, using helicopters and light aircraft.

Hungary
Member of the Warsaw Pact, but possesses a relatively small air force. Front-line strength comprises MiG–21 fighters and Su–7s for ground-attack.

India
Buys aircraft from both East and West as well as building its own types. MiG–21s are constructed under licence, the first examples having been bought off the shelf, and the Indian-developed Ajeet is taking over from the Gnat on which it is based. Ground-attack squadrons operate Hunters, Su–7s and the indigenous Hindustan Aeronautics Marut, with Canberras used as bombers. The domestically designed Kiran jet trainer is being supplemented by the Polish Iskra, and the Il–38 May maritime-patrol aircraft is the latest acquisition from the Soviet Union. India's aircraft industry also provides basic trainers, transports and helicopters. The Navy has one aircraft carrier, *Vikrant*, from which Sea Hawks and Alizés are operated.

Indonesia
Now operates aircraft supplied by the US and Australia, with all Russian equipment grounded. The only jet combat types are Commonwealth Sabre fighters.

Iran
One of the world's most powerful air arms, and the only non-US operator of the F–14 swing-wing fighter. The present Phantoms and F–5Es are due to be supplemented by new lightweight fighter-bombers, and other modern equipment includes P–3F maritime-patrol aircraft, Boeing 707 and 747 tanker/transports, Hercules and Friendship transports, and one of the world's largest helicopter forces.

Iraq
Most aircraft have traditionally been supplied by the Soviet Bloc, but Western arms are now being bought. The most modern Russian type is the MiG–23 fighter, backed up by MiG–21s and –19s. Ground-attack machines include MiG–17s, Su–7s and Hunters, with Tu–16s and Il–28s used for bombing.

Ireland
This small defence force operates armed Magister light strike/trainers and a number of light aircraft fitted to carry stores.

Israel
A modern, powerful and well equipped air force with extensive recent combat experience. Ground-attack is carried out by some 500 Phantoms and Skyhawks, with Mirages, the Kfir J79-powered Mirage development and F–15 Eagles

flying as fighters. Israel Aircraft Industries builds the Arava light transport as well as Kfir, but virtually all other aircraft are supplied by the US. These include E–2C Hawkeyes for early-warning, Hercules transports, Boeing 707 tanker/transports and helicopters.

Italy
Member of Nato, with a small but healthy aircraft industry supplying many of its needs. The F–104S version of the Starfighter, developed by Aeritalia, is to be supplemented by the tri-national Panavia Tornado. The G.91 is used in a number of versions for training and ground attack, and the G.222 medium transport is being introduced to complement the larger Hercules. Macchi's MB.339 jet trainer has been ordered to follow the MB.326, and light aircraft are supplied by a number of companies. Atlantics and Trackers carry out maritime reconnaissance.

Ivory Coast
No combat aircraft are operated, the air force's roles being restricted to transport and liaison.

Jamaica
Light transports and helicopters are used for patrol, communication and liaison, but no armed types are operated.

Japan
Japan's aircraft industry is following licence production of US types such as the Phantom, Starfighter and Neptune with its own developments. These include the T–2 trainer and the FST–2 attack aircraft developed from it, together with the C–1 transport and the series of Shin Meiwa flying boats and amphibians. The Starfighters are due to be replaced by Eagles, Hawkeyes have been ordered for early-warning duties and a new maritime-patrol aircraft is required. Japan also supplies most of its own primary trainers, light aircraft and helicopters.

Jordan
A comparatively small but expanding force, with front-line equipment comprising Starfighters, F–5As and F–5Es. These are supplemented by a small transport force and a number of helicopters and trainers, both jet-powered and piston-engined.

Jugoslavia
More than 100 MiG–21s form the major part of the intercepter element, and the Orao – being developed jointly with Romania – is likely to be the main ground-attack type in the future. The helicopter fleet includes licence-built Gazelles, and a variety of Russian and Western transports are operated.

Kenya
Jet equipment comprises a small number of Hunter fighter-bombers and some Strikemaster light strike/trainers. The training fleet is being expanded.

Korea (North)
This Russian-equipped force operates the usual array of MiG and Sukhoi combat types, plus Il–28s and Soviet transports and helicopters.

Korea (South)
Almost totally US-equipped, with Sabre fighters complemented by Phantoms and F–5s for ground-attack. The Sabres are likely to be replaced by F–16s.

Kuwait
Modern jet equipment consists of Skyhawks and Mirage F.1s, the former supplementing the force of Hunters and Strikemasters with the latter taking over from Lightning intercepters.

Laos
US-supplied equipment is largely non-operational, following the Communist take-over. Russian aircraft may now be in service.

Lebanon
Hunters and Mirages are the only jet combat aircraft, although Syria may pass on some Russian equipment.

Libya
Operates modern Soviet aircraft in the form of MiG–23s and Tu–22s in addition to a variety of Mirages. Training aircraft, transports and helicopters have been supplied by Russia, the US, France and Jugoslavia.

Malagasy
No combat types, operating only a selection of light transports and helicopters.

Malawi
Operates only a handful of transports.

Malaysia
Commonwealth Sabres have been replaced by F–5Es, with Canadair CL–41 Tebuans doubling as light strike aircraft in addition to their role as trainers.

Mali
Supplied with Russian equipment, including MiG–17s and –15s.

Malta
This helicopter force has recently introduced its first fixed-wing light transports.

Mauritania
Has added Skyvans and Defenders to its force of French-supplied transports.

Mexico
No modern combat aircraft, relying on obsolescent types such as Vampires and Shooting Stars.

Mongolia
Uses Russian-supplied MiG–15s, transports and helicopters.

Morocco
Mirage F.1s and F–5Es are due to supplement the force of early-mark F–5s, armed Magisters and Russian fighter-bombers (now in storage). Modern transports and helicopters are operated.

Nepal
Operates transports and helicopters only.

Netherlands
An important member of Nato, operating more than 100 Starfighters as intercepters and for ground attack. These will be supplemented and replaced by F–16s built under licence in co-operation with Belgium, Denmark and Norway. Canadair NF–5s are also operated.

New Zealand
Small but up-to-date force, operating Skyhawks and Strikemasters. The Hercules fleet has been augmented by the purchase of ex-RAF Andovers, and P–3B Orions patrol the surrounding seas.

Nicaragua
Uses piston-engined and early jet types for ground-support and bombing, with more modern transports and helicopters.

Niger
A former French colony, supplied with a selection of transports.

Nigeria
MiG–21s have been added to the Russian aircraft supplied earlier, with the West contributing transports, trainers and helicopters.

Norway
Nato's northernmost member, and one of the alliance's four European participants to have ordered the F–16. This type will replace Starfighters and F–5s in the 1980s. Other aircraft include maritime-patrol Orions and Hercules transports.

Oman
Jaguar International fighter-bombers are augmenting the force of Hunters and Strikemasters used for ground-attack.

Pakistan
Operates aircraft from many sources, including Iran (surplus F–5s), France (Mirages and second-hand Atlantics), China (MiG–19s) and the US (B–57 bombers). A large number of trainers and helicopters are also used, and licence production of overseas types is building up.

Panama
Operates no combat aircraft but has a comparatively modern transport fleet.

Papua New Guinea
Uses transport aircraft donated by Australia.

Paraguay
Primarily engaged in transport and liaison duties, armed trainers being the only combat aircraft.

Peru
The first South American customer for Russian combat aircraft, having ordered swing-wing Su–20s. Other jet types include Mirage 5s, Canberras, Hunters and A–37s.

Philippines
Operates Sabre fighters and F–5 fighter-bombers, with transports and a variety of smaller aircraft supplied by several countries.

Poland
The largest Soviet Bloc air force after that of Russia itself. Some 200 ground-attack Su–7s are being supplemented by the Su–20 development, taking over from MiG–17s. About 300 MiG–21 fighters are also on strength.

Portugal
A Nato member, but lacking modern combat aircraft. The only aircraft committed to the alliance are Neptune maritime-patrollers. Sabres are used for interception, with G.91s for ground-attack.

Qatar
Four Hunters are the sole combat aircraft.

Rhodesia
Operates Canberras, Hunters and Vampires on ground-attack missions, backed up by a number of lighter aircraft and helicopters.

Romania
Member of the Warsaw Pact, operating the normal force of MiG and Sukhoi types for interception and ground-attack. Romania also has Alouette IIIs, used in the anti-tank role.

Rwanda
A small number of Magisters comprise the only jet equipment.

Salvador
Ex-Israeli Ouragans and Magisters have been supplied for fighter and strike duties, to add to a varied transport and training fleet.

Saudi Arabia
This rapidly expanding force is introducing US aircraft to augment its British-supplied types, including Lightnings and Strikemasters. Latest acquisitions comprise F-5E fighter-bombers, gunship helicopters and additional Hercules for transport and aerial refuelling.

Senegal
A small transport and liaison force with no combat aircraft.

Sierra Leone
Uses primary trainers and helicopters only.

Singapore
The attack force of Hunters and Strikemasters is being supplemented by Skyhawks modified to Singaporean requirements, and a new intercepter type is being sought.

Somalia
Largely equipped with Russian aircraft, including MiG-21s. Somalia also provides base facilities for Soviet aircraft.

South Africa
Various marks of Mirage III are used for interception and ground-attack, and these are being supplemented by Mirage F.1s in both roles. Canberras and Buccaneers are also on strength, with MB.326s being employed both for training and attack. Atlas Aircraft Corporation builds several types under licence, including the Mirages, MB.326s (known as Impalas) and a number of smaller types.

South Yemen
Operates Communist-supplied aircraft, including MiG-21s.

Soviet Union
Operates some of the world's most advanced aircraft. Swing-wing Backfire bombers are supplementing the force of Tu-16s, Tu-22s, Tu-95s and Mya-4s used for bombing and aerial refuelling,

the latter role also being carried out by Il-76 tankers. Variable-geometry Su-19 fighter-bombers and MiG-21 attack aircraft are the latest additions to the fighter-bomber force, which also has Su-17s and MiG-23s as well as older types such as Su-7s and MiG-17s. Perhaps most impressive of all is the MiG-25 Foxbat, operated both as a fighter and for reconnaissance. Other recce types include the Yak-28. The intercepter force has Su-9s, -11s and -15s in addition to some of the types already mentioned, plus Tu-28Ps. The same design bureau's Tu-126 is the Russian equivalent of AWACS, although not as advanced, and the Navy has Il-38s and a variety of flying-boats/amphibians for maritime-patrol in addition to many of the Air Force's types. The latest aircraft revealed to Western eyes is the Yak-36 vertical take-off fighter-bomber operated from *Kiev*-class aircraft carriers. Combat aircraft are backed up by massive fleets of transports, trainers and helicopters.

Spain
A well equipped force operating Phantoms and Mirages – IIIs and F.1s – with F-16s on order. F-5s are used for attack and reconnaissance, and Casa is developing the new C.101 jet trainer. The Navy operates Matadors (AV-8As) from the carrier *Dedalo*.

Sri Lanka
The only combat unit is a MiG-17 squadron, supported by jet trainers supplied by Russia and Britain.

Sudan
Supplied with combat aircraft by both Russia and China, but much equipment is grounded.

Sweden
Moving towards a force comprising only three combat types – Draken, Viggen and Saab 105 – all supplied by Swedish industry. Various marks of Viggen are used as fighters, for attack and on reconnaissance missions, over both land and sea.

Switzerland
The F-5E is being procured to replace the large force of obsolescent Venom fighter-bombers and to supplement the Hunters. Mirage IIIs are used as intercepters and for reconnaissance.

Syria
A major recipient of Russian aircraft, including MiG-23s and some 200 MiG-21s. MiG-17s and Su-7s are also used, and helicopters have been supplied by France.

Tanzania
Operates combat aircraft donated by China, including F-8s (MiG-21s). The transport and training fleets are composed of Western types.

Thailand
Almost all aircraft are of US origin, including F-5s, A-37s, Shooting Stars and a multitude of propeller-driven types.

Togo
Operates a varied fleet on transport and communication duties, plus a small number of Magisters.

Tunisia
F-5Es are replacing elderly Sabres, with MB.326s doubling as trainers and light strike aircraft.

Turkey
Rapidly building up strength, with Phantoms and Italian-built F-104S Starfighters bolstering the force of earlier Starfighters, Delta Daggers, Super Sabres and F-5s. A substantial transport fleet is operated, and more combat types – perhaps built in Turkey – are planned.

Uganda
Russia has supplied most of the combat aircraft, including MiG-21s.

United Arab Emirates
A small force operating helicopters. Further aircraft are under the control of member emirates.

United States
The Air Force's latest types include the F-15 Eagle air-superiority fighter, F-16 air-combat fighter and A-10 attack aircraft. Other newcomers are the E-3A AWACS and the winner of the AMST competition between the YC-14 and YC-15. Further in the future is the B-1 strategic swing-wing bomber. These will augment and partially replace B-52s operated by Strategic Air Command, which also has the smaller FB-111. Reconnaissance types include the SR-71 Blackbird and U-2. Tactical Air Command operates Phantoms, Corsairs, Thunderchiefs, F-111s and many other types, with the Air National Guard acting as a reserve. Military Airlift Command includes the C-5A Galaxy among its big-lifters and is stretching its StarLifters to increase payload. The US Navy has introduced the F-14 Tomcat shipboard fighter and plans the F-18 to take over from some Phantoms, Corsairs and Skyhawks. Other specialist USN aircraft include the Intruder heavy attack type, Orion and Viking maritime-patrollers and Hawkeye early-warning aircraft. The Marine Corps has AV-8A Harriers in addition to Navy types and plans to buy AV-8Bs to replace them, while the Army is by far the world's largest helicopter operator.

Uruguay
The single combat squadron operates Shooting Stars, and Trackers are used for shore-based anti-submarine missions. Several types of transports and helicopters are also on strength.

Venezuela
Mirages, Sabres and F-5s are used as fighters, with Canberras and Broncos for attack. A wide variety of transports, trainers and helicopters are also operated.

Vietnam
Equipped with aircraft of Russian and Chinese origin. Has expanded its operations to include the whole of Vietnam, following the withdrawal of US forces from the South.

Yemen
Western types are replacing Russian-supplied equipment.

Zaire
Mirage fighter-bombers have bolstered the combat element, which also includes MB.326 light strike/trainers and propeller-driven types. Modern transport aircraft are operated.

Zambia
The major combat force comprises MB.326s, supported by piston-engined trainers which can also carry stores.

War Machines

BELOW: *The French Morane-Saulnier Type L parasol scouting monoplane was an early attempt to combine the monoplane's speed with the strength and reconnaissance capabilities of the biplane.*

BOTTOM: *The B.E.2c, designed by Britain's Royal Aircraft Factory, was one of the most widely used reconnaissance aircraft of all time. It was extremely stable, making it an excellent observation platform.*

Reconnaissance aircraft

Military commanders have always wanted to know what the enemy was doing. The invention of the balloon in the late 18th century provided the first opportunity for reconnaissance to be made from the air, and tethered balloons and kites were widely used for observation. They had the disadvantage, however, that they could not provide more than a local view of the enemy's movements, and they were cumbersome to set up and operate.

Mobile airborne platforms were much better suited to the task, with both aeroplanes and airships being quickly adopted for this role. In 1911 a small force of Italian aircraft was used for observation in the dispute with Turkey about control of Libya, and in the spring of 1912 these aircraft carried out the first photographic reconnaissance.

Initial developments

When World War I began in 1914 the main task of aircraft on both sides was to glean information for use by the army and navy. As the air war developed, reconnaissance types played the central role, with the early fighters and bombers supporting them. Fighters were intended to protect the reconnaissance aircraft and to shoot down the enemy's airborne observers, while bombers were used to attack the bases from which reconnaissance aircraft and airships were operating. Knowledge of the enemy's movements at sea was especially important, and the German Navy's Airship Division, for instance, was intended mainly for reconnaissance over the North Sea.

Observers could not remember everything they saw on a long mission, so cameras were installed to bring back a complete record. France, with a strength of 160 aircraft at the beginning of the war, set up specialized photo-reconnaissance units. Main types were Morane-Saulnier parasols and the pusher Farmans. Strategic aerial reconnaissance proved itself definitively, when on 3 September 1914, French airmen noted a growing gap between the German First and Second Armies near the Marne. Knowledge of the fatal opening led to the Allied victory in the subsequent battle.

The German Army encouraged aerial observation, and especially photography, from the very beginning. Germany produced the world's best lenses and had an extensive camera industry. Soon after the war began the German High Command had a complete photographic record of the Western Front which could be updated every two weeks. By 1916 almost every German Army headquarters had its own detachment of three specially equipped camera aircraft, and types such as the L.F.G. Roland C.II were even

designed specifically for photo-reconnaissance. General Ludendorff, the German Commander-in-Chief, said: 'Complete photographic reconnaissance with no gaps must be ensured. This is of decisive importance.' By the time of the last great offensive of the war, the German Army Air Service was taking about 4,000 photographs a day.

Britain relied on lumbering observation aircraft such as the Royal Aircraft Factory

B.E.2c, with a maximum speed of little more than 113km/h (70mph). They were extremely stable, allowing details on the ground to be recorded without the pilot having to concentrate on flying a high-performance machine. But they were sitting ducks for German fighters. The German Fokker E I fighter entered service in 1915, armed with a machine-gun synchronized to fire through the propeller disc, and it was the B.E.2cs which took the brunt of their attack. Of the 80 kills scored by Manfred von Richthofen (the Red Baron), for example, 47 were reconnaissance aircraft.

By 1918 R.E.8s had replaced the B.E.2cs. More than 2,000 R.E.8s were used on the Western Front alone, mainly for artillery spotting (reporting by radio to correct the gunners' aim). The de Havilland D.H.9, with a range of nearly 500km (300 miles), could photograph strategic targets east of the Rhine, and the RAF ended the war with about 9,000 airborne cameras in service.

Germany prepares for World War II

Most of the hard-won expertise in airborne reconnaissance techniques was dispersed soon after the war. Germany was defeated, and the Allies had no need for the elaborate network of interpreters and collators which is part and parcel of any comprehensive intelligence network. As the aviation industry gradually built up again in Germany, however, emphasis was once more placed on the reconnaissance units. The first was formed in November 1936 to act as the aerial-observation wing of the Condor Legion in Spain.

About 80 units, comprising one-fifth of all German military aircraft, were operational when World War II began in September 1939. Reconnaissance squadrons were divided into short-range units, for tactical army support, and a long-range strategic element. The main strength of the army-support squadrons was the Henschel Hs 126 high-winged monoplane carrying fully automatic cameras in a fuselage bay. Almost 260 were in service at the beginning of the war. The *Luftwaffe* also operated a large number of long-range Dornier Do 17P reconnaissance aircraft and had more than 5,000 ground processing and interpretation staff dispersed in support of the Army's *Blitzkrieg* strategy.

Development of specialized aircraft

Britain's Royal Air Force, in contrast, was ill equipped. Credit for building up the RAF's reconnaissance forces belongs largely to Squadron Leader Sidney Cotton, who had been carrying out clandestine photographic missions before the outbreak of war. Within a few weeks of the start of hostilities he was appointed head of the newly formed Photographic Development Unit (PDU) at Heston, and the following month he managed to obtain two Supermarine Spitfires to augment his force of converted Bristol Blenheims. The requirement was for an aircraft which could exceed 483km/h (300mph) at 9,145m (30,000 ft) to avoid anti-aircraft fire and Messerschmitt Me 109 fighters. A camera fitted with a 12·7cm (5in) lens was mounted in each wing of one of the Spitfires. This plane, the Spitfire PR.1A, could reach nearly 644km/h (400mph) when stripped of its guns and armour-plating. It was painted duck-egg blue to make it difficult to see against a sky background. Later experiments showed that the best colour for high-altitude aircraft was a Prussian blue known universally as 'PR blue' (PR = Photographic Reconnaissance). Surprisingly, pale pink was the most effective colour for camouflage when an aircraft was operating against a background of sun-lit clouds.

March 1940 saw the appearance of the Spitfire PR.1C, the first with a fuselage-mounted camera. In the late summer of that year it was thought that the Germans might be assembling an invasion fleet in the Baltic, and Cotton enlisted the help of the Chief of the Air Staff in obtaining his first specialized reconnaissance Spitfire, the PR.1D. Filling the wing leading edges with 523 litres (115 Imp gal) of fuel gave the aircraft a range of 2,815km (1,750 miles) and the PR.1D, nicknamed 'the Bowser' because it was considered to be a flying petrol tanker, made its first sortie at the end of October.

Cotton's approximate opposite number in the *Luftwaffe*, Oberstleutnant Rowehl, experimented throughout 1939 to find the best photo-reconnaissance machine. In his position as head of the German High Command's secret reconnaissance wing he tried pressurized and unarmed variants of the Junkers Ju 86 medium bomber, and the Dornier Do 217. The Ju 86P–1 and P–2 were fitted with three automatic cameras, and in the summer of 1940 a P–2 was coaxed up to 12,500m (41,000ft). The Spitfire PR.1 could reach only 9,755m (32,000ft) and was far more easily observed by the enemy.

The long-range Do 217A–Os had their fuselages extended to house two vertical cameras, and the *Luftwaffe* thus obtained excellent high-altitude photographs of every important RAF airfield and British city. By

Type: Royal Aircraft Factory B.E.2c
Engines: One 90hp RAF 1a
Armament: One or more machine guns, up to 100kg (220lb) of bombs
Maximum speed: 116km/h (72mph)
Climb: 66m/min (218ft/min)
Ceiling: 3,048m (10,000ft)
Range: about 370km (230 miles)
Weight: 972kg (2,143lb)
Span: 11·28m (37ft)
Length: 8·31 (27ft 3in)
Height: 3·40m (11ft 2in)

the end of 1940 these aircraft were operating over the Soviet Union in preparation for Operation Barbarossa, the invasion of Russia.

Designers did not strive for higher cruise altitudes merely because fighters would then have to climb further to make an interception. At altitudes between 8,230 and 12,190m (27,000 and 40,000ft), depending on humidity and temperature, the water vapour in the exhaust from an aero engine will condense to form a visible trail. There is little point in painting an aircraft to merge with its background if it is producing a vapour trail, so machines which could cruise undetected in the stratosphere were continually being sought. There was also the added advantage that any fighter climbing to intercept such an aircraft would itself make a vapour trail, giving warning of its approach.

Morale in the *Luftwaffe* declined as interpreters were transferred to other posts and venerable aircraft were not replaced. Planners concentrated on a range of exotic but unsuccessful designs, although one specialized reconnaissance type – the Arado Ar 234 could have had a decisive impact if it had been deployed earlier during the war. Its range and ceiling were modest, but two turbojets gave it a top speed of more than 740km/h (460mph).

The Soviet Union had used aerial reconnaissance to good effect during World War I, with the Sikorsky Ilya Mourometz carrying two observation officers on sorties up to 240km (150 miles) behind the German lines. Photo-reconnaissance missions were later carried out during the Russo-Finnish war, but at the time of the German invasion in 1941 fewer than one Russian aircraft in 20 was equipped for such work. The force was soon built up, however, with modified Lavochkin and Yakovlev fighters being employed on short-range army-support missions and converted bombers being used on strategic sorties.

The United States made extensive use of bombers for reconnaissance, including the Boeing B–17 (as the F–9), Consolidated B–24 (F–7 and US Navy PB4Y), Boeing B–29 (F–13) and Douglas A–20 (F–3). Maritime-patrol types also carried out surveillance missions, and more than 1,000 Lockheed P–38 Lightnings were modified specifically for reconnaissance. The most important Japanese aircraft in this category was the Mitsubishi Ki–46, a twin-engined type with a top speed of 600km/h (375mph), allowing the defensive armament to be dispensed with until Allied fighters could match its performance. Converted bombers such as the Mitsubishi G4M1 were also employed in this role after being replaced by more modern designs in their primary capacity.

The Royal Air Force's PDU, renamed Photographic Reconnaissance Unit (PRU) in July 1940, continued to operate Spitfires, but other types were used in different theatres. In November an American-built Martin Maryland operating from Malta plotted the position of 5 Italian Navy battleships, 14 cruisers and 27 destroyers in Taranto harbour. The Fleet Air Arm was able to disable half the Italian battle fleet with only 11 torpedoes, making this one of the most graphic

demonstrations of the value of reconnaissance in warfare. Hawker Hurricanes and Bristol Beaufighters also served as recce aircraft in the Middle East.

In the spring of 1941 the first Spitfire PR.IVs were delivered. These were production 'Bowsers', having the fuselage of the Mk V fighter, special wings and a Merlin 45 engine. The leading edges held 605 litres (133 Imp gal) of fuel, giving a range of 2,900km (1,800 miles), and cameras were fitted in the wings and fuselage. The reconnaissance units were always pressing for greater range, and the first production de Havilland Mosquito to leave the line in 1941 was a recce variant. With a range of more than 3,200km (2,000 miles) and a top speed exceeding 612km/h (380mph), the Mosquito was exactly what the Air Force needed.

The Allies had good cause to thank the reconnaissance crews for their work during the war. The discovery of German radar installations, the V1 and V2 revenge weapons and many other objectives of strategic importance depended on fast and accurate reconnaissance work. Specialist targets such as the dams which supplied water to the Ruhr could not have been attacked successfully without an excellent knowledge of their defences, and the necessary information was supplied to a large extent by the reconnaissance crews.

A new kind of war in Korea

With the end of hostilities, however, the intricate wartime reconnaissance network began to disintegrate, just as it had in 1919. The United States Air Force (USAF) toyed with specialized aircraft such as the twin-boom Hughes XF–11, but strategic reconnaissance remained the responsibility of converted – and still armed – bombers such as the Con-

vair RB–36 and Boeing RB–47. The RB–47, with up to seven cameras in its bomb bay, could photograph 2·6 million square km (1 million square miles) in a single three-hour flight. When the Korean War broke out in 1950 the USAF found itself with jet reconnaissance aircraft in the form of modified fighters, but the cameras left over from World War II were designed for slower operating speeds and could not perform adequately. Also, the North Koreans and Chinese moved by night, and the standard of night photography was not good. A rapid re-equipment programme was needed.

Soon after the end of World War II the US Army carried out experiments with captured A4 (V2) ballistic rockets, one of which was fitted with a 35mm film camera. These tentative beginnings led to what is now probably the most advanced field of 'aerial' observation – reconnaissance satellites.

The U–2

At the July 1955 summit conference President Eisenhower proposed an 'Open Skies' policy as a means of defuzing international tension. The United States and Russia would, under this plan, allow each other to carry out unrestricted reconnaissance flights over their territory. Marshal Bulganin rejected the proposal, but in the previous December the USAF had already given the go-ahead for an aircraft suitable for high-level surveillance missions. This was the Lockheed U–2, designed by Kelly Johnson and built virtually by hand at the company's secret 'Skunk Works' in Burbank. The U stood for 'Utility', one of the many steps taken to disguise the real purpose of the aircraft. The first U–2 made its maiden flight in August 1955, and the later U–2B, with its glider-like wings and lightweight construction, could cruise at well

FAR LEFT ABOVE: *The giant Convair B–36J was powered by four turbojets as well as six Wasp Major piston engines.*

FAR LEFT BELOW: *The twin-engined Mitsubishi Ki–46 was the most important land-based Japanese reconnaissance aircraft of World War II.*

LEFT: *The Russian Tupolev Tu–20 Bear is a typical example of a former strategic bomber finding a new lease of life in the recce role. A McDonnell Douglas Phantom acts as escort.*

BELOW: *The Boeing B–17 Flying Fortress – this example is a B–17F – is remembered mainly as a bomber but was also used, as the F–9, for long-range reconnaissance.*

BOTTOM: *The Dornier Do 217 medium bomber was one of the Luftwaffe's major reconnaissance types in the early part of World War II. A Do 217E is illustrated.*

RIGHT: *The Grumman OV–1 Mohawk was used extensively by the United States Army in Vietnam. It can carry pods housing Infra-Red (IR) sensors or Sideways-Looking Airborne Radar (SLAR), or both, to map large areas of enemy-held countryside. Moving-Target Indication (MTI) allows mobile targets to be picked out from the background on the radar.*

FAR RIGHT: *The McDonnell RF–101 Voodoo was a reconnaissance version of the normal fighter, with the cameras housed in the distinctive chisel-shaped nose. RF–101s were heavily involved in surveillance of Cuba during the 1962 crisis, making low-level runs over the island to detect missile sites and other military installations.*

over 21,335m (70,000ft) for more than 6,435-km (4,000 miles).

In April 1960 a set of U–2 prints revealed what looked like the first Russian ICBM (Intercontinental Ballistic Missile) installation. A U–2 was accordingly ferried from Incirlik Air Force Base in Turkey to Peshawar in Pakistan, ready for a long-range overflight covering about 4,700km (2,900 miles) of the Soviet Union. At 1100hr the aircraft, flown by Gary Powers, was knocked into a spin by the explosion of a surface-to-air missile detonated by a proximity fuze. Powers bailed out and was captured by the Russians. At his trial, it was revealed that the U–2 carried equipment capable of taking 4,000 pairs of photographs covering a strip 160km to 200km (100 miles to 125 miles) wide and 3,540km (2,200 miles) long.

High- and low-level reconnaissance

The news that a U–2 had been knocked down by a missile while flying at 20,725m (68,000ft) came as a blow to Britain as well as to the United States. The RAF was only just introducing its English Electric Canberra PR.9, which had a broad-chord centre section to the lengthened wing and uprated Avon engines, allowing it to cruise at 18,285-m (60,000ft). The USAF later exploited the Canberra even further, in the form of the license-built RB–57F with a wingspan of 37·2-m (122ft). Its range was reported to be 6,435-km (4,000 miles) and its cruising altitude 30,480m (100,000ft).

The RAF had developed the art of low-level high-speed photography in Palestine and Malaya from 1950. Canberra PR.3s and PR.7s replaced the venerable Mosquitoes, but the unarmed Supermarine Swift PR.6, which was to have taken over from the Gloster Meteor PR.10, was cancelled.

Russia, like Britain and the United States, continued to use converted bombers for high-level reconnaissance. Tupolev Tu–20 Bears, Myasischev Mya–4 Bisons and Tupolev Tu–16 Badgers became familiar sights to Western fighter pilots sent up to escort them away from their airspace.

Cuban Crisis

U–2s did not fade from the scene after the Powers incident. In August 1962 a U–2 from Laughlin Air Force Base at Del Rio in Texas discovered that Russian surface-to-air missiles were being installed in Cuba. Overflights were stepped up, and the presence of Soviet SS–4 Sandal intermediate-range ballistic missiles, which could be fitted with nuclear warheads, was detected. So began the Cu-ban crisis. Aerial reconnaissance really came into its own, with Strategic Air Command Boeing B–47s and B–52s spotting the movements of ships in the western Atlantic, carrier-based Vought RF–8A Crusaders of the US Navy making low-level runs over the island, USAF McDonnell RF–101 Voodoos carrying out similar missions and the U–2s continuing surveillance from on high. On 27 October one of the U–2s was shot down by a surface-to-air missile, and the situation became very grave. The next day, however, the Russians agreed to dismantle the SS–4 sites and low-level operations by RF–101s confirmed that their word was being kept.

Capability extended by new sensors

By the mid-1960s the United States was heavily engaged in the war in Vietnam. Reconnaissance was no longer based on aircraft making high-speed dashes at low level or cruising at high altitude, out of reach of enemy intercepters or missiles. Missions of this type were still very important, but the aircraft had become just one part of a complicated surveillance network.

The normal complement of optical cameras had now been joined by infra-red sensors capable of detecting minute heat differences. Images recorded on film allowed interpreters to say whether a particular aircraft parked on the apron of an enemy air base had just returned from a mission, whether it had recently emerged from its hangar and was being prepared for a sortie, or if it had been standing outside all day and was therefore probably either a dummy or unserviceable. All this could be derived by noting different heat patterns – hot engines showed up a different colour, and an aircraft newly emerged from a cool hangar would also stand out against the warmer background of the aerodrome's tarmac.

Infra-red sensors could also be made to produce an image like a television picture. Such Forward-Looking Infra-Red (FLIR) equipment allowed lorries to be spotted at night by their warm engines, or ships could be detected because of the warm wake which remained visible for hours afterwards. Radar could produce maps at night when optical cameras could not be used without dropping flares and announcing the presence of a reconnaissance aircraft. At dawn and dusk Low-Light-Level Television (LLLTV) came into its own, and image-intensifiers allowed objectives to be found in almost total darkness. Also in use are air-delivered sensors such as Acoustic and Seismic Intrusion Detection and Commandable Microphone.

Vietnam War

Powered aircraft developed from sailplanes were used to gather intelligence at low altitude over the jungle without being heard, and special listening probes derived from naval sonobuoys could be dropped to listen for enemy movements. Men were increasingly removed from the danger areas completely, with pilotless drones carrying out missions over heavily defended areas. These drones, which came to be known as Remotely Piloted Vehicles (RPVs), could bring back a record of their flight, or even relay it directly to ground controllers while still in mid-air.

Modified fighters and bombers such as the RF–101 Voodoo and B–57G of the USAF, alongside the Navy's North American RA–5C Vigilante, were joined by types developed specifically for the war in Vietnam. The Rockwell OV–10 Bronco, powered by a pair of turboprops, met the Light Armed Reconnaissance Aircraft (LARA) specification, while the larger Grumman OV–1 Mohawk could be fitted with radar or infra-red pods, or both, to map large areas of enemy-held countryside. The little Cessna O–1 Bird Dog, carrying a Forward Air Controller (FAC) for spotting potential targets, was joined by the Cessna O–2 with more advanced sensors and greater capability. Light-armed helicopters also played their part, finding targets to be attacked by other helicopters or fixed-wing aircraft.

SR–71 Blackbird

After the United States ended its bombing of North Vietnam in January 1973, only two reconnaissance types were permitted to continue overflights. One of these was the Teledyne Ryan AQM–34L remotely piloted vehicle and the other was the Lockheed SR–71 Blackbird. The Blackbird is a remarkable vehicle – the ultimate in a search for ever higher and faster reconnaissance aircraft. Built mainly of titanium, and designed by the same 'Skunk Works' which was responsible for the U–2, the SR–71 can cruise at more than Mach 3 (three times the speed of sound) at a height of 24,400m (80,000ft) or more. In September 1974 one flew from New York to London in less than two hours, at an average speed of more than 2,900km/h (1,800mph). Maximum range at this sort of speed is some 4,825km (3,000 miles). The Blackbird's cameras, radars and infra-red sensors can map 155,000 square km (60,000 square miles) in an hour, and its missions have included keeping an eye on trouble spots in other parts of the world, such as the Middle East, as well as in Vietnam.

A Saab SF37 Viggen photo-reconnaissance aircraft. Note pods under wings.

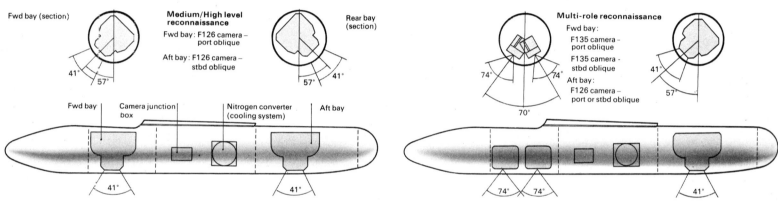

Reconnaissance Pods

Modern reconnaissance aircraft can contain any combination of sensors selected from optical cameras, including those used at night in conjunction with some form of illumination; infra-red; ultra-violet; radar; or television. Specialized reconnaissance types generally carry their surveillance equipment internally, for example in a lengthened nose, but many multi-role aircraft are fitted with one or more pods containing the sensors. There are arguments in favour of and against both methods; probably the biggest disadvantage of pod-mounting is that it reduces the space available for weapons or external fuel tanks.

An example of an advanced reconnaissance pod is that developed by EMI for the Royal Air Force's Phantoms. The streamlined pod, 7·32m (24ft) long, contains two forward-looking cameras, infra-red linescan equipment, two night cameras, four oblique cameras and a Sideways-Looking Reconnaissance Radar (SLRR). The full fan of cameras gives horizon-to-horizon coverage, and exposure rate can be set at 4, 6, 8, or 12 frames per second; one of the last two values is normally chosen, depending on the operational height. Exposures are controlled automatically.

The infra-red linescan uses heat-sensitive detectors to pick out objects on the ground. A typical detector material is cadmium mercury telluride, which operates in the band of wavelengths between 8 and 14 microns (a micron is a millionth of a metre). These wavelengths are slightly longer than those of visible light but are much shorter than radio or radar. When the sensors are cooled, for example by being bathed in liquid nitrogen at only 77°C above absolute zero, they can pick up radiation from objects hotter than themselves. This is recorded on film, the image being made up of lines from each of many detectors which are scanned by rotating mirrors – hence the word linescan. Hot objects, such as human bodies, jet engines or gun barrels, appear darker than their surroundings. This allows interpreters to work out, for example, whether a particular parked aircraft has just returned from a mission or whether it has been standing idle all day. The coverage given by the linescan equipment extends over an area equivalent to about three times the height of the aircraft in each direction.

The radar gives a coverage of some 8km (5 miles) at low level and twice that distance from a height of 1,830m (6,000ft), with a consequent reduction in picture quality. The images are recorded on film rather than being shown on a cockpit display.

Accurate low-level reconnaissance depends on good navigation, because only a single run can be made over the target. The run in to the objective, at 835km/h (450kt) or more at a height of 75m (250ft) or less, begins at an Initial Point (IP) between 60 seconds and 90 seconds from the target. Once the target has been photographed the aircraft moves on to the next objective or returns to base, where technicians retrieve the film – including that from the infra-red linescan and radar – and take it to the Reconnaissance Interpretation Centre (RIC) for processing and examination. Some types of pod carry on-board processing equipment to save time. Up to 230m (750 ft) of film may have to be dealt with, and the first strips are ready about 90 seconds after they enter the RIC. They are examined by the aircraft crew and Photographic Interpreters (PIs) for points of interest and an immediate report is then made.

The exacting requirements demanded of modern reconnaissance cameras are demonstrated by the constraints imposed on the pod intended for the Panavia Tornado multi-role combat aircraft. The maximum allowable diameter is 60 cm (24in), but this cramped space is sufficient for a forward-facing camera, a long-range oblique camera, a fan of three for low-level operations and infra-red linescan. The forward-facing unit provides 40° coverage across the line of flight and is adjustable in depression angle between 15° and 20°. The film capacity must be sufficient to allow a search to be made along a 41-km (29-mile) line from a height of 60m (200ft), with a 60 per cent overlap on the area covered by successive frames. This assumes a velocity/height (V/H) ratio of 5, which equates to a speed of Mach 0·9 at that height.

The long-range oblique camera has an even more demanding role. It must be able to resolve objects only 2m (6·5ft) across at a range of 40km (25 miles) from a height of 15,250m (50,000ft). At a height of 900m (3,000ft) it is required to pick out objects 30cm (1ft) in diameter at a distance of 8km (5 miles). Film capacity must be sufficient for 322km (200 miles) at low level with 60 per cent forward overlap. All cameras have data recorders for latitude, longitude, height, roll angle, heading and time.

The requirements of high-level strategic reconnaissance are just as exacting, and the USAF's Lockheed SR–71 Blackbird can photograph 259,000km^2 (100,000 square miles) in an hour.

BELOW: *Kelly Johnson's Lockheed U–2, built at the famous Skunk Works, is one of the most famous of all surveillance aircraft. Gary Powers was shot down while flying a U–2.*

BOTTOM: *The English Electric (now BAC) Canberra was one of the most successful bombers of the 1950s and is still used extensively for reconnaissance throughout the world.*

TOP RIGHT: *The Lockheed SR–71A Blackbird can cruise at Mach 3, its sensors scanning 155,000km² (60,000 square miles) an hour from a height of 24,400m (80,000ft).*

Some modern reconnaissance aircraft

For tactical reconnaissance the USAF has the McDonnell Douglas RF–4C Phantom, which has replaced the RF–101 Voodoo. The radar and cameras are housed in an extended nose, making the aircraft 82cm (33in) longer than the Phantoms used as fighter-bombers. More than 500 have been built, and the rear-seat operator is responsible for the sideways-looking radar, infra-red sensor and forward- and sideways-looking cameras. Until recently the Royal Air Force has also used Phantoms for reconnaissance, but it chose to develop a pod-mounted selection of sensors instead of installing its equipment directly in the aircraft. There are many arguments both for and against pod mountings, and neither method has a clear-cut advantage. The responsibility for tactical reconnaissance in the RAF has now been transferred to the Anglo-French SEPECAT Jaguar, which also carries its equipment in a pod.

Sweden has developed specialized variants of its Saab Viggen (Thunderbolt) fighter-bomber, the SF37 and SH37, for reconnaissance over both water and land, and other well equipped air forces also use modified fighters for reconnaissance such as the French Dassault Mirage and the American Northrop F–5.

Soviet reconnaissance

If the Blackbird is the pride of the USAF reconnaissance fleet, then the Soviet Union can fairly claim to have a counterpart in the Mikoyan MiG–25 Foxbat B. This variant of the Foxbat A intercepter can cruise for a short time at about Mach 3·2 and has a service ceiling of about 24,400m (80,000ft) – almost exactly the same as the figures for the SR–71. The Foxbat's range is appreciably shorter, but is sufficient for overflights of Iran and Israel to have been made as a matter of routine. The reconnaissance MiG–25 has five cameras as well as mapping radars.

The Soviet Air Force's tactical reconnaissance is based on the Mikoyan MiG–21R and RF versions of this widely deployed fighter-bomber. A pod mounted under the centre of the fuselage carries infra-red sensors and oblique or forward-facing cameras. Yakovlev Yak–28s are also used for recce work, and the Cub C variant of the Antonov An–12 transport carries pods for electronic intelligence purposes.

Electronic intelligence-gathering

The prefix 'E' (for 'Electronic') is becoming ever more important in the reconnaissance business. 'E' aircraft are used for Elint (gathering *el*ectronic *int*elligence), which involves listening to the radar and radio transmissions of a potential enemy in order to build up a 'library' of information so that appropriate Electronic Countermeasures (ECM) can be developed to jam those transmissions, which are the eyes and ears of any modern battle commander.

Future trends

So what of the future? Perhaps the two most significant areas of development are RPVs and Airborne Warning And Control System (AWACS). A typical example of the strides being made in automatic reconnaissance is the Boeing Compass Cope project. Scheduled to enter service in about 1980, this RPV will be capable of cruising literally all day at an altitude of about 21,335m (70,000ft), with up to 907kg (2,000lb) of sensors continuously scanning the world beneath. The Boeing E-3A AWACS is a modified 707 airliner carrying a gigantic saucer-shaped radome on its back. Its crew of specialists can analyze and interpret the movements of both enemy and friendly aircraft over half of Europe at any one time, and instructions can then be sent out to ground commanders and to intercepters. The US Navy has a similar aircraft in the carrier-based Grumman E-2C Hawkeye, and Russia operates the Tupolev Tu-126 Moss, which closely resembles AWACS but which is not as advanced.

ABOVE CENTRE: *The Rockwell OV-10A Bronco has large windows for good visibility.*
ABOVE: *A Lockheed DC-130A Hercules mother aircraft carrying Ryan Model 154 drones.*

ABOVE RIGHT: *The Boeing E-3A AWACS (Airborne Warning And Control System) is dominated by the rotodome containing the revolving aerial of its very powerful search radar.*

BELOW: *The two-seat Breguet Br.19 replaced the highly successful Br.14 and was itself an outstanding French two-seat bomber. More than 1,000 were built in France alone, and some were still in service in 1940.*

RIGHT: *The de Havilland D.H.4 was the first British aircraft designed from scratch as a daylight bomber, being able to outfly most of its adversaries. More than 6,000 were built in all, most in the United States.*

Bombers

The use of fixed-wing aircraft for bombing dates from 1 November 1911, when a Rumpler Taube of the Italian Army's aviation service dropped bombs on North African townships during Italy's dispute with Turkey about control of Libya. Specialist bombers thus predated fighters by some three years, and by the outbreak of World War I several countries, including France, Russia and Italy, had developed suitable aircraft for this role. The first bombing raid of the war was carried out on 14 August 1914, when Voisins of France's *Aviation Militaire* attacked the Zeppelin hangars at Metz-Frascaty. In the following month the Voisin force was reorganized specifically to carry out bombing missions, and some 600 of the type were eventually built for the *Aviation Militaire*. In addition to service with the French throughout the war, Voisins were also bought by Britain and Italy and later constructed under licence.

French bombers in World War I

Voisins were used for strategic daylight bombing during the first year of the war, before being relegated to night operations when results did not meet expectations. This pattern was to be repeated many times until the appearance of the Breguet 14, which could hold its own on daylight missions. A major reason for the success of Voisin's pusher biplanes was the use of a steel airframe which could carry increasingly powerful engines. The Voisin 1, which entered service in early 1914, was powered by a 70hp Gnôme rotary. By late 1915, however, the Voisin 5 had a 150hp air-cooled radial engine. This gave a maximum speed of 105km/h (65mph), a ceiling of 3,500m (11,500ft) and an endurance of 3½hr. Three hundred and fifty Voisin 5s were built.

French bombers had consistently proved to be too slow and ill armed for daylight operations until the appearance of the Breguet 14, the initial reconnaissance version of which was followed by the bomber variant. It served with the French forces on day and night missions throughout the last year of the

war, and it equipped the first day bombing squadron of the American Expeditionary Force from June 1918. With the introduction of the Breguet 14 the bomber crews became the elite, and morale soared. On 4 June 1918 a force of Breguet 14s dropped 7,200 bombs on German troops massing for an attack, virtually wiping them out.

Extensive use was made of aluminium alloy, resulting in a light but strong structure, and the 300hp water-cooled Renault engine gave a top speed of 177km/h (110mph). The aircraft could carry 32 bombs of 8kg (17lb) each on racks protruding from the leading edge of the lower wing, and it had a maximum endurance of 2¾hr. More than 8,000 had been built when production ended in 1926.

Britain also began strategic bombing in August 1914, when the Royal Flying Corps attacked the airship sheds at Düsseldorf, Cologne and Friedrichshafen. The major emphasis throughout 1915 and 1916 was on tactical operations, but in the spring of 1916 the Royal Naval Air Service formed a strategic-bomber force comprising Sopwith 1½-Strutters for daylight operations and Short Bombers and Caudron G.4s for night missions. They attacked production centres such as the Mauser works, German naval forces, railway nerve centres and the airfields from which Gothas were operating on their bombing raids over Britain. These types were later superseded by Handley Page 0/100s and de Havilland D.H.4s.

The D.H.4, much maligned both at the time and since, was nevertheless a fine aeroplane. It entered service early in 1917 as the first British aircraft designed from the outset for high-speed bombing in daylight, and it was sufficiently manoeuvrable and powerful to out-fly or out-climb enemy fighters, allowing it to be operated without an escort. With a Rolls-Royce Eagle III water-cooled Vee engine of 250hp installed, it could achieve a top speed of 188km/h (117mph) and reach a ceiling of 4,875m (16,000ft). A variety of other powerplants were fitted, however, including the 375hp Eagle VIII, which gave a top speed of 230km/h (143mph) and allowed the D.H.4 to show a clean pair of heels to virtually any fighter. The maximum bomb

load was only 210kg (460lb), but endurance was a reasonable 3½hr. Nearly 1,500 of the type were built in Britain, plus almost 5,000 in the United States. The latter had Liberty engines and two forward-firing Marlin guns, and more than 1,800 of them saw service with US bombing units in Europe.

In the spring of 1917 the RFC chose the F.E.2b as its standard medium night bomber, and in October of that year Major-General Trenchard formed the strategic-bomber wing operating F.E.2bs, D.H.4s and Handley Page 0/100s. This was later enlarged, and in June 1918 it became the Independent Force. The 0/400, developed from the 0/100, had entered service in the spring of 1918 as a day bomber based in France. It was transferred to night operations in the autumn, and by the end of the war some 250 were on strength.

0/400 and V/1500

The 0/400 was powered by a pair of Rolls-Royce Eagle VIII engines, delivering 360hp and conferring a top speed of nearly 160km/h (100mph). By then, heavy bombers were beginning to approach the size which came to characterize aircraft used for this role – the 0/400 was 19·2m (63ft) long, had a span of 30·5m (100ft), was 7·7m (22ft) high and had a maximum take-off weight of 6,033kg (13,300lb). Endurance was 8hr. The 0/400's successor, the V/1500, was designed as the first British strategic bomber, but it was just too late to see action during the war. It was intended to bomb Berlin from bases in East Anglia, carrying a 450kg (1,000lb) weapon load. It could transport up to 3,400kg (7,500-lb) over a short distance, and the normal load was to be up to 30 bombs weighing 113kg (250 lb) each or two of the new 1,500kg (3,300lb) weapons. At the beginning of World War I the standard bomb size had been 10kg (20lb), so this was an area which saw great strides during the four years of the conflict.

The V/1500 was the biggest British bomber yet: 18·9m (62ft) long, 38·4m (126ft) across the wings and 7m (23ft) high. Its maximum take-off weight was 13,600kg (30,000lb) – more than twice that of the 0/400 – and endurance was 6hr. The four uprated Eagle

BELOW: *The Voisin was the most widely used French bomber in the first two years of World War I, and more than 2,000 were built in all. The type had a steel airframe to which increasingly powerful engines could be attached, but the pusher arrangement fell from favour when fighters evolved and could move in unopposed from the rear. Voisins were sturdy and dependable, however, and the gunner/bomb-aimer had an excellent view from his front cockpit.*

VIII engines of 375hp each gave a maximum speed of 145km/h (90mph) and up to six Lewis guns, including one in the tail, were carried for self-defence. The Vickers Vimy was a contemporary of the Handley Page bomber, being designed to attack Berlin from bases in France, but it likewise failed to see war service and became best known for its use on pioneering and record-breaking flights such as Alcock and Brown's crossing of the Atlantic and Ross and Keith Smith's race to Australia, both in 1919. Large numbers of D.H.9s and B.E.8s were also used during the war, but not so effectively.

German airships and giant aircraft

The Imperial German Military Aviation Service had in September 1914 formed a strategic bombing force to attack England from Belgium, but the 100hp two-seaters with which it was equipped proved to be unsuitable for sustained overwater operations. They carried out the first large-scale night attack, against Dunkirk in January 1915, but after they were transferred to the Eastern Front during that spring the responsibility for attacks on Britain fell even more heavily on the shoulders of the airship crews. In the early part of the war both Germany and Austro-Hungary relied heavily on Zeppelins and other airships as their main bombing vehicles, and the German Naval Air Service continued with lighter-than-air operations when the military arm turned to aircraft.

When Germany began daylight raids with aircraft in early 1917, the RFC and RNAS were forced to pull back aircraft from the front for use on home-defence duties. One of the mainstays of the long-range bomber fleet was the Gotha series. The G V, which took over from the G IV as a night bomber in August 1914, could carry 300kg (660lb) of weapons across the English Channel, representing about half its total load. The two Mercedes water-cooled in-line engines of 260hp each gave a maximum speed of 140km/h (87mph). The G V's ceiling was 6,400m (21,000ft) and its range 840km (520 miles). About 230 of the earlier G IV model were built, but there were far fewer G Vs.

The main force of Gothas and AEG bombers was backed up by smaller numbers of Friedrichshafen and Zeppelin types. The Friedrichshafen G III, which was used mainly as a night bomber against French and Belgian targets as well as in the offensive against Britain, had the same engines as the Gothas and virtually identical take-off weight – 4,000kg (8,800lb) – and speed. Ceiling was 4,570m (15,000ft) and endurance 5hr. The G III appeared in early 1917, and more than 300 were eventually built. Its normal bomb load was 500kg (1,100lb), of which one-fifth could be carried internally, and the three-man crew was provided with one or two Parabellum machine guns in the front and rear cockpits for self-defence.

The giant Zeppelin Staaken R VI had double the engine power of the Gothas and Friedrichshafens, allowing a bomb load of 2,000kg (4,400lb) to be carried over a short range. Endurance could be as much as 10hr with smaller payloads. The R VI's wings spanned 42·2m (138ft 6in), the fuselage was 22·1m (72ft 6in) long and maximum take-off weight was 11,790kg (26,000lb). The type bombed France and Britain from September 1917, but it was the only one of the Zeppelin R series to enter production and a mere 18 were built.

Use of bombers by other air arms

The Imperial Russian Air Service had the distinction of operating the first four-engined bomber in the world, the Sikorsky Ilya Mourometz. The type equipped a specialist bomber group which began offensive operations from a Polish base in February 1915. Although fewer than 80 were built, they had a significant impact. Many different engines were tried, the Type V being equipped with Sunbeam water-cooled models producing 150hp each, and the low top speed of only 120km/h (75mph) was offset by the use of extremely effective Russian-designed bomb sights and formidable defensive armament. Up to seven machine guns could be fitted, and the only Ilya Mourometz to be shot down in air combat accounted for three enemy fighters before succumbing.

When Italy joined the war in May 1915 it already had a bomber force in the shape of Caproni Ca 2s. They were sufficiently reliable for missions over rugged country, and operations against Austro-Hungary began on 15 August 1915. Austro-Hungary retaliated with standard reconnaissance two-seaters manufactured by the Lloyd and Lohner concerns. Their missions include a daylight raid on Milan in February 1916. Gothas were later introduced.

Between the wars

In the years from 1919 to 1939, bombers progressed from fabric-covered wooden biplanes to all-metal monoplanes. The Junkers D.1, which first flew in 1916, had many of the features that did not become standard until the 1930s – all-metal construction, cantilever-monoplane layout – but few were built because of production difficulties. Post-war cuts in defence spending and the lack of an official re-equipment policy meant that innovation was generally kept to a minimum and well established layouts were retained.

French bombers

France ended World War I with more military aircraft than any other state, and despite post-war cutbacks the *Aviation Militaire* retained nearly 40 bomber squadrons equipped with the Breguet 14, 16 and later the 19. The two-seat Br.19 light bomber, which replaced the Br.14, had a fabric-covered metal framework. One of the most successful metal biplanes, it entered service in 1925 and was still operation in small numbers 15 years later. A variety of powerplants with outputs of up to 550hp gave a top speed of about 230km/h (143mph) and a range of 800km (497 miles). Up to 440kg (970lb) of bombs could be carried, and four machine guns were fitted for offensive use as well as self-defence. Some 1,100 were built in France and the type was widely constructed under license.

The duralumin Lioré et Olivier LeO.20 three-seat twin-engined night bomber was widely deployed with French squadrons during 1927–37, rivalling the Farman F.160 to F.168 series. The three-seat single-engined Amiot 122 BP3 bomber/escort biplane, also constructed from light alloy, served during 1928–35 and could carry as great a load as the much larger twins. One of the earliest stressed-skin bombers was the Amiot 143, a twin-engined high-wing monoplane. The Bloch 210, developed from the Model 200 five-seat night bomber introduced in 1934, was used in support of Republican forces during the Spanish Civil War as was one Bloch 200. Other bombers were the Farman 60, 63 and 221, and the LeO 206.

Developments in Italy and Germany

Italy reduced its military strength after World War I but set up an independent air service in 1923. Single-engined Caproni Ca 73s replaced multi-engined bombers and the later Ca 101 and 111 high-wing monoplanes were among types used in Ethiopia. Smaller European countries such as Czechoslovakia and Holland were also active in bomber development. The Czech Aero A 11, which entered service in 1923, was produced in many variants. It carried a crew of two at 215km/h (133mph) over 750km (466 miles),

Type: Breguet 14 A2
Engines: One 300hp Renault
Armament: Three 7·7mm (0·303in) machine guns,
    32 bombs of 8kg (17·6lb) or 10kg (22lb)
Maximum speed: 184km/h (296mph)
Climb: 260m/min (792ft/min)
Ceiling: 6,100m (20,000ft)
Range: 700km (435 miles)
Loaded weight: 1,310kg (2,888lb)
Span: 14·91m (48ft 11·5in)
Length: 8·87m (29ft 1in)
Height: 3·0m (9ft 10in)

Type: Handley Page 0/400
Engines: Two 360hp Rolls Royce Eagle VIIIs
Armament: Three 7·7mm (0·303in) Lewis guns, eight
    113kg (250lb) bombs or 16 51kg (112lb) bombs
Ceiling: 2,591m (8,500ft)
Range: 1,046km (650 miles)
Loaded weight: 6,350kg (14,000lb)
Span: 30·48m (100ft)
Length: 19·16m (62ft 10in)
Height: 6·70m (21ft 11.75in)

BELOW: *The fast and manoeuvrable Hawker Hart was the Royal Air Force's standard light bomber in the first half of the 1930s.*
BELOW CENTRE: *The Vickers Virginia, a conventional wooden biplane, was the RAF's main heavy night bomber for 13 years from 1924. The engines were a pair of Napier Lions.*

BOTTOM LEFT: *The de Havilland D.H.9 was used extensively in World War I and survived into the 1920s, being replaced by the Wapiti.*
BOTTOM RIGHT: *Dornier's Do 17, originally designed as an airliner, joined the Luftwaffe in 1937 and became, along with the Heinkel He 111, one of the mainstays of the bomber force.*

although its bomb load was only 50kg (110-lb). More than 400 of the later Letov S–238 were built, and a number captured by the Germans were transferred to the Bulgarian and Slovak air forces, the latter using them during the invasion of Poland and Russia. In Holland, Fokker produced types such as the C.V series, which served from the mid-1920s until the late 1930s. A light bomber and reconnaissance aircraft, it was very reliable and easy to fly. The type was designed to accept a variety of wings and powerplants for different roles, and it was bought by a dozen countries as well as being built under licence.

In Germany, the aircraft industry re-established itself after World War I and the Dornier Do 23, developed from the Do F mail and freight transport of the late 1920s, was the first medium bomber to equip the newly formed *Luftwaffe*. The very advanced Heinkel He 70, which made its maiden flight in December 1932, was designed and built in just over six months but the twin-engined Do 17 was preferred for long-range duties. The *Luftwaffe* used the Spanish Civil War to test its equipment and techniques, discovering for example that the defensive armament of the Ju 86 was inadequate when faced by modern fighters. Also used as a bomber in that conflict was the Ju 52/3m 'Iron Annie', later to become famous as a transport.

Advances in Britain

In Britain, the Royal Air Force had been formed as the first independent air arm in Europe by merging the RFC and RNAS. It was assumed by the British Government that no major war would break out for at least ten years, so the RAF's strength was reduced from 188 squadrons to 33, and types such as the D.H.9A, D.H.10 Amiens and Vimy continued to see action in India and the Middle East. The first post-war two-seat light day bomber was the Fairey Fawn, which served during 1923–26. It was handicapped, however, by having to conform to restrictive official specifications and its performance was inferior to that of its predecessor, the D.H.9A.

In 1917 it had been officially decreed that the standard new British aero engine would be the ABC Dragonfly, a nine-cylinder radial intended to produce 400hp. It proved to be a technical disaster, so when Richard Fairey decided to develop a light bomber as a private venture he went to the United States for the powerplant. He chose the in-line Curtiss D12, which had helped give the Curtiss seaplane its victory in the 1925 Schneider Trophy. The engine, built under licence as the Fairey Felix, gave the Fox a top speed of 250km/h (156mph) when it appeared in 1925. This was faster than most contemporary fighters, and the Fox also had the edge in manoeuvrability, but only one RAF squadron was equipped with the aircraft – fitted with Rolls-Royce Kestrels in the production version – and it was in Belgium that the type achieved its well deserved acclaim. Later variants, powered by Hispano-Suiza engines as well as Kestrels, were capable of 360km/h (225mph), and the Belgian production line turned out nearly 200 to add to the 28 built in Britain.

The RAF's elderly D.H.9A was replaced by the Westland Wapiti, using the same wing and undercarriage as its predecessor. The prototype and initial production machines had fabric covering on the wings and rear fuselage, but later variants were all-metal. The main production version was the Mk IIA, powered by a 500hp Bristol Jupiter, and 415 were built. The air-cooled Jupiter, originally a back-up for the Rolls-Royce Eagle, dominated the aero-engine world in the 1920s and was built under license in no fewer than 16 countries. In 1918 it turned out between 375 and 400hp. Later it produced more than 500hp and the Kestrel, developed from it, was capable of more than 1,000hp by 1938. The Wapiti Mk V had a lengthened fuselage and was exported to several countries as well as being built under licence in South Africa. It was developed into the Wallace, of which only about 100 were built and which served solely with Auxiliary squadrons. The Mk II version was powered by a 680hp Pegasus IV engine, and in 1933 a Wallace was one of two aircraft to make the first flight over the summit of Everest, the world's highest mountain.

The mainstay of the RAF's fleet of heavy night bombers from 1924 to 1937 was the Vickers Virginia, a conventional wooden biplane. It was powered by two 450hp Napier Lions, this engine being the other powerplant originally developed as a back-up for the Rolls-Royce Eagle. A water-cooled 'Vee', as opposed to the air-cooled Jupiter, it produced up to 1,320hp in racing form and was also used in the Handley Page Hyderabad. The Virginia Mk X, powered by 580hp Napier Lions, had a gross take-off weight of 7,983kg (17,600lb) and could carry 1,360kg (3,000lb) of bombs. It cruised at 160km/h (100mph) and carried a crew of two, using three 0·303in machine guns for self-defence. The Avro Aldershot also entered RAF service in 1924, and in the same role, but it saw only limited service because the Air Staff were opposed to single-engined heavy bombers. The Aldershot nevertheless had a respectable 900kg (2,000lb) bomb load.

One aircraft which enjoyed a reasonable production run was the Fairey III series used by the RAF, Fleet Air Arm and a number of overseas air forces. The most numerous version was the IIIF, which entered RAF service in 1927 on light bombing and general duties. The first British metal heavy bomber

was the Handley Page Hinaidi, developed from the Hyderabad. It entered service in 1929 and served until 1933, when it was replaced by the Heyford. This latter aircraft was unusual in having the fuselage attached to the upper rather than lower wing, and it also featured a rotating ventral dustbin turret which was housed inside the fuselage when not in use.

In 1928 the RAF had introduced its first medium bomber, the Boulton-Paul Sidestrand, which was sufficiently fast and manoeuvrable to be used in daylight. In 1934 it was replaced by the same manufacturer's Overstrand, the first British bomber with a power-operated nose turret. Apart from these two examples, all British day bombers were single-engined two-seaters until the monoplanes arrived in the late 1930s. The standard RAF light bomber during 1930–37 was the Hawker Hart, which has been described as 'one of the most technically and strategically significant' bombers designed in the ten years following the end of World War I. Nearly 1,000 were built, about half being used as trainers. Its top speed of 280km/h (175mph) was better than that of many fighters, and the Hart was also highly manoeuvrable. It was replaced on an interim basis from 1935–38 by the Hind, the RAF's last biplane bomber. Nearly 600 were built, and the type was widely exported. It in turn was superseded from 1937 by the Fairey Battle and Bristol Blenheim all-metal cantilever low-wing monoplanes. The Fairy Hendon of 1936 had been the first RAF twinengined cantilever monoplane, but its metal basic structure had fabric covering.

The RAF's bomber force in the 1930s also included the Vickers Vildebeest, delivered from 1932 to replace the Hawker Horsley torpedo bomber of mixed wood and metal construction. The Horsley had itself taken over from the Fairey Fawn. The Vildebeest still equipped two squadrons of Coastal Command at the outbreak of World War II. The Handley Page Harrow heavy bomber was unusual in having a mixture of fabric and metal covering, but the private-venture Vickers Wellesley was even more innovative. It was constructed on the geodetic principle developed by Dr Barnes Wallis, using a basketwork of members carrying loads in compression or tension but not bending. This was covered with an unstressed fabric skin, allowing battle damage to be repaired by replacing deformed members. The Wellesley entered service in 1937, but only 136 were built because the Wellington, using the same method of construction, was already becoming available.

Bomber aircraft of the Soviet Union

The Soviet Air Force was re-established in 1924, and Russian industry began to turn out a vast number of aircraft to equip it. About 6,000 Polikarpov R–5s were built between 1928 and the late 1930s, the type being used in the Spanish Civil War, against Japanese in Mongolia during 1938 and 1939, and in the 1939–40 Winter War with Finland. The assault version carried 500kg (1,100lb) of bombs plus seven 7·62mm machine guns. The Polikarpov U–2 was even more remark-

able, more than 20,000 being built between the late 1920s and 1952. Until the outbreak of World War II, it served on general-purpose duties but then, as the U–2VS, it was used for light bombing and close support. The U–2VS could carry 250kg (550lb) of bombs and was defended by a 7·62mm machine gun. Its operations included the defence of Stalingrad, and rocket projectiles were later carried in place of bombs.

The first Russian metal bomber was the Tupolev R–3 of 1926. A two-seat single-engined biplane, it was covered in corrugated aluminium sheeting. In the following year the TB–1 twin-engined monoplane appeared, setting the pattern for Russian bomber design until the end of the 1930s. It had a crew of six and carried 3,000kg (6,614 lb) of bombs. The Tupolev TB–3 entered service in 1932 and remained operational throughout World War II, about 800 being built. It was powered by four Hispano-Suiza engines of 730hp each. Various Hispano-Suiza V12s of outputs ranging from 600 to 1,200hp were the standard powerful engines used in Russian combat aircraft until 1941. The TB–3 followed the tradition of the Ilya Mourometz as a four-engined bomber, several years before America's Boeing B–17 came on the scene. It could carry 2,200kg (4,850lb) of bombs, some internally and some externally, was equipped with six 7·62mm machine guns for self-defence and took part in experiments with parasite fighters. The later Tupolev SB–2 entered service in 1936 and operated throughout the war as a night bomber. Production exceeded 6,000.

United States bombers

The United States Army Air Service was set up in April 1918, but with the coming of peace its money was cut by Congress and only 27 squadrons could be established instead of the planned 87. Of these 27, a mere four were assigned the bombing role and but a single squadron was equipped with the Martin MB–2. The MB–2 was a development of the MB–1, the design of which had been influenced by features of Handley Page and Caproni types built under licence during the war. The MB–1's radius of action, at 280km (175 miles), was only half that of its European contemporaries and the bombload was a paltry 455kg (1,000lb), so it was developed into the MB–2 – regarded as the United States' first indigenously designed bomber – by fitting strengthened and slightly larger wings which raised the payload to 818kg (1,800lb). The MB–2 replaced 0/400s from 1919 and remained in service until 1927.

The MB–2 was superseded by a series of

aircraft designed by Huff-Daland (later Keystone). The layout of the B–4A – followed by the B–5A and B–6A – was changed from single-engined to twin for safety reasons and to give the crew a better view and freedom of action by leaving the nose clear. This was at approximately the same time as the Avro Aldershot was failing to find favour because of its single engine. In fact the Keystone bombers offered little improvement on their predecessors.

British D.H.4s, built under licence as Boeing DH–4As, continued to operate as light bombers. More than 5,000 were built in the United States, many being converted to the improved DH–4B and 4M standards. They remained in service as bombers until 1928 and were finally retired in 1932.

From then on the pace of development began to accelerate, and the heavy bomber was transformed within the space of a decade. The Douglas Y1B–7 of 1930 (later B–7) was the first US monoplane bomber. In the following year the Boeing YB–9 made its appearance. This was an all-metal cantilever low-wing monoplane with a semi-retractable landing gear and variable-pitch propellers for its two engines. It could carry a 1,025kg (2,260lb) bombload entirely within its semi-monocoque fuselage. Only seven YB–9s were built. Although chronologically a little earlier than the B–9, the Martin B–10 has a significant place in US Army history. The use of powerful 775hp Wright R–1820–3 engines, combined with streamlining, gave the B–10B a 343km/h (213mph) top speed at 1,980m (6,500ft) – faster than most contemporary fighters. A fully retractable landing gear and enclosed cockpit were fitted, and the B–10, of which more than 150 were built (including the B–12 and B–14), became the first mass-produced US monoplane all-metal bomber. It was also the first to have a gun turret.

This series was replaced at the end of the 1930s by the Douglas B–18, developed from the DC–2 and DC–3 airliners. The switch to monoplane design in the civil field had begun with the Douglas DC–2, Boeing 247 and Lockheed Electra airliners. The B–18A could carry a maximum bombload of 2,950kg (6,500lb) and had a speed of 345km/h (215 mph). It was powered by two 1,000hp Wright R–1820–53 Cyclones, one of the new breed of air-cooled radials – alongside the Pratt & Whitney R–1830 Twin Wasp – which had been becoming increasingly dominant in US combat aircraft. The B–18 was later overshadowed by the longer-ranged and much more expensive Boeing B–17 Flying Fortress four-engined bomber, which had flown in 1934 as the Model 299 but which was not ordered until 1938.

Japan prepares for war

Across the Pacific, the country that was to bring the new generation of US bombers into action had been building up its own forces. Japan had flown against German and Austro-Hungarian forces on the coast of China during World War I and against Russian forces in Siberia from 1918 to 1921, using imported and license-built types. Japanese companies employed European designers to help build up an indigenous industry, and also asked

overseas concerns to design types for production in Japan. The Kawaski Type 87 heavy bomber, for example, was designed by Dornier and powered by a pair of 500hp BMW engines. Only 28 were built, and the Mitsubishi 2MB1 (Type 87 light bomber) did not fare much better, with production totalling 48 units. The latter aircraft, a three-bay biplane, was powered by a single Hispano-Suiza water-cooled engine of 450hp and was replaced by an adaptation of the Kawasaki Type 88 reconnaissance biplane in 1929, only two years after entering service.

Designed by Dr Richard Vogt, later of Blohm und Voss, the Type 88–II – as it was designated in the light bombing role – could carry a payload of only 200kg (440lb) and was rather slow, but it could withstand heavy punishment. More than 400 were built as light bombers, many serving in the Manchurian conflict. This campaign showed up

the deficiencies of the Japanese bombers, so the Army ordered three new aircraft in the Type 93 series: the Mitsubishi Ki–1 twin-engined heavy bomber, the Mitsubishi Ki–2 twin-engined light bomber and Kawasaki's Ki–3 single-engined light bomber. The two Mitsubishi aircraft were all-metal designs influenced by Junkers. The four-seat Ki–1 had a gross take-off weight of 8,165kg (18,000 lb) and was powered by two 940hp water-cooled Ha–2 engines. The three-seat Ki–2 grossed at 4,535kg (10,000lb) and was fitted with a pair of 450hp air-cooled Bristol Jupiters, while the two-seat fabric-covered Ki–3 – the last Japanese Army Air Force biplane bomber – was powered by a single water-cooled BMW IX engine of 800hp and had a maximum take-off weight of 3,100kg (6,834lb).

The first and third of the series were slow and unreliable, mainly because of problems with their water-cooled engines, and they were soon withdrawn from front-line service. The Ki–2 was popular, however, especially in the later Mk II version with retractable landing gear and two 550hp Ha–8 engines, and was used widely up to the outbreak of World War II. The JAAF's first really modern bomber was the Mitsubishi Ki–21 (Type 97 heavy bomber), which replaced the Ki–7. An all-metal monoplane powered by two 950hp Ha–5 engines, it had a gross weight of 9,700kg (21,400lb) and was the principal Army bomber in the Chinese and Pacific wars. More than 2,000 were built. The Ki–3 was replaced by the Kawasaki Ki–32 (Type 98 light bomber) and Mitsubishi Ki–30 (Type 97 light bomber). The former, a mid-wing monoplane powered by an 850 hp in-line Ha–9, proved unpopular with its crews because of the unreliability of its engine. The Ki–30, also a mid-wing monoplane, introduced wing trailing-edge flaps and an internal bomb-bay and was powered by a

conventional 950hp Ha–5 air-cooled radial engine. Both types, with combat ranges greater than 1,600km (1,000 miles), were widely used on strategic missions against China.

The Ki–2 was eventually replaced by the Kawasaki Ki–48 twin-engined light bomber, of which 2,000 were built. It was short on range, however, and had a small bombload. In its operations against China the Ki–21 was shown to have inadequate range and poor defensive armament and it was superseded by the Nakajima Ki–49 (Type 100). Eight hundred were built, but these aircraft proved difficult to handle and there was still no Japanese bomber capable of carrying an adequate payload.

Meanwhile the Japanese Navy had been building up its land-based forces as well as its

carrier fleet. In the early 1930s it had asked Mitsubishi to design a twin-engined biplane torpedo-bomber. The resulting G1M (Type 93) was withdrawn from service, after only a handful had been built, because of stability and engine problems. The Navy turned to the Hiro arsenal for a replacement, but the resulting G2H (Type 95) also had serious defects. Mitsubishi had developed a mid-wing twin-engined reconnaissance aircraft with retractable landing gear which first flew in May 1934, and this led to the G3M (Type 96) medium bomber. It entered service in 1937 and was used in the war against China, bombing cities from bases in Japan and Formosa. It also took part in World War II, more than 1,000 having been built by the end of 1943. The final version had two 1,200hp Kinsei engines. The G3M was replaced by the Mitsubishi G4M (Type 1), of which some 2,500 were constructed. Armour-plating was sacrificed for the sake of extra range, and self-sealing fuel tanks were not fitted – a common

failing of Japanese military aircraft at that time – so the bomber was apt to catch fire once hit by gunfire.

German bombers of World War II

Germany was undoubtedly the country which made the greatest strides in bomber design during World War II, even if many of the more ambitious proposals failed to see the light of day or appeared too late to affect the course of the war. For example, a *Luftwaffe* medium bomber such as the Dornier Do 17Z of 1939 could carry 1,000kg (2,205lb) of bombs at 360km/h (225mph) and 4,000m (13,125ft) altitude. Five years later the jet-powered Arado Ar 234B light bomber could carry 1,500kg (3,300lb) at twice the speed and height of the earlier aircraft.

The first chief of staff of the *Luftwaffe*, Lt-

Gen Wever, supported long-range strategic bombing and began the 'Ural Bomber' project in 1935. After his death in June 1936, however, he was succeeded by Gen Kesselring, who believed that the primary role of the *Luftwaffe* was tactical support of the Army. He therefore concentrated on short-range, lightly armed day bombers, and although the *Luftwaffe* had a front-line strength of 1,750 bombers in September 1939 it lost about 2,000 aircraft and 5,000 crew on daylight attacks on Britain before the force was transferred to night operations.

Germany's mainstay bombers during the Battle of Britain in the summer of 1940 were the Dornier Do 17 and Heinkel He 111. The former, originally designed as a commercial transport, was first delivered in early 1937; by the outbreak of war some 370 were operational. They were first used in the Polish campaign, later bombing convoys in the English Channel before being switched to attack RAF airfields and British cities. The Do 17Z–2, powered by a pair of 1,000hp Bramo radial engines and carrying a crew of four or five, cruised at a mere 300km/h (186mph) at an altitude of 4,000m (13,125ft) when fully laden and had a tactical radius of only 320km (200 miles) in this condition. Maximum internal bombload was 1,000kg (2,205lb), and six machine guns were fitted for self-defence. During the spring of 1941 Do 17s were used for anti-shipping operations in the eastern Mediterranean, and by the time of Operation Barbarossa, the invasion of Russia in July that year, only one unit was equipped with the type. Do 17s were later used as glider tugs and were replaced in the bombing role by Do 217s and Junkers Ju 88s (see below).

The Heinkel He 111 remained in service so long mainly because no suitable replacement could be found; production exceeded 7,300, with peak output being reached in 1939 and 1943. It was used widely in the invasions of Poland, Denmark and Norway, and in attacking Britain's Royal Navy North Sea fleet. It suffered heavy losses in the Battle of Britain, however, and by mid-1940 was being replaced by Ju 88s. Defensive armament, despite including cannon as well as machine guns, was insufficient for the unescorted missions on which the He 111 was employed. Bombload, at 2,500kg (5,500lb), was also inadequate, and the 2,050km (1,275 miles) range at 385km/h (240mph) and 5,000m (16,400ft) altitude was too short for effective strategic operations.

The He 111 continued occasional night bombing, anti-ship strikes and mine-laying, was used during Barbarossa and in the spring and summer of 1942 was employed on torpedo strikes against Arctic convoys, flying from Norwegian bases. The type was increasingly used as a transport and glider tug on the Eastern Front, and in the summer of 1944 was given the new role of air-launching V1 flying bombs. More than 1,200 of these missiles were fired from He 111s.

The Do 217, scaled up from the Do 17, had both longer range and a better bombload than its predecessor. It entered service in 1941, carrying out missions over Britain and against ships in the North Sea in the spring of 1942. From August 1943 the type attacked shipping in the Bay of Biscay and Mediterranean, using Hs 293 and Fritz–X guided bombs. More than 1,300 were operated as bombers and missile carriers, with a further 300-plus being used as night fighters and intruders. The Do 217M night bomber was powered by two Daimler-Benz engines of 1,750hp each at take-off, giving a cruise speed of 400km/h (250mph) and a range of 2,400 km (1,500 miles) on internal fuel. Bombload was 4,000kg (8,800lb), of which 2,500kg (5,500lb) was internal, and six machine guns were fitted for self-defence.

The Junkers Ju 88, of which more than

entered service, and the need for a bomber able to attack any British target from bases in France and Norway receded as the tide turned against Germany. The Heinkel He 177 Greif (Griffon) heavy bomber evolved too late and also failed to live up to its promise for a variety of reasons. The original design was very advanced, but shortage of a suitable 2,000hp powerplant meant that its designer, Siegfried Günter, was compelled to rely on the expedient of coupling two 1,000 hp Daimler-Benz engines together, using two of the units to power the He 177. They proved unreliable and were prone to overheating.

15,000 were built, was one of the outstanding aircraft of the war and operated in a wide variety of roles. In many ways it was the German equivalent of the Mosquito. The Ju 88A–4 was powered by a pair of Junkers Jumo in-line engines rated at 1,340hp each, had a normal range of 1,790km (1,110 miles) and carried 1,800kg (4,000lb) of bombs plus a combination of machine guns and cannon. A slightly larger development, the Ju 188, entered service in 1942. The two 1,775hp Jumo engines of the Ju 188A–2 version provided a maximum speed of 520km/h (325 mph).

The search for a high-altitude bomber to replace the Ju 88 and He 111 – the 'Bomber B'– lasted four years and failed to turn up an effective answer. The various proposals, such as the Ju 288, Do 317 and Fw 191, never

Mention must also be made of the Arado Ar 234B Blitz, the second jet-powered aircraft to enter *Luftwaffe* service and used as a bomber as well as for reconnaissance. In March 1945 the type took part in an all-jet attack on the Ludendorff bridge over the Rhine at Remagen, with Messerschmitt Me 262 fighter-bombers strafing the flak emplacements. Only 210 were completed, but they ushered in the era of the jet bomber.

British bombers of World War II

The RAF substantially modernized its bomber force in the late 1930s. Deliveries of Bristol Blenheim light bombers began in January 1937, and over the next few years the aircraft was widely exported and built under license. Despite being some 64km/h (40mph) faster than contemporary fighters

when it appeared, the Blenheim was not as successful as might have been expected. The Mk I, of which more than 1,500 were built, was followed by nearly 2,000 Mk IVs and some 200 of the original aircraft were converted into night fighters. The Mk IV was built in Canada as the Bolingbroke, where 629 were used for coastal patrol and target-towing. Douglas Bostons and de Havilland Mosquitoes replaced the Blenheims in Europe from 1942, but the type continued to serve in the Middle East and Far East until the end of the following year. The Mk IV was powered by a pair of 920hp Bristol Mercury XV radials, giving a speed of 428km/h (266mph) over a range of 2,350km (1,460 miles). The Blenheim could carry 599kg (1,320lb) of bombs and was fitted with a defensive armament of five 0·303in Browning machine guns.

Bristol used its experience with the Blenheim to develop the Beaufort torpedo bomber, which entered service with RAF Coastal Command in December 1939. More than 1,100 were built, the type being replaced in 1943 by the Beaufighter, based on the Beaufort and regarded – in its radar-equipped Mk X form – as one of the best maritime strike fighters of its day.

The distinction of carrying out the first RAF bombing raid of the war went to Bristol Blenheims and Vickers Wellingtons, which attacked the German Fleet in the Schillig Roads, off Wilhelmshafen, on 4 September 1939. The Wellington was transferred to night operations that December as the main

RAF bomber until the arrival of the four-engined heavy types. It was also the first aircraft to drop the 1,814kg (4,000lb) blockbuster bomb. The most numerous version was the Mk X, produced from 1943. Powered by two 1,675hp Bristol Hercules VIs or XVIs and carrying a crew of six, it had a maximum take-off weight of 16,555kg (36,500lb) and carried 2,040kg (4,500lb) of bombs as well as eight 0.303in Brownings for self-defence.

One of the mainstays of Bomber Command in 1939 was the Armstrong Whitworth Whitley. In its initial role as a night bomber and leaflet-dropper it became the first British aircraft of World War II to bomb Berlin and to attack Italy. Whitleys later operated with Coastal Command on reconnaissance and anti-submarine duties, as well as being used to drop paratroops. The major production version was the Mk V, of which some 1,500 were delivered between 1939 and June 1943. This was powered by a pair of Rolls-Royce Merlin Xs of 1,145hp each, giving a speed of 357km/h (222mph) and a range of 2,655km (1,650 miles) with 1,360kg (3,000lb) of bombs. Maximum load was 3,175kg (7,000lb).

Handley Page's first monoplane bomber, the Hampden, was faster than the Whitley, had a good range and bombload, and was easy to fly. Eight squadrons were equipped with Hampdens at the outbreak of war, operating them as heavy day bombers, but inadequate defensive armament caused the aircraft to be transferred to night operations and in 1942 they were passed on to Coastal Command as torpedo bombers.

The first Allied four-engined bomber of the war was the Short Stirling, which entered service at the end of 1940 and began operations over enemy territory the following February. The engines of the Mk I version were 1,590hp Bristol Hercules XI radials, giving a speed of nearly 418km/h (260mph) and a range of 3,100km (1,930 miles). A payload of nearly 6,400kg (14,000lb) could be carried, maximum gross weight being 26,950-kg (59,400lb). The Stirling was well defended—it carried eight machine guns and could absorb punishment, but most had been transferred to night operations by the beginning of 1942 and a year later the type was outdated as a bomber.

The RAF's main 'heavies' from 1942 were the Handley Page Halifax and Avro Lancaster. The former was designed to meet the same specification as the Avro Manchester, the twin-engined bomber on which the Lancaster was based. The Halifax entered service at the end of 1940, and as well as operating over Germany it was also the only RAF four-engined bomber to serve in the Middle East. More than 6,000 were produced, the most numerous version being the Mk III. This was powered by four 1,615hp Bristol Hercules XVIs and had a range of 1,600km (1,000 miles) at a maximum of 454km/h (282mph). A bombload of about 5,900kg (13,000lb) could be carried, and normally eight Browning machine guns were fitted for self-defence.

Nearly 7,400 Lancasters were built, the first entering service at the beginning of 1942. The type took part in many famous raids, including the dam-busting mission by 617 Squadron in May 1943, the aircraft carrying Barnes Wallis's 'bouncing bombs'. In November 1944 thirty-one Lancasters, each carrying a 5,450kg (12,000lb) Tallboy bomb, sank the German battleship *Tirpitz* in a Norwegian fjord. The Lancaster Mk I (Special) was fitted with the even larger – 10,000kg (22,000lb) – Grand Slam. Maximum take-off weight with a Grand Slam aboard was 31,750kg (70,000lb), slightly more than when the normal load of 6,350kg (14,000lb) was carried. The four Rolls-Royce Merlins of up to 1,640hp each gave a top speed of 462km/h (287mph) and a maximum range of 2,670km (1,660 miles) with normal

FAR LEFT ABOVE: *The Handley Page Halifax entered service with the RAF in 1940.*
FAR LEFT BELOW: *The first Allied four-engined bomber of World War II was the Short Stirling.*
BELOW LEFT: *The Savoia-Marchetti S.M.79 Sparviero (Hawk) medium bomber comprised well over half the Italian Air Force's bomber fleet at the outbreak of World War II.*

BELOW: *The Vickers Wellington medium bomber used the Barnes Wallis geodetic method of construction and was the first aircraft to drop the 1,814kg (4,000lb) blockbuster bomb.*
BOTTOM: *The Avro Lancaster, one of the classic aircraft, was developed from a failure – the underpowered twin-engined Manchester. The 'Lanc' dropped Barnes Wallis's bouncing bombs.*

bombload. A formidable defensive armament of ten machine guns was installed.

The de Havilland Mosquito was designed as a light bomber, despite its use in a multitude of other roles. More than 13,000 were built, with the aircraft entering service in 1941 and still performing useful hack duties well into the 1960s. The Mk XVI high-altitude bomber with its pressurized cabin was powered by a pair of 1,680hp or 1,710hp Rolls-Royce Merlins, a top speed of 668km/h (415mph) and ceiling of 12,190m (40,000ft) allowing defensive armament to be dispensed with. The two-crew Mosquito had a range of 2,205km (1,370 miles) in this variant and could carry a 1,811kg (4,000lb) bombload.

Developments in France, Italy and Russia during World War II

French bombing activities in World War II were obviously limited, as the country was invaded in 1940. On the night of June 7–8 in that year, however, a Centre NC223.4 four-engined bomber – originally designed as a transatlantic mailplane – became the first Allied plane to bomb Berlin in World War II.

When Italy joined the war in 1940 its air force had nearly 1,000 bombers, of which well over half were Savoia-Marchetti S.M.79 Sparviero (Hawk) medium bombers. These trimotors, were thought by many to be among the best land-based torpedo bombers of the war. They could carry 1,250kg (2,750 lb) of bombs internally or two torpedoes. Also active as a medium bomber around the Mediterranean and on anti-ship duties was the

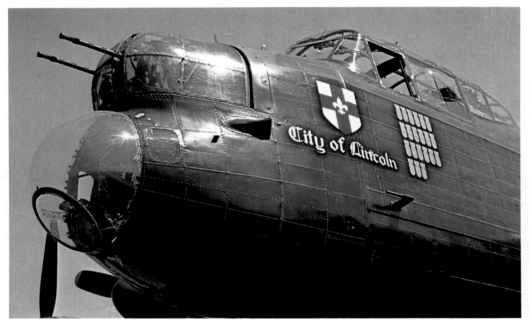

Cant Z.1007*bis* Alcione (Kingfisher), production of which began in 1939. It also was a trimotor, powered by 1,000hp Piaggio radials, and it carried four machine guns for self-defence as well as up to 2,000kg (4,410lb) of bombs or two torpedoes.

Fiat's B.R.20 Cicogna (Stork) medium bomber operated briefly against British targets from bases in Belgium in 1940 but was soon withdrawn, and only a handful of the production run of some 600 remained in service at the time of the Italian surrender in 1943. The four-engined Piaggio P.108B heavy bomber, of which only about 160 were

built, entered service in 1942 and was employed against Mediterranean targets including Gibraltar. It could carry 3,500kg (7,700lb) of bombs.

On the Eastern Front two Russian medium bombers which served throughout the war were the Ilyushin Il–4 and Tupolev 2B–2*bis*. The former was the first Russian aircraft to bomb Berlin and was also widely used as a torpedo bomber in the Baltic, its payload being either 2,000kg (4,410lb) of bombs or a single torpedo. Two 1,100hp radial engines gave the Il–4 a range of about 4,000km (2,485 miles). The SB–2*bis*, also twin-engined and with a crew of three, had a smaller bombload – 600kg (1,320lb). The Soviet Air Force did not invest in strategic bombers as heavily as did the RAF and US forces, but the four-engined Petlyakov Pe–8 was used to attack German and Balkan targets with up to 4,000 kg (8,820lb) of bombs. From the same manufacturer came the much smaller Pe–2 light bomber, which served on all Russian fronts from 1941 to 1945. Power was provided by a pair of Klimov in-line engines of 1,000hp each, giving an impressive top speed of 540 km/h (335mph). The two-crew aircraft could carry 1,000kg (2,205lb) of bombs. Towards the end of the war the Pe–2 was replaced by the Tupolev Tu–2, regarded as one of the best Russian designs of the period. The four-man aircraft, powered by a pair of 1,850hp Shvetsov radials, could carry 2,270kg (5,000 lb) of bombs and was defended by two 23mm cannon and five machine guns.

America's long-range bombers

The United States produced bombers in massive quantities to meet the needs of its own forces and those of its allies in the Pacific, North Africa, the Middle East and Far East as well as in Europe. More than 12,700

Boeing B–17s were built, of which nearly 8,700 were the B–17G model. Four 1,200hp Wright Cyclones gave a speed of 462km/h (287mph) and a range of about 3,220km (2,000 miles) with a 2,720kg (6,000lb) bombload. The B–17G, with its crew of ten, could carry a maximum bombload of nearly 8,000 kg (17,600lb) over short distances and was armed with 13 0.50in machine guns for self-defence.

The Consolidated B–24 Liberator was built in greater numbers than any other US aircraft – more than 18,000 were completed – and is said to have dropped 635,000 tons of bombs and destroyed more than 4,000 aircraft in its career. Operated by the RAF and Commonwealth air forces as well as by the US, the Liberator saw service as a transport and reconnaissance aircraft in addition to its bombing role. The B–24J, of which 6,678 were built, was powered by four 1,200hp Pratt & Whitney Twin Wasps and could carry its 12 crew for 3,380km (2,100 miles). Normal maximum bombload was 3,990kg (8,800lb), although 5,800kg (12,800lb) could be carried over short ranges, and 10 machine guns were installed for self-defence.

Medium bombers included the North

American B–25 Mitchell and Martin B–26 Marauder, both of which had a normal bombload of 1,360kg (3,000lb). The Mitchell was also very heavily defended, the B–25H carrying 14 machine guns. Production ran to 4,300-plus and 5,000-plus respectively. The principal Mitchell variant was the B–25J powered by two 1,700hp Wright Cyclones. The B–26 used 2,000hp Pratt & Whitney Twin Wasps. A 1,180kg (2,600lb) bombload was carried by the Douglas A–20 Havoc – half internally and the rest externally – of which more than 7,000 had been built when production ended in September 1944. Also known as the Boston, it was used by the RAF as well as the US and was widely employed as a torpedo bomber by the Soviet Union.

The heaviest combat aircraft of the war was the Boeing B–29 Superfortress, which entered service in the early summer of 1944. Intended as a strategic bomber for use against Germany, it in fact operated only against Japan. Maximum take-off weight of the B–29A was 64,000kg (141,100lb) and the four immensely powerful – 2,200hp each – Wright Cyclones gave a speed of 575km/h (357mph) and a normal range of 6,600km (4,100 miles). Bombload was normally 5,440kg (12,000lb)

and the defensive armament, largely remotely controlled by the standard crew of 10, comprised a 20mm cannon as well as 10 machine guns. It was a B-29, the *Enola Gay*, which dropped the atomic bomb on the Japanese city of Hiroshima.

Japanese bombers

The Japanese Navy's land-based bombers gave a good account of themselves early in the war, G3Ms sinking the battleships HMS *Repulse* and *Prince of Wales* in December 1941. The later G4M was used both for normal bombing and for torpedo operations, and from October the Navy's torpedo units began operating what was in fact an Army aircraft, the Mitsubishi Ki-67 Hiryu (Flying Dragon). Some 700 were built, and it was regarded as the Army's best bomber of the war. Two Mitsubishi Ha-104 radials of 2,000hp each gave a top speed of 540km/h (335mph), and the range was an impressive 3,780km (2,350 miles). A 20mm cannon and four machine guns were carried in addition to the 795kg (1,750lb) of bombs.

1945 to the present

The B-29, with its operational ceiling of more than 9,000m (30,000ft), radar-controlled defences and pressurized crew positions, bridged the gap between World War II heavy bomber and strategic jet types. Nine B-29 squadrons operated in the Korean War, and by 1951 most Strategic Air Command front-line units had re-equipped with the B-50 development powered by Pratt & Whitney Wasp Majors. Top speed approached 650km/h (400mph). The B-29 was also built in Russia between 1946 and 1949 as the Tupolev Tu-4 Bull, and the defensive armament of the next generation of Russian

bombers was based on that fitted to the Tu-4.

An American legacy from World War II was the Convair B-36, the requirement for which was originally drawn up when it seemed likely that the whole of Europe would be overrun and strategic missions would have to be flown direct from the United States. The B-36, which first flew in August 1946 and entered service two years later, was therefore enormous. Its wings spanned 70·1m (230ft), it was 49·4m (162ft) long and a crew of 15 was embarked. Design range was 16,100km (10,000 miles) with a bombload of 4,500kg (10,000lb). In fact, the B-36B carried a normal bombload of 32,660kg (72,000lb) over a range of 13,150km (8,175 miles). The six 3,500hp Pratt & Whitney Wasp Majors buried in the wings gave a speed of 600km/h (372mph) at 12,200m (40,000ft), but this was insufficient so four turbojets were added in the B-36D version to raise the speed to 690km/h (430mph). A total of 350 B-36s was built, with the type equipping 33 Strategic Air Command squadrons at its peak.

The United States had a monopoly on intercontinental strategic bombers for a decade after the end of the war, until the Tupolev Tu-20 Bear entered service in 1956. The Bear is unusual in being a turboprop, the four engines delivering nearly 15,000hp each to give a top speed of more than 800km/h (500mph). Maximum take-off weight of the Bear is about 170,000kg (375,000lb); most of the type have now been converted for reconnaissance and missile mid-course guidance. The smaller Tu-16 Badger medium bomber, using defensive armament based on that in the Tu-4, entered service two years earlier. Roughly equivalent to the American B-47 and British Valiant, it is powered by a pair of turbojets. In Russian terms, small numbers

of Myasischev Mya-4 Bisons, the Soviet Union's first four-jet strategic bomber, were also deployed in the late 1950s, but are now used mainly as flying tankers.

In the US the mixed-powerplant B-36 led on to the all-jet Boeing B-47, of which more than 2,000 had been delivered when production ended in 1957. The six-engined B-47 had much lower drag than had been predicted, giving it a sufficient turn of speed to outrun many contemporary fighters. Boeing followed the B-47 with the B-52 Stratofortress, which entered service in 1955. The original Pratt & Whitney J57 turbojets, each of 5,080kg (11,200lb) thrust, were more economical than earlier engines, and in later models the fuel capacity was greatly increased, which reduced the need for aerial refuelling. The turbofan-powered B-52H has a range of 16,093km (10,000 miles) with two Hound Dog stand-off missiles, and some 200 aircraft out of the total production run of 744 have been converted to operate the SRAM air-to-surface missile which is used to attack defences in the bomber's path as well as the main target. The B-52 can also carry a conventional weapon load such as 54 340kg (750lb) bombs internally plus a further 12

OPPOSITE PAGE
LEFT: *Widely regarded as the Japanese Army's best bomber of World War II, the Mitsubishi Ki-67 Hiryu (Flying Dragon).*
CENTRE: *The Soviet Tupolev Tu-2 light bomber, which replaced the Pe-2.*
RIGHT: *The Consolidated B-24 Liberator was built in larger numbers than any other US aircraft – more than 18,000.*
BELOW: *The Boeing B-52, developed as a strategic bomber, was also used on tactical missions in Vietnam.*
THIS PAGE
BELOW: *The B-29 Superfortress saw extensive action during World War II.*

LEFT: *The Handley Page Victor, with its distinctive crescent wing, was one of the Royal Air Force's three types of V-bomber. The others were the Vickers Valiant and Avro Vulcan.*
BELOW LEFT: *Designed as a successor to the B–52, the Rockwell B–1 has variable geometry to allow it to operate from small air bases yet fly supersonically at altitude.*
BELOW: *The delta-winged Dassault Mirage IV is France's strategic bomber, carrying free-fall nuclear bombs from nine bases dispersed around France for protection.*

under the wings. In missions over Vietnam B–52s carried loads of 31,750kg (70,000lb) or more.

The Soviet Union introduced its Ilyushin Il–28 Beagle medium bomber in 1950 and Britain's English Electric Canberra followed a year later. The Canberra was also built under licence in the US as the Martin B–57. The RAF's three V-bombers – the Vickers Valiant, Avro Vulcan and Handley Page Victor – were introduced during the mid-1950s, replacing the Lincoln derivative of the Lancaster. Britain's primary nuclear strike role has since been taken over by Polaris submarines, with the remaining Victors and Vulcans being used for reconnaissance, tanking and tactical bombing. France retains a strategic nuclear bomber in the form of the Dassault Mirage IV carrying free-fall weapons.

The USAF introduced the first supersonic strategic bomber, the Convair B–58 Hustler, in 1960. This three-man aircraft, built mainly of stainless steel, had a range of more than 8,000km (5,000 miles) on internal fuel. A belly-mounted pod containing fuel for the outward journey, together with the nuclear weapons, was jettisoned over the target to allow the B–58 to return home 'clean'. The Hustler was retired in 1970.

The only other bomber operated alongside Strategic Air Command B–52s is the General Dynamics FB–111, of which there are two squadrons. These aircraft can also carry the SRAM missile as well as bombs. In Russia the Yakovlev Yak–28 tactical bomber was introduced in 1963–64 and was followed in 1965 by the Tupolev Tu–22 Blinder. This was intended as a Tu–16 successor but did not have sufficient range when supersonic.

The most modern bombers developed by the superpowers are the Tupolev Backfire and Rockwell B–1. Both use variable geometry, swinging most or part of the wing to the position best suited to the speed and altitude required for a particular stage of the flight. The Backfire is already in service, and when the B–1 reaches the squadrons the USAF will have the most potent bomber ever built.

Bombs

The first bomb designed specifically to be dropped from an aeroplane was the German APK of 1912, a simple cast-iron sphere filled with explosive. At 5kg (11lb) or 10kg (22lb), it was too light to have any great effect and was not used in World War I. It led on, however, to the Carbonit series of weapons employed throughout 1914 and 1915. These weighed up to 50kg (110lb) and had begun to take on the streamlined shape which later became characteristic. The pear-shaped body was fitted with a steel nose to assist target penetration and carried a stabilizing tail unit.

Britain's equivalent, the 9-kg (20-lb) Hale bomb, was developed for the Royal Naval Air Service and carried by its Avro 504s during early wartime raids on Zeppelin sheds. Soon afterwards, versions weighing up to 45kg (100lb) were in use by the Royal Flying Corps as well as the RNAS. France adopted modified artillery shells of 75mm, 90mm and 155mm calibre and fitted with tail fins and fuses by Canton-Unné. Although the French later developed weapons specifically for aircraft use, the 75-mm shell was the most widely employed bomb throughout the war.

As the war progressed and bombers became larger it was possible to carry heavier weapons. By 1918 the four standard British bombs were the 9-kg (20-lb) Cooper, which replaced the Hale weapon of the same weight;

the Woolwich Royal Laboratory's bombs of 23kg (50lb) and 51kg (112 lb); and the Royal Flying Corps weapon of 104kg (230lb). Heavier bombs, weighing up to 816kg (1,800 lb), were dropped on occasion from the Handley Page 0/100 and 0/400, and a development weighing 1,500kg (3,300lb) was built for the same company's V/1500 but never used in action.

Germany's 300-kg (660-lb) PuW bomb of 1915 was extremely advanced for its day, having a steel rather than cast-iron casing. Its canted fins produced a high rotational speed, allowing the weapon to be armed centrifugally in the manner of an artillery shell instead of by a propeller. The PuW's streamlined shape reduced aerodynamic drag, and the weapon was carried horizontally in racks or in a bomb bay. The Allies, in contrast, transported their weapons on the fuselage sides or underneath the aircraft. The Germans also produced the heaviest bomb used operationally during the war – a monster of 1,000kg (2,200lb) dropped by Zeppelin (Staaken) Giants on London.

Other World War I weapons included Le Prieur rockets, used mainly against Zeppelins; Ranken darts, otherwise known as flechettes – steel darts some 13cm (5in) long which were dropped from drums containing 500; and incendiaries which de-

veloped from petrol-filled canisters to specialized weapons burning at very high temperatures.

By the end of World War II, bomb development had reached an advanced stage. Weapons were available for specific purposes, such as piercing heavy naval armour or concrete bunkers. General-purpose bombs between 45kg (100lb) and 900kg (2,000lb) were commonplace, and in the spring of 1941 the first 1,800-kg (4,000-lb) weapon was dropped on Emden by a Wellington. Three years later the 5,450-kg (12,000-lb) Tallboy, an 'earthquake bomb' developed by Dr Barnes Wallis, entered service and in 1945 it was joined by the 9,980-kg (22,000-lb) Grand Slam. The first Grand Slam destroyed two spans of the Bielefeld railway viaduct when dropped from a Lancaster of the RAF's 617 Squadron, the same unit which two years previously had attacked the Mohne, Eder and Sorpe dams with Barnes Wallis's 'bouncing bombs'.

A weapon which made its debut in 1944 was napalm, a jellied mixture of naphtha and palm oil (hence its name) in a droppable canister. It is ignited on contact with a target, such as fuel dumps or soft-skinned vehicles, and adheres to everything that it touches.

Torpedoes were first used in action by the RNAS in 1915, against

Turkish shipping. By the later stages of World War II the US Mk 13 torpedo had been improved as a result of experiences in the Pacific and could travel in excess of 73km/h (40 kt) for several miles. It could seek out its target and carried a proximity fuse to detonate the 272-kg (600-lb) warhead. Weighing 900kg (2,000lb) and measuring 3.96m (13ft) long by 56cm (22in) in diameter, it could be dropped at altitudes of 300m (1,000 ft) and speeds of 555km/h (300kt) compared with the precise launching at 15m (50ft) required by the Mk 7.

World War II also saw the service introduction of the atomic bomb. Since the first such weapons were dropped on Hiroshima and Nagasaki, the maximum yield of air-dropped nuclear weapons has risen from about 20 kilotons to 25 megatons or more, and thermonuclear bombs have replaced the first fission weapons. Conventional bombs are available with low-drag profiles in weights up to 1,360kg (3,000lb) and others are fitted with parachutes or flip-out brakes to allow the aircraft to drop them from extremely low levels without risk of being damaged by the explosion. Cluster bombs dispense hundreds of bomblets in a cloud to cover a target, and a host of guided missiles (see chapter 10) have been developed for airborne use. Other air-launched weapons include grenades, rockets and mines.

Fighters

At the beginning of World War I in 1914 there were no specialized fighters, only a handful of scouts capable of 145km/h (90-mph) at best. Aircraft were regarded as being useful only for observation – if indeed they were thought to have any worthwhile military application at all. The first Royal Flying Corps aircraft assigned an offensive role were unarmed and intended to attack Zeppelins by ramming them; this was not greeted with much enthusiasm by the crews, who were not supplied with parachutes. Aircraft of both sides flew over enemy territory on reconnaissance missions, reporting back information such as troop movements and trench positions for use by the army. They acted also as artillery spotters, correcting the aim of ground gunners. But very soon it was realized that there could be another role for aircraft; machines on surveillance missions soon found themselves coming under attack by enemy two-seaters in which the observer carried a hand-aimed rifle or pistol. So began the development of air-to-air fighting.

Aircraft acquire machine guns

At the beginning of 1915 air warfare took a big step forward with the introduction of aircraft machine guns. Before the war Colonel Isaac Newton had fitted a machine gun on a Wright biplane of the US Army Signal Corps, but he met with so little official enthusiasm that in 1913 he left the country in disgust and set up a factory in Liège, Belgium. Lewis's machine gun was paralleled by developments in Britain, France and Germany. The Vickers 0·33in and German weapons were variants of the Maxim infantry machine gun, while

TOP LEFT: *The two-seat Vickers F.B.5 Gunbus equipped the first British all-fighter squadron in France – in July 1915 – and helped counter the 'Fokker scourge'.*

ABOVE: *France's SPAD S.XIII carried twin Vickers machine guns, twice the armament of its predecessor, and the powerful Hispano-Suiza engine gave a reasonable top speed.*

TOP CENTRE: *The Fokker Eindekker series carried the first synchronized machine guns.*
TOP RIGHT: *The Bristol Scout was Britain's first type with synchronized guns.*

France produced the Hotchkiss. The German 7·92mm LMG.08, operated like the Vickers by the pilot, was commonly known as the Parabellum, and the LMG.08/15 was an observer's gun in the same mould as the Lewis.

It was left to the French to pioneer aerial fighting in their *Escadrilles de Chasse*, formed to protect reconnaissance aircraft and to escort bombers. These squadrons were equipped with Morane Type Ns, with a machine gun firing forward through the propeller, and two-seat parasol-wing Type Ls, in which the observer was similarly armed.

Before the war Franz Schneider of LVG and Raymond Saulnier of Morane-Saulnier had worked on interrupter gear which would allow guns to be fired through the propeller disc without damaging the blades. The equipment was installed in an LVG E.VI in 1915, but the aircraft was destroyed on its way to the front. In his experiments with interrupter gear, Saulnier had been troubled by faulty ammunition and, as a result, had fitted steel wedges to the propeller of his aircraft in order to deflect any bullets striking the blades. Roland Garros, who adopted the steel-wedge

idea on a Morane scout, accounted for five victims in under three weeks, largely because the enemy did not expect to be attacked with forward-firing weapons. On 18 April 1915, however, Garros was shot down and the secret was revealed.

German designers tried to reproduce the arrangement but were unsuccessful, possibly because steel-jacketed bullets were being used, but three of Anthony Fokker's engineers went one better and developed an interrupter mechanism along the lines of those pioneered before the war. This was installed

Type: Bristol F.2B
Engines: One 275hp Rolls Royce Falcon III
Armament: Two or three 7·7mm (0·303in) machine guns, up to 1 2 9·1kg (20lb) bombs
Maximum speed: 182km/h (113mph)
Climb: 258m/min (826ft/min)
Ceiling: 5,486m (18,000ft)
Weight: 1,292kg (2,848lb)
Span: 11·96m (39ft 3in)
Length: 7·87m (25ft 10in)
Height: 2·97m (9ft 9in)

in a Fokker E.I – E = Eindekker (monoplane) – and accounted for its first victim on 1 August. The Eindekkers were used at first to escort two-seat observation aircraft and for local defence, but the Germans soon realized that they had a superior weapon and, stung by criticism following sustained unhindered bombing raids by Voisins and Farmans, began to fight back for the first time.

The 'Fokker scourge'

The most famous of the Eindekker series was the E.III, and the six months or so of domination by this type was known by the Allies as the 'Fokker scourge'. In fact the E.I with its 89hp engine giving a top speed of only 128 km/h (80mph) was not a particularly impressive machine, but – as has so often been the case since – superior armament made up for basic deficiencies. Numerous methods of

mounting a forward-firing gun had been tried before the Eindekkers appeared. As early as May 1915 a Martinsyde biplane had been fitted with an upward-firing gun on the centre section of the top wing, so that the stream of bullets missed the propeller disc, and this method was later used on the Nieuport XI (*Bébé*). Another solution was to mount a Lewis gun so that it fired abeam at 45°, its bullets thus clearing the propeller.

The Eindekkers' success forced the French to abandon their daylight bombing missions by December 1915, but their main victim was the British B.E.2c two-seat observation aircraft. In the summer of 1915 the Germans had introduced the C series of observation types, such as the Rumpler C.I, Albatros C.I and Aviatik C.I, in which the observer occupied the rear cockpit instead of the front. This allowed them to carry a 'sting in the tail' in the form of an LMG.08/15 machine gun (commonly known as a Spandau, after its place of manufacture). The C series were a great improvement on the Bs, and their 160 hp Mercedes D.III engines, coupled with the fact that the Spandau was superior to the Hotchkiss, gave them quite an edge. Placing the observer at the rear gave him a much better field of fire and, although the aircraft were vulnerable to frontal attacks, the generally slow and unmanoeuvrable pusher biplanes encountered at first did not provide formidable opposition.

The British, however, refused to learn and continued to turn out great numbers of extremely stable and hence unmanoeuvrable

B.E.2cs with the observer hemmed in at the front. He fired the Lewis gun from his shoulder or from one of the mountings disposed about his cockpit.

The British temporarily overcame the problem of firing through the propeller by producing a series of pusher aircraft, thus removing the problem altogether. The first British all-fighter squadron in France had already received the new F.B.5 Gunbus – a two-seat pusher – in July 1915, and single-seat fighters joined them in February 1916. The D.H.2 and F.E.8 – both single-seat pushers – helped put an end to the Fokker scourge, and the two-seat pusher F.E.2b with its 120hp or 160hp Beardmore engine further augmented the force.

By the spring of 1916 the ageing Eindekkers were being replaced. Immelmann, for one, had extracted the last ounce of aggression by fitting three Spandaus to his aircraft. The interrupter gear was not completely reliable, however, and it was a quite common occurrence for a pilot to shoot off his own propeller. The Germans re-equipped with Halberstadt D.I biplanes and Pfalz monoplanes, together with two-seat LFG Roland C.IIIs which, at 165km/h (103mph), were extremely fast for their day. In March 1916 the Bristol Scout, the first British aircraft with synchronized guns, appeared in France. And by the time of the Battle of the Somme in July the Sopwith 1½-Strutter, the first British tractor two-seater with the observer at the rear, had at last entered service. The 1½-Strutter was slow, but its forward-firing

Type: Fokker Dr.1
Engines: One 110hp Le Rhône rotary
Armament: Two 7·92mm (0·312in) Spandau machine guns
Maximum speed: 165km/h (103mph)
Initial climb: 220m/min (720ft/min)
Ceiling: 6,100m (20,000ft)
Range: about 210km (130 miles)
Loaded weight: 586kg (1,292lb)
Span: (upper wing) 7·19m (23ft 7in)
Length: 5·77m (18ft 11in)
Height: 2·95m (9ft 8in)

Vickers and rear-mounted Lewis gun largely overcame this deficiency.

More disappointing were the B.E.12, based on the B.E.2, and the R.E.8. The latter was insufficiently manoeuvrable to escape enemy attacks, and when it first entered service was prone to spin and had an unreliable engine – an unfortunate combination. The most effective British two-seater remained the F.E.2 series, especially the F.E.2ds fitted with 250 hp Rolls-Royce Eagles. The D.H.2s and F.E.2s reigned supreme until towards the end of 1916, even though the former were capable of no more than 123km/h (77mph) at 3,050m (10,000ft). The F.E.8 proved to be obsolete by the time it joined the fighting, but generally the pushers, with an unobstructed forward view and a high rate of fire from their unsynchronized guns, proved to be good enough.

Not to be outdone, France contributed the single-seat Spad S.VIII and various Nieuport developments. The former, which entered service in September 1916, was strong and fast – 190km/h (118mph) – but carried only a single gun. It was later developed into the S.XIII, however, with twin Vickers and an Hispano-Suiza 8B engine of 220–235hp, giving a top speed of 220km/h (138mph). The Nieuport 16 and 17 retained the single Lewis gun on top of the upper wing, and the design was later copied by the Germans in the Albatros D.III, D.V and D.Va.

The Fokker biplanes developed to replace the Eindekkers were disappointing, but the Halberstadt D.II and D.III, together with the Albatros D.I and D.II with their twin Spandaus, wrested back the initiative for the Germans. From then on, superiority in the air swung back and forth between the contestants for the duration of the war. The S.E.5, with its Hispano-Suiza engine, could achieve 182km/h (114mph) at 3,000m (10,000ft) compared with the D.H.2's 123km/h (77-mph), and Sopwith produced the remarkable series of Pup, Triplane and Camel. The Pup, developed from the Tabloid, had a low wing loading and was consequently very manoeuvrable, being able to out-turn an Albatros D.II. The Triplane went one better, with improved rate of climb and better visibility, while the Camel eventually destroyed nearly 1,300 enemy aircraft to become the most successful fighter of World War I.

In the F.1 Camel – the first British fighter with twin Vickers – weight was concentrated as near as possible to the centre of gravity. This, combined with powerful controls, conferred excellent manoeuvrability. With a 110 hp Le Rhône, the Camel had a maximum speed of 195km/h (122mph) at sea level, and engines of up to 150hp could be fitted. The torque of the powerplant gave the Camel its famous lightning turn to the right, but it also led to an undeserved reputation for unsafe handling during take-off and landing. The F.2B Bristol Fighter was one of the types fitted with a powerful Rolls-Royce engine, in this case a 275hp Falcon, which gave a top speed of 193km/h (123mph) at 1,210m (4,000ft). Indeed, by the end of World War I the two-gun fighters were as nimble as the lighter single-gun aircraft of 1916–17 and could often reach 192km/h (120mph).

FAR LEFT: *Germany's Albatros scouts – a D.I is illustrated here – were an improvement on the first generation of biplane fighters but were less manoeuvrable than types such as the Sopwith Pup. The D.II, with its twin Spandaus, was nevertheless formidable.*
LEFT: *The French Nieuport 17 carried on the sesquiplane layout, with the lower wing reduced to a bare minimum. A single Lewis gun was mounted on top of the wing and needed no interrupter gear. This arrangement was copied in the Albatros D.III, V and Va.*
BELOW: *The Royal Aircraft Factory's S.E.5 (Scouting Experimental No 5) was one of several types designed round the Hispano-Suiza engine, which gave the S.E.5 a top speed half as fast again as that of the single-seat pusher D.H.2.*

Germany, too, was not to be outdone, producing such types as the Fokker D.VIII, armed with two Spandaus and having excellent performance at altitude. The type was strong and agile, being powered usually by an Oberursel rotary engine of 110hp which gave a maximum speed of 185km/h (116 mph). Aircraft had begun to be adapted for more specialized roles such as ground attack, one example being the Hannover CL.IIIa, which carried out close-support missions as well as acting as an escort fighter. It was compact and often mistaken for a single-seater – sometimes with disastrous results, because a rearward-firing Parabellum was carried in addition to the fixed Spandau. This kind of specialization was carried further after the end of the war.

French inter-war fighters

The European countries followed much the same development path – ever more powerful and faster biplanes of conventional configuration, then the major step to modern monoplanes. In many cases the transition came too late, since the performance of most other fighters had to be judged against that of the Messerschmitt Bf 109. The first French monoplane fighter with an enclosed cockpit and retractable undercarriage was the Morane-Saulnier M.S. 405, which made its maiden flight in August 1935. The M.S. 406 development entered service in 1939, and more than 1,000 had been completed when France fell in the summer of 1940. An 86ohp Hispano-Suiza 12Y engine gave a top speed of 490km/h (304mph), and the armament of two 7·5mm machine guns and a 20mm cannon allowed M.S. 406 pilots to account for more than 250 enemy aircraft, including some Bf 109s.

Another fighter used extensively towards the end of the Battle of France was the Bloch MB. 152, late examples of which were fitted with a 1,100hp Gnome-Rhône 14N–25 radial engine and had a maximum speed of 512km/h (318mph). Armament comprised a pair of 7·5mm machine guns and two 20mm cannon, but the weapons were not always reliable. Nearly 700 MB.152s were built, in addition to 85 of the earlier MB.151, and the type served in Romania after the fall of France. On a larger scale was the Potez 631 three-seat heavy fighter, one of the 63 series which also included developments for bombing, attack and reconnaissance. Powered by a pair of 700hp Gnome-Rhône 14 radials, it lacked the speed which could have made it a potent fighting machine – armament comprised two 20mm cannon and up to eight 7·5mm machine guns. France's best fighter was undoubtedly the Dewoitine D.520, which entered service too late to be decisive but accounted for more than 100 victims in the Battle of France. It was slower than the Bf 109, but more manoeuvrable.

Italian inter-war fighters

Italy's best known scout of World War I had been the S.V.A.5, which carried out long-range missions against Austria. Its 220hp engine gave it an impressive top speed of 228 km/h (143mph). The biplane tradition continued via the single-seat Fiat C.R.32, which entered service in 1933 and was also widely exported. Its 600hp Fiat A.30 gave a top speed of 350km/h (217mph) and armament comprised the virtually mandatory pair of machine guns. Later Fiat biplanes such as the C.R.42 saw extensive war service.

Czech and Polish inter-war fighters

The standard Czech pre-war fighter was the single-seat Avia B–534 biplane which entered service in 1935. A 650hp Hispano-Suiza 12Ybrs engine propelled the aircraft at up to 363km/h (225mph). Of similar vintage was Poland's P.Z.L. P–11c, a single-seat monoplane advanced for its time but hopelessly outclassed against the *Luftwaffe* in 1939. In Holland, Fokker's single-seat monoplane D.XXI of 1937, with its fixed undercarriage and maximum speed of 435km/h (270mph), was also no real match for the invading forces. The same manufacturer's G–1A heavy fighter, which appeared two years later, was the first modern type with twin booms, allowing it to carry the formidable armament of nine machine guns in a central fuselage nacelle. Two 830hp Bristol Mercurys gave a speed of 475km/h (295mph), but the aircraft was too late to save Holland.

Russia's Polikarpov I–16 Ishak (Little Donkey) of 1936 was the first monoplane fighter with a fully enclosed cockpit and retractable undercarriage, but by 1941 it was outclassed by the Bf 109. The *Luftwaffe* had also espoused biplanes, operating the Heinkel He 51 and Arado Ar 68 in the Spanish Civil War, but the monoplane Bf 109 had made its maiden flight in 1935 and by the outbreak of World War II the biplane fighters had been retired.

British inter-war fighters

A rapid run-down of fighter strength in Britain followed the Armistice in 1918, with the Sopwith Snipe and some Bristol Fighters forming the backbone of the remaining force. The Snipe, with its two forward-firing machine guns and a top speed of 191km/h (119 mph), had reached the Western Front in September 1918. Its equipment included electrical heating, oxygen and pilot armour, indicating just how far the fighter had come in four years of war. The Snipe was the RAF's only home-defence fighter between April 1920 and October 1922, and it remained the force's major type until the mid-1920s. It was also used in Iraq from 1922, when the RAF took control there, and was still operational in the Middle East as late as 1926.

A modest expansion programme was authorized in 1923, allowing 52 squadrons to be allocated to air defence alone. The Gloster Grebe and Hawker Woodcock replaced the Snipe, but they were no more than extensions of the same formula, with fabric-covered wooden fuselages, bulky uncowled radial engines, wooden propellers and twin Vickers machine guns mounted directly in front of the pilot's face. The Gloster Gamecock and Bristol Bulldog followed, along with contemporaries such as the Armstrong-Whitworth Siskin, but the principles stayed the same – despite the fact that the Bulldog remained in service until 1936.

Bulldog deliveries to No 3 Squadron began in June 1929, the IIA being powered by a 440hp Bristol Jupiter VIIF and having a top speed of 286km/h (178mph). It was the RAF's main interceptor in the early and mid-1930s. Engine powers and thus maximum speeds increased steadily throughout this period. The Hawker Fury was the first British fighter capable of more than 320km/h (200 mph), its 525hp Rolls-Royce Kestrel producing up to 333km/h (207mph). The Fury was widely exported but did not enter full production for the RAF until 1936, five years after becoming operational, and by then it was obsolete. The V12 Kestrel, which was

also the powerplant for the Hart bomber and its derivatives, had each bank of cylinders cast in a single block rather than separately and was thus slimmer and had a better power-to-weight ratio than its predecessors.

The two-seat Hawker Demon, whose ancestry can be traced right back to the Bristol Fighter, was a contemporary of the Fury. The logical progression of ever-faster single-seat fighters continued with the Gloster Gauntlet, a popular and manoeuvrable type which served from 1935 to 1939. Its 640hp Bristol Mercury VI gave a top speed of 370 km/h (230mph). Then came the type which in many ways represented a transition. The Gloster Gladiator, which entered service in January 1937, was the RAF's last biplane fighter and only now was the standard World War I armament of two machine guns doubled to four. An 840hp Bristol Mercury IX gave the Gladiator a top speed of 407km/h (253mph), but this was soon to be put in the shade by the new generation of monoplane fighters, which had armament doubled again to eight Brownings and top speeds in excess of 480km/h (300mph).

The Hawker Hurricane prototype flew in November 1935 and the first Spitfire followed it four months later, but by the time of the 1938 Munich crisis only two of the RAF's 30 fighter squadrons – including Auxiliaries – were equipped with Hurricanes, and Spitfires had yet to enter service. By the summer of 1940, however, these types had replaced the biplanes in time – but only just in time – for the Battle of Britain.

American inter-war fighters

In the United States, the Army Air Corps had to content itself almost exclusively with European types during World War I, but in the early 1920s 200 Boeing-built MB–3As were ordered to add to the original 50 Thomas Morse MB–3s. This constituted the largest single order for US military aircraft for the next 17 years. The MB–3A was powered by a Wright-Hispano engine of 300hp, giving a top speed of 225km/h (140mph) and a remarkable rate of climb – from take-off to 3,000m (10,000ft) in under five minutes. Despite suffering from engine overheating, a cramped cockpit and maintenance difficulties, it was an impressive beginning for the Army Air Corps series of pursuit ships (derived from the French practice of calling their fighters *avions de chasse*).

Boeing followed the MB–3A with the PW–9, of which more than 100 were built. That company's main rival, Curtiss, produced the Hawk series, which remained in service until 1939. The best known model was the P–6E of 1932, with an engine of up to 600hp giving a top speed of 318km/h (197mph).

Meanwhile Boeing had moved on to the P–12, similarly armed with a pair of 0·303in machine guns. The P–12E variant, entering service in 1932, was fitted with a 525hp Pratt & Whitney Wasp and could achieve 305km/h (190mph). The Air Corps retained the P–12 until 1934, and the type served the US Navy for a further two years. US pursuit ships then took a major step forward at the same time as the first really modern bombers also made their appearance. The Boeing P–26, of which 111 were ordered in 1933, was the first US monoplane fighter and the first of all-metal construction. Dubbed the Peashooter by its pilots, it was one of the fastest fighters of its time. The 600hp Pratt & Whitney Wasp of the P–26A drove it through the air at 376km/h (234mph). The P–26 was used in China against Japanese forces and later took part in the early stages of World War II.

In 1935 there was a brief resurgence of the two-seat fighter. Two USAAC squadrons were equipped with Consolidated PB–2s, but in the following year the single-seat Seversky P–35 appeared. It was an improvement on the P–26, its 950hp Pratt & Whitney R–1830 giving a top speed of 450km/h (280mph) and a range of nearly 1,600km (1,000 miles), but it still carried two guns only and had no protective armour. It did, however, form the basis for the P–47 Thunderbolt.

Japanese inter-war fighters

In the years after World War I the Japanese Army relied on imported fighters and overseas designs built under license. Then in 1931 the Nakajima NC single-seat high-wing monoplane was ordered as the Army Type 91. Powered by a 450hp Bristol Jupiter, it saw widespread use in Manchuria as the main fighter of the early 1930s; 450 were built. Kawasaki, defeated in the competition in which the Type 91 was selected, designed the single-seat KDA–5 biplane, powered by a 750hp BMW. It was later adopted by the Army as the Type 92, and 380 were constructed. Kawasaki went on to develop the Ki–10 which, as the Type 95, was the Army's last combat biplane. Nearly 600 were produced and saw widespread combat, but the Army realized in 1935 that fabric-covered biplanes were outdated and therefore launched a competition to find a successor. The winner was the Nakajima Ki–27 (Type 97 fighter), of which more than 3,300 were built and which remained in front-line service until the beginning of the Pacific war. A low-wing all-metal monoplane, it was light and manoeuvrable. Its excellent record in the Sino-Japanese war hid the fact, however, that modern fighters needed armour plating and self-sealing fuel tanks, with the result that later types proved vulnerable in combat.

German fighters of World War II

In September 1939 the *Luftwaffe* had a front-line strength of 1,200 fighters, including the formidable Messerschmitt Bf 109. As the war progressed, and the advantage swung away from Germany, greater emphasis was placed on intercepters and night fighters than on bomber escorts, and in the last year output was concentrated almost entirely on last-ditch defenders. The Bf 109E was the *Luftwaffe's* standard single-seat fighter for the first three years of the war and was able to outfight or outrun virtually all opposition. From the summer of 1942 the Bf 109G, powered by a Daimler-Benz DB 605D producing 1,800hp with water-methanol injection and giving a speed of 685km/h (428mph), entered service in Russia and North Africa before being de-

ployed in every other theatre. With its standard armament of a cannon and two machine guns the Bf 109, like the Spitfire, saw action throughout the war.

From 1941 it was joined by the Focke-Wulf Fw 190, widely regarded as Germany's best fighter. Its introduction has been compared with the 'Fokker scourge' of 1915, and it was more than a match for the contemporary Spitfires. The Fw 190 was armed to the teeth – four 20mm cannon plus two machine guns – and later versions could carry a 30mm cannon firing through the propeller boss. Early Fw 190s, powered by an air-cooled BMW radial, were Germany's first radial-engined monoplane fighters, but in the Fw 190D–12 of 1945 a Jumo 2,060hp 213F liquid-cooled in-line engine replaced the earlier power-plant and conferred a top speed of 730km/h (453mph). The long-nosed Fw 190D was also developed into the Ta 152 – after its designer, Kurt Tank – in which the installation of a 2,300hp (with boost) DB 603 engine pushed the speed up to 745km/h (463mph). The Ta 152, armed with a 30mm cannon and four of 20mm, equipped only a handful of squadrons at the end of hostilities but might have been decisive if widely deployed earlier in the war.

The Bf 110, Messerschmitt's first twin-engined design, served throughout the war but was increasingly used for intercepting bombers and as a night fighter after its mediocre display in the Battle of Britain. The first fighter version of the much more successful multi-role Junkers Ju 88 was the Ju 88C,

armed with three 20mm cannon and the same number of machine guns. A fourth crew member was added in the specialist Ju 88G night fighter, and the Ju 88H–2 was employed as a long-range escort. Many Dornier Do 217E–2 bombers were converted to the night-fighting role from 1942, becoming Do 217J–1s and J–2s, the latter being radar-equipped. Do 217Ms were also converted into 217N night fighters. All were armed with four 20mm cannon and up to five machine guns.

Messerschmitt's proposed Bf 110 successor, the Me 210, was a failure and the Me 410 Hornisse (Hornet) developed from it was not much better, even when operated as a heavy

FAR LEFT: *The Boulton-Paul Defiant II was the world's first fighter to dispense with forward-firing armament and had to rely instead on a power-operated gun-turret.*
FAR LEFT BELOW: *The Focke-Wulf Fw 190 was an outstanding fighter, fast and heavily armed with cannon and machine guns.*
LEFT: *The Supermarine Spitfire was the only British type in production throughout World War II.*
BELOW: *The Messerschmitt Bf 109 was the Luftwaffe's standard single-seat fighter in the first half of World War II.*
BOTTOM: *The Gloster Gladiator was the first RAF fighter to carry four machine guns, but it was outclassed by German types.*

LEFT: *The revolutionary Messerschmitt Me 163B Komet, powered by a rocket engine, was a last-ditch bomber intercepter.*

CENTRE LEFT: *The twin-jet Messerschmitt Me 262 could have had a decisive effect if it had been used as a fighter rather than a bomber.*

BOTTOM LEFT: *The Heinkel He 162 Salamander was built from 'non-strategic' materials and was to be flown by hastily trained young pilots.*

TOP RIGHT: *The Gloster Meteor was the only Allied jet aircraft to see action in World War II, but it never met the Me 262.*

CENTRE RIGHT: *The Hawker Hurricane shared the laurels with the Spitfire in the Battle of Britain. It was a robust gun platform.*

fighter with a 50mm cannon in the bomb bay as well as four 20mm weapons. A specialist night fighter which could have been devastating if official bickering had not disrupted its development was the Heinkel He 219 Uhu (Owl). Powered by a pair of 1,900hp DB 603s, giving a speed of 670km/h (416mph), it carried the ultimate in firepower – six 30mm and two 20mm cannon. Yet another victim of bad planning and muddled thinking was the Me 262, the first jet aircraft to enter service. Adolf Hitler ordered that it should be used as a bomber, despite the fact that this negated its speed advantage over Allied piston-engined types. Only when Germany's position was hopeless did he give the Me 262 priority over all other projects.

Last-ditch attempts to hack down the overwhelming bomber fleets were typified by the Me 163B Komet and Heinkel He 162 Salamander. The former, the only rocket-powered aircraft ever to see service, could reach its service ceiling of 12,100m (39,700ft) in 3·35 minutes under 1,700kg (3,750lb) of rocket thrust. It carried a pair of 30mm cannon but its high speed – 960km/h (596mph) – and endurance of only eight minutes combined to make interceptions difficult. The undercarriage was jettisoned to save weight, and more Komets were lost as a result of explosions following landings on skids than were shot down by the Allies. More than 350 Me 163s were built, but it was the same story all over again – too little and too late. Equally remarkable – and hopeless – was the He 162, otherwise known as the Volksjäger (People's Fighter). Making its maiden flight only ten weeks after the beginning of design work, the Salamander was planned to be produced by the thousand from non-strategic materials such as wood. It was to be flown by young pilots with the minimum of training, but it proved difficult to handle and only a hundred-odd were built.

British fighters of World War II

At the outbreak of war in September 1939 the re-equipment of RAF Fighter Command with the new generation of monoplanes was well under way. Front-line fighter strength was more than 1,000, of which well over half comprised Hawker Hurricanes (18 squadrons) and Supermarine Spitfires (nine squadrons). The former type shot down nearly half the enemy aircraft accounted for by the RAF in the first year of war, and it made up 60 per cent of Fighter Command in the Battle of Britain. Early models were armed with eight machine guns, with later variants carrying 12 of these weapons or four 20mm cannon.

Type: Supermarine Spitfire
Engines: One Rolls Royce Merlin III 12-cylinder
Armament: Eight 7·7mm (0·303in) Browning Mk II
    machine guns
Maximum speed: 502km/h (312mph)
Initial climb: 762m/min (2,500ft/min)
Ceiling: 10,360m (34,000ft)
Range: 925km (575 miles)
Loaded weight: 2,640kg (5,820lb)
Span: 11·23m (36ft 10in)
Length: 9·12m (29ft 11in)
Height: 3·48m (11ft 5in)

Type: Messerschmitt Bf 109
Engines: One Daimler-Benz DB601A 12-cylinder
Armament: Two 20mm (0·787in) MG FF cannon, two
    7·9mm (0·311in) MG 17 machine guns
Maximum speed: 541km/h (336mph)
Initial climb: 1,000m/min (3,280ft/min)
Ceiling: 10,500m (34,450ft)
Range: 660km (410 miles)
Loaded weight: 2,665kg (5,875lb)
Span: 9·87m (32ft 4·5in)
Length: 8·64m (28ft 4in)
Height: 2·49m (8ft 2·3in)

The Hurricane was slightly slower than the Messerschmitt Bf 109, so its major role in the summer of 1940 was bomber interception. It was later used for a wide variety of other missions, including ground attack and operation from catapult-equipped merchant ships, with more than 14,500 of all variants being built.

The Spitfire, one of the classic aircraft of all time, ran to more than 40 versions and was the only British aircraft to remain in production throughout the war. More than 2,000 were on order in September 1939, and production exceeded 20,000, making the Spitfire the most widely produced British aircraft of all time. The first variants were powered by the ubiquitous Rolls-Royce Merlin – the same engine was used in the Hurricane as well as many other types – and later models had the follow-on Griffon installed, giving a top speed of more than 724km/h (450mph) in the fastest fighter version. The original armament of eight machine guns was replaced by four cannon in some of the later models.

A contemporary of the Hurricane and Spitfire was the Boulton-Paul Defiant, the world's first fighter to dispense with forward-firing armament and rely on a power-operated gun turret behind the cockpit. The Defiant entered service in early 1940 but was not particularly successful, being relegated to night-fighting in August 1941 and then to target-towing.

Two other major types widely used as night fighters among a multiplicity of roles were

the Bristol Beaufighter and de Havilland Mosquito. The former, equipped with an early version of AI (Airborne Interception – later known as radar), strengthened the night-fighter force from November 1940. It combined a high speed, 515km/h (320mph), with a range of 2,415km (1,500 miles) and carried the devastating armament of four 20mm Hispano cannon and seven machine guns. The Beaufighter was later replaced as a night fighter by the de Havilland Mosquito.

Also armed with four Hispanos was the Hawker Typhoon, which entered service in September 1941 to counter Focke-Wulf Fw 190s. The 2,200hp Napier Sabre engine gave a top speed of 663km/h (412mph) to the Typhoon IB, and the aircraft later served extensively in the ground-attack role.

The Tempest followed the Typhoon, with the Sabre uprated to 2,420hp and speed increased to 700km/h (435mph) in the Tempest II. The Mk V was the only version to see war service, and between June and September 1944 Tempests shot down 638 V1 flying bombs before moving into Europe and accounting for 20 Me 262s among a large number of other victims.

Also used against V1s from July 1944 was the Gloster Meteor, the only Allied jet aircraft to become operational during the war. In the F.4 version, which entered service in 1948, the two Rolls-Royce Derwent turbojets of 1,590kg (3,500lb) thrust conferred a maximum speed of 885km/h (550mph) at an operational ceiling of approximately 9,150m (30,000ft).

Italian fighters of World War II

The other European Axis power, Italy, was not so well prepared at the beginning of the war. Its weak link was the force of obsolescent biplane fighters and underpowered monoplanes, and it was not until German-designed engines began to appear in 1942 that the quality improved. The single-seat biplane Fiat C.R.42 Falco (Falcon) served as an escort and night fighter from 1940 until replaced by monoplanes at the end of 1941. More than 1,750 had been built when production ended, but the 840hp Fiat A.74 gave a top speed of only 440km/h (274mph). The same engine powered the Fiat G.50 Freccia (Arrow) and Macchi C.200 Saetta (Lightning) monoplanes, which could achieve 472 km/h (293mph) and 502km/h (312mph) respectively. Like most Italian fighters, they were light and easy to handle but underarmed (they carried no cannon) and underpowered. Production ran to 730 G.50s, including 450 of the *bis* version, and more than 1,090 C.200s.

The C.200 was developed into the C.202 Folgore (Thunderbolt), powered by a 1,200 hp Daimler-Benz in-line engine in place of the heavy and drag-inducing Fiat A.74. This type entered service in 1941, and then both it and the G.50 were re-engined with license-built 1,475hp DB605As to become the C.205V Veltro (Greyhound) and G.55 Centauro respectively. These fighters at last had adequate top speeds–645km/h (400mph) and 620km/h (385mph) – but did not enter service until 1943 and were consequently too late to affect the course of the war.

Aces

The ace system originated in France during World War I, any pilot with five confirmed victories in air combat being mentioned in an official communiqué. The United States later adopted the practice of conferring 'ace' status on a pilot with five aerial victories, but the Germans regarded ten as the cut-off point and the British shied away from singling out individuals. Methods of verifying scores also varied, so the totals given here cannot strictly be compared.

* = *approximate total.*
† = *radar operator.*
Note: *other jet aces include Pakistani and Israeli pilots.*

World War I

Name	Nationality	Score
Rittmeister Manfred von Richthofen	German	80
Capitaine René P. Fonck	French	75
Major E. C. Mannock	British	73*
Major W. A. Bishop	Canadian	72
Oberleutnant Ernst Udet	German	62
Major R. Collishaw	Canadian	60
Major J. T. B. McCudden	British	57
Captain A. W. Beauchamp-Proctor	South African	54
Capitaine Georges M. L. J. Guynemer	French	54
Captain D. P. MacLaren	Canadian	54
Oberleutnant Erich Loewenhardt	German	53
Major W. G. Barker	Canadian	52
Captain P. F. Fullard	British	52
Major R. S. Dallas	Australian	51
Captain G. E. H. McElroy	Irish	49
Leutnant Werner Voss	German	48
Captain A. Ball	British	47
Captain R. A. Little	Australian	47
Hauptmann Bruno Loerzer	German	45
Lieutenant Charles E. J. M. Nungesser	French	45
Leutnant Fritz Rumey	German	45
Hauptmann Rudolph Berthold	German	44
Leutnant Paul Bäumer	German	43
Major T. F. Hazell	Irish	43
Leutnant Josef Jacobs	German	41
Capitaine Georges F. Madon	French	41
Hauptmann Oswald Boelcke	German	40
Hauptmann Godwin Brumowski	Austro-Hungarian	40
Leutnant Franz Buchner	German	40
Major J. Gilmour	British	40
Captain J. I. T. Jones	British	40
Oberleutnant Lothar von Richthofen	German	40
Leutnant Karl Menckhoff	German	39
Leutnant Heinrich Gontermann	German	39
Lieutenant Willy Coppens de Houthulst	Belgian	37
Captain F. R. McCall	Canadian	37
Captain W. G. Claxton	Canadian	36
Captain J. S. T. Fall	Canadian	36
Leutnant Max Müller	German	36
Captain H. W. Woollett	British	36
Captain A. C. Atkey	Canadian	35
Lieutenant Maurice Boyau	French	35
Leutnant Julius Buckler	German	35
Leutnant Gustav Dörr	German	35
Captain S. M. Kinkead	South African	35–40*
Hauptmann Eduard Ritter von Schleich	German	35

Also

Maggiore Francesco Baracca	Italian	34
Captain Edward V. Rickenbacker	US	26
Major A. A. Kazakov	Russian	17*

(*The above three pilots were the top scorers of their nationalities*)

World War II, Spanish Civil War, Russo-Finnish Winter War and Japanese action on the Asian mainland

Germany (day fighters)

Major Erich Hartmann	352
Major Gerhard Barkhorn	301
Major Gunther Rall	275
Oberleutnant Otto Kittel	267
Major Walter Nowotny	258
Major Wilhelm Batz	237
Major Erich Rudorffer	222
Oberst Heinz Bär	220
Oberst Hermann Graf	212
Major Heinrich Ehrler	209*

Germany (night fighters)

Major Heinz-Wolfgang Schnauffer	121
Oberst Helmut Lent	102
	(plus 8 by day)
Major Heinrich Prinz zu Sayn-Wittgenstein	84
Oberst Werner Streib	65
	(plus 1 by day)
Hauptmann Manfred Meurer	65
Oberst Gunter Radusch	64
Hauptmann Heinz Rökker	64
Major Rudolph Schönert	64
Major Paul Zorner	59

Also

Major Wilhelm Herget	57
	(plus 14 by day)

Japan

Warrant Officer Hiroyoshi Nishizawa	JAAF	87
Lieutenant Tetsuzo Iwamoto	JNAF	80*
Petty Officer 1st Class Shoichi Sugita	JNAF	70*
Lieutenant Saburo Sakai	JNAF	64
Warrant Officer Hiromichi Shinohara	JAAF	58
Petty Officer 1st Class Takeo Okumura	JNAF	54
Master Sergeant Satoshi Anabuki	JAAF	51
Lieutenant Mitsuyoshi Tarui	JAAF	38
Warrant Officer Isamu Sasaki	JAAF	38
Petty Officer 1st Class Toshio Ohta	JNAF	34

Russia

Ivan N. Kozhedub	62
Aleksandr I. Pokryshkin	59
Grigori A. Rechkalov	58
Nikolai D. Gulayev	57
Arsenii V. Vorozheikin	52
Kirill A. Yevstigneyev	52
Dmitri B. Glinka	50
Aleksandr F. Klubov	50
Ivan M. Pilipenko	48
Vasilii N. Kubarev	46

British Commonwealth

Squadron Leader M. T. St J. Pattle	South African	51*
Group Captain J. E. Johnson	British	38
Wing Commander B. Finucane	Irish	32
Group Captain A. G. Malan	South African	32*
Flight Lieutenant G. F. Beurling	Canadian	31⅓
Wing Commander J. R. D. Braham	British	29
Wing Commander R. R. S. Tuck	British	29
Wing Commander C. R. Caldwell	Australian	28½
Group Captain F. R. Carey	British	28*
Squadron Leader N. F. Duke	British	28

United States

Major Richard I. Bong	USAAF	40
Major Thomas B. McGuire	USAAF	38
Commander David S. McCampbell	USN	34
Lieutenant Colonel Gregory Boyington	USMC	28
Colonel Francis S. Gabreski	USAAF	28
Major Robert S. Johnson	USAAF	28
Colonel Charles H. MacDonald	USAAF	27
Major Joseph J. Foss	USMC	26
Lieutenant Robert M. Hanson	USMC	25
Major George E. Preddy	USAAF	25

Finland

Lentomestari Eino Ilmari Juutilainen	94
Kapteeni Hans Wind	78
Majuri Eino Luukkanen	54
Lentomestari Urho Lehtovaara	44
Kapteeni Risto Olli Puhakka	43
Lentomestari Oiva Tuominen	43
Lentomestari Nils Katajainen	36
Luutnantti Kauko Puro	35
Luutnantti Lauri Nissinen	32½
Majuri Jorma Karhunen	31

Also

Captain Prince Constantine Cantacuzene	Romanian	60
Commandante Joaquin Garcia Morato y Castano	Nationalist Spanish	40
Leutnant Cvitan Galic	Croatian	36
Second Lieutenant Rotnik Rezny	Slovakian	32
Sergeant Joseph Frantisek	Czech	28
Capitano Franco Lucchini	Italian	26
Capitaine Marcel Albert	French	23
Wing Commander Stanislav F. Skalski	Polish	21*

(*The above pilots were the top scorers of their nationalities*)

Korean War

Captain Joseph McConnell Jr	USAF	16
Major James Jabara	USAF	15
Captain Manuel J. Fernandez	USAF	14½
Major George A. Davis Jr	USAF	14
Colonel Royal N. Baker	USAF	13

Vietnam War

Colonel Tomb	Vietnamese People's Air Force	13
Captain Nguyen Van Bay	Vietnamese People's Air Force	7*
Captain Charles D. DeBellevue	USAF	6†

TOP LEFT : *Charles Nungesser.*
TOP RIGHT : *Edward Rickenbacker.*
CENTRE LEFT : *Manfred von Richthofen.*
CENTRE RIGHT : *Stamford Tuck.*
BOTTOM LEFT : *W A Bishop.*
BOTTOM RIGHT : *Oswald Boelcke.*

Russian fighters of World War II

In the early months following the invasion by German forces, beginning in July 1941, the USSR relied on fighters such as the Lavochkin LaGG–3 and the Mikoyan MiG–1/MiG–3 series. The latter were very fast for their time – 650km/h (405mph) – but suffered from a number of shortcomings and were relegated to reconnaissance by the end of 1943. The all-wood LaGG–3 was strong but not particularly manoeuvrable, being used for roles such as escorting ground-attack types. It was replaced by the La–5, one of two new fighters making their combat debut at the Battle of Stalingrad in October 1942 (the other being the Yakovlev Yak–9). The La–5 was in effect an LaGG–3 with the power increased from 1,100hp to 1,600hp. The later La–7, which carried three 20mm cannon in place of the La–5's two, could achieve 660km/h (413mph) with a 1,775hp powerplant. The Yak–9, of which many thousands were built, was light and easy to handle. The smaller Yak–3, which followed it in 1944, could reach 645km/h (403mph) and was widely used as an escort for ground-attack types.

American fighters of World War II

More than 50 per cent of the US Army Air Force's fighter strength in the first half of World War II was made up of two types, the Bell P–39 Airacobra and Curtiss P–40 Warhawk/Kittyhawk series. Both were powered by variants of the Allison V–1710 engine ranging from 1,040hp to 1,360hp. The P–39 was unusual in having the powerplant mounted centrally in the fuselage and driving the propeller through an extension shaft. It was also one of the first production fighters with a tricycle undercarriage. The type entered service with the RAF in October 1941, and about 9,500 – of which some 5,000 were supplied to the Soviet Union – were eventually built. The most numerous version was the P–39Q, of which nearly 5,000 were produced. This carried four 0·50in machine guns, in addition to the 37mm cannon, whereas previous variants had been armed with a mixture of 12·7mm and 0·30in weapons. The Curtiss P–40 series, which followed the P–36 Mohawk, was the first mass-produced US single-seat fighter. More than 14,000 were built, being supplied to the RAF (which called it the Tomahawk), Dominion air forces and the Soviet Union as well as to the USAAF. More than 5,200 P–40Ns alone, armed with six 0·50in machine guns, were constructed.

Nearly 10,000 Lockheed P–38 Lightnings were built, this type being responsible for destroying more enemy aircraft in the Pacific war than any other fighter. Nearly 4,000 of these were P–38Ls, capable of 665km/h (415 mph), and the radar-equipped P–38M night fighter saw service in the closing stages of the war. The Douglas A–20 Havoc was also used as a night fighter, but the first US aircraft designed specifically for this role was the Northrop P–61 Black Widow, which became operational in the summer of 1944.

Two remarkable fighters which did sterling duties as long-range bomber escorts as well as their other duties were the Republic P–47 Thunderbolt and North American P–51 Mustang. Originally designed as a lightweight fighter, the P–47, affectionately known as the Jug, turned out to be the biggest and heaviest single-seat fighter then built. The 9,615kg (21,200lb) P–47N, with strengthened and extended wings for Pacific operations, was almost as heavy as the twin-engined Beaufighter. It was powered by the 2,800hp engine which had given the earlier P–47M a top speed of more than 750km/h (470mph). Most of the lighter P–47Ds, of which 12,000 were built, had the Pratt & Whitney Double Wasp of 2,300hp, giving a speed of 687km/h (429mph). The Mustang was designed originally to a British specification and was powered by a Rolls-Royce/Packard Merlin engine. It was later adopted by the USAAF, and nearly 8,000 of the P–51D model alone were built. Its 1,590hp powerplant conferred a top speed of 703km/h (437mph); armament comprised up to six 0·50in machine guns. The P–82 (later F–82) Twin Mustang, a pair of P–51s joined in Siamese twin-fashion, entered service just before the end of the war and later operated as a long-range escort.

Japanese fighters of World War II

Across the Pacific, Japan had introduced its first low-wing monoplane fighter, and the first with an enclosed cockpit, in mid-1937. The Nakajima Ki–27 (Type 97 Fighter), of which more than 3,300 were built, was a main Japanese Army Air Force fighter until replaced by the Ki–43 at the end of 1942. The same manufacturer's Ki–43 Hayabusa (Peregrine Falcon) became the most widely produced JAAF fighter, nearly 5,800 being built. Late models had nearly twice the power of the Ki–27, raising top speed from 458km/h (285mph) to 512km/h (320mph). The Ki–43, armed with two machine guns, saw service in every theatre of the Pacific war. Nakajima's Ki–44 Shoki (Demon), of which more than 1,200 were constructed, was heavy and unpopular with its pilots but had a good rate of

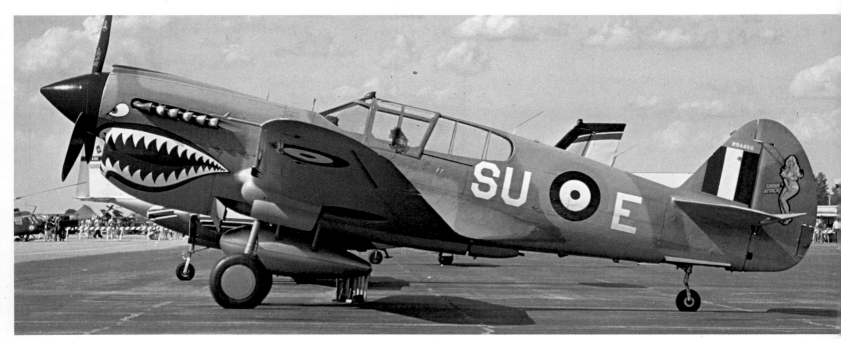

climb and, at 600km/h (375mph), was fast.

The Kawasaki Ki–45 Toryu (Dragon Slayer) entered service in October 1941 as a JAAF night fighter and was widely used in the south-west Pacific and the defence of Japan, about 1,700 being built. It was heavily armed, carrying one 37mm and two 20mm cannon. The same manufacturer's Ki–61 Hien (Flying Swallow) followed in the late summer of 1942, and its close resemblance to the Messerschmitt Bf109, coupled with the fact that an in-line engine was most unusual in a Japanese aircraft, gave rise to speculation that the Ki–61 might be a German type built under license. In fact, its engine was a licence-built version of the German Daimler-Benz DB601A. It was armed with two 20mm cannon and a pair of machine guns, and had a top speed of 556km/h (385mph). About 2,750 were built, and a shortage of in-line engines led to some being fitted with radials from the beginning of 1945 for use in the defence of Japan. These were designated Ki–100.

The formidable Nakajima Ki–84 Hayate (Gale) entered service only a year before the end of the war, but more than 3,500 were built and they made their mark. Later versions carried four cannon, two 20mm and the others 30mm, and the 1,900hp engine was capable of propelling the aircraft at 612km/h (380mph). The same company's J1N1 had a chequered career, being designed as a fighter, seeing service on reconnaissance duties and finally, as the Gekko (Moonlight), operating as a night fighter with primitive radar. Not to

ABOVE FAR LEFT: *North American P–51B Mustang.*
TOP LEFT: *The Yakovlev Yak-3 entered service with the Soviet Air Force in 1944.*
TOP RIGHT: *Lavochkin's LaGG–3, built of wood, was strong but relatively unmanoeuvrable.*

CENTRE: *The Curtiss P-40 was known as the Tomahawk in the Royal Air Force.*
ABOVE: *The Curtiss P–36 Mohawk laid the foundations for the P–40, the first US mass-produced fighter, with more than 14,000 built.*

LEFT: *The Kawasaki Ki–61 (Flying Swallow), which entered service with the Japanese Army Air Force in the summer of 1942, closely resembled the German Bf109.*
BELOW: *The Republic P–47M Thunderbolt affectionately known as the Jug, had a top speed of more than 750km/h (470mph). The Thunderbolt was the heaviest single-seat fighter of its time.*
BELOW CENTRE: *The heavily armed Kawasaki Ki–45 Toryu (Dragon Slayer) was used by the Japanese throughout the south-west Pacific and in the defence of Japan itself.*
BOTTOM: *More than 3,500 Nakajima Ki–84s were built, even though the type did not enter service until the summer of 1944.*

Guns and Cannon

also adopted heavy cannon, and used guns of up to 37mm in its first jet fighters. Japan was slow in introducing weapons of heavier calibre – a 12·7-mm machine-gun was requested by pilots in 1939 but not received for two years, and the 20-mm cannon did not appear until 1944.

The first major innovation for some time in aircraft gun armament was the General Electric M61 Vulcan, introduced in the Lockheed F–104 Starfighter and since adopted as the standard fighter gun for the US forces. A six-barrelled 20-mm weapon, it uses the Gatling-gun principle to spit out up to 6,000 rounds per

it fires shells weighing 360 grams (three-quarters of a pound). The combination of high velocity and weight gives the shell six-and-a-half times the kinetic energy at impact of a round from the previous-generation Aden or DEFA 30-mm cannon fitted to such types as the Hawker Hunter, Harrier and Hawk, and the Dassault Mirage series. The time of flight to 1,000m (3,300ft) is 1·23 seconds, and the drop in trajectory at that distance is only as much as that experienced in earlier 30-mm weapons at 400m (1,300ft).

For air-to-ground operations the latest state of the art is represented by the General Electric GAU–8/A Avenger fitted in the Fairchild A–10. The muzzle velocity, 1,050m/sec (3,450ft/sec), is not much greater than that of the Vulcan but the shell's flight time is reduced by 40 per cent because of improved ballistics. The Avenger's 30-mm shell weighs 0·7kg (1·6lb) and a single hit will destroy a tank. Sufficient ammunition is carried for ten two-second bursts at the maximum firing rate of 4,000 rounds per minute.

The aircraft machine-gun was introduced at the beginning of 1915, armament previously having been restricted to hand-held pistols and rifles. Typical observers' guns were the US 0·303-in Lewis and the German 7·92-mm LMG.08/15. Ammunition was fed to the air-cooled Lewis gun from a revolving drum containing 47 rounds at first and 97 in later versions. Cartridge cases were collected in a receptacle to prevent damage to the aircraft which would have been possible if they had been ejected overboard. By 1918 the Lewis's rate of fire had reached 850 rounds per minute, while the Parabellum could fire 700 rounds a minute. The most commonly used pilots' guns, the British 0·303-in Vickers and the German 7·92-mm LMG.08, were both developments of the Maxim infantry machine-gun. The LMG.08, almost universally referred to as the Spandau (after its place of manufacture), was slightly heavier than the 10kg (22lb) of the similar Parabellum.

Other weapons included France's 8-mm Hotchkiss, which produced a lot of drag and used an ammunition drum containing only 25 rounds; it was replaced by the Lewis gun. The Austrian 8-mm Schwarzlose had a short range and low rate of fire, and Italy's 9-mm Villa Perosa was not particularly successful, despite having two barrels and a high muzzle velocity. Some Voisins were fitted with 37-mm or 47-mm Hotchkiss cannon for ground-attack work, and these weapons were also employed occasionally in the air-to-air role, but not to any great effect.

Gun development between the wars was generally slow, and a pair of

forward-firing Vickers machine-guns remained the standard armament of RAF fighters until the mid-1930s. The US forces espoused the machine-gun even longer. Hitting power was improved from the mid-1930s, however, by the introduction of 0·50-in heavy machine-guns to supplement or replace the 0·30-in weapons. It was not until after the beginning of the Korean war that the switch to cannon armament became general. The cannon fires a heavier shell than the machine-gun, and range and muzzle velocity are also generally greater. The destructive effect is enhanced by the use of explosive rather than solid shells.

French, British and German fighters usually used 20-mm cannon at first, but calibres of up to 75-mm could be found in ground-attack types and the *Luftwaffe* tried a 50-mm weapon for air-to-air work. Russia

minute at a muzzle velocity of 1,000 m/sec (3,300ft/sec). The Soviet Union has recently fitted a 23-mm weapon operating on the same principle to some of its latest fighter-bombers.

A modern example of a single-barrel cannon is the Oerlikon KCA developed to arm the Swedish Air Force's new JA37 Viggen fighter. A 30-mm weapon with a muzzle velocity of 1,030m/sec (3,400ft/sec) and a rate of fire of 1,350 rounds a minute,

TOP LEFT: *The observer of an FE-2b and his Lewis gun.*
TOP RIGHT: *A 50-calibre machine gun arming a Boeing B-29.*
CENTRE LEFT: *The six-barrelled 20-mm Vulcan gun.*
CENTRE: *Tail of a Boeing B-29.*
CENTRE RIGHT: *The GAU-8 cannon mounted in the Fairchild A-10.*
ABOVE LEFT: *Standard forward-firing machine gun.*
ABOVE RIGHT: *7·62-mm guns in the Fairchild AU-23A.*

199

be outdone, the Japanese Navy introduced the Kawanishi N1K2–J Shiden (Violet Lightning), a land-based fighter with a rapid rate of climb and good manoeuvrability. It was too late to affect the course of the war, however.

Post-World War II fighters

Although piston-engined fighters remained in service after World War II and for a few years new ones were developed – the last Russian propeller fighter, the Lavochkin La–11, did not enter service until 1948 – the post-war era is definitely the age of the jet. Britain and Germany had established an early lead, but this was soon lost to the United States and Russia, both of whom absorbed experience and hardware previously developed by British and German engineers. Europe re-emerged later as a centre of jet-fighter production, while other countries such as Japan, India and Israel have since joined the exclusive band.

The first US jet was the Bell P–59 Airacomet, which made its maiden flight in October 1942, but its performance was unimpressive and it was relegated to training duties. Lockheed's F–80 Shooting Star just failed to see war service, but it became assured of a place in aviation history when, on November 8, 1950, Lt Russell Brown, USAF, shot down a MiG–15 over Korea in what is thought to have been the first-ever all-jet combat. The Republic P–84 Thunderjet first flew as early as February 1946, but it was destined to be the USAF's last straight-

winged subsonic fighter. Wartime work in Germany had proved that swept wings were more efficient for high-speed flight, and the North American P–86 Sabre was redesigned to take a swept wing before its maiden flight in October 1947. Republic went on to build more than 4,400 Thunderjets, armed with six 0·50in machine guns or unguided rockets, and a further 2,700 of the swept-wing F–84F Thunderstreak development were constructed.

Meanwhile the Soviet Union built a number of jet-fighter designs, beginning with the Yakovlev Yak–15 and MiG–9, which both made their first flights on the same day in April 1946. The former's single RD–10 centrifugal-flow turbojet of 900kg (1,980lb) thrust gave it a top speed of just over 800km/h (500mph); the MiG–9, however, was powered by a pair of axial-flow turbojets. The Lavochkin La–15, another jet design, entered service in 1949 but it was the MiG–15 which really made a permanent mark in history.

MiG–15s and F–86 Sabres tangled over Korea in a faster, more sophisticated repeat of the Spitfire-versus-Bf 109 dogfights of the Battle of Britain. The Russian aircraft, armed with one 37mm and two 20mm cannon, outgunned the Sabre with its six 0·50in machine guns (later variants carried four 20mm weapons and, ultimately, 24 2·75in folding-fin rockets). The MiG–15 was also more manoeuvrable above about 10,000m (33,000ft), but at low levels the Sabre had the edge. The decisive difference between the two

TOP: The Republic F–84 Thunderjet failed to see service during World War II but made its name in Korea.
ABOVE LEFT: The MiG–15 had just about everything its pilots could ask – speed, manoeuvrability and heavy armament.
ABOVE: The North American F–86 Sabre was outgunned by MiG–15s in Korea, but the battle-hardened US pilots won through.
TOP RIGHT: The de Havilland Vampire was under development from early in World War II but entered service only in 1946.
TOP FAR RIGHT: North American's F–100 Super Sabre was supersonic in level flight.
ABOVE CENTRE RIGHT: The Hawker Hunter is still used throughout the world.
BELOW CENTRE RIGHT: The variable-geometry Dassault G.8 with its wings swept back.
BOTTOM RIGHT: The experimental G.8 with its wings swept forward for low-speed flight and during take-off and landing.

turned out to be that the USAF pilots were battle-hardened veterans, whereas those flying the MiGs were comparatively raw recruits. The USAF and USN claimed to have shot down 792 MiG–15s over Korea, giving a kill ratio of more than ten to one. The improved MiG–17 joined its stablemate in 1952, and the combined production run of these two types is estimated at nearly 20,000.

The Lockheed F–94 Starfire, developed from the F–80, joined the USAF inventory in 1950 but by then supersonic fighters were becoming the name of the game, North American took the Sabre, swept the wings back by a further 10°, made many other changes and improvements, and turned out the F–100 Super Sabre. It entered service in 1954 as the first operational fighter able to exceed the

Type: McDonnell Douglas F–4 Phantom
Engines: Two General Electric J–19–17 turbojets
Armament: Four AIM–7 sparrow missiles, one 20mm
(0·787in) M61 multi-barrel gun, up to 7,260kg
(16,000lb) of bombs
Maximum speed: 1,464km/h (910mph)
Climb: 8,534m/min (28,000ft/min)
Ceiling: 19,685m (60,000ft)
Range: about 2,810km (1,750 miles)
Loaded weight: 27,500kg (60,630lb)
Span: 11·7m (38ft 5in)
Length: 19·2m (63ft)
Height: 4·96m (16ft 3in)

*General Dynamics built two of these YF–16
prototypes for a US Air Force competition – which
the type won – and now has orders for 1,000
production F–16s.*

Type: Mikoyan MiG–21
Engines: One Tumansky R–11 rated at 5,100kg (11,240lb)
Armament: One or two 30mm (1·181in) NR–30 guns, two K13 missiles
Maximum speed: 2,070km/h (1,285mph)
Initial climb: 11,000m/min (36,090ft/min)
Ceiling: 18,000m (59,050ft)
Range: 1,800km (1,118 miles)
Loaded weight: 8,500kg (18,740lb)
Span: 7·15m (23ft 5·5in)
Length: 14·3m (46ft 11in)
Height: 4·5m (14ft 9in)

speed of sound in level flight. The Pratt & Whitney J57 turbojet ultimately produced nearly 7,700kg (17,000lb) of thrust, enough to propel the Super Sabre at a little over 1,350km/h (850mph), or Mach 1·3. The USAF continued its practice of switching to cannon rather than machine guns, four 20 mm weapons being installed. More than 2,200 F–100s were built. In Russia, the MiG–19 entered service in 1955, providing the other superpower with its first supersonic fighter.

Britain lagged behind, relying on developments of the wartime Gloster Meteor and de Havilland Vampire, although the latter type did not enter service until 1946. The more advanced Supermarine Swift and Hawker Hunter became operational in 1954, but both were essentially subsonic and the former was soon confined to photo-reconnaissance duties. The Hunter, with its four 30mm Aden cannon, was nevertheless a fine fighter and remains in service today. Britain's first supersonic intercepter – and first Mach 2 warplane – was the outstanding BAC Lightning, which remained in front-line RAF service until American-built Phantom II F–4s replaced it in the mid-1970s.

Europe's first swept-wing jet fighter was the Swedish SAAB J29, nicknamed the Flying Barrel, which entered service in 1951. Its de Havilland Ghost engine gave it a top speed of 1,024km/h (636mph) and it carried an armament of four 20mm cannon. The first production European fighter which was supersonic in level flight, France's

Dassault Super Mystère B.2, did not enter service until 1958. Its SNECMA Atar turbojet of 3,400kg (7,500lb) thrust gave it a speed of Mach 1·25. The Super Mystère's ancestry can be traced back through the Mystère IVA, which saw action during the Suez crisis of 1956; the earlier Mystère IIC, which was basically a swept-wing version of the Ouragan; and the Ouragan itself. France followed the Super Mystère with the Mirage III; and Sweden introduced the SAAB Draken in 1960. All these types are capable of Mach 2, but this milestone had already been reached by the Lockheed F–104 Starfighter and the MiG–21. The Starfighter, designed originally as a day fighter with stunning performance in response to the USAF's demands after its experience in Korea, was later converted into a multi-role type with ground-mapping radar. It was the first aircraft to be armed with the General Electric M61 Vulcan six-barrelled Gatling gun, giving an extremely high rate of fire.

Several countries developed specialized fighters designed to operate at night and in bad weather, necessitating installation of radar and provision for two crew members. The USAF's Northrop F–89 Scorpion was a typical early example; France's Sud-Ouest Vautour carried four 30mm cannon and rockets. Canada contributed the Avro CF–100, and Russia relied on the Yakovlev Yak–25. The RAF's specialist in this field, the Gloster Javelin, was the first twin-jet with a delta wing when it entered service in 1956. In the United States, Convair had carved

out a niche in the delta-wing market, developing the supersonic F–102 Delta Dagger and the F–106 Delta Dart. The latter, powered by a J75 engine of 11,130kg (24,500lb) thrust, entered service in mid-1959 with a top speed of Mach 2·3.

The present generation of jet fighters is of extremely high performance. The Hawker Siddeley Harrier, the world's first operational V/STOL (Vertical/Short Take-Off and Landing) aircraft, entered service with the RAF in 1969 and, under the designation AV–8A, also equips the US Marine Corps. France's Dassault Mirage F.1 followed three years later, and Sweden has the SAAB Viggen (Thunderbolt). The latest USAF fighters, the twin-engined McDonnell Douglas F–15 Eagle and single-engined General Dynamics F–16, are both powered by the Pratt & Whitney F100 advanced turbofan engine of about 10,800kg (23,800lb) thrust. Both are extremely manoeuvrable fighters with a very impressive rate of climb, and they have been ordered in large quantities. Britain, Germany and Italy are developing the Panavia Tornado, a multi-role combat aircraft which includes air-to-air fighting among its duties, and Russia's newest types, the MiG–23 Flogger and MiG–25 Foxbat, are potent enough to cause the West more than a few headaches. When the F–15 set up a series of new time-to-height records, the MiG–25 grabbed them back soon afterwards, and the MiG–23 with its variable-sweep wings looks set fair to take over from the MiG–21 as one of the world's standard fighters of the next decade.

RIGHT: *The Lockheed F–104 Starfighter, nicknamed the 'missile with a man in it', carries a 20-mm Vulcan cannon and can fly at more than twice the speed of sound.*

BELOW: *The variable-geometry MiG–23 Flogger fighter is one of the Soviet Air Force's latest combat types. It can carry missiles as well as its built-in gun.*

BELOW RIGHT: *The Swedish SAAB Draken, with distinctive double-delta wing, has equipped the Swedish Air Force since 1960. It is capable of Mach 2.*

BOTTOM: *The Dassault Super Mystère B.2 was the first production European fighter able to exceed the speed of sound in level flight, but it did not enter service until 1958.*

FAR RIGHT ABOVE: *The Hawker Harrier entered service in 1969, becoming the world's first operational V/STOL combat aircraft.*

FAR RIGHT CENTRE: *The multi-role combat aircraft prototype, the MRCA–02 Tornado, developed by Britain, Germany and Italy.*

FAR RIGHT BELOW: *The Junkers CL.1 is regarded as the best German ground-attack aircraft of World War I.*

Attack aircraft

The definition of an attack aircraft has never been clearly laid down. Some authorities include under this heading all bombers which do not deliver their weapons in level flight – in other words dive-bombers are counted as attack aircraft. This is debatable – for example, essentially low-level types such as the BAC/Dassault-Breguet Jaguar drop their bombs in level flight but would be counted as attack aircraft even if they carried no cannon armament as well. Perhaps the best definition of an attack aircraft is one which is designed specifically or primarily to attack ground targets with guns, rockets or guided weapons, or which is intended to deliver free-fall bombs from low level.

Almost every fighter aircraft has at one time or another been used to drop bombs. In fact, the McDonnell Douglas Phantom II, officially designated F–4 (F = Fighter), has been very often used to carry a heavier bomb load than could be lifted by erstwhile 'heavy bombers'.

World War I
Ground attack, otherwise known as close support or army co-operation, began to emerge as a specialist task in the last year or

so of World War I. From the very beginning it was obvious that the forward-firing guns in the early fighters could be used effectively against surface targets as well as against other aircraft, especially as the main role of aircraft at that time was to support the army and not to fight an air war *per se*. In those days of small bombs it was also very difficult to distinguish between specialist bombers and observation types which dropped bombs as a secondary role.

Germany's CL types were intended originally as escorts for C-type observation aircraft, but it was soon found that their forward-firing machine guns made them extremely

useful for ground attack. From the middle of 1917, the Halberstadt CL.II was widely used for harassing ground forces, the observer being supplied with four or five small grenades or mortar bombs, weighing about 10kg (22 lb), which he dropped by hand. Similar missions were later carried out by the Halberstadt CL.IV and the Hannover CL.IIIa. In early 1918 Albatros and AEG J types, the latter developed from the C.IV, entered service as specialized ground-attack aircraft. The AEGs, of which some 600 were built, carried twin Spandaus mounted in the floor of the rear cockpit, pointing downwards at about 45°. The engine and crew were protected by 390kg (86olb) of armour plating, and an experimental single-seat version with six downward-firing guns was also constructed. It was found, however, that such armament was very difficult to aim accurately at low level.

Junkers developed the J.I to replace the interim J types, and the same manufacturer's CL.I was widely regarded as the best German ground-attack aircraft of the war. Grenades were stored in racks alongside the rear cockpit, but the type's introduction was too late to have any great effect.

On the Allied side, some 200 Voisin 4s were built with a forward-firing Hotchkiss 47mm cannon for strafing. The later Voisin 8 LBP could be fitted with either this weapon or one of 37mm. Some F.E.2bs were converted for ground attack, with a Vickers one-pounder installed in place of the Lewis machine gun, and the Martinsyde G.100/102 Elephant was employed in a light bombing role after being found unsuitable as a fighter. The Bristol Fighter could carry 12 bombs of 9kg (20lb) each. The D.H.5 was used from the autumn of 1917 as an attacker with 11kg (25lb) of bombs under its fuselage, and the S.E.5 had the same payload. The R.E.8 could carry four weapons of 30kg (65lb) each.

The first specialized British ground-attack aircraft was the Sopwith Camel, which incurred heavy losses when used as a light bomber with four weapons of 9kg (20lb) under its fuselage. An experimental version with downward-firing machine guns was tried, and experience gained with the Camel led to the Sopwith Salamander. Designated the T.F.2 (T.F. = Trench Fighter), the Salamander was similar to the Snipe but carried 295kg (65olb) of armour around the pilot and the fuel, plus a pair of forward-firing Vickers machine guns supplied with 1,000 rounds each. This development was too late to see widespread service.

World War II
In the inter-war years, with money generally at a premium, air forces tended to concentrate on fighters and bombers rather than ground-attack types. Those specialized aircraft that were developed for this role were not bought in large numbers. In the United States, Curtiss produced the A–3 version of the O–1B, which had an additional machine gun in each lower wing to supplement the pair in the nose, and later turned out the A–8/A–10/A–12/ Shrike series of all-metal low-wing monoplanes armed with four 0·30in machine guns and able to carry four bombs of 45kg (100lb)

LEFT: *The Italian Air Force used the Breda Ba65 as a specialist ground-attack type in the invasion of Abyssinia and later in North Africa.*
BELOW LEFT: *The Luftwaffe's Junkers Ju 88s were used for strafing as well as fighters. The Ju 88Ps (this is a P–2) were fitted with heavy-calibre cannon under the fuselage.*
BELOW: *The Henschel Hs 129 was designed from the start as a tank-buster, carrying three cannon and two bombs. The B–2/R4 version mounted a devastating 75mm cannon.*
RIGHT: *Another fighter which was as good or better on ground-attack duties was the Hawker Hurricane.*
CENTRE RIGHT: *The Soviet Air Force placed great emphasis on ground attack, one of its main types used in this role being the Petlyakov Pe–2.*
BELOW RIGHT: *The infamous Junkers Ju 87 Stuka was used effectively in the Spanish Civil War and in World War II. The dive-bomber versions (this is a B–1) were followed by Stukas with heavy guns.*

or two weighing 14kg (30lb). Northrop A–17/A–33s entered service with the USAAC in 1936 but were soon withdrawn and eventually passed on to South Africa via Britain.

Italy used the Breda Ba65, armed with four machine guns, as a specialist ground-attack aircraft in the invasion of Abyssinia and later in North Africa, while the *Luftwaffe* tested its Henschel Hs 123 biplane in Spain during the civil war. This type later saw service during the invasion of Poland and on the Russian front, the Hs 123C version having two additional machine guns in the lower wings for strafing. Another type used successfully in Spain and Poland was the Junkers Ju 87 Stuka dive-bomber. The Stuka, with its distinctive cranked wings and high-pitched whine during the attack, came to symbolize the inhumanity of modern warfare. It fared badly against eight-gun fighters such as the Hurricane and Spitfire, however, and lost much of its aura of omnipotence. As a dive-bomber the Stuka could carry a weapon load of 1,800kg (4,000lb) in addition to four 7·9mm machine guns; later specialist ground-attack developments included the heavily armour-plated Ju87D–3 and D–4, with underwing gun packs, and the anti-tank Ju87G fitted with a 37mm cannon under each wing.

The Stuka's 'tank-busting' role was taken over in North Africa and on the Russian front by the Henschel Hs 129, designed specifically for this role. It carried a single 30mm and two

20mm cannon, machine guns and two bombs of 50kg (110lb) each. In the B–2/R4 variant the 30mm weapon was replaced by one of 75mm. Eight hundred Hs 129s were built. The Ju 88 was also employed in the anti-tank role, the Ju 88P having one or two heavy-calibre cannon in a housing under the fuselage, and the later Ju 188S specialized in low-level operations with a variety of weapons including ventrally mounted 50mm cannon. Smaller fighters were also pressed into service in the ground-attack role, the Fw 190F – developed from the Fw 190A fighter – having extra armour-plating and fewer guns. On fighter-bomber missions the Fw 190G could carry a 500kg (1,100lb) or 1,000kg (2,200lb) bomb, and the Bf 109F was transferred from air-to-air operations when Bf 109Gs were introduced. The 109Fs were in this case armed with rocket projectiles; later on, the 109G was also employed on ground-attack work. Hitler's apparent insistence that the jet Me 262 be used for attack roles resulted in misuse of an aircraft which was undoubtedly far more successful as a pure fighter.

From October 1941 the RAF used 'Hurri-bomber' versions of the Hurricane IIB and IIC, the aircraft carrying a 114kg (250lb) bomb under each wing. These were followed in mid-1942 by Mk IIDs armed with a pair of 40mm cannon under a strengthened wing. Each shot pulled the Hurricane's nose down by 5°, so the aircraft then had to be re-aimed, but the type was used with great success in the Western Desert. Rocket-carrying vari-

ants of the Mks IIB, IIC and IV became available from September of the following year, and the Hurricanes supplied to Russia were modified to carry a crew of two for ground-attack work. These aircraft were operated by the French *Normandie* squadron operating in Russia, as well as by the Soviet Union itself. Another type which doubled as a fighter and attacker was the Bristol Beaufighter. Some Mk VIs were operated as 'Flakbeaus' armed with eight rockets or up to 45kg (1,000lb) of bombs. Similarly, the Mosquito F.B.XVIII could carry eight rockets and two 225kg (500lb) bombs as well as a 57mm (six-pounder) gun under its nose. The earlier F.B.VI, of which more than 1,000 were built, could also be fitted with eight 27kg (60lb) rocket projectiles.

Two very effective types used against tanks, trains and shipping were Hawker's Typhoon and Tempest. Their four built-in Hispano 20mm cannon were augmented by eight rockets and up to 900kg (2,000lb) of bombs.

The French Air Force's specialized two-seat ground-attack Potez 633s saw action in the Battle of France, but were too sparsely deployed to have any great effect. Liore-Nieuport 401s and 411s were also used at this time. The United States' fighters in the early part of the war, especially the Bell P–39 and Curtiss P–40, were also operated as fighter-bombers. The former could carry a 225kg (500lb) bomb, the latter as many as three of the same weight or one under the fuselage and six of 9kg (20lb) each under the wings. The P–38L version of the Lockheed Lightning, of which nearly 4,000 were built, carried ten 127mm (5in) rockets, as could the North American P–51D Mustang and late models of the Republic P–47 Thunderbolt. Five hundred A–36As, specialized ground-attack Mustangs with dive-brakes above and below the wings, had been supplied earlier.

On the larger side, a formidable attacker was the Douglas A–20 Havoc. Most of the 2,850 A–20Gs were supplied to Russia, where they were an invaluable addition to the air-to-surface strike force. They were fitted with up to eight nose-mounted 0·50in machine guns, or two of these weapons and four 20mm cannon, and could carry a bombload of up to 1,814kg (4,000lb). The A–20 was developed into the A–26B (later B–26) Invader, a heavily armoured attacker with six machine guns in the nose; the fire from these could be augmented by locking the upper turret in the forward position and firing its guns under control of the pilot. Even heavier was the disappointing North American B–25G/H series, armed with a massive, nose-mounted 75mm cannon as well as up to 14 0·50in guns. Some B–25Js were fitted with no fewer than 18 0·50in machine guns, plus eight rocket projectiles, for ground attack.

The Soviet Union's best known attacker was the Ilyushin Il-2 *Shturmovik*, which was designed specifically for that role. It entered service in 1941 as a single-seater armed with two 20mm cannon and a pair of forward-firing 0·30in machine guns. The pilot was protected by armour-plating, but the aircraft was found to be vulnerable from the rear. In 1942, therefore, a two-seater with a pair of rearward-firing 0·30in weapons for self-defence was introduced. The Il–2 was one of the first types to use rocket projectiles – up to eight weighing 25kg (56lb) each – and could carry 400kg (880lb) of bombs. It had the lowest wartime attrition rate of any Russian combat aircraft. The machine-gun-armed Petlyakov Pe–2 was also used for ground attack, as was the Tupolev Tu–2 that replaced it. Fighters such as the Polikarpov I–16, Lavochkin LaGG–3 and Yakovlev Yak–3 were employed on strafing duties and could be fitted with rockets, while Yak–9Ts were armed with 75mm cannon for anti-ship operations.

In Japan the Mitsubishi Ki–46–IIIB was a ground-attack adaptation of the type normally used for reconnaissance, and about 2,000 of the same manufacturer's specialized Ki–51 – sometimes called the Japanese Stuka – were built. The Kawasaki Ki–102, only a small number of which were completed by the end of the war, was formidably armed with a 57mm cannon, two of 20mm, a 0·50in machine gun and 500kg (1,100lb) of bombs. Kawasaki's earlier Ki–45 had also been heavily armed, carrying one 37mm and two 20mm cannon or a 75mm weapon for anti-ship strike. This form of attack was the forté of Japanese *Kamikaze* pilots in the Pacific. With some success they tried to stem the tide of Allied shipping by the simple expedient of crashing into it. This was a desperate tactic and another case of that war-time cliché: 'too little, too late'.

Type: Ilyushin Il–2
Engines: One 1,300hp M–38 Vee-12 liquid-cooled
Armament: Two 20mm (0·787in) and two 7·62mm
  (0·299in) guns, eight 82mm (3·228in) rockets and four
  100kg (220lb) bombs
Maximum speed: 452km/h (281mph)
Climb: 150m/min (490ft/min)
Ceiling: 6,500m (21,325ft)
Range: 600km (373 miles)
Loaded weight: 5,872kg (12,947lb)
Span: 14·6m (47ft 11in)
Length: 12m (39ft 4·5in)
Height: 3·4m (11ft 2in)

Post-war developments

In the immediate post-war years most effort was concentrated on applying the new jet engines to ever faster fighters and bigger bombers. Specialized ground-attack types were generally ignored, with the result that the outbreak of the Korean War in 1950 caught all combatants with ageing attack forces. In fact, jet power was not necessary for this role because a stable weapon platform was usually more important than a high top speed. United Nations forces continued to rely on such types as the North American Mustang and Douglas B–26 (formerly A–26) Invader. Probably the most effective close-support aircraft was the Douglas A–1 Skyraider, which remained in production from the end of World War II until 1957, so difficult was it to find something better to replace it. The Skyraider had an endurance of up to ten hours and could be fitted with a wide variety of weapons on 15 attachments. A typical load was a dozen high-velocity 127 mm (5in) rockets, two 450kg (1,000lb) bombs and a napalm canister. A–1s, of which more than 3,000 were built, could be flown with 6,350kg (14,000lb) of underwing stores in addition to their four 20mm cannon in the wing. For really hard targets such as bridges they could mount 12in Tiny Tim rockets. Both the A–1 and B–26 were later used in Vietnam.

As had been the case in the war, virtually all fighters were also used for air-to-surface missions. Types such as the Republic F–84 and North American F–86 carried bombs in addition to their built-in cannon and machine guns, while the Soviet Union employed Mikoyan MiG–17s and –19s against ground targets. The Russian practice of fitting large cannon–up to 37mm–for air-to-air work gave the fighters a good punch against tanks, but design of the aircraft made them suitable for high-speed flight and bombload was severely limited. Britain had produced the de Havilland Venom, armed with four 20mm cannon and up to 900kg (2,000lb) of bombs, and in the Hawker Hunter provided a true multi-role aircraft tailored to the needs of many emerging air forces. The Hunter combined 30mm cannon with heavy rockets–16 of 27kg (60lb) each, for example –and bombs. In France, the Sud-Ouest Vautour could carry 3,200kg (7,000lb) of bombs as well as four 30mm cannon; the Dassault Super Mystère, mounted bombs and rockets plus its two 30mm guns.

The United States continued to develop fighters which performed equally well, if not better, as bombers. The North American F–100 Super Sabre is still in use, toting up to 2,720kg (6,000lb) of bombs and delivering a hail of shells from its four 20mm cannon. The McDonnell Voodoo, in its F–101C variant, was modified for ground attack. The M61 Vulcan six-barrelled Gatling gun was first brought to bear on surface targets in the Lockheed F–104G Starfighter. By then a wide range of missiles were available, allowing attacks to be made with pin-point accuracy from outside the range of the target's defences. The Republic F–105D Thunderchief also packs the punch of a Vulcan gun, and despite its fighter designation can carry, internally and externally, a load of 6,350kg (14,000lb). With a typical arrangement of 16 bombs of 340kg (750lb) each under its wings, the F–105 bore much of the responsibility for USAF tactical bombing in Vietnam. The F–105G version operated on Wild Weasel missions, attacking enemy radars with missiles which homed on to their radiation.

In the late 1950s the aircraft gun came to be regarded as old-fashioned, and many new fighters were designed around missile armament only. Early versions of the McDonnell F–4 Phantom, for example, relied on Sidewinder and Sparrow air-to-air missiles. It was soon realized, however, that the gun added versatility and in many close-in dog-fighting cases was superior to the missile. The F–4E version of the Phantom therefore incorporates a Vulcan, enhancing its effectiveness in the air-to-surface role as well as in air combat. In fact, the Phantom is no mean bomber in its own right, being able to carry a load of 7,257kg (16,000lb).

In the 1950s, Fiat (now Aeritalia) developed the G.91 to meet a NATO requirement for a light strike fighter, and in its twin-engined G.91Y variant it can carry 1,800kg (4,000lb) of bombs, missiles or machine gun pods in addition to the pair of built-in cannon. Russia also produced a ground-attack specialist in the form of the Sukhoi Su–7, carrying rockets and cannon. This type has seen extensive action in the Middle East, where it equips the air forces of many Arab states.

France's Dassault Mirage III can be employed on ground-attack duties, carrying a pair of 450kg (1,000lb) bombs or missiles in addition to two DEFA 30mm cannon in a gun pack. Dassault has also developed the same basic aircraft into the Mirage 5, with simplified electronics, more fuel, easier maintenance and a far bigger – 4,000kg (8,800lb) – weapon load. In Sweden, SAAB followed the Lansen with the Draken, a multi-role type able to act as a fighter-bomber as well as a Mach 2 intercepter.

Vietnam

The war in Vietnam changed the face of the American armoury. Attack aircraft of all shapes and sizes proliferated; Republic F–105s delivered guided and unguided ordnance by the ton, light aircraft weighed in with rockets and machine guns, and in between came the specialized attackers. The USAF took the Navy's LTV A–7A Corsair II carrier-based fighter-bomber and turned it into the A–7D – a bomb truck designed to deliver up to 6,800kg (15,000lb) at a time. The Cessna T–37 trainer was beefed up, given twice the thrust and became the A–37B, with a multi-barrelled 0·30in Minigun and 2,270 kg (5,000lb) of bombs. A requirement for a light armed reconnaissance aircraft resulted in the Rockwell OV–10A Bronco, carrying four 0·30in machine guns and 1,100kg (2,400lb) of other weapons.

More unusual were the converted transport aircraft used to pour a hail of fire on to

BELOW: *The Anglo-French BAC/Dassault-Breguet Jaguar serves with four air forces.*
BELOW CENTRE: *The Blackburn Buccaneer S.1 operated from Royal Navy aircraft carriers.*

BOTTOM CENTRE: *France and Germany are collaborating on the Dassault/Dornier Alpha Jet.*
BOTTOM: *Sweden's SAAB Viggen is used for anti-ship attacks and against land targets.*

ground targets. The Douglas AC–47D, known unofficially as 'Puff the Magic Dragon', could carry three 0·30in Miniguns each able to fire 6,000 rounds a minute out through the side of the fuselage. At a later stage, Fairchild AC–119s and Lockheed AC–130s were fitted with cannon and Gatling guns for the same role.

The European battlefield

The Soviet Union has 20,000 tanks available for a thrust against Western Europe, and NATO's ground-attack aircraft would have the task of helping to stop such an assault. Land-based types would also be called on to assist carrier aircraft in missions against shipping. The RAF deploys the Hawker Siddeley Buccaneer, Harrier and BAC/Dassault-Breguet Jaguar in these roles. The Buccaneer S.2, designed originally for the Royal Navy, can carry four 450kg (1,000lb) bombs internally and an additional 5,450kg (12,000lb) of various weapons under its wings – these could include rockets or Martel guided missiles. Being designed specifically for low-level attack, it is a stable weapon platform ideally suited to such a task. The V/STOL (Vertical/Short Take-Off and Landing) Harrier can be fitted with two pods containing 30mm Aden cannon plus underwing stores such as a pair of 450kg (1,000lb) bombs and two containers each holding 19 68mm rockets. The RAF's Jaguar, carrying the computer-based NAVWASS (Navigation and Weapon-Aiming Sub-System), is designed to fly a ground-hugging mission to make surprise, one-pass attacks using its two built-in Aden guns and up to 4,500kg (10,000lb) of weapons such as the BL755 cluster bomb, which dispenses 147 bomblets in a cloud.

France also uses Jaguars, with different weapons, as well as ground-attack Mirage IIIs and some Mirage 5Fs. Germany's Lockheed F–104Gs are to be replaced by the Panavia Tornado multi-role combat aircraft, being built in collaboration with Britain and Italy. A British variant of the swing-wing Tornado will be used as an intercepter but the basic common version is designed for ground attack, anti-shipping duties and reconnaissance. Germany is also co-operating with France, in this case on the Dassault-Dornier Alpha Jet light attack/trainer. In the *Luftwaffe* the Alpha Jet will replace G.91s, capable of being fitted with a pod containing a Mauser 27mm cannon, the same gun as used in Tornado, or up to 2,200kg (4,850lb) of bombs or other weapons on a total of five pylons. The Alpha Jet has been ordered by Belgium as well as its two sponsoring countries. Britain's Hawker Siddeley Hawk – which the RAF uses as an advanced flying and weapons trainer – is competing in the same export market in a version which can carry up to 2,270kg (5,000lb) of mixed weapons.

Belgium is also one of several countries, including Holland, Denmark and Norway, to have ordered the General Dynamics F–16 for ground-attack duties as well as air combat. Sweden continues to produce modern weapons of extremely high quality, including the SAAB AJ37 Viggen for anti-ship strike in

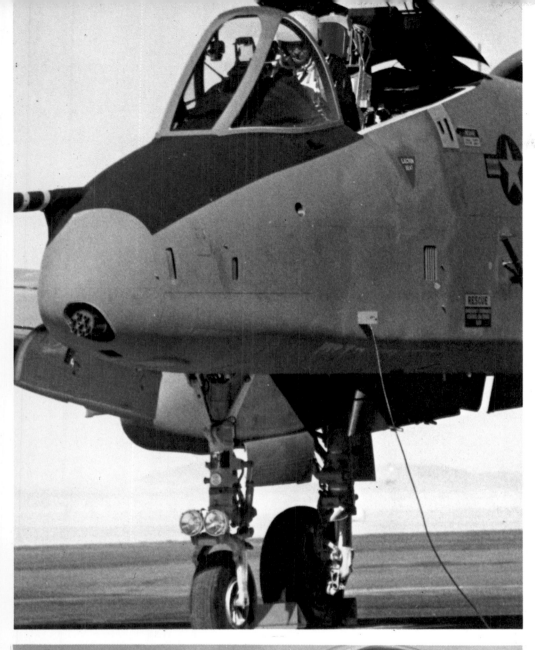

the Baltic as well as overland operations.

The McDonnell Douglas F–15 Eagle, primarily a fighter, can nevertheless carry more than 5,450kg (12,000lb) of bombs, but the USAF's main tank-buster in Europe is to be the Fairchild A–10. Its top speed is modest – a significant departure from the 'fast is good' thinking which has largely prevailed since World War II – but it is a stable and yet highly manoeuvrable weapon-delivery platform. The A–10 is built round 'a General Electric GAU–8/A Avenger seven-barrelled cannon, which can fire 1,350 rounds of armour-piercing ammunition at a rate of 4,000 rounds a minute and with a muzzle velocity of 1,050m/sec (3,450ft/sec). The shells weigh 0·73kg (1·6lb) each and can disintegrate a tank. The A–10 also has 11 pylons for up to 7,250kg (16,000lb) of guided and unguided ordnance.

Light strike aircraft

The development of small yet powerful and economical jet engines has led to a new breed of aircraft, the light strike types. These often double as trainers, and are cheap enough to give even small air forces a potent attack force. At the top end of the scale is the Northrop F–5, developed from the T–38 trainer. The most modern versions, the F–5E and two-seat F–5F, are really too heavy to be included under this heading, indicating the growth potential of even small aircraft. The F–5E can carry four Maverick air-to-surface missiles on special lightweight launchers, as well as a pair of built-in 20mm cannon and two Sidewinder missiles for self-defence. Maximum external weapon load is 3,175kg (7,000lb).

On the smaller side, alongside the Hawk and Alpha Jet mentioned above, are the BAC Strikemaster, SAAB 105G and Aermacchi MB.326/339 series, together with a range of types built in Eastern Europe. They can usually carry about 1,350kg (3,000lb) of bombs in addition to rockets, missiles, cannon or machine guns. Perhaps the nearest modern aircraft to the attack types of World War II is the Argentinian FMA I.A.58 Pucara twin-turboprop, which carries two 20 mm cannon and four 0·30in machine guns internally and which has three pylons for external loads.

The future

The Soviet Air Force is deploying a new generation of specialized attack aircraft and multi-role fighter-bombers, including the Sukhoi Su–19 Fencer, similar to but smaller than the General Dynamics F–111 of the USAF; the Mikoyan MiG–23 Flogger; and the Su–17 variable-sweep development of the Su–7.

Similarly, the NATO countries are busy introducing aircraft which outshine previous types in almost every department. And not all the big strides are being made in the field of large, complicated and expensive warplanes. The new breed of light strike/trainers, such as the Hawk and CASA C.101, use economical turbofan engines and save fuel as well as offering performance which is much improved over that of their heavyweight predecessors of as little as a decade ago.

TOP: *The Fairchild A–10 is the first specifically ground-attack type developed for the US Air Force in the past two decades. Its main armament is the 30-mm Avenger cannon.*

ABOVE: *BAC took the Jet Provost trainer and developed it into the Strikemaster, armed with a pair of machine guns. The Strikemaster is able to carry bombs or rockets.*

Carrier-based aircraft

From the very earliest days of fixed-wing flying it seemed natural to use water as a runway – it was generally flat, unrestricted and readily accessible. Glenn Curtiss made the first flight in a practical seaplane during February 1911 (a seaplane has floats, whereas a flying boat has a planing boat-like hull). It is significant that Curtiss's flight took place from alongside a warship, the cruiser USS *Pennsylvania* anchored in San Diego Bay, as military planners were to prove more enthusiastic about seaplanes than about aircraft with normal undercarriages but based aboard ship. It must be remembered, however, that Curtiss's pioneering flight immediately followed two other very significant events. In November 1910 a Curtiss biplane piloted by Eugene Ely, a demonstration flyer, had taken off from a platform on the bows of the light cruiser USS *Birmingham*, anchored off Virginia. This was the first time that an aircraft had been operated from a ship, and two months later Ely made the first shipboard landing, touching down on a platform built on the stern of the cruiser *Pennsylvania* anchored in San Francisco Bay.

In 1898 US Naval officers had been on an inter-Service board set up to investigate the possibilities of Langley's Aerodrome, which at one time looked likely to be the first successful aeroplane. It was a failure, however, and interest waned until two naval officers attended a demonstration of the Wright Model A to the US Army in 1908. In September 1910 a Captain Chambers was appointed officer in charge of aviation for the US Navy, and he ordered two aircraft from Glenn Curtiss. By the time the first of these, the A–1 Triad, flew in July 1911, Chambers had arranged Ely's demonstrations and two Lieutenants had been taught to fly.

the conflict, 19 months later, the number had grown to more than 2,000. The only ship-borne wheeled aircraft, however, was a Sopwith Camel operated from a turret on the battleship *Texas*.

British naval aviation had begun in the spring of 1911, when three Royal Navy officers and one from the Royal Marines Light Infantry were taught to fly at the Isle of Sheppey. In October of that year the Admiralty bought the two Short pusher biplanes being used for instruction, and in the same month a naval flying school was set up at Eastchurch under Lt C. R. Samson, one of the original four students. The following January Samson flew a Short S.27 from a platform on the stationary battleship HMS *Africa*, and in May he took off from the battleship *Hibernia* while she was under way, this being the first sortie from a moving vessel. The Royal Flying Corps had been set up the previous month, and in July 1914 its naval wing became the Royal Naval Air Service.

Pups had first been embarked on the converted Isle of Man packet *Manxman*, which joined the fleet at the end of 1916. The Pups were modified for anti-Zeppelin patrols and were also used in deck-arresting trials at the Isle of Grain and for the development of flotation gear, as well as equipping a total of five aircraft carriers and seven cruisers.

Sopwith Camels later replaced the Pups, serving on five aircraft carriers, two battleships and 26 cruisers. The 2F.1 shipboard variant had an upward-firing Lewis gun in place of the starboard Vickers, and the wings were of shorter span. The type became operational in the spring of 1918, and 340 were built. Some acted as diver-bombers with two 23kg (50lb) bombs under the fuselage. On 17 July 1918 six Camels operating from *Furious* destroyed the Zeppelins L.54 and L.60 in their shed at Tondern.

carried 28 seaplanes or flying boats and four catapults. It remained in service until 1950. Both Germany and Italy were later to lay down carriers, but they were never completed. The first flush-deck carrier, HMS *Argus*, had joined the British fleet just before the end of World War I. She carried the Sopwith/Blackburn Cuckoo, the first purpose-designed torpedo bomber. The single-seat Cuckoo was powered by a 200hp Sunbeam Arab engine, giving a top speed of 140 km/h (87mph), and it could carry a 450kg (1,000lb) torpedo. The cruiser *Cavendish* was converted in the same way as the *Furious* to become the *Vindictive*, and the *Furious* herself was given a flush flight deck at the end of the war. The world's first purpose-built carrier was HMS *Hermes*, and the first with the superstructure offset to starboard as an island was *Eagle*, completed in 1920.

British inter-war carrier aircraft

The Fairey Flycatcher, the Fleet Air Arm's first specialist carrier-borne fighter, entered service in 1923. The RFC and RNAS had been amalgamated to form the Royal Air Force in April 1918, and to a certain extent naval aviation entered the wilderness. The Blackburn Skua, for example, entered active service just before World War II but had

In 1914 seven pilots and five aircraft participated in two detachments aboard the cruisers USS *Birmingham* and *Mississippi*, being used to observe Mexican positions. In July 1915 the Office of Naval Aeronautics was set up within the Navy Department, and the Naval Flying Corps (150 officers and 350 men) was authorized in August 1916. When the United States entered World War I in 1917, the NFC had 54 aircraft. By the end of

The Royal Navy was soon joined by those of the United States and Japan in operating aircraft carriers, and France had the *Béarn*. The French had begun experiments with carrier-based aircraft as early as 1918 when Lieutenant de Vaisseau Georges Guierre flew a Hanriot HD 1 from a platform on board the battleship *Paris*.

In 1932 the French Navy commissioned a seaplane carrier, the *Commandant Teste*, which

TOP: *The Fleet Air Arm's first specialist carrier-based fighter was the Fairey Flycatcher, which entered service in 1923. It carried a pair of synchronized machine guns and remained in service for a decade.*

ABOVE: *Nearly 2,400 examples of the popular Fairey Swordfish torpedo bomber were built, and the type outlasted its intended successors. The 'Stringbag' saw action at Taranto, where the Italian fleet was badly damaged, and took part in the sinking of the* Bismarck.

Catapults and Arrester Gear

Various ways of accelerating aircraft on take-off have been tried from the earliest days of aviation. In 1904–05 the Wright brothers used a tower supporting a block-and-tackle arrangement which carried a weight to give the aircraft its initial impetus when released. The first true catapult launch was made by Lieutenant Ellyson at the Washington Navy Yard in 1912; a wheeled dolly supporting his aircraft was propelled along a track by compressed air. Deck-mounted catapults were widely used on seaplane carriers and true aircraft carriers, although the low flying speed of aircraft right up to the time of World War II meant that a normal take-off could generally be made.

In 1934 the US Naval Aircraft Factory began developing a flush deck catapult, using a bridle to accelerate the aircraft and do away with the need for launching dollies. France, Britain and Germany also worked on catapults, but Japan lagged behind despite her rapid building programme for carriers. The need for an effective catapult became critical when escort carriers were developed during World War II. These were converted merchant ships with confined flight decks, a low top speed and a tendency to wallow badly in heavy seas. The use of catapults confers many other advantages also, including the ability to carry more aircraft, launch at night without extensive deck lighting, and conduct operations with less regard for wind direction.

A modern US Navy carrier such as the USS *John F. Kennedy* has four catapults, two at the bow and a pair at the waist. The longest one is 99m (325ft) and the other three are 81m (265ft). They operate under constant steam pressure, valves opening at different rates to give variations in acceleration according to launch weight. An aircraft taxis up to the catapult and its nose-tow launch bar, which replaces the bridle (strop) used previously, engages the shuttle. A T-bar forms the weak link between the aircraft and a hold-back bar which ensures that there is no slack in the system; it snaps when the catapult fires. Some aircraft, such as the Grumman F–14 Tomcat, use a different arrangement – a reusable rod which stretches and disengages on firing. The aircraft is launched with its engines at full power and is accelerated to its single-engine safe flying speed plus a margin of about 30km/h (18·75mph).

Arrester gear

When Eugene Ely made the first landing aboard a ship he was brought to rest by 22 ropes laid across the deck and attached to 23-kg (50-lb) sandbags at each end. Hooks between the aircraft wheels engaged the ropes.

A development of this eminently practical method was later used on the US Navy's first aircraft carrier, the *Langley*, with the addition of longitudinal wires to engage hooks on the axle and keep the aircraft straight.

An improvement of the sandbag arrangement was introduced by running the arrester cables to weights at the bottom of towers. When the aircraft snagged the wires the weights were lifted, automatically applying tension. The Norden gear introduced by the US Navy carried this a step further, the cables being wound at each end round a drum fitted with a brake to ensure that paying-out was slow and smooth. An electric motor rewound the drum after use. The problem of wire being paid out unequally if an aircraft landed off the centre-line was solved by using a drum at one end of the cable only.

This is the essence of the modern arrangement. In the *John F. Kennedy*, the four steel-cable arrester wires are each 3·8cm (1·5in) thick and 33m (110ft) long. They are attached to 640-m (2,100-ft) purchase cables driven by engines below deck. The tension of the arrester wires is adjusted for each aircraft according to its weight, so that all are brought to rest in the same distance. Pilots always aim for the third wire.

During World War II just about the most important man on a carrier was the Landing Signals Officer (LSO). He hand-signalled with 'paddles' (light-coloured discs) to indicate to pilots how they were doing on the approach. Modern carriers still carry LSOs in case the automatic equipment breaks down, but his paddles have been replaced by the Manually Operated Visual Landing Aid System (MOVLAS) – a series of lights which he illuminates to aid pilots on the approach. Normally, landings are made with the aid of a combination of lenses and coloured lights. The pilot flies to keep the image of a yellow light positioned between two horizontal bars of green lights. This ensures that he is approaching at the correct vertical angle, and he aligns his aircraft with the deck centre-line markings to keep himself correctly positioned in azimuth.

ABOVE LEFT: *A biplane making a landing on HMS* Furious *in 1917.*
ABOVE RIGHT: *A Grumman Avenger landing on an aircraft carrier. A similar type of arrester cable is in general use today.*
BELOW LEFT: *A French Etendard IV on the aircraft carrier* Foch *before launching.*
BELOW RIGHT: *A Chance-Vought Crusader being prepared for launch by catapult.*

Type: Fairey Swordfish I
Engines: One 690hp Bristol Pegasus III M3 nine-
    cylinder radial
Armament: Two 7·7m (0·303in) machine guns, up to
    66okg (1,500lb) of bombs or torpedoes
Maximum speed: 222km/h (138mph)
Initial climb: 372m/min (1,220ft/min)
Ceiling: 5,867m (19,250ft)
Range: 879km (546 miles)
Loaded weight: 3,410kg (7,510lb)
Span: 13·87m (45ft 6in)
Length: 10·87m (35ft 8in)
Height: 3·76m (12ft 4in)

been requested as a Flycatcher replacement in 1924. The Flycatcher itself, armed with two synchronized 0·303in machine guns and powered by a 400hp Armstrong Siddeley Jaguar giving a top speed of 214km/h (133 mph), remained in service until the early 1930s. The Blackburn Dart followed the Cuckoo as a torpedo bomber and eventually led to the last of the Blackburn biplane torpedo bombers, the Shark. It was first delivered for service aboard HMS *Courageous* in May 1935, and replaced by the Swordfish in 1938.

The Fairey IIIF Mk III was a popular general-purpose type which entered service in 1928 and remained operational until 1940. Operated as a three-seater by the Royal Navy (the RAF's Mk IV had two seats), the IIIF was replaced by a developed version known as the Seal by the Navy and Gordon by the RAF. The Seal differed from its predecessor in being powered by an Armstrong Siddeley Panther rather than a Napier Lion. Ninety were built, the type serving on several carriers from 1933 until being replaced by the Blackburn Shark in 1935–38. Fairey continued its naval tradition with the Swordfish, affectionately known as the Stringbag. Deliveries began in February 1936, and nearly 2,400 were built; in fact the Swordfish outlived its intended replacements. The 750hp Bristol Pegasus 30 gave a top speed of 224km/h (139 mph), and if desired a number of small bombs could be carried in place of the normal 680 kg (1,500lb) mine or 730kg (1,610lb) torpedo. The Swordfish was used as a floatplane

in addition to its role as a carrier-based aircraft, and took part in many famous engagements during World War II.

American inter-war carrier aircraft
The US Navy's first aircraft carrier, a converted 11,000-ton collier renamed the USS *Langley*, was commissioned in September 1922. The first US aircraft designed specifically for carrier operations was the Naval Aircraft Factory TS–1, used aboard the *Langley* and as a seaplane. It entered service in 1922 and was later built as the Curtiss F4C. A 200hp Wright J4 engine gave a maximum speed of 198km/h (123mph), and armament comprised a single 0·30in machine gun. Curtiss's later F6C–4 Hawk fighter equipped a single squadron on *Langley* until the beginning of 1930, only 31 being built. A 410hp Pratt & Whitney R–1340 conferred a top speed of nearly 250km/h (155mph), and armament was doubled to a pair of machine guns. The same basic powerplant, but uprated to 425hp, was installed in the Boeing F2B–1 single-seat shipboard fighter, deliveries of which began in January 1928 to equip the *Saratoga*. The slightly modified F3B–1 followed seven months later, serving aboard the *Langley* and later the *Lexington* and *Saratoga*. Production of the F2B–1 and F3B–1 totalled 32 and 74 respectively, and the latter type remained in service until 1932.

The next in the series, the F4B–1, was likewise powered by an R–1340 (this time of 450 hp) and had a top speed of 283km/h (176 mph) compared with the F3B's 254km/h

(158mph). Deliveries of the 27 F4B–1s began in June 1929, the aircraft equipping *Lexington* and *Langley*. They were followed by 46 F4B–2s from early 1931 (*Saratoga* and *Lexington*), 21 F4B–3s from the end of that year (*Saratoga*) and 92 F4B–4s from July 1932 (*Langley* and *Saratoga*). The F4B–4's R–1340 engine of 550 hp gave it a speed of just over 300km/h (188 mph), and the type remained in service until 1937. All F4Bs were armed with a pair of 0·30in machine guns or with one weapon of that calibre and one of 0·50in.

Curtiss, meanwhile, followed the unsuccessful F8C–4 Helldiver two-seat fighter, of which 25 were built and which served aboard the *Saratoga*, with the F11C single-seat fighter. Twenty-seven F11C–2s were delivered from February 1933, equipping one squadron on *Saratoga*, and in March of the following year their designation was changed to BFC–2 to reflect their fighter-bomber role. They remained in service until February 1938. The next off the line, 27 BF2C–1s (formerly F11C–3s) which served aboard *Ranger* for a few months from October 1934 until being withdrawn because of undercarriage failures, were the US Navy's last Curtiss fighters. One of the companies which inherited the Curtiss mantle was Grumman. The two-seat FF–1, of which 27 were built, was the US Navy's first fighter with a retractable undercarriage. Its 700hp Wright R–1820 gave a speed of 332km/h (207mph), and armament comprised a forward-firing 0·30in machine gun plus two more on flexible mountings in the rear cockpit. The FF–1s were later modified

RIGHT: *The Chance Vought F4U Corsair was the most powerful naval fighter of its day, more than 12,000 being built by three companies.*
BELOW RIGHT: *The Boeing F4B–4 shipboard fighter served aboard the US Navy carriers* Langley *and* Saratoga *from 1932.*
BELOW: *A Chance Vought Ve–7 off the USS* Langley, *the first American aircraft carrier, converted from a collier, which entered service with the US Navy in September 1922.*

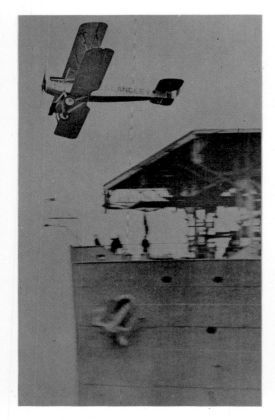

to FF–2 standard with dual controls. The type served aboard the *Lexington* for three years from 1933.

Grumman then moved on to a series of single-seat fighters. The F2F 'Flying Barrel', a scaled-down FF–1, was the first of its type to have a fully enclosed cockpit. It served from 1935 to 1940, at various times equipping the *Ranger*, *Lexington*, *Yorktown* and *Wasp*. The F3F–1 had a longer fuselage and wings to improve manoeuvrability, and was powered by a 650hp Pratt & Whitney R–1535 Twin Wasp. It was in service for four years from 1936, on the *Ranger* and *Saratoga*. The F3F–2, with the Wright R–1820 of 950hp, entered service aboard the *Enterprise* in 1938. At the end of that year it was joined by the F3F–3, capable of 425km/h (264mph). The F3F series were the last American biplane fighters, and were finally replaced by the Wildcat (see below) in October 1941.

While Curtiss, Boeing and Grumman were supplying fighters, Martin produced a series of bombers. The T3M–1 biplane torpedo/bomber/scout, based on the earlier CS–1/2 but having a steel-tube fuselage and uprated Wright T–3B engine, was delivered from September 1926. Wheels or floats were interchangeable. It was followed in mid-1927 by the T3M–2, in which the crew was carried in three individual cockpits and the power-plant was changed to the 770hp Packard 3A–2500, giving a speed of 175km/h (109mph). One hundred were built, and embarked aboard the *Lexington* and *Langley*. In August 1928 the T4M–1 entered service on

the *Lexington* and *Saratoga*. It had the less powerful 525hp Pratt & Whitney R–1690 Hornet, but the top speed was 183km/h (114 mph). The Great Lakes company later took over production, the aircraft being redesignated TG–1 and TG–2 as they were improved. The latter served from 1930 to 1937 as the US Navy's last biplane torpedo bomber. Its 620hp Wright R–1820 gave it a maximum speed of 204km/h (127mph). Before the take-over Martin had also built 32 BM–1 and BM–2 two-seat dive/torpedo bombers, which were embarked on the *Lexington* and *Langley* for six years from 1931.

Great Lakes used the experience gained during production of the TG–2 to design the BG–1 two-seat dive-bomber. The 60 aircraft served from October 1934 until 1938 aboard the *Ranger* and *Lexington*. They were powered by a 750hp Pratt & Whitney R–1535 and could carry a 450kg (1,000lb) bombload. Results with the Curtiss F8C–4 had been unsatisfactory, so the Vought SBU two-seat scout bomber entered service in 1935. It could carry a 225kg (500lb) bomb and was powered by a 700hp Pratt & Whitney R–1535 which gave a maximum speed of 330km/h (205mph).

The distinction of being the last combat biplane built in the United States (production ended in April 1940) went to the Curtiss SBC Helldiver scout bomber. Deliveries of the SBC–3, of which 83 were built, began in July 1937 and the first of 174 SBC–4s followed in 1938. The latter, powered by a 950 hp Wright R–1820 giving a top speed of

380km/h (237mph), could carry a 450kg (1,000lb) bomb and two squadrons of Helldivers were still operational aboard the *Hornet* at the time of Pearl Harbor.

Japanese inter-war carrier aircraft

The Japanese Navy's first aircraft carrier, the 9,500-ton *Hosho*, was commissioned in 1922 and could carry 19 aircraft. It was followed in 1927 and 1928 respectively by *Akagi* and *Kaga*, converted from unfinished 34,000-ton battle-cruisers. The Navy's first fighter squadrons operated the Mitsubishi 1MF (Type 10 Carrier-based Fighter), a single-seat biplane capable of 220km/h (138mph) on its 300hp Hispano-Suiza engine. The 2MR was developed from it to become the Type 10 Carrier-based Reconnaissance Aircraft, of which more than 150 were built, and Mitsubishi was also responsible for the 2MT (Type 13 Carrier-based Attacker), a two/three-seat biplane of which nearly 450 were constructed.

The 1MF was replaced by the Nakajima A1N1–2 (Type 3 Carrier-based Fighter), powered by a 420hp Bristol Jupiter. Designed for Nakajima by Gloster in Britain, who called it the Gambet, 150 were modified for naval use from 1929 by Eng Takao Yoshida. The 2MT was superseded by the Mitsubishi 3MR4, otherwise known as the B1M1–2 and designated Type 89 Carrier-based Attacker. A three-seat biplane designed by Blackburn, who also built a prototype, it was powered by a 600hp Hispano-Suiza. Just over 200 were constructed, from 1932.

TOP LEFT: *The Grumman TBF Avenger torpedo bomber, which replaced the Devastator, was one of the most successful torpedo bombers.*
TOP RIGHT: *The Aichi D3A2 dive-bomber took over from the D3A1, which had caused havoc at Pearl Harbor, and served until 1944.*

ABOVE CENTRE: *The Grumman F4F Wildcat was the US Navy's standard fighter at the time of the Japanese attack on Pearl Harbor.*
ABOVE: *The Vought F4U–2 carried a radar in one wingtip, and in October 1943 it carried out the US Navy's first radar interception.*

The Type 3 Carrier-based Fighter was replaced by a development of itself, the Nakajima A2N1–3, designated the Type 90 Carrier-based Fighter and powered by a 580hp Kotobuki II. In all, 106 were built.

Type 3 fighters and Type 13 attackers took part in the Shanghai conflict of January and February 1932, the first time that Japanese aircraft had been involved in air combat. The Navy aircraft operated from the carriers *Notoro, Hosho* and *Kaga*. Experience gained in these operations showed that the Type 89 torpedo bomber was in need of replacement and a design competition led to selection of the Yokosuka Arsenal B3Y, an improved version of the Type 13 with a 600hp Type 91 engine, which then entered service as the Type 92 Carrier-based Attacker. It saw widespread service at the beginning of the Sino-Japanese war, but the engine proved to be unreliable and the Navy therefore ordered about 200 Yokosuka 84Ys (Type 96 Carrier-based Attackers) powered by an 840hp Hikari. The Type 96 had a good range and was relatively trouble-free; it also proved to be the Japanese Navy's last fabric-covered biplane torpedo bomber.

News of American interest in dive-bombers led to Japanese Navy procurement of the Aichi AB–9, also known as the D1A1 (Type 94 Carrier-based Bomber), its first aircraft of this kind. It had a 580hp Kotobuki II and could achieve 500km/h (310mph) in the dive, but its payload was only 300kg (660lb). It was very reliable, however, and was developed into the Type 96 which was used extensively in the Sino-Japanese war. Total production of the Type 94/Type 96 was 590. In the Mitsubishi A5M (Type 96 Carrier-based Fighter) Japanese Navy pilots found the answer to their prayers. A low-wing, fixed-undercarriage monoplane, it was fast – 450 km/h (280mph) – and light, weighing less than 1,800kg (4,000lb) fully loaded. It could climb to 3,000m (10,000ft) in less than four minutes and was extremely manoeuvrable, with an endurance of more than three hours. The powerplant was a 560hp Kotobuki V, and armament comprised a pair of 0·303in machine guns; nearly 1,000 were built. Its successor, the Zero, was even better (see page 218).

World War II

In 1939 the US Navy's standard fighter was the Grumman F3F, a biplane but nonetheless able to reach 4,700m (15,000ft) in just over six minutes. A two-stage supercharger gave it a speed in excess of 416km/h (260mph), and the type introduced the heavy 0·50in machine gun as a permanent fixture. The US Navy's first monoplane fighter, and the first capable of exceeding 480km/h (300mph), was the Brewster F2A introduced in 1941. It was otherwise not very impressive, however, and by the time of Pearl Harbor the standard USN fighter was the Grumman F4F Wildcat. This had already been in service with the Fleet Air Arm for more than a year as the Martlet, the aircraft being 'inherited' after the fall of France. With a 1,200hp Pratt & Whitney Twin Wasp, the F4F–3 had a top speed of 523km/h (325mph), and armament comprised four 0·50in machine guns. It was replaced from January 1943 by the F6F Hellcat, able to extract a speed of 605km/h (376mph) from its 2,000hp Pratt & Whitney R–2800 Double Wasp and with an extra two guns. More than 12,000 were built, the type also equipping the Fleet Air Arm.

The last US piston-engined fighter, and at the time the most powerful naval fighter ever built, was the Chance Vought F4U Corsair. Again, more than 12,000 were built, including those turned out by Brewster and Goodyear, and the type was responsible for destroying more than 2,000 enemy aircraft as well as surface ships and submarines. The Corsair entered service in 1943, and the F4U–4 fighter variant could reach 718km/h (446mph) from its 2,450hp Pratt & Whitney R–2800 Double Wasp. It also had a range of just over 2,400km (1,500 miles) and could carry two 450kg (1,000lb) bombs or eight rockets as well as six machine guns.

The Douglas TBD Devastator torpedo bomber, designed initially to equip the USS *Ranger*, was the US Navy's first carrier-based monoplane to be produced in quantity. Deliveries for embarkation on *Saratoga* began in November 1937, and by the time of Pearl Harbor the type equipped a further five carriers. Its 800hp Pratt & Whitney R–1830 Twin Wasp gave the Devastator a top speed of only 208km/h (129mph), and the type was withdrawn after being badly mauled during the Battle of Midway in June 1942. The TBD was replaced from the spring of that year by the Grumman TBF Avenger, one of the most successful torpedo bombers of the war. The

three-crew Avenger had a power-operated gun turret and could carry a 22in torpedo internally. Its 1,700hp Wright R–2600 Double Cyclone gave it a top speed of more than 435km/h (270mph) and its range was an impressive 1,600km (1,000 miles) with a full weapon load.

The Douglas SBD Dauntless dive-bomber was obsolescent by the time of Pearl Harbor, yet was kept in service because no suitable replacement could be found. It could absorb heavy punishment and had the lowest attrition rate of any US carrier-based type operating in the Pacific. The Dauntless could carry 450kg (1,000lb) of bombs or half that weight of depth charges, and had a range of 1,770km (1,100 miles). Nearly 6,000 were built from 1939 to mid-1944. The Curtiss SB2C Helldiver joined the fleet in November 1943 and could carry 450kg (1,000lb) of bombs or a torpedo internally. Nearly 1,000 SB2C–1s were followed by SB2C–3s with an uprated (1,900hp) Wright Cyclone R–2600, and by SB2C–4s with underwing bomb and rocket attachments. The two-crew Helldiver had a top speed of 473km/h (294mph) and a maximum range of nearly 3,200km (2,000 miles). It carried two 20mm cannon and a machine gun in addition to its complement of bombs.

In December 1942 the Imperial Japanese Navy attacked Pearl Harbor with 353 warplanes from six aircraft carriers. The air armada comprised the 'unholy trinity' of D3A dive-bombers, B5N torpedo bombers and A6M fighter-bombers. The Aichi D3A was produced in two versions, the D3A1 from

1937 to 1942 and the D3A2 from that year until 1944. Nearly 1,300 were built in all. The later variant was powered by a 1,300hp Mitsubishi Kinsei 54, conferring a top speed of 426km/h (266mph). The payload was 370 kg (816lb) and maximum range was nearly 1,600km (1,000 miles). The three-crew Nakajima B5N served from 1937 to mid-1944, also in two versions. The B5N1 was powered by a 770hp Hikari 3, giving a top speed of 369km/h (229mph), and was armed with a 0·303in machine gun in addition to its bombload of 800kg (1,760lb). It was replaced by the Nakajima B6N2 Tenzan (Heavenly Mountain), of which more than 1,200 were built. It carried a crew of three, was capable of 480km/h (300mph) and had a range of 1,450km (900 miles). Its weapon load was a single torpedo or six 100kg (220lb) bombs externally in addition to a pair of 0·303in machine guns. The D3A dive-bomber was replaced by the Yokosuka D4Y Suisei (Comet), which in its D4Y2 form was powered by a 1,400hp Atsuta 32 and could achieve 575km/h (360mph). More than 2,300 were built, including land-based and reconnaissance versions.

The outstanding Japanese aircraft of World War II was probably the Mitsubishi A6M Reisen, commonly known as the Zero (it was the Navy's Type O carrier-based fighter). The Japanese Navy issued its specification for a new fighter in October 1937, and pre-production Zeros were used in China from August 1940. Very few problems were encountered, and the A6M2 had replaced all A5Ms by the time of Pearl Harbor. This was

Type: Mitsubishi A6M5 Zero-Sen
Engines: One Nakajima NK1F Model 21 14-cylinder
   two-row radial
Armament: Two 7·7mm (0·303in) machine guns, two
   20mm (0·787in) cannon, up to two 60kg (132lb)
   bombs
Maximum speed: 565km/h (351mph)
Initial climb: 855m/min (2,805ft/min)
Ceiling: 11,740m (38,520ft)
Range: 1,884km (1,171 miles)
Loaded weight: 2,960kg (6,510lb)
Span: 11m (36ft 1in)
Length: 9·12m (29ft 11in)
Height: 3·51m (11ft 6·5in)

a devastating fighter based on the Japanese Navy's 20 years of experience. It was fast – 520km/h (325mph) – and highly manoeuvrable, could reach 4,700m (15,000ft) in five minutes and was comparatively heavily armed (two 20mm cannon and two 0·303in machine guns). More than 10,000 were built in all, the major version being the A6M5. In this variant a Nakajima Sakae 21 gave a top speed of 560km/h (350mph), and a 0·50in machine gun replaced one of the 0·303in weapons.

Seven new aircraft carriers were ordered for the Fleet Air Arm in 1938, but at the outbreak of war the force was deficient in both ships and aircraft. Its two fighter types were the Blackburn Skua, which had to double as a dive-bomber, and the biplane Gloster Sea Gladiator. The Skua had been very advanced for its day when it was designed in 1934, being an all-metal monoplane with a retractable undercarriage, but it was a heavy two-seater and was underpowered. The Blackburn Roc, supposedly a fighter derivative of the Skua, was on the point of entering service, but if the Skua was disappointing, the Roc was disastrous. A four-gun power-operated turret replaced the Skua's four wing-mounted 0·303in Brownings and a rearward-facing Lewis. The Roc had a maximum speed of 354km/h (220mph), making it slower than the Sea Gladiator, and it took no less than 25 minutes to reach 4,700m (15,000ft).

In June 1940 the Fleet Air Arm's first eight-gun fighter, the Fairey Fulmar, joined the fleet. It was also underpowered, its 1,080hp Merlin giving it a top speed of only 448km/h (280mph), but it carried a lot of ammunition for its eight Brownings and had a four-hour endurance. It was replaced by the Fairey Firefly and Supermarine Seafire from 1943. The former was powered by a Rolls-Royce Griffon of up to 1,990hp, giving it a maximum speed of 509km/h (316mph), and it had a 1,600km (1,000-mile) range. Armament comprised four 20mm cannon plus bombs or rockets. More than 1,200 Seafires were built, the most important version being the Mk III, with folding wings, which entered service in 1943. The Royal Navy also made extensive use of US fighters and bombers.

An unusual application of maritime air power was the deployment of Hawker Sea Hurricane Mk IAs – known as 'Hurricats' – on merchant ships equipped with catapults. The fighter had to be ditched after each mission, but this tactic was successful in combating maritime-patrol aircraft such as the Focke-Wulf Condor. The Mk IB also served as a normal carrier-based fighter equipped with arrester gear.

The Fairey Swordfish soldiered on in a variety of roles, and in 1943 the force was joined by the Mk II, with a strengthened wing for firing rockets, and the Mk III, carrying ASV (Air-to-Surface-Vessel) Mk X radar. It was planned to replace the Swordfish with the Fairey Albacore, which entered service in March 1940 but flew only from shore bases for the first year of its career. Its first carrier action was from HMS *Formidable* at the Battle of Cape Matapan in March 1941, and this was also the first time that the type dropped torpedoes in anger. Eight hundred Albacores were built, and they also served on convoy-escort duties in the Baltic and on anti-submarine operations in the Mediterranean and Indian Ocean. The type was in fact outlasted by the Swordfish.

The Royal Navy's first monoplane torpedo bomber was the Fairey Barracuda. It entered service in September 1942, supported the Salerno landings a year later and attacked the *Tirpitz* in April 1944. More than 2,500 were built.

Post-war carrier aircraft

The US Navy emerged from World War II as one of the most powerful fighting arms anywhere. Grumman supplied the F7F Tigercat and F8F Bearcat to follow its long line of piston-engined carrier fighters, but the jet age had dawned and Grumman's next effort was the straight-winged F9F Panther powered in its initial version by a licence-built Rolls-Royce jet engine of 2,270kg (5,000lb) thrust. The USN's first jet fighter had been the

as a night fighter and missile-armed intercepter. Vought's F7U Cutlass tailless twin-engined intercepter was also less than successful, but the company's F–8 Crusader did more than make amends. It was the first carrier-borne aircraft capable of exceeding 1,600km/h (1,000mph) in level flight, having a top speed of about Mach 1·7. The F–8 served from the late 1950s to the mid-1970s, carrying an armament of four 20mm cannon and Sidewinder missiles.

The McDonnell Douglas Phantom II, described in the attack section, was originally designed as an all-missile-armed naval fighter, and it gave sterling service until replaced by the Grumman F–14 Tomcat. One of the world's most advanced fighters, the variable-geometry Tomcat can attack six airborne targets simultaneously with Phoenix missiles, and it also carries Sparrows, Sidewinders and a Vulcan 20mm cannon. The present attack force is made up of Vought A–7 Corsair IIs and Grumman A–6 In-

truders. These can deliver bombs or guided missiles at great range from the carrier, attacking targets far inland if necessary. A development of the Intruder, the EA–6B Prowler, accompanies the attack force to jam enemy radars and guide the strike aircraft round hostile defences.

In the Lockheed S–3A Viking the US Navy for the first time has a carrier aircraft able to carry out the complicated task of seeking out and destroying submarines at great ranges and without aid from the ship or other aircraft. Another compact type is the Grumman E–2C Hawkeye early-warning aircraft, a flying radar station which extends the eyes and ears of the ship and its fighter defenders.

When the McDonnell Douglas/Northrop F–18 enters service in the early 1980s it will take over some work both from the Tomcats and the attack aircraft, acting as a multi-role fighter-bomber. Further in the future are a wide range of VTOL (Vertical Take-Off and Landing) types, which may one day dispense with the need for a long flight deck, catapults and arrester gear. The Royal Navy's Hawker Siddeley Sea Harrier is only the first step in this process.

After World War II the Fleet Air Arm operated navalized versions of many RAF aircraft, such as the de Havilland Sea Mosquito torpedo bomber, Sea Hornet all-weather/night fighter, Sea Venom two-seat all-weather fighter and Hawker Sea Fury

McDonnell FH–1 Phantom, also straight-winged and with a pair of Westinghouse turbojets in the roots. It was succeeded by the F2H Banshee, virtually a scaled-up Phantom with more power and greater range. Both the Banshee and Panther carried four 20mm cannon, and both acquitted themselves well in the Korean War as fighter-bombers.

The Panther was replaced by the F9F–6 Cougar, in effect a swept-wing development of its predecessor but also with a new tail. The company's later F11F Tiger, designed as a day intercepter, was late in entering service and was overshadowed by the F–8 Crusader (see next column). Another type in action over Korea – alongside piston-engined machines such as the F4U–4 and –5 Corsair, and AD Skyraider – was the Douglas F3D Skynight, a radar-equipped night fighter powered by a pair of belly-mounted Westinghouse turbojets. Douglas was additionally responsible for the F4D Skyray tailless intercepter/fighter and later produced the A–3 Skywarrior and A–5 Vigilante nuclear bombers, since adapted for reconnaissance duties. Sandwiched between these was the A–4 Skyhawk light bomber, still in production in the mid-1970s.

North American developed the F–86E Sabre into the FJ–2 Fury for the US Navy, and followed it with the FJ–3 and FJ–4/4B. McDonnell built the F3H Demon, but it was dogged by troubles and was eventually used

LEFT: *The Grumman F–14 Tomcat is the US Navy's most lethal carrier-based fighter.*
BELOW: *The Supermarine Scimitar operated from Royal Navy aircraft carriers in the 1950s.*

BELOW CENTRE: *Dassault has developed the Super Etendard naval strike fighter from the earlier Etendard by redesigning the wing, installing a new engine and radar.*

BOTTOM: *The Dassault-Breguet Alizé anti-submarine aircraft operates from the French Navy's carriers* Foch *and* Clemenceau. *The improved Iguane radar is being fitted.*

single-seat fighter-bomber. The Royal Navy's first purpose-built carrier-borne jet fighter was the Supermarine Attacker, armed with four 20mm cannon and powered by a Rolls-Royce Nene of 2,300kg (5,100lb) thrust. The same engine was installed in the similarly armed Hawker Sea Hawk, which was in turn replaced by the innovative Supermarine Scimitar, with its four 30mm cannon, area-ruling, powered controls and blown flaps. The Scimitar's powerplant of two Rolls-Royce Avon turbojets was the same as that in the twin-boom de Havilland Sea Vixen fighter, armed with cannon and later missiles. The Fleet Air Arm's last purpose-designed fixed-wing type was the Blackburn (now

Hawker Siddeley) Buccaneer anti-ship aircraft, since also supplied to the RAF (see attack section). In the torpedo strike role the Blackburn Firebrand was replaced in May 1953 by the Westland Wyvern, with its 4,110hp turboprop, and the Fairey Gannet now operates in the early-warning capacity.

Emphasis has now switched away from large aircraft carriers, and the Royal Navy is receiving vertical take-off Sea Harriers to operate from the new through-deck cruisers. If the British carrier force is shrinking, however, that of the Soviet Union is expanding. Its first carrier, the *Kiev*, entered service in 1976 and is equipped with a new type of VTOL strike fighter believed to have

emerged from the Yakovlev design bureau. France is also deploying new aircraft on its carriers. The Dassault Etendard strike fighter has been modernized to become the Super Etendard, powered by a Snecma 8K50 engine and fitted with Agave radar, Sagem inertial navigation system, laser ranger, five weapons pylons and two 30mm cannons.

Maritime-patrol aircraft

There are three basic types of maritime-patrol aircraft: land-based machines employed to seek out and destroy enemy shipping and additionally carry out reconnaissance; flying boats and seaplanes which carry out similar tasks from coastal bases or seaplane carriers; and fleet spotters operated from capital ships. The first category is now easily the biggest, but seaplanes and flying boats played an important part in both World Wars.

Germany operated no flying boats, relying on seaplanes. The Friedrichshafen series was much used from coastal bases and seaplane carriers, nearly 500 being built. The Austro-Hungarian Navy's principal type was the single-engined Loehner L flying boat used against Allied shipping in the Adriatic and to attack Italian land-based targets. It carried a crew of two and 200kg (440lb) of bombs or depth charges. Franco-British Aviation produced a range of flying boats for the French, British, Italian and Russian navies. The role of ship-based seaplanes is described in the carrier aviation section.

The most successful of the Allies' big flying boats was the Felixstowe F.2A, derived from the Curtiss America series but having an improved hull design. Deliveries began in November 1917 and the type accounted for a number of submarines and airships during its North Sea patrols. The F.2A was very manoeuvrable, and its armament of up to seven machine guns was enough to deter even single-seat fighters. An endurance of up to nine hours was possible, and two bombs of 100kg (220lb) each could be carried. The pair of 345hp Rolls-Royce Eagle VIIIs gave a top speed of just over 150km/h (95mph).

World War II

Britain turned out a range of big biplane flying boats including the Supermarine Stranraer, Saro London and Short Singapore. The Short Sunderland was a military development of the C-class Empire boats and entered service in the summer of 1938. More than 700 were built, and they became known as 'Flying Porcupines' because of their heavy defensive armament – a pair of 0·50in machine guns and up to a dozen of 0·30in. In later versions the four Bristol Pegasus engines were replaced by 1,200hp Pratt & Whitney R–1830 Twin Wasps. The Sunderland carried a crew of up to 13, had a maximum range of about 4,800km (3,000 miles) and a bombload of 900kg (2,000lb).

Another aircraft well liked by its crew was the Consolidated PBY Catalina, which established an enviable reputation for ruggedness, reliability and adaptability. More than 2,000 were built for the US Navy and a further 650-plus went to the RAF, the type serving in virtually every theatre of World War II; 749 of an amphibious version, the Canso, were built in Canada for the RCAF. Late models were powered by a pair of 1,200hp Pratt & Whitney Twin Wasps and could transport their crew of eight over 5,000km (3,100 miles). Defensive armament usually comprised two 0·50in and two 0·30in machine guns. In Germany the Blohm und Voss Bv 138 was employed for long-range reconnaissance, convoy patrol and U-boat co-operation. Powered by three 880hp Junkers Jumos, it had a range of more than 4,000km (2,500 miles) and could deliver six 50kg (110lb) bombs and four depth charges.

Italy had some 200 Cant Z.501 Gabbiano (Gull) parasol-winged single-engined flying boats in service at the outbreak of war, while the Soviet Union employed the monoplane flying boat Beriev Be–2 (MBR–2) on duties such as coastal reconnaissance. One of the most successful flying boats of World War II was the Kawanishi H8K2, of which 167 were built. It replaced the obsolescent H6K, which had a crew of nine and could carry a 1,600kg (3,500lb) payload over a range of 5,000km (3,100 miles). The H8K2 could carry 2,000kg (4,400lb) of weapons, plus five 20mm cannon and four 7·7mm machine guns for self-defence, and had a maximum range of 6,400km (nearly 4,000 miles).

World War II seaplanes included the four-crew Heinkel He 115, of which more than 300 were constructed. Powered by a pair of 900hp BMW radials, it was used in such roles as U-boat co-operation over ranges of up to 2,000km (1,250 miles). The He 115's offensive warload comprised 1,000

kg (2,200lb) of bombs, mines or torpedoes. It also carried a pair of 7·9mm machine guns for protection. Italy contributed the Cant Z.506B Airone (Heron), which served throughout the war. It had a crew of five, and its three 750hp Alfa Romeo engines could power it over a range of 2,300km (1,430 miles). Two machine guns – one of 7·7mm calibre and the other of 12·7mm – were carried, and the Airone's warload was up to 1,200kg (2,640lb) of bombs or torpedoes.

Many types were used partly or exclusively for fleet spotting and general reconnaissance from heavy warships. The ungainly Supermarine Walrus entered service in July 1936 and equipped Royal Navy battleships and cruisers until succeeded by the same manufacturer's Sea Otter. The standard German Navy catapult seaplane for many years was the twin-float Arado Ar 196, of which more than 400 were built. Up to four were carried by a battleship, one of the famous vessels to use the type in battle being the *Graf Spee*. The two-crew Ar 196, which had a range of 1,070km (665 miles), was also used for coastal patrol. It was fitted with two 20mm cannon and a pair of machine guns, and could carry a 50kg (110lb) bomb under each wing.

Japan built more than 1,400 Aichi E13A1s for ship-based reconnaissance and general duties, the type carrying out the pre-Pearl Harbor surveillance and serving throughout the Pacific. It was succeeded by the E16A1 Zuiun (Auspicious Cloud), used as a dive-bomber as well as for reconnaissance. Its armament consisted of two 20mm cannon and a pair of machine guns, including one of 13·2mm calibre. Battleships and cruisers of the US Navy carried the two-seat scout/observation Curtiss SOC Seagull. The SOC–1 version, of which 135 were built, entered service in November 1935 as the USN's last Curtiss biplane.

The Allies used many bombers, such as the Armstrong Whitworth Whitley, Boeing B–17, Bristol Beaufort, Consolidated B–24, Handley Page Halifax and Vickers Wellington, for maritime patrol in addition to their main role, but all the major combatants also developed specialist land-based maritime aircraft. The Avro Anson, although perhaps better known as a trainer, was originally designed for shore-based reconnaissance and served in this capacity from March 1936 until replaced by Lockheed Hudsons from 1942. The Anson's performance was fairly modest, range being 1,225km (760 miles) and its payload 163kg (360lb). Defensive armament consisted of two 0·303in machine guns. The Lockheed A–28/A–29 Hudson, which replaced the Anson, was developed from the

ABOVE LEFT: *The Consolidated PBY Catalina was one of the most famous and well liked World War II maritime-patrol aircraft.*
ABOVE CENTRE: *Lockheed developed the Hudson from the Model 14 airliner to meet a British requirement for a maritime patroller to replace the Avro Anson from 1942.*
ABOVE RIGHT: *The Junkers Ju 290 never lived up to expectations as a successor to the famous Focke-Wulf Condor, but it served in a variety of roles during World War II.*

Model 14 airliner to meet a British requirement. First deliveries were made in the summer of 1939, and RAF Coastal Command alone operated more than 2,000. The Hudson, powered by two 1,200hp Wright R–1820 Cyclones, also served with many other air forces and saw action in every theatre of the war. It carried a 635kg (1,400lb) payload and five crew over ranges up to 4,500km (2,800 miles), and was armed with as many as seven 0·30in machine guns.

Lockheed then developed the PV–1 Ventura, again from an airliner (the Model 18 Lodestar), to meet Britain's request for a Hudson replacement. It entered RAF service in 1942, while 1,600 were operated by the US Navy as PV–1s. In Canada, Venturas supplemented Liberators on coastal patrols. When the type was adopted by the USAAF it was designated B–34. The PV–1, powered by two Pratt & Whitney R–2800 Double Wasps of 2,000hp each, carried a crew of four and had a range of 1,750km (1,100 miles). Defensive armament was six machine guns of 0·50in calibre, and the PV–1 could carry a 22in torpedo, bombs or depth charges up to a total of 1,600kg (3,500lb). The PV–2 Harpoon had an additional four machine guns, 225kg (500lb) of payload and 1,450km (900 miles) of range.

Perhaps the most famous maritime-patrol aircraft of the war was the Focke-Wulf Fw 200 Condor. Originally designed as a commercial transport, it was delivered from the spring of 1940 and began attacking shipping from Danish bases.

The Fw200C had seven or eight crew, five 7·9mm machine guns and a 20mm cannon for self-defence and could carry up to 2,100kg (4,625lb) of bombs, although 1,500 kg (3,300lb) was more normal. The four BMW-Bramo engines produced 1,000hp each at sea level, and the Condor could cruise at 250km/h (160mph) for 3,500km (2,200 miles), giving an endurance of 14 hours. Maximum range was 6,400km (nearly 4,000 miles). The Junkers Ju 290 was proposed as a Condor successor, and it did operate on U-boat co-operation missions as well as launching anti-ship glide bombs.

Type: Tupolev Tu–16 Badger
Engines: Two Mikulin AM–3M single-shaft turbojets
Armament: Six 23mm (0·906in) cannon, up to 9,000kg
    (19,800lb) of bombs
Maximum speed: 945km/h (587mph)
Climb: about 1,250m/min (4,100ft/min)
Ceiling: 13,000m (42,650ft)
Range: 4,800km (3,000 miles)
Loaded weight: about 68,000kg (150,000lb)
Span: 33·5m (110ft)
Length: 36·5m (120ft)
Height: 10·8m (35ft 6in)

Post-war developments

Only two countries, Russia and Japan, now produce large maritime-patrol flying boats. The United States' involvement ended with the Martin P–6 SeaMaster, a jet-powered mine-layer which made its maiden flight in 1955. The final version, which first flew four years later, was powered by four Pratt & Whitney J75 turbojets of 7,950kg (17,500lb) thrust each. Martin's previous design, the P–5 Marlin developed from the wartime Mariner, was more conventional. More than 200 were built, a pair of Wright R–3350 Turbo Compound engines of 3,400hp each giving a speed of 400km/h (250mph) and a range of 3,220km (2,000 miles). The ultimate basic variant, the P–5B, made its maiden flight in 1954 and ended its career as the SP–5B with advanced sensor equipment. Weapons and sonobuoys were carried in the engine nacelles, each of which could accommodate two torpedoes, or a pair of 907kg (2,000lb) bombs; a combination of smaller weapons could be carried on underwing pylons, taking maximum load up to 3,630kg (8,000lb). Self-defence in the SP–5A was provided by a radar-directed twin 20mm cannon in the tail.

The Soviet Union produced the Beriev Be–6 flying boat in 1949. It was powered by a pair of 2,300hp Shvetsov radials and had a range of about 4,800km (3,000 miles). All armament – four depth charges, bombs, etc – was carried externally, and 23mm cannon were installed in the nose and in the dorsal position. This was followed in 1960 by the Be–10, powered by two turbojets of some 6,400kg (14,110lb) thrust each. It can achieve a speed of about 900km/h (560mph) and a range of 2,100km (1,300 miles). This time the two 23mm cannon are mounted in a tail turret. The more recent Be–12 amphibian is powered by two 4,000hp Ivchenko AI–20D turboprops, giving a range of 4,000km (2,485 miles). Sensors include a nose-mounted radar and a MAD (magnetic anomaly detector) sting in the tail, and a range of weapons can be carried on six pylons as well as in the internal bay.

Japan's big flying boat is the Shin Meiwa PS–1, which is used for anti-submarine patrol. The design philosophy is unusual in that a dunking sonar is employed rather than the more common sonobuoys which are sown and then interrogated from the aircraft. The PS–1 has high-lift devices to give it STOL (Short Take-Off and Landing) performance – it can clear a 15m (50ft) obstacle after a take-off run of less than 300m (1,000ft), and can touch down as slowly as 76km/h (47mph) – and is designed to operate in rough seas. Power is provided by four General Electric T64 turboprops built under licence in Japan, and patrol endurance is up to 15 hours. A wide variety of weapons may be carried.

The vast majority of modern maritime-patrol missions, however, are carried out by aircraft operating from land bases or from aircraft carriers. Some carrier-based types, such as the Fairey Gannet and Breguet Alizé, can also fly from shore bases, but long-range work is left to airliner-sized machines. Early post-war patrol aircraft included the Avro Shackleton and Lockheed P–2 Neptune. The Shackleton was based on the Lancaster/Lincoln series of bombers, and in its MR.3 variant was powered by a pair of Viper turbojets in addition to four Rolls-Royce Griffon piston engines of 2,500hp each. The Shackleton, which entered service in 1951, had a maximum range of 5,800km (3,600 miles) and could carry 12 450kg (1,000lb) bombs or a variety of other ordnance such as nine depth charges, three torpedoes and 12 sonobuoys. The Neptune predated its British counterpart by some three or four years. Later versions, beginning with the P–2H, also used auxiliary turbojets – two Westinghouse J34s of 1,540kg (3,400lb) thrust each – in addition to a pair of 3,500hp Wright R–3350 Turbo Compounds. Maximum range and speed were 3,540km (2,200 miles) and 565km/h (350mph) respectively, and more than 1,000 Neptunes were built. In Japan, Kawasaki produced the P–2J variant with licence-built 2,850hp General Electric T64 turboprops and IHIJ3 auxiliary turbojets of 1,400kg (3,085lb) thrust.

The Wright Turbo Compound had further applications in the Lockheed C–121 series, based on the Constellation airliner, and in Canadair's CL–28 Argus. The C–121s were used for a wide variety of duties, but the Argus was developed specifically for maritime patrol. It incorporated parts of the Bristol Britannia airliner, with a new fuselage and a change of powerplant. A search radar

ABOVE: *The Breguet Atlantic is a European collaborative, anti-submarine type. It entered service in 1965.*

BELOW LEFT: *Britain's Hawker Siddeley Nimrod is the world's only long-range, jet-powered anti-submarine and maritime-patrol aircraft.*

BELOW RIGHT: *The United States Navy's standard shore-based anti-submarine type is the Lockheed P-3 Orion.*

was installed in a chin-mounted bulge, and a MAD sting in the tail. Maximum range was just over 9,000km (5,600 miles), speed 505km/h (315mph) and weapon capacity 1,800kg (4,000lb) in two internal bays plus 3,450kg (7,600lb) on pylons. The Argus entered service in 1958 and is still in use, but is to be replaced by the Lockheed Aurora.

A smaller type which has been operated from shore bases as well as from carriers is the Grumman S-2 Tracker. Powered by a pair of 1,525hp Wright R-1820s, it has a normal patrol range of 1,450km (900 miles) and can carry weapons such as four torpedoes or rocket projectiles. The same manufacturer's HU-16 Albatross, which also uses the same powerplant, is a general-purpose type which includes anti-ship operations among its duties. Maximum range is 5,280km (3,280 miles) when external fuel tanks are carried.

The current generation of specialist maritime-patrol types comprises the Lockheed P-3C Orion, Hawker Siddeley Nimrod, Dassault-Breguet Atlantic and Ilyushin Il-38. All except the Atlantic were adapted from airliners: the Electra, Comet and Il-18 respectively. The original P-3A entered service in 1962, and more than 400 of the Orion series have since been built. The type's maximum weapon load is a little over 9,000kg (20,000lb), of which more than a third can be carried internally. Power is provided by four Allison T56 turboprops of 4,900hp each, giving a patrol endurance of up to 18 hours. The Nimrod is the only jet-powered type in this class. Four Rolls-Royce Spey turbofans

of 5,445kg (12,000lb) thrust each are installed to allow a high-speed dash to be made to the search area, but two of these can be shut down if necessary to conserve fuel on a long mission. At 925km/h (575mph), the jet-powered Nimrod's top speed is naturally appreciably higher than that of its competitors, and normal endurance is 12 hours. The Nimrod entered service in 1969.

The Atlantic, built by a European consortium, entered service in December 1965 and remained in production for ten years. A Mk 2 version is now being developed to take its place. The Mk 1, powered by a pair of 6,105hp Rolls-Royce Tyne turboprops, has an exceptionally long endurance of 18 hours at 320km/h (200mph); it normally cruises at 555km/h (345mph). The CSF radar is installed in a retractable 'dustbin' and the customary MAD boom is mounted in the tail. Weapons and sonobuoys are carried both internally and on underwing pylons. The Il-38 is the most recent of the quartet, having become operational in 1970. Its range of about 7,250km (4,500 miles) is appreciably shorter than that of the Tu-16 Badger, and it is likely that the Il-38 is not a direct replacement for the older type. Four 4,250hp Ivchenko turboprops confer a cruise speed of about 650km/h (400mph), and the payload is made up of an assortment of sonobuoys and weapons, in very much the same way as in its Western counterparts.

The field of maritime-patrol aircraft is a very stable one in that designers are not continually striving for more speed, payload

or manoeuvrability—merely improved equipment in the same basic shell. The service life of each type therefore tends to be very long, with updating going on almost all the time. The present generation will thus remain operational for a good many years. Despite its lack of glamour, however, maritime patrol is a vital role and one which becomes ever more important as the technology of submarines and surface vessels advances.

Trainers

Many World War I front-line aircraft were allocated to training duties once they had been overtaken in performance by the next generation. In some cases one specific subtype, such as the B.E.8a, was used exclusively for training. The war, however, also saw the introduction of aircraft designed for this role from the outset. One of the most famous of these was the Curtiss JN series, widely known as Jennies. More than 5,500 of the JN-4 variant alone were built, in Britain and Canada as well as the United States. Probably the best known trainer of this era was the Avro 504, although its early career was as a light bomber and ground-attack machine.

The first version intended specifically for instruction was the 504J introduced as late as the autumn of 1916; it became the Royal Flying Corps' first basic trainer. The later 504K was adapted to take a wide variety of engines and the type remained in production for more than ten years, in excess of 10,000 being built. Some were still in service at the outbreak of World War II.

The inter-war years saw the development of several basic trainers. In Russia the Polikarpov Po–2 – which was to cause headaches for jet-fighter pilots in Korea more than 20 years later – made its maiden flight as the U–2 in 1928. Britain's similar de Havilland D.H.82 Tiger Moth followed soon after, entering service with the RAF in February 1932. In France there were several Morane-Saulnier types, chiefly the 230, from 1930 to 1939.

Monoplanes soon followed. North American developed the AT–6 Texan (known as the Harvard in service with air forces of the British Commonwealth) as a cheap trainer with the handling characteristics of a fighter. About 15,000 were built. The RAF's first monoplane basic trainer was the Miles Magister. The Arado Ar 96B was adopted as the *Luftwaffe's* standard primary and advanced trainer in 1940, and in the same year production began in America of the Fairchild PT–19/23/26 series. Built in Canada as the Cornell, the PT–26 replaced the Fleet Finch and de Havilland Tiger Moth as the standard elementary trainer of the British Commonwealth Air Training Plan.

The RAF's first twin-engined monoplane trainer was the Airspeed Oxford, which joined the Central Flying School in November 1937. Production exceeded 8,700, but this figure was easily beaten by the Avro Anson, with more than 11,000. The 'Faithful Annie' was used initially for maritime reconnaissance, but it was much more widely employed as a crew trainer. In Germany the twin-engined Siebel Si 204D replaced the Focke-Wulf Fw 58 in this role, carrying five students in addition to its normal crew. The type was built in Czechoslovakia and France to leave German production capacity available for front-line aircraft.

The United States forces' main transitional and advanced trainers were the plywood Beech AT–10 Wichita and the Cessna AT–17 Bobcat. The RAF introduced the single-engined Miles Master as an advanced trainer in the spring of 1939, and more than 3,300 of them were turned out. Japan's main twin-engined advanced trainer was the Tachikawa Ki–54. Radio/navigation instruction was carried out with such types as the D.H. Dominie, a military version of the Dragon Rapide small biplane airliner; the Mitsubishi K3M high-wing monoplane which had been adapted from a Dutch design in 1931/32; and the single-engined Percival Proctor.

The Bristol Buckmaster, one of the fastest and most powerful trainers of its time, served the RAF for ten years from 1945. Its two 2,500hp Bristol Centaurus VIIs conferred a top speed of 566km/h (352mph). The first jet aircraft in this category also made its appearance – the Bell P–59 Airacomet. It was intended to be a fighter in its own right, but mediocre performance led to it being employed for instruction of pilots destined to fly the Lockheed P–80 Shooting Star.

The Shooting Star itself, as the two-seat T–33, was to become one of the most successful post-war jet trainers. The piston-

ABOVE: *The ubiquitous Polikarpov Po–2.*
BELOW: *BAC's Jet Provost.*
BOTTOM LEFT: *A North American Harvard.*

ABOVE: *An Avro Anson trainer.*
BOTTOM RIGHT: *The USAF's aerobatic team, the Thunderbirds, fly the Northrop T–38 Talon.*

engined North American T–28, designed to seating rather than the tandem arrangement used previously. The world's first jet trainer to enter production, however, had been France's Fouga Magister.

In Britain the Percival Provost succeeded the Prentice, and in turn was replaced by the succeed the Texan, was itself replaced by the Cessna T–37. This was the first USAF jet *ab initio* trainer, and introduced side-by-side Jet Provost, loosely based on its piston-engined forebear. The Yakovlev Yak–11, 'Russia's Harvard', had entered service in 1947 and was replaced by the Czech Aero L–29 Delfin, selected as the Warsaw Pact's standard basic jet trainer. This in turn has been followed by the L–39 Albatross.

The United States Navy is buying turbo-prop Beech T–34C Mentors to replace the earlier piston-engined variants in the T–34 series, while the Service's standard multi-stage jet trainer is the Rockwell T–2 Buckeye. The same engines as in the Buckeye – General Electric J85 turbojets – also power

the USAF's Northrop T–38 Talon advanced trainer, the first in the world capable of supersonic speeds. Sweden's SAAB 105G is a further application of the J85. Another much-used engine is the Rolls-Royce Viper, installed in the Italian Macchi MB.326/MB.339 series and other overseas trainers as well as in the Jet Provost.

Hawker Siddeley has developed the Hawk to replace both the Gnat and the Hunter as an advanced flying and weapons trainer. Head-on competition comes from the Franco-German Dassault-Breguet/Dornier Alpha Jet. The jet trainer/light-strike market is a booming one, with one of the latest contenders being the turbofan-powered Spanish CASA C.101.

Another lucrative sector is that of modern basic trainers. The Scottish Aviation Bulldog, the SAAB Supporter and the New Zealand Aerospace Industries CT/4 Airtrainer, as well as many other adaptations of light civil aircraft, have all been prominent in the world market.

BELOW: *Lockheed's C–5 Galaxy is the United States Air Force's biggest transport aircraft. It would be used to ferry troops and outsize equipment from US bases to Europe and the Pacific in times of war.*

BELOW: *The DHC–5 Buffalo is one of several Canadian short take-off transports.*
BOTTOM: *The McDonnell Douglas YC–15 was developed for the USAF competition to find a replacement for the Lockheed Hercules.*

RIGHT: *The four-engined Tupolev ANT–6, designated TB–3 when used as a bomber and G–2 in the transport role, could carry 30 paratroops. It was obsolescent by the time Russia entered World War II.*

Type: Douglas Dakota
Engines: Two 1,200hp Pratt & Whitney R–1830–92 engines
Armament: Usually three 7·62mm (0·299in) mini guns or many other types
Maximum speed: about 370km/h (230mph)
Initial climb: about 366m/min (1,200ft/min)
Ceiling: 7,000m (23,000ft)
Range: 3,420km (2,125 miles)
Loaded weight: 14,060kg (31,000lb)
Span: 28·96m (95ft)
Length: 19·66m (64ft 6in)
Height: 4·98m (16ft 4in)

CANADIAN ARMED FORCES

Transport aircraft

Although many World War I bombers could double as transports, their accommodation was strictly limited and large-scale movement of troops and equipment by air was impossible. After the war specialized transport adaptations of heavy bombers appeared, but it was the airlines that paved the way by demanding more speed, accommodation and comfort. Modified bombers such as the Vickers Victoria and its successor, the Valentia, were easily outclassed by the new generation of all-metal monoplane airliners. These included the famous Douglas DC–2/DC–3 series, which later became the military C–47 Skytrain and C–53 Skytrooper. More than 10,000 were built as wartime transports, and the type was constructed under license in Russia as the Lisunov Li–2, with 1,000hp Shvetsov radial engines replacing the pair of 1,200hp Pratt & Whitney R–1830 Twin Wasps. The C–47s and C–53s, which entered service in 1941, were used as ambulances and glider tugs in addition to carrying troops and equipment. They were known as R4Ds by the US Navy and by the RAF as Dakotas – a name that has stuck ever since.

During World War II, the United States was given prime responsibility for building transports, allowing Britain's aircraft industry to concentrate on combat types. Bombers and patrol aircraft as well as civilian machines were used as the basis for transports, examples being the Consolidated LB–30 and C–87 Liberator Express versions of the B–24 bomber and the Consolidated PB2Y–3R flying boat, able to carry 44 troops or 7,260kg (16,000lb) of cargo.

The RAF operated a number of home-designed types as well as those supplied by the US. These included the Handley Page Harrow; designed as a transport for 20 troops, then operated as a bomber, it finally reverted to its original role when replaced by Wellingtons. The latter type was itself one of a series of bombers used also as transports when superseded in the offensive role, another widely used model being the Short Stirling (Mks IV and V). The 50 or so Bristol Bombays built in the 1930s combined bombing and transport duties.

Germany produced one of the war's outstanding transports in the trimotor Junkers Ju 52/3m, but even this started life as a bomber in the Spanish Civil War. 'Iron Annie' or 'Auntie Ju' took part in many airborne invasions, carrying up to 18 paratroops, and about 3,500 were built. Its proposed successor, the Ju 352 Herkules, proved to be little or no improvement. The Blohm and Voss Bv 222 Wiking (Viking), designed as a transatlantic passenger flying-boat, could carry 110 fully equipped troops and had a range of 6,000km (3,730 miles). It was overshadowed, however, by the Me 323. Derived from the Me 321 Gigant (Giant) glider, the Me 323 was powered by six 990hp Gnome-Rhône radials and could carry 130 troops or 10,000kg (22,000lb) of equipment. Only 40 of the specialist Arado Ar 232 were built, but the type could carry 4,500kg (9,920lb).

Italy's Savoia-Marchetti S.M.81 Pipistrello (Bat) served as a bomber in Abyssinia

and Spain but was later relegated to transport duties, and the S.M.83 Canguro (Kangaroo), able to carry 40 troops, was the country's largest wartime transport. A third trimotor, the Fiat G.12T, was also used.

The Russian Air Force employed a variety of erstwhile bombers as transports. These included the four-engined Tupolev ANT–6, which as the G–2 could carry 30 paratroops; the Petlyakov Pe–8; and the PS–41 version of the Tupolev SB–2.

Two of the Japanese Army Air Force's major transports were the Kawasaki Ki–56 and Mitsubishi Ki–57. The former was copied from the US Lockheed Super Electra, more than 700 replicas being followed by 100-plus of the Ki–56 built to Japanese standards, and some 500 of the 11-passenger Ki–57 were constructed. The Ki–57 resembled the company's Ki–21 bomber, some of which were also used as transports, and other dual-role types included the Ki–49, Ki–54 (up to nine passengers) and the Japanese Naval Air Force's G3M and G4M.

Post-war transports

The Avro York, using a new fuselage and tail attached to the Lancaster's wings and engines, gave sterling service during the Berlin Airlift, and the demands of the Korean War occupied a fleet of Boeing C–97s (134 troops) and Douglas C–124 Globemasters (200 troops, or bulky equipment which could not previously be carried by air). Smaller types with twin piston engines included the twin-boom Fairchild C–119 Packet (Wright R–3350s, 62 troops) and Nord Noratlas (2,000hp Bristol Hercules), plus the Fairchild C–123 Provider which was still going strong in the Vietnam War. Updating of the USAF's transport fleet resulted in the introduction of turboprop types – the 200-troop Douglas C–133 Cargomaster (four Pratt & Whitney T34s) and the Allison T56-powered Lockheed C–130 Hercules, able to carry 92 troops or 20,000kg (44,100lb) of equipment.

Strategic transports kept getting bigger. The Lockheed C–141 StarLifter, powered by four Pratt & Whitney TF33 turbofans of 9,525kg (21,000lb) thrust each, can swallow 154 troops or 31,750kg (70,000lb) of cargo and has a range of 6,440km (4,000 miles).

The stretched C–141B is being produced by modifying the present fleet. Another type powered by four TF33s is the Boeing C–135, the military version of the 707 airliner. The biggest military transport ever is the Lockheed C–5A Galaxy, which has two decks able to accommodate 120,200kg (265,000lb) of cargo made up of 270 fully equipped troops, two tanks, five armoured personnel carriers or a selection of awkward and bulky machinery. The Galaxy, powered by four General Electric TF39 turbofans of 18,600kg (41,000lb) thrust each, has a range of just over 6,000km (3,750 miles). The RAF's strategic freighter until 1976 was the Short Belfast, which could carry 270 troops or 35,380kg (78,000lb) of equipment. The Soviet Union relies on mammoth lifters such as the Antonov An–22, capable of transporting 45,000kg (99,200lb) of cargo on the power of four 15,000hp Kuznetsov turboprops and with a maximum range of 11,000 km (6,835 miles). Recently the Russian Air Force has introduced the turbofan Ilyushin Il–76, with a payload of 40,000kg (88,185lb) and a range of 5,000km (3,100 miles).

On the smaller side are the Antonov An–12, powered by four 4,000hp Ivchenko turboprops and having a typical load of 100 paratroops; the collaborative European C.160 Transall with two Rolls-Royce Tyne turboprops of 6,100hp each, able to carry 93 troops and with a maximum range of 4,550km (2,830 miles); and the Japanese Kawasaki C–1, which uses a pair of Pratt & Whitney JT8D turbojets. Battlefield transports include the 44-troop Aeritalia G.222 and 41-passenger de Havilland of Canada DHC–5 Buffalo, both using a pair of General Electric T64 turboprops. The British equivalent is the Hawker Siddeley Andover, a military derivative of the HS.748 airliner powered by a pair of Rolls-Royce Dart turboprops.

One of the most interesting developments for the future has been spawned by the USAF's competition to find a Hercules successor. Both contestants in the AMST (Advanced Medium STOL Transport) fly-off, the Boeing YC–14 and McDonnell Douglas YC–15, incorporate many new ideas which will benefit both military and civilian passengers for many years to come.

Civil and Maritime Aviation

Airlines and Airliners

In the first decade of this century, to be precise on 16 November 1909, the world's first airline was founded. This was Deutsche Luftschiffahrts AG, generally known as Delag, with headquarters at Frankfurt-am-Main, Germany, and its purpose was to operate passenger flights with Zeppelin airships and to train Zeppelin crews. Count Ferdinand von Zeppelin had flown his first rigid airship, LZ 1, at Manzell on Bodensee (Lake Constance) on 2 July 1900, but it was not a complete success. But on 19 June 1910, his seventh airship, the 147·97m (485ft 6in) long LZ 7 *Deutschland* (*Germany*) made its first flight. It had been ordered by Delag and, although short-lived, was the first powered aircraft to carry passengers.

Delag had plans for a system of Zeppelin-operated air services, built a number of airship stations with sheds, and even published maps of the routes, but activities were limited to voyages from these stations and no scheduled services were operated. By the time

PREVIOUS PAGES: *A biplane class racer.*

World War I began Delag had operated seven passenger Zeppelins, made 1,588 flights covering 172,535km (107,211 miles) and carried 33,722 passengers and crew without injury.

It was on the other side of the Atlantic, in Florida, that the only pre-World War I scheduled air services were operated. On 4 December 1913, the St Petersburg–Tampa Airboat Line was established, and at 10·00hr on New Year's Day 1914 a single-engined 75hp Benoist biplane flying boat, piloted by Tony Jannus, left St Petersburg for the cross-

ing of Tampa Bay and alighted at Tampa 23 minutes later to complete the world's first scheduled airline service. The city of St Petersburg subsidized the service, and traffic demand made necessary the use of a second flying boat. Operations continued until the end of March, 1,024 passengers being carried.

The next important step in establishing air services was taken in Britain, when the Royal Air Force set up a Communication Wing to provide fast transport, mainly between London and Paris, for members of the Government and other officials attending the Peace Conference. Using mostly D.H.4s, 4As and, later, Handley Page O/400 twin-engined bombers, regular London–Paris services began on 10 January 1919. This was the start of cross-Channel air services, and it is claimed that the modified O/400 *Silver Star* carried the first non-military cross-Channel passengers and also made the first passenger night flight across the Channel. The RAF services continued until September 1919, 749 flights were made with 91 per cent regularity, and 934 passengers and 1,008 bags of mail were carried.

BELOW LEFT: *The St Petersburg–Tampa Airboat Line's Benoist Flying Boat leaving St Petersburg, Florida, at the start of the world's first scheduled air service, on 1 January 1914. This was the only scheduled airline service to operate before World War I, and there were soon enough passengers to merit the use of a second flying boat.*

BOTTOM LEFT: *S. Instone and Company's D.H.4 at Hounslow in October 1919. This aeroplane was later converted to a cabin D.H.4A. D.H.4s were originally built in 1917 as day bombers and used by both the British and the Americans. After the war many of them were modified for civil airline and airmail duties.*

BELOW: *One of the Royal Air Force Airco D.H.4As used on the Communications Squadrons' first cross-channel services. These aircraft were designed by de Havilland and were powered by 375hp Rolls-Royce Eagle engines. They were mainly used to transport Government members and other officials.*

The start of commercial air transport

Aircraft Transport and Travel (AT and T), although founded in 1916, had to wait for the return of peace and for government permission before it could begin commercial operation. However, all was eventually ready, and a civil Customs airport was established at Hounslow, near the present London Airport at Heathrow, for the start of scheduled services on 25 August 1919. At 12.40 that day Major Cyril Patteson took off with four passengers in a de Havilland 16 on the first scheduled London–Paris service. On that same morning at 09.05 Lieut E. H. 'Bill' Lawford had left Hounslow for Paris in an AT and T D.H.4A with one passenger and some goods; Lawford's flight has often been reported as the inaugural service, but this is not true.

A second British airline, Handley Page Transport, had been formed on 14 June that year, and on 25 August one of the company's O/400s flew from London to Paris with journalists. Regular Paris services did not begin until 2 September, when Lt-Col W. Sholto Douglas (later Lord Douglas of Kirtleside) flew an O/7 from Cricklewood to Le Bourget.

Handley Page opened a London–Brussels service on 23 September 1919, and a London–Amsterdam service on 6 July 1920, although AT and T had already begun a London–Amsterdam service on 17 May in conjunction with the Dutch KLM.

A third British airline was that operated by the Aerial Department of the shipowners S. Instone and Co. This company had begun a private Cardiff–Hounslow–Paris service on 13 October 1919, for the carriage of staff and shipping documents, and on 18 February 1920, began a public London–Paris service when Capt F. L. Barnard flew a D.H.4A on the inaugural service. From 12 December 1921, operations were under the title The Instone Air Line.

By the end of 1920 the British airlines were in financial trouble. French companies had begun Paris–London services in September 1919, and the Belgian SNETA had begun flying between Brussels and London in June 1920. These British companies were now competing with each other and with sub-sidized continental companies for very limited traffic. At the end of October Handley Page ceased operating the Amsterdam route, in November gave up regular operation of the Paris route, and then on 17 December AT and T stopped all its operations.

On 28 February 1921, all British air services came to an end through lack of finance. As a result, small Government subsidies were granted to Handley Page and Instone and they resumed London–Paris services in the second half of March at the same £6 6s single fare as the French airlines. The situation was not helped when the Daimler Airway began London–Paris services on 2 April 1922, so that three British airlines and two French competitors were all fighting for the same traffic; in the year ending 31 March 1922, a total of 11,042 passengers had crossed the Channel by air, 5,692 flying in British aircraft and 4,258 in French.

From April 1922 government subsidies were granted to Daimler, Instone and Handley Page for the Paris route and to Instone for a London–Brussels route which was opened on 8 May. However, it soon became

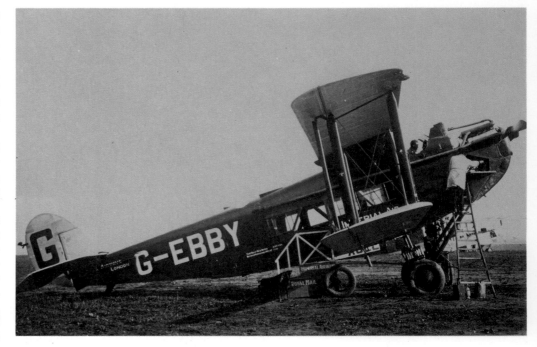

obvious that the competitive operations could not continue, and in October a revised scheme was introduced and routes allocated. Daimler was allocated £55,000 for a Manchester–London–Amsterdam route with a connection to Berlin; Instone £25,000 for London–Brussels–Cologne; Handley Page £15,000 for London–Paris; and British Marine Air Navigation (not then formed) £10,000 for a Southampton–Channel Islands–Cherbourg flying boat service. The Southampton–Guernsey service opened on 25 September 1923, but no regular service was flown to Cherbourg.

Operations on these lines, with some changes, continued, and Handley Page opened a London–Paris–Basle–Zürich service in August 1923; but the financial situation was still unsatisfactory and the government decided to set up a national airline. This came into existence on 31 March 1924, as Imperial Airways with £1 million capital and guarantee of a subsidy of £1 million spread over ten years. Imperial Airways took over the fleets, staff and operations of the four earlier airlines and was due to begin operation on 1 April but unfortunately a pilots' strike prevented the working of any services until 26 April.

Most of the aircraft used by the pioneer British airlines were of two families: Airco and Handley Page. AT and T, having close associations with Airco, chose de Havilland designs. The RAF Communication Squadrons had used single-engined D.H.4 two-seat bombers, and some of these were converted to D.H.4As with two passenger seats over which there was a hinged cover with windows. AT and T had four of these aircraft and eight D.H.16s, which were four-passenger adaptations of the D.H.9 bomber design. Both types were of wooden construction, powered by 350/365hp Rolls-Royce Eagle water-cooled engines, and cruised at about 160km/h (100mph).

Following the D.H.4A and D.H.16, de Havilland designed the purely civil D.H.18, with 450hp Napier Lion engine and eight seats. This type appeared in 1920 and was used by AT and T and Instone. A much improved development was the Lion-powered eight-passenger D.H.34 which first flew on 26 March 1922, and went into service with Daimler Airway on 2 April! It also served with Instone and one was exported to Russia.

ABOVE LEFT: One of the fleet of more than 100 Breguet 14s used by the Latécoère line to develop the air services between Toulouse and West Africa. Mail containers can be seen beneath the lower wings. The services of this line were gradually extended during the early 1920s, and carried both mail and passengers.
TOP: The famous Instone Vickers Vimy Commercial City of London. The Instone house flag appears on the nose. This aeroplane flew mainly on the London–Brussels–Cologne route.

ABOVE: One of the Daimler Airways' de Havilland D.H.34s, seen after passing to Imperial Airways in the spring of 1924.
ABOVE RIGHT: The twin-engined Farman Goliath. This type of aircraft was widely used by the early French airlines on many of their European routes and made a Paris–London return night flight in June 1922. They were also used on the first regular scheduled international passenger service, operated by Farman from Paris to Brussels. This was a weekly flight starting in March 1919.

The RAF Communication Squadrons had also used the large Handley Page O/400 with two Eagle engines and a span of 30·48m (100ft). A few had passenger cabins in place of the bomb cells, while others only had the military equipment removed and seats installed. Handley Page Transport used O/400s with austere cabins, but developed a number of sub-types with improved accommodation. These included the O/7, O/10 and the O/11 freighter. In all of these aircraft two passengers could be carried in the open nose cockpit. The maximum weight was 5,470kg (12,050lb), cruising speed about 112km/h (70mph) and passenger accommodation was 14 in the O/7, 12 in the O/10 and 5 in the cargo O/11.

Based on the O/400 series, Handley Page

designed and built the W.8 with reduced span, better passenger accommodation and single fin and rudder in place of the O/400's box-like structure. The sole W.8, with 12 to 14 seats and Lion engines, first flew on 4 December 1919, saw limited service with Handley Page Transport and was followed in 1922 by three 12/14-seat Eagle-powered W.8bs.

On 30 April 1920, Instone took delivery of an aeroplane that was destined to become the best known of all in those pioneering days. It was the Vickers Vimy Commercial named *City of London*. This was basically the same as the modified Vimy bombers which in 1919 made the first nonstop transatlantic flight and the first England–Australia flight, but incorporated a new fuselage having seats operations until the following year, starting a Paris–London service with Farman Goliaths on 29 March.

The network of French air routes rapidly expanded and services were begun between France and Corsica and France and North Africa. But the great French dream was an air service to South America, and Pierre Latécoère, the aircraft manufacturer, set about its achievement. The route through Spain to West Africa was opened in stages for the carriage of mail and operated as far as Casablanca by April 1920. Services were initially worked under the title Lignes Aériennes Latécoère, but in April 1921 the name was changed to Cie Générale d'Entreprises Aéronautiques, to be succeeded by Cie Générale Aéropostale in 1927. Operating

Type: Farman F.60 Goliath
No of passengers: 12
Engines: Two 260hp Salmson CM.9s
Cruising speed: 120km/h (75mph)
Ceiling: 4,000m (13,120ft)
Range: 400km (248 miles)
Weight: 4,770kg (10,515lb)
Span: 26·5m (86ft 10in)
Length: 14·33m (47ft)

for as many as ten fare-paying passengers.

British Marine Air Navigation, for its cross-Channel services, used three wooden Supermarine Sea Eagle amphibian flying boats. These had a Lion or Eagle engine with pusher propeller and a small six-seat cabin in the bows. Only the three Sea Eagles were built, and two passed to Imperial Airways along with the Vimy Commercial, the three H.P.W.8bs, seven D.H.34s and, unairworthy, a D.H.4A and an O/10.

France quickly set about the development of air services after the war, formed a number of airlines and made plans for trunk routes to South America and the Far East. On 8 February 1919, a Farman Goliath flew from Paris to Kenley, near London, with 11 military passengers. It is often claimed that

this was the start of French cross-Channel services, but, although this is untrue, France did open the first regular scheduled international passenger service as early as 22 March 1919, when Farman began a weekly Paris–Brussels service.

Early in 1919 an association of French aircraft manufacturers established Compagnie des Messageries Aériennes (CMA), and this airline developed a system of air services beginning with a daily link between Paris and Lille from 1 May. Breguet 14 single-engined biplanes were used and it was this type with which CMA began Paris–London services on 16 September, later working in pool with Handley Page Transport.

Compagnie des Grands Express Aériens was also founded in 1919, but did not begin

under severe climatic conditions and crossing stretches of desert where a forced landing could mean death or torture for the crew at the hands of hostile tribesmen, the line was pushed forward through Agadir, Cap Juby, Villa Cisneros, Port Étienne and St Louis to Dakar – the full route to West Africa being opened in June 1925.

French airlines were also looking towards the Orient, and the first step was the founding, on 23 April 1920, of Cie Franco–Roumaine de Navigation Aérienne. This airline opened the first sector of its eastward route, from Paris to Strasbourg, on 20 September 1920. Prague was reached in that October and Warsaw in the following summer. In May 1922 the Paris–Strasbourg–Prague–Vienna–Budapest route was opened,

Civil and Maritime Aviation

RIGHT: *A Luft-Verkehrs Gesellschaft C VI of the Deutsche Luft-Reederei airline at Gelsenkirchen. This was very probably on the occasion of the inauguration of an air service.*

BELOW: *German airlines also began to spring up very soon after the end of World War I. One of the smaller ones, Rumpler-Luftverkehr, first opened a service from Augsberg to Berlin via Munich, Nuremberg and Leipzig, in 1919. Ex-military Rumpler C1 biplane fighters were used on the route. In this photograph the passengers are seen just before climbing into the open rear cockpit.*

BOTTOM: *KLM (Royal Dutch Airlines) established its operations during the early 1920s with fleets of Fokker monoplanes. On the left is a Fokker F.II and in the background the F.III.*

BELOW RIGHT: *A Blériot Spad 33 of Cie Franco-Roumaine de Navigation Aérienne, seen at Le Bourget, Paris, in the early 1920s. There were several versions of this aircraft which could accommodate from four to six passengers and attain a speed of 170km/h (106mph).*

BOTTOM RIGHT: *Post Office DH–4s, US-built versions of the de Havilland two-seat bomber, at Omaha on the US transcontinental mail route.*

FAR RIGHT: *The first all-metal civil aircraft, the Junkers F 13, appeared in June 1919. It was one of the first specially designed transport aeroplanes. A low-wing cantilever monoplane, the aircraft was powered by a single 185hp B.M.W. engine and could carry four passengers. A number of airlines used the aircraft, including some float-plane versions, throughout the 1920s.*

Bucharest was reached in September and on 3 October the entire route was open to Constantinople (now Istanbul). This route across Europe involved flying in mountainous terrain and through some of the continent's worst weather, and therefore represented a great achievement. Up to 1923 all flights were made with single-engined aircraft and confined to daylight, but in that year three-engined Caudron C.61s were introduced and night flying was pioneered with the first such service between Strasbourg and Paris on 2 September 1923, and between Bucharest and Belgrade on 20 September. On the first day of 1925 the company's name was changed to CIDNA, and by the end of 1927 the line was operating no less than 76 aircraft.

Night flying was also pioneered on the Paris–London route in June 1922 when Grands Express made a return night flight with a Goliath, but it was not until April 1929 that regular night services were flown over the route – by Air Union, which in 1923 had been created by the merger of CMA and Grands Express.

The numerous French pioneer airlines employed a very wide range of aircraft. Wartime Salmson 2–A.2 and Breguet 14 single-engined reconnaissance and bomber biplanes were used in large numbers, Latécoère employing well over 100 of the latter on the route to West Africa.

Franco-Roumaine used Salmsons and some single-engined Potez biplanes before acquiring a main fleet of Blériot Spad cabin biplanes. The first of these was the Spad 33 of 1920, and it was developed into a whole family of similar aircraft with seats for four to six passengers and a variety of engines including, in later models, the air-cooled Jupiter. More than 100 of these attractive little biplanes were built, and some could cruise at 170km/h (106mph).

Widely used by the Farman Line, CMA, Grands Express and some non-French airlines, was the Farman Goliath. This was designed as a twin-engined bomber but converted to have two passenger cabins with seats for up to 12 passengers. The wing span was 26·5m (86ft 10in), most had two 260hp Salmson water-cooled radial engines, and cruising speed was about 120km/h (75mph).

Germany also made an early start in establishing regular services. Numerous com-

panies began operating, but the two most important were Deutsche Luft-Reederei (DLR) and Deutscher Aero Lloyd. DLR began Europe's first sustained regular civil daily passenger services when it opened the Berlin–Weimar route on 5 February 1919. The operation grew rapidly and employed a large fleet of ex-military single-engined biplanes, mostly the L.V.G. C VI with room for two passengers in the open rear cockpit, but there were also numbers of A.E.G. J IIs and some twin-engined A.E.G. G Vs and Friedrichshafen G IIIas.

Junkers began flying a Dessau–Weimar service in March 1919 with a modified J 10 two-seat attack aircraft. This was a low-wing cantilever monoplane of all-metal construction with corrugated metal skin, and is almost certainly the first all-metal aeroplane to have operated an air service. In 1921 Junkers set up Junkers-Luftverkehr to operate air services and promote its F 13 cabin monoplane. The F 13 was the first all-metal aeroplane designed and built as a transport, having an enclosed cabin for four passengers, and made its first flight on 25 June 1919. More than 300 were built, in many versions.

In January 1926 Deutsche Luft Hansa was created by the merging of Aero Lloyd and Junkers-Luftverkehr and operations began on 6 April. Thereafter Luft Hansa (written as one word from the beginning of 1934) was the German national airline, but numbers of small airlines continued to exist.

Although short-lived, there was one German airline operation which must be mentioned. This was the postwar revival of Delag, with ambitious plans for airship services within Germany and on international routes, and two new Zeppelins, the LZ 120 *Bodensee* (*Lake Constance*) and LZ 121 *Nordstern* (*North Star*) were built. The *Bodensee* flew on 20 August 1919, and with accommodation for 21 to 27 passengers began working a Friedrichshafen–Berlin service on 24 August, flying in opposite directions on alternate days. *Bodensee* flew until December, made 103 flights (including one from Berlin to Stockholm) and carried 2,253 revenue passengers, but the Inter-Allied Control Commission would not allow the service to restart in 1920.

Numerous other European countries began air transport operations. In Belgium SNETA did pioneering work leading to the formation

RIGHT: *The Fokker F.XII* Leeuwerik (Lark) *was the first of the type to fly over the Amsterdam–Batavia route operated by KLM.*
BOTTOM: *Imperial Airways' Handley Page H.P.42* Hannibal *at Baghdad. A biplane with wings mounted above the fuselage, the H.P.42 used four 475hp radial engines and could carry up to 38 passengers in a luxurious interior.*
FAR RIGHT: *Imperial Airways' Armstrong Whitworth Argosy* City of Glasgow *seen over London.*

Type: Junkers F13
No of passengers: 4
Engines: One 185hp BMW IIIa
Cruising speed: 140km/h (87mph)
Ceiling: 4,000m (13,120ft)
Range: 700km (435 miles)
Weight: 1,730kg (3,814lb)
Span: 17·75m (58ft 2·75in)
Length: 9·6m (31ft 6in)

of Sabena in 1923. KLM Royal Dutch Airlines was founded in October 1919. Although it did not initially operate its own services, KLM was to play a major part in developing world air transport and still operates under its original title. DDL – Danish Air Lines – was another very early European airline, beginning a Copenhagen–Warnemünde seaplane service on 7 August 1920. Today DDL is a constituent of SAS – Scandinavian Airlines System.

United States concentrates on the mail

The first stage in opening up US nationwide air mail services was the start on 15 May 1918, of a mail service linking Washington, Philadelphia and New York. Curtiss JN–4 biplanes were used, flown by Army pilots.

The Post Office took over the US Aerial Mail Service on 12 August 1918. Specially built Standard JR–1B mailplanes were introduced and by the end of the year the service had achieved an average 91 per cent regularity. The Washington–New York mail service was closed down at the end of May 1921, by which time the entire transcontinental mail service was in being.

Late in 1918 the Post Office acquired a large number of war-surplus aircraft, including more than 100 US-built DH–4Bs with 400hp Liberty engines. This fleet made it possible to start establishing the coast-to-coast service and on 15 May 1919, the Chicago–Cleveland sector was opened, saving 16hr on the Chicago–New York journey. On 1 July the New York–Cleveland sector was opened, with through New York–Chicago flights from September, and the San Francisco–Sacramento section was opened on 31 July. On 15 May 1920, the mail route was opened from Chicago to Omaha via Iowa City and Des Moines, and the full route came into operation on 8 September with the opening of the Sacramento–Salt Lake City and Salt Lake City–Omaha stages. Branch lines were also opened between Chicago and St Louis and Chicago and the twin cities Minneapolis/St Paul.

In order to save time it was decided to make experimental flights in each direction, with night flying over some stages. On 22 February 1921, two aircraft took off from each end of the route and so began a saga that is now part of American history. One of the eastbound aircraft crashed in Nevada, killing the pilot, and only one of the westbound aircraft managed to reach Chicago because of extremely bad weather, and at that point the flight was abandoned. The surviving eastbound mail was taken over at Salt Lake City by Frank Yeager, who flew through the night to Cheyenne and North Platte, where he handed over to Jack Knight for the flight to Omaha. Because of the termination of the westbound flight there was no aircraft at Omaha, and Knight secured a place in history by flying on to Chicago. Ernest Allison flew the last stage to New York, and the total coast-to-coast time was 33hr 20min.

In 1922 a start was made on lighting the mail route. The aerodromes were equipped with beacons, boundary and obstruction lights and landing-area floodlights. At the regular stops there were revolving beacons of 500,000 candle-power, and at emergency landing grounds 50,000 candle-power beacons. Flashing gas beacons were installed every three miles along the route, and by the end of 1925 the entire 3,860km (2,400 miles) of route had been lit at a cost of some $550,000.

During 1926/27 the Post Office Department turned over its air mail services to

private contractors. When the Post Office's own operations ceased it had flown more than 22 million km (13¾ million miles) with 93 per cent regularity and carried more than 300 million letters; but there had been 4,437 forced landings due to weather and 2,095 because of mechanical trouble. Worse still, there had been 200 crashes with 32 pilots killed, 11 other fatalities and 37 seriously injured.

Pioneering the trunk routes

In spite of sparse ground facilities, harsh climatic conditions, and low-performance aircraft, Britain, Belgium, France and the Netherlands were all eager to establish air communication with their overseas territories, and this was to lead to the opening of trunk routes which ultimately grew into our present globe-encircling system uniting what were remote corners of the world.

The first attempt to operate commercial air services in the tropics was that by the Belgian SNETA in the Congo (now Zaïre) when it opened the first stage of the Ligne Aérienne Roi Albert (King Albert Air Line) between Kinshasa and N'Gombé on 1 July 1920, using a three-seat Lévy-Lepen flying boat with a 300hp Renault engine. The N'Gombé–Lisala sector was inaugurated on 3 March 1921, and by that July the entire Congo River route was open between Kinshasa and Stanleyville (now Kisangani).

In Britain, at the end of October 1919, the Advisory Committee on Civil Aviation had recommended the establishment of trunk air routes linking the Commonwealth with the United Kingdom. They stated that 'the proper place for initial action' was the route to India and ultimately thence to Australia, 'to be followed by a service to South Africa...' and in October 1926 there was an agreement between Air Ministry and Imperial Airways for operation of an Egypt–India service. But things did not quite work out like that.

In March 1921 there was a Cairo Conference to examine administration and control of mandated territory, and Sir Hugh Trenchard, Chief of the Air Staff, proposed policing Mesopotamia (now Iraq) with air forces instead of the orthodox ground forces. The proposal was adopted and this in turn led to the establishment of the Desert, or Baghdad, Air Mail to speed communication between the United Kingdom and Baghdad. In June a survey was made of the route, landing grounds were marked out in the desert at intervals of 25 to 50km (15 to 30 miles) and a furrow was ploughed over some sectors as a navigational aid to the pilots. The route between Cairo and Baghdad was opened by the RAF on 23 June 1921, and maintained until commercial operations began in January 1927.

Ground and air surveys were made of the route between Cairo and India, and a fleet of special aircraft was ordered for Imperial Airways so that commercial service could replace the Desert Air Mail and implement the plan for a service to India. The route from Cairo involved long desert stages, several mountain crossings and the use of comparatively high-elevation aerodromes in extreme temperatures. The limited range and low speed of the aircraft also meant that aerodromes had to be provided at frequent intervals. Perhaps the most serious obstacle was political, for it was the task of obtaining permission to overfly and land in various countries that was to delay the opening of services, and for many years prevent through flights from the United Kingdom.

It should be realized that the early aircraft found the Alps a formidable barrier; they had to fly round them over France or the Balkans, and this still applied to many transport aircraft into the 1950s. France was in dispute with Italy, and would not allow British aircraft to fly via France into Italy and this, apart from a few experiments, enforced a railway sector in British trunk air routes until late in the 1930s. Persia did not wish to allow air services through her territory, and so the first British trunk air route was confined to the Cairo–Baghdad–Basra sectors.

Five de Havilland 66 Hercules biplanes were specially built for the route. These had three 420hp Bristol Jupiter air-cooled engines, accommodation for eight passengers, cruised at 176km/h (110mph) and had a range of about 640km (400 miles).

On 7 January 1927, one of the Hercules left Basra to open the fortnightly service to Cairo via Baghdad and Gaza. It arrived in Cairo on 9 January and three days later the first eastbound service left Cairo.

Eventually Persian permission was granted for a coastal route, and this enabled Imperial Airways to open its long awaited England–India service. The Armstrong Whitworth Argosy *City of Glasgow* took off from Croydon on 30 March 1929, and carried its passengers and mail to Basle. From there they travelled by train to Genoa, then in a Short Calcutta flying boat to Alexandria and on to Karachi in a Hercules. The Egypt–India sector involved eight scheduled intermediate stops, the total journey took seven days and the single fare was £130.

The service was extended to Jodhpur and Delhi in December 1929, and in association with Indian Trans-Continental Airways to Calcutta in July 1923, to Rangoon that October and to Singapore by the end of the year. Because of political and operational difficulties the route was transferred from the Persian to the Arabian shore of the Gulf in October 1932.

The setting up of a route through Africa was much more difficult. The continent rises slowly from the coast and then steeply from

southern Sudan to over 1,525m (5,000ft) at Nairobi and about 1,830m (6,000ft) at Johannesburg. Temperatures can be extremely high, and tropical storms of great intensity led to flooding of aerodromes as well as severe turbulence in flight. Aircraft performance falls off sharply in high temperatures and at high elevations. Ants were also apt to build quite solid obstructions on landing areas. In the 1920s and early 1930s Africa posed a formidable challenge to the operation of air services. However, all the problems were tackled, aerodromes constructed, rest houses built and fuel supplies laid down, and on 28 February 1931, the inaugural service to Central Africa left Croydon, although at that stage passengers were only carried to Khartoum.

The Central Africa service which left Croydon on 9 December 1931, was extended experimentally to Cape Town for the carriage of Christmas mail, a Hercules being used south of Nairobi. It was this type which operated the Nairobi–Cape Town sector when the entire route was brought into opera-

Type: Fokker F.VIIb–3m
No of passengers: 8–10
Engines: Three 215hp Armstrong Siddeley Lynxes
Cruising speed: 150km/h (93mph)
Ceiling: 4,400m (14,435ft)
Range: about 1,000km (620 miles)
Weight: 4,500–5,000kg (9,920–11,023lb)
Span: 21·71m (71ft 2·75in)
Length: 14·5m (47ft 7in)

tion in the following January.

In 1925, while employed with the French company CIDNA, Maurice Noguès made a Paris–Teheran survey flight with a Blériot Spad 56, and in 1927 CIDNA began negotiations for the extension of its services to Beirut, Damascus, Aleppo and Baghdad. Noguès later transferred to Air Union's Ligne d'Orient which was founded in 1927, that organization joined with Air Asie to form Air Orient, a regular Marseilles–Beirut mail service was started in June 1929 and the route was extended to Baghdad at the end of the year. On 17 January 1931, the entire line to Saïgon was opened with a ten-day schedule, although at first passengers were carried only as far as Baghdad. In 1938 the route was extended to Hong Kong, and in 1939 260km/h (161mph) three-engined Dewoitine D.338 monoplanes were working the entire route, by then operated by Air France.

On 1 October 1931, KLM inaugurated a regular Amsterdam–Batavia (now Jakarta) passenger service using Fokker F.XIIs. These aircraft had luxury-type seats for 4, although in Europe they could carry 16 passengers. The scheduled journey time was ten days and the flying time 81hr for what was almost certainly at that time the world's longest air route. In 1932 Fokker built five slightly larger F.XVIIIs to replace the F.XIIs, and the new aircraft had sleeper seats. In 1934 a KLM Douglas DC-2 took part in the England–Australia race and, carrying three passengers, covered the 19,795km (12,300 miles) to Melbourne in just over 90hr. In June 1935 DC-2s were introduced on the Far East service with a six-day schedule.

Consolidation in Europe

In Europe the pioneer years of air transport continued through the 1920s and, according to definition, into the 1930s. For most of this time many routes were operated only in the summer, and night services were only gradually introduced. There was steady development of aircraft, particularly in Germany and the Netherlands, and the air-cooled engine largely replaced the water-cooled engine, with its attendant plumbing problems and heavy radiators. Radio came into increasing use, airport lighting was developed, and Germany, in particular, gave considerable attention to developing ways of navigating and landing in bad weather.

The British national airline operated a very small European route system. Nevertheless, Imperial Airways did improve its fleet, at first with developments of the early Handley Pages but from 1926 with a small number of three-engined Armstrong Whitworth Argosy 18/20-seat biplanes. Unlike their British predecessors, these had metal structures although they still employed fabric covering.

A much greater improvement in standards came in 1931 when Imperial Airways began using a fleet of Handley Page H.P.42 Hannibal and H.P.45 Heracles biplanes. These were large four-engined aircraft with Jupiter engines, 38 seats on European services and 16 to 24 on the Egypt–India and Egypt–Central Africa routes. On Heracles two

stewards were carried, full meals were served, and during peacetime this fleet operated with perfect safety. The only problem was their low speed of around 160km/h (100mph).

The Handley Pages remained in operation until World War II although some smaller and faster aircraft had been added to the fleet by this time, including the beautiful de Havilland Albatross monoplanes, known as the Frobisher class by Imperial Airways, which cruised at 335km/h (210 mph).

In 1937 a second British operator, British Airways, began using fast Lockheed Electras on European services and later added Lockheed 14s. They flew to Germany, Poland and Scandinavia as well as Paris and, in terms of speed, Imperial Airways was shown in a bad light. It was finally agreed to amalgamate the two airlines and BOAC – British Overseas Airways Corporation – resulted.

France continued expansion of its air routes and used a wide variety of indigenous aircraft, mostly biplanes, including the

OPPOSITE PAGE

LEFT: *An Air France Lioré et Olivier 213. It was painted red and gold and bore the fleet name* Rayon d'Or *(Golden Ray).*

CENTRE: *Air France's Dewoitine D.338* Ville d'Orleans *(City of Orleans) at Le Bourget Airport, Paris, embarking passengers for Lyons, Marseilles and Cannes. In the background the Bloch 220* Provence *is positioned to operate a London service. The photograph was taken in 1938 or 1939, and the large letter F on the roof of the Dewoitine was for recognition while flying through the war zone in the Far East.*

RIGHT: *A Savoia Marchetti S.73 of Sabena, built under licence by SABCA in Belgium.*

THIS PAGE

ABOVE LEFT: *The Ad Astra Aero base at Zürich-horn in the early 1920s, with a Macchi M.3 flying boat on the slipway.*

ABOVE RIGHT: *Swissair's Fokker F.VIIa CH 157 on the ice in front of the Grand Hotel, St Moritz. This aircraft had originally been one of the Balair fleet. This design was the first notable civil aircraft from the Royal Netherlands Aircraft Factory after its very successful models of WWI.*

BELOW: Nordmark, *one of Lufthansa's Focke-Wulf FW.200 Condors, seen at Tempelhof Airport, Berlin, shortly before World War II. It was a four-engined monoplane capable of a speed of about 368km/h (230mph).*

single-engined Breguet 280T and twin-engined Lioré et Olivier 21. But CIDNA had introduced the three-engined low-wing Wibault 280T monoplane on its Paris–Istanbul route and Air Union had at least two on the London–Paris route before Air France was formed in 1933 as the successor to these airlines and Aéropostale, Air Orient and the Farman Line.

The new organization introduced a further wide range of types including the twin-engined Potez 62 and Bloch 220 and the three-engined Dewoitine series.

Sabena expanded its routes with Fokker F.VIIb–3ms, and later introduced three-engined Savoia Marchetti monoplanes. KLM used a whole series of Fokker monoplanes for its European passenger and cargo network, including the four-engined F.XXII and F.XXXVI which appeared in 1935 and 1934 respectively. But the Fokkers, with their wooden wings and welded steel-frame fuselages and, except in one case, non-retractable undercarriages, were outmoded by the Douglas DC–2 and DC–3, and KLM became the first European operator of these advanced aeroplanes.

It was Germany, in the form of Lufthansa, which dominated the air transport map of Europe. When the airline was founded it took over 162 aircraft of 19 different types. The largest batches of standard, or reasonably standard, aeroplanes were 46 Junkers-F 13s, 19 Fokker-Grulich F.IIs and 13 F.IIIs. There were also numbers of Dornier Komets, and it was one of these that operated the airline's first service. Three-engined Junkers-G 24s were used for the first night service on 1 May 1926, and three-engined Rohrbach Rolands pioneered trans-Alpine services from 1928.

Lufthansa expanded rapidly and in its third year had a European network of more than 33,000km (20,500 miles) over which it flew 10 million km (6,214,000 miles) and carried 85,833 passengers and 1,300 tons of cargo, mail and baggage. The airline had the biggest domestic network of services in Europe, and also served most of the continent's main cities.

In 1932 Lufthansa began operation of that very famous aeroplane, the Junkers-Ju 52/3m. This was a three-engined low-wing monoplane with accommodation for 17 passengers, was of all-metal construction with corrugated skin and, although not particularly fast, was extremely reliable. Lufthansa was to use about 230 with a maximum of 78 at any one time. The Ju 52/3m was widely used as a civil and military transport; nearly 5,000 were built, and most prewar European airlines used them at some time – two on floats working in Norway until 1956.

Lufthansa also introduced a number of limited-capacity high-speed aircraft including the four-passenger single-engined Heinkel He 70, commissioned on *Blitz* (*Lightning* or *Express*) services in Germany in June 1934, and the twin-engined ten-passenger He 111 which had a smoking cabin and began service in 1936. The four-engined 40-passenger Junkers-Ju 90 and 25/26-passenger Focke-Wulf Fw 200 Condor were prevented by war from showing their full potential.

Almost every European country operated its own air services. Austria's Ölag was founded in 1923 and flew Junkers aircraft. Poland began very early, using mostly French and German aircraft; LOT was founded in 1929 and flew Junkers and Fokker types and a few Polish designs, and later adopted the Lockheed Electra and Model 14. Czechoslovakia's CSA and CLS used Czechoslovak aircraft and Fokkers before CLS adopted the DC–2 and CSA the Savoia Marchetti S.73. Hungary used Fokkers and Junkers; Greece used Junkers types; Rumania used a mixture of British, Czechoslovak, French and German aircraft; and Yugoslavia used mostly British and French aircraft. Most of these airlines operated domestic services and services to other European destinations, although LOT had a route to Palestine.

Spain began mail services in October 1921, when CETA began operating D.H.9s between Seville and Spanish Morocco. In 1925 UAE was formed and, using Junkers aircraft, opened services linking Madrid with Seville and Lisbon. A Madrid–Barcelona route was opened in 1927 by the original Iberia using Rohrbach Rolands, but in March 1929 the three pioneer Spanish companies were amalgamated to form CLASSA, in turn superseded in 1932 by LAPE, which operated domestic and international services with Fokker F.VIIb–3ms, Ford Trimotors and, later, Douglas DC–2s.

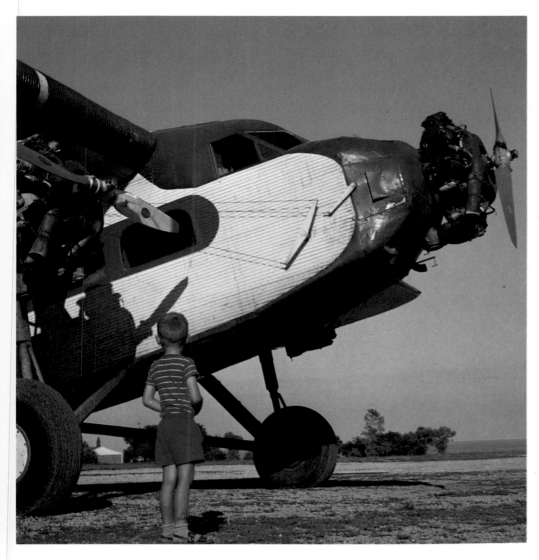

FAR LEFT BELOW: *Frobisher, one of Imperial Airways all-wood de Havilland monoplanes. It is seen at Croydon with a Douglas DC–3 approaching.*
LEFT: *The Ford Trimotor, generally known as the 'Tin Goose', because of its outer skin constructed of corrugated metal.*

A number of small Swiss companies were founded and at the end of 1919 one of these was renamed Ad Astra Aero. Initially it operated a number of small flying boats from the Swiss lakes, but did not begin regular scheduled operations until June 1922 when it began Geneva–Zürich–Nuremberg services with Junkers F 13s. This airline expanded its operations, mostly with Junkers aircraft, and, in 1931, amalgamated with Balair to form Swissair. Balair had begun services in 1926 and was equipped with Fokkers. Since its inception Swissair has been one of Europe's most technically progressive airlines, has introduced a range of advanced aircraft and been among the first to adopt such types as the DC–2 and DC–3. It was Swissair's introduction of the Lockheed Orion monoplane with retractable undercarriage in May 1932 that led Germany to produce the high-performance Heinkel He 70 and Junkers Ju 60 and Ju 160.

Scandinavian air transport differed from that in other parts of Europe because of terrain and the difficulty of providing aerodromes. DDL, formed in Denmark in 1918, began operation with a seaplane, but otherwise was able to develop its routes with landplanes but Sweden and Norway had to rely mainly on seaplanes.

Type: Ford Trimotor
No of passengers: 13–15
Engines: Three 420/450hp Pratt & Whitney Wasps
Cruising speed: 196km/h (122mph)
Ceiling: 6,045m (18,600ft)
Range: 901km (560 miles)
Weight: 6,123kg (13,500lb)
Span: 23·72m (77ft 10in)
Length: 15·36m (50ft 3in)

BELOW LEFT: *One of the high-speed Lockheed Orions introduced by Swissair in May 1932 on the route from Zurich to Vienna via Munich. A single-engined low-wing monoplane, it could carry up to six passengers at a maximum speed of about 360km/h (225mph).*
BELOW CENTRE: *DDL's (Danish Air Lines) first Junkers Ju.52/3M, Selandia, at Kastrup Airport, Copenhagen. This aircraft first flew in 1932 and remained in production throughout the 1930s and World War II. An all-metal, low-wing monoplane, it used three B.M.W. radial engines to attain a top speed of 288km/h (180mph).*

BELOW RIGHT: *One of Aero O/Y's Junkers F.13s fitted with skis for winter operation. This was the first all-metal civil aircraft, and first appeared in 1919. A low-wing cantilever monoplane, the aircraft was powered by a single 185hp B.M.W. engine and could carry four passengers. A number of airlines used the aircraft throughout the 1920s.*
BOTTOM: *The first Short Calcutta flying boat, seen on the Medway at Rochester, England, before delivery. It first entered service with Imperial Airways in 1928, and it was used principally on the Mediterranean section of the air route to India.*

RIGHT: *One of Ala Littoria's Savoia-Marchetti S.66 twin-hulled flying boats alighting on the Tiber near Ostia, close to Rome's present Leonardo da Vinci Airport. This was one of a series of flying boats built by the company during the 1920s and 1930s, while it was primarily a manufacturer of sea planes. The S.66 was a development of the S.55. It was equipped with three Fiat engines of 550 or 750hp and could accommodate up to 18 passengers. Some 24 were built and used in service by, among others, Aero Espresso, SAM and SANA. A few survived to be used in World War II.*

AB Aerotransport – Swedish Air Lines – began services in June 1924 between Stockholm and Helsinki using Junkers F 13 floatplanes. As traffic grew a three-engined Junkers G 24 was added and in August 1932 a Ju 52/3m floatplane – almost certainly the first regular airline operation of the Ju 52/3m, even before Lufthansa. Lack of a land aerodrome at Stockholm forced seaplane operation to continue until May 1936, when Bromma Airport was opened. However, ABA had established services to Denmark, Germany, Amsterdam and London from the airport at Malmö on the west coast. ABA was an early operator of DC–3s, acquiring three in 1937. Like Swissair, ABA was a technically advanced airline, as its fleet composition shows, and it also opened the first experimental night mail service in Europe when, on the night of 18/19 June 1928, an F 13 with onboard sorting facilities flew from a military aerodrome near Stockholm to London in four stages via Malmö, Hamburg and Amsterdam.

The real beginning of air transport in Norway came with the founding in 1932 of DNL. A coastal route from Oslo through Kristiansand, Stavanger and Bergen was established into Arctic Norway. It was mainly operated by the Ju 52/3m on floats, although a few other types were used, including Short Sandringham flying boats after World War II.

Aero O/Y, in Finland, began its services in 1924 with a Helsinki–Reval route. F 13 seaplanes were used, followed by a G 24 and Ju 52/3ms, and pre-World War II operations were mainly confined to routes across the Baltic and the Gulf of Finland. In winter many of the aircraft had to be fitted with skis because ice prevented the use of seaplanes. Aero O/Y now operates as Finnair.

Most of the pioneer Italian services, too, were operated by marine aircraft, but Transadriatica, based in Venice, began operation in 1926 with a fleet of F 13 landplanes and, with three-engined G 24s, opened a Venice–Munich service in 1931.

Avio Linee Italiane was founded in 1926, used Fokkers on its early services, and had established a route to Munich by 1928 and Berlin by 1931. It also opened a Venice–Milan–Paris service and in June 1938 extended this to London, with Fiat G.18s.

Ala Littoria was formed in 1934 to take over most of the Italian airlines and it operated numbers of Savoias and other Italian aircraft but long remained a large operator of flying boats and seaplanes, although flying three-engined Caproni landplanes on its services to Italian East Africa.

Marine aircraft in Europe
Much use of marine aircraft was made in Europe in the pioneer years of air transport. There was an erroneous belief that seaplanes and flying boats offered greater security on overwater crossings.

Britain used flying boats on the trans-Mediterranean section of the Empire routes. France and Italy, with many Mediterranean and Adriatic routes, were Europe's biggest users of commercial seaplanes and flying boats, although Germany used such aircraft on coastal resort services and in the Baltic.

When the England–India route was opened in 1929, Imperial Airways used Short Calcutta flying boats on the trans-Mediterranean section. They were 12-passenger metal-hulled biplanes with three 540hp Bristol Jupiter engines, and the first example flew in February 1928. The Calcutta was followed by the Short Kent, of similar configuration but with four 555hp Jupiter engines and improved accommodation for 16 passengers. There were only three Kents, they comprised the Scipio class and entered service in May 1931.

In July 1936 Short Brothers launched the first of the S.23 C class flying boats, the *Canopus*. These had been designed for implementation of the Empire Air Mail Programme and were very advanced high-wing all-metal monoplanes powered by four 920hp Bristol Pegasus engines, had accommodation for 16 to 24 passengers and a top speed of just on 320km/h (200mph). *Canopus* made the

BELOW LEFT: Canopus, *the first Short C class flying boat, seen on the slipway at Rochester in 1936. Each of this fleet of 'Empire Boats' as they were called, was powered by four 910hp Bristol Pegasus engines and accommodated 24 passengers with their luggage, plus two tons of mail and freight. Their cruising speed was 264km/h (164mph) and the maximum speed of 322km/h (200mph) was as fast as many fighters of the time if not faster.*
BELOW: *One of SANA's Dornier Wal flying boats used on both European and international routes during the 1930s.*

first scheduled flight of the type, from Alexandria to Brindisi on 30 October 1936. Eventually they were to work the entire routes between Southampton and Sidney and Southampton and Durban, and some remained in service until after World War II.

Sandringham and Solent developments of the C class operated some of BOAC's post-war routes, and the last British flying boat services were those operated by Aquila Airways' Solents to Madeira until the end of September 1958.

The German resort services were mostly flown by small seaplanes and the Baltic services by Dornier Wals. The first Dornier Wal flew in November 1922 and, because of Allied restrictions on German aircraft production, most early Wals were built in Italy and Italian airlines employed them in considerable numbers. The Wal was an all-metal monoplane with the wing strut mounted above the hull and braced to the stabilizing sponsons, or sea wings. Two engines were mounted back to back on top of the wing,

and the passengers occupied a cabin in the forward part of the hull. There were many versions of the Wal, with different engines, weights, performance and accommodation, but the early examples had seats for eight to ten passengers and were usually powered by Rolls-Royce Eagle or Hispano Suiza engines. SANA was the biggest operator of passenger Wals, and put them into service in April 1926 on a Genoa–Rome–Naples–Palermo service.

There were three major flying boat constructors in Italy – Cant, Macchi and Savoia Marchetti. The Cants were biplanes, mostly of wooden construction, and SISA used the single-engined four-passenger Cant 10*ter* on its Trieste–Venice–Pavia–Turin service, which opened in April 1926, and on its Adriatic services. To supplement them SISA had a fleet of three-engined ten-passenger Cant 22s. Aero Espresso used a twin-engined eight-passenger Macchi M.24*bis* biplane flying boat on its Brindisi–Athens–Istanbul service.

Although the biplane served well into the

1930s, it was the Italian monoplanes that proved of most interest. In 1924 Savoia built a twin-hulled monoplane torpedo-bomber to the design of Alessandro Marchetti, and from this developed a passenger aircraft for Aero Espresso's then planned Brindisi–Istanbul service. This was the S.55C with thick-section 24m (78ft 9in) span wooden wing, accommodation for four or five passengers in each hull, triple rudders and two tandem-mounted 400/450hp Isotta-Fraschini engines. These aircraft went into service in 1926 and were followed in 1928 by the more powerful S.55P version, of which SAM had 14 or 15 on trans-Mediterranean services.

Developed from the S.55 was the 33m (108ft 3¼in) span S.66 of 1932. This had three 550 or 750hp Fiat engines mounted side by side, and the twin hulls could accommodate up to 18 passengers. It is believed that 24 were built. They were operated by Aero Espresso, SAM and SANA, and some passed to Ala Littoria, working services between Italy and Tunis, Tripoli and Haifa, and some survived to be taken over for war service.

In a completely different category was the Cant Z.506 which saw widescale service with Ala Littoria on Mediterranean and Adriatic routes. This was a three-engined twin-float low-wing monoplane with seating for 12 to 16 passengers.

As early as 1923 L'Aéronavale started using twin-engined four-passenger Lioré et Olivier 13 wooden flying boats between Antibes and Ajaccio, and in May that year a Latécoère affiliate opened a Marseilles–Algiers service with them. More than 30 were built.

Also in 1923, CAMS had begun production of a series of civil and military flying boats designed by Maurice Hurel. One of them was the wooden CAMS 53 biplane with two tandem 500hp Hispano Suiza engines and a small cabin for four passengers. It was introduced by Aéropostale on the Marseilles–Algiers route in October 1928.

The biggest French biplane flying boat in passenger service was the 35·06m (115ft) span Breguet 530 Saïgon, with three 785hp

Hispano Suiza engines, three-class accommodation for 19 to 20 passengers and a maximum weight of 15,000kg (33,069lb).

As a replacement for its CAMS 53s, Air Union had also ordered a fleet of four-engined 10 to 15 passenger Lioré et Olivier H242 monoplane flying boats. These had their 350hp Gnome Rhône Titan Major engines in tandem pairs above the wing, and 14 went into service with Air France beginning in 1934.

The last trans-Mediterranean flying boat services of Air France were those operated to Algiers immediately after the war by two Lioré et Olivier H246 four-engined 24 to 26 passenger monoplanes.

Mail and passenger services in the USA

On 1 March 1925, Ryan Airlines opened its Los Angeles–San Diego Air Line with modified Standard biplanes and a Douglas Cloudster, and this is claimed to have been the first regular passenger service wholly over the US mainland to be maintained throughout the year.

The first major legislative step in creating an airline industry was the passing of the Contract Air Mail Act (known as the Kelly Act) in February 1925. This provided for the transfer of mail carriage to private operators, and it was followed in May 1926 by the Air Commerce Act, which instructed the Secretary of Commerce to designate and establish airways for mail and passengers, organize air navigation and license aircraft and pilots. This Act came into force at midnight on 31 December 1926.

The history of United States air transport over the next few years was extremely complex, with numerous airlines competing for mail contracts. Some were small concerns, but others were backed by large financial organizations and closely linked with the aircraft manufacturing industry. Here only the briefest details of this intricate picture can be given.

The first five mail contracts were let on 7 October 1925, and 12 airlines began operating the services between February 1926 and April 1927 as feeders to the transcontinental mail route which was still being operated by the Post Office.

The Ford Motor Company had begun private daily services for express parcels between Detroit and Chicago on 3 April 1925, using single-engined all-metal Ford 2–AT monoplanes. Ford secured Contract Air Mail Routes (CAM) 6 and 7 covering Detroit–Chicago and Detroit–Cleveland and was the first to operate, beginning on 15 February 1926. Passengers were carried from August that year.

Next to start was Varney Air Lines, on CAM 5, between Pasco, Washington State, and Elko, Nevada, via Boise, Idaho. Leon Cuddeback flew the first service on 6 April 1926, using one of the airline's fleet of Curtiss-powered Swallow biplanes, but the operation was immediately suspended until the Swallows could be re-engined with air-cooled Wright Whirlwinds.

Also in April 1926 Robertson Aircraft Corporation began flying the mail on CAM 2 between St Louis and Chicago, and this operation is claimed as the first step in the eventual creation of the present American Airlines. Western Air Express began working CAM 4 between Los Angeles and Salt Lake City with Douglas M–2 biplanes, and opened its first passenger service over the route on 23 May that year.

CAM 1, New York–Boston, was awarded to Colonial Air Transport, but the services did not start until June 1926 and passenger service, with Fokkers, began almost a year later in April 1927.

PRT – Philadelphia Rapid Transit Service – obtained CAM 13 for Philadelphia–Washington and operated three flights a day from 6 July 1926. Whereas most of the mail carriers used passengers as fill-up load or ignored them altogether, PRT, with its Fokker F.VIIa–3ms, catered for passengers and used mail as fill-up.

The prize routes were those covered by CAM 17, from New York to Chicago, and CAM 18, San Francisco to Chicago. National Air Transport (NAT) was founded in May 1925, secured CAM 17, and began operating it with Curtiss Carrier Pigeons on 1 September 1927, having opened CAM 3, Chicago–Dallas, on 12 May the previous year. NAT was not very interested in passenger traffic and soon acquired a fleet of 18 ex-Post Office Douglas mailplanes; but, later, did buy Ford Trimotors.

Boeing, however, secured the San Francisco–Chicago route and was very interested in passengers. The company built a fleet of 24 Model 40A biplanes for the route. They were powered by 420hp Pratt & Whitney Wasp engines and could carry pilot, two passengers and 545kg (1,200lb) of mail, and were superior in payload and performance to the aircraft operated by NAT and most other mail carriers. By midnight on 30 June 1927, the Boeing 40s were deployed along the route and service began the following day.

Western Air Express (WAE) had hoped to get the San Francisco–Chicago mail contract, but Boeing's tender was much lower. Instead WAE developed a Los Angeles–San Francisco passenger service with Fokkers and

established a high reputation for reliability and safety.

In 1926 and 1927 two events took place which had a marked effect on the growth of air transport in the United States. The first was the appearance of the Ford Trimotor, which first flew in June 1926. This was an all-metal high-wing monoplane powered by three 200/300hp Wright Whirlwind engines, and had accommodation for 10 or 11 passengers in its original 4–AT version. Later came the 5–AT with 400/450hp Pratt & Whitney Wasps and seats for 13 to 15. The other event, in May 1927, was Lindbergh's flight from New York to Paris. This was the first solo flight across the North Atlantic, and it created enormous interest in aviation.

Brief mention must be made of three other airlines. Pacific Air Transport was organized by Vern Gorst in January 1926 and opened service over CAM 8, Seattle–San Francisco–Los Angeles, on 15 September; Maddux Air Lines opened a Los Angeles–San Diego passenger service with Ford Trimotors on 21 July 1927; and Standard Airlines under Jack Frye began a Los Angeles–Phoenix–Tucson passenger service with Fokker F.VIIs on 28 November 1927.

The Standard Airlines operation, by using a rail connection, provided a 70-hour air-rail transcontinental service from February 1929 and further development cut the time to 43hr 40min. Boeing Air Transport acquired Pacific Air Transport in January 1928, and this gave Boeing a connection between the Chicago–San Francisco route and Seattle. Boeing's passenger traffic was developing, but its aircraft were unsuitable, so the company built the three-engined Model 80 with Pratt & Whitney Wasps and accommodation for 12 passengers. Four Boeing 80s were built and began service in October 1928, to be followed by ten more powerful Model 80As with 18 seats.

In May 1928 Transcontinental Air Transport (TAT) was formed, and began planning a transcontinental route using Ford Trimotors on which meals could be carried, although the first air stewardesses appeared on Boeing's Model 80s in 1930. TAT came to an agreement with the railways for an air-rail coast-to-coast service. It began on 7 July 1929. Westbound passengers left New York's Pennsylvania Station in the *Airway Limited* and travelled overnight to Port Columbus in Ohio, where a special combined air-rail terminal had been built. From there they flew to Waynoka in Oklahoma where they transferred to the Atchison, Topeka and Santa Fe Railroad for the night journey to Clovis in New Mexico. The final stage by air took them to Los Angeles, and from there they could continue free to San Francisco by train or by Maddux Air Lines. The New York–Los Angeles journey took exactly 48hr and the fare ranged from $337 to $403 one way. In November that year TAT acquired Maddux.

In the east, on 1 May 1928, Pitcairn Aviation began operating CAM 19 between New York and Atlanta with Pitcairn Mailwings and, using the lighted airway, did some night flying. That December the airline took over Florida Airways' Atlanta–Miami route, and the company became Eastern Air Transport in January 1930. The route was extended to Boston and passengers were carried over part of it from August. In December 1930 Curtiss Condors were introduced, and were also used by TAT. These were large twin-engined biplanes with 600hp Curtiss Conqueror engines and 18 seats. They led in 1933 to the T–32 model, which could carry 12 passengers in sleeping berths.

In 1929 Walter Folger Brown became Postmaster General, and he had strong views

on how US airways should be developed. The Post Office contract for the central transcontinental route – CAM 34 New York–Los Angeles – was up for tender, but before TAT could secure the contract Brown forced the merger of TAT with Western Air Express, thus forming Transcontinental and Western Air (TWA). The new airline began the first coast-to-coast all-air through service on 25 October 1930, using Ford Trimotors on the New York–Los Angeles route with a nightstop at Kansas City and an overall time of 36hr.

American Airways, formed on 25 January 1930, obtained the southern route CAM 33 via Nashville and Dallas by a series of route extensions and company take-overs.

Then in July 1931 United Air Lines was organized to take over officially Boeing Air Transport, NAT, PAT and Varney, which for some time had been working under the United title.

Thus, by mid-1931, the Big Four had been created out of nearly 30 airlines of varying

OPPOSITE PAGE
LEFT: *A Ryan Los Angeles–San Diego Air Line Standard biplane of 1925.*
CENTRE: Maiden Dearborn IV, *one of the Ford 2–ATs operated by the Ford Motor Company on the routes from Detroit–Chicago and Detroit–Cleveland.*
RIGHT: *One of National Air Transport's fleet of Curtiss Falcon mail planes, used on the New York to Chicago route during the 1920s.*
THIS PAGE
ABOVE LEFT: *One of the Boeing Air Transport fleet of Boeing 40Bs, a development of the Model 40As introduced in 1927. The aircraft bears CAM 18 on its fuselage, the number of the San Francisco–Chicago contract mail route. It could carry both passengers and mail and was powered by a 420hp Pratt & Whitney Wasp radial engine.*
ABOVE CENTRE: *One of the four-engined Fokker F.32s used by Western Air Express, before it was amalgamated with Transcontinental Air Transport to form TWA. These aircraft were used on the Los Angeles to San Francisco passenger service route, which they operated with great reliability and safety.*
ABOVE RIGHT: *A Pitcairn PA–5 Super-Mailwing of Colonial Western Airways, used on the CAM 20 Cleveland to Albany route.*

Type: Boeing 247D
No of passengers: 10
Engines: Two 550hp Pratt & Whitney Wasps
Cruising speed: 250km/h (155mph)
Ceiling: 5,600m (18,400ft)
Range: 780km (485 miles)
Weight: 5,738kg (12,650lb)
Span: 22·56m (74ft)
Length: 15·65m (51ft 4in)

size. They were American Airways, Eastern Air Transport, TWA and United Air Lines.

Although this is but a brief summary of the early development of US air transport, mention must be made of the Ludington Line and of two more transport aircraft. Ludington was an airline which really believed in passengers, and on 1 September 1930, began a service 'every hour on the hour' from 08.00 to 17.00hr over the Newark (New York)–Camden (Philadelphia)–Washington route, mainly with Stinson Trimotor monoplanes. In the two years before the company was taken over by Eastern it carried 124,000 passengers.

An event of great importance was Boeing's production of the Model 247 ten-passenger low-wing all-metal monoplane with two Pratt & Whitney Wasp engines and retractable undercarriage. This can be claimed as the prototype of the modern airliner. The Boeing 247 first flew on 8 February 1933, 60 were ordered for the United group, and they went into service with Boeing Air Transport, National Air Transport and Pacific Air Transport and became United Air Lines' standard equipment up to the end of 1936. The Boeing 247 was able to climb with one engine inoperative and cruise at 250km/h (155mph), and it made obsolete all other US airline equipment.

Boeing 247s were not available to non-United group airlines, and so TWA asked Douglas to produce a competitive aircraft. This was the DC–1, of similar layout to the Boeing. It first flew on 1 July 1933, and TWA ordered 20 of the improved production DC–2s.

But before the DC–2 could enter service, in July 1934, President Roosevelt, believing that some airlines had been unduly privileged in securing contracts, cancelled all the mail contracts on 9 February 1934, thus ending an important chapter in US airline history. Under White House instructions the last mail flight had to be completed on 19 February. That day, as a dramatic gesture, Jack Frye of TWA and Eddie Rickenbacker flew the DC–1 from Los Angeles to Newark, via Kansas City and Columbus, in a transcontinental record time of 13hr 4min.

Development in the Commonwealth

On 12 November 1919, Capt Ross Smith and Lieut Keith Smith with two crew took off from Hounslow in a Vickers Vimy and made the first flight to Australia. They arrived at Darwin on 10 December, after which they continued across Australia to Sydney, Melbourne and Adelaide. In preparation for the flight across Australia a route was surveyed, aerodromes prepared and fuel and oil provided. Responsible for this work on the Darwin–Longreach section were W. Hudson Fysh and P. J. McGinness, and it was these men, with others, who founded Queensland and Northern Territory Aerial Services (QANTAS) on 16 November 1920.

It was to Norman Brearley's West Australian Airways that the honour went of starting the first subsidized air service in Australia. On 4 December 1921, a Bristol Tourer took off from Geraldton, the railhead north of Perth, to inaugurate a weekly mail service to Carnarvon, Onslow, Roebourne, Port Hedland, Broome and Derby. The route was extended to Perth in January 1924, and from Derby to Wyndham in July 1930. In 1929 a weekly Perth–Adelaide service began using de Havilland Hercules biplanes, and Vickers Viastra monoplanes were introduced in 1931, covering the journey in less than 24hr.

On 2 November 1922, QANTAS opened its first scheduled service when P. J. McGinness flew an Armstrong Whitworth F.K.8 from Charleville to Longreach with mail, and on the next day Hudson Fysh flew on with mail and one passenger to Cloncurry.

QANTAS steadily expanded its operations in Queensland, and in 1931 took part in the first experimental England–Australia mail flights, carrying the mail from Darwin to Brisbane. QANTAS was chosen as the partner to Imperial Airways to carry passengers and mail between Singapore and Brisbane when the England–Australia service opened in December 1934. A new company, Qantas Empire Airways (referred to hereafter as Qantas), was registered in January 1934 with Imperial Airways and QANTAS each holding half the share capital.

Qantas ordered a fleet of D.H.86 four-engined biplanes for the Brisbane–Singapore operation, but, when the first service left Brisbane on 10 December 1934, they had to use a single-engined D.H.61 and D.H.50 because of the late delivery, and Imperial Airways worked the Darwin–Singapore sector until February 1935. Passengers were carried over the entire England–Australia route from April.

In September 1932 the Holyman brothers began a Launceston–Flinders Island service with a Fox Moth, and soon after merged with another concern to form Tasmanian Aerial Services, which a year later became Holyman's. In October 1935 Adelaide Airways began operations, and sometime that year Airlines of Australia began services based on Brisbane and Sydney. Then, in July 1936, Australian National Airways (ANA) was incorporated to include Holyman's, Adelaide Airways, Airlines of Australia and West Australian Airways.

Also in 1936 came an insignificant event which, years later, was to have a major influence on Australian air transport. Reginald Ansett had been refused a licence for a bus service between Hamilton and Melbourne, so, on 16 February 1936, he began an air service between these points, for which a licence was not required. After World War II Ansett was to get control of ANA and take over other companies to form Australia's largest private airline.

In Canada, during 1920, about 12,070km (7,500 miles) of landplane and seaplane routes were surveyed, the first flight to penetrate the Northwest Territories was made in the following year, and in 1923 the first air mail flight was made between Newfoundland and Labrador.

On 11 September 1924, Laurentide Air Service and Canadian Pacific Railway established an air service linking the railway at Angliers with the Quebec goldfields at Rouyn. This was the first regular air service introduced in Canada for the carriage of

passengers, mail and freight.

Much of Canada's early air transport was on these lines, with air services linking remote areas with the nearest railhead. In summer the aircraft operated as landplanes and seaplanes, but the harsh winter climate enforced a change to skis.

Many concerns were involved in these early operations, mostly using single-engined aircraft. On 26 December 1926, Western Canada Airways began operations at Sioux Lookout and regular services were begun to Rolling Portage and Red Lake mining districts, and over the next few years a fairly extensive route network was established. On 3 March 1930, the airline began the nightly *Prairie Air Mail* service over the Winnipeg–Calgary and Regina–Edmonton routes. The initial service was flown by a Fokker Universal, and these were the first scheduled night flights in Canada.

On 25 November 1930, Canadian Airways Ltd began operations, having been formed

244

by Canadian Pacific Railway, Canadian National Railway, Western Canada Airways and a group of airlines controlled by Aviation Corporation of Canada. The new concern established services in many parts of the country and undertook a lot of mail and freight carriage. But although it linked many pairs of cities, it did not provide a transcontinental service.

However, work went ahead on preparing airports and navigational services for a transcontinental route and on 10 April 1937, Trans-Canada Air Lines (TCA) was created by a Government Act. Survey flights over the route began from Vancouver in July 1937 and on 1 September that year TCA began operation with a Vancouver–Seattle service flown by Lockheed Electras. Early in 1938 Vancouver–Winnipeg mail and cargo services began, and that October the route was extended, for cargo only, to Toronto, Ottawa and Montreal, mail being carried from the beginning of December.

On 1 March 1939, the full-scale official transcontinental mail service was inaugurated, and passengers were carried from 1 April on this route and on the Lethbridge–Calgary–Edmonton route. TCA now operates as Air Canada.

The other major Canadian airline is CP Air, which was formed on 30 January 1942, as Canadian Pacific Air Lines. This was founded as a subsidiary of Canadian Pacific Railway, and represented the merger of Arrow Airways, Canadian Airways, Dominion Skyways, Ginger Coote Airways, Mackenzie Air Service, Prairie Airways, Quebec Airways, Starratt Airways, Wings Ltd and Yukon Southern Air Transport. The initial CPA fleet consisted of 77 single- and twin-engined aircraft.

On 31 July 1929, Mrs F. K. Wilson founded Wilson Airways in Nairobi, and when Imperial Airways' Central Africa route was opened Wilson Airways operated connecting flights between Kisumu, on Lake Victoria,

and Nairobi, using a Puss Moth. In August 1932 Wilson Airways began Nairobi–Mombasa–Tanga–Zanzibar–Dar-es-Salaam mail services, and subsequently developed a network of services in the region.

With the introduction of the Empire Air Mail Programme in 1937, Imperial Airways introduced flying boats via a coastal route to Durban, and Wilson Airways opened a weekly Kisumu–Nairobi–Moshi–Dodoma–Mbeya–Mpika–Broken Hill–Lusaka mail service to connect with Imperial Airways at Kisumu.

In 1931 two airlines were formed in Central Africa, Rhodesian Aviation and Christowitz Air Services (in Nyasaland). The former opened a weekly Bulawayo–Salisbury service, subsidized by the Government of Southern Rhodesia and the Beit Trustees. The service was only operated as required and used South African-registered Puss Moths. Christowitz opened a Blantyre–Beira service, also using a Puss Moth. In 1933 Rhodesian Aviation began a weekly passenger and goods service over the Salisbury–Gatooma–Que Que–Gwelo–Bulawayo–Johannesburg route with a Fox Moth and Christowitz began a Salisbury–Blantyre service. Then in October 1933 Rhodesia and Nyasaland Airways (RANA) was formed. This acquired the assets of Rhodesian Aviation, taking over the Salisbury–Johannesburg service, which was terminated at Bulawayo, and in February 1934 the Christowitz Salisbury–Blantyre service. RANA also developed new routes and, like Wilson Airways, operated services connecting with Imperial Airways flying boat operations.

The first Government air mail flight in the world took place in India when, on 18 February 1911, Henri Pequet, in a Humber biplane, flew mail from Allahabad to Naini Junction about 8km (5 miles) away. The first actual mail service in India began on 24 January 1920, when the RAF opened a weekly service between Bombay and Karachi. This was maintained for only a few weeks, and there was no Indian air service until 15 October 1932, when Tata Sons opened a Karachi – Ahmedabad – Bombay – Bellary – Madras mail service to connect with Imperial Airways' England–Karachi flights. The Tata aircraft was a Puss Moth, and it was flown from Karachi to Bombay by J. R. D. Tata.

In May and June 1933 two airlines were formed in India. The first, Indian National Airways (INA), was established to participate as a shareholder in the second, Indian Trans-Continental Airways, and to develop services in northern India. Indian Trans-Continental was set up to operate the trans-India route in association with Imperial Airways, beginning the Karachi–Calcutta service on 7 July 1933, with Armstrong Whitworth Atlanta monoplanes.

On 1 December 1933, INA started a weekly Calcutta–Rangoon service with Dragons, and on the same day opened the first daily air service in India – between Calcutta and Dacca.

INA and Tata Air Lines (as successor to Tata Sons) continued to expand their opera-

tions, Tata opening a Bombay–Delhi service on 6 November 1937, and INA establishing a Karachi–Delhi service a year later.

A number of short-lived air services were operated in New Zealand during the 1920s, and in 1930–31 Dominion Airways operated a Desoutter monoplane on about 100 flights between Hastings and Gisborne before the loss of the Desoutter ended the undertaking. Air Travel (NZ) started a Hokitika–Okuru service with a Fox Moth on the last day of 1934, East Coast Airways began a twice daily Napier–Gisborne service with Dragons in mid-May 1935, and at the end of that December Cook Strait Airways opened a Wellington–Blenheim–Nelson service with two Dragon Rapides.

The year 1935 saw the founding of Union Airways of New Zealand as an offshoot of Union Steam Ship Co, and this airline began a daily Palmerston North–Blenheim–Christchurch–Dunedin service on 16 January 1936, with D.H.86s. The airline commissioned

three Lockheed Electras in June 1937 and put them on a daily Auckland–Wellington service. Union Airways purchased East Coast Airways in July 1938, and the following March opened a Palmerston North–Napier–Gisborne–Auckland service. After the war Air Travel (NZ), Cook Strait Airways and Union Airways were all absorbed by the newly founded New Zealand National Airways Corporation.

South Africa was slow in setting up any form of air transport, and it was only in March 1925 that the South African Air Force began a weekly experimental mail service over the Cape Town–East London–Port Elizabeth–Mossel Bay–Durban route, using D.H.9s. Only 32 flights were made, with 276 bags of mail, and it was not until more than four years later that a private air service began when Union Airways opened a subsidized Cape Town–Port Elizabeth service with extensions to Durban and Johannesburg.

Type : Junkers Ju 52/3m
No of passengers : 15–17
Engines : Two 1,000hp Wright Cyclones
Crusing speed : 296km/h (184mph)
Ceiling : 5,486m (18,000ft)
Range : 915km (568 miles)
Weight : 9,200kg (20,282lb)
Span : 29·25m (95ft 11·5in)
Length : 18·9m (62ft)

During 1930 the administration of South West Africa concluded an agreement with Junkers to form South-West Africa Airways and operate a weekly passenger, freight and mail service between Windhoek and Kimberley. This and a number of other services were begun in 1931 using F 13s and Juniors.

A change in policy came with the founding, on 1 February 1934, of South African Airways (SAA), which began operation with aircraft and staff taken over from Union Airways. SAA introduced Junkers–Ju 52/3ms, and these were the first multi-engined aircraft used by a South African airline.

At the beginning of February 1935 SAA took over South-West Africa Airways. The airline steadily expanded its network and on 1 April 1936, took over the Cape Town–Johannesburg sector of the England–South Africa route. Junkers–Ju 86s were added to the fleet in 1937, and by the time all civil flying was suspended in May 1940, SAA had opened routes to Lusaka, Broken Hill, Nairobi, Kisumu and Lourenço Marques.

BELOW: *The* Graf Zeppelin *at Recife, Brazil. This airship made a historic flight round the world in 1929, taking 21 days for the journey. During this trip it became the first aircraft of any type to make a flight across the Pacific Ocean.*

CENTRE: *One of Air France's South Atlantic Farman F.2200s,* Ville de Montevideo. *This was a large four-engined aeroplane.*
BOTTOM: *A Wilson Airways' de Havilland D.H.84 Dragon at Zanzibar.*

The South Atlantic

Having opened the air route between Toulouse and Dakar, France set about establishing services between Natal in Brazil and Buenos Aires. Airports were prepared and radio equipment installed, at an estimated cost of $1·5 million. Aeropostal Brasileira and Aeroposta Argentina were established as subsidiaries of Aéropostale, and the Natal–Buenos Aires services was opened in November 1927. The dream of a service linking France and South America finally came true on 1 March 1928, when the entire route from Toulouse to Buenos Aires was opened for mail, with a transit time of eight days, but the ocean sector had to be operated by ships.

In 1928 Aeroposta Argentina opened services from Bahía Blanca, south of Buenos Aires, to the oil centre of Comodoro Rivadavia 950km (590 miles) further south, and from Buenos Aires to Asunción in Paraguay. In July 1929 the great barrier of the Andes was conquered with the opening of the Buenos Aires–Santiago service, and French

air services had reached the Pacific coast.

For several years the services in South America were operated by a series of single-engined Latécoère monoplanes, the Laté 17, 25 and 26, and open-cockpit Potez 25 biplanes. Much of the flying was done at night and weather was frequently appalling. On the route to Comodoro Rivadavia there were very strong winds to contend with, but it was the service through the Andes which called

for a very high standard of flying and a great amount of bravery. One incident is enough to illustrate the character of the route. In June 1930 Henri Guillaumet left Santiago in a Potez 25 with the mail for Europe. He encountered blinding snowstorms and violent turbulence and was forced to land close to Laguna Diamante at an elevation of 3,500m (11,480ft). The little biplane overturned, but Guillaumet survived and it took

BELOW: *One of the Latécoère 25 aircraft operated by Aeroposta Argentina. A single-engined monoplane, this type was used on the routes from north to south of the continent and also for the hazardous journeys across the Andes.*

CENTRE: *The four-engined Blériot 5190 flying boat Santos-Dumont. This aircraft made its first crossing of the South Atlantic from Dakar to Natal on 27 November 1934, and began regular service with Air France on this route early in 1935.*

BOTTOM: *Lufthansa's 10-ton Dornier Wal Boreas being lifted on to the catapult of the depot ship Schwabenland. This aircraft used two engines, which were placed in line, one driving a pusher propeller and the other a tractor propeller.*

him five days and four nights to struggle to safety.

Great as were the achievements of what was known as The Line, the South America route could not be regarded as satisfactory until the entire route could be covered by air. The first attempt was made in 1930, when on 12–13 May Jean Mermoz flew the ocean crossing from St Louis, Sénégal, to Natal in 21hr in the Latécoère 28 seaplane *Comte de la Vaulx*. But a single-engined floatplane was not a suitable aircraft for the ocean crossing, and the French Government ordered the three-engined Couzinet 70 *Arc-en-Ciel* landplane and the four-engined Blériot 5190 flying boat *Santos-Dumont*.

On 16 January 1933, Mermoz flew the *Arc-en-Ciel* from St Louis to Natal in 14hr

27min. After modifications, as the Couzinet 71, it began regular South Atlantic mail flights at low frequency from 28 May 1934, completing eight ocean crossings by the end of the year. Flown by Lucien Bossoutrot, the *Santos-Dumont* made its first crossing, from Dakar to Natal, on 27 November 1934, and began regular service with Air France early in 1935. It made at least 22 ocean crossings and cut the Toulouse–Buenos Aires time to 3 days 20hr.

The construction of the big Blériot flying boat had been delayed by financial problems, and as a result it had been beaten into service by the four-engined Latécoère 300 flying boat *Croix du Sud* (*Southern Cross*). This boat made its first crossing on 3 January 1934, and continued as far as Rio de Janeiro. Thereafter it shared the route with the *Arc-en-Ciel* and made six crossings by the end of the year; but on 7 December 1936, radio contact was lost with the *Croix de Sud* about 4hr after it left Dakar. The flying boat, its famous commander Jean Mermoz, and his crew disappeared and were never found.

The overall success of the *Croix du Sud* led to construction of three similar Latécoère 301s, and these began service early in 1936.

Air France also employed a number of large four-engined Farman landplanes on the South Atlantic route, beginning with the F.220 *Le Centaure*, which made its first Dakar–Natal flight on 3 June 1935. In November 1937 the last of these, the F.2231 *Chef Pilote L. Guerrero*, owned by the French Government, flew from Paris to Santiago in an elapsed time of 52hr 42min and made the Dakar–Natal crossing in 11hr 5min.

Although passengers were carried on the route to West Africa and in South America, none were carried on these prewar ocean crossings.

and the entire route from Berlin to Buenos Aires was scheduled for four to five days. The 10-ton Wal was introduced on the route and, after trials over the North Atlantic in 1936, the much-improved Do 18s began working over the South Atlantic. Four-engined Do 26s made 18 mail crossings before war stopped the service, and during their operations the Wals made 328 crossings.

The third country to begin South Atlantic air services was Italy. Ala Littoria Linee Atlantiche was set up as the Atlantic division of Ala Littoria, and had begun taking delivery of a special fleet of Savoia Marchetti S.M.83 three-engined monoplanes before Linee Aeree Transcontinentali Italiane (LATI) was established to operate the services. After proving flights, a regular

BELOW LEFT: *Two of SADTA's Junkers W 34s on a river in Colombia. The airline used these aircraft on several of the routes in the northern part of South America from 1919 onwards. It was founded with German capital immediately after World War I and gradually built up until eventually in 1940 it became part of the new airline Avianca.*
RIGHT: *One of the Boeing Model 314 flying boats, more usually known as 'Boeing Clippers'. This resulted from their individual names, such as Yankee Clipper, bestowed upon them by Pan American Airways. A total of 12 were built, 6 as 314s with 1,500hp Wright Double Cyclone engines, and a further 6 314As with increased passenger accommodation and 1,600hp engines.*

Germany used different methods in establishing its services to South America. Luftschiffbau Zeppelin decided to use the LZ 127 *Graf Zeppelin* on the route and on 18 May 1930, this airship left Friedrichshafen on a trial flight to Rio de Janeiro. This was followed by further trials in 1931. As a result the airship left Friedrichshafen on 20 March 1932, to open a regular service to Recife in Brazil, and this flight carried paying passengers – the first ever to fly on a transocean air service. Four flights were made that spring and five at fortnightly intervals in the autumn, with the last three continuing to Rio de Janeiro. In 1933 the *Graf Zeppelin* made 9 flights over the route, in 1934 twelve, in 1935 sixteen, and in 1936 nine, with an additional seven by the larger *Hindenburg*. From March 1935 this service was operated by Deutsche Zeppelin-Reederei, which was founded by Lufthansa and the Zeppelin company.

Germany's second method of flying to South America was to use landplanes between Germany and Africa and in South America and flying boats over the ocean. A system was devised for catapulting the flying boats from depot ships because they could not take off under their own power with sufficient fuel and while carrying a payload. The Dornier 8-ton Wal was used initially and the first experimental crossing made on 6 June 1933, when the *Monsun* was catapulted from the depot ship *Westfalen*. Regular mail services began in 1934, when *Taifun* made the first crossing on 7–8 February,

Rome–Rio de Janeiro service was inaugurated in December 1939. Avoiding British and French territory, the route was via Seville, Villa Cisneros, the Cape Verde Islands, Natal and Recife.

US air mail upheaval and a new start

After President Roosevelt's cancellation of the mail contracts and the last mail flight on 19 February 1934, the US Army Air Corps was given the task of flying the mail. The 43,450km (27,000 mile) network of mail routes was reduced to 25,750km (16,000 miles), and about 150 aircraft of various types were allocated to the operation. The weather was bad, the crews were inexperienced and ten pilots were killed before the last flight on 1 June.

The President admitted that he had been wrong, and in April 1934 the Postmaster General, James Farley, called in the airlines to find ways of salvaging what remained of the nation's airways. Temporary mail contracts were awarded, and among the conditions required to qualify for a contract was the stipulation that no contract carrier could be associated with an aircraft manufacturer.

The Big Four were reorganized as American Airlines, Eastern Air Lines, TWA Inc and United Air Lines, and of the 32 new mail contracts they were awarded 15, with TWA and United both getting mail contracts for transcontinental routes – Newark–Los Angeles and Newark–Oakland respectively. Eastern got three important routes, Newark–New Orleans, Newark–Miami and

Chicago–Jacksonville, while American's routes included Newark–Chicago and Newark–Boston. By combining Newark–Fort Worth and Forth Worth–Los Angeles they gained a transcontinental route, although it was not as direct as TWA's and United's.

Latin America

Most of the early airlines in South America were established by German nationals and with German capital, the first being SCADTA, which was founded in Colombia in 1919. This airline had a fleet of Junkers–F 13 seaplanes and, after a period of experimental operation, opened a regular service in 1921 over the Magdalena River route linking the port of Barranquilla with Girardot, the railhead for Bogotá. The distance was 1,046km (650 miles) and the flight took 7hr, compared with a week or ten days by steamer. New routes were added and more modern equipment acquired until finally, in 1940, the airline was merged with another small company to form today's Avianca.

The next airline to be formed, again by Germans, was Lloyd Aéreo Boliviano (LAB). Equipped with F 13s, this company was founded in August 1925, and by the end of the year was running regular services between Cochabamba and Santa Cruz, taking three hours against the surface time of four days. This company was almost certainly the first to operate Junkers–Ju 52/3ms, although it did so on military operations during the Gran Chaco war in 1932. LAB is still the Bolivian national airline.

In 1927 two German influenced airlines were founded in Brazil, Varig and Syndicato Condor. Condor opened a Rio de Janeiro–Pôrto Alegre–Rio Grande do Sul service in October, and during the year handed over the Pôrto Alegre–Rio Grande sector to Varig. Both companies used German aircraft, mostly Junkers, with floatplanes predominating, and built up a route system, initially in the coastal regions. In 1942 Condor was reorganized as Serviços Aéreos Cruzeiro do Sul and, although retaining its identity, was taken over in 1975 by Varig, which remains the principal Brazilian airline and now operates intercontinental services.

In Peru Elmer Faucett founded Compañia de Aviación Faucett in 1928, and by the following year had established air services extending the length of the country, from

Ecuador in the north to Chile in the south. Faucett was unusual in that it built many of its own aircraft, based on Stinson single-engined monoplanes. Although now under different ownership, Faucett is still operating.

A military air service was introduced in Chile in 1929. This ran north from Santiago to Arica near the Peruvian border. It was taken over by Linea Aérea Nacional (LAN) in 1934, at first flying mail and then passengers, and since that time a considerable route system has been developed, including transatlantic services. LAN is the only airline to serve Easter Island, which it includes on its Chile–Tahiti route.

The Unites States airline which became deeply involved in Latin America was Pan American Airways. This company, led by Juan Trippe for nearly 40 years, began regular contract mail services between Key West and Havana on 28 October 1927, using Fokker F.VIIa–3m monoplanes, and carried passengers from January 1928. PAA developed a network of services in the Caribbean, mostly using Sikorsky amphibians, and its routes reached as far as Cristóbal in the Panama Canal Zone. Extension southward down the west coast of South America was blocked by the Grace shipping line; so in 1929 Panagra was formed, with Pan American and Grace each holding 50 per cent of the shares. Panagra secured a mail contract for the route from Cristóbal to Santiago, Chile, and across the Andes to Buenos Aires. The first mail left Miami on 14 May 1929, and from Cristóbal was flown by Sikorsky S–38 and then Fairchild FC–2 to Mollendo in Peru, where the route then terminated. The extension to Santiago was inaugurated on 21 July and, after the acquisition of Ford Trimotors, Buenos Aires was reached on 8 October and Montevideo on 30 November. A speeding up of the services in April 1930 enabled mail to travel from New York to Buenos Aires in 6½ days. Passengers were carried to Santiago from 15 August 1931, and through to Montevideo on 5 October.

Although Pan American had to settle for a half share in South American west coast operations, the company would not compromise on the east coast. In March 1929 NYRBA (New York, Rio and Buenos Aires Line) was founded, and that August it began a Buenos Aires–Montevideo service. The

BELOW: *Pan American Airways' Martin M–130 flying boat* China Clipper, *which flew on the trans-Pacific route. It carried mail from November 1935, and up to 14 passengers from October 1936.*
BOTTOM: *A Panagra Fairchild FC– 2 flying over the Andes.*
BELOW RIGHT: *One of NYRBA Line's 14 Consolidated Commodore flying boats, which were used on the east coast. By February 1930 the entire route from Miami to Buenos Aires had been opened.*
CENTRE RIGHT: *Pan American Airways' flying boat, the Sikorsky S–40* Southern Clipper. *Although amphibians, the S–40s were normally operated as pure flying boats. This type was designed specially for NYRBA Pan American as an aircraft with a longer range and bigger payload than the Consolidated Commodore. These features were needed for long routes over the sea.*
BOTTOM RIGHT: *One of Mexicana's Douglas DC–3s from the post-war period.*

Hornets, tail units carried on twin booms, and accommodation for 32 passengers.

A much more advanced and more important flying boat was the Sikorsky S–42, powered by four 700hp Hornets and having accommodation for up to 32 passengers. The S–42 cruised at 274km/h (170mph) and had a normal range of 1,930km (1,200 miles). Ten examples of three models were built, and the type was introduced on the Miami–Rio de Janeiro route on 16 August 1934.

It was also in 1934 that VASP came into being and today, with Cruzeiro, Transbrasil and Varig, this company operates the Ponte Aérea (Air Bridge) between Rio de Janeiro and São Paulo, with 370 flights a week in each direction.

In Central America a New Zealander,

1939 Yerex founded British West Indian Airways (BWIA), and the airline opened its first service, Trinidad to Barbados via Tobago, in November 1940, using a Lockheed Lodestar.

Mexico has had a large number of airlines, its first being Cia Mexicana de Aviación (CMA), which began work in August 1924, carrying wages to the oil fields near Tampico with Lincoln Standard biplanes. This operation was devised to circumvent the activities of bandits. Under the title Mexicana, CMA is now a major international airline. Mexico's other major airline, Aeromexico, was created in 1934 as Aeronaves de Mexico. During the course of its long history this airline has absorbed a considerable number of other Mexican carriers.

next month a mail and passenger service was started between Buenos Aires and Santiago with Ford Trimotors – five weeks ahead of Panagra's trans-Andes service.

Before the east coast route could be opened to the United States it was necessary to obtain suitable aircraft. There were long overwater sectors and few landing grounds, so a fleet of 14 Consolidated Commodore flying boats was ordered. These were large monoplanes powered by two 575hp Pratt & Whitney Hornet engines, and could carry 20 to 32 passengers. They cruised at 174 km/h (108mph), and had a range of 1,600km (1,000 miles). Four had been delivered by the end of 1929 and on 18 February 1930, the entire route between Miami and Buenos Aires was opened, the 14,485km (9,000 miles) being flown in seven days. NYRBA also set up NYRBA do Brasil to undertake local operations in Brazil.

Pan American desperately wanted the east coast route, and finally managed to acquire NYRBA in September 1930, when it took over the Commodores – including those still on order – and changed NYRBA do Brasil to Panair do Brasil. Postmaster General Brown awarded Pan American the mail contract for the east coast route, FAM–10, on 24 September 1930.

Through NYRBA Pan American had acquired a fleet of Commodores, it urgently needed long-range aircraft with bigger payloads, and the need was met by three specially designed Sikorsky S–40s. These were large flying boats with four 575hp Pratt & Whitney

Lowell Yerex, was responsible for much of the early air transport development. In 1931 he founded Transportes Aéreos Centro-Americanos (TACA) in Honduras, and built up a main airway linking British Honduras with the capitals of Costa Rica, Guatemala, Honduras, Nicaragua, Panama and Salvador. In 1933 he opened the first service between Tegucigalpa and San Salvador. Networks of routes were set up in the Central American republics, and eventually TACA associated companies were established in Colombia, Costa Rica, Guatemala, Honduras, Mexico, Nicaragua, Salvador and Venezuela.

Today this vast TACA empire has shrunk to the present TACA International, which in the spring of 1976 was operating three BAC One-Elevens and three DC–6As. In

Conquering the Pacific

The first air crossing of the Pacific was not made until 1928, when Charles Kingsford Smith, C. T. P. Ulm, Harry Lyon and James Warner flew from Oakland, across the Bay from San Francisco, to Brisbane in Queensland in the three-engined Fokker F.VII *Southern Cross.* They left Oakland on 31 May and arrived in Brisbane on 9 June with a flight time of 83hr 38min.

In July 1931 Charles Lindbergh and his wife made a survey of a northern route in a Lockheed Sirius single-engined seaplane, flying to Japan via Alaska, Siberia and the Kuriles, but political problems prevented the establishment of such a route.

The only alternative was to use island stepping-stones which were United States territory, and bases were therefore prepared on Wake Island and Guam to enable a service to operate from San Francisco to Manila via Honolulu, Wake and Guam. This gave stages of 3,853km (2,394 miles) from San Francisco to Hawaii, 3,693km (2,295 miles) to Wake, 2,414km (1,500 miles) to Guam and 2,565km (1,594 miles) to Manila.

To obtain aircraft for the operation of a regular service, Pan American issued a specification for a flying boat capable of flying 4,023km (2,500 miles) against a 48km/h (30mph) headwind while carrying a crew of four and at least 136kg (300lb) of mail. To this specification Martin built three M–130 flying boats, each powered by four 800/950hp Pratt & Whitney Twin Wasp engines. The boats had a span of 39·62m (130ft), weighed

23,700kg (52,252lb) fully loaded and could carry 41 passengers, although only 14 seats were installed for the Pacific route. Cruising speed was 253km/h (157mph) and the range 5,150km (3,200 miles), or 6,437km (4,000 miles) if only carrying mail.

The M–130s were named *China Clipper*, *Philippine Clipper* and *Hawaii Clipper*, and the first was delivered in October 1935. The *China Clipper*, under the command of Capt Edwin Musick, inaugurated the trans-Pacific mail service when it left Alameda on 22 November 1935, and it alighted at Manila 59hr 48min later. Paying passengers were carried from 21 October 1936.

Early in 1937 the Sikorsky S–42B *Hong Kong Clipper* was delivered, and that spring it made a survey of the southern Pacific

route to Auckland, subsequently being used to extend the trans-Pacific operation from Manila to Hongkong, the first service being on 27–28 April. This gave Pan American a direct link to China through the China National Aviation Corporation's Hongkong–Canton–Shanghai service. From that time the Martin M–130s were completing the San Francisco–Manila out and back flights in 14 days.

On 23 December 1937, Pan American inaugurated a San Francisco–Auckland service via Hawaii, Kingman Reef and Samoa, but the S–42B, with its commander, Edwin Musick, and crew, was lost on the second flight and the service had to be suspended. But on 12 July 1940, a fortnightly service was opened via Hawaii, Canton Island and New Caledonia using one of the new Boeing 314s, with passengers being carried from 13 September.

The modern airliner

The principal passenger aircraft in use in the United States in the late 1920s and early 1930s were Fokker F.VIIs and Ford Trimotors. They had accommodation for 8 to 15 passengers, but cruised at only a little over 160km/h (100mph), and for much of the time very few of their seats were occupied. Some people believed there was a need for smaller and faster aeroplanes, and as a result there was a period when numerous airlines were operating fleets of small single-engined monoplanes capable of cruising at more than 241km/h (150mph).

John Northrop and Gerrard Vultee designed a very clean four-passenger high-wing monoplane known as the Lockheed Vega. It was a wooden aeroplane, powered by a Wasp engine, and it first flew in July 1927. The Vega entered service with International Airlines on 17 September 1928, and subsequently there were several versions, including one with a metal fuselage. Cruising speed was 217–241km/h (135–150mph), and the type was used by a number of airlines, including Braniff and TWA. Very similar was the parasol-winged Lockheed Air Express, which was produced for Western Air Express and is believed to have entered service in 1929.

The last of Lockheed's single-engined high-speed transports was the six-passenger Orion, which had a low-mounted wing and retractable undercarriage. It went into service with Bowen Air Lines in May 1931. With either a Wasp or Cyclone engine the Orion cruised at 289–313km/h (180–195 mph), and is claimed as the first transport aircraft capable of 320km/h (200mph). American Airways, Northwest Airways and Varney Speed Lines were among the Orion users, two were exported to Swissair, and Air Express Corporation operated them on a US transcontinental freight service, achieving coast-to-coast times of 16–17hr.

The most advanced of these single-engined monoplanes was the Vultee V–1A, which could carry eight passengers and cruise at 340km/h (211mph). The Vultee had an 850hp Wright Cyclone engine, was of all-metal construction and had a retractable undercarriage. American Airlines introduced the type in September 1934.

There were also two Boeing prototypes. These were the Model 200 and 221, both named Monomail. They were all-metal low-wing monoplanes, each powered by a 575hp Pratt & Whitney Hornet. The Model 200 was originally a single-seat mail and cargo carrier. It first flew on 6 May 1930, and its semi-retractable undercarriage made possible a cruising speed of 217km/h (135mph). This first Monomail was followed in August 1930 by the slightly longer Model 221 with non-retractable undercarriage and a cabin for six passengers. It went into service with Boeing Air Transport, and as the Model 221A was later lengthened to provide two extra seats. The original Monomail was modified to Model 221A standard and put into service on the Cheyenne–Chicago route. Experience gained with these aircraft was incorporated in the twin-engined Model 247, described earlier.

On 19 February 1934, the Douglas DC–1 had made its dramatic coast-to-coast flight, and TWA had already ordered 20 of the 14-passenger production DC–2s. These were each powered by two 720hp Wright Cyclones, giving a maximum cruising speed of 315km/h (196mph) and a range of just over 1,600km (1,000 miles). The first DC–2 was delivered to TWA on 14 May 1934, and four days later made a proving flight from Columbus to Pittsburgh and Newark. On 1 August DC–2s began transcontinental operation over the Newark–Chicago–Kansas City–Albuquerque–Los Angeles route to an 18hr schedule. Apart from providing much improved transcontinental services, the Newark–Chicago sector was the first nonstop operation over the route.

On 5 May 1934, American Airlines had begun transcontinental sleeper services with Curtiss Condors, and had also used them to build up frequency on its New York–Boston route. Condors were no match for the DC–2, and so American Airlines asked Douglas for a sleeper development of the DC–2.

Douglas enlarged the DC–2 by widening and lengthening its fuselage and added 3·04m (10ft) to its wing span. Powered by two 1,000hp Cyclone engines and having 14 sleeping berths, this new type was known as the DST – Douglas Sleeper Transport.

American Airlines had ordered 10 DSTs, but after its first flight on 17 December 1935, increased the order and changed it to cover eight DSTs and 12 dayplanes – DC–3s with 21 seats. The first DST was delivered at the beginning of June 1936 and, used as a dayplane, went into service on the New York–Chicago route on 25 June. American took delivery of its first DC–3 in August, and on

15 September was able to inaugurate its DST *American Mercury* skysleeper transcontinental service with an eastbound schedule of 16hr.

Thus was launched one of the world's great transport aeroplanes, the DC–3, of which by far the biggest percentage was powered by 1,200hp Pratt & Whitney Twin Wasps. It was to be built in numerous civil and military versions, with a total of 10,655 produced in the United States and others being built in Japan and, under licence, in the Soviet Union. After the war large numbers of surplus military DC–3s became available to civil operators, and in the postwar years almost every airline operated them at some period. There are still several hundred flying.

Lockheed also embarked on production of a series of fast twin-engined monoplanes. The first was the ten-passenger Model 10A Electra with 450hp Pratt & Whitney Wasp Junior engines and a cruising speed close to 322km/h (200mph). The Electra was introduced on 11 August 1934, by Northwest Airlines. The original British Airways had 7, and also bought 9 of the more powerful 12-passenger Model 14s, which were about 64km/h (40mph) faster. The Lockheed 14 was also known as the Super Electra and the Sky Zephyr and, like the Electra, was first operated by Northwest Airlines, from September 1937.

The major United States airlines required an aeroplane with greater capacity and range than the DC–3 and, in March 1936, the Big Four and Pan American each came to an agreement to share the cost of developing the four-engined Douglas DC–4E, with a span of 42·13m (138ft 3in) and a maximum weight of 30,164kg (66,500lb). It was powered by 1,450hp Pratt & Whitney Twin Hornets, and cruised at 322km/h (200mph). The DC–4E had a nosewheel undercarriage, the first on a big transport, triple fins, and production models were to be pressurized. United Air Lines ordered six 52-passenger sleeper DC–4Es in July 1939, having put the prototype into experimental operation in the previous month. But the aeroplane was found to be unsuitable, the order was cancelled, and the only example exported to Japan.

The last American transport landplane to go into service before the Japanese attack on Pearl Harbor was the Boeing 307 Stratoliner. Although only ten were built, it has an important place in history as the first pressurized aeroplane to go into airline service. The Stratoliner was a low-wing monoplane with a wing span of 32·64m (107ft 3in), powered by four 900hp Wright Cyclones and

LEFT: *One of TWA's Lockheed Orions, with, in the background, one of the airline's single-seat Northrop Alpha mail-planes. The Orion was the first Lockheed aircraft to be fitted with fully retractable landing gear. Very successful in the US, it was also exported to Europe.*
CENTRE: *A metal-fuselage Lockheed Vega used on Braniff Airways' Chicago–Dallas services.*
RIGHT: *One of American Airlines' Vultee V–1A fleet. This was a single-engined, eight-passenger monoplane airliner.*

LEFT: *The Boeing Model 200 Monomail, an all-metal low-wing monoplane fitted with semi-retractable landing gear.*
BELOW: *A Douglas DC–3 of CP Air. A 21-seater plane with a maximum speed of 320km/h (200mph) and a range of up to 2,400km/h (1,500 miles), it was an immediately successful plane from its introduction in 1936.*
BOTTOM: *Progenitor of the ubiquitous DC–3 Dakota, the DC–1 was the Douglas Aircraft Company's answer to the Boeing 247.*

having a maximum weight of 19,051kg (42,000lb). It cruised at 354km/h (220mph) and had a range of 3,846km (2,390 miles). This design employed the wings, nacelles, powerplant and tail surfaces of the B–17 Flying Fortress bomber, but had a completely new circular-section fuselage with pressurized accommodation for 33 passengers and 5 crew. The first aircraft flew on the last day of 1938, but was lost before delivery to Pan American. PAA had three, TWA five, and Howard Hughes had a modified aircraft for record breaking.

TWA introduced the Stratoliner on its transcontinental route on 8 July 1940, and cut eastbound times to 13hr 40min; Pan American based its Stratoliners in Miami for Latin American operations; but at the end of 1941 these aircraft were ordered into war service, with TWA's fleet being used over the North Atlantic. After the war the TWA aircraft, much modified, were put back into civil operation with 38 seats and increased

take-off weight. Some Stratoliners were sold to Aigle Azur in 1951, and some saw service in Latin America and the Far East for several years, a few remaining in use until the mid-1960s.

United Kingdom domestic airlines

When sustained air services were established in the United Kingdom, most that were to prove successful were based on routes which involved a water crossing. In the spring of 1932 British Amphibious Air Lines began irregular operation of such a route, between Blackpool and the Isle of Man, using a Saunders-Roe Cutty Sark amphibian. From June until the end of September the service operated regularly, and there was a bus connection between Blackpool and a number of towns in Yorkshire.

In April 1932 Hillman's Airways opened a service between Romford and Clacton, and by June had achieved a frequency of every three hours from 09.00 until dusk. A de

Havilland Fox Moth was used for the first time on this route.

June 1932 saw the start of a ferry service between Portsmouth and Ryde. This was operated, at very low fares, by Portsmouth, Southsea and Isle of Wight Aviation, using a three-engined Westland Wessex monoplane. The company was to work up a network of services in the south of England, use a wide variety of aircraft and carry a thousand passengers a day at some periods before World War II closed down all operations.

Two other events of importance in 1932 were the opening of a twice-daily Bristol–Cardiff service, which began on 26 September and was operated by Norman Edgar with a Fox Moth; and the first flight of the de Havilland D.H.84 Dragon on 24 November. Norman Edgar's service was to develop into a sizeable operation under the title Western Airways, and the Dragon was to make possible economic short-haul airline operations in the United Kingdom and

RIGHT: *The Portsmouth, Southsea and Isle of Wight Aviation's Westland Wessex at Portsmouth Airport. This was a light airliner used on short range routes.*
OPPOSITE PAGE
ABOVE: *The fleet and staff of Midland and Scottish Air Ferries lined up at Glasgow's Renfrew Airport. The nearest aircraft is the Avro Ten.*
BELOW LEFT: *Six of Jersey Airways' de Havilland Dragons on the beach in Jersey in April 1934. The D.H.84 Dragon was an eight-passenger transport biplane using two de Havilland Gipsy Major engines.*
RIGHT: *Jersey Airways' de Havilland D.H.89 Dragon Rapide St Ouen's Bay at Jersey. This, the most famous of the Dragon class, was also a twin-engined eight-passenger aeroplane and was first introduced into service in 1934. It was used during World War II under the name of* Dominie.

Type: Douglas DST/DC–3
No of passengers: 14(DST)/21(DC–3)
Engines: Two 1,000hp Wright cyclones
Cruising speed: 296km/h (184mph)
Ceiling: 7,300m (24,000ft)
Range: 2,880km (1,790 miles)
Weight: 10,886kg (24,000lb)
Span: 28·96m (95ft)
Length: 19·66m (64ft 6in)

many other parts of the world. The Dragon was a six-passenger biplane with two 130hp de Havilland Gipsy Major engines, and 115 were built in the United Kingdom and 87 in Australia. The first Dragon was delivered to Hillman's on 20 December 1932.

The entry of the railways into UK airline operation took place in 1933, and the same year witnessed the start of air transport in Scotland and the beginning of large-scale air services to the Channel Islands. On 12 April the Great Western Railway (GWR) began a public service, twice each way on weekdays, between Cardiff and Plymouth, with a stop at Haldon to serve Torquay and Teignmouth. The aircraft used was a Westland Wessex chartered from Imperial Airways. The service was extended to Birming-

ham in May, the frequency cut to once a day, and at the end of September closed for the winter.

On the day that the GWR began its services, Spartan Air Lines began a service between Cowes and Heston with a Spartan Cruiser three-engined monoplane, and when it was withdrawn at the end of the summer 1,459 passengers had been carried. This operation was continued in 1934, grew considerably, and became part of the railway group's operations.

Of much greater importance was the founding of Highland Airways by Capt E. E. Fresson on 3 April 1933. On 8 May this airline opened a regular service linking Inverness and Kirkwall, in Orkney, via Wick. A Monospar S.T.4 monoplane was

used and, in spite of some appalling weather, set such a high standard of regularity that a year later the airline was awarded the first domestic mail contract. The airline extended its routes to include Aberdeen and Shetland and operated the first Orkney inter-island services.

In Glasgow, John Sword had established Midland and Scottish Air Ferries (M&SAF), and on 8 May it made its first recorded ambulance flight, from Islay to Glasgow. The air ambulance is still an essential element of Scottish air transport. Regular passenger services were begun on 1 June over the Glasgow–Campbeltown–Islay route, with Dragons, and M&SAF were to develop a number of routes before closing down at the end of September 1934.

periods they catered for holiday traffic.

Hillman's Airways had opened a London–Liverpool–Isle of Man–Belfast service on 16 July 1934, and this was extended to Glasgow on 1 December, when the company got the mail contract instead of RAS.

Following the ending of Midland and Scottish Air Ferries' operations in September, George Nicholson gave up his short-lived Newcastle–Carlisle–Isle of Man service, moved to Glasgow and founded Northern and Scottish Airways. Operations began on 1 December with twice-weekly Glasgow–Campbeltown–Islay services, and the company steadily developed, with Skye being served from 5 December 1935. By July 1936 a circular route was linking Glasgow with Skye, North Uist and South Uist. Most

services were flown by Dragons or Spartan Cruisers, and in August 1937 the company amalgamated with Highland Airways to form Scottish Airways, the link between the two networks coming in May 1938, when a Glasgow–Perth–Inverness–Wick–Kirkwall–Shetland service began.

On 30 September 1935, three domestic airlines, Hillman's Airways, Spartan Air Lines and United Airways, were merged to form Allied British Airways. The name was changed to British Airways on 29 October, and in the following August the company absorbed British Continental Airways. British Airways operated some domestic routes and controlled a number of United Kingdom domestic airlines, but its main effort was concentrated on developing services to the continent.

E. Gandar Dower founded Aberdeen Airways, later renamed Allied Airways (Gandar Dower) Ltd, and operated services in Scotland, including routes to Orkney and Shetland, and on 12 July 1937, started a service between Newcastle and Stavanger. Between March 1935 and the summer of 1936 Crilly Airways operated a number of domestic services; North Eastern Airways developed routes down the eastern side of the country between London and Scotland; Blackpool and West Coast Air Services operated over the Irish Sea; and there were others which operated for varying periods.

Although Aer Lingus is the Irish national airline, its beginning was closely involved with the United Kingdom domestic operations. The airline was founded on 22 May 1936, and a week later began a daily Dublin–Bristol service. In the same month it started working between Dublin and the Isle of Man, and in September opened a Dublin–Liverpool service and extended its Bristol service

On 18 December 1933, Jersey Airways began a daily Portsmouth–Jersey service. There was no airport on Jersey until 1937, so the fleet of Dragons operated from the beach at St Aubin's Bay near St Helier. Sometimes the whole fleet was on the beach at the same time, because schedules were governed by the tides and the fleet flew in a loose formation.

Having suffered as a result of increasing road competition, the four mainline railways had obtained rights to operate domestic air services. On 21 March 1934, they registered Railway Air Services, with the London Midland and Scottish Railway, London and North Eastern Railway, Great Western Railway, Southern Railway and Imperial Airways as the shareholders and Imperial

Airways responsible for undertaking flying operations. The first RAS service was opened on 7 May. This was the previous year's GWR operation, and the route was extended to Liverpool and operated by a Dragon. At the end of July RAS began a Birmingham–Bristol–Southampton–Cowes summer service, but the main RAS operation was to be the *Royal Mail* trunk route linking London, Birmingham, Manchester, Belfast and Glasgow. This was to be operated with D.H.86s and the opening was set for 20 August, but the weather was atrocious and only part of the route could be flown. Full working began the next day. This route, with modifications, continued throughout the years up until the war, but RAS's other routes were mainly confined to summer months, during which to London. All these operations were in association with Blackpool and West Coast Air Services, and under the title 'Irish Sea Airways'. Dragons were used on the first three routes, and D.H.86s flew to London.

A variety of aircraft served the United Kingdom routes, but the biggest contribution was made by the de Havilland biplanes – the D.H.84 Dragon, D.H.86 and D.H.89 Dragon Rapide. The Dragon Rapide had first flown in April 1934; it was a much-improved Dragon with two 200hp Gipsy Six engines, there were seats for six to eight passengers, and the cruising speed was about 210km/h (130mph). Several hundred Dragon Rapides were built; they served airlines in many parts of the world and a few are still flying on short routes today.

The Empire air mail programme

In December 1934 HM Government announced that from 1937 all letters despatched from the United Kingdom for delivery, along what were then the Empire routes, would, as far as practicable, be carried by air without surcharge. The carrier was to be Imperial Airways, with certain sectors to be covered by Commonwealth airlines.

A fleet of 28 Short S.23 C class flying boats was ordered, and 12 Armstrong Whitworth A.W.27 Ensign landplanes, although some of the latter were for European operation. The first C class flying boat was launched at Rochester on 2 July 1936, making its first flight on 4 July, and the first Ensign flew on 24 January 1938.

The Ensigns were large, high-wing monoplanes powered by four 850hp Armstrong Siddeley Tiger engines, and had accommodation for 27 passengers on Empire routes and 40 on European. Cruising speed was 274km/h (170mph) and range 1,287km (800 miles). The Ensigns suffered numerous troubles and, although introduced in Europe towards the end of 1938, played little part in Empire operations until they had been re-engined with Wright Cyclones during World War II.

The C class flying boats began operation in October 1936, and the first stage of the Empire Air Mail Programme was inaugurated on 29 June 1937, when the *Centurion* left Southampton with 1,588kg (3,500lb) of unsurcharged mail for the Sudan, East and South Africa.

On 23 February 1938, the Mail Programme was extended to cover Egypt, Palestine, India, Burma and Malaya when the *Centurion* and the Qantas 'boat *Coolan-gatta* left Southampton. By early April the schedules had been improved to give a Southampton–Karachi time of 3 days, a Singapore time of 5½ days and Sydney time of 9½ days. At that time the all-up mail did not apply to Australia, and the flying boats did not work through to Australia until June.

The Mail Programme was extended to Australia, New Zealand, Tasmania, Fiji, Papua, Norfolk Island, Lord Howe Island, Nauru, Western Samoa and certain other Western Pacific territories with the departure of *Calypso* from Southampton on 28 July 1938. Not all these places were served by air, the mail sometimes being sent over its last stages by sea.

The North Atlantic

Today there are some 30 airlines operating scheduled passenger services across the North Atlantic, and in 1975 the airlines made more than 80,000 scheduled flights over the ocean, carrying 8,782,176 passengers and more than half a million tons of cargo. In 1947 the airlines carried 209,000 passengers across the North Atlantic, whereas 415,000 travelled by sea. In 1957 the numbers using sea and air services were just about equal, at slightly over one million by each type of transport, and in 1958 the airlines carried 1,292,000, while sea passengers had dropped to 964,000. In 1970 the airlines carried 10,038,000 passengers on scheduled and charter services while sea traffic had fallen even further, to 252,000. Total North Atlantic airline passengers in 1975 numbered nearly 12½ million.

It is not surprising that from the earliest days of aviation there were dreams of North Atlantic services, but the problems of making these dreams reality were formidable. The Great Circle distance between the present Shannon Airport, in Ireland, and Gander, in Newfoundland, is 3,177km (1,974 miles), and that is the shortest direct ocean crossing. North Atlantic weather is notoriously bad, with frequent fog in the Newfoundland area, and very strong westerly prevailing winds add considerably to the still-air distance.

The first aerial crossing of the ocean was made in May 1919 by US Navy flying boats, NC–1, NC–3 and NC–4. They left Newfoundland on 16 May, and the NC–4, commanded by Cdr Albert Read, reached the Azores after a flight of 15hr 18min. Thereafter it continued via Portugal and Spain to alight at Plymouth on 31 May.

On 14 June John Alcock and Arthur Whitten Brown took off from Newfoundland in a modified Vickers Vimy bomber, and they landed at Clifden in Ireland the next day after spending 16hr 27½min in the air and making the coast-to-coast crossing in 15hr 57min. It was the first non-stop flight across the North Atlantic. Then on 2 July the British airship R34 left East Fortune, in Scotland, and flew to Long Island. The airship was commanded by Maj G. H. Scott and carried 28 officers and men and one stowaway, and the flight took 108hr 12min. The return flight took 75hr 3min. This was the first out and return flight over any ocean, the first North Atlantic crossing by an airship and the first westward flight by any aircraft.

It was not until April 1928 that an aeroplane crossed the Atlantic Ocean from east to west, when Baron von Hünefeld, Cmdt J. Fitzmaurice and Hermann Köhl flew from Ireland to Greenly Island off Labrador in the Junkers–W 33 *Bremen*.

As early as 1928 Pan American Airways began investigating possible North Atlantic routes. Numerous surveys were made, including one by Lindbergh, who studied a northern route via Greenland and Iceland, making his flight in a Lockheed Sirius seaplane. The very big problem was aircraft range, and Pan American and Imperial Airways did not begin trial flights until 1937.

France began designing a large transatlantic flying boat in 1930. During the design stage it had to be considerably modified, and emerged in January 1935 as the Latécoère 521, to be named *Lieutenant de Vaisseau Paris*. The Laté 521 was a 42-tonne monoplane powered by six 800/860hp Hispano Suiza engines. It was designed to carry 30 passengers on Atlantic routes or 70 over the Mediterranean, and its range was 4,000km (2,485 miles). Its first successful North Atlantic flight, from Biscarosse to New York via Lisbon and the Azores, was made in August 1938, and it subsequently made trial flights over various North Atlantic routes.

Germany undertook North Atlantic trial flights during 1936 using two Dornier Do 18 twin-engined flying boats – *Zephir* and *Aeolus*. These were catapulted from the depot ship *Schwabenland* near the Azores, and from it the *Zephir* flew to New York in 22hr 12min

on 11 September, arriving with 10 hours' reserve fuel. By 20 October, when the trials ceased, the two Do 18s had flown 37,637km (23,386 miles) on eight flights over various North Atlantic routes. In the periods August–November 1937 and July–October 1938 a further 20 flights were made by three Blohm und Voss Ha 139 four-engined seaplanes operating from the *Schwabenland* and the *Friesenland*.

But the honour of operating regular North Atlantic air services still went to Germany, when the Zeppelin LZ 129 *Hindenburg* began operation in 1936. Operated by Deutsche Zeppelin-Reederei, the *Hindenburg* left Friedrichshafen for New York with the first paying passengers on 6 May 1936, and on its return flight landed at Frankfurt, which became the regular European terminal. Ten return flights were made before the service was suspended for the winter, and so great was the demand that the airship's passenger accommodation had to be increased from the original 50. During that first season 1,309 passengers were carried, and the fastest flight from Lakehurst, New Jersey, to Frankfurt was made in 42hr 53min.

A programme of 18 return services was announced for 1937, and on 3 May the airship left Frankfurt with 97 passengers and crew. But on 6 May (local time) fire broke out as the ship was landing at Lakehurst, 35 people lost their lives, and German Zeppelin services came to an end, although three new Zeppelins had been ordered and the LZ 130 was test flown in September 1938.

Germany did not re-establish North Atlantic air services until 1955, but in August 1938 made a spectacular non-stop flight from Berlin to New York in 24hr 56min and back in 19hr 55min. This flight was made by a special Focke-Wulf Condor, and was the first across the ocean by a four-engined landplane.

The first regular service by heavier-than-air craft to be operated over part of the North Atlantic began on 16 June 1937, when Imperial Airways opened a Bermuda–New York service with the C class flying boat *Cavalier*, and Pan American started working a reciprocal service with the Sikorsky S–42 *Bermuda Clipper*.

Then on 5–6 July that year the two airlines made their first North Atlantic survey flights. The special long-range C class 'boat *Caledonia*, commanded by Capt A. S. Wilcockson, flew from Foynes on the Shannon to Botwood in Newfoundland in 15hr 3min, and the Sikorsky S–42 *Clipper III* (Capt H. E.

FAR LEFT ABOVE: *In the summer of 1939 Jersey Airways used the prototype de Havilland D.H.95 Flamingo. This aircraft was a twin-engined high-wing airliner designed for short-range routes.*
FAR LEFT BELOW: *The Blohm und Voss Ha 139a Nordmeer (North Sea) with, in the background, the Nordwind (North Wind) on board the depot ship Friesenland. This flying boat was used on the North Atlantic route, where the depot ship stationed off the Azores could retrieve, refuel and catapult the aircraft off. In 1937 14 scheduled flights were operated successfully by this method.*

ABOVE: *The Dornier Do 18 flying boat* Aeolus *which made several trial flights across the North Atlantic during 1936. The route was from Berlin to New York, with a refuelling stop in mid-Atlantic alongside the depot ship* Schwabenland. *Mail was carried on these trips but there were no passengers on these experimental flights.*
LEFT: *A Heinkel He 58 seaplane, used to carry transatlantic mail from ship to shore. It was launched in mid-ocean from a catapult on board ship, and carried mail from both merchant ships and passenger liners, such as the* Europa.

Gray) flew in the opposite direction. *Caledonia* continued to Montreal and New York, and the Sikorsky flew on to Southampton.

Neither the C class 'boats nor the S–42 were suitable for commercial operation because they did not have the ability to carry sufficient fuel and a payload. Pan American ordered the large Boeing 314 for its services, and Imperial Airways undertook experiments designed to increase the range of its aircraft. One experiment involved refuelling in the air. An aircraft can carry a greater load than it can lift off the ground or water, so modified C class 'boats were built which could take off with a payload and then receive their main fuel supply from tanker aircraft via a flexible hose.

The other experiment involved launching a small aircraft from the back of a larger one. The Short-Mayo Composite Aircraft was therefore built. This consisted of a modified C class 'boat, on top of which was mounted a small floatplane. Take-off could be achieved with the power of all eight engines and the lift of both sets of wings, and then at a safe height the aircraft would separate, the smaller mailplane flying across the ocean and the flying boat returning to its base. The launch aircraft was the Short S.21 *Maia*; the mailplane the S.20 *Mercury*, powered by four 340hp Napier Rapier engines and having a crew of two. The first separation took place successfully near Rochester on 6 February 1938, and on 20–21 July the *Mercury* made the first commercial crossing of the North Atlantic by a heavier-than-air craft when,

commanded by Capt D. C. T. Bennett, it flew from Foynes non-stop to Montreal in 20hr 20min carrying mail and newspapers. From Montreal *Mercury* flew on to Port Washington, New York, but it played no further part in North Atlantic air transport.

On 4 April 1939, Pan American's Boeing 314 *Yankee Clipper* arrived at Southampton on its first proving flight from New York, and on 20 May the same aircraft left New York on the inaugural mail service. Flying via the Azores, Lisbon and Marseilles it arrived at Southampton on 23 May and left

BELOW: *Coriolanus, the last of the Q.E.A. Empire flying boats, was able to carry about 24 passengers plus mail at a cruising speed of 264km/h (165mph).*
BOTTOM: *The Short-Mayo composite aircraft on the Medway at Rochester. It consisted of a Short S.21 Maia flying boat and a Short S.20 Mercury seaplane. The S.21 flying boat carried the smaller seaplane on top of its fuselage, releasing it to complete the journey with mail and newspapers.*
BELOW RIGHT: *The Short S.30 C class flying boat Cabot being refuelled from a Handley Page Harrow tanker during tests over Southampton Water in July 1939.*

Type: Short S.23 C class
No of passengers: 16–24
Engines: Four 920hp Bristol Pegasus XCs
Cruising speed: 264km/h (164mph)
Ceiling: 6,500m (20,000ft)
Range: 1,223km (760 miles)
Weight: 18,370kg (40,500lb)
Span: 34·75m (114ft)
Length: 26·82m (88ft)

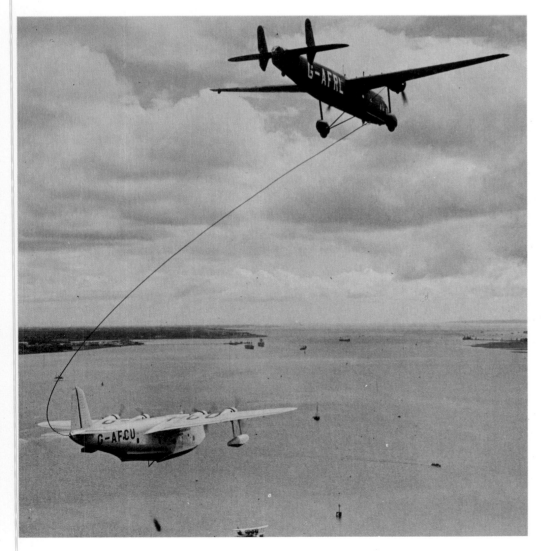

on the first westbound service the next day.

The northern mail route was opened on 24 June by the same aircraft, and on 28 June the *Dixie Clipper* left Port Washington on the inaugural southern-route passenger service – the first by a heavier-than-air craft. On 8 July, with 17 passengers, the *Yankee Clipper* left Port Washington on the inaugural service over the northern route, via Shediac, Botwood and Foynes. The single fare was $375.

On 4 August Britain began a weekly experimental mail service between Southampton and New York via Foynes, Botwood and Montreal, using S.30 C class flying boats which were refuelled in flight from Handley Page Harrow tankers based at Shannon and Botwood. The first service was flown by the *Caribou*, commanded by Capt J. C. Kelly Rogers. The full programme of 16 flights was completed on 30 September in spite of war having started. Because of the war Pan American terminated its services at Foynes, and then withdrew altogether on 3 October.

BOAC, as successor to Imperial Airways, operated the C class flying boat *Clare* on four round trips between Poole, in Dorset, and New York via Botwood and Montreal during the period 3 August–23 September 1940, and one round trip by the *Clyde* during October. These flights, most of which were made while the Battle of Britain was in progress, carried mail, despatches and official passengers, but the first truly commercial British North Atlantic services did not begin until 1 July 1946.

Airlines at war

BOAC had the wartime task of maintaining communication between the United Kingdom and the Commonwealth. This was largely achieved in spite of the German occupation of Europe and Axis control of much of the Mediterranean. The C class flying boats operated the *Horseshoe* route between Durban and Sydney via the Middle East, and connection to this route was provided by services between the United Kingdom and West Africa and thence via a trans-African route to Khartoum. The *Horseshoe* services were maintained until Japan cut the route at the beginning of 1942, after which they terminated at Calcutta. But by a brilliant operational feat Qantas reopened the route by introducing a service between Perth and Ceylon. This began on 10–11 July 1943, and was operated by Consolidated Catalina flying boats, which had to maintain radio silence while flying the 5,654km (3,513 miles) overwater route. On the inaugural flight the *Altair Star* took 28hr 9min from Koggala Lake to the Swan River, but the longest crossing made took 31hr 35min. Qantas also played a very important part in the fighting around New Guinea and suffered heavy casualties.

In May 1941 the Atlantic Ferry Organization of the Ministry of Aircraft Production began operating the North Atlantic Return Ferry service. This was flown with Consolidated Liberators, and had the task of returning crews to North America after they had delivered military aircraft to the United Kingdom. In September that year BOAC took over the operation.

BOAC also maintained North Atlantic services over various routes with three ex-Pan American Boeing 314s, operated a considerable number of vital routes in the Middle East, and flew regularly between Scotland and Sweden – flying unarmed aircraft across occupied Norway to maintain essential communication and import much-needed ball bearings to Britain. It was on this last operation that the airline used the all-wood de Havilland Mosquito. An outstanding BOAC operation was the evacuation of 469 British troops from Crete to Alexandria in April and May 1941 by the flying boats *Coorong* and *Cambria* in the course of 13 return flights.

The war had a major effect on many of the United States airlines. Within the US they had to maintain vital services with what fleets they were allowed to keep – mostly DC–3s – and they had to provide a wide range of services for the government. Until that time Pan American had been the only US airline to operate outside North America, and it undertook global operations. But many others undertook long-haul transoceanic flying for the armed services, mostly with military Douglas DC–4s (the C–54 Skymaster). TWA operated North Atlantic flights with Boeing Stratoliners, and American Export Airlines began a New York–Foynes service on 26 May 1942, with Sikorsky VS–44 flying boats.

One of the epic operations of the war was that over the 'Hump'. This was the supply route from India across the mountains into

China from 1942 until 1945. This was really a military operation, but was flown by the crews of several US airlines, and of US Air Transport Command and China National Aviation Corporation. DC–3s were used as well as some Consolidated C–87 Liberator transports, but the bulk of the work was done by Curtiss C–46 Commandos. The scale of the 'Hump' operation can be appreciated from the fact that 5,000 flights, carrying 44,000 tons, were made in one month. At some stages of the operation aircraft were taking off at two-minute intervals.

Finally, mention must be made of the New Zealand–Australia link. Before the war three C class flying boats had been ordered for Tasman Empire Airways (TEAL), although the airline was not founded until April 1940,

with New Zealand, Australia and the United Kingdom holding the shares. Only two boats, *Aotearoa* and *Awarua*, were delivered, but not until March 1940, and on 30 April *Aotearoa* flew the first Auckland–Sydney service. In June 1944 the 1,000th Tasman crossing was completed, and throughout the war these two flying boats provided the only passenger service of any kind between the two countries.

The return to peace

The war had brought about three major changes in air transport. These were the design and construction of higher-capacity longer-range aircraft capable of transoceanic operation, the large-scale construction of land airports, and worldwide operations by United States airlines. A further change was to follow

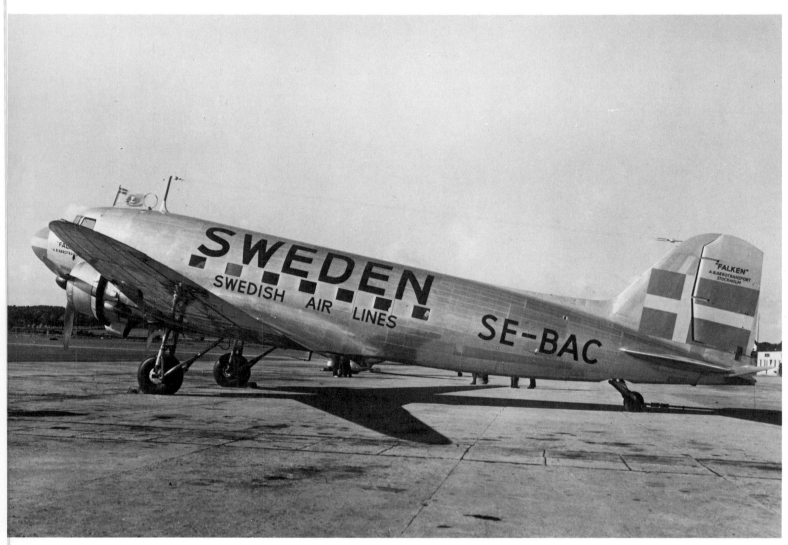

FAR LEFT ABOVE: *Pan American World Airways'
Douglas DC–4 Clipper Union. This was the first
four-engined Douglas airliner and it went into service in
1939, but with the beginning of World War II many
DC–4s were used by the USAAF under the designation
C–54.*
FAR LEFT BELOW: *BEA's first Vickers-Armstrongs
Viking service leaving Northolt for Copenhagen
on 1 September 1946. This was the first post-war
British airliner design, and was based on the Wellington
wing and tail.*
LEFT: *A Scottish Airways' de Havilland Dragon
Rapide, in wartime camouflage and with red, white
and blue identification stripes, at Stornoway in
Lewis. The eight-passenger Dragon Rapide stayed in
production throughout World War II serving civil and
military users all over the world.*
BELOW: *AB Aerotransport (Swedish Air Lines)
Douglas DC–3 Falken declares its Swedish
nationality. Later ABA DC–3s were painted orange
overall.*

shortly, as the overseas territories of European countries gained their independence and set up their own international airlines.

Most of the immediate postwar airline operations was undertaken with the DC–3, most of them war surplus, but the four-engined Douglas DC–4, mostly ex-military Skymasters, began to appear in some numbers and to be used to inaugurate transatlantic services, although with intermediate fuelling stops.

In Britain the decision had been taken to nationalize the air transport industry, with three corporations each having its own area of responsibility. BOAC already existed and, on 1 August 1946, British European Airways Corporation (BEA) and British South American Airways Corporation (BSAA) were

established under the Civil Aviation Act which was passed in 1946.

BOAC was to be responsible for all long-distance services except those to South America, BEA's sphere was mainly Europe and the United Kingdom, and BSAA was to operate all services to Latin America. BOAC had already opened a number of European routes and set up a BEA Division, and these were handed over on 1 August. But the domestic airlines retained their identities until early 1947, working the routes on behalf of the new BEA. Before the war there had been no British air services to South America, but in January 1944 British Latin-American Air Lines had been founded by a number of shipping companies. The name was changed to British South American Airways in

October 1945 and, following a series of proving flights, BSAA opened regular London–Buenos Aires services with Avro Lancastrians on 15 March 1946 – the first scheduled operations from the new Heathrow Airport. A route had been opened down the west coast of South America to Santiago in Chile, and the east coast route was also extended to that city by the time the company was changed to a State corporation.

BSAA was later absorbed into BOAC, and over the years numerous private companies were to establish regular air services. Finally, in 1972, BEA and BOAC were to be amalgamated to form British Airways, while British Caledonian Airways – resulting from the mergers of several private airlines – was to become the second major British airline,

Type: Lockheed Constellation
No of passengers: 44–81
Engines: Four 2,200/2,500hp Wright Cyclone R–3350s
Cruising speed: 480km/h (298mph)
Ceiling: 7,620m (25,000ft)
Range: 2,832km (1,760 miles)
Weight: 47,627kg (105,000lb)
Span: 37·49m (123ft)
Length: 29·01m (95ft 2in)

with responsibility for South American operations from October 1976.

Throughout Europe the airlines were rebuilding, mostly with DC–3s on short routes and DC–4s on intercontinental services. Air France, Sabena, KLM, Swissair and others established transatlantic services and other long-haul routes into Africa or the Far East. Sweden established SILA to operate Atlantic services and then eventually formed SAS – Scandinavian Airlines System – as a consortium of Danish, Norwegian and Swedish airlines. Some airlines were established with outside help – Alitalia was set up in Italy with BEA assistance, and TWA was to be involved in assisting airlines in Greece, Ethiopia and Saudi Arabia.

In Eastern Europe the prewar CSA in Czechoslovakia and LOT in Poland restarted services, and in Bulgaria, Hungary, Rumania and Yugoslavia airlines were set up with Soviet participation – BVS in Bulgaria, Maszovlet in Hungary, TARS in Rumania and JUSTA in Yugoslavia. JAT was also established in Yugoslavia. Later these East European airlines became completely nationally owned as TABSO (later Balkan Bulgarian Airlines), Malév (Hungary) and Tarom (Rumania). JUSTA ceased to exist in 1948 and Tarom was renamed LAR at the end of 1976. These airlines developed domestic and international services and in the cases of CSA, JAT, LAR and LOT have North Atlantic services.

The year 1955 saw the rebirth of Lufthansa, and it has now developed into one of the line, developed its system, opened up networks of services in the New Guinea area, introduced round-the-world services and pioneered the Indian Ocean route to South Africa. ANA was the main Australian domestic operator and, on behalf of the newly formed British Commonwealth Pacific Air Lines, worked a Sydney–San Francisco–Vancouver service until BCPA could undertake its own operations. But a change in Australian civil aviation policy in 1945 was to have a profound effect on ANA. The Australian National Airlines Act of 1945 led to the founding of the State-owned Trans-Australia Airlines (TAA), and all main domestic air services had to be shared equally between TAA and ANA. Over the years Ansett had been acquiring various Australian airlines, and in October 1957 acquired ANA to form Ansett-ANA, now renamed Ansett Airlines of Australia. These two major operators, each carrying more than four million passengers a year, give a very high standard of service and have, with Qantas, outstanding safety records.

In New Zealand the newly created New Zealand National Airways ran the domestic services, and TEAL (now Air New Zealand) developed its services between New Zealand and Australia, retaining flying boats until June 1954. TEAL also opened a number of South Pacific routes – on which flying boats survived even longer – and eventually a trans-Pacific service to the United States.

India's airlines rapidly developed after the war, new companies were formed, and

world's major airlines. In East Germany a separate Deutsche Lufthansa had been established the previous year, but it was forced to abandon this name and since 1963 has worked as Interflug, which had been set up in 1958 to work services between East Germany and Western Europe.

The United States rebuilt its domestic networks and started developing worldwide services on a big scale. Pan American resumed commercial North Atlantic services, and was joined by TWA and American Overseas Airlines (AOA), successor to American Export Airlines. TWA opened up routes to the Middle East and Far East, and AOA was absorbed by Pan American which even-

tually inaugurated round-the-world services. United Air Lines and Pan American found lucrative traffic between the USA and Hawaii, and Northwest Airlines established a northern Pacific route to the Orient. Braniff opened services to South America and in more recent times National Airlines opened a Miami–London route.

In Canada Trans-Canada Air Lines and Canadian Pacific Air Lines made rapid progress, both building up services to Europe and the latter establishing routes to Australia and Japan. They are Canada's biggest airlines and now trade as Air Canada and CP Air respectively.

Qantas, as Australia's international air-

FAR LEFT CENTRE: *The Qantas de Havilland Canada Otter Kerowagi on the hillside aerodrome at Wau, New Guinea, in 1959.*
FAR LEFT BELOW: *The Douglas DC–6 prototype, a development of the DC–4, with a pressurized fuselage and more powerful engines. The C–118 was a military transport version of the DC–6.*
TOP: *Transatlantic services to the UK were started by Pan American on 4 February 1946 and by TWA on the following day, both using the Lockheed L–1049. Illustrated are the L–1049C Super Constellation, the first civil version with turbo-compound engines, and the much larger L–1649 Starliner which entered service in 1957.*
ABOVE: *A TWA Lockheed Super Constellation over New York. This aircraft is typical of the final stage of development of the long range piston-engined airliners that preceded the jet age.*

in July 1946 Air-India was founded as the successor to Tata Air Lines. In March 1948 Air-India and the Indian Government formed Air-India International, and this airline began a Bombay–Cairo–Geneva–London service on 8–9 June 1948, using Lockheed Constellations. Now State-owned as Air-India, this airline enjoys a remarkable reputation for efficient operation and has a jet-operated network stretching from New York through India to Japan and Australia. By 1953 India had eight domestic airlines operating an extensive route system with a total fleet of nearly 100 aircraft, but on 1 August that year they were amalgamated to form the State-owned Indian Airlines Corporation which now carries in excess of three million passengers a year.

With the creation of Pakistan in August 1947, that country rapidly had to develop its air transport in order to provide communication between its widely separated west and east wings (the latter is now Bangladesh). The first airline was Orient Airways, which had been founded in India the previous year on the initiative of Jinnah, the founder of Pakistan. This airline established vital services including the supply routes through the Indus Valley and the world's highest mountains to Gilgit and Skardu. Pakistan International Airlines (PIA) was set up, and with three Lockheed Super Constellations began Karachi–Dacca nonstop services in June 1954 and Karachi–Cairo–London services on 1 February 1955. The airline was reorganized as a corporation with majority government holding in March 1955, and took over Orient Airways.

South African Airways greatly expanded operations after the war, worked the *Springbok* services to London in association with BOAC, opened a trans-Indian Ocean route to Australia, another to Hongkong and one to New York via Ilha do Sul.

In January 1947 the Governments of Kenya, Tanganyika, Uganda and Zanzibar established East African Airways, initially with a fleet of six de Havilland Dragon Rapides. Owned by Kenya, Tanzania and Uganda, East African Airways was a jet-equipped airline flying regional services, and routes to Europe, India and Pakistan. It was on the point of dissolution in early 1977.

Starting in 1951, Japan Air Lines began in a small way with the help of Northwest Airlines, which supplied aircraft and crews – Japanese nationals still being forbidden to fly as pilots. This airline rapidly established itself, and is now widely regarded as a major international carrier, having a very extensive route system and carrying about nine million passengers a year. There is now an enormous volume of air traffic in Japan, and this is shared between JAL, All Nippon Airways, TOA Domestic Airlines and a few small companies. Japan Asia Airways was formed to operate services to Taiwan after JAL began operating to China.

A new generation of transport aircraft
In the first full year of peace after World War II, the scheduled services of the world's airlines carried 18 million passengers, double

BELOW: *The flight deck of a Boeing 377 Stratocruiser, showing the control panel. This was Boeing's first post-World War II commercial airliner, entering service in 1947. Four 3,500hp Pratt & Whitney radial engines gave the aircraft a maximum speed of about 560km/h (350mph) and a range of up to 6,400km (4,000 miles). Only 55 civil versions were built.*

BOTTOM LEFT: *The Douglas DC–4 Sverker Viking of SAS (Scandinavian Airlines System).*
BOTTOM RIGHT: *A Pakistan International Airlines' Douglas DC–3 at Chitral in the Hindu Kush, one of the many examples of DC–3s still in service with airlines throughout the world many years after their first introduction in 1936. They are mainly used on short routes.*

the 1945 total, and in 1949 the total for the year was 27 million. For some time to come the passenger total was to double every five years, and after a while cargo tonnage was to grow even faster.

These enormous traffic totals were largely due to the production of a remarkable series of transport aeroplanes – mostly designed and manufactured in the USA. Ever since the war the DC–3 has played a major role, although its numbers have declined; but even in the early 1940s it was obvious that larger, longer-range aircraft were required.

The four-engined Douglas DC–4E prototype had been abandoned as unsuitable in 1938, but Douglas designed a smaller, unpressurized DC–4. Before any could be delivered the United States was at war, and DC–4s were put to military use, mostly as C–54 Skymasters. US airlines gained experience with these aircraft, flying them on military duties, but had to wait for peace before they could acquire surplus ex-military aircraft and some of the 79 civil examples built after the war.

The DC–4 was a low-wing monoplane with nosewheel undercarriage and four 1,450hp Pratt & Whitney R-2000 engines. Initially it had 44 seats, but high-density seating for up to 86 was later installed. American Overseas Airlines introduced the DC–4 on New York–Hurn (for London) services at the end of October 1945. There were two intermediate stops and the scheduled time was 23hr 48min. On 7 March 1946, DC–4s went into US domestic service on the New York–Los Angeles route with American Airlines. Subsequently they were used by most US carriers and by many airlines throughout the world. A total of 1,242 civil and military DC–4s was built.

The DC–4 was a magnificent aeroplane, but it was unpressurized and its cruising speed of 352km/h (219mph) was no match for the other US wartime transport, the Lockheed Constellation. This had been designed for TWA as a long-range aircraft, but it did not fly until January 1943. TWA and Pan American had each ordered Constellations, but the small number built went to the United States Air Forces as C–69s, entering service in April 1944.

After the war civil production was resumed and the military aircraft were brought up to

BELOW: *Sleeping accommodation on a Boeing 377 Stratocruiser. The double deck provided space for between 50 and 100 passengers, depending on whether the aircraft was fitted with the comfortable 'flying boat' style of seating or had a more densely packed interior. It usually appeared on services which had a high proportion of first class travellers.*

BOTTOM LEFT: *Capital Airlines' red and white Lockheed Constellation Capitaliner United States. This type entered service with several airlines in 1948 including Pan Am and TWA.*

BOTTOM RIGHT: *Before being taken over by Pan American in 1950, American Overseas Airways operated Boeing Stratocruisers on North Atlantic services.*

civil standard. Pan American began a Constellation service between New York and Bermuda on 3 February 1946, and in the same month TWA introduced Constellations on its New York–Paris and New York–Los Angeles services. The original Constellation had four 2,200/2,500hp Wright Cyclone R–3350 engines and 44 seats – later increased to as many as 81 in some configurations. It had a pressurized cabin, and at 480km/h (298mph) its cruising speed was at least 127km/h (79mph) higher than the DC–4's. Several improved models were built, and total production amounted to 233.

The superior performance of the Constellation led Douglas to build the comparable DC–6, with pressurized cabins and a maximum cruising speed of just over 482km/h (300mph). The DC–6 had the same 35·81m (117ft 6in) span as the DC–4 but was longer, had accommodation for 50 to 86 passengers, and was powered by four 2,400hp Pratt & Whitney R–2800 engines.

American Airlines and United Air Lines were the first to operate DC–6s, introducing them on 27 April 1947, on the New York–Chicago and transcontinental routes re-

spectively. Its eastbound transcontinental scheduled time was 10hr. It was used by many major airlines and 170 were built.

In Montreal Canadair produced versions of the DC–4 and DC–6 modified to take Rolls-Royce Merlin liquid-cooled engines.

Douglas followed the DC–6 with the longer fuselage DC–6A and DC–6B, which had increased range. The DC–6A was a cargo aircraft mainly used by the US Air Force and Navy, but the DC–6B proved to be one of the finest piston-engined passenger aircraft ever produced. It entered service on 29 April 1951, on American Airlines' transcontinental route, began service with 54 seats but, later, in high-density configuration could seat 102 passengers. The DC–6B cruised at 507km/h (315mph) and had a range of just over 4,830km (3,000 miles). It was used by a large number of airlines, a total of 288 being built.

Lockheed developed the Constellation into the L.1049 Super Constellation, with 5·48m (18ft) increase in fuselage length and 2,700hp Cyclone engines. It went into service as a 66-seat aircraft with Eastern Air Lines on 17 December 1951.

At about that time Curtiss-Wright's 3,250/3,400hp Turbo-Compound engine became available, and both Douglas and Lockheed developed their aircraft to make use of the new engine. Douglas slightly lengthened the DC–6B, but retained the same wing and produced the longer range DC–7, while Lockheed retained the basic Super Constellation airframe to produce the Turbo-Compound-powered L.1049C, D, E, G and H.

The DC–7 was the first aircraft capable of operating US transcontinental services in both directions without stops, and American Airlines introduced it on non-stop New York–Los Angeles services on 29 November 1953, scheduled to take 8hr 45min on the westbound flight, and 8hr eastbound – although it did not always make these times. Only 110 DC–7s were built, all of which were initially purchased by US airlines. Some later served as DC–7F freighters.

TWA had begun non-stop coast-to-coast services with L.1049C Super Constellations between Los Angeles and New York on 19 October 1953, but these had to stop at Chicago for fuel on westbound flights. However, the L.1049G, with wing tip fuel tanks, enabled TWA to match American Airlines' non-stop performance in both directions.

The DC–7 was developed into the longer-range DC–7B. This entered service in 1955, but only 112 were built–108 for US airlines and four for South African Airways.

The DC–7 and L.1049G had made US transcontinental non-stop operation a practical undertaking, but at that time non-stop North Atlantic operation in both directions was rarely possible. In order to attain this desirable goal, Douglas added 3m (10ft) to the span of the DC–7 and increased its fuel tankage. It thus became the DC–7C Seven Seas with 7,412km (4,606 miles) range and North Atlantic non-stop capability. Pan American introduced them on the route on 1 June 1956, and numerous other airlines adopted the type, 121 being built.

Lockheed went further than Douglas and designed a completely new 45·72m (150ft) span one-piece wing, containing fuel for more than 9,655km (6,000 miles), and mated this with the Super Constellation fuselage to form the L.1649A Starliner, with up to 99 seats. It entered service with TWA on the New York–London service on 1 June 1957.

These two very advanced piston-engined aircraft also made possible one-stop services between Europe and Japan over the Polar route, with a call at Anchorage in Alaska. SAS was first with the DC–7C on the Copenhagen–Tokyo route on 24 February 1957, and Air France followed about a year later, with L.1649As flying between Paris and Tokyo.

In addition to the Douglas and Lockheed types, there was one other large American four-engined airliner – the Boeing Stratocruiser. This was bigger than the other types, and had a lounge and bar on a lower deck. It had seats for up to 100 passengers, was powered by four 3,500hp Pratt & Whitney Double Wasp engines, and entered service over the North Atlantic with Pan American in 1949. Only 55 civil Stratocruisers were built, and they earned a poor reputation

Type: Vickers-Armstrong Viscount 720
No of passengers: 40–47
Engines: Four 1,740hp Rolls-Royce Dart propeller-
    turbines
Cruising speed: 521km/h (324mph)
Ceiling: 8,380m (27,500ft)
Range: 3,200km (2,000 miles)
Weight: 29,318kg (64,500lb)
Span: 28.56m (93ft 8.5in)
Length: 24.96m (81ft 10in)

because of engine and propeller problems. In spite of this they were popular with crews and passengers, and maintained BOAC and Pan American first-class North Atlantic services until the introduction of jet aircraft in 1958.

In the immediate postwar years there was an urgent need for a twin-engined short-haul aeroplane to replace the DC–3, and several countries designed aircraft to meet this requirement. In the United States, Martin and Convair both produced aircraft in this category. They were low-wing monoplanes with nosewheel undercarriages and 2,500hp Pratt & Whitney R–2800 engines.

The 42-seat Martin 2–0–2 was unpressurised and entered service in autumn 1947 with Northwest Airlines in the United States and LAN in Chile. The type was involved in a number of serious accidents, and one suffered a wing failure which led to the type being withdrawn. After strengthening the 2–0–2 returned to service in 1950 as the Martin 2–0–2A. It was followed by the 48 to 52-seat pressurized Martin 4–0–4, which entered service with TWA in October 1951. A total of 149 aircraft of both models was built for several airlines.

Much greater success was enjoyed by the Convair-Liner. The CV–240, with 40 seats and pressurized cabin, entered service in June 1948 with American Airlines. It quickly found favour, and 176 civil examples were built. The improved 44-passenger CV–340 followed in 1952, and in 1956 the 52 to 56 seat CV–440 Metropolitan made its debut.

More than 1,000 civil and military Convair-Liners were built, of which more than 240 were later re-engined with propeller-turbines.

In Britain in the early postwar years BOAC was using DC–3s, Avro Lancastrians and Yorks developed from the Lancaster bomber, and Short flying boats. But plans had been made for new aircraft, and two of them flew before the end of 1945. They were the Vickers-Armstrongs Viking, developed from the Wellington bomber, and the Bristol 170 Freighter/Wayfarer.

The Viking was a mid-wing monoplane with two Bristol Hercules engines, unpressurized cabin, and a tailwheel undercarriage. It cruised at about 320km/h (200 mph), and on entering service with BEA on 1 September 1946, had 27 seats. For several years it was the airline's principal type. It also served with many other airlines, and 163 were built.

The Bristol 170 was very different. It was a high-wing monoplane with a slab-sided fuselage, non-retractable undercarriage and two Hercules engines. The Wayfarer was a passenger aircraft, but the Freighter undertook the duties which its name implied – the best known operation being Silver City Airways' cross-Channel vehicle ferries, which it and the longer-fuselage Superfreighter undertook for many years. The type also operated cargo services between North and South Island in New Zealand.

A very handsome British aeroplane was the high-wing Airspeed Ambassador, with two 2,625hp Bristol Centaurus engines and

pressurized cabin. It had accommodation for 47 to 49 passengers and was introduced into scheduled service as the Elizabethan by BEA in March 1952. Only 20 were built.

France's first postwar transport aircraft to enter airline service was the 33-seat Sud-Est SE.161 Languedoc which, as the Bloch 161, had made its first flight in September 1939, but could not be produced until after the war. It was originally powered by four Gnome Rhône engines, but most had Pratt & Whitney R–1830s. A total of 100 Languedocs was built, entering service with Air France on the Paris–Algiers route in May 1946 and serving a number of airlines in Europe and the Middle East.

Italy continued to produce three-engined Fiats and four-engined Savoia Marchetti S.M.95s. One of the latter inaugurated Alitalia's Rome–London service on 3 April 1948, but these types made no significant contribution to air transport outside Italy.

There is one other European transport

FAR LEFT BELOW: *One of Finnair's Convair CV–340s at Helsinki. Soon after the end of World War II Convair began to produce a series of twin-engined, short-range airliners which were exported to a number of European airlines in addition to being used by American operators.*
BELOW: *A Vickers-Armstrong Viscount of Trans-Australia Airlines. This aircraft was the first successful turboprop airliner.*

BOTTOM LEFT: *A Vickers-Armstrong Viking of Indian National Airways. The design of its wing and tail was based on that of the Vickers Wellington bomber, and the prototype made its first flight in June 1945. It was soon in service with BEA and many independent airlines. Two 1,675hp Bristol Hercules 634 radial engines produced a maximum cruising speed of 366km/h (210mph) and a range of up to 1,840km (1,150 miles).*

BOTTOM RIGHT: *A Bristol 170 Freighter flying with the port engine shut down and the propeller feathered. This high wing monoplane started its development during the closing years of World War II and made its first flight in December 1945. Most production models went to military users, and a few were used for car-carrying transport by commercial operators. All-freight versions had a clam-shell nose-door.*

aircraft of the postwar era worthy of mention. This was the Swedish Saab Scandia, a low-wing monoplane with 32 to 36 seats and two 1,800hp Pratt & Whitney R–2180 engines. It first flew in November 1946 and 18 were built, including six by Fokker.

Turbine power

In Britain the Brabazon Committee was set up in December 1942 to make recommendations for the development of postwar transport aircraft. Among its recommendations was the design and production of a North Atlantic turbojet aeroplane, Brabazon Type IV, and a short-haul propeller-turbine type, Brabazon Type IIB.

The Type IV evolved through a number of designs to become the de Havilland Comet – the world's first turbojet airliner. Two types were designed to meet the Type IIB recommendation: the Armstrong Whitworth Apollo, of which only two prototypes were built, and the Vickers-Armstrongs Viscount. Tur-

bine power was to change the whole standard of airline flight by reducing vibration and interior noise levels. In the case of the turbojet, flight times were to be approximately halved in one step.

The prototype Viscount, the V.630, made its first flight on 16 July 1948. It was a low-wing monoplane with a pressurized cabin for 32 passengers, and was powered by four 1,380hp Rolls-Royce Dart turbines driving four-blade propellers. Although the V.630 was considered too small to be economic, BEA did use it to operate the first ever services by a turbine-powered aeroplane. On 29 July 1950, it flew from Northolt, west of London, to Le Bourget, Paris, carrying 14 revenue passengers and 12 guests. The V.630 stayed on the Paris route for two weeks and then, from 13 August until 23 August, operated over the London–Edinburgh route on the world's first turbine-powered domestic services.

Rolls-Royce increased the power of the

Dart and enabled Vickers to stretch the Viscount to become a 47 to 60 seat aircraft as the V.700. BEA placed an order for 20 and regular Viscount services began on 18 April 1953, when RMA *Sir Ernest Shackleton* operated the London–Rome–Athens–Nicosia service. The Viscount immediately proved a success, being produced in several versions and sold in many parts of the world, including the USA and China. It frequently doubled the airline's traffic, and 445 were built.

The Comet 1 was a very clean low-wing monoplane with four 2,018kg (4,450lb) thrust de Havilland Ghost turbojets buried in the wing roots. There was accommodation for 36 passengers in two cabins and pressurization enabled it to fly at levels over 12,190m (up to 40,000ft). The first prototype flew on 27 July 1949, and soon made a number of spectacular overseas flights. BOAC took delivery of ten Comet 1s and on 2 May 1952, operated the world's first jet service – over the London–Johannesburg route. With their cruising speed of 788km/h (490mph) Comets covered the 10,821km (6,724 miles) in less than 24hr. On London–Singapore they cut the time from 2½ days to 25hr, and reduced the London–Tokyo time from 86hr to 33¼hr.

Air France and UAT introduced Comets, and they were ordered by several other airlines. But exactly a year after their introduction a Comet broke up in flight near Calcutta, and in January 1954 another disintegrated and fell into the sea near Elba. After modifications the Comet was put back into service, but less than three weeks later, on 8 April, a third Comet broke up, and the type was withdrawn from service.

Fatigue failure of the pressure cabin was said to have been the cause of the last two failures, and some fuselage redesign resulted. Comet 2s, already under construction, were modified and went to the RAF. Work went ahead on the Rolls-Royce Avon-powered Comet 4 with longer fuselage, seats for up to 81, and additional, wing-mounted, fuel tanks.

BOAC ordered 19 Comet 4s and on 4 October 1958, operated the first ever North Atlantic jet services, the London–New York flight being made in 10hr 22min with a fuel stop at Gander. The eastbound flight was made nonstop in 6hr 11min. A shorter-span longer-fuselage Comet 4B, with seats for up to 101, was introduced by BEA on 1 April 1960, and in the same year the Comet 4C was commissioned – this combined the Comet 4 wings with the Comet 4B fuselage. A total of 74 Comet 4-series aircraft were completed.

The second European turbojet airliner to enter service was the French Sud-Aviation SE.210 Caravelle. It was a twin-engined aircraft and the first to have its turbojets mounted on either side of the rear fuselage. The Caravelle was designed primarily for operation between France and North Africa. It first flew on 27 May 1955, was powered by two 4,762kg (10,500lb) thrust Rolls-Royce Avons and, as the Caravelle I, had seats for up to 80 passengers. The Caravelle I entered service with Air France in May 1959 on the

specification early in 1947 for a Medium Range Empire (MRE) transport, and Bristol designed the Type 175 with four Centaurus piston engines to meet the requirement. Subsequently it was agreed that Bristol Proteus propeller-turbines would be used and in this form, as the Britannia, the prototype flew on 16 August 1952. The Britannia was a large low-wing monoplane with seats for up to 90 passengers and a take-off weight of 70,305kg (155,000lb).

BOAC introduced this Britannia 102 on the London–Johannesburg route on 1 February 1957, and the longer-range Britannia 312 on London–New York services on 19 December 1957. The latter were the first North Atlantic services by turbine-powered aircraft. The Britannia was an extremely good aircraft, but it appeared much too late and only 85 were built.

Canadair produced a number of Britannia variants, one of which, the CL–44, went into airline service. These aircraft generally resembled the Britannia, but had 5,730hp Rolls-Royce Tyne propeller-turbines and lengthened fuselages. Known as the CL–44D, and provided with swing-tail fuselage for cargo loading, the type entered service with the US cargo carrier Seaboard World Airlines in July 1961. Then came the CL–44J, with even longer fuselage and accommodation for up to 214 passengers, for the cheap-fare North Atlantic services of the Icelandic airline Loftleidir.

The large propeller-turbine aircraft built for BEA was the Vickers-Armstrongs Van-

was powered by four 3,750hp Allison 501 engines. The Electra first flew on 6 December 1957, and entered service with American Airlines and Eastern Air Lines in January 1959.

The most successful of all the western propeller-turbine transports has been the Fokker F.27 Friendship. This is a high-wing monoplane powered by two Rolls-Royce Darts and normally accommodating about 48 passengers. The first prototype flew on 24 November 1955, and the aircraft went into production in the Netherlands and also in the United States as the F–27, built by Fairchild (later Fairchild Hiller).

The type first entered service in the United States, with West Coast Airlines, on 28 September 1958. In Europe Aer Lingus began operating the Dutch-built aircraft on Dublin–Glasgow services on 15 December 1958. Numerous versions have been built, including the 56-passenger FH–227, more than 650 have been ordered and the type is still in production at Amsterdam.

Britain's attempts to break into this market have been less successful. Handley Page produced the twin-Dart Herald, which was very similar to the F.27, but only 48 were completed. More successful was the low-wing Avro (later Hawker Siddeley) 748, also Dart-powered, which entered service in 1962 and is still in production. More than 300 civil and military examples have been built, about 50 of these being assembled or constructed in India.

There has also been one Japanese turbine-

Paris–Rome–Istanbul route, and with SAS between Copenhagen and Cairo.

Numerous versions of the Caravelle were produced, up to the 128-passenger Caravelle 12B, and they were operated in many parts of the world, including the United States, where United Air Lines had 20. The Caravelle was an exceptionally fine aeroplane, and of the 280 built nearly 200 are still in service.

Although BOAC introduced the pure-jet Comet as early as 1952, the airline was to commission a large propeller-turbine aircraft nearly five years later, and BEA began using a similar type several months after it had introduced Comets. BOAC issued a

guard, also powered by Tynes. It could carry 139 passengers and had considerable underfloor cargo capacity. The Vanguard first flew on 20 January 1959, and began operation with BEA on 17 December 1960, with regular operation from March 1961. About a month earlier it had entered service with Trans-Canada Air Lines, the only other customer for new Vanguards. Only 43 were built, and both airlines converted some into freighters.

Only one type of large civil propeller-turbine aeroplane, the Lockheed L.188 Electra, was built in the United States. This was smaller than the Vanguard, having accommodation for up to 99 passengers, and

powered transport, the NAMC YS–11. This is a 46 to 60 passenger low-wing monoplane powered by two 3,060hp Dart engines. It first flew on 30 August 1962, and entered airline service in Japan in April 1965. More than 180 have been built and, apart from serving with several Asian airlines, they have been exported to the USA, South America, Canada, Europe and Africa.

The first 'big' jets

Not until the Comet 1 had been withdrawn from service did the first United States turbojet transport make its maiden flight. At Seattle, in Washington State, on 15 July 1954, a large brown and yellow swept-wing

ABOVE LEFT: *A BOAC Bristol Britannia 102, a turboprop airliner famed for its low level of noise and therefore very popular with passengers.*
ABOVE CENTRE: *The Aer Lingus Fokker F.27 Friendship* St Fergal, *used on short-range European routes. The first prototype flew in 1955.*

ABOVE RIGHT: *One of Piedmont Airlines' Japanese NAMC YS–11s, powered by two Rolls-Royce 3,060hp turboprop engines, which give a maximum cruising speed of 475km/h (297mph) and a range of up to 2,360km (1,475 miles).*
OPPOSITE PAGE
LEFT: *An HS 748 of Royal Nepal Airlines.*

ABOVE RIGHT: *A Lockheed L–188 Electra II. This was a medium-range turboprop airliner which came into service in January 1959, with several US airlines and KLM.*
CENTRE RIGHT: *A de Havilland Comet 4B of BEA, a version of the Comet 4 which made the world's first transatlantic jet flight.*

monoplane with four pod-mounted engines took to the air and began a new era in air transport. It was the Boeing 367–80, known affectionately as the Dash 80, and was in fact the prototype Boeing 707. This was a much more advanced aeroplane than the Comet: its wings were swept back 35°, and it embodied the experience gained with Boeing B–47 and B–52 jet bombers.

Pan American placed the first order, and the type went into production as the Model 707–100 with the customer designation 707–121. The production aeroplane had a span of 40·18m (131ft 10in), a length of 44·04m (144ft 6in), accommodation for up to 179 passengers, and a maximum weight of 116,818 kg (257,000lb). It was powered by four 5,670kg (12,500lb) thrust Pratt & Whitney JT3C turbojets, cruised at 917km/h (570 mph) and had a maximum range of 4,949km (3,075 miles) with full payload. The 707–121 entered service with Pan American on the North Atlantic in October 1958.

Type: Sud-Aviation Caravelle
No of passengers: 80
Engines: Two 5,533kg (12,200lb) thrust Rolls-Royce Avon 531 turbojets
Cruising speed: 821km/h (510mph)
Ceiling: 10,000m (32,800ft)
Range: 2,419km (1,503 miles)
Weight: 48,000kg (105,822lb)
Span: 34·3m (112ft 6·25in)
Length: 32m (105ft)

RIGHT: *A Convair CV–880, a four-engined, medium-range jet airliner with a swept wing. Sixty-five were built, mostly for US domestic airlines, but the market had already been captured by the Douglas DC–8 and Boeing 707.*
BELOW: *A Douglas DC–8 of Braniff Airways. This was designed as a rival to the Boeing 707 and de Havilland Comet 4 jet airliners, and has been very successful, both in the passenger and freight versions.*
FAR RIGHT ABOVE: *A Boeing 707–400 of Air India. Originally intended purely for American domestic routes, the 707–400 is in fact now used on routes throughout the world.*
FAR RIGHT CENTRE: *A Boeing 720B of Pakistan Airlines, a smaller version of the 707–320, uses Pratt & Whitney JT3C–7 turbofans.*
FAR RIGHT BELOW: *One of BEA's de Havilland Trident 3Bs. The booster engine can be seen at the base of the rudder.*

This original Boeing 707 was followed by a whole family of 707 passenger and cargo variants, with different lengths and weights, and turbofan power. The passenger-carrying 707–320B and passenger/cargo 707–320C models are still in production. Also developed was the short-to-medium-range version known as the Boeing 720 or, with turbofans, 720B. By the end of October 1976, 920 Boeing 707s and 720s of all models had been ordered, and they had flown more than 30 million hours and carried just under 522 million passengers.

The second United States jet transport was the Douglas DC–8. It closely resembles the Boeing 707, and has likewise been produced in several versions. The first DC–8 flew on 30 May 1958, and the JT3C-powered DC–8–10 entered service with Delta Air Lines and United Air Lines on 18 September 1959. Then followed the –20 with more powerful JT4A engines, the –30 long-range aeroplane with the same engines, the –40 with Rolls-Royce Conway bypass engines and the –50 with JT3D turbofans. There were also freight, convertible, and mixed passenger/cargo versions. All had a span of 43·41m (142ft 5in) and a length of 45·87m (150ft 6in). Maximum seating was 177 and maximum weight varied between 120,200kg (265,000lb) and 147,415kg (325,000lb).

In 1966 the Series 60 DC–8 appeared. This was built in three main versions, the –61 with the same span as earlier models but a length of 57·09m (187ft 4in), seating for up to 257 and take-off weight of 147,415kg

(325,000lb); the –62 with 45·23m (148ft 5in) span, 47·98m (157ft 5in) length, seats for 201 and take-off weight of 151,952kg (335,000lb); and the –63, combining the wing of the –62 with the fuselage of the –61. This had a maximum weight of 158,755kg (350,000lb) and seats for up to 269.

The DC–8–61 was put into service between Los Angeles and Honolulu by United Air Lines on 25 February 1967; the DC–8–62 entered service on the Copenhagen–Los Angeles route with SAS on 22 May 1967; and the DC–8 –63 was introduced by KLM on the Amsterdam–New York route in July 1967. There were cargo and convertible versions of the Series 60 aircraft, and a total of 556 DC–8s of all models was built before production ceased in 1972.

The third United States constructor of large commercial jet transports was the Convair Division of General Dynamics, which produced two types. The first was the CV–880. It was smaller than the Boeing and Douglas types, its narrower fuselage having a maximum seating capacity of 130. It was powered by four 5,080/5,285kg (11,200/11,650lb) thrust General Electric CJ–805 engines, had a maximum weight of 87,770kg (193,500lb) and cruised at up to 989km/h (615mph). It was designed for TWA, but first went into service with Delta Air Lines on 15 May 1960, over the Houston–New York, New York–New Orleans and New York–Atlanta routes. Only 65 were built.

The second Convair was the CV–990 (named Coronado by Swissair). It was

designed for American Airlines and closely resembled the CV–880, but had 7,257kg (16,000lb) thrust General Electric CJ–805–23B turbofans, seating for up to 158 and a maximum cruising speed of 1,005km/h (625 mph). Distinctive external features were the four canoe-like shock bodies which extended aft of the wing. The CV–990 entered service with American Airlines and Swissair in March 1962. Total production was 37.

Britain made an attempt to break into the so-called 'big' jet market, but with little success. The aircraft was the Vickers-Armstrongs VC10, which was in the same category as the Boeing 707 but had its four 9,525kg (21,000lb) thrust Rolls-Royce Conway bypass engines mounted in pairs on each side of the rear fuselage, and a high-mounted tailplane and elevators. The VC10 was designed for BOAC and was required to operate from restricted, hot and high runways which demanded specially good take-off and landing performance. Indeed, the VC10 could undertake some operations which were impossible for the early Boeings.

The standard VC10 could carry up to 139 passengers, had a maximum weight of 141,520kg (312,000lb), and a maximum cruising speed of 933km/h (580mph). The VC10 went into service on the London–Lagos route on 29 April 1964, and was followed by the Super VC10 which was 3·96m (13ft) longer, had more powerful Conways, seating for up to 163 and a maximum take-off weight of 151,952kg (335,000 lb). Super VC10s were introduced on the London–New York route on 1 April 1965. Only 54 of both were produced.

Medium- and short-range jets

In the summer of 1956 BEA issued a specification for a 965km/h (600mph) aircraft to meet its short- to medium-range route requirements. The de Havilland 121 Trident was selected, and the Aircraft Manufacturing Co, comprising de Havilland, Fairey and Hunting, set up to build the aircraft, but de Havilland then became part of the Hawker Siddeley Group. The design was changed to meet differing BEA demands before the first aircraft made its initial flight on 9 January 1962.

The Trident is a low-wing monoplane with high T-tail and three rear-mounted Rolls-Royce Spey bypass engines. BEA ordered 24 Trident 1s with 4,477kg (9,850lb) thrust engines, 88 seats, a maximum weight of 52,162kg (115,000lb), cruising speed of 941km/h (585mph) and typical full-payload range of 1,448km (900 miles) with full fuel reserves. The first revenue flight by a Trident was made on 11 March 1964, and full scheduled services with Tridents began on 1 April 1964.

The Tridents have given good service and played a major role in the development of automatic landing, using a triplex system to provide a very high standard of reliability and safety. The first automatic landing by an aircraft on a passenger service was made on 10 June 1965, by a Trident landing at Heathrow on arrival from Paris.

The Trident 1E with uprated engines, leading-edge slats and seating for up to 139 passengers in high-density layout flew in November 1964. Fifteen were built, and customers included Air Ceylon, Iraqi Airways, Kuwait Airways and PIA. Then came the Trident 2E of which 15 were built for BEA, 33 for China and two for Cyprus Airways. This had 5,411kg (11,930lb) thrust Speys, increased span, seats for 97 in BEA service, a take-off weight of 64,863kg (143,000 lb) and increased range. This version entered service on 18 April 1968.

The last major version of the series was the Trident 3B. This has a tail-mounted 2,385kg (5,250lb) thrust Rolls-Royce RB.162 booster engine to improve take-off performance, is 5·0m (16ft 5in) longer than the earlier Tridents, has a maximum weight of 70,305kg (155,000lb) and accommodation for up to 180 passengers. BEA ordered 26, and began using them in March 1971. Finally came the Super Trident 3B with 3,628kg (8,000lb) weight increase and maximum-payload range of 3,380km (2,100 miles) and seats for 152 passengers. Two Super Tridents were ordered by CAAC in China, bringing the Trident total to 117.

In the same category as the Trident and of very similar layout is the Boeing 727. Design began in June 1959, but Boeing regarded the decision to go into production as a major gamble. However, the decision has been completely justified by the fact that 727 sales exceed those for any other Western jet transport by a very large margin, 1,352 having been ordered by October 1976.

The Model 727 has the same fuselage cross-section as the Boeing 707, 32 degrees of sweep on the wing, which is fitted with triple-slotted flaps and leading-edge slats, and much better take-off and landing performance than the original Tridents. The 727–100, powered by three 6,350kg (14,000 lb) thrust Pratt & Whitney JT8D–1 turbofans and having accommodation for a maximum of 131 passengers, made its first flight on 9 February 1963, and entered service with Eastern Air Lines and United Air Lines at the beginning of February 1964.

Numerous versions of the Boeing 727 have been produced, the latest being the Advanced 727–200, which is 6.09m (20ft) longer. This is powered by 6,577/7,257kg (14,500/16,000 lb) thrust JT8Ds and can carry up to 189 passengers. Maximum take-off weight is now 94,318kg (207,500lb) compared with 72,570 kg (160,000lb) for the original aeroplane. Up to the end of October 1976 Boeing 727s of all versions had flown more than 22 million hours and carried more than 873 million passengers while serving over 80 airlines.

In addition to the Boeing 707s, 720s, 727s, Douglas DC–8s, Convairs and Tridents, there was considered to be a need for about 1,000 smaller twin-jet aircraft. The first designed to meet this requirement was the British Aircraft Corporation's BAC One-Eleven, powered by two rear-mounted Speys and having accommodation for up to 89 passengers. The first announcement about the BAC One-Eleven was made in May 1961,

when it was stated that British United Airways had ordered ten. The first aircraft flew on 20 August 1963, but was lost in a deep stall, and it was not until April 1965 that the production Series 200 entered service with BUA and Braniff International Airways. The Series 200 was followed first by the increased-range Series 300 and then by the similar Series 400, which was specially adapted to meet US conditions and entered service with American Airlines on 6 March 1966.

Then came the Series 500, with more powerful Speys, 1·52m (5ft) increase in span, 4·21m (13ft 10in) increase in length, seating for up to 109 passengers and a take-off weight of 44,450kg (98,000lb) compared with 35,605 kg (78,500lb) for the Series 200. BEA ordered 18 of the bigger version and introduced the type on 17 November 1968. There is also the short-field Series 475, which has been ordered in small numbers, bringing the total sales to more than 220.

Douglas also produced an aircraft in this class and of similar appearance. This was the DC–9, which first flew on 25 February 1965, and entered service with Delta Air Lines on 8 December the same year. As the DC–9–10, powered by two 6,350kg (14,000 lb) thrust Pratt & Whitney JT8D–1 turbofans, the aircraft has a span of 27·25m (89ft 5in), a length of 31·82m (104ft 4¾in), accommodation for 80 passengers and a maximum weight of 41,140kg (90,700lb).

As with most previous Douglas types, success was assured by producing a family of aeroplanes to suit varying requirements, and the DC–9 was stretched by nearly 4·57m (15ft) to produce the 105-seat 28·47m (93ft 5in) span DC–9–30. This larger type flew on 8 August 1966, and entered service on 1 February 1967, with Eastern Air Lines on its shuttle operations. The correctness of the decision to stretch the DC–9 is shown by the fact that about 600 of the more than 840 ordered have been DC–9–30s or DC–9–30F or CF freighters or passenger/cargo aircraft.

Two special versions of the DC–9 were produced to meet the needs of SAS. These were the –40 with just over 1·82m (6ft) longer fuselage, 6,803kg (15,000lb) thrust JT8D–11 engines, 115 seats and a maximum weight of 51,710kg (114,000lb); and the –20, which combined the –10 fuselage with the –30 wing to achieve short-field performance. SAS bought 45 DC–9–40s and introduced them in March 1968, followed by ten DC–9–20s, which were commissioned in January 1969.

The latest version of the DC–9 is the –50, which first flew on 17 December 1974, and entered service with Swissair on 24 August 1975. This has a length of 40·7m (133ft 7in), accommodation for up to 139 passengers, and a maximum take-off weight of 54,884kg (121,000lb).

When the DC–9 was announced, BAC and Douglas expected to share a market for 1,000 aircraft. This total has been exceeded, although BAC got only a low share. But in spite of this Boeing produced a competitor which up to the end of October 1976 had itself attracted 489 orders. The decision to build the Boeing 737 was taken in February 1965, the type first flew on 9 April 1967, and it entered service early in 1968 with Lufthansa and United Air Lines.

Because the Model 737 retains the fuselage cross-section of the Boeing 707 and 727, it appears to be very stubby, having a length of only 28·57m (93ft 9in). It also differs in having its two 6,350kg (14,000lb) thrust Pratt & Whitney JT8D turbofans attached close beneath the wings. The tailplane is attached to the fuselage, and there is a tall single fin and rudder. Maximum weight is 42,410kg (93,500lb) and maximum seating 99. Like the other Boeings, the 737 has been developed into a family, and the Advanced 737–200 has a length of 30·48m (100ft), is powered by 7,257kg (16,000lb) thrust JT8D–17 engines, weighs up to 53,070kg (117,000lb) and can accommodate a maximum of 135 passengers. By the end of October 1976, 474 Boeing 737s had been delivered and they had flown more than 5¼ million hours and carried 356,890,000 passengers with more than 60 operators.

In the Netherlands, Fokker (now Fokker-

ABOVE LEFT : *One of British Caledonian's fleet of BAC One-Eleven jet airliners, used on international routes.*
TOP : *A Boeing 727 belonging to Royal Nepal Airlines. This aircraft has a maximum speed of 1,080km/h (630mph) and a range of about 3,200km (2,000 miles).*
ABOVE CENTRE : *A Fokker–VFW F.28 Fellowship, a medium-range jet airliner with a cruising speed of 843km/h (527mph).*
ABOVE : *A Douglas DC–9 of Aviaco, used on routes in Spain and Portugal, and some services to North Africa.*

Type: Boeing 707
No of passengers: 179
Engines: Four 5,625kg (12,500lb) thrust Pratt &
  Whitney JT3C turbojets
Cruising speed: 917km/h (570mph)
Ceiling: 12,800m (42,000ft)
Range: 4,949km (3,075 miles)
Weight: 116,573kg (257,000lb)
Span: 39·9m (130ft 10in)
Length: 44·04m (144ft 6in)

VFW) designed a jet successor to the F.27 Friendship. This was the F.28 Fellowship, which flew on 9 May 1967, and entered service with the Norwegian airline Braathens SAFE on 28 March 1969. The F.28 is a low-wing monoplane powered by two rear-mounted Rolls-Royce Speys. It was designed to operate from short rough runways and, to achieve good low-speed handling, the wing sweep was restricted to 16 degrees. An unusual feature of the F.28 is its rear-fuselage air-brake.

The original, or basic, version, known as the Mk 1000, had a span of 23·58m (77ft 4¼in), a length of 27·4m (89ft 10¾in), a maximum weight of 28,125kg (62,000lb) and accommodation for 65 passengers when operating from a 1,220m (4,000ft) runway. The Mk 2000 is 2.26m (7ft 5in) longer and has 79 seats; the Mk 3000 and Mk 4000 have 1·49m (4ft 11in) greater span and uprated engines, and will replace the Mks 1000 and 2000 on the production line; the Mk 6000 has the increased span and, like the Mk 4000, a longer fuselage with up to 85 seats. F.28s are truly international aeroplanes, components being built in the Netherlands, Germany and Britain. By October 1976 a total of 116 F.28s had been ordered by 33 operators in 23 countries.

Different to other jet transports is the VFW-Fokker VFW 614, designed for low-density traffic, short-haul routes, and to have the ability to operate from runways of under 1,220m (4,000ft). It is a low-wing monoplane with modest sweepback, and its two 3,527kg (7,760lb) thrust Rolls-Royce/Snecma M 45H bypass engines are mounted on pylons above the wing. The VFW 614 has a span of 21·5m (70ft 6in), a length of 20·6m (67ft 6in), a maximum take-off weight of 19,950kg (43,982lb) and accommodation for 40 to 44 passengers. Maximum cruising speed is 702km/h (436mph) and range with 40 passengers and fuel reserves 1,200km (745 miles). The VFW 614 first flew on July 14 1971, has been ordered in small numbers and went into service with Cimber Air in Denmark late in 1975.

More independence creates new airlines

As related earlier, the granting of independence to India and other countries led to the creation of new airlines or the expansion of existing ones. In 1949 the Netherlands East Indies became Indonesia and Garuda Indonesian Airways was created in the following year, to become a major airline with a wide network of domestic and regional services, services to Europe and the Far East, and an annual passenger volume in excess of two million. In more recent times numerous other Indonesian airlines have been founded, including Merpati Nusantara and Bouraq Indonesia Airlines.

In 1957 Malaya became independent and formed the Federation of Malaysia, which later included Borneo, Sabah and Sarawak. Malayan Airways, founded in 1947, gave way to Malaysia-Singapore Airlines, but Singapore withdrew from the Federation and two separate airlines were formed: Malaysian Airline System, mainly equipped

with Boeing 737s and Fokker F.27s, and Singapore Airlines, which has established an outstanding reputation with its Boeing 747 services to Europe.

Most of the countries which became independent in the period 1956–1965 were in Africa, and many of these had been French territories. In the north, Morocco and Tunisia became sovereign states in 1956 and Algeria in 1962, but these countries already had well-established airlines – Royal Air Maroc, Tunis Air and Air Algérie.

French Equatorial Africa in 1960 became the Central African Republic, Chad, Congo (Brazzaville) and Gabon, and together with Cameroun, Dahomey (now Benin), Ivory Coast, Mauritania, Niger, Sénégal and Upper Volta, formed Air Afrique as a joint airline. This has an extensive route network, including services between Dakar and New York, and operates DC–8s, DC–10s and Caravelles. Cameroun withdrew from Air Afrique in 1971 and set up Cameroon Airlines, with Boeing equipment, but Togo later joined the Air Afrique group.

Of the British territories, the Gold Coast became Ghana in 1957 and formed Ghana Airways; Nigeria became independent in 1960 and replaced WAAC (Nigeria) with Nigeria Airways; Sierra Leone became independent in 1961 and Sierra Leone Airways is operated with assistance from British Caledonian Airways; Gambia became independent in 1965 and its Gambia Airways is also connected with BCAL; Air Malawi and Zambia Airways were created after the break-up of the Central African Federation.

The Belgian Congo became independent in 1960 and in the following year founded Air Congo as the national airline. The country's name was changed to Zaïre and the airline became Air Zaïre in 1971. The airline has a large network of domestic and regional services and operates to Europe. Its jet fleet includes Caravelles, DC–8s, DC–10s and Boeing 737s.

Although Libya became an independent state in 1951 it did not form an airline until 1964. It was founded as Kingdom of Libya Airlines and began flying Caravelles between Benghazi and Tripoli and to several neighbouring countries and Europe. F.27s were used on some domestic services. In 1969 the carrier was renamed Libyan Arab Airlines, and now operates a fleet which includes several Boeing 727s.

Various Australian airlines operated in New Guinea and Papua and between those territories and Australia, and when Air Niugini was founded in 1973 as the national carrier of Papua New Guinea, Ansett, Qan-

tas and TAA all became shareholders. Services began on 1 November 1973, with DC–3s and F.27s.

One of the latest of the independent national airlines is Royal Brunei Airlines, which was founded in November 1974 and began services to Hongkong, Kota Kinabalu, Kuching and Singapore on 14 May 1975.

Wide-bodied fleets

In 1960 the world's airlines, excluding those of China and the Soviet Union, carried 106 million passengers, and in 1966 this figure had nearly doubled, standing at 200 million. This rapid increase in traffic called for larger fleets of aircraft, and these added to airport and airway congestion. One way of absorbing the traffic growth without increasing aircraft movements was to build much bigger aircraft. At the same time these aircraft would reduce seat-mile costs and ease the noise problems in the vicinity of airports – an aspect of air transport which was begin-

TOP LEFT: *One of Royal Air Maroc's fleet of Boeing 737–2B6s. These are small, two-engined jets similar to the 707 and 727 in many respects and available in a cargo version as well as the all-passenger model.*

TOP RIGHT: *A Boeing 737–2H7C belonging to Cameroon Airlines.*

ABOVE: *Part of an economy class cabin in a Boeing 747 'jumbo jet', with a film being projected onto small screens. This was the first production aircraft to use one of the quieter advanced technology engines, though these are not in fact as quiet as the more sophisticated engines which are now in use on the Airbuses. It is the world's largest civil aircraft and the first of the modern range of wide-bodied jets.*

OPPOSITE PAGE

ABOVE LEFT: *A Boeing 737–298C operated by Air Zaïre, mainly on routes within Africa, and to several destinations in the Middle East.*

ABOVE RIGHT: *A Royal Brunei Boeing 737. This aircraft, being a small, medium-range jet, has been found very useful by a large number of small airlines throughout the world.*

ning to reach generally intolerable levels.

The first of this new generation was made known in April 1966, when Boeing announced that it would build the Model 747 and that Pan American had placed an order for 25. In one step the Boeing was doubling the capacity, power and weight of the transport aeroplane.

In general appearance the Boeing 747 was similar to the Boeing 707, but was scaled up to have a wing span of 59·63m (195ft 8in), a length of 70·51m (231ft 4in) and a height from the ground to the top of the fin of 19·32m (63ft 5in). The maximum interior width is just over 6m (20ft), and the ceiling height 2·43m (8ft). Seating on the main deck can be nine- or ten-abreast (in tourist class) with two fore and aft aisles, and this feature has caused the term 'wide-body' to be applied to this category of airliner. The flight deck is on an upper level, and behind this is a passenger cabin which serves as a first-class lounge in most 747s. A stairway

connects the two levels. Three cargo and baggage holds have a total volume of 175·28m³ (6,190cu ft), which is about equal to the entire volume of a cargo Boeing 707.

The original engines in the Boeing 747 were four 18,597kg (41,000lb) thrust Pratt & Whitney JT9D–1 turbofans, with a diameter of just under 2·43m (8ft). The first quoted maximum take-off weight was 308,440kg (680,000lb), and landing weight 255,825kg (564,000lb). The first Boeing 747 flew on 9 February 1969, and when the type entered service with Pan American on the New York–London route on 22 January 1970, the brake-release weight had already risen to 322,956kg (712,000lb).

Pan American's aircraft had 58 first-class and 304 economy-class seats, the maximum payload was 56,245kg (124,000lb) and the maximum cruising altitude 13,715m (45,000 ft). In spite of its size the aircraft was completely orthodox in appearance, except that it had four four-wheel main undercarriage

units in order to spread the load on runways, taxiways and airport aprons. Maximum seating was originally quoted as 490.

The Model 747 underwent rapid development, with increased power and consequently higher permissible weights, and the 747–200B with 22,680kg (50,000lb) thrust Rolls-Royce RB.211s, 23,585kg (52,000lb) Pratt & Whitney JT9D–70s or 23,815kg (52,500lb) General Electric CF6–50Es has a brake-release weight of up to 371,943kg (820,000lb) and has taken off at about ten tons above this weight.

The Boeing 747 has also been built as the all-cargo 747F, with upward-swinging nose for front-end loading and a payload of up to 113 tons, and as the 747C, which can have all-cargo or all-passenger configuration or a combination of both.

In September 1973 Boeing flew the 747SR with structural reinforcement to allow high-frequency operation over short routes, which imposes greater stress on the structure – particularly the wings and undercarriage. This model can carry 500 passengers, 16 on the upper deck, but its take-off weight is limited to 272,154kg (600,000lb). Seven Boeing 747SRs were built for Japan Air Lines' domestic services, and they began operation on 10 October 1973.

All these Boeing 747s had the same external dimensions, but, on 4 July 1975, Boeing flew the first Model 747SP (Special Performance). This has a shortened fuselage, measuring 14·73m (48ft 4in) less in length than the other 747s, but its fin is 1·52m (5ft) higher.

Type: Boeing 747
No of passengers: 385
Engines: Four 22,680kg (50,000lb) thrust Pratt & Whitney JT9D turbojets
Cruising speed: 937km/h (582mph)
Ceiling: 13,715m (45,000ft)
Range: 8,047km (5,000 miles)
Weight: 351,532kg (775,000lb)
Span: 59·64m (195ft 8in)
Length: 70·51m (231ft 4in)

It has been designed for very long-range operation over routes where traffic volume does not require the larger-capacity 747s. The 747SP can carry up to 321 passengers in mixed-class configuration, with 32 on the upper deck, and can fly 11,105km (6,900 miles) with full passenger payload. Pratt & Whitney, General Electric or Rolls-Royce engines can be used and maximum brake-release weight is 299,370kg (660,000lb).

The enormous range potential of the 747SP was shown during a world tour before entering service. It flew non-stop from New York to Tokyo with 200 on board, a distance of 11,152km (6,930 miles) in 13hr 33min; non-stop from Sydney to Santiago, Chile, 11,495km (7,143 miles) in 12hr 14min; and

non-stop from Mexico City to Belgrade, 11,595km (7,205 miles) in 12hr 56min.

Pan American took delivery of its first 747SP on 5 March 1976, and at the end of April introduced the type on non-stop services between Los Angeles and Tokyo and New York and Tokyo. The latter was the longest scheduled non-stop service until Pan American began a non-stop San Francisco–Sydney service in December 1976 – a distance of 11,582km (7,197 miles). On a delivery flight in March 1976 a South African Airways 747SP flew non-stop from Paine Field, near Seattle, to Cape Town – 16,560 km (10,290 miles) in 17hr 22min.

To the end of October 1976, 313 Boeing 747s had been ordered, 291 had been de-

livered and they had flown just under 4 millions hours and carried more than 127 million passengers. In 6¾ years of service only one had been involved in a fatal accident.

The Boeing 747 was too big for some airlines which required large-capacity aircraft, and McDonnell Douglas and Lockheed both built very similar three-engined aircraft to meet this need. In layout both were wide-bodied aircraft with two wing-mounted engines and one tail-mounted, although the two companies adopted different methods of mounting the rear engine. In the Douglas DC–10 the rear engine is built into the fin structure, but in the Lockheed L.1011 Tri-Star it is within the fuselage with the air intake above the fuselage forward of the fin.

The first DC–10 flew on 29 August 1970. This was the Series 10 version with 18,145kg (40,000lb) thrust General Electric CF6–6D turbofans, seating for 270 passengers in basic mixed-class configuration or a maximum of 345 in economy class, a maximum brake-release weight of 195,043kg (430,000lb) and a still-air range of 6,727km (4,180 miles). Span of the –10 is 47·34m (155ft 4in), and length 55·55m (182ft 3in). This version entered service on 5 August 1971, on American Airlines' Los Angeles–Chicago route, and on 14 August on United Air Lines' San Francisco–Washington route.

On 28 February 1972, the DC–10–20 made its first flight. This version, later re-designated –40, has a 1·82m (6ft) increase in span, 22,680kg (50,000lb) thrust Pratt & Whitney JT9D–25W engines, a brake-release weight of 251,742kg (555,000lb), and a still-air range of 9,060km (5,630 miles). The DC–10–40 was built for Northwest Airlines, and entered service on 16 December 1972.

The most used DC–10 is the –30 model which first flew on 21 June 1972. This has the increased span of the –20/40, is powered by 23,133kg (51,000lb) thrust CF6–50C engines, has the same weight as the –20/40 but a range of 9,768km (6,070 miles). The DC–10–30 first went into service with Swissair on North Atlantic services on 15 December 1972. There are also cargo and convertible versions of the DC–10, and by autumn 1976 a total of 246 had been ordered.

The Lockheed L.1011 TriStar, which first flew on 16 November 1970, has exactly the same span as the DC–10–10 but is slightly shorter at 54·43m (178ft 7½in). It was the first aircraft to be powered by the Rolls-Royce RB.211, which in its –22B form develops 19,050kg (42,000lb) of take-off thrust. The TriStar can carry 272 passengers in mixed-class configuration, 330 in coach class or up to 400 in economy class. Maximum take-off weight is 195,043kg (430,000 lb), and the range with 272 passengers and full fuel reserves is 6,275km (3,900 miles). Maximum payload is 38,782kg (85,500lb). The TriStar entered service on 26 April 1972, with Eastern Air Lines and 159 had been ordered by the autumn of 1976, with options

FAR LEFT ABOVE: *The Boeing 747SP–44 (Special Purpose) Matroosberg, of South African Airways. This is a very long-range version with a comparatively short body.*
FAR LEFT BELOW: *The latest wide-bodied airliner is the Airbus Industrie A300B.*
LEFT: *One of Middle East Airlines' Boeing 747–2B4Bs, with the Cedar of Lebanon crest on its tail. This airline now operates an extensive route network throughout the Middle East and to Africa, Asia and Europe. It suffered a setback in December 1968, when an Israeli attack on Beirut airport destroyed six of its airliners.*
BELOW: *Another of the big wide-bodied jets is the Lockheed Aircraft Corporation's L–1011 TriStar, powered by the advanced technology RB.211 turbofan engine developed by Rolls-Royce.*
BOTTOM: *This dramatic view of Lufthansa's McDonnell Douglas DC·10–30 Düsseldorf landing at Hong Kong shows clearly the mounting of the rear engine.*

held on a further 50. Included in these orders are Saudi Arabian Airlines' L.1011–200s with 22,680kg (50,000lb) thrust RB.211–524 engines, and six L.1011–500s ordered by British Airways. These last six are to be longer range aircraft with 21,772kg (48,000 lb) thrust RB.211–524B engines, 24,493kg (54,000lb) additional fuel, a take-off weight of 224,980kg (496,000lb) and a range of 9,817km (6,100 miles) with full passenger payload of 246. The L.1011–500 will be 50m (164ft 2in) in length. Flight trials are due to begin in 1978 with entry into service in 1979.

The fourth type of wide-bodied airliner is the Airbus Industrie A300B, which is slightly smaller than the DC–10 and TriStar, with a span of 44·84m (147ft 1in) and a

ABOVE: *An Aeroflot Antonov An–22 at Le Bourget, arriving for the 1965 Paris Air Show.*
RIGHT: *An Ilyushin Il–18 taxiing in at Heathrow Airport, 1959, one of the first aircraft to have a forward positioned entrance.*
BELOW RIGHT: *A Tupolev Tu–134 of Balkan Bulgarian Airlines. This aircraft is a development of the Tupolev Tu–124, with the engines moved from the wings to the tail and a 'T' tailplane fitted. It is a medium-range airliner.*

ABOVE FAR RIGHT: *An Aeroflot Tupolev Tu–114 at John F. Kennedy International Airport, New York in June 1959. For many years the world's largest airliner, it was based on the Tu–20 bomber. There is also a military version.*
BELOW FAR RIGHT: *An early Tupolev Tu–104A, the first Soviet turbojet transport aircraft. This model carried 70 passengers and was powered by two wing-mounted 9,720kg (21,385lb) thrust Mikulin AM–3M–500 turbojets.*

length of 53·62m (175ft 11in). Unlike the other wide-bodied aircraft, the A300 is twin-engined, being powered by two wing-mounted 23,133kg (51,000lb) thrust General Electric CF6–50C turbofans. Maximum cabin width is 5·35m (17ft 7in) and seating ranges from 251 in mixed class to 336 in high-density nine-abreast layout.

The Airbus is an international product with French, German, Dutch and Spanish partners, involving government backing. Hawker Siddeley designs and builds the wings in Britain, but without government support. The wing is claimed to be of the most advanced design in service.

The A300 first flew on 28 October 1972, and the B2 version entered service on the Paris–London route with Air France on 23 May 1974. It has a maximum take-off weight of 142,000kg (313,000lb), a cruising speed of 870km/h (541mph) and a range of up to 3,860km (2,400 miles). The B4 model has increased fuel capacity, a maximum take-off weight of 157,500kg (347,100lb) and a range of 6,000km (3,728 miles).

By autumn 1976 a total of 34 A300s had been ordered and options taken on a further 23, and Airbus had announced its intention of offering airlines the B4FC freighter conversion with a large cargo door and a payload of more than 40 tonnes over distances of up to 3,500km (2,175 miles).

In the Middle East there has been fantastic growth in air transport. This is due to large-scale development of Middle East countries made possible by oil revenue, but tourism has also played a part, particularly in Egypt and Lebanon. Most of the Middle East airlines have grown in the past 20–30 years from small local or regional carriers into major international airlines.

Soviet air transport

In 1921 or 1922 there were a few experimental air services in the Soviet Union, and in 1923 three air transport undertakings were formed. But before the formation of Soviet concerns, a Königsberg (now Kaliningrad)–Kowno–Smolensk–Moscow service had been opened, on 1 May 1922, by the joint Soviet-German airline Deruluft, using Fokker F.III single-engined monoplanes. This company, with various types of aircraft and with varying routes, was to operate between Germany and the USSR until 1937.

The three undertakings set up in 1923 were Dobrolet, Ukrvozdukhput in the Ukraine, and Zakavia. These organizations developed a number of routes, mainly with German aircraft, and in 1930 the first two were re-organized as Dobroflot, Zakavia already having been taken over by Ukrvozdukhput in 1925. In 1932 Aeroflot was created when all Soviet air services came under the Chief Administration of the Civil Air Fleet.

Until the German invasion of the Soviet Union in June 1941, Aeroflot gradually built up its network, and by 1940 had a route system measuring 146,300km (90,906 miles) and that year carried nearly 359,000 passengers and about 45,000 tons of cargo and mail.

During the war Aeroflot was engaged on essential tasks, and when peace returned, faced the job of re-establishing and expanding its nationwide operations and building up an international route system. Its success is illustrated by the fact that Aeroflot now serves some 3,500 places in the USSR, operates to 65 other countries and, in 1975, carried more than 100 million passengers.

During the war the Soviet Union had received considerable numbers of military

DC–3s from the United States, and in 1939 had already begun licence production of these under the designation PS–84, changed in September 1942 to Lisunov Li–2. In the early post-war years these Li–2s and ex-military DC–3s formed the backbone of the Aeroflot fleet, and some were supplied to neighbouring Communist countries.

But even while the war was being fought, Sergei Ilyushin's design bureau began work on the USSR's first postwar transport aeroplane–the Il–12. This was a low-wing 21/32-seat monoplane powered by two 1,650/1,775hp Shvetsov ASh–82FN engines. It had a nosewheel undercarriage, but was unpressurized. The type was introduced by Aeroflot on 22 August 1947, large numbers were built, and on the last day of November

1954 the Il–12s were joined by the improved but very similar Il–14.

In the mid-1950s the Il–12s were taking 33hr to fly from Moscow to Vladivostok, with nine intermediate stops, and on the Moscow – Sverdlovsk – Novosibirsk – Irkutsk route they took 17hr 50min with 14hr 35min flying time. These aeroplanes were obviously not acceptable for the distances which had to be covered and in 1953, as part of a major modernization plan, the first Soviet jet transport was designed. This was the Tupolev Tu–104, which first flew on 17 June 1955, and went into service on the Moscow–Omsk–Irkutsk route on 15 September 1956, with a schedule of under seven hours.

The Tu–104 had a low-mounted swept-back wing, swept tail surfaces and two 6,750

kg (14,881lb) thrust Mikulin RD–3 or AM–3 turbojets close in to the fuselage. The pressurized cabins seated 50 passengers. The Tu–104 had a span of 34·54m (113ft 4in), a loaded weight of 71,000kg (156,528lb) and a cruising speed of 750/800km/h (466/497mph).

The Tu–104 transformed Soviet long-distance air services, but it was not particularly economic and was therefore followed by the 70-passenger Tu–104A and 100-passenger Tu–104B. It is believed that between 200 and 250 examples were built and many are still in service after 20 years.

The Soviet aircraft industry next designed three types of propeller-turbine transport aircraft. Two of these were for heavy-traffic routes and the third was a long-range aircraft. Ilyushin produced the Il–18, which was to prove of major importance to Aeroflot, about 600 being put into service. This was a low-wing monoplane powered by four 4,000hp Ivchenko AI–20 engines, and initially having accommodation for 80 passengers. The Il–18 made its first flight on 4 July 1957, when it bore the name Moskva (Moscow), and it went into service on the Moscow–Alma Ata and Moscow–Adler/Sochi routes on 20 April 1959. Several versions of Il–18 were built, including the Il–18V which has accommodation for up to 110, a maximum take-off weight of 61,200kg (134,922lb), a cruising speed of 625/650km/h (388/404mph) and a maximum-payload range of 2,500km (1,552 miles). About 100 Il–18s were sold to non-Soviet airlines.

The Antonov An–10 was of similar size to the Il–18, but was a high-wing monoplane designed to operate from poor aerodromes. Like the Il–18, the An–10 had four 4,000hp Ivchenko AI–20 engines, and when it entered service, on the Moscow–Simferopol route, on 22 July 1959, had 85 seats. The improved An–10A which followed had 100–110 seats. The number of An–10s and An–10As built is not known, but they did carry 10 million passengers in just under seven years, until all were withdrawn following a fatal accident at Kharkov on 18 May 1972. A freighter version, with rear under-fuselage loading, was developed as the An–12. Large numbers were produced for both civil and military use and the type operates many of Aeroflot's cargo services at home and abroad.

The long-range aeroplane was unlike any

other to be used in airline service. It was the Tupolev Tu–114, developed from the Tu–95 bomber. The 51·1m (167ft 7¾in) wing was low-mounted, swept-back 35 degrees and carried four massive Kuznetsov NK–12M turbines, each of 12,000hp and driving 5·6m (18ft 4½in) diameter eight-blade contra-rotating propellers. Later the 15,000hp NK–12MV was installed. Fully loaded, the Tu–114 had a take-off weight of 175,000kg (385,809lb), and for nearly a decade it was the biggest aeroplane in airline service. It was also the fastest propeller-driven airliner ever in service, having a maximum speed of 870km/h (470mph).

The Tu–114 entered service on the Moscow–Khabarovsk route on 24 April 1961; went onto the Moscow–Delhi route in March 1963; opened the first Soviet transatlantic service, to Havana, on 7 January 1963; and the first to North America when it began operating to Montreal on 4 November 1966. Tu–114s began working joint Aeroflot-Japan

Air Lines Moscow–Tokyo services on 17 April 1967, and bore JAL's name and badge as well as Aeroflot's. This large aircraft could carry 220 passengers, but standard seating was for 170 or, on intercontinental routes, 120. Only about 30 Tu–114s were built and most have now been replaced.

Having re-equipped with medium- and long-range turbine-powered aircraft, Aeroflot set about the task of modernizing its short-haul fleet and introduced two new types in October 1962. One was the Tu–124, which was virtually a three-quarter-scale Tu–104, and the other was the Antonov An–24, which resembled the Fokker Friendship. The Tu–124, with two 5,400kg (11,905lb) thrust Soloviev D–20P turbofans, had accommodation for 44 to 56 passengers and entered service on the Moscow–Tallinn route. There was much criticism of the Tu–124, only about 100 were built, and it was replaced on the production lines by the similar, but rear-engined, 64/80-seat Tu–134 and Tu–134A,

TOP LEFT: *A Yakovlev Yak–40 tri-jet, the first Soviet airliner to be given a certificate for operations in the West. The Yak–40 can operate from bush airfields.*

TOP RIGHT: *A Polskie Linie Lotnicze 'LOT' Antonov An–24. The An–24, a high-wing monoplane, is powered by two 2,100hp Ivchenko AI–24 propeller-turbines.*

ABOVE: *One of Aeroflot's twin-engined Tupolev Tu–134 airliners. It replaced the Tu–124.*
RIGHT: *One of British Airways' Concordes, the Anglo-French supersonic transport aircraft.*

which are now used in quite large numbers, some having been exported to East European airlines.

The An–24, with two 2,100hp Ivchenko AI–24 propeller-turbines, is a high-wing monoplane. It has been built in several versions and in very large numbers, and it has accommodation for up to 50 passengers. There are cargo versions, including the An–24TV and An–26, and the An–30 survey aircraft. Numbers of An–24s have been exported.

As Aeroflot began developing its long-haul international and intercontinental routes, it required a jet transport to replace the Tu–114. To meet this requirement Ilyushin designed the Il–62, which closely resembles the British BAC VC10. The Il–62 has four rear-mounted Kuznetsov or, in the Il–62M, Soloviev turbofans, and normal seating for 186. The Il–62 first flew in January 1963, but its development was prolonged and it did not enter service until March 1967, on domestic routes. On 15 September 1967, Il–62s began working the Moscow–Montreal services and on 15 July 1968 the extension to New York was opened.

Aeroflot has a vast number of local services, and a modern aeroplane was required to replace the Li–2s, Il–14s and smaller aircraft on these operations. The type chosen was the Yakovlev Yak–40, a unique tri-jet with the ability to operate from small, rough fields and carry up to 32 passengers. The Yak–40 flew in October 1966, went into service in September 1968 and has been exported to several countries including Afghanistan, Germany and Italy. The engines are 1,500kg (3,306lb) thrust Ivchenko AI–25 turbofans. It is reported that 2,000 Yak–40s are being built, and it is believed that nearly half that number have been delivered.

On 4 October 1968, a new Soviet airliner, also a tri-jet, made its first flight. This was the Tu–154, which has been designed to replace the large numbers of An–10s, Il–18s and Tu–104s. It has been reported that more than 600 were ordered for Aeroflot, and the type entered service on the Moscow–Simferopol and Moscow–Mineral'nye Vody routes on 15 November 1971.

For future re-equipment two other Soviet types are known to be under development: the 120-passenger Yak–42, which first flew in March 1975, and the 350-passenger Il–86.

Supersonic transport
In Britain and France the decision was taken to produce jointly an airliner capable of cruising at more than Mach 2, about 2,143 km/h (1,332mph). This was the enormously costly Concorde project, with Aérospatiale and the British Aircraft Corporation being responsible for the airframe and Rolls-Royce and Snecma for the engines. The Concorde is a slim delta-winged aircraft with four 17,260kg (38,050lb) thrust Olympus 593 turbojets, a span of 25·37m (83ft 10in), a length of 61·94m (203ft 9in) and a maximum take-off weight of 181,436kg (400,000lb).

The first Concorde flew on 2 March 1969, and on 21 January 1976, the first supersonic passenger services were inaugurated – Air France flying the Paris–Dakar–Rio de Janeiro route and British Airways the London–Bahrein route. Air France also put Concordes on the Paris–Caracas route, and on 24 May 1976, Concordes of Air France and British Airways made simultaneous arrivals at Dulles Airport, Washington, inaugurating services from Paris and London respectively. Only nine Concordes have been ordered for airline service, five for British Airways and four for Air France.

The Soviet Union was actually first to fly a supersonic transport, its Tupolev Tu–144 making its first flight on the last day of 1968. Superficially the Tu–144 resembles the Concorde, but has so far not proved to be so successful. One was lost in an accident at the 1973 Paris Air Show and, although the type began operating a Moscow–Alma Ata cargo service on 26 December 1975, there is no news of its entry into passenger service.

The United States held a design competition for a supersonic airliner, and selected the 298-passenger variable-geometry Boeing 2707 with four General Electric engines. This aircraft would have been 96·92m (318ft) long, spanning 53·08m (174ft 2in) with the wing swept forward and 32·23m (105ft 9in) with the wing swept back 72 degrees for supersonic flight. This design was then replaced by a pure-delta type, but finally the whole supersonic project was considered to be uneconomic and, after a long series of design hold-ups, it was cancelled.

TOP: *The Soviet Union's Tu–144 was the first supersonic transport to fly.*
ABOVE: *A full-scale mock-up of the Boeing 2707 supersonic transport project.*

IATA Airlines

IATA the *International Air Transport Association – is the postwar successor to the original IATA, the International Air Traffic Association founded in 1919. IATA's aims are to promote safe, regular and economical air transport for the benefit of the peoples of the world; to foster air commerce and to study the problems connected therewith; to provide means for collaboration among the air transport enterprises engaged directly or indirectly in international air transport service; and to co-operate with the International Civil Aviation Organization (ICAO) and other international organizations.*

At mid-1976 there were 110 IATA member airlines, and they carry 84 per cent of the world's scheduled air traffic, excluding that of China and the Soviet Union.

The badges or logos of the member airlines are shown here, with the exception of that of Aerolineas Cordillera of Chile, for which information is not available. Passenger figures are for 1975 unless otherwise stated. Fleet figures are the latest available.
Note: All figures for kilometres/miles flown should be multiplied by 1,000.

Aerial Tours

Aerial Tours (Papua)
Founded 1965
Fleet 16

Aer Lingus/Aerlinte (Ireland)
Founded 1936
Passengers 1,475,720
Fleet 13
Kilometres/miles flown 18,799/11,681
Freight tonnes/tons carried 44,803/44,086

Aerochaco (Argentina)
Passengers 25,496
Fleet 3

Aerolineas Argentinas (Argentina)
Founded 1949
Passengers 1,977,447
Fleet 22
Kilometres/miles flown 45,196/28,067
Freight tonnes/tons carried 19,868/19,550

Aeromexico (Mexico)
Founded as Aeronaves de Mexico 1934
Passengers 2,777,185
Fleet 27
Kilometres/miles flown 53,233/33,058
Freight tonnes/tons carried 22,445/22,086

Air Afrique (Central African Republics)
Founded 1961
Passengers 426,197
Fleet 12

Air Algérie (Algeria)
Founded 1953
Passengers 1,575,975
Fleet 24
Kilometres/miles flown 25,525/15,851
Freight tonnes/tons carried 6,704/6,597

Air Canada (Canada)
Founded as Trans-Canada Air Lines 1937
Passengers 10,394,102
Fleet 120
Kilometres/miles flown 190,270/118,158
Freight tonnes/tons carried 115,554/113,705

Air Ceylon (Sri Lanka)
Founded 1947
Passengers 117,371
Fleet 6
Kilometres/miles flown 4,095/2,543
Freight tonnes/tons carried 643/633

Air France (France)
Founded 1933
Passengers 7,981,436
Fleet 124
Kilometres/miles flown 185,766/115,361

AIR GUINEE

Air Guinée (Republic of Guinée)
Founded 1960
Passengers 56,858 (1974)
Fleet 7

Air-India (India)
Founded as Air-India International 1948
Passengers 662,902
Fleet 14
Kilometres/miles flown 28,640/17,785
Freight tonnes/tons carried 33,076/32,547

Air Liberia (Liberia)
Founded 1974
Fleet 5
Kilometres/miles flown 487/302
Freight tonnes/tons carried 20/19·7

Air Malawi (Malawi)
Founded 1964
Passengers 126,558
Fleet 6

Air Mali (Mali)
Founded 1960
Passengers 50,462
Fleet 6

Air Malta (Malta G.C.)
Founded 1973
Passengers 205,243
Fleet 2

Air New Zealand (New Zealand)
Founded as Tasman Empire Airways 1940
Passengers 744,603
Fleet 12
Kilometres/miles flown 24,691/15,333
Freight tonnes/tons carried 19,924/19,605

Air Niugini (Papua)
Founded 1973
Fleet 23
Kilometres/miles flown 7,216/4,481
Freight tonnes/tons carried 5,433/5,346

Air Siam (Thailand)
Founded 1965. Ceased operations early 1977
Passengers 456,568
Fleet 3
Kilometres/miles flown 7,359/4,570
Freight tonnes/tons carried 6,673/6,566

Air Zaire (Zaire)
Founded as Air Congo 1961
Passengers 439,706
Fleet 21

Alia – Royal Jordanian Airlines (Jordan)
Founded 1963
Passengers 379,911
Fleet 10
Kilometres/miles flown 9,703/6,026
Freight tonnes/tons carried 5,770/5,678

Alitalia (Italy)
Founded 1946
Passengers 5,806,132
Fleet 82
Kilometres/miles flown 106,190/65,944
Freight tonnes/tons carried 108,937/107,194

Allegheny Airlines (USA)
Founded as All-American Airways 1937
Passengers 10,268,867
Fleet 83
Kilometres/miles flown 111,933/69,510
Freight tonnes/tons carried 47,381/46,623

American Airlines (USA)
Founded 1934
Passengers 20,827,620
Fleet 232
Kilometres/miles flown 441,412/274,117
Freight tonnes/tons carried 284,352/279,802

Angola Airlines (Angola)
Founded as DTA 1938
Fleet 14

Ansett Airlines of Australia (Australia)
Founded as Ansett Airways 1936
Passengers 4,047,371
Fleet 40
Kilometres/miles flown 57,476/35,693
Freight tonnes/tons carried 59,820/58,863

Ariana Afghan Airlines (Afghanistan)
Founded 1955
Passengers 79,963
Fleet 3
Kilometres/miles flown 3,754/2,331
Freight tonnes/tons carried 3,302/3,249

Austrian Airlines (Austria)
Founded 1958
Passengers 912,120
Fleet 11
Kilometres/miles flown 15,035/9,337
Freight tonnes/tons carried 8,696/8,557

Avianca (Colombia)
Founded as SCADTA 1919
Passengers 2,384,904
Fleet 20
Kilometres/miles flown 29,580/18,369
Freight tonnes/tons carried 59,444/58,493

AVNA Airlines (South Africa)
Founded 1965
Ceased operations 1976
No other information available

Braniff International Airways (USA)
Founded as Braniff Airways 1930
Passengers 8,541,046
Fleet 85
Kilometres/miles flown 163,572/101,578
Freight tonnes/tons carried 68,156/67,066

British Airways (United Kingdom)
Founded 1972 by merger of BEA and BOAC
Passengers 12,372,320
Fleet 153
Kilometres/miles flown 235,786/146,423
Freight tonnes/tons carried 179,134/176,268

British Caledonian Airways (United Kingdom)
Founded 1970
Passengers 1,012,498
Fleet 27
Kilometres/miles flown 22,773/14,142
Freight tonnes/tons carried 13,180/12,969

**British West Indian Airways
(Trinidad and Tobago)**
Founded 1948
Passengers 369,043   Fleet 9
Kilometres/miles flown 12,042/7,478
Freight tonnes/tons carried 9,262/9,114

Cameroon Airlines (Cameroun)
Founded 1971
Passengers 249,007
Fleet 7

**Ceskoslovenské Aerolinie–CSA
(Czechoslovakia)**
Founded 1923
Passengers 1,505,803   Fleet 41
Kilometres/miles flown 22,680/14,084
Freight tonnes/tons carried 5,914/5,819

Chicago Helicopter Airways (USA)
Founded as Helicopter Air Service 1949
Passengers 3,076
Fleet 4
Kilometres/miles flown 45/28

Commercial Airways/Comair (South Africa)
Founded as Commercial Air Services 1946
Passengers 39,666 (1974)
Fleet 6
Kilometres/miles flown 917/569
Freight tonnes/tons carried 765/753

CP Air (Canada)
Founded as Canadian Pacific Air Lines 1942
Passengers 2,495,256
Fleet 28
Kilometres/miles flown 65,894/40,920
Freight tonnes/tons carried 32,077/31,564

Cruzeiro (Brazil)
Founded 1942
Passengers 1,493,403
Fleet 25
Kilometres/miles flown 27,112/16,837
Freight tonnes/tons carried 13,520/13,304

Cubana (Cuba)
Founded 1930
Passengers 711,103
Fleet 31

Cyprus Airways (Cyprus)
Founded 1947
Passengers 136,615
Fleet 11
Kilometres/miles flown 2,423/1,505
Freight tonnes/tons carried 2,519/2,479

Delta Air Lines (USA)
Founded as passenger airline 1929
Passengers 26,767,661
Fleet 189
Kilometres/miles flown 338,070/209,941
Freight tonnes/tons carried 200,915/197,700

DETA – Mozambique Airlines (Mozambique)
Founded 1936
Passengers 261,718
Fleet 7
Kilometres/miles flown 7,802/4,845
Freight tonnes/tons carried 5,637/5,547

**East African Airways
(Kenya, Tanzania and Uganda)**
Founded 1946. Ceased operations 1977
Passengers 708,435   Fleet 19
Kilometres/miles flown 18,079/11,227
Freight tonnes/tons carried 10,007/9,847

Eastern Air Lines (USA)
Founded 1938
Passengers 27,626,504
Fleet 242
Kilometres/miles flown 426,850/265,074
Freight tonnes/tons carried 189,996/186,956

Eastern Provincial Airways (Canada)
Founded 1949
Passengers 603,944
Fleet 10
Kilometres/miles flown 7,765/4,822
Freight tonnes/tons carried 5,026/4,946

East-West Airlines (Australia)
Founded 1947
Passengers 469,937
Fleet 9

Ecuatoriana (Ecuador)
Founded 1947
Passengers 108,093
Fleet 2
Kilometres/miles flown 3,221/2,000
Freight tonnes/tons carried 1,388/1,366

Egyptair (Arab Republic of Egypt)
Founded as Misr-Airwork 1931
Passengers 916,866
Fleet 18
Kilometres/miles flown 17,579/10,917
Freight tonnes/tons carried 9,012/8,868

El Al (Israel)
Founded 1948
Passengers 678,248
Fleet 13
Kilometres/miles flown 25,530/15,854
Freight tonnes/tons carried 29,076/28,611

Ethiopian Airlines (Ethiopia)
Founded 1945
Passengers 244,253
Fleet 13
Kilometres/miles flown 11,162/6,932
Freight tonnes/tons carried 8,223/8,091

Finnair (Finland)
Founded as Aero O/Y 1923
Passengers 1,984,686
Fleet 30
Kilometres/miles flown 30,069/18,673
Freight tonnes/tons carried 13,322/13,109

The Flying Tiger Line (USA)
Founded as National Skyway Freight Corp 1945
Cargo airline
Fleet 19
Kilometres/miles flown 36,380/22,592
Freight tonnes/tons carried 267,148/262,874

Garuda Indonesian Airways (Indonesia)
Founded 1950
Passengers 2,080,942
Fleet 39
Kilometres/miles flown 43,639/27,100
Freight tonnes/tons carried 24,605/24,211

Ghana Airways (Ghana)
Founded 1958
Passengers 150,019
Fleet 4
Kilometres/miles flown 3,892/2,417
Freight tonnes/tons carried 1,069/1,052

Iberia (Spain)
Founded 1940
Passengers 9,811,256
Fleet 85
Kilometres/miles flown 122,398/76,009
Freight tonnes/tons carried 136,527/134,343

Icelandair - Flugfelag Islands (Iceland)
Founded 1937
Passengers 303,793
Fleet 7
Kilometres/miles flown 4,836/3,003
Freight tonnes/tons carried 6,753/6,645

Indian Airlines (India)
Founded 1953
Passengers 3,219,857
Fleet 45
Kilometres/miles flown 44,284/27,500
Freight tonnes/tons carried 20,921/20,586

Iran Air (Iran)
Founded 1962
Passengers 1,950,054
Fleet 21
Kilometres/miles flown 29,781/18,494
Freight tonnes/tons carried 14,550/14,317

Iraqi Airways (Iraq)
Founded 1945
Passengers 387,569
Fleet 9
Kilometres/miles flown 7,776/4,829
Freight tonnes/tons carried 2,672/2,629

Japan Air Lines (Japan)
Founded 1951
Passengers 8,888,422
Fleet 72
Kilometres/miles flown 132,260/82,133
Freight tonnes/tons carried 178,017/175,169

JAT – Jugoslovenski Aerotransport (Yugoslavia)
Founded 1947
Passengers 2,664,701   Fleet 29
Kilometres/miles flown 29,054/18,043
Freight tonnes/tons carried 14,343/14,114

KLM Royal Dutch Airlines (Netherlands)
Founded 1919
Passengers 3,130,322
Fleet 51
Kilometres/miles flown 89,255/55,427
Freight tonnes/tons carried 127,712/125,669

Kuwait Airways (Kuwait)
Founded as Kuwait National Airways 1953
Passengers 624,827
Fleet 7
Kilometres/miles flown 10,284/6,386
Freight tonnes/tons carried 11,248/11,068

Ladeco (Chile)
Founded 1958
Passengers 61,871
Fleet 6
Kilometres/miles flown 1,684/1,046
Freight tonnes/tons carried 1,910/1,879

Libyan Arab Airlines (Libya)
Founded as Kingdom of Libya Airlines 1964
Passengers 558,455
Fleet 8
Kilometres/miles flown 7,852/4,876
Freight tonnes/tons carried 3,489/3,433

Linea Aerea Nacional – LAN (Chile)
Founded 1932
Passengers 464,147
Fleet 17
Kilometres/miles flown 19,225/11,957
Freight tonnes/tons carried 14,280/14,052

LOT – Polish Airlines (Poland)
Founded 1929
Passengers 1,454,473
Fleet 39
Kilometres/miles flown 24,427/15,169
Freight tonnes/tons carried 10,695/10,524

Lufthansa (Germany)
Founded (original company) 1926
Passengers 9,369,194
Fleet 90
Kilometres/miles flown 174,692/108,483
Freight tonnes/tons carried 250,280/246,276

Mexicana de Aviacion (Mexico)
Founded 1924
Passengers 3,100,671
Fleet 21
Kilometres/miles flown 36,597/22,727
Freight tonnes/tons carried 29,250/28,782

MEA – Middle East Airlines (Lebanon)
Founded 1945
Passengers 1,037,322 (1974)
Fleet 21

Mount Cook Airlines (New Zealand)
Founded 1920
Passengers 94,231
Fleet 31

National Airlines (USA)
Founded 1934
Passengers 4,264,730
Fleet 55
Kilometres/miles flown 69,457/43,133
Freight tonnes/tons carried 29,253/28,785

New York Airways (USA)
Founded 1949
Passengers 281,119
Fleet 4
Kilometres/miles flown 687/427
Freight tonnes/tons carried 136/134

New Zealand National Airways (New Zealand)
Founded 1945
Passengers 2,188,545
Fleet 24
Kilometres/miles flown 21,136/13,125
Freight tonnes/tons carried 35,998/35,422

Nigeria Airways (Nigeria)
Founded 1958
Passengers 430,306 (1974)
Fleet 15

Olympic Airways (Greece)
Founded 1957
Passengers 2,832,646
Fleet 43
Kilometres/miles flown 35,117/21,808
Freight tonnes/tons carried 18,732/18,432

Pakistan International Airlines – PIA (Pakistan)
Founded 1955
Passengers 1,451,812   Fleet 21
Kilometres/miles flown 31,268/19,417
Freight tonnes/tons carried 31,166/30,667

Pan American World Airways (USA)
Founded 1927
Passengers 7,431,263
Fleet 118
Kilometres/miles flown 245,176/152,254

Panga Airways (Papua)
Founded as Crowley Airways 1949
Passengers 32,000
Fleet 11

Philippine Air Lines (Philippines)
Founded as Philippine Aerial Taxi Co 1932
Passengers 2,758,424
Fleet 49
Kilometres/miles flown 40,512/25,158
Freight tonnes/tons carried 52,490/51,650

Qantas (Australia)
Founded 1920
Passengers 1,402,759
Fleet 25
Kilometres/miles flown 65,276/40,536
Freight tonnes/tons carried 29,999/29,519

Quebecair (Canada)
Founded as Rimouski Airlines 1947
Passengers 577,484
Fleet 16

Sabena (Belgium)
Founded 1923
Passengers 1,585,421
Fleet 32
Kilometres/miles flown 47,802/29,685
Freight tonnes/tons carried 68,675/67,576

Saudia – Saudi Arabian Airlines (Saudi Arabia)
Founded 1945
Passengers 1,835,733
Fleet 26
Kilometres/miles flown 27,518/25,344
Freight tonnes/tons carried 18,323/18,030

SAS – Scandinavian Airlines System (Denmark, Norway and Sweden)
Founded 1946
Passengers 6,667,908   Fleet 75
Kilometres/miles flown 112,851/70,080
Freight tonnes/tons carried 112,407/110,608

South African Airways (South Africa)
Founded 1934
Passengers 2,878,258
Fleet 41
Kilometres/miles flown 56,532/35,106
Freight tonnes/tons carried 36,760/36,172

Sudan Airways (Sudan)
Founded 1946
Passengers 255,158
Fleet 10

Suidwes Lugdiens (South Africa)
Founded as South West Air Transport 1946
Passengers 30,214
Fleet 28
Kilometres/miles flown 1,178/732
Freight tonnes/tons carried 207/204

Swissair (Switzerland)
Founded 1931
Passengers 4,690,971
Fleet 57
Kilometres/miles flown 83,084/51,595
Freight tonnes/tons carried 85,010/83,650

Syrianair – Syrian Arab Airlines (Syria)
Founded 1961
Passengers 341,087
Fleet 6
Kilometres/miles flown 9,058/5,625
Freight tonnes/tons carried 2,972/2,924

Talair (Papua)
Founded as Territory Airlines 1952
No other information available

TAP (Portugal)
Founded 1944
Passengers 1,388,490
Fleet 26
Kilometres/miles flown 36,066/22,397
Freight tonnes/tons carried 24,795/24,398

THY – Turkish Airlines (Turkey)
Founded as DHY 1933
Passengers 1,777,821
Fleet 21
Kilometres/miles flown 19,200/11,923
Freight tonnes/tons carried 11,683/11,496

Trans-Australia Airlines – TAA (Australia)
Founded 1946
Passengers 4,212,465
Fleet 40
Kilometres/miles flown 57,327/35,600
Freight tonnes/tons carried 46,448/28,844

Transbrasil (Brazil)
Founded as Sadia 1955
Passengers 1,265,710
Fleet 20
Kilometres/miles flown 19,654/12,205
Freight tonnes/tons carried 43,881/43,179

Trans-Mediterranean Airways (TMA) (Lebanon)
Founded 1953
Cargo airline
Fleet 8
Kilometres/miles flown 21,431/13,309
Freight tonnes/tons carried 83,304/81,971

Trans-West Air Charter (Australia)
Founded 1967
Passengers 13,872
Fleet 22
Kilometres/miles flown 448/278
Freight tonnes/tons carried 355/349

Trans World Airlines – TWA (USA)
Founded as Transcontinental and Western Air 1930
Passengers 15,854,002
Fleet 228
Kilometres/miles flown 424,795/263,798
Freight tonnes/tons carried 222,178/218,623

Tunis Air (Tunisia)
Founded 1948
Passengers 782,007
Fleet 10
Kilometres/miles flown 10,688/6,637
Freight tonnes/tons carried 3,897/3,835

United Airlines (USA)
Founded 1931
Passengers 29,347,289
Fleet 363
Kilometres/miles flown 520,216/323,054
Freight tonnes/tons carried 361,155/355,377

United Air Services (South Africa)
Founded 1965
Passengers 18,495
Fleet 7
Kilometres/miles flown 664/412
Freight tonnes/tons carried 38/37

UTA – Union de Transports Aériens (France)
Founded 1949
Passengers 621,818
Fleet 17
Kilometres/miles flown 32,821/20,382
Freight tonnes/tons carried 51,465/50,642

Varig (Brazil)
Founded 1927
Passengers 3,014,027
Fleet 56
Kilometres/miles flown 88,580/55,008
Freight tonnes/tons carried 96,358/94,816

VASP (Brazil)
Founded 1933
Passengers 1,999,785
Fleet 33
Kilometres/miles flown 33,788/20,982
Freight tonnes/tons carried 12,499/12,299

VIASA (Venezuela)
Founded 1961
Passengers 484,849
Fleet 13
Kilometres/miles flown 18,046/11,207
Freight tonnes/tons carried 24,658/24,263

Zambia Airways (Zambia)
Founded 1967
Passengers 234,083
Fleet 15

General Aviation

General Aviation (GA) is defined as all flying other than military and airline. It embraces private and business flying, all air sport, air taxi, agricultural, photographic survey and bush flying. The aircraft which GA uses are generally the smaller types, but not always. The King of Saudi Arabia's private Boeing 747, for example, strictly counts as a GA aeroplane as do the range of several dozen other airliners which are in private hands and are used as personal transports. There are more than 200,000 GA aircraft in the world, three-quarters of them in the United States. For comparison, there are about 10,000 airliners in the world. GA accounts for about 40 million flying hours a year, more than three times the airlines' total. Of this, 16 per cent is 'aerial work' flown by specialized commercial operators (agricultural, air survey, construction, photographic, etc.), and the remaining 84 per cent is flight instruction, transport and recreation. More than three-quarters of all GA flying is transport.

About 88 per cent of the GA fleet consists of single-engined lightplanes, the majority of them used for pilot training and personal flying. Some ten per cent are twin-engined piston types used for personal or business transport. There are slightly fewer than 2,000 business jets flying, which represents less than 1 per cent of the total in numbers but much more than that in terms of cost. There are about 6,000 GA helicopters. GA is easily the fastest-growing segment of aviation, with a growth rate which varies markedly with the world economy but which averages about six per cent a year. One reason for this growth is that the airlines tend to serve fewer and fewer airports as their fleets change from relatively large numbers of smaller jets to smaller numbers of the new wide-body types. In the USA only 425 airports out of a total of some 12,700 are now served by the airlines, leaving 12,275 served only by GA.

ABOVE: *The Beagle Pup was a British trainer that was manufactured briefly in the 1960s. It had a cruising speed of 200km/h (125mph).*
BELOW: *The 1930 de Havilland Puss Moth was one of the first monoplanes for the private owner. 250 were built.*

BOTTOM: *The very successful Britten-Norman Islander is an inexpensive STOL light twin that sells all over the world.*
CENTRE RIGHT: *The Piper Seneca flies at over 320km/h (200mph) on two 200hp engines. The engines rotate in opposite directions.*

Of the approximately one million licensed pilots in the 'free' world, three-quarters are also in the United States. (All these figures exclude the USSR and China, and many of the world's smaller states who do not file returns with the International Civil Aviation Organization.) Second in the league is Canada, with 50,000 pilots and 16,000 aircraft. France is the European country where flying is most popular, with some 37,000 pilots and 6,000 GA aircraft. Australia has some 27,000 pilots and 4,000 aircraft. In South America both Argentina and Brazil have more than 20,000 pilots and 3,000 or 4,000 aircraft. As might be expected, these are all countries where distances are large and personal incomes relatively high. Britain has about 20,000 GA pilots and 3,000 GA aircraft; prosperous West Germany has only half as many pilots, but twice as many aircraft.

GA manufacturers

The United States also completely dominates the manufacture of GA aircraft: it produced about 15,000 in 1976, with a value of $1,125 million – and nearly a quarter of these were for export. Britain pioneered the private aeroplane in 1925 with the de Havilland Moth, and enjoyed a thriving lightplane industry up until 1939. But the UK now manufactures only the Islander/Trislander utility aircraft and the Hawker Siddeley 125 business jet in the general aviation field. Some GA aircraft are built in Europe and South America, but in general the world flies American types. Cessna, Piper and Beechcraft are the Big Three of GA manufacturing. Cessna

TOP RIGHT: *The 6-seat Cessna Centurion is as fast as many twin-engined designs. The turbocharged version reaches 8,700m (28,500ft).*
ABOVE: *The Beech Baron is a luxurious twin-engined plane for the private owner. One version has a pressurized cabin.*

Type: Cessna 172
Accommodation: Four
Engines: One 150hp four-cylinder Lycoming
Cruising speed: 217km/h (135mph)
Ceiling: 3,993m (13,100ft)
Range: 1,022km (635 miles)
Loaded Weight: 1,043kg (2,300lb)
Span: 10·92m (35ft 10in)
Length: 8·21m (26ft 11in)

is the biggest, building some 8,000 aircraft a year. Grumman and Rockwell are the next largest manufacturers of GA aircraft. Like Cessna, they both manufacture the full spectrum of GA types, from little two-seat trainers through more powerful single-engined aircraft and twins up to business jets. But the most successful manufacturer of business jets, Gates Learjet, builds no other type of aircraft.

Three-quarters of the aircraft which the American GA industry builds are single-engined types; some 14 per cent have more than one piston engine; eight per cent are agricultural designs; two per cent are turbo-prop-powered; and one per cent are jets.

In France the state-owned company Aerospatiale, a partner in the international enterprises that build Concorde and the A300B Airbus, also manufactures a range of smaller types including the Corvette business jet, a range of helicopters, and the Rallye light aircraft, noted for its slow-flying and safety qualities. The Dassault-Breguet combine builds the Mystère/Falcon business jets as well as the renowned Mystère jet fighters. Reims Aviation builds and markets American Cessna lightplanes under license from the American Cessna company. Avions Pierre Robin in Dijon builds high-performance touring lightplanes of its own design. Wassmer at Issoire builds light aircraft of fibreglass – the only powered plastic aircraft presently being manufactured in the world. The CAARP factory at Beynes near Paris, partners in the CAP aerobatic sport aircraft, is

Type: Piper Cub
Accommodation: Two
Engines: One 75hp flat-four Franklin, Continental or Lycoming
Cruising speed: 140km/h (87mph)
Ceiling: 3,505m (11,500ft)
Range: 354km (220 miles)
Loaded weight: 553kg (1,220lb)
Span: 10·73m (35ft 2·5in)
Length: 6·82m (22ft 4·5in)

TOP LEFT: *This Rockwell Shrike Commander is used by the British Airports Authority for checking radio navigation aids.*
FAR LEFT: *The Grumman American Cheetah is a fast tourer for the private owner. It can carry four people at 237km/h (147mph).*
CENTRE LEFT: *The Rallye, built by the French company, Aérospatiale, is noted for its safe flying characteristics.*
LEFT: *Also French is the Dassault Falcon business jet. Like most modern business jets, it has fan rather than pure jet engines.*
ABOVE: *The Cessna Skymaster; twin booms behind the rear propeller carry the tail.*
BELOW: *The Rockwell Quail Commander is an American agricultural plane built in Mexico. It can spray liquids or chemical dusts.*

interesting in that it is effectively a workers' cooperative.

In Australia the state-owned Government aircraft factory builds the twin-turboprop Nomad utility aircraft. In Canada the Canadair company has built the CL–215, a unique twin-engined amphibious waterbomber used for fighting forest fires in France, Greece, Spain, West Germany and Quebec; and will be building the Learstar 600 business jet. The Canadian de Havilland company builds a range of advanced Short Take-Off and Landing STOL small transport aircraft.

Continental and Lycoming, both now divisions of large industrial groups (respectively, Teledyne and Avco) are the principal manufacturers of piston engines for GA aircraft. General Electric, Garrett Air Research, Canadian Pratt & Whitney and Rolls-Royce are the leading manufacturers of turbine engines in this field. Some half-dozen companies manufacture the navigation and communication equipment for GA aircraft. These systems, collectively called avionics (*aviation electronics*), may well account for a third of the total cost of the aircraft, and it is not unusual for even simple family aircraft to be as well equipped with radios as an airliner. The GA fleet also supports many businesses in the sales, maintenance and flying-instruction fields.

The modern lightplane

The earliest aircraft for the private owner were made of wood or metal structures with fabric covering. Almost all are now built entirely of light alloy, with thin metal skins contributing to the strength of the primary structures. These structures need to be light to allow a good load of passengers, baggage and fuel to be carried.

Modern piston aero engines are almost invariably four- or six-cylinder with the cylinders lying flat, horizontally opposed in pairs, and air-cooled. Dual ignition systems are universal. With the necessity for these engines to be extremely reliable, manufactured cost is unfortunately relatively high. Wing flaps and dual controls for the pilots are standard on practically all types. The smaller aircraft have fixed landing gear and fixed-pitch propellers.

Even the least expensive training types have quite comprehensive instrumentation: airspeed indicator, altimeter, two gyro-driven attitude instruments and customary engine instruments such as an rpm gauge. They also generally have radios for navigation and communication. The faster single-engined types and almost all twins have retractable landing gear, constant-speed propellers, duplicated radios and, often, duplicated flight instruments. The more powerful engines have fuel injection rather than carburettors, and cowl flaps to vary the flow of cooling air. All but the smaller types now have autopilots. The basic radios – VHF communication, VHF Omni-Range (VOR) and Airborne Direction-Finding (ADF) navigation sets – are supplemented in the more expensive aircraft by radar transponders, Distance-Measuring Equipment (DME), computer-based area-navigation systems and weather radar. Turbine-powered GA aircraft are generally

as well equipped as most airliners and are operated in flight in much the same way.

The increasing complexity of systems and equipment, particularly in the larger and newer aircraft, makes correspondingly increased demands on the skill and training of the pilots. The required levels of these qualities may not always be in evidence, particularly in non-professional GA pilots. Largely for this reason, GA's accident record is consistently worse than that of the airlines and the military. The manufacturers do a fine job in building inherently safe aircraft, but the abilities of those who fly them do not always match the capabilities of their machinery. Most GA accidents are ascribed fairly to 'pilot error'; and the largest proportion of these accidents are the result of pilots attempting to fly in weather worse than they can safely cope with. Yet travel by GA aircraft is still generally safer than travel by automobile.

Pilot training

One of the most useful and important GA activities is pilot training. Even those flying schools which exist to train airline pilots are effectively GA operations using GA aircraft types; and most military pilot trainees in most countries undergo at least some basic instruction or ability-grading in GA aircraft. These training aeroplanes are usually low-powered two-seaters of modest performance but correspondingly small fuel consumption.

Training for a private pilot's license varies around the world but almost invariably consists of ground instruction in such subjects as principles of flight, navigation, aviation law, flight planning and basic airframe, engine and instrument construction, all usually proceeding in parallel with airborne instruction. At least half of the flying is 'dual', i.e. with an instructor. Solo flying begins at the instructor's discretion, usually after 12 to 15 hours of dual flying, though often less. Gaining a commercial pilot's license takes longer, perhaps one or two years, and naturally involves more elaborate training.

The basic pilot's license generally qualifies the holder to fly single-engined aircraft in good weather and to carry non-paying passengers; further training and tests are required to fly multi-engined aircraft, or floatplanes, or in cloud using only instruments, or to give flying instruction. For the heavier piston-engined and all the turbine-powered types, a 'rating' on the license is required for that particular aircraft type as well. But the majority of amateur pilots never proceed beyond the first license. A Commercial Pilot's License (CPL) is required before a pilot may fly for hire or reward, whatever the aircraft type; there are hardly any exceptions to this rule.

Some airlines and governments sponsor young citizens for commercial pilot training. Third-world countries often have a state airline but no commercial-pilot training schools, or even a reservoir of ex-military pilots on which to draw. These countries must send their trainees abroad, usually to schools in the United States or Britain. One factor here is that English is the worldwide language of

TOP LEFT: *A Cessna AGtruck at work. Like all modern agricultural aircraft, it has a very strong and well-padded cockpit designed to keep the pilot from injury in a crash.*
LEFT: *The instrument panel of a Piper Seneca. Flight instruments are on the left, with some duplicated on the right for the second pilot. Engine controls are on a centre pedestal, with radios for both communication and navigation purposes located above them.*
ABOVE: *The Australian Nomad is a twin turbo-prop STOL bush aeroplane. It can carry a dozen passengers in and out of unprepared or short strips. The pilots have a notably good field of view from the cockpit.*
RIGHT: *Typical of aeroplane designs for the home-builder is the Taylor Monoplane, a tiny single-seater powered by a Volkswagen car engine. A home-built aeroplane is cheap, but may take years of spare time to complete.*

commercial aviation.

The ultimate goal of many who choose a flying career is to become an airline pilot – for one thing, it is very much the best paid kind of flying. Young men, and women, who cannot obtain sponsorship or who do not wish to serve in the military can sometimes obtain employment with an airline if they build up flying experience and ratings in other ways. This is usually done by working in GA, either as an instructor or in charter and air-taxi flying.

To learn to fly in Europe, one ordinarily begins by joining a flying club, an institution offering the social amenities of a club and a bar/restaurant as well as providing flying training and aircraft hire. In North America one would go to a Fixed-Base Operation (FBO), likely to be a larger business offering aircraft sales and maintenance as well as tuition and rentals, but without social facilities. The odd name came about because the earliest FBOs in America began in the 1920s with 'barnstorming' pilots, trying to make a living out of passenger rides and display flying, growing tired of a wandering life and deciding to put down roots and set up shop on one airfield. Thus they had opted for a fixed base.

Bush pilots

Bush pilots still abound in northern Canada, in Alaska and the outback of Australia. Here there are few or no highways and railways; local knowledge – of the communities, the terrain and the weather – is as important to

a bush pilot as his peculiar flying skills. Special abilities are required in the North to operate aircraft in the extreme cold of winter. Bush aircraft often fly on skis in winter and floats in summer, and on wheels hardly at all.

Agricultural flying

Agricultural flying, principally spraying insecticides, fungicides and top dressings, is the province of specialist light aircraft which have evolved to meet the requirements peculiar to this expanding branch of GA. Dusters and sprayers have gear under their wings and hoppers to feed them, as well as specially armoured cabins to protect the pilot in a crash. Accidents are not infrequent, as might be expected in flying which is all done at extremely low level. Such aircraft are designed to use short landing strips. Aerial treatment is most often employed for those crops whose nature makes them unsuitable for land vehicles: potatoes in East Anglia, cotton in the Sudan and the Mississippi delta, bananas in the tropics, for example. Aerial top-dressing is used extensively in New Zealand for hill country pastures which comprise about two-thirds of the country's farmland and whose terrain makes them otherwise inaccessible. One of the most popular agricultural aircraft is the Fletcher FU–24, built by N.Z. Aerospace Industries. More than 90 per cent of North America's rice crop is now seeded by air. There are some 24,000 agricultural aircraft in the world, treating 200 million hectares (494,200,000 acres) of land. One 'ag-plane' can do more in one hour than a tractor can accomplish in a day, and using only a tenth of the fuel.

Flying doctor

There are 'flying-doctor' services in Australia and parts of Africa as well as South America, where sparse populations and poor surface transport make it impossible except by air to get medical help quickly to people who need it. Such services are usually allied to an extensive ground radio network.

Amateur fly-ins

Not all light aeroplanes are professionally manufactured; there is a thriving movement for home-built and often home-designed aircraft. These types are usually in a purely sporting or recreational vein and it is a minority market largely avoided by the major manufacturers' who prefer the mass transport and training markets. Home-builders are often hobbyists who enjoy working with their hands, and who are attracted by the much lower costs of a home-built aeroplane (with no factory labour involved). The design and workmanship of such craft must, however, still be approved by the relevant authority, although the certification requirements are easier than those applied to manufactured types. Further cost savings are possible in amateur aircraft by using mass-produced automobile engines such as the air-cooled and relatively light Volkswagen units.

The size of the amateur-built aeroplane movement has seen spectacular growth in the past two decades; the annual US get-together of the movement, held at Oshkosh

in Wisconsin, now attracts more than a quarter of a million visitors and 1,200 amateur-built aircraft. There are also annual fly-ins for home-built aircraft in France and England. At the 1976 fly-in in the USA a team of 80 enthusiasts built and flew an aeroplane from scratch during the nine-day event, but three or four years is a more typical completion time for an amateur working on his own in his spare time. Home-built designs seldom have a performance to match those of production types – but some do: at least one has flown around the world, while another has a 523km/h (325mph) cruise speed on a single 200hp engine.

Also popular is the maintenance in flying trim of historic or antique aircraft, many of them discovered as mouldering skeletons and lovingly restored to fitness. An additional appeal here is that such aircraft usually appreciate in value.

Private flying is undeniably expensive, and it is evident that its already impressive growth rate would be even faster were it not for the costs. Helicopters are even more expensive than fixed-wing aeroplanes. Yet GA aircraft (particularly the smaller types) are relatively fuel-efficient. Another attraction is that, unlike road vehicles, they are not subject to legal restrictions on speed. A Cessna 172 carries four people, cruises at 225km/h (140mph) in a straight line while returning 6·8km per litre (16 miles to a US gallon) of fuel. In the United States, where automobiles often have a fuel consumption worse than that, and where there is an overall 88km/h

(55mph) speed limit on all highways, flying becomes an attractive alternative to road travel for journeys of 160km (100 miles) or more. It has been suggested that the speed limit has been a powerful factor in GA's recent boom in America. It should also be said that there are often tax benefits in aircraft purchase for wealthy men or businesses.

Most attempts to reduce the costs of aircraft ownership involve some kind of shared utilization. Private pilots rent an aeroplane from a flying club as and when they wish. Thus club aircraft have higher utilization and so lower fixed costs. Alternatively several pilots can share the ownership of a personal aeroplane. Businesses can simply rent aircraft as air taxis when they have the need. The trend throughout this century, however, is for personal flying to come within the grasp of even more people, and GA's remarkable growth may be expected to continue.

Air Sport

Aerobatics

'Aerobatics' is the proper word for what most laypeople think of as 'stunting' or 'stunt-flying': flinging an aeroplane around the sky, turning it upside down for the sheer pleasure and excitement of it. The basic aerobatic manoeuvres are the loop, roll, spin and stall-turn. From these, and variations and combinations of them performed from both erect and inverted flight, an expert pilot can construct an intricate sequence of manoeuvres which at its best becomes a kind of aerial choreography. There are contests in which competitors fly in turn, to be judged by experts on the ground. These are at every level of flying, from club competitions through national to a world aerobatic championship held every two years. Aerobatic flying is also the principal activity at most air shows and air displays.

The sport is almost as old as flying itself. The Russian pilot Petr Nesterov is usually credited with having been the first man to loop-the-loop, on 20 August 1913, at Kiev and in a French Nieuport monoplane. The French pilot C. A. Pégoud began giving aerobatic demonstrations that same year in a 50hp Gnome Blériot, which people flocked to watch. In the USA, Lincoln Beachey started public aerobatic flying soon afterwards. By the end of World War I it is probable that nearly every aerobatic manoeuvre known today had been worked out by military pilots.

Aerobatic aircraft today are special types with extra-strong airframes to withstand the acceleration forces involved, which may exceed 6g (six times gravity), and with powerful engines and large control surfaces. Special fuel and oil systems allow the engine to run when inverted. Pilots wear strong harnesses to hold them in their seats while upside-down and often wear parachutes in case of structural failure. Aerobatics as a sport is relatively dangerous – perhaps about as dangerous as motor racing – and for this reason novices are advised to practise with a skilled instructor, wear a parachute, and to fly only at considerable altitude until expert.

There is a notation shorthand for the sport, called the 'Aresti cryptographic system', which enables a sequence of manoeuvres to be drawn simply on paper.

The commonest manoeuvres are the loop (a vertical circle), slow roll (rotation through inverted back to level while flying at the same height), flick or snap roll (horizontal spin), stall-turn or hammerhead (a sideways reversal of direction from a vertical climb), tail-slide (backwards recovery from a steep climb), and Cuban eight (loops linked by descending half-rolls). Rarely performed but most spectacular of all is the Lomcevak,

a series of inverted flick rolls which culminates with the aeroplane tumbling end-over-end.

Air Racing

Air racing is easily the fastest competitive sport on earth, with speeds in the *Unlimited* class (actually limited to piston-engined aircraft, which in practice are almost all World War II fighter types) in excess of 650km/h (400 mph). This is pylon racing, at low level around a course delineated by tall pylons on the corners, where judges look for pylon 'cuts' (turning inside the pylon, which costs the pilot a lap). In addition, there are occasional straight-line point-to-point races see page 432 for some of the most important of these).

The United States is the real home of air racing, where the biggest meeting is the annual National Air Races held near Reno, Nevada, every September. In addition to the *Unlimited* class, there are also *T–6* class races (limited to stock North American AT–6 or Harvard aircraft – the type was a prominent World War II advanced trainer); *Sport Biplane* class races for biplanes of limited engine displacement; *Formula One* races for tiny fixed-landing gear monoplanes of limited engine displacement; and *Formula V* races for aircraft with Volkswagen car engines. Pylon races for jet aircraft have also been held, but the enormous operating costs of these, and the great disparity in speeds, have not yet made this form of exciting but expensive jet racing popular.

Formula One racing has in recent years spread to Europe. The costs of *Formula One* aircraft are reasonably low and speeds, on a nominally 100hp engine, relatively high at more than 320km/h (200mph). Handicap racing is a popular form of the sport with handicappers computing probable race speeds and promulgating a different start time for each aircraft. The aim is to have them all cross the finish line together – an impossible result that is never in practice achieved. Handicap racing attracts a variety of different types of aircraft, from tiny homebuilts through ordinary production lightplanes (the majority) up to the occasional piston or even jet fighter aircraft. The appeal of handicap racing is that it allows virtually any pilot to enter any aircraft; and it does not require commercial sponsorship to be financially viable.

The most spectacular aerobatic demonstrations are those of military teams.
RIGHT: *The RAF's Red Arrows in a 'twizzle', with each aircraft rolling in turn, changing the formation from echelon to line astern.*
TOP RIGHT: *A Red Arrow Gnat jet trainer.*
INSET: *Gaily coloured racing biplane.*

Ballooning

Ballooning is the oldest kind of flying, almost 200 years old as against the powered aeroplane's 75 years. Except for some war applications – such as the use of tethered balloons as observation posts, and of free balloons to get messages and important people out of besieged Paris in 1870 – ballooning has always been an essentially sporting form of flight.

The very first balloons were hot-air filled; hydrogen balloons soon followed, and this gas largely supplanted hot air as a lifting substance until recent years and the invention of propane-gas burner systems. These offer a light, safe, simple and quite inexpensive source of hot air and allow the balloon to be airborne as little as 20 minutes after arrival at the launch site, whereas a hydrogen-gas balloon takes hours to fill.

Balloons, like aeroplanes, require airworthiness certificates, and the pilot-in-command needs a private pilot's licence (balloons). For this, a candidate needs a minimum of 12 hours' flying in balloons and to pass a simple medical, written papers and a flight test. Tuition is generally available from balloon manufacturers, balloon schools and already licensed pilots.

Ballooning was popular until World War I, and then declined until the 1960s when a great resurgence began which still continues. Today there are about 600 balloons flying in the USA and 320 in the rest of the world – almost all propane-fuelled. The first world championships were held in New Mexico in 1972, with tests of the balloonists' abilities to ascend, maintain a set height and descend in timed steps measured by a barograph.

Calm summer evenings are the most popular time for a balloon flight, which begins with the big envelope laid out on the grass, downwind of its basket (usually still made of wicker, though some are of metal or glass-fibre) and the burner assembly. After a careful inspection of the whole balloon, the pilot light is lit and the main gas valve opened to generate a flame of some 1,093·3°C (2,000°F) and several feet long. The open neck of the balloon must be held open by hand at first; soon the envelope begins to swell with warm air. Crew members tug and heave at shroud lines, and may even run inside the envelope to help distend it properly.

Eventually the envelope contains enough hot air to lift itself and pull the basket upright. All the flight crew climb aboard, and after another long burn of 30 seconds or so the balloon lifts off. It is now a two-ton bubble of air heated to about 37·8°C (100°F), its buoyancy derived from the lower density of the hot air it contains. Further burns are required from time to time to maintain this buoyancy as the hot air cools.

Besides the burner valve, the balloonist also has a vent valve to release a small amount of hot air if he is climbing too fast; a rip panel to release a large amount quickly after landing; and a trail rope to slow his descent and forward speed before landing. He will also carry a welder's spark in case he has to relight the pilot burner – though even in the case of total burner failure the balloon should still hold its shape and descend slowly as a parachute.

Hang gliding

The current renaissance of hang gliding derives from work by the US National Aeronautics and Space Administration (NASA) on developing a foldable wing for spacecraft re-entering the atmosphere. NASA scientist Francis Rogallo invented an A-shaped fabric wing on a rigid frame, which has proved excellent for hang gliding. The present renewed interest in the sport began, like so many others, in Southern California but it has now spread throughout the world. Some of the more advanced gliders resemble conventional aeroplanes, but most are still variations of the original Rogallo delta wing.

A typical hang glider consists of a tough Terylene sail attached to a strong tubular A-frame, from which the pilot hangs in a harness. In front of him is a small triangular sub-frame which is rigidly attached to the main frame; the pilot holds this with both hands and steers the glider by swinging his

LEFT: Hot air ballooning is growing rapidly in popularity, with almost a thousand such balloons flying throughout the world.
INSET: *A propane burner is used to heat the air in the balloon, generating a flame up into the balloon's envelope.*
BELOW: *Hang gliding is the least expensive way to go flying, and closest to man's dream of being a bird. The gliders derive their shape from space research.*

body about under it, thus moving the whole aircraft's centre of gravity. Some larger gliders have two harnesses and thus allow the dual instruction of novice pilots.

Hang gliders have poor glide ratios in comparison with conventional sailplanes, and thus require strong updrafts for continued flight. Favoured sites are those where a moderate to strong wind blows up and across a ridge of high ground. Most hang gliding is simple slope-soaring at low altitudes, though some experts have managed to climb sufficiently in slope lift to find thermals at high altitudes.

There are world and national contests for hang gliding, as with other aerial sports. The great appeal of hang-gliding is that it is the cheapest form of flying; and, of all forms and ways of flying, it is the closest to Man's dream of 'being a bird'. It is also the only form of air sport which is good exercise: the glider, weighing about 17kg (35–40lb) has to be carried back up the hill after every flight. Neither the craft nor the pilot is required to be licensed.

Development work in hang glider design is concentrated on improving the efficiency of the basic Rogallo shape, and on improving its glide angle without impairing its natural docility and controllability. Whereas at first the pilot always hung vertically upright in his harness, the more advanced types now allow him to hang prone, thus reducing the drag of his body shape.

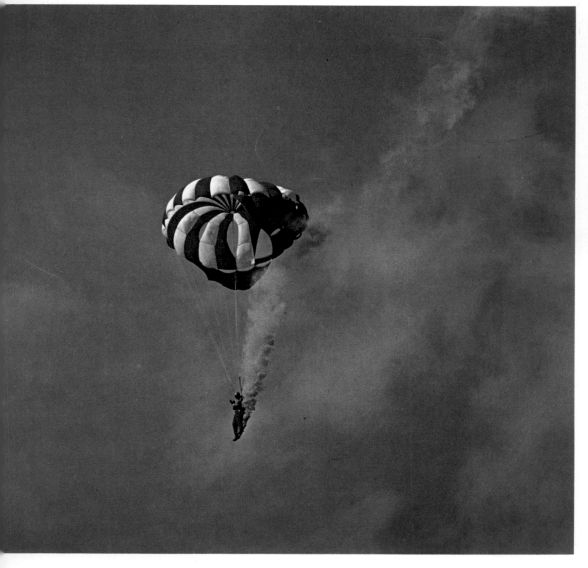

Parachuting

The first successful parachute descent was made by the Frenchman André Jacques Garnerin, jumping from a balloon at about 1,000m (3,280ft) near Paris on 22 October 1797. Captain Albert Berry made the first descent from an aeroplane, in America on 1 March 1912, when he jumped from a Benoist aircraft at about 500m (1,640ft) over St Louis.

Parachutes have saved the lives of possibly some 100,000 aviators in stricken aircraft. A handful of lucky men have even survived falls from high altitude *without* parachutes. One, Lt Col I. M. Chissov, a Russian, fell 7,000m (23,000ft) and survived, though he was badly injured. A British bomber crewman, Flt Sgt Nicholas Alkemade, jumped from his blazing aircraft without a parachute at about 5,500m (18,000ft) and survived without a single broken bone. The first emergency parachute descent was by a Polish balloonist, Jodaki Kuparento, after his balloon caught fire on 24 July 1808. One American in modern times has made more than 7,000 jumps; two Americans once made 81 jumps in 8hr 22min; and five RAF parachuting instructors once jumped together from 12,614m (41,383ft), falling free for more than 11,900m (39,000ft).

Perhaps the most astonishing parachute descent ever was that made by Capt Joseph Kittinger of the United States Air Force, who jumped from the gondola of a huge helium balloon at a height of 31,150m (102,200ft) over New Mexico on 16 August 1960. He fell free for 4min 38sec, through 25,817m (84,700ft), reaching a peak speed at about 18,300m (60,000ft) of almost 1,000 km/h (620mph), representing a Mach number of 0.93. The step by his balloon gondola's door was inscribed 'the highest step in the world', and his jump was the highest ever made, with the longest free fall. His parachute, with a barometric operating device, opened automatically.

Sport parachuting is a fast-growing sport, part of its appeal being that, unlike most other forms of air sport, it does not require a long and expensive training period. Early jumps are made with a static line attached to the aircraft to open the jumper's parachute automatically. Free fall comes later.

There are local, national and world contests in parachuting, when accuracy of touchdown is measured and style while manoeuvring in free fall is judged.

Jumpers must wear two parachutes, one a reserve in case of a malfunction. Touch-down speeds are often low enough to allow experts to perform a stand-up landing in low winds. Landing is not like jumping from a particular height of, say, 3m (10ft) because the upper body, still sustained by the parachute, slows after the feet have touched. The important point to master in landing is not so much the vertical speed but rather the horizontal component caused by wind.

Soaring

Soaring – gliding, using several sorts of up-current in the air to stay aloft – was first developed after World War I. The peace treaty forbade defeated Germany from having powered aircraft, but did not ban gliders. In 1921 a German glider soared for 13 minutes, finally beating the Wright Brothers' 1911 time of 9 minutes 45 seconds. In 1922 a German pilot made the first soaring flight of more than an hour; in 1926 another was drawn up into a thunderstorm and made the first soaring flight away from his launch site. By 1935 the sport had advanced so that four contestants in a competition in Southern Germany flew more than 500km (300 miles) into Czechoslovakia. World records today reflect the extraordinary efficiency of modern sailplanes and the skills of their pilots. The record for distance in a straight line is 1,461 km (908 miles). The absolute altitude record is 14,102m (46,266ft).

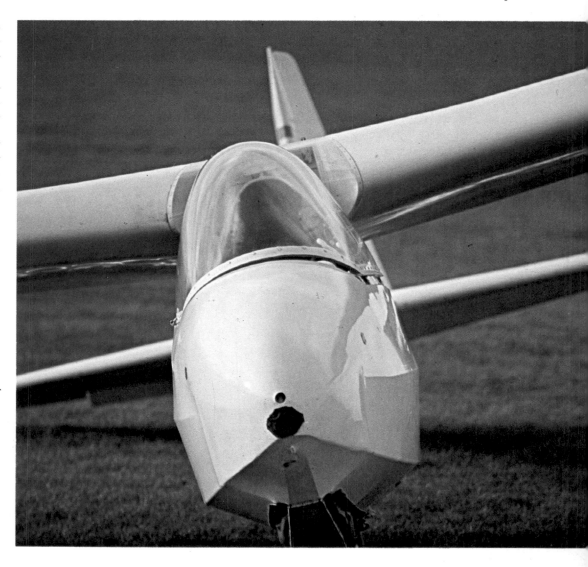

Modern high-performance gliders are easily the most efficient aircraft of all, employing some of the most advanced aerodynamics and modern structures. Many are built largely of glass-fibre plastics – the only aircraft that are. German designers and manufacturers are still in the forefront of the craft. Minimum still-air sink rates may be less than 0·6m/sec (2ft/sec), and glide ratios can approach 50:1. Such sailplanes have very long, narrow wings (to reduce induced drag) and require the pilot to lie back in an almost-prone position to reduce the fuselage frontal area. Most have wings and tailplanes which are quickly detachable so that they can be fitted in a long, narrow trailer for towing behind a car.

Aero-towing behind powered aircraft to a release height of about 700m (2,000ft) or winch-launching to about 250m (800ft) are the commonest methods of launching today, with car towing used to a lesser extent. A fairly recent development is the powered sailplane, which uses a small motor (usually a modified Volkswagen car engine) to climb to a useful height, when the engine is shut down and the aircraft is flown as a glider.

As with powered aircraft, all glider training is by dual instruction in two-seaters. Gliding clubs offer low-cost accommodation and catering, and encourage members to stay the weekend. Costs generally are kept low by the requirement for considerable voluntary assistance from members in all aspects of club life. The most basic qualifications are national certificates, after which there are international silver, gold and diamond badges for advanced performance. A Silver C, for example, requires a flight of at least five hours, a height gain of 1,000m (3,281ft), and a straight-line distance flight of at least 50km (31 miles). A Gold C requires five hours, 3,000m (9,842ft) height gain and 300km (186 miles) distance, which may be an out-and-return or a triangular flight. Diamonds may be added to a Gold C badge for a height gain (recorded on a barograph) of 5,000m (16,404ft); or a triangular or out-and-return flight of 300km (186 miles); or a distance flight of 500km (311 miles).

Gliding contests usually involve flying set tasks, typically out-and-return flights with photographs required of the turning points, these tasks being chosen by the contest judges having regard to the prevailing weather.

Gliders soar by using different kinds of rising air (it occasionally being possible to employ all kinds in a single flight). One is slope-soaring, riding the updraft of air over a hill ridge on a breezy day. The commonest 'lift' is that found in thermals – large bubbles of relatively warm air rising from near the surface of the earth as the sun heats it. (An extreme form of thermal lift is that under and inside a building thunderstorm.) Wave lift is found in mountainous regions where a strong, unstable air stream flows across the mountains; 'standing' waves form in the air, and these remain stationary with respect to the mountain ranges. Such lift is often very strong and smooth, and it can persist well into the stratosphere.

Flying Boats

The development of water-borne aircraft began very soon after the first successful landplane flights: after all, two-thirds of the earth's surface is water, and there are an enormous number of lakes, rivers and sheltered inlets which provide potential natural water aerodromes. Maritime aircraft seemed for a long time to have a big future: they were employed extensively for oceanic reconnaissance duties in both world wars, against submarines and for rescue work in World War II, and as long-range civil transports in the 1930s and 1940s. Yet today hardly any flying boats still exist; and the only water-borne aircraft currently in use in any numbers are a few light floatplanes operating in thinly-populated parts of the world, where land airports are few and lakes numerous.

Several factors combined to bring about the decline of the flying boat, most of them related to economics. Helicopters proved able to carry out air-sea rescue and anti-submarine roles in all weathers and, sometimes, more cheaply. All the world's cities, even those that were seaports, proved only too willing to build land airports with vast runways to attract landplane airliner services. Flying boats, with their big stepped hulls, could not be made to fly as fast as the slender airliners, and this became more marked as speeds rose. Because of their inherently higher drag they were more costly in fuel, and the boats also remained susceptible to damage from collision with floating debris, from waves when operating out at sea, and to the corrosive effects of salt water on aluminium alloys.

Yet flying boats had their attractions. Their big hulls allowed passengers a degree of room and comfort unknown in most landplanes. They were beautiful to watch, during take-off and landing, and still invoke affection among passengers and aviation enthusiasts.

ABOVE: *Henri Fabre's* Hydravion *was the first successful floatplane. Built in 1910, it was powered by one 50hp seven-cylinder Gnome rotary engine, driving a pusher propeller, giving a maximum speed of 90km/h (55mph).*
RIGHT: *The Short Sunderland, which first flew with the RAF in 1937. It carried seven to ten Browning and Vickers machine guns and a bomb load of 700kg (2,000lb).*
BELOW: *The Dornier DO X, the world's largest aircraft when it was built in 1929. It had a maximum speed of 215km/h (134mph), and a range of 1,700km (1,056 miles). It could carry up to 150 passengers.*

ABOVE: *The Navy Curtiss NC–4, the first aircraft to cross the Atlantic, did so in several stages. It was powered by four 400hp Liberty V–12 engines, two pusher, two tractor, giving a maximum speed of 145km/h (90mph) and a range of 2,360km (1,470 miles).*
BELOW: *The Saunders-Roe (Saro) Princess, a very large flying boat intended as a high capacity transatlantic transport aircraft. It first flew in August 1952, powered by ten Bristol Proteus turboprops, eight of which were coupled in pairs to contra-rotating propellers. These engines gave a cruising speed of 580km/h (360mph) and a range of 8,480km (5,270 miles).*

Early history

Henri Fabre, member of a family of Marseilles shipowners, developed the first aeroplane to take off from water. His very first Hydravion, built in 1909, had three engines coupled to drive a single propeller, and could not be coaxed into flight at all. His second design was also freakish in layout. It was of canard form, with the tail surfaces at the front and the wing and engine (driving a pusher propeller) at the back. The fuselage consisted simply of two wooden girders, astride the top one of which Fabre sat, his feet dangling down to a pair of pedals which warped the wings for lateral control, and his hands grasping a stick which moved the front elevator and rudder. The craft sat on three tiny floats which were almost wholly submerged when at rest. The flying surfaces resembled sails in that their fabric was taughtened to the end of each rib by spring hooks, and could be detached and reefed up. Only one surface of the wing was covered.

In this odd device, Fabre became the first man to take off from and land back on water, on 28 March 1910. His first flight covered some 500m (1,640ft) over the calm water of the harbour at La Mede near Marseilles. Not only had Fabre been first to succeed where many better-known aerial experimenters completely failed; but it was also his first flight. He succeeded because his exquisitely-built craft was extremely light in weight, and powered by one of the very first Gnome rotary engines, which was relatively light, but gave a powerful 50hp.

Fabre apparently lacked the funds to continue experimenting, though he continued to make floats for other experimenters. In 1911 he made some floats for a Voisin biplane landplane, which was thus transformed into the world's first amphibious aeroplane.

Glenn Curtiss

The great American pioneer of water-borne aircraft was Glenn Curtiss. He began his aviation experiments with wheeled landplanes, evolving a simple but efficient pusher biplane with hinged surfaces – ailerons – for roll control. As early as November 1908 he had tried (unsuccessfully) to turn his pioneering aeroplane, *June Bug*, into a seaplane by mounting it on floats and renaming it the *Loon*, after a species of water bird.

On 31 May 1910, he flew non-stop from Albany to New York City in a landplane fitted with a cork-filled canvas tube, a nose hydro-ski and wing-tip balance floats for flo-

BELOW: *Henri Fabre's 1910 50hp* Hydravion *was the first aircraft in the world to take off from water. It flew tail first.*
BELOW CENTRE: *This twin-engined Curtiss* America *flying boat was intended to fly the Atlantic in 1914, but war intervened.*

BELOW CENTRE: *Henry Ford (right) visited the Curtiss plant in 1912, and is here shown an 'aerial yacht' by Curtiss.*
BOTTOM: *Eugene Ely, flying a Curtiss pusher biplane, flew from San Francisco and landed near the cruiser* Pennsylvania.

tation should he be forced to land on the Hudson river on the way. He foresaw the value to the US Navy of a true hydro-aeroplane, and tested a variety of floats on his biplane. With none of these could he achieve speeds sufficient for take-off from water.

The next winter he moved from the bitter cold of upstate New York to San Diego in California; and there, on 26 January 1911, he finally made his first take-off from water, in a pusher biplane employing a single central float with stabilizing outriggers.

On 14 November 1910, a (wheeled) Curtiss pusher flown by Eugene Ely became the first aeroplane ever to take off from a ship – the USS *Birmingham* moored in Hampton Roads, Virginia. On 18 January 1911, Ely completed the achievement by landing on the deck of the USS *Pennsylvania* in San Francisco Bay.

Curtiss flew the first aircraft with parallel twin floats, and demonstrated their natural lateral stability. He flew with a passenger; developed an amphibious wheel-and-float aeroplane; and had his seaplane lowered to the surface from a warship, flown, and then winched back aboard afterwards. On 12 January 1912, he flew the first successful boat-hulled aeroplane.

It was Curtiss who stumbled on the idea of a stepped hull to break the water's suction during take-off – a device which has been used on every successful seaplane and speedboat ever since. By 1912 he was manufacturing a two-seat Aeroyacht, and in the same year a boat-hulled Curtiss Model F hydroaeroplane became the first aeroplane ever to fly with the newly-invented Sperry gyroscopic autopilot. At least 150 Model Fs were eventually ordered by the US Navy.

BELOW: *The Curtiss NC–4 flying boat was the first aircraft to fly the Atlantic, in 1919.*
BOTTOM: *The Macchi M.5 was a fighter flying-boat of World War I. With a 160hp V–12 engine, it was manoeuvrable.*

BELOW: *Felixstowe F–2As, big patrol craft used by the Royal Navy in World War I, carried up to seven machine guns.*
BOTTOM: *The 12-engined Dornier Do X first flew in 1929, and once carried 169 people.*

RIGHT: *The twin-engined Dornier Wal.*
BELOW RIGHT: *Formations of Savoia Marchetti S–55As flew the Atlantic in the early 1930s.*
BOTTOM RIGHT: *The Macchi MC72 held both the world air and seaplane speed records.*

World War I

During the war maritime aircraft were extensively used by both sides for reconnaissance duties and to drop bombs and launch torpedoes. Seaplane carriers were also used by both sides. Britain's first was a 7,500 ton converted collier which was also the first Royal Navy ship to bear the name HMS *Ark Royal*. Others were converted cross-Channel steamers fitted with cranes and carrying about four aircraft each. The German merchant raider *Wolf* sank 28 Allied vessels in the Indian and Pacific Oceans, helped by the Friedrichshafen seaplane that she carried. This was the most famous of all the Friedrichshafen *FF* seaplanes, the *FF* 33e *Wolfchen*.

By the end of the war some very large flying boats were being built; by Zeppelin-Lindau in Germany whose boats were designed by Claude Dornier; Curtiss in America; and derivatives of Curtiss designs in Britain. The wing spans of some of these craft approached that of a modern Boeing 707; the Navy Curtiss NC flying boats, for example, spanned 38·40m (126ft). They were most literally flying 'boats', with a speedboat-style hull instead of a fuselage; the biplane wings, engines and tail surfaces were held above this hull by a web of struts and bracing wires.

Some 43 per cent of their all-up weight of 12,700kg (28,000lb) was useful load (a remarkable ratio for aircraft of any age), and could include some 4,500kg (10,000lb) of fuel. The prototype had three 400hp Liberty engines, but subsequent aircraft had four engines, giving a speed of between 107 and

137km/h (66 to 85mph). The engines had electric starters, for the propellers were too big to be turned by hand.

They were ready too late to take part in the war, but they achieved fame as participants in the US Navy's great 1919 project to make the first aerial crossing of the Atlantic. The attempt involved enormous surface vessel support; there were 68 navy destroyers, one stationed every 80km (50 miles) along the route to assist the flying boats by radio, smoke signal and pyrotechnic guidance.

Three of these 'Nancy boats' set off from Newfoundland on 16 May 1919, and one of them, the NC–4 commanded by Lieutenant Commander Albert C. Read, arrived safely in Lisbon on 27 May, via refuelling stops on the Azores, reaching Plymouth, England, on 31 May. The other two 'Nancies' came down in the open Atlantic; NC–1 sank after her crew had been rescued, but NC–3 taxied 322km (200 miles) to the Azores.

The Dornier Do X

An even slower Atlantic crossing was made by the huge Dornier Do X 12-engined flying boat, which took ten months to travel from Lake Constance to New York, where it arrived on 27 August 1931.

The Do X was the biggest aeroplane in the world in its time, spanning 48m (157ft 6in) and having a maximum weight of 56,000kg (123,459lb), and carrying aloft on one test flight 169 people – then a world record – comprising of 10 crew, 150 passengers and no less than 9 stowaways. (However, the aircraft's intended usual complement was no more than approximately 70 passengers). The Do X's hull had three decks, and contained a bar, smoking and writing rooms, a bathroom, a lounge and sleeping quarters, and a kitchen and dining room.

At first she was powered by twelve 525hp Siemens-built copies of the British Bristol Jupiter air-cooled engine. These were mounted in six back-to-back pairs on an auxiliary extra wing above the main wing. It was quickly found that the rear engines, mounted in the disturbed airflow from the front engines and the stub wing, tended to overheat, and there was a loss of lift and excessive drag. In an attempt to cure this, 12 American Curtiss Conqueror liquid-cooled engines of 600hp each were installed to replace the Jupiters, and the auxiliary wing was deleted. The Do X burned 1,828·57 litres (400 gallons) of petrol an hour to cruise at 175km/h (110mph), her maximum speed was 210km/h (130mph), and her ceiling when loaded was 3,200m (10,500ft).

Dornier Wal
Dornier Wals were much more successful. They served with several early airlines, and two were used by Roald Amundsen on his 1925 attempt to reach the North Pole, one reaching 87° 43′ North – the farthest north any aeroplane had been – on 21 May 1925. Ramon Franco, brother of General Franco was the first to fly a Dornier Wal across the South Atlantic in 1926, and another was flown across the North Atlantic to Chicago in August 1930 by Wolfgang von Grunau, the first east-west Atlantic crossing by a flying boat.

Other long-distance flights
Many epic long-distance flights were made in lighter aircraft fitted with floats. Perhaps the most remarkable were those of Francis Chichester, (later Sir Francis), who made the first solo air crossing of the Tasman Sea from New Zealand to Australia, between 28 March and 6 June 1931, in a little de Havilland Gipsy Moth seaplane, which he rebuilt *en route* after it had sunk at Lord Howe Island. Between 3 July and 14 August he made the first-ever solo flight between Australia and Japan, again in his seaplane.

An Italian design, remarkable because of its unorthodox configuration was the Savoia-Marchetti S.55, a twin-hulled flying boat with an open cockpit, very thick wings, twin engines installed back-to-back and canted at a striking angle, and a tailplane carried on wire-braced booms. In 1926 S.55s set up 14 world records for speed, altitude, and distance with payload. In 1927 and 1928 they made long flights across the Atlantic (both north and south). In January 1931 12 S.55s led by the Italian Air Minister Marshal Italo Balbo made a flight in formation (though three aircraft crashed during the voyage) from Rome to Rio. In 1933 Balbo led a formation of 24 S.55s to Chicago for the World's Fair, making the journey of almost 10,000km (6,000 miles) in just under 49 hours.

Undoubtedly some of the greatest waterborne aircraft ever built were those designed to compete in the Schneider Trophy Races, described in Chapter 21. One of these machines was probably one of the greatest seaplanes ever built, although it was not completed in time to compete in the last contest, held in 1931. This was Italy's Macchi-Castoldi M.C. 72, which had a pair of V-12 Fiat engines mounted back-to-back in tandem, driving a pair of contra-rotating propellers. This installation solved the outstand-

ing problem which had plagued other Schneider designers: the effects of torque when their throttles were opened for take-off. The controllable pitch propeller had not been perfected in those days, and the Schneider racers had enormous fixed-pitch propellers of exceedingly coarse pitch. When the throttle was first opened and before the craft had gathered forward speed one float would dig in, and try to turn the machine in a circle. This was also the moment when the spray was worst, preventing the pilot from seeing where he was going. But there was no such problems with the Macchi M.C. 72, which

could make a straight take-off run under full control the whole time, because the contra-rotating propellers were free from torque. Four M.C.72s were built, three crashing and killing their pilots; but the fourth, piloted by Warrant Officer Francesco Agello, set several remarkable speed records, including one of 709km/h (440mph), established on 23 October 1934, (by which time the aeroplane's double engine was developing more than 3,000hp). This remained an outright world speed record until 1939, and a seaplane record until it was beaten by a Russian turbo-prop-powered Beriev Be–10 in August 1961.

Transport Flying Boats

LEFT: *The 1934 Sikorsky S–42 was a 32-passenger flying boat designed for Pan American.*
FAR LEFT INSET: *Short Solents were used by BOAC in the late 1940s. Twelve were built.*
CENTRE LEFT INSET: *42 of these Short 'C' Class boats entered service with Imperial Airways in the 1930s.*
LEFT INSET: *Two Breguet 530 Saigons served with Air France in the mid-1930s.*

Amphibious Aircraft

BELOW LEFT: *The Grumman Goose amphibian is a 1936 design which continues to give good service.*
BELOW FAR LEFT INSET: *Pan American used Sikorsky S–38 ten-passenger, twin-engined amphibians to expand its services through Latin America.*
BELOW CENTRE LEFT INSET: *A few Douglas C–47s were experimentally fitted with amphibious floats, used as fuel tanks, in World War II.*
BELOW LEFT INSET: *More than 700 Supermarine Walruses served in World War II, mostly rescuing British pilots from coastal waters.*

World War II

Maritime aviation played a huge role in World War II – particularly in the form of carrier-borne landplanes, and most particularly in the Pacific Ocean war with Japan. Carrier flying, however, is described elsewhere in this book. (See pages 212–219.) Waterborne aircraft also operated in the war in large numbers; one type, the Consolidated PBY Catalina originally a 1935 design, was built in three countries (the USA, Canada, and the USSR) in a number totalling about 3,500 – the largest production run of any fly-

ABOVE: *The Martin PBM Mariner served as a transport, reconnaissance, air-sea rescue and anti-submarine aircraft with the US Navy in World War II.*

ing boat in history. Some PBYs are still flying today as water bombers.

Flying boats and floatplanes were employed for oceanic patrol duties, in particular reconnaissance and anti-submarine work, and for rescue duties at sea.

Germany operated several Dornier derivatives of the Wal, as well as the Heinkel He–59 twin-engined floatplane and Blohm und Voss flying boats, including the large six-engined Bv 222 Wiking – the largest flying boat in service with any nation in World War II. They also built a prototype of an even

ABOVE CENTRE: *More than 3,500 Consolidated PBY Catalinas were built in the USA, Canada and the USSR; the type was the most prominent maritime aircraft of World War II.*

bigger boat, the 60·17m (197ft 4¾in) span Bv 238, with six 1,750hp engines.

A very large US boat was the Martin Mars, with a maximum take-off weight of 65,770kg (145,000lb). Originally a long-range patrol aircraft ordered by the US Navy in 1938, the Mars served principally as a cargo transport. Four were retired by the US Navy in 1950, and operated in Canada for many years thereafter as civil forest-fire water bombers. In naval service Mars flying boats set several records, including carrying 9,300kg (20,500 lb) of payload over 7,564km (4,700 miles) to

TOP: *Three Blohm und Voss Ha 139 seaplanes were used by Lufthansa for transatlantic mail flights in the late 1930s. This shows one on the German depot ship* Schwabenland.

Hawaii and back in 1944, and in carrying the largest number of passengers then flown, 301 plus a crew of 10, on a flight over California on 19 May 1946.

The principal British type was the Short Sunderland, a development of the pre-war Empire civil boats. This large machine had a span of 34·38m (112ft 9½in), a take-off weight (in the Mk III version) of 26,000kg (58,000lb), a maximum endurance of 13½ hours and maximum speed of 330km/h (205 mph) on four Bristol Pegasus 1,050hp engines.

Hughes Hercules

Even more grandiose, and still one of the largest aeroplanes ever built, was the wooden Hughes H.2 Hercules, a 97·54m (320ft) span colossus powered by eight 3,000hp Pratt & Whitney piston engines, and designed to carry 700 passengers or freight and to weigh 177·16 tonnes (180 tons) at take-off. The H.2 was intended for production should a shortage of metal alloys develop; in the event there was no such shortage, and the war was over before the craft was ready. The prototype only made one flight, a hop of about a mile over Los Angeles harbour on 2 November 1947, when it was flown by the aircraft's sponsor, the millionaire Howard Hughes.

Saro Princess

Three prototypes of a gigantic new flying boat intended for commercial service were constructed in Britain between 1943 and 1953. The Saunders-Roe Princess was almost as large as the Hughes H.2, with a 66·75m (215ft) span and 149,685kg (330,000lb) take-off weight. It had the largest pressurized hull ever built, fully electric ('fly-by-wire') signalling to the controls, and was designed to carry a 18,000kg (40,000lb) payload at a cruising speed of 579km/h (360mph) at 11,278m (37,000ft). Power plants were ten 3,780hp Proteus propeller-turbine engines, eight of them coupled in pairs and driving contra-rotating propellers.

There were also two other fascinating Saunders-Roe projects: the Duchess, a four-jet passenger flying boat; and the P.192, a fantastic dream of a 1,000 passenger five-deck 24-jet-engined flying boat, to fly between England and Australia.

Jet flying boats

The Saunders-Roe Company experimented in the early post-war years with a jet fighter flying boat, the SR/A1: the aircraft proved too slow (805km/h: 500mph) to be competitive with landplane fighters, which were already some 160km/h (100mph) faster. A later design for a waterborne jet fighter was the Convair XF2Y–1 Sea Dart which did

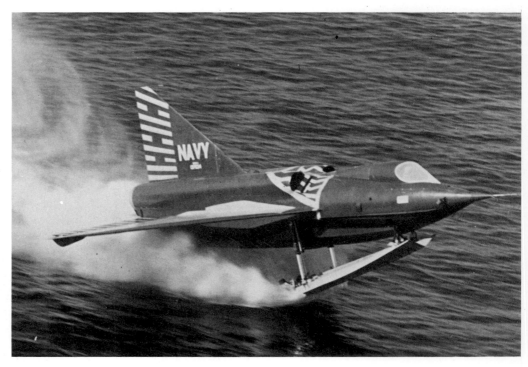

FAR LEFT: *The largest flying boat in the world in its day, the Martin Mars served as a cargo transport with the US Navy in the 1940s. In the mid-1950s four were modified to serve as fire-fighting water bombers in Canada.*
CENTRE LEFT: *Short Sunderlands served as patrol and anti-submarine craft in World War II. They were heavily armed, with up to ten machine guns.*
LEFT: *The ten-engined Saunders-Roe Princess was intended as a transatlantic airliner for BOAC; but engine problems and the development of landplane airliners doomed the project.*

BELOW LEFT: *The Saunders Roe SR/A1 was the world's first jet fighter flying boat. It was planned for service in the Pacific in World War II, but did not fly till 1947. Three were built and test-flown; with a maximum speed of only 800 km/h (500mph) they were too slow to succeed as fighters.*
BOTTOM LEFT: *The 1952 Convair XF2Y–1 Sea Dart was a revolutionary attempt to build a seaborne combat jet fighter, floating on a boat hull but rising on extendable hydroskis for take-off and landing. It is the only waterborne aircraft to have flown faster than sound. Only two were built, and one crashed.*

BELOW: *The Japanese Shin Meiwa PS–1 is one of the only two large flying boats of recent design in service today. It can operate in very rough water and has a notably wide range of operating speeds.*
BELOW CENTRE: *Two Martin XPM–1s were built in the late 1950s as prototypes of a bomber and mine layer for the US Navy; both crashed, and although three production Seamasters were built, the programme was abandoned.*
BOTTOM: *The twin-turboprop Beriev Be 12 amphibian is in service with the Soviet Navy and is comprehensively equipped with radar and electronic detection devices.*

not have a conventional boat hull but instead rose up for take-off on hydro-skis. This project, too, was abandoned after only four examples had been built. The type remains the only supersonic seaplane.

The US Navy remained interested in flying boats for some years; their 1952 design competition led to the Martin Seamaster four-jet patrol flying boat; however two prototypes crashed during flight testing, and only six other prototypes and three production aircraft were built, the programme being abandoned in 1960.

Japanese PS–1

Two major powers have, however, continued with military flying boat programmes. The Japanese Maritime Self-Defence Force operates the Shin Meiwa PS–1 four-turboprop anti-submarine and search-and-rescue flying boat and amphibian; and the manufacturer continues to evaluate passenger and water-bomber versions of the aircraft. The PS–1 employs a boundary layer control system, driven by a fifth engine, using blown flaps and control surfaces and has an automatic flight control system as well. Its long narrow hull serves both to reduce the high aerodynamic drag inherent in a flying boat design, and also enables it to operate in very rough water, in wind speeds of 47km/h (29 mph) and wave heights of up to 4m (13ft). An unusual spray suppression device is a long groove built into the chine of the hull forebody. The aircraft has a high maximum speed of 547km/h (340mph); yet its touchdown speed is only 76km/h (47mph) and it can take off in 305m (1,000ft) to clear 15m (50ft).

In the search-and-rescue role the amphibian version can take off from a land base, fly 1,100km (684 miles) out to sea at a cruising altitude of 3,050m (10,000ft) at a speed of 425km/h (264mph) and then search at low level for five hours. The aircraft is then able to land on the water and spend an hour picking up survivors before returning to base.

The water-bomber version could carry as much as 16,257kg (35,840lb) of water, picking this up through hull scoops while contacting the water surface for only 20 seconds at a speed of 55 knots (34mph).

Russian flying boats

The Soviet Naval Air Force also continues to operate twin-turboprop Beriev Be–12 amphibians; the same design bureau earlier produced the piston engined Be–6 and the twin-jet Be–10 flying boats. The Be–12 holds a number of world records, including an altitude record in its class of 12,185m (39,977ft).

Canadair CL–215

A recent civil amphibious design is the Canadair CL–215, powered by two 2,100hp Pratt & Whitney R–2800 piston engines. This Canadian design is intended primarily as a water bomber for use against forest fires, and is in service with the Canadian, French, Spanish and Greek governments – the Spanish aircraft are additionally equipped for search and rescue duties. The CL–215 can attack brush or forest fires with a variety of fire retardants: these include pre-mixed chemicals ground-loaded at a land aerodrome; short-term retardants mixed automatically with water scoop-loaded while taxying at speed across a lake; plain water scooped from any lake or the ocean; and pre-loaded foams for attacking oil fires. The aircraft can carry 5,455 litres (1,200 gallons) of water and can fill its tanks in under 20 seconds while skimming the water at 111km/h (69mph). It needs only a 1,220m (4,000ft) stretch of water for this purpose; on several occasions CL–215s have made more than 100 drops totalling almost 545,500 litres (144,110 gallons) of water in a single day. While fighting forest fires in Provence, full loads of water have been scooped from the Mediterranean in 2m (6ft) swells. Other flying boats have also been used for airborne fire-fighting and forestry protection. The Ontario Provincial Air Service pioneered these operations in 1924 with 13 HS2L flying boats, and now has about 50 aircraft, making it the largest service of its kind in the world.

Operating and piloting techniques

Operating and piloting techniques for water aircraft are interesting, and notably different from those of landplanes.

On the water with the motor cut or idling a seaplane always tends to weathercock into wind; power is always needed to turn it out of wind. At low power it tends either to creep into wind or drift back, depending on the relative strengths of wind, current and propeller thrust. The pilot should hold up-elevator at all times on the water, except towards the end of the take-off run. Taxying is always done at low speeds, except where there is a considerable distance to cover and when wind and water allow fast taxying 'on the step'. To get on the step the throttle is opened with the stick held hard back. At first the bows of the floats generate a considerable amount of spray – this reaches a peak at about 24km/h (15mph). As speed is gained the bows of the floats begin to rise out of the water and the spray moves back behind and below the propeller and the cabin. The aeroplane may then be taxied at speed. It is important not to stay at the in-between speeds where spray goes through the propeller, since in time it may cause damage: consequently seaplanes should be taxied either fast or very slowly.

When starting a turn out of the wind, wind and centrifugal force oppose each other, and turning is therefore easy. Turns through downwind require more care, as wind and centrifugal force are now combined to try to upset the craft. Furthermore, the downwind float may tend to dig in as the ship lists, causing more drag and requiring more rudder and more power to overcome it. If the wind is strong enough the downwind wingtip may even dig into the water, making capsizing a real possibility. Under such conditions it is best to close the throttle completely whereupon the sea plane will slow down and then weathercock into wind by itself.

To beach the ship cross-wind it is desirable to come at the shore at a modest speed; if this is attempted too slowly the aircraft may weathercock around out of control just when it should be beaching. Furthermore, the bow wave from the floats serves to cushion the shock of contact with the shore if this is done at constant power. If power is reduced at the last minute the bows tend to drop with a bump just as contact is made.

It is easiest to come up to a boat, buoy or raft into wind; where possible manoeuvres on the water should be done downwind of one's objective, which is then approached straight and into wind at minimum speed. A straight-in approach also enables the pilot to feel out the effect of wind and water on the aircraft's heading while still out in the open, and to find the slowest (and therefore safest) speed at which to maintain positive control.

Modern floatplanes have retractable water rudders connected to the main rudder circuits, which make manoeuvring appreciably easier. They hang down below the floats, and can be retracted during the take-off and landing runs to avoid any risk of damage to them from floating objects and vibration.

On breezy days and in confined spaces it is often easiest to manoeuvre a seaplane downwind by sailing it much like a boat. Here again the water rudders should be retracted, since they will tend to oppose the turning moment of the air rudder as the ship drifts backwards. Cutting one magneto will further reduce the propeller thrust at idle and help the plane drift backwards, as will lowering the flaps and opening the cabin door. The plane can be steered when sailing backwards by slightly increasing power and turning the air rudder.

In open water on a windy day 'step turns' are a useful if tricky means of turning downwind. From weathercocked into wind, the pilot slams open the throttle and pulls hard back on the stick to get the craft partially planing. Power is then reduced, but the heels of the floats are kept well dug in for stability. The ship may then be turned out of wind and all the way round to downwind, steering with the rudder and taking great care to keep the tilting force of the wind and centrifugal force neatly in balance.

Take-off and landing, performed into wind, are, by comparison with manoeuvring on the water, comparatively easy. For take-off the water rudders are raised, throttle opened wide and the stick pulled all the way back. As speed is gained the bows of the floats rise to a certain height and then flatten out. By now the aircraft is starting to plane, and the stick should be eased forward to a neutral position so the float heels do not dig in. Soon the seaplane is running on the central part of the float bottoms alone – this is the minimum drag condition allowing fastest acceleration to take-off speed. Once this stage is reached a slight back-pressure on the stick will allow

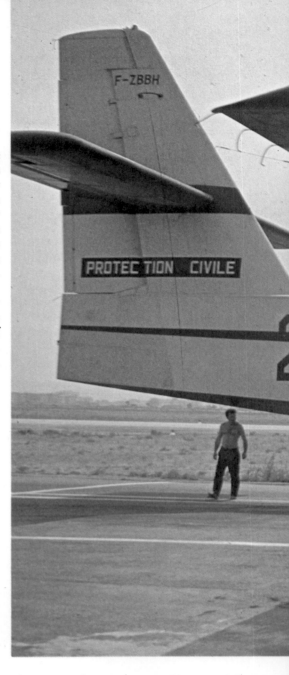

the plane to leave the water. If too much back pressure is applied the float heels may dig in again and slow the aircraft down. Similarly, attempting the take-off run with the nose too low wets more of the floats and delays the actual take-off. One quickly learns to feel the angle at which the aircraft will be best able to plane.

Water landings are similar to wheel landings, except that there is a broader range of safe attitudes at touchdown. On rough water the landing should be full-stall with maximum flap.

Special techniques are employed for landing on very calm water, particularly on misty days, for then water and sky merge imperceptibly so that it is quite impossible to judge one's height above the surface. In such conditions (called 'glassy water'), one tries to land alongside a shoreline, a boat or some other floating object to give one depth perception. Otherwise one simply sets up a very shallow descent on instruments with power, at low airspeed and waits until the floats make (hopefully) gentle contact with the surface – which may well be the first indication of just where it is.

As part of his preflight inspection, the seaplane pilot checks the bilges of each watertight compartment to be sure none is leaking. However, if he is mooring the aeroplane he may deliberately flood some compartments to make the craft heavy and less likely to lift in a wind. If a float is ever accidentally holed (by floating timber or a submerged rock) the craft must be beached at once.

Operation from seawater brings special problems, since salt is highly corrosive to aluminium. Seawater-based craft are usually hauled up the ramp at the day's end and hosed down with fresh water; land-based

time goes by. Fibreglass floats are now available which do not corrode; however, they are not yet as tough and resistant to damage as those made from light alloy.

The weight and drag of float assemblies mean floatplanes are inherently inferior in performance to landplanes. Yet in a few regions such as northern Canada and Alaska, which are inaccessible to other aircraft, the floatplane is still supreme.

ABOVE: *The Canadair CL–215 is a piston-engined amphibian widely employed as a water bomber for attacking forest fires.*
BELOW LEFT: *Pioneer bush fliers in Canada had little in the way of airport facilities and so operated on floats in summer and skis in winter. Here a Fairchild 71 of Canadian Pacific Airways is seen with a variety of stores for one of the remote areas.*
BELOW: *This Cessna floatplane operates a service for wealthy commuters from suburban Long Island to Wall Street, New York City.*

amphibians should be landed in fresh water after sea operations to wash the salt water from them. Seaplane structures are carefully corrosion-proofed during manufacture, yet this proofing tends to wear away in spots as

The construction of flying boats presents unusual technological problems. Flying boats must be able to float as well as to move along the water surface at near-flying speeds. Basically, two approaches have been developed: float construction and hull construction. In the former, floats or pontoons are substituted for wheels; in the latter, the aircraft is built with a boat-like structure.

FAR LEFT: *The He 45 was a general purpose military aircraft used for training and reconnaissance.*

BELOW FAR LEFT: *This Tiger Moth is used for training British Seaplane Club members in floatplane handling techniques.*

BELOW LEFT: *The Macchi M—12 was a World War I Italian seaplane. A three-seat coastal patrol flying boat, it had fore and aft gun positions connected by a tunnel in the fuselage so that both could be manned by one gunner. Side or wing tip floats were necessary to keep this single-hulled aircraft upright.*

BELOW: *The Short Shrimp was typical of seaplanes of the early inter-war period. Of twin-float construction, it also had a tail float attached directly to the underside of the rear fuselage. The tail float carried a hollow water rudder containing a spring-loaded drop-plate to improve steering while taxiing.*

LEFT: *Fifty-seven Supermarine Stranraers were built. They served with the RAF and RCAF from 1936 to 1940.*

ABOVE: *This twin-float Gloster IIIA biplane came second in the 1925 Schneider Trophy race.*

Lighter-than-Air

Balloons

It can be argued that the balloon is the most significant aircraft ever invented by man. Its original importance lay in the fact that for the very first time it enabled him to leave the surface of the Earth and travel freely in the air above, albeit at the whim of the breeze.

First demonstration of balloon flight

It has long been believed that the French brothers Etienne and Joseph Montgolfier were the originators of the hot-air balloon, the type of lighter-than-air craft with which man first achieved flight. But recent research has shown that in 1709 the Brazilian priest Bartolomeu de Gusmão demonstrated a model hot-air balloon at the court of King John V of Portugal. According to one Salvador Ferreira, the model balloon was constructed of thick paper and inflated by hot air. This came from 'fire material contained in an earthen bowl' which, as shown in a contemporary painting, was suspended beneath the open neck of the envelope.

On 8 August 1709, Gusmão presented his model balloon for examination by a distinguished and unimpeachable gathering which included the King, Queen Maria Anna, the Papal Nuncio and Cardinal Conti (later Pope Innocent III), together with princes, nobles, diplomats and other members of the court. It is recorded that the balloon rose to a height of 3·66m (12ft) before two valets, who feared it might set the curtains alight, ter-

PREVIOUS PAGES:
Hot-air balloons.

ABOVE: *The balloon built by the Montgolfier brothers, made of paper and filled with hot air. Its first ascent was made on 5 June 1783 at Annonay near Lyons.*
BELOW LEFT: *A drawing of the Montgolfier balloon, showing the hot air rising into it and (below) a plan of the balloon and its burner.*
BELOW RIGHT: *Lunardi's second balloon in which he, Mr Biggin and Mrs Sage (the first English lady aeronaut) ascended from St George's Fields on 29 June 1783. He had previously made an ascent on 13 May.*

minated its flight by knocking it to the ground. Thus, almost three-quarters of a century before the Montgolfiers, the principle of the hot-air balloon had already been demonstrated.

The Montgolfier brothers

Many stories, doubtless fanciful, have been told to explain the way in which Etienne and Joseph Montgolfier discovered that hot air rises, and how they concluded that if contained in an envelope of sufficient size it would have enough 'lift' to raise passengers into the air.

The choice of paper for the envelope of their first balloon must have seemed natural to the brothers, who were paper-makers by trade. The balloon, fairly rigid, stood over a pit containing wool and straw which when ignited filled the balloon's envelope with hot air. On 25 April 1783, the first successful Montgolfière took to the air at Annonay near Lyons in France. It is reported to have risen to a height of about 305m (1,000ft) and travelled about 91m (3,000ft) horizontally before it fell to the ground as the air in the envelope cooled.

The brothers gave a public demonstration at Annonay on 4 June 1783, when a new balloon rose to about 1,830m (6,000ft). This success resulted in a summons to the capital, so that King Louis XVI could see the Montgolfier's invention for himself. A balloon some 13m (42ft) in diameter was constructed especially for the event, and a basket hung

beneath it to carry the world's first aerial voyagers: a cock, a duck and a sheep.

The balloon was launched at the Court of Versailles on 19 September 1783, climbing to approximately 550m (1,800ft) before the astonished gaze of King Louis, Marie Antoinette and their court. It landed about 3·2km (2 miles) away, and there was some concern when the cock was discovered to be a little the worse for his adventure. Had he been weakened by the great altitude at which the balloon had flown? Further investigation suggested that he was probably suffering from the effects of being trampled or sat on by the sheep.

The moment was fast approaching for manned flight, for which the Montgolfiers created a magnificent new balloon 15m (49 ft) in diameter. Superbly decorated in a blue-and-gold colour scheme, it was emblazoned with the royal cipher, signs of the zodiac, eagles and smiling suns. Around its open neck was attached a wicker gallery capable of accommodating one or two men. In this vehicle the 26-year-old François Pilâtre de Rozier made a tethered flight to 26m (85ft) on 15 October 1783 and remained airborne for about 4½ minutes.

Just over a month later, on 21 November 1783, de Rozier and his passenger, the Marquis d'Arlandes, became the first men in the world to be carried in free flight by a balloon. They rose from the garden of the Chateau La Muette in the Bois de Boulogne, Paris, and were airborne for 25 minutes before landing

ABOVE: *A print showing the inflation of a* Charlière
(Charles' hydrogen balloon) in about 1783.
ABOVE RIGHT: *The Montgolfier balloon over
Versailles on 19 September 1783, carrying a cock,
a duck and a sheep.*
RIGHT: *The* Charlière *hydrogen balloon which
came down at Gonesse near Paris on 27 August 1783,
and was attacked and destroyed by the local inhabitants.*
BELOW RIGHT: *The hot air balloon in which
Pilâtre de Rozier and the Marquis d'Arlandes
made the first free balloon flight by man.*

about 8·5km (5·3 miles) from their departure
point.

The first hydrogen balloon

A couple of decades before the Montgolfier
flights, in 1766, the British scientist Henry
Cavendish had isolated a gas which he called
Phlogiston. Weighing only 2·4kg (5·3lb) per
28·3m³ (1,000cu ft) by comparison with 34·5
kg (76lb) for the same volume of air at standard temperature and pressure, it seemed
likely to prove invaluable for lighter-than-air
flight.

By 1790 this gas had been named hydrogen by the French chemist Lavoisier. Seven
years earlier on 27 August 1783, Professor
Jacques A. C. Charles had launched successfully a small, unmanned Phlogiston-filled
balloon. Flown from the Champs-de-Mars,
Paris, it was airborne for about 45 minutes
before coming to earth some 25km (15·5
miles) away at Gonesse. There it was attacked
with pitchforks by panic-stricken villagers,
who believed it to be some strange device of
the devil and who were not satisfied until it
had been torn to shreds.

To construct the envelope of the balloon,
Professor Charles had sought the assistance
of two brothers named Robert. They had devised a method of rubberizing silk to make
it leak-proof. With their help, following the
successful flight of the model, Charles designed and built a man-carrying balloon.
This balloon of 1783 was essentially the same
as a modern gas-filled sporting design, and in

it Professor Charles and one of the Robert brothers, Marie-Noel, became the first men in the world to fly in a hydrogen-filled balloon. Ascending in front of an estimated 400,000 people from the Tuileries Gardens in Paris on 1 December 1783, they completed successfully a flight of 43·5km (27 miles) in two hours. The balloon was 8·6m (28·2ft) in diameter and had a volume of about 325·5m³ (11,500cu ft).

The balloon goes to war

The success of the *Charlière*, as Charles's craft was named, generated tremendous interest in the balloon as a sporting vehicle, a money-spinner for showmen and daredevils, a possible means of exploration and, of course, as a weapon of war. Within days of de Rozier's first flight in the Montgolfier's hot-air balloon, he had taken up one André Giraud de Vilette as a passenger. Afterwards, in a letter to the *Journal de Paris* de Vilette commented on the ease with which he had viewed the environs of Paris. 'From this moment,' he wrote, 'I was convinced that this apparatus, costing but little, could be made very useful to an army for discovering the positions of its enemy, his movements, his advances, and his dispositions . . .'

Not surprisingly, the French were the first to take the balloon to war. Four military balloons – the *Entreprenant*, *Celeste*, *Hercule* and *Intrepide* – were constructed and a Company of Aérostiers formed as a component of the Artillery Service under the command of Captain Coutelle. On 26 June 1794, Coutelle ascended in the balloon *Entreprenant* during the battle of Fleurus in Belgium. Information signalled by Coutelle is believed to have played a significant part in the defeat of the Austrians. This flight represented the first operational use of an aircraft in war.

The spread of ballooning

Before the balloon's military debut, the first ascent by a woman had been recorded, as had first flights in Britain, Italy and America, and the first aeronaut, François de Rozier and a companion, Jules Romain, had been killed in a ballooning accident on 15 June 1785, while attempting a crossing of the English Channel from Boulogne in a combination hydrogen and hot-air balloon. The cause of the accident was unknown, but as the envelope was destroyed by flame it was believed that hydrogen had ignited during the venting of gas to control altitude.

The Channel had already been crossed, however, on 7 January 1785, by Jean-Pierre Blanchard of France and the American Dr John Jeffries. They took off from Dover, Kent, on a bitterly cold day and in a balloon which had only a small margin of lift when laden with the two men and their equipment. To avoid a ducking they had to throw overboard everything possible, including most of their clothes, but the two half-frozen gentlemen landed safely in the Forêt de Felmores, France, some two and a half hours later.

Balloons in America

Jean-Pierre Blanchard was well known as a

LEFT: *M. Charles and M. Robert descending in the presence of the Duc de Charle at Nesle on 1 December 1783, after making the first aerial voyage in a hydrogen balloon. It rose again with M. Charles alone in it and then descended after a trip of three miles.*
BELOW LEFT: *A military observation balloon in use at the siege of Mayence, 1794.*
BELOW: *Blanchard and Jeffries' historic cross-Channel flight on 7 January 1785, from Dover to the forest around Guines, near Calais, took two and a half hours to complete.*

ABOVE: *A tethered hydrogen balloon used by the French for observation purposes at the battle of Fleurus in Belgium on 26 June 1794, when they defeated the Austrians.*
RIGHT: *Jean-Pierre Blanchard making a flight over Berlin on 27 September 1788. He was one of the best known early balloonists after his cross-Channel flight.*
BOTTOM: *Another of Blanchard's pioneering balloon flights. In this picture he is shown at Lille, France, during a parade. A large crowd stand admiring.*

balloonist in Europe before his crossing of the English Channel. Dr Jeffries must have then suggested that he visit America, because eight years later Blanchard arrived in Philadelphia, where arrangements were made for a flight from the yard of the old Walnut Street Prison. At the appointed time, 10AM on 9 January 1793, a large part of the city's population turned out to witness the historic event. They numbered among them President George Washington, as well as John Adams, Thomas Jefferson, James Madison and James Monroe, all four of whom were subsequently to become presidents of the United States.

The president handed Blanchard a letter asking 'all citizens of the United States, and others, that in his passage, descent or journeyings elsewhere, they oppose no hindrance or molestation to the said Mr Blanchard.' After wishing him a safe journey, the president joined the assembled thousands to watch the balloon rise easily into the sky. Some 46 minutes later Blanchard landed safely about 24km (15 miles) away.

Ballooning in America expanded rapidly after this first demonstration. But unlike the French government, those in authority in America could visualize no military employment for the balloon. One significant flight caused ballooning in the United States to be regarded in an entirely new light. On 2 July 1859, John Wise, John La Montain and O. A. Gager flew 1,770km (1,100 miles) from St Louis, Missouri, to Henderson, New York.

This achievement brought the realization that long-distance travel by balloon was possible, and a number of people discussed seriously and planned a transatlantic flight. Among them was a flamboyant showman named Thaddeus Sobieski Constantine Lowe. He made a balloon 39·6m (130ft) in diameter with a reported gross lift of 20 tons. Named the *Great Western*, this balloon was weakened during a trial flight on 28 June 1860, and finally burst when the gas pressure proved too much. Finding that the *Great Western* was beyond repair, Lowe, still intent on flying across the Atlantic, built a second balloon, which was named the *Enterprise*.

Balloons in the American Civil War

In April 1861 the first shots of the American Civil War were fired. On 15 April President Abraham Lincoln called for troops and four days later balloonist James Allen and a friend were among those who volunteered, taking along two balloons. They were the spiritual fathers of today's enormous US Air Force, making their first military ascent on 9 June 1861. Other balloonists to join the Union Army included John Wise, John La Montain and Thaddeus Lowe.

On 18 June 1861, the latter demonstrated the potential of captive balloons for military reconnaissance. Climbing to a height of 152m (500ft) in the *Enterprise*, Lowe, a telegraph operator and an official of the telegraph com-

pany Balloon Corps of the Army of the Potomac.

But this first 'air force' was to last only 18 months. Though Lowe was a powerful driving force, the majority of his men were apathetic. When he resigned in May 1863 Lowe had made more than 3,000 ascents. His departure marked the end of the Balloon Corps, and almost 30 years were to pass before the US Army renewed its interest in military aviation.

Balloons in the Siege of Paris

When Paris was encircled by the Prussian army in September 1870 Chancellor Bismarck believed that the beleagured city would surrender quickly, being completely isolated from the rest of the world. But he had

pany sent the first air telegraph through a wire trailing to the ground. In it he told President Lincoln: 'This point of observation commands an area nearly 50 miles (80km) in diameter. The city, with its girdle of encampments, presents a superb scene...'

The president was suitably impressed, but it was not until early August 1861 that Lowe received his first official instructions. Ordered to construct a balloon of 708m³ (25,000cu ft) capacity, he flew the *Union* within three weeks. On 24 September Lowe made military history. He observed the fall of artillery fire from the *Union* and transmitted corrections by telegraph. The results were so good that Lowe was almost immediately tasked with providing four more balloons and crews to form the

not counted on the balloon as a means of carrying important passengers and dispatches out of Paris.

Under the leadership of Gaspard-Felix Tournachon the balloonists of Paris formed the *Compagnie d'Aérostiers Militaires*, intending to use captive balloons to observe Prussian army movements. On 23 September 1870, the balloon *Neptune* took off from the Place St Pierre. Piloted by Jules Duruof, *Neptune* landed three hours later at Evreux, some 97 km (60 miles) away. The 125kg (275lb) of mail and dispatches carried out of the city by Duruof was then sent on its way by more conventional means. The world's first airmail service had been inaugurated.

At the beginning of the siege there were

only five or six balloons in the city, so arrangements were made to mass-produce further examples. 'Production' lines were started at the Gare d'Orléans and at a derelict music hall in the Elysées-Montmartre. New pilots were also needed, and circus acrobats and sailors – selected because they were likely to have a good head for heights – were trained to fly the balloons out of Paris.

The balloons offered only a one-way service, leaving Paris in the direction of the wind. Messages from outside were brought into Paris by carrier pigeons flown out in the balloons. The number of communications a single pigeon could carry was very limited until a Monsieur Barreswil hit on the idea of photographing and reducing the letters and dispatches so that one bird could transport many more messages. Once delivered, these 'microfilms' could be enlarged to readability. During World War II this idea was to be developed into the Airgraph system to cater for the large volume of forces (and later civilian) airmail.

By the end of the siege, when a final sortie flown on 28 January 1871, carried news of the armistice, some 64 balloons had taken 155 passengers and crew to safety and 2½ to 3 million letters had reached destinations outside Paris. In the other direction, some 60,000 messages had been carried by 60 pigeons.

The siege gave rise to one other invention: the anti-aircraft gun. Not surprisingly, the Prussians were infuriated at the sight of im-

portant people and vital information floating to safety over their heads. Krupps, the famous armament manufacturers, responded by producing a special anti-balloon gun which could be elevated to fire at balloons passing over at altitude.

Military balloons in Britain

Although the first balloon flights in Britain took place in 1784, it was not until 1878 that the British Army showed any interest, allocating £150 for the construction of a balloon. Captains J. L. B. Templer and H. P. Lee were responsible for developing the *Pioneer*, which in 1879 became the first balloon to enter the Army's inventory. The first balloon to be actually used by the Army was Captain Tem-

pler's own *Crusader*, which entered service shortly afterwards.

On 24 June 1880, a balloon detachment was involved in military manoeuvres at Aldershot, Hampshire. Four years later the first British balloon detachment ordered to fly in support of military operations was sent to Bechuanaland. Arriving in Cape Town on 19 December 1884, this unit comprised 2 officers, 15 other ranks and 3 balloons. But order was restored in the colony without a shot having to be fired, and they never saw action.

In 1885 a detachment was sent to the Sudan, and in 1899 a balloon was used to keep an eye on the movements of the Boers besieging Ladysmith.

LEFT: *Auguste Piccard designed this airtight, pressurized and air-conditioned gondola to be suspended from a balloon, in which he set an altitude record of 16,201m (53,153ft) in 1932. The previous year he had made the first flight into the stratosphere.*
BELOW LEFT: *The Italian Avorio-Prassone.*
BELOW RIGHT: *Not far from the British detachment in Flanders with their spherical observation balloon (late 1914) was a Belgian detachment complete with a German Drachen kite balloon.*

ABOVE: *The balloon detachment of the Prussian Army in 1884 at Tempelhof Field Berlin, with their partly inflated balloon.*
RIGHT: *A tethered kite balloon used for observation purposes by the German Army, seen here partially inflated.*
BELOW FAR RIGHT: *A row of barrage balloons in 1940. They were used by the British at possible targets such as airfields to present a hazard to enemy aircraft, and to deter them from mounting low-level attacks.*

Development of military balloons

The conventional spherical balloon is quite at home when travelling freely with the wind. But when restrained by a rope anchored to the ground it can spin and buck so badly that the observation crew can soon lose interest in everything but a rapid return to the ground.

To overcome this problem the kite balloon was developed and brought close to perfection by the Germans August von Parseval and H. B. von Sigsfeld. They took the partly controllable sausage-shaped observation balloon of the time and added a tail fin to keep it pointing steadily into the wind. The French army officer Captain Caquot later developed this design by improving the streamlining of the basic shape and introducing three inflated tail fins disposed at 120° intervals, with one pointing vertically downward. Like the single fin of the von Parseval Drachen, they were inflated by an airscoop facing into the wind. The Caquot type was used extensively for aerial observation both on land and at sea during World War I. By the beginning of World War II the balloon had long since been superseded by heavier-than-air craft in this role. Instead, barrage balloons were used in large numbers to present a hazard to enemy aircraft and deter low-level attacks.

One unusual military application of the balloon came during World War II, when the Japanese tried to attack North America from the home islands. Launched into the jetstream winds prevailing at a fixed altitude, bomb-carrying balloons proved capable of crossing the Pacific. They were equipped

with an ingenious barometric device which worked in conjunction with an automatic gas-discharge valve to keep the balloon at the desired altitude of between 9,144m (30,000ft) and 11,582m (38,000ft). The higher daytime temperature would have caused the balloon, if unchecked, to ascend until it burst as the gas expanded. The valve discharged gas, and so reduced buoyancy and caused the balloon to descend. When the required altitude was reached the barometric device energized an electrical ballast-discharge circuit, causing the balloon to rise again. Enough ballast was carried for the 9,978km (6,200 miles) Pacific crossing. When the last of this had been jettisoned, the weapon load of two incendiary bombs and one 15kg (33lb) anti-personnel device was released during the next low-level cycle. A small explosive charge was detonated to destroy the balloon.

It was calculated that weapon-release would occur over the not insignificant target represented by the North American continent. Of about 9,000 balloons launched, between 11 and 12 per cent are believed to have completed the crossing. Despite this comparatively large number of weapons over the target, the damage was confined largely to fires in open areas and proved of little consequence.

Only six people were killed in the campaign, and the bomb-carrying balloons were finally countered by a complete ban on radio and newspaper reports. As a result, the Japanese were unaware of the operation's technical success and called it off. Had they known that one in eight of these weapons were reaching the target they might have launched many more, equipping them with a far more potent payload.

Scientific use of balloons

Balloons have also played a significant part in scientific research from the earliest days. J. A. C. Charles made recordings of air temperature and changes in barometric pressure during his first ascent in a hydrogen balloon on 1 December 1783. In 1784 Jean-Pierre Blanchard and Dr Jeffries made similar recordings.

In 1804 the French scientist Gay-Lussac made two flights to investigate the way in which the Earth's magnetic field varied with increasing altitude. In Britain James Glaisher made 28 ascents for scientific purposes during 1862 to 1866. On one occasion Glaisher became unconscious with the balloon still ascending at an altitude which he estimated at 8,839m (29,000ft). He survived, but the companions of Gaston Tissandier were not so lucky; they died during an ascent in 1875. (See page 139). In Germany, Professor Assman continued the work begun by Glaisher, achieving more significant results with his more highly developed instruments. By 1932 the Swiss physicist Auguste Piccard had climbed 16,201m (53,153ft) in a sealed capsule suspended beneath his free balloon, having made the first flight into the stratosphere during the previous year. Some great heights have been reached, notably 34,668m (113,740ft) by US Navy reservist Commander Malcolm D. Ross on 4 May 1961. Unmanned balloons also have meteorological uses; some small ones indicate wind direction and speed, others carry instrument packages for transmitting data to earth.

Airships

In the 18th and 19th centuries the balloon had made many things possible, but there were some serious problems to be overcome if men were to travel easily by air from point to point. These shortcomings can be summarized briefly: the balloon could travel only in the direction of the wind; and at the end of each flight all the costly lifting gas had to be valved off to allow the balloon to be packed and transported back to its home base. Such disadvantages were acceptable to sportsmen, but they made the balloon completely impractical for most military or commercial tasks. What was needed was an independent source of power to render balloons navigable.

Steerable balloons: the first ideas

Once airborne the balloon is wedded to the wind, moving in the same direction and at the same speed. It has no independent motion within the airstream which would allow the rudders or sails proposed by many inventors to affect its direction of movement. So despite some ingenious plans to utilize muscle power, the evolution of a steerable balloon had to await the development of a compact power unit. By propelling the vehicle independently of the wind, such an engine would make it possible for rudders and elevators to control direction.

While balloonists waited for a suitable powerplant they came to realize that the spherical balloon was hardly ideal in shape for steering anywhere. They therefore began to streamline it into a spindle shape not so different from more modern solutions. But

ABOVE: Pétain's giant multiple airship built in 1850. It was constructed of several balloons linked together by a single undercarriage. It was a design very much ahead of its time, but in fact never flew.
BELOW: A drawing of an airship suspended from copper spheres in which a vacuum has been created, designed by Francis Lana, a Jesuit physicist, in 1670. It had a sail and oars for propulsion.

FAR RIGHT CENTRE: Details for a proposed 'aerostatic machine' or airship designed by Meusnier in 1785. This model never got beyond the drawing board.
FAR RIGHT BELOW: The first successful airship constructed by Henri Giffard in 1852. It was powered by a small steam-engine also designed by Giffard, which developed approximately 3hp. He flew in it from Paris to Trappes on 24 September 1852.

the early experimenters were disappointed to find that despite this 'ideal' shape, muscle-powered oars or propellers were incapable of steering their prototype airships.

The first practical airships

The autumn of 1852 saw French engineer, Henri Giffard, preparing for flight a vehicle which has the distinction of being the first powered and manned airship. He had constructed an envelope 43·9m (144ft) in length, pointed at each end and with a maximum diameter of 11·9m (39ft). Capacity of the envelope was 2,492m³ (88,000cu ft), and from it were slung a car containing the powerplant and pilot.

The power source was a steam engine designed by Giffard which weighed about 45kg (100lb) and developed approximately 3hp. The engine, boiler, three-blade propeller and an hour's supply of water and fuel weighed 210kg (463lb). The propeller, 3·35m (11ft) in diameter, was driven at a maximum speed of 110rpm. The airship was to be steered by what Giffard called a keel, a triangular vertical sail mounted at the aft end of the long

TOP: *The airship* La France *designed by Renard and Krebs in 1884, which made the first fully controlled flight by an airship.*
ABOVE: *Masse's design for an airship propelled and controlled by oars.*
RIGHT: *The nacelle and engines of the airship built by the French Tissandier brothers in 1883. It was driven by a 1·5hp electric motor. This illustration (engraved from a photograph) shows the brothers in it.*

horizontal pole to which the gondola was attached. It was effectively a rudimentary rudder.

On 24 September 1852, Henri Giffard piloted his airship from the Paris Hippodrome to Trappes some 27km (16·8 miles) away at an average speed of 8km/h (5mph). This flight must have been made in virtually still air if it was in fact steered: control must have been marginal at such a low speed, and the airship would have been carried away if there had been any wind at all. Giffard's craft was nonetheless the first true airship.

The next important development came from the German Paul Hänlein, who in December 1872 flew a small airship at Brünn in Central Europe. Its 6hp gas engine was fuelled by the coal gas which filled the envelope. Designed by Etienne Lenoir, this powerplant was a development of his basic single-cylinder gas engine, first demonstrated in 1860. Hänlein's airship was not a success, but it is remembered for its powerplant, the first internal-combustion engine to take to the air. In 1883 the Tissandier brothers of France built and flew an airship powered by a 1·5hp electric motor. It was driven by primitive batteries which together with the motor weighed about 200kg (440lb), giving an improbably low power:weight ratio of 1hp:293lb. Despite this, the Tissandier airship was at that time marginally the most successful.

The following year saw the most important of the early airships, *La France*, designed by Captains Charles Renard and A. C. Krebs

of the French Corps of Engineers. With an envelope of 1,869m³ (66,000cu ft) capacity, it was 50·3m (165ft) long and had a maximum diameter of 8·23m (27ft). Beneath the envelope was suspended a lightweight gondola which extended for about two-thirds of the length of the vessel. It comprised a framework of bamboo covered by silk, and in it was mounted the powerplant, a 9hp electric motor drawing on specially developed batteries. This drove a four-blade tractor propeller of 7m (23ft) diameter. A total powerplant weight of 857kg (1,890lb) gave a power:weight ratio of 1:210. Though still impractically low, this figure nevertheless represented a considerable advance on the Tissandier engine.

On 9 August 1884, Renard and Krebs lifted off in *La France* from Chalais-Meudon, France. They completed a circular course of about 8km (5 miles), reaching a maximum speed of 23·5km/h (14·6mph) en route. This is regarded as the first fully controlled powered flight by a manned airship anywhere in the world. *La France* made a further six flights later that year and in the following one.

Development of the Airship

In spite of these achievements, electric motors powered by storage batteries were clearly impractical. Like the pioneers of heavier-than-air flight, those who believed that the airship represented the best method of air transport had to await the availability of a light and compact power source. Their patience was rewarded when an airship powered by a single-cylinder Daimler petrol engine was flown successfully on 12 August 1888. This was designed by the German Dr Karl Wëlfert, who was later to die in an airship. A flame from the petrol engine's exhaust is believed to have ignited gas being vented from the envelope.

Next on the scene with an airship powered by an internal-combustion engine was the Brazilian Alberto Santos-Dumont. He achieved a first successful flight in Paris on 20 September 1898, in a craft powered by a small motor-cycle engine. This little power-plant drove his *No 1* along quickly enough in relation to the day's light breeze that he could steer the craft in the chosen direction.

But it was his *No 6* of 1901 that brought Santos-Dumont real fame. In it he won the 100,000 franc prize offered by M Deutsch de la Meurthe, a wealthy member of the Aéro Club, for a flight of about 11·3km (7 miles) from the *Parc d'Aérostation* at St Cloud, around the Eiffel Tower and back. *No 6* was pointed at both ends and had an overall length of 33m (108ft 3in), a maximum diameter of 6m (19ft 8in) and a hydrogen capacity of 622m³ (21,966cu ft). Suspended from

the envelope was a lightweight girder keel supporting the small control basket which accommodated the pilot, engine, tanks, pusher propeller and triangular rudder. Power-plant was a Buchet petrol engine based on the Daimler-Benz design and fitted with a water-cooling system. Developing about 15hp, it drove a crude two-blade pusher propeller.

The first Zeppelin

The airships discussed so far belonged to the classes known as non-rigids and semi-rigids. In the former the shape of the envelope was maintained by gas pressure alone; in the latter a rigid keel permitted a lower gas pressure. One of the drawbacks of these two types was that diminishing gas pressure brought a

change in the shape of the vessel, and a serious pressure reduction could lead to the collapse of the forward end of the envelope. The resulting drag usually proved too much for the feeble powerplants of the day and was likely to thwart any attempts to steer the vehicle.

Though it was appreciated that a rigid airship would be far more practical, the weight penalty imposed by a rigid frame or envelope was unacceptable in the early years of airship development. The Austrian David Schwarz nevertheless designed an airship with a rigid aluminium-sheet envelope – reported to be 0·2mm (0·008in) thick – attached to a light-weight tubular framework braced by internal steel tension wires. Overall length was 47·55 m (156ft) and gas capacity 3,681m³ (130,000 cu ft). Power was provided by a 12hp Daimler petrol engine driving four propellers, two of which were for propulsion and two for directional control. When the airship flew for the first time, on 3 November 1897, the belt drives to the propellers were found to be useless. The ship drifted for about 6·5km (4 miles) before landing heavily and breaking up in the wind.

Meanwhile, a significant figure had taken the stage in Germany, Count Ferdinand von Zeppelin. Visting America during the Civil War, he had taken to the air for the first time in one of the Army's balloons at St Paul, Minnesota. Impressed by this flight, influenced by a lecture on airship travel by the German Postmaster-General, and concerned at the comparative success of Renard and Krebs' *La France*, Count Zeppelin was convinced that it was his duty to provide Germany with a fleet of military airships.

In 1899 he began the construction of his first rigid airship, *Luftschiff Zeppelin 1*, (LZ1) in a floating shed on Lake Constance. Like many pioneers before and after him, the Count seems to have believed erroneously that in the event of a heavy landing the surface of the lake would prove more forgiving than the ground.

Zeppelin's airship was truly a giant for its day, measuring 128m (420ft) in length and having a maximum diameter of 11·73m (38 ft 6in). Its 11,327m³ (400,000cu ft) of gas was contained in 17 separate cells, an entirely new feature. Only its engines were less than huge: the two Daimlers together produced a mere 30hp for a weight of 771kg (1,700lb), giving a power:weight ratio of 1:57. Although this represented a great improvement on the airship *La France*, the enormous LZ1 needed large reserves of power if it was to be controllable in anything but still air. When the Zeppelin flew for the first time, on 2 July 1900, it was apparent immediately that it was grossly underpowered. Instead of flying at the expected 45km/h (28mph), the LZ1 had a maximum speed of only 26km/h (16 mph). This would have given marginal controllability if the vessel had been equipped with efficient aerodynamic controls. Miniature rudders at bow and stern were expected to provide directional control, and a 250kg (551lb) weight could be slid fore and aft on a track between the two gondolas to take care of vertical control.

Not surprisingly, after two more test flights giving a total airborne time of two hours, LZ1 was scrapped in 1901. It was not until four years later than von Zeppelin began construction of the LZ2, but by then an important airship had been built and flown in France.

BELOW: *A Lebaudy dirigible. This particular one was built for the British Army and is here seen leaving its hangar. In 1903 the first Lebaudy airship made the first controlled air journey by a practical dirigible, from Moisson to the Champ-de-Mars, Paris, a distance of 61km (38 miles). The airships were designed by Paul and Pierre Lebaudy.*

BELOW CENTRE: *One of the five airships designed and constructed by Ernest Willows, seen on 20 September 1913. They were all comparatively small dirigibles.*
BOTTOM: *The Spencer airship ascending at Ranelagh in Great Britain in 1903, watched by a crowd of admiring onlookers.*

is considered to be the first-ever controlled air journey by a practical dirigible. The Lebaudy airship subsequently suffered serious damage at Chalais Meudon. It was repaired and handed over in 1906 to the French government. Other examples were built for the French Army, Britain and Russia each acquired one, and a final example was built under licence in Austria.

Airship pioneers in America

The first true powered dirigible to be built in the United States was Captain Thomas S. Baldwin's *California Arrow*. With an envelope 15·85m (52ft) in length and powered by a two-cylinder motor-cycle engine built by Glenn H. Curtiss, it was flown for the first time on 3 August 1904, at Oakland, California, piloted by Roy Knabenshue. When Brigadier General J. Allen of the US Army subsequently saw it in flight at St Louis, Missouri, he was so impressed that he per-

The first controlled air journey

Under the guidance of an engineer, Henri Julliot, the brothers Paul and Pierre Lebaudy designed and completed an airship at Moisson, Seine-et-Oise, in 1902. It was strange in appearance, with an envelope 57·9 m (190ft) in length and pointed sharply at each end. Beneath the envelope – made of two-ply rubberized material and with a capacity of 2,000m³ (70,629cu ft) – was a steel-tube structure carrying a basketwork gondola to contain the powerplant and crew. The German-manufactured engine developed about 35hp, driving two pusher propellers.

First flown early in 1903, it made a number of successful local flights and, on 12 November 1903, was flown 61km (38 miles) from Moisson to the Champs-de-Mars, Paris. This

suaded the War Department to request tenders for the supply of a dirigible.

Baldwin's tender proved to be the lowest and on 20 July 1908, a 29·26m (96ft) dirigible powered by a 20hp Curtiss engine was delivered to Fort Myer, Virginia. When accepted on 28 August 1908, it was designated Dirigible No 1. The pilots trained to fly it were Lieutenants Frank P. Lahm, Benjamin D. Foulois and Thomas E. Selfridge. The Baldwin ship remained in service for three years before being scrapped, and was for all practical purposes the one and only US Army dirigible. Its engine and propeller can be seen to this day in the Smithsonian Institution.

At about this time the wealthy and eccentric journalist Walter Wellman hired Melvin Vaniman and Louis Godard to design and build a dirigible for a flight to the North Pole. The resulting *America* was 69·49m (228ft) long, had a capacity of 9,911m³ (350,000cu ft) and was powered by a single 80hp engine. A canvas-covered hangar for the airship was completed at Dane's Island, Spitzbergen, in September 1906. A year later, a first attempt to reach the Pole ended when the *America* was forced down in a snowstorm. The airship was recovered and fitted with a second engine, and another polar flight was tried two years later, but unfortunately this also proved a failure.

A transatlantic attempt followed in 1910, with the *America* lifting off from Atlantic City, New Jersey, on 15 October. Three days later the five-man crew was rescued off New England by a British ship, the RMS *Trent*.

Airship developments in Britain

The earliest practical British airship was the first of five designed and constructed by Ernest Willows between 1905 and 1914. Willows' *No 1* was only 22·56m (74ft) in length and was powered by a 7hp Peugeot engine. *No 3* achieved the first airship flight across the English Channel, travelling from London to Paris. The largest Willows ship, *No 5*, had only 1,416m³ (50,000cu ft) of gas capacity, and they were distinguished (with the exception of *No 1*) by their swivelling engines, which assisted in manoeuvring the vessels laterally and vertically.

Britain's first military airship, British Army Dirigible No 1, was built by the Balloon Fac-

tory at Farnborough, Hants. Known unofficially as *Nulli Secundus*, this non-rigid had an envelope 37·19m (122ft) in length, 7·92m (26ft) in diameter, and with a capacity of 1,557m³ (55,000cu ft). No suitable engine was available, so Balloon Factory commanding officer Colonel J. E. Capper obtained an Antoinette engine of about 50hp from Paris. This was installed along with the crew positions in a small car suspended beneath the envelope. *Nulli Secundus* flew for the first time on 10 September 1907, piloted by Colonel Capper and with the colourful Samuel F. Cody as engineer. A month later this airship flew from Farnborough to London, causing great excitement when it circled St Paul's Cathedral. Its maximum speed of about 26 km/h (16mph) ruled out a return journey that day, however, and a landing was made in the grounds of the Crystal Palace.

Redesigned in the following year, *Nulli Secundus* acquired a triangular-section fabric-covered keel which made her a semi-rigid, and the addition of pointed ends to the envelope provided another 28·3m³ (1,000cu ft) of capacity. These changes improved maximum speed to 35km/h (22mph).

She was followed by the *Beta* (unofficially *Baby*), which measured 25·6m (84ft) in length and 7·52m (24ft 8in) in diameter, and had a capacity of 623m³ (22,000cu ft). The original pair of 8hp Buchet engines were later re-

placed by a single 25hp radial engine driving two propellers. *Beta* was also rebuilt, and when flown in May 1910 had a gas capacity of 934m³ (33,000cu ft) and a British-built Green in-line engine developing 35hp. In this form *Beta* could carry a crew of three and had a powered endurance of about five hours. The first practical airship to serve with any of Britain's armed services, *Beta* was flown at night in June 1910 and in a summer of activity was reported to have flown some 1,609km (1,000 miles) without any serious problems.

Later military airships included *Gamma* of 1912, which demonstrated a maximum speed of 51km/h (32mph); the 1912 *Delta*, capable of 71km/h (44mph); and *Eta* of 1913, reported to have a speed of 67·5km/h (42mph) and an endurance of up to ten hours.

ABOVE: *The British airship* HMA Gamma, *built in 1912, seen here leaving its hangar. This was a non-rigid military dirigible in service with the British Army, which attained a maximum speed of 51km/h (32mph).*
LEFT: *Baldwin's Dirigible no. 1, constructed for the United States Army Signal Corps in 1908, and here seen in flight at Fort Myer, Virginia. It remained in service until 1911 and was the only practical non-rigid airship used by the US Army.*
BELOW: *The first British Naval airship* Mayfly *outside its shed on 23 September 1911. The structure was not sufficiently strong, and while being manoeuvred on the water by means of winches, it broke in two. It was returned to the shed and later dismantled without ever having flown; however, it did provide the builders with valuable experience.*

Airship development in Italy

Italy, the only other European nation actively interested in the development of airships, started by building a number of nonrigids and semi-rigids for the army's Corps of Engineers. The most important of these was the Forlanini semi-rigid of some 3,680m³ (129,995cu ft) capacity, which first flew in 1909. Airships of this type were to serve with the Italian Army for some years, although they could hardly be classed as highly successful experiments.

Flight and control of an airship

The endurance of an unpowered hydrogen balloon of any size depends largely on the amount of ballast it can carry. With its envelope completely full of gas, such a balloon is ballasted so that the weight of the crew, equipment and ballast are just enough to keep it on the ground. The discharge of a small amount of ballast will cause the balloon to rise, and as atmospheric pressure decreases the gas will expand and the volume of the envelope increase. Gas is able to vent off to prevent undue stress on the envelope, and eventually a height will be reached at which the balloon is in equilibrium. Further ballast must then be dropped if the balloon is to climb. If it is to descend, more gas must be valved off, and a second climb will call for the dropping of more ballast. Finally, when all the ballast has been discharged, the flight must be terminated.

A dirigible – a navigable airship – is affected by very different problems arising from the powerplant which gives it airspeed and directional control. Like the balloon, the dirigible can ascend vertically from the ground. Then, at a suitable height, the engines can be started and the ship can be steered in the required direction. The climb from ground level to the height at which the engines are started is made possible by the static lift provided by the gas within the envelope. Once the engines are started and the vessel is moving fast enough for its aerodynamic controls to be effective, the nose can be pitched up and dynamic lift created. In the same way, a negative dynamic force can be created by pitching the nose down.

USS Akron, 1931

An airship usually carries water ballast, as opposed to the sand carried normally by balloons. But just as with balloons, airships have to discharge ballast if they are to rise from the ground under static lift.

If the airship is of the non-rigid or semirigid type, the envelope will contain a number of ballonets which are filled with air by a pump or via scoops placed in the slipstream of the propellers. They maintain pressure within the envelope so that it retains its aerodynamic shape. An envelope pressurized with gas alone would vent it off throughout the ascent. Then, on descent, the remaining gas would be compressed under the increasing atmospheric pressure. The envelope's internal pressure would fall, possibly causing a drag-inducing change in its aerodynamic form.

To prevent this, about 95 per cent of the envelope's volume is taken up by lifting gas, with the air-filled ballonets occupying the remaining 5 per cent. Air is vented off instead of gas as the airship climbs, and gas plus air maintain the aerodynamic shape. At optimum altitude the lifting gas will fill the envelope at the desired pressure, and the ballonets will be completely empty. The height to which an airship can climb without losing any lifting gas is known as its pressure altitude.

This simple arrangement becomes complicated when it is necessary to fly higher than the pressure altitude, and by the fact that the engines consume fuel. The airship will climb if ballast is discharged. Lifting gas will however have to be vented off as atmospheric pressure decreases. Secondly, the

upper gangway

gun platform

bulkhead

helium gas cell

observation platform

winch platform

lower gangway

bow cabins

main frames

flutter tie wires

aeroplane compartment & crew quarters

gas cell & shear wires

control car

as fuel is consumed. Thus Paul Hänlein's airship, with an engine fuelled by lifting gas from the envelope, was not quite as short-sighted a design as it first appears.

It was also proposed that as the airship's engines consumed liquid fuel, reducing gross weight, the hydrogen that had to be valved off to maintain equilibrium should be mixed with liquid fuel in the engines' carburation system. The vented gas would not therefore be a total loss, being added instead to the fuel stock and so helping to increase range. One of the features of the German *Graf Zeppelin* of 1928 was the use of a fuel known as *blaugas*, a petroleum vapour some 20 per cent heavier than air. This gas was stored in separate cells occupying some 30,000m³ (1,059,434cu ft), and the vessel's gross weight changed little as fuel was consumed. The later *Hindenburg* was equipped to take in water when flying through heavy rain to increase her ballast reserves.

Airships in World War I

By building the airships which operated with the pioneering airline, Delag, the designers of the Zeppelin Company learned a great deal that was to prove of enormous value in the development of military airships for the German Army and Navy.

While Delag was developing its airship services, a new design had appeared in Germany. A rigid airship designed by D. Johann Schütte and Heinrich Lanz, the Schütte-Lanz SL.1 made its first flight on 17 October 1911. Measuring 128m (420ft) in length and 17·98m (59ft) in diameter, the SL.1 had a capacity of about 16,672m³ (700,000cu ft). Its pair of 270hp engines gave a maximum speed of about 56km/h (35mph). One of the SL.1's most advanced features was an improved streamline shape, which had an important influence on the development of the Zeppelin airships when Schütte-Lanz became a part of the Zeppelin Company. But a second revolutionary idea, the use of wood for the SL.1's rigid frame, did not survive the amalgamation of the companies.

There was one other significant airship company in Germany: the concern established to build the non-rigid airships designed by Major von Parseval. These non-rigids had

LEFT: *A partially inflated airship belonging to the Italian Army, used in the war against Turkey of 1911–12. This type rendered valuable service in exploration missions over unknown territory.*
BELOW LEFT: *One of the German Zeppelin rigid airships in trouble on the Belgian coast in 1915. It had to make a forced landing after suffering heavy damage from anti-aircraft fire during raids on the south coast of England. The first airship raids against London were launched in January 1915. The German Army ceased offensive airship operations in September 1916 after suffering serious losses in a bombing raid. The Navy, however, continued their raids on London until 1918.*

ABOVE: *A cutaway diagram of the Goodyear airship* Akron, *built for the United States Navy in 1931. It was 239 m (785ft) in length and 41·4m (133ft) in diameter, and was powered by eight Maybach VL–II engines, giving a total of 4,480hp. It could attain a speed of 128km/h (79mph). On 3 April 1933 it crashed at sea off Barnegat, killing 73 people out of the 76 on board.*
BELOW: *The airship* Parseval III *at Munich in 1909. This was one of a number of non-rigid dirigibles constructed by Major August von Parseval, during the first years of the 20th century when his designs vied with Zeppelin's rigid airships for the attention of the German Navy.*

gross weight of the vessel will decrease as the engines consume fuel, and the airship will climb steadily unless gas is vented off. Changes in air temperature and temperature inversion present further control problems to the airship designer.

Here, very briefly, are some of the ways in which these problems can be overcome. If the lifting gas is heated on the ground, a volume of gas smaller than that normally required will expand to fill the envelope. The heating system can then be switched off as the airship starts its climb, and the falling gas temperature and external air pressure more or less cancel one another out. With such a system, lifting-gas pressure falls at about the same rate as external atmospheric pressure, making it unnecessary to vent gas during the climb above pressure altitude. An efficient means of condensing the water in the exhaust gas from the engines would provide additional ballast to keep the ship in equilibrium pressure envelopes and were considered unsuitable for operational military use, but a small number were used for training.

Germany's principal military airships during World War I were the Zeppelins of the German Navy, which earned a fearsome reputation with their bombing raids on Britain. Though this was due more to the inadequacy of Britain's home defences than the accuracy and weight of the attacks, the Zeppelins were intensively developed, from the L3, with which Germany began the war, to the L70 and L71.

The L3 was 158m (518ft 4in) long, 14·78m (48ft 6in) in diameter and had a volume of 22,500m³ (794,575cu ft). Powered by three engines giving a total of 630hp, the L3 had a maximum speed of about 75km/h (46·5mph).

Four years later, Zeppelin attacks on Britain ended after the loss of the L70 and *Fregatten Kapitän* Peter Strasser, Chief of the German Naval Airship Division. L70 fell to the de Havilland D.H.4 patrol seaplane of Major Egbert Cadbury and Captain Robert Leckie on 5 August 1918. The L70 was 211m (692ft 3in) long and 23·9m (78ft 5in) in diameter, and had a volume of 62,178m³ (2,195,800cu ft). Its engines developed a total of 1,715hp and were reported to have speeded the airship through the air at 130km/h (81mph) during a trial flight.

Military airship development in Britain and France followed a different pattern, for neither nation envisaged those craft as war-winning strategic weapons. The two Allies proposed to use the airship mainly for naval patrol, a role in which it was to give valuable service, especially for Britain.

France, pioneer of the dirigible, used about 25 airships – 21 non-rigids and 4 semi-rigids – during World War I. The former were mainly of the Astra-Torres type, a design in which the three lobes of the envelope ran from stem to stem. Designed by a Spaniard, Torres Quevedo, they were built and developed by the French *Astra Société des Constructions Aéronautiques*. The internal rigging of the Astra-Torres passed within the folds of the lower lobes, considerably reducing the parasite drag generated by the rigging. The other French manufacturer worthy of mention was Clément-Bayard, which built a small number of non-rigid airships of the Lebaudy type. The majority of the French airships were used

FAR LEFT: *The Gondola of a Zeppelin airship used in attacks against England.*
LEFT: *The French airship* Alsace *in 1915 after a forced landing.*
BELOW: *One of the US Navy's airships built by the Goodyear company.*
BELOW RIGHT: *An airship moored at Barrow-in-Furness in 1918. It is secured by the nose and free to swing round with the wind.*
ABOVE RIGHT: *The British Naval Airship C.23a starting off on submarine patrol.*
CENTRE RIGHT: *The rigid airship R.23, put into commission in 1916 as a training ship.*
BELOW FAR RIGHT: *Messrs Armstrong's airship shed at Barlow, Yorkshire, about 1917.*

mainly for patrols over the Mediterranean Sea.

The RNAS, which became the main user of dirigibles among Britain's military services, began the war with a Parseval, an Astra-Torres and a Lebaudy. The RNAS urgently required a fleet of semi-rigids for coastal anti-submarine patrols, and an experimental vessel was built from the spare envelope of a Willows airship and the shortened fuselage and powerplant of a Royal Aircraft Factory B.E.2C aeroplane. It proved an immediate success and a whole family of related non-rigids—or Blimps as they became known—evolved from this first successful experiment. Designations for these types included Sea Scout (SS), Coastal (C) and North Sea (NS), and there were variants of each. Undoubtedly the most successful was the N.S. class, which had an envelope of Astra-Torres form, length of 79·86m (262ft), diameter of 17·37m (57ft) and a capacity of 10,194m³ (360,000cu ft). A completely enclosed gondola 10·67m (35ft) in length and 1·83m (6ft) high accommodated the crew of ten. The two 240hp engines were mounted in a completely separate car and gave a maximum speed of about 93km/h (58mph), making it an effective patrol aircraft.

The success of the Royal Navy's scouting airships lay not so much in their ability to carry out attacks as in their efficiency in tracking U-boats and calling up surface vessels to harass or destroy them.

The United States entered the war comparatively late and did not feel the same urgency about developing airships for a military role. During the war a number of blimps were built for the US Navy, mainly by the Goodyear Tire and Rubber Company, which continues to build airships to this day. The main US user of lighter-than-air craft in World War I was the US Army which deployed large numbers of kite balloons on the Western Front to observe enemy movements and direct artillery fire.

The only other combatant to make any significant use of airships was Italy, which employed a small number of non-rigids and semi-rigids on naval duties. Largest of the semi-rigids were the three built by Forlanini, which were 71·32m (234ft) long, 17·68m (58ft) in diameter, and with a volume of 11,330m³ (400,113cu ft).

Post-war development of the airship

Britain was left after the war with a small number of indifferent rigid airships, and with the R.33 and R.34 just about to enter service. Both were modelled on the German Zeppelin L.33 that was forced to land at Little Wigborough, Essex, on 24 September 1916. While R.33 is renowned mainly for her struggle to regain her base at Pulham, Norfolk, after being damaged and blown across the North Sea, R.34 has an important place in aviation history. Between 2 and 6 July 1919, this vessel carried out the first North Atlantic crossing by an airship, taking just over 108 hours. The return west–east crossing was completed between 9 and 13 July in just over 75 hours. The only other really successful British airship was the R.100. (See p. 339.) Built at the same time as the R.100 was the R.101, which crashed and was destroyed in late 1930.

Germany, forbidden by the Versailles Treaty to build aeroplanes, lost little time in starting up a post-war airship service. Delag was resuscitated and on 24 August 1919, a new purpose-built passenger-carrying airship, the *Bodensee*, started to operate between Friedrichshafen and Berlin. So successful was this service that a second vessel, the *Nordstern*, was called for. But before it could enter service the Allies put a stop to the operation.

At the end of World War I most of Germany's Zeppelin airships had been destroyed by their crews instead of being surrendered to the Allies in accordance with the Armistice agreement. America had been due to receive at least one of the Zeppelins and was seeking

ABOVE: *HM Airship R33 moored to a 30·5m (100ft) high mooring mast at Pulham Airship Station, 31 March 1921.*
ABOVE RIGHT: *Building an airship at Short Bros. works. The wooden frame showing the spiral tube. (Inset) Girls at work on the frame of a gondola.*

ABOVE: *The* Graf Zeppelin *at Los Angeles in 1929. It made an historic round-the-world flight in 21 days 7 hours 34 minutes.*
ABOVE RIGHT: *Dr Hugo Eckener in the R.101's control cabin with the airship's designer and the commander of the R.100.*
LEFT: *On 11 May 1936 the* Graf Zeppelin *landed at Frankfurt – the first airship to use the new airport.*
BELOW FAR LEFT: *The R.34 outside its shed at Pulham on 4 July 1919, after a trans-atlantic flight.*
BELOW: *The Zeppelin LZ.126* Los Angeles *which served with the US Navy from 1924 to 1932, here moored over water.*

financial compensation. In Germany, meanwhile, the fortunes of the Zeppelin Company were at a low ebb. Count von Zeppelin had died in 1917, and direction of the company had passed to Dr Hugo Eckner, the Count's close associate from the early days of rigid airships. Eckner suggested to the Americans that his company should build them a new airship. That way America would get her airship, and Zeppelin would stay in the forefront of airship development. The resulting LZ.126 began flight tests in the summer of 1924 and, on 12 October 1924, was flown across the Atlantic from Friedrichshafen to Lakehurst, New Jersey, in a time of 79 hours.

The uneventful Atlantic crossing was to be typical of this airship's service life. Designated ZR.3 and named USS *Los Angeles* in US Navy service, she accumulated 5,368 flight hours before being retired in 1932. She was subsequently recommissioned and used occasionally before being scrapped altogether in 1939.

Zeppelin was to build two more superb vessels, the *Graf Zeppelin* and the *Hindenburg*. The former, designated officially LZ.127, was 236m (774·28ft) long and had a maximum diameter of 30·5m (100·07ft). Volume was 105,000m³ (3,708,020cu ft), of which 30,000 m³ (1,059,434cu ft) was occupied by blaugas fuel and the remaining 75,000m³ (2,648,586 cu ft) by the hydrogen lifting gas. Power was provided by five 530hp Maybach engines each mounted in a separate gondola. Luxury accommodation was provided for 20 passengers, and up to 12 tons of mail or other cargo could be carried.

First flown on 18 September 1928, the *Graf Zeppelin* made a round-the-world flight in 21 days, 7 hours and 34 minutes between 8 and 29 August 1929. She last flew during 1939 off the east coast of England, unsuccessfully attempting to monitor British radar installations. Before being scrapped finally in 1940, LZ.127 had completed 590 flights, including 140 Atlantic crossings, carried 13,100 passengers, and travelled 1,695,252km (1,053,396 miles) in 17,178 flying hours.

But even while the *Graf Zeppelin* was going from success to success, an even larger sister ship was being created by the Zeppelin Company. When completed in March 1936 the LZ.129 (or *Hindenburg*) was the world's largest rigid airship: 245m (803·81ft) in length, with a maximum diameter of 41m (134·51ft) and a volume of approximately 200,000m³ (7,062,895cuft). Its four 1,000hp Daimler diesel engines gave a maximum speed of 130km/h (81mph), and this giant vessel could accommodate 75 passengers and a crew of 25. Entering service in the summer of 1936, the *Hindenburg* carried out a number of North and South Atlantic crossings. Then, on 6 May 1937, a tongue of flame broke out at the top of the envelope near the stern as the great ship was approaching the mooring mast at Lakehurst, New Jersey. Within a matter of seconds *Hindenburg* was a blazing mass of wreckage from which 62 of the 97 people on board miraculously escaped with their lives.

This disaster, coming on the heels of the R.101 tragedy and accidents to two other large dirigibles in US service, marked the end of German attempts to create a worldwide fleet of commercial transport airships. It also put a full stop to the furtherance of development work in this field by other nations, notably Italy and the United States.

The most successful of the large, non-rigid Italian airships built after the war was the N.1, later named *Norge*. In this ship a crew of 16, including the American Lincoln Ellsworth, Colonel Umberto Nobile and the Norwegian explorer Roald Amundsen, reached the North Pole on 12 May 1926. The entire flight, about 4,830km (3,000 miles) from Spitzbergen to Teller, Alaska, took 71 hours.

A little more than two years later Umberto Nobile led a polar expedition of his own in a similar semi-rigid, the N.4 *Italia*. The *Italia* and her crew reached the North Pole on 24 May 1928, only to crash into the pack ice about 282km (175 miles) north-east of Spitzbergen on the morning of 25 May. The rescue of some of the survivors was an epic of courage

TOP, ABOVE LEFT AND ABOVE RIGHT: *The airship* Norge *was used by Nobile and Amundsen on their expedition to the North Pole in May 1926.*
BELOW: *The airship* Italia *at King's Bay, Spitzbergen, at the beginning of Nobile's polar expedition of 1928.*
BELOW RIGHT: *The United States Naval Airship K.3 being tethered to its mooring mast at Lakehurst, New Jersey.*

RIGHT: *The* Hindenburg *in flames at Lakehurst, New Jersey, on 6 May 1937. It had been designed for helium, but eventually used hydrogen when helium was not available, and thus leading to the Lakehurst tragedy.*
BOTTOM RIGHT: *The* Hindenburg *(Zeppelin LZ.129) on a flight over New York in 1936. It contained cabins for 75 passengers, a salon and a dining-room, as well as an airtight smoking room.*

in which many lives were lost, including that of Roald Amundsen.

The United States Army and Navy have at differing times been the world's major operators of military airships. The US Army's heyday lasted from 1921 to 1935, with the Navy taking over during World War II. In 1921 an agreement between the Army and Navy resulted in the former concentrating on the use of non-rigid and semi-rigid types for coastal and inland patrol, a division which lasted until the termination of US Army lighter-than-air operations in 1936.

As well as some notable rigid airships, the US Navy acquired a total of 241 non-rigids between 1917 and 1958. Some of these were excellent, fast vessels: the final examples of the N series, delivered between 1958 and 1960, had lengths of 122·83m (403ft), volumes of 42,929m³ (1,516,000cu ft), and maximum speeds of 145km/h (90mph). Of the Navy's rigid airships, the most successful was the German-built ZR–3 USS *Los Angeles*. Built subsequently in America by the Goodyear-Zeppelin Corporation were the 239·27m (785

RIGHT: *The US Navy airship* Macon *in flight escorted by Curtiss Sparrowhawk fighters. It was built in America by Goodyear-Zeppelin in 1933 and crashed two years later at sea off Point Sur, with only two people dead and 81 survivors.*
BELOW RIGHT: *The Goodyear airship* Defender, *one of the fleet now maintained by the company for publicity purposes.*
BOTTOM RIGHT: *With scarcely a hum, a 9m (30ft) prototype of Britain's flying saucer hovers overhead in a giant aircraft hangar at Cardington. The battery-powered aircraft is about 2·5m (8ft) in height, and helium, a non-inflammable gas sealed in plastic bags, gives the craft its buoyancy. A full size version of the Skyship is planned to carry cargo and passengers.*

ft) ZRS–4 *Akron* and ZRS–5 *Macon*. Fighter aircraft were carried inside and could be launched and recovered on a trapeze. Both of these airships were lost at sea: the *Akron* on 4 April 1933, with the loss of all but three of her crew; the *Macon* on 11 February 1935, with the loss of only two lives. This brought and end to the Navy's rigid airship programme.

Airships survive in the jet era

Although the USA no longer uses airships for military purposes, Goodyear has retained a fleet of four non-rigids for publicity purposes. Goodyear can claim to have built more airships than any other company in the world. Its 301st, the *Columbia III*, was completed in 1975.

Hot-air airships have been flown by Cameron in Britain (1973) and Raven Industries in America (1975). The *Albatross*, which first flew in October 1975, was designed by a husband and wife team, Brian and Kathy Boland.

Non-rigid airships designed in recent years include the WDL–1, a 55m (180ft 5in) helium-filled airship built by WDL in Essen-Mülheim, West Germany, and first flown in August 1972. British non-rigids include the 23·16m (76ft) helium-filled *Santos-Dumont* constructed by Anthony Smith and first flown in May 1974; the 25m (82ft) Skyships Ltd *Skyship 1*, which was nearing its first flight in late 1976; and the 50·29m (165ft) Aerospace Developments Type B, which was scheduled to fly in early 1977. Japan had several versions of the Fuji Model 500, small research airship, undergoing flight test in 1976, and other examples were also being built. Airships under construction in the United States include B and G Airships' semi-rigid BG–1 *Dolphin*, which is 29·63m (97ft 2in) long; Tucker Airship Company's TX–1 semi-rigid, which is 27·74m (91ft) long and scheduled to fly for the first time in 1977; and one rigid, a 68·58m (225ft) ship with a gross volume of 7,079m³ (250,000cu ft) being built by Conrad Airship Corporation.

Some of these craft have been built 'just for fun', while others are intended for roles which – in a period of aviation history when money and fuel are both in short supply – their designers believe can best be carried out by airships. These tasks include maritime patrol; cargo carriage to points of difficult access; aerial survey and photography; meteorological and pollution measurement; distribution of seeds, fertilizers and insecticides; logging; and advertising.

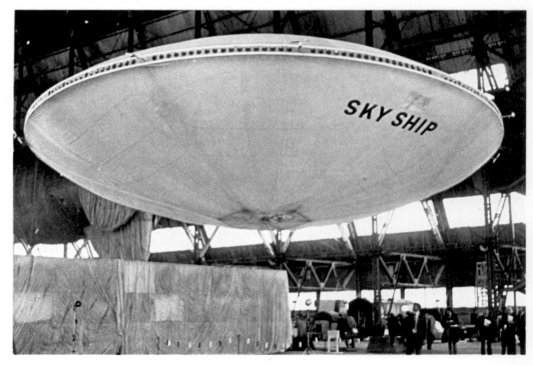

R.100

In an attempt to resolve the question of whether the large, rigid airship was the ideal long-range commercial transport vehicle for the mid-1920s, Britain's first Labour government under Ramsay MacDonald promoted a programme of airship development. A sum of £1·3 million was allocated over a three-year period to cover the building of new sheds and mooring masts in Canada, Egypt, England and India; a limited amount of research into airship structures and aerodynamics; and the construction of two large intercontinental-range airships. Designated R.100 and R.101, these were to be designed and built respectively by the Airship Guarantee Company and the Air Ministry's Royal Airship Works at Cardington, Bedfordshire.

The Airship Guarantee Company, a subsidiary of Vickers Aircraft Company, represented the private-enterprise sector of the industry. Its design team – headed by the great inventor and engineer Barnes Wallis and including N. S. Norway (also known as the author Nevil Shute) as chief calculator, and a skilled metallurgist, Major P. L. Teed – found themselves based at the disused RNAS station at Howden, Yorkshire. Howden possessed a shed just large enough to accommodate the giant airship which Barnes Wallis was beginning to create on his drawing board.

The contract for the construction of R.100 was placed on 22 October 1924, and required the company to design and build the airship for a fixed price of £350,000; to demonstrate its capability with a return flight to India (a destination altered later to Canada); and to achieve a maximum speed of 113km/h (70 mph). A penalty clause provided for the deduction of £1,000 for each 0·8 km (0·5mph) that demonstrated maximum speed fell short of the specified maximum.

Duralumin – a light alloy composed of aluminium, copper, manganese, magnesium and silicon – had been developed in Germany by this time. Appreciating its potential as an aircraft-construction material, Vickers obtained world rights for the manufacture of duralumin outside Germany. Easily worked in its normalized state, duralumin hardens with age until it has almost as much tensile strength as an equal mass of steel, while weighing only one-third as much.

Already widely experienced in the design and building of airships, Barnes Wallis realized that a rigid duralumin frame would be both strong and significantly lighter than existing structures. At that time, however, there was no method of producing extruded tubes of duralumin with a thin section and large diameter. Typically, Wallis set about designing and building a machine to produce such tubes. They were fabricated in the end by helically winding thin-gauge flat strip and riveting it at close centres along the continuous overlap.

The giant craft slowly took shape, hanging from the roof of the Howden shed as the metallic jig-saw puzzle was pieced together. The hydrogen lifting gas was to be contained in 15 gas bags, the 14th and 15th of which were interconnected. The three-ply bags, made of cotton lined with two plies of gold-beaters' skin, were made by the Zeppelin Company at Friedrichshafen.

To ensure that the bags would not be chafed by their containing frames, Wallis devised a network of flexible wires which both restrained the bags and allowed them to expand and contract as the conditions of flight changed. From this arrangement evolved the geodetic method of construction, which he was later to develop and apply successfully to the production of military aeroplanes.

Three decks for the passengers and crew were located in the lower part of the hull between the fifth and sixth structural frames. The lower deck housed the crew; the upper deck provided a gallery lounge and the majority of the double and four-berth cabins; the remainder of the cabins were situated on the centre deck. In all, a hundred passengers could be carried in great comfort. The rest of the centre deck was occupied by a dining room that could seat 56 persons at a time. Having eaten, they could then take the air on the 12·2m × 4·6m (40ft × 15ft) viewing promenades on either side of the dining room.

The R.100 was powered by six 650hp Rolls-Royce Condor IIIA engines mounted in tandem pairs in three cars. One car was set centrally on the undersurface of the hull some 12·2m (40ft) ahead of the lower vertical fin, with the other two placed low on each side of the hull about 39·6m (130ft) aft of the passenger accommodation. In each car the forward engine drove a tractor propeller, the aft engine a pusher, and in addition each rear engine was fitted with reversing gear to facilitate

mooring operations.

On 16 December 1929, the R.100 flew for the first time, from Howden to Cardington under the command of Major G. H. Scott. Flight trials were completed at Cardington, and between 29 July and 16 August 1930, the airship, with a crew of 44, was flown to Canada and back. The outward flight took 78 hours against prevailing headwinds, the homeward crossing only 58 hours.

A little less than two months later, on 4 October 1930, the government-built R.101 crashed at Beauvais, France, on its maiden intercontinental flight, bringing British airship development to an end. The highly successful R.100 was taken out of commission and scrapped without making another flight.

These figures are taken from the original specification drawn up by Mr B. N. (now Sir Barnes) Wallis and from the hand-written reports of N. S. Norway during the airship's trials.

Length overall 219·4m (719·8ft)

Length of hull 216·2m (709·29ft)

Height overall 21·7m (136·8ft)

Maximum diameter 41·55m (136·33 ft)

Gross volume 141,585m³ (5,000,000 cu ft)

Fineness ratio 5·3

Fin area (total) 1,059m² (11,400 sq ft)

Hull weight 53,668kg (118,318lb)

Gross lift 159,052kg (350,650lb)

Fuel and oil 29,075kg (64,100lb)

Water ballast 19,586kg (43,180lb)

Maximum trial speed 131·16km/h (81·5mph)

Rotorcraft

The development of rotorcraft, which term includes both helicopters and autogyros, or gyroplanes as they are sometimes called, has always been in a world of its own. Apart from ballooning, it was mainly with moving wings designed to emulate the flapping of bird flight that man made his first attempts to fly. From the legendary experiments of Icarus and the sketches of Leonardo da Vinci, right through to the notable contributions of Sir George Cayley in the 19th century, most of the proposed flying machines had some means of flapping or rotating the wings to produce lift.

Initially, the practical problems of mechanical complexity were quite insuperable, and it is only within the past 100 years that any significant attempts have been made to depart from the moving-wing concept. Then, as it came to be more clearly discerned that so many of the finest natural fliers – such as the eagle and the albatross – seldom flapped their wings, the fixed-wing philosophy began to make great strides. But there were still some adherents of rotating wings who were not deterred in their search for vertical take-off and landing. To them, the aeroplane was a highly dangerous form of flight and, although they were habitually ridiculed, there was a great deal of evidence to support their contentions. Most of the frequent aeroplane crashes of the early 20th century occurred during the critical manoeuvres of take-off and landing at comparatively high forward speeds.

The group of rotorcraft pioneers contracted as many gave up the complexities and turned to the much simpler fixed-wing aeroplane, but during the first 20 years of this century a handful of designers did meet with some limited success. Among the helicopters to fly successfully in that period, the Breguet-Richet No 1 was credited, on 29 September 1907, with being the world's first man-carrying helicopter to become airborne, albeit under restraint from tethering ropes controlled by the ground crew. This machine had a gross weight of 578kg (1,274lb) and was lifted by four biplane rotors of 8m (26ft 3in) diameter each and driven by a single Antoinette engine of 45bhp. It remained airborne for only about one minute outside the Breguet aircraft works at Douai, France, and reached a height of only about 0·6m (2ft).

On 13 November of that same year and also in France, at Lisieux, the Cornu tandem-rotor helicopter became the world's first rotating-wing aircraft to achieve unrestrained free flight, with the designer himself at the controls. This maiden flight deserves its place in history even though, at less than 30 seconds, it was of even shorter duration than Breguet's. The machine weighed 260kg

PREVIOUS PAGES:
The Mil Mi–6, Nato code-name 'Hook', can carry up to 65 armed troops, and, as a freighter, it has a 12,000kg (26,455lb) payload capacity.

342

ABOVE: *This sketch of Sir George Cayley's 'Aerial Carriage', of 1843 vintage, reveals that he had a remarkable insight into the problems of rotating wing flight almost a century before the first practical helicopters began to emerge. The first Focke and Weir helicopters followed this configuration.*
BELOW: *Credited with achieving the world's first free flight by a man-carrying helicopter, this Cornu design remained airborne for less than a minute with the designer at the controls. The short flight was not long enough to give him time to become accustomed to the handling characteristics, even if control provision had been adequate. The fragile machine crashed and broke up on landing.*

ABOVE RIGHT: *A 1910 attempt to build a contra-rotating helicopter by Vuitton. Like other attempts of its day, it was not successful.*
BELOW RIGHT: *The Cierva C–19 Mk IV was the world's first autogyro to be put into quantity production. It was flown successfully by private pilots in a number of flying schools during the early 1930s and was the first type to demonstrate that rotating wing flight could be a practical proposition.*
BELOW FAR RIGHT: *The Cierva C–40 was the last autogyro design to be produced by the company. Detail design was by Dr James Bennett, based on Cierva's final research work before his untimely death. The rotorhead mechanism embodies means to provide for vertical 'jump' take-off.*

(573lb) and was powered by a 24hp Antoinette engine which drove the two twin-bladed 'paddle-wheel' rotors through a belt-and-pulley transmission system. To outward appearances, it gave the impression of having been built from parts of several bicycles and its short flight ended, regrettably, in the collapse of its frail tubular framework following a heavy landing. Still, it was a world first.

World War I brought a temporary halt to experiments but in the period that followed there were other limited successes. In France, the quadruple-rotor Oemichen helicopter,

which was additionally fitted with five small variable-pitch propellers for control purposes, actually achieved a world helicopter distance record with a flight of just over 500m (1,640ft) in 1924. Another quadruple-rotor machine, the de Bothezat helicopter, was also being flight-tested in the USA by the US Army Air Force and achieved a maximum duration of 1min 40sec. Both were incredibly complicated mechanical contraptions. Hardly less complicated was the Pescara helicopter which was lifted by twin co-axial, contra-rotating biplane rotors. This machine, built in France by a Spanish designer, proved itself superior to the Oemichen by increasing the world helicopter distance record to just about 800m (2,640ft). It was no wonder that the helicopter proponents were ridiculed by fixed-wing aeroplane pioneers. The Atlantic had already been flown non-stop by Alcock and Brown in a Vickers Vimy bomber.

The Cierva autogiro
The breakthrough in rotating-wing design came with the invention by the Spaniard Juan de la Cierva of the autogyro. By 1925, he had proved the validity of his concept beyond all doubt and was invited to England to con-

Cierva's invention was based on a quite novel design philosophy which emerged from the mathematical analysis he made of contemporary helicopter designers' problems. They were then all using their various forms of rotor system with the blades set at a high positive pitch angle, rotated by the application of power to the drive shafts on which they were mounted. In effect, they were large propellers which screwed themselves upward against the resistance of the air. There were two principal problems. On the one hand, the application of engine power to turn the rotor drive shaft produced an equal and

work in a simple rotor system satisfied him that, if the blades were to be set at a *low* positive pitch angle and started in rotational motion, the rotating system could be towed through the air in such a way that the blades would maintain a constant rotational speed in a state of equilibrium, without any application of power.

Autorotation
He termed this phenomenon autorotation and applied it in practice by building a single rotor and mounting it on a pylon above a conventional aeroplane fuselage. Instead of a complex transmission system there was simply one bearing at the head of the pylon which allowed the rotor to turn freely. There were a few teething troubles initially but he soon developed an arrangement that worked satisfactorily. Take-off in the early machines was achieved by hand-starting the rotation of the blades and then accelerating across the aerodrome, pulled by a conventional engine-driven propeller. As forward speed increased on the take-off run, rotor rpm also increased until the state of equilibrium was reached. At this stage, which was normally after a run of a few hundred metres to reach a speed of some 48km/h (30mph), sufficient lift was being generated by the spinning blades for the machine to become airborne.

It was an elegant solution to the problem of flight with rotating wings. A simple, single rotor system could be used because, as it was freely rotating, there was no torque to counteract. The extended flight-test and develop-

tinue his research and development work with British sponsorship. During the next ten years, the English company he formed produced a succession of autogyro prototypes which established all the design theory and data on which the helicopter industries of the world were subsequently founded. Tragically, Cierva himself was killed at Croydon in 1936, at the premature age of 41, without seeing the extent to which his invention would be developed. Ironically, he was a passenger in a fixed-wing airliner when he lost his life; it was just such a crash as he had devoted his whole working life to eliminate.

opposite reaction which would turn the fuselage in the opposite direction when airborne. Known as torque reaction, this is a phenomenon familiar to all engineers. To avoid it, rotors on early helicopters were used in pairs, turning in opposite directions to counteract the torque.

Following from this need to use pairs of rotors came the requirement for complex mechanical transmission systems to transmit the engine power and then elaborate structures to support the systems. Cierva's discovery was that none of this was necessary. His calculations of the aerodynamic forces at

ment work which the first practical autogyro made possible yielded, in due course, a vast accumulation of technical data on which future improved designs could be based. Subsequent refinements to the system included mechanical means to start the rotor before take-off and means of precise control of its tip-path plane for safety in landing.

The latest forms of autogyro under development just before Cierva's untimely death had progressed still further. Methods were developed to enable the mechanical drive system to overspeed the rotor on the ground before take-off so that a sudden increase of blade pitch under the pilot's control would cause the machine to jump vertically without any forward run. The vertical jump was sustained for just long enough to allow the machine to gain normal forward flying speed under the influence of propeller thrust.

The autogyro was never able to hover but it could fly much more slowly than a fixed-wing aircraft, down to less than 40km/h (25

BELOW: *These Cierva C–30s, lined up outside the manufacturers' flying school, were the most popular autogyros produced. Several hundred were built in England and Europe. Like the C–40, they have no wings but this type was not able to take off vertically. It needed a short forward run.*

BOTTOM LEFT: *A historic picture of Igor Sikorsky with one of his early attempts at helicopter design, in 1910. Hardly surprising, it never flew.*
BOTTOM RIGHT: *The world's first helicopter to demonstrate extended precision hovering flight was the Focke Fa–61.*

BELOW FAR RIGHT: *Igor Sikorsky at the controls of his VS–300, the world's first practical single rotor helicopter. This photograph was taken in 1939. The tethering ropes were to prevent the machine overturning on its initial hovering trials.*

mph) without losing height, and could land with virtually no forward speed. If forward speed were reduced below this value in the air, the machine would begin to sink gently towards the ground. Rotor speed remained constant during the gliding descent, akin to the spinning descent of a sycamore seed. Since the control system governed the rotor's angle of tilt, and not that of the fuselage, the pilot was able to maintain full and precise control right to the point of touchdown.

Cierva C–30

The most effective of the many autogyros developed during the 1930s was the Cierva C–30, of which several hundred were produced by manufacturing licensees of the Cierva Autogiro Company in the UK and Europe. Modified versions of the type were also produced in the USA. The C–30 was a two-seat machine of some 862kg (1,900lb) gross weight and was powered by a 140bhp Armstrong Siddeley Genet Major radial engine. A power take-off from the rear of the engine crankshaft was used as a mechanical starting system for the three-bladed, 11·28m (37ft) diameter rotor. The two seats were arranged in tandem as open cockpits, with the pilot at the rear. The forward cockpit was located immediately below the rotorhead with its supporting pylon straddling the cockpit coaming. In this way, the weight of the passenger was exactly on the centre of gravity so that flying trim did not alter when the machine was flown solo.

The fuselage was a fabric-covered, tubular-steel structure, substantially the same as that of the Avro Cadet biplane, a successor to the famous 504K. The C–30 was, in fact, designed around this fuselage as Avro was Cierva's UK licensed manufacturer. From a production viewpoint it was advantageous to use an existing fuselage, although it was of course the rotor system rather than the fuselage which led to the C–30's success.

The fully articulated rotor was mounted universally on the pylon so that it could be tilted in any direction in response to movement of the pilot's hanging control column. Rotor blades were of aerofoil section and their construction was based on a tubular-

Type: Cierva C-30
Accommodation: Two
Engines: One 140hp Armstrong Siddeley Genet Major
    seven-cylinder radial
Cruising speed: 129km/h (80mph)
Ceiling: 2,438m (8,000ft)
Range: 402km (250 miles)
Loaded weight: 862kg (1,900lb)
Rotor diameter: 11·28m (37ft)
Length: 6·01m (19ft 8·5in)

steel spar with spruce ribs and plywood covering. Blade chord was 25cm (10in) and the pitch angle was fixed at 2° positive. Normal rotational speed in the autorotative condition was 200rpm.

Design modifications to the standard fuselage included the fitting of a long-travel, soft-oleo landing gear, to accommodate the unique autogyro landing characteristics, and a steerable tailwheel operated by the pilot's rudder pedals. The tailplane was also of unique design. Fitted with upswept tips, the aerofoil camber was positive on the starboard side and negative on the port side to provide a movement about the longitudinal axis (anticlockwise when viewed from the rear) and thus counteract propeller torque in forward flight.

Design maximum speed was over 160km/h (100mph). It was not always possible to achieve this, particularly at full load, but the type had a useful cruising speed in the order of 130km/h (80mph) and carried fuel for just over two hours' endurance. The Cierva C-30 was sold widely for private and club flying and a number were also bought by the military agencies of several countries, mainly for army reconnaissance evaluation. Another military role, for which their slow-flying capabilities were found to be singularly well suited during World War II, was the calibration of ground radar stations.

If the war had not erupted when it did, it is more than likely that the pattern of progress might have been very different. In the years immediately preceding the outbreak

of war, however, there was a small handful of designers who, having derived benefit from the accumulated knowledge of autogyro rotor design, were beginning to show promising results with new helicopter projects. Prominent among them were Heinrich Focke in Germany, James Weir in Scotland, who had earlier been instrumental in sponsoring Cierva's developments in England, and Igor Sikorsky in the USA. Sikorsky had, in fact, built two unsuccessful helicopters in Europe in 1909, at the tender age of 19 years, and had then changed to fixed-wing aeroplane design after emigrating to America. He was prompted to look at the possibilities of helicopter design again by Cierva's autogyro successes which he enthusiastically acknowledged.

Pioneer helicopters

Three projects – the Focke-Achgelis Fa-61, the Weir W-5 and W-6, and the Sikorsky VS-300 – began to attract the interest of their respective military authorities in the late 1930s. They were all more complex than the autogyros, which by then were flying in quite large numbers, but the ability to sustain hovering flight was of special value in a variety of military roles. Even the vertical-jump take-off facility of the latest autogyros then flying was not considered by the military to be a suitable substitute for a hovering capability. Nor was the subsequent wartime use of autogyros on a scale sufficient to deflect their interest. So it was that the helicopter, when it finally began to emerge as a practical flying machine, was initially developed largely under military sponsorship and specifically as a military vehicle. This factor has influenced all its subsequent progress.

The demands made by the military upon the pioneer constructors were unbridled. There was a war to be won and the fledgling helicopter was seen to have enormous potential as a reconnaissance vehicle for swiftly moving ground forces. Initially, the interest came mainly from the US Army and the British Royal Navy. Government money was poured into development contracts with the result that by 1945 Sikorsky's Main and Tail Rotor (MTR) design had become firmly established as the classic configuration. Following the VS–300 prototype, three new designs were developed and put into limited production by the same company to meet military orders. These were the Sikorsky R–4, R–5 and R–6. The first and last were two-seaters, supplied to special units for pilot training and operational evaluation, while the R–5 was a larger helicopter with a lifting capacity of about 508kg (1,120lb). It was the world's first helicopter designed for a specific military role, having been ordered off the drawing board by the Royal Navy to operate from the decks of independently routed merchant vessels on anti-submarine patrol duties.

Other American companies had also been engaged in experimental work. Notable among them was Bell Aircraft, which was developing its own design of MTR helicopter. Its principal unique feature was a gyro-stabilized two-bladed rotor having one common flapping hinge for the two blades. Bell termed it a tetering or see-saw rotor, and it has become well known throughout the world as a feature of most Bell helicopters.

Post-war developments

After World War II, the established helicopter constructors turned their attention towards a possible commercial market. Bell was first to be awarded a commercial helicopter certificate of airworthiness, in 1946. This was for the Model 47, which remained in production for 27 years in many two- and three-seat variants. Sikorsky was not far behind, with a four-seat civil version of the R–5 designated S–51. It quickly became apparent, though, that the helicopter was anything but a motor car for the man in the street. Such was the cost structure established by the initial pressure of military procurement that manufacturers found the civil versions they were producing could be operated economically only in a limited number of highly specialized roles. Commercial sales were thus few and, with military interest becoming less intense, the crucial question of the hour was: 'Is the helicopter here to stay?'

In agricultural roles such as crop-spraying, for example, the high cost of the helicopter put it at a considerable disadvantage compared with fixed-wing aircraft. Commercial helicopter operators found themselves unable to penetrate more than about 20 per cent of the market, which comprised mainly those areas in which it was too difficult for the fixed-wing crop-sprayers to operate. The same applied in other aerial-work roles, par-

ticularly in survey and construction engineering support. In some applications, however, mainly those concerned with operations in remote areas or mountainous terrain, the helicopter was able to perform time-saving miracles. In such uses its apparently high cost was immaterial since to do the job any other way would have cost even more.

Unfortunately, the opportunities to engage in such specialized work were few, and progress in developing commercial uses for the helicopter was painfully slow for the first few years after World War II. There was, nevertheless, still something of a helicopter euphoria during this period, with new projects making their appearance in countries all over the world. In Europe, the pre-war French and British pioneers applied themselves to further development, seeking to make up for the time lost during the war years.

In France, during this period, three groups in the nationalized aircraft industry were engaged in rival helicopter projects. SNCA du Nord began in 1947 but its interest sur-

vived only a few years. SNCA du Sud Ouest had acquired as part of German war reparations the services, for a few years from 1946, of members of a wartime Austrian design team. They had successfully built and flown the word's first jet-rotor helicopter, designed by Friedrich von Doblhoff in 1943. The Sud Ouest projects were thus all in the Single Jet-driven Rotor (SJR) category and led to the development of the SO–1221 Djinn helicopter, the only jet-rotor helicopter to go beyond the prototype stage into quantity production.

Other members of von Doblhoff's team went to Fairey Aviation in Britain, which led to the development of a Gyrodyne derivative with a jet-driven rotor and, from this, to the Rotodyne. Von Doblhoff himself went to the USA and joined McDonnell Aircraft Corporation to develop a ram-jet helicopter. No jet-rotor helicopter, however, has ever achieved any marked degree of commercial operating success.

Even the SO 1221 Djinn helicopter, the agricultural version of which is pictured here, was not a great success commercially. Production was discontinued after just over 100 had been built. A lightweight two-seater, the type was used mainly for pilot training and crop spraying. Its rotor was driven by what is known as 'cold' jets at the blade tips. This was, simply, compressed air bled from the compression chamber of the Turbomeca Palouste turbine engine. The air was ducted through a rotating seal at the rotorhead and thence through hollow spars to the blade tip nozzles.

Other forms of jet driven rotor have made use of pulse jets, pressure jets and ram jets. These all involve the ducting of fuel through the head and blades, to be burnt in small combustion chambers at the blade tips. Hence the contrasting term, 'hot' jets. Many such experimental helicopters have been built and some have flown extremely well; but the fuel consumption has always been prohibitive.

The third French company, SNCA du Sud Est, followed more conventional lines in the development of MTR designs, and produced the series of helicopters which have dominated French involvement in the field. The SNCA du Sud Est and Sud Ouest were later amalgamated in Sud Aviation, which itself was subsequently regrouped under what is now the single French nationalized aircraft constructor, Aérospatiale. Among the wide range of helicopters Aérospatiale produce, three, the Puma, Gazelle and Lynx, are manufactured jointly with Westland Aircraft Ltd under the Anglo-French collaboration agreement.

In Britain after World War II, the original Cierva Autogiro Company re-formed with many of its former key engineering staff and began the development of two new designs. The first to fly, the Cierva W–9, was a two-seat single-rotor helicopter but, instead of following exactly the classic MTR configuration, it used a laterally deflected jet at the tail in place of the tail rotor for torque compensation. Concurrently, the company was also building a much larger machine, the triple-rotor Cierva W–11 Air Horse, which flew

RIGHT: *The Fairey Rotodyne was an advanced design concept to attain high cruising speeds but the prototype was never developed to the production stage, largely for financial reasons.*
BELOW: *The French Djinn helicopter was the only jet-rotor helicopter to be produced in quantity. The duct from the turbo-compressor to the rotor head is clearly visible. This one has a spray boom fitted.*
BOTTOM: *Turbine powered, five-seat Gazelle helicopter, currently in production by Aérospatiale and Westland Aircraft. Main rotor torque, in this type, is counteracted by a ducted fan in the tail fin named a fenestron.*

Type: Aerospatiale AS 350 Ecureuil
Accommodation: Five/six
Engines: One Turbomeca Ariel turbine or
    Lycoming LTS 101 turbine
Cruising speed: 219km/h (136mph)
Ceiling: 5,800m (19,030ft)
Range: 800km (497 miles)
Loaded weight: 1,900kg (4,190lb)
Rotor diameter: 10·67m (35ft)
Length: 13m (42ft)

successfully at its design gross weight of 7,938kg (17,500lb).

This, in its day, was the largest helicopter in the world, with a cargo compartment 5·79m (19ft) in length capable of carrying wheeled vehicles. Volumetric capacity was in the region of 22·65m³ (800cu ft) and entry was by means of a ramp through clam-shell doors at the tail. The Air Horse was powered by a single water-cooled Rolls-Royce Merlin engine of 1,620bhp, the same engine that powered the famous Spitfire fighter. That the Air Horse did not mature to a successful conclusion was due mainly to lack of appreciation by the sponsoring British government of the need for a much higher level of funding to support so sophisticated a design.

Three other British aircraft constructors also entered the rotating wing field at the end of World War II: Westland Aircraft negotiated a manufacturing licence with Sikorsky to build the S–51 in Britain; Bristol Aeroplane Company began the development of a new MTR design with a cabin for five passengers; and Fairey Aviation Company developed a novel Compound Helicopter (CMP) project, also able to carry five passengers, named the Gyrodyne. All three were powered by the same type of engine, the Alvis Leonides nine-cylinder radial of 525 bhp. The Fairey Gyrodyne, with its novel compound design for superior cruising speed, was the first rotorcraft to take the world helicopter speed record above the 200km/h (124mph) mark. Over a 3km (1·86 miles) course, it attained 201km/h (124·9mph).

American initiative

In spite of inevitable setbacks in the comparatively early stages, helicopter projects grew both in number and variety, and nowhere was the profusion of new ideas so great as in the United States. At one time, just before 1950, there were more than 70 different active helicopter projects in America. Many were being built by small engineering companies or by individuals in private garages. Of these, only a few ever left the ground; many never progressed beyond the stage of being a gleam in their hopeful inventors' eyes.

One notable exception was the project of a young Californian graduate, Stanley Hiller Jr, who built his own back-yard Co-axial, Contra-rotating Rotor (CXR) helicopter in 1944. He was fortunate in having links with a major industrial corporation which helped him to surmount the initial hurdles. He was later to develop his own servo-paddle rotor control system. Hiller Helicopters Inc, which he formed, produced more than 1,000 helicopters based on this design feature during the ensuing two decades. Among other American companies, the two which had been predominant in pre-war autogyro development were also involved with new helicopter projects. Pitcairn Autogiro Company, which had been taken over by the giant Firestone Tyre & Rubber Company, produced a conventional MTR helicopter, but with a novel rotorspeed governor, while Kellett Aircraft Corporation concentrated its studies on what was then the unusual Twin Intermeshing-Rotor (TIR) configuration. The same de-

sign was also favoured by Kaman Aircraft Corporation, which developed it to build several hundred helicopters for the USAF.

The tandem-rotor helicopter was introduced because it was thought that limitations in feasible rotor diameters necessitated multiple rotors to lift heavier payloads. Piasecki Helicopter Corporation was the first to produce a practical Twin Tandem-Rotor (TTR) design, and derivatives of its first tandem-rotor machine, the XHRP–1 (jocularly known as the 'Flying Banana'), were still in production by Boeing Vertol in the mid-1970s. Among other configurations developed in the USA during the 1945 to 1950 period, SJR designs with rotors driven variously by pulse jets, pressure jets and ram jets all made their appearance – and, as often as not, their disappearance shortly thereafter.

By 1950, most of the weaker brethren had disappeared, leaving about 10 or 12 companies to form the nucleus of what was then a Cinderella industry struggling for recognition in a highly competitive aviation market.

Korean War

It was the outbreak of war in Korea, in the mid-summer of 1950, that provided the next major impetus to transform this small group of manufacturers into the thriving helicopter industry which now exists. The US Air Force and US Navy units equipped with the few hundred helicopters which had been delivered for evaluation were despatched to Korea for trials under active service conditions. Their performance was far beyond the wildest expectations of the most optimistic military strategists.

The series of helicopter types principally involved were, initially, the Sikorsky H–5, derived from the S–51, Bell H–13 and Hiller H–23. Later, these were supplemented by the Sikorsky H–19 series, a larger machine capable of lifting ten men or a load of almost a ton, and the Piasecki HUP–1 series, a TTR design based aboard US Navy aircraft carriers and used for ship-to-shore work. These helicopters, in their performance of otherwise impossible rescue missions, confirmed beyond any doubt that rotating-wing aircraft were here to stay. With their unique versatility and independence of prepared landing strips, they were able to save the lives of thousands of soldiers, wounded or stranded behind enemy positions. This in itself was enough to ensure their unreserved acceptance as a new ancillary to fighting armies. Perhaps even more significant was the potential that the success of such rescue operations revealed.

Military tacticians were quick to realize that if the helicopter could quite easily infiltrate behind enemy lines to rescue wounded soldiers, it could equally penetrate with offensive personnel, weapons and supplies to mount attacks from almost any unexpected quarter. By the time the Korean war had ended, American military strategy had been completely re-orientated in line with this new philosophy. The new US Army was to be composed largely of highly mobile task forces mounted, supplied and supported entirely from the air by fleets of helicopters designed specifically for the variety of operational tasks involved. At the same time, the helicopter's potential in marine warfare, as an anti-submarine weapon and to support marine commando raids ashore, was realized.

The new philosophy was pioneered by the American armed forces and quickly taken up by those of other nations throughout the world, including the Soviet Union where the history of rotating-wing development had had early origins but not the same degree of practical development as elsewhere.

With military procurement pressure once again calling the tune, the helicopter industry made rapid strides in the decade following the Korean war. Military agencies were then in a much better position to write operational specifications for helicopters to fulfil special duties for which active-service experience had shown the need. Thus, with specific targets to achieve and the money to spend in terms of development contracts, helicopter construction was suddenly transformed into a boom industry and the various new designs began to roll off the production lines in their hundreds.

TOP LEFT: *The Sikorsky H–5 and its civil equivalent, the S–55, was the first helicopter to have a lifting capacity in the region of one tonne.*
TOP RIGHT: *The Cierva Air Horse was the world's largest helicopter in its day but it was not a successful design and only two were built.*
ABOVE CENTRE: *The Piasecki HRP–1 was the first practical tandem rotor helicopter.*
ABOVE: *One of Germany's successful wartime helicopters, the Flettner Fl–282 was the first to use a twin intermeshing rotor system.*
LEFT: *One of the small servo rotor 'paddles' is visible above the rotor head of this Hiller H–23B.*

349

Rotorcraft Configurations

Configuration Code & Category

RTG Running Take-off Autogyro
STG Short Take-off Autogyro
VTG Vertical Take-off Autogyro
Freely rotating rotor, with forward propulsion by conventional propeller thrust. The rotor is tilted backward with respect to the flight path at all times. No rotor torque and no hovering capability.

AGG Autogyro Glider
Freely rotating rotor, usually started by hand. The equivalent of propeller thrust is supplied by a tow rope. In high winds, the AGG can be made to take off as a kite with an anchored tow rope.

MTR Main and Tail Rotor helicopter
Both lift and propulsion are provided by a single main rotor. The functions of the small tail rotor are to counteract main-rotor torque and to provide control in yaw. Both rotors are engine-driven through a gearbox and shaft system at a constant speed ratio, tail-rotor rpm being approximately five times main-rotor rpm.

TTR Twin Tandem-Rotor helicopter
The twin rotors are contra-rotating to counteract torque and in some types they may overlap slightly. In such cases a synchronizing transmission shaft between the two rotor heads ensures that the two rotors keep a uniform speed so that blades cannot foul each other.

TSR Twin Side-by-side Rotor helicopter
The twin rotors are contra-rotating to counteract torque and are mounted on lateral outriggers which may, but need not, be lifting surfaces. The rpm of the two rotors are synchronized but the blades do not normally overlap. A conventional tail unit often supplements rotor control.

TIR Twin Intermeshing-Rotor helicopter
This is a cross between the TSR and CXR configurations. It avoids the mechanical complexity of co-axial gear systems but needs precise synchronization of the contra-rotating rotors. At the same time, the greater swept area increases rotor efficiency.

CXR Co-axial contra-rotating Rotor helicopter
The twin rotors are contra-rotating to counteract torque. Cyclic and collective pitch is applied to the two rotors in unison. Control in yaw is achieved by differential collective-pitch variation between the rotors so that the resulting difference in torque produces a turning moment.

CMP Compound helicopter
A single lifting rotor provides the means of sustentation alone, while separate means of propulsive thrust is used to combine the propulsion and anti-torque functions. The plane of the rotor remains substantially parallel to the flight path in normal cruising flight to reduce aerodynamic drag for higher speeds.

CVT Convertiplane
The thrust produced is used in the vertical sense for take-off and to reach a forward speed at which the conventional fixed wing can take over the lift function. The vertical thrust is then converted, usually by mechanical means, into horizontal thrust for high-speed propulsion. For landing it is converted back again.

SJR Single Jet-driven Rotor helicopter
This may be similar in appearance to the MTR, but without the tail rotor as there is no torque when the rotor is rotated by jet propulsion at the blade tips. If a separate means of propulsive thrust is embodied in the design, the SJR can also be a VTG or a CMP.

Typical Features

Most autogyros come within these three categories. Different types are obviously different in appearance but there is little to distinguish the categories from each other as variations in take-off performance are normally achieved through refinements to the rotorhead design. The distinctions become apparent only in a detailed inspection of the rotorhead mechanism.

Introduced by Focke Achgelis during World War II. The Fa–330 single-seater was built in quantity for use by German submarines on aerial spotting duties. Post-war versions, designed for towing behind a motor car or boat, became popular for pleasure flying in the 1950s and could be converted to ultra-light RTGs (*q.v.*) by the addition of an engine and propeller.

The classic helicopter configuration followed by the great majority of all helicopter constructors. This configuration is now equally applicable to the entire size range, from ultra-light single-seaters to the giant 50,800kg (112,000lb) helicopter cranes.

Developed originally to provide greater lifting capacity when it was thought that single rotors would not be practicable in the sizes calculated to be necessary. This early hypothesis has since been disproved by progressive experience but the TTR configuration is still retained by Boeing Vertol types and there have been many other examples.

This was the original configuration adopted by Focke and Weir but it has hardly been used since, except in Russia. The TSR configuration, however, is suitable for some convertible helicopters, such as the tilt-rotor projects. One example of these, the Bell XV–15, is under development in the USA. If convertible, they are categorized as CVTs (*q.v.*).

A variation on the TSR configuration to reduce the overall width and eliminate the structural weight of the outriggers. First used by Flettner in Germany and followed by Kellett and Kaman in the USA. There are still a few of the last-mentioned types in current operation. TIRs are known jocularly as 'egg-beaters', but the configuration has not been used for new projects since the 1950s.

This was the original Bréguet-Richet configuration. It has the advantage of compactness but aerodynamic interference between the downwash from the two rotors can cause problems. The possibility of mechanical interference between the blades is overcome in the latest example, by Cierva Rotorcraft, with an inter-rotor transfer link system.

In this category, the means of sustentation and the means of propulsion are designed to retain their separate functions throughout the flight envelope. The category was pioneered by the Fairey Gyrodyne and can be said to include any helicopter fitted with supplementary means of increasing horizontal propulsive thrust.

Tilt-wing and tilt-rotor aircraft come within this category. In the Canadair CL–84 the whole wing, engines and propellers are power-tilted to convert from one flight regime to another. In the Bell XV–15, the rotors and gearboxes on the wing tips are tilted while the wing itself remains fixed. Both fly as conventional aircraft in normal cruising flight.

Pioneered by Frederick von Doblhoff in Austria, the jet-driven rotor system has been applied many times in experimental helicopter projects. Only one, however, the French Djinn helicopter, has ever been put into quantity production and even this was for only a comparatively short period.

Cierva Autogyro

Focke–Achgelis FA–330

Bell Jet Ranger

Boeing Vertol CH.47 Chinook

Bell XV–15

Kaman H–43 Huskie

Cierva

Fairey Cyrodyne

Canadair CL–84

Djinn

The turbine engine

Another coincident factor, which had a particularly important influence on the rapid rate of development from the mid-1950s onward, was the advent of the turbine engine and its application to helicopters. In fixed-wing aircraft, the shaft turbine as a powerplant to drive a conventional propeller – known as the turboprop – was not the sweeping success for which its designers had hoped. This was largely because it was so quickly superseded by the turbojet, which could produce much higher speeds and thereby justify its much higher costs.

For helicopters, though, the shaft turbine proved ideal. It had a much lower installed weight than the piston engine, which more than offset the greater fuel loads which had to be carried. Consequently, helicopter designers found for the first time that they had abundant power available. Moreover, the normal operating characteristics of the turbine, which permitted extended running without fear of damage at up to about 85 per cent power, was particularly well suited to a helicopter's requirement for long periods of continuous hovering in certain military roles. The high initial cost and high fuel consumption were no drawbacks to the military, while the much shorter warm-up period before take-off and smoother operation in flight were considerable advantages.

So, with the power available, much bigger helicopters were soon found to be practicable. Earlier fears of limitations to the size of rotor systems proved groundless in practice, and

Aerospatiale's boat-hulled Super Frelon seen in an air/sea rescue exercise.

the helicopter grew up. Before 1950, apart from the Cierva W–11 Air Horse prototype, of 7,938kg (17,500lb) gross weight, the biggest production helicopters powered by piston engines were in the region of 2,500kg (5,510lb) gross weight, with a lifting capability of some 680kg (1,500lb). Ten years later, at the outset of the Vietnam conflict in the early 1960s, transport helicopters like the Boeing Vertol CH–47A Chinook were in the air at gross weights of some 15,000kg (33,070 lb). The Chinook, with twin Lycoming tur-

bines providing 5,300shp total installed power, had a useful load capability of more than 7 tons.

Speeds too had risen. Before 1950, the world helicopter speed record stood at 201 km/h (124·9mph). By 1963, a French MTR helicopter, the Sud Aviation Super Frelon, had taken it to 341km/h (211·9mph).

In addition to the technological progress, production quantities were also increasing substantially. Four major American constructors, Bell, Boeing Vertol, Hiller and Sikorsky, were all in the big league, each with more than 1,000 helicopters produced. Bell, in fact, was well in the lead with more than 3,000. Large numbers were also being built in Europe and the Soviet Union. Some indication of the extent to which the USA had by then developed the new strategic philosophy of helicopter mobility is that in the US Army alone there were some 5,000 qualified helicopter pilots. Their largest training school was equipped with more than 200 light helicopters, mainly of Bell and Hiller manufacture, and staffed by nearly 150 flying instructors.

Looking to the future at that time, the US Army sponsored a Light Observation Helicopter (LOH) design competition among the already extended industry, the prize for which was to be a production contract for 3,000 turbine-powered helicopters. With military contracts of such proportions in progress and in prospect, it was not surprising that helicopter constructors could spare but scant effort to meet the admittedly

Type: Boeing Vertol CH–47C Chinook
Accommodation: 30–40
Engines: Two 3,750hp Lycoming T55–L–11 turbo-shafts

Cruising speed: 259km/h (161mph)
Ceiling: 4,570m (15,000ft)
Range: 370km (230 miles)

Loaded weight: 20,865kg (46,000lb)
Rotor diameter: 18·29m (60ft)
Length: 15·54m (51ft)

small needs of commercial operators. Progress was nevertheless made in commercial applications and a few constructors did set up small sales organizations to supply civil adaptations of the military helicopters which comprised their main production. Their selling price was high, but for specialized tasks they could be operated on a cost-effective basis. After some 15 years of consistent, if slow, growth, there were by 1960 about 1,000 helicopters operated commercially by some 300 companies throughout the world. More than half the companies, though, may have been operating only one, two or possibly three small helicopters.

Specialized tasks

The multiplicity of tasks undertaken by these civil operators impinged upon almost every sphere of industrial and commercial activity. The thousands of kilometres flown on such tasks as overhead power-line construction and patrol, or the innumerable hours flown on crop-spraying and other agricultural work, would rarely be noticed except by those directly concerned. Similarly, the constant aerial support work done for offshore oil prospectors became commonplace.

By its very nature, the greatest proportion of all such operations was performed in remote areas and received little publicity. Only when a helicopter was used for spectacular work in a populous area did its unique attributes become more widely known. Typical of such a single feat was the placing of the cross on the summit of the rebuilt Coventry Cathedral by an RAF Belvedere. Following this remarkable demonstration of precision lifting, aerial crane work became more widely accepted as part of the commercial helicopter's repertoire. In particular, larger machines were used to lift air-conditioning equipment on to the flat roofs of 'hi-rise' buildings, a job which helicopters still are not infrequently called upon to do.

The growth of this particular application, combined with military needs for heavy-lift helicopters, led to the development of aircraft designed specifically for aerial crane work. In the Sikorsky S–60 and S–64 crane helicopters, provision is made in the aft of the cabin for a third set of pilot's controls, with the seat facing rearwards. When the actual lifting is to be done, the helicopter is flown with the normal controls into the hover approximately above the load. The captain then leaves his usual seat and takes over the hover with the third, aft-facing, set of controls. In this position he is looking directly downward on to the load for the precision manoeuvre and can instruct the second pilot, over the intercomm, to take over and resume normal flight as soon as the load has been secured or released, as the case may be.

Mainly because of their high cost, these specialized helicopters have not yet come into general use with commercial operators, whose fleets are made up mostly of small and medium-sized machines with gross weights ranging between some 1,360kg (3,000lb) and 6,350kg (14,000lb). Some of the larger operators, with big oil-rig support contracts, may exceed this upper figure if they have Sikorsky S–61 series helicopters engaged on this work.

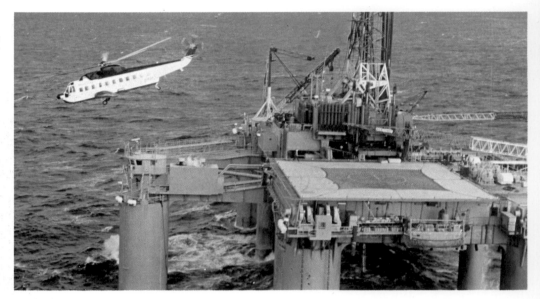

Passenger transport

The one area in which the civil helicopter had not made any significant headway up till the early 1960s was the carrying of passengers. There were a few meritorious attempts, mainly in the USA, to set up helicopter airline services and these met with some, if qualified, success. The routes flown provided direct links between the principal airports of the area served – Los Angeles, San Francisco, Chicago and New York – and the outlying suburbs. Their success was qualified in that, although the adapted military transport helicopters themselves were technically capable of providing the services, their operating economics were such that the companies needed some measure of government subsidy. There have been a few isolated exceptions, but most were forced eventually to close down for this reason. In Europe, a helicopter airline service centred on Brussels, operated by the Belgian airline SABENA, was discontinued but a British Airways service between Cornwall and the Scilly Isles has continued.

In its smaller sizes, too, the helicopter was as far from becoming an effective means of personal transport for the man in the street as it had ever been. In fact, by 1960 the dream of a back-garden flying machine for the masses had been completely abandoned. It was still hoped, though, that the unique vertical take-off and landing ability would enable executive transport and aerial taxi work to become an important addition to the helicopter's extensive range of applications.

One of the first helicopters to be developed specifically for this latter role was the Bell Model 47J, named the Ranger. This was not a new design but an adaptation of the earlier Model 47G, of which it used all the dynamic components. In other words, it was a 47G in

all its rotating mechanisms but had a newly styled four-seat cabin in place of the earlier type's transparent plastic bubble which enclosed a bench seat for three, including pilot, sitting side-by-side. The bench was retained in the 47J for the three passengers, but the cabin was extended forward to provide space for a fourth, separate, seat for the pilot. The fuselage was more streamlined, with a stressed-skin monocoque structure instead of the open tubular-steel framework of the 47G.

With these improvements, the 47J Ranger was able to attain slightly higher speeds, up to a maximum of some 169km/h (105mph), and the type was used quite widely for passenger transport. In contrast, however, contemporary light fixed-wing aircraft of equivalent size and power could offer something like twice the speed at about one-third of the cost, so the helicopter was again operating in a strictly limited field. At that time, few more than 100 helicopters of this kind were in regular operation for company transport use and, in most cases, they were for a highly specialized requirement which virtually precluded the use of fixed-wing aeroplanes.

The position changed dramatically with the introduction of the small turbine engine, a by-product of the American LOH design competition previously mentioned. The turbine engines first used as helicopter powerplants produced some 1,000shp. Two types were used initially, the General Electric T58, with a power range between 900shp and 1,100shp, and the Lycoming T53 of some 1,000shp to 1,100shp. Both were free-shaft turbines, more details of which can be found in the engine section of this volume. These two power units gave rise to the development of helicopters such as the Bell UH–1A Iroquois series, a ten-seat MTR helicopter of 3,856kg (8,500lb) gross weight; the Kaman

H–43B, a TIR aircraft of similar size; and, with a twin turbine installation, to the 25-seat Vertol 107 TTR transport helicopter and the 28-seat Sikorsky S–61 series, the latter still in production in 1977. All these types were flying by 1960.

Although the 1,000shp turbines were regarded as small by contemporary fixed-wing standards, they were far too large for use in the four- or five-seat aircraft in the 1,300 to 1,400kg (2,850 to 3,085lb) gross-weight category. The French company Turboméca was developing a range of smaller fixed-shaft turbines producing some 400shp, but it was the Allison T63 free-shaft unit, designed specifically for the US Army LOH project, which provided the major breakthrough. It had a power-turbine spool no bigger than a two-litre oil can but produced 250shp at its best operating speed.

All three finalists in the LOH competition, the Bell OH–4A, Hiller OH–5A and Hughes OH–6A, used this Allison T63 turbine. The declared winner was the Hughes OH–6A, a four-seater with a gross weight of 1,089kg (2,400lb) and a maximum speed of some 241 km/h (150mph), and mass-production of the type was set in motion. Of the other two, Bell developed its OH–4A prototype, which had been built to full civil airworthiness standards as one element of the design competition conditions, into what was to become the Model 206A JetRanger. A refined version of this type now constitutes the mainstay of light executive helicopter fleets. The additional speed conferred by the turbine engine was enough to make helicopter transport worthwhile to a much wider field of prospective users. Against a stiff headwind, the earlier 160km/h (100mph) helicopters were often no faster than a good motor car for conventional journeys. The extra 80km/h (50mph) of the turbine helicopter placed it well ahead in any wind conditions. Later, Hughes was also to produce a civil version, known as the Hughes 500, of the company's own turbine-engined competition winner.

Vietnam and its aftermath

When the Vietnam War began, the American armed forces were fully reorientated to the new military strategy of helicopter mobility. They were also partially equipped with a variety of light, medium and heavy transport helicopters, all turbine-powered, to put the new tactics into effect. The strategy met with virtually instant success, to the extent that some historians have dubbed the war in Vietnam 'The Helicopter War'. That the final outcome did not bring with it a conventional military victory for the new tactics was no fault of the helicopters.

The effect on the American helicopter industry of the initial successes in active service was extremely rapid expansion. Helicopters of all types were ordered in thousands; at one stage, Bell had one of the Beechcraft aeroplane factories almost exclusively engaged in producing fuselage and other components under sub-contract to meet the military demands. Experience in Vietnam also had a corresponding effect in other countries as

military strategists began to follow the American lead. The idea of an army going into action without helicopter support became totally outmoded.

The advances made during the ensuing decade and into the 1970s were largely a matter of degree. For example, the UH–1A Iroquois, designed by Bell as the Model 204, originally entered service just before 1960 as a ten-seat utility helicopter powered by a 1,100shp Lycoming T53–L–11 turbine. Its gross weight was 3,856kg (8,500lb), rotor diameter 13·41m (44ft) and disposable load 1,805kg (3,980lb). Through the years, 15 variants of the design have been produced, amounting to some 10,000 helicopters of this one series. The latest derivative, Bell's Model 214, has a maximum gross weight of 7,258kg (16,000lb) and a lifting capacity for external loads of up to 3,629kg (8,000lb). The rotor diameter has gone up to 15·24m (50ft) and the powerplant is a 2,930shp Lycoming T55–O8D turbine derated to 2,050shp for normal sea-level operation. This leaves a substantial power reserve available for high-altitude operation, maintaining sea-level performance up to about 6,000m (19,685ft).

Another current variant of the series, the 15-seat Bell 212, has a twin turbine installation for greater safety. The powerplant in this variant is the Canadian Pratt & Whitney PT6T–3, rated at 1,800shp total, in two coupled turbines either of which will sustain level flight if the other fails. The Model 212 rotor diameter is slightly smaller than that of the 214 at 14·69m (48ft 2½in) and the gross weight is 5,080kg (11,200lb).

Some indication of these advances' full extent can be gauged from the fact that the Lycoming T55 turbine in the model 214 is the same basic power unit used in a twin installation to power the 15-ton Boeing Vertol CH–47 Chinook helicopter. The Chinook itself is another typical example of the degree of advance made during the decade of the Vietnam war. The first prototype made its début in 1961 as a 14,969kg (33,000lb) gross-weight TTR military transport helicopter. It was powered by twin Lycoming T55–L–7 turbines of 2,650shp each and had a disposable load capacity of 6,804kg (15,000lb). It was the first big helicopter in which the rear loading door opened downwards to form a drive-on ramp for loading wheeled or tracked vehicles into the cabin, which was 9·14m (30ft) long. Diameter of the two tandem rotors was 17·98m (59ft).

In the latest Chinook, the CH–47C Model 234, the maximum gross weight has grown to 22,680kg (50,000lb) and the disposable load can now be more than 11,340kg (25,000lb). The rotor diameter has remained substantially the same but the systems and transmission have all been modified and strengthened to take the considerably greater power output from the twin Lycoming T55–L–11C turbines. These are rated at a maximum of 3,750shp each, with emergency reserve up to 4,500shp each. Altogether, Boeing Vertol and the Piasecki Helicopter Corporation (which it absorbed) have produced more than 2,500 tandem-rotor helicopters.

Sikorsky Aircraft, which has also graduated mainly into the construction of large

LEFT: *Latest of the Bell Iroquois series, known affectionately to thousands of pilots as 'Huey', is the 214.*
BELOW LEFT: *Another advanced concept is the Westland Lynx's hingeless rotor system.*
RIGHT: *The Bell LongRanger.*
BELOW RIGHT: *The Bell HueyCobra gunship firing one of its stub-wing-mounted rockets. The forward cockpit (left inset) is used by the second pilot who is also gunner/observer. The right insert shows the quick-firing gun mounted in a power-controlled turret.*
BOTTOM RIGHT: *Army version of the MBB Bo105 with pilot's cockpit (inset).*

helicopters, has produced even more, though not of tandem-rotor design. This company pioneered the boat-hulled helicopter with its S-61 series and has consequently been concerned mainly with production of aircraft for maritime applications. One of the latest versions of the S-61, known as the SH-3D Sea King, is in service with many navies for anti-submarine and air-sea rescue operations. One of their much publicized applications has been the retrieval of American astronauts on their splash-down return from space missions in the Atlantic or Pacific oceans. The Sea King is built under licence in several countries, in England by Westland Aircraft. Their version has a gross weight of 9,525kg (20,995lb). Disposable load is 2,350kg (5,180 lb). The machine is powered by twin Rolls-Royce Gnome H.1400-1 turbines, rated at 1630shp each, driving an 18m (59ft) diameter 5-bladed rotor. The Gnome turbines are derived from the General Electric T.58 turbines which power the American-built version. In addition to all-weather navigation systems, the Sea King's equipment can include full sonar detection apparatus plus four torpedoes and four depth charges. It is operated by a crew of four.

At the other end of the size range, the helicopter war in Vietnam brought out the light observation helicopters in their thousands. First the Hughes OH-6A Cayuse and, later, the Bell OH-58A Kiowa, derived from the original OH-4A which was itself the forerunner of the five-seat civil JetRanger. Bell's latest JetRanger variant, known as the Long-Ranger, has a passenger cabin 0·61m (2ft) longer than that of the JetRanger to provide space for two extra seats. The rotor is of 1·12 m (3ft 8in) greater diameter and the power unit, an Allison 250-C20B turbine, has a maximum continuous rating of 370shp as opposed to the 270shp of its predecessor. Gross weight of the seven-seat LongRanger is up to 1,814kg (4,000lb) whereas the JetRanger's gross weight is 1,452kg (3,200lb). Both types are still in full production.

Helicopter gunship
One more significant concept emerged from the implementation of the new military strategy in Vietnam. This concerned a much faster, heavily armed helicopter which could give close support and protection to troop-transport and supply armadas moving into forward battle zones. US Army commanders in the field found that aerial support available from conventional fixed-wing fighter squadrons was sometimes too remote and inflexible to be sufficiently effective for their specialized requirements. So the idea of the helicopter

recent attempts to revive the autogyro, commonly in the form of ultra-light single-seaters designed principally for amateur flying. There has been some progress in this field, though not without its problems, and the popularity of these diminutive rotorcraft has been spasmodic.

There is no reason why the autogyro could not be developed to a standard comparable in its own way with that of the present-day helicopter. It would never, however, be capable of sustained hovering flight, and it has always been precisely this facility from which the helicopter has derived its operating superiority. Enormous sums of money have been spent in reaching the present stage of development. The millions of flying hours accumulated by the tens of thousands of helicopters in current operation have yielded knowledge which has elevated the helicopter

gunship was born, the best known example of which is probably the Bell AH–1 Huey-Cobra. This design uses all the dynamic components of the latest Bell UH–1 utility helicopter in a slender, streamlined fuselage to give it a speed of up to 354km/h (220mph). It carries a crew of two, pilot and air gunner/observer, and can be armed with a range of missiles, rockets, rapid-firing machine-guns and other weapons. The type was in quantity production before the end of the Vietnam war and proved extremely effective on active service.

After Vietnam, attention was once more turned towards civil applications, the most significant current trend being the design of light and medium-sized twin-turbine helicopters able to operate in full Instrument Flight Rules (IFR) conditions. This has entailed the development of special instrumentation, autostabilizers and navigation aids and has resulted in the production of such sophisticated executive transport helicopters as the West German five-seat Messerschmitt-Bölkow-Blohm (MBB) BO105, the Italian eight-seat Agusta A.109 or the American ten-seat Bell 222. The twin-engine reliability common to all three is essential to meet the requirements of IFR operation in air traffic control zones and also to fly into heliports located at the centre of populous areas. All three follow the classic MTR configuration and all are capable of speeds of about 240 km/h (150mph) or better.

Mil V–12

One helicopter which merits special mention, as the largest in the world, is the Russian V–12 heavy transport helicopter, designed by the Mil bureau. In the 1960s, Mikhail Mil produced what was then the world's largest helicopter, designated Mi–6. It was a conventional MTR helicopter with a rotor diameter of 35m (114ft 10in) and powered by twin TV–2BM turbines producing 5,500shp each. Its gross weight was about 40,642kg (89,600lb), almost twice the weight of its nearest rival.

The V–12 is twice this size again, having been produced by combining two Mi–6 rotors, each with its twin-turbine power supply, in a giant Twin Side-by-side Rotor (TSR) configuration. The rotors with their power units are mounted at the ends of two inversely tapered outrigger booms, through which transmission shafts couple the two pairs of turbines through a common gearbox in the upper fuselage. Power can thus be transferred from either side in the event of partial failure. The capacious cargo compartment measures over 29·43m (90ft) in length, 4·27m (14ft) in height and width. These are the same dimensions as those of the Antonov An–22 cargo transport aircraft, so it seems that the helicopter is intended to carry some of the same outsize loads. Lifting capability is more than 40,642kg (89,600lb).

Right at the other end of the size range, there should also be mentioned the many

engineer to a status of scientific parity with his fixed-wing counterpart.

Further design refinements, mainly to increase reliability, component life and comfort can be expected. Hingeless rotor systems such as in the new Westland Lynx and MBB BO105 are examples, as is the new nodal-beam suspension system being introduced by Bell to reduce the effects of unavoidable vibration. Some marginal increases in cruising speeds may also be introduced to advantage. The use of 'exotic' materials will certainly increase. In the early days, rotor blades were manufactured on a tubular spar with wooden ribs and stringers, and covered in fabric. Today, extruded alloy spars are used, with stainless steel and glass-reinforced plastics also embodied. Titanium is beginning to replace steel for certain rotorhead components, and many more developments along these lines are on the way.

With its present-day sophisticated systems, and especially with its requirement for an extremely high degree of precision engineering, the helicopter is probably one of the most expensive means of transport yet devised by man. Its great saving grace is that, in its unique sphere, it is also one of the most effective.

TOP LEFT: *The latest Agusta A–109 twin turbine helicopter and cockpit (inset).*
ABOVE LEFT: *The world's largest helicopter is Russia's Mil Mi–12.*
ABOVE: *The Bo–105 hingeless rotorhead system.*

Rotorhead Design

The heart of all rotorcraft, whatever the configuration, lies at the centre of the rotorhead. Through the geometry of this rotating mechanical assembly, all the power and all the major control functions are passed to the rotor system while back through it, as appropriate to the design, comes the principal response to aerodynamic effects.

All the basic principles of aerodynamics explained in the first chapter of this volume apply equally to the individual blades of the rotor system; but there is added complexity of effect due to the more complex motions of the blades with respect to the fuselage. In hovering flight, each blade is generating a constant lift proportional to the square of its own rotational speed throughout its 360° cycle of rotation. As soon as the machine begins to move forward, however, each blade produces lift proportional to the square of its rotational speed plus the forward speed on one side of the rotor and minus the forward speed as it passes round on the opposite side. The two sides are termed the advancing and retreating sides of the rotor disc.

Lift asymmetry between the advancing and retreating sides, which would obviously cause lateral instability, is avoided in most rotorhead designs by the inclusion of a flapping hinge on the hub, inside the blade root attachment. This allows a blade to flap upwards in response to its increasing lift as it comes into the influence of the higher-velocity airflow on the advancing side. This upward movement reduces the blade's angle of attack and, consequently, its lift. The reverse occurs as it passes round to the retreating side and flaps downward again in response to the lower-velocity air, increasing angle of attack and lift. Blade lift is thus automatically equalized between the two sides of the disc. In Cierva's original autogyros, plain steel bearings were used for the flapping hinges. Later, roller bearings took their place while, in the latest helicopter designs, elastomeric bearings needing no lubrication are used. The equivalent effect in so-called rigid-rotor helicopters is achieved through the medium of a flexible section at the root end of the blade spar itself.

Equalization of lift over the swept area is also influenced by the rotor control system. In flight, the blades are held in position between the effects of lift and centrifugal force, the latter being approximately five or six times greater than the former. The overall rotor lift can be taken to act through a point at the hub centre and control of flight attitude is effected by means of tilting the rotor so that its overall lift vector moves away from the vertical, remaining perpendicular always to the plane of the spinning blades. The helicopter thus tilts with the rotor and then begins to move into the direction of tilt.

Tilting the rotor for control purposes is achieved either by mounting the hub on a universal joint and tilting it through a lever mechanism connected to the pilot's controls, or by fitting a universally mounted swashplate below the hub which is likewise connected to the pilot's controls. In this case, pitch-change bearings (to allow the blades torsional freedom about their longitudinal axes) are fitted in the blade-spar roots and connecting rods link the tiltable swashplate to pitch-control arms on the blades.

In the case of the tilting-hub method, as used in the early autogyros, a forward tilt of the hub

introduced by pilot control reduces the pitch angle of the advancing blade with respect to the fuselage because it inclines the flapping hinge axis. At the same time, the same hub inclination increases the pitch angle of the retreating blade. A forward rotor tilt thus follows the forward hub tilt because the blades are made to fly low in the forward sector of the disc and high at the rear.

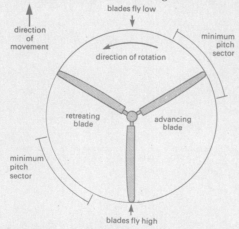

In addition, asymmetry of lift is influenced by the input of such a control tilt because the magnitude of blade lift is dependent both on the pitch angle and on the air velocity. Since the reduction of pitch resulting from the forward hub tilt takes effect in the advancing sector of the disc, and vice versa on the retreating side, the advancing blade loses lift while the retreating blade gains lift from the effect of the hub inclination. The flapping effect and the forward tilt effect are therefore working in harmony to equalize blade lift on the advancing and retreating sides of the rotor. Although the blade pitch change introduced by the control tilt does minimize the flapping motions of the blades, the flapping hinges are nonetheless necessary as some residual flapping still occurs which would otherwise lead to undesirable blade-root stresses and vibration.

The same applies to the alternative method using the tilting swashplate, which is known as

cyclic pitch control. A forward tilt of the swashplate causes the blade pitch arm connecting rods to be pulled down on the advancing side while, at the same time, they are being pushed up on the retreating side. This reduces the pitch angle of each blade with respect to the hub when advancing and increases it again when retreating, by twisting it about its pitch-change bearing. In this case, the effect on rotor tilt is accentuated. The cyclic variation of blade pitch is in the order of 10°, from a datum setting plus 5° on the retreating side to datum minus 5° in the advancing sector. Control movements to tilt either the swashplate or the universally mounted hub are made through a bearing assembly, since they are rotating with the rotorhead whereas the control-lever mechanism is mounted on the fuselage structure.

Use of the tilting-swashplate method also allows the introduction of what is known as collective pitch control. Its primary function is to provide for control of movement in the vertical sense at take-off and landing. Superimposed on the rotorhead cyclic pitch-control mechanism is another assembly which permits the swashplate itself to be raised or lowered, irrespective of its angle of tilt. Thus the connecting rods to the blade-pitch

arms can also be pushed up or down in unison, either to increase or decrease the pitch angle of all blades simultaneously. Associated engine-control linkages ensure that as the connecting rods move the blade-pitch arms upwards, increased power is applied to the rotor drive-shaft, and vice versa. This power control is often applied through the medium of an engine-speed governor, particularly with turbine-powered helicopters.

The range of collective pitch control available on a typical helicopter would be from 2° positive (the autorotative pitch) to about 14° positive. For take-off, the collective pitch lever would normally be raised to give a setting of some 10° on the blades, at which point the machine would lift off. To sustain forward flight, a continuous forward tilt is applied to the rotor through the controls; higher speeds are attained by increasing collective pitch and power. In this condition, the individual blades will be changing their pitch continuously at a rate of something like eight times per second, as they pass through their cycle of rotation. In the event of engine failure, the pilot action is to reduce collective pitch to the lowest value, whereupon the helicopter becomes an autogyro and glides gently downwards with the rotor in autorotation.

In the autogyro itself, blade pitch is normally fixed at the 2° setting and the rotor is not tilted forwards to provide propulsive thrust. This comes from the conventional propeller. In both the helicopter and the autogyro, lateral tilting of the rotor is used for sideways and turning control.

Reference to the section on aerodynamics will show that the reduction of blade lift resulting from its upward flapping motion is governed by the reduction in the blade's effective angle of attack. The reduced lift following a reduction of blade pitch angle represents a different means of achieving the same objective. The difference between angle of pitch and angle of attack is explained in the glossary.

There remains one further degree of freedom which may be allowed to the blades in some rotorhead designs. This is achieved by including drag hinges, also known as lead-lag hinges, which permit the blades limited motion with respect to each other in the plane of rotation. For a combination of aerodynamic and mechanical reasons, the blades tend to speed up very slightly as they pass through the advancing sector of the disc and slow down again as they traverse the retreating sector. These minor accelerations and decelerations with-

in the spinning rotor would give rise to vibrations if not suitably suppressed. Drag hinges are normally located between the flapping hinges and pitch-change bearings, but in some cases the flapping and drag hinges are coincident. Some designs dispense with drag hinges in favour of providing suitable stiffness in the blade spars themselves.

Rotors fitted with both flapping and drag hinges are known as fully articulated since the combination of the two constitutes the equivalent of a universal joint. Rotors with flapping hinges only are termed semi-articulated. The addition of hydraulically operated servo controls, in the larger helicopters, does not necessarily affect the geometry of the rotorhead, but other design refinements may do so. For example, if the flapping-hinge axis is designed to be set at an angle of less than 90° to the blade's longitudinal axis, when the blade flaps upwards the motion will also have in it an element of pitch reduction. The so-called rigid-rotor helicopters, which at the time of writing comprise only a small proportion of all rotorcraft, would be better described as hingeless-rotor machines. They function on much the same principles, using flexible members in place of hinges in order to reduce complexity.

V/STOL

The introduction of the turbojet engine, towards the end of World War II, came at a time when every available effort was being made by both sides to channel this new invention into a fighter aircraft. As events transpired, neither side was able to bring the first jet fighters into service until the war was virtually over.

After hostilities ceased, engine designers had more time to think of other future possibilities and vertical take-off, for both military and civil aircraft, was one obvious application. Even the early jet engines could develop a thrust of higher value than their own weight. By the time the Rolls-Royce Nene turbojet came into service, in the early 1950s, its maximum thrust of some 1,814kg (4,000 lb) was roughly twice its own weight. There was thus ample margin for the additional weight of a supporting framework.

To evaluate the feasibility of controlling such a concept, Rolls-Royce mounted two Nenes horizontally in a tubular-steel engine test-bed and modified the engine tailpipes to direct the jet efflux vertically downwards. When it first flew, in 1953, the four-legged framework created a worldwide sensation and was promptly dubbed the 'Flying Bedstead'.

Gross take-off weight of the machine was 3,264kg (7,196lb). Maximum vertical thrust from the two Nenes was about 3,629kg (8,000 lb) so there was no doubt about its vertical take-off capability. The main experimental purpose of the test rig was to evaluate the system devised for attitude control in hovering flight. Compressed air was bled from the two engine compressors, at 3·2kg (7lb) per second, into a common collector box and then ducted into four downward-facing nozzles, one positioned forward, one aft and one at either side.

The fore and aft nozzles each had a 10cm (4in) diameter orifice and produced some 132kg (290lb) average thrust at a 4·27m (14 ft) arm from the centre of gravity. To control pitch attitude, their thrust could be varied differentially by diverter valves connected to the pilot's control column. The nozzles could also be swivelled differentially from side to side by the rudder pedals, to provide control in yaw. The lateral nozzles were approximately half the diameter and half the distance from the centre of gravity, producing some 15·9kg (35lb) thrust each. This, too, could be varied differentially by lateral movement of the pilot's control column. The aggregate of all the control thrust remained constant and continuous during hovering flight and so it contributed slightly to vertical lift. After a few inevitable teething troubles had been overcome, the system worked reasonably well. About 380 tethered flights and 120 free

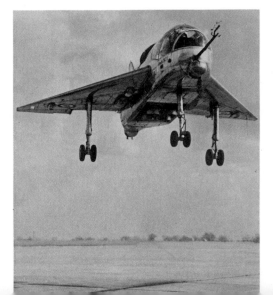

flights were made during the comprehensive tests that followed.

The success of the 'Flying Bedstead' conjured up futuristic visions of Vertical Take-Off and Landing (VTOL) airliners operating direct between the centres of the world's capital cities, without the need for aerodromes and all the travelling delays associated with them. It was the fixed-wing aircraft designers' answer to the helicopter, then still in the throes of demonstrating its basic practicability. The vision spurred Rolls-Royce into the development of a special series of lightweight turbojet engines with a remarkably high power:weight ratio; in the first of the series, the RB.108, it was 8:1. The RB.108 was rated at 1,002kg (2,210lb) maximum take-off thrust for a basic dry weight of only 122kg (269lb). It was designed specifically for a vertical-lift application with provision for deflecting the angle of the jet efflux by a few degrees to aid control when hovering in flight.

The first use made of this power unit was by Short Brothers & Harland in the SC–1 delta-wing research aircraft. Powered by five RB.108s, four mounted vertically in two pairs for lift and one mounted horizontally for propulsive thrust, the SC–1 became the world's first fixed-wing jet-powered VTOL aircraft to achieve vertical take-off, in 1958. The first full transition—from the hover to fully wingborne forward flight and then back to the hover sustained only by the lift jets—was made in 1960.

Provision was made in the SC–1 for the

two pairs of lift engines to be swivelled fore and aft of the vertical. After take-off, they were swivelled aft a few degrees so that their thrust supplemented that of the propulsive engine in the transition to forward flight. On the approach to land, the lift engines could be swivelled forward a few degrees to provide a braking effect in the transition back to hovering flight. All five engines were fitted with a compressor bleed from which high-pressure air was fed into a common duct for hovering control. The duct system terminated in four small ejector nozzles, one at each wing tip, one at the nose and one at the tail, similar to the system used on the 'Flying Bedstead'.

The SC–1 was intended as the forerunner of a single-seat VTOL fighter which would use a more powerful version of the RB.108 engine for propulsive thrust. It was also intended as the scaled-down prototype of a much larger VTOL airliner. There was, however, another jet-lift system under concurrent development by Hawker and this, known as the vectored-thrust system, eventually proved superior.

Based on the Bristol Siddeley BS.53 Pegasus turbofan engine (see Chapter 4 for details), the vectored-thrust system was first tried in the Hawker P.1127, a developed version of which prototype was later named the Kestrel when it joined a trinational evaluation squadron of British, American and West German composition. Whereas in the Short SC–1 the greater part of thrust available was shut down during wing-borne flight, in the

vectored-thrust system of the Kestrel it could all be used to attain much higher forward speeds. The efflux from the turbofan engine was ejected through four swivelling nozzles, two forward and two aft on either side of the fuselage under the wing. For vertical take-off and landing, the nozzles were swivelled to direct the jets vertically downward, while for forward flight the nozzles were swivelled to the rear to give horizontal thrust.

First hovering trials of the P.1127 began in 1960 and the first full transition from vertical take-off to conventional forward flight and then back to vertical landing was achieved in the following year. By 1964, the aircraft had attained supersonic speed in a shallow dive and more powerful, truly supersonic, versions were under development.

Meanwhile, in Europe, the French company Marcel Dassault was developing a VTOL adaptation of one of its Mirage fighters. By replacing the SNECMA Atar turbojet with a smaller Bristol Siddeley Orpheus turbojet, space was made in the fuselage for installing eight Rolls-Royce RB.108 lift jets, mounted vertically in four pairs. This aircraft, called the *Balzac*, began flight trials in 1962 and was the forerunner of the Mirage III–V prototypes, which in turn were de-designed to lead on to a Mach 2 VTOL fighter-bomber. The production version of the Mirage III–V was planned to have a SNECMA-developed afterburning TF–306 (based on the Pratt & Whitney TF30) as its much more powerful main propulsion unit, and eight Rolls-Royce RB.162 jets for vertical lift. The RB.162 was a developed version of the RB.108 and produced just over twice the thrust, 2,109kg (4,650lb). Development of the Mirage III–V was however discontinued after an unfortunate series of accidents, despite the prototypes having made successful transitions from hovering to forward flight and vice versa, and having achieved supersonic speed.

The more powerful Rolls-Royce lift jets were also chosen by the German company Dornier, which produced an ambitious project for a VTOL transport aircraft. It was designed as a high-wing monoplane with a cruising speed of 750km/h (466mph). Collaborators in the project were Vereinigte Flugtechnische Werke (VFW). The prototype, designated Do31E, had two banks each of four RB.162s to provide a total lift thrust of some 16,000kg (35,274lb), mounted in wing-tip pods. This was supplemented at take-off by the vectored thrust of twin Bristol Siddeley Pegasus 5 turbofans which combined to add some 10,433kg (23,000lb) to

TOP LEFT: *A tilt duct VTOL project developed in France by S.NCA du Nord. Only one machine was built.*

TOP: *A Fiat G/95A hovering rig built for research purposes in Italy. It was powered by Rolls-Royce lift jets.*

FAR LEFT: *This hovering rig was built by Dornier in Germany. The long puff jet arms relate to the wing span of the Do–31E prototype (above).*

LEFT: *The Ryan XV–5A fan-in-wing research aircraft was one of the concepts developed in the American attempts at VTOL design.*

ABOVE RIGHT: *The Lockheed Hummingbird, designated XV–4A by the US Army, employed an induced flow principle to achieve VTOL characteristics.*

RIGHT: *The Ryan X–13 Vertijet had no landing gear but took off from and landed on this adjustable hydraulic ramp. It proved impracticable.*

the static lift thrust. The production version was planned to have still higher take-off thrust, with ten RB.162 lift jets, and its gross weight was to be about 23,500kg (51,808lb).

Control in hovering flight was by a combination of differential thrust on the lift jets, for lateral control, and small 'puffer' nozzles at the tail for fore-and-aft control. Two of the tail nozzles were directed downwards and two upwards, all four being fed by ducted high-pressure air bled from the lift engines. Control in yaw was by differential inclination of the lift-engine nozzles.

To test this proposed control system, Dornier built an open-framework hovering rig powered by four Rolls-Royce RB.108 lift jets. This test rig had much longer arms than the original 'Flying Bedstead'. Its overall dimensions were similar to the wing span and length of the actual Do31E prototype so that control movements would be comparable with those to be expected in the actual aircraft when it flew, which was in 1967. The hovering rig flew in 1964 but the main project was later discontinued. Nevertheless, both Dornier and VFW retain an interest in Vertical/Short Take-off and Landing (V/STOL) aircraft. A similar hovering rig was built by Fiat, in Italy, but was abandoned in 1966 before free flight was attempted.

Another German project, developed by the Entwicklungsring Sud research group formed by Bölkow, Heinkel and Messerschmitt in 1960, adopted yet another design configuration. In this project designated VJ–101C, a small high-wing monoplane of 6,010 kg (13,250lb) gross weight had six Rolls-Royce RB.108 lift jets installed in three pairs. One pair was mounted vertically in the fuselage, immediately abaft the pilot's cockpit, while the second and third pairs were in swivelling wing tip pods. For vertical take-off, all six lift jets were used, with the wing tip pods swivelled into the vertical position. To make the transition into forward flight, the wing tip pods were swivelled forwards through a 90° arc until their efflux provided horizontal thrust. As forward speed increased, with the wing taking over the lift function, the forward pair of lift engines was shut down. The prototype VJ–101C started flight trials in 1963 but the project was abandoned in the following year.

Concurrently, a variety of different projects was in the course of development in the USA. In 1963, Lockheed produced and flew its XV–4A jet-lift VTOL fighter prototype, powered by twin Pratt & Whitney JT12A–3 turbojets rated at 1,497kg (3,300lb) static thrust each. Named Hummingbird, the XV–4A was a mid-wing monoplane. The two engines, mounted horizontally in nacelles alongside the centre fuselage, were arranged to provide either horizontal or vertical thrust. For vertical take-off, the efflux from both engines was diverted through ducting into rows of downward-facing nozzles in the centre-fuselage compartment between the engine nacelles known as the nozzle chamber. Above and below the chamber, long doors in the upper and lower fuselage skin could be opened to allow free downward flow of the efflux, coupled with induced flow of ambient air through the upper doors to mix with and

augment the jet efflux. The angle of the fixed nozzles was such that the aircraft hovered in a nose-up attitude. As in a helicopter, the application of forward control lowered the nose and thus introduced a rearward component of vertical thrust which imparted forward acceleration.

At approximately 145km/h (90mph), sufficient lift was being produced by the wing to allow the efflux from one of the turbojets to be diverted back to the direct propulsive function; conventional wing-borne flight was then established. This would be followed by diverting the second engine to direct horizontal thrust and closing the nozzle chamber doors. Design maximum speed was 837km/h (520mph). The system functioned reasonably well, but performance was not sufficient to warrant continuation of the project.

Ryan Aeronautical conceived a different way of achieving vertical take-off. Using what was known as the fan-in-wing system, the XV–5A prototype obtained its vertical thrust from two 1·59m (5ft 2½in) diameter,

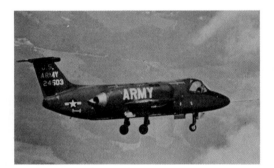

36-blade lift fans mounted horizontally in the wings. A third, smaller, lift fan was mounted in the nose for control purposes. Around the periphery of each fan were fitted small turbine blades, or scoops, on to which the efflux from the twin General Electric J85–5 turbojets impinged to produce a fan speed of 2,640rpm at the full rated power of 1,206kg (2,658lb) static thrust on each engine.

Hinged semi-circular doors in the upper and lower wing surfaces above and below the fans were opened during the take-off. Below each fan there was also a series of transverse louvres, adjustable under pilot control. A thumb-wheel on the control column was used to rotate these louvres and so deflect the fan thrust rearwards to gain forward speed from the hovering position. Differential rotation of the louvres could be demanded through the pilot's normal controls to provide roll and yaw control in the hovering and slow-speed phases. Conventional wing-borne flight was established in this aircraft at approximately 225km/h (140mph), whereupon the turbojet efflux was transferred from the peripheral scoops on the fans to normal tail-pipe ejection and the fan doors were closed.

Flight trials of the Ryan XV–5A began in 1964 but, although the concept proved practicable, it too was later abandoned. Ryan was also involved in the experimental development of a 'tail-sitter' jet aircraft, the X–13, which was designed to take off vertically from a gantry. This, however, proved impracticable for a number of reasons. More successful was the company's contribution, with Hiller

LEFT: *Ling Temco Vought XC–142A military transport tilt wing aircraft. The project was designed by a consortium of American companies, including Hiller and Ryan, for the US Air Force. It flew successfully on test but has not been built in quantity.*
BELOW: *Canadair's CL–84 tilt wing aircraft has a horizontal co-axial rotor system designed by Cierva Rotorcraft mounted abaft the rudder. It provides fore-and-aft control in the hover and is stopped and locked in cruising flight.*
BOTTOM: *US Marine Corps Harrier Squadron. US manufacturing licencees for the type are McDonnell Douglas and the USMC designation is AV–8A.*
ABOVE RIGHT: *The Curtiss Wright X–19 tilt propeller VTOL research aircraft. It flew successfully but the mechanical complexity of the design was too great for practical operations.*
BELOW RIGHT: *Russian Forger A VTOL fighters and KA–25 helicopters pictured on the flight deck of the new Russian commando assault ship* Kiev. *The picture was taken by an RAF reconnaissance aircraft in the Mediterranean.*
FAR RIGHT: *Hawker Siddeley Harrier VTOL supersonic fighter. The design was developed from the original P–1127 and the Kestrel and it is now in production in both a land-based version and a naval variant known as the Sea Harrier.*

Helicopters, to the Ling-Temco-Vought XC–142A tilt-wing project for a military transport. Powered by four 2,850shp General Electric T64–1 shaft turbines, driving 4·72m (15 ft 6in) diameter variable-pitch propellers, the XC–142A was designed to carry up to 7,112kg (15,680lb) of wheeled vehicles and other cargo in its 9·14m (30ft) long cabin. Its maiden flight was in 1964, but it too never entered production.

Other North American companies concerned with tilt-wing projects have been Boeing Vertol and Canadair, the latter company's twin-engined CL–84 having been longest in development. The use of ducted fans or ducted propellers has been yet another concept in the USA's search for a vertical take-off capability. It has been proved feasible by Hiller, Piasecki and others, but is hardly practical for general service. Bell Aerosystems, an associate of the helicopter constructor, developed a project for an aircraft in which four ducted propellers mounted on two stub wings were capable of being tilted through 90° to provide either vertical or horizontal thrust. Powered by twin General Electric T58 shaft turbines of 1,250shp each, the machine was known as the X–22A. A similar aircraft, using four tilting propellers without the ducts, was built by Curtiss Wright and designated X–19A.

Between 1950 and 1970, the US military authorities sponsored the development of almost any apparently feasible VTOL system for practical evaluation. None of the methods, however, was as reliable as the British vectored-thrust principle, so it has transpired that a developed version of the Hawker Siddeley Kestrel has been adopted for operational service with the US Marine Corps and Spanish Navy as well as with Britain's Royal Air Force (RAF).

Named the Harrier, this single-seat V/

STOL close-support and reconnaissance aircraft is powered by a single Rolls-Royce Pegasus 11 turbofan developing 9,752kg (21,500lb) thrust. It is a shoulder-wing monoplane with pronounced anhedral both on the wings and tailplanes and with the leading edges of both swept back to an angle of about 40°. The first fixed-wing V/STOL aircraft to enter service in the world, some 105 Harriers had been ordered for the RAF by the mid-1970s, 110 for the US Marine Corps and 12 for the Spanish Navy.

Two new variants of the type are now under development. In Britain, Hawker Siddeley is building the Sea Harrier, substantially the same as its land-based progenitor but with a new nose section to house a multi-mode radar. The type is due to enter Royal Navy service in 1979 and will operate from a new class of anti-submarine cruisers.

In the USA, Hawker Siddeley's licensee McDonnell Douglas is developing a variant designated AV–8B, which will retain the Harrier's fuselage and vectored-thrust engine but will have an entirely new and larger wing made substantially of composite materials. The AV–8B will also be endowed with strakes and other lift-improvement devices designed to eliminate 'suck-down' effects when the aircraft is hovering near the ground.

That the VTOL fighter is now firmly established as a weapon with formidable potential is evidenced by the recent appearance in Russian naval service of the Yakovlev Yak–36 Forger, which uses an almost unique lift- and lift/cruise-engine formula. A single lift and propulsion engine has two vectoring nozzles, one on each side of the fuselage beneath the trailing edge of the wing. This is supplemented for vertical take-off and landing by two lift jets mounted in tandem just aft of the cockpit. This layout, though demonstrably effective in vertical operations, is for a number of reasons operationally unsuitable for short take-offs, such as the Harrier is able to make with a bigger payload than it can manage in vertical take-off.

Whether the vision of VTOL airliners will ever materialize must be left for the future to record. One of the greatest practical difficulties to be overcome may well be the noise generated at take-off and landing which, at current values, would be totally unacceptable in any city centre. It is by no means impossible, though, that some of the current principles may be applied to shorten the take-off runs of conventional jet or even supersonic airliners, in an endeavour to keep the size of tomorrow's international airports within reasonable bounds.

Short Take-off and Landing (STOL) Aircraft

For a wide range of aerial transport operations in which neither the vertical take-off capability nor high cruising speeds are essential, another quite specialized category of aircraft has evolved. This is the Short Take-off and Landing (STOL) aircraft which operates to the greatest advantage in the less well-developed regions of the world, often taking off from and landing on small, rough airstrips with few, if any, ground facilities.

Jet lift VTOL aircraft can, of course, be operated in an STOL mode. In other words, if space and a suitable surface are available for a running take-off to be made with the vectored thrust nozzles swivelled to a setting between the vertical and horizontal positions, this technique will permit greater loads to be carried. A typical application for such a technique could be for missions where longer range requires additional fuel to be carried. After its initial running take-off and flight to its operating area, the machine's VTOL capabilities will have been restored as the extra fuel load will, by then, have been consumed. The same technique can also be applied to

many helicopters and some convertiplanes, such as tilt-wing aircraft, to enable them to supply forward bases at long range. If the vertical take off or hovering capability is *never* to be required, though, the STOL aircraft is much more economic.

Background to the development of this category of aircraft is to be found in the growth of 'bush flying' during the 1920s, mainly in the northern territories of Canada and the Australian outback. Here, the principal attributes required of an aircraft have always been ruggedness, reliability and economy of operation; high speed is not so important. For safety in these desolate regions, where any reasonably level open space has to serve as an airfield, short take-off runs and low landing speeds are essential.

As the rapid improvement of aircraft in the years following World War I began to result in progressively higher cruising speeds, landing speeds increased proportionately and airfields had to be made correspondingly larger. To meet the bush fliers' special needs, some aircraft manufacturers introduced a variety of aerodynamic devices, such as special flaps, slots and the like, to improve wing efficiency. Aircraft so fitted were found to possess greatly improved handling characteristics at low speeds and a better load carrying performance for an equivalent installed power.

Through the years, many such aircraft types have been produced and some have made substantial contributions to man's pioneering in the remote regions of the world.

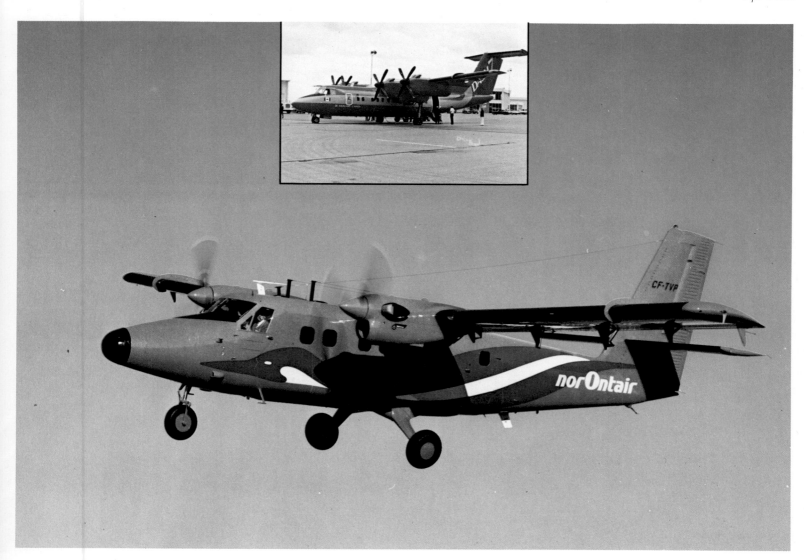

There has also been a good deal of military interest in STOL machines for general army transport and aerial reconnaissance duties. Today, sophisticated developments of the basic STOL theme, such as the sugmentor wing concept designed by de Havilland Aircraft in Canada, are being applied to much larger aircraft which are designed to have both civil and military functions.

Augmentor wing

The augmentor wing concept involves the use of full span slats at the leading edge, to delay the onset of turbulence over the wing's upper surface in an exaggerated nose-up attitude. This is combined with the use of full span double slotted flaps at the trailing edge, capable of downward deflection to an angle of 75°. The flaps are divided into three approximately equal length sections on each wing, the outboard sections serving also as ailerons. These are drooped to an angle of 30° when the inboard flaps are extended to 60° deflection and beyond. The drooped ailerons thus add considerably to the flap effect. They have a differential movement of plus or minus 17° on either side of the drooped datum position.

To supplement their effect still further, an air distribution duct system carries air bled from the Rolls-Royce Spey turbofan engines and expels it over and through the trailing edge flaps, to mix with and deflect downward the main airstream over the wing. Chokes in the airflow augmentor system can restrict the fan air outflow area at the flaps to control

ABOVE LEFT: *Of original Swiss design, the Pilatus Turbo-Porter can take off in 130m (426ft) with a payload of 940kg (2,072lb) in still air. Its high lift wing has a full span hinged trailing edge, the inner sections being double slotted.*
LEFT: *Produced by de Havilland Canada, the STOL DHC–5 Buffalo is being modified to embody the latest augmentor wing concept and boundary layer control systems. It is designed as a military transport with rear loading ramp for vehicles.*

ABOVE: *In current production by de Havilland Canada, the Twin Otter is designed for use particularly in remote regions where airstrip conditions may be very poor. Powered by twin turboprop engines, the type has full span flaps with drooped ailerons to achieve STOL characteristics.*
INSET ABOVE: *Latest in the long line of DHC STOL aircraft is the four-engined Dash 7 which more than doubles the Twin Otter payload while keeping the same STOL characteristics.*

the lift of the flap system. The outboard chokes can be linked to the pilot's controls, to supplement the roll effect of the ailerons at slow forward speeds, and all four chokes can be used simultaneously as a 'lift dump' at the moment of touch down. In addition, the high pressure fan air is used for a boundary layer control system at the flaps, to delay airflow separation at slow speeds.

Various versions of the system, either in whole or in part, are embodied in current de Havilland Canada designs such as the DHC–5 Buffalo, DHC–6 Twin Otter and DHC–7 Dash–7. The full system, as described here, is being developed by the company in collaboration with the Canadian and US governments in a DHC–5D Buffalo procured by the US National Aeronautics and Space Administration. NASA's designation of the test aircraft is XC–8A.

STOL aircraft have progressed considerably during the last quarter century. In contrast to the earlier single engined machines which, typically, could carry up to 6 or 7

passengers or a payload of about 1 tonne, the Twin Otter has accommodation for a crew of 2 and 20 passengers (or a 2-tonne payload), while the Dash–7, with four engines, has accommodation for 50 passengers or over 5 tonnes payload. The military transport Buffalo will carry 41 equipped troops, at speeds up to 420km/h (261mph), or stores up to 8,164kg (18,000lb). It was designed to have a load capability compatible with the Boeing Vertol Chinook helicopter. Like the Chinook, the Buffalo has a rear loading ramp for wheeled vehicles.

Typical take-off distance to become airborne that these big STOL aircraft can achieve is only about 300m (984ft) in still air. Landing rund for those types fitted with fully reversible pitch propellers may be as little as half this distance. While the concept may not be suitable for airliners flying the trunk air routes of the world, there can be little doubt that STOL aircraft will be coming into much more general use on short-haul routes as development proceeds.

Rocketry and
Space Exploration

Rockets and Guided Missiles

The Chinese are believed to have been the first to use missiles which fly by the reactive effect of their hot exhaust gases. Mongols besieging the town of Kai-fung-fu, north of the Yellow River, in 1232 felt the impact of 'arrows of flying fire' which the townsfolk launched in large numbers. The arrows were described as making a noise like thunder and travelling a great distance, spreading fire and destruction where they fell. There is no mention in the early literature of these fire-arrows being launched from a bow, and it seems likely that the Chinese stumbled upon the reactive effect after incendiary arrows (which had tubes of burning compounds bound to the shaft) were observed to fly faster and farther than conventional arrows.

Accounts exist of rocket-propelled fire-arrows being used in the siege of Siang-yang-fu in 1271, and the Mongols themselves seem to have introduced them into Japan. They were launched from Mongol ships during the battle of Tsu Shima in 1274 and were used again during the land attack on Iki Shima.

The next five centuries saw rockets being

used as fireworks and sometimes as weapons. One can trace the history of such devices – particularly fireworks – from China through the Mongolian intervention in Japan to Korea, Java and India.

Although mention of the use of saltpetre in explosive mixtures had been made in Arab literature of the 13th century, it was Roger Bacon, an English Franciscan monk, who established the proper mixture ratios of sulphur, saltpetre and charcoal which put 'gunpowder' on the map. Such refinements led, in about 1300, to the first crude firearms which used the principle of a tube, closed at one end, from which a ball was propelled by

PREVIOUS PAGES:
The development of Spacelab is a joint European–US programme. It will begin its first mission in 1980.

the sudden explosive ignition of gunpowder.

For a long time the war rocket was relatively neglected. It was not until the latter part of the 18th century, when British troops in India came under fire from Indian-built rockets in the two battles of Seringapatam of 1792 and 1799, that impetus was given to further development.

The Indian rockets used by the troops of Haidar Ali, prince of Mysore, had iron tubes bound by leather thongs to a bamboo stabilizing stick. They weighed between 2·7 and 5·4kg (6 and 12lb) and travelled over 915m (3,000ft). The rockets bounced and skittered over the ground and were particularly damaging to the British cavalry.

Congreve rockets

It was this encounter with rockets in India that led to more serious work in England through the efforts of Col William (later Sir William) Congreve, who began with the aim of doubling the range of the Indian rockets. His 14·5-kg (32-lb) weapon was iron-cased with a conical nose cap, measured 107cm (42in) in length and had a diameter of 10cm (4in). It contained a 3·17kg (7lb) charge. The 4·57m (15ft) stabilizing stick was detachable. It slipped into metal straps on the rocket head.

Under Congreve experiments were begun at the Royal Laboratory at Woolwich to develop incendiary rockets for use against the French during the Napoleonic Wars. The first major engagement took place in 1806 when some 2,000 Congreve rockets were dis-

charged against the town of Boulogne. They were fired from 18 boats which had been quietly launched from parent ships and rowed into the bay.

The following year a still more spectacular rocket attack was launched on Copenhagen which left much of the town ablaze. Congreve rockets were in action again in 1813 at the battle of Leipzig, and later that year Danzig fell after a series of rocket attacks.

In the war of 1812 between Britain and the United States, Congreve rockets repelled American troops in the battle of Bladensburg (1814) and were effective against infantry, cavalry and ships. The sight of the rockets bombarding Fort MacHenry inspired Francis Scott Key to write 'The Star-Spangled Banner' which later became the American national anthem. Warheads were of two types, those which discharged carbine balls with a shrapnel effect, and those with an incendiary mixture which started fires. In the end a whole family of Congreve rockets had been produced ranging from 8·2, 10·9, 14·5 and 19kg (18; 24, 32 and 42lb) to 'blockbusters' of 45·4 and 136·2kg (100 and 300lb). Rockets were referred to as 'pounders' – the 'pounder' designation actually referred to the weight of a lead ball that would fit into the internal diameter of a rocket.

Although Congreve made considerable advances in manufacture, rockets were still relatively inefficient and lacking in accuracy. A major disadvantage was the long balancing stick which inevitably accounted for a large part of the rocket's total dead weight.

William Hale, another British subject, eliminated the balancing stick by placing exhaust deflectors to impart spin at the nozzle end. These spin-stabilized rockets were used in various campaigns, notably by the Austrian rocket corps and the Dutch colonial service.

Some 2,000 were made in the US for use in the Mexican War. In the US Ordnance Manual of 1862 the 7·26kg (16lb) Hale rocket was credited with a range of 2km (1·25 miles).

Congreve also made spin-stabilized rockets later in his career. By the turn of the century, however, the black powder rockets were being outclassed by new developments in field artillery.

The rocket pioneers

The next big advances were of a more theoretical nature. In 1881 a Russian explosives expert, Nikolai Ivanovich Kilbalchich, was arrested and sentenced to death for his part in an assassination plot against Tsar Alexander II. While awaiting execution he sketched a design for a man-carrying platform propelled by gunpowder cartridges fed continuously to a rocket chamber. The chamber, mounted in a gimbal frame, could be swung manually on its axis to change the platform's path of flight as it rose into the air.

Kilbalchich's sketches were not discovered until after the Russian Revolution of 1917. In the meantime, a Russian genius of humble birth – Konstantin Tsiolkovsky – had greatly advanced rocket theory. By 1883 he was convinced that a rocket would work in the vacuum of space by the recoil effect of its exhaust gases. In 1903 he published his first treatise on space travel, in which he boldly advocated the use of liquid propellants.

During the early years of the 20th century Tsiolkovsky filled his notebooks with advanced ideas for rockets and with the arithmetic of space travel. He considered a whole range of liquid propellants including liquid oxygen and liquid hydrogen, liquid oxygen and gasolene or kerosene. He recommended controlling the thrust by regulating the flow of liquids by valves and proposed cooling the combustion chamber in which they burned by passing one of them through a double wall or jacket.

He proposed stabilizing rockets by the gyroscopic effect of a rotating flywheel and controlling their flight outside the atmosphere by means of rudders, or jet-vanes, working in the rocket's exhaust or by swivelling the nozzle. In this the Russian pioneer was anticipating *thrust vector control* in which a rocket is steered by changing the direction of its exhaust. In modern rockets this is either done by moving vanes in the exhaust gases, swivelling the rocket nozzle, or injecting fluid into a fixed nozzle from the side.

Tsiolkovsky also drew attention to the

ABOVE: *Robert H. Goddard was the great American rocket pioneer. The picture shows him loading a solid-fuel rocket of bazooka type in 1918. In 1926 he launched the world's first liquid fuel rocket.*
LEFT: *Modell B rocket to explore the upper atmosphere proposed by Hermann Oberth in 1923. Although never built, it inspired the rocket experimenters of the VfR ('German Society for Space Travel').*

ABOVE: *From this tower on 17 July 1929 Goddard launched a 'weather rocket' with a barometer, thermometer and camera. Instruments were recovered by parachute.*
BELOW: *By the mid-thirties Robert H. Goddard was already launching liquid fuel rockets at Roswell, New Mexico. This four-chamber L–7 rocket climbed 61 metres (200ft) on 7 November 1936.*

potential value of rockets built on the 'step' principle. The first step, or stage, would propel the top stages until its propellants were used up. The next stage would fire when the first had been separated, and so on until the final stage and its cargo (payload) would reach the speed required to complete the journey.

If speed is great enough and the rocket is flying parallel with the Earth above the atmosphere, Tsiolkovsky calculated, 'the centrifugal force cancels gravity and after a flight which lasts as long as oxygen and food supplies suffice, the rocket spirals back to Earth, braking itself against the air and gliding back to Earth. . . .'

Though he never built a rocket, Tsiolkovsky combined in these few ideas the basic requirements for large rocket missiles and space travel. His theories were soon to be corroborated by rocket pioneers in other countries, notably Robert Esnault-Pelterie in France (1913), Robert H. Goddard in the United States (1919) and Hermann Oberth in Germany (1923).

It was Goddard who launched the world's first liquid-propellant rocket at Auburn, Massachusetts, on 16 March 1926. Fuelled by gasolene and liquid oxygen, it flew for just 2·5 seconds and landed 56·08m (184ft) from the launch stand. Its average speed was 103km/h (64mph).

Next to succeed – but only just – was a German, Johannes Winkler, whose rocket made a brief hop of just over 3m (10ft) near Dessau on 21 February 1931. Three weeks later, however, the same rocket ascended 305m (1,000ft). It was fuelled with liquid methane and liquid oxygen.

Wernher von Braun

The year 1927 had seen the foundation of the *Verein für Raumschiffarte.V.(VfR)*, the German Society for Space Travel. For the rocket enthusiasts it was a time when small amateur groups could still make important contributions by building and firing rockets. The *VfR* concentrated on the improvement of liquid-fuel motors, launching its Mirak and Repulsor rockets from a converted ammunition depot in Reinickendorf – a Berlin suburb – which they called the *Raketenflugplatz* (rocket flying field).

Leading members of the *VfR* included Hermann Oberth, Walter Hohmann, Guido von Pirquet, Max Valier, Rudolf Nebel, Klaus Riedel, Kurt Hainish and Willy Ley. A youth of 18 who joined in 1930 was to become a legend in his own time: Wernher von Braun.

By now the liquid-fuel rocket had been firmly established and in August 1931 the *VfR* launched a Repulsor rocket to an altitude of 1,006m (3,300ft) which floated back to the ground by parachute. The experiments at the *Raketenflugplatz* began to attract international attention, but Germany was in the grips of an economic depression and membership of the *VfR* fell significantly. Money ran short and the Berlin authorities – quite understandably – objected to rockets being fired within the city limits.

It was clear that further progress would have to depend on gaining some kind of government support. Accordingly, in the summer of 1932, Nebel and von Braun set up a demonstration for the German Army near Kummersdorf. It was an appropriate moment. Hitler was a rising star (he came to power in 1933) and the Army recognized that rockets were outside the scope of the Versailles Treaty which forebade the manufacture of aircraft in Germany. By the end of the year work at the *Raketenflugplatz* had ended and von Braun had received an invitation to conduct experimental work for his doctor's thesis on rocket combustion at the Army's proving ground.

Other early experiments

By that time the *VfR* had fired the enthusiasm of people in other countries and March 1930 saw the foundation of the American Interplanetary Society (later the American *Rocket* Society), which carried out a wide range of experimental work with liquid-fuel rockets before World War II. The British Interplanetary Society, barred from making rocket experiments under the Explosives Act of 1875, nevertheless made a number of significant theoretical contributions to rocket flight, including the first engineering concept of a vehicle for landing on the Moon. The Society, founded in October 1933, is still active today.

Small groups of rocket enthusiasts (unknown to the Germans, Americans or British) also were at work in the Soviet Union and on 17 August 1933 a small rocket fuelled by liquid oxygen and solidified gasolene (gasolene and colophony, a dark-coloured resin obtained from turpentine) placed in the combustion chamber reached a height of 400m (1,312ft). This rocket, known as the GIRD 09, was designed by M. K. Tikhonravov and built by a team which included Sergei P. Korolev, an engineer who was later to achieve fame as the chief designer of Soviet spaceships.

TOP: *Mirak 2 rocket built by the VfR ('German Society for Space Travel') in 1931. The rocket motor was inside the liquid oxygen tank, left, and the fuel in the tubular extension.*
ABOVE: *The automobile manufacturer Fritz von Opel experimented with rocket propulsion and flew this rocket glider at 153km/h (95mph) on 30 September 1929. It had a cluster of 16 solid fuel Sander rockets.*

ABOVE: *Second rocket motor built by the American Interplanetary Society.*
RIGHT: *GIRD X was the first Soviet rocket to use a liquid oxidant and a liquid fuel. On 25 November 1933 it soared nearly 4,900m (16,076ft).*

How a Rocket Works

It is essential to appreciate from the beginning that a rocket is, quite simply, another form of heat engine. It burns fuel to produce heat and can, in its most simple form and without any moving parts, transform this heat energy into motion. In so doing, the rocket conforms to the principle of reaction, expressed by the scientist Sir Isaac Newton as his Third Law of Motion: every action produces an equal and opposite reaction.

This may, at first, seem difficult to understand, but one of the easiest ways to learn how a rocket works is to think about a rubber balloon. If it has been blown up, and the neck through which it was inflated tied to prevent air from escaping, then

all forces
balance – equilibrium

forces now unbalanced
causing motion to the left

the balloon is full of air at an inner surface pressure equal to that of the atmospheric pressure on the outer surface.

So that the balloon can maintain its shape, without being distorted in any way by the atmospheric pressure, the air within the rubber envelope exerts an equal pressure on every point of the inner surface. It is thus in equilibrium:

provided there is no leak, change of temperature or atmospheric pressure, it will maintain its form and volume.

If we now release the tie securing the neck of the balloon, we open a channel to atmosphere and the air rushes out. At all other points within the balloon air continues to press against the inner surface – only at the orifice of the neck has the air nothing to push against. The balloon is no longer in equilibrium and, if released, will fly off in a direction diametrically opposite to the point at which the air is escaping.

Perhaps you think that the escaping air is pushing against the atmospheric air that surrounds it. It is fairly easy to prove that this is not the case. At sea level under conditions known as the International Standard Atmosphere (ISA), the air has a pressure of $71 \cdot 8 \text{kg/m}^2$ ($14 \cdot 7 \text{lb/sq in}$) and a relative density of $1 \cdot 0$. At a height of 6,705m (22,000ft) the pressure has already fallen to only $30 \cdot 3 \text{kg/m}^2$ ($6 \cdot 21 \text{lb/sq in}$) and its relative density to less than $0 \cdot 5$. At 18,590m (61,000ft) the pressure is less than 5kg/m^2 (1lb/sq in) and the relative density is only $\cdot 0897$.

As we climb higher into space, both pressure and density cease to have any significance, and this is a good point at which to carry out our balloon experiment yet again. This time it will need very little pressure to inflate it to the same size as at sea level, and when we release the tie at the neck we shall find that, despite the much reduced inner pressure, it will travel away from the air release point at an even greater speed. This is because, firstly, the air flowing from the balloon has no atmospheric pressure to slow its egress, which means that the 'opposite reaction' will be greater. Secondly, the bulky volume of the

balloon travelling through the air meets with no resistance from a dense atmosphere and can, therefore, move more easily.

All ordinary firework rockets work in precisely the same way: instead of air for propulsion, they burn within their casing combustible material which produces a large volume of gas. The rocket continues to react to the expulsion of this gas until all the gas producing materials are consumed. And because the rocket can carry its own oxidant (oxygen source) and fuel to burn with the oxygen, it is quite independent of atmospheric oxygen and can operate in the vacuum of space. In this respect it differs com-

igniter   tube   throat insert   nozzle

section through
charge

pletely from the aero-engine which is an air-breathing engine, able to operate only within Earth's atmosphere, and only to altitudes at which it can obtain adequate supplies of atmospheric oxygen to permit combustion of its hydrocarbon fuel.

Weapon-carrying ballistic rockets usually burn solid propellants. Because it is more difficult to control the thrust of solid-propellant motors, liquid oxidants and fuels have proved better for space vehicles, since liquid-propellant motors can be shut down and re-ignited to permit positioning and control.

ABOVE LEFT: *Forces acting in a balloon.*
LEFT: *Firework rocket*
ABOVE: *Solid rocket motor with case-bonded charge.*
BELOW: *Pressure-fed rocket with regenerative cooling.*
BELOW RIGHT: *Pump-fed rocket with regenerative cooling.*

ABOVE: *The US Airforce Titan rocket.*

high pressure gas
bottles

valves

oxidant
tank

fuel
tank

valves

combustion
chamber

nozzle

exhaust gas

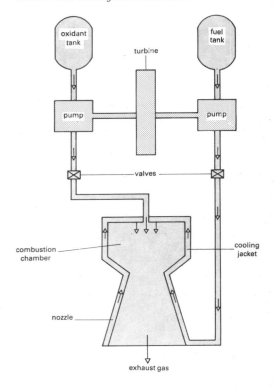

oxidant
tank

turbine

fuel
tank

pump   pump

valves

combustion
chamber

cooling
jacket

nozzle

exhaust gas

The V–2

The major advances in the 1930s, however, were taking place in Germany. In a remarkably short space of time the Army was making significant experiments in a bid to raise the efficiency of rocket motors. The work was under the direction of Captain Walter Dornberger (a qualified engineer) and Wernher von Braun. The first rocket Aggregate One, or A–1, was used for static tests only. It was just over 1·5m (4·9ft) long and had a diameter of 30·5cm (12in). The motor, fuelled by alcohol and liquid oxygen, was regeneratively cooled and had a design thrust of 300kg (660 lb). When ignited, the rocket blew up because an explosive mixture had accumulated in the combustion chamber, a problem which afflicted many of the early liquid-fuel rockets.

Success, however, was not to be long delayed. In December 1934, from the island of Borkum in the North Sea, two A–2 rockets fuelled by liquid oxygen and alcohol climbed to altitudes of about 2,400m (7,900 ft). Stability was maintained by the action of a 'brute-force' gyro set between the propellant tanks.

This double success led to more money becoming available to the researchers, who already had plans for a larger A–3 rocket with several important technical innovations. A three-axis gyro-control system worked exhaust vanes and fin-mounted rudders; a liquid-nitrogen pressure system replaced a thick-walled nitrogen bottle as a means of pressurizing the propellant tanks. New alcohol and oxygen flow valves were designed to eliminate ignition explosions. The rocket also had the virtue of not needing a launching ramp. Because of the new stabilization system, it could be launched vertically, 'standing on its fins'.

Although firings carried out from the Baltic island of Griefswalder Oie were disappointing – in the first, the recovery parachute opened prematurely only five seconds after lift-off – they were successful enough to show the merit of the basic design.

While this work was going on in Germany, Goddard was making similar progress near Roswell, New Mexico. On 28 March 1935, he fired a gyro-stabilized rocket to an altitude of 1,463m (4,800ft) and over a distance of 3,962m (13,000ft). The average speed was 885km/h (550mph). The flight path of the rocket was corrected by the gyro working steerable vanes in the exhaust. The rocket was 4·51m (14·8ft) long and had an empty weight of 35·61kg (78·5lb).

With the resurgence of German militarism, huge sums of money became available to von Braun's research team, from both the German Army and the Luftwaffe. This allowed work to begin in 1935 on a large experimental rocket establishment near the village of Peenemünde on the Baltic coast.

The major project was to be a large artillery rocket for which the designation A–4 had already been chosen. To achieve it, features of the design would be tested on a small-scale A–5 rocket. Launched at Griefswalder Oie in mid-1938, without the guidance system, the rockets reached heights of 12,875m (42,240ft). Over the next two years different control techniques were tried and

some A–5s, launched on inclined trajectories to achieve maximum range, were made to fly along radio guide beams to improve their accuracy.

Thus was born the concept of the A–4 rocket, designed to carry a 1,000kg (2,205lb) warhead over a distance of 275km (170 miles). This involved major advances in almost every department of rocket engineering. The A–4, which weighed more than 12,500kg (27,557lb), did not, however, achieve immediate success at Peenemünde. The first example, set upright on its fins on a small launch table, failed to lift off as the thrust of its engine gradually faded; it toppled over and exploded. The second A–4, held stable by its gyro-controlled exhaust vanes, flew perfectly for more than 45 seconds, then began to oscillate from side to side and finally broke apart in the air.

After necessary strengthening modifications had been made, the third A–4 made a perfect ballistic flight, reaching a maximum height of 85km (53 miles) before splashing into the Baltic some 190km (118 miles) from the launch pad. The date was 3 October 1942 – World War II had already been in progress for three years. In the eyes of the German High Command, the rocket had now become something far more important than a mere artillery weapon. Before adequate trials could be carried out, Hitler ordered the A–4 into large-scale production as a means of bombarding London and Britain's Home Counties.

Mobile A–4 batteries were organized and

TOP LEFT: *Forerunner of the German A–5 and A–4 (V–2) rockets was the A–3 static-tested at Kummersdorf in 1936. When launched in 1937 at Griefswalder Oie, a tiny island in the Baltic, three rockets went out of control and crashed soon after lift-off due to troubles with the gyro-control system. However, they gave the Germans experience with three-axis gyros and exhaust rudder control.*
TOP RIGHT: *First A–4 (V–2) rocket to perform successfully is prepared for launching at Peenemünde. On 3 October 1942 it travelled 190km (118 miles) reaching a peak altitude of some 85km (53 miles). Two others had misbehaved. In the spring of 1942, the first toppled over on the launch pad and exploded. Four weeks later the second made a smooth take-off, penetrated the so-called 'sound barrier' but then went out of control.*
ABOVE: *A–4 rocket being raised into the vertical firing position on the Meillerwagon transporter-erector. After a hurried test programme at Peenemünde, the first production models appeared early in 1943. In June 1944, an A–4 fired from Peenemünde went off course and crashed in Sweden. The debris, brought to England, gave vital clues to the rocket's capability.*

rockets were deployed at coastal sites. The A–4 attack on London began on 8 September 1944, from a site near the Hague in Holland; and at last the Goebbels propaganda ministry was able to reveal the existence of the V–2–Retaliation Weapon No 2 – against which there was no available defence.

Some 4,320 V–2s were launched between 6 September 1944 and 27 March 1945. Of these some 1,120 were directed against London and the London Civil Defence area, killing 2,511 people and seriously injuring nearly 6,000 more.

When the war in Europe ended, the full extent of the V–2 operation was at last open to inspection, including the extensive underground factory in the Kohnstein Hills, near Nordhausen, where V–1 flying bombs and V–2 rockets had been made on a production line basis. The principals at Peenemünde, in the face of the Russian advance, had fled westward, preferring to place themselves in the hands of the Western Allies. General Dornberger and von Braun surrendered to the welcoming and open arms of the US 7th Army on 2 May 1945.

Wernher von Braun's interrogation report showed the depth of progress that had been achieved by the Peenemünde team, and that it had kept alive the spaceflight ideal despite the pressures of the military establishment. In order to improve the range of the V–2, test

rockets had been fitted with swept-back wings to see if they would glide in the upper atmosphere. One had flown with some degree of success in 1944, and drawings existed for a version in which a pressure cabin replaced the warhead so that a man could fly in space. Even more ambitious was the A–9/A–10 project in which an improved A–4, with dart-like wings, was to be launched in flight from the nose of a huge liquid-fuel booster to fly some 5,000km (3,100 miles).

Although the scheme never got beyond the design stage in 1942, it was a clear indication of the shape of things to come. In his interrogation report, von Braun described a coming era when multi-stage rockets would launch artificial satellites, allow the construction in orbit of giant space platforms and put men on the Moon. Within a quarter of a century, he would be making his own prophecies come true.

Other war-time developments

The V–2 was only part of the story, for the arts of war had taken steps in many other directions. Much of the rocket work in Germany had been devoted to countering Allied air raids on the homeland though, in practice, few of the new weapons saw service by the war's end.

From Peenemünde came the ground-to-air missile Wasserfall (Waterfall), which outwardly resembled a scaled-down V–2 with

stubby cruciform wings. The need to keep the missile fully fuelled and ready for operations, however, led to the use of Visol, a by-product of petroleum, as the fuel which ignited in the combustion chamber on contact with the oxidant, nitric acid. Like the V–2, Wasserfall took off vertically from a simple platform.

This supersonic missile was expected to intercept bombers at a slant range of 48km (30 miles) and at an altitude of 9,650m (31,650ft), steering being effected by graphite vanes acting in the exhaust in combination with aerodynamic rudders. Guidance depended on the missile centering itself in a radar beam directed at the target. Early trials, however, were restricted to visual sighting and radio control by 'joystick' from the ground. It was proposed to fragment the entire rocket body from the detonation of 90kg (200lb) of high explosive to achieve a devastating shrapnel effect.

Another promising German ground-to-air missile of the period was the Hs–117 Schmetterling (Butterfly), which had the appearance of a small swept-wing monoplane. Ramp-launched, it was accelerated into flight by solid-fuel rocket boosters mounted above and below the fuselage. One version used a BMW liquid-propellant rocket motor of 159 kg (350lb) thrust. It flew at subsonic speed and was expected to make its kill at heights up to 8,850m (29,050ft), again under joy-

BELOW: *A requirement to increase the range of the V–2 led to the A–4b. This was basically a strengthened V–2 fitted with sweptback wings and enlarged aerodynamic rudders. From this von Braun believed a spaceplane could be developed to carry a pilot 644km (400 miles) in 17 minutes.*

BELOW RIGHT: *The first successful launch of an A–4b took place at Peenemünde on 24 January 1945. This was probably the first winged guided missile to fly faster than sound. However, on the downward leg of the trajectory, a wing broke off and the extended-range experiment was frustrated.*

BOTTOM: *Also developed at Peenemünde was the Wasserfall surface-to-air missile. Based on the aerodynamics of the A–5 and its A–4 big brother, it used storable propellants which ignited on contact (nitric acid and Visol, a petroleum by-product). It came too late to be used in the war.*

stick control by the ground operator.

The techniques of control were highly advanced for their day. Not only did Schmetterling have a kind of Machmeter to control the flight velocity but self-homing systems were under development. One was an infrared device with a 20° cone of sensitivity; a gyro-stabilized iconoscope ('electric eye') was designed to operate in conjunction with a proximity fuze using the radar principle.

The Russians, meanwhile, had made important advances of their own. Before World War II, Korolev had worked on a rocket-powered flying bomb (Project 212) following experiments with a rocket-powered glider. Ramp-launched from a rocket-propelled carriage, the small monoplane was designed to carry a 30kg (66lb) warhead a distance of some 50km (31 miles). Its ORM-65 rocket engine, designed by Valentin Glushko, burned kerosene and nitric acid.

Although test launchings got underway in 1939, the flying bomb was not put into production. Korolev had been working on a much improved cruise missile (Project 212A) which embodied some very advanced features of rocket propulsion and guidance, but the war caused such projects to be abandoned in favour of less sophisticated weapons such as the Katyusha barrage rockets and air-launched rocket bombs.

Initial post-war developments

At the end of the war, Germany stood head and shoulders above all others in the technology of rockets and guided weapons, and major efforts were made by America and Russia to round up as many rocket specialists as could be found. Many of the principals, including von Braun and a large part of his Peenemünde team, were encouraged to continue their work in the United States. Others were taken to Russia and put to work in collectives which worked in isolation from mainstream Soviet technology so that secrets could be preserved.

In the meantime, work in America, spurred by the pioneering efforts of Goddard (who died in August 1945), had led to a research group at the California Institute of Technology to developing in 1944 to 1945 a small rocket called Wac-Corporal. It was powered by a nitric acid/aniline engine of 680kg (1,500lb) thrust. Launched from a tower by a solid-fuel booster, the rocket sent a payload of instruments to an altitude of 70km (43·56 miles).

Like some of the German anti-aircraft missiles and the rocket motors developed in Russia the propellants were self-igniting and of a type which could be stored in the tanks of a rocket. This was to lead to a series of missiles for the US Army which could be held at instant readiness. It was also to result in experiments in which Wac-Corporals mounted as second stages of modified V–2s were to show the prospect for reaching the greater speeds and altitudes required for long-range ballistic rockets and space travel. On 24 February one such vehicle, blasting off from White Sands, New Mexico, sent the smaller Wac to a record height of 393km (244 miles). The rocket's maximum speed was 8,286km/h (5,150mph). Others of the series

were launched from Cape Canaveral by the US Army Ordnance to obtain maximum horizontal range.

In the Cold War era the rocket age was exploited with a new frenzy. Guided missiles of many kinds were developed in both offensive and defensive roles, with the major powers striving to match blow for blow each new technical advance.

Surface-to-air missiles

One of the first operational missiles to employ storable liquids was America's MIM–3A Nike-Ajax, the ramp-launched anti-aircraft missile which took off with the assistance of a three-finned solid-fuel booster. The missile itself had triangular cruciform wings and steerable nose vanes and was powered by a nitric acid/aniline motor. Guidance was by radio command. One radar tracked the target aircraft and another tracked the missile. A computer continuously integrated the two plots and caused steering signals to be sent to the missile, vectoring it towards the

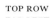

TOP ROW

FAR LEFT: *Captured German V–2 carries an American Wac-Corporal rocket as second stage: White Sands, New Mexico, February 1949.*

THIRD LEFT: *Early version of the US Army's Nike-Ajax surface-to-air missile on test at White Sands, New Mexico.*

SECOND LEFT: *US Navy Talos surface-to-air missiles on shipboard launcher.*

LEFT: *Bomarc surface-to-air missile of USAF Air Defense Command which could attain Mach 4 speeds and altitudes above 30,480m (100,000ft).*

MIDDLE ROW

FAR LEFT TOP: *Members of a Soviet SA–4 Ganef surface-to-air missile battery train in conditions of mock gas attack.*

FAR LEFT BOTTOM: *Soviet training exercise with SA–2 Guideline surface-to-air missile.*

CENTRE: *The Russian SA–5 Gammon high-altitude air defence weapon.*

SECOND RIGHT TOP: *Seacat, Britain's close-range anti-aircraft missile is launched from the Swedish ship* Sodermanland.

SECOND RIGHT BOTTOM: *Masurca, an early French surface-to-air missile, was first deployed on the frigates* Suffren *and* Duquesne.

RIGHT: *Bloodhounds of No 30 Surface-to-Air Missile (SAM) Squadron at RAAF Base, Williamtown, New South Wales, Australia.*

BOTTOM ROW CENTRE: *US Army's earliest family of air-defence missiles: left to right, Nike Ajax, Nike Hercules and Nike Zeus.*

target. When fairly close, the missile became self-homing, responding to ground-radar reflections from the target.

Its Russian counterpart, (SA–2, NATO code-name Guideline – Russian missiles are identified by their NATO code names throughout) burned nitric acid and a hydrocarbon fuel and was also guided by automatic radio command. Evidence of the effectiveness of this weapon came on 1 May 1960, when it brought down Lt Francis Gary Powers in his high-flying U–2 reconnaissance aircraft.

Other anti-aircraft weapons followed in quick succession. In America the MIM–14A Nike-Hercules gave more height and range, as did the LIM–49A Nike-Zeus, which had a small nuclear warhead. Bomarc, an aircraft-like missile with cropped delta wings, had twin underslung ramjets and a rocket booster. It could reach a speed twice that of sound and heights of 18,288m (60,000ft) and had a range comfortably exceeding 161km (100 miles).

Russia's response to Nike-Zeus was the SA–5 Gammon, claimed to be effective against both high-flying aircraft and missiles. Anti-aircraft missiles for the Soviet Fleet were the SA–N–1 Goa and SA–N–2 Guideline. US naval weapons in the same class were Talos, Tartar and Terrier.

Britain, too, gave priority to anti-aircraft defence. Early developments were the solid-fuel Thunderbird and the ramjet-powered Bloodhound, both of which responded to semi-active radar homing. For air defence at sea there were the close-range Seacat, the longer-range Seaslug and, later, Sea Dart. From France came Masurca, a two-stage solid-fuel missile which first appeared as a beam-rider and then with self-homing capability. A missile which depends on semi-active radar homing incorporates a seeker which locks onto radar reflections from a target which is being illuminated from another source, e.g. a ground radar or, in the case of an air-to-air missile, the fire-control radar of the launch aircraft. *Active radar hom-*

ing missiles carry both a radar transmitter and a seeker and therefore are able to home on the target reflections of their own transmissions.

Man-portable guided weapons have also made their mark for the self-defence of Army units against low-level air attack. America's tube-mounted Redeye, launched from the shoulder, was designed to home automatically on the engine heat of an attacking aircraft. Russia's equivalent – the SA–7 Grail – is believed to have a slant range of 2·9 to 4·0km (1·8 to 2·5 miles). Britain has produced the Blowpipe, a similar weapon but which the operator steers along his line of sight by radio signals.

The post-war years also saw a major growth in arms exports as the leading powers manoeuvred on the chessboard of world influence. The Russian surface-to-air missile SA–2 Guideline, as well as becoming established in the Warsaw Pact countries, was supplied to Cuba, Indonesia, North Vietnam and certain Middle East countries. A Mk 2 version supplied to Egypt was in action against the Israeli Air Force during the 1967 Six-Day War.

In the Yom Kippur War of 1973, Israeli pilots faced Soviet anti-aircraft weapons deployed in depth. While batteries of SA–2 Guideline missiles engaged their aircraft at long range, SA–3 Goa took on low-flying targets. A relatively new anti-aircraft missile, the SA–6, was fired from triple mounts on tracked vehicles which advanced with the Egyptian infantry, giving them effective cover. Of 104 Israeli aircraft lost in 1973, 100 are said to have fallen to missiles.

Significant Missiles of the Post-War Era

Abbreviations: H.e., high explosive (chemical); KT, kiloton, the explosive power, or yield, of 1,000 tons of TNT; LOS, line-of-sight; MT, megaton, equivalent to the explosive power of 1,000,000 tons of TNT; MIRV, multiple, independently targetable re-entry vehicle; NA, not available; RV, re-entry vehicle; SAC, semi-active command; SAR, semi-active radar; SD, snap down; SU, snap up; TTR, target-tracking radar; TVC, thrust vector control. Data shown in *italics* provisional.

Surface-to-air missiles

Designation/Country	Length m/f	Diameter cm/in	Span cm/in	Weight kg/lb	Range km/miles	P, Propulsion; G, Guidance; C, Control; W, Warhead
Crotale (France) Tube-launched from tracked AFV	2·89 (9·4)	15 (5·9)	54 (21)	80–85 (176–187)	0·5–8·5 (0·3–5·3)	**P:** Solid rocket. **G:** Radio command. **C:** Cruciform canard vanes. **W:** H.e., fragmentation, IR proximity fuze.
Roland I (Germany) * Radar, Roland II.	2·40 (7·9)	16 (6·3)	50 (20)	65 (143)	0·2–6·3 (0·1–3·7)	**P:** Solid rocketboost/sustainer. **G:** Infra-red autogathering, then SAC to LOS*. **C:** Deflector in motor exhaust. **W:** H.e., with 65 projectile charges, proximity fuze.
RBS 70 (Sweden) Tube-launched by infantryman from tripod stand. Altitude: 3km (1·86 miles)	1·32 (4·33)	10·6 (4·17)	NA	23·5 (51·8)	5 (3·1)	**P:** Solid rocket boost (jettisonable), solid rocket sustainer. **G:** Laser beam rider. Target tracking by stabilized optical system. **C:** Cruciform rear fins. **W:** H.e., prefragmented, impact or laser proximity fuze.
Bloodhound Mk 2 (UK) Speed: M2+. Altitude: NA	7·67 (25·2)	54·6 (21·5)	282 (111)	NA	80+ (50+)	**P:** Four solid rocket boosters, 2 Thor ramjets. **G:** Constant wave semi-active radar homing. **C:** Twist and steer, pivoting wings. **W:** H.e., proximity fuze.
Blowpipe (UK) Speed: 1·5. Altitude 1,500m (4,920ft). Tube launched from shoulder.	1·34 (4·4)	7·6 (3)	27·4 (10·75)	NA	3 (1·9)	**P:** Solid rocket boost/solid sustainer. **G:** Radio command line-of-sight. **C:** Cruciform canard fins. **W:** H.e., fragmentation or shaped charge, impact fuzes.
Rapier (UK) Speed: M2+. Altitude: 3,000m (9,840ft).	2·24 (7·3)	12·7 (5)	38 (15)	42·5 (94)	0·5–7 (0·3–4·3)	**P:** Dual-thrust solid rocket. **G:** SAC to LOS, optical or with Blindfire radar. **C:** Cruciform rear fins. **W:** H.e., hollow charge, impact fuze.
Seacat/Tigercat (UK) Seacat on wide variety of ships including cruisers, destroyers, frigates. Tigercat is land based version.	1·47 (4·8)	19 (7·5)	64 (25·2)	63–68 (139–150)	5+ (3·1+)	**P:** Dual thrust solid. **G:** Radio-command to line-of-sight (TV autogathering). **C:** Cruciform wings. **W:** H.e., proximity fuze.
Sea Dart (CF-299) (UK) Speed: M3·5. Altitude: 25,000m (82,020ft). RN type 42 destroyers. Type 82 destroyer.	4·36 (14·3)	42 (17)	91 (36)	550 (1,213)	80+ (50+)	**P:** Solid rocket boost, Odin ramjet. **G:** Semi-active radar. **C:** Cruciform rear fins. **W:** H.e., fragmentation, proximity fuze.
Seaslug Mk 2 (UK) Altitude: 15,000m+ (49,213ft). Last four RN County-class destroyers.	6·1 (20·0)	41 (16·1)	144 (57)	NA	45+ (28+)	**P:** Four solid rocket boosts, solid sustainer. **G:** Beamrider, infra-red auto-gathering/command line-of-sight. **C:** Cruciform rear fins. **W:** H.e., proximity fuze.
Seawolf (PX 430) (UK) Speed: 800m/sec+ (2,625ft/sec+). Shipbourne with six-barrelled auto-controlled launcher. RN County-class GM destroyers Type 22 frigates etc.	*2·0* *(6·56)*	19 (7·5)	*56* *22*	*80–84* *(176–185)*	5 (3·1)	**P:** Dual thrust solid rocket. **G:** Semi-active command to line-of-sight/TV plus TTR. **C:** Cruciform rear fins. **W:** H.e., impact + proximity fuzes.
Thunderbird Mk 2 (UK) Speed: M2+. Altitude NA.	6·34 (20·8)	53 (21)	162 (64)	NA	50–80 (31–50)	**P:** Four solid-rocket boosts, solid sustainer. **G:** Semi-active radar homing. **C:** Cruciform rear fins. **W:** H.e., proximity fuze.
Improved Hawk MIM-23B (US) Speed: M2·5. Altitude: 30/18,000m (98/59,000ft)	5·08 (16·6)	37 (14·5)	120 (47)	625 (1,378)	40 (25)	**P:** Dual thrust solid. **G:** Semi-active constant wave radar. **C:** Elevons on long chord cropped delta wings. **W:** H.e., blast fragmentation.
Nike Hercules MIM-14B (US)	12·70 (41·6)	88 (34·6)	*228* *(90)*	4,800 (10,584)	30/150 (19/93·2)	**P:** Four × solid rocket boosts, solid sustainer. **G:** Radar command. **C:** Elevons on long chord delta wings. **W:** H.e., fragmentation or nuclear, command detonation.
Red Eye FIM-43A (US) Altitude: 2,500m (8,200ft).	1·2 (3·6)	7·0 (2·75)	14·0 (5·51)	8·2 (18)	3·4 (2·1)	**P:** Dual thrust rocket. **G:** Infra-red homing, optical aiming. **C:** Cruciform flip-out canard vanes. **W:** H.e., fragmentation, smooth casing.
SAM-D XMIM-104A (US) Replacement for Hawk and Nike-Hercules. Speed: M3.	5·18 (17·0)	40·6 (16·0)	92 (36·2)	NA	NA	**P:** Solid rocket. **G:** Semi-active radar homing. **C:** Cruciform rear fins. **W:** H.e., or nuclear.
Standard ER RIM-67A (US) Speed: M2·5+. Altitude: 20,000m+ (65,620ft). Four missiles on M730 tracked vehicle.	8·23 (27·0)	35 (13·8)	157 (61·8)	*1,360* *(3,000)*	56 (35)	**P:** Solid rocket boost, solid sustainer. **G:** Semi-active radar. **C:** Cruciform rear fins. **W:** H.e., proximity fuze.

Stinger **XFIM–92A** (US)	1·52 (5·0)	7·0 (2·75)	9·0 (3·5)	15·1 (33·3)	4·8 (3·0)	**P:** Dual thrust solid. **G:** Infra-red homing proportional navigation. **C:** Cruciform flip-out vanes. **W:** H. e., fragmentation, smooth casing.
Guideline **SA–2** (USSR) Altitude: 18,288m+ (60,000ft+)	10·6 (34·7)	51 (20)	170 (67)	2,300 (5,070)	40–50 (25–30)	**P:** Solid rocket booster, liquid sustainer. **G:** Automatic radio command, radar tracking of target. **C:** Cruciform steerable fins. **W:** H.e., 130kg (286lb).
Goa **SA–3** (USSR) Altitude: 12,192m (40,000ft+).	6·7 (22·0)	45·7 (18)	122 (48)	NA	25–30 (15–18)	**P:** Two-stage solid rocket. **G:** Radio command, radar terminal homing. **C:** Cruciform steerable foreplanes. **W:** H.e.
Ganef **SA–4** (USSR) Altitude: 18,000m (59,000ft). Two mounted on tracked launcher.	9·1 (30·0)	80 (32)	228·6 (90)	1,000 (2,200+)	70 (42)	**P:** Integral ramjet, four wrap-round solid rocket boosters. **G:** Radio command. **C:** Cruciform steerable wings. **W:** H.e.
Gammon **SA–5** (USSR) Altitude: 30,000m (98,425ft).	16·4 (54·0)	86 (34)	365 (144)	NA	160+ (100+)	**P:** Solid boost, solid sustainer. **G:** Radio command, semi-active radar homing. **C:** Cruciform steerable fins plus wing-mounted ailerons. **W:** H.e.
Gainful **SA–6** (USSR) Speed: M2·8. Altitude: 100/18,000m (328/59,055ft). Triple launcher on modified PT 76 tank.	6·2 (20·3)	33·5 (13·2)	124 (48·8)	550 (1,212)	59·5 (37)	**P:** Integral solid fuel ramjet, solid rocket boost. **G:** Radio command, semi-active radar homing. **C:** Cruciform steerable wings? **W:** H.e., 80kg (176lb).
Grail **SA–7** (USSR) Speed: M1·5. Altitude: 45/1,500m (148/4,920ft)	1·35 (4·4)	7 (2·75)	NA	NA	2·9–4·0 (1·8–2·5)	**P:** Solid rocket boost/sustainer. **G:** Infra-red homing, optically aimed. **C:** Cruciform flip-out steerable(?) wings and tail fins. **W:** H.e., 2·5kg (5·5lb), probably fragmentation.
Gecko **SA–8** (USSR) Altitude: 50–6,000m (164–4,920ft). On six-wheeled amphibious vehicle.	3·2 (10·5)	20·2 (8·25)	64 (25)	NA	12·0 (7·5)	**P:** Dual thrust solid rocket. **G:** Radar command. **C:** Cruciform canard fins and foreplanes. **W:** H.e.
Gaskin **SA–9** (USSR)	NA	NA	NA	NA	5 (3·1)	**P:** Solid rocket motor. **G:** Infra-red homing. **C:** Cruciform wings and tail fins. **W:** H.e., Twin-quad canister on modified BRDM Scoutcar.

Air-to-air missiles

Rb 72 (Sweden)	260 (102·3)	17·5 (6·9)	60 (24)	110 (242)	8 (5)	**P:** Solid rocket. **G:** Infra-red. **C:** Cruciform rear fins. **W:** H.e.
Magic **R.550** (France) Dog-fight missile, high-g manoeuvres.	274 (107·8)	15·7 (6)	66 (26)	90 (198)	0·3–7·0 (0·2–4·3)	**P:** Solid rocket. **G:** Infra-red (fast reacting, all-aspect). **C:** Cruciform canard fins. **W:** H.e., impact + IR proximity fuze.
Super R.530 (France) Altitude: 21,300m (70,000ft). Speed: M4·5+.	354 (139)	26 (10)	90 (35·4)	200 (441)	29–35 (18–22)	**P:** Dual thrust solid rocket. **G:** Semi-active radar. **C:** Cruciform rear fins. **W:** H.e. + proximity fuse.
Red Top (UK) Speed: M3·0.	327·7 (129)	22·1 (8·75)	91 (35·8)	150 (330)	11 (7)	**P:** Solid rocket. **G:** Infra-red, (lead collision). **C:** Cruciform rear fins. **W:** H.e.
Skyflash (UK) Based on Sparrow air-frame.	366 (144)	20·3 (8·0)	102·3 (40·3)	192·8 (425)	25·5 (15·8)	**P:** Solid rocket. **G:** Advanced semi-active radar seeker (SU and SD capability). **C:** Cruciform wings. **W:** H.e. + radar proximity fuze.
Falcon **AIM 26B, HM 55, R627** (US) Speed: M2·0.	213 (84)	27·9 (11·0)	61 (24)	115 (253)	8–10 (5–6)	**P:** Solid rocket. **G:** Semi-active radar homing. **C:** Cruciform rear fins. **W:** H.e. (AIM–26B), nuclear (AIM–26A).
Phoenix **AIM–54A** (US) Speed: M5·0+. On F–14A.	396 (156)	38 (15)	91·4 (36)	380 (838)	200+ (124+)	**P:** Solid rocket. **G:** Cruise: semi-active radar, active radar final 16km (10 miles). **C:** Cruciform rear fins. **W:** H.e., proximity + contact fuzes.
Sidewinder IC **AIM–9C/D** (US) Speed: M2·5.	292 (114)	12·7 (5)	63·5 (25)	84 (185)	10–18 (6–11·2)	**P:** Solid rocket. **G:** Semi-active radar (AIM–9C), infra-red (AIM–9D). **C:** Cruciform triangular canard fins. **W:** H.e. + contact fuzes.
Sparrow **AIM–7E** (US) Speed: M4·0. Also surface-to-air application.	365 (144)	20 (8)	102 (40)	205 (452)	25–50 (15–31)	**P:** Solid rocket. **G:** Semi-active, constant-wave radar. **C:** Cruciform wings. **W:** H.e., proximity plus contact fuzes.
Acrid **AA–6** (USSR) Speed: M2·2.	590 (232) IR 628 (247) SAR	36 (14·2)	225 (88·5)	650–850 (1,433–1,874)	37 (10)	**P:** Solid rocket. **G:** Infra-red or radar homing. **C:** Cruciform canard fins and wing-mounted surfaces. **W:** H.e., 100kg (220lb).

						Details
Apex **AA–7** (USSR)	430 (169)	24 (9·45)	105 (41·3)	NA	28 (17)	**P:** Solid rocket. **G:** Infra-red or radar homing. **C:** Cruciform rear fins. **W:** H.e.
Aphid **AA–8** (USSR)	210 (83·7)	NA	NA	NA	5–8 (3·1–5)	**P:** Solid rocket. **G:** Infra-red or radar homing. **C:** Cruciform canard fins (?). **W:** H.e.

Air-to-ground missiles

						Details
AS–30 (France) Also 'fire-and-forget' AS 30 laser version. *When launched at M0·9 at low level.	3·78 (12·4)	34·2 (13·5)	100 (39·4)	520 (1,146)	2–3 (1·2–1·86) 12 (7·4)*	**P:** Solid rocket boost, solid rocket sustainer. **G:** Radio command, late models SAC to LOS. **C:** Deflectors in motor efflux. **W:** H.e., 230kg (507lb) general purpose or semi-armour piercing fuze.
Martel **AS–37** (France) Martel AJ163 (length 3·9m [12·8ft]), is radio command/TV guided.	4·16 (13·7)	40 (15·7)	120 (47)	530 (1,168)	30 (18·6)	**P:** Solid rocket boost, solid rocket sustainer. **G:** Passive radar homing. **C:** Cruciform rear fins. **W:** H.e., 150kg (330lb), proximity fuze.
Bullpup A **(AGM–12B)** (US)	3·20 (10·5)	30·5 (12)	101 (40)	258 (571)	11 (6·8)	**P:** Storable liquid rocket (pre-packaged). **G:** Radio command. **C:** Cruciform canard fins. **W:** H.e., 113kg (250lb).
Maverick **(AGM–65)** (US)	2·46 (8·07)	30·5 (12)	71 (28)	210 (463)	25–30 (15·5–18·6)	**P:** Solid rocket. **G:** Automatic TV homing or IR or semi-active laser. **C:** Cruciform rear fins. **W:** H.e., 59kg (130lb).
Shrike **(AGM–45A)** (US)	3·05 (10)	20·3 (8)	91·4 (36)	177 (390)	16 (10)	**P:** Solid rocket. **G:** Passive radar homing. **C:** Cruciform wings. **W:** H.e., fragmentation.
Standard Arm **(AGM 78)** (US)	4·57 (15)	30·5 (7·7)	109 (240)	816 (1,800)	25 (15·5)	**P:** Dual-thrust solid rocket. **G:** Passive radar homing. **C:** Cruciform rear fins. **W:** H.e.
Kipper **AS–2** (USSR) Speed: M1·2. Belly-mounted on TU–16. Badger C. Also anti-shipping role.	9·5 (31)	NA	4·6 (15)	NA	180–210 (112–130)	**P:** Underslung turbojet. **G:** Radio command, mid-course; radar homing. **C:** Aircraft type. **W:** H.e.
Kitchen **AS–4** (USSR) Speed: M2+. Belly-mounted on Tu–22 Blinder B.	11·3 (37)	NA	245 (96)	6,000+ (13,228+)	300 (186)	**P:** Storable liquid rocket. **G:** Inertial plus mid-course (?). **C:** Aircraft type. **W:** H.e.

Ballistic missiles, tactical

						Details
Frog 7 (USSR) On ZIL–135 erector- launcher.	9·1 (29·8)	55 (21·6)	NA	NA	60 (37)	**P:** Dual thrust solid. **G:** Spin-stabilized, (unguided). **C:** Cruciform fixed fins. **W:** H.e., chemical or nuclear.
Lance **MGM–52C** (US)	6·10 (20·0)	56 (22)	198 (78)	1,530 (3,373)	70–120 (43–74·5)	**P:** Single-stage storable liquid rocket. **G:** Simplified inertial. **C:** Fluid injection into single nozzle. **W:** Nuclear 10 KT or h.e. cluster.
Pershing **MGM–31A** (US) Deployed on erector-launcher. Being replaced by terminally guided Pershing 2.	10·5 (34·5)	101·6 (40)	NA	4,535 (10,000)	160–640 (160–460)	**P:** Two-stage solid, Thiokol XM105, Thiokol XM106. **G:** Simplified inertial. **C:** Efflux deflectors, stage 1; steerable fins, stage 2. **W:** Nuclear 60–400KT.

Anti-tank missiles

						Details
Harpon (France)	121·5 (47·8)	16·4 (6·4)	50 (19·7)	30·4 (67)	500–3,000 (1,640– 9,842)	**P:** Solid rocket boost/sustainer. **G:** Wire, automatic command to line-of-sight. **C:** Deflectors in sustainer exhaust. **W:** H.e., shaped charge.
Swingfire (UK)	107 (42·0)	17 (6·7)	37 (14·5)	34 (75)	140–4,000 (459–13,123)	**P:** Solid rocket boost/sustainer. **G:** Wire command to line-of-sight. **C:** Jetavator. **W:** H.e., 6·8kg (15lb) hollow charge. Container launched.
Tow **BGM–71** (US)	117 (46·0)	15·2 (6)	34 (13·4)	24·5 (54)	65–3,750 (213–12,303)	**P:** Solid rocket boost/sustainer. **G:** Wire command to line-of-sight, automatic optical tracking. **C:** Flip-out fins. **W:** H.e., shaped charge. Tube launched.
Sagger **AT–3** (USSR)	87 (34·2)	12 (4·7)	46 (18·1)	11 (24·2)	500–3,000 (1,640– 9,842)	**P:** Solid rocket. **G:** Wire command to line-of-sight. **C:** Not available. **W:** H.e., shaped charge.

Anti-ship missiles

	Length m (ft)	Diameter cm (in)	Span cm (in)	Weight kg (lb)	Range km (miles)	
Exocet MM–38 (France) Speed: Mo·93–0·95.	5·20 (17)	35·0 (13·8)	104 (41)	735 (1,620)	5–40+ (3·1–25+)	**P:** Solid rocket, boost and sustainer. **G:** Cruise: inertial plus radio altimeter; attack: active radar seeker. **C:** Cruciform rear fins. **W:** H.e., 165kg (364lb), hexolite in steel block, delay fuze.
Kormoran (W. Germany)	4·40 (14·4)	34·4 (13·5)	100 (39·3)	600 (1,323)	35+ (22+)	**P:** Solid rocket, boost and sustainer. **G:** Cruise: autopilot plus radio altimeter; attack: active radar seeker. **C:** Cruciform rear fins. **W:** H.e., 160kg (353lb), clustered projectile charges, delay fuze.
Gabriel (Israel)	3·35 (11)	32·5 (12·8)	138·5 (54·5)	400 (882)	20+ (12+) 40+ (25+)	**P:** Solid rocket, boost and sustainer. **G:** Cruise: autopilot; radio altimeter; attack: radar/electro-optical. **C:** Cruciform rear fins. **W:** H.e., 150kg (331lb).
Sea Skua (CL 834) (UK)	2·8 (9·2)	22·2 (8·7)	67 (26·3)	200 (441)	14 (9)	**P:** Solid rocket. **G:** Semi-active homing responsive to target illumination by radar. **C:** Cruciform canard fins. **W:** H.e., 35kg (77lb).
Harpoon AGM–84A/RGM–84A (US)	4·58 (15·0) 3·84 (12·6) air launch	34·3 (13·5)	91·4 (36)	667 (1,470) 522 (1,151) air launch	110 (68)	**P:** Solid rocket, boost turbojet cruise 300kg (661lb) thrust. **G:** Cruise: advanced autopilot; attack: active radar seeker. **C:** Cruciform fins. **W:** H.e., 227kg (500lb), shaped charge, contact, delay fuze.
Scrubber SS–N–1 (USSR) Speed: Mo·9. Operational 1958–59.	7·6 (25·0)	100 (39·3)	460 (180)	4,080 (9,000)	110–185 (68–115)	**P:** Solid rocket, boost turbojet cruise. **G:** Cruise: autopilot/radio command; attack radar or IR homing. **C:** Aircraft-type. **W:** H.e. On Kildin and Krupny class destroyers.
Styx SS–N–2 (USSR) Speed: Mo·9. Operational 1960. On Komar and Osa fast patrol boats.	6·25 (20·5)	75 (29·5)	275 (108·2)	2,500–3,000 (5,513–6,615)	40+ (25+)	**P:** Solid rocket, boost turbojet cruise. **G:** Cruise: autopilot/radio command; attack: command active radar. **C:** Aircraft-type control (ailerons + rudders). **W:** H.e.
Shaddock SSC–1/ SS–N–3 (USSR)	10·9–13·8 (35·7–42)	100 (39·3)	210+ (82·6+)	11,790 (26,000)	450+ (280+)	**P:** Two × solid rocket boost; turbojet cruise. **G:** Cruise: radio command; attack: radar or IR homing. **C:** Aircraft-type. **W:** H.e., or nuclear KT range. M2·0–2·5.

Cruise or Stand-off missiles, strategic

Hound Dog AGM–28B (US) Speed: M2+.	13·0 (42·5)	71·1 (28)	370 (146)	4,603 (10,104)	1,207 (750)	**P:** Pratt & Whitney J52–P–3, turbojet 3,400kg (7,496lb) thrust. **G:** Inertial. **C:** Aircraft-type. **W:** Single thermonuclear IMT.
SRAM AGM–69A (US)	4·27 (14)	45 (17·7)	NA	1,000 (2,205)	64–161 (40–100)	**P:** Two-pulse solid. **G:** Inertial plus terrain avoidance. **C:** Cruciform rear fins. **W:** Single thermonuclear 200KT.
ALCM AGM–86A (US) Speed: Mo·55 cruise. Mo·7 attack.	4·3 (14·0)	61 (24)	NA	860 (1,896)	1,207+ (750+)	**P:** Single Williams Research F 107 turbofan, 300kg (661lb) thrust. **G:** Inertial and terrain comparison. **C:** Aircraft-type. **W:** Single thermonuclear.
Tomahawk YBGM 109 (US) Speed: Mo·7 attack. Modified 391cm (154in) Tomahawk adapted for air-launching. Also land-launched and ship-launched versions.*	5·56 (18·3)	52 (20·5)	228 (90)	NA	2,414+ (1,500+) 3,600* (2,237)*	**P:** Teledyne F 106 turbofan, 300kg (661lb) thrust + solid booster. **G:** Inertial and terrain comparison. **C:** Cruciform rear fins. **M:** Thermonuclear or H.e.

Ballistic missiles, strategic, land based

Scarp SS–9 (USSR) Silo hot launch. No. in service 1976: 200+.	35·0 (115)	300 (118)	NA	12,000 (7,456)	**P:** Two-stage storable liquid. **G:** Inertial. **C:** Steerable vernier motors. **W:** Mod: 3 FOBs. Mod: 4 3 MRVs or test MIRVs.
Sego SS–11 (USSR) Service entry 1966. Silo hot launch.	19·5 (64)	240 (94)	NA	10,500 (7,456)	**P:** Two-stage storable liquid. **G:** Inertial. **C:** Not available. **W:** Single RV 1–2 MT (Mod. 1), three MRVs 300–500 KT each. (Mod. 3).
Scaleboard SS–12 (USSR) Service entry 1969. Mobile on MAZ 543 carrier.	11·0 (36)	NA	NA	700–800 (435–497)	**P:** Single-stage rocket. **G:** Inertial. **C:** Steerable aerodynamic rudders (?). **W:** Nuclear or h.e.
Scapegoat SS–14 (USSR) Mobile on Scamp transporter-erector (modified JS III tank chassis).	10·6 (35)	140 (55)	NA	4,000 (2,485)	**P:** Two-stage solid. **G:** Inertial. **C:** Not available. **W:** Thermonuclear.
SS–16 (USSR) Silo hot launch. Also mobile role.	20 (66)	200 (79)	NA	9,000 (5,592)	**P:** Three-stage solid. **G:** Inertial. **C:** Not available. **W:** Single RV IMT + or 3 MIRVs and penetration aids.
SS–17 (USSR) Silo cold launch. Number in service mid-1976: 30 (in modified SS–11 silos).	24 (79)	260 (102)	NA	10,000 (6,214)	**P:** Two-stage storable liquid. **G:** Inertial. **C:** Not available. **W:** Four? IMT KT MIRVs.

SS–18 (USSR) Silo cold launch. No. in service late 1976: 50. Mod 2 entered service late 1976.	37 (121)	340 (132)	NA	Mod 1 10,500+ (6,525+) Mod 2 9,250+ (5,748+)		**P:** Two-stage storable liquid. **G:** Inertial. **C:** Not available. **W:** Mod. 1. Single RV 40–50 MT; Mod. 2. Eight to ten MIRVs 1–2 MT each.
SS–19 (USSR) Silo cold launch. No. in service late 1976: 140.	24 (79)	260 (102)	NA	10,000 (6,214)		**P:** Two-stage storable liquid. **G:** Inertial. **C:** Not available. **W:** Six MIRVs 400–500 KT.
SS–20 (USSR) Employs first two stages of SS–16. Max. range lightweight thermo-nuclear warhead.	16 (55)	200 (79)	NA	2,400–7,000 (1,491–4,350)		**P:** Two-stage solid. **G:** Inertial. **C:** Not available. **W:** Single IMT RV or 3 MIRVs.
Minuteman II LGM–30F (US) Silo-launched.	18·2 (60)	183 (72)	31,750 (70,000)	11,000+ (6,835+)		**P:** Three-stage solid; lift-off thrust 91,000kg (200,621lb) × 60sec. **G:** Inertial. **C:** 4 moveable nozzles (stages 1 and 3); fluid inertion into single fixed nozzle (stage 2). **W:** Single RV 1–2MT plus penetration aids.
Minuteman III LGM–30G (US) Silo-launched.	18·2 (60)	183 (72)	34,475 (76,000)	13,000+ (8,078+)		**P:** Three-stage, solid (improved stage 3). **G:** Inertial. **C:** As Minuteman II. **W:** Three MIRVs of 200 KT each plus penetration aids.
Titan II LGM 25C (US) No. in service: 54. Silo launched.	31·4 (103)	305 (120)	149,690 (330,000)	15,000 (9,320)		**P:** Two-stage storable liquid. **G:** Inertial. **C:** Gimballed engines, both stages. **W:** Single RV 10MT plus penetration aids.
SSBS S3 (France) Silo launched.	13·7 (45)	150 (59)	25,800+ (56,880+)	3,000+ (1,864+)		**P:** Two-stage solid; lift-off thrust 55,000kg (121,254lb) × 76sec. **G:** Inertial. **C:** 4 Gimballed nozzles (stage 1); Freon injection into single fixed nozzle. **W:** Single RV IMT plus penetration aids.

Ballistic missiles, strategic, submarine based

Polaris A–3 UGM–27C (US/UK)	9·75 (32)	137 (54)	15,850 (35,000)	4,626 (2,875)		**P:** Two-stage solid. Lift off thrust 36,287kg (80,000lb). **G:** Inertial. **C:** 4 rotating nozzles (stage 1), fluid injection into single fixed nozzle (stage 2). **W:** Three MRVs, 200 KT each.
Poseidon C–3 UGM–73A (US)	10·36 (34)	188 (74)	29,484 (65,000)	4,626+ (2,875+)		**P:** Two-stage solid. **G:** Inertial. **C:** One gimballed nozzle each stage. **W:** 10 MIRVs 50 KT each at 5,200km (3,231 miles), or 14 50 KT at 4,000km.
Trident I C–4 UGM–93A (US)	10·36 (34)	188 (74)	32,000 (70,560)	7,000 (4,350)		**P:** Three-stage solid. **G:** Inertial + stellar navigation. **C:** Not available. **W:** Eight MIRVs 100 KT.
Sawfly SS–N–6 (USSR) In Yankee-class nuclear submarines: 16 per vessel.	12·8 (42)	175 (68·9)	18,000–20,000 (39,690–44,100)	2,400 (1,491) 3,000 (1,864)		**P:** Two-stage storable liquid rocket. **G:** Inertial. **C:** Not available. **W:** Thermonuclear IMT.
SS–N–8 (USSR) In Delta-class nuclear submarines; 12 in Delta 1, 16 in Delta 2.	14+ (45·9+)	180–200 (70·8–78·7)	20,000+ (44,100)	7,800 (4,847)		**P:** Two-stage storable liquid rocket. **G:** Inertial + stellar navigation. **C:** Not available. **W:** Thermonuclear 1–2 MT.
SS–NX–17	NA	NA	NA	NA		**P:** Two-stage solid rocket. **G:** Inertial + stellar navigation (?). **C:** Not available. **W:** Thermonuclear, single RV or MIRVs.
SS–NX–18 Replaces SS–N–8 in Delta 1 and 2 class submarines.	NA	NA	NA	8,046+ (5,000+)		**P:** Two-stage storable liquid rocket. **G:** Inertial + stellar navigation (?). **C:** Not available. **W:** Thermonuclear, MIRVs.
MSBS M2/M20 (France) In French ballistic submarines, 16 per vessel.	10·4 (34·1)	150 (59)	20,000 (44,100)	1,864 (3,000)		**P:** Two-stage solid rocket. **G:** Inertial. **C:** Four gimballed nozzles, stage 1; Freon injection into single fixed nozzle, stage 2. **W:** Thermonuclear, 500KT in M2 and 1 MT in M20.

Anti-ballistic missiles

Galosh ABM–1 (USSR) 64 launchers at four sites defend Moscow.	18–19 (59–62)	240–270 (945–106)	NA	NA	300 (186)	**P:** Multi-stage rocket, 4 first stage nozzles. **G:** Radar command. **C:** Not available. **W:** Probably nuclear.
Spartan XLM–49A (US) 'Safeguard' system high-altitude, area defence.	16·8 (55·2)	107 (42)	3·0 (9·8)	13,000 (28,660)	460 (750)	**P:** Three-stage solid rocket, Thiokol TX 500, TX 454, TX 239. **G:** Radar command. **C:** Aerodynamic cruciform fins/fins and gas-jets on final stage. **W:** Nuclear.
Sprint 1 (US) 'Safeguard' system high-acceleration terminal defence. Sprint 2 under development.	8·3 (27)	137 (54)	NA	3,402 (7,500)	40+ (25+)	**P:** Two-stage solid rocket. **G:** Radar command. **C:** Thrust vector control and aerodynamic cruciform fins, stage 2. **W:** Nuclear.

LEFT: *US Army Lance was designed to replace the tactical missiles Honest John and Sergeant. It employs pre-packaged liquid propellants. Maximum range is about 120km (75 miles).*
BELOW: *MGR–3 Little John, the compact, solid-fuel, air-transportable, artillery rocket, could have either a nuclear or conventional h.e. warhead.*
BELOW RIGHT: *The highly successful French SS–11 wire-guided anti-tank missile. More than 160,000 were produced for many countries.*

CENTRE LEFT: *Soviet FROG tactical missiles during manoeuvres in Minsk. It is operated by Warsaw Pact countries, Egypt and Syria.*
CENTRE RIGHT: *Soviet troops photographed on manoeuvres with SCUD B tactical missiles. Missiles are elevated for vertical firing from a small launch table at the back on the lines of the German V–2.*
BOTTOM: *The Vigilant anti-tank missile was a British development. It was easily carried and with it one man could destroy a heavy tank single-handed.*

Tactical missiles

Battlefield weapons include large, unguided and spin-stabilized rockets with conventional high explosive, chemical or nuclear warheads launched from tracked or wheeled chassis. American examples are the MGR–1B Honest John, MGR–3A Little John and MGM–52B/C Lance. Russia has produced a whole family of such weapons known to the West as Free Rocket Over Ground (FROG). More complex missiles of medium range – some able to attack near battlefield areas – also quickly made their mark.

From the beginning Russia concentrated on giving tactical missiles high mobility by mounting them on cross-country vehicles which could be driven off the road and concealed in woods and forests. The missiles, raised into a vertical firing position by the carrier vehicle's hydraulic erector, are placed on a small launch table and fired from the vehicle by remote control. Typical examples bear the NATO code-name Scud A and Scud B; Scaleboard has much greater range. America produced Redstone, Corporal, MGM–29A Sergeant and MGM–31A Pershing.

Early missiles were beam-riders, centring themselves on radio beams aligned with the target; others were guided by radio com-

mand. Such systems, however, are vulnerable to electronic counter-measures and they were rapidly superseded by inertial guidance systems with pre-set target instructions which could not be 'jammed'. The MGM–13B Mace – an American battlefield missile in the form of a ramp-launched pilotless aircraft – had a Goodyear Atran terrain/map-comparison guidance system, a forerunner of the highly advanced terrain-comparison systems used in America's latest hedge-

hopping cruise missiles.

France too has developed its own surface-to-surface battlefield missile, Pluton. This highly effective solid-fuel weapon has inertial guidance and operates from the AMX–30 tracked launcher.

Nor has the infantryman been neglected. To meet the challenge of the new battle tanks, a whole range of anti-tank missiles have become operational with the world's armies. The MGM–51A Shillelagh – developed for

BELOW: *The US Army Sergeant. This medium-range artillery missile became operational in 1962, was air-transportable and could be rapidly emplaced and fired by a six-man crew. The faster reaction time achieved over earlier missiles reflected the use of a solid propellant, reduced ground handling equipment and the use of digital electronics. The project originated at the Jet Propulsion Laboratory which had previously developed the liquid-propellant Corporal surface-to-surface missile.*

BELOW: *Mace, a modernized 'flying-bomb' of aircraft scale, was towed to the launch site on a vehicle which served the double purpose of transporter and launcher. The powerplant was an Allison J33–41 turbojet. Launch was assisted by an under-tail solid rocket booster. Now superseded by medium-to-long range tactical ballistic missiles and specialized strike aircraft, Mace was deployed on Okinawa in the Far East and in West Germany. It could carry a nuclear warhead more than 1,900km (1,200 miles).*

BOTTOM: *The French tactical missile Pluton is operated from a tracked carrier known as the AMX–30. The vehicle also embodies the associated data processing and control equipment. Range is 10 to 120km (6·25 to 74 miles). Warhead can be either nuclear or conventional high explosive.*
INSET: *A French Harpon missile being fired from its carrier. The wire-guided missile can be used against tanks and fortifications and has an automatic system of guidance which confers deadly accuracy.*

the US Army – was launched from a combination gun/launcher carried by a variety of vehicles, including the General Sheridan lightweight, armoured reconnaissance vehicle and the M60A1E2 medium tank. The missile itself had flip-out fins and was steered by deflecting the exhaust of the sustainer rocket according to signals from a microwave guidance system. The operator kept his optical sight fixed on the target and the missile responded automatically. The same gun/launcher could fire conventional 152mm (6in) ammunition.

Another significant US anti-tank weapon is the MGM–71A Tube-launched, Optically sighted, Wire-guided (TOW). The missile and its tripod-mounted launcher can be operated by two men. Its effective range is 1,830m (6,000ft). In Vietnam, TOW was mounted in launch pods carried by Huey helicopters. All the 'gunner' had to do was hold a target such as a supply truck in the cross-hairs of his stabilized sight. The pilot could do limited evasive manoeuvres after missile launch and the weapon would still score a bullseye at a range of 3,000m (9,840ft). In four weeks, two helicopters registered 47 kills, including the destruction of 24 Communist tanks.

Equally effective is the British anti-tank missile Swingfire. Powered by a two-stage rocket motor, it covers 4,000m (13,120ft) in 25 seconds, though even this is not as fast as either TOW or the Euromissile HOT. Command signals generated by a thumb control stick are transmitted over fine wires (breaking strain 10·4kg [23lb]) and the missile is programmed automatically to the operator's line of sight. Path changes are effected by a swivelling tail-end 'jetavator'. The High-Explosive Anti-Tank (HEAT) warhead consists of a copper cone backed by a shaped charge which can punch a hole through 56cm (22in) of armour.

When Egyptian troops stormed across the Suez Canal on 6 October 1973, special units engaged Israeli tanks with Russian-built Sagger missiles, which they unpacked from suitcase-like containers. With this weapon, the infantryman attaches the warhead to the missile and unfolds the guidance fins. A launch rail is set up on the container's lid and Sagger mounted on it. Wire connections can then be run out to a firing unit which the operator uses to launch and steer the missile in conjunction with an optical sight and a joystick. With this and other weapons some 200 Israeli tanks were destroyed in one day.

Air-to-air missiles
During World War II, Germany expended much effort on air-to-air guided weapons. The 90·7kg (200lb) Henschel Hs 298 was actually put into production in 1945 just as the war was ending. It took the form of a small swept-wing monoplane powered by a

TOP LEFT: *Shillelagh is launched from the same 152mm gun that fired conventional ammunition.*
TOP: *Probably the world's most effective long-range air-to-air missile is the AIM–54A Phoenix which arms the USN F–14A Tomcat and other high performance interceptors.*
ABOVE: *TOW anti-tank missile being fired from a Bell Huey helicopter.*
LEFT: *One of the world's most effective anti-tank weapons is Swingfire which became operational with the British Army in 1969. There are man-portable versions and launchers for mounting on combat reconnaissance vehicles and helicopters.*

dual-thrust solid-fuel motor, with fast- and slow-burning propellants for boost acceleration and sustained flight, one inside the other. Its maximum speed was about Mach 0·8. Launched at a distance of up to 1·6km (1 mile) from the target, it was radio-controlled and had a warhead which was detonated by a proximity fuze.

A more advanced weapon was the Ruhrstahl X–4, which had a crude form of self-homing and a maximum range of some 3·2 km (2 miles). Like some other German guided weapons, it was impervious to radio jamming since control signals were transmitted through fine, 0·2mm (0·008in) insulated wires which unwound from bobbins on the wings and connected it to the launch aircraft.

The missile, which had cruciform wings, was spin-rotating and controlled by solenoid-operated spoilers on the tail fins. In normal flight these vibrated at 5 cycles per second

but, in order to change the flight path, were made to operate asymmetrically by control signals from the launch aircraft. The smaller X–7 variant was designed by the same team for air-launching against ground targets.

The lessons learnt in Germany were quickly applied by the United States, the USSR, Britain and France. Early examples of American air-to-air missiles were the AIM–4E/F Falcon, which armed the F–101, F–102 and F–106 interceptor/fighters, and the AIM–7E Sparrow IIIB, which became standard armament on the F–4 Phantom. Both employ semi-active radar homing and depend on continuous-wave radar beams being directed from the launch aircraft and they respond to the reflections from the target. Sidewinder, on the other hand, had an Infra-Red (IR) seeker which steered the missile towards any heat source of a certain intensity, such as an engine or its exhaust.

The Soviet Union replied with a large

ABOVE: *Another formidable anti-tank missile is the Soviet AT–3 Sagger which Egyptian forces used with devastating effect against Israeli tanks during the Yom Kippur War. Apart from two-man infantry deployment, it is also mounted on a number of vehicles.*
BELOW: *Saab 37 Viggen attack aircraft with some alternative war-loads: on the aircraft three 600kg (1,320lb) Saab 04E air-to-surface missiles; in front two 300kg (660lb) Saab 05A ASM's, four AAM's (Falcons and Sidewinders), and four pods with 36 135mm air-to-surface rockets and other external stores.*

TOP: *Sparrow III on a modified UH–2C Seasprite helicopter for tests at the Naval Air Station, Point Mugu, California. This highly successful US air-to-air missile, which became operational in 1958, has appeared on a large number of the western world's interceptors and strike aircraft. It has since appeared in many variants for air, sea and ground-launched applications.*
ABOVE: *HOT – the high-speed, long-range anti-tank missile – launched from a 'Jagdpanzer Rakete' tracked combat vehicle. Developed jointly by France and West Germany, it can be fired by the infantry from ground positions and from vehicles, ships and helicopters.*

RIGHT: *Soviet AA–2 Atoll air-to-air missile on MiG–21PFM interceptor of the Indian Air Force. The weapon closely resembles the US Sidewinder and has similar infra-red guidance. Typical mounts are the MiG–21 Fishbed, MiG–23 Flogger and MiG–25 Foxbat. It has been produced in quantity for the Warsaw Pact countries and has been widely exported – to North Korea, North Vietnam, Egypt, Syria, Cuba, Iraq and Finland, and built in India under licence.*
BELOW: *Buccaneer strike aircraft with four Martel air-to-surface missiles, developed jointly by France and Britain. One version (AS.37) homes automatically into enemy radars, the other (AJ.168) is guided from the launch aircraft by television. Aircraft operating Martel include the Jaguar, Harrier, Mirage III–E, Buccaneer, Nimrod, Atlantique, and Sea King helicopter.*

solid-fuel missile (NATO code-name Alkali) which armed all-weather versions of the MiG–19. Like Sparrow and Falcon, it homed on the reflections from the target of the interceptor's radar signals.

Russian designers have generally tended to develop two versions of their air-to-air missiles, one with semi-active radar homing and the other with an IR homing head. Both versions are then flown on the same interceptor to enhance the probability of a kill. Two versions of Anab, for example, are carried by the Yak–28P, Su–9 and Su–11 all-weather interceptors. The Tu–28P can accommodate four of the larger AA–5 Ash missiles, two with radar homing and two with IR.

Britain, too, was well to the fore with missile armament during the 1950s and 1960s. Firestreak, an IR-homing pursuit course weapon, became operational on Lightning and Sea Vixen interceptors. It was followed by the IR-guided Red Top, which could attack from virtually any direction by virtue of a lead-collision IR guidance system.

France's first-generation air-to-air missile, the Matra R.511, depended on fairly crude semi-active radar homing and was carried by Vautour and Mirage IIIC interceptors. It was superseded by the Matra 530, a much more effective weapon not limited to pursuit-course attack. Like the Russian Anab and Ash, it was produced in both IR and semi-active radar homing versions.

One of the most promising of the new breed of air-to-air weapons is Skyflash, which has been adapted in Britain from the well tried Sparrow airframe. Using a new and advanced semi-active radar seeker, it is designed to engage targets from sea level to high altitudes and can 'snap down' to inter-

ABOVE CENTRE: *The French describe their R–550 Magic as a 'dog-fighter'. At the tail are rectangular fins and aft of the nose two sets of vanes one fixed, one steerable. In close-range air combat Magic is capable of making high-g turns exceeding those of the most manoeuvrable piloted aircraft. It is in service with the French forces on several types of aircraft.*

ABOVE: *Firestreaks mounted on the missile pack of a Lightning interceptor. The first-generation British infra-red guided missile was limited to pursuit-course engagements but regularly demonstrated a success rate of over 85 per cent in trials. It was superseded by Red Top which is faster, has greater range and can make its attack from almost any angle.*

cept low-flying aircraft. It is claimed to be particularly effective in electronic-warfare environments where the enemy is operating 'jammers' and other devices.

The Matra Magic 'dogfight' missile, which can manoeuvre at very high g levels, is another highly promising example.

Air-to-surface missiles

Germany played a leading role in developing anti-shipping guided missiles in World War II when glide-bombs were used against Allied merchant shipping. The Hs 293, which took the form of a small monoplane, had an underslung rocket motor which gave a thrust of 590kg (1,300lb) for 12 seconds. The maximum speed was about 600km/h (375mph).

Released at 8 to 9·7km (5 to 6 miles) from the target, the Hs 293 was radio-controlled from the launch aircraft, where the pilot visually tracked a flare in the tail of the missile. Experiments were also made with a crude television system to give the crew of the launch aircraft a missile-eye view of the approaching target. There was even a scheme to control such relatively long-range glide missiles by wire transmission to prevent the Allies jamming the control signals. An enlarged version, developed in 1944, was the Hs 295.

The Hs 294 was a more advanced weapon, designed to attack warships in a spectacular manner. After being visually guided by radio from the launch aircraft, the missile entered the sea within some 45·7m (150ft) of the target ship, shedding the wings and rocket motor to complete the attack under water. It was then exploded below the waterline either by the action of a proximity fuze or automatically at a predetermined depth.

Air-to-surface (tactical)

The need to pick off point targets in Vietnam – especially bridges defended by anti-aircraft missiles, and single vehicles carrying supplies from the North – led the Americans to introduce the so-called 'smart' bomb. Paveway was a conventional bomb fitted with a laser seeker and extra control surfaces. A laser beam aimed at the target by a supporting aircraft meant the bomb, released from an attack aircraft such as a Phantom, could steer itself towards the bright spot of laser energy reflected from the target. This allowed it to score a direct hit. From such devices have come a whole range of precision guided missiles which allow launch aircraft to leave the scene immediately the weapon has been released.

Another example of precision guidance is found in the AGM–65A Maverick. It has a small television camera which focuses on the target, steering the missile on to it with lethal effect.

A European example of a precision tactical missile is Martel, which exists in two versions. One, built in Britain, is TV-guided; the other, built in France, homes on to radar emissions.

So effective are such techniques that TV-guided Mavericks have been launched against ground targets from radio-controlled pilotless drones, removing the human element entirely from the attack zone.

TOP: *The Sky Flash air-to-air missile, installed on an RAF McDonnell Douglas F-4 Phantom. The all-weather missile, based on the US AIM–7E Sparrow, has totally new British electronic equipment and can be launched at sub-sonic or supersonic speeds. It is designed to intercept a target flying faster and at higher or lower altitudes than the launch aircraft.*

ABOVE: *Falcon air-to-air missiles in production for the US Air Force. Since the weapon first entered service in 1955 there has been a whole family of missiles with variations in guidance system, body design, propulsion and warheads. The two basic types have infra-red and semi-active guidance respectively. Versions of Falcon are licence-built in Sweden.*

bers to 'hedge-hop' and attack at low level.

Russia is also prominent in this league. As early as 1961 a stand-off missile, about 15m (50ft) long and resembling a swept-wing turbojet fighter, made its appearance beneath the fuselage of a Tu–95 Bear B. It was given the NATO code-name Kangaroo. Designed to attack peripheral targets within the NATO area, it was guided by radio from the launch aircraft.

Smaller winged missiles were developed mainly for anti-shipping duties. Two turbojet missiles which bear the NATO codename Kennel are carried by the Tu–16 Badger B on underwing pylons. A small radar mounted above the engine air intake in the nose allows the weapon to home on to its target automatically. A land-based version for coastal defence is called Samlet.

A more recent air-launched weapon is the rocket-powered Kelt, two of which can be carried under the wings of the Tu–16 Badger G. Yet another winged missile for antishipping use is Kipper, which is bellymounted on the Tu–16 Badger C. It resembles a swept-wing aircraft with an underslung turbojet.

New Soviet cruise missiles are now anticipated by the West, which expects that they will profit from the latest advances in turbojet and rocket/ramjet technology. The Tupolev Backfire B bomber, for example, can accommodate two large stand-off missiles beneath the fixed portions of its variable-geometry wings.

Intercontinental ballistic missiles

Marshal Zhigarev, Commander-in-Chief of the Soviet Air Forces, had pressed the importance of inter-continental rockets as early as 1946. Before such ambitions could be realized, much research and development was needed to improve rocket technology in four major areas: propulsion, structures, guidance and warheads.

The Russians began by improving the German V–2. Starting in 1945, the Gas Dynamics Laboratory/Experimental Design Group (GDL–OKB) sought to expand the know-how embodied in the RD–1/RD–3 family of rocket engines, variants of which had also been used for the assisted take-off of aircraft. Performance of the original V–2 was improved by modifying the engine cooling system, reducing the water content of the fuel, increasing the chamber pressure and temperature, and lengthening the nozzle.

By the end of 1947 the first launchings were being made of improved V–2 rockets built by Soviet engineers on Soviet soil. A secret launch base was used at Kapustin Yar (literally 'cabbage crag'), south-east of Stalingrad (now Volgograd).

The Russian version of the German missile had an RD–101 rocket engine. The same basic vehicle was later to appear as a geophysical rocket, the V–2–A. Experience with this vehicle led to the first Soviet short-range ballistic missile, known to the West as the SS–3 Shyster and to the Russians as Pobeda (Victory). The missile first appeared in a Red Square military parade in 1957, but US radar stations in Turkey had long since detected its early trials and listened in to its

TOP: *AGM–28A Hound Dog strategic missile was designed to be released from the B–52 bomber some 965km (600 miles) from a target. It carried a thermonuclear warhead.*

CENTRE: *Soviet SS–4 Sandal was the medium-range ballistic missile with which Premier Khruschev confronted President Kennedy during the Cuban crisis of October 1962.*

ABOVE LEFT: *Subsonic cruise missiles are carried by long range bombers of the Soviet Naval Air Force for attacking ships and coastal targets. Photograph shows the Tu–16 Badger with two AS–1 Kennel missiles on underwing pylons. It is turbojet powered and has a maximum range of about 150km (93 miles). Above the engine intake is a small radome. The weapon has been largely superseded by the rocket-powered AS–5 Kelt.*

ABOVE RIGHT: *Line-up of Blue Steel missiles at RAF Scampton. The large stand-off missile was carried by RAF Mk 2 Vulcan and Victor aircraft of RAF Bomber Command as part of the UK nuclear deterrent. Towards the end of its operational life crew training was directed towards penetrating hostile airspace at low level. Blue Steel was superseded in the deterrent role by the RN Polaris submarines.*

Air-to-surface (strategic)

Efforts to enhance the ability of strategic bombers to reach their targets led to air-launched 'stand-off' missiles which fly on as the bomber turns away. Among the first of such weapons was the AGM–28B Hound Dog carried by Boeing B–52Gs and Hs of the US Air Force's Strategic Air Command. Powered by an underslung turbojet, this 4,355kg (9,600lb) winged missile had a range of some 1,110km (690 miles). It carried a thermonuclear warhead and flew under inertial control.

Blue Steel, the British equivalent, was carried by Victor B.2s and Vulcan B.2s of RAF Bomber Command. It was powered by a Stentor two-chamber rocket engine fuelled by kerosene and High Test Peroxide. One chamber was for cruising flight, the other for a high-speed dash. The missile was 10·7m (35ft) long, had a maximum diameter of 127 cm (50in) and a wing span of 3·96m (13ft). It was particularly effective in allowing bomtelemetry, radio signals which carry coded data.

The engine, developed between 1952 and 1953, was the RD–103 which burned kerosene and liquid oxygen to produce a vacuum thrust of some 50,000kg (110,230lb). America's equivalent was the US Army's Redstone, developed by the von Braun team at Redstone Arsenal, Alabama.

Next to appear in Russia was the SS–4 Sandal, powered by a four-chamber RD–214 engine of 74,000kg (163,140lb) vacuum thrust. Developed between 1955 and 1957, this engine had variable thrust in flight, achieved by adjusting the supply of propellants to the gas generator of the turbopumps. It was this missile which featured in the Cuban missile crisis of 1962, when Nikita Khruschev tried to put pressure on the United States by stationing offensive missiles on its 'doorstep'. Reconnaissance photographs of Cuba showed that concrete had been poured for launch pads with support vehicles and missiles drawn up around the sites. The United States was within range of a missile capable of carrying a nuclear warhead over 1,770km (1,100 miles). Operational flexibility had been greatly improved compared with earlier missiles because Sandal employed storable liquids – nitric acid and kerosene – and could thus be held ready, fully fuelled, for long periods.

Although the Cuban sites were dismantled at the end of the confrontation, and the missiles returned to the Soviet Union, the episode proved to be the final justification for the

TOP LEFT: *The US Army's Redstone surface-to-surface missile was based on experience gained from the German V–2. It had steerable refractory vanes operating in the rocket efflux.*
TOP RIGHT: *Soviet geophysical rockets in the 'Cosmos' pavilion at the USSR Exhibition of Economic Achievement, Moscow. In the foreground is a Soviet version of the German V–2 (NATO code name*

Scunner) modified with a jettisonable instrument-carrying nosecone and ejectable instrument canisters on the body. At left is the later geophysical rocket based on the early ballistic rocket Shyster. The nosecone is open to reveal a spherical instrument container.
ABOVE: *While the United States and the Soviet Union were negotiating the basis of a SALT 2 agreement to limit the number of strategic delivery systems, the USSR*

was building bigger missiles to achieve a much greater throw-weight of nuclear explosives within agreed numerical ceilings. This chart shows the scale of the build-up compared with contemporary US weapons. From left to right: Titan II, SS–7, SS–5, SS–8, SS–4, Minuteman II, SS–11, SS–9, Minuteman III, SS–13, SS–16, SS–19, SS–17, SS–18. For details see missile table, pages 379 to 383.

BELOW: *Thor intermediate-range ballistic missiles were stationed in eastern England between 1958 and 1963. They were operated by the Royal Air Force but the US Air Force had authority over the thermonuclear warheads. When Atlas and Titan ICBMs brought the USSR within range from bases in the United States, Thor was withdrawn from England. The British Government planned to replace it with Blue Streak installed in underground silos but this was cancelled in 1960.*

build-up of missile forces in the United States. Already, Thor intermediate-range missiles stood ready at four RAF bases in eastern England pending the development of the big Intercontinental Ballistic Missiles (ICBMs) which could reach Soviet targets from launch sites in the United States. These rockets, fuelled with liquid oxygen and kerosene, had a range of some 2,775km (1,725 miles), putting Moscow into the front line of any nuclear exchange. Thor, instead of employing exhaust vanes to steer, had an inertial guidance system which issued commands to the rocket motor itself; the engine was gimbal-mounted and thus the thrust direction was changed for course corrections.

In the meantime the Russians had built a second major test centre north of Tyuratam in Kazakhstan. The big intercontinental rocket was rolled ponderously out to the launch pad for its first firing. In 1957 came the triumphant (if terse) announcement from the *Tass* news agency: . . . a super long-distance international ballistic multi-stage rocket flew at . . . unprecedented altitude . . . and landed in the target area.

It was many years before the West was to be acquainted with the design, although the broad features were known to Western intelligence. At lift-off, no fewer than 20 main

thrust chambers fired, as well as 12 smaller swivel-mounted engines for control. Sixteen of the main chambers were in four strap-on boosters which were thrown off sideways as the vehicle left the atmosphere. The central core of the rocket, powered by four main chambers, drove the vehicle to its final cut-off velocity as four Vernier motors responded to commands from the inertial guidance system. The warhead separated successfully and continued to its target on a ballistic trajectory.

The engine of the central core was the RD–107 of 96,000kg (211,650lb) vacuum thrust. Each of the four boosters had an RD–108 engine of 102,000kg (224,870lb) vacuum thrust. All of them burned liquid oxygen and kerosene. Launch pads for these huge rockets were elaborate and extremely vulnerable to nuclear attack. At the test centre they comprised a large reinforced-concrete platform linked with the preparation building by a standard-gauge railway. Rockets assembled horizontally on a transporter-erector were transferred to the launch pad by diesel locomotive. After being elevated into a vertical position on the pad, they were fuelled from rail-mounted tankers moved up on adjacent track.

America's reply to Korolev's ICBM was

the 1½-stage Atlas, which broke new ground by having thin but pressurized stainless-steel tanks which withstood the thrust loads of the rocket engines without heavy reinforcement. Fuel (kerosene) and oxidant (liquid oxygen) were kept in separate compartments.

The original Atlas tank, 18·29m (6oft) long and 3·05m (1oft) diameter had no internal framework and comprised the entire airframe from propulsion bay to nosecone. At the base was a single gimbal-mounted rocket engine with two small swivel-mounted engines outboard for roll control and Vernier adjustment of velocity. In a jettisonable skirt – into which the main sustainer engine projected – were two thrust chambers drawing their propellants from the same tanks.

All engines burned at lift-off, producing a total thrust exceeding 163,295kg (360,000lb). The outboard engines were jettisoned with the skirt after 145 seconds of flight. The sustainer accelerated Atlas to a velocity of about 24,140km/h (15,000mph), when it was shut off by the guidance system. Launch tests began at Cape Canaveral, Florida, as the Russians were preparing to launch their first ICBM at Tyuratam – but early success was to be denied. In June 1957, a test missile blew up soon after take-off and the following September another went off course and dis-

LEFT: *Titan II – the largest and most powerful ICBM in the US inventory – is launched from an operational type of silo at Vandenberg AFB, California. Top left, twin jets of smoke roar from vents on either side of the 44.5m (146ft) deep silo as the engines ignite. Top right, the nosecone appears above ground level. Left to right, bottom row, the missile rises quickly out of the silo until the full 31·4m (103ft) length appears. The total number of missiles of this type deployed in the United States at present is 54.*

BELOW: *The 18.3m (60ft) tank for an Atlas intercontinental ballistic missile is moved to the final assembly area of the manufacturing plant in San Diego, California. The thin-skinned stainless steel tank is pressurized to maintain its shape. During final assembly the tank was mounted to the propulsion section and other systems – guidance and control, power supply, telemetry, etc – were added. Although no longer an operational weapon, Atlas has been used widely in US space programmes.*

BELOW: *An Atlas ICBM blasts off from the US Air Force Missile Test Centre at Patrick Air Force Base, Florida. The weapon is long retired from operational service, its role being taken over by the Titan II and missiles of the Minuteman family. Towards the end of its life, Atlas provided targets for US anti-ballistic missiles launched on test from Kwajalein Atoll in the Pacific. Atlas also performed flawlessly in all the Mercury manned orbital flights, and was used in the launch vehicles Atlas-Agena and Atlas-Centaur.*

integrated completely in the atmosphere.

Only the booster engines were live in these initial tests. But when Atlas was launched with all engines firing, on 2 August 1958, success was complete; the rocket splashed into the Atlantic some 4,000km (2,500 miles) downrange. Although testing was far from complete, the US Defence Department lost no time in ordering the missile into production and Atlas D became operational on 'soft' sites in the United States in 1959.

In the meantime, a two-stage ICBM of more conventional design had been tested in January with a dummy top stage. The rocket – Titan I – employed the same propellants as Atlas and the engine gave a lift-off thrust of some 136,080kg (300,000lb). The vulnerability of missiles on open sites to nuclear attack, however, had already made clear the need for protective measures. Efforts to improve the reaction time of Atlas D led to above-ground 'coffin sites' at Vandenberg Air Force Base (AFB), California, and at Warren AFB, Wyoming. These offered a degree of protection from blast effects. The missiles were stored horizontally and fuelled behind protective walls before being elevated into a vertical launch position.

Titan I was stored in a deep underground silo. When the launch command was given, the silo doors opened and the rocket was raised to the surface by an elevator. Like Atlas, however, Titan I suffered the disadvantage of having to have liquid oxygen loaded on board immediately before launch; this added precious minutes to its reaction time, which was about 15 minutes. An improved version of Atlas, the F model, was tested in 1961. This too was designed for protection in an underground silo.

In the Soviet Union, the two-stage ICBM known to the West as SS–7 Saddler, became operational in 1961. Unlike some other missiles of the period, it was omitted from Red Square military parades. Evidence from reconnaissance satellites showed it to be a two-stage missile over 30·5m (100ft) tall and some 3m (9·84ft) in diameter. It was thought to employ storable liquid propellants.

The Russians were then discovered to be installing missiles in underground silos from which they could be launched direct, the exhaust flame being diverted through vents on two sides of the silo. This rocket was thought capable of delivering a 5-megaton (MT) warhead over a range of more than 10,460km (6,500 miles). Another two-stage rocket of similar range, the SS–8 Sasin, became operational in 1963.

Strenuous efforts were being made in the United States to develop ICBMs which could be launched from inside their silos. By 1963, the two-stage Titan II was in service. This used fuel and oxidant which (as in some contemporary Russian missiles) ignited on contact. This big ICBM stands 31·39m (103 ft) high, has a range of more than 8,047km (5,000 miles) and carries a warhead of over 5-MT yield. With propellants stored in the missile, Titan II has a reaction time of one minute from its fully hardened underground silo. Fifty-four of them are still operational at air force bases in Arizona, Kansas and Arkansas.

Russia replied to the new Titan with another two-stage rocket, also employing storable propellants and silo-launched. This is the ICBM known in the West as the SS–9 Scarp, which entered service in 1965 and has since appeared in four different versions. The so-called Mod 1 version carries a single re-entry vehicle of about 20-MT yield; Mod 3 has been used to test Fractional Orbit Bombardment System (FOBS) vehicles.

The missile build-up of the 1960s, however, was only beginning. The need to achieve faster-reacting missiles which could be held at instant readiness underground, or deployed in mobile launch systems, led to solid-fuel rockets of high performance. At the same time, advances in inertial guidance and reductions in the size and weight of thermonuclear warheads allowed ICBMs of high destructive power to be designed very much smaller than Atlas and Titan.

In the United States, the Minuteman I ICBM was officially declared operational in December 1962, only four years after the programme began. Eleven months later, Minuteman Wing I at Malmstrom AFB, Montana, and Wing II at Ellsworth AFB, South Dakota, were fully operational and missiles were being installed at Minot AFB, North Dakota. No fewer than 1,000 silos were built for Minuteman ICBMs, which lie hidden below ground in the wheat and cattle country of North and South Dakota, Wyoming, Montana and Missouri. Each flight of ten missiles is controlled from a metal capsule located 15m (50ft) underground and which is manned 24 hours a day, on a rota basis, by two officers of Strategic Air Command.

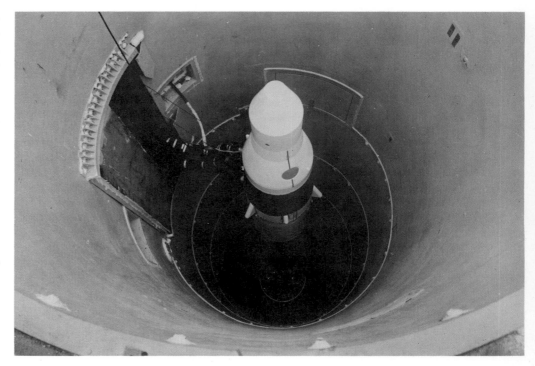

The original three-stage missiles have now been replaced by new models of increased range, accuracy and warhead power. The latest version, Minuteman III, carries three Multiple, Independently targetable Re-entry Vehicles (MIRVs). The MIRVs are carried in a post-boost 'bus' and are discharged against different targets according to instructions from a computer in the missile.

The Soviet counterpart of Minuteman I is the silo-launched SS–13 Savage, which entered service in 1968. It is believed to carry a single warhead of between 1- and 2-MT yield or three Multiple Re-entry Vehicles (MRVs) which explode in the same general area as each other but which are not individually guided towards specific targets.

Soviet designers developed the SS–13 on a modular basis. The second and third stages were used in a tracked transporter-erecter (Scamp) to achieve a mobile system which can be driven to different parts of the country and operated from points of concealment, among trees or in mountain passes for example. Some have been deployed near the border with China. A longer-range development of the same launch technique is Scrooge, which carries a larger missile (possibly also derived from the SS–13) in a long tubular container. The SS–11 Sego liquid-propellant rocket, however, although in the same general class as the SS–13, had greater performance and was produced in greater numbers.

France joined the 'ballistic club' in August 1971, when the first squadron of nine two-stage, solid-fuel *Sol-Sol Balistique Stratégique* (SSBS) missiles became operational in silos on the Plateau d'Albion in Haute Provence, Southern France. These S1 missiles could launch a 150-kT warhead a distance of 3,000 km (1,864 miles). Two years later a second squadron of nine S2 missiles became operational. These have a range of 3,150km (1,957 miles). In 1979 to 1980, these early missiles are to be replaced by the slightly smaller but more effective S3, which is designed to carry a 1·2-MT thermonuclear warhead. Manufactured at the French Atomic Centre at Pierrelatte, warheads of this type have been tested amid environmentalists' protests at the *Centre d'Expérimentation du Pacifique*, Fangataufa Atoll, near Mururoa.

China, too, began to build ballistic missiles in the 1960s. The first examples appear to have been based on the Soviet Shyster/Sandal-class medium-range missiles. They have a range of over 1,700km (1,056 miles), can carry either h.e. or nuclear warheads and have been operational, according to intelligence reports, since about 1966.

By the end of the decade it was clear that missiles of longer range were on the way. First to be tested was a single-stage rocket known in the West as the CSS–2 which employed storable liquid propellants and had a range of some 4,000km (2,485 miles). A multi-stage variant of this rocket is thought to have launched China's first artificial satellite on 24 April 1970.

The mid-70s saw the introduction of multi-stage ICBMs of limited range – the CSS–3. Installed in underground launch cells in north-west China they are capable of reaching Moscow and the European part of the USSR. A modification of this rocket is believed to be responsible for launching China's largest observation satellites which eject data capsules for recovery, e.g. China 4 on 26 November 1975 and China 7 on 7 December 1976.

The latest development, the CSSX–4 – a true ICBM with a range of some 11,000km (6,835 miles) – brings the United States within range of thermonuclear warheads. It is expected to be operational about 1980 in limited numbers.

Tests of nuclear warheads are made at Lop Nor in Sinkiang Province. The first atomic test took place there on 16 October 1964, the first thermonuclear (hydrogen-bomb) test on 17 June 1967. Subsequent tests have indicated that the warheads of China's ICBMs will have an estimated explosive yield of some 3 MT.

The main missile test centre – from which the Chinese also launch their satellites – is at Chuang Ch'eng-tze in the sparsely-populated, rolling wastes of Inner Mongolia.

Submarine-launched Ballistic Missiles
The increasing vulnerability of land-based ICBMs to thermonuclear attack led to the super-powers installing ballistic missiles in submarines. America began with Polaris A–1, which first became operational aboard the Fleet Ballistic Missile (FBM) submarine USS *George Washington* on 15 November 1960, with a full complement of 16 missiles. By 4 October 1967, the forty-first FBM submarine, USS *Will Rogers*, had set out on patrol.

Thirty-three of these vessels were assigned to the Atlantic Fleet and eight to the Pacific, target selection and assignment being under the control of the Joint Chiefs of Staff. The first five vessels, which originally carried Polaris A–1, were re-fitted to carry the longer-range Polaris A–3; most of the 616-class vessels have since been converted to accommodate the larger-diameter Poseidon C–3 missile.

Broadly, the development history of these two-stage sea-going missiles reflects the in-

TOP FAR LEFT: *A Minuteman ICBM installed in its silo. The total force of 1,000 missiles deployed in the United States comprises 450 LGM–30F (II) and 550 LGM–30G (III). The original Minuteman I is no longer in service.*
CENTRE FAR LEFT: *Russia's equivalent of the USAF's Titan II is the SS–9 Scarp. It can carry a single 20–25 megaton warhead or three 5 megaton multiple re-entry vehicles (MRVs).*
BOTTOM FAR LEFT: *The three-stage SS–13 Savage which employs solid propellants was Russia's answer to Minuteman I but only about 60 missiles were ever deployed – at Plesetsk south of Archangel.*
ABOVE LEFT: *The French constructed underground launch silos on the Albion Plateau in Haute Provence. This is one of their Sol-Sol Balistique Stratégique (SSBS) missiles on a fully enclosed transporter-erector.*
ABOVE: *The increasing vulnerability of land-based ICBMs to nuclear attack led to sea-based missiles. Here a Polaris is being loaded aboard the nuclear submarine USS George Washington.*
LEFT: *This Soviet tracked carrier bears the NATO code name Scamp; it contains the two-stage missile Scapegoat. Weapons of this type are operational on the Chinese border.*

creasing demand for more range, payload and accuracy. The Polaris A–2, slightly longer than the original, led to the A–3 which was a big advance on both earlier models. The Navy-industry team described it as 'an 85 per cent new missile', with 60 per cent more range and only a minimal increase in overall size. In fact, it had the same diameter of 137 cm (54in) and was just 30·5cm (12in) longer. The maximum effective range was about 4,635km (2,880 miles).

Britain abandoned the Blue Streak Intermediate-Range Ballistic Missile (IRBM) in April 1960 in favour of the American Skybolt air-launched ballistic missile. Skybolt, however, was subsequently cancelled by the Americans, and by the Nassau agreement of December 1962 Britain was to buy Polaris missiles, without warheads. By the end of 1969 the base at Faslane on the Clyde in Scotland had been built and all four of the British-produced Polaris submarines had been commissioned.

They have been named HMS *Resolution* (launched September 1966), HMS *Renown* (February 1967), HMS *Repulse* (November 1967) and HMS *Revenge* (March 1968). Each carries 16 Polaris A–3s with warheads of British design and manufacture. Like their American contemporaries, each submarine thus has more firepower at its disposal than the total of conventional explosives used in World War II.

Russia, too, was in the race and, after gaining experience with large and primitive solid-propellant missiles carried in both diesel- and nuclear-powered submarines (in two and three vertical launch tubes extending from the base of the hull through an extended bridge fin), much improved missiles began to appear.

Russian Yankee-class nuclear submarines have 16 SS–N–6 Sawfly missiles apiece in the pressure hull. The two-stage Sawfly has appeared in three versions: Mod 1 has a single re-entry vehicle of about 1–MT yield; Mod 2 has improved performance; and Mod 3 has three MRVs. Late models have a range of some 3,000km (1,865 miles).

Greater surprises were in store when high-resolution photographs of Soviet submarine yards were secured by US Air Force reconnaissance satellites. At Severdovinsk they uncovered the new Delta-class submarines which carry the SS–N–8 ballistic missile. This can achieve ranges of 7,885km (4,900 miles) and 12 are carried in Delta 1 vessels, 16 in Delta 2s.

For a submarine-launched missile, SS–N–8 performance is outstanding. Test firings carried out from a submarine in the Barents Sea in October 1974 resulted in high-accuracy impacts in the central Pacific, suggesting that the United States could be attacked from as far away as the North Sea.

The SS–N–8 is believed to obtain a mid-course navigational fix from a stellar-inertial guidance system. It is thought to employ a storable liquid propellant of the type which the Americans dismissed as too dangerous in their own FBM submarines in the face of counter-launched missiles, torpedoes and nuclear depth charges.

America's counterpart of the Delta 2 sub-

FAR LEFT: *Polaris A–3 starts a ballistic test down the Atlantic Missile Range. The weapon can be distinguished from its predecessors by the bullet-shaped nosecone; it had new rocket motors, control systems and guidance package. Range exceeds 4,020km (2,500 miles).*
CENTRE LEFT: *Armed with multiple, separately targeted warheads, Poseidon C3 has greater ability to penetrate enemy defences. It is carried by 31 of the US Navy's FBM submarines which have 16 launch tubes each.*
FAR LEFT BELOW: *Britain's Blue Streak intermediate range ballistic missile was intended to be launched from silos in Britain and the Middle East. The project was cancelled in 1960 due to soaring costs and the increasing vulnerability of land-based missiles.*
LEFT: *Skybolt ballistic missiles on a B–52 bomber. Britain was preparing to operate the weapon from V-bombers when America cancelled the project. Instead, Polaris missiles were offered for use in British-built nuclear submarines.*
BELOW: *This Soviet two-stage silo-launched IRBM is code-named Sasin by NATO. It was being phased out of service in 1976 to make way for newer land-based and sea-based missiles.*
BOTTOM: *Test model of the French MSBS ballistic missile bursts from the sea at the Toulon test centre. A small fleet of French nuclear-powered submarines has since put to sea with 16 missiles apiece. The M–1 missile has a range of 2,590km (1,400 miles).*

marine is the Trident, which is planned to carry no fewer than 24 missiles with ranges of between 7,400–7,800km (4,600–4,850 miles). Each UGM–93A Trident I missile can carry eight MIRV warheads of 100-kT yield. Associated with Trident is the world's most advanced re-entry vehicle, the General Electric Mk 500 Evader. This is the first Manoeuvrable Re-entry Vehicle (MARV), which can make abrupt directional changes in flight in order to confuse anti-ballistic missile defences.

The Chinese also have begun to develop their own ballistic missiles for launching from nuclear powered submarines.

France, too, has a fleet of FBM nuclear-powered submarines, each of which carries 16 two-stage solid-fuel *Mer-Sol Balistique Stratégique* (MSBS) missiles of French design and manufacture. The M1 and M2 versions carry a 500-kT warhead with ranges of 2,593km (1,610 miles) and 3,148km (1,955 miles) respectively. The M1 was installed in the submarines *Le Redoutable* and *Le Terrible*, and the M2 in *Le Foudroyant*. M20 missiles with 1–MT thermonuclear warheads are carried in *L'Indomptable*. The fifth and sixth French missile submarines, *Le Tonnant* and *L'Inflexible*, to be commissioned in 1979 and 1983, will carry the larger M4 missile with six or seven multiple re-entry vehicles, each having a 150-kT yield.

Anti-ballistic missiles

The 'missile race' caused the super-Powers to seek ways of protecting vital targets from the worst effects of a nuclear attack. Since most ICBMs have multiple warheads and/or eject decoys, this is no easy task and a determined attack would surely saturate any practical defence system.

In the United States the Safeguard Anti-Ballistic Missile (ABM) system was developed

LEFT: *America's fast-reacting anti-missile missile is Sprint. The photograph shows a prototype on test. It is designed to destroy incoming warheads which have already succeeded in penetrating the first line of defence supplied by the long-range Spartan ABM.*
RIGHT: *Spartan is the long-range component of the US anti-ballistic missile system, Safeguard, established at Nekoma, North Dakota in November 1974. Its short range counterpart is Sprint. The first operational test was made in August 1970 when a Spartan, launched from Kwejalein Atoll, scored a direct hit on a Minuteman I. Other successes followed, but the Nekoma site was deactivated in 1975 as an economy measure.*

LEFT: *Inside this casing is Russia's long-range anti-missile missile which bears the NATO code name Galosh. 64 missiles were installed at four sites on the perimeter of Moscow in the late 1960's. Modifications have since been made to associated radars to make the system effective against China's long-range missiles which have the Soviet capital within range from sites in north-west Sinkiang.*

largely as a means of protecting Minuteman ICBM bases. The first sites were earmarked for Malstrom AFB, Montana, and Grand Forks AFB, North Dakota, each complex having 100 missiles – 30 long-range LIM–49A Spartan and 70 short-range Sprint. (However, see below).

Controlled by a Missile Site Radar (MSR) the three-stage Spartan is silo-launched to intercept missile re-entry vehicles above the atmosphere. The third stage is ignited by ground command at a time which depends on the precise path of the incoming warhead as worked out by fast computers on the ground. Interception, carried out automatically by radar command, ends with the detonation of a thermonuclear warhead.

The two-stage Sprint was meant to catch ICBM warheads which had eluded Spartan *after* they had entered the atmosphere. In consequence it has a very high acceleration and is launched from its underground cell by a separate charge, the first stage igniting in mid-air. Rapid course changes after launch are brought about by a thrust vector control system by fluid injection into a single propulsion nozzle, and then during second stage flight by aerodynamic controls.

Associated with Safeguard are Perimeter Acquisition Radar (PAR) located at strategic points around the United States which provide the MSRs with preliminary tracking data. Supporting data comes from radars external to the United States and US Air Force early warning satellites which can detect the launch of ICBMs and Submarine-Launched Ballistic Missiles (SLBMs) from geo-stationary orbit by sensing energy emitted in the rocket's exhaust.

Similar developments have, of course, taken place in the Soviet Union. Four sites of 16 ABM–1 Galosh anti-ballistic missiles defend Moscow. They operate in conjunction with two Try Add radar sites which contain target tracking and guidance/interception radars. Advance warning of missile attack depends on large Hen House phased-array radars in peripheral areas of the country and Dog House acquisition radars near the capital.

A new SH–4 exo-atmosphere ABM and a Sprint-type high-acceleration ABM have been tested together with more advanced radars. Advance warning satellites have also reached the test stage.

SALT negotiations

The enormous build-up of thermonuclear weapons by the major Powers in the 1960s led to the Strategic Arms Limitation Talks (SALT). A five-year agreement signed by the United States and the Soviet Union on 26 May 1972, allowed the USA 1,054 land-based ICBMs, 44 FBM submarines and 710 SLBMs. The USSR could deploy 1,618 land-based ICBMs, 62 FBM submarines and 950 SLBMs. There was no restriction, however, on the number of warheads a missile could carry. Strategic bombers were also left out of the equation, and no limits were placed on medium-range missiles of the type which could easily threaten to destroy Western Europe.

Curbs were also placed on anti-missile missiles. Under Salt 1, each super Power was allowed two ABM complexes with 100 missiles apiece. This allowed the Russians to preserve their Moscow ABM defences and, if desired, to place ABM's at one other location. America elected not to set up an ABM system near Washington but continued with the installations near the Minuteman base at Grand Forks, North Dakota, other sites under construction at this time being aban-

Fu
Poc

Magnetic Compass

BELOW: *America's superior technology led to a major breakthrough in the mid 1970s in the shape of precision-guided cruise missiles. The winged missiles (next page) follow the contour of the earth at low level to strike their targets with deadly accuracy. They are a far cry from their predecessor – the Fieseler Fi 103, or V–1 flying bomb, used by the Germans during World War II for the indiscriminate bombardment of London and south-east England. It was powered by an Argus As 014 pulse-jet engine. At a pre-set range the V–1 was put into a dive cutting off the supply of fuel to the engine. The cut-out of the engine gave people in the area a few seconds in which to take cover before the missile hit the ground and exploded. Data: length 7·3m (24ft 5in); wing span 5·4m (17ft 8in); launch weight with 568 litres (150 gal) fuel 2,203kg (4,959lb); thrust 300kgf (660lbf); warhead 848kg (1,870lb); speed 563km/h (350mph); range 260km (161 miles).*

Air Intake Grid

Fuel Feed Pipe

Air Bottle

Trailing Aerial

Automatic Pilot

Electrical Supply

Air Charging Valve

Fuel Tank

Warhead

V-1 Flying Bomb

doned despite heated public debate.

The *status quo* was recognized in 1974 when a rider was added to the 1972 Treaty which limited each country to just one ABM complex. In 1975, however, the Grand Forks ABM sites were mothballed as an economy measure – just as they were becoming operational leaving Moscow with the only 'alert' ABM complex.

Efforts to embrace a wider concept of strategic arms limitations in the interests of détente led to a second round of negotiations (SALT 2), which resulted in President Ford and Russian Communist Party chairman Brezhnev meeting in Vladivostok on 23 to 24 November 1974. This meeting ended with

the so-called Vladivostok Accord, in anticipation of a ten-year agreement under which both countries would place a ceiling of 2,400 on all strategic nuclear-delivery systems – land-based, airborne and submarines. At most, 1,320 could have MIRV warheads.

The SALT negotiators in Geneva were left to work out the details of an agreement which, if all went well, was expected to be signed by mid-1975. Under the Accord, the USSR had already won one major concession. The much larger ICBMs that Russia was already bringing into service to replace the ageing SS–7, SS–8, SS–9, SS–11 and SS–13 were capable of carrying heavier warheads than contemporary American ICBMs. Al-

though they would be restricted in the number of MIRV warheads, many would have a throw-weight of thermonuclear explosive greater than US equivalents.

The Russians, too, had recently begun to deploy the Backfire B supersonic bomber. Although they claimed it did not have a strategic role, if refuelled in the air it could easily fly to the United States and return. American apprehension was hardly lessened by the knowledge that this formidable aircraft could accommodate two large stand-off missiles on underwing pylons.

The Russians, for their part, were greatly concerned about progress the Americans were making with the Air-Launched Cruise

Missile (ALCM) to be carried by B–52s and the planned B–1 strategic bombers. No fewer than eight ALCMs could be accommodated in a B–52's weapon-bay rotary launcher, with 12 more under the wings. The B–1 could carry 24, all internally.

Compact stowage of the Boeing ALCM – which began flight-tests from a B–52 over White Sands, New Mexico, early in 1976 – is achieved by folding the wings and tail surfaces and retracting the engine inlet into the back of the fuselage. After the ALCM is released from the bomber its engine inlet pops up, the tail surfaces spring open, the turbofan engine ignites and the wings swing out like knife-blades.

The ALCM's great attributes are small size and ability to dive almost to tree-top level when penetrating enemy territory. On the way to a target a programmer commands course changes so that the missile can fly round known defence positions, at the same time up-dating its 'navigator' to give precise instructions for the final run-in to the pre-set target.

Work on cruise missiles for the US Navy had also progressed in 1976 to the point of test firings of the General Dynamics Tomahawk. Designed for launching from the torpedo tubes of submarines, a variant of Tomahawk has also been fitted to the rotary launcher of a B–52 to see if the one basic missile could serve both sea- and air-launched applications.

In the submarine role, a solid-fuel boost motor ignites underwater and the missile is steered to the surface by thrust-vector control. Once the missile has emerged from the sea, explosive devices separate the covers from the turbofan engine inlet and three folded fins spring into place. Wing-slot covers eject and high-aspect-ratio wings swing out into flying position. Tomahawk then proceeds to its target using terrain-matching techniques of the kind described for the Boeing ALCM. A variant utilizing a different guidance system can be used against ships.

Strenuous efforts have been made by Soviet SALT 2 negotiators to limit the range of cruise missiles to 600km (373 miles). The issue has however been complicated by the fact that most important Soviet strategic targets lie well inland, while many of those in the USA are in or near coastal areas.

When Jimmy Carter became President of the United States in January 1977, high priority was given to achieving an early resumption of the SALT 2 negotiations. At the President's first full press conference, he expressed willingness to complete the negotiations without reaching agreement on the controversial trade-off between the Russian Backfire bomber and the US Cruise missiles. There were also hopes that the limits placed on the number of nuclear delivery systems could be reduced below the figures in the 'Vladivostok Accord'.

Mr. Carter also called upon the Soviet Union to halt deployment of its latest medium-range ballistic missiles aimed at targets in Western Europe. Central to this argument was the SS–20 on its mobile launcher which, at least in early versions, did not have inter-continental range and thus lay outside the scope of the current SALT negotiations. The US, he said, would be willing to respond by halting development of similar weapons.

TOP FAR LEFT: *The US Navy Tomahawk. Three versions were planned for strategic, anti-ship and land-based roles. First flight with the terrain-comparison (Tercom) guidance system was made on 27 January 1977.*

TOP LEFT: *Russia was well to the fore with cruise missiles in the early Sixties. Here a Styx surface-to-surface missile is put aboard a fast patrol boat of the Soviet Navy.*

ABOVE: *Deploying the Air Launched Cruise Missile (ALCM). Top, location of rotary launcher in B–52 strategic bomber. Below, how the ALCM opens out from the packaged configuration after release.*

ABOVE RIGHT: *B–52 bomb bay showing rotary launcher containing eight packaged ALCM's. Alternative arrangements are possible with extended range missiles.*

LEFT: *Another Soviet anti-shipping cruise missile bears the NATO code name Shaddock. The coastal defence version is carried on an eight-wheeled vehicle which resembles a road tanker. Other versions of Shaddock are installed in similar weather-proof containers aboard ships of the Soviet Navy.*

INSET LEFT: *For launch the tank-like containers is elevated by hydraulic jacks and the missile is fired from above the cab with the help of attached rocket boosters.*

RIGHT: *The new-generation American flying-bomb which disturbed the SALT 2 negotiations with the USSR. Called the Air-Launched Cruise Missile (ALCM) it can fly a precise course to its target at tree-top level that avoids radar.*

Space Exploration

RIGHT: *Sputnik ('Fellow Traveller') 1, the world's first artificial satellite. It was launched on 4 October 1957 from the Tyuratam-Baikonur cosmodrome by Russia's newly-developed intercontinental ballistic missile designed by Dr S P Korolyov. It was little more than an orbiting radio transmitter with long 'whip' aerials, and weighed 83·6kg (184lb). The casing had a diameter of 58cm (22·8in). The orbit ranged between 215 and 939km (134 and 588 miles) inclined at 65·1 deg to the equator, and this spherical satellite reached a velocity of over 28,400kph (17,750mph). Sputnik 1 burned up in the atmosphere after 92 days on 4 January 1958. The same basic rocket that launched this satellite was later fitted with a top stage to launch Russia's cosmonauts, see page 403.*

FAR RIGHT: *A month later came an even bigger surprise for the new 'Space Age' world with the orbiting of the dog Laika in a small pressure cabin. Laika was fed and watered automatically and sensors attached to the body gave basic medical data which was relayed to Earth by radio. Sputnik 2, which remained attached to the orbiting carrier rocket, circled the Earth for 5½ months, then burned up as it came into contact with the Earth's atmosphere. The Russians had made no plans for recovery but Laika had long since lost consciousness and died as the air supply ran out. The photograph shows a replica of the spacecraft as it appeared on the nose of the launch vehicle. Laika's pressure cabin is the cylinder at the bottom; the radio transmitter is housed in the smaller section above.*

Russia shook the world on 4 October 1957, by launching the world's first artificial satellite. This signal event in world history had been made possible by the big intercontinental ballistic missile developed by the team under Sergei P. Korolev. The satellite itself, called *Sputnik 1*, weighed 83·6kg (184lb). It took the form of a polished aluminium sphere of 0·58m (1·9ft) diameter with long whip antennae. The distinctive 'bleeps' of its radio transmitter, picked up by radio stations around the globe, signified the dawn of a new age.

America's position in the field of rocketry was seriously challenged, and President Eisenhower felt the need to re-assure the American public, on television and radio, that the nation's defences were sound. In Moscow there was unsuppressed glee. Enthusiastically, *Pravda* commented that 'The launching of the first satellite proved that ... the possibility of flying to the Moon is reasonable and justified.'

In the United States efforts were redoubled to bring to the launch pad at Cape Canaveral the three-stage Vanguard rocket which had previously been announced as part of America's contribution to the International Geophysical Year (1957–58). The objective was the launching of a 9kg (19·8lb) scientific satellite. The first rocket with all stages 'live' was ready on the launch pad on 6 December 1957. Within its nose cap was a test satellite of 13·3cm (6·4in) diameter, which weighed just 1·47kg (3·25lb).

However, when Vanguard's engine was ignited it failed to develop sufficient thrust, and instead of blasting off into space the rocket toppled over and erupted in a sea of flames. The tiny satellite, thrown clear of the inferno was still bleeping.

Almost immediately the Eisenhower administration agreed to allow the US Army Ballistic Missile Agency to develop their Jupiter C rocket as a satellite launcher. The concept had already been worked out by rocket scientist Dr Wernher von Braun and his associates, and it took a remarkably short time to bring it to the pad.

On 1 February 1958, the rocket – Juno I – lifted off from Cape Canaveral to put into orbit America's first artificial satellite, *Explorer 1*. The satellite swung round the Earth in a wide, elliptical orbit and the data it sent back led to the discovery that the Earth is girdled by electrically-charged particles from the Sun, trapped by the Earth's magnetic field (ie, the Van Allen radiation belts, named after the scientist who devised the experiment).

Soon afterwards a Vanguard rocket succeeded in placing a 1·47kg (3·25lb) test satellite into orbit, which Nikita Khruschev promptly dubbed America's 'grapefruit' satellite. Further salt was rubbed into the wound when, two months later, Russia launched *Sputnik 3*, a big cone-shaped geophysical laboratory nearly 100 times as heavy as *Explorer 1*.

By then a major re-think of space policy was taking place in America, leading to the National Aeronautics and Space Act which was passed on 29 July 1958. This opened the way for the formation, from the nucleus of the existing National Advisory Committee for Aeronautics (NACA), of an important new body, the National Aeronautics and Space Administration (NASA), inaugurated on 1 October 1958. All space-related functions were to be transferred to NASA over the next four years, and the civilian space agency was thus able to acquire the services of the Army Ballistic Missile Agency and von Braun's concepts for large (Saturn) launch vehicles. In March 1960 von Braun was appointed director of NASA's Marshall Space Flight Center at Huntsville, and additional funds were given to support the Saturn rocket programme.

In the meantime, the Russians had not been idle. On 12 April 1961, they pulled off the supreme achievement of putting a man into orbit – using a modification of the same type of rocket that had launched the first sputniks. That man was Yuri Gagarin. He travelled in a ball-like re-entry capsule, attached to a service module which kept the craft supplied with air (oxygen and nitrogen at about 1 atmosphere pressure). The cone-shaped service module had small thrusters for changing the craft's attitude in space and a retro-rocket which, fired at a backward angle, braked it for re-entry. Only the cosmonaut's capsule returned to Earth; the service module, which separated before re-entry, was burned up by friction in the atmosphere.

Gagarin made one circuit of the Earth in 108 minutes, proving that a human being

BELOW: *The lifting power of the big Russian ICBM received still greater emphasis in May 1958 with the launching of Sputnik 3, a cone-shaped geophysical laboratory. It weighed 1,327kg (2,926lb), but otherwise failed to set any new records.*
RIGHT: *America's Vanguard 2 satellite in place on the launch vehicle before fitment of the jettisonable nosecone. Launched on 17 February 1959 into a high elliptical orbit it should circle the Earth for more than 100 years before it eventually burns itself out in contact with the Earth's denser atmosphere.*

BELOW: *Before America launched a man into Earth orbit, sub-orbital tests were made in Mercury capsules. This Redstone rocket launched the future astronaut Alan Shepard on a 15-minute flight over the Atlantic on 5 May 1961.*
BOTTOM: *The Vostok launcher. Russia kept the big rocket that launched Yuri Gagarin into orbit on 12 April 1961 secret for six years. A replica was eventually shown to the world at the Paris Air Show in 1967.*

could survive in space at least for relatively short periods, despite the high accelerations experienced at take-off and re-entry, a period of weightlessness and exposure to radiation while in orbit.

America was still some way from a similar achievement, having restricted initial tests to ballistic lobs over the Atlantic. On 5 May 1961, Alan Shepard, in the Mercury capsule *Freedom 7*, was launched by a Redstone rocket to reach a height of 187km (116 miles) and travel a maximum distance of 478km (297 miles). Just over two months later Virgil 'Gus' Grissom made a similar flight in the capsule *Liberty Bell* splashing down 488km (303 miles) downrange. Although his capsule became waterlogged and sank, he was rescued in good shape by helicopter. (Grissom was later to lose his life with Ed White and Roger Chaffee in the Apollo spacecraft fire at Cape Canaveral on 27 January 1967.)

These early American experiments had one advantage over those carried out by Russia. The astronauts themselves used hand controls for changing the attitude of their spacecraft in flight, providing valuable experience for America's first attempt to place a man into orbit. The opportunity fell to John Glenn, who lifted off from Cape Canaveral on 20 February 1962, aboard the capsule *Friendship 7* on the nose of a modified Atlas ICBM. Glenn completed three orbits of the Earth in a flight which lasted 4 hours 55 minutes. Although the Russian Gherman Titov had already made a spaceflight lasting over 25 hours, Glenn's flight was a milestone booster adapter   afterbody   escape system

forebody

in American space exploration history.

More American and Russian manned flights followed in swift succession. Valentina Tereshkova, the first spacewoman, made a spaceflight of nearly 71 hours in June 1963. Russia launched a three-man spacecraft, *Voskhod 1*, in October 1964, and less than five months later Russia's Alexei Leonov 'space-walked' from the orbiting *Voskhod 2*.

America followed this with the two-man Gemini spacecraft, from which Ed White spacewalked in June 1965, manoeuvring in space with the help of a hand-held 'gas-gun'. In *Gemini 7* Frank Borman and James Lovell remained aloft for nearly two weeks, during which they flew close to *Gemini 6*, manned by Walter Schirra and Tom Stafford. Manned spacecraft docked with Agena 'targets' in orbit, and astronauts perfected the art of spacewalking.

Events were now moving swiftly towards a major American challenge. On 25 May 1961, President Kennedy told a joint session of Congress, 'I believe that this nation should commit itself to achieving the goal, before the decade is out, of landing a man on the Moon and returning him safely to Earth ...' Thus was born Project Apollo.

Unmanned Moon probes

Before men could land on the Moon it was necessary to send unmanned probes to ex-plore its surface. Russia succeeded first in

TOP: *The first American to orbit the Earth was Colonel John Glenn on 20 February 1962. His Mercury capsule complete with escape tower weighed 1,935kg (4,265lb) and was just under 8m (26ft) long. Glenn made three orbits of the Earth before landing in the Atlantic some 338km (210 miles) north-west of San Juan, Puerto Rico. When he re-entered the atmosphere there was concern that the capsule's heat shield may have become detached. Flaming chunks of debris, glowing bright orange, streaked past his window. In fact, it was the retro-rocket pack which had failed to jettison and was instead burning up – not the heat shield.*
BELOW: *Although Soviet cosmonauts normally land on Russian soil they have to be ready to make an emergency landing on water. For example, the Soyuz 23 cosmonauts inadvertently splashed down in a Russian lake. This photograph shows Alexei Leonov during a training session in a Soyuz capsule.*

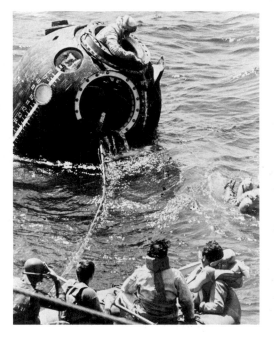

crash-landing an object (*Lunik 2*) on the Moon, in 1959. In the same year they sent *Lunik 3* around the Moon to photograph the hidden side. Another major achievement was the landing of *Luna 9* in February 1966, which sent the first television pictures from the Moon's surface.

America sent Ranger spacecraft, which photographed the Moon continuously until they crash-landed on it. The three-legged Surveyor craft examined the soil by means of a mechanical scoop operated under remote control from Earth. Another American spacecraft, Lunar Orbiter, photographed large areas of the Moon from orbit. These robot forays proved that the Moon's surface was safe for a manned landing, and allowed landing sites to be selected for the forthcoming Apollo missions.

Men around the Moon

At last – in the face of circumlunar flights by Russian unmanned Zond spacecraft – NASA gave the go-ahead to launch three men into lunar orbit aboard *Apollo 8*. During Christmas 1968 Frank Borman, James Lovell and William Anders gave television viewers on Earth their first sight of the Moon's bleak surface from a distance of 112·6km (70 miles).

This was the turning point in the 'Moon Race'. After a final dress rehearsal by the *Apollo 10* astronauts, a manned landing was at last in sight.

After separating from the *Apollo 11* command ship in lunar orbit, Neil Armstrong and Edwin Aldrin began their descent onto the Moon's Sea of Tranquillity, skirting a boulder field to put their Lunar Module safely on to the surface. The date was 20 July 1969.

A large part of the world, linked by television, watched the misty image of Neil Armstrong slowly descend the ladder to jump lightly on to the virgin moondust. He was soon joined by Aldrin. The two men, quickly adjusted to low gravity conditions. They set up scientific instruments and obtained 21·8kg (48lb) of moon samples.

At the end of their nearly 22-hour stay, they blasted off in the ascent stage of the Lunar Module, leaving the descent stage behind. A metal plaque records their visit: 'Here, men from planet Earth first set foot upon the Moon, July 1969 AD. We came in peace for all mankind.'

By the end of 1972, five more Apollo craft

LEFT: *Astronaut emerges from an Apollo spacecraft after a docking test with a Lunar Module in Earth orbit. Before this stage was reached, American astronauts had gained considerable experience with Gemini spacecraft which they docked with unmanned Agena targets. With these craft they also practised the art of space-walking which a Russian cosmonaut was actually first to achieve in March 1965.*
BELOW: *'Fish-eye' view of technicians preparing a Gemini spacecraft within the servicing gantry at Cape Canaveral. The spacecraft is on the Titan II launch vehicle. The two-man spacecraft rapidly shortened the Russian lead in space, and led on rapidly to Project Apollo and thence the Moon.*
BELOW CENTRE: *Overhead view of a Gemini spacecraft showing the 'snug fit' of the two cosmonauts inside it. In one of these craft Frank Borman and James Lovell, Jr. lived for nearly two weeks in orbital flight before returning to earth to face a daunting array of advanced medical tests.*

BELOW: *Gemini capsule was bell-shaped like Mercury with a blunt heat shield to protect it from frictional heating as it re-entered the atmosphere at high speed. In the small end were recovery parachutes. Landing was at sea, although the capsule was built to withstand an accidental 'grounding'.*
BELOW CENTRE: *Ed White was the first American to spacewalk on 3 June 1965. After the Gemini cabin had been depressurized the space-suited astronaut was able to climb out of a hatch and float in space on the end of an umbilical hose. He used a gas-gun to control his movements.*
BOTTOM: *First unmanned spacecraft to land on the Moon and send TV pictures was Luna IX. After being braked by a retro-rocket the egg-shaped capsule separated from its mothercraft bouncing and rolling on the lunar surface. Petal-like covers sprung open to erect the craft and reveal a small television camera and research instruments. This successful soft landing occurred on 3 February 1966.*

had landed and 12 men had left footprints in the Moon.

More than 380kg (837·7lb) of lunar rock and soil were brought to Earth by the six successful missions, ranging from loose soil and surface rocks to core samples from *mare* ('lunar seas') and highlands. The mare rocks turned out to be relatively rich in titanium and iron, and the highland rocks had a greater abundance of aluminium. A typical *Apollo 11* soil sample contained: oxygen (40 per cent), silicon (19·2 per cent), iron (14·3 per cent), calcium (8·0 per cent), titanium (5·9 per cent), aluminium (5·6 per cent) and magnesium (4·5 per cent).

Of the rocks taken from the first four landing sites, none was older than 4,200 million years nor younger than 3,100 million years. The soils were older than the rocks, and dated back 4,500 or 4,600 million years. The age of the crater Copernicus, dated by material found in its 'rays', appeared to be only about 850 million years.

A total of 166 man-hours had been spent in surface exploration at six different sites, and the astronauts had travelled more than 96km (59·6 miles). Five Apollo Lunar Surface Experiment Packages – science stations powered by nuclear energy – continued to send data to Earth years after the astronauts had departed. A total of 60 major scientific experiments in geology, geophysics, geochemistry and astrophysics were left behind on the Moon. Another 34 were conducted in lunar orbit from the command ships.

In the light of this tremendous achievement, one must inevitably ask what had happened to the Russian challenge. In 1968–69 cosmonauts seemed to be on the brink of making circumlunar flights. By linking up separate spacecraft modules in orbit, they might even – eventually – have landed on the Moon. The immense success of the Apollo programme, however, put Soviet plans for manned moonflight into abeyance, and effort was concentrated on perfecting automatic Moon samplers, able to land, collect soil and rock specimens, and bring them back to Earth. Even as the *Apollo 11* astronauts were preparing to land, a robot spacecraft, *Luna 15*, was being manoeuvred in lunar orbit under control from a Russian ground station. There was speculation that this was an attempt to obtain a Moon sample and fly it to Earth in a final bid to up-stage Apollo. In the event, the probe crash-landed.

Apollo Space Mission

ABOVE: *The last three Apollo missions to the Moon carried electric-powered lunar rovers which the astronauts removed folded up from storage space in the base of the Lunar Module. The 'moon-cars' greatly extended the radius of exploration and allowed the astronauts to collect a much wider range of moon samples for analysis by selected scientists at centres around the world.*

In September 1970 *Luna 16* soft-landed, drilled 35cm (13·8in) into the Moon's surface, transferred a 100 gramme (3·5oz) core sample to a capsule and blasted it back to Russia. Two months later *Luna 17* succeeded in landing a Lunokhod roving vehicle, which the Russians steered over the lunar surface by remote radio control.

Interplanetary probes

Similar means of robot exploration were developed in the United States. With the 'Moon Race' won, Congress looked with disfavour on more manned missions as new priorities and the unpopular war in Vietnam began to engage its attention. Any long-term prospects of astronauts pressing on to Mars were abandoned.

Instead, research was directed to developing an increasing number of ingenious automatic vehicles to range deeper into the Solar System. Built at a fraction of the cost of manned spacecraft, they could be sent to places where men dare not go: deep into the crushing atmosphere of Venus, for example, and through the intense radiation belts of Jupiter.

In 1962 America had already flown *Mariner 2* past Venus and probed the planet with instruments which indicated surface temperatures above the melting point of lead. Russia then parachuted instrument capsules through the planet's thick carbon dioxide atmosphere to find that its surface pressure was 90 to 100 times that on Earth. There was strong competition between Russia and America to probe the secrets of Mars, with fly-by and orbital missions. The US *Mariner 9* spacecraft became the first artificial satellite of the Red Planet on 13 November 1971, as a dust storm raged on Mar's surface. When the dust storm cleared *Mariner 9*, scanning from orbit, discovered huge volcanoes, canyons and features like ancient dried-up river beds.

At the same time Russia was attempting to land instrument capsules. The first was destroyed on impact; the second came down in the region between Electris and Phaethontis (about 48 deg S, 158 deg W), but failed just as it began to send a picture.

In 1974 *Mariner 10* flew past Venus on its way to Mercury, showing for the first time that the tiny planet nearest the Sun had a moon-like surface of craters, mountains and valleys.

Pioneers 10 and *11* swung around the giant planet Jupiter before departing on different paths. The first is due to leave the Solar System in 1987; the second is headed for the ringed planet Saturn, which it should reach in 1979. Calculations show that *Pioneer 10* will reach the environs of the star Aldebaran in the constellation of Taurus after some 1,700,000 years. Both craft carry pictorial greetings to any extra-terrestrial intelligence that may find them in the remote future, giving information on the senders, their home planet known to them as Earth, and its position in the Galaxy.

In 1973 Russia again launched a spacecraft to Mars, using the powerful Proton D–I–e rocket and spacecraft of a new generation – *Mars 4, 5, 6* and *7*. The results were disappointing. One arrived in orbit around Mars; the others flew past, one doing so unintentionally when its braking engine failed to fire. However, the biggest setback was the loss of the two landing capsules released by the *Mars 6* and *7* mothercraft as they approached the planet.

Despite these costly setbacks, Russia pressed on and, in November 1975 two large automatic spacecraft succeeded both in landing capsules on Venus and going into orbit. The capsule of *Venera 9* plunged into the planet's atmosphere at 10·7km/sec (6.6 miles/sec) and at an angle of 20 degrees. When speed had dropped to 250m/sec (820ft/sec) the probe threw off clamshell protective covers and deployed a parachute. After it had floated down to a height of 50 km (31 miles) from the surface, the parachute jettisoned and the capsule was slowed in the thickening atmosphere by a disc-like drag brake attached to the body. It hit the surface at 7–8m/sec (23–26ft/sec), the landing shock being absorbed by a ring of crushable metal. The capsule transmitted data (via its orbiting mothercraft) for 53 minutes, including the first picture to show surface conditions on Venus.

Clearly visible was a level surface strewn with sharp-edged rocks 30 to 40 cm (12 to 16in) across, which might have come from volcanoes. Atmospheric pressure at the surface was about 90 atmospheres, and the temperature 485°C (905°F).

The capsule released by *Venera 10* came down some 2,200km (1,367 miles) from the first landing site, transmitting for 65 minutes and sending a picture showing outcrops of rock among rock debris. There the atmosphere was 92 atmospheres, which suggested that the craft had dropped into a lower lying region.

Two years later America sent two Viking spacecraft into orbit around Mars, on 19 June and 7 August 1976 respectively. The first released its landing craft onto the dry plains of Chryse Planitia on 20 July, seven years to the day since men first walked on the Moon. Photographs received on Earth showed a scattering of rocks; the surface had a red-brown colouring and the sky was a pinkish hue. The thin carbon dioxide atmosphere had a pressure of 7·69 millibars.

On 3 September 1976, the Lander of Viking 2 made its touchdown in Utopia Planitia some 200km (125 miles) west of the crater *Mie*, which has a diameter of about 100km (62 miles). It is believed that some of the rocks in the pictures came from this impact crater.

In a highly successful series of experiments, both robot Landers scooped up Martian soil and transferred samples to an onboard biology laboratory for automatic analysis. The results revealed that the main constituents of Mars' soil were iron, calcium, silicon, titanium and aluminium. But whether the reactions of treated soil samples are evidence of chemical or biological activity remain an open question. The results indicated a surprising amount of water and oxygen in the soil, but there was no certain evidence of organic material.

Meanwhile, the Viking Orbiters had made extensive photographic surveys of the sur-

LEFT: *History was made on 16 July 1969 when the first men destined to walk on the Moon blasted off from Cape Canaveral. The task set by President Kennedy in 1961 was brilliantly fulfilled. A million people witnessed the launching and it is estimated that 590 million others watched on television around the world as Neil Armstrong made his momentous 'One small step . . .' speech.*

LEFT INSET: *The first man to leave footprints in the moondust was Neil Armstrong who later took this picture of his companion Edwin Aldrin. The two men landed on the Sea of Tranquillity in the Lunar Module Eagle on 20 July 1969 while the third member of the team, Michael Collins, remained aboard the orbiting command ship* Columbia *taking charge of Earth Communications.*

TOP: *America's Mariner 10 made a tour of the inner planets in 1973–75. After taking photographs of the Earth and the Moon, it swung past Venus and on to Mercury, the tiny planet nearest the Sun. Mercury was found to have a moon-like landscape with craters, mountains and valleys – also a distinctive magnetic field. Previous launches of the successful Mariner series had already probed the secrets of Mars.*

INSET: *Lunokhod looked like something out of a Jules Verne fantasy. In fact, it was a highly functional electric-powered robot with TV 'eyes' which sent pictures to a Russian control station. When its batteries needed re-charging the lid opened to expose solar cells which generated electricity from sunlight. Throughout its long lunar life this vehicle was to be directed successfully from Earth.*

ABOVE: *Lunokhod 1 was landed on the Sea of Rains by the Luna 17 carrier in November 1970. After being driven off ramps under remote control from Earth, it was steered on a series of journeys lasting 322 Earth days. The Russians claim it travelled a distance of 10,542m (34,588ft), sending back TV pictures and scientific data, and travelling on gradients up to 30 deg in the Mare Ibrium.*

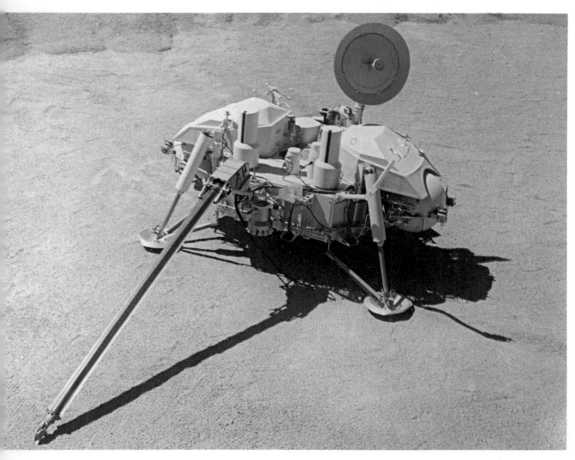

face, using two high-resolution cameras which provided spectacular new details of the ancient river beds, the equatorial canyon and the polar caps. Temperature measurements revealed that, contrary to expectations, the latter consist mainly of water ice and not dry ice (frozen CO_2).

Earth satellites

The results of deep space astronomy conducted from unmanned Earth satellites and manned space stations have been no less exciting. Orbiting above the Earth's hazy and turbulent atmosphere, they have opened up a 'new' universe to which we were practically blind – a universe of fantastic spectral range extending far beyond visible light and radio waves to X-rays, ultraviolet and gamma rays. Astronomers have begun to make fundamental discoveries about supernovae (exploding stars), pulsars (pulsating stars), neutrons (superdense stars), 'black holes' and quasars (quasi-stellar objects). The effect of changing conditions of the Sun upon the Earth's environment has also been under constant study.

Not all the work is in the interests of pure science. Meteorological satellites keep us informed from day to day of the world's changing weather conditions and give advance warning of destructive storms like hurricanes and typhoons. Early examples of such satellites were Tiros and Nimbus (US) and Meteor (USSR). They send television pictures of cloud, ice and snow cover on the day and night sides of the Earth, and also provide data on the thermal energy reflected and emitted by the Earth and its atmosphere, important for the greater understanding of meteorological conditions.

At the same time the super-powers lost no time in exploiting the military potential of space – especially by the use of photo-reconnaissance satellites and satellites able to provide advance warning of missile attack.

Earth satellites have also become 'radio stars', to assist the precision navigation of ships and aircraft in all weathers, and networks of military satellites have been established to maintain reliable, fade-free communications with naval vessels. *Elint* (electronic intelligence) missions are also carried out from orbit, with satellites 'listening in' to defence radars and communications, logging their codes and frequencies.

After America, for some obscure reason, had shelved development of an anti-satellite rocket (Saint), the Russians began testing 'killer' satellites within the Cosmos programme which fragmented close to orbiting targets. Other military test satellites were observed to eject re-entry vehicles at the end of a single orbit. These were the so-called Fractional Orbit Bombardment System (FOBS) vehicles which, launched in anger, could attack the United States through the 'back door' of the South Pole.

Nonetheless, enormous efforts have been made by the super-powers to apply the fruits of space technology to human need. More and more people are becoming involved in Space in their ordinary work – geologists, oilmen, doctors, farmers, ecologists, teachers and others. And although few of them are likely ever to see a rocket blast off from a launch centre, they will be called upon to use their skills, via space, to help solve some of mankind's most terrifying problems – poverty and famine, over-population, illiteracy, pollution, and perhaps even the energy crisis.

It all began with a space age communications explosion sparked by a technical memorandum which the 'space prophet' Arthur C. Clarke placed before the Council of the British Interplanetary Society (BIS) in 1945.

That brief document, headed: 'The Space Station: Its Radio Applications' heralded the greatest 'revolution in global communications of all time. It described how three satellites, spaced at equal distances apart in 24-hour 'stationary' orbit high above the equator, could serve to spread communications around the world, and showed how a single satellite could broadcast directly to several regions simultaneously.

Clarke wrote: 'No communications development which can be imagined will render the chain obsolete, and since it fills what will eventually be an urgent need, its economic value will be enormous.'

Although Clarke and the BIS did all they could to promote the scheme, it was left to America to put the 24-hour satellite into commercial practice with *Early Bird* built by the Hughes Aircraft Company in 1965. Today's communications explosion is the result. Matching the Earth's rotation above the Atlantic, Pacific and Indian Oceans are big, drum-shaped satellites of the Intelsat network, any one of which can relay up to 6,000 telephone calls, or 12 colour television programmes or a combination of the two.

By 1975 the chain linked North and South America, Europe and Africa, and girdled the Far East via 111 antennae at 88 Earth stations in 64 countries. (By the use of land-lines from the existing Earth stations, the system actually reaches more than 100 countries on a full time basis).

Since 1965 transoceanic telephone traffic has grown from an estimated three million calls a year to more than 50 million in 1974, and it is predicted that calls will increase to 200 million by 1980. Indeed, because of satellites, a three-minute telephone call between New York and London is 55 per cent cheaper today than when *Early Bird* entered service. And satellites are the only way to send television around the globe.

The ripples of Clarke's idea are spreading continually. Indonesia, for example, ordered from Hughes a domestic satellite system of the kind pioneered in Canada and America. Unlike satellites which span oceans and link continents, a domestic satellite focuses its power into a beam that concentrates coverage onto a specific nation. The Indonesian satellite *Palapa* (a name which signifies national unity) opened its service to 130 million people in the world's largest archipelago on 17 August 1976, in celebration of the Republic's 31st year of independence. It provides telephone, television, radio, telegraph and data services to the populated areas of 5,000 of the nation's 13,000 islands, which stretch over 5,000km (3,107 miles). Plans were also set in hand to use the satellite to broadcast educational television programmes throughout Indonesia.

The big test of the social applications of space technology began in 1974 in a programme co-ordinated by the US Department of Education and Welfare. The powerful ATS–6 'umbrella' satellite was placed in geostationary orbit just west of the Galapagos Islands in the Pacific to transmit educational and medical services directly to low-cost television receivers in scores of isolated communities in the United States.

LEFT: *America triumphed by landing two Viking robots on Mars in 1976. The first came down on* Planitia Chryse *on 20 July, the second on* Planitia Utopia *on 3 September. Each took samples of the reddish Martian soil with a mechanical scoop and analysed them. Although there were strong chemical reactions, there was no positive sign of any animal or vegetable life.*

BELOW: *Technicians of the British Aircraft Corporation check the antennae mast of Intelsat 4, one of the world's most advanced communications satellites.*

CENTRE BELOW: *GEOS 1 was to have been Europe's first geo-stationary satellite for research into the Earth's magnetosphere. A launch mishap left it stranded in an unplanned orbit.*

ABOVE: *Tiros 3, an American meteorological satellite, used to transmit pictures of cloud cover and the Earth's terrain to assist in meteorological research and the understanding of weather patterns.*

BELOW: *Comsat 1, a USA communications satellite in geo-stationary orbit used to relay telephone calls and TV broadcasts.*

Teachers participating in the experiment were able to see instructors, pictures and charts 'bounced' to them from the satellite across hundreds of miles, and to ask questions as if they were in the same lecture hall. The satellite allowed doctors in city hospitals to 'visit' patients in remote regions of Alaska, monitor their medical condition and advise locums of specialized medical treatments. Medical data, including electro-cardiograms and X-rays, were sent to doctors over the space link.

The same versatile platform was later moved eastward, by operating a small rocket motor aboard the satellite, to take up a position some 35,880km (22,295 miles) above Lake Victoria in East Africa. From this lofty vantage point, it broadcast directly to children and adults in some 5,000 towns and villages in seven states of India.

Wernher von Braun one of the creators of that experiment claimed that 'ATS-6 could turn out to be the most important advance since movable type as a means of reaching people now separated by vast geographical, economic and cultural barriers. Its successors may indeed eradicate illiteracy from the face of the Earth.'

All the time space investment is producing new opportunities for social advance. 'If I had to chose one spacecraft, one Space Age Development, to save the world,' said NASA Administrator Dr James C. Fletcher, 'I'd pick ERTS and the satellites which I believe will be evolved from it later in this decade.' He was speaking about the first of two observation satellites – later re-named Landsat – which take special photos of the Earth. Rocketed into polar orbits some 925km (575 miles) high, they circle the globe every 103 minutes. Every 18 days they view the same spot anywhere in the world at the same local time of day.

The 952kg (2,100lb) Landsats carry television cameras as well as radiometric scanners, to obtain data in various spectral ranges of visible light (red, blue and green) and infrared, which show up hidden features on the ground. The data obtained relates to crop species, crop quality, moisture content of the soil, and soil fertility over wide areas. This in turn helps to find the best places to develop new land for farming and the best time to plant and harvest crops for maximum yield.

Satellite observation also promises to achieve an early prediction of the total harvest, so that food supplies are known in advance and can be set against future need. An early discovery was that crops and forest areas damaged by blight or insects showed up blue-black in the satellite photos and healthy vegetation pink or red.

Landsat observations have also shown how controlled grazing of cattle in the drought and famine-stricken Sahel region of Africa can lead to the reclamation of desert land for productive use. And in cases of severe flooding – along the Mississippi and in devastated areas of Bangladesh, for example – the satellite images have given vital information for the resettlement of whole communities.

India is now moving into the field of space technology with determination. Having had a scientific satellite launched by the Russians in April 1975, India is now building her own satellites and launch vehicles for meteorological study and storm warning, Earth resource observation and help with agriculture. If, for instance, the onset of the monsoon rains can be predicted by satellites – information which is crucial to the transplantation of rice – millions of dollars a year could be saved. And in these regions the saving of a rice crop is not just a financial gain; it could mean the ultimate difference between life and death.

Other developing countries are catching on fast. Kenya, Zaire, Iran and Venezuela were among the first to set up ground stations so that resource data supplied by America's Landsats could be applied without delay in their own particular territories. Already the Landsats have made important discoveries in many parts of the world in the search for deposits of minerals and fossil fuels.

An early revelation was the 'geological inference' that the oil and gas deposits of the Alaskan North Slope are much larger than had been previously believed. The satellites obtained multi-spectral images of previously invisible 'large lineaments and structural breaks' bearing no relationship to surface geology. It is such hidden features, discernible only by satellite, that are providing fresh hope of discovering oil and mineral deposits throughout the world.

In retrospect, it is that sort of data, streaming back to us from spacecraft sent to explore the Moon, Mars and other planets, that has been most valuable. It has prepared the way for a spectacular and much needed rediscovery of our own planet. And, what is even more remarkable, these benefits are coming from only a small share of the one cent of the tax dollar which currently supports the space programme in the United States.

Space stations

The desire to gather information on Earth's natural resources and expand other useful areas of science and technology, led to the first manned space stations. After teething troubles with test models, the Russians launched a series of 18·5-tonne (18·2-ton) Salyut orbital laboratories. Cosmonauts docked with the stations at intervals in Soyuz ferries to carry out various research tasks, which ranged from photographing the Earth's resources to making experiments in biology, medicine and industrial processing under conditions of weightlessness. Telescopes were carried to observe the Sun and the stars from above the atmosphere.

The much larger Skylab space station launched by America on 14 May 1973, carried out a wide range of similar experiments which included use of the Apollo Telescope Mount to increase knowledge of the Sun and its influence on Earth's environment. Metals were melted in a small electric furnace, and experiments made in the growth of crystals of a kind which could be of value to the electronics industry. Photographs of the comet Khoutek were taken by astronauts.

Skylab was made from the S–IVB stage of a Saturn rocket. Fitted out with two-storey accommodation, it included a large workshop area for experiments and, on the 'lower floor', a wardroom and living area including a combined washing and toilet compartment and separate sleeping compartments.

Although damaged during the launching – accomplished by a two-stage *Saturn V* – the first two boarding parties of three men each were able to carry out running repairs. The workshop's external meteoroid shield and one of the large solar 'wings' had been torn off by air pressure as the rocket passed through the atmosphere; the other 'wing' was held fast by a piece of torn metal. Not only was the first boarding party able to erect a temporary sunshade over part of the workshop to reduce the temperature, but the astronauts were able to climb out of the station to cut away the obstruction and release the jammed solar 'wing'. The second team brought a larger sunshield which they erected without great difficulty. In the end Skylab exceeded all expectations, with three highly successful astronaut missions lasting 28, 56 and 84 days respectively.

Not long after, Russia and America pooled their resources in a joint space experiment which entailed astronauts and cosmonauts training in each others' countries. This was the celebrated Apollo-Soyuz Test Project (ASTP).

The mission got underway in July 1975, when a three-man Apollo spacecraft docked with a two-man Soyuz 225km (140 miles) above the Earth. Both craft had been modified to make their life support and docking

BELOW: *Detached S-IVB stage of a Saturn rocket photographed from Apollo 7 spacecraft in Earth orbit. The Skylab space-station was based on a modification of the S-IVB. Within the big hydrogen fuel tank compartments were built to provide two-floor accomodation for three astronauts. An experiment chamber, which occupied the upper third of the tank, allowed the astronauts to float about freely doing various zero-g experiments. Below this was the crew work area and living quarters which featured every possible refinement to make this cramped space an endurable working environment.*

TOP: *An infra-red view of Italy taken by NASA's Landsat-I Earth Resources Satellite. To obtain cloud-free shots for this series of pictures, the photographs were taken over a period of over a year, between 1972 and 1973 as the satellite cruised in polar orbit.*

ABOVE: *Skylab was badly damaged when it was launched on 14 May 1973. It arrived in orbit minus a solar 'wing' with the meteoroid shield ripped off and the other 'wing' jammed shut by a piece of torn metal. The first boarding party had to carry out emergency repairs. Astronauts spacewalked to extend the remaining solar 'wing'. They also fixed a sunshade to prevent Skylab from overheating. In the end near disaster was turned to triumph in a series of spectacular experiments. At the time of this flight, Skylab took the record for the heaviest object to ever have orbited the Earth.*

systems compatible. The crews visited one another and carried out joint experiments before separating their ships and landing in their respective recovery areas. The project proved the feasibility of space rescue missions and the ability of nations to co-operate in the joint construction and supply of space stations and in their peaceful use.

The space shuttle
Meanwhile, a revolutionary new space vehicle which promises to bring down the cost of space travel was taking shape in America. Unlike conventional rockets, which fall to destruction each time a spacecraft is launched, this winged craft – blasting off like a rocket and flying home like an aeroplane –

can be re-used 100 times or more. Called the Space Shuttle, it consists of the winged Orbiter, about the size of a DC–9 airliner, a large external tank and two powerful solid rocket boosters. The Orbiter has a crew of three – pilot, co-pilot and mission specialist.

Launched vertically from the pad like a normal rocket, it rides on the large external tank which supplies the ascent propellants (liquid oxygen and liquid hydrogen). The two solid fuel rockets, mounted on the sides of the tank, assist during the lift-off and jettison when the craft has climbed some 45km (28 miles). They are intended to be recovered after parachuting into the sea. Some of them will be used again after being cleaned and re-filled with propellant.

The big tank is jettisoned just before the 'spaceplane' arrives in orbit under the thrust of small manoeuvre engines. This is the only part which does not return to Earth, as it burns up in the atmosphere during re-entry.

On certain missions the Orbiter will carry the European Spacelab, an entirely new concept in manned space stations. Unlike Salyut and Skylab, which had to be abandoned in space along with their costly instruments, Spacelab – which remains fixed inside the spaceplane's cargo bay – will return to Earth after each mission. Up to four specialists can ride as payload into orbit with the astronaut flight crew for missions lasting 7 to 30 days.

To return from orbit, the spaceplane is turned to a backward angle so that its manoeuvre engines can serve as retro-rockets. It descends through the atmosphere at a high angle of attack, and is protected from the high temperatures of frictional heating by special surface insulation. At the end of its flight the Orbiter will fly across Florida at high speed, to circle round and land without power on a 4·8km (3 mile) runway at the Kennedy Space Center.

The Shuttle is the key to a major new effort in manned spaceflight for the 1980's. It could lead to large space stations built up piece by piece from modules carried up in the cargo bay.

Moving factories into space may seem like science fiction. But this is now a very likely development, following the experiments carried out in weightlessness aboard the Skylab and Salyut space stations. The electronics industry should be among the first to benefit from the ability to manufacture high-purity crystals and other special products vital to the age of computers and other electronic products.

Medicine may also have a bright space future. The extremely stable, gravity-free environment should be ideal for highly delicate separation methods, used to isolate biological materials in order to obtain pure preparations of cells for transplantation. It should also be possible to prepare concentrated antibodies for treatment of certain diseases, and to purify vaccines by eliminating those contaminants that can cause serious medical side-effects.

In space stations it should be possible to melt and solidify metals while floating free of container walls, using electromagnetic, electro-static or acoustic fields to suspend and shape them. New products made in this way could include foam steels, ultra-lightweight/high strength alloys and even combinations of dissimilar materials like steel and glass.

LEFT AND BELOW : *The Space Shuttle is intended to reduce costs by making flight into orbit more like normal air travel. It takes off vertically like a rocket with crew and cargo and flies home like an aeroplane. When it is not carrying Spacelab, it can launch satellites or retrieve them from orbit for repair or servicing. The scale drawing shows the Shuttle Orbiter mounted on the External Tank with the two Solid Rocket Boosters alongside. Overall length is 56·1m (184ft). At over twice the cost of the Apollo project, America's Space Shuttle will – by 1990 – lead the way to 'space colonies'.*
CENTRE : *Europe joins this exciting project in the most practical way possible – by supplying the interior laboratory which fits into the Shuttle's cargo bay. Inside four scientists can work in the orbiting Spacelab in shirt-sleeve comfort.*

Significant Space Missions

Manned spacecraft

Spacecraft/country	Date	Crew	Weight kg (lb)	Earth orbit parameters Perigee km (miles)	Apogee km (miles)	Incl. to equator deg.	Notes
Vostok 1 (USSR)	12 April, 1961	Yuri Gagarin	Sphere-cylinder 4,725 (10,419)	169 (105)	315 (196)	64·95	First man in space. One Earth orbit. Flight time 108min.
Freedom 7 (US)	5 May, 1961	Alan Shepard, Jr	Cone-frustum 1,829 (4,032)	Sub-orbital trajectory reaching 187km (116 miles) altitude, 478km (297 miles) range.			First American in space. Flight time 15min 22secs. Mercury MR–3.
Liberty Bell 7 (US)	21 July, 1961	Virgil Grissom	Cone-frustrum 1,829 (4,032)	Sub-orbital trajectory reaching 190km (118 miles) altitude, 487km (303 miles) range.			Craft sank after splashdown. Flight time 15min 37secs. Mercury MR–4.
Vostok 2 (USSR)	6–7 August 1961	Gherman Titov	Sphere-cylinder 4,730 (10,430)	166 (103)	232 (144)	64·93	First flight to exceed one day. 17 orbits. Flight time 25·3hr.
Friendship 7 (US)	20 February, 1962	John Glenn, Jr	Cone-frustum 1,352 (2,981)	159 (99)	265 (165)	32·54	First American in orbit. Three orbits. Flight time 4hr 55min 23sec. Mercury MA–6.
Aurora 7 (US)	24 May 1962	Scott Carpenter	Cone-frustum 1,349 (2,975)	154 (96)	260 (162)	32·5	Repeated Glenn's flight. Flight time 4hr 56min 5sec. Mercury MA–7.
Vostok 3 (USSR)	11–15 August 1962	Andrian Nikolayev	Sphere-cylinder 4,730 (10,430)	166 (103)	218 (135)	64·98	First television from manned spacecraft. Flight time 94hr 22min.
Vostok 4 (USSR)	12–15 August 1962	Pavel Popovich	Sphere-cylinder 4,730 (10,430)	169 (105)	222 (138)	64·95	First time two manned craft in orbit simultaneously. Approached to about 5km (3 miles) of Vostok 3. Flight time 70hr 57min.
Sigma 7 (US)	3 October 1962	Walter Schirra, Jr	Cone-frustum 1,370 (3,201)	153 (96)	285 (177)	32·55	Almost doubled previous US flight time. Flight time 9hr 13min 11sec. Mercury MA–8.
Faith 7 (US)	15–16 May 1963	Gordon Cooper, Jr	Cone-frustum 1,370 (3,020)	161 (100)	267 (166)	32·54	First extended US flight. Flight time 34hr 19min 49 sec. Mercury MA–9.
Vostok 5 (USSR)	14–19 June 1963	Valery Bykovsky	Sphere-cylinder 4,730 (10,430)	162 (101)	209 (130)	64·97	Longest flight to date. Flight time 119hr 6min.
Vostok 6 (USSR)	16–19 June 1963	Valentina Tereshkova	Sphere-cylinder 4,713 (10,392)	168 (104)	218 (135)	65·09	First woman in space. Flight time 70hr 50min.
Voshkod 1 (USSR)	12–13 October 1964	Konstantin Feoktlstov Vladimir Komarov Dr Boris Yegorov	Sphere-cylinder 5,320 (11,731)	177 (110)	377 (234)	64·90	First three-man crew in space. Flight time 24hr 17min.
Voskhod 2 (USSR)	18–19 March 1965	Pavel Belyayev Aleksei Leonov	Sphere-cylinder 5,682 (12,529)	167 (104)	475 (295)	64·79	Leonov took first space walk (about 10min). Flight time 26hr 2min.
Gemini 3 (US)	23 March 1965	Virgil Grissom John Young	Cone-frustum 3,220 (7,100)	160 (99)	240 (149)	33·00	First US two-man flight. Flight time 4hr 53min.
Gemini 4 (US)	3–7 June 1965	James McDivitt Edward White, II	Cone-frustum 3,540 (7,800)	162 (101)	281 (175)	32·53	White walked in space for 21min. Flight time 97hr 56min 11sec.
Gemini 5 (US)	21–29 August 1965	Gordon Cooper, Jr Charles Conrad, Jr	Cone-frustum 3,180 (7,011)	197 (122)	303 (188)	32·61	Tested man in prolonged weightlessness. Flight time 190hr 55min 14sec.
Gemini 7 (US)	4–18 December 1965	Frank Borman James Lovell, Jr	Cone-frustum 3,200 (7,056)	215 (134)	321 (199)	28·87	Endurance flight of nearly two weeks – a record that stood for 4½ years. Flight time 330hr 35min 31sec.
Gemini 6 (US)	15–16 December 1965	Walter Schirra, Jr Thomas Stafford	Cone-frustum 3,800 (8,379)	258 (160)	271 (168)	28·89	Approached to nearly 30cm (1ft) of Gemini 7, thus achieving first 'rendezvous' (close formation flight) of manned orbiting spacecraft. Flight time 25hr 51min 24sec.
Gemini 8 (US)	16 March 1966	Neil Armstrong David Scott	Cone-frustum 3,789 (8,355)	159 (99)	265 (165)	28·91	First docking (joining) of manned–unmanned craft in orbit; ended early because of malfunction. Flight time 10hr 41min 26sec.
Gemini 9 (US)	3–6 June 1966	Thomas Stafford Eugene Cernan	Cone-frustum 3,680 (8,114)	270 (168)	272 (169)	28·86	Demonstration of extended walk, rendezvous. Flight time 72hr 21min.

Mission	Date	Crew	Shape / mass kg (lb)	Perigee km (miles)	Apogee km (miles)	Inclination	Notes
Gemini 10 (US)	18–21 July 1966	John Young Michael Collins	Cone-frustum 3,630 (8,004)	160 (99)	268 (167)	28·85	Retrieved scientific experiment package during rendezvous with unmanned orbiting Agena craft. Flight time 70hr 46min 39sec.
Gemini 11 (US)	12–15 September 1966	Charles Conrad, Jr Richard Gordon, Jr	Cone-frustum 3,630 (8,004)	161 (100)	280 (174)	28·83	Docking tests. Flight time 71hr 17min 8sec.
Gemini 12 (US)	11–15 November 1966	James Lovell, Jr Edwin Aldrin, Jr	Cone-frustum 3,630 (8,004)	243 (151)	310 (193)	28·78	Aldrin walked in space 129min. Flight time 94hr 34min 31sec.
Soyuz 1 (USSR)	23–24 April 1967	Vladimir Komarov	Sphere-cylinder + 2 'wings' 6,000 ? (13,230?)	198 (123)	211 (131)	51·64	Komarov, killed in re-entry crash, becomes history's first space flight fatality. Flight time 26hr 40min.
Apollo 7 (US)	11–22 October 1968	Walter Schirra, Jr Donn Eisele Walter Cunningham	Cone-cylinder 14,690 (32,391)	231 (144)	297 (185)	31·63	First US three-man flight. Flight time 260hr 9min 3sec.
Soyuz 3 (USSR)	26–30 October 1968	Georgiy Beregovoi	Sphere-cylinder + 2 'wings' 6,000? (13,230?)	177 (110)	203 (126)	51·66	Beregovoi, at 47, oldest man in space, manoeuvred near unmanned Soyuz 2. Flight time 94hr 51min.
Apollo 8 (US)	21–27 December 1968	Frank Borman James Lovell, Jr William Anders	Cone-cylinder 28,400 (62,622)	191 (119)	191 (119)	32·60	First men to visit vicinity of a celestial body by coming to within 112·6km (70 miles) of the Moon. First circumnavigation of Moon by men. Flight time 147hr 0min 42sec.
Soyuz 4 (USSR)	14–17 January 1969	Vladimir Shatalov Aleksei Yeliseyev Yevgeniy Khrunov	Sphere-cylinder + 2 'wings' 6,625 (14,608)	161 (100)	215 (134)	51·73	First docking of two manned craft; first crew transfer between orbiting craft. Flight time 71hr 22min.
Soyuz 5 (USSR)	15–18 January 1969	Boris Volynov Aleksei Yeliseyev Yevgeniy Khrunov	Sphere-cylinder + 2 'wings' 6,585 (14,520)	210 (130)	233 (145)	51·69	Soyuz 4 and 5 docked and transferred two cosmonauts by EVA from Soyuz 5 to Soyuz 4. Flight time 72hr 40min.
Apollo 9 (US)	3–13 March 1969	James McDivitt David Scott Russell Schweickart	Cone-cylinder 22,030 (48,576)	203 (126)	229 (142)	32·57	First in-space test of Lunar Module (Moon landing craft); first crew transfer between craft through interior connection. Flight time 241hr 0min 54sec.
Apollo 10 (US)	18–26 May 1969	Thomas Stafford John Young Eugene Cernan	Cone-cylinder 28,870 (63,658)	183 (114)	184 (114)	32·56	Stafford and Cernan flew in separated Lunar Module to within 15km (9·4 miles) of Lunar surface, in final rehearsal for Lunar landing. Flight time 192hr 3min 23sec.
Apollo 11 (US)	16–24 July 1969	Neil Armstrong Edwin Aldrin, Jr Michael Collins	Cone-cylinder 28,800 (63,504)	183 (114)	184 (114)	32·51	First Lunar landing by men, Armstrong and Aldrin on Sea of Tranquillity. Stay time 21hr 36min 21sec. Flight time 195hr 18min 35sec.
Soyuz 6 (USSR)	11–16 October 1969	Georgiy Shonin Valeriy Kubasov	Sphere-cylinder + 2 'wings' 6,577 (14,502)	192 (119)	231 (144)	51·68	Soyuz 6, 7 and 8 operated as a group flight without actually docking. Flight time 118hr 21min.
Soyuz 7 (USSR)	12–17 October 1969	Viktor Gorbatko Anatoliy Filipchenko Vladislav Volkov	Sphere-cylinder + 2 'wings' 6,570 (14,487)	210 (130)	223 (139)	51·65	See above. Flight time 118hr 43min.
Soyuz 8 (USSR)	13–18 October 1969	Vladimir Shatalov Aleksei Yeliseyev	Sphere-cylinder + 2 'wings' 6,646 (14,654)	201 (125)	227 (141)	51·65	See above. Flight time 118hr 51min.
Apollo 12 (US)	14–24 November 1969	Charles Conrad, Jr Alan Bean Richard Gordon, Jr	Cone-cylinder 28,790 (63,482)	183 (114)	199 (124)	32·56	Second manned landing on Moon. Conrad and Bean on Ocean of Storms. Stay time nearly 31hr 31min. Flight time 244hr 36min 25sec.
Apollo 13 (US)	11–17 April 1970	James Lovell, Jr John Swigert Fred Haise	Cone-cylinder 28,890 (63,702)	186 (116)	186 (116)	32·56	Explosion of oxygen tank in Service Module prevented planned Moon landing. Astronauts safely recovered after circumnavigation of Moon. Flight time 142hr 54min 41sec.
Soyuz 9 (USSR)	1–19 June 1970	Andrian Nikolayev Vitaliy Sevastyanov	Sphere-cylinder + 2 'wings' 6,500 (14,332)	176 (109)	227 (141)	51·64	Longest-duration manned spaceflight to date. Flight time 424hr 59min.
Apollo 14 (US)	31 January– 9 February 1971	Alan Shepard, Jr Edgar Mitchell Stuart Rossa	Cone-cylinder 29,229 (64,450)	186 (116)	186 (116)	32·56	Third manned landing on Moon, Shepard and Mitchell on Fra Mauro. Stay time 33hr 31min. Flight time 216hr 1min 57sec.
Soyuz 10 (USSR)	22–24 April 1971	Vladimir Shatalov Aleksei Yeliseyev Nikolai Rukavishnikov	Sphere-cylinder + 2 'wings' 6,575? (14,497?)	209 (130)	258 (160)	51·60	Docked with Salyut 1 space station, launched 19 April 1971, but crew did not board. Flight time 47hr 46min.

Mission	Date	Crew	Shape / Weight kg (lb)	Perigee km (miles)	Apogee km (miles)	Incl.	Remarks
Soyuz 11 (USSR)	6–29 June 1971	Georgiy Dobrovolsky, Vladislav Volkov, Victor Patsayev	Sphere-cylinder + 2 'wings' 6,565? (14,476?)	189 (111)	209 (130)	51·57	Docked with Salyut 1 for 22 days. Crew died as they returned to Earth when faulty valve allowed air to escape from cabin. Flight time 570hr 22min.
Apollo 15 (US)	26 July–7 August 1971	David Scott, James Irwin, Alfred Worden	Cone-cylinder 30,340 (66,900)	169 (105)	173 (108)	32·56	Fourth manned landing on Moon, Scott and Irwin on Hadley-Apennine region. First use of Lunar Roving Vehicle. Stay time 66hr 55min. Flight time 295hr 11min 53sec.
Apollo 16 (US)	16–27 April 1972	John Young, Charles Duke, Jr, Thomas Mattingly, II	Cone-cylinder 30,358 (66,939)	169 (105)	178 (111)	32·56	Fifth manned landing on Moon, Young and Duke on Descartes region. Set up first astronomical observatory. Used Lunar Roving Vehicle. Stay time 71hr 2min. Flight time 265hr 51min 5sec.
Apollo 17 (US)	7–19 December 1972	Eugene Cernan, Harrison Schmitt, Ronald Evans	Cone-cylinder 30,340 (66,900)	169 (105)	178 (111)	32·56	Sixth manned landing on Moon, Cernan and Schmitt on Taurus Littrow region. Used Lunar Roving Vehicle. Stay time 75hr. Flight time 301hr 51min 59sec.
Skylab 2 (US)	25 May–22 June 1973	Charles Conrad, Joseph Kerwin, Paul Weitz	Cone-cylinder 13,780 (30,385)	156 (97)	359 (223)	50·04	First astronauts to board Skylab Space Station, carried out repairs. Flight time 672hr 49min 49sec.
Skylab 3 (US)	28 July–25 September 1973	Alan Bean, Jack Lousma, Owen Garriott	Cone-cylinder 13,860 (30,561)	159 (99)	230 (143)	50·03	Second crew to board Skylab Space Station. Flight time 1427hr 9min 4sec.
Soyuz 12 (USSR)	27–29 September 1973	Vasily Lazarev, Oleg Makarov	Sphere-cylinder 6,570? (14,487?)	181 (112)	229 (142)	51·58	Test of improved Soyuz for Salyut ferry missions, with chemical batteries replacing solar 'wings'. Flight time 47hr 16min.
Skylab 4 (US)	16 November 1973–8 February 1974	Gerald Carr, Edward Gibson, William Pogue	Cone-cylinder 13,980? (30,826?)	154 (96)	224 (139)	50·04	Third and final crew to board Skylab Space Station. Man's longest space-flight to date. Flight time 2017hr 15min 32sec.
Soyuz 13 (USSR)	18–26 December 1973	Pyotr Klimuk, Valentin Lebedev	Sphere-cylinder + 2 'wings' 6,570? (14,487?)	188 (117)	247 (153)	51·57	Conducted experiments in biology, astrophysics and Earth resource observation. Flight time 188hr 55min.
Soyuz 14 (USSR)	3–19 July 1974	Pavel Popovich, Yuri Artyukhin	Sphere-cylinder 6,570? (14,487?)	195 (121)	217 (135)	51·58	Docked with Salyut 3 for 353hr 33min. Flight time exceeded 370hr.
Soyuz 15 (USSR)	26–28 August 1974	Gennardy Sarafanov, Lev Demin	Sphere-cylinder 6,570? (14,487?)	173 (108)	236 (147)	51·62	Failed to dock with Salyut 3 on 27 August because of fault in automatic control system. Flight time 48hr 12min.
Soyuz 16 (USSR)	2–8 December 1974	Anatoly Filipchenko, Nikolai Rukavishnikov	Sphere-cylinder + 2 'wings' 6,680? (14,729?)	184 (114)	291 (181)	51·80	ASTP flight test. Tested docking system of Soyuz and reduction of cabin pressure as required for joint docking experiment. Flight time 143hr 4min.
Soyuz 17 (USSR)	11 January–9 February 1975	Alexei Gubarev, Georgi Grechko	Sphere-cylinder 6,570? (14,487?)	185 (115)	249 (155)	51·63	Docked with Salyut 4 for 677hr 8min. Flight time 709hr 20min.
Soyuz 'anomaly' (USSR)	5 April 1975	Vasily Lazarev, Oleg Makarov			Sub-orbital		Attempt to reach Salyut 4 failed, due to launch vehicle third stage malfunction. Cosmonauts recovered safely in Western Siberia.
Soyuz 18 (USSR)	24 May–26 July 1975	Pyotr Klimuk, Vitaly Sevastyanov	Sphere-cylinder 6,570? (14,487?)	186 (116)	230 (143)	51·69	Docked with Salyut 4. Flight time 1,511hr 20min.
Soyuz 19 (USSR)	15–21 July 1975	Alexei Leonov, Valery Kubasov	Sphere-cylinder + 2 'wings' 6,680 (14,729)	186 (116)	220 (137)	51·78	ASTP mission. Docked with Apollo CSM/DM for about 2 days for crew exchanges and joint experiments. Flight time 142hr 31min.
Apollo 18 ASTP (US)	15–24 July 1975	Thomas Stafford, Vance Brand, Donald Slayton	Cone-cylinder 13,860? (30,561?)	170 (106)	228 (142)	51·76	See above. Flight time 217hr 28min.
Soyuz 21 (USSR)	6 July–24 August 1976	Boris Volynov, Vitaly Zhdobov	Sphere-cylinder 6,570? (14,487?)	246 (153)	274 (170)	51·59	Docked with Salyut 5 on 7 July. Flight time 1,182hr 24min.
Soyuz 22 (USSR)	15–23 September 1976	Valery Bykovsky, Vladimir Aksyonov	Sphere-cylinder + 2 'wings' 6,570? (14,487?)	185 (115)	296 (184)	64·75	Intercosmos mission. Carried MKF–6 multi-spectal cameras made in East Germany. Flight time 189hr 54min.
Soyuz 23 (USSR)	14–16 October 1976	Vyacheslav Zudov, Valery Rozhdestvensky	Sphere-cylinder 6,570? (14,487?)	188 (117)	224 (139)	51·61	Failed to dock with Salyut 5 on 15 October because of fault in automatic control system. Flight time 48hr 6min.

Soyuz 24 (USSR)	7 25 February 1977	Viktor Gorbatko Yuri Glazkov	Sphere-cylinder 6,570? (14,487?)	218 (135)	281 (175)	51·60	Docked with Salyut 5 on 8 February. Flight time 424hr 48min.

Orbital data refers to *initial* orbits only before any subsequent manoeuvres.

Moon Probes Some significant launchings

Space probe/ country	Launch date	Launch vehicle	Weight kg (lb)	Notes
Pioneer (US)	17 August 1958	Thor-Able 1	38·0 (83·8)	First attempt to put probe into orbit around the Moon. First stage of launcher exploded. USAF project.
Pioneer 1B (US)	11 October 1958	Thor-Able 1B	38·3 (84·4)	Second attempt to put probe into orbit around the Moon. Third stage cut off speed 206km/h (128mph) too slow – probe rose 113,756km (70,700 miles) and fell back to Earth. USAF project.
Pioneer 2 (US)	7 November 1958	Thor-Able	39·6 (87·3)	Third attempt to put probe into orbit around the Moon. Able second stage failed to ignite. Probe rose to height of only 1,549km (963 miles). USAF project.
Pioneer 3 (US)	6 December 1958	Juno II	5·87 (12·94)	Attempt to obtain elementary pictures of Moon during fly-by. Fourth stage cut-off speed 37,982km/h (23,606mph) – too low. Rose 107,246km (66,654 miles) and fell back to Earth. US Army project.
Luna 1 (USSR)	2 January 1959	A–1	361 (79·6)	Probable attempt to impact Lunar surface. Passed within 5,955km (3,700 miles) of Moon and continued into Solar orbit.
Pioneer 4 (US)	3 March 1959	Juno II	5·87 (12·94)	Attempt to obtain elementary pictures of Moon during fly-by at distance of 32,187km (20,000 miles). Missed Moon by 60,015km (37,300 miles). Passed into Solar orbit.
Luna 2 (USSR)	12 September 1959	A–1	390 (860)	First man-made object to hit Moon – fell between craters *Archimedes*, *Aristillus* and *Autolcycus* (about 1°W, 30°N).
Luna 3 (USSR)	4 October 1959	A–1	278·5 (6,141)	First circumlunar flight – in effect flight was elongated Earth-orbit distorted by Moon's gravitational field. Probe passed 7,886km (4,900 miles) behind Moon taking photos and returning images to Earth by television.
Ranger 7 (US)	28 July 1964	Atlas-Agena D	365·6 (806)	Obtained 4,316 television pictures during last 13min before impact Sea of Clouds. (10° 38′S, 20° 36′W).
Luna 9 (USSR)	31 January 1966	A–2–e	Total vehicle 1,583 (3,490) Landing capsule only 99·8 (220)	First unmanned space probe to land on Moon and send data, Ocean of Storms. (7° 8′N, 64° 33′W). Sent 360° panorama of still pictures showing rocks up to 10–20cm (3·9–7·8in) across.
Luna 10 (USSR)	31 March 1966	A–2–e	245 (540)	Achieved Lunar orbit 349 × 1,017km (217 × 632 miles) × 71·9° to equator.
Surveyor 1 (US)	30 May 1966	Atlas-Centaur	998 (2,200)	First fully-controlled soft-landing on Moon, Ocean of Storms (2°27′S, 43°13′W). Survey camera sent 11,150 high-resolution photos of Lunar surface up to 2·4km (1·5 miles) from landing site.
Lunar Orbiter 1 (US)	10 August 1966	Atlas-Agena 10	385 (849)	Obtained high-resolution photos of potential Apollo landing sites from Lunar orbit 191 × 1,867km (119 × 1,160 miles) inclined at 12·2° to equator.
Luna 11 (USSR)	24 August 1966	A–2–e	1,640 (3,616)	Achieved Lunar orbit 159 × 1,200km (99 × 746 miles) × 27° to equator.
Luna 12 (USSR)	22 October 1966	A–2–e	1,640 (3,616)	Achieved Lunar orbit 100 × 1,739km (62 × 1,081 miles) × 15° to equator. Television system sent 1,100-line pictures showing craters up to 15m (49·2ft) across.
Luna 13 (USSR)	21 December 1966	A–2–e	Total vehicle 1,590 (3,501) Landing capsule only 99·8 (220)	Landed Ocean of Storms 18°52′N, 62°3′W. Camera distinguished objects as small as 1·5–2·0mm (0·38–0·50in).
Surveyor 3 (US)	17 August 1967	Atlas-Centaur	998 (2,200)	Soft-landed Ocean of Storms (2°56′S, 23°20′W). Mechanical scoop worked by radio control from Earth allowed scientists to dig Lunar top-soil and photograph results. Camera obtained nearly 6,320 photos of landing site.
Zond 5 (USSR)	14 September 1968	D–1–E	NA	First circumlunar flight, returning to USSR. Achieved minimum Lunar distance of 1,950km (1,212 miles). Re-entry capsule splashed into Indian Ocean (32°38′S, 65°33′E).
Zond 6 (USSR)	10 November 1968	D–1–E	NA	Circumlunar flight, returning to USSR by aerodynamic 'skip' in Earth's atmosphere. Achieved minimum Lunar distance of 2,418km (1,503 miles).
Luna 15 (USSR)	13 July 1969	D–1–E	NA	Manoeuvrable spacecraft in Lunar orbit as US astronauts attempted first Moon landing. Crash-landed two hours before Apollo 11 astronauts left the Moon.
Luna 16 (USSR)	12 September 1970	D–1–E	1,880 (4,145)	First automatic unmanned Lunar landing returning 100g Moon sample to Earth. Landed Sea of Fertility (0·41°S, 56·3°E).
Luna 17 (USSR)	10 November 1970	D–1–E	Lunokhod 1 756 (1,667)	Landed first remote-controlled Moon rover, Lunokhod 1, Sea of Rains (38° 18′N, 35°W). Travelled total distance of 10,542m (34,588ft), sending television pictures and testing soil en route.

Interplanetary Probes Some significant launchings

Space probe/ country	Launch date	Launch vehicle	Weight kg (lb)	Notes
Venera 1 (USSR)	12 February 1961	A–2–e	643·5 (1,418·9)	Passed within 100,000km (62,000 miles) of Venus on 19–20 May 1961, but communications lost 27 February.
Mariner 2 (US)	27 August 1962	Atlas-Agena B	202·7 (447)	Passed within 34,830km (21,643 miles) of Venus on 14 December. Instruments scanned planet for 35min. Surface temp 428°C.
Mars 1 (USSR)	1 November 1962	A–2–e	893·5 (1,970)	Passed within 998 and 10,783km (620 and 6,700 miles) of Mars on 19 June 1963, but communications lost on 21 March.

Zond 1 (USSR)	2 April 1964	A–2–e	950 (2,094)	Passed within 99,779km (62,000 miles) of Venus on 19 July. Communications lost.
Mariner 4 (US)	28 November 1964	Atlas-Agena D	260·8 (575)	Passed within 8,690km (5,400 miles) of Mars on 14 July 1965. Sent 21 pictures of Martian surface. Radio occultation experiment indicated surface pressure of 10–20 millibars.
Zond 2 (USSR)	30 November 1964	A–2–e	950 (2,094)	Passed within 1,497km (930 miles) of Mars. Communications lost.
Venera 2 (USSR)	12 November 1965	A–2–e	963 (2,123)	Passed within 24,000km (14,913 miles) of Venus on 27 February 1966. Communications lost at time of fly-by.
Venera 3 (USSR)	16 November 1965	A–2–e	960 (2,116)	Crashed on Venus without sending data.
Venera 4 (USSR)	12 June 1967	A–2–e	1,106 (2,438)	Capsule parachuted into atmosphere of Venus on 18 October, but transmission stopped above surface, indicating 280°C temperature, 22 atmospheres pressure.
Mariner 5 (US)	14 June 1967	Atlas-Agena D	245 (540)	Passed within 3,991km (2,480 miles) of Venus on 19 October. Instruments scanned planet. Found temperatures near surface of 'about' 267°C. Magnetic field 0–1/300th that of Earth.
Venera 5 (USSR)	5 January 1969	A–2–e	1,120 (2,470) including 405 (893) capsule	Capsule parachuted into atmosphere of Venus on 16 May. Stopped transmitting above surface.
Venera 6 (USSR)	10 January 1969	A–2–e	1,120 (2,470) including 405 (893) capsule	Capsule parachuted into atmosphere of Venus on 17 May. Stopped transmitting above surface.
Mariner 6 (US)	24 February 1969	Atlas-Centaur	413 (910)	Passed within 3,427km (2,130 miles) of Mars on 30 July. Obtained 24 near-encounter pictures, 12 medium and 12 high resolution during 17min period. Atmospheric pressure 6–7 millibars.
Mariner 7 (US)	27 March 1969	Atlas-Centaur	413 (910)	Passed within 3,427km (2,130 miles) of Mars on 4 August. Obtained 33 near-encounter pictures, 17 medium and 16 high resolution. One showed moon Phobos as minute speck.
Venera 7 (USSR)	17 August 1970	A–2–e	1,180 (2,602)	Capsule parachuted into atmosphere of Venus on 15 December. First confirmed landing on Venus. Faint signals from surface lasted about 23min, indicating temperature of 475 ± 20°C and atmospheric pressure of 90 ± 15atm.
Mars 2 (USSR)	19 May 1971	D–1–E	4,650 (10,253)	Second artificial satellite of Mars on 27 November. Orbit 1,380 × 25,000km (858 × 15,535 miles) inclined 48°54' to equator. Capsule, released before orbit entry, crashed on Mars.
Mars 3 (USSR)	28 May 1971	D–1–E	4,650 (10,253)	Third artificial satellite of Mars on 2 December 1971. Capsule released before orbit entry, landed in dust storm between *Electris* and *Phaethontis* (approx. 45°S, 158°W). Stopped transmitting after 20sec (included fragment of panoramic television pictures which showed no detail).
Mariner 9 (US)	30 May 1971	Atlas-Centaur	1,031 (2,273)	First artificial satellite of Mars on 13 November 1971. Orbit 1,398 × 17,916km (868 × 11,133 miles), inclined at 64·3° to equator. Photographed huge equatorial canyon, volcanoes, features like dried-out riverbeds, etc. Returned 7,329 pictures.
Pioneer 10 (US)	3 March 1972	Atlas-Centaur/ TE–M–364–4	258 (570)	Passed within 130,000km (81,000 miles) of Jupiter December 1973 to obtain close-up pictures of banded gas clouds and 'red spot'. Will escape from Solar System.
Venera 8 (USSR)	27 March 1972	A–2–e	1,180 (2,602) including 495 (1,091) capsule	Capsule landed on Venus on 22 July 1972. Transmitted for 50min. Surface pressure 90kg/cm² (1,280lb/m²), temperature 470°C, 97% CO_2 and not more than 2% nitrogen.
Pioneer 11 (US)	6 April 1973	Atlas-Centaur/ TE–M–384–4	258 (570)	Passed within 42,800km (26,600 miles) of Jupiter on December 1974 and diverted to Saturn fly-by September 1979. Returned photos and data of Jupiter.
Mars 4 (USSR)	21 July 1973	D–1–E	NA	Passed within 2,200km (1,367 miles) of Mars on 10 February 1974. Braking engine failed to fire.
Mars 5 (USSR)	25 July 1973	D–1–E	NA	Fourth artificial satellite of Mars on 12 February 1974. Orbit 1,760 × 32,500km (1,094 × 20,196 miles) inclined at 35° to equator.
Mars 6 (USSR)	5 August 1973	D–1–E	NA	Craft flew past Mars after releasing capsule. Radio transmission lost just before capsule reached surface of Mars, about 24°S, 25°W.
Mars 7 (USSR)	9 August 1973	D–1–E	NA	Landing capsule mis-directed – missing Mars by 1,300km (808 miles). Mother craft continued in Solar orbit.
Mariner 10 (US)	3 November 1973	Atlas-Centaur	408·2 (900)	Passed within 5,768km (3,584 miles) of Venus before passing Mercury within 740 km (460 miles) on 29 March 1974. Second approach within about 48,280km (30,000 miles) on 21 September 1974. Third approach within 320km (199 miles) on 16 March 1975. All passes returned photos and data.
Helios 1 (Germany/US)	10 December 1974	Titan III-Centaur/ TE–364–4	367 (810)	Passed within 45 million km (28 million miles) of the Sun on 15 March 1975.
Venera 9 (USSR)	8 June 1975	D–1–E	4,936 (10,884)	Released 1,560kg (3,440lb) landing capsule and swung into orbit of 1,510 × 112,200km (938 × 69,721 miles) × 34°10' inclination on 22 October 1975. First artificial satellite of Venus. Capsule transmitted from surface for 53min, including television pictures, surface pressure 90atm, temperature 485°C. Landed within Beta region 30°N, 293° longitude.
Venera 10 (USSR)	14 June 1975	D–1–E	5,033 (11,098)	Released 1,560kg (3,440lb) landing capsule and swung into orbit of 1,620 × 113,900km (1,007 × 70,777 miles) × 29°30' inclination on 25 October 1975. Capsule transmitted from surface for 65min including television pictures. Surface pressure 92atm, temperature 465°C. Landed 15°N, 295° longitude.
Viking 1 (US)	20 August 1975	Titan III/ Centaur	2,313 (5,100) orbiter 1,089 (2,400) lander	Swung into orbit around Mars on 19 June 1976. Lander touched down on *Chryse Planitia* (22·46°N, 48·01°W) on 20 July 1976. Sent first pictures from Martian surface, tested the soil, obtained meteorological data, etc.
Viking 2 (US)	9 September 1975	Titan III/ Centaur	2,313 (5,100) orbiter 1,089 (2,400) lander	Swung into orbit around Mars on 7 August 1976. Lander touched down on *Utopia Planitia* (47·97°N, 225·67°W) on 3 September 1976. Sent pictures from Martian surface, tested the soil, obtained meteorological data, etc.

Facts, Feats
and Records

Great Flying Feats

On 13 January 1908 at Issy Les Moulineaux in France Henry Farman flew the first circular flight in Europe, thus winning the 'Grand Prix d'Aviation' donated by two French benefactors. He covered a distance of 1km (·625 miles) in a modified Voisin biplane and remained airborne for 1 minute 28 seconds. Though a mere hop by modern standards this was the most impressive flight that had been made in Europe to that date. Yet in America the Wright Brothers, before they temporarily gave up flying in 1905, had already covered 40·25km (25 miles) in one flight and stayed up more than half an hour at a time; and they could turn and fly figure

PREVIOUS PAGES:
Gnat fighters of the Red Arrows aerobatic team.

eights with ease. In Europe no one knew or believed this until, in 1908, the Wrights returned to flying, and gave their first demonstrations in public. Wilbur took a Flyer to France, while Orville stayed home to fly their new two-seat Flyer for the US Army.

The Wrights' achievement

Wilbur's first flight in Europe was a two-minute circuit of Le Mans race-course on 8 August 1908. He astonished spectators with the degree of control he had over his machine. 'One of the most exciting spectacles in the history of applied science,' wrote one. 'Good grief!' exclaimed another, 'We are beaten . . . we don't exist.' When he finished his French demonstrations at Auvours on the last day of 1908 Wilbur Wright had made

more than 100 flights, with flying-time of more than 25 hours; he had taken up passengers on more than 60 occasions; had attained an altitude of 110m (360ft); and had made one flight of more than 2 hours.

Orville's flights in America began impressively, but ended tragically on 17 September with structural failure of his Flyer while aloft.

Louis Blériot

One of the French experimenters most inspired by watching Wilbur's demonstrations was Louis Blériot. His 1909 Type XI monoplane was his first really successful design, and in it he made a cross-country flight of 42km (26 miles) from Etampes to Chevilly on 13 July. On 25 July he made the first aerial crossing of the English Channel. This flight won him the £1,000 prize offered by the London *Daily Mail* newspaper to the first person to achieve this feat as well as attracting extraordinary publicity around the world. It brought home to people for the first time that the aeroplane might in time become a formidable weapon of war. Blériot's flight was also a feat of great courage: the 37 minutes it took was about as long as his frail 25hp 3-cylinder Anzani engine had ever run without stopping. He had no compass or real means of navigation for the misty crossing and he was still suffering the effects of an injury received in an earlier crash. (His arrival on the Cliffs of Dover was in truth another crash-landing.) The feat earned him a fortune. In addition to the £1,000 newspaper prize he soon had orders for more than 100 of his Type XI monoplanes. The design of the XI was interesting in that it incorporated many features that we have since come to take for granted in aeroplane design: monoplane wings, tractor propeller directly attached to the engine crankshaft, hinged tilting stick and rudder pedal controls, and a covered-in fuselage structure. (The Wright Flyers by contrast had none of these features.)

ABOVE: *Two important early aircraft which were seen at the Reims Air Show in 1909. Top, the Voisin biplane; bottom, the Blériot 12 monoplane.*
BELOW: *A reconstruction of Blériot's famous Type XI monoplane.*
BOTTOM LEFT: *Wilbur Wright repairing his launching rail at Le Mans, 1908.*
BOTTOM RIGHT: *Louis Blériot and his Type XI monoplane at Dover after his historic cross-Channel flight on 25 July 1907.*

Reims air show

The first flying meeting took place soon after Blériot's Channel crossing, between 22 and 29 August at Reims in France. It was sponsored by local champagne interests and 38 aircraft were entered. Of these, 23 actually got airborne to make 120 flights. Speed records were established by Blériot and the American Glenn Curtiss of between 75 and 77km/h (47 to 48mph); an Antoinette monoplane climbed to 155m (508ft); and the distance prize was won by Henry Farman, who covered 180km (112·5 miles) in 3 hours 5 minutes. Among the many impressed visitors was Lloyd George, who commented: 'Flying machines are no longer toys and dreams . . . the possibilities of this new system of locomotion are infinite.' However, as much as the many fine flights made at Reims, most visitors were impressed by the general appalling unreliability of the engines.

1909–1910

On 7 September 1909 the first pilot of a powered aeroplane was killed and on 22 September the second, and on 6 December, the third. Since the beginning of the 19th century five men and one woman had been killed in parachuting accidents; two experimenters in glider crashes; and a considerable number in balloons. There were no less than 32 aviation fatalities in 1910. That year, however, also saw more than 20 aviation meetings held, in Europe, the USA and Egypt; the first night-flying accomplished, in the Argentine; and the first lady to qualify as a pilot, Baroness de Laroche. The Hon C. S. Rolls, the wealthy sportsman who was involved in the founding of Rolls Royce cars, made the first out-and-return non-stop Channel crossing on 2 June 1910 and lost his life on 12 July during a meeting at Bournemouth when his French-built Wright Flyer broke up in the air. On 17 August a French-American pilot, J. B. Moisant, crossed the Channel carrying his mechanic as a passenger.

The Peruvian pilot, Georges Chavez, flying a Blériot monoplane made the first aerial crossing of the Alps, through the Simplon pass, although he lost his life at the end of the attempt while trying to land at Domodossola. Curtiss biplanes made several remarkable flights in the USA: from Albany to New York City; and New York to Philadelphia and back when radio was used for the first time. Eugene Ely took off in a Curtiss biplane from a platform built on the USS *Birmingham* – another first in aviation. Glenn Curtiss himself made the first bombing tests, dropping dummies onto flagged buoys which marked the outline of a warship.

FAR LEFT: *Farman, using the aeroplane as a sporting vehicle, here makes a graceful turn round a pylon in the type of biplane used by Grahame-White in 1910.*
BELOW FAR LEFT: *Not all early flights met with success. This is Baroness de la Roche's wrecked Voisin in July 1910.*
LEFT: *The Paulhan triplane, one of the new types of military aeroplanes exhibited at the Reims show in 1911.*
BELOW: *Tryggve Gran's aeroplane at Cruden Bay, Scotland before the start of its flight across the North Sea in July 1914.*
BOTTOM LEFT: *W. Newell with his parachute at Hendon. He was the first man to make a parachute drop from an aeroplane over Great Britain, on 9 May 1914.*
BOTTOM RIGHT: *Georges Chavez at the start of his flight over the Alps which ended in disaster when he crashed on landing.*

by William Randolph Hearst, but arrived outside the specified 30-day limit. Another American pilot flew a Curtiss 90 miles over water–from Key West to Havana, Cuba. Curtiss flew the first practical seaplane in 1911. And Orville Wright made a nine-minute flight in a glider which remained a soaring world record for ten years. Near the end of the year a *Concours Militaire* was held at Reims, for the display of aeroplanes that might be used in war. And one *was* used, for the first time, when an Italian pilot, in a Blériot, made an hour-long flight on 22 October 1912 to observe Turkish positions near Tripoli. The first air mail flights were made. The first parachutist to drop from an aeroplane was Captain Albert Berry in the USA, and American Harriet Quimby became the first woman to fly the Channel. In England Frank McClean flew a Short float-plane through Tower Bridge and was promptly in trouble with the police (as has been every other pilot to try it since) when he landed on the Thames by Westminster.

1911

By 1911 aviation had become an enormously popular public spectacle, and the first air races were held that year. The first non-stop flight from London to Paris was made on 12 April in a Blériot by Pierre Prier, who flew the 402km (250 miles) in a little less than 4 hours. There were races (in stages) from Paris to Rome and Madrid and a return trip to Paris via London, Brussels and Amiens. In America Calbraith P. Rodgers made the first coast-to-coast flight in a Wright biplane. The 6,437km (4,000 miles) took him 82 flying hours in 82 stages over a period of 49 days. He had 19 crashes en route and was followed all the way by a special train containing spares as well as his wife and mother. He had hoped to win a $50,000 prize for the journey offered

1912–1918

During 1912 and 1913 the world airspeed record was raised no less than ten times by two French pilots, Jules Vedrines and Maurice Prévost, flying very advanced Deperdussin monocoque racers. The first such record set was Vedrine's 145km/h (90mph) on 13 January 1912. By 29 September next year Prévost had achieved 203km/h (126mph).

Two outstanding flights of 1913 were the first air crossing of the Mediterranean, by Roland Garros in a Morane-Saulnier monoplane. He flew 729km (453 miles) from southern France to Tunisia in just under 8 hours. The first flight from France to Egypt was made, in stages, by Vedrines in a Blériot. The Norwegian pilot Tryggve Gran was the first man to fly the North Sea, in a Blériot, on 30 July 1914.

Civil flying generally ceased in Europe during World War I. But South America was far from the conflict and two remarkable record flights were made there. The Argentinean Army pilot Teniente Candelaria made the first crossing of the Andes from east to west on 13 April 1918. He flew a Morane and reached an altitude of about 3,960m (13,000 ft). A Chilean pilot, Teniente Godoy, crossed the Andes from west to east on 12 December in a Bristol monoplane.

1919

Substantial prize money had already been put up before the war for the first air crossing of the Atlantic Ocean. As soon as the war was over many began to plan for the attempt. Newfoundland, the easternmost province of Canada, had never seen an aeroplane, but, in the spring and summer of 1919, it became a familiar dateline for press reports of preparations for the transatlantic crossing. When the two British aviators John Alcock and Arthur Whitten Brown arrived as latecomers in the race they were hopefully asked to pay $25,000 for the temporary lease of one small meadow when land could be bought there for 35 cents an acre! The prize for the first successful crossing was £10,000 (then $50,000), put up by the *Daily Mail* in 1913 for the first flight between England and America to be completed within 72 hours.

Meanwhile the US Navy planned an ambitious Atlantic crossing with 3 huge Curtiss flying-boats aided by a string of destroyers stationed every 80·5km (50 miles) across the ocean. Two of the flying-boats were wrecked during the attempt, but the third, the NC–4, left Newfoundland on 8 May. She landed twice to refuel, in the Azores and in Portugal, and finally arrived in England on 31 May – the first Atlantic crossing by any aircraft. It was a formidable achievement, with 6,315km (3,925 miles) covered in 57 hours 16 minutes flying time at an average airspeed of 126·8km/h (78·8mph)

News of the US Navy's attempt stampeded two landplane crews also in Newfoundland into making ill-advised and hasty starts from there on 18 May. First off were Harry Hawker and MacKenzie Grieve in a Sopwith biplane named, appropriately, the *Atlantic*. An hour later followed Frederick Raynham and William Morgan (who had lost a leg in the war) in a Martinsyde. They crashed on take-off, but survived. Nothing was heard of Hawker and Grieve for a week; then a Danish tramp steamer which had no radio signalled to a semaphore station in the Hebrides that she had picked up the Sopwith's crew who had ditched alongside her after experiencing trouble with the aircraft's engine.

Alcock and Brown left Newfoundland on 14 June. They were flying a converted twin-engine Vickers Vimy bomber fitted with extra fuel tanks. It was so overloaded that spectators watching its take-off run were convinced it would crash. Even when airborne and headed out to sea they were still struggling for altitude. Later, flying higher but in cloud, they lost control of the aircraft and it fell into a spin from which it was only recovered just above the waves. They also became badly iced-up, with rime clogging the engine air intakes. Brown crawled out between the biplane wings to each engine in turn to clear them. Another hazard awaited them even after they had arrived safely over Ireland: the green field on which they chose to land was in fact a soft peat bog, and the Vimy went over on its nose in a crash-landing. Nevertheless, Alcock and Brown made the first ever non-stop Atlantic crossing, flying 3,041km (1,890 miles) in 16 hours 28 minutes. Subsequently, both were knighted by King George V for the feat. Sir John

Alcock did not have long to enjoy his fame for he lost his life on 19 December that year while flying in bad weather over France.

In July 1919 the Atlantic was crossed for the first time by an airship, the British R-34. It set out from Scotland on 2 July, captained by Major G. H. Scott of the RAF and carrying Lieutenant Commander Zachary Lansdowne of the US Navy as an observer. The R-34 also carried the first transatlantic aerial stowaway, a rigger who, disgruntled at being left off the crew roster, had hidden among the gas-bags. The airship battled headwinds, and over Newfoundland met thunderstorms that threatened to wrest control of it from the crew, who radioed for help from the US Navy. The crew recovered control and made their way unaided to Long Island, where they landed at Montauk (with just two hours' fuel remaining) on 6 July. The R-34 was the first big airship – 202·69m (665ft) long – to be seen in the United States and attracted huge crowds during its short stay. Just before midnight on 9 July it took off, circled the Empire State Building with its searchlights playing, and set off on the return journey. It arrived back in England in 75 hours 3 minutes, helped by good tailwinds.

Thus within two months the Atlantic was crossed four times, by relatively crude and frail machines and yet without a single life being lost on any of the attempts.

A Vimy was used later that year when two Australians, brothers Ross and Keith Smith, made the first flight from England to Australia, in just under 28 days, from 12 November to 10 December. Their flight from Hounslow to Darwin covered 18,175km (11,294 miles). It earned them knighthoods and a £10,000 prize donated by the Australian government. There is another and more tragic coincidence with Alcock and Brown's flight: Sir Ross Smith was killed in an accident not long afterwards, near Brooklands in England on 13 April 1924 while flying a Vickers Viking – the same type in which Sir John Alcock had been killed.

TOP LEFT: *The crew of the US Navy Curtiss NC–4 flying boat which made the first transatlantic flight during May 1919, making seven stops on the way. Three other aircraft set out at the same time, but were not successful.*
CENTRE LEFT: *The British airship R.34, shown here as it came in to land at Mineola, Long Island, on 6 July 1919. It was the first aircraft of any type to make a double crossing of the North Atlantic.*
LEFT: *Alcock and Brown standing by their Vickers Vimy a few days after their Atlantic flight on 14–15 June 1919. They made the crossing from St John's, Newfoundland, to Clifden, County Galway, Ireland.*
TOP: *The United States Navy Curtiss NC–4 flying boat that made the first transatlantic crossing, photographed here as it was entering the harbour at Lisbon, Portugal, where it stopped to refuel.*
ABOVE: *The Vickers Vimy converted bomber in which Ross and Keith Smith won the £10,000 prize offered by the Australian Government for the first flight from Great Britain to Australia, seen here with the crew.*
RIGHT: *The Vickers Vimy was a favourite plane with the first long distance fliers. Here the model in which Alcock and Brown made the first non-stop Atlantic crossing takes off from Newfoundland.*

1920–1925

A Vimy was also the chosen mount of Pierre van Ryneveld and Christopher Quintin Brand when they set off from Brooklands for South Africa on 4 February 1920. When they crashed at Wadi Halfa the South African government provided them with another Vimy in which to continue. This in turn they crashed at Bulawayo on 6 March and it was replaced by a DH–9. They arrived at Wynberg Aerodrome, Cape Town, on 20 March . . . the first men to fly from England to South Africa. They too received knighthoods and £5,000 prize-money.

In the United States, the first coast-to-coast crossing in a single day was accomplished by James H. Doolittle in a DH–4. He flew from the east coast of Florida to San Diego, California, on 4 September 1922 with one refuelling stop in Texas. His flying time was 21 hours 19 minutes over a distance of 3,480km (2,163 miles). (Doolittle, then an Army lieutenant, was to go on to greater fame as a racing pilot and later still organizer and leader of the first US bombing raid on Tokyo during World War II.)

On 2–3 May 1923 two other US Army aviators, Lieutenants O. G. Kelly and J. A. MacReady, flew a Fokker T.2 monoplane from Long Island to San Diego for the first non-stop coast-to-coast flight. They covered 4,050km (2,516 miles) in 26 hours 50 minutes. A little later they established a new world endurance record for aeroplanes by staying aloft in the Fokker for 36 hours 5 minutes over a 4,052km (2,518 miles) measured

ABOVE: *The de Havilland DH–4B flown by Smith and Richter being refuelled in mid-flight by another DH–4.*
ABOVE INSET: *The crew of the first mid-air refuelling flight in June 1923 at Rockwell Field, California.*
RIGHT: *One of the Douglas World Cruisers which made the first round-the-world flight in 1924.*
ABOVE FAR RIGHT: *Charles Lindbergh standing in front of his aeroplane,* Spirit of St Louis, *a modified version of a Ryan monoplane mail carrier.*
FAR RIGHT: *Another view of the* Spirit of St Louis, *in which Lindbergh made the first solo crossing of the North Atlantic on 20–21 May 1927.*

course. The record was beaten on 27–28 August the same year when two other US Army aviators, Captain L. H. Smith and Lieutenant J. P. Richter, kept a DH–4B aloft for 37 hours 15 minutes using in-flight refuelling – their DH–4 was flight-refuelled 15 times from another DH–4.

In 1924 the US Army mounted an even more elaborate exercise than that of the US Navy's transatlantic flight of 1919 – the first around-the-world flight. Four Douglas World Cruisers, open-cockpit single-engined biplanes, were used. Of these two finished the flight – flying 42,398km (26,345 miles) in 363 hours 7 minutes of flying time.

This American project was not the first attempt to fly around the world. Sir Ross Smith had been killed testing a Vickers

amphibian preparing for such an attempt in 1922. An Englishman, Norman Macmillan, using a DH–9 landplane and then a Fairey III–C seaplane, had got as far as the Bay of Bengal in 1922, before the Fairey was wrecked in a storm. They planned a second attempt in 1923, but abandoned it when their supply yacht was arrested in San Pedro, California, for breaches of the US prohibition laws. A French expedition was mounted in 1923 with 5 aircraft and 14 personnel, but they did not get far. There were three other attempts proceeding at the same time as the successful American one: that of Squadron Leader Stuart MacLaren of the RAF, who actually saw the Douglas World Cruisers fly overhead while he was on the water in Burma waiting out a storm; that of Lieutenant Antonio

Locatelli of the Italian Air Service, who flew with the Americans on one leg, but got no further than Iceland; and that of Major Pedro Zanni of Argentina, who crashed his first aeroplane in French Indochina in August and his spare in Japan in May 1925.

There is a point in all this that is insufficiently emphasized by most historians. Most great flying feats and record flights become achievable due to technical advances and that if whoever *did* first achieve them had *not* succeeded, some other aviator, not far behind him, surely would have.

Charles Lindbergh

It was thus, though it is none the less praiseworthy for that, with the flight that is perhaps the single greatest feat in flying history: Charles Lindbergh's first solo Atlantic crossing, from New York to Paris, on 20–21 May 1927. Technically, it was made possible by the development of the Wright Whirlwind engine which possessed a reliability, power: weight ratio and fuel efficiency of a new order. The financial spice for such a flight was a $25,000 prize put up in 1919 by Raymond Orteig. Before Lindbergh's flight six men had already died in the many attempts on the Orteig prize. France's two greatest surviving fighter aces of World War I, René Fonck (who survived) and Charles Nungesser (who vanished in mid-Atlantic with his navigator), were among the failed contenders for the prize.

Lindbergh chose to make his flight solo in a single-engined plane in contrast to several of

his rivals who had chosen trimotors or twins with multi-man crews. Lindbergh's decision was based on the consideration that the weight he would save by flying alone on one engine would be more useful as extra fuel capacity. He commissioned a modified version of a Ryan monoplane mail-carrier, named *Spirit of St Louis*. He designed and controlled the modifications (principally to increase its fuel capacity) himself. Throughout his preparations he doubted that he would be ready in time to cross the Atlantic before his competitors and kept an alternate set of charts of the Pacific.

His take-off roll, which began at 07.52 on 20 May 1927 was one of the great cliffhangers of all time. The earth was soft with rain, and spectators followed in cars with fire

extinguishers convinced they would be needed since his plane was accelerating so slowly. Lindbergh just staggered over the wires at the end of the field, and set off at low altitude northwestward. Lindbergh battled ice, an involuntary spin in mid-ocean (as had Alcock and Brown) and the craving to sleep. When he arrived over Le Bourget airfield near Paris in the darkness of his second night aloft, at 22.24 on 21 May, traffic jammed every access road from all directions and such a wave of humanity poured over the field that he could hardly find space to land without injuring someone. He had been airborne 33 hours 39 minutes (after having hardly had any sleep the previous night) and had flown 5,810km (3,610 miles) non-stop, averaging 173km/h (107·5mph). His aircraft, which

hangs today in the National Air & Space Museum in Washington, had a performance that was extraordinary then and is still remarkable now. With a 14m (46ft) span, 975·5kg (2,150lb) empty weight and 237hp engine, it could carry 1,700 litres (450 US gallons) of fuel, for a range of about 7,000km (4,350 miles). Its useful load was thus considerably greater than its empty weight. It offered Lindbergh (the only pilot who ever flew it) no direct forward visibility for the huge fuel tank was where the windshield should have been. He could only peer obliquely forward through side panels.

Perhaps the major significance of Lindbergh's feat was that it enthused many ordinary people, who had never given aviation much attention, with flying's possibilities.

BELOW: *The Fokker F.VIIB–3M trimotor* Southern Cross, *in which Charles Kingsford Smith and a crew of three made the first full crossing of the Pacific by air, between 31 May and 9 June 1928, from Oakland to Brisbane.*

BELOW RIGHT: *Bert Hinkler working on his Puss Moth, in which he flew from Toronto via New York and South America to Africa, the first solo flight across the South Atlantic.*

BOTTOM: *Jim Mollison and Captain Broad, a test pilot, standing in front of Mollison's aeroplane, the* Heart's Content, *in which he made the first east-west crossing of the Atlantic during 18–19 August 1932.*

RIGHT: *The LZ 127* Graf Zeppelin *arriving at Hanworth in August 1931. This airship made the first and only airship flight round the world during August 1929, in a total time of 21 days, 7 hours and 34 minutes.*

BELOW FAR RIGHT: *Members of the crew of Byrd's Antarctic expedition grouped in front of the Curtiss-Wright plane which was used by the expedition for aerial surveys.*

BOTTOM RIGHT: *Amelia Earhart standing by her Lockheed Vega monoplane. She was the first woman to make a solo crossing of the North Atlantic, during 20–21 May 1932, from Newfoundland to Northern Ireland.*

1927–1929

In the same year as Lindbergh's flight, on 28–29 June, two US Army Lieutenants, Albert F. Hegenburger and Lester J. Maitland, in a Fokker C–2 trimotor, made the first non-stop flight from the USA westwards to Hawaii. They flew 3,874km (2,407 miles), from Oakland to Honolulu, in 25 hours 50 minutes.

The South Atlantic was also first flown non-stop that year, on 14–15 October, when Dieudonné Costes and Joseph Le Brix of France flew a Breguet XIX from Senegal to Brazil covering 3,420km (2,125 miles) in 19 hours 50 minutes.

The first solo flight between England and Australia was made by H. J. L. 'Bert' Hinkler in a prototype Avro 581 Avian (7–22 February 1928). An Avian III was used by Lady Heath to make the first solo flight by a woman from South Africa to London (12 February–17 May 1928). At about the same time another woman pilot was setting out in the opposite direction, from London for South Africa. Lady Bailey, flying a Cirrus II Moth, left London on 9 March 1928 and returned on 16 January 1929 having in that period flown round Africa, crashed her Moth and replaced it with another.

Charles Kingsford Smith with a crew of 3 made the first full crossing of the Pacific by air between 31 May and 9 June 1928 in a trimotor Fokker F.VIIB–3M, *Southern Cross*. Flying from Oakland to Brisbane via Honolulu and Fiji, they covered 11,890km (7,389 miles) in 83 hours 38 minutes flying time. Kingsford Smith captained the same Fokker for the first air crossing of the Tasman Sea. He flew from Sydney to Christchurch in 14 hours 25 minutes on 10–11 September of that year.

Two RAF pilots, G. Jones Williams and N. H. Jenkins, made the first non-stop flight from England to India, in a Fairey Long-range Monoplane, between 24–26 April 1929. They flew 6,647km (4,130 miles) in 50 hours 37 minutes – more than 2 days and nights aloft without landing.

Graf Zeppelin

The first, and only, airship flight around the world, and one of the most romantic journeys ever, was made by the *Graf Zeppelin*, captained by Dr Hugo Eckener, between 8–29 August 1929. It was only the second world flight by any aircraft. German airships were noted for their comfort, good food and fine wines, and it is reported that, with the clocks on board being advanced 1 hour every 7, the approximately 20 passengers, some of whom had paid $9,000 for the trip, complained they were being fed too often!

Commander Byrd

The first flight over the South Pole took place on 28–29 November 1929 in a Ford 4–AT Trimotor commanded by Commander R. E. Byrd of the US Navy and flown by Bernt Balchen with two other crew members. The flight, from and returning to the expedition's base at 'Little America' on the edge of Antarctica, took 18 hours 59 minutes. It is interesting that no less than 10 aircraft were in Antarctica with various expeditions that summer. The first aerial expedition to the South Pole (a British one) had been planned as early as 1920.

Byrd, with Floyd Bennett as co-pilot, had earlier made the first-ever flight over the North Pole, out of and back to Spitsbergen, on 9 May 1926 in a Fokker F.VIIA–3M. He had been greatly assisted on this occasion by the Norwegian explorer Roald Amundsen, who had been the first man ever to reach the South Pole.

1930s

Long-distance and over-ocean records continued to be set throughout the 1930s. Clyde Pangborn and Hugh Herndon, in a Bellanca, made the first non-stop flight from Japan to the USA between 3–5 October 1931. The flight, from Tokyo to Washington state, lasted 41 hours 13 minutes. The great American woman pilot, Amelia Earhart, made the first female solo crossing of the North Atlantic from Newfoundland to Londonderry, in a Lockheed Vega monoplane during 20–21 May 1932. James Mollison made the first solo east–west Atlantic crossing, from Dublin to New Brunswick on 18–19 August 1932 in a de Havilland Puss Moth. Mollison had set an Australia-to-London speed record in 1931 in a Moth, and from London to Cape Town in 1932, both times using the same aeroplane. In 1933 Mollison made the first solo east–west crossing of the South Atlantic, in the course of a marathon flight which took him from Lympne, England to Natal in Brazil in a time of 3 days, 10 hours 8 minutes.

Mollison was married to the British aviation heroine Amy Johnson, who had made in 1930 an impressive solo flight – the first by a woman – from England to Australia. She flew a de Havilland D.H.6DG Gipsy Moth. Jim and Amy Mollison flew the North Atlantic together during 22–24 July 1933 in a twin-engined DH Dragon, from Pendine in Wales to a crash-landing at Bridgport, Connecticut.

A world long-distance record, and the first-ever non-stop flight from England to South Africa, was made by Squadron Leader O. R. Gayford and Flight Lieutenant G. E. Nicholetts in a Fairey Long-range Monoplane between 6–8 February 1933. They flew 8,595km (5,431 miles) in 57 hours 25 minutes.

The first solo flight around the world was made by the one-eyed American pilot Wiley Post between 15–22 July 1933. Piloting a Lockheed Vega, *Winnie Mae*, he flew 25,099km (15,596 miles) in 7 days 18 hours 49 minutes.

Sir Charles Kingsford Smith accompanied by P. G. Taylor made the first flight from Australia to the USA between 22 October–4 November 1934 flying a Lockheed Altair. Amelia Earhart used a Lockheed Vega monoplane to make the first solo flight from

LEFT: *Amy Johnson (Mrs Jim Mollison) in the cabin of her aircraft* Desert Cloud *in November 1932.*
LEFT INSET: *Amy Johnson setting out in her small biplane for the lone flight from Croydon to Australia on 5 May 1930. It was the first such flight by a woman.*

Significant Air Races

Race	Date	Place/Course	Winner	Aircraft	Speed/time
First Gordon Bennett aeroplane race	29 October 1910	Belmont Park, N.Y./100km (62.2 miles)	Claude Graham-White	100hp Gnome-Blériot	1hr 1min 4.74sec
Circuit of Europe	18 June–7 July 1911	Paris–Reims–Liege–Spa–Liege–Verloo–Utrecht–Breda–Brussels–Roubaix–Calais–Dover–Shoreham–London–Shoreham–Dover–Calais–Amiens–Paris	Lieutenant de Vaisseau Conneau	Blériot	
Daily Mail Circuit of Britain	22–27 July 1911	Brooklands–Hendon–Harrogate–Newcastle–Edinburgh–Stirling–Glasgow–Carlisle–Manchester–Bristol–Exeter–Salisbury Plain–Brighton–Brooklands/1,625km (1,010 miles)	Lieutenant de Vaisseau Conneau	Blériot XI	22hr 28min
Daily Mail First Aerial Derby	8 June 1912	Hendon–Kempton Park–Esher–Purley–Purfleet–Epping–High Barnet–Hendon/130km (81 miles)	T. O. M. Sopwith	Blériot	Av. 94km/h (85.5mph) 1hr 23min 8.4sec
First Kings Cup Air Race	8–9 September 1922	Croydon–Glasgow–Croydon	Captain F. L. Barnard	DH–4A	198.9km/h (123.6mph) 6hr 32min 50sec
First Pulitzer Trophy Race	1920	Mitchel Field, Long Island, N.Y./closed-circuit	Lieutenant Corliss C. Moseley	638hp Verville-Packard	251.87km/h (156.5mph)
Last Pulitzer Trophy Race	1925	Mitchel Field, Long Island, N.Y./closed-circuit	Lieutenant Cyrus K. Bettis	620hp Curtiss R3C–1	400.72km/h (248.99mph)
First Thompson Trophy Race	August 1930	Chicago/closed-circuit	Speed Holman	450hp Laird Solution	324.9km/h (201.9mph)
Last Thompson Trophy Race	1949	?Cleveland	Cleland	4,000hp F2G–1 Corsair	639.04km/h (397.07mph)
First Bendix Trophy Race	4 September 1931	Burbank–Cleveland	James Doolittle	535hp Laird Super Solution	358.94km/h (223.03mph)/ 11hr 16min 10sec
Last Bendix Trophy Race		Rosamond Dry Lake, California–Cleveland	Joe DeBona	2,270hp P–51 C	756.63km/h (470.136mph)/ 4hr 16min 17sec
MacRobertson Race	20–23 October 1934	England–Australia/18,329km (11,333 miles)	Charles W. A. Scott/ Tom Campbell Black	DH–88 Comet	255.7km/h (158.9mph)/ 70hr 54min 18sec
Schlesinger Air Race	29 September–1 October 1936	Portsmouth–Johannesburg/9,897km (6,150 miles)	C. W. A. Scott/ Giles Guthrie (only finishers)	Vega Gull	186.7km/h (116mph)/ 2 days 4hr 56min
Circuit of the Alps	25 July 1937	Zurich International Flying Meeting/125 miles	Oberst Karle Franke	Me–109V13	387km/h (240.9mph)
London–Christchurch (NZ) Air Race	8–9 October 1953	London–Christchurch, New Zealand/19,623km (12,193 miles)	Flight Lieutenants R. L. E. Burton and D. H. Gannon	English Electric Canberra	795.887km/h (494.48mph)/ 23hr 51min 10sec
Daily Mail Transatlantic Air Race	4–11 May 1969	London–New York	Lieutenant Commanders Brian Davies and Peter Goddard, RN	McDonnell-Douglas F–4K	4hr 36min 30.4sec flying time

The Schneider Trophy

When the French armaments industrialist Jacques Schneider first put up his trophy for seaplane races in 1912 he can hardly have envisaged that it would become a tournament of enormous world-wide interest and that the competing aircraft, despite the extra drag from their huge floats, the size of which was fixed by the principles of buoyancy, would become the fastest machines in the world at the time. Their designers extended the frontiers of high-speed flight as they wrestled with the problems of minimum-drag airframes, control-surface flutter, propeller torque and cooling the big engines. The early Schneider races were all biplanes, strut- and wire-braced. By the time the series ended in 1931 the superiority of the low-drag monoplane for high-speed flight had been proved and solutions provided for the design of thin-winged monoplanes, necessary for faster aircraft.

Britain had won the last pre-war contest in Monaco in 1914. The first post-war race, held at Bournemouth in 1919, was declared null and void. Italy won the 1920 and 1921 contests at Venice; but Britain won the contest again at Naples in 1922. In 1923, at Cowes, it was won by a US Navy-sponsored team of 465hp Curtiss CR–3 racers. The Americans declined to hold a race in 1924 after all European entries had been withdrawn; but they won the 1925 contest with a 600hp Curtiss R3C–2 flown by Lieutenant James Doolittle at 374km/h (232mph). The 1926 contest was won by the 882hp Italian Macchi M.39. Britain won the 1926 race at Venice with a Supermarine S.5 of the RAF's High Speed Flight, flown by Flight Lieutenant S. N. Webster, who during the contest set a world seaplane speed record of 455 km/h (283mph). This same S.6B, flown by Flight Lieutenant G. H. Stainforth on 29 September 1931, set up a world absolute speed record of 658km/h (490mph).

Thereafter it was agreed by the competing nations, in view of the costs and work involved, to hold the contest every other year. Flying Officer H. R. D. Waghorn won the 1929 contest at Spithead, in a Supermarine S.6 at 528km/h (328mph). The S.6s were powered by a special Rolls Royce V–12 engine that developed almost 2,000hp, and was a forerunner of the Merlin. The British government, in view of the poor economic state of Britain, declined to sponsor a team for the 1931 contest. A private individual, Lady Houston, donated £100,000 to allow Britain to host the race. However, no other nation was ready to take part and unlike the USA in 1924, Britain chose to win the contest, an uncontested 'walkover', with an S.6B powered by a 2,350hp Rolls-Royce racing engine. Under the original terms of the contest Britain thereby retained the trophy, having won it three times running.

The aircraft that competed for the Schneider Trophy were somewhat freakish craft, and seaplanes rather than landplanes only because the contest rules required that they be so. Their handling was tricky, they were dangerous to fly, and many of them crashed. Yet despite all that they made a great contribution to the development of aviation. One example will suffice. The Supermarine designer R. J. Mitchell later used the experience he gained from his Schneider racers to help in the design of the Spitfire, a decisive factor in the outcome of the Battle of Britain – an event which surely changed history.

LEFT: *Lieutenant James H. Doolittle standing on the float of the Curtiss R3C–2 flying boat in which he won the 1925 Schneider Trophy at Baltimore, USA. He won with an average speed of 374·3km/h (232·5mph), which pushed up the winning speed by over 88km/h (55mph) more than in the previous contest.*

BELOW: *The Supermarine S.6 N247 in which Flying-Officer H. R. Waghorn won the Schneider Trophy in 1929 at Cowes. The S.6's average speed was an astonishing 528·9km/h (328·6mph), and its victory was the second consecutive one for Britain, leaving only one more to be gained to win the trophy outright, which Britain did in 1931.*

Date	Place	Winner	Country	Aircraft	Engine	Speed km/h (mph)
16 April 1913	Monaco	Maurice Prévost	France	Deperdussin	160hp Gnome	73·63 (45·75)
20 April 1914	Monaco	Howard Pixton	Britain	Sopwith Schneider	100hp Gnome Mono	139·66 (86·78)
10 September 1919 (Contest later declared null and void)	Bournemouth	Guido Janello	Italy	Savoia S.13	250hp Isotta-Fraschini	176·66 (109·77)
21 September 1920	Venice	Luigi Bologna	Italy	Savoia S.12	550hp Ansaldo	172·55 (107·22)
7 August 1921	Venice	Giovanni di Briganti	Italy	Macchi M.7	250hp Isotta-Fraschini	189·74 (117·90)
12 August 1922	Naples	Henri Biard	Britain	Supermarine Sea Lion II	450hp Napier Lion	234·48 (145·70)
28 September 1923	Cowes	David Rittenhouse	USA	Curtiss CR–3	465hp Curtiss D–12	285·46 (177·38)
26 October 1925	Baltimore	James Doolittle	USA	Curtiss R3C–2	600hp Curtiss V–1400	374·28 (232·57)
13 November 1926	Hampton Roads	Mario de Bernardi	Italy	Macchi M.39	882hp Fiat AS.2	396·70 (246·50)
26 September 1927	Venice	S. N. Webster	Britain	Supermarine S.5	900hp Napier Lion VIIA	453·28 (281·66)
7 September 1929	Calshot	H. R. Waghorn	Britain	Supermarine S.6	1900hp Rolls-Royce 'R'	528·87 (328·63)
13 September 1931	Calshot	J. N. Boothman	Britain	Supermarine S.6B	2350hp Rolls-Royce 'R'	547·31 (340·08)

Hawaii to the US mainland on 11–12 January 1935. Amelia Earhart's solo flight lasted 18 hours 16 minutes.

Jean Batten of New Zealand made the first solo South Atlantic crossing by a woman on 13 November 1935 flying a Percival Gull. She used the same aircraft to make the first flight from Britain to New Zealand by a woman, in the fastest time ever of 11 days 45 minutes (5–16 October 1936).

Other events of that time foretold the way aviation was headed. The prototype Me 109 first flew in September 1935; the first Hurricane on 6 November; and the first Spitfire on 5 March 1936. A development of the Me 109, the 109R, flown by Fritz Wendel, set a world speed record of 781·97km/h (486 mph) on 29 April 1939. This remained the world record for piston-engined aircraft for 30 years. The first successful helicopter, the Focke-Wulf Fw–61V1, made its first flight on 6 June 1936. Frank Whittle ran the first gas turbine aero engine on 12 April 1937. The first jet aircraft to fly was the Heinkel He–178, on 27 August 1939. The first British jet, the Gloster E.28/39, did not make its maiden flight till 15 May 1941. Germany also flew the first rocket-propelled aircraft, a modified glider named the *Ente* piloted by F. Stamer. The flight lasted a minute, on 11 June 1928.

Post-war achievements

A rocket-powered aircraft, air-launched from under the wing of a bomber, made the first manned supersonic flight. The Bell X–1 was flown by Major Charles Yeager on 14 October 1947. Rocket aircraft remain those which have flown fastest and highest, even within the atmosphere. A North American X–15A–2 research aircraft, air-launched from under the wing of a B–52 jet bomber and piloted by W. J. Knight, reached a speed of Mach 6·72 (7,297km/h/4,534mph) on 3 October 1967. The highest altitude achieved during the X–15 programme was 107,860m (354,200ft), reached by J. A. Walker on 23 August 1963.

The first non-stop flight around the world was made by a piston-engined Boeing B–50 Superfortress in March 1949, captained by James Gallagher and manned by a crew of 18. The *Lucky Lady II* flew about 36,225km (22,500 miles) at an average speed of 378·35km/h (235mph), and was refuelled in the air four times: over the Azores, Saudi Arabia, the Philippines and Hawaii. Three 8-jet Boeing B–52 bombers flew around the world in formation and non-stop in 1957, covering 39,147km (24,325 miles) in 45 hours 19 minutes – less than half the time the B–50 had taken only 8 years earlier. The B–52s were refuelled four times, and followed a route that took them over the Atlantic to Morocco, to Dharan, across India and Ceylon, and home to California via Guam. Each aircraft carried a crew of 9 instead of the usual 6, and one tail gunner set a record of a kind as the first man to circumnavigate the world facing backwards.

The world has been circumnavigated since World War II by innumerable pilots, including at least one in a homebuilt aeroplane. Among the women who have flown around the world is Miss Sheila Scott who achieved her feat in 33 days 3 hours, between 18 May–20 June 1966, in a single-engined 260hp Comanche. Her other records include flying from London to New York in 24 hours 48 minutes on 4–5 May 1969; and from London to South Africa in 3 days 2 hours 14 minutes, between 6–9 July 1967. The world has been circumnavigated over the North and South Poles by, among others, Max Conrad flying solo in a light twin. This pilot has made a number of remarkable long distance solo flights. He holds a world class record for distance, at 11,211·83km (6,967 miles) in a single-engined Comanche. At the age of 62 he flew solo from Cape Town to St Petersburg, Florida, in a Twin Comanche.

The more important world records since World War II have generally been competed for by air forces and governments, with private individuals lacking the financial resources to embark on such ventures. A number of memorable world records have, however, been set in recent years. The Lockheed test pilot Darryl Greenamyer, in a privately sponsored project, flying his much-modified Grumman Bearcat Special *Conquest One*, took the world airspeed record for piston-engined aircraft, achieving 776·449 km/h (483·041mph) on 16 August 1969.

James R. Bede, flying a sailplane which he had converted to motor power, gained the world record for distance around a closed circuit for piston-powered aeroplanes, when he covered 17,083km (10,615 miles) between 7–10 November 1969 in 70 hours 15 minutes.

In September 1975 a Lockheed SR–71A aircraft, en route to participate in the Farnborough Air Show, set a record of 1 hour, 54 minutes 56·4 seconds for the New York to London sector of its flight – a distance of 5,584km (3,470 miles). It returned to Los Angeles 9,085km (5,645 miles) in just 3 hours, 47 minutes 35·8 seconds. The same type of aircraft holds the world airspeed record at 3,523km/h (2,189mph), and the (sustained) altitude record of 26,213m (86,000ft). Yet it is less than 70 years since Louis Blériot made that first crossing of the 30·6-km (19-mile) wide English Channel and when the world speed and altitude records were a mere 77·3km/h (48mph), and just over 152·4m (500ft) in altitude.

FAR LEFT: *The New Zealand girl Jean Batten arriving at Croydon after her solo flight from Australia to Britain which ended after 15 days on 29 April 1935.*
CENTRE LEFT ABOVE: *Sheila Scott in the cockpit of her single-engined Piper Comanche, in which she later flew round the world, between 18 May and 20 June 1966.*
CENTRE LEFT BELOW: *The veteran American pilot Max Conrad checking up on his engine after landing safely in Rome at the end of a non-stop flight from Chicago.*
LEFT: *The Bell X–1, a rocket-powered aircraft which made the first manned supersonic flight on 14 October 1947, air-launched from under the wing of a bomber.*
BELOW: *The North American X–15A–2 research aircraft, which has attained a speed of Mach 6·72 (7,927km/h, 4,534mph) and a maximum height of 107,860m (354,200ft).*

Air Crimes

Crimes connected with aviation fall into four main categories: theft, smuggling, sabotage and hijacking. They may be categorized as follows:

Theft

Unless the villain is a pickpocket, or one prepared to snatch hand-luggage from the overhead rack, theft rarely occurs *within* an aircraft. It is in the terminal and its environs that theft flourishes. In the terminal itself the loss of luggage is commonplace, either before departure, after arrival, or at some transit airport. There have been enormous losses by bullion robberies from airport warehouses, as well as pilfering from stacks of cargo awaiting shipment, which offer tempting opportunities for amateur and professional alike.

Terminal car parks – where automobiles are left for extended periods – are also targets for thieves, who know that in many instances the theft may not be reported for two or more weeks after the event. The only safeguard against theft, whatever form it takes, lies in constant and increased vigilance by police, security patrols and by the public generally.

Smuggling

Smuggling, in some form or other, whether it be watches, drugs, diamonds, currency, or any other dutiable or forbidden items, has flourished since the beginning of international air travel, and customs officers at airports throughout the world remain constantly alert for such attempts. Hiding places for would-be smuggled items frequently display imagination – inside hats and babies' nappies, hidden in hollow heels and wooden legs, and concealed around the figures of stout men and women, who become surprisingly thin when examined by customs officials.

Some smugglers are prepared to gamble with their lives. For example, some attempt to smuggle drugs by swallowing liquid cannabis contained in rubber contraceptives. Although smuggling by swallowing is an old practice, this idea is comparatively new – only about two years old, in fact. Although this idea originated in America, customs investigators in Europe are concerned because the idea is fast spreading on their side of the Atlantic. Some cannabis smugglers give themselves away by refusing a cup of tea or drink of water when being quizzed by investigators. The drugs are usually swallowed in India just before a flight, and nothing else must be swallowed until they are passed naturally – usually in the United States. Liquid swallowed could bring about an embarrassing situation, or worse still, cause death by perforation of the contraceptive. Light aircraft have also been used frequently for smuggling cocaine and marijuana from South America, Mexico, Jamaica and elsewhere into the United States and Canada.

Another comparatively new form of smuggling is that of human beings – mainly illegal immigrants – into the United States and into Britain. Many succeed with the connivance of staff already employed at international airports. Many attempts have been very ambitious. On one occasion a chartered airliner arrived at Heathrow, London, from the East; its passengers, all carrying musical instruments, were ushered through customs, gaining entry as an orchestra. Two weeks later the airliner returned to take them back, but not one member of the 'orchestra' was seen again.

Sabotage

This may be regarded as the most cowardly of all crimes, especially when innocent men, women and children lose their lives in the explosion or subsequent crash, as so often happens. Saboteurs fall into three categories: those with strong political or ideological motives; those who threaten sabotage in the hope of gain – either in cash or the release of persons from custody; and demented, compulsive murderers.

From their very nature, aircraft are particularly vulnerable to sabotage, and almost any concessions can be wrung from the operating companies – at least when the lives of passengers and crew are in jeopardy.

The important subject of sabotage, and how to combat it, was discussed at a conference organized by the International Civil Aviation Organization (ICAO) in the summer of 1970. This conference, held in Montreal, revealed that there had been 14 sabotage or armed-attack cases during the 18 months prior to the end of June 1970. A six-point manifesto was issued, in which one item called for 'concerted action' in suppressing such criminal acts. Today, although acts of sabotage appear to be less frequent, it is possible that some aircraft whose disappearance is marked down as 'cause unknown', could be traced to an act of sabotage.

Hijacking

Of all modern aviation crimes, 'hijacking' is the most recent. Isolated incidents of aerial piracy have been brought to the notice of the public since 1930, but the first official statement concerning this crime came from the Tokyo Convention of September 1963, held to discuss 'Offences Committed on Board Aircraft'. The Convention stated that '. . . if a person on board unlawfully or by force or threat of force seized an aircraft, or wrongly interfered with the control of it in

LEFT INSET: *French anti-hijack commandos waiting for action at Orly Airport, Paris, where terrorists were holding seven hostages on 20 January 1975.*
RIGHT INSET: *The British Airways Super VC-10 at Schiphol Airport, Amsterdam, on 5 March 1974, after it had been set alight by Arab terrorists who hijacked it.*
BELOW: *A Pan Am plane at Rome, after terrorists had killed more than 20 people with machine-guns and fire-bombs.*

THIS PAGE: *Jugoslovenski Aerotransport... [illegible]. The Croatian nationalists who hijacked a TWA Boeing 727 from America to Paris.*

flight, all parties to the Convention should have an obligation to take all appropriate measures to restore control of the aircraft to its lawful commander or to preserve his control of it'.

While outlawing the crime, the Tokyo Convention proposals were considered by most to be inadequate. It discussed the release of passengers, crew and aircraft, but laid down no penalties for the hijacker himself.

By 1963 – the year of the Tokyo Convention – the number of hijack incidents had fluctuated through the years as follows: 1947, 1; 1948, 7; 1949, 6; 1951, 1; 1952, 2; 1953 and 1956, 1 each; 1958 and 1959, 7 each; 1960, 8; 1961, 11; 1962 and 1963, 3 each. Then, as if in contempt of the Tokyo Convention, the number of incidents began to grow from 7 in 1967 to a fantastic 92 in 1969. The years 1968 to 1972 were those of the 'Havana hijackings', which were to become so frequent that they finally lost their newsworthiness and continued virtually unnoticed by all but the airlines and the unfortunate passengers involved. These Cuban hijackings involved the flying of aircraft from the USA to Havana. Not all were successful, as this table shows:

1968	35 hijackings, of which 29 were to Cuba (including 3 failures)
1969	92 hijackings, of which 58 were to Cuba (including 12 failures)
1970	85 hijackings, of which 36 were to Cuba (including 3 failures)
1971	61 hijackings, of which 21 were to Cuba (including 7 failures)
1972	62 hijackings, of which 11 were to Cuba (including 2 failures)

Originally the Cuban authorities allowed the passengers to return home, although they had to wait for another aircraft to be flown out specially. Before the hijacked aircraft could be released, landing and other charges had to be met. This was changed in February 1969 and passengers were afforded a virtual 'turn around' at Havana Airport for the return flight.

The most spectacular of the many hijacks to Cuba at that time was that of a US Boeing 747 on a New York to Puerto Rico flight, which was diverted to Havana with 378 passengers. The aircraft was actually inspected at the airfield by Cuba's leader, Fidel Castro, who admitted that he had never had the opportunity to see a Jumbo jet before.

In 1970 President Nixon spoke out against hijacking saying: 'Piracy is now a new challenge for the community of nations. Most countries, including the United States, found effective means of dealing with piracy on the high seas a century and a half ago. We can, and we will, deal effectively with piracy in the skies today.' This was the first time that a leader of one of the world's great powers had made specific reference to hijacking and offered recommendations to combat it.

Hijackings to other parts of the world continued but were becoming rarer. Nevertheless, in October 1969, a most unusual hijack occurred. Ex-US Marine Raffaele Minichiello boarded a TWA Boeing 707 at Los Angeles and when airborne, demanded to be flown to Rome, backing up his request with a rifle. The Boeing was refuelled at Denver, New York and Bangor, (Maine) then took off for Italy. After a 17-hour non-stop flight of 11,263km (7,000 miles) the aircraft touched down in Rome. The hijacker escaped but was later arrested, without resistance, in a country church.

In March 1970, seven Japanese extremist left-wing students hijacked a Boeing 707 on a Tokyo to Fukuoka flight and demanded to be flown to Pyongyang, North Korea. The pilot was ordered by radio to land at Kimbo, Seoul, where elaborate attempts were made to delude the students that they had actually landed at Pyongyang. Western signs were concealed, a large 'Welcome to North Korea' poster covered the fascia of the airport building, and the few soldiers to be seen were in North Korean uniforms. Nevertheless the hijackers were suspicious and the aircraft finally took off for Pyongyang. On arrival the North Korean authorities were furious at having 'such men forced on us'. The aircraft was released immediately and flown back to Tokyo.

The ICAO Montreal Conference of 1970 proposed sanctions against those countries which aided or sheltered hijackers. This was a great advance on the insipid proposals of the Tokyo Convention of seven years earlier, yet three months later the most expensive hijack in history took place. On 6 September 1970, a TWA Boeing 707 on a Frankfurt to New York flight with 145 passengers and a crew of 10 and a Swissair DC–8 flying from Zurich to New York, were both hijacked and flown to a desert airfield north of Amman, Jordan. On the same day a Pan Am 747 on an Amsterdam to New York flight with 158 passengers and 18 crew was also hijacked, flown to Cairo, and blown up on the following day. On 9 September a British BAC VC–10 with 105 passengers and 10 crew flying from Bombay to London, was hijacked and flown to the desert airfield near Amman. After more than 300 passengers and crew had been released the three aircraft were blown up, at an estimated loss of 50 million dollars.

Following this serious incident, a number of governments and airlines considered following Israel's practice of using armed guards and closed-circuit television to enable pilots to keep an eye on passengers. The adoption of the El Al system, whereby incapacitating gas could be pumped into the aircraft's air-conditioning system, was also considered. Magnetometers were immediately installed at airports to check passengers' clothing and hand-luggage for metal objects, a system that has definitely prevented many attempts at both hijacking and sabotage.

The year 1971 saw an appreciable decrease in hijackings, more than half of the attempts being foiled. The trend continued into 1972 due to an overall tightening of security throughout the world. During a three-month period at Heathrow Airport, London, checks revealed 19 pistols, shotguns and rifles, 300 rounds of ammunition, 160 replicas or toy firearms plus 400 knives, swords, axes, bayonets and open razors. By 1973 airport officers had been granted stronger legislative powers for search, arrest and detention than afforded any other peace-time corps.

Nevertheless, hijackings still persist – but with far less regularity. One that took place in September 1976 had every indication of being well organized. A hijacked TWA Boeing 727 was diverted to France, the pilot being forced to fly at 609 metres (2,000ft) over London whilst leaflets printed in English were dropped, and over Paris where French leaflets were similarly scattered. They called for independence for the Croatians of Yugoslavia. When the hijackers surrendered on arrival in Paris, their dynamite and detonators were found to be made of modelling clay.

Significant Post-War Hijackings

The first recorded incident of hijacking occurred in 1930, followed by two in 1931. They were all politically motivated and were connected with the Peruvian revolution of the time. There was then a cessation of such incidents until 1947.

1947
The pilot of a Romanian aircraft was shot dead after refusing to fly it to Turkey. It was the first fatality in hijacking.

1948   7 July
A Cathay Pacific Consolidated Catalina on flight Macau–Hong Kong crashed into the Canton River Delta after its pilot had been shot by an armed passenger. Of the 23 passengers, 10 were killed and 12 listed as missing. This was the world's first non-political hijack.

1964   7 May
San Francisco control tower received the message, 'We are being shot'. The aircraft, a Fairchild F-27, crashed, and in the wreckage was found a revolver and six empty cartridges. Forty-four occupants were killed.

1969   29 August
A TWA Boeing 707 was hijacked over Southern Italy by two Arabs as the aircraft was on a New York to Lydda flight. The pilot was forced to land at Damascus and the aircraft was evacuated and destroyed on the ground. The hijacking was a reprisal for a US sale of 50 Phantom jet fighters to Israel.

13 September
An Ethiopian Airlines Douglas DC-6 flying from Addis Ababa to Djibouti was seized by three hijackers. One was shot and wounded by a security officer on board, the other two were arrested.

31 October
A TWA Boeing 707 was hijacked over California and diverted half-way across the world.

1970   17 March
As an El Al DC-9 approached Boston Airport, an armed passenger ordered the pilot to fly east. Both pilot and co-pilot were shot whilst struggling with hijacker, who was overcome and shot. The co-pilot died on the way to hospital.

30 March
The hijacking of a Japanese Boeing 707 on a flight from Tokyo to Fukuaka led to an elaborate hoax in South Korea.

1 July
While flying from San Paulo to Buenos Aires, an attempt to hijack a Sud-Aviation Caravelle of Cruzeiro was made by four persons. The pilot was shot and injured. The Brazilian Air Force intervened and forced the aircraft to return to Rio where, on landing, police immobilized the aircraft by machine-gunning the tyres. Using a smoke and tear-gas screen, they then forced their way into the aircraft and captured the hijackers.

6–9 September
Three airliners were hijacked and an attempt made on a fourth in the most spectacular hijacking of all time. Eventually four airliners were destroyed by terrorists.

1971   30 March
A Philippine airliner flying Manila to Davoa was hijacked by five armed Filipino students, and the aircraft diverted to China. The authorities made the hijackers apologize to passengers.

23 July
An armed man seized a TWA airliner bound for Chicago, forcing it to return to La Guardia, New York. He then held a stewardess as hostage and ordered a TWA maintenance man to drive them to Kennedy Airport. The hijacker ordered an aircraft to fly him to Italy, but was shot dead by FBI marksmen.

25 November
A Northwest Airlines aircraft was seized by a passenger known as 'D. B. Cooper' prior to touchdown at Seattle. The passengers were allowed to disembark, and the hijacker then collected 200,000 dollars ransom and a parachute. The aircraft was ordered to fly to Reno, but on arrival the hijacker was missing, having parachuted out *en route*.

1972   2 February
Five members of an ultra-militant wing of the Popular Front for Liberation of Palestine (PFLP) hijacked a Lufthansa Boeing 747. After releasing the 182 passengers, the hijackers offered the lives of 5 crew members for 5 Palestinian commandos held by Germany. A ransom of five million dollars was subsequently paid by Lufthansa.

9 May
Three Palestine guerillas threatened to blow up a Sabena Boeing 707 with 95 occupants unless Israel freed some 100 Palestinian guerillas. The hijackers were overcome by 15 'technicians' with guns concealed in their boots.

30 May
Three Japanese walked into the passenger terminal at Lydda, Israel, pulled rifles from their luggage and fired indiscriminately, killing 20 people and wounding 50. One attacker committed suicide by throwing himself on his own grenade, one was caught, and the other escaped.

9 June
Ten Czechs (seven men, three women) hijacked an aircraft of Czechoslovakian State Airline, seeking asylum in West Germany. The pilot was killed in the struggle. The aircraft, on a Marienbad to Prague flight, landed in Weiden.

2 July
An Asian tried to hijack a Pan Am flight to Hanoi, but was overpowered and shot dead by a passenger. His 'bombs' were two lemons wrapped in tinfoil.

12 July
A National Airlines Boeing 727 was hijacked while making its final approach to Kennedy Airport, New York, with 113 passengers and crew of 5. It was forced to return to Philadelphia, and the passengers were held on board in stifling heat for nine hours. A ransom of 600,000 dollars was paid, then the two remaining crew members (the pilot and two others being injured) and four stewardesses were transferred to a new aircraft which flew to Lake Jackson, Texas, where the hijackers surrendered.

18 August
A hijacker cycled through a hole in the airport fence at Reno, Nevada and forced a United Airlines Boeing 727 to fly to Vancouver, Canada, where he demanded 15 gold bars and 2 million dollars in cash. The gold was handed over and the aircraft then flew on to Seattle, Washington, where the cash was being gathered by FBI. The hijacker was shot later by FBI men in Tacoma.

8 December
Six hijackers (four men, two women) died in a mid-air battle with security guards aboard an Ethiopian Airlines Boeing 720B as a grenade tore a hole in the side of the aircraft. Nine other people were treated in hospital.

1973   30 May
A Colombian Lockheed Electra with 80 passengers was hijacked by 2 armed men who ordered the pilot to head for Cuba and demanded the release of all political prisoners in Colombia and 200,000 dollars ransom for the passengers. The Colombian government rejected the demand, and the aeroplane finally landed at Buenos Aires on 5 June after the longest hijack flight on record.

25 November
A KLM Boeing Jumbo on flight from Amsterdam to Tokyo with 280 passengers was hijacked at Beirut by three armed Arabs. After being diverted to Damascus for refuelling, permission was sought to land at Cairo, Baghdad, Kuwait, Bahrain and Aden. All refused, and the aircraft finally landed at Dubai, where the hijackers surrendered.

1974   24 January
Three men and a woman hijacked a helicopter in Eire and forced the pilot to fly them to Strabane at gun point. They tossed out two milk-churns filled with explosive. No damage was done, but it was the first 'air raid' on Northern Ireland.

15 September
A Boeing 727 informed radio control at Danang that a hijacker was on board. The aircraft tried to land at Phan-Rang, but overshot the runway and exploded on touching the ground, killing 67 passengers and the crew of 9.

21 November
Four Palestinian guerrillas forced a British Airways BAC VC-10 to fly to Tunis, where the 40 occupants were held hostage until 25 November as ransom for the release of 15 Palestinians serving sentences for hijacking. A compromise was reached, the passengers were released in exchange for seven Palestinians. The guerrillas then finally surrendered to the Tunisian authorities.

6 June
A helicopter pilot was forced at knife-point to sweep down into a prison yard near Jackson, Michigan, to rescue a convict. A waiting car took him to safety.

1976   27 January
Three men and a woman hijacked an Air France A300–B with 247 passengers and 12 crew aboard soon after take-off from Athens. The pilot was forced to land at Entebbe, Uganda. The hijackers were joined by six more Palestinians and asked for the release of 'freedom fighters' imprisoned in various countries. A successful rescue operation was made by the Israeli government using three Lockheed Hercules C–180 transport aircraft. The passengers and crew were flown to Israel after a brief refuelling stop in Nairobi, Kenya.

12 September
A TWA Boeing 727 on a flight from New York to Chicago was hijacked, 52 passengers and 7 crew were held hostage at Charles de Gaulle Airport, Paris. A Boeing 707 was forced to accompany the hijacked aircraft, whose pilot was inexperienced in trans-Atlantic travel. A 'leaflet raid' followed before the hijackers gave themselves up in Paris after negotiations.

Air Disasters

From the day that man made his first tentative attempts to become airborne in a heavier-than-air machine, it was inevitable that the first fatal accident should soon follow. That doubtful honour fell to Lieutenant Thomas Selfridge, who was killed while flying as a passenger with Orville Wright, when their Wright Biplane crashed at Fort Myer on 17 September 1908. He thus became the world's first powered aeroplane occupant to be killed whilst flying.

The increasing number of fatalities is allied to the incredible progress of aviation in general. They have grown from the first, isolated accidents to large and then even larger accidents which the press inevitably describes as 'disasters', to the natural indignation of aviation officials.

Yet curiously, a comparison of passenger miles travelled per accident reveals that flying has become progressively safer over the years. Accident statistics relating to British regular air transport show that between August 1919, when the first regular air transport service was inaugurated, and the end of 1933, the number of aircraft miles flown per accident resulting in death or injury to occupants increased from 574,535km (357,000 miles) during the period 1919 to 1924, to 3,759,400km (2,336,000 miles) during the period 1930 to 1933. A typical 'serious accident' of 1933 occurred when an Imperial Airways' aircraft flying from Cologne to London caught fire and crashed at Dixmude, the crew of 3 and all of its 12 passengers being killed.

A large proportion of early accidents was attributed to the inability of some aircraft to cope with sudden stresses. A report of 1912 stated that most mishaps were caused by 'frames broken by sudden deflecting forces thrown upon them from the rotating machinery due to an unusually quick change in the direction of the axis of rotation of the driving mechanism'. More than half of the casualties caused by men falling to the ground in aeroplanes are traceable to this instability, known as the 'gyroscopic effect'.

In World War I, 'unusually quick changes in direction' often made the difference between life or death, and this resulted in the development of far more robust and handier machines. By then the greatest single contributory cause of fatal accidents was that of 'stalling'. This occurs when flying speed is lost, and the smooth airflow over the upper surface of a wing (aerofoil surface) breaks up, causing a breakdown of the low-pressure area above the wing, an increase in drag and a sudden loss of lift. The wing is said to have stalled. The effect is for the nose to drop and the aircraft to lose height. Unless the aircraft has sufficient altitude to regain flying speed

in its dive, enabling the pilot to regain control, it will crash. On take-off an aircraft with a tailwheel-type landing gear may not even get off the ground if the nose is raised too high, as the wing will be in a stalled condition. Aircraft with tricycle-type landing gear are, generally, in an ideal attitude of minimum drag for their take-off run. When flying speed is attained, the climb-out from the runway is under conditions of high lift from the wing.

Types of accidents

Aircraft accidents today, other than those caused by sabotage or air piracy (hijacking), fall into 23 categories:
Airframe failure; Aquaplaning/Hydroplaning; Bird strike/ingestion; Cargo breaking loose; Collision with high ground; Collision with water; Crew incapacitation; Door, windows opening/falling off in flight; Electrical system failure/malfunction; Failure of power units; Flying control system malfunctions; Fuel contamination; Fuel exhaustion, starvation, mismanagement; Hail damage; Ice/snow accretion – airframe/engine; Inflight fire/smoke; Instruments incorrectly set, misread, failure, malfunction; Lightning strike; Major powerplane disruptions/loss of propeller in flight; Mid-air collision with another aircraft; Over-running/Veering off runway; Third-party accidents; Tyre burst after retraction.

ABOVE: *The debris of one of the propellers from a crash in Switzerland, 10 April 1973.*
BOTTOM RIGHT: *The wreckage of a Brazilian plane at Orly airport, Paris, in July 1973.*

Despite all these possibilities, and no matter by what yardstick the safety of airline operations is measured, air travel is very safe. Jet operations alone – comprising some 90 per cent of all flying done today – have improved tenfold since 1959, when jet transport was established. A rate of one jet aircraft loss in every 50,000 hours was recorded in that first 'jet year'. By 1976 it had improved to about 1 in 560,000 hours flown. Assuming an average sector length of three hours (a 'sector' is the average time between a take-off and a landing), and that each passenger averages two sectors, a passenger should have to make 84,500 journeys before he is likely to be involved in an accident. Even flight crews on long-haul operations, whose time in the air is much greater than that of the passengers, would have to live to be about 400 years old before they were likely to be involved in a fatal accident.

The last decade has shown a remarkable improvement in safety standards. In 1966 4,480 million km (2,784 million miles) were flown as against 7,550 million km (4,691 million miles) in 1975. In 1966 there were 31 fatal accidents and 1,001 passengers killed, representing 0·33 fatal accidents for every

440

Major Air Disasters

*Note : Only those with 100 or more fatalities are shown.
Obviously, as aircraft developed, so the seating capacity increased,
and individual disasters grew larger by comparison. The first
disaster with a 100+ fatality occurred in 1956*

Date	Aircraft	Location	Fatalities Total	Pass	Crew
1956					
30.6	Lockheed L–1049	Arizona, USA	128	64	6
	Douglas DC–7			53	5
1960					
16.12	Lockheed L–1049	New York, USA	133	39	5
	Douglas DC–8			77	7
				(Others, 5)	
1962					
4.3	Douglas DC–7C	Cameroons	111	101	10
16.3	Flying Tiger Super Constellation	Between Guam and Philippines	107	96	11
3.6	Boeing 707–328	France	130	122	8
22.6	Boeing 707	Guadeloupe	112	102	10
1963					
1.2	Vickers Viscount 754	Turkey	104	11	3
	Douglas C–47			3	3
				(Others, 87)	
3.6	Douglas DC–7C	Alaska	101	95	6
29.11	Douglas DC–8F	Canada	118	111	7
1965					
20.5	Boeing 720B	Egypt	119	114	5
1966					
24.1	Boeing 707–437	France	117	106	11
4.2	Boeing 727	Japan	133	126	7
24.12	Canadair CL–44	South Vietnam	111	0	4
				(Others, 107)	
1967					
19.4	Bristol Britannia 313	Cyprus	126	117	9
11.11	Ilyushin Il–18	Russia	130	n.a.	n.a.
1968					
20.4	Boeing 707 344C	S.W. Africa	123	111	12
1969					
16.3	Douglas DC–9	Venezuela	154	74	10
				(Others, 70)	
20.3	Ilyushin IL–18	Egypt	100	93	7
1970					
15.2	Douglas DC–9	Argentina	102	97	5
3.7	de Havilland Comet 4	Spain	112	105	7

Date	Aircraft	Location	Fatalities Total	Pass	Crew
1970					
5.7	Douglas DC–8	Canada	109	100	9
9.8	Lockheed Electra L–188A	Peru	101	99	0
				(Others, 2)	
1971					
30.7	Boeing 727	Japan	162	155	7
4.9	Boeing 727	Alaska	111	104	7
1972					
7.1	Sud-Aviation Caravelle	Spain	104	98	6
14.3	Sud-Aviation Caravelle	Muscat & Oman	112	106	6
5.5	Douglas DC–8	Sicily	115	108	7
18.5	Antonov An–10	Russia	108	n.a.	n.a.
18.6	Hawker Siddeley Trident	England	118	109	9
14.8	Ilyushin Il–62	Germany	156	148	8
2.10	Ilyushin Il–18	Russia	100	n.a.	n.a.
13.10	Ilyushin Il–62	Russia	174	164	10
3.12	Convair CV–990A	Tenerife	155	148	7
1973					
22.1	Boeing 707	Nigeria	176	170	6
21.2	Boeing 727	Sinai Desert	106	n.a.	n.a.
10.4	Vickers Vanguard	Switzerland	108	104	4
11.7	Boeing 707	France	123	116	7
22.12	Sud-Aviation Caravelle	Morocco	106	99	7
1974					
5.3	Douglas DC–10	France	345	334	11
22.4	Boeing 707	Bali	107	96	11
4.12	Douglas DC–8	Sri Lanka	191	182	9
1975					
24.6	Boeing 727	New York	113	107	6
3.8	Boeing 707	Morocco	188	181	7
19.8	Ilyushin Il–62	Nr. Damascus	126	115	11
1976					
5.3	Ilyushin Il–18	Russia	127	109	11
				(Others, 7)	
10.9	Douglas DC–9	Yugoslavia	176	108	5
	Hawker Siddeley Trident			54	9
13.10	Boeing 707	Bolivia	100+	0	3
				(Others, 100+)	
1977					
27.3	Boeing 747 (KLM)	Tenerife	561	229	15
	Boeing 747 (PanAm)			308	9

100,000 aircraft hours flown, or 0·44 fatalities per million passenger-km. In 1975 there were 21 accidents and 473 passengers killed, representing the related factors of 0·17 and 0·07 respectively.

The human factor

Such has the standard of design and manufacture improved that today something like 80·5 per cent of all accidents are the result of human error. Broken down into percentages, these comprise: crew 62 per cent; operational (procedures etc) 15 per cent; maintenance 3·5 per cent; non-operational sabotage 6·5 per cent; material or system failure 8 per cent; and weather 4·5 per cent.

The Lovelace Foundation's Department of Aerospace and Environmental Medicine studied a number of approach and landing accidents in an attempt to identify common factors. Of the 197 critical elements catalogued, 117 were grouped under 'man', 12 under 'machine' and 68 under 'environment'. This is further shown by an analysis of jet losses during two significant periods.

Aircraft situation when accident occurred	*1962–1971*	*1972–1975*
Take-off and initial climb	20%	18·25%
Climb	13%	2%
Cruise	4%	6%
Descent	9%	10%
Approach	35%	36·5%
Landing	12%	18·25%
On ground (during maintenance, etc.)	4%	8%
Test and training	3%	—
Missed approach	—	1%

The International Air Transport Association (IATA) has identified so-called 'human factors' as a major causal element in accidents. The term 'human factors' is used to describe events where the flight crew would seem to have failed to act as they should have done, thereby contributing to an accident. Intensive work on this problem over a period of years culminated in the 20th IATA Technical Conference, held in Istanbul in November 1975. This Conference led to a number of recommendations which, it is believed, will play an important role in reducing the number of 'human factors'-related accidents.

International co-operation

Some countries insist that certain occurrences are reported regularly and investigated thoroughly. By this it is hoped to prevent recurring problems in both machinery and operating practices. These are, of necessity, 'after the event' actions.

Today there are a number of exchange schemes where airlines share their experiences freely, albeit on a confidential basis. IATA, America's Air Transport Association (ATA) and the UK Flight Safety Committee all have similar schemes. These provide a forum where any airline operator who has experienced an occurrence from which he has learned a lesson, or which has caused him to change his procedures or drills, can report to the others participating in the scheme.

Most countries have some form of Flight Safety Committee, a group which includes representatives of their country's airlines, manufacturers, insurers and ministries. IATA's Regional Technical Offices spend a great deal of their time persuading governments to install and maintain modern navigation and landing aids. It is well known that a very large majority of accidents occur in the descent, approach and landing phase, and by providing pilots with these facilities at all airports, the incidence of this class of accident should be substantially reduced.

Whilst IATA basically consists of airlines, ICAO is comprised of governments and well over 100 are represented. The constitution of ICAO is the Convention on International Civil Aviation, drawn up by a conference in Chicago in November/December 1944, and to which each ICAO member state is a party.

One of its chief activities is standardization, the drafting of international standards and procedures covering the whole field of aviation, including airworthiness, search and rescue, accident inquiry, and so on.

IATA maintains an incident exchange scheme known as the 'Safety Information Exchange'. This provides for exchange between IATA Members (and more recently non-IATA airlines) of anonymous reports on accidents and serious incidents – particularly the latter. There is a great deal to be learned from incidents, that is to say, unusual or alarming in-flight events which did not lead to an accident, but nevertheless taught some safety lesson. Incidents occur much more frequently than accidents, and the lessons they teach are often just as important as those learned from accidents themselves. The incident exchange scheme therefore immensely broadens the foundation for future preventive action.

'The little black box'

One important instrument that has helped investigators to reach their conclusions more quickly and accurately than before is the tell-tale device popularly known as 'the little black box', introduced as long ago as 1924. The title is very much a misnomer as, for the most part, flight recorders are painted in brilliant colours such as fluorescent scarlet or orange, to make them easier to locate amid aircraft wreckage. The vital information concerning time, speed, pitch attitude, altitude, magnetic heading and vertical acceleration, plus other significant data, is produced through a sophisticated programme of digital flight data recording. As many as 125 channels a second from 60 separate sources can be recorded.

Equally important is the introduction of machines that prevent mid-air crashes. Systems currently in use are basically of two types; those used by the Air Traffic Control system on the ground, to indicate to the controller that he has a conflict, or those in the aircraft that interrogate all the aircraft nearby to establish if collison potential exists. In the former case the Air Traffic controller would pass the necessary avoidance instructions or, as in the B–CAS System, it could also be carried on board the aircraft and displayed to the pilot. In the latter case, it is necessary to have compatible equipment in *every* aircraft. This has to be set against a common time base which needs to be incredibly accurate. The 'on board' systems tell the pilot to turn, climb or dive to avoid the conflict.

The search for improved safety standards never ceases. It is partly because of this search that ICAO came into being, in an attempt to achieve cooperation and coordination wherever commercial aircraft fly. The success which international civil aviation has achieved in the past two decades has already proved that nations *can* work together effectively for the public good . . . and do.

FAR LEFT : *Crash experts examine the wreckage of the BEA Trident which crashed at Staines on 18 June 1972, killing all 118 on board.*
LEFT : *The scattered remains of the Boeing 707 which crashed at Kennedy Airport on 25 June 1975.*
ABOVE : *One of the worst air disasters was the Turkish Air Lines DC–10 which crashed in the Forest of Ermenonville near Paris, in March 1974.*

Aviation Law

The emergence and development of aviation has created complex social relationships among individuals, corporations, governmental authorities and between States. These social relationships require legal regulation. The conduct of the different subjects in these social relationships has to conform to rules established by an appropriate authority, and the same authority enforces these rules in order to achieve harmonious development of relationships and to avoid possible conflicts and dangers to the society.

'Air law' may be defined as a functional and interdisciplinary branch of the legal system. It deals with the rights and duties of different subjects with respect to the airspace and the aeronautical use thereof, and with respect to aircraft and its operations. It falls both in the category of *international law* (i.e., rules created by and applicable to sovereign States in their mutual relations) and *national legislation* (i.e., legal rules issued by an appropriate authority of a state and enforced by the judicial and other authorities of that state). The national legislation comprises private law, administrative law, labour law, criminal law, etc. Due to the international character of aviation and the need for world-wide uniformity of legal regulation, the national legislation is to a large extent modelled on or derived from international agreements and other sources of international law.

The following are just a few examples of the spectrum of problems governed by air law on national or international level: licensing of the flight personnel; rules of the air; registration and nationality markings of the aircraft; certification of airworthiness of aircraft; operation of the aircraft; establishment, equipment and operation of airports; aeronautical communications; search and rescue in case of aircraft in distress; investigation of accidents; economic regulation and licensing of operators; rules on contract of carriage in respect to passengers, cargo and mail, including problems of liability and insurance; protection of aviation against unlawful acts (hijacking, sabotage); protection of the environment against noise, sonic boom and pollution; and so on.

The 'aircraft' is internationally defined as 'any machine that can derive support in the atmosphere from the reactions of the air, other than the reactions of the air against earth's surface. A hovercraft derives its support from the reactions of the air against the earth's surface. Consequently it is not an 'aircraft', and is not governed by the international air law conventions or by the national air legislation.

The Roman law maxim *'cuius est solum eius est usque ad coelum'* (who owns the land, owns it up to the skies), generally considered as historically the first rule of air law, is hardly more than a clarification of the scope of the proprietary rights of the landowner, and was never intended to regulate the art of flying. Law cannot be expected to develop faster than the social relationships it is supposed to regulate.

The law-maker and the law-enforcer closely followed the aviators from their earliest exploits. The historians seem to agree that the first real legal regulation of aviation is contained in an ordinance of a certain M. Lenoir – a *lieutenant de police*

ABOVE: *In June 1972 a suicide squad composed of three Japanese terrorists attacked the airport at Lydda, Israel, killing 26 people and wounding over 50. Only one of the terrorists, Kozo Okamoto, was caught. He is seen here during his* interrogation by Israeli police when it was announced that he was to be tried by an Israeli military court. In front of him are ranged some of the weapons used in the massacre.

in Paris – which prohibited balloon flights without special permit from 23 April 1784 – some five months after the first manned flight of a hot-air balloon over Paris. In January 1822 the New York Supreme Court issued the first recorded judicial decision in an aviation case – a balloonist was found liable for damage caused on the plaintiff's land by a forced landing of the balloon (incidentally, the damage was caused mostly by a crowd of curious onlookers, who rushed to the place of landing and damaged the plaintiff's fences).

In the first years of this century most developed countries had some form of legal regulations for the safety in air navigation, customs regulations applicable to foreign aviators, penalties and jurisprudence. In practice, if not by law, many states clearly started to assert their sovereign rights in the airspace above their territories. The first international incident occurred in August 1904, when Russian border guards shot down a German balloon allegedly overflying Russian territory.

The cardinal disputed question at the outset of development of air law was the legal status of the airspace above national territory. At the beginning of the 20th century three basic theories were advocated:

Freedom of the air: by analogy with the regime of the high seas, it was argued that the airspace was a common property of mankind and not subject to appropriation or claims of sovereignty.

Complete and exclusive sovereignty: according to this theory the airspace above the territory of a state was to be considered an integral part of that state's sovereign territory.

Mixed theory: this theory recognized the 'freedom of the air' while safeguarding certain rights of the state in its national airspace.

Whatever merits these theories may have had, it was the practice of states that determined the sovereign character of the airspace above state's territory. There was an abortive attempt, in Paris in 1910, to prepare an international convention on air navigation. However, World War I interrupted further diplomatic negotiations, aircraft proved to be a formidable new weapon and states resorted to unilateral – and surprisingly uniform – practice. All international boundaries were closed to all aircraft of the belligerents, and all neutral states strongly protested against any violation of their airspace, and in numerous cases had the intruding aircraft shot down. Thus, by 1918, the international practice recognized unequivocally the legal principle of state sovereignty in the airspace.

The milestones in the development of public international air law are the following conventions:

International Convention on Air Navigation (Paris, 1919): This Convention recognized that every state has complete and exclusive sovereignty over the airspace above its territory, and provided for the freedom of innocent passage of civil aircraft of other contracting states over the state territory. It also established the International Commission for Aerial Navigation (ICAN) as an international organization, the function of which was to exercise the legislative, administrative and judi-

cial functions set out under the Paris Convention.

Ibero-American Convention on Air Navigation (Madrid, 1926): Essentially identical with the Paris Convention, the Madrid Convention was to group Spain and Latin American countries into an organization similar to ICAN, but with equal voting power for all states.

Pan-American Convention (Havana, 1929): Accepted by 16 states at the 6th Pan-American Conference, this was also modelled on the Paris Convention, and included detailed technical legislation as well as some rules of private air law.

Convention on International Civil Aviation (Chicago, 1944): 135 states are presently Parties to this Convention (generally known as 'Chicago Convention'), which is the backbone of the current public international air law. Part I of the Convention sets out the rules applicable to air navigation. The Convention recognizes that each state has complete and exclusive sovereignty over the airspace above its territory (land areas and territorial waters adjacent thereto). Aircraft of other contracting states are entitled to make non-scheduled flights into or over the territory of a state and make stops for non-traffic purposes without the necessity of obtaining prior permission, but subject to certain limitations. Consequently, the Convention does not recognize (unlike the Paris Convention) the right of 'innocent passage' as such. No scheduled international services may be operated over or into the territory of a state except with special permission or other authorization of that state. Such authorization is usually contained in bilateral agreements on air traffic services, in which states contractually agree on a mutual exchange of commercial rights for the operation of their airlines. There are presently over 2,000 such bilateral agreements.

The Chicago Conference in 1944 also adopted the **International Air Services Transit Agreement** (generally known as 'two freedoms' agreement), in which contracting states agreed to grant to other contracting states, in respect of scheduled international air services, the privilege to fly across their territory without landing and the privilege to land for non-traffic purposes (e.g., refuelling, maintenance, but not to take on or put down passengers, mail or cargo). This agreement is presently in force for 92 states.

The **International Air Transport Agreement** (also known as 'five freedoms' agreement) was also adopted by the Chicago Conference. In addition to the above-mentioned 'two freedoms' this also grants the commercial 'freedoms' (privilege to put down passengers, mail and cargo originating from the territory of the state of registry of the aircraft, the privilege to take on passengers, etc. destined for such territory and, finally, to take on or put down passengers, etc. coming from or destined to the territory of any contracting state). Only 12 states are parties to this agreement, and states prefer to negotiate the granting of the traffic rights on a bilateral basis.

The Chicago Convention deals in detail with many technical and economic aspects of international civil aviation, and in Part II establishes the International Civil Aviation Organization (ICAO) and sets its constitutional rules.

The International Civil Aviation Organization (ICAO), created by the Chicago Convention, came into being on 4 April 1947. It is a specialized agency in the United Nations system and its membership – 135 states – makes it practically universal. The Headquarters of ICAO is in Montreal, Canada, and Regional Offices are located in Paris (European Office), Dakar (African Office), Bangkok (Far East and Pacific Office), Cairo (Middle East and Eastern African Office), Mexico City (North American and Caribbean Office) and Lima (South American Office).

The aims and objectives of the Organization are to develop the principles and techniques of international air navigation, and to foster the planning and development of international air transport to insure the safe and orderly growth of international civil aviation throughout the world, encourage the arts of aircraft design and operation for peaceful purposes, promote safety of flight in international air navigation and to promote generally the development of all aspects of international civil aeronautics.

The supreme body of ICAO is the Assembly, which meets every three years. The executive body is the Council, a permanent body composed of 30 states elected by the Assembly. The Air Navigation Commission is a permanent body of 15 technical experts appointed by the Council from among persons nominated by contracting states. The Air Transport Committee dealing with economic matters is composed of Representatives on the Council. The Legal Committee of ICAO was established by the Assembly, and is open to participation by all states. The President of the ICAO Council is elected by the Council, and is an international civil servant; he has no vote in the Council. The chief executive officer is the Secretary General who is appointed by the Council.

From the legal point of view, the essential function of ICAO is the formulation and approval of international standards and recommended practices in the field of civil aviation. These standards are approved by the Council and designated as Annexes to the Chicago Convention. All contracting states undertake to collaborate in securing the highest practicable degree of uniformity in regulations, standards, procedures, etc., but may file a difference if they find it impracticable to comply in all respects with any international standard or procedure. So far the Council of ICAO has approved 17 Annexes to the Chicago Convention containing international standards and recommended practices.

The International Air Transport Association (IATA) is a non-governmental organization of airlines, and was created in 1945 to succeed the International Air Traffic Association of 1919. It was incorporated in Canada by Act of Parliament and has the status of a corporation, to which Canadian law attributes an international character. IATA is sometimes compared with an international cartel of airlines – particularly because of its rate-making functions. However, since in many states the airlines are subject to anti-trust legislation, and since the tariffs and rates are subject to governmental approval, IATA should not legally be considered as a business cartel.

Apart from technical and economic regulation of the airline industry, IATA performs important functions in the legal field by establishing uniform air transport documents and general conditions of carriage which are accepted uniformly in the tariffs of a great majority of world airlines.

The international character of civil aviation necessitates a high degree of uniformity of legal regulations. The unification of law is best achieved by multilateral international agreements, the rules of which are transformed into the national legislation of contracting states. Since the establishment of ICAO, all agreements in this field have been prepared by the ICAO Legal Committee and adopted by Diplomatic Conferences convened and held under the auspices of ICAO. The following air law conventions have been adopted so far.

Warsaw Convention for the Unification of Certain Rules Relating to International Carriage by Air (1929). This Convention, to which 108 states are parties, is the most widely accepted unification of private law. It unifies the rules on documentation in the carriage of passengers, baggage and cargo (passenger ticket, baggage check and air waybill). Secondly, it unifies the regime of liability of the carrier. The carrier is liable on the basis of fault, but there is a presumption of fault and the burden of proof is reversed. The extent of liability of the carrier is limited to 125,000 Poincaré francs (less than US $10,000) in respect of passengers, and to 250 francs (about US $20) per kilogramme of baggage or cargo. Finally, the Convention unifies the question of jurisdiction by defining the courts before which an action may be brought.

The Convention was amended in 1955 by **The Hague Protocol**, which simplified the documentation and doubled the limit of liability in respect of passengers. In 1961 a Supplementary Convention was adopted at *Guadalajara*, which extends the applicability of the Warsaw Convention to the 'actual' (as distinct from 'contractual') carrier. In 1966 the Warsaw Convention was *de facto* amended by a private agreement of air carriers ('**Montreal Agreement, 1966**') with respect to carriage to, from or via the territory of the USA.

For such carriage the carrier is absolutely liable with respect to passengers, and the limit of liability is $75,000.

The **Guatemala City Protocol** of 1971 (not yet in force) further simplified the documentation requirements with respect to passengers, introduced the principle of absolute liability and increased the limit of liability to about US $100,000.

The **Montreal Protocols** of 1975 (not yet in force) would furthermore replace the gold value clause (Poincaré franc) in the system of the Warsaw Convention by the Special Drawing Rights of the International Monetary Fund.

Geneva Convention on the International Recognition of Rights in Aircraft (1948). The purpose of this Convention, to which 38 states are parties, is to ensure protection of rights in aircraft (such as the right of creditors), when the aircraft and its equipment are situated in another country or where the registration of the aircraft is changed from one country to another.

Rome Convention on Damage Caused by Foreign Aircraft to Third Parties on the Surface (1952). There are 28 states parties to this Convention, which introduces the regime of absolute liability for damage caused by aircraft on the surface. The liability is limited and the amount varies with the weight of the aircraft. The Legal Committee of ICAO is now studying a possible amendment of the Rome Convention in order to make it clear that it would deal only with 'physical impact' damage and not with damage caused by noise, vibrations or sonic boom. The system of the limits of liability will also be reviewed. The preparation of a new separate instrument on liability for damage caused by noise and sonic boom is under study in ICAO.

Under the auspices of ICAO three Conventions in the field of criminal law have been prepared, the last two of them dealing with criminal acts against the safety of civil aviation such as 'hijackings'. They are the **Tokyo Convention on Offences and Certain Other Acts Committed on Board Aircraft** (1963); the **Hague Convention for the Suppression of Unlawful Seizure of Aircraft** (1970) and the **Montreal Convention for the Suppression of Unlawful Acts Against the Safety of Civil Aviation** (1971). For further details see the Chapter on Air Crimes on pages 436–439.

LEFT : *Some of the passengers from an airliner hijacked to Damascus on 29 August 1969. It was a TWA Boeing 707 on a flight to Lydda, and was forced to land at Damascus by two Arab terrorists, who then destroyed the aircraft there after allowing the passengers to be evacuated. This attack was another example of hijacking for political reasons – the terrorists declared that it was a reprisal for the recent sale by the United States of 50 Phantom jet fighters to the Israeli armed forces.*

Famous Names

Ader, Clement (1841–1925)
French pioneer, whose bat-winged *Éole* monoplane became, on 9 October 1890, the first man-carrying aeroplane to achieve a powered 'hop' into the air.

Alcock, Sir John (1892–1919)
Who, with Lieutenant Arthur Whitten-Brown (later Sir Arthur) as navigator, achieved the first non-stop crossing of the North Atlantic in a Vickers Vimy bomber, 14 to 15 June 1919.

Aldrin, Edwin (1930–   )
Astronaut and crew member of the *Apollo XI* spacecraft which carried the first men to land on the Moon's surface, on 21 July 1969.

Amundsen, Roald (1872–1928)
Renowned explorer, a member of the crew of 16 of the Italian airship *Norge* which flew over the North Pole on 12 May 1926.

Archdeacon, Ernest (1863–1957)
Whose prize awards did much to foster European aviation, was the first passenger to be carried in an aeroplane in Europe, on 29 May 1908.

Arlandes Marquis d'
First aerial passenger in history, who accompanied Pilâtre de Rozier in a Montgolfier hot-air balloon on 21 November 1783.

Armstrong, Neil (1930–   )
Commander of the *Apollo XI* spacecraft which carried the first men to the Moon, and the first man to step on the lunar surface on 21 July 1969.

Bacon, Roger (1214–1292)
English scientist-monk who, so far as is known, was the first person to write in a scientific manner about the possibility of manned flight. His *Secrets of Art and Nature*, in which he first put forward such ideas, was written about 1250.

Bader, Sir Douglas (1910–   )
Famous British fighter ace of World

War II, who achieved his 22 credited victories while flying with two artificial legs. His legs were terribly injured and amputated following a pre-war flying accident.

Balbo, General Italo (1896–1940)
Italian Air Minister, who led two mass flights of Savoia-Marchetti flying-boats across the South and North Atlantic in 1931 and 1933 respectively.

Balchen, Bernt (1899–1973)
Pilot of the Ford Trimotor *Floyd Bennett*, which recorded the first flight over the South Pole on 29 November 1929.

Baldwin, F. W. (Casey)
First British subject (a Canadian) to fly a heavier-than-air machine. This flight was made at Hammondsport, N.Y., 12 March 1908, in an AEA Red Wing.

Ball, Albert (1896–1917)
First great British fighter ace of World War I, was credited with his 47th victory on 6 May 1917. He died on the following day when his aircraft crashed after following a German single-seater scout aircraft into dense cloud.

Banks, F. Rodwell (1898–   )
Of the Ethyl Export Corporation, whose specialized knowledge of aviation fuels played an important part in the development of the Rolls-Royce racing engines and, subsequently, of the Rolls-Royce Merlin.

Barber, Horatio (1875–   )
Pilot of a Valkyrie monoplane which, on 4 July 1911, carried the first recorded consignment of air-freight between Shoreham and Hove in Sussex.

Barnard, F. L.
Commodore of Britain's early Instone Airline, who won the first King's Cup Air Race on 9 September 1922. Captain Barnard was flying Sir Samuel Instone's de Havilland D.H.4A *City of York*.

Batten, Jean (1909–   )
Pioneer woman pilot from New Zealand, whose exploits included the first solo air crossing of the South Atlantic by a woman, 11–13 November 1935.

Beachey, Lincoln
Daring pioneer pilot in America, first became famous for an airship flight around the Washington Monument on 13 June 1906.

Béchereau, Louis
Responsible primarily for the design of the streamlined, circular, monocoque wooden fuselage of the highly successful French Deperdussin monoplanes of 1912/1913.

Bell, Alexander Graham (1847–1912)
Famous inventor born in Edinburgh, was associated with Glenn Curtiss and Thomas E. Selfridge in Bell's Aerial Experiment Association which, in 1903 to 1905, carried out successful aeroplane experiments in America, following the work of the Wright brothers.

Bennett, D. C. T. (1910–   )
Piloted the upper, Short S.20 *Mercury* seaplane, component of the Short-Mayo composite, from Foynes, Ireland to Montreal, Canada on 21

to 22 July 1938, the first commercial use of composite aeroplanes.

Bennett, Floyd (1890–1928)
Pilot of the Fokker F.VIIA/3m monoplane *Josephine Ford* which, on 9 May 1926, became the first aeroplane to fly over the North Pole.

Birkigt, Marc (1878–1953)
Swiss engineer who in 1904 founded with Damien Mateu the Hispano Suiza Motor Company. During World War I the company turned to production of aero-engines. Another famous product of the company was the 20mm Hispano gun.

Bishop, R. E. (1903–   )
Designer of the de Havilland D.H.106 Comet 1, which on 2 May 1952, operated the world's first passenger service by a turbojet-powered aircraft.

Bishop, William A. ('Billy') (1894–1956)
Canadian ace pilot of World War I, credited with 72 confirmed victories. Awarded Britain's highest military honour, the Victoria Cross, he rose subsequently to the rank of Honorary Air Marshal in the Royal Canadian Air Force.

Black, Tom Campbell
Co-pilot of the de Havilland D.H.88 Comet which won the 1934 MacRobertson race from Mildenhall, England, to Melbourne, Australia, in a time of 71 hours.

Blériot, Louis (1872–1936)
French aviator pioneer who, flying a Blériot XI monoplane of his own design, made the first crossing of the English Channel in an aeroplane, on 25 July 1909.

Boeing, William (1881–1956)
Co-pilot with Eddie Hubbard of the Boeing C–700 seaplane which made the first international air mail flight from Canada to America, on 3 March 1919, he was the founder of the now famous Boeing Company.

Boothman, John N. (1901–1957)
A member of the Royal Air Force High Speed Flight of 1931, and pilot of the Supermarine S.6B racing seaplane which won the Schneider Trophy outright for Great Britain on 13 September 1931.

Brabazon of Tara, Lord (Moore-Brabazon, J. T. C.) (1884–1964)
First Englishman to make an officially recognized aeroplane flight in England, on 30 April 1909, and holder of the first Aviator's Certificate in Great Britain, awarded by the Aero Club on 8 March 1910.

Braun, Dr Werner von (1912–1977)
German rocket pioneer, under whose

supervision was developed the world's first ballistic rocket missile, the V–2 (A–4), first launched successfully on 3 October 1942. He was one of the leading American space scientists.

Breguet, Louis (1880–1955)
French pioneer of rotary-wing flight. In association with Professor Richet he designed and built a helicopter which, on 29 September 1907, was the first to lift a man from the ground. This was not a controlled flight, the aircraft being stabilized by four men with poles.

LeBris, J. M. (1808–1872)
A French sea captain who studied bird flight on his ocean voyages. In 1856 he completed construction of a glider which was launched from a horse-driven cart. A second aircraft, built in 1868, was launched frequently, with ballast instead of a human pilot.

Butler, Frank Hedges (1856–1928)
Aware of the encouragement which early aviation activities in Europe were receiving from the Aéro-Club de France, was the first to suggest the formation of an Aero Club in Britain. This was duly registered on 29 October 1901.

Byrd, Richard E. (1888–1957)
American explorer, first man to fly over both North and South Poles, on 9 May 1926, and 29 November 1929, respectively.

Cabral, Sacadura
Who, together with Gago Coutinho, achieved the first aeroplane crossing of the South Atlantic in 1922. Their arrival in Brazil, on 16 June, marked the end of an epic three-month journey involving three aircraft.

Camm, Sir Sydney (1893–1966)
Famous British aircraft designer, who joined the H. G. Hawker Engineering Company in the early 1920s. Knighted in 1953 for his services to aviation, his name will always be associated in aviation history with the Hawker Hurricane of World War II.

Capper, J. E. (1861–1955)
Officer Commanding the Balloon Sections of the British Army in 1903 and pilot of the first British Army airship, *Nulli Secundus*, which flew for the first time on 10 September 1907.

Castoldi, Dr Ing Mario
Famous aircraft designer, whose work is associated with the Italian company Aeronautica Macchi. He is known universally for the superb racing seaplanes which he designed to compete in the Schneider Trophy Contests.

Cavendish, Henry (1731–1810)
British scientist who isolated the gas hydrogen in 1766. The discovery of this lightweight gas, which Cavendish called Phlogiston, or inflammable air, led to the development of practical lighter-than-air craft.

Cayley, Sir George (1773–1857)
British inventor, now regarded universally as the 'Father of Aerial Navigation'. As early as 1799 he engraved on one side of a silver disc – now in

London's Science Museum – a diagram showing the forces of lift, drag and thrust.

Chadwick, Roy (1893–1947)
Famous aircraft designer of the British A. V. Roe Company, renowned for the design of the Avro Lancaster bomber which played a significant role in World War II.

Chanute, Octave (1832–1910)
American railway engineer, who became one of three great pioneer designers of gliders. He began to build hang gliders in 1896.

Charles, Professor J. A. C. (1746–1823)
Designed and built the first hydrogen-filled balloon. This made the first ascent, unmanned, of a hydrogen balloon on 27 August 1783. He was also one of the first men to be carried aloft in such a balloon on 1 December 1783.

Chavez, Georges (1887–1910)
Peruvian pioneer pilot, made the first aeroplane flight over the Alps, in a Blériot monoplane, on 23 September 1910. Success turned to disaster, for Chavez was killed when his aircraft crashed when landing at Domodossola, Italy.

Chichester, Sir Francis (1901–1971)
British aviator, sailor and navigator extraordinary, achieved the first solo flight in a seaplane between New Zealand and Japan in 1931.

Cierva, Juan de la (1886–1936)
Spanish designer of rotary-wing aircraft, whose C–4 *Autogiro* flew successfully for the first time at Getafe, Spain, on 9 January 1923.

Coanda, Henri (1885–1972)
Romanian aviator engineer who, in 1910, built the world's first jet-propelled aeroplane. This was not powered by a turbojet, but by what today would be called a ducted-fan. He subsequently became a significant aircraft designer with the British & Colonial Aeroplane Company (later Bristol).

Cobham, Sir Alan (1894–1973)
Gained early renown for a number of long distance flights, including a 8,047m (5,000 mile) circuit of Europe in 1921, London to Cape Town and return in 1926 and a 37,015m (23,000 mile) flight around Africa in 1927.

Cochrane, Jacqueline
Who, flying a North American F–86 Sabre fighter aircraft on 18 May 1953, became the first woman in the world to pilot an aeroplane at a speed faster than sound.

Cody, Samuel Franklin (1861–1913)
Born an American, made the first officially recognized aeroplane flight in Britain, in the *British Army Aeroplane No. 1*, which he designed and built. This flight, of 424m (1,390ft) was made on 16 October 1908. Cody later became a British citizen.

OPPOSITE PAGE
TOP LEFT: *Douglas Bader (left)*.
TOP RIGHT: *Floyd Bennett (left)*.
CENTRE: *Jean Batten*
BOTTOM LEFT: *Neil Armstrong (left)*.
BOTTOM RIGHT: *Louis Blériot*.
THIS PAGE
ABOVE LEFT: *Dr Werner von Braun (right)*.
ABOVE CENTRE: *Georges Chavez*.
ABOVE RIGHT: *Octave Chanute*.
BELOW LEFT: *Richard E Byrd*.
BELOW RIGHT: *Samuel F Cody*.

Conrad, Max
American pilot who made numerous record long-distance flights in light aircraft, including Casablanca–Los Angeles, non-stop in 58.5 hours. Between 1928 and 1974 he logged 52,929 hours' flying time, a world record.

Cornu, Paul
Pioneer designer of rotary-winged aircraft, achieved the first free flight of a man-carrying helicopter on 13 November 1907. This was in a twin-rotor aircraft of his own design, flown at Lisieux, France.

Costes, Dieudonné
With Joseph le Brix, achieved the first non-stop crossing of the South Atlantic flying the Breguet XIX *Nungesser-Coli* on 14 to 15 October 1927.

Coutelle, Capitaine J.-M.-J.
(1748–1835)
Commander of the French Company of Aérostiers in the Artillery Service who, on 26 June 1794, carried out military reconnaissance from the tethered observation balloon *Entreprenant* at the battle of Fleurus – the first operational use of an aircraft in warfare.

Curtiss, Glenn H. (1878–1930)
American pioneer designer and aircraft builder. He made the first official public flight in America of more than 1km (0·62 miles) on 4 July 1908. His Curtiss Aeroplane and Motor Company was to become famous for the design and construction of naval aircraft.

Dassault, Marcel
French aircraft designer who, under the original name of Marcel Bloch, was responsible for the design of a number of bomber aircraft which equipped the French Air Force during the inter-war period and at the beginning of World War II. During the war his brother Paul, a General in the French Army, adopted the Resistance code-name of d'Assault. After the war, in 1946, both brothers adopted the family name Dassault, and Marcel rebuilt his aircraft company under this name. From this company has come some of the most advanced fighter and bomber aircraft to be produced by the post-war French aircraft industry.

Delagrange, Léon (1873–1910)
French pioneer pilot who accomplished the first aeroplane flight in Italy in May 1908, and in which country he flew the world's first woman aeroplane passenger on 8 July 1908. On 17 September 1908, he flew non-stop for 30min 27sec at Issy-les Moulineaux, then the longest duration recorded in Europe.

Doolittle, James H. (1896–   )
Renowned American pilot, who has contributed much to aviation. He made the first one-day transcontinental crossing of the United States in 1922, won the 1925 Schneider Contest at Baltimore, made the first instrument landing in fog in 1929 and became a national hero when he led a raid on Tokyo in April 1942.

Dornier, Dr Claude (1884–1969)
German pioneer designer and aircraft builder, first employed in the development of large all-metal flying-boats for Count von Zeppelin. This early work culminated in the evolution of some superb flying-boats in the between-wars period,

some of which remained in service until 1970.

Douhet, Giulio (1869–1930)
Italian exponent of air power whose outspoken criticism of Italy's conduct of World War I earned him a court-martial. Subsequently restored to command, his book *Command of the Air* is a classic argument for strategic bombing.

Dunne, J. W. (1875–1949)
British pioneer designer of tailless aircraft. His then-advanced designs were aimed at producing an automatically-stable aircraft. His first really successful aircraft – the Dunne D.5 – flew in 1910.

Durouf, Jules
French balloonist, pilot of the first balloon to ascend from besieged Paris, on 23 September 1870, to initiate the world's first 'airline' and 'airmail' services.

Earhart, Amelia (1898–1937)
American pioneer pilot, the first woman to achieve a solo North Atlantic flight in May 1932. Subsequently she made the first solo flight from Hawaii to California in 1935. She disappeared over the Pacific during a round-the-world flight attempt in 1937.

Eckener, Dr Hugo (1868–1954)
Early associate of Count von Zeppelin. After the death of the latter he headed the Zeppelin Company and was responsible for development and construction of the LZ.126 later *Los Angeles*, *Graf Zeppelin* and *Hindenburg*.

Ellehammer, Jacob C. H.
(1871–1946)
Danish inventor who designed and built an early aeroplane with which he achieved 'hopping' flight in 1906.

It was powered by a 20hp, three-cylinder, radial air-cooled engine of his own design.

Ely, Eugene
American pilot with the Curtiss Aeroplane & Motor Company who achieved the first aeroplane take-off from a ship, the *USS Birmingham*, on 14 November 1910. On 18 January 1911 he piloted the first aeroplane to land on a ship, the *USS Pennsylvania*, anchored in San Francisco Bay.

Esnault-Pelterie, Robert
(1881–1957)
French aircraft designer and founder of the R.E.P. Aircraft Company, his developed R.E.P. 2 *bis* monoplane flying successfully on 15 February 1909. He is better remembered as a pioneer researcher into the possibility of space flight.

Fabre, Henri (b. 1883)
French pioneer of the seaplane, whose Hydravion became the first aircraft to take off from water on 28 March 1910. Fabre was to become well-known as a designer and constructor of seaplane floats.

Farman, Henry (1874–1958)
British-born pilot and aircraft builder who became a naturalized French citizen in 1937, and was the first Briton to establish an internationally ratified world distance record. A distance of 771m (2,530ft), it was achieved in a Voisin aircraft on 26 October 1907.

Flynn, Reverend J. (1880–1951)
Founder of the Australian Flying Doctor Service which was inaugurated on 15 May 1928.

Fokker, Anthony H. G.
(1890–1939)
Aviation pioneer, pilot and founder

of the companies which today bear his name in Germany and the Netherlands. His name is perpetuated in aviation history not only for World War I fighter aircraft, but for a superb family of transport aircraft which have contributed much to civil aviation.

Gagarin, Yuri (1934–1968)
Russian cosmonaut, was the first man to orbit the Earth in spaceflight, in the *Vostok 1* spacecraft, on 12 April 1961.

Garnerin, André Jacques (1769–1823)
A Frenchman, recorded the first successful parachute descent from a vehicle in flight on 22 October 1797. He descended from a balloon which was at a height of about 915m (3,002ft).

Garros, Roland (1888–1918)
Made the first air crossing of the Mediterranean on 13 September 1913 flying a Morane-Saulnier monoplane. This French pilot has another niche in aviation history, recorded in World War I, when he used a crude method of firing a machine-gun through the propeller disc to make head-on attack possible.

Giffard, Henri (1825–1882)
French pioneer airship builder, whose steam-engine powered vessel, in which he flew from Paris to Trappes on 24 September 1852, is regarded as the world's first successful airship.

Glenn, John (1921–   )
American astronaut who, on 20 February 1962, became the first American to orbit the Earth. His three-orbit flight in the Mercury

capsule *Friendship 7* marked the start of US attempts to catch up on Russia's lead in space technology.

Goddard, Robert H. (1882–1945)
American pioneer of rocket propulsion for space flight. His research and development of high energy liquids led to the launch of a liquid-propellant rocket of his own design, the world's first, on 16 March 1926.

Grahame-White, Claude (1879–1959)
Pioneer British pilot and competitor in many of the early aviation races; developer of the aerodrome at Hendon, north London, which became the venue of many important aviation meetings, and is now the site of the Royal Air Force Museum.

Green, Charles (1785–1870)
British balloonist and showman who, by 1854, had made well over 500 ascents. His *Royal Vauxhall* balloon, first flown in August 1836, could carry 12 persons when the envelope

was filled with coal gas, and as many as 28 when pure hydrogen was used for lift.

Guidoni, A.
One of the significant names in Italian aviation history, he pioneered the naval torpedo-carrying aeroplane. His first successful launch of a 340kg (750lb) torpedo was made in February 1914.

Gusmão, Bartolomeu de (1686–1727)
Luso-Brazilian priest who, on 8 August 1709, demonstrated before King John V of Portugal and his court a practical model of a hot-air balloon which rose to a height of about 3·6m (11ft).

Hamel, Gustav (1889–1914)
Pioneer aviator, and pilot of the Blériot monoplane which, on 9 September 1911, carried the first official air mail in Britain, between Hendon and Windsor.

Handley Page, Sir Frederick (1885–1962)
British aviation pioneer, founder of Handley Page Ltd in 1909 and builder of Britain's first strategic bomber aircraft in World War I. His name will be perpetuated in aviation history for the Handley Page slot, an aerodynamic feature contributing to aircraft safety since its demonstration in 1920.

Hargrave, Lawrence (1850–1915)
Australian pioneer of kite design, whose development and perfection of the box-kite in 1893 was an important contribution to the construction of early European aircraft.

Havilland, Sir Geoffrey de (1882–1965)
One of the best-known British aviation pioneers, whose career extended from the very beginning of powered flight to the advent of the jet age. His name is linked in aviation history with the D.H.60 Moth that his company produced in 1925, and which fostered the private flying movement around the world.

Hawker, Harry G. (1889–1921)
Australian pioneer pilot, contender and recipient of a £1,000 consolation prize in the *Daily Mail* Hydro-Aeroplane Trial of August 1913. He was a founder of the H. G. Hawker Engineering Company at Kingston-upon-Thames, Surrey, and his name is perpetuated in today's Hawker Siddeley Aviation group.

Heinkel, Professor Ernst (1888–1958)
German pioneer aircraft designer. Amongst a whole series of superb aircraft, he is likely to be best remembered for the Heinkel He 178, the world's first turbojet-powered aircraft, which flew for the first time on 27 August 1939.

Henson, William Samuel (1805–1888)
Early British disciple of Sir George Cayley, he designed and patented a heavier-than-air craft, the *Aerial Steam Carriage*, in 1843. Although never built in full-size form, it incorporated many advanced ideas.

Hill, G. T. R. (1895–   )
British designer of tailless aircraft

who, like J. W. Dunne, sought to evolve an extremely stable aircraft. Most advanced was the Pterodactyl Mk V, built by the Westland Aircraft Company, which flew in 1932.

Hinkler, H. J. L. ('Bert') (1892–1933)
Australian pilot who made the first solo flight from England to Australia, between 7 and 22 February 1928. Later, between 27 October and 7 December 1931, he made the first solo flight in a light aircraft, a de Havilland Puss Moth, from New York to London.

Hughes, Howard (1905–1976)
American millionaire and movie magnate, in 1935 built an advanced racing aircraft designated H–1, with which, on 13 September 1935, he established a new landplane speed record of 567·026km/h (352·388 mph). He was later to build the Hughes H.2 *Hercules*, a 180-ton giant flying-boat which he flew once only, on 2 November 1947.

Immelmann, Max (1890–1916)
Renowned German pilot of World War I, whose name is always linked with those of Oswald Boelcke and Manfred von Richthofen. This legendary trio developed German fighter tactics. Immelmann died after achieving 15 victories in air combat.

Jatho, Karl (1873–1933)
German pioneer designer and constructor, whose powered aeroplane made a number of short 'hops' in 1903, including one of about 18·30m (60ft) recorded on 18 August 1903.

Johnson, Amy (1903–1941)
British airwoman who became famous by achieving the first female solo flight from England to Australia between 5 to 24 May 1930 flying a de Havilland Gipsy Moth.

Junkers, Professor Hugo (1859–1935)
German aircraft designer and pioneer of all-metal aircraft construction, whose Junkers J.I, the world's first all-metal cantilever monoplane, flew for the first time on 12 December 1915.

OPPOSITE PAGE
TOP: *Leon Delagrange (fifth from right)*.
LEFT ABOVE: *Dieudonné Costes*.
LEFT BELOW: *Glenn Curtiss*.
CENTRE LEFT: *James Doolittle*.
CENTRE RIGHT: *Amelia Earhart*.
RIGHT: *Henry Farman (right)*.
THIS PAGE
TOP: *Yuri Gagarin*.
LEFT ABOVE: *Roland Garros*.
LEFT BELOW: *Rev Dr John Flynn*.
CENTRE LEFT: *John Glenn*.
CENTRE RIGHT: *Max Immelmann*.
RIGHT: *Amy Johnson*.

Kingsford-Smith, Sir Charles
(1899–1935)
Australian pioneer pilot whose famous flights include the first trans-Pacific crossing, between 31 May and 9 June 1928; the first crossing of the Tasman Sea, 10/11 September 1928; and the first aeroplane flight from Australia to the United States between 22 October and 4 November 1934.

Knight, W. J.
Pilot of the North American X-15A-2 rocket-powered research aircraft which, on 3 October 1967, he flew at a speed of 7,297km/h (4,534mph), making the X-15 the fastest aeroplane ever flown.

Krebs, A. C. (1850–)
Associate of Charles Renard, whose electric-motor-powered airship, *La France*, flew for the first time on 9 August 1884.

Langley, Samuel Pierpont
(1834–1906)
American railway surveyor and civil engineer, who demonstrated successful steam-powered model aeroplanes in 1896. A full-size man-carrying aircraft was developed from these in 1903, but two attempts to launch the *Aerodrome*, as it was called, proved unsuccessful.

Latécoère, Pierre (1883–1943)
French aircraft manufacturer and founder of the Lignes Aériennes Latécoère, which he established to forge an air route between France and South America. On 12 May 1930 a Latécoère 28 floatplane *Comte de la Vaulx* first completed the trans-Atlantic route which had been Pierre Latécoère's dream.

Latham, Hubert (1883–1912)
French pioneer pilot, renowned for his two unsuccessful attempts to beat Louis Blériot in achieving the first crossing of the English Channel in a heavier-than-air craft.

Levavasseur, Léon (1863–1922)
French pioneer aviation engineer and designer of the graceful Antoinette monoplanes and Antoinette engines which contributed importantly to the early development of aviation.

Lilienthal, Otto (1848–1896)
German pioneer glider-builder and pilot, one of the most important names in aviation history. Before his death on 10 August 1896 – the result

of a flying accident the previous day – he had made thousands of flights and had recorded meticulously the results of his theoretical and practical research work.

Lindbergh, Charles (1902–1974)
American airmail pilot who, on 21 May 1927, landed at Paris after a 33½-hour flight non-stop from New York. This historic flight was the first solo non-stop flight across the North Atlantic, and brought everlasting fame to Lindbergh.

Link, Edward Albert
American inventor of a ground-based flight trainer which could reproduce the behaviour and response to controls of an aeroplane in flight. His first trainer, sold in 1929, has led to the complex flight simulators used by commercial and military pilots today.

Lippisch, Professor Alexander
(1894–)
German aircraft designer responsible for much research into advanced aerofoils. He designed the DFS 194 which, powered by a 272kg (600lb) thrust Walter rocket, was the first successful liquid-rocket-powered aircraft, flown in 1940 by Heini Dittmar, and he contributed to the development of tailless and delta aircraft.

McCurdy, John A. D.
Canadian engineer who made the first successful controlled flight in a heavier-than-air machine AEA Silver Dart in the British Commonwealth by a British subject. Baddeck, N.S., 23 February 1909.

Manly, Charles M. (1876–1927)
Associate of American Samuel Pierpont Langley, and designer of the remarkably advanced five-cylinder radial air-cooled petrol engine which powered Langley's *Aerodrome*.

Maxim, Hiram Stevens
(1840–1916)
American who, while resident in England, designed and built a giant flying-machine of 31·70m/104ft) wing span. Powered by two 180hp steam-engines of his own design, and launched along a special railway track in 1894, it lifted at a speed of 64km/h (40mph) but broke its restraining guard rails and came to a halt.

Mayo, R. H. (1890–1957)
Technical general manager of British

Imperial Airways, who proposed a piggy-back concept to help achieve a North Atlantic mail service. The resulting Mayo composite, a Short 'C Class' flying boat carrying a specially-built four-engined seaplane, achieved its first separation on 6 February 1938.

Mermoz, Jean (–1936)
Pilot of the French Lignes Aériennes Latécoère and later Cie Générale Aéropostale, renowned for his pioneering flights across the South Atlantic. He disappeared without a trace on 7 December 1936 during his 24th trans-Atlantic flight.

Messerschmitt, Willy
(1898–)
Famous German aircraft designer who as early as 1921 collaborated in the design of a successful glider. It was followed by other gliders and a series of lightplanes before his creation of the Me 108 Taifun in 1934, Messerschmitt's first all-metal aircraft. Then came what must be regarded as his masterpiece, the Me 109 fighter, often claimed as the most famous German aircraft of all time. It was to record distinguished service with the Luftwaffe throughout the war, and remained in service with foreign air arms for almost 20 years.

Mitchell, R. J. (1895–1937)
British aircraft designer of the Supermarine Aviation Works, Southampton, Hants, responsible for the design of the S.4, S.5, S.6, S.6A and S.6B racing seaplanes which gained the Schneider Trophy for Britain. These aircraft had an important influence on Mitchell's Spitfire design.

Mitchell, William E. ('Billy')
(1880–1936)
Controversial exponent of air power, and commander of all US Army fighter squadrons at the Western

THIS PAGE
TOP LEFT : *Sir Charles Kingsford Smith*.
ABOVE CENTRE : *Charles Lindbergh*.
ABOVE : *Hiram Maxim (centre front)*.
LEFT : *Otto Lilienthal*.
OPPOSITE PAGE
TOP LEFT : *Jim Mollison*.
TOP CENTRE : *Hermann Oberth*.
TOP RIGHT : *Umberto Nobile (right)*.
CENTRE LEFT : *Billy Mitchell*.

Front in World War I. Court-martialled in 1926 for his outspoken views, he resigned his commission. In 1946, ten years after his death, he was posthumously awarded the Congressional Medal of Honour.

Mollison, J. A. (1905–1959)
British long-distance pilot, first to make a solo east–west crossing of the North Atlantic, on 18/19 August 1932. He was also the first man to fly solo east–west across the South Atlantic and the first man to cross both North and South Atlantic.

Montgolfier, Etienne (1745–1799) and **Joseph** (1740–1810)
French makers of the world's first hot-air balloon capable of lifting a man, and whose balloon, launched on 21 November 1783, was the first to carry men in free flight.

Mozhaiski, Alexander F. (1825–1890)
Russian designer of an odd-looking monoplane which, powered by two steam-engines, achieved a short 'hop' of 20 to 30m (66 to 98ft) in 1884 after take-off down an inclined ramp.

Nesterov, Lieutenant
Pilot of the Imperial Russian Army who, on 27 August 1913, was the first pilot in the world to execute the manoeuvre known as a loop, flying a Nieuport Type IV monoplane.

Nobile, Umberto (1885–   )
Italian designer of the semi-rigid airship *Norge* in which he, together with Lincoln Ellsworth and Roald Amundsen, flew over the North Pole on 12 May 1926. Nobile was later to build the *Italia*, which was lost after flying over the Pole on 24 May 1928.

Oberth, Hermann (1894–   )
Austrian pioneer of the theory of rocket power and the problems of interplanetary navigation. His thesis *The Way to Space Travel* is regarded as a basic classic of the theory of astronautics.

Ohain, Pabst von (1911–   )
German pioneer of jet propulsion who, financed by Ernst Heinkel, demonstrated his first turbojet engine of about 250kg (551lb) thrust in September 1937. His experiments were in no way influenced by the work of Frank Whittle in Britain.

Opel, Fritz von (1899–1971)
German tycoon of the motor industry, who financed development of several rocket-powered aircraft. Most successful was the Opek-Sander-Hatry Rak. 1, first flown by von Opel on 30 September 1929.

Parke, Wilfred
British naval pilot, was the first to demonstrate the method of recovery from a spin on 25 August 1912. Prior to that time spinning aircraft had almost invariably crashed.

Paulhan, Louis (1883–1963)
French pioneer pilot and winner of the *Daily Mail* £10,000 prize for the first flight from London to Manchester. Paulhan, flying a Farman biplane, became involved in a race with Claude Grahame-White, who was equally anxious to win the prize, but Paulhan was the victor, landing at Didsbury at 05·32am on 28 April 1910.

Pégoud, Adolphe (1889–1915)
The first pilot in the world to demonstrate an aircraft in sustained inverted flight, at Buc, France, on 21 September 1913.

Pénaud, Alphonse (1856–1880)
French inventor who built and flew a successful rubber-driven model aeroplane in 1871. He was the first to establish some basic aerodynamics, including the suggested use of control surfaces on wings and tail.

Phillips, Horatio (1845–1924)
Little-known British designer who patented, in 1884, a wing section which contributed to the design of modern aerofoil sections. His multiplane of 1907 had some 200 narrow-chord wings of venetian-blind form and was reported to have flown for a short distance, but this claim is unsubstantiated.

Pilcher, Percy (1866–1899)
British pioneer glider builder and pilot, inspired and given practical help by the German Otto Lilienthal. Pilcher, like his mentor, died when one of his gliders crashed, on 2 October 1899, the first Englishman to lose his life in an heavier-than-air craft.

Platz, Reinhold
German aircraft designer, who was responsible for the basic design of the Dr I triplane and D VII biplane fighter aircraft built during World War I by the German Fokker aircraft factory.

Porte, John C.
A member of the British Royal Naval Air Service, who developed from the Curtiss *America* flying boat – which he had assisted to design – a superb series of RNAS flying boats during World War I, known as Felixstowe 'boats.

Post, Wiley (1899–1935)
Renowned American long-distance pilot who, flying the Lockheed Vega monoplane, *Winnie Mae*, made the first solo round-the-world flight between 15 and 22 July 1933.

Prévost, Maurice
French pioneer pilot and winner of the first Schneider Trophy Contest, held at Monaco on 16 April 1913. His low average speed of 73·63km/h (45·75mph) was due to his having to complete an extra lap to comply with the rules of the contest.

Reitsch, Hanna
Famous German airwoman, and the first woman in the world to pilot a helicopter. She demonstrated the Focke-Achgelis Fw 61 twin-rotor helicopter in the Deutschland-Halle in Berlin in 1938.

Renard, Charles (1847–1905)
French airship pioneer who, with the assistance of A. C. Krebs, designed and built the first practical airship. Powered by an electric motor, it reached a speed of 19km/h (12mph) when first flown on 9 August 1884.

Roe, Sir Alliott Verdon (1877–1958)
British pioneer aircraft designer, constructor and pilot, and founder of the famous aircraft Company which bore his name. On 13 July 1909 he flew his Roe I triplane to become the first Briton to fly an all-British aeroplane.

Rolls, The Hon. Charles S. (1877–1910)
Associate of Henry Royce in the founding of Rolls-Royce Limited, accomplished the first double crossing of the English Channel in a French-built Wright biplane on 2 June 1910. He was killed on 12 July 1910 when his aircraft crashed at Bournemouth.

Royce, Sir Henry (1863–1933)
Co-founder with C. S. Rolls of Rolls-Royce Limited, he authorized development of the Buzzard in-line engine as a power plant for the British Schneider Trophy contender of 1929. This led to the evolution of the Rolls-Royce Merlin engine.

Rozier, Francois Pilâtre de (1754–1785)
First man in the world to be carried aloft in a tethered Montgolfier balloon on 15 October 1783; first to make a free flight, in company with Marquis d'Arlandes, on 21 November 1783; and the first to die in a ballooning accident on 15 June 1785.

Santos-Dumont, Alberto
(1873–1932)
Brazilian aviation pioneer resident in Paris, was first to fly round the Eiffel Tower in his No. 6 dirigible, and the first to achieve a manned, powered and sustained aeroplane flight in Europe in his *14 bis* tail-first biplane on 12 November 1906.

Schneider, Jacques (1879–1928)
Son of a French armaments manufacturer, in 1912 he offered a trophy for international competition to speed the development of waterborne aircraft. The resulting Schneider Trophy Contests had significant influence on the design of high-speed aircraft.

Scott, Charles W. A.
(1903–)
Pilot of the de Havilland D.H.88 Comet who, together with Tom Campbell Black, won the 1934 Mac-Robertson England–Australia air race. Charles Scott had, in 1931, made two record-breaking solo flights, England to Australia and Australia to England, in a de Havilland Gipsy Moth.

Scott, Sheila
British record-breaking woman pilot of the post World War II years. Between 18 May and 20 June 1966 she completed a solo round-the-world flight in a record time – the longest solo flight by any pilot of any nationality, and the first round-the-world flight by a British pilot.

Seguin, Laurent and Louis
French designers of the Gnome rotary engine which, from 1908, was the most important of early aircraft engines. The performance of the Gnome rotaries was surpassed by

new designs evolved during World War I.

Shepard, Alan B. (1923–)
First American to travel in space, was launched in a sub-orbital trajectory in the Mercury capsule *Freedom 7* on 5 May 1961. In his 486km (302 mile) flight he attained a height of 185km (115 miles).

Short, Eustace (1875–1932),
Horace (1872–1917) **and**
Oswald (1883–1970)
British pioneers who founded the nation's first aircraft factory. By early 1909 they were building their first six Short-Wright biplanes under licence. The company exists to this day, under the title of Short Brothers & Harland, and is still designing and building aeroplanes.

Sikorsky, Igor A. (1881–1972)
Russian pioneer aircraft designer and builder, creator of the world's first four-engined aircraft, the *Bolshoi*, which flew on 13 May 1913. Later becoming a naturalized American citizen, he concentrated on the development of rotary-winged aircraft, his VS–300, which was first flown on 14 September 1939, being developed into what is now regarded as the world's first practical single-rotor helicopter.

Smith, Sir Keith (1890–1955) **and**
Sir Ross (1892–1922)
Australian brothers who, between 12 November and 10 December 1919, achieved the first flight from England to Australia in a Vickers Vimy bomber. The brothers won a prize of £10,000 from the Australian Government, and both were knighted.

Smith-Barry, R. R.
Founder of the School of Special Flying at Gosport, Hampshire, in July 1917, marking the beginning of the

superb flying training which became a feature of the Central Flying School of the Royal Air Force.

Sohn, Clem (d. 1937)
American 'bird-man' who devised webbed 'wing' and 'tail' which enabled him to manoeuvre in semi-gliding 'flight' after jumping from an aircraft, landing finally by parachute. He was killed on 25 April 1937 when his parachute failed to open fully.

Sopwith, Sir Thomas
(1888–)
British pioneer pilot and founder of the Sopwith Aviation Company at Kingston-upon-Thames, Surrey; later a director and subsequently Chairman of the Hawker Siddeley Group.

Sperry, Lawrence B. (1892–1923)
American designer of gyro-stabilizing mechanisms to control an aircraft in flight. His earliest device was fitted to a Curtiss flying boat in 1912.

Stringfellow, John (1799–1883)
British associate of W. S. Henson in the construction of the 6.10m (20ft) span, Aerial Steam Carriage. Stringfellow was responsible in particular for its steam-engine power plant.

Sukhoi, Pavel Osipovich
(1895–)
Contemporary of Andrei Tupolev at the TsAGI (Central Aero and Hydrodynamic Institute), he has been concerned primarily with the design of fighter aircraft. The greatest success of his design bureau has come in the years since 1953, with the development of a family of jet fighters, the most interesting feature of which is the steady and economic improvement of the type, extending from the Su–7 of 1956 to the latest Su–19

twin-engined variable-geometry fighter-bomber which has the NATO reporting name *Fencer*.

Tank, Kurt
Contemporary with Germany's Willy Messerschmitt, Kurt Tank achieved similar fame as an aircraft designer with the Focke-Wulf company. His first significant design was the Fw 56 Stösser trainer of 1933, but he is remembered especially for the Fw 190, regarded as the most advanced fighter aircraft in the world when it entered active service in 1941. It proved, beyond dispute, the efficiency of the radial-engined

fighter. Also famous, in a quite differing military role, was the Fw 200 Condor adopted for maritime patrol.

Temple, Félix du (1823–1890)
French naval officer who designed and built a powered monoplane aircraft which, piloted by an unknown young sailor in 1894, gained the distinction of being the first manned aircraft to achieve a brief 'hop' after launch down a ramp.

Tereshkova, Valentina (b. 1937)
Russian cosmonaut, the first woman to travel in space, in *Vostok 6*, 16 to 18 June 1963, completing 48 orbits of the Earth before landing.

Thomas, George Holt
(1869–1929)
British founder of Aircraft Transport and Travel Ltd., first British airline to be registered (on 5 October 1916). On 25 August 1919 this company inaugurated the world's first daily scheduled international commercial airline service.

Trenchard, Hugh (1873–1956)
British soldier turned aviator, regarded as the 'Father of the Royal Air Force', who fought strenuously to keep it an independent service. He was to become Lord Trenchard, Marshal of the Royal Air Force.

Trippe, Juan T. (1899–)
Airline pioneer and founder of Pan American World Airways System in 1927. Before then Trippe had organized Long Island Airways with seven World War I aeroplanes. For many years Pan American dominated American civil aviation.

Tsiolkovsky, Konstantin (1857–1935)
Russia's 'father of astronautics' who, as early as 1898, suggested the use of liquid propellants to power space rockets. He first discussed the principle of reaction, proved theoretically that a rocket would work in a vacuum, and made the first serious calculations relating to interplanetary travel.

Tupolev, Andrei Nikolaevich (1888–1972)
Most famous internationally of all Soviet aircraft designers, he helped to found the TsAGI (Central Aero and Hydrodynamic Institute) in 1918, becoming the head of its aircraft design department in 1920. His design and development of the Tu–104 jet-powered airliner earned him the Lenin Prize and the Gold Medal of the FAI, and in 1970 he was made an Honorary Fellow of the Royal Aeronautical Society. Apart from the creation of some important bomber and civil transport aircraft, the Tupolev design bureau's Tu–144 was the world's first supersonic airliner to fly.

Turnbull, W. R.
Canadian engineer who tested aerofoils in a wind tunnel he built in 1902. He may have been the first to recommend dihedral to increase stability. He developed the first controllable pitch propeller between 1916 and 1927.

launch, Gabriel recorded the first flight from water by a manned aircraft on 6 June 1905.

Walden, Henry W.
Designer and builder of the first successful monoplane aircraft to fly in America. This was the Walden III which, powered by a 22hp Anzani engine, made its first flight on 9 December 1909.

Wallis, Sir Barnes N. (b. 1887)
British aviation engineer and designer, designer of the rigid airship R.100, originator of geodetic construction, inventor of the skip bomb which breached the German Moehne, Eder and Sorpe dams, and of the earthquake bombs which helped to bring Allied victory in Europe. Post World War II he developed the variable-geometry wing.

Twiss, L. P. (1921–)
Pilot of the Fairey Delta 2 research aircraft which, on 10 March 1956, set the first world speed record established at over 1,609km/h (1,000mph). His average speed for the two runs over the selected course was 1,822km/h (1,132mph).

Vinci, Leonardo da (1452–1579)
Italian genius born in 1452 who is renowned in aviation history for drawings which show his early designs for a rotary-wing aircraft and a parachute. He believed from his observations of bird flight that man would be able to achieve flight by his own muscle power.

Voisin, Charles (1882–1912) **and Gabriel** (1886–)
French pioneer aircraft builders. Flying a boxkite glider towed by a

Watt, Sir Robert Watson (1892–1973)
Leader of the British research team which, in the three years prior to the outbreak of World War II, designed and created a radar system for the detection and location of enemy aircraft.

Wenham, F. H. (1824–1908
His classic paper *Aerial Locomotion* was read to the Aeronautical Society in 1866. One of the leading theorists of his day, he also built the world's first wind-tunnel in conjunction with John Browning.

Whittle, Sir Frank (1907–)
British designer of the aircraft gas turbine engine, who ran the first aircraft turbojet engine in the world on 12 April 1937. It later powered the Gloster Meteor jet fighter.

Willows, E. T. (–1926)
British designer of some small, but successful, semi-rigid airships, the first of which flew in 1905. He patented the design of swivelling propellers to simplify control of an airship in flight.

Wright, Orville (1871–1948) **and Wilbur** (1867–1912)
The proud names of the two American brothers renowned in aviation history for designing, building and flying the first man-carrying aeroplane in the world to achieve powered, controlled and sustained flight, on 17 December 1903.

OPPOSITE PAGE
TOP LEFT: *Alberto Santos-Dumont.*
TOP RIGHT: *John Stringfellow.*
BOTTOM LEFT: *Sheila Scott.*
CENTRE: *Sir Ross and Sir Keith Smith.*
BOTTOM RIGHT: *Valentina Tereshkova.*
THIS PAGE
TOP: *The French brothers Charles and Gabriel Voisin.*

Yakovlev, Alexander (b. 1906)
One of the younger generation of Soviet aircraft designers, he completed his first military design in 1939. This had the designation Ya–22, but became better known as the Yak–4. His first important military aircraft was the Yak–1 fighter, seen at the October Day flypast in 1940, and of which it is believed that about 9,000 were built. Since those days the Yakovlev design bureau has been responsible for aircraft ranging from basic trainers, the important Yak–40 civil transport, and military aircraft which includes the VTOL combat aircraft (*Forger*) first seen aboard the Soviet carrier/cruiser *Kiev* in the summer of 1976.

Yeager, Charles (1923–)
United States Air Force pilot who, on 14 October 1947, piloted the Bell XS–1 rocket-powered research aircraft at a speed of 1,078km/h (670mph) (an equivalent of Mach 1·015) at a height of 12,802m (42,000ft). His was the first supersonic flight in history.

Zeppelin, Ferdinand von (1838–1917)
Founder of the German Zeppelin Company at Friedrichshafen on Lake Constance. His first rigid airship, the LZ.I, flew for the first time on 2 July 1900.

FAR LEFT: *Andrei Tupolev.*
LEFT: *Sir Barnes Wallis.*
ABOVE LEFT: *Wilbur Wright.*
ABOVE RIGHT: *Count Ferdinand von Zeppelin.*
BELOW: *A group of aviation pioneers photographed in 1909. The Short brothers Oswald, Horace and Eustace, are second, third and fourth from the left.*

Chronology

1709-1914

1709
8 August
Bartolomeu de Gusmão demonstrated the world's first model hot-air balloon.

1783
25 April
First flight of a Montgolfier hot-air balloon capable of lifting a man.
4 June
First public demonstration by the Montgolfiers of a small hot-air balloon.
19 September
A Montgolfier balloon carried a sheep, a duck and a cockerel into the air, the first animals to fly.
15 October
First man carried in tethered flight in a Montgolfier hot-air balloon.
21 November
First man carried in free flight in a Montgolfier hot-air balloon.

1 December
First men carried in free flight in a hydrogen balloon.

1784
4 June
First woman carried in free flight in a Montgolfier hot-air balloon.

1785
7 January
First crossing of the English Channel by balloon.

1793
9 January
First free flight of a manned hydrogen balloon in America.

1794
26 June
Observation balloon used at battle of Fleurus, the first operational use of an aircraft in war.

1797
22 October
First successful parachute descent from a balloon made by Frenchman A. J. Garnerin.

1849
22 August
First air raid by balloons: the Austrians launched pilotless balloons against Venice, armed with time-fuse-controlled bombs.

1852
24 September
First flight of the world's first powered and manned airship.

1861
1 October
American Army's Balloon Corps was formed.

1866
12 January
Foundation of the Aeronautical Society of Great Britain (later the Royal Aeronautical Society).

1870
23 September
First balloon ascent from besieged Paris at the height of the Franco-Prussian War.

1884
9 August
The dirigible *La France* made the world's first flight of a powered, manned and controlled airship.

1890
9 October
Clément Ader's bat-winged *Éole* monoplane made a brief hop.

1896
10 August
Death of Otto Lilienthal as the result of a gliding accident.

1898
In this year the Aero Club de France was founded.

1899
2 October
Death of Percy Pilcher as the result of a gliding accident.

1900
2 July
Count von Zeppelin's first rigid airship made its first flight.

1901
19 October
Alberto Santos-Dumont flew his No. 6 dirigible round the Eiffel Tower, Paris.
29 October
Foundation of the British Aero Club (later Royal).

1903
17 December
Wright brothers achieve world's first powered, controlled and sustained flight by a man-carrying aeroplane.

1905
12 October
Foundation of the *Fédération Aeronautique Internationale* (FAI).

THIS PAGE
TOP LEFT: *The siege of Fleurus, 1794.*
TOP RIGHT: *Santos-Dumont's airship.*
ABOVE FAR LEFT: *The first Montgolfière.*
ABOVE LEFT: *Garnerin and parachute.*
FACING PAGE
TOP LEFT: Nulli Secundus II.
TOP RIGHT: *Chavez over the Alps, 1910.*
CENTRE: *S. F. Cody in his aircraft, 1909.*
BELOW: *Cody and one of his designs.*

2 August
The US Army bought its first aeroplane from the Wright brothers.
22 August
World's first international aviation meeting held at Reims, France.
30 October
First official aeroplane flight in Romania made by Louis Blériot flying a Blériot monoplane.
9 December
First official aeroplane flight in Australia. Colin Defries flew an imported Wright biplane over the Victoria Park Racecourse at Sydney.

1906
12 November
Alberto Santos-Dumont makes first powered and sustained flight by a man-carrying aeroplane in Europe.

1907
10 September
First flight of *Nulli Secundus*, first British army airship.
13 November
Paul Cornu's helicopter made world's first flight by a manned rotary-wing aircraft.

1908
16 October
First officially recognized aeroplane flight in Britain made by S. F. Cody.

1909
14 May
First flight of over 1·6km (1 mile) in Britain recorded by S. F. Cody.
25 July
First aeroplane flight across the English Channel made by Louis Blériot in his Type XI monoplane.
25 July
First official aeroplane flight in Russia, made by Van den Schkrouff flying a Voisin biplane at Odessa.
29 July
First official aeroplane flight in Sweden, made by French pilot Legagneux flying a Voisin biplane.

1910
8 March
Frenchwoman Mme la Baronne de Laroche became the first certificated woman pilot in the world.
10 March
First night flights in an aeroplane made by Frenchman Emil Aubrun.
28 March
First successful powered seaplane, built and flown by Henri Fabre, takes off from water.
2 June
First 'there and back' double crossing of the English Channel by an aeroplane, flown by the Hon C. S. Rolls.
27 August
First transmission of radio messages between an aeroplane and a ground station made by James McCurdy in America.
11 September
First crossing of the Irish Sea, from Wales to Ireland (Eire) made by Robert Loraine in a Farman biplane.
23 September
Georges Chavez made the first aeroplane flight over the Alps in a Blériot monoplane.
14 November
A Curtiss biplane flown by American pilot Eugene Ely was the first aircraft to take off from a ship.

1911
18 January
Eugene Ely, flying a Curtiss biplane, recorded the first landing of an aeroplane on a ship.
18 February
World's first official air mail flight at Allahabad, India, flown by Frenchman Henri Pequet.
12 April
Pierre Prier, flying a Blériot monoplane, made the first non-stop flight from London to Paris.
18 June
The Circuit of Europe, the first real international air race, started from Paris.
1 July
First flight of the US Navy's first aeroplane, a Curtiss A–1 Hydroaeroplane.
22 July
First 'Round Britain' air race started from Brooklands, Surrey.

1911
17 September–5 November
First coast-to-coast flight across the United States made by Calbraith P. Rodgers in a Wright biplane.
19 September
First official air mail flight in Great Britain, made by Gustav Hamel in a Blériot monoplane, which carried air mail between Hendon and Windsor.
23 September
First official air mail flight in the United States, made by Earl L. Ovington flying a Blériot monoplane.

22 October
First use of an aeroplane in war, Italian Capitano Piazza making a reconnaissance of Turkish positions in his Blériot monoplane.

1912
13 April
The British Royal Flying Corps was constituted by Royal Warrant.
12 November
A Curtiss A–1 Hydroaeroplane, flown by Lt Ellyson, was launched by a compressed-air catapult.

1913
16 April
First Schneider Trophy Contest was won at Monaco by Maurice Prevost.
13 May
First flight of a four-engine aeroplane, the *Bolshoi* biplane designed by Igor Sikorsky, at St Petersburg, Russia.
23 September
First flight across the Mediterranean Sea made by Roland Garros in a Morane-Saulnier monoplane.

1914
1 January
Inaugural date of the world's first scheduled service by an aeroplane, the Benoist Company's St Petersburg to Tampa service in Florida, USA.
1 August
Beginning of World War I.
30 August
Bombs were dropped on Paris, the first to be dropped from an aeroplane on a capital city.

1915-1933

1915
19 January
First air raid on Britain by Zeppelin airships.
3 March
NACA, National Advisory Committee for Aeronautics, predecessor of NASA, established in America.
31 May
Zeppelin LZ.38, an airship of the German Army, made the first Zeppelin attack on London.
12 December
The Junkers J.1, the world's first all-metal cantilever monoplane, flew for the first time.

1916
15 March
First use of US Army aircraft in military operations, in support of a punitive expedition into Mexico.
31 May
A British naval seaplane spotted for the British fleet at the Battle of Jutland, the first use of an aeroplane in a major fleet battle.
12 September
The Hewitt-Sperry biplane, in effect the world's first radio-guided flying-bomb, was tested in America.
5 October
First British airline company, Aircraft Transport and Travel Ltd, registered by George Holt Thomas.

1917
20 May
First German submarine (U–36) sunk as the direct result of action by an aircraft.
2 August
A Sopwith Pup, flown by Sqdn Cdr E. H. Dunning, made the first landing of an aeroplane on a ship under way.

1918
11 March
The first regular and scheduled international air mail service in the world began, between Vienna and Kiev.
1 April
British Royal Air Force formed.
13 April
First flight across the Andes, from Argentina to Chile, made by Lt Luis C. Candelaria.
24 June
First official air mail flight in Canada, from Montreal to Toronto, by a Curtiss JN–4, flown by Capt B. A. Peck, RAF.
12 August
First regular air mail service inaugurated in America, with a New York to Washington route.

1919
3 March
First American international air mail service established between Seattle and Victoria, British Columbia.
8–31 May
First crossing of the North Atlantic by air achieved by Lt Cdr A. C. Read of the US Navy, flying a Navy/Curtiss NC–4 flying-boat.
14–15 June
First non-stop crossing of the North Atlantic by air, achieved by Capt John Alcock and Lt Arthur Whitten Brown in a Vickers Vimy bomber.
2–6 July
First crossing of the North Atlantic by an airship, the British R.34 made a return flight between 9–13 July.
7 August
First flight across the Canadian Rocky Mountains, from Vancouver to Calgary, made by Capt E. C. Hoy.
25 August
World's first scheduled daily international commercial airline service began, Aircraft Transport and Travel's London to Paris service.
1 November
America's first scheduled international commercial air service began, between Key West, Florida, and Havana, Cuba, by Aeromarine West Indies Airways.
12 November–10 December
First flight from England to Australia completed by Australian brothers Keith and Ross Smith.

1920
4 February–20 March
First flight from England to South Africa made by Lt-Col P. van Ryneveld and Sqdn Ldr C. Q. Brand, using three aircraft.
7–17 October
First trans-Canada flight, from Halifax, N.S., to Vancouver, B.C., by aircraft and airmen of the Canadian Air Force.
16 November
QANTAS (Queensland and Northern Territory Aerial Service), Australia's famous international airline, was first registered.

1921
22 February
Inaugural flight of America's first coast-to-coast air mail service, between San Francisco and New York.
5 December
Australia's first regular scheduled air services inaugurated by West Australian Airways.

1922
4 September
First coast-to-coast crossing of the US in one day achieved by Lt J. H. Doolittle flying a de Havilland D.H.4B.
2 November
First scheduled service operated by Australia's QANTAS, between Charleville and Cloncurry.

1923
9 January
Spaniard Juan de la Cierva's first successful rotating-wing aircraft, the C–4 *Autogiro*, made its first flight.
2–3 May
First non-stop air crossing of the US accomplished by Lts O. G. Kelly and J. A. Macready flying a Fokker T–2 monoplane.

US Army Air Service, made the first successful round-the-world flight.
1 July
Inauguration of America's first regular transcontinental air mail service.

1926
16 March
American R. H. Goddard launched the world's first liquid-propellant rocket.
9 May
First flight of an aeroplane over the North Pole, the Fokker F.VIIA/3m *Josephine Ford* piloted by Floyd Bennett.

27 June
First successful in-flight refuelling of an aeroplane, made during the setting of a world endurance record by the US Army Air Service.
4 September
The *Shenandoah*, America's first helium-filled rigid airship, made its first flight.

1924
1 April
Establishment of Imperial Airways, Britain's first national airline.
6 April–28 September
Two out of four Douglas DWC floatplanes, flown by pilots of the

28–29 November
First aeroplane flight over the South Pole, made in a Ford Trimotor, the *Floyd Bennett*, piloted by Bernt Balchen.

1930
5–14 May
The first solo flight from England to Australia was made by a woman pilot, England's renowned Amy Johnson flying a de Havilland Gipsy Moth.

15 May
An aircraft of Boeing Air Transport carried the first airline stewardess, Ellen Church, on a commercial flight.

1931
13 March
First successful firing of a solid-fuel research rocket in Europe, by Karl Poggensee near Berlin.

13 September
Schneider Trophy won outright for Britain, by a Supermarine S.6B seaplane flown by Flt-Lt J. N. Boothman.

3–5 October
First non-stop flight from Japan to America made by Clyde Pangborn and Hugh Herndon in a Bellanca aircraft.

1932
20–21 May

1927
20–21 May
First non-stop solo crossing of the North Atlantic, from New York to Paris, achieved by Charles Lindbergh in the Ryan monoplane *Spirit of St Louis*.

28–29 June
First non-stop flight between America and Hawaii, made by Lts A. F. Hegenberger and L. J. Maitland in the Fokker C–2 monoplane *Bird of Paradise*.

14–15 October
First non-stop aeroplane crossing of the South Atlantic, from Saint-Louis, Senegal, to Port Natal, Brazil, made by Capt D. Costes and Lt-Cdr J. Le Brix in the Breguet XIX *Nungesser-Coli*.

1928
7–22 February
Sqdn Ldr H. J. L. Hinkler made the first solo flight from England to Australia.

15 May
Inauguration date of the Australian Flying Doctor Service.

31 May–9 June
First flight across the Pacific Ocean, from San Francisco to Brisbane, made by Capt C. Kingsford Smith and C. T. P. Ulm, in the Fokker F.VIIB/3m *Southern Cross*.

11 June
First flight of the world's first rocket-powered aircraft in Germany.

8 October
The first cinema film was projected in an aircraft in flight.

1929
30 March
First commercial air route between London and Karachi, India, inaugurated by Imperial Airways.

24–26 April
First non-stop flight from England to India, made by Sqdn Ldr A. G. Jones Williams and Flt-Lt N. H. Jenkins in a Fairey Long-range Monoplane.

8–29 August
First airship flight around the world, made by the German *Graf Zeppelin* commanded by the famous Dr Hugo Eckener.

FACING PAGE
TOP : *Airship R.34 at its moorings, 1919.*
CENTRE : *First in-flight refuelling.*
BELOW LEFT : *First American air mail service.*
BELOW RIGHT : *The first round-the-world flight.*
THIS PAGE
TOP : *De Havilland US mail carrier.*
ABOVE CENTRE : *Wiley Post and his Lockheed Vega*, Winnie Mae, *1933.*
ABOVE : *The* Graf Zeppelin *at Lakehurst, New Jersey, in 1929.*
LEFT : *The Australian Flying Doctor Service in action.*
BELOW : *The Russian Polikarpov I–16.*

Amelia Earhart achieved the first solo crossing of the North Atlantic by a woman.

1933
6–8 February
First non-stop flight from England to South Africa, made by Sqdn Ldr O. R. Gayford and Flt-Lt G. E. Nicholetts flying a Fairey Long-range Monoplane.

3 April
First aeroplane flights over Mount Everest, a Westland PV–3 flown by the Marquess of Clydesdale and a Westland Wallace flown by Flt-Lt D. F. McIntyre.

15–22 July
American pilot Wiley Post, flying the Lockheed Vega *Winnie Mae*, made the first solo round-the-world flight.

31 December
First flight of Russia's Polikarpov I–16, first monoplane fighter with enclosed cockpit and retractable landing gear to enter squadron service.

1934-1977

1934
8-9 August
First non-stop flight from Canada to Britain by J. R. Ayling and L. G. Reid, from Wasaga Beach, Ont., to Heston.
20 October
Start of the MacRobertson Air Race from England to Australia.
22 October-4 November
First flight from Australia to the United States.
8 December
Inauguration of the first regular weekly air mail service between England and Australia.

1935
11-12 January
First solo flight by a woman from Honolulu, Hawaii, to America.
13 April
Inauguration of the first through passenger service by air from England to Australia.
6 November
First flight of the Hawker Hurricane, Britain's first monoplane fighter with enclosed cockpit, retractable landing gear and armament of eight machine-guns.
22 November
First scheduled air mail flight across the Pacific Ocean, San Francisco to Manila, Philippines.

1936
March
First Spitfire flight.
26 June
The Focke-Wulf Fw 61 twin-rotor helicopter, the first entirely successful powered rotary-wing aircraft in the world, made its first flight.

1937
12 April
Frank Whittle in Britain successfully ran the world's first aircraft gas turbine engine.
6 May
The German airship *Hindenburg* destroyed by fire in America.

1938
26 June
The first through flying-boat service from England to Australia was operated by Short C Class 'boats of Imperial Airways.
20-21 July
First commercial aeroplane flight across the North Atlantic, flown by the *Mercury* upper component of the Short-Mayo composite.

1939
28 June
Inauguration of Pan American's weekly New York to Southampton service, flown with Boeing Model 314 flying boats.
5 August
Imperial Airways began an experimental Southampton to Montreal and New York mail service with Short C Class flying boats, which were refuelled in flight.
27 August
The German Heinkel He 178, the world's first aircraft to fly solely on the power of a gas turbine engine, made its first flight.
2 September
Beginning of World War II.

1941
5 April
First flight of the Heinkel He 280, the world's first aircraft designed specifically as a turbojet-powered fighter.

15 May
The first British aircraft powered by a turbojet, the Gloster Whittle E.28/39, flew for the first time at Cranwell, Lincolnshire.
20 May
The Luftwaffe's largest airborne assault of the war was launched against the island of Crete.
2 October
The German Messerschmitt Me 163, the world's first rocket-powered combat aircraft, was flown at a speed of 1,004km/h (624mph) during early tests.

1942
7-9 May
The Battle of the Coral Sea, the first naval battle in history which was fought entirely by carrier-based aircraft.
3 October
First successful launching of a German V-2 (A-4) ballistic rocket.

1943
9 September
The Italian battleship *Roma* was hit and sunk by a German Ruhrstahl/Kramer X-1 radio-guided armour-piercing bomb.

1944
12 July
Britain's first jet fighter, the Gloster Meteor Mk.1, began to enter service with the Royal Air Force.
3 October
Germany's first jet fighter, the Messerschmitt Me 262, began to enter operational service.

1945
14 March
First operational use of the British *Grand Slam* bomb, weighing 9,980kg (22,000lb).
6 August
First military use of an atomic bomb, when a nuclear device was exploded over the Japanese city of Hiroshima.
3 December
A de Havilland Vampire I, used for deck-landing trials aboard HMS *Ocean*, was the first jet fighter to operate from the deck of an aircraft carrier.

1946
24 July
First manned experimental use of an ejection seat: the 'guinea pig', Bernard Lynch, ejected at 515km/h (320mph).

1947
14 October
The Bell XS-1 rocket-powered research aircraft became the first aircraft in the world to exceed the speed of sound, piloted by Charles Yeager, USAF.

1948
26 June
Beginning of the Berlin Airlift.

1950
25 June
Beginning of the Korean War.
29 July
A Vickers Viscount made the world's first scheduled passenger service to be flown by a turboprop-powered airliner.

1951
21 February
A British English Electric Canberra bomber achieved the first non-stop unrefuelled crossing of the North Atlantic by a jet-powered aircraft.

1952
2 May
The world's first regular passenger service flown by a turbojet-powered airliner, the de Havilland Comet 1.

1953
18 May
American airwoman Jacqueline Cochrane, flying a North American

F-86 Sabre, became the first woman in the world to fly at supersonic speed.

1954
15 July
First flight of America's first turbojet-powered commercial aircraft, the Boeing 707.

1956
21 May
The world's first airborne hydrogen bomb was dropped on Bikini Atoll in the Pacific Ocean.

1957
4 October
First man-made satellite, *Sputnik 1*, launched into Earth orbit by Russia.
19 December
First transatlantic passenger service flown by a turboprop-powered airliner.

1958
4 October
First transatlantic passenger service flown by turbojet-powered airliner, the de Havilland Comet 4.

1961
12 April
Russian spacecraft *Vostok 1* launched into Earth orbit carrying Russian cosmonaut Yuri Gagarin, the first man to travel in space.

1963
16 June
Russian cosmonaut Valentina Tereshkova, launched into Earth orbit in *Vostok 6*, became the first woman to travel in space.

1966
3 February
Russia's *Luna 9* spacecraft soft-landed on the Moon's surface and transmitted the first pictures of the lunar scene.
20 June
British airwoman Sheila Scott landed at Heathrow after setting a new woman's record of 33 days 3 mins for a round-the-world flight.

1967
3 October
North American X–15A–2 rocket-powered research aircraft was flown at a speed of 7,279km/h (4,534mph) by W. J. Knight.

1968
31 December
Russia's Tupolev Tu–144 prototype made its first flight, the first super-sonic commercial transport aircraft to fly.

1969
9 February
First flight of the world's first wide-body turbojet-powered airliner, the Boeing Model 747.
2 March
The 001 prototype of the Anglo–French Concorde supersonic transport aircraft made its first flight at Toulouse, France.
1 April
The Hawker Siddeley Harrier, the world's first V/STOL close support aircraft, first entered squadron service.

FACING PAGE
TOP : *The Messerschmitt Me–262*.
ABOVE CENTRE : *The E28/29*.
CENTRE LEFT : *Hindenburg*.
CENTRE RIGHT : *Bell X–1 under B–29*.
BOTTOM : *Mercury part of Short-Mayo*.
THIS PAGE
TOP : *The Hawker Kestrel*.
BELOW : *Vostok launcher at Le Bourget*.
BOTTOM LEFT : *North American X–15*.
BOTTOM RIGHT : *The Lunar Rover*.

21 July
Neil Armstrong, US astronaut, became the first man to step on the Moon's surface.

1970
12 September
Launch of Russia's unmanned spacecraft *Luna 16*, which landed on the Moon, collected soil samples, took off from the Moon under remote control and was recovered success-fully on 24 September.

1971
31 July
A Boeing Lunar Roving Vehicle was driven on the Moon's surface for the first time.

1974
14 August
First flight of a Panavia MRCA (now Tornado) multi-role combat aircraft prototype.
23 December
First flight of a Rockwell Inter-national B–1 strategic bomber prototype.

1976
21 January
Concorde SST introduced into international commercial airline service simultaneously by Air France and British Airways.
20 July
Touchdown on Mars of the first Viking Lander.

1977
7–25 February
Russia's two-manned Soyuz 24 docked with the Salyut 5 spacelab during a flight lasting 424 hr 48 min.

Vought Corsair o2U–1–biplane.

Glossary

Absolute ceiling
The maximum altitude above sea-level at which a heavier-than-air craft can maintain level flight.

Accumulator
A reservoir to supply a fluid under pressure.

ADF
Automatic direction finder. An automated system of radio direction finding (RDF), *(q.v.)*.

Aerobatics
Manoeuvres, other than those necessary for normal flight, carried out voluntarily by an aircraft's pilot.

Aerodrome
An area intended for the take-off and landing of aircraft, and including generally the associated buildings and equipment for the operation of aircraft.

Aerodynamics
The science dealing with air in motion and the reactions of a body moving in air.

Aerodyne
See aeroplane.

Aerofoil
A suitably shaped structure which, when propelled through the air, generates lift.

Aeronautics
Dealing with flight within the Earth's atmosphere.

Aeroplane
A heavier-than-air aircraft.

Aerostat
A lighter-than-air aircraft.

Afterburner
A thrust-augmenting feature of a gas turbine engine.

AI
Airborne interception. An airborne radar system evolved to assist in the location and interception of hostile aircraft.

Aileron
Movable control surface hinged to aft edge of each wing, usually adjacent to wingtip, to control rolling movements.

Airbrake
An aerodynamic surface which can be deployed in flight to increase drag.

Aircraft
Vehicles, both lighter- and heavier-than-air, which derive their flight capability from reactions of the air.

Airfield
See aerodrome.

Airfoil
See aerofoil.

Airframe
The name given to an aircraft's structure, excluding the power plant.

Airlift
The carriage of personnel or supplies by air.

Airplane
See aeroplane.

Airscrew
See propeller.

Airship
Popular name for a steerable lighter-than-air craft. More accurately a dirigible.

Airstrip
A natural surface adapted – often in an unimproved state – for the operation of aircraft. Located usually in a forward area, such strips are sometimes reinforced by steel netting.

Aldis lamp
Signalling device, projecting a narrow beam of light, visible only at the point to which it is aimed by a sight.

Altimeter
A height recording instrument.

Altitude
Height.

Amphibian
A heavier-than-air craft which can operate from land or water surfaces.

Analogue computer
A computing device, based on the principle of measuring as opposed to counting.

Angle of attack
The angle at which an aerofoil surface meets the oncoming airstream.

Angle of incidence
The angle at which an aerofoil surface is attached to a fuselage in relation to the longitudinal axis.

Anhedral
The angle which an aerofoil surface makes to the fuselage when the wing or tailplane tip is lower than the root attachment.

Area rule
A concept for shaping an aircraft for minimum drag in supersonic flight.

Artificial horizon
A gyro-stabilized flight instrument which shows graphically pitching and rolling movements of the aircraft, to aid the pilot to maintain level flight.

ASI
Air-speed indicator (see IAS).

Aspect ratio
The ratio of the span to the mean chord of an aerofoil surface.

Astrodome
Transparent dome on fuselage upper surface to permit celestial navigation.

Astronaut
Crew member of a spacecraft.

Astronautics
Dealing with flight in space.

ASW
Anti-submarine warfare.

Automatic pilot
A gyro-stabilized system to maintain an aircraft in steady flight.

Autopilot
See automatic pilot.

Autorotation
The continued automatic rotation of a rotary wing by means of air flowing through it due to forward or downward motion of a gyroplane.

APU
Auxiliary power unit carried within an aircraft for such tasks as main engine starting, ground air conditioning, and the provision of electric, hydraulic or pneumatic power in the air or on the ground.

Ballast
Carried in an aerostat to permit variation of lift.

Ballistic missile
One which becomes an unguided free-falling body in the unpowered stage of its flight, and subject to ballistic reactions.

Ballonnet
An air-filled compartment in the envelope of an airship, used to maintain a desired gas pressure at varying altitudes.

Balloon
An unsteerable lighter-than-air craft.

Biplane
A fixed-wing aircraft with two superimposed wings.

Blimp
Small non-rigid, occasionally semi-rigid, airship.

Convair F–102A – one of the first applications of the area rule.

Mirage III – delta wing.

Boundary layer
The thin stratum of air in contact with the skin surface of the airframe.

Buffet
Irregular oscillations imposed upon an aircraft's structure by turbulent airflow or conditions of compressibility.

Bungee
A tensioning device, usually of rubber cord. Used commonly for landing gear shock-absorption of simple, lightweight aircraft.

Cabin
An enclosed compartment for the crew and/or passengers of an aircraft.

Camber
The curvature of an aerofoil surface.

Canard
An aircraft which has its main wing or lifting surface at the aft end of the airframe.

Cantilever
Describing a beam or other structural member which is supported at one end only.

CAT
Clear air turbulence. Invisible, and sometimes violent whirlpools of air, created usually by the shearing action between jet streams or other high velocity winds, and a larger mass of slow moving air.

Ceiling
Operating height of an aircraft.

Centre of gravity
(CG), the point of a structure at which the combined total weight is considered to act.

Centre of pressure
The point at which the left of an aerofoil surface is considered to act.

Centre-section
The central portion of a wing.

Chaff
Narrow metallic foil strips dropped by an aircraft to confuse an enemy's radar system. Known also by its original British code name Window.

Chord
The distance from the leading- to trailing-edge of an aerofoil.

Cockpit
An open compartment in an aircraft's fuselage to accommodate a pilot, other crew member, or passenger.

Constant-speed propeller
One in which the pitch angle of the blades is changed constantly in flight to maintain engine revolutions at their optimum for maximum torque.

Cosmonaut
Term used by the Soviet Union to describe a crew member of a spacecraft.

Cowling
Usually the fairing which encloses a power plant.

Delta wing
One which, viewed in plan, has the appearance of an isosceles triangle: the apex leads, the wing trailing-edge forming the flat base of the triangle.

Digital computer
A computing device, based on the principle of counting as opposed to measuring.

Dihedral
The angle which an aerofoil surface makes to the fuselage when the wing or tailplane tip is higher than the root attachment.

Dirigible
See airship.

Ditch
To set down a landplane on water, due to emergency conditions.

Dive brake
A drag-inducing surface which can be deployed to reduce the speed of an aircraft in a dive, sometimes to prevent structural limitations being exceeded, and to improve controllability. A similar aerodynamic device used to steepen an aircraft's glide path is termed an air brake.

DME
Distance measuring equipment, a navigational aid.

Dope
A cellulose base paint used to waterproof and/or render taut the fabric covering an aircraft.

Drag
The resistance of an aerofoil to its passage through the air, creating a force parallel to the airstream.

Drag chute
A heavy-duty parachute attached to an aircraft's structure which can be deployed to reduce its landing run.

Drift
The lateral movement of an aircraft away from its true heading.

Drone
A pilotless aircraft controlled remotely from the ground, known also as an RPV (*q.v.*).

Drop tank
An auxiliary tank, generally containing fuel, which can be jettisoned if required.

ECM
Electronic countermeasures. Airborne electronic equipment designed to neutralize or reduce the effectiveness of an enemy's radar or other devices which employ or are affected by electromagnetic radiations.

Elevator
Movable control surface hinged to the aft edge of the tailplane (stabilizer) to permit control about the aircraft's lateral axis.

Elevons
Control surfaces which on a tailless aircraft combine the duties of ailerons and elevators.

Elint
Electronic intelligence, regarding the location, volume, direction and type of an enemy's electronic devices.

Envelope
The gas container of a lighter-than-air craft, or of air in a hot-air balloon or airship.

Exhaust-gas analyser
An instrument to determine and indicate the ratio of fuel to air fed into an engine.

FAA
Fleet Air Arm (UK).

FAC
Forward air controller. An officer operating in a forward position with a land force, and with suitable radio equipment to call in attack or bomber aircraft for close-support operations.

Fairing
An addition to a structure to reduce its drag coefficient.

Fillet
A faired surface to maintain a smooth airflow at the angular junction of two components for instance between wing and fuselage.

Fin
Fixed vertical surface of tail unit, to provide stability about the aircraft's vertical and longitudinal axes.

Flap
Usually a hinged wing trailing-edge surface which can be lowered partially to increase lift, or fully to increase drag.

Flaperon
Control surface which can serve the dual functions of a flap or aileron.

Flight deck
Term for a separate crew compartment of a cabin aircraft.

Flight envelope
An aircraft's performance range characteristics.

Flight plan
A written statement of the route and procedures to be adopted for other than local flights.

Flight simulator
Permits the practice of flight operations from a ground-based training device. Some are for general flight routines, but many are configured for training in the operation of a specific aircraft.

FLIR
Forward-looking infra-red, which allows a pilot to see land surface features under no-visibility conditions.

Floatplane
An alternative name for a seaplane, i.e. an aircraft which operates from water and is supported on the water's surface by floats.

Flutter
An unstable oscillation of an aerofoil surface.

Flying-boat
A heavier-than-air craft which operates from water, and in which the hull or body is the main flotation surface.

Flying wires
Bracing wires of a non-cantilever wing which take the load of the wing in flight.

Fully-feathering propeller
One in which, in the event of engine failure, the leading-edge of each blade can be turned to face the airstream. This prevents windmilling and minimizes drag.

Fuselage
The body of an aircraft.

GAM
Guided air missile. A guided and generally self-propelled weapon, designed to be air-launched from an aircraft.

Piper Super Cub – high wing.

GAR
Guided air rocket. A guided, rocket-propelled weapon, designed to be air-launched from an aircraft.
GCA
Ground controlled approach. Landing procedure when a pilot receives radio instructions for his approach and landing from a ground-based controller who monitors the operation by radar.
Glider
An unpowered heavier-than-air craft.
Gosport tube
Flexible speaking tube used for communication between instructor and pupil in early training aircraft.
Ground effect
The effect upon an aircraft of the cushion of air compressed against the ground by a helicopter's rotor or a low-flying fixed-wing aircraft.
Gyroplane (gyrocopter, 'Autogiro')
An aircraft with an unpowered rotary wing.
Harmonize
To align a fighter aircraft's guns and gunsight to produce a desired pattern of fire at a given range.
Helicopter
An aircraft with a powered rotary wing.
Helium
A valuable lifting gas for lighter-than-air craft which is not inflammable.
High-wing monoplane
One in which the wing is mounted high on the fuselage.
Horizontally-opposed engine
In which two banks of in-line cylinders are mounted horizontally opposite to each other on a common crankcase.
HUD
Head-up display, which projects performance and/or attack information on to an aircraft's windscreen for constant appraisal by the pilot.
Hull
The fuselage or body of a flying-boat.
HVAR
High velocity aircraft rocket.

Hydrogen
The lightest known lifting gas, for lighter-than-air craft; unfortunately highly inflammable.
IAS
Indicated air-speed, from an ASI, which progressively reads lower as altitude increases and air density decreases.
ICBM
Intercontinental ballistic missile (see ballistic missile).
Icing
The process of atmospheric moisture freezing upon the external surfaces of an aircraft.
IFF
Identification, friend or foe; an electronic interrogation device.
ILS
Instrument landing system, to permit safe landing in conditions of bad visibility.
ILS marker
A radio marker beacon of an instrument landing system.
Inertia starter
Starting device of many piston-engines, the inertia of a hand- or electrically-driven flywheel being connected to the engine by clutch.
In-line engine
In which cylinders are one behind another.
INS
Inertial navigation system. This relies upon the ability of three highly sensitive accelerometers to record, via a computer, the complex accelerations of an aircraft about its three axes. From this information the computer can continually integrate the aircraft's linear displacement from the beginning of the flight, pinpointing the position of the aircraft at all times.
Interdiction
The prevention of, or interference with, an enemy's movements and communication.
Interference drag
Drag induced by conflicting airstreams over adjacent streamlined structures.

ISA
International Standard Atmosphere. An agreed standard of sea-level pressure and temperature (1,013·2 millibars at 15°C) to facilitate the comparison of aircraft performance figures.
JATO
Jet-assisted take-off. The augmentation of an aircraft's normal thrust for take-off, by the use of a jet engine.
Kinetic heating
The heating of an aircraft's structure as a result of air friction.
Kite
A tethered heavier-than-air craft sustained in the air by lift resulting from airspeed in a horizontal wind.
Landing weight
The maximum weight at which an aircraft is permitted to land.
Landing wires
Bracing wires of a non-cantilever wing which support the wing when it is not in flight.
Landplane
A heavier-than-air craft which can operate from land surfaces only.
Leigh-light
An airborne searchlight used for ASW operations in World War II.
Lift
The force generated by an aerofoil, acting at right angles to the airstream which flows past it.
Longeron
A primary longitudinal member of a fuselage structure.
Loran
Long-range navigation, a navigational aid.
Low-wing monoplane
One with the wings attached at or near the bottom of the fuselage.
Mach number
The speed of a body as measured by the speed of sound in the medium in which that body is moving. Hence, Mach 0·75 represents three-quarters of the speed of sound. The speed of sound in dry air at 0°C (32°F) is about 331m (1,087ft) per second (1,193km/h; 741mph). Named after the Austrian physicist Ernst Mach.

Mean chord
The area of an aerofoil divided by its span.
Mid-wing monoplanes
One with the wings attached midway on the fuselage.
Minimum control speed
The lowest practicable speed at which an aircraft can be flown and controlled.
Monocoque
Aircraft structure in which the skin carries the primary stresses.
Monoplane
A fixed-wing aircraft with one set of wings.
NACA
National Advisory Committee of Aeronautics (US, predecessor of NASA).
NASA
National Aeronautics and Space Administration (US).
NATO
North Atlantic Treaty Organization.
Navigation lights
Mounted on the exterior of an aircraft so that its dimensions and position can be seen at night.
Omni
Omnidirectional radio range, a navigational device giving bearing from the transmitter, irrespective of the location or heading of the aircraft.
Ornithopter
Name given to a flapping-wing aircraft. Only model ornithopters have so far, proved capable of flight.
Parachute
A collapsible device which, when deployed, is used to retard the descent through the air of a falling body. Worn originally by aircrew for escape from a stricken aircraft, the parachute has since been adopted for paratroopers (parachute equipped troops), and for such uses as the dropping of cargo and supplies, recovery of spacecraft, and to reduce the landing run of high-speed aircraft.
Parasite drag
Induced by structural components which make no contribution to lift.

Parasol monoplane
One in which the wing is mounted above the fuselage.

Pitch
The movement of an aircraft about its lateral axis, i.e. that which extends from wingtip to wingtip, resulting in up and down movements of the tail.

Pitot head
Comprising two tubes, one to measure impact pressure, the other static pressure. They are used in conjunction with an airspeed indicator which registers airspeed from the pressure difference between the two tubes.

Planing
The condition when a flying-boat's hull or seaplane's floats are supported by hydrodynamic forces.

Pressurization
A condition in an aircraft's cabin, cockpit or a compartment, where the air is maintained at a pressure higher than that of the surrounding air. This is to compensate for the lower pressure at high altitude, permitting the normal respiratory and circulatory functions of crew and passengers at heights abnormal to the body.

Port
To the left of, or on the left-hand side of an aircraft.

Propeller
Rotating blades of aerofoil section, engine driven, to create thrust for the propulsion of an aircraft. Sometimes called an airscrew.

Pulse jet engine
Essentially an aerodynamic duct with a series of spring-loaded inlet valves at the forward end. Works on intermittent combustion principle and will run in a static condition.

Pusher propeller
A propeller mounted aft of an engine.

RAAF
Royal Australian Air Force.

Radar
A method of using beamed and directed radio waves for location and detection of a variety of objects, and for navigational purposes.

Radial engine
In which the radially disposed cylinders are fixed and the crankshaft rotates.

RAE
Royal Aircraft Establishment (UK).

RAF
Royal Air Force.

Ramjet engine
Essentially an aerodynamic duct in which fuel is burned to produce a high-velocity propulsive jet. It requires acceleration to high speed before any thrust is produced.

RATO
Rocket-assisted take-off. Describes the augmentation of an aircraft's normal thrust for take-off, by the use of a rocket motor.

RCAF
Royal Canadian Air Force.

RDF
Radio direction finding. A method of obtaining by radio the bearing of an aircraft to two or three ground stations to determine its position.

Reversible-pitch propeller
One in which the blades can be turned to provide reverse thrust to reduce an aircraft's landing run.

RFC
Royal Flying Corps (UK, predecessor of RAF).

Rib
A component of an aerofoil structure, shaped to locate the covering or skin of such structure in the desired aerofoil section.

RNAS
Royal Naval Air Service (UK, predecessor of FAA).

RNZAF
Royal New Zealand Air Force.

Rocket engine
One which consists simply of an injector, combustion chambers and exhaust nozzle, and which carries with it a liquid or solid fuel and an oxidizer, allowing it to operate outside of the Earth's atmosphere.

Roll
The movement of an aircraft about its longitudinal axis, i.e. that which extends through the centre-line of the fuselage, representing a wing-over rolling movement.

Rotary engine
In which radially disposed cylinders rotate around a fixed crankshaft.

Rotor
A rotary-wing assembly, comprising the rotor blades and rotor hub, of an autogyro or helicopter.

RPV
Remotely piloted vehicle (see Drone).

Rudder
Movable control surface hinged at aft edge of fin to permit directional control.

SAAF
South African Air Force.

Sailplane
An unpowered heavier-than-air craft designed for soaring flight.

Scanner
The antenna of a radar installation which moves (scans) to pick up signal echoes.

Scarff ring
Movable mounting for a machine-gun.

Seaplane
A heavier-than-air craft which operates from water, and in which floats provide the flotation surface.

Semi-monocoque
Aircraft structure in which frames, formers and longerons reinforce the skin in carrying the load stresses.

Skin
The external covering of an aircraft's structure.

Skin friction
Drag induced by rough or pitted skin surfaces.

Slat
An auxiliary aerofoil surface, mounted forward of a main aerofoil.

Slot
The gap between a slat and the main aerofoil surface, which splits the airflow at the wing leading-edge to maintain smooth airflow at greater angles of attack.

Spacecraft
A vehicle to travel in space – that is outside the Earth's atmosphere – which can be manned or unmanned.

Spar
A principal structural member of an aerofoil surface.

Specific fuel consumption (sfc)
The amount of fuel required per hour by an engine per unit power.

Spoilers
Drag-inducing surfaces used for both lateral control and for lift dumping to improve braking and reduce landing run.

Stall
Describes the condition of an aerofoil surface when its angle of attack becomes too great and the smooth air flow over the upper surface breaks down, destroying lift.

Starboard
To the right of, or on the right-hand side of an aircraft.

Short SC–1 – VTOL.

Step
A break in the smooth undersurface of a flyingboat hull or seaplane float to resist suction and facilitate planing.

STOL
Short take-off and landing.

Streamline
To shape a structure or component so that it will cause minimum aerodynamic drag.

Stringer
An auxiliary, lightweight structural member, the primary use of which is to establish the desired external form of a structure before covering or skinning.

Strut
Usually a tube or rod in compression, frequently separating the wings of a biplane.

Subsonic
Flight at speeds below the speed of sound.

Supercharger
A form of compressor to force more air or fuel/air mixture into the cylinders of a piston-engine (to super charge) than can be induced by the pistons at the prevailing atmospheric pressure.

Supersonic
Flight at speeds above the speed of sound.

SV-VS
Soviet Military Aviation Forces (*Sovietskaya Voenno-Vozdushnye Sily*).

Swept wing
In which the angle between the wing leading-edge and the fuselage centre-line is less than 90 degrees.

Tabs
Small auxiliary surfaces which are used to trim an aircraft so that the pilot does not have to offset manually loads induced by control surfaces.

Tailplane
(Stabilizer) horizontal aerofoil surface of tail unit, fixed or with small angular adjustment, to provide longitudinal stability.

Thickness/chord ratio
The thickness of an aerofoil expressed as a ratio of the wing chord.

Thrust
A force generated by propeller or jet efflux which propels an aircraft through the air. For stable forward flight the forces of thrust and drag must be equal.

Tractor propeller
The term for a propeller mounted forward of an engine.

Transonic
Relating to the phenomena arising when an aircraft passes from subsonic to supersonic speed.

Triplane
A fixed-wing aircraft with three superimposed wings.

Turbofan
A gas turbine in which air is ducted from the tip of the fan blades to bypass the turbine. This air, added to the jet efflux, gives high propulsive efficiency.

Turbojet
A gas turbine engine which produces a high velocity jet efflux.

Turboprop
A gas turbine which, through the medium of reduction gearing, also drives a conventional propeller.

Turboshaft
A gas turbine which, through the medium of a gearbox, drives a power take-off shaft. Used most commonly for rotary-wing aircraft.

USAAC
United States Army Air Corps (US, predecessor of USAAF).

USAAF
United States Army Air Forces (US predecessor of USAF).

USAAS
United States Army Air Service (US, predecessor of USAAC).

USAF
United States Air Force.

USMC
United States Marine Corps.

USN
United States Navy

Variable-geometry wing
One which can be swept or spread in flight to provide optimum performance for take-off/landing, cruising and high-speed flight.

Variable-pitch propeller
One in which the pitch angle of the blades can be changed in flight to give optimum performance in relation to engine load.

Vee-engine
In which two banks of in-line cylinders are mounted at an angle on a common crankcase.

V/STOL
Vertical and/or short take-off and landing.

VTOL
Vertical take-off and landing.

Wing warping
Early method of lateral control in which a flexible wing was twisted, or warped, to provide control similar to that of an aileron.

Yaw
The movement of an aircraft about its vertical axis, i.e. that which passes vertically through the junction of the lateral and longitudinal axes, representing movement of the tail unit to port or starboard.

Air Museums

The major international air shows of the world are those held in alternate years at Paris, France (1977 and 'odd' years) and Farnborough, England (1978 and 'even' years). The Paris Show is organized by the Union Syndicale des Industries Aeronautiques et Spatiales, and is normally held during the first week in June. This has been staged at Le Bourget Airport, Paris, for many years, although it may be transferred to a new site in a few years' time. The Farnborough Show is arranged by the Society of British Aerospace Companies, and has been held at its present site since shortly after World War II. The Farnborough display usually takes place during the first week in September.

Other important trade shows are held at Hannover in the Federal German Republic – this takes place during the first week in May in the same year as Farnborough shows – and at Iruma, near Tokyo in Japan, during October.

Surprisingly the USA does not have a regular showpiece to display the products of its aerospace industry, but there are two specialist shows held annually. These are the annual conventions of the National Business Aircraft Association – the location of this varies but it is held late in September – and of the Experimental Aircraft Association – which is held at Oshkosh, Wisconsin, during the first week in August. The latter is a gathering of amateur aircraft constructors from all over the United States and beyond. Other regular events in the USA are the National Air Races, held at Stead Field, Reno, Nevada, during September, and the Confederate Air Force annual air show, a unique gathering of surviving World War II aircraft types, held in October, at Harlingen, Texas.

There are many major aviation museums in countries all over the world. Much effort has been put into preserving and restoring significant historical aircraft, especially in the last ten years, a period which has seen the growth of many new museums in Europe, the USA and elsewhere. Although some of this work is comparatively recent, it is fortunate that much of the world's early aviation heritage had already been preserved for posterity – for example, 6 original Wright biplanes still exist in museum collections, together with over 30 Blériot monoplanes, and – from a more modern era – more than 70 Supermarine Spitfires.

The tabulation below includes all major museums that have aircraft on display and are open to the public, with the location of each, the number of aircraft actually on display, and some indication of the particular specialization of each.

ARGENTINA

Museo Nacional de Aeronautica, Aeroparque Airport, Buenos Aires. Twenty aircraft, relating to the history of the Argentine Air Force and aircraft industry, from a Comper Swift of 1930 to an I.A.35 Huanquero of 1957.

AUSTRALIA

Camden Museum of Aviation, P.O. Box 72, Kogarah, New South Wales.
Twenty-two aircraft, almost all of military types, from a D.H. Moth of 1927 to two Sea Venom jet fighters of 1955.
Moorabbin Air Museum, P.O. Box 242, Mentone, Victoria. (At Moorabbin airfield.)
Ten aircraft of both military and civilian types, dating from a D.H. Moth of 1929 to a Gloster Meteor jet fighter of 1951.
Warbirds Aviation Museum, Mildura Airport, Mildura, Victoria. Ten aircraft, all military types.

BELGIUM

Musée de l'Armée et d'Histoire Militaire, Palais du Cinquantenaire, Brussels.
Sixty aircraft relating to the history of Belgian military and civil aviation.

BRAZIL

Air Museum, Campo dos Afonsos, Rio de Janeiro.
Ten aircraft, connected with the history of Brazilian military aviation.

CANADA

Calgary Centennial Planetarium, Mewata Park, Calgary, Alberta.
Six relatively modern aircraft are displayed here.
Canadian National Aeronautical Collection, Rockcliffe Airfield, Ottawa, Ontario.
An excellent and varied collection with forty exhibits dating from 1918 to the present day, ranging from a Sopwith Camel to a Vickers Viscount. Products of the Canadian aircraft industry and aircraft which have served with Canadian airlines and the Armed Forces are comprehensively covered. About four aircraft each at Ottawa International Airport, the National War Museum, and the Museum of Science and Technology, all in Ottawa.
Canadian Warplane Heritage, Hamilton Civic Airport, Hamilton, Ont.
Fairey Firefly, Vought Corsair, B-25 Mitchell and about six other World War II aircraft, all in flying condition or being restored to it.

CZECHOSLOVAKIA

Letecka Expozice Vojenskeho Muzea, Prague-Kbely.
Forty aircraft, including gliders, light aircraft, fighters, bombers and helicopters, mostly dating from World War II or later.

National Technical Museum, Kostelni Str. 42, Prague 7.
Thirteen aircraft, dating from a 1910 Blériot, to a Mraz Sokol light aircraft of 1947.

DENMARK

Egeskov Museum, DK-5772, Kvaerndrup. (South of Odense.)
Thirteen aircraft, mostly light aircraft and gliders owned by the Royal Danish Aero Club.

FRANCE

Musée de l'Air, Aeroport du Bourget, Paris; and 8 rue des Vertugadins, Chalais Meudon, Hauts-de-Seine.
Two separate exhibitions, with a total of over sixty aircraft on display, together giving a comprehensive view of French aviation history, with extra exhibits from other countries.

GERMAN FEDERAL REPUBLIC

Deutschesmuseum, 800-München (Munich).
Fifteen aircraft, covering the history of German aviation, from an early Lilienthal glider to a Dornier DO 31 vertical take-off transport.
Hubschraubermuseum (Helicopter Museum), Bückeburg. (Near Minden.)
Seventeen helicopters of German, British, French and US manufacture mostly being modern designs.
Luftwaffen Museum, 2082-Uetersen, Holstein. (Near Hamburg.)
Twenty aircraft, mostly related to the post-1955 history of the Luftwaffe, but also including a Messerschmitt Bf109 and Heinkel He 111.

HOLLAND

Aviodome, National Aeronautical Museum, Schiphol Airport, Amsterdam.
Seventeen aircraft, covering the history of Dutch aviation, from a replica Fokker Spin (Spider) of 1911 to a Fokker S.14 jet trainer of 1951.
Luchtmacht Museum, Soesterburg Air Force Base. (Between Utrecht and Amersfoort.)
Twelve aircraft connected with the history of the Royal Netherlands Air Force, mostly of World War II or more modern design.

INDIA

Indian Air Museum, Palam Airfield, New Delhi.
A collection of seventeen aircraft relating to the history of the Indian Air Force, from a unique Westland Wapiti of 1935 to a Folland Gnat jet fighter.

ITALY

Museo Aeronautico Caproni di Taliedo, Via Durini 24, Milano.
Thirty-two aircraft, mostly of Italian (and many of Caproni) design. Oldest is a Caproni Ca.6 of 1910, newest a Bernardi Aeroscooter of 1961.

Museo Nazionale della Scienza e della Technica, Via San Vittore 21, Milano.
Twenty aircraft, mostly of Italian design, dating from 1910 to 1950.

NEW ZEALAND

Museum of Transport and Technology, Western Springs, Auckland 2.
Twenty aircraft, both military and civilian types, from the Pearse monoplane of 1904 to a de Havilland Vampire of 1952.

POLAND

Army Museum, Warsaw.
A display of nine military aircraft ranging from a Yak-9 of 1942 to a MiG-15 of 1954.
Museum of Aeronautics and Astronautics, Kracow.
Thirty-three aircraft, ranging from a replica Blériot XI to a Yakovlev Yak-23 jet fighter.

ROMANIA

Central Military Museum, Bucharest.
Eleven aircraft of Romanian, Italian, Russian and Canadian design, from a replica Vuia monoplane of 1906 to a MiG-15 jet fighter.

SOUTH AFRICA

South African National Museum of War History, Erlswold Way, Saxonwold, Johannesburg.
Nine aircraft are displayed, all being British or German types used in World War II.

SWEDEN

Air Force Flymuseer, F13M Malmslätt, near Linköping.
Over forty aircraft are held at this Royal Swedish Air Force base, including a wide variety of Swedish, British, German, Italian and American designs relating to the history of the Air Force.

SWITZERLAND

Verkehrshaus, Lidostrasse 5, CH-6006 Lucerne.
Thirty aircraft, dating from the Dufaux biplane of 1910 to modern jets such as a Swissair Convair 990 airliner, covering the complete spectrum of the history of the Swiss aircraft industry.

THAILAND

Royal Thai Air Force Museum, Don Muang Air Force Base, Bangkok.
Twenty-eight aircraft of types used by the Royal Thai Air Force, from a Boeing P-12 of 1931 to a North American F-86 Sabre of 1953.

UNITED KINGDOM

Cosford Aerospace Museum, Royal Air Force Cosford, Shropshire. (Near Wolverhampton.)
Twenty-five aircraft, most of which are World War II or modern types, ranging from a Spitfire to a TSR-2.

Fleet Air Arm Museum, RNAS Yeovilton, Ilchester, Somerset.
Forty-five aircraft connected with the history of the Fleet Air Arm, mainly being World War II or modern types, and also including the first British Concorde.

Historic Aircraft Museum, Aviation Way, Rochford, Southend-on-Sea, Essex. (Adjacent to Southend Airport.)
Thirty aircraft, mostly of World War II or more modern design, but also including some pre-war D.H. Moths.

Imperial War Museum, Lambeth Road, London SE1.
Fourteen aircraft, including missiles. Another thirty-six, ranging from a 1917 R.E.8 to a Concorde, are at Duxford Aerodrome, Cambridgeshire, together with over twenty of the Duxford Aviation Society's mainly civil collection. Annual flying display.

Lincolnshire Aviation Museum, Old Station Yard, Tattershall, Lincolnshire.
Ten aircraft, dating from a Mignet Flying Flea of 1936 to a Vampire T.11 jet trainer of 1953.

Mosquito Aircraft Museum, Salisbury Hall, London Colney, Hertfordshire.
Ten aircraft, all of de Havilland manufacture, of which the most famous is the prototype Mosquito.

Newark Air Museum, Winthorpe Airfield, Newark, Nottinghamshire.
Twelve aircraft relating to aviation history in Nottinghamshire and Lincolnshire.

Royal Air Force Museum, Aerodrome Road, Hendon, London NW9 5LL.
Forty aircraft, all related to the history of the Royal Air Force and the British aircraft industry, ranging in age from a Blériot XI of 1910 to a Lightning supersonic jet fighter.

Royal Scottish Museum (Museum of Flight), East Fortune Airfield, near Haddington, Lothian.
Fifteen aircraft, related to the history of aviation in Scotland, dating from a D.H. Dragon Rapide of 1935 to modern jets.

Science Museum, Exhibition Road, South Kensington, London SW7 2DD.
Twenty-five aircraft depicting milestones in aviation technology, including types as varied as a Cody biplane of 1912 and a Rolls-Royce 'Flying Bedstead' vertical take-off test rig of 1954.

Shuttleworth Collection, Old Warden Aerodrome, near Biggleswade, Bedfordshire.
Twenty-five aircraft, mostly in flying condition, including all airworthy aircraft in the UK over fifty years old, and examples of most RAF training types from the Avro 504 to the Hunting Provost. Regular monthly flying displays in summer.

Skyfame Museum, Staverton Airport, Gloucestershire. (Between Gloucester and Cheltenham.)
Fifteen aircraft, mostly World War II and modern types, including the unique Saro A.1 jet fighter flying-boat and a rare Hawker Tempest.

Strathallan Collection, Strathallan Airfield, Auchterarder, Tayside.
Fifteen aircraft, mostly still in flying condition, and the majority being World War II types. Included are a Lancaster and a Mosquito. Annual flying display, usually held in July.

Torbay Aviation Museum, Higher Blagdon, Paignton, Torbay, Devon.
Twenty aircraft, mostly modern types, including light aircraft, jet fighters and helicopters.

UNITED STATES OF AMERICA

Aerospace Park, 413 West Mercury Boulevard, Hampton, Virginia 23666.
Ten aircraft, all American helicopters or jet fighters, except for one Hawker Siddeley XV–6A Kestrel VTOL prototype.

Air Force Museum, Wright-Patterson Air Force Base, Fairborn, Ohio 45433 (near Dayton).
A truly massive collection of 115 aircraft, concentrating on USAF aircraft types, but also including European and Japanese types, and ranging from a Wright Brothers Model B to a prototype North American XB–70 Valkyrie supersonic bomber.

Airpower Museum, Antique Airfield, Blakesburg, Iowa 52536. (Between Blakesburg and Ottumwa.)
Ten aircraft, mostly classic and vintage light types dating from the 1930–40 era, and mostly in flying condition.

Bradley Air Museum, Bradley International Airport, P.O. Box 44, Hebron, Connecticut 06248. (North of Hartford, near Windsor Locks, and North of Route 20).
Thirty aircraft, of which the majority are relatively modern types, ranging from a Boeing B–17G to a Douglas C–133B.

Confederate Air Force, Harlingen Industrial Airport, Harlingen, Texas 78550.
A museum of flying aircraft, largely devoted to US designs of World War II, but also including European World War II types and post-war US designs, the latter in a static exhibition. Usually about forty aircraft may be seen, although often airworthy aircraft may be involved in displays elsewhere in the USA. Annual air display normally held early in October.

Experimental Aircraft Association Air Museum, 11311 West Forest Home Avenue, Franklin, Wisconsin 53132. (Franklin is a suburb of Milwaukee.)
An impressive collection of ninety-five aircraft tracing the development of the light aircraft, both home-built and factory made, featuring both historic and modern designs, and displays of constructional techniques.

Florence Air and Missile Museum, Florence Municipal Airport, Florence, South Carolina 29501.
Fifteen modern US military aircraft are displayed, together with a collection of missiles.

Flying Circus Aerodrome, Route 17, Bealton, Virginia 22712. (Between Warrenton and Fredricksburg).
Twelve flying aircraft ranging from a replica Sopwith Pup to a Stampe SV.4 and Stearman. Weekend flying displays in summer.

Flying Tiger Air Museum, P.O. Box 113, Paris, Texas 75460. (On Highway 82, at airport.)
Twelve aircraft, mostly in flying condition and concentrating on World War II types. Offers flying training to would-be owner-pilots of Mustangs and similar types.

Frederick C. Crawford Auto-Aviation Museum, 10825 East Boulevard, Cleveland, Ohio 44106.
Primarily an automobile museum, with eight aircraft on display ranging from a Curtiss A–1 of 1910 to a P–51K Mustang of 1944.

Glenn H. Curtiss Museum, Hammondsport, New York 14840. (North-West of Elmira, North of Route 17.)
This museum houses eight aircraft, mostly of Curtiss design.

Greenfield Village and Henry Ford Museum, Dearborn, Michigan 48121.
Twenty aircraft, the oldest being a Blériot XI. Most date from the inter-war period.

Harold Warp Pioneer Village, Minden, Nebraska 68959. (South of Route 80 at Kearney.)
Fifteen aircraft, mostly of the 1910–1930 period, including a Curtiss Jenny and a Pitcairn autogiro.

Hill Country Transportation Museum, 15060 Foothill Avenue, Morgan Hill, California 95037. (South of San Jose.)
Thirty aircraft, mostly vintage and classic light aircraft types.

History and Traditions Museum, Lackland Air Force Base, San Antonio, Texas 78236.
Thirty aircraft, all relevant to the history of the USAF.

Movieland of the Air, Orange County Airport, Santa Ana, California 92707.
Thirty aircraft, many of which have featured in a variety of aviation films in the hands of Frank Tallman and remain in flying condition.

Museum of Flight, Seattle Centre, 305 Harrison Street, Seattle, Washington 98109.
Twelve gliders and powered aircraft, from a replica Wright 1902 glider to a prototype Northrop YF–5A jet fighter.

Museum of Science and Industry, Lake Shore Drive and 57th Street, Jackson Park, Chicago, Illinois 60637.
Ten aircraft ranging from a 1917 Curtiss Jenny to a 1940 Supermarine Spitfire set against the background of a major science and technology museum.

National Air and Space Museum, Smithsonian Institution, Washington D.C., 20560.
Sixty-five aircraft, including many famous and historic examples, from the original Wright Flyer to the North American X–15 rocket-powered research design of 1956, are on display in the new museum on the Mall in Washington, opened on 4 July 1976. In addition, more aircraft from the reserve collection may be viewed at the storage facility at Old Silver Hill Road, Silver Hill, Maryland.

Old Rhinebeck Aerodrome, P.O. Box 57, Route 1, Rhinebeck, New York 12572 (North of Poughkeepsie).
Twenty-five aircraft, mostly in flying condition, and representing the early days of aviation, with many original or replica World War I designs. Regular flying displays are held on Sundays in the summer.

Pate Museum of Transportation, P.O. Box 711, Highway 377, Fort Worth, Texas 76101. (South-West of city, between Benbrook and Cresson.)
Twelve modern US designs displayed as part of a larger exhibition.

Pima County Air Museum, Old Vail Road, Tucson, Arizona 85731. (Adjacent to the South side of Davis-Monthan Air Force Base.)
Fifty aircraft, mostly of US military origin.

Planes of Fame, Chino Airport, Chino, California 91710. (East of Los Angeles, to South of the Pomona Freeway, Route 60.)
Thirty aircraft varying in age from a rare Boeing P–12E fighter of 1932 to a Lockheed T–33A of 1953.

San Diego Aerospace Museum, 1649 El Prado, Balboa Park, San Diego, California 92101.
Thirty-five aircraft varying from a replica Wright Flyer to various jet fighters of the 1950s.

SST Aviation Exhibit Center, Kissimmee, Florida 32749.
Twelve aircraft, mostly light civilian types, in an exhibition dominated by the mock-up of the abandoned Boeing 2707 supersonic transport.

Strategic Aerospace Museum, 2510 Clay Street, Bellevue, Nebraska 68005. (Located at Offutt Air Force Base, South of Omaha.)
Thirty aircraft, including a collection of strategic bomber types loaned by the USAF Museum. A Convair B–36 is undoubtedly the most impressive exhibit.

USAF Armament Museum, Eglin Air Force Base, Valparaiso, Florida 32542.
Ten complete aircraft shown as part of an exhibition of aircraft armament dating from World War I until now.

US Army Aviation Museum, Fort Rucker, Alabama 36360. (North of Ozark, North-West of Dothan.)
Sixty aircraft, almost all of which have been associated with US Army Aviation, ranging from a Piper L–4 Cub to a Lockheed AP–2E Neptune.

US Army Transportation Museum, Fort Eustis, Virginia 23604. (North of Newport News.)
Twenty aircraft and helicopters relating to US Army aviation.

US Marine Corps Museum, Quantico Marine Corps Base, Quantico, Virginia 22134.
There is an aviation annex to the main military museum at this base, located at the Marine Corps Air Station – this contains twenty-five aircraft related to US Marine Corps history.

US Naval Aviation Museum, Naval Air Station Pensacola, Pensacola, Florida 32508.
Sixty aircraft related to the history of US Naval aviation.

USS Alabama Battleship Commission, Battleship Parkway, Mobile, Alabama 36601.
Nine aircraft, mostly of World War II origin and including a rare Vought OS2U Kingfisher.

Victory Air Museum, Polidori Airfield, Gilmer Road, Mundelein, Illinois 60060. (North of Chicago.)
Twenty military aircraft, mostly of World War II vintage.

Wings of Yesterday, P.O. Box 130, Santa Fe, New Mexico 87501.
Twenty aircraft, mostly in flying condition, and ranging in variety from a Stinson Detroiter trimotor to a rare A–36 Mustang.

URUGUAY

Air Museum, Avenida de 31 Marzo, Montevideo.
Seventeen aircraft, dating from an Escafet 2 of 1910 to a Lockheed F–80 Shooting Star jet fighter.

Index

Page references in *italic* refer to captions in **bold** to three-views.

Acknowledgments

The publishers would like to thank the following individuals and organizations for their kind permission to reproduce the photographs in this book. In particular special thanks is given to John W. R. Taylor and Michael J. H. Taylor for the material used from their superb collection of prints and transparencies. Any photographs not listed below are from this collection. Aer Lingus 272 centre; The Aeroplane 238, 454–455 below; Aerospatiale 385 inset; Air Canada 136; Air France 19 below, 123 above right, 236 centre, 248 below, 249 above and centre, 273 above right; Air Ministry 168–169, 171 left, 343 below left; Air Portraits 193 above; American Airlines 243 right, 256 above left; Basil Arkell 343 below right, 345 below, 346 above and below, 347 above and centre left, 351 above, 352, 353 above left, above centre, centre left and below centre, 354 above, 355 left inset and right inset and below inset, 356 above, above inset and right, 360 above left and below right, 362 centre, (Peter Shepherd) 459 centre; Associated Press 74 above centre, 85, 87 below, 154–155, 155 centre, 338 below; Associated Newspapers 339 below; Australian News and Information Bureau 49 below, 132, 133 top right, 155 below; Avoco Lycoming 75 below; Ron Barnfield 125 above right; Bell Helicopter Co. 355 centre; Lewis Benjamin 290 below; Bildarchiv Preussischer Kulturbesitz 33 above, 34 inset, 34–35, 35 inset, 50 above right, 316 above, 317 above right, centre right and below right, 319 above right, centre left and below left, 320 above, 321 left, 324 above, 454 above left, 455 above left and centre; Boeing Company 104–105, 243 left, 247, 255 left, 268 above, 269 above, 275 centre, 276–277 above, 278 above left, above right, and below, 279 above left, 280 above left, 280–281 above, 391 below, 401 below; Douglas Botting 339 above; British Aircraft Corporation 272 left, 411 above left and below left; British Airways 264 below, 285 left, 141 below; C E Brown 235, 260 above, 263; David Calkin 314–315; Camera Press Ltd. 195 above centre, centre right, below left and below right, 446 above left, 449 centre right; J Charleville/SAF 96 centre left; CP Air 311 below left; D D L 240 above centre; Daily Telegraph 298 inset, (Mike Sheil) 298; Dassault-Breguet Aviation 74 below; William Gordon Davis 38 below, 183 above, 326 left, 427 below, 453 above centre right; Dornier-Werke GmbH 241 above right, 261 above; Douglas Aircraft Co 254–255 above, 257 above; E S A/Spacelab 366–367, 414 below; Robert Estall 133 top left; Mary Evans Picture Library 40 above; Finnair 240 above right, 270; Flight International 63 above right, 142 left, 160 below; 176 below, 177 above right, 184 above, 189 above, 271 below right, 433 right; Fokker 234 above, 276 centre right; Ford Motor Company 242 centre; F P G/McFadden Air Photo 306 below; Kenneth Gatland 369 inset and below, 375 below, 376 above left and above right, 384 centre left and below, 385 above right, 391 above right, 392 left, 393 left and right, 396 above left, 397 below, 405 centre right, 409, 414 above, 447 above left, 459 above; General Dynamics Corporation 281 centre; James Gilbert front jacket, endpapers, 4–5, 8–9, 20, 21 left and right, 103 below, 104 left centre, 186 above, 187 above centre, 226–227, 290 above, 291 above left and below right, 292 above and centre, 293 centre left, 294 below, 295 above, 296 inset, 300 right, 301 above and below, 306 above centre inset and below centre inset, 311 below right, 312–313, 340, 341; Golden Ray 236 left, Goodyear Aerospace Co. 330–331 above, 338 centre; Bill Gunston 73 above right; Clive Hart 12 right, 14 left, 17 left, 23 below, 24 above left and above right, 26–27, 28 above left, above centre and above right, 29 above and below right, 30 above, 33 below, (Smithsonian Institution) 22 above and below, 23 above, 27 above, 29 below left, (Science Museum, Crown Copyright) 24 below, (British Museum) 28 below left and below right; F Haubner 282; Hawker Siddeley Aviation 2–3, 95 below, 273 left, 362–363, 388 left, 389 above; Mike Hooks 120 below, 121 below, 122, 123 below left, below right, 124, 125 left and below right, 126 above right, above left and below, 127 above left, above centre, above right and below, 128, 129 left, centre and right, 130 above and below, 131 above centre and below, 133 below, 134 above and below, 134–135, 137 above and below; Angelo Hornak (From "Early Flying Machines 1799–1909" by Charles Gibb-Smith. Published by Eyre Methuen) 17 above right, 25 above left, centre left, 37 above, 39 above, (From "History of Rocketry and Space Travel" by Werner Von Braun and Frederick Ordway. Published by Nelson) 368 left, above, centre and below right, 369 above, above centre and below centre, 370 above left, above centre, above right and below, 371 above, below left, 373 left and above right, 375 above, 451 above centre; P Howard 139, 140 left, 141 above, 143 right, 144 above left and below; Hudson's Bay Company 245 above right; Leslie Hunt 167 centre, 190 below, 191 above and centre; Robert Hunt Library 39 centre and below; Imperial War Museum 65 above right, 119, 148–149 below, 171 below right, 172, 174 above, 181 below left and below right, 182 above left, 187 above and below, 189 below, 304 below left and above right, 321 below right, 322 below left and below right, 328 above and centre, 329 above, 333 above, centre, below left and below right, 334 above left, 373 below right; Italian Air Ministry 177 above left; Keystone Press Agency 121 above left, 133 centre, 154 above, 436 inset, 437 inset, 436–437, 438, 439, 440, 441, 442, 442–443, 443, 444, 445; K L M 232 below left; Howard Levy 103 above, 182 below, 186 centre and below, 295 right, 347 below, 355 above, 405 below; Library of Congress 48 below; Lockheed 267 above, 396 above right; Lufthansa 232 above left, 232–233 above, 248 above, 249 below, 281 below, 304 below right, 307 above; McDonnell Aviation Corporation 74 above, 164 right; Harry McDougall 239; Mansell Collection 12 left, 13, 53 below left, 318 below; Martin Marietta 410; Otto Menge 307 above centre; Ministry of Defence 163 above, 363 right; 386 below left; Minnesota Historical Society 322 above left; J G Moore Collection 91 above, 181 above centre; Kenneth Munson 63 below right; Musee de L'Air 160 below; N A M C 272 right; N A S A 412 left, 446 below left; Port Authority, New York and New Jersey 283 above; High Commissioner for New Zealand 121 above right; Norsk Teknisk Museum 336 above, centre left and centre right, 425 centre; Novosti Press Agency 145 below, 197 above left and above right, 395 below, 397 centre, 400 above right and inset, 402 left and right, 403 left, 404, 409 inset, 449 above centre left, 452 below right, 453 left, 457 below right; Panagra 252 below; Pan Am 264 above; Photri 110 above, 145 above right, 405 above centre, above right and centre left, 408 and 408 inset, 411 right, 413 right, 459 below right; Popperfoto 104 above, 113 below, 148–149 above, 151, 178 below left, 325 above left, 334 below, 336 below right, 337 above, 339 below, 422–423, 422 inset, 426 centre, 430 below, 430–431 above, 432, 432 inset, 434 below right and above right, 446 below right, 448 above left and centre right, 452 centre and above right, 453 above right, 456 above; Pratt and Whitney 58 left; QANTAS Air Lines 41 below, 245 above left; Radio Times Hulton Picture Library 10–11, 15 left, 17 right, 36 below, 42 above, centre left, below left and right, 43 above, below left and below right, 46 above and below, 47 below, 50 above left and below left, 51 above left, 50–51 centre, 51 centre right and below right, 52 centre and below, 53 above and below right, 54 above, 76–77 below, 101 above, 316 below right, 317 above left, 318 above, 324 below, 325 below left, above right, centre right and below right, 328 below, 329 below, 334 above right and inset, 342 above and below, 343 above, 424 below, 425 below left, 426 above and below, 427 centre, 448 below left; Pierre Regout 230 below right; John Rigby 6–7, 87 above, 146–147, 177 below, 280 below, 293 centre right, 297 above, 420–421; Herbert Rittmeyer 95 above, 99 centre, 197 centre, 291 above right, 353 above centre left; Rockwell International 180 below; Rolls Royce, Aero Division 84, 84 inset; Ronan Picture Library 454 below right; Ryan 242 left; SABENA 236 right, SAS-ABA 265 below; Satour 133 above; The Science Museum 25 right and below, 30 below left, 32 above left, 32–33 below, 41 above, 48–49, 450–451; Short Bros 240 below; Smithsonian Institution 37 below, 47 above, 162 below, 320 below, 447 above right, 450 below; Spectrum 30 below right, 31, 71 centre left, 123 above left, 193 centre, 224 left, 296–297, 300 left, 403 below, 405 left, 413 left; Tom Stack and Associates 335 above left; Tony Stone Associates Ltd 299; John Stroud 1, 78 below, 92 above, 228 above and below, 229, 230 left and above right, 231 above, 232–233 centre, 233 right, 234 below, 237 above, 240 above left, 241 above left and below, 246 above and below, 250 below, 252 above, 253 below, 254 centre and right, 256 below, 257 above, 258 above, 259 above left, below left and right, 260 below, 265 above, 266 above, 268 below right, 269 below left and below right, 271 below left, 283 below, 284 above left and above right, 306 above right, 458 below centre; Suddeutcher Verlag 40 below, 50 centre and below right, 51 above right, 316 below left, 319 above left, 321 above right, 322 above right, 323 above and below, 327 above and below, 330 below, 331, 332 above left and above right, 334–335, 335 above right and centre left, 337 below, 425 above and below right, 431 centre and below, 434 left, 435 below, 446 centre and above right, 447 below left, above centre and below right, 448 below right, 449 above left and below right, 450 centre, 451 above left, 452 above left, 454 below left, 455 above right, 456 below left, 457 below centre; Swiss Air 237 above left and above right; Teledyne Ryan Aeronautical 67 centre, 167 below left and below right; TWA 243 centre, 254 left; United Airlines 232–233 below, 242 right; US Airforce 303 centre right, 329 centre, 372, 428 above and inset, 456 centre; US Army 398 above; US Navy 303 below, 332 below; Vought 448 centre left; John Warwick 326 right; Gordon S. Williams 244–245, 253 centre, 307 below centre.

Illustrations drawn by Mike Badrock, The County Studio, Bill Hobson, Nigel Osborne and Tom Stimpson.

SOLDIER

www.rbooks.co.uk

SOLDIER

The Autobiography of General Sir Mike Jackson

GENERAL SIR MIKE JACKSON

BANTAM PRESS

LONDON • TORONTO • SYDNEY • AUCKLAND • JOHANNESBURG

TRANSWORLD PUBLISHERS
61–63 Uxbridge Road, London W5 5SA
A Random House Group Company
www.rbooks.co.uk

First published in Great Britain
in 2007 by Bantam Press
an imprint of Transworld Publishers

A CIP catalogue record for this book
is available from the British Library.

ISBN 9780593059074 (cased)
9780593059081 (tpb)

Maps by Encompass Graphics

Addresses for Random House Group Ltd companies outside the UK
can be found at: www.randomhouse.co.uk
The Random House Group Ltd Reg. No. 954009

The Random House Group Limited supports The Forest Stewardship Council (FSC), the
leading international forest certification organisation. All our titles that are printed on
Greenpeace approved FSC certified paper carry the FSC logo.
Our paper procurement policy can be found at
www.rbooks.co.uk/environment

Mixed Sources
Product group from well-managed
forests and other controlled sources
www.fsc.org Cert no. TT-COC-2139
© 1996 Forest Stewardship Council
FSC

Typeset in 11.5/15pt Times New Roman by
Falcon Oast Graphic Art Ltd.

Printed in the UK by
CPI Mackays, Chatham, ME5 8TD.

4 6 8 10 9 7 5 3

This book is dedicated to the British soldier
and his family, past, present and future.

Contents

List of Maps

Preface

What follows is an autobiography. It focuses more on my life in the Army than on my personal life. But my own experiences, reactions and observations provide the thread running through the book. If what I have written seems to some egocentric, this is the reason why.

I should like to stress that I make no claim to have written a history of the events I have lived through. I am aware that there is much else that could be included, were I writing a different sort of book. But to do so would be in a sense dishonest. I have tried to describe how these events seemed to me at the time, and to distinguish clearly the occasional afterthought reached with the benefit of hindsight.

There are many people with whom I've worked closely during my military career who are not mentioned by name in the pages that follow. To do so would be to burden the narrative with a weight of detail it could not support. These people know who they are, and I hope they know that I'll always be grateful to them for their advice, encouragement and support – particularly my various Chiefs of Staff, Military Assistants and ADCs. That they are not all named in this text does not mean that they are not remembered.

This book is therefore both a story and a statement. The story begins with youthful adventure and ends in rather less youthful high command. The statement is what that journey taught me. I also hope that this book might even inspire some of its younger readers to undertake a similar journey.

Acknowledgements

My heartfelt thanks go to all those people who have kindly helped and encouraged me along the way, and without whom I doubt the book would have been written. I would particularly like to thank all those who read and commented on the text, including: Edwin Glasgow QC, Major General David Howell (Director of Army Legal Services), Major General (Retd) Andrew Ritchie and William Shawcross; and of course various members of my family, but especially Mark, my elder son, who has been invaluable in scrupulously giving me the grass-roots view. Among those who shared their memories with me were Brigadier Mark Carleton-Smith, Lieutenant Colonel Ed Smyth-Osbourne, Major (Retd) Milos Stankovic and Lieutenant General Sir Freddie Viggers.

I am particularly grateful to Brigadier James Everard and Major General (Retd) Jonathan Bailey for lending me their Kosovo diaries, and to Brigadier (Retd) Nick Ridley for lending me his account of Warrenpoint. All three of these generously allowed me to make use of their material.

ACKNOWLEDGEMENTS

I should also like to thank Alex Bedford for stepping in at short notice to help with corrections, and Micola Neville for introducing her. Jeremy Cartwright kindly downloaded an early typescript in the Rift Valley in Kenya. Derek Askew helped out by copying photographs from my scrap-books and other memorabilia.

Paul and Sarah Horsley generously lent us Ebbi, their beautiful villa in Tuscany, for a week at the beginning of the process, which allowed me to concentrate on the book free from other distractions.

I am most grateful to Adam Sisman for his professional and patient assistance with the text; to all the capable staff at Transworld, and particularly my editors Bill Scott-Kerr and Simon Thorogood, for their helpful comments on the typescript; to Gillian Somerscales for her excellent copy-editing; and to Sheila Lee for her part in the picture research.

Thanks are also very much due to Colonel Ben Bathurst and Nick Gurr of the MOD's Directorate General of Media and Communication for their rapid examination of the text for errors of security and fact.

For the avoidance of any doubt I want to make it clear that I have not always taken the advice I received, and I bear sole responsibility for the book's contents.

I particularly want to thank Annabel Merullo for encouraging me to write the book and helping me to place it; and my agent Christopher Little for delivering on what he promised.

Last, and greatest, of my debts is to Sarah, who has played a pivotal part at every stage of the preparation of the book, particularly with the picture research – and, as a soldier's wife, in the past twenty-two years of my life.

List of Abbreviations

ACE	Allied Command Europe
ADC	aide-de-camp
AFOR	Albania Force
AFSOUTH	(NATO's) Allied Forces Southern Europe
AG	Adjutant General
ARRC	(NATO's) Allied Rapid Reaction Corps
CCF	Combined Cadet Force
CDS	Chief of the Defence Staff
CGS	Chief of the General Staff
CINCEUR	Commander in Chief US European Command
CinCLand	Commander in Chief Land Command (British Army)
CINCSOUTH	(NATO's) Commander in Chief Southern Europe
CJO	Chief of Joint Operations
CO	commanding officer
COMAFOR	Commander Albania Force
COMARRC	Commander Allied Rapid Reaction Corps
COMBRITFOR	Commander British Forces
COMKFOR	Commander Kosovo Force
CSCE	Conference on Security and Co-operation in Europe
DEFRA	Department of Environment, Food and Rural Affairs
DfID	Department for International Development
DIPTEL	diplomatic telegram

DPR (Army)	Director of Public Relations (Army)
DPR (Navy)	Director of Public Relations (Navy)
DS	directing staff
DSACEUR	(NATO's) Deputy Supreme Allied Commander Europe
DZ	dropping zone
EOD	explosive ordnance disposal
EP	entitled person
ETA	estimated time of arrival
FLOTUS	First Lady of the United States
FRU	Force Reconnaissance Unit
FRY	Federal Republic of Yugoslavia
FYROM	Former Yugoslav Republic of Macedonia
GOC	General Officer Commanding
ICRC	International Committee of the Red Cross
ICTY	International Criminal Tribunal for Yugoslavia
IEBL	(Bosnia) Inter-Entity Boundary Line
IED	improvised explosive device
IFOR	(Bosnia) Implementation Force
IRA	Irish Republican Army
ISAF	(Afghanistan) International Security Assistance Force
KFOR	Kosovo Force
KLA	Kosovo Liberation Army
KVM	Kosovo Verification Mission
JIC	(Kosovo) Joint Implementation Committee
JIC	(UK) Joint Intelligence Committee
MA	military assistant
MAFF	Ministry of Agriculture, Fisheries and Food
MOD	Ministry of Defence
MRF	Military Reaction Force
MTA	Military–Technical Agreement
MUP	Ministarstvo Unutrasnjih Poslova (Serb special police)
ODA	Overseas Development Agency

OTC	Officers' Training Corps
P Coy	Pegasus Company
Pifwic	person indicted for war crimes
PJHQ	Permanent Joint Headquarters
POTUS	President of the United States
PPS	pre-parachute selection course
PRT	Provincial Reconstruction Team
RUC	Royal Ulster Constabulary
RUF	(Sierra Leone) Revolutionary United Front
SACEUR	(NATO's) Supreme Allied Commander Europe
SFOR	(Bosnia) Stabilization Force
SHAPE	Supreme Headquarters Allied Powers Europe
SITREP	situation report
SRSG	Special Representative of the (UN) Secretary-General
TA	Territorial Army
Tac HQ	Tactical Headquarters
TAOR	tactical area of operational responsibility
UCK	Ushtria Clirimtare e Kosovës (Kosovo Liberation Army)
UDR	Ulster Defence Regiment
UNHCR	United Nations High Commission for Refugees
UNMIK	United Nations Interim Administration Mission in Kosovo
UNPROFOR	(Bosnia) United Nations Protection Force
UNSCR	UN Security Council Resolution
VJ	Vojska Jugoslavia (Serbian Armed Forces)
VTC	video conference
WMD	weapons of mass destruction
ZOS	Zone of Separation

1

Schoolboy

I am a soldier. I have held every rank in the British Army from officer cadet to four-star general. I am now retired, but my almost forty-five years of service ensure that I remain a soldier at heart. My father was a soldier, my elder son has been a soldier and my younger son is thinking about becoming a soldier. My father-in-law, my brothers-in-law and my son-in-law have all been soldiers – so the Army is something of a family tradition. But my father didn't push me in that direction, and what I have said to my sons is that it is your life, and therefore your call, and you must decide what you want to do with it. I am pleased that both of them have decided to follow the path I took, but I would have been entirely content had they chosen otherwise.

My father George Jackson served in the Army for forty years, without ever rising beyond the modest rank of major. He suffered a serious heart attack in the early 1950s and that put the kibosh on any further promotion. The Army was pretty ruthless about such matters then. My father never showed any resentment at this setback. If it ever went through his mind that he might leave the Army, he never mentioned it to me. He was a great gentleman, very courteous, and scrupulously honest; a delightful man, who always had a wry smile on his lips, perhaps indicative of his humorous attitude to life. I liked him and I respected him; to me he was always 'Pop'. My mother too was very loving, and ours was a happy, secure home. My parents were not strict in the Victorian sense, but they did set rules, and I grew up with a definite sense of what was right and what was wrong.

Pop was a tall, lean, dark man with a long nose, all features which he handed on to me. He sported a neatly trimmed moustache, a practice I have not emulated! Pop was an active and practical man, who'd been a member of the Boys' Brigade and who was very fond of playing football. In adulthood he became a keen motorcyclist. Mother was dark too, slight but none the less forceful, a strong, bright-eyed Yorkshire woman, who had been quite a beauty in her youth. She loved walking, and in her teens had done a great deal of hiking in the Peak District.

My father joined the Army in 1935 as a private soldier, becoming a trooper in the Household Cavalry. I can remember his telling me about being a member of the Sovereign's Escort at the coronation of King George VI, which sounded very impressive to a young boy. He didn't make the big leap to commissioned rank until about halfway through the Second World War, when he became an officer in the Royal Army Service Corps. I suspect that my parents waited until my father was commissioned to get married.

George was the youngest of five children of Charles Henry Jackson, the skipper of a deep-sea line-fishing vessel working out of Grimsby. My grandfather, whom I sadly never knew, had lost his father when he was only four and, having been sent to work on a Lincolnshire farm at the age of ten, had run away to sea in his late teens. The life of a long-line fisherman then was very hard, sailing small vessels up to Iceland and along the

Greenland coast even in winter, often under brutal masters and in cruel conditions, defying icebergs and heavy seas in the search for cod and halibut up to 20 stone in weight. Such a harsh life left him unmarked, however, for Pop said that no family ever had a better father. My grandfather was patient, loving and fair; everyone who knew Charles Jackson respected him and his word, and looked upon him as a gentleman. In the First World War he served as a master of a minesweeper. In the Second World War, though by then well into his sixties, he again volunteered for service with the Royal Navy and was made master of a small vessel working out of Scapa Flow.

My parents must have met during the early part of the war when both were in their mid-twenties, though unfortunately I know almost nothing about the circumstances beyond the fact that Pop was then living in Bristol, and since my mother's death late in 2006 there is now no one left alive to tell me. My mother Ivy was from Sheffield, where her father, Tom Bower, had been an engineer in the steel industry who had lost his job in the Depression. She was a year older than my father, born five months before the outbreak of the First World War, and the only child of her parents, which was unusual for the period. (Her own mother had been one of eleven siblings.) An intelligent girl, she won a scholarship to Sheffield Grammar School, and when she met my father she was working as a curator at the Sheffield Museum.

Along with so many British soldiers, my father spent the early part of the war kicking his heels. He and my mother married on 7 March 1942, soon after he received his commission. I was born two years later, at my mother's home in Sheffield, just ten weeks before my father finally went into action on D-Day, 6 June 1944. He was second-in-command of a squadron of amphibious vehicles (DUKWs) whose function was to ferry men and materiel ashore. His squadron commander was killed on the first run in to 'Gold' Beach, so my father had to take command from then on. For him, as for so many others, D-Day was a baptism of fire. For his actions then and subsequently he was awarded the Belgian *Croix de guerre* and was mentioned in dispatches. Like so many of his generation, he was reluctant to talk about his experiences and, judging that it would make him uncomfortable, I didn't seek to push him to do so.

I don't know much about what Pop did for the rest of the war except that he took part in the Allied advance through north-west Europe, finishing up on VE-Day in Germany. After the war he was posted to Palestine, in the Mandate days, before the creation of the State of Israel. British soldiers were trying to keep the peace between Arabs and Jews, and might be attacked by either; it was no place for wives and children. So my early years were spent in Sheffield with my mother's family, and then in Aldershot when Pop came back from Palestine. In 1948 he was posted to Libya, an Italian colony which had been occupied by the British during the war, and which would become an independent kingdom in late 1951. My first memory is of sailing out by troop-ship with my mother to join him. I can dimly remember our cabin, and the fact that both of us were very seasick as the ship sailed through the Bay of Biscay. In Libya the sun seemed to shine every day. We lived in the capital, Tripoli, where I attended the British Forces primary school. I can remember the name of our street, the Via Generale Cantore. We had an Alsatian, Roly – too good-natured to be a proper guard dog – and a pre-war Lancia with running boards, no doubt a legacy of the Italian occupation. In 1949 my sister Lynne was born in the British Military Hospital in Tripoli.

My parents enjoyed their overseas postings and, unlike some British people of their generation, always embraced 'abroad'. But after two years in Libya we came back to England when my father was posted to a Territorial Army unit in London. We lived in Army quarters, a large flat in Putney. I attended the local primary school on the west side of Putney High Street. A few years later my father was posted to a staff job in Nottingham, and not long afterwards to Germany, but by this time I had already started boarding at Stamford School, a single-sex establishment situated as you might expect in the town of Stamford, in southern Lincolnshire. Many Service families send their children to boarding schools, to achieve continuity of education while their parents are posted from place to place. The Army makes a contribution to the fees in recognition of this.

I was still only a small boy of eight when I went away to school. We slept in big dormitories with the windows left wide open, even in winter. I can remember waking in the morning to find snow on the bed. St Peter's, the junior boarding house, was on the other side of town from the main school, so every morning and then again in the late afternoon we youngsters would set off in a long crocodile, escorted by one of the house-masters.

At breakfast, we all gathered in the dining hall where each form sat at a different long table, waiting for the arrival of the Headmaster and his wife before beginning to eat. The Head was known to us as 'Eee-Hee', because of his funny little laugh; boys home in on such things. Eee-Hee, whose real name was Basil Deed, always had a bowl of porridge for breakfast. He would read *The Times* for what seemed quite a long time, and then scoff his porridge in double-quick time before going back to his newspaper. We used to time him, and it became quite a thing to see how fast Eee-Hee would get his porridge down on any particular morning.

I don't remember being homesick, and in general I was quite happy at school. We were all in the same boat, after all. There was a fagging system in place which required small boys to 'fag' for their seniors, running errands and generally acting as drudges: perhaps a little archaic, but it taught you to obey orders unquestioningly. Like boys everywhere we fought, but I don't remember any bullying. Being taller than most, I was able to look after myself.

At the end of term I would travel back to my family, and once my father had been posted to Germany, this meant taking the boat from Harwich to the Hook of Holland and then boarding a special military train that wandered through the garrison towns of northern Germany. I can still remember the sense of adventure of one occasion when I went by plane, the first time I had ever flown. Like any first-time flyer, I found it all very exciting. A family friend had met me at King's Cross off the train from Peterborough and driven me to the West London Air Terminal, where I was handed over to the care of an air hostess. She and the steward fussed over me during the flight – the fate of an unaccompanied minor is not a bad one!

I suppose I was a typical 1950s schoolboy: a Boy Scout who read *Eagle* and *Hotspur*, made Airfix models and spent long hours playing with my model railway. Family holidays were spent camping throughout western Europe, travelling in Pop's old Mercedes, and after that in his lovely pale-green BMW, so big that Mother needed a sandbag under her foot to reach the pedals. At school I played rugby and tennis, a sport I still enjoy, and took part in middle-distance and cross-country running. I enjoyed swimming, too; the school opened a pool soon after I joined – unheated, of course! Perhaps I was a bit rowdy. When I was eleven my housemaster warned my parents that my behaviour 'must improve'; the following term he reported that I was 'noisy and impetuous', and the next term that I was 'wild and scatterbrained'. I was often walloped for 'ragging' by prefects, who were entitled to administer corporal punishment, using a cane. But by the time I was almost thirteen the housemaster informed my parents that I was 'sobering down and growing up'. Eventually I became a house prefect, which in retrospect was good preparation for my future life as an officer, in that it gave me some experience of maintaining discipline and taking responsibility for others.

In my early teens I joined the school cadets, the Combined Cadet Force (CCF), which encompasses all three Services. We didn't have a navy section, as Stamford was some way from the sea, but we certainly did have an air section. I remember a most improbable Heath Robinson glider, which boys would fly across the playing field only a few feet above the ground. I chose to go into the army section, probably because of my father. I used a .22 cadet rifle and practised on an indoor range, but to this day I have never managed to become more than a very run-of-the-mill shot. I enjoyed the CCF camps, which meant going away for ten days or so with boys from several other schools, sleeping in tents or huts and spending our days under the supervision of a handful of regular Army soldiers. I remember one in Scotland, at Cultybraggan, and another in Aldershot. This was my first taste of soldiering. We undertook tactical exercises under the direction of the regular soldiers – one group setting out to capture a hill, for example, while another group was tasked to defend it. 'Go left flanking!' the sergeant might bellow as we schoolboys advanced across the heather, taking advantage of any piece of natural cover, often flinging ourselves forward on to the wet ground. In those days there were no cadet rifles; we carried the heavy Lee Enfield No. 4s, bolt-action rifles loaded with blanks. When you fired there was a satisfying crack and a smell of cordite, but no recoil and, of course, no bullet.

It's fair to say that I wasn't an outstanding scholar at Stamford. If I excelled at anything, it was modern languages. I have always been interested in the structure of words and in etymology generally, and I found that I had a facility for languages. Perhaps I have a good ear. My mother was a talented musician, a pianist who might well have made music her career had she not met my father and got married, and she too was good at languages. She encouraged me to take up the violin, which I persisted with throughout my years at school, though I think that hearing me scratch away used to drive her crazy. I did a bit of choral singing as well, and I particularly remember the excitement of putting on a performance of Handel's *Messiah* with the girls of Stamford High School. We also put on a French play with Stamford High, Molière's *Le Malade imaginaire*. Any contact with girls was of course very welcome!

French was compulsory, and I also took German, largely I suspect because my parents were living in Germany and I could practise my German in the holidays. More unusually, I also did Russian. Stamford was very go-ahead in offering Russian at O and A level in the late 1950s, when there was something almost exotic about it. From the late 1940s onwards the Russians had been the enemy, as they would be for forty years; the Soviet Union was a formidable opponent, very powerful and very menacing, and at the same time somewhat mysterious, hidden behind an 'Iron Curtain'. So there was a slight sense of forbidden fruit in studying Russian.

The sixth form at Stamford was grouped by study area, so that one had a modern language set, a science set, and so on. I decided to go with my strengths, studying French, German and Russian at A level, taking my exams in the summer of 1961, when I was seventeen.

It was about this time that I decided to join the Army. It's difficult to remember now what led to this decision. It was just one of those things that I seemed to have been thinking about for some time. Perhaps it had always been there in some way or other. I suppose that for me joining the Army meant a life of adventure, an escape from the humdrum alternative of working in an office. I was intrigued by the idea of putting myself on the line, of seeing how far I could push myself. And becoming a soldier offered the prospect of seeing something of the world. It's perhaps hard for young people now to realize how rare the opportunities for overseas travel were in those days if you weren't wealthy. My parents didn't push me into it, and I don't think that I had joined the CCF intending to join the Army in due course. But it was obvious to me that my father found his Army career satisfying, and I'm sure that my experiences in the CCF had a considerable influence in demonstrating the pleasures of soldiering.

Not many of the other boys at school were interested in a Service career, though there was one I recall, a bit younger than me: John Drewienkiewicz, known subsequently by his Army nickname, DZ, who would go on to have a successful military career, rising to become a major general. Our paths would cross again many years later when he was number two in the Kosovo Verification Mission.

My headmaster was a bit sniffy about my decision to join the Army. 'You know, Jackson,' he told me, 'you really should go to university.' There was a sense then, although it's completely changed now, that the Army was not the place for the brightest. I took it as quite a compliment that he thought I might be a candidate for university entrance, because in the early 1960s only a very small minority, perhaps about 5 per cent of all school pupils, had any form of tertiary education. But I had made up my mind and nothing he could say would alter it, though I did agree to go back to school for a term after taking my A levels as an insurance policy, in case the Army gave me the thumbs-down.

By this time my father had been posted to Malta, where I spent the 1961 summer holidays after my A levels. I remember sitting around the kitchen table with my parents and talking my career choice over with them, the application papers to join the Army as a regular commissioned officer spread out in front of us. I put in my papers, and in early November I was called before the Regular Commissions Board at Westbury, in Wiltshire. I would be away for three nights. I suppose I must have been quite nervous, aware that the stakes were high: I had been warned that around half of all candidates were failed by the Board. I took the train down to London and then another train out to Westbury, dressed in the suit that I would wear in the evenings. At Westbury station I was picked up by a minibus together with several other youngsters and driven to Leighton House, the home of the Regular Commissions Board (now known as the Army Officer Selection Board). The main building was a Georgian mansion, surrounded by lesser outbuildings, one of which provided the candidates' quarters.

There were about fifty of us on that three-day course, divided into three or four groups. We all wore colour-coded tabards with numbers on them – rather like the ones competitive runners wear – and throughout the course we would be addressed by number rather than by name. As well as standard intelligence tests, we were given a range of tasks, when there would be at least one member of the staff watching and listening to everything we did and said. One of the tasks was to give a 'lecturette' in front of the assembled company: five or ten minutes on the subject of your choice – which in my case was Malta.

Rather more taxing were tests of the kind widely used in the military, and nowadays often also on management courses. The scenarios differ but the same principles apply. In the Army these are known as command tasks: for example, working as a team to get a burden – a heavy oil drum or something like that – over some notionally bottomless chasm. You're given some planks and ropes but nothing quite fits, and the goal is to work out what to do. For some of these tasks a leader is appointed, while others are so-called leaderless. In all cases the observers watch the dynamics of the group to see who emerges with the bright ideas, who is a team player or who isn't.

Back at school, the eagerly awaited envelope arrived a few days later. There was a place for me at the Royal Military Academy, Sandhurst, starting in January 1962.

I passed the good news on to my parents, but I can't

remember how. Telephoning abroad back in those days was a nightmare. For one thing, you often had to wait hours until a line was available. If you were calling from a payphone, you had to insert exactly the right change, then press buttons A and B in the right sequence. If you pressed the wrong one, or pressed them in the wrong order, you risked losing all your money. I probably decided that it was easier to send them a telegram.

The rest of my last term at Stamford was fairly relaxed. The pressure was off, and this gave me the opportunity to study other subjects I hadn't been able to give a lot of time to before, like art. Unlike my son Mark I am no good at painting, but I enjoyed calligraphy. Our art master was quite a character, and oddly enough it was he who first suggested I read Clausewitz, the great philosopher of war. He said, 'You're going to be in the Army, boy, you must read Clausewitz's *Vom Kriege*, "On War".' So I did. I confess that I found it intellectually challenging. This was my first introduction to the theoretical side of warfare. Like so many others before and since, I was particularly struck by Clausewitz's dictum that 'war is nothing but the continuation of politics with the admixture of other means'. It was a concept that would resonate throughout my career as a soldier.

Before going to Sandhurst I had to enlist as a soldier, because as an officer cadet you are a soldier, not an officer. I was summoned to the nearest recruiting office, in Leicester, where with one hand on a Bible and standing in front of a uniformed officer I swore an oath of allegiance to the Queen, Her heirs and successors. Then I signed my so-called 'attestation paper', and that was it: I was a soldier. I was given one day's pay and sent away on unpaid leave until the date I was due to report to Sandhurst.

2

Cadet

Very early, perhaps even on my first evening at Sandhurst, we were given a talk about what it means to be an officer. The Royal Military Academy's motto is germane: 'Serve to Lead'.

An officer is a leader of men. He has to exert the authority to ensure immediate obedience when necessary. To do so effectively it is essential for him to earn the respect of the men under his command. Of course, he has to show himself to be physically fit, able to do the things he asks his soldiers to do. Courage is another obvious requirement, moral as well as physical. If an officer loses the confidence of his soldiers then obviously he is in some trouble; so he's got to have a good brain in his head, he's got to show good judgement and he needs to be decisive, to show the men that he knows the job and is able to make up his mind about things, quickly if need be. But there's another side to this too. An officer has got to look after his soldiers, not in a patronizing sense, but to ensure their welfare, safety and, where possible, comfort. He is responsible for them in every aspect.

The training at Sandhurst is designed to produce officers who understand the range of qualities required of them and who are capable of exhibiting these in practice. To those who aren't used to it, the combination of military discipline, rigid adherence to standards of dress and behaviour, and hard physical training may seem strange – though less so if you've been educated at a British boarding school. A certain degree of humility is necessary; you have a lot to learn. Being shouted out by a sergeant reinforces this message. There's an Army tradition that at Christmas the officers and NCOs serve the men their lunch, a symbolic gesture of the principle enshrined in the Academy motto.

The big day arrived in January 1962 when I presented myself at Sandhurst, just north of Camberley, on the border between Berkshire and Surrey. I remember how imposing it seemed: large and handsome buildings set in several hundred acres of grounds, with parkland, woods and ornamental lakes. I was excited to be there, keen to make a good fist of it.

Back then there were two intakes to the Royal Military Academy every year, in January and September. Cadets took a two-year course, with three terms in each year, following the academic model. We worked a five-and-a-half-day week, with Saturday afternoons and Sundays free, though we were not allowed out for the first few weeks. In those days, more than half of the course was academic, with lectures, tutorials, essays and examinations, very much on university lines and taught by civilian academic staff. We studied science, mathematics, languages, international affairs and military history. In recent years the curriculum has changed, to reflect the fact that the great majority of the intake will be graduates, and the course has been shortened from two years to one, with a more condensed academic syllabus.

Some things were much like school. For example, there were three colleges, Old, New and Victory, much like school houses. Old College is a magnificent stucco-fronted Georgian building in the Palladian style, with a grand entrance of massive Doric columns supporting an ornate pediment. I was housed in New College, itself a large and imposing red-brick building dating from the Edwardian era. Slightly to my surprise, I found that I had my own room, which I quickly discovered had to be kept immaculate because, like everything else, it would get inspected. It was small, equipped with a single bed, a wardrobe, a hand-basin and a bookshelf, and heated by a heavy cast-iron radiator: all pretty basic, perhaps, but to me, accustomed to sleeping in large dormitories at boarding school, it seemed very comfort-able. There were endless roll calls; I heard ours so often that I could soon recite the names of the cadets in my platoon by rote. On arrival, every cadet was assigned to one of four companies in each college, named after battle honours of the British Army – I was assigned to Ypres Company – and within the company to the junior platoon of about fifteen to twenty cadets (about half the size of a regular Army platoon). Each company consisted of four platoons at different stages in their training, and each platoon had an officer as the platoon commander and a platoon sergeant, both regular Army: ours were Captain David Martin, a jovial gunner, and Sergeant Ford, a Grenadier Guardsman, a small but fierce man with a bristling moustache.

A sizeable minority of cadets were from overseas; in my company there were cadets from Jamaica, Malaysia, New Zealand, Nigeria, Pakistan, Sierra Leone and Thailand – and two from Iraq; in my platoon, we had a Sikh from Malaysia, Sarjit Singh, a very good man, and Sam Mboma from Sierra Leone. Poor Sam chose the wrong side of an attempted coup and was executed only a few years after leaving Sandhurst. As for the British cadets, I'm always wary of making assertions when I don't have the hard evidence, but I would have thought that two-thirds or more of them were public schoolboys, whereas nowadays the proportion is more like one-third. Society was more hierarchical then than it is today, and this fact alone may have deterred many good candidates from state schools from applying to Sandhurst. I would maintain that the Army has always been open to talent, however. The First World War general Sir William Robertson may have dropped his aitches, but he rose from private soldier to become Chief of the Imperial General Staff. My own view has always been that I don't give a damn where somebody comes from; if he's good, he's good, and that's the end of the matter. I loathe snobbery in any form.

Unlike today, there were no women at Sandhurst at that time. The then Women's Royal Army Corps was completely separate, and female officer cadets had their own nearby but separate college.

To say that there was a lot to get used to would be an understatement. For one thing, everything seemed to have to be done at the double, and we were inspected all the time to make sure we'd done everything properly. Then there was the novelty of being addressed by grown men as 'Sir' (I was still only seventeen). All the warrant officers and senior NCOs would address you as 'Sir', even if they prefixed this with an unflattering description, such as: 'You horrible lazy idle officer cadet, Sir.'

I remember very early on being on parade and addressed by the great Academy Sergeant Major, the senior warrant officer for the entire British Army. 'Now that you are at Sandhurst,' he barked at us, 'I will call you Sir and you will call me Sir, because I am a warrant officer. But there's one difference: you will mean it and I most certainly won't.' This was the legendary Jackie Lord, the Academy Sergeant Major for most of my time at Sandhurst. A tall, lean man with a well-trained moustache and piercing eyes, he stood ramrod-straight. Lord had been a Grenadier Guardsman; having joined Airborne Forces on their formation, he had fought at Arnhem and had been captured. The story is told that, by the time his prisoner-of-war camp was liberated, Jackie Lord had rounded up the remaining Germans and put them in custody, and was ready at the front gate with an immaculate salute and a guard of honour when the Allied liberators arrived. He was a hell of a man, much admired and respected by all the cadets.

Right at the beginning we were issued with our kit. Sandhurst has its own uniform, given that none of the cadets at this stage is a member of any particular regiment. We were issued with a smart full dress uniform, known as 'Blues', khaki serge battle-dress (which despite its name wasn't worn in the field), combat kit (which was), a peaked cap for smart wear and a beret for field and non-smart wear, and several pairs of very stiff boots: best boots that had to be kept highly polished, and boots for the field. In those days they were hobnailed, believe it or not, and you had to put the studs in yourself to a set pattern. The boot had to be soaked first to make the leather supple enough, and then you banged in the studs with a hammer. Boots were inspected like everything else. The sergeant would bark, 'Mr Jackson, Sir, let me see your boots' – then, 'Those boots are fucking idle, Sir. Show again.'

We spent a lot of time cleaning our kit, and usually we'd sit doing this together, in and out of each other's rooms, or at tables in the corridor, chattering away with one another. The shared tedium of it all helped build a sense of comradeship.

Cadets were issued with their own weapon, the standard rifle of the day, which was known as the SLR, the self-loading rifle. 'This is yours, look after it very well, Sir,' I was instructed. We kept our rifles in our rooms when not in use, with the bolt extracted and locked in a small safe. Nowadays this would be an unacceptable arrangement; the complete weapon must be kept in a secure armoury.

The first term's training was all military, essentially the same as any recruit going into the Army gets: basic weapon handling, basic fieldcraft, basic infantry tactics, basic communications – and of course we began square-bashing. We learned all the drill: how to present arms, how to stand at ease, how to march in step and keep an exact distance from the next man while turning our heads to give the salute. The man on the inside of the row has to remain looking forward to ensure that the rest continue to march straight ahead. The slightest mistake and we had to do it all over again. There's plenty of hard physical exercise ('beasting' as it's known in the Army): cross-country runs, route marches, a lot of gym work, boxing, swimming and so on. Much of this is done on a competitive basis between the companies, encouraging an *esprit de corps*. Then there's the assault course. All assault courses are basically the same: there'll be a number of obstacles, such as rope swings and ditches. Some you can only really handle as a team. The high wall is one of those. You won't get over it on your own because it's too high for an individual to jump to the top, so you have to shove up one or two blokes, who, having got up there, lie on their bellies with their legs dangling on the other side and their arms reaching down, ready to catch people and hoick them up as they take a running jump at it. Plenty land face down in the mud. You're carrying your kit and being chivvied all the time, naturally.

It was soon borne in on us that to a large extent we would stand or fall by our ability to work as a team. In that respect the platoon is a microcosm of the Army as a whole. The sense that you're all in it together is very important. And of course that sense forms among a platoon of officer cadets as it forms in any other unit: you help each other through some of the difficult bits, and where somebody's a bit weak you'll offer to give them a hand.

Inevitably there were some cadets who dropped out, and a few who failed to come up to scratch, those who were told that there was no point in continuing. If you were struggling to keep up you might get 'back-termed', which meant you had to do the last term again and pick up the course with the next intake coming through. Fortunately this didn't happen to me.

In the battlefield exercises, some cadets would be given command appointments such as platoon or section commander for, say, the following twelve hours, and ordered to carry out some major tactical task. The permanent staff watch this sort of exercise particularly closely, because if there is any doubt about a cadet's suitability, this is where it shows. A cadet platoon commander might be charged with taking his platoon from point A to point B, and then ambushed on the way by the enemy (another platoon firing blanks). How do you handle that? Some guys freeze: Bloody hell, I've been ambushed, what do I do next?

Each December we travelled abroad for a big exercise. In my first year we went to Cyprus, which at that time of year has a climate much like England in early summer. In the second year we went to Libya, which was interesting for me personally because of course I remembered living there as a boy. We also did an exchange exercise with the French military academy, St Cyr: one year they came to us and then the next we went to them. I chatted with some of the French cadets, who impressed me as competent, professional and committed. This was a pleasant surprise, because in those days the prevailing wisdom was primarily to see the French as having been defeated by the Germans in 1940 and by the Viet Minh in the early 1950s.

Once the first term was over we were allowed out at weekends, after the Saturday morning parade on Old Building Square. The parade itself would usually take an hour or so, and afterwards we would be itching to get off. But sometimes, instead of the hoped-for 'Well, gentlemen, that's it, off you go for your weekend,' we would hear the Academy Sergeant Major utter the dreaded words: 'That was terrible. Go round again.' A groan would go out, as cadets realized that they would not be able to catch the planned train or make the arranged rendezvous.

By this time I had a car, a green 1937 Morris 8 Tourer known as 'Esmeralda' that I had bought for £20 – one of a collection of old bangers belonging to cadets, many of them pre-war, parked around the back of New College. I often had to crank-start the engine, but in general Esmeralda behaved herself. Those cars were so simple that even with minimal mechanical skills you could more or less maintain them.

Camberley was handily placed for heading up to London. There was a pub in South Kensington that we cadets frequented, The Bunch of Grapes, and often that would be the first – and last – port of call. We drank a lot of beer, and chased the girls in West London flat-land. Often we could go from party to party until very late on a Saturday night. We had a lot of fun in those days. Work hard, play hard: that was our formula.

It's been largely superseded, but there was then at Sandhurst a sort of prefect system: so-called 'cadet government'. Only in a minor way was this a disciplinary body, but cadets were ranked: cadet corporal, cadet sergeant, junior under-officer and senior under-officer. The senior intake provided a complete cadet command structure, which shadowed the real officers at Sandhurst: the senior under-officer shadowed the company commander, three junior under-officers shadowed the platoon commanders of the following three intakes, and so on. I made it to junior under-officer, one short of the highest rank – quite pleasing.

A few days before the end of my time at Sandhurst the order of merit for our intake was published. A typed list was pinned up on the notice board, and everybody crowded around to examine it, inevitably with much leg-pulling. I was ranked fifth in the overall order of merit – 'jammy bastard', as one of my friends kindly put it. I sent my parents a telegram to let them know how I'd done. A day or two later came the prizegiving; I must have been a real inky swot in those days, because I won two prizes, for languages and military law.

On the morning of 19 December 1963, I was one of two hundred or so officer cadets in our 'Blues' who passed out on the Sovereign's Parade. General Sir Gerald Lathbury, the then Quartermaster General, took the salute on behalf of the Queen from the top of a dais. He had commanded the 1st Parachute Brigade at Arnhem, and was now Colonel Commandant of the Parachute Regiment, the tribal elder. We marched past in slow time and then in quick time, saluting as we passed the general. At last we marched up the wide stone steps of the grand entrance of the Old College, between the massive Doric columns and on through the open doors. In accordance with tradition, the Adjutant followed us up the steps mounted on his charger.

After the parade came a formal lunch. There was an end-of-term feeling, and when lunch was over we handed in our kit and then let off a bit of steam. It was a tradition for each platoon on commissioning day to pose for a photograph in the most ridiculous dress they could find; perhaps because we'd just got back from Libya, we chose a French North African theme, with guys dressed as legionnaires, matelots and other outlandish figures. In the evening we changed into our smart new regimental mess kit uniforms, ready for the Commissioning Ball that evening, attended by lots of pretty girls. For some reason I had two girls to escort that evening, one of whom I contrived to pass on to another cadet whose date had stood him up. Our rank as second lieutenants would be shown by a star, known as a pip, one on each epaulette. But we would not actually become commissioned until midnight, by which time most of the regular staff would be long gone – ever since the time when a newly commissioned young officer had tried to place his sergeant under arrest. And so the form was to cover each pip with a piece of tape. At midnight, to the popping of champagne corks, off came the tapes, and from that moment on we were all officers.

The one really big decision that any cadet has to make at Sandhurst is which part of the Army he's going to join. The regimental system is fundamental to the British Army (although something of a mystery to foreigners). The different components of the Army are known as the Arms and Services: broadly speaking, the Arms comprises the fighting elements – for example, the Royal Armoured Corps, the Infantry, the Royal Artillery, the Royal Engineers – and the Services the support and logistic elements, for example, the Royal Army Medical Corps and the Royal Logistic Corps. Furthermore, the Royal Armoured Corps and the Infantry in turn each comprise a number of regiments. British soldiers give their first loyalty to their own corps or regimental cap-badge, and only then to the Army as a whole. The British Army can therefore be seen as a federation of warrior tribes, each with its own history, hierarchy, customs, dress and so on. It is a peculiarly British structure, but one which self-evidently works well for the British Army.

I'd been attracted by the Parachute Regiment right from the start. The Paras had a reputation as a can-do organization, offering the young soldier the prospect of plenty of action. On enlisting in the Army you formally have to join one tribe or another, even if you are bound for Sandhurst. When I went to the recruiting office in Leicester after being accepted by the Regular Commissions Board I had chosen to enlist in the Parachute Regiment. Clearly it was in my mind even then that serving with the Paras would be an exciting challenge.

As my time at Sandhurst wore on, however, I came to the view that I could best use my languages in the Intelligence Corps. So when I filled out preference forms about halfway through my second year, that became my first choice, and in due course I was accepted and commissioned into the Corps.

After leaving Sandhurst, I was ordered to report to the Intelligence Corps training centre (then called a 'depot') at Maresfield, near Uckfield in Sussex, after completing twenty-five days' commissioning leave. To celebrate becoming an officer, I bought myself a used sports car, a green, soft-top Sunbeam Alpine, not very reliable but a lot more glamorous than my old Morris 8.

To be frank, Maresfield was a bit of an anti-climax after Sandhurst. I seemed to be treated as a sort of general dogsbody, doing the boring tasks nobody else wanted to do. This didn't last very long, however, because after three months I was sent on the fifteen-week infantry platoon commanders' course. The Intelligence Corps had, and still has, a commendable policy of ensuring its young officers get some combat-arm experience by spending a year or two as a platoon commander with an infantry battalion, and one had to do the course as preparation for that. The course takes the young subaltern beyond the very basic level of tactics he learned at Sandhurst and prepares him to join an infantry battalion as a platoon commander. So there were young officers on the course from every different infantry regiment, dressed in a startling variety of different uniforms and headgear.

The first part of the course was at the long-since closed Small Arms School at Hythe, on the Kent coast. This was primarily about weapons and was taught mainly by senior NCOs. The second part was all about infantry tactics, taught mainly by officers, and took place at what was then the School of Infantry at Warminster, on the edge of Salisbury Plain. It was an intensive course and we spent a lot of it in the field, some of the time carrying out practical tasks such as digging slit trenches – hard work in the chalk of the Plain. The exercises included 'all phases of war', i.e. advance, attack, defence, withdrawal. Sometimes these exercises were scripted very tightly, and at other times there was more scope for improvisation, what we call 'free play'. Umpires decided the casualties, handing out tags labelled 'gunshot wound' or whatever. We also learned how an infantry battalion works in the field, with its three manoeuvre companies, its support company equipped with anti-tank weapons and mortars, and its administrative company which runs the battalion's logistics.

Before I reached the end of the platoon commanders' course I was summoned to Birmingham University for an interview. While still at Sandhurst I had decided to apply to university to read Russian Studies, even though getting a place would mean postponing by another three or four years the day when I would begin real soldiering. Back then, as I have said, only a handful of the cadets at Sandhurst had degrees, but the Army took the view that a proportion of its officer corps ought to be graduates and therefore it funded a limited number of university places annually for newly commissioned young officers: about forty out of an annual intake of around four hundred, so around 10 per cent of the total.

My original A-level grade in Russian had been pretty poor, and as Sandhurst offered the opportunity to take A levels, I had decided to have another go. My Russian teacher was a splendid character, Count Constantinoff, a small and wizened old man who used to tell rather tall stories about sledges and wolves in the snow when he was in his cups. As a White Russian he had fought in the Civil War against the Reds, and only got out when it was clear that the Whites had lost.

I re-sat my Russian A level and obtained a better grade. Even with my improved Russian, however, my grades – a D and two Cs – were still not good enough for Oxford, which turned me down, rather to the disappointment of my parents. With hindsight, this was probably fortunate, because as a result I took a degree which interested me rather more and which I think has stood me in rather better stead. The Oxford degree focused on Russian literature, and while I had studied the Russian classics – Pushkin and Tolstoy, in particular – I felt that if there were something broader, that would be better for me. That's why I was attracted by a course in Russian Studies, whereby you studied the language as much as a means to read source material in Russian as for its own linguistic sake. At that time only two or three universities in Britain were offering such a course. In the first year, one would study straightforward politics, economics and sociology, and then in the second and third years one would move on to apply those disciplines to what was then the Soviet Union, and its history. I felt that it might be useful to 'know thine enemy'.

Birmingham accepted me, so a month or two after completing the platoon commanders' course, off I went to begin life as a student. The mid-1960s was an interesting time to be at university. A new Labour Government under the leadership of Harold Wilson had come in, after a long period of Tory rule. Change was in the air: there was the beginning of a youth counter-culture which rejected established values. Young men were starting to grow their hair long and dress in some pretty outlandish clothes. Students were in general left-inclined and pretty anti-war. Many of them were viscerally opposed to the use of force, whatever the circumstances. As a serving young Army officer I suppose I must have seemed an object of some curiosity to most of them, but I made no attempt to disguise who I was or what I thought.

My time at Birmingham coincided with an escalation of the Vietnam War. Professional interest led me to follow events as closely as I could. The strong opposition to the war felt by the majority of my fellow students was obvious. I wasn't opposed to the war in principle, and I did share the American belief that the march of Communism needed to be resisted. I can remember speaking at a formal debate in the Students' Union; the subject was a rather general pacifist proposition along 'King and Country' lines, but of course Vietnam was always in the background. Unsurprisingly, the vote went against us. Wilson made it clear early on that he was not going to deploy British troops to Vietnam to support our American allies. The British Army had mixed feelings about this. On the one hand, there was relief that British soldiers were not going to be sent into what was obviously a very difficult and dangerous situation. On the other hand, there was a sense of an opportunity missed.

I was two or three years older than most of my

contemporaries at Birmingham, and perhaps a little more mature: certainly better off, thanks to my second lieutenant's pay. I used to go up to London quite a lot. Having a bit more money to spend as well as a sports car was no bad thing for my social life.

I lived in digs, in Edgbaston, just down the road from the university, as the only tenant of a middle-aged landlady, a widow as I remember. She would cook me breakfast, and then I would normally eat lunch and my evening meal in the university refectory. They were comfortable lodgings, though my landlady was very proper and there was no question of being able to bring girls back. To keep fit I used to swim and go pounding round the streets of Edgbaston in my Army boots. I kept my military hand in by doing the odd weekend exercise with the Officers' Training Corps (OTC), and I went on their camp on Dartmoor for a fortnight in the summer vacation. It was pretty tame stuff after what I was used to, but I enjoyed it all the same. I was relieved to be in the company of people who didn't disapprove of my choice of career. It must be admitted, too, that the OTC bar served some of the cheapest beer in Birmingham.

Russian Studies was not everybody's cup of tea, and only a handful of students took the course. We were taught in small groups or in one-to-one tutorials. It was a degree requirement to spend part of your second long summer vacation in Russia, to improve your spoken language as much as anything else. But the Ministry of Defence thought this was a bad idea and told me I couldn't go. I'm not sure what they thought might happen. Maybe they were worried that I might be seduced by some KGB beauty – not that I knew any secrets to betray. It was disappointing, because when you spend so much time studying a country, you want to go and see it for yourself. I didn't argue against the ruling, however. I had to get a special dispensation from the University Senate to relieve me of the obligation to fulfil that aspect of the course. In its place they sent me on a language immersion course at a summer school in Chester, a poor substitute. I was quite envious when my fellow undergraduates came back at the end of their stay and told me what I had missed. Ironically, ten years later I would be sent to the Soviet Union, courtesy of the MOD.

I got married in 1966, while still at university. It seemed very much the right thing to do at the time, but we were both rather young, even by the ways of the time. As the marriage regretfully broke down in the early 1980s, I will say no more, beyond that I became the father of two much-loved children, Amanda, who was born in 1971 when I was serving in Northern Ireland, and Mark, born in Scotland a couple of years later.

In 1967 I graduated with second-class honours. I didn't attend the actual graduation ceremony, because by the time it took place I was halfway across the world, with my wife and parents in Hong Kong, where my father had been posted not long before. We had flown out to join them under what is called an 'indulgence', a scheme that allowed you to take up an empty seat on any RAF aircraft for a nominal sum. I had applied for an indulgence and one came up, irritatingly the day before the graduation ceremony. Thankfully the university agreed to grant me my degree *in absentia*, so off we went to Hong Kong for a few weeks. I found it a vibrant, exciting place, though there was a sense of unease about the upheaval just across the border in Communist China. It was a treat to stay with my parents, who lived on the second floor of an apartment block with a big balcony overlooking Repulse Bay, one of the most beautiful beaches in Hong Kong. Then we flew back to England, and on 7 August 1967 I reported to the Parachute Regiment depot in Aldershot to begin my infantry attachment.

3

Subaltern

The Parachute Regiment considers itself to be special. It attracts a certain sort of soldier, with a lust for adventure and excitement, and terrier-like commitment and determination. The Regiment prides itself on its fighting qualities and its wholly professional approach. It is a young regiment, founded in the Second World War, and some see it as still having the brashness of youth. If that might have had some truth forty years ago, I believe it to be without foundation today. The Paras have come of age, matured by operational reality and experience. Officers of the Regiment – and never more so than now – have achieved high rank in the Army in competition with others of their peer group. The Paras provide over half of the regular Special Air Service – a statistic which vividly emphasizes their fighting qualities.

The Parachute Regiment, the infantry of the Army's Airborne Forces, has the unique ability to deploy directly to its objective over strategic distances, independent of any need for ports, airfields and other infrastructure in the theatre of operations. The airborne role is a dramatic one, not least because it carries with it inherent risk, but also because it provides the ability to surprise the enemy, to dislocate him. Helicopter-borne operations can produce a similar effect, but they can only be mounted at short, tactical ranges.

The Regimental motto is 'Utrinque Paratus', which means 'ready for anything' – a neat pun on 'Para'.

I had opted to join the Intelligence Corps, and at this stage I still had every intention of returning to them once I had completed my infantry attachment. But it was no coincidence that I opted to do my infantry training with the Parachute Regiment. I'd had the Paras in mind right back when, as a schoolboy, I went to Leicester to enlist – and in my second year at Sandhurst I had volunteered for the basic beginner's parachute course at RAF Abingdon, though this was more because I thought it would be fun than with any thought to the future. The course began with a fortnight's concentration on drills and landing techniques. As part of this you jumped from a platform about 10 yards high, wearing a harness attached through a pulley to an air fan, which slowed your descent so that you dropped to the ground as if wearing a parachute. Afterwards you did eight proper parachute jumps, the first two from a small cage dangling below a tethered balloon, in those days an old Second World War barrage balloon (this means of training went out of service years ago).

I wouldn't be honest if I didn't admit to being a little apprehensive the first time I jumped, but it was exciting too. The feeling of letting go when you step into space is so intoxicating that some people get hooked on it. And when you hit the ground you feel exhilarated. In some ways it's more daunting to jump from a balloon because the whole thing is that much more clinical, as deliberate as stepping off a cliff. In a military aircraft, on the other hand, it can feel somewhat claustrophobic. You're packed in like sardines, you've been sitting in an uncomfortable position for hours, it's hot and sweaty, and there's a hell of a lot of noise, especially once they open the door and the red light comes on. Low-level flying can be particularly unpleasant, with many people being airsick. It's a relief to get out into the fresh clean air. And as soon as you leave the plane you're in the propeller backwash – whereas if you step out of a balloon you fall vertically.

After a couple of jumps from the static barrage balloon, the other six training jumps were from aircraft. In those days we jumped from a Hastings or a Beverley, the four-engine transports of the day. There was a very clear drill on the ground beforehand, so we knew exactly what was coming. One of the drills to help you cope with the turbulence on leaving an aircraft involved using the so-called 'knacker-cracker', a cable running between two towers. You're harnessed to a slide, and after you jump off, you get bounced around as you slide – which can be quite painful in the nether regions if you haven't got the harness just so!

In the aircraft you're seated in a row with your back against the aircraft frame. Twenty minutes before jumping, you stand up and hook up your parachute to a static line above head height. About five minutes before you jump, one of the crew opens the door and after a short while the red light comes on. Then the light turns green and an RAF 'dispatcher' orders the first man in the line to jump – and so on, until it's your turn. You're on your feet, waiting in line. There's no time to hesitate: you just have to follow the man in front to the door and jump. The time interval between each man and the next is no more than a second.

Landing is not as difficult as one might imagine. Your vertical speed on hitting the ground is not that great; they say the impact is not much more than that of jumping off a kitchen table. That's in still air, of course; if you've got a brisk wind, that will give you lateral movement as well. But in still air you can sometimes remain on your feet when you land – the so-called 'stand-up' landing.

You did the first few jumps from an aircraft without your kit, but the training course was progressive, so after two or three jumps, you then started jumping with all your equipment.

Jumping with all your kit is another matter altogether. It might weigh fifty or sixty pounds, more in some cases: a heavy pack filled with everything you will need on the ground, your weapon strapped alongside your pack in a canvas sleeve, and your webbing with your ammunition. Just carrying it makes you feel like a beast of burden. But this is what you've been training for – to be able to land in a potentially hostile environment and fend for yourself when you reach the ground. Of course, it would be dangerous to land carrying so much extra weight; so the pack is not on your back, but hooked on to your parachute harness in front, with a quick-release mechanism that operates once the parachute opens, so that the pack falls on a length of rope perhaps 15 feet below you. There's a bit of a jerk when it reaches the end of the line, but then it dangles below you for the rest of the drop, and hits the ground first.

You finished by doing a night drop, which concentrates the mind because you can't see the ground unless the moon is very bright. As you drop you don't know how high you are, so it's important to keep a good landing position throughout. Just before you land you hear the thump of your pack hitting the ground, which gives you about a second's warning.

On successful completion of the Sandhurst parachute course, you were awarded a little parachute emblem – known as the 'light bulb' because that's what it looks like – which you wore on your lower sleeve. Afterwards we undertook a live jump as part of the Sandhurst exercise we carried out against St Cyr, the French military academy.

To qualify for Airborne Forces, you first have to pass the pre-parachute selection course (PPS) run by Pegasus Company (P Coy), so that was the next thing on my horizon in the late summer of 1967. It's a hard, physically demanding course: somewhat different from the SAS selection course, but none the less very tough. It is designed (a) to make sure each individual has a high level of fitness, and (b) to put him under stress and see how he copes with it. By no means everyone makes it through. For the duration of the course an officer is just a member of his squad, being shouted at by a sergeant along with all the others. As it turned out I was the only officer in my squad, which meant I came in for particular attention from our squad sergeant, a Geordie called Les Peacock. Sergeant Peacock was small, wiry, and extremely fit.

In those days, the course took place in Aldershot and in South Wales, near Crickhowell, where the Black Mountains meet the Brecon Beacons. The location has since moved to Yorkshire, but the format remains the same. There are speed marches (known as 'tabbing') over the hills, when you've really got to move; log races between teams carrying big heavy logs; what's called 'milling' – individual boxing, without any Queensberry Rules; the assault course; and other similar delights. The last thing you do is the stretcher race. You're in a squad of eight; the stretcher is loaded to simulate the weight of a wounded man, and you take it in turns to carry this, four at a time. It's very hard work, but there's a wonderful feeling when you get to the end and know that you've finished.

Once I'd passed the PPS that September, the Great Men who decide these things told me that I had to go back to RAF Abingdon and do the same basic parachute course all over again. I felt that this was unnecessary, but they said there had been too long a gap since I had last parachuted while still at Sandhurst more than four years earlier. So I went through the whole course once more. At the end of it I emerged with my red beret and parachute wings, indicating that the wearer has qualified to become a member of Airborne Forces.

I was now a full lieutenant, and almost six years after

enlisting had at last reached the stage when I was going to command real soldiers, in a real battalion in the field army. This is a moment every young Army officer looks forward to, with a mixture of anticipation and trepidation. I would be commanding a platoon of thirty-odd guys, some of them no doubt older than me and all serious soldiers, while I was a raw young man who wasn't even a proper Parachute Regiment officer.

The Regimental Headquarters of the Parachute Regiment posted me to the Second Battalion, 2 Para. On joining, I replaced the cap-badge of the Intelligence Corps with that of the Parachute Regiment – naturally a very proud moment. At the time, the whole Parachute Brigade – consisting of the three Parachute battalions and other airborne units from the Artillery, the Engineers, and so on – was in Germany on a very large exercise, so off I went to join them in the field. When I got there I was told, 'Right, you're going to B Company and you're going to command No. 4 Platoon.' Unusually, there would be no officer/officer handover, because the platoon sergeant had been in temporary command of this particular platoon. I was coming in over his head, which might have been a bit tricky.

The relationship between a new officer and the platoon sergeant is one that has been played out thousands of times over the centuries. The sergeant is almost inevitably older and vastly more experienced; typically he may have served ten years or more. In comes the young officer who has a lot to learn, but at the end of the day he is the one who has the authority. It is a very important part of the platoon sergeant's job, not only to be second-in-command of the platoon, but also to bring on his young officer, to show him the ropes.

No matter how much training you may have received, there's no template to show you how to work with your platoon sergeant. Everybody has to work it out for himself. So much of it is a matter of chemistry, of establishing the right relationship with this particular individual. Any young officer in those circumstances who starts to throw his weight around will become rather 'unloved'. You've got to walk a tightrope: you must show on the one hand that you are the boss, and on the other that you value your sergeant's opinion. There must be a bit of distance, even if it's only psychological. Physically you can be in a slit trench with the guy, you are sleeping next to him, you are crapping next to him: you can't be too standoffish in the field, but you mustn't be too matey either.

The sort of thing you might do is to have a quiet conversation with your platoon sergeant, maybe over a beer, certainly not in front of the soldiers, after you've been serving together three or four months or perhaps after a big exercise. 'How am I doing?' you might ask. If you give him the opening, you can have that conversation. But it's a delicate balance. Soldiers don't like being bullshitted. Some young officers make the error of trying to 'curry favour', and they soon learn that soldiers don't like that either.

In this case there was a further twist in the tale, in that the platoon sergeant I inherited soon moved on to other duties, to be replaced by . . . Sergeant Peacock! As it turned out this was a stroke of luck, because he knew me from the selection course, and if he hadn't thought then that I was OK, I wouldn't have passed. In fact we got on very well. He was a very dedicated and professional soldier, with a nice dry sense of humour, a remarkable man who finished up a lieutenant colonel. Many years later, I bumped into him on one of my last visits as Chief of the General Staff. I was at Bovington saying goodbye – and, lo and behold, there he was: Les Peacock. He was working as a retired officer down at the Royal Armoured Corps Centre. We had ten or fifteen minutes reminiscing together before I had to leave.

After the exercise in Germany was over I came back with the rest of the Battalion to Aldershot, where the Parachute Brigade was based at the time. Then early in 1968 2 Para headed out to the Far East for four months' jungle training. Malaysia seemed wonderfully warm after an English winter. We were based at a place called Kota Tinggi, about 20 miles north of the town of Johor Baharu, right at the southern tip of Malaysia, at the end of the causeway which links Singapore to the mainland. This was only my second time in the Far East – the first being my visit to Hong Kong to see my parents the year before – and the sights, the sounds and the smells all seemed very exotic. Malaysia and Singapore were then comparatively backward and undeveloped – very different from the way they are today.

Independent Malaysia was at this point just five years old. After the end of the Second World War, British and Commonwealth troops had fought a long counter-insurgency campaign in the Malay Peninsula against Communist guerrillas. The Malayan Emergency had lasted from 1948 until 1960, ending in the defeat of the Communists. The campaign had featured large in the Sandhurst military history syllabus. General (later Field Marshal) Sir Gerald Templar had been appointed High Commissioner, with extraordinary powers: one of his policies had been to move people out of the areas penetrated by guerrillas into protected areas, thus denying the insurgents a population to support their activities. In 1968, when we arrived in Malaysia to do our training, the US Army was already heavily engaged in what had begun as a counter-insurgency campaign in Vietnam. Interestingly enough, my company commander in Malaysia was Sam Conn, an American officer with experience of Vietnam, serving with us under a longstanding exchange arrangement whereby there's always a Parachute Regiment officer with an airborne unit of the American Army and an American airborne officer with one of our parachute battalions. We were fascinated to hear of Sam's Vietnam experiences. At the time I questioned the American tactics, and wondered whether they were not too reliant on technology and firepower. Now I am not so sure that they could have done anything else, given the political constraints on them and the growing unpopularity of the war at home.

This was a period of dramatic developments in the Vietnam War. In January 1968 the North Vietnamese had launched what came to be known as the Tet (New Year) Offensive, a massive surprise attack involving half a million men. North Vietnamese troops reached the gates of the American Embassy in the South Vietnamese capital of Saigon before being repulsed. The Commander of US Land Forces, General William Westmoreland, requested a further two hundred thousand reinforcements. Faced with a storm of criticism at home, the American President, Lyndon Baines Johnson, announced at the end of March that he would not be seeking re-election, as well as directing a halt to the bombing of North Vietnam. There was no bigger scalp than that of an American President; the North Vietnamese had suffered a military defeat, but scored a political victory. For military strategists considering how best to respond to Communist insurgency, there was plenty to think about in the spring of 1968.

Before going out to Malaysia, we had practised jungle tactics in thick woods back at home. There were soldiers in the Battalion who had operational experience of fighting in the jungle during the Borneo campaign in the early 1960s, when the British Army and its Commonwealth allies had successfully resisted Indonesia's attempt to take over the country. This had been largely infantry versus infantry fighting in the jungle – 'low intensity' operations, as opposed to high intensity, which involves tanks, artillery, air power: the full panoply.

Jungle warfare is the essence of infantry soldiering in many ways. You *can* use artillery, but it's not very effective because you can't tell where the rounds are landing. Usually you can't see very far, sometimes only three or four yards ahead. Then you have to decide: do you use tracks or do you not? If you follow a track, you're likely to make faster progress; but you may walk into an ambush, or step on a booby-trap. We tried to avoid unnecessary noise when moving through the jungle. Of course we carried machetes, and sometimes we were forced to use them, but only if there was no alternative. The area we were operating in was mostly secondary jungle, which is much thicker and harder to move around in than the original primary rainforest. It's hot and steamy, and you have to carry everything you need with you. In particular, you always have to think about your water requirements. Navigation in the jungle is very difficult. Before the days of GPS you had to navigate solely by dead reckoning, using a compass and a map and reading the contours. Two soldiers are nominated to count paces, and you have to check their counts one against the other: 'Right, how far have we come? Two hundred and fifty yards, OK, move off on a bearing of one-fifty.' If you get lost, well, Sir gets his leg pulled a bit. Serving in the jungle is a good way to get to know your soldiers because you're all living on top of each other.

One agreeable aspect of serving in the jungle is that you get eight hours' sleep every night. Sleep in the field is normally in short supply, because much operational activity takes place at night. But in the jungle the night is so dark that movement is almost impossible without using a torch.

Less agreeable were the leeches, thoroughly unpleasant creatures which would fasten on your legs and elsewhere. We took to wearing condoms after a young officer friend of mine found a leech disappearing up a precious part of his anatomy.

I was still commanding the same platoon I joined in Germany. The odd soldier came and went, but basically it was my gang, and I found the experience very satisfying. And we had a bit of fun, too. I remember nights out with other young officers in Singapore when we'd go on what the Navy calls 'a run ashore'. Though everyone knew I'd be leaving for the Intelligence Corps sooner or later, I was made to feel one of the tribe. Of course I used to get teased a bit – 'Where's the intelligence?', that sort of thing – but it was all very good-humoured.

While out in Malaysia we were warned that we would not be going home at the end of that tour. The Battalion was ordered to Hong Kong, then of course still a British colony, to reinforce the garrison. We flew there by RAF Hercules from Singapore. I remember that my parents came to meet me at Kai Tak airport.

On our arrival in Hong Kong, the tension was palpable. There had been unrest in the Colony the previous year, no doubt a spillover from events across the border. The Cultural Revolution in China was in full ferment. It was a bizarre period of upheaval in that vast country. China then was very different from the economic powerhouse of today. The Chinese leader Mao Zedong seemed semi-detached from the Government. His encouragement of ground-level revolutionary activism had unleashed violent forces, and the whole country seemed danger-ously unstable. The Chinese were attempting to foment trouble – even revolution – in Hong Kong, and there were fears that fanatical Red Guards might pour across the border.

The Battalion was given the task of securing the border with mainland China. Of course, if the Chinese had really wanted to invade we could not have stopped them. They had a huge army millions strong, whereas the entire British garrison was then four or five battalions, just a few thousand men. We would have fought, but we would have been quickly overwhelmed.

B Company's focus was on a place called Mam Kam To, one of the few points where you could cross by road into mainland China. Here a river formed the border. A simple barrier controlled access over the bridge. We were on a small hillock overlooking the crossing, in a makeshift *Beau Geste*-style fort. On the far side was an area where the peasant farmers would bring their produce to sell to traders from Hong Kong, who would be up there with small trucks and carts to collect it and bring it back to the city. Every morning these Chinese farmers would have what we used to call the Red Book session. They would all line up and chant and wave their copies of Mao's *Little Red Book*. It was the most extraordinary business.

The People's Liberation Army sentries patrolling the border took no part in these sessions. Not that we had any contact with them either. They were very disciplined, with precise orders how to react, depending on how close you came. So, for example, a sentry would be standing at ease with his weapon on the ground: when you approached within, say, thirty yards, he'd come to attention, and then within twenty yards he would hoist his weapon across his chest. You could tease them, just by approaching and retreating: very unkind really.

The barrier at Mam Kam To consisted simply of a red-and-white striped barber's pole, hinged at one end. I can still remember the first of the printed 'Orders for War' we were given, dating from many years earlier: '1. Close the barrier.'

In those days all you could see on the other side of the border were paddy fields stretching into the distance. Now there are skyscrapers everywhere you look.

As an American, Sam Conn had not been allowed by his superiors back home to accompany us to Hong Kong, and so for about a month, until his relief arrived, I took over command of B Company, about a hundred men, because I was the senior platoon commander. It was quite a privilege, given that I was still only a lieutenant of twenty-four.

And then I had another little stroke of luck. One of the tasks laid on the Battalion by the local Brigade Headquarters was to produce a young officer as a watchkeeper in the operations room back at Headquarters British Forces in Kowloon: POLMIL it was called, because it was run jointly with the police. Lieutenant Colonel Richard Dawnay, who was the Battalion commanding officer, asked me if I'd like to take it on and see a bit more of my parents. Of course, I said, I'd love to. So I spent a month actually living with my parents and commuting by duty vehicle to the Headquarters, where I did night duty manning the phones. After writing up the evening's report, you didn't have to stay awake: it was a sleeping duty, which meant that you'd only have to get up if the phone rang. So I got a reasonable amount of kip and then I had the days to myself.

The unrest was mainly confined to Kowloon, the urban area on the mainland; Hong Kong Island was more isolated from the trouble, both literally and metaphorically. But it was obvious to me that the vast majority of the population didn't want anything to do with Mao; on the contrary, what they wanted was to make money, and of course the Hong Kong Chinese are very good at that. It was pretty raw capitalism, with its downsides as well as its upsides. But I loved the energy, the colour, and the bustle; Hong Kong was an exciting place to be.

By the time 2 Para was withdrawn from Hong Kong, the crisis in China was coming to an end. Mao himself declared the Cultural Revolution over, and the Red Guards were disbanded. When the Battalion returned to Aldershot I was due to go back to the Intelligence Corps, but my return was delayed because 2 Para were again deployed early in 1969.

The British operation in Anguilla is an extraordinary tale, with many elements of comic opera; it would have made ideal material for Gilbert and Sullivan. Some people referred to it ironically as 'Harold Wilson's finest hour'. To those who wanted to see it that way, the story seemed to encapsulate the shrunken horizons of Britain in the late 1960s. While America was fighting a major war against Communist infiltration in South-East Asia, Britain was dealing with a little local difficulty on a tiny Caribbean island.

The origin of the problem was one of the many loose ends being tied up as Britain withdrew from Empire. At the time, there was a bit of a Whitehall fashion for putting federations together as a prelude to independence. The planners at the Foreign and Commonwealth Office tried it in Southern Africa, tying together Rhodesia and Nyasaland, and that didn't work terribly well. They tried to create a federation of all the British colonies in the Caribbean, which quickly fell apart. And following this collapse, they wanted to create a federation of three small islands in this particular bit of the Caribbean, St Kitts, Nevis and Anguilla – inevitably dominated by the first, as it was the biggest. The Anguillans, all six thousand of them, didn't like being lorded over by Kittitians, and they feared that with independence they would no longer be able to appeal to the British for protection. So, instead of demanding independence, the Anguillans insisted on remaining a colony. They made representations to London, which allowed matters to drift for a couple of years.

Then things began to get out of hand. There was talk of the Mafia establishing a foothold in this part of the Caribbean. A few dodgy characters appeared on Anguilla, including a fellow called Spector, Dr Spector, who – far from being an evil mastermind of the type faced by James Bond – was said to be a convicted abortionist from Cleveland, Ohio. A local politician made threatening noises, warning that he had caches of arms at his disposal to resist any attempt at imposing a solution on the island. Eventually a junior FCO minister was dispatched to Anguilla to persuade the inhabitants to accept the federation plan. On the very day of his arrival he sent a message back to London saying that he was under siege. It was alleged that shots were fired, though nobody was hit and no property seemed to have been damaged. The junior minister left the island shortly afterwards.

The British Government decided that it would have to act to restore law and order and to re-impose its authority by direct rule. So a force was speedily assembled to do this, based on 2 Para, because at that juncture we were the Spearhead Battalion

– that is, the battalion nominated to be at very high readiness for any unexpected eventuality. It was 2 Para's good luck that they were on the Spearhead roster when the decision was made. We were all very keen to take part, however ludicrous the politics of it all, because soldiers always want to take part in operations. It is what we're trained for, after all.

It was clear that one company would be left behind. And of course there was great competition inside the Battalion to avoid drawing the short straw. Much to our chagrin, it was decided that B Company would be the one to suffer that terrible fate 'Left out of Battle', while the rest of the Battalion would form the invasion force, accompanied by a contingent of 120 policemen provided by the Metropolitan Police. We at Aldershot witnessed the strange sight of groups of senior police officers arriving to coordinate their planning.

At first the plan was to parachute into Anguilla. That was rejected as being overdramatic, and it was decided that the force should be flown out to Antigua and then taken to the island on board two frigates, HMS *Minerva* and HMS *Rothesay*. They steamed through the night, arriving offshore while it was still dark, only a week after the envoy had left so hurriedly. At dawn the force set out for the shore in small rubber boats. Richard Dawnay, the commanding officer, was up on the bridge of one of the two frigates, waiting anxiously for news. Flashes were seen on the beach, though there was no sound of gunfire. A moment later the radio burst into life, reporting contact: several journalists, no injuries. The flashes had come from the photographers' cameras.

As it turned out there was no opposition at all, and not a shot was fired during the whole operation. Most of the islanders were hugely pleased to see British soldiers, because most of them had never wanted to become independent. The world found the whole affair rather comical. Somewhat undignified photographs appeared in the press of large naked policemen disporting themselves in the tropical waters. A boatload of prostitutes arrived from the nearby island of St Martin and were promptly sent back again, despite their protests that they had come to offer their services to the islanders and not to the servicemen.

In due course it was decided that the force in Anguilla should be downsized, and at the same time that there should be a *roulement*, i.e. that the existing force deployed there would hand over to B Company, to spread the operational experience around the Battalion. Richard Dawnay came home and his second-in-command, Major Norrie Giles, went out to replace him, as a 'local' (i.e. temporary) lieutenant colonel, to give the Army that extra bit of clout. He needed a small staff, and since by that time I'd been a platoon commander for eighteen months or so, I was chosen to be the adjutant of the force in Anguilla, on promotion to acting captain. So that was good news, both for Norrie Giles and for me.

I'd never been to the Caribbean before. We staged through Antigua, where the logistic base was, and then flew on to Anguilla by RAF Hercules, landing on a dirt airstrip. It's a flat island, scrub-covered, with some glorious beaches. I paid a nostalgic visit to Anguilla early in 2007 to find it transformed into a high-end tourist destination; but then it was rather dilapidated, with just a couple of ramshackle beach hotels, and very little infrastructure. By the time B Company arrived, any tension there had been before had eased. A British Commissioner had been installed and things were starting to return to normal. The soldiers continued to patrol the island, to get to know the locals and to deal with any remaining unrest, but there were no incidents at all that I can remember. A squadron of Royal Engineers was already on the island repairing the roads, building a new school and constructing a deep-water jetty. The police, dressed in their British helmets but mercifully not in their serge tunics, did what police do normally. We played cricket with the locals and were thrashed every time. 'This has been most useful for the airborne soldier,' Lieutenant Colonel Giles was quoted as saying in an interview given to a reporter from the *Aldershot News* shortly before we left, in September 1969: 'It has taught him citizenship.'

As a postscript: St Kitts and Nevis became fully independent in 1983, while Anguilla remains a British Overseas Territory. The island is now stable and thriving. Comic opera it may well have been, but the operation served to stabilize the situation and to provide Anguilla with the foundation of a prosperous future.

After the Anguilla operation my time with 2 Para was over. This was very sad for me. As my infantry attachment continued, I had asked myself increasingly whether I'd made the right choice in opting for the Intelligence Corps. I was more and more drawn to the active life of an infantryman, and I loved serving with the Paras. I relished their commitment, their professionalism, their unpretentiousness and their energy. I'd made a lot of good friends, and there was a buzz about the Parachute Regiment which was heady stuff to me. So I made up my mind to ask for a formal transfer. Richard Dawnay was encouraging. The Army has a system of annual confidential reports on every serving officer, which are collected in a book, to be used by the selection boards when a candidate is being considered for promotion; he wrote in mine that 'by inclination, character, and physique' I was 'far more suited to an infantry environment than to his present Corps', i.e. the Intelligence Corps. The Parachute Regiment had obviously decided that I was OK: if I wanted to join them, they were happy to have me.

But the Intelligence Corps didn't like the idea at all. To them, this was poaching. And I wasn't the only one who'd decided to leave. Of course, it was the risk they took in having this commendable scheme whereby their young officers go on an infantry attachment. So there was a bit of irritation when I announced that I wanted to make the transfer. The upshot was that they insisted I went back to the Intelligence Corps and soldiered on, at least for a time: their argument was that I needed to gain more experience of intelligence work before I could make an informed decision. By this time their depot had moved from Maresfield in Sussex to Ashford in Kent, so that's where I went next. And the first thing I had to do was to go on an Intelligence Corps young officers' course, because even though at twenty-five I was by this time not quite so young, I had yet to receive any intelligence training.

I left 2 Para in July 1969 as an acting captain. My date for substantive promotion was December that year. Now, there are rules about this: you can only maintain acting rank if you are working in a post which is allocated to that rank, and of course being a student on a course is not a captain's post per se. The purists would say, 'Well, you lose your acting rank and you're a lieutenant again.' But it's a bit hard to go down, having gone up; so a deal was struck that I would be a 'local captain', i.e. unpaid, until my substantive promotion came through in December. Army logic, perhaps.

The following three months were spent learning how the Intelligence Corps operates. From what I can remember the course focused on operational intelligence: how do you find out about what the enemy's doing over the next hill? Some of it was interesting, some less so, though really I was just marking time. I hope I gave it a fair shot and wasn't resentful about being made to do it. But the longer I stayed, the clearer I was that I wanted to transfer back to the Paras.

The first job I was given, and the last as it turned out, had nothing to do with intelligence per se. I was posted to be second-in-command of the depot at Ashford, which was really about training recruits for the Intelligence Corps – important enough, but nothing special. If the Corps had really wanted to keep me they might have given me something more exciting to do, so perhaps they'd given up on me by then. I had the sense that they didn't really approve of me; an earlier annual report had criticized my 'tendency to ebullience and flamboyant behaviour'. During my time with the Intelligence Corps I was sent on what was then called the 'Junior Division of the Staff Course', a three-month course intended to equip captains to become junior staff officers, and to initiate them into all-arms tactics – that is, tactics in operations involving all elements of the Army's various Arms and Services.

As time wore on I became more and more frustrated. Things had to be brought to a head. I asked for an interview with the Director of the Intelligence Corps. He must have guessed why I wanted to see him, because he gave me a less than encouraging look when I walked into his office and saluted.

'What's all this about, Mike?' he asked as I sat down.

I put the case that I had put forward the year before, when I'd been persuaded into staying on. 'Sir, I thought then that I'd made the wrong choice,' I explained, 'and now I'm convinced of it.'

He ran through the same old arguments for my remaining with the Corps.

'Look, Sir,' I said to him, 'I've given it a try, just as you asked me to. I've been back with the Corps for the best part of a year and I'm more convinced than ever that I made the wrong choice. I hope you will let me go, but you are probably going to lose me either way, because if I can't go back to the Parachute Regiment, I don't think I'll stay in the Army. I'll go and do something else.'

I fear this was bluff: I didn't have a Plan B. But I really wanted to move on. And I knew that, at the end of the day, he couldn't stop me. Every officer and soldier has the right to transfer between regiments if he wants to, though a great deal of pressure may be put on him to stay. With some reluctance, the Director of Intelligence agreed to let me go. On 9 November 1970 I received a posting order transferring me permanently to the Parachute Regiment. I reported back to the Regimental HQ, and they sent me off to join the 1st Battalion, which was already two months into an eighteen-month tour in Northern Ireland. This would be a residential tour, living with our families in Palace Barracks, Holywood, 10 miles east of Belfast. Like most people in Great Britain, I had not known much about Northern Ireland until the unrest had begun a couple of years before, but since then the Province had been in the media spotlight: as a result one was very conscious of the street violence and the fact that the Army had become heavily committed in trying to restore order. I was excited to be posted there. Northern Ireland was an operational theatre which offered an opportunity to see some action.

4

Troubles

The 'Troubles' in Northern Ireland seemed to go on so long that few people now recall how they started. Of course, there has been trouble between Protestant and Catholic in Ireland going back at least three centuries. But the modern 'Troubles' began in 1968, that year of upheaval – of *les événements* in Paris, of the 'Prague Spring', of the mass protests throughout America against the Vietnam War. Ironically, this was the only year since the Second World War in which no British soldier was killed on operations. Marches by the Catholic Civil Rights Association sparked Protestant reaction, and a spiral of violence began, with serious rioting in the main urban areas of Belfast and Londonderry. Houses were burned to the ground, families were driven from their homes, and civilians were killed in firefights between paramilitary groups set up on both sides of the religious divide. Rightly or wrongly, the Catholics felt that the police (the Royal Ulster Constabulary or RUC) sided with the majority Protestant or 'Loyalist' population and stood aside when Catholics needed defending. When

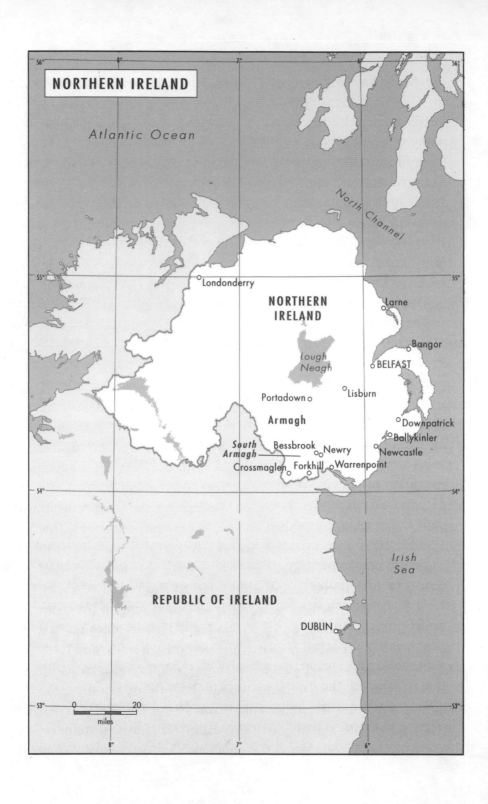

NORTHERN IRELAND

Atlantic Ocean

North Channel

Londonderry

NORTHERN IRELAND

Larne

Lough Neagh

Bangor

BELFAST

Portadown

Lisburn

Armagh

Downpatrick

South Armagh

Bessbrook

Newry

Ballykinler

Newcastle

Crossmaglen

Forkhill

Warrenpoint

Irish Sea

REPUBLIC OF IRELAND

DUBLIN

0   20

miles

the Army was first deployed on the streets of the Province late in 1969, at the urgent request of the Northern Ireland Government, the troops were welcomed and even cheered by many of the Catholic population, who saw them as protection from Protestant thugs. Looking back, I don't see that the British Government had any choice but to act as it did. However, the Irish Government, which had not then surrendered its constitutional claim to the Province, declared that the deployment of British troops on the streets of Ulster was unacceptable. British ministers described their intervention as a 'limited operation', with the idea that the soldiers should be withdrawn as soon as law and order was restored.

There was no reason for the soldiers to take one side or the other; so far as the Army was concerned, they had come to the Province simply to re-establish order, not for any political purpose. But it was impossible to avoid politics in Northern Ireland. So many things were sensitive, even the names of places. To call the Province itself by its ancient name, Ulster, could be an irritant to the Nationalists. The Royal Ulster Constabulary was therefore condemned by its very title. (It has recently been renamed, with a conscious effort at neutrality, the Police Service of Northern Ireland.) Whether you called the Province's second city Derry or Londonderry marked you out as Catholic or Protestant.

British soldiers entered a febrile situation. This was the first time that troops had been operationally deployed within the United Kingdom since the advent of a properly constituted police force. The Army was on a very steep learning curve in dealing with these intractable problems of civil disorder, not on some far-flung island but on domestic British territory, under the scrutiny of the ever-present press and television. To do so effectively required methods and skills that had not then been developed. There were new weapons, too: CS gas, then relatively untried, and baton rounds (generally known as rubber bullets), designed to disable without causing serious injury.

There is a story, perhaps apocryphal, perhaps not, from those early days when troops were first deployed to deal with rioters in Northern Ireland. It is said that the old colonial techniques of riot control were still being used, because they knew nothing else. I can remember watching a training film at Sandhurst in the early 1960s called *Keeping the Peace*, showing troops in box formation, the platoon commander surrounded by a square of soldiers. There was an escalatory procedure: first you addressed the crowd with a loudhailer, ordering them to disperse; next you unfurled the banner reading 'disperse or we fire'; and so on. The story has it that the first such banner unfurled in Northern Ireland was greeted with total incomprehension: apparently the phrase 'disperse or we fire' was written in Arabic, because the last time it had seen daylight had been in Aden.

By the time I arrived in Northern Ireland towards the end of 1970, the conflict had developed into a three-way struggle between Catholic paramilitaries, Protestant paramilitaries and the Security Forces. Soldiers were regularly taunted and stoned by young hooligans when they tried to impose order, in particular to prevent the traditional parades marching through areas where their presence was bound to provoke resentment. The Army had already largely lost the confidence of the Catholics, often described as 'Nationalists' because many of them were assumed to favour a united Ireland. Marches which had begun as a legitimate protest against social deprivation had become politicized. Soldiers were beginning to be shot at by snipers. The imposition of a curfew in the Falls Road area of Belfast in July 1970, and the subsequent violent reaction, had ended in several deaths and numerous injuries.

On 6 February 1971, Gunner Robert Curtis was shot dead in North Belfast by an Irish Republican Army (IRA) terrorist, the first British soldier to be killed in the Troubles. A line had been crossed: a British soldier had been killed on the streets of the United Kingdom, almost certainly by a fellow UK citizen. It was a shock, though we had all realized that this was bound to happen sooner or later. I was only a few hundred yards off at the time – close enough to hear the gunfire – taking part in the same operation, to contain rioting in the largely Catholic area of the Ardoyne.

The Northern Ireland Prime Minister went on television to announce that the Province was 'at war' with the IRA. But if this was a war, it was a war in which the Security Forces were at a disadvantage: they were, quite properly, required to operate within the law, while their opponents were literally outlaws. British soldiers serving in Northern Ireland were not immune from criminal prosecution for acts carried out on active service. They were given special powers to enter private property, stop vehicles, and so on – but in response to unlawful violence, they were permitted by law only to use 'reasonable force', a vague term that wasn't a great deal of help to the soldier on the ground. Nor could he rely on his commanding officer, because – particularly in this kind of situation – it was unusual for a soldier to be given an order to open fire; most commonly he had to make this decision for himself. As a result of the imprecision of the law, every soldier was issued with a set of rules of engagement, printed on a yellow card, to carry with him. Thus, for example, a soldier was entitled to return fire if he could see a weapon being used.

The violence got steadily worse. In March 1971, three off-duty soldiers in civilian clothes were lured to their deaths by women they had met in a pub. A soldier's Catholic girlfriend had her hair shaved by Republicans, and then was tarred and feathered and left tied to a lamp-post. Increasingly the IRA resorted to bombings rather than taking on the Army directly. A senior NCO in the Parachute Regiment, Sergeant Michael Willetts, sacrificed himself to save the lives of children by throwing himself on an IRA bomb at a Belfast police station. He was awarded a posthumous George Cross.

The increased risk to soldiers necessitated the introduction of further restrictions on off-duty activities, particularly within the most dangerous areas of the city itself. Outside these, however, life went on almost as normal. Only a dozen or so miles from the centre of Belfast, for example, was the largely Protestant seaside town of Bangor, where the boys used to go for a night out with no security concerns.

At this time 1 Para was the reserve battalion for 39 Brigade, one of three brigades stationed in the Province and responsible not only for the city of Belfast, but also for a considerable rural hinterland. Each of the ten or more battalions of 39 Brigade, minus 1 Para, was responsible for its own 'patch' within the Belfast area. As the reserve battalion, 1 Para was brought in wherever more troops were needed. At that stage we had four companies within the Battalion, and there was a cycle of readiness, so that the lead company was on, say, fifteen minutes' notice to move, the second company had thirty minutes, the third had an hour, and we would rotate through. My role for my first few months with 1 Para was as community relations officer/unit press officer. As such, I worked directly for the commanding officer, Lieutenant Colonel Mike Gray (later Lieutenant General), who had been my first company commander in 2 Para. My job didn't take me out on routine patrol, but I was out on the streets a great deal, because the press were everywhere, often crouching alongside soldiers to avoid being hit by bullets or stones. Some of the press were more sympathetic than others, but I didn't encounter any outright hostility. Everything we did was filmed by television cameras; the Army hadn't experienced anything like this before. A young corporal might give an interview in the street – 'I was here, I got shot at, I fired back' – and the public loved it: here was one of the boys, telling it as it was. This was my first real exposure to the media and, often flying by the seat of my pants, I found it very stimulating. I relished the challenge – not least because the job took me out on to the streets wherever there was trouble.

Like any other soldier serving in Northern Ireland, I got used to having bricks and petrol bombs thrown at me, and to abuse from passing civilians, particularly women, who would shout and spit. It was irksome, but best ignored. The first time I came under fire with live rounds was during the winter of 1970–1. I was with C Company, which had been given the job of protecting the Springfield Road police station, in the heart of West Belfast. We were lined up in anti-riot formation, wearing protective helmets with visors and carrying transparent shields to ward off missiles, while rioters pelted us with stones and petrol bombs. Even in this dangerous situation, there were press about. We were attempting to disperse the crowd with rubber bullets when I heard the sudden crack and thump of incoming rounds. The crowd vanished as we took cover. It was a strange sensation to be under fire. Of course there was an element of fear, and an adrenalin thrill as well; on the other hand, we had trained so much for this that it seemed oddly familiar. There is a sense of immunity – 'it's not going to happen to me' – so that when a soldier is hit by enemy fire, his first reaction is often surprise. It doesn't do to think too much about the possibility. I carried a pistol, but never used it except in training. The best people to return fire are not officers, who have other things to think about, but soldiers, whose job this is, and who are usually rather better at it.

In the spring of 1971 the IRA split into two wings, the old 'Official' IRA and the new, more militant and more radical 'Provisional' IRA, which soon emerged as the main enemy. Our role as regular soldiers was to deter the terrorists at a local level. The phrase used was 'framework operations', the aim being to create a situation within which, as much as possible, normal civilian life could continue. The boys on the ground would of course return fire if anyone opened fire on them, but there were other units who would take on the terrorists less openly. The Force Reconnaissance Unit (FRU), 14 Intelligence Company, the Military Reaction Force (MRF) – these were all cover names for covert armed units. Intelligence and the response to it were handled on a very tight, need-to-know basis. Even when I became a brigade commander, I would not necessarily be in the loop. There would be a directive that uniformed troops were to keep out of a particular area between this time and that time because it had to be 'sanitized' for a particular operation. I didn't always know what was going on, but I didn't always need to know.

The Commander of 39 Brigade was Brigadier (later General) Frank Kitson, a soldier with a very distinguished record of counter-insurgency operations in Kenya, Malaya, Oman and Cyprus. An incisive thinker and military theorist, he had just completed a year at University College, Oxford, on a Defence Fellowship, that is, a sabbatical period of study. Kitson was a small man with a piercing stare and a high, nasal voice, notorious for his dislike of small talk. The story is told of a dinner party at which some ambitious young wife sat next to him. Her opening gambit was to say with a smile, 'General, I've been bet I'll get at least half a dozen words out of you,' to which Frank replied, 'You've just lost,' and didn't say another word to her for the remainder of the evening. He had a reputation as cold and remote, but he commanded enormous respect among those who served under him. Kitson was not the most senior officer in the Province – as one of the three regional brigade commanders he reported to the General Officer Commanding, Northern Ireland (GOC, NI) – but within his area of responsibility he was the sun around which the planets revolved, and he very much set the tone for the operational style.

Kitson had used his year as an Oxford Fellow to write a book. *Low Intensity Operations*, published soon after I arrived in

Northern Ireland, was to make him a hate figure for the far left, for in it Kitson detailed the pioneering techniques he had used to counter Communist insurgents and guerrillas in a colonial setting. His essential point was that counter-insurgency and intelligence-gathering needed to be integrated, and he advocated aggressive methods in the pursuit of these aims. Most controversially, he argued that internal subversion and civil disorder in the UK would loom large among the threats to be faced in the future. He envisaged that the unrest in Northern Ireland might spread to the mainland, requiring the rapid intervention of the Army to retrieve the situation. To some retired Army officers of a right-wing bent, such ideas would not seem so far-fetched in the 1970s, when strikes paralysed the economy and the sovereignty of the elected Government appeared to be threatened. But no serving officer I encountered took talk of such a scenario seriously.

The security situation in Northern Ireland deteriorated throughout 1971. There were almost seven thousand violent incidents that year, including 261 attacks on police stations and more than a thousand bombings. At Palace Barracks we developed an extraordinary operational routine. More often than not, trouble took place during the evening and the early hours. We would be relaxing in the officers' mess, watching television, reading the newspaper or having a drink, when we'd hear a bomb exploding in Belfast, even though this was a few miles off. Maybe the windows would shake. We'd look at our watches, reach a decision on the critical issue of whether we had time for dinner, and not long afterwards the phone would ring, requesting support, so off would go the lead company. Later the second company might be called out too. This became an almost nightly occurrence. Typically we might be out until the small hours of the morning.

The so-called 'Civil Rights' marches continued, as did the

so-called 'Loyalist' marches, defying a ban introduced earlier in the year. These marches provoked further civil disorder. Riots were often used as a 'come-on' by the IRA to lure soldiers into an ambush. After a while, we learned that rioters apparently dispersing could be a signal that IRA gunmen were about to open fire.

The British Government was coming under intense pressure from the Northern Ireland Government to introduce internment without trial. Internment had been used in Northern Ireland before, during a previous, very short-lived IRA campaign in the mid-1950s, when both Dublin and Stormont had introduced it. I think that within the Northern Ireland Government there was a feeling based on a kind of collective memory: 'Well, it worked last time; it will work this time.' The difference this time around, however, was that there was no stomach for it south of the border. Terrorists would be able to find shelter in the Republic, safe from arrest. The round-up might catch a few of them, but most would escape the net. Meanwhile, many innocent people would be interned. The outrage at such injustice would undermine our attempts to isolate the men of violence. Internment was a blunt weapon which served to exacerbate rather than ameliorate the situation.

In midsummer the Northern Ireland Government had its way when London yielded, over-riding objections from the Security Forces. At dawn on 9 August 1971 a huge operation to round up suspected terrorists began. More than three hundred were taken away on that first morning. The reaction to internment by the Nationalist community was predictably violent: widespread rioting, shootings, bombings, and attempts to establish no-go areas with barricades constructed from burnt-out cars, rubble and anything else that came to hand. Northern Ireland seemed to be teetering on the brink. There were many firefights, and 39 Battalion was fully engaged. Frank Kitson would not accept no-go areas; as a consequence, 1 Para conducted a series of operations to remove barricades and re-establish some semblance of law and order. At first light each morning for a week or so, we would be in a different barricaded area. The job done and handed over to the local unit, we would return to Palace Barracks around lunchtime, sort ourselves out, get the briefings done for the next day and then get to bed before repeating the operation elsewhere the following morning. These intensive days were not without incident: when dealing with the barricaded Ballymurphy estate, for example, we found that the barricade across the Springfield Road had been booby-trapped, and in the course of the operation the Battalion fought a fierce three-hour gun battle with an estimated twenty gunmen. I was just around the corner, dealing with the press. Serving in Northern Ireland was sometimes surreal.

In the early summer I had taken over as the adjutant, a sought-after post for a young captain. The adjutant is the commanding officer's right-hand man, and so a pivotal figure in a battalion. This was my first staff job, albeit at unit level, meaning that I was assigned to a commander's staff rather than in command of a unit myself. The Army seeks to provide officers with broad experience, meaning that as they move up the career ladder officers switch back and forth between staff jobs and regimental commands. Much of the adjutant's job concerns personnel matters, including the administration of discipline: doing the paperwork, arranging the hearings and reading out the charges to an accused soldier. He has no disciplinary powers himself: those, of course, are the prerogative of the commanding officer and the company commanders. The adjutant does have the task of keeping rowdy young officers in order, but that's about the limit of it. In those days we had no operations officer, so I fulfilled this function too. But I kept the press job as well, because there was nobody else available. It was a particularly busy time in this respect, because we were very much in the spotlight. Nevertheless I was able to return to England briefly to undertake a specialist anti-terrorist training course under the auspices of MI6.

Because as unit press officer my name often appeared in the press I began to receive hate letters, saying for example that I'd been sentenced to die by a sniper's bullet – but they were very crude and I just laughed them off. I didn't show these to my wife.

Soon after I became adjutant a new battalion commander was appointed: Lieutenant Colonel Derek Wilford, who was not Parachute Regiment by origin, but an officer of the Royal Anglian Regiment. There is a system whereby both officers and soldiers can volunteer to do a tour with Airborne Forces (and if they are infantry, therefore with the Parachute Regiment), and this is what Derek Wilford did. I had known him previously when he had served as a company commander in 2 Para before taking command of the 1st Battalion. Wilford was a slim man, already greying in his late thirties, and a dynamic, positive, confident leader. He made it very clear that he would always support the men under his command, and as a result the soldiers adored 'the Colonel'. He struck me as intelligent and thoughtful. You'd sometimes come across him reading a volume of poetry.

During that winter, as the security situation steadily deteriorated, we received a succession of high-level visitors, including Lord Carrington, then Secretary of State for Defence, and General Carver, who had just taken over as Chief of the General Staff (CGS), the head of the Army. Christmas brought two visitors of a different kind, who had come to Northern Ireland to provide cheer to the troops: the comedian Frankie Howerd, and the reigning Miss World, Eva Reuber-Staier. As adjutant, I ensured that the onerous task of escorting Eva to the Combined Service Entertainment (CSE) show that year fell to me. Meanwhile we kept our parachute training going, making a weekly drop on Slemish Mountain in County Antrim, where St Patrick had lived and preached.

*

By the beginning of 1972 1 Para had been in Belfast for almost eighteen months, far longer than most of the other battalions, which were then on four-month tours. Our distinctive maroon berets made us immediately recognizable to the civilian population, and we had acquired a reputation for tough, uncompromising soldiering, going in hard and ready. We became particularly experienced at crowd dispersal: we developed the tactic of driving our squat armoured personnel carriers (nicknamed, for reasons obscure to me, 'pigs') into the middle of a rioting crowd before the soldiers debussed and set about the rioters, normally with batons. It was aggressive stuff, but it didn't always find favour with some other units. When they found themselves up against a problem without enough manpower to deal with it, we would arrive to support them, sort it out, get back in our vehicles and shove off back to Palace Barracks, leaving them to deal with the aftermath.

A front-page story in the *Guardian* in early January 1972 suggested that some other units had asked us to keep out of their areas, but this was strongly denied by HQ Northern Ireland. Another story in the following day's *Daily Telegraph* quoted 'Captain Mike Jackson' as describing attempts to stir up trouble between different units of the Army as 'contemptible'. I arranged for the *Daily Express* to run an interview with Derek Wilford headed 'My men are not thugs'.

All this came to a head in an incident towards the end of January, when C Company of 1 Para was deployed to assist soldiers from the Royal Green Jackets. I was not present myself, but I heard about it immediately afterwards from some of the officers involved. The Green Jackets were responsible for security at a place called Magilligan Point, an old army training centre at the end of a peninsula on the north coast, which had been converted into a temporary internment camp. On this particular day there had been a march from Londonderry to protest against internment, in defiance of the ban. A barbed-wire fence had been erected across the peninsula to keep out the demonstrators, but unfortunately this fence stopped at the high-water mark. It was low water when the marchers arrived at the fence, and some of the demonstrators strayed on to the beach in an attempt to go around the edge of the wire. There was real concern that they might try to release the internees. C Company responded with a spirited baton charge. The subsequent mêleé was captured on television, including a sequence in which it appeared that a soldier was kicking a marcher who was on the ground.

In the week that followed, bombs exploded within the compound housing our barracks at Holywood. Fortunately there were no casualties as a result, but this lapse in security caused a furore.

The following Sunday, 31 January 1972, would become notorious as 'Bloody Sunday'. What exactly happened on that day remains in dispute. There was an inquiry shortly afterwards presided over by Lord Chief Justice Widgery, but the findings were bitterly contested. Lord Saville's subsequent inquiry has yet to report. The controversy centres on the question of how British soldiers came to open fire on apparently unarmed civilians. It would be quite wrong of me to attempt to answer this question – indeed, as I write it is still *sub judice*, nearly ten years after the second inquiry was set up. I can only describe the events as I witnessed them, as fairly and as accurately as possible.

A 'Civil Rights' march had been organized for that Sunday afternoon, and it was anticipated that this would be much larger than usual, perhaps ten thousand people. Of course it was illegal, but as usual that didn't seem to worry the marchers. Headquarters Northern Ireland decided to reinforce 8 Brigade with 1 Para for the operation to handle the march, probably because of our long experience in Belfast at handling public disorder on the streets.

Londonderry, Northern Ireland's second largest city, felt quite different from Belfast. While there was a significant Catholic minority in West Belfast, in Londonderry Catholics were in the majority. Londonderry lies very close to the border with the Republic, and the west side, on the far bank of the River Foyle and lying outside the city walls, was pretty well exclusively Catholic. This was known as the 'Bogside': here Nationalists had declared 'Free Derry', a barricaded 'no-go' area for the Security Forces, openly policed by armed and hooded IRA men. A community alert system was used to mobilize the IRA to repel incursions by the Security Forces. Women would sound the alarm by banging dustbin lids. The Irish flag flew over 'Free Derry', which to all intents and purposes was no longer part of the United Kingdom.

The point had been reached where the Army's street maps showed a big black dotted line, known as the 'containment line', beyond which the police and the Army hardly ventured. There was a bit of waste ground on this boundary known as 'Aggro Corner', where young hooligans considered it good sport to come in the early evening and 'brass up' the troops holding the containment line, hurling stones and petrol bombs, anything they could find. This became known as the 'five o'clock follies'. You would see it on television, night after night, soldiers wearing shin guards and carrying big shields, standing there and getting pelted. Some referred to these as matinee performances, because they seemed so obviously staged. As in Belfast, there were occasions on which snipers exploited such riots in order to fire at soldiers. On the very morning of Bloody Sunday, a young officer died of wounds received from such a sniper attack days before.

Londonderry lay within the area of responsibility of 8 Brigade, commanded by Brigadier Andrew McLelland. By comparison with 39 Brigade, it was 8 Brigade's practice to use CS gas in large quantities, while in Belfast we hardly used it at all. Although circumstances in Londonderry were quite different from those prevailing in Belfast, there was a sense in 39 Brigade that 8 Brigade hadn't been firm enough. We were very disapproving of the fact that a 'no-go' area had been allowed to come into being. The violence would never end unless the perpetrators were arrested.

The city centre, including the Guildhall and many other fine old buildings, was just outside the no-go area. This was the city's commercial heart. The Chamber of Commerce was very concerned about widespread destruction if lawless marchers were allowed to over-run the city centre. Once the mob was in, shops and offices would be in danger, and with them the livelihoods of owners and employees alike. As a result 8 Brigade had erected barricades along the containment line to keep demonstrators out of the city centre.

The basic plan was to hold the marchers on the containment line to protect the city centre; but it was also decided to take advantage of the opportunity to arrest the worst of the hooligans. This would be our task. It was a snatch operation, of the type we did all the time. The main difficulty was to stop people running away: to put a cork in the bottle. We had evolved a tactic of going in behind the crowd or of coming in at the flank to cut them off. Clearly this was a large operation which would require a large number of troops. We envisaged using three companies, in a pincer movement, to surround the rioters and cut off their retreat, arrest them, bundle them into the pigs and take them off for handover to the RUC.

Derek Wilford gave us a briefing shortly before the march. His attitude was confident and professional. There was a sense that we might be heading for some sort of set-piece confrontation: it seemed unlikely that there wouldn't be at least some aggro. But it's worth stressing that the Battalion's mission was to capture rioters in the immediate vicinity of the barricades, which of course meant going over the containment line.

'BLOODY SUNDAY'
30TH JANUARY 1972

0 — 100
metres

N

City Wall

"FREE DERRY CORNER"

Lecky Road

Barrier 17

Rossville Flats

Rossville Street

Barricade

Glenfada Park

Barrier 16

Harvey St

Chamberlain Street

High St

Barrier 15

Barrier 14

PARAS ADVANCE

"AGGRO CORNER"

RIOTERS

City Centre
200 – 300m

Tac HQ

William Street

PATH OF MARCHERS

Barrier 13

Little James St

Barrier 12

Barrier 11

Barrier 9

Great James Street

The barriers mark the 'Containment line'.

The Colonel had thought long and hard about how to get in, how to get over the containment line into the area where the rioters would be. The main difficulty was vehicle access. Of course we anticipated that the IRA might react when we 'invaded their turf'. We had to be prepared to be attacked at any time. However, there was no sense in which we planned to use the arrest operation to 'teach the IRA a lesson'. That was not on the agenda.

I drove up to Londonderry early on Sunday morning in a vehicle we knew as the 'Gin Palace', a rather ancient box-bodied truck which served as a mobile HQ. It was fitted out inside with chairs, desks, map boards and communications equipment. Nowadays there is always an operations officer in the Battalion HQ, but then the adjutant usually fulfilled this role when the Battalion deployed, so more often than not I would be stuck in the Gin Palace during operations. However, on this occasion the Colonel asked me to accompany him, effectively to act as his 'gofer'. I remember being with him and the small group that formed his tactical HQ in a room on the first or second floor of a building looking south over the waste ground, towards the gable end of the dominating Rossville Flats, thought to be an IRA stronghold. We were in position by 14.30 hours, about an hour before the march was expected to pass. I recall going across to the window to get a better view. Derek snapped at me, 'Get back, you bloody fool, they could have snipers in those flats!'

A little later, there was a shot which holed a drainpipe close to the building in which we were standing. I cannot now be certain whether I actually heard the shot or whether I heard about it subsequently on the radio. But from this point we had every reason to believe that at least one individual out there had a weapon and that therefore we might come under fire again. About 15.55 hours we heard over the radio that Support Company had identified and shot a man attempting to detonate a nail bomb.

We heard reports over the radio of the marchers coming downhill. Then they came into view and we saw them pass by. There was a lot of shouting and chanting. The vast majority of them did not linger by the barricades, but moved on beyond the Rossville Flats to 'Free Derry Corner', a well-known gathering place, where they were addressed by various speakers. But the hooligans hung back by the barricades so they could take on the soldiers. This is what we had anticipated. The thugs and the marchers were now separated, so we could get behind the thugs and isolate them. I remember groans from those present when soldiers at the barricades began to use CS gas, because this made it likely that we would have to use our respirators, at least initially. They were uncomfortable and smelly, and worse still, they restricted your vision, which made you feel more vulnerable to snipers. In fact the gas had cleared by the time the snatch operation took place.

Our main force was further back with the pigs, poised to go forward into the waste ground and scoop up the hooligans. We were kept waiting for what seemed a long time for the order to go – Brigade Headquarters was concerned that there should be adequate separation between the violent and non-violent elements of the marchers. The Colonel became impatient. There were various communications over the radio, in which he expressed his desire to get a move on. He said something to the effect of 'They are all where we want them now.' Eventually, at 16.10 hours, we were given the order to go.

Through the window I saw our Support Company's vehicles moving towards the Rossville Flats, about two hundred yards off. The barricades had been pulled to one side to allow vehicle access. Now they were debussing in the shadow of the flats. Some soldiers were carrying batons ready to make arrests, their rifles slung across their backs, but some had their weapons ready to cover the others. There was nothing unusual about this; on the contrary, it was standard drill for some soldiers to cover those making arrests. Almost immediately it became apparent that they thought they had come under fire. They began zig-zagging from side to side and looking for cover.

Derek Wilford was a commander who liked to be forward among his soldiers, to see what was happening for himself. After a few minutes, he decided to do just that. We tore down the stairs together, round the corner and out into the street, and then sprinted across the waste ground. There was a lot of noise. I saw soldiers hunched up, trying to make their bodies as small as possible. As I dashed forward with my head down I had the defi-nite impression that someone was firing at me from a vantage point somewhere ahead. When you are used to the sound of gunfire you can estimate the range and the direction it is coming from. You first hear a crack, which is the sound of displaced air as the bullet passes close to you; then a thump, the delayed noise of the rifle being fired. The thump gives you an indication of the direction, the time gap between the crack and the thump gives you a sense of range.

It took us about thirty seconds to reach the gable end of the Rossville Flats, where Support Company Headquarters had taken cover. I remember the surge of relief when I reached them. The mood among the soldiers was tense. Major Ted Loden, the company commander, was one of them, and I remember his making it very clear that he and his company had been under fire. It seemed that most of the shooting stopped soon after we reached the Rossville Flats.

My view of what was happening was constricted. I didn't see any soldiers firing their weapons, nor did I draw my own pistol. Nor did I see any gunmen firing at us. It was a confused situa-tion. People were running here and there. The ground was scattered with debris left behind by the demonstrators. I noticed a low barricade across the road. I can recall 'losing' Derek Wilford, and I think he ran across the road, but after a while he was back. Everything seemed to calm down and go quiet. The

Colonel was working out what to do. I heard him say something into the radio to the effect of 'What do you want me to do now?' After a few minutes the order was given by HQ 8 Brigade to pull back behind the containment line. This was about twenty or thirty minutes after we had gone in. But I do have a clear memory of seeing a pig with bodies lying in the back. These were three civilians who had been shot near the gable end of the flats.

My next clear memory of that day is of being back in a factory building in Drumahoe, just outside the city, which we had been allocated as a holding area. It was early evening, and it was becoming clear that there had been a large number of fatalities. In fact, thirteen civilians had been shot dead, and a fourteenth died later. I was deeply shocked, because although the British Army had shot a number of persons in the past, there had never been deaths on this scale. To this day it remains the most tragic such episode in the whole sad history of the Troubles.

I was left with some very mixed and worrying feelings. I imagine that others in the Battalion felt the same. I hated the thought, as some commentators would state straight away, that our soldiers might have lost control. It would be very unprofessional to have done that, and in the Army one is very proud of professionalism. I knew these men, and I knew their quality. So far as I was concerned the Paras were tough, but they were disciplined. I found it difficult to accept that there could have been any mass breach of discipline. Other people would suggest that there had been some sort of conspiracy, a hypothesis which the facts do not sustain. Though the two theories were mutually inconsistent, some tried to argue both at once: that there had been some sort of conspiracy and that the soldiers had run amok. But however incredible the accusations, it was a terrible thought that we might have killed innocent people, whatever the stress of the moment, and whatever the provocation. There was no doubt in my own mind that we had come under fire, and in those circumstances it was legitimate to return fire at properly identified targets. The question remains whether the response of some of our soldiers was proportionate or not, considering the nature of the threat.

In the factory that evening, the standard 'after action' drills were cutting in. There were a lot of military policemen around. It was – and is – an absolute rule in Northern Ireland that military police take statements from any soldiers who have fired live rounds. Every soldier is allocated a certain number of live rounds, and has to account for them to his platoon sergeant. The rounds have batch numbers so that they can be identified after firing. As adjutant, I helped in the administration of the statement-taking exercise, making a list of those who needed to be interviewed. There was absolutely no question of briefing the soldiers about what they should say.

I remember speaking to a staff officer at HQ 8 Brigade over the telephone. Such was the scale of the casualties, he said, that there could well be a special inquiry. The Brigade HQ required statements from Derek Wilford and each of the company commanders. My job was to act as a scribe, interviewing each of them, writing out a statement and then getting him to read it through before signing it. The work took most of the night. In the process it became clear that the only soldiers from 1 Para who had fired their weapons came from Support Company, and that quite a large number of rounds had been fired.

The announcement of an inquiry presided over by the Lord Chief Justice was made very quickly afterwards. Lord Widgery decided to hold his inquiry in the Province at Coleraine on the north coast, so that he would have ready access to witnesses. I was not called upon to give evidence myself, but back at Palace Barracks I was involved in some of the administration, dealing with witness requests from the inquiry and arranging helicopter flights to Coleraine. Part of the preparation for Widgery was that each soldier who had fired his weapon had to indicate where he was when he fired and where his target was. I remember large charts spread out on the floor, with soldiers marking their positions and their targets in blue and red.

Widgery reported his findings within a couple of months or so of Bloody Sunday. His inquiry pretty much exonerated the Army, and concluded that there had been no general breakdown in discipline, though it also concluded that some of the firing 'bordered on the reckless'. As soon as it was published, the Widgery Report was criticized as a whitewash. It failed to assuage the anger of the relatives of those shot on the day, or to quell the speculation, which continued to poison attempts to reach a peaceful settlement in the Province.

In 1998, the recently elected Labour Prime Minister Tony Blair announced the setting up of a new inquiry under the Law Lord, Lord Saville. At the time of writing this inquiry has yet to publish its findings, though the cost to the British taxpayer is said to be approaching an astonishing £400 million. I myself testified before the inquiry on two occasions in 2003, and until Lord Saville has concluded his contemplations on the matter I am constrained in how much I can say. The fact that the Saville Inquiry has taken so long to report and consumed so much public money is perhaps in itself evidence of the difficulty in establishing the truth of the events on that tragic day.

I found the charge that the Paras had 'run amok' on 'Bloody Sunday' difficult to accept. A decade later the self-discipline and the humanity of the Parachute Regiment soldier would be tested on the far side of the world. One of the closing battles of the Falklands War, the Battle of Wireless Ridge, was fought by 2 Para. This was a completely different environment from Northern Ireland, where we were always operating among civilians: the Falklands was straight force on force; the Army's job was to kill the enemy and win the war. Come daylight, 2 Para had pushed the Argentines off the ridge, the final piece of high ground they occupied. To the west was Tumbledown Mountain, which the Scots Guards had taken the same night, at some cost. After fierce fighting on Tumbledown, the Argentine soldiers broke and ran. My friend David Chaundler, who was in command of 2 Para, described the scene to me afterwards. From the ridge looking south-east, you could see Port Stanley about three miles off. To the south-west, the eastern slopes of Tumbledown Mountain were covered in Argentine soldiers fleeing towards the town. And of course, the gunner forward observation officers were firing artillery at them as they fled. It was a 'turkey shoot', though legitimate within the laws of international conflict. David Chaundler ordered the guns to cease firing. It was a big decision, because no formal surrender had been taken at that point, and theoretically the soldiers he spared might have regrouped to fight us again; but he chose to stop the killing, in the interests of common humanity. And the guns of the British Army fell silent.

5

Behind the Curtain

Though Frank Kitson was a brusque man, he knew his soldiering. He would have understood that Derek Wilford was feeling bruised and battered and worried about what had happened that Sunday in Londonderry. Shortly after we got back to Belfast, Kitson came to see the Colonel. To reach the office of the commanding officer one had to pass through that of the adjutant, so I greeted the brigadier and ushered him in, before leaving the two of them alone together. Kitson has a very distinct nasal voice, so it would have been difficult not to over-hear what he was saying even if I had been trying not to. 'Well, Derek,' Kitson began, 'you'd better tell me what happened.' So I heard the Colonel describe the snatch operation across the containment line into 'Free Derry'. Kitson was generally supportive, but when Wilford had finished, he offered a trenchant comment. 'What I don't understand is why, having got that far in, you didn't go on and sort the whole bloody mess out.'

Kitson expressed himself pretty brutally, but he had a point.

There was no doubt that we could have gone on to retake the 'no-go' area, though this would almost certainly have resulted in more deaths.

In the aftermath of Bloody Sunday, a crowd in Dublin burned down the British Embassy while the Gardai stood by and watched. In February the IRA took their bombing campaign to mainland Britain, exploding a bomb at the officers' mess of the Parachute Brigade HQ in Aldershot, killing six civilians and a Catholic padre. The following month the Provisional IRA detonated a huge bomb in the centre of Belfast that killed six people and injured a hundred and fifty more, many of them horrifically. A young lance corporal from 1 Para was photographed cradling in his arms a young woman who had just lost both her legs in the explosion. The Official IRA attempted to assassinate John Taylor, Northern Ireland's Minister for Home Affairs; despite being shot six times, he survived. On the streets, thousands of Protestant paramilitaries paraded in uniform, and let it be known to sympathetic journalists that they had built up a large stockpile of weapons. In Belfast, 1 Para intervened to break up a running battle between Protestant and Catholic gunmen which left eight people dead. The Province appeared to be heading for civil war. Less than two months after Bloody Sunday, the British Government decided that enough was enough, suspending the Stormont Parliament and imposing direct rule. A temporary truce was agreed while senior British politicians held secret talks with representatives of the IRA – but no agreement was reached, and in the summer the bombing campaign resumed with a vengeance when twenty-six IRA bombs exploded in Belfast, killing eleven people. With grim symmetry this day, 21 July 1972, became known as 'Bloody Friday'.

By this time 1 Para had reached the end of its eighteen-month tour and we had returned to the mainland; but we had barely settled back in Aldershot before we were recalled to Northern

Ireland for a mammoth operation to remove the no-go areas, mainly in Londonderry, as Frank Kitson thought should have been done long before. Heavy Royal Engineer armoured vehicles were brought over from Germany by landing craft to clear the barricades. In all, twenty-one thousand troops took part in Operation Motorman, the greatest number of British soldiers committed to any one operation since 1945. As there was a shortage of available barracks, we were garrisoned initially on HMS *Maidstone*, a Royal Navy ship in Belfast dock that had previously served as an internment centre. I spent much of my time aboard ship running the operations room. Fearing a bloodbath, the authorities had made no secret of the imminent operation. The IRA decided not to stand and defend 'Free Derry', melting away before we arrived. In the event there were few civilian casualties, and no soldiers were injured. The most violent response occurred at Claudy, a small village not far from Londonderry and the border with the Republic, where nine people died after three terrorist car bombs exploded in succession. At first companies of 1 Para were farmed out to other battalions, but after a while we were given our own 'patch' in northern Belfast, straddling the two communities. We remained in the Province for a few more months and finally got out in November. It had been a long haul.

The Battalion's next deployment was to be a six-month UN tour in Cyprus, but I was told that I wouldn't be going with them. Instead I was off to Scotland to join 15 Para, one of the then three Territorial Army battalions in the Parachute Regiment that supplemented the three regular battalions. It was quite a wrench to leave 1 Para after the shared experience of dramatic events, and disappointing to miss the operational tour in Cyprus – but the TA was an important part of the Army of which I knew little, and the job carried with it welcome promotion to acting major. The Army's career structure is designed to give officers a broad range of experience as they move up the ladder. In any event, I've always taken the view that whatever I'm asked to do, I'll give it a good try.

A TA unit has a small number of regular Army staff who are the oil in the engine. The commanding officer can be either regular or TA, but the so-called training major, who writes all the training programmes and plans all the exercises, is always a regular officer – and that was me. My new battalion was widely spread: Battalion Headquarters, A and Support Companies in Glasgow, B Company in Aberdeen, C Company in Edinburgh.

Part-timers TA soldiers may be, but they too are professional, and 15 Para trained hard. A demanding weekend's programme would begin with a parade in the TA Centre on Friday evening after work, following which the troops would move to a local airport, where several RAF Hercules aircraft would be waiting: then fit parachutes, emplane, take off at 23.00 hours, fly south and jump on to Salisbury Plain at 01.00 hours the next morning, going straight into a 36-hour exercise. The exercise would finish at 13.00 or 14.00 on Sunday afternoon, and after a quick clear-up we would be driven to RAF Lyneham to fit parachutes, emplane and jump back into Scotland around 17.00 or 18.00 hours on the Sunday evening. Then home to bed, and back to work on Monday morning. That's real commitment. Yes, they got paid for it, but not a huge amount of money.

There is an ill-informed view that the Territorial Army is only playing at soldiers. For myself, I've always been a great admirer of the TA. They bring a lot of colour to the Army, because they have a foot in both the civilian and military camps. There is a slogan, 'One Army' – i.e. not a regular army and a territorial army but a single army – and in my view that says it all. There is a tendency nowadays to refer to the TA as reservists, perhaps founded on the idea that, as a title, 'Territorial Army' may be old hat. But plenty of people continue to think the name an honourable one.

In those days the TA essentially had one job, which was to fill out the order of battle – to do or die against the Warsaw Pact in north-west Europe. For the forty years up to 1989, the core strategic requirement for the British Army was to play its part in NATO's defence of western Europe, and most of the fighting Army was dedicated to this task. That role would be overtaken by events when the Cold War came to an end. Now the TA plays an important part in helping the regular Army to sustain current operations. It's not always easy, of course. Although the Reserve Forces Act 1996 gives the Army the legal power to mobilize TA soldiers, compulsory mobilization is kept to a minimum in peacetime. Much depends on an individual TA soldier's circumstances. If he works for himself, he can come to his own decision. The real rub comes if you get a TA soldier who is a key player in a small family firm, when it's obviously very difficult for him to go off for a six-month tour. Some of the big firms are extremely generous with their employees' time, and actually see the TA as a benefit, not a detriment. I remember a conversation with a senior executive of a large manufacturing company. 'Thank you very much,' I said to him, 'for letting your chap go to Iraq for six months.' His reply was quite unexpected. 'I'm the one who should thank you. I sent out a shop-floor worker, and I got back a foreman.'

Many TA soldiers join a part of the Army which has no relation to their civilian life, just to have the change. But we also try to make use of an individual's skills where appropriate. For example, there are many people in the TA Royal Signals who work for BT. And we have a wonderful group of railway repairers, maintainers and train crews within the Royal Logistic Corps who have been used in at least two operations that I can recall, Kosovo and Iraq. Almost by definition they are professional railwaymen in civil life; they can repair railways, they can run railways and they can drive trains, all of which can be extremely useful at times. But we only need them on an occasional basis. It would be a very expensive capability to maintain within the regular Army, and therefore it makes sense to keep that expertise within the TA and draw on it when you need to.

The regular defence medical services were severely reduced in the cuts that followed the ending of the Cold War. Now the Army relies very heavily on TA medics – which means in effect the National Health Service, because that's where most of them work normally. The MOD has chosen not to employ many of the top specialist surgeons needed operationally in full-time service; so TA medical personnel can mean the difference between life and death for a wounded soldier.

I became a strong advocate for the TA, though I suspect that while with 15 Para I may have ruffled a few feathers. 'If he has a fault,' read a comment in my generally favourable annual report for 1973, 'it is that because of his extrovert nature and that he is so capable, he occasionally gives some of those less endowed the impression that he is arrogant.'

There was one tragic incident during my two and a half years with the TA which still casts a shadow over my memory of this period.

Exercise 'Bold Guard' in September 1974 was a very big NATO manoeuvre, involving American, British, Danish and German forces. We were rehearsing one of the Battalion's possible war contingencies: what we would do in a time of tension, or indeed if the Warsaw Pact actually attacked. The specific purpose here was to put an airborne force into Germany in a reinforcement role – and, on the assumption that runways had been knocked out, to deploy as quickly as possible: by parachute. We in 15 Para were due to make the second of two battalion parachute drops with 'heavy drop platforms' carrying our vehicles, following a drop the previous day by 2 Para. We were flying from RAF Lyneham, a journey of two or three hours in a large stream of C130 Hercules aircraft. Once the Battalion reached Lyneham, my job as training major was done. I took on the role of umpire, observing what went on and adjudicating on tactical engagements. We were all loaded with heavy packs, carrying weapons, ammunition and supplies sufficient for an eight-day exercise: approximately eighty pounds in weight per man. The dropping zone (DZ) chosen was in northern Germany near the border with Denmark, immediately south of the Kiel Canal, which links the North Sea to the Baltic. During the Anglo-German naval race before the First World War, the canal had been dug wide and deep, deep enough to take battleships. It might seem strange to choose a DZ so close to such an obvious hazard, but it was always hard to find the amount of space necessary for a drop; this DZ met the required safety criteria, and precautions had been taken in the event of anyone dropping into the water. In the event, these precautions proved tragically inadequate.

The drop was to have taken place in the morning, but because of local fog over the canal it was postponed to 21.00 hours, not long after last light, the same day. The run-in was north–south, i.e. the stream of thirty-six RAF Hercules aircraft flew at right angles over the canal before the drop. As always, flares in the shape of an 'A' (the 'Alpha') had been positioned to show where the first parachutist should land, about 350 yards south of the canal bank. If all goes as intended, the first man out lands on or very close to the Alpha. The first one out of the aircraft is not normally the commanding officer; where he drops varies, but often it's in the middle of the 'stick', depending how one wants to rendezvous on the ground. The lighting in the aircraft is subdued to promote night vision. As you approach the DZ, the dispatcher gets the line of parachutists to their feet. The doors on both sides open, and there's a rush of air into the aircraft. When the green light is illuminated, it's time to go.

In the event we jumped from rather higher than we need have

done, from a thousand feet, and the speed of the light southerly wind had been underestimated because of undetected wind shear. This meant that both the personnel and vehicle drops began a few seconds early.

I was one of the first few out of my aircraft. I could see the Alpha clearly, and I could tell straight away that I was going to drop short. I could see the canal, too, because there was a large ship going past, all lit up like a Christmas tree. At that point I knew with a horrible sense of foreboding that something had gone very wrong, because the canal was supposed to have been closed to shipping before the drop. I pulled down very hard on the rigging lines to try to steer the parachute away from the water. In the event, I splashed down in the shallows, and was able to wade ashore easily.

I was lucky. Fourteen paratroopers landed further out into the canal, along with three heavy equipment platforms. They would have felt the shock of the cold water, followed immediately by the pull of their heavy packs dragging them down. We had trained for this contingency, of course. If you find yourself dropping towards water, the drill is to get rid of your equipment by emergency release, and then to get out of your parachute just before you hit the surface: you bang the quick release box to undo the harness. You keep hold of the straps until the last moment, and then release them as you splash down, so that you won't get dragged under by a water-logged parachute. But at night it's difficult to judge how high you are, and obviously you don't want to let go of your parachute too early.

Some of those who landed in the water managed to make it to the shore, or were rescued by the German safety boats which had been standing by as a precaution, but six men drowned. It was particularly upsetting for me, because these were men I knew. When the bodies were recovered it was found that not all of them had been able to jettison their packs. Like the rest of us they were all wearing lifejackets, but none of them had been inflated in time. One man's parachute was wrapped around the propeller of the ship that I had seen from the air.

In a further tragedy, the German engineer colonel whose job it had been to provide the safety boats and to liaise with the authorities to close the canal hanged himself the day afterwards.

The Battalion quite rightly got on with the exercise. Intense activity is a powerful antidote to shock and grief. But instead of acting as umpire, I stayed behind for the next few days to liaise with the German police, the British military police, and an RAF board of inquiry which arrived the following day. I camped by the canal, living on my field rations, while I watched German frogmen make a systematic search of the canal bottom. My abiding memory of that time is of bodies lined up on the bank. I had the unpleasant task of identifying the corpses: to do so I had to reach down, unzip the combat jackets, extract the dog tags and verify the name and number stamped on each with the young military police officer standing beside me.

Earlier in the year I had sat the staff promotion examination. This was a crucial stage in any officer's career. The Staff College was the intellectual powerhouse of the Army, taking 120 of the 400 or 500 or so officers in each age group and grooming them for senior ranks in the future. If you were accepted by the Staff College, you had a chance of making general; if not, the odds were against you.

In those days everybody had to take the basic exam to be promoted to the rank of major, and those applying to the Staff College had to take additional papers. Candidates were also assessed by the so-called 'book' of their confidential reports, a system which continues to the present day. Each year a report is written on every officer and NCO in the Army by his or her superior in the chain of command, with comments from at least one other officer further up the chain. These reports assess both performance over the past year and potential for promotion, and are collected with past reports in the 'book'.

The Army is a meritocracy. Officers benefit from careful career planning. Career progression is very tightly structured – quite properly, in my view. At each stage some move forward, while others fall by the wayside. Officers are assessed for promotion by annual selection boards, a system that continues all the way up to the top of the Army: No. 5 Board looks at candidates for promotion to major, No. 4 at candidates for lieutenant colonel, and so on up to No. 1 Board, which looks at candidates for promotion to general. The Army is rightly proud of this rigorous system, designed to be as objective as possible, avoiding any possibility of nepotism or favouritism. Each member of the board works alone to score each candidate on the basis of his 'book'; if there's a wide discrepancy between any two scores, the relevant board members are asked to mark again, and to continue to do so until the discrepancy is reduced to the acceptable level. Then the scores are aggregated to produce an order of merit, and those with the highest aggregate scores are the ones selected for promotion. The boards are also responsible for appointments. The Military Secretary, who is the officer responsible for career matters, circulates a list of posts coming up as their holders are promoted or move on in some other way, you indicate your interest, and the boards decide who goes where.

Promotion lists are distributed under embargo down the chain of command. Each list is printed on differently coloured paper: the list of promotions to major is beige, to lieutenant colonel pink, to colonel blue and to brigadier green. There isn't an annual list for generals because there are so few such appointments; these are made as and when required. For obvious reasons the lists are known as the 'beige list', the 'pink list', and so on.

Typically, an officer will hear news of his promotion or future appointment from his commanding officer, at whatever level, an

Aged nineteen, in full dress uniform ('Blues') on Sandhurst commissioning day, 19 December 1963.

My father and mother in Bristol 1941, the year before they married, and before my father had obtained his commission.

Sitting with my mother on the running board of our pre-war Lancia near our home in Tripoli, late 1940s. Our dog Roly poses on the pavement.

Candidates on the officer selection course at the Regular Commissions Board, November 1961. I am in the middle of the back row, no. 35.

Ypres Company cleaning parade, Sandhurst, 1962. Sarjit Singh polishes a boot in the foreground; Sam Mboma is seated in the middle of the picture, and I am standing in the corridor behind him.

With my father, a keen motorcyclist, in Tripoli, 1949.

As a young officer, behind the wheel of the green Sunbeam Alpine that I bought second-hand in the mid-1960s.

Shortly after being commissioned, with my mother and sister Lynne in Germany.

Preparing to jump on the basic parachute training course, RAF Abingdon, September 1967. I am seated fourth along the row.

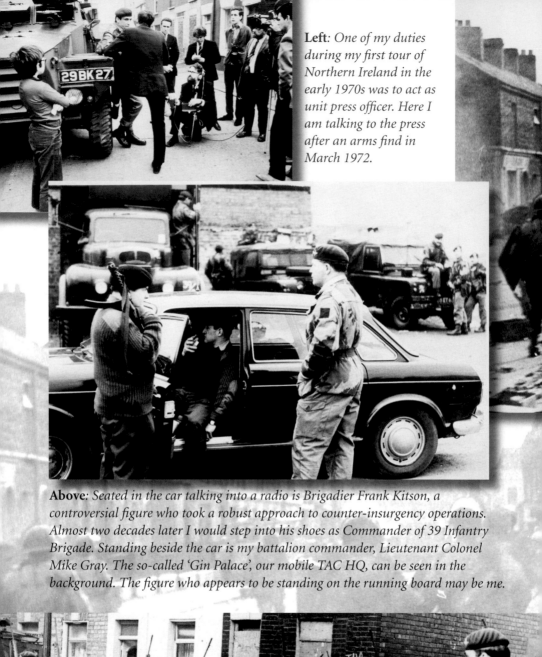

Left: *One of my duties during my first tour of Northern Ireland in the early 1970s was to act as unit press officer. Here I am talking to the press after an arms find in March 1972.*

Above: *Seated in the car talking into a radio is Brigadier Frank Kitson, a controversial figure who took a robust approach to counter-insurgency operations. Almost two decades later I would step into his shoes as Commander of 39 Infantry Brigade. Standing beside the car is my battalion commander, Lieutenant Colonel Mike Gray. The so-called 'Gin Palace', our mobile TAC HQ, can be seen in the background. The figure who appears to be standing on the running board may be me.*

9 August 1971, the day internment without trial was introduced in Northern Ireland.

Left: *Security operations in Belfast, 1971. I am standing at the right of the picture; my commanding officer, Lieutenant Colonel Derek Wilford, is standing just to the left of the lamp-post.*

Above: *A young woman who has lost both legs in a huge IRA explosion is comforted by Lance Corporal Wayne Evans, central Belfast, 20 March 1972.*

About to enter the Russian Sector of Berlin at the legendary 'Checkpoint Charlie'. My young daughter Amanda stands beside the family car.

Right: *Briefing senior officers in my role as Chief of Staff of the Berlin Brigade. In the centre of the picture is Brigadier Charles Grey, and on his left is Major General Roy Redgrave. At this stage I was still a mere major.*

Below: *A training exercise which provided a close view of the Berlin underworld. We explored the city sewers as a possible means of tactical movement for fighting in built-up areas.*

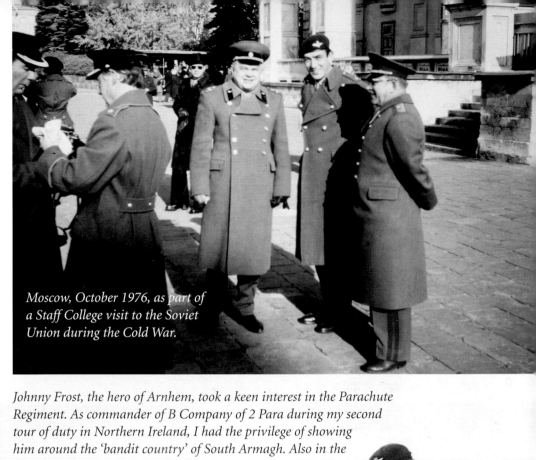

Moscow, October 1976, as part of a Staff College visit to the Soviet Union during the Cold War.

Johnny Frost, the hero of Arnhem, took a keen interest in the Parachute Regiment. As commander of B Company of 2 Para during my second tour of duty in Northern Ireland, I had the privilege of showing him around the 'bandit country' of South Armagh. Also in the picture is Lieutenant Colonel Colin Thomson.

Warrenpoint, August Bank Holiday 1979, when two coordinated bombs were detonated by the IRA, inflicting the highest number of casualties suffered by the British Army in a single incident since the Second World War.

Above: *The vehicle destroyed by the full force of the first explosion.*

Right: *My notes on hearing the first report of the incident.*

Below: *The scene of the carnage. On the left is the tidal estuary of the Newry River, which forms the border with the Irish Republic; in the foreground is the crater formed by the first explosion; and on the right of the dual carriage-way is the ruined gate-lodge where the second bomb detonated. I set up my HQ in the stone tower opposite.*

announcement often accompanied by a congratulatory drink. Those promoted to major general and above will receive a personal telephone call from the CGS. It does occasionally happen that an officer at this level will decline to take up a posting, but the system is so refined that such an occurrence is rare.

In April 1974 I received a letter from the Ministry of Defence confirming that I had qualified both for promotion to the rank of major and for entry into the Staff College when I finished my tour with the TA. In the autumn of the following year I began a three-month course at the Royal Military College of Science, at Shrivenham near Swindon, as a precursor to my Staff College year. This was a crash course on military technology: armoured vehicles, explosives, that sort of thing. Science was never my strongest suit, and I scraped through with a C grade. 'Major Jackson had some difficulty keeping pace with the technical aspects of the course,' my report read afterwards. Not my finest hour.

At the beginning of 1976 I became a student at the Staff College. This was based at Camberley in Surrey, another large mid-Victorian building built in a style somewhat reminiscent of Haussmann's Paris, with dormer windows projecting from the roofline.

Years later, when I was myself on the Directing Staff (DS) at Camberley, I used to say to my students at the beginning of the year, 'I hope you've enjoyed everything you've done in the Army before this moment, but frankly it counts for little enough in terms of your future, because you start again here. What happens to you in the future will be almost exclusively deter-mined by how well you do on this course.'

The Staff College syllabus was broad: basic staff duties; conventional tactics; counter-revolutionary warfare, as it was then called; 'out-of-area operations', meaning operations outside what was then considered as the main theatre in north-west Europe; joint operations, i.e. with the Navy and the

Air Force; how the MOD works and other non-Army matters. The syllabus reflected the Army's core roles as they were then defined. The emphasis was understandably on how the Army should play its part in the defence of north-west Europe, but the course also took account of possible unexpected challenges in the future – such as we would face when Argentina invaded the Falkland Islands.

Students are taught in groups of ten, known as 'syndicates', by a member of the DS; these are all lieutenant colonels, supposedly picked from the most promising in that rank within the Army. There's a lot of writing involved: students learn how to write operation orders, and to prepare what is called a brief, i.e. a paper a staff officer would give to his boss as an aide-memoire or decision-making tool. For example: 'The divisional commander will be coming to see you next week; we know he wants to talk about these subjects and here are some notes on them; these issues may arise; etc.'

Your written work is very carefully marked, and a report is written on your performance at the end of each term. What the DS are looking for all the time is the power of analysis, i.e. the ability to digest complex material rapidly, to identify what's really important, and then to express your thoughts – whether verbally or in writing – in succinct and lucid English. It was a great wartime leader, Major General 'Windy' Gale, commanding the 6th Airborne Division, who stated very succinctly and lucidly that the one purpose of communication is to take a thought from one human being's brain and to transmit it to the brain of others with the minimum possibility of misunderstanding, confusion or ambiguity. You also take part in map exercises, where there are no troops involved, and by which you practise the intellectual process of handling quite large formations. There are visiting speakers as well, of all sorts. In my time as a student at the Staff College they ranged from General Sir John Hackett, a brigade commander at Arnhem, to the left-wing union leader Hugh Scanlon. Ken Livingstone has also visited several times over the years, always ensuring good cut-and-thrust at question time.

We learned more about battle procedure: the sequence of warning orders, operations orders and confirmatory orders. It's a top-down process, and the procedure is the same at every level, from corps right down to platoon. For example, a battalion commander might receive from his brigade commander a warning order, telling him to get ready to do something. There will be a task – e.g. 'capture hill 123' – probably some timings – 'by first light on Wednesday' – and any other relevant information available at that point. When a battalion commander receives such a warning order – whether in writing or verbally – he will immediately then think, 'Right, what does this mean, what are my options?' The ensuing mental exercise of analysing the mission, evaluating the various factors involved (the ground, the enemy, time and space, etc.) and developing possible solutions was then known as 'the appreciation of the situation' (the Army has subsequently adopted the American term 'the estimate'), and putting it down on paper was one of the skills taught in the written work. The point is to lay out clearly each stage in your thinking so that it can be examined critically, and any flaws detected and eliminated. If at all possible, the commanding officer should make a reconnaissance. The outcome of the process is a series of possible courses of action, along with a list of the advantages and disadvantages of each. The commander must now make his decision. What will then emerge will be a battalion scheme of manoeuvre: e.g. 'A and B Companies, you are to attack the objective from the right flank; C Company, you are in reserve but be prepared to exploit tactical success.' The timings are very important: everything revolves around H-Hour, the moment when the action commences. Hours are expressed as H+3 or H−3. The same applies to dates: a campaign or an operation commences on D-Day, and dates are expressed as D−1, D+2, and so on.

As soon as he's worked out his preliminary thoughts, the commander will issue his own warning order to the companies in the battalion – 'Be prepared for so-and-so' – with timings and probably some logistic information at that point. So everybody is starting to think about the task that they've been given, and as the orders come down through the ranks, right down to section level, they become more and more specific and more and more limited.

It's always the preferred option for the commander to give his orders personally, because he can then discuss face-to-face any questions his subordinates may have. Almost certainly, at the level of brigade and upwards, these oral orders will be supplemented by a written operation order, which will provide all the supporting detail. As you go further down, the requirement for written orders diminishes. There is also a mechanism for feedback up the chain of command, known as the 'back-brief'.

The final part of this sequence is the confirmatory order, which is not always given, depending on the circumstances. So the commander at any level has the authority to proceed without receiving a confirmatory order, unless he's been told to wait for one.

All these principles and procedures are set out in the commander's field manual, a type of aide-memoire, which provides a useful checklist of details, particularly if you're tired and under pressure.

One of the teaching methods used at the Staff College and elsewhere is the TEWT, the tactical exercise without troops. You are set a tactical problem and given all the necessary information (perhaps on your own, perhaps as a small group of two or three). You go out and walk the ground and form a plan, which you subsequently present to the other students, and they are invited to comment. It isn't a question of getting it right or wrong; this is a means of getting students to think about operational planning and execution, at whatever level. The TEWTs are jocularly contrasted with NEWDs (night exercises without darkness) and JEWTs (jungle exercises without trees).

All students at the Staff College were roughly the same age, in their early thirties, and at the same level, senior captains or newly promoted majors. In addition, there were a handful of officers from the RAF, the Royal Navy and the Royal Marines, plus fifty-odd students from overseas. This can lead to some strange encounters afterwards. During the Falklands War, an Argentine graduate from Camberley would surrender to a fellow Staff College graduate.

There is a system whereby each overseas student has a British student as a sponsor. I looked after one of the Germans, an officer called Rudiger Drews who became a good friend of mine. Many years later, when I was head of KFOR in Macedonia, he visited my HQ in Skopje in his capacity as the three-star general commanding the German land forces. Another of the foreigners I got to know pretty well was Itzik Mordechai, a veteran of the 1973 Yom Kippur War who became a major general and later the Israeli Minister of Defence. So there is a bit of a Staff College old boy network.

It was professionally stimulating to be at the Staff College, of course, but one abiding memory of that year at Camberley is that hardly any of us seemed to have any money. Here we were, 120 of the allegedly most promising officers in the Army, all – except the odd one with family means – flat broke. The economy in 1976 was in a terrible state; annual inflation soared to over 20 per cent. We seemed to be always worrying about how we were going to manage. I can remember being delighted to get my posting overseas, both because of the job, of course, but also because I would qualify for Local Overseas Allowance, which I think saved my financial bacon. By this time I had two young children, and we were living in married quarters within the college grounds, boxy 1960s houses nicknamed 'Legoland'. My parents were just up the road, literally ten minutes away, close enough to see their grandchildren regularly. They had come back from Hong Kong in 1970, when my father retired from the Army. He then took what's known as a retired officer's job at a local Army training centre.

There comes a memorable day two-thirds of the way through the year at Staff College when the syndicate DS doles out brown paper envelopes to the students, each of which contains a posting order. This is the moment you find out what you're going to be doing for the next two years. It's known as black bag day, for reasons that are lost in the mists of time. Someone described it as 'the annual pit-head disaster, complete with wailing wives' – because of course the students' wives may have their own views about the postings, not always positive.

The jobs on offer are very varied. Some students open their brown paper envelopes and groan. Others, confronted by an indecipherable alphabet soup, mutter, 'What the hell's that? I don't even understand what the job is.' I was delighted because I had been appointed Chief of Staff of the Berlin Brigade: a plum job in a fascinating place. Perhaps not the ripest plum; a purist would have said that I'd have been better off with a brigade in West Germany, because that was where the real centre of gravity of the British Army was to be found. But I certainly wasn't complaining; I was very pleased and excited to be heading for Berlin, and so were all the family.

At Christmas 1976, right at the end of the course and following longstanding tradition, we staged a pantomime, produced, directed and put on by the students. Ours was loosely based on the Cinderella story; I remember that I had a small part in the second row of the male chorus. In the time-honoured tradition of the genre, the script was extremely irreverent, with plenty of leg-pulling of the Commandant and his DS, and Ugly Sisters who needed a shave. The overseas students watched in bemused amazement. So this is the conclusion of the great British Army staff course? Some kind of comic opera?

The mid-1970s saw various moves to try to reduce the tension between East and West. The buzz word of the time was détente, meaning an easing or relaxing. As part of the so-called Helsinki Accords of 1975, it was agreed that there should be bilateral UK–Soviet military exchange visits, staff college to staff college, starting in 1976. There was considerable excitement in Camberley at this prospect. I saw this as a great opportunity. I had missed out once on a visit to the Soviet Union; I wasn't going to miss out again. I decided to corner the Commandant, Major General John Stanier, whenever I had a chance. There are moments in your life when you have to blow your own trumpet, because no one else will blow it for you. This was one of them. The opportunity arose at some social occasion, the kind of envi-ronment in which it is easiest for a young major to talk informally to a major general – particularly a somewhat august and patrician general like John Stanier.

'General,' I said, taking the plunge: 'We hear there's a trip to Russia coming up.'

'Yes,' he replied, 'looks like that.'

'Well,' I persisted, 'you do know, don't you, that I'm the only student who speaks Russian?' I wasn't entirely sure of that, but since only two places had been allocated for students, all the rest having been grabbed by the Ministry of Defence and DS, I said it anyway. It seemed to work, because I was chosen to be one of the two student members of the party, the other being John le Quesne from the Royal Electrical and Mechanical Engineers.

Nowadays, when Russia is largely seen as just another foreign country much like any other, this visit might seem unexcep-tional. But in 1976, with the Cold War still icy, it was unusual for anyone to go there, let alone a British Army officer. The Soviet Union was a totalitarian state, secretive and forbidding. Its citizens were rigidly and sometimes brutally controlled, and constantly monitored. Just to converse with a Russian was quite something.

Everything was to be done strictly according to the published programme. In mid-October we flew by Aeroflot to Moscow. We were picked up from the airport in a fleet of long black Zil cars and driven to a pretty basic Ministry of Defence hotel on the Lenin Hills, quite near Moscow University. After a gruesome evening meal, the senior escorting officer announced that we would now go and tour Moscow by night, as the programme indicated. We were in uniform, and assumed we would change into civilian clothes for our tour of the capital, as we would have done had we been in London. When this was put to our senior minder, there was considerable surprise. 'We are military,' he replied, making it clear that we were expected to wear uniform throughout. Strap-hanging on the Moscow underground and strolling across Red Square in British Army uniform was an interesting experience – though I can't pretend that we noticed any particular reaction from the Muscovites. Perhaps they thought we were officers from the army of some more obscure member of the Warsaw Pact.

The next morning John le Quesne and I laid a wreath at the Tomb of the Unknown Soldier at the Kremlin Wall. We would do quite a lot of wreath-laying on that trip. After an appointment with Colonel General Makarov, the Chief of the Main Directorate of Military-Educational Establishments, we were driven to the Frunze, the Moscow staff college, which turned out to be a very imposing neoclassical building in the centre of the city. You entered a very large vestibule, and on the left as you went in there were racks and racks of coat hooks, though we never saw a single student in the whole place. Maybe they were away on an exercise, but more likely they were being kept out of our way. Inevitably, the British military attaché in Moscow was a member of our party, and of course it was part of his job to find out as much as he could about the Soviet armed forces. I noticed his eyes roving across the coat racks and his lips moving, and I realized that he was surreptitiously counting the coat hooks. One of the Russians spotted what he was doing at the same moment. 'My dear Brigadier,' he interrupted with a smile, 'five hundred and sixty-four.' Everyone laughed hard at that point. The ice was thawing.

We were given lunch at the Frunze, with many vodkas and much toasting. The Commandant was an ancient old boy, and we got the impression that he wasn't very well; but he came in for lunch and reminisced about the old days, becoming very maudlin, almost to the point of tears, telling a long story about his horse being shot from beneath him (the Red Army still having cavalry in the Second World War). That evening there was a lively cocktail party in the residence of the military attaché, and the next day we were given a tour of the Kremlin. One obligatory engagement, of course, was a trip to see the embalmed body of Lenin in his mausoleum. We arrived there to be confronted with a huge queue, and we imagined that we were in for a long wait in the October cold. But we needn't have worried, because we were marched directly to the head of the queue. Before we entered, one of the escorting officers indicated that he had something to say. We all gathered round expectantly. 'I am required by law to ask if any of you have any explosives about your persons,' he said very solemnly, 'because if you have you must surrender them before you go in.'

I was very struck by the Soviet Armed Forces Museum, which was organized by rooms depicting different stages of the Second World War. We British could hardly fail to notice that of these thirty or forty rooms only one was given to the Anglo-American Allies – just one, dealing with the Normandy invasion. This was how Russians perceived what they know as the Great Patriotic War: they believed that what the Western Allies did was peripheral, that the war had been fought and won largely by Soviet forces. I wondered how my father would have responded to that.

After an evening performance of *Nutcracker* at the Bolshoi, we caught the overnight train for Leningrad, the Red Arrow express. John le Quesne and I shared a compartment. Before we had left England the security authorities had given us a fairly stern wigging to beware of being subverted; to beware especially of Olga, the beautiful spy. John and I were teasing each other about this very subject when the compartment door opened and a woman's head appeared – but it belonged to a babushka, a grandmother with her samovar, enquiring whether we would like any tea.

The next morning we arrived in Leningrad, now once again known by its pre-revolutionary name of St Petersburg, and were taken to visit a Sandhurst equivalent, the wonderfully named Leningrad Higher All Arms Twice Red Bannered School. This time the cadets paraded for us, and General John Stanier, a polished public speaker, addressed them. I can't now remember exactly what he said, but no doubt it was something anodyne about building bridges, and I expect that he referred to the great wartime alliance against the Nazi menace.

After the obligatory tour around the sights of Leningrad – and the glorious Summer Palace just outside the city – we were taken that evening to the opera, something very modern and not to my taste. But I was interested by the theme: the life and achievements of Peter the Great. It was clear that he was still a great hero in Soviet Russia, even though he had been a tsar.

By the time the opera ended it was already late, and we were due to return to Moscow by the night train, which left at 23.55. It must have been the first night, because the applause went on and on, with ovation after ovation. Our Russian hosts began looking at their watches, caught in an awful dilemma: we couldn't miss the train, that would be a terrible loss of face; but nor could we walk out while the audience was still applauding this great work of Soviet art. Eventually we were hustled out into another convoy of big black cars, and driven hell-for-leather across the city. As the lowliest members of our party, John le Quesne and I were in the last of these. Suddenly a taxi shot out of a side street and drove into the side of us. Our driver, who had been silent until now, became very voluble. We had visions of being left behind in Leningrad while the rest of the party took the train to Moscow. Fortunately, neither car was seriously damaged. As ours drove away, John and I looked back to see the poor old taxi driver up against the wall, being given a hard time by members of our police escort. We made the train by the skin of our teeth. Arriving in Moscow the following morning, we were met by one of the senior Russians, whom by this time we had got to know quite well. After the usual greetings I mentioned the crash and expressed the hope that the taxi driver was OK. I received a stony-faced denial: 'There was no crash.'

I found this response an insight into the real Soviet Union. The accident was certainly unprogrammed, and obviously embarrassing – so it didn't happen. For me it had been fascinating to be in Russia, to get a sense of the Soviet Union from the inside, to snatch a peep behind the curtain. Back in 1939 Churchill had described the Soviet Union as 'a riddle wrapped in a mystery inside an enigma' – and almost forty years later its citizens were still just as difficult to fathom. I was always trying to understand the Russian paradox. Did they think of themselves principally as Russians or as Soviet citizens? As Marxists or patriots? Europeans or Asiatics? They were such a cultivated people, yet their government was so brutal. In so many ways they were like us – yet in as many others they were not like us at all.

6

City on the Edge

The fall of the Berlin Wall is already receding into history. For young people, it must be hard to imagine Europe as it was for almost half a century after the end of the Second World War: divided down the middle, from the Arctic to the Black Sea. The border was sealed; the peoples of the eastern side were imprisoned, and those who tried to escape were frequently shot in the attempt.

This absolute divide between East and West was most apparent in Berlin, then a city like none other. Right up until 1989 Berlin remained an anomaly, still under military occupation as it had been since 1945. As all of Germany had once been, so Berlin remained, carved by the victorious Allies into Zones of Occupation as prescribed by the Yalta Conference of early 1945. There was a British Sector, an American Sector, a French Sector – and, on the eastern side of the city, a Russian Sector, by far the largest of the four. These arrangements had been frozen in the Cold War that had begun almost immediately after the Germans were defeated. It had been intended that Berlin should be a unified city administered jointly by the four Allied powers, but very soon after the end of the war the Russians had walked out of the quadripartite institutions, in particular the Kommandatura, the military government. The Kommandatura continued to meet monthly, year after year, with an empty place at the table left for the Russians should they ever decide to return – which they never did.

West Berlin was an island, isolated more than a hundred miles within Russian-occupied territory, accessible only along restricted road and rail links, and by three narrow air corridors. In 1948 the Russians had sealed the land links and tried to starve West Berlin into submission, but a continuous airlift had kept the city supplied until, over a year later, the Russians relented and lifted the blockade. Germany divided into two separate states, the Federal Republic in the West and the 'Democratic' Republic in the East, with formidable armies stationed in each, under the umbrella organizations of NATO and the Warsaw Pact respectively. But Berlin continued to be administered in the same way, because any changes would have upset the delicate balance prevailing in the city. For example, the Western forces in Berlin were not under the NATO chain of command, because their status had been defined under the Potsdam Agreement between the Allied Powers in the summer of 1945, pre-dating NATO which did not come into being until 1949. The Western Allies refused to recognize East Germany, so all road traffic up 'The Corridor', as it was known, was regulated by the Russians.

Within Berlin, civilians could move fairly freely between the sectors until 1961, when mass emigration of skilled workers to the West prompted the building of a wall between the Russian Sector and the others, preventing any further passage across the city. This infamous wall became a dramatic symbol of Communist oppression. Along the west bank of the River Spree, which in the vicinity of the Reichstag formed the boundary between the Soviet and the Western sectors, was a row of crosses, in memory of people who had been shot dead by guards while trying to reach the West. In 1963 President Kennedy flew into Berlin and famously declared his solidarity with the people of the city: 'Ich bin ein Berliner.'

So Berlin continued from decade to decade, and so it was when I was posted there in January 1977. The house which I was going to take over from my predecessor being not yet available, I drove out alone, the rest of the family following by air two weeks later. In any event, I thought it would be fun to drive across Europe in my recently acquired Rover 2000. This was the first new car I'd ever owned; as I was going abroad I was able to buy it tax-free, and the garage did me a good exchange deal on the old car. I took the overnight boat from Harwich to the Hook of Holland, arriving at six o'clock in the morning, and then drove east the whole day. Of course, to reach West Berlin you had to drive through East Germany. Afterwards I'd drive that route between the West German border and Berlin so many times that I would come to think nothing of it, but that first time was memorable.

Crossing the Inner German Border was an elaborate ritual. The form was to report first to the Royal Military Police post at Helmstedt, with all your documents: your ID card, your passport and your posting order. The military police would fill out transit documents and give them to you, along with very detailed maps. You'd be warned not to stray from the prescribed route, and not to drive too fast, because it would be very embarrassing if you were arrested for speeding by the East German police (the 'Vopos'), given that we did not recognize their status. After that you were on your own. Having left the military police post, you would negotiate various chicanes and other obstacles until you reached the Soviet checkpoint. There you had to park your car, get out and walk across towards a little office building. The sentry would salute you, and you would salute him back, even if you were in plain clothes. On the outer wall of the building was just a little counter with a hole in the wall through which you shoved your papers. A hand would take them away. You waited, hoping everything would be in order, and after a while the papers would re-appear at this hole, duly stamped. Then you could set off.

It was late on a wet January afternoon and getting dark when I set out along the East German autobahn to Berlin for the first time. There seemed to be no traffic at all. It was uncanny to drive through dripping forests as the light was going, with no headlights behind me and none coming towards me. Bloody hell, I thought: into the heart of darkness go I.

After driving for two hours I arrived at the Berlin Russian checkpoint (known as Bravo), where I had to go through the same rigmarole as at the inner German border, and then on through the Allied checkpoint, and eventually there I was, in West Berlin. I drove straight to the officers' mess of the Berlin Brigade Headquarters for what I felt was a very well-earned whisky.

My appointment as Chief of Staff of the Berlin Brigade was what the Army calls an 'all-arms' staff job, i.e. where one's tribal identity is of no consequence to the job itself, and where one serves alongside officers and soldiers from many other tribes. My brigade commander, Charles Grey, was a Sapper, for example. The Brigade Headquarters was in the administrative building of the 1936 Olympic stadium, an imposing edifice in the Nazi neoclassical style, designed by Hitler's architect Albert Speer. There were amazing facilities, including two huge swimming pools, one outdoor, one indoor: all free, of course, because under international law we were still the occupying power, though we did not use that term to avoid any possibility of offending the Germans. The Brigade consisted of three infantry battalions, two of them based in Spandau, which is almost a satellite town but still within the perimeter of West Berlin, and the other right up against the East German border on the other side of the Havel, the long thin lake which runs north–south through the city. In support we had engineers, a logistics base, communications, a military hospital – in fact, all the infrastructure one could want, including schools, one of which my two children attended.

The four-thousand-strong Berlin Infantry Brigade was the sole British force in Berlin, and one of three Allied brigades, one per Western ally. In a unique arrangement the three brigade commanders reported to three major generals, the commandants of the Allied Sectors. Our commandant was Roy Redgrave, a cousin of the left-wing actors Vanessa and Corin. The strategic role of the Allied Forces in Berlin, and thereby the British Brigade, was to play their part in deterring and, if need be, resisting a Warsaw Pact attack. Of course, if it came to resistance we probably wouldn't last very long, because we were completely outnumbered. But our presence was symbolic, a powerful signal of the West's determination to remain in Berlin.

Operating as we were in such a confined area, organizing military exercises was not easy. For some exercises – armoured manoeuvres or parachuting, for example – we would have to decamp to the Federal Republic. But we were able to conduct set-piece exercises in the great forest, the Grünewald, and put much effort into maintaining our ability to ferry across the Havel, because that would be important if the bridges were destroyed. The West Berliners were very tolerant of any disruption resulting from our activities, because they were well aware that their continuing freedom depended on our presence. Our exercises led to some comic incidents. In summer young Germans like to prance around naked in the sunshine, and Berliners were no exception. On more than one of our exercises we burst out of the wood into a large clearing at the centre of the Grünewald to find bare Berliners disporting themselves.

British soldiers concealed in camouflaged gear encountered German girls playing volleyball with everything on view – very good for morale!

We also had what were known as 'crash-outs': no-notice exercises, designed to test the speed of our reactions. As the Chief of Staff I would plan these, keeping the details on an absolute close hold, so that only about four or five people knew when the hooters would sound. Typically, this would be at about 01.00 or 02.00 hours, so of course on such occasions I wasn't the most popular man in Berlin. The boys were expected to be out of barracks within an hour, and they always were; for them, it was almost a point of honour which battalion was first out. I remember one occasion when we were given the opportunity to exercise in a derelict area of the city that was about to be demolished. This would provide a rare opportunity to practise house-to-house fighting, what is known in the Army as FIBUA ('fighting in built-up areas'). I planned the exercise to simulate a counter-attack on an enemy-held urban position, negotiating very discreetly with the *Stadt* authorities to avoid giving any warning of the crash-out.

If war came, our job was to hold West Berlin until we were relieved. Short of general war, had the autobahn corridor been cut, there was a plan for an Allied armoured division to fight its way up the corridor towards us. Of course, being surrounded by enemy territory made us vulnerable to attack from all sides. When I arrived in Berlin, each Western Ally had its own plan to defend its own bit of the city, but there was no fully coordinated defence plan. I found my brigade commander a difficult boss, but he clearly saw the need for an integrated defence concept; he pushed this hard, and it was eventually accepted. I did a great deal of work on this new plan, and in the process learned a lot about multinational operations which would come in useful later in my career, not least the friction that can result when national interests do not entirely coincide.

The main obstacle to any integrated plan was establishing an integrated chain of command, and this was particularly difficult for the French. They were always slightly prickly about their position in Berlin anyway – perhaps a legacy of their difficult experience in the war. France had been a founding member of NATO in 1949, but traditionally disliked the idea of American predominance. In 1966, de Gaulle had withdrawn French forces from the integrated NATO military structure, though they remained political members of the Alliance. The NATO political headquarters, which had been in Fontainebleau, moved to Brussels; the military HQ, Supreme Headquarters Allied Powers Europe (SHAPE), moved to Mons, also in Belgium. A French corps remained stationed in Germany, based in the Black Forest as it had been since 1945, but throughout the Cold War period we in the British Army (and no doubt the other NATO members) could never be sure what the French would do if it came to the crunch. They would say, 'Of course we will be there' – but there was always this uncertainty, because they weren't part of the integrated forces and therefore they weren't part of integrated planning.

So the development of an integrated plan for the defence of West Berlin was a very delicate business. Obviously the US Commandant in Berlin would have to be *primus inter pares*, but the French found that difficult. And there was a further complication: the Allied forces in Berlin were not part of NATO, and so the plan needed to be coordinated with the NATO chain of command in West Germany. The Allied armoured division forcing its way down the autobahn to relieve West Berlin would be under NATO control. So getting our Gallic Allies on board required considerable diplomacy, and my A-level French was often tested – but we had just about cracked it by the time I moved on.

I remember the drama when a British Army convoy, heading back to West Germany, took the wrong turning on the autobahn. They had seen a sign saying Frankfurt, and thought,

'That's fine, we know Frankfurt'; but it turned out that they had taken the turning not for the familiar Frankfurt am Main, which is in the Rhineland, but for Frankfurt an der Oder, which is on the Polish border. So there was a British Army convoy driving east through Warsaw Pact territory: the kind of thing that in those days made people very nervous indeed. The convoy had actually reached Frankfurt an der Oder, clearly about to invade Poland, before somebody twigged. Sector Headquarters were going spare: 'What the hell's going on? Can't these people map-read?'

One enjoyable way to get into and out of Berlin was by rail. Each of the three Western Allies had a train service to the West: the American train went to Frankfurt, the French to Strasbourg and the British to Brunswick. We could ride on each other's without payment. Trains ran every day, no matter how few passengers there were, because the train service was, like so much else about Berlin, of symbolic importance. Each train was guarded by six soldiers, with an officer commanding, a duty that was handed out in turn to units throughout the Brigade. This was the only duty I ever volunteered for: not for altruistic reasons, but because I enjoyed it and found it interesting. You would leave Charlottenburg station early in the morning, and very quickly the train would reach the East German border. As the officer in charge, you had to have 'movement orders' ready for every passenger on the train, together with either passports (for families and civilians) or military ID cards (for servicemen). With all of these documents in your possession you would disembark, walk down the platform, and present them to a Russian officer – Russian, not East German – who sometimes would take a long time and peer at each and every one and sometimes would just say 'Fine'. Some would even offer a glass of vodka, and maybe there would be some idle chat. There was a civilian interpreter in tow – but being a Russian-speaker I could to some extent dispense with his services, which would immediately establish more of a rapport: people are always appreciative if you can speak their language, however haltingly. Some few hours later, around midday, after passing through a further set of Russian and then Allied controls on the border between the two Germanies, the train would reach Brunswick, where passengers would disembark, perhaps to catch a connecting train. There were two or three hours of free time in Brunswick to have a wander round and do whatever you wanted – perhaps shop a little, take a stroll by the river, visit an art gallery, or just sit in a café – before the train left on its return journey at around four o'clock in the afternoon. Meals on board were provided free of charge, in a restaurant car run for some historical reason by a group of elderly Polish displaced persons. As officer commanding the train you were made a bit of a fuss of: you'd be served with a full English breakfast soon after you left, then (having had lunch in Brunswick) afternoon tea just as the train set out on the way back, and some hours later dinner. Wine didn't cost very much, and so you arrived back at Charlottenburg in the early evening feeling absolutely no pain at all, after a very good day out.

Living in Berlin was exciting. Every morning you got up with a spring in your step. Of course, it helped that I was a reasonably competent German-speaker. I remember talking to a good friend of mine, a German, and saying to him, 'What a wonderful city this is, what an amazing place. Despite all its problems,' I said, 'life here is like nowhere else.' And he replied, '*Jawohl, heute leben, besonders heute abend – morgen, wer weisst, vielleicht die Russen*' ('Live today, especially tonight – tomorrow who knows, perhaps the Russians'). That was very much the Berlin philosophy.

And life was good. We were quartered in Charlottenburg, very close to the Olympic stadium, in a comfortable house on the south side of the long straight road which heads west out of Berlin. It was very pleasant, set in well-tended gardens surrounded by mature trees. I had to wait until I was made a general before I would be allocated quarters as good as that again. One was extremely fortunate.

Under the terms of the Potsdam Agreement, the Western Allies had absolute right of access to East Berlin, as the Russians did to West Berlin, because Berlin was considered as a single city. All ranks were encouraged to exercise this right, and of course it was a fascinating thing to do. The old classical heart of Berlin, all the museums, the beautiful old opera house – all this was in the East. The only condition was that you had to go in uniform. My first venture into the Soviet Sector was on one of the bus tours organized by the British authorities every Saturday morning. We passed through the only access point for Allied personnel, the infamous Checkpoint Charlie, the funnel for all our traffic between East and West. This was the front line of the Cold War, a place immortalized in thousands of books and films and magazine articles. Passing through the checkpoint was a potential problem, because we did not recognize the authority of the East German guards. For those wearing it, the uniform itself was sufficient proof of identity, but other members of the family would make a slight concession by holding their passports open against the car window. Once through the checkpoint, we were taken to see the sights: the Brandenburg Gate, Hitler's bunker and so on. That first trip into East Berlin was just to get my bearings really, but I liked it and afterwards I would go often, usually with the family. Everything seemed very cheap there. While West Berlin used the Deutschmark – then one of the strongest currencies in the world – East Berlin had the Ostmark, the East Mark, which was another matter altogether. The official exchange rate was around four to one, but you could go into any bank in West Berlin and get fifteen or sixteen Ostmarks for your

Deutschmark – so your Western currency went a long way in East Berlin. Unfortunately, there wasn't much worth buying, except cheap LPs, Meissen porcelain if you could find any, cameras, binoculars and children's clothes.

Often at the weekend we'd wander around Alexanderplatz, which was the big central area, do a bit of shopping, and then find somewhere to have a half-decent lunch. In the evenings you could go to the opera for next to nothing, and there were two or three places we knew where one could have dinner afterwards, dressed in full mess kit, bow tie, medals, the whole shebang. One favourite restaurant was called the Ganymede; its interior was like a relic of the 1930s, with potted palms and a little string orchestra. Once, as we came in after the opera with four or five other British couples, the string orchestra struck up 'God Save the Queen'! The East Berlin restaurants would pretend to serve lurid cocktails and offer an elaborate menu when in reality there would only be Wiener schnitzel or whatever, accompanied by some vinegary East European red wine. It would be difficult to over-estimate the vivid contrast between West and East Berlin: the change as one drove back through Checkpoint Charlie from the darkness and the gloom of the East to the bright lights and *joie de vivre* of the West was abrupt and extraordinary.

Occasionally you would see Russians in West Berlin doing what we did, exercising their right of access and no doubt spending such money as they had on Western goodies. Sadly, we had very little contact with Russians, except on a very formal basis. One exception to this was the summer party given by the British Military Liaison Mission (known as Brixmis).

At the end of the Second World War, all four Allies had agreed that they should have military liaison missions, one commander in chief to another, with right of access throughout occupied Germany. Thus the British mission had right of access throughout East Germany, as did the French and American missions; and likewise, the Soviet mission had right of access throughout West Germany. Once the Cold War started these liaison missions became essentially intelligence-gathering operations, but they retained a semblance of their old liaison function. The British Mission's HQ was an elegant *fin de siècle* house in Potsdam, only half an hour from the British Sector in West Berlin, but in East Germany. Members of the Mission lived with their families in the West, but this Headquarters was kept in Communist-controlled territory as a symbolic gesture. And every summer a reception would be held in the garden there. Many Russians would be invited, and some of the other Allied Grands Fromages as well. I was invited *ex officio*, and very intrigued to be attending. Apart from anything else, we got there not by going through Checkpoint Bravo, which was the one on the main autobahn from West Germany, but by going across Glienicke Bridge, the spy exchange bridge. So there we were, on a warm summer's evening, all in uniform of course, with the Pimm's flowing, and I was enjoying the rare opportunity to use my rusty Russian. Towards the end of the party, when I was probably not entirely sober, I found myself talking to some Russian officer. I hadn't taken on board who he was until I suddenly noticed his five-pointed star on a ribbon: the emblem of a marshal of the Soviet Union. I had been banging on to the Soviet Commander in Chief in Germany. I stopped in mid-sentence, aghast. He looked at me with a rather quizzical expression for a moment, and then said, 'How very interesting, Major,' before turning on his heel and walking off.

The only other place where I would have 'face time' with Russians was at Spandau Prison, a grim fortress built of dark red bricks with turrets and watchtowers. This was another of those bizarre Berlin anomalies, a prison with only one prisoner: Rudolf Hess, 'the loneliest man in the world'. Only once or twice did I ever catch sight of him, a stooping, gaunt, frail figure strolling in the garden alone. Hess had been Hitler's deputy; now he was the last surviving Nazi leader, and as such was deemed to be potentially a focus around whom neo-Nazi groups attempting to revive the glories of the Third Reich could rally. For the Russians in particular, his continued incarceration was a matter of the utmost importance.

Hess was guarded by a platoon of thirty soldiers from each of the four Allied powers in turn. Each platoon would be on duty for a month, before handing over to the next. It was a dreary duty, and the soldiers used to hate it. But on handover day there would be a lunch, for the incoming and outgoing platoon commanders, plus other representatives of all four Allies. As the Brigade Chief of Staff, I used to work out the rota, so I would be invited, as would my opposite numbers: American, French and Russian. There would be between a dozen and twenty young officers, four or five from each country, and all at roughly the same level. It was an opportunity to mix informally, and of course it helped that I could speak some Russian. I recall idly remarking to one Russian officer, 'What a dreadfully boring duty this is!' and the Russian getting quite cross with me. 'No,' he said, 'this is a very honourable duty. You should not forget what Hess represents, and all those who died in order to remove people like him.'

From time to time Hess, who was already in his mid-eighties and who had been in prison almost half his life, would need medical treatment. Again, I was responsible for making the arrangements, since the prison was in the British Sector. He would be treated in the British military hospital, about three miles up the road towards the city centre. He would be taken there by convoy, with a military escort and representatives from all three other Allies in attendance, watching everything that we did – particularly the Russians. Like so many other aspects of Berlin, Spandau Prison was surreal.

*

Ceremonial was an important part of life in Berlin. There was the annual Allied Forces Day Parade, when contingents of the three Western garrisons would march through the centre of West Berlin, close to the Wall itself. The British also celebrated the Queen's Birthday with a larger parade every summer in the grounds of the Olympic stadium complex. The Great and the Good of Berlin would be invited to watch. One year, despite several rehearsals, Charles Grey got his word of command wrong; the result was a bugger's muddle on the parade ground and huge embarrassment all round. Against my strong advice, he instigated one of those early-morning crash-out exercises only thirty-six hours afterwards. We all can and do make mistakes, but this lost him any sympathy he might originally have enjoyed.

My appointment as Chief of Staff of the Berlin Brigade had been for two years, concluding at the end of 1978. The next step along the usual Army career path was to go back to the Regiment as a company commander, and at the beginning of 1979 I was posted to the 2nd Battalion, 2 Para – which coincidentally was coming towards the end of a tour in Berlin, so the Jackson family was able to stay on there another six months. I was given B Company to command, the company I had joined when first posted to the Regiment as a young lieutenant. Among the hundred-odd men now under my command were some from my original platoon, including 'Banzai' Burton, who had succeeded Sergeant Peacock as my platoon sergeant while I was still a platoon commander, and who now was to be B Company Sergeant Major.

We were conducting one of our field exercises, in a rural area which was outside the city but still part of the British Sector, when the Prince of Wales visited the Battalion in his capacity as Colonel in Chief of the Parachute Regiment. It was the beginning of a long relationship with the heir to the throne, culminating in the six years I served as Colonel Commandant of the Regiment. Soon afterwards I learned with much pleasure that I had been awarded the MBE, for my 'exceptional contribution' to the new integrated Allied plan for the defence of West Berlin.

Bizarrely, most of my last six months in Berlin was taken up with special training for Northern Ireland, which is where 2 Para were headed again. Civilians might ask themselves whether this was a welcome posting. The fact is that, as a soldier, you take what you're given. Some of this preparation was carried out at 'Tin City', a mocked-up urban environment the size of an English village constructed predominantly of corrugated iron in Sennelager, West Germany. We undertook various kinds of minor tactical training: patrolling, anti-ambush drills, anti-bomb drills – and what we called 'judgemental shooting': training in when we were authorized to open fire according to the rules of engagement stipulated on the 'yellow card'.

We left Berlin in June and, after summer leave, reassembled at the Army camp at Ballykinler, a small village at the southern end of County Down, right on the coast. This would be another two-year residential tour, with the families housed within the barracks' perimeter for their own security. Ballykinler was a pretty place, in sight of the Mourne Mountains and with a glorious sandy beach, but isolated: Downpatrick, the nearest town, was 7 miles away, and it was 25 miles to Lisburn, the main military base.

The primary role of 2 Para on this posting was to act as reserve battalion to 3 Infantry Brigade, headquartered in Dungannon, whose tactical area of operational responsibility (TAOR) took in the south-east of the Province, including South Armagh. Our particular role was to support the South Armagh *roulement* battalion – headquartered at Bessbrook, about twenty minutes' flying time from Ballykinler – which when we arrived in Ballykinler was the 1st Battalion, the Queen's Own Highlanders. At any one time 2 Para provided at least one company to serve under their command, on a monthly rotation. For most of 2 Para's tour, the South Armagh company was based at the tiny village of Forkhill, in the old police station, which had been expanded with Portakabins and other temporary buildings and was protected by a high fence.

For me this tour would prove totally different from my tour with 1 Para seven years before. Our patrols then had been almost entirely in built-up areas. Now we would be operating in the fields and villages of South Armagh, the region that had become notorious as 'bandit country'.

7

Bandit Country

The landscape of South Armagh is exceptionally beautiful. Rough moorland studded with glacial moraines covers the hills, which look down over a patchwork of green fields. Armagh is the smallest of the six counties of Ulster, and very rural, noted for its orchards. There are no big towns or busy roads here. Modest villages huddle in the valleys; tracks end abruptly at small farmsteads. Only a small painted cross on the road surface informs the traveller that he has reached the border with the Republic.

This seems like a peaceful place, quiet and tranquil. So it is again, perhaps. But until recently, these lanes and hedgerows were laced with menace. The lush green countryside had been a battleground between the Security Forces and the IRA since the Troubles began, with innumerable bombings, shootings and mortar attacks. Lack of vigilance here could prove fatal.

The people of South Armagh never accepted partition. The locals were always staunchly Republican, resenting the border that legally if not culturally had divided them from the rest of

Ireland since 1920. Smuggling in and out of the Republic was so commonplace as to be mainstream, encouraged by the absurd agricultural subsidies in both countries. I well remember stopping a large truck somewhere on a lane in South Armagh to search the vehicle. The driver had a load of pigs on board which he had brought in from the Republic.

'Right, so where are they going?' I asked him.

He told me that he was taking them to Warrenpoint, the small port just south of Newry. Was he hoping to sell them there?

'Not exactly,' he answered. 'I'll just be taking them there and bringing them back again.'

Puzzled, I asked why.

'Because when we cross this way I get a subsidy from the British Government for doing it, and then when I cross back I can get a subsidy from the Irish. Then I take the pigs back to the fella I've rented them from.'

'Give me that again,' I said. 'You're joking, aren't you?' But he wasn't.

An unhealthy contempt for the forces of the British state prevailed throughout this close-knit community. South Armagh was a stronghold of the IRA, which enjoyed the sympathy if not the active support of local people. Even priests could be part of the conspiracy, and it was rumoured that a local doctor had laughed as he walked past a badly wounded British soldier. In this part of the Province terrorists could be sure of shelter and assistance, and if threatened with capture it was easy for them to slip across the border into the Republic. IRA gunmen carried out a series of atrocities here, some in response to killings by Loyalist death squads. In 1976, for example, a minibus carrying men home from work had been stopped at a bogus vehicle checkpoint near Bessbrook. The Catholic driver was allowed to go, but the passengers, all Protestants, were massacred with automatic weapons. Ten men died at the scene; one survived, despite being shot eighteen times.

South Armagh was particularly dangerous for the Security Forces. Almost half of all the British soldiers murdered by the IRA in the first decade of the Troubles had been killed in this sparsely populated rural backwater, only about a hundred miles square. Scores of policemen and Ulster Defence Regiment (UDR) part-timers had died here too. This was enemy territory, with a sullen and hostile population; behind every pair of eyes lurked a potential spy. What we were involved in here was counter-insurgency, of the type the Army had conducted in Malaya and elsewhere, but fought in what should have been a sleepy corner of the British Isles.

The South Armagh IRA specialized in ambushes, exploding roadside bombs as Security Force vehicles were passing. Many of these were detonated by a signal carried along dug-in wires, but they had also developed bombs that could be detonated by radio, which were harder to deal with and involved much less risk for the bomber. There were also frequent gun attacks on British foot patrols, using long-range sniper fire. The IRA had recruited a large number of 'scouts' whose job it was to watch the Security Forces and record their habits, with the aim of identifying potential targets. They placed their bombs in locations where they knew soldiers were likely to pass. Travelling overland in South Armagh became so dangerous that the Army had to use helicopters to move troops and supply its bases, just as the Americans had done in Vietnam. The landing site in the village of Bessbrook became the busiest heliport in Europe, more so than those supplying the North Sea oil rigs. Everything was transported by helicopter – even the rubbish. Army helicopters would take off and land every few minutes, flying at rooftop level to reduce the risk of missile or small-arms attack.

Our job was to put boots on the ground, to support the beleaguered police and to show that the rule of law still held in South Armagh. We almost always patrolled on foot; paradoxically, it was safer that way. Vehicles on the whole have to use roads or tracks, and it was simplicity itself for the IRA to put an explosive device in a culvert under the road or dig it into the verge and leave it there, sometimes for months, until an Army vehicle happened to come past. On foot, you could choose your own route. You never went through a gateway because that was an obvious place for an improvised explosive device (IED). Instead, you always went from one field to another by forcing your way through the blackthorn hedges, despite the inevitable scratches and discomfort. The IRA used both command wire and radio signals to detonate IEDs; neither was simple to defeat, whether by physical or technical means.

Another reason for patrolling on foot was that the soldiers were spaced out, so if a bomb was detonated it was unlikely that many of them would be within range. In a vehicle, on the other hand, you're packed in, and the likelihood is that if a bomb explodes several of you will be killed at once.

Every patrol would be carefully planned in advance, with possible firing points identified and covered. Sometimes we'd carry out a 'route clearance', searching a road for bombs in advance of a convoy, checking every culvert for IEDs. The Belfast–Dublin railway was a favourite target for the IRA. For them it was a propaganda coup to be able to close this line, so they tried to sabotage it whenever possible. One especially vulnerable place was the infamous Kilnasaggart Bridge, where the railway crossed over a road only three or four hundred yards from the border. We tried to protect this by maintaining a presence on the ground, but of course this made the soldiers a target.

As well as bombs, the South Armagh IRA would use homemade mortars, but their range was only two to three hundred yards and they were not very accurate, so they would only use them to attack static targets like exposed bases – and there were not many of these in South Armagh.

In many ways this was a cat-and-mouse game, particularly where IEDs were concerned. Those of us operating overtly – the so-called 'Green Army' – were not there primarily to flush out the IRA, but if they attacked us, it was game on. There were some fierce gun battles, some lasting an hour or more. But most often it would be frustrating: if you didn't hit one of your attackers in your opening burst of fire, you probably wouldn't hit them at all, because the terrorists had their escape route planned in advance. A car would be waiting, and they'd race off towards the border, which would be only a few minutes' drive away. Even if we did hit someone we wouldn't necessarily know it, because the wounded would be whisked away for treatment in the South. Sometimes they would open fire on us from across the border, and in those circumstances we were permitted to return fire into the Republic; but of course then you'd have even less chance of knowing whether you'd hit one of them.

We had no formal contact with the Irish Army. If we were doing an operation right up against the border, a request would be put in for a Security Forces presence on the other side to deter IRA activity. This would always be done through the RUC, who would talk to the Garda, who in turn might call on the Irish Army for support. By and large the Irish Security Forces were cooperative at a local level. Officially they were not supposed to fraternize with us, but sometimes I might have a brief chat with an Irish Army officer at the border.

The IRA in South Armagh were not to be underestimated. They knew the lie of the land extremely well and they were pretty cunning. Operations in the area were a real battle of wits. It was said that if you stopped thinking, you'd start dying. Our job, operating alongside the police, consisted of 'framework operations', routine patrols, searches, manning vehicle checkpoints and so on, just to show that we had the presence, the boots on the ground. In many ways the real war of attrition against the IRA was carried out by covert forces of one sort or another, working 'on very close hold', meaning on a strict need-to-know basis. Some of the time we didn't even know when they were around. To avoid the risk of mistaken identity and a blue-on-blue ('friendly fire') contact, the standard procedure was to impose a so-called 'out-of-bounds area'. For example, we might be told that an area of two or three square kilometres was out of bounds to us, and mark this on our maps. Sometimes a quick reaction force would be put on standby, in case things went wrong and the covert operation needed backup. Occasionally when we'd stop a covert vehicle at a checkpoint, the driver would produce ID showing that he was a member of the Security Forces.

The four companies of 2 Para rotated on roughly a monthly basis between Forkhill, guard duty at Ballykinler, and specific operations such as reinforcing Newry and protecting the railway line. Rural patrols from the company base would be out for several days at a time. Living in an improvised base like Forkhill was cramped, unpleasant and uncomfortable; for one thing, there never seemed to be enough hot water. The boys had to sleep in dormitories, with beds crammed in close to each other and very little storage space for clothes and other personal possessions. But at least the food was consistently good, thanks to the excellent Army chefs. Occasionally we would join a 'surge' operation in a different part of the South Armagh TAOR, when troops would flood an area in the hope of making arms finds and deterring terrorist attacks. After a month or so on deployment, it would be a relief to get back to barracks in Ballykinler. We would always hold a company party the night we got in – an opportunity for the boys to let off steam. As the evening wore on, we would belt out what had become the company song: 'You'll Never Walk Alone'.

In between all of this there was some time for leave. This kind of *roulement* was essential to morale, but of course it made us more vulnerable to attack every time a company moved into or out of a deployment. Even helicopters were not entirely invulnerable to IRA attack; and there were insufficient helicopter hours to avoid road moves outside South Armagh. It was a road move between Ballykinler and Newry – not in South Armagh proper – which provided the IRA with the opportunity for their single most devastating attack in their long campaign against the British Army.

The August Bank Holiday Monday of 1979 was hot and sunny, coming at the end of a month of fine weather. B Company had been conducting operations along the railway line for several days, and we had come into the HQ of the Queen's Own Highlanders at Bessbrook to sort ourselves out and grab some rest. The plan was to stay there a night or two before going back to the railway line. We set up an ops room, while anyone not on duty wandered off in various directions: to the Naafi to get something to eat, to find a bunk for a kip or a shower for a wash. Bessbrook was a huge building; originally a Victorian textile mill, it had been heavily reinforced and reconstructed to house up to a thousand men. Its windowless corridors were lined with pipework, and the constant throbbing of generators gave one the feeling of being in a ship below the waterline.

Meanwhile 2 Para's Support Company in Newry was due to be relieved by A Company later that day. My opposite number Major Peter Fursman, commanding A Company, was already in Newry in the process of taking over from Major Barry Rogan, commanding Support Company. We were all company commanders together, and good friends. The main body of A Company would be coming in by road, which was always a concern; the operations room back in Ballykinler had identified a number of different routes, and would pick one of them at random to try to vary any pattern we might have been setting. This time, the random choice was to result in mayhem.

The convoy of a Land Rover and two four-ton lorries carrying a platoon of about twenty-six soldiers from A Company was sent south along the coast and then up the eastern shore of the estuary of the Newry River. For several miles above the port of Warrenpoint, the river estuary funnels into a tidal lough several miles long and about two hundred yards wide known as Narrow Water, which marks the border with the Republic. A dual-carriageway road ran along the eastern (Northern Irish) shore, while thick woods came down to the water's edge on the Republic side. It was an ideal place for an ambush. The woods provided cover for the terrorists, who had a clear view of traffic passing along the road on the other side of the estuary. There were no obstacles to interfere with a radio signal detonating a bomb on the eastern shore. Being already in the Republic, the terrorists had a good chance of escaping after making their attack.

The Army had long recognized the vulnerability of this stretch of road and frequently put it out of bounds. However, there were only a few routes into Newry from Ballykinler, and if we were to avoid establishing a predictable pattern which would be vulnerable to ambush elsewhere, we had to use this one from time to time. The IRA had in all probability targeted the Royal Marines, who often used this route after conducting their regular checks on the container port at Warrenpoint docks.

In studying the Army's procedures following a bomb attack, IRA analysts had noticed that we would invariably set up an incident control point near the scene of an explosion, from which we would evacuate casualties and collect forensic evidence. They had decided to exploit this procedure by placing two bombs close to each other, the second located where they thought the incident control point was likely to be. The first bomb was hidden beneath straw bales in a trailer which had been parked the previous night in a lay-by. The second bomb was hidden about two hundred yards further along the road towards Newry, in the gate-lodge to a large country house situated higher up the slopes of the Narrow Water valley. Opposite the gate-lodge, on a small promontory that projected almost halfway across the lough, was one of a series of stone towers built in Elizabethan times to defend the east coast of Ulster. It was a noted local beauty spot.

We in B Company were relaxing back at Bessbrook when the dreadful news of Lord Mountbatten's murder came through at about midday. He and members of his family had been heading out to sea on a fishing-trip from Mullaghmore, the village in County Sligo, on the west coast of the Republic, where the Mountbattens had spent every summer for the previous thirty years. Apparently a radio-controlled device had been hidden in his boat and then triggered by somebody on the shore. As well as the Earl, three others had been killed: his fourteen-year-old grandson Nicholas Knatchbull; the boy's grandmother, Lady Brabourne; and Paul Maxwell, a fifteen-year-old local boy who had been acting as boatman. Several further members of the family, including Mountbatten's daughter, were in hospital being treated for their injuries. Service in Northern Ireland hardens one to atrocities, but even so everybody was deeply shocked by the cruel murder of such a distinguished figure, and the wanton killing of his companions. The news subdued us all, eliminating the normal exuberance you usually feel after completing an operation in the field. But if this was bad, it was about to get much worse.

Later in the afternoon, shortly before five o'clock, I was having a cup of tea in the officers' mess downstairs at Bessbrook when the intercom buzzed. It was my colour sergeant. 'I think you'd better come upstairs,' he said. 'Now.' I raced up to the ops room, two steps at a time. He looked up at me with a sombre expression. It was not a clear picture, he informed me – it never is in these early stages – but he had heard a report on the Battalion radio net from Royal Marines in the area that there had been some sort of explosion on the main road from Warrenpoint to Newry. I had a sinking feeling in the pit of my stomach as I realized that 2 Para was involved.

The bomb in the lay-by had been detonated at 16.40 hours as the rear lorry of the convoy was passing. It took the full force of the explosion and was hurled on to its side. The other lorry driver put his foot down and drove on before parking under the cover of some trees, while the Land Rover swerved across the central reservation and turned around to face the direction from which it had come, towards the smoking debris of the trailer and the wrecked rear lorry. Here the platoon commander set up an incident control point, while he tried frantically to raise Bessbrook on the radio, without success. Radio communications between Bessbrook and the company at Newry had broken down, and the resulting inability to talk to the troops on the ground greatly complicated the Battalion HQ's ability to control the incident and provide support. The crew of a Wessex helicopter on a routine mission intercepted the soldiers' distressed and increasingly desperate transmissions, and contacted Bessbrook. The helicopter was ordered to return to the Battalion HQ, collect a medical team and the four-man Battalion quick reaction force, and take them to Warrenpoint.

Bodies of the soldiers who had been riding inside the lorry were scattered across the road, many of them in flames. All this time the air was filled with the crackle of ammunition and blasts of explosive detonating in the ruined lorry, mixed with the screams of the wounded lying across the road. The surviving soldiers were very jittery. Convinced that they were being shot at from the other side of the water, they returned fire, killing an innocent tourist and wounding another. One soldier became aware of movement behind a roadside wall; pointing his gun, he shouted an order to come out with hands held high. Several shocked children appeared; they had been picnicking with their mother.

Lieutenant Colonel David Blair, commanding officer of the Queen's Own Highlanders at Bessbrook, was himself airborne in a small Gazelle helicopter when he heard the news. He quickly decided that his presence was needed on the ground. Meanwhile, in Newry, Barry Rogan dispatched his own eight-man quick reaction force to the scene in two Land Rovers, and a few moments later he and Peter Fursman followed in two further Land Rovers. On arrival they made the fateful decision to set up the incident control point at the gate-lodge, parking their vehicles beside the building and positioning two Land Rovers on either side of the incident, to prevent civilians entering the area. The Wessex helicopter landed on the central reservation of the dual carriageway, between the wrecked vehicle and the gate-lodge. The medical team alighted immediately, followed by the quick reaction force from Bessbrook. A few moments later a soldier returned to the helicopter to tell the crew to expect only two casualties, as the other six men who had been travelling in the lorry were all dead. About five minutes later the first stretcher was on board, and the other was alongside the Wessex, which was ready for take-off.

It was now almost 17.00 hours. Colonel Blair's Gazelle helicopter had dropped him and his signaller in the grounds of the country house before leaving. These two ran down the drive to join Peter Fursman and his mobile HQ at the gate-lodge. At this moment the watching terrorists detonated the second bomb. The building disintegrated in a huge explosion, disappearing in a cloud of dust and smoke. Lumps of granite were hurled through the air. The Wessex shifted slightly in the shock wave, which blew out one of its Perspex windows. It was then bombarded with fragments of stone. One boulder as big as a football came down through the rotor blades, bouncing off the nose of the aircraft. Though severely damaged, the helicopter managed to take off and fly low over the trees towards Bessbrook.

By this time I was in the Battalion ops room trying to follow what was happening on the Queen's Own Highlanders battalion net. I realized with a sense of mounting dread that there had been many casualties. I still have the scrap of paper on which I scribbled some notes. They read: '1st explosion W[arren]p[oin]t docks, Wessex [bringing] cas[ualties], 2nd 200 yds, all cas[ualties], still some dead, contact 2 hits claimed, one body in the river.' There was still much confusion about what had happened: the Royal Marines' initial contact report had implied an explosion at Warrenpoint docks. Details became clearer over the next few minutes. It was feared that both Peter Fursman and David Blair were dead. Barry Rogan had been bowled over by the second bomb, but miraculously had escaped serious injury.

Brigadier David Thorne, Commander of 3 Brigade, arrived at Bessbrook from his HQ in Dungannon and took control of the situation, issuing orders very rapidly. The Queen's Own Highlanders urgently needed a new battalion commander, and as bad luck would have it Colonel Blair's second-in-command, Major Jeremy Mackenzie, was in Hong Kong reconnoitring their next deployment. The senior company commander, Major Nick Ridley, was in Crossmaglen, 15 miles to the south-west. Thorne made ready to fly to Crossmaglen, where he would promote Ridley to local lieutenant colonel on the spot, ordering him to fly immediately to Bessbrook to take command of the Battalion. Then he noticed me.

'Hello, Mike,' he said. 'What are you doing here?'

I explained that we were untasked, having just come off an operation.

'Right,' he said. 'You're the people to do this, because it's a company from your battalion that's been attacked. Get down to Warrenpoint and sort it out.' Within minutes I was flying to the scene with my immediate command team, followed in fairly short order by the rest of the company. Our job was to relieve the soldiers on the ground and contain the scene until the clear-up operation was completed. I was anxious that there might be further bombs. I remember saying to 'Banzai' Burton, 'We want to be bloody careful that there isn't a third one around here somewhere.'

I arrived at the incident within half an hour of the second bomb explosion. As we circled before landing I could see two craters and large scorch-marks on the road marking where the bombs had been. The gate-lodge had been completely destroyed, with large lumps of granite scattered as far as a hundred yards off. The police and the ambulance service were already on the scene. We landed on the road about three hundred yards south-east of the first bomb-crater (see sketch-map), reckoning that this was a spot with nothing distinct about it that might have caused the IRA to identify it as a potential target. Other helicopters were evacuating the wounded. We relieved the Queen's Own Highlanders' quick reaction force and the survivors of the two bomb blasts. I found Barry Rogan, now the senior officer on site, his forehead covered by a field dressing; after a quick briefing, he handed over the situation to me and returned to his company HQ in Newry.

I knew what I had to do as incident commander under those circumstances: deter further attack, put a cordon around the whole area, preserve the scene of the crime, help the investigative agencies to do their job, and keep all other people out. I set up my HQ in the stone tower opposite the wrecked gate-lodge, after having had it thoroughly checked out for any further IEDs. Only then could I take stock. It was a horrifying scene. There

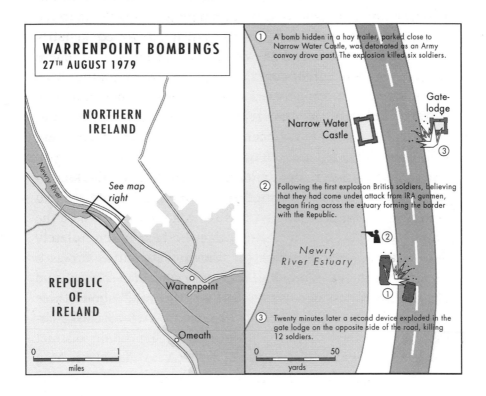

WARRENPOINT BOMBINGS
27TH AUGUST 1979

NORTHERN
IRELAND

Newry River

See map
right

REPUBLIC
OF
IRELAND

Warrenpoint

Omeath

0   1
miles

① A bomb hidden in a hay trailer, parked close to Narrow Water Castle, was detonated as an Army convoy drove past. The explosion killed six soldiers.

Gate-lodge

Narrow Water Castle

③

② Following the first explosion British soldiers, believing that they had come under attack from IRA gunmen, began firing across the estuary forming the border with the Republic.

Newry River Estuary

②

①

③ Twenty minutes later a second device exploded in the gate lodge on the opposite side of the road, killing 12 soldiers.

0   50
yards

was human debris everywhere, in the trees, on the grass verge and in the water: mostly unidentifiable lumps of red flesh, but among them torsos, limbs, heads, hands and ears. I had seen the effect of bombs before, of course, but never carnage on this scale. When a bomb goes off, the air inside the body is compressed, and often forces its way out through the joints. There were some very gruesome sights. All that was left of the driver of the rear lorry was his pelvis, which had been welded to the seat by the intense heat. In these circumstances your emotions shut down and the training takes over. Soldiers try to remain as professional as possible. If anyone felt sickened by what he saw, he would go into the bushes so as not to be seen vomiting by his mates.

Around 18.00 hours the newly promoted Nick Ridley arrived, and we spent some time together assessing the situation before he flew back to Bessbrook. The Garda had been alerted and were in the process of securing the far side of the lough. It later emerged that they had detained two men, but had released them for lack of evidence.

It stayed light late that warm summer evening. An eerie silence descended, as the drone of helicopters and vehicles faded. It seemed unbelievable that something so terrible could have happened in such a beautiful spot. Gradually the specialists arrived: CID, the forensic team, the weapons intelligence people, search teams, divers – the whole gamut. At this stage we still did not know the precise number of casualties, and we were trying to work out who was missing by a process of elimination. It was almost impossible to identify who had been killed, because there were so few remains. I remember one of the divers from the Royal Engineers asking me quietly to come and look at something he'd found in the water. It was a human face that had been blown clear of the man's skull. The line of a moustache was still visible. The diver asked me if I recognized the man. I felt a shiver of horror. 'Of course I do,' I said in a shaky voice.

'He's a good friend of mine.' It was Peter Fursman; that was all we ever found of him. David Blair was identified only by the crown and the star on his epaulette.

I was told that back at Ballykinler it was like the Village of the Damned, while the wives and families waited to hear who had been killed. Apparently there was a rumour that I was one of the dead.

The final body count was eighteen soldiers killed, sixteen Paras and two from the Queen's Own Highlanders. Six more Paras were seriously wounded. This was the highest number of soldiers killed in any single incident during the whole bloody history of the Troubles. Lieutenant Colonel David Blair was one of the most senior officers killed. The loss to the Paras in a single contact was the worst since Arnhem in 1944. The death toll might have been even higher but for some miraculous escapes. One soldier survived uninjured despite being blown 30 feet through the air; another remained unscathed even though he was taking cover behind a bush beside the lodge-gates when the second bomb exploded.

We maintained the cordon for five days while the emergency services carried out their grisly work, painstakingly clearing the human remains, gathering forensic evidence and removing the debris. Astonishingly, they found the window of the Wessex helicopter intact; I eventually sent it back up to RAF Aldergrove, where I think it's still on display.

The clear-up was very hard for the soldiers, because these were their mates. All the time we were down there by the water's edge I was anxious about the danger of further sniper attacks from the far side. I charted the possible enemy positions for a shoot and placed my cordon accordingly, though of course we could not fully protect those involved in the clear-up.

I still have ugly pictures in my head from that terrible day. Once you've seen such appalling sights, you can't close your mind to them. But I don't have nightmares; fortunately my temperament isn't like that. My attitude is: move on, put that away, because if you get bogged down in thinking too much about it, you might start losing your own courage – and that wouldn't do at all.

Peter Fursman's widow, Christine, said she wanted to see where her husband had died. Lieutenant Colonel Colin Thomson, 2 Para's commanding officer, was very unsure about this, but Christine was insistent. I took it upon myself to escort her around the site of the bombing; it seemed to me that I owed it to them both. For me this was the hardest moment of the whole incident. Christine's fortitude was tremendously affecting; I felt close to tears myself as I watched her holding back her own. I was very anxious that there might still be body parts lying around, but if she did catch sight of anything of that kind, she didn't react. Peter and I were the same age and the same rank. We'd been friends for years, and spent a lot of time together. It occurred to me later that if the cards had come off the pack in a different order it could have been B Company rather than A Company travelling along the road that day, and then it might have been Peter who would have pulled my face out of the water.

Humphrey Atkins, the Secretary of State for Northern Ireland, visited us at the scene the next day, and on the Wednesday Mrs Thatcher, only three months into her tenure as Prime Minister, flew to the Province. She first visited the wounded in hospital, and then spent some hours in Belfast before flying on to South Armagh. Nick Ridley and I briefed her on what had happened in the presence of the Secretary of State, the GOC, Lieutenant General Sir Timothy Creasey, Brigadier David Thorne and Barry Rogan. I was impressed by the way she listened carefully and asked pertinent questions. At the end she instructed the Secretary of State that increased effort should be put into developing new technology to counter the threat of bombs detonated by remote control, and directed him to establish a much closer relationship with the Garda. Both these initiatives were to prove valuable in countering the IRA threat over the two decades that followed.

A month after the Warrenpoint killings, a memorial service was held at the garrison church in Aldershot, attended by the Prince of Wales in his capacity as Colonel in Chief of the Regiment. I was among many 2 Para personnel who flew back to England for the ceremony. The church was packed with wives, girlfriends, parents and other family members. The Prince of Wales read the lesson, and then the names of the dead were read out, before the Last Post sounded. We resolutely sang 'Onward Christian Soldiers', followed by the National Anthem. Finally the Regimental Colours were carried from the church, followed by Prince Charles and the families of the fallen.

I received a letter from Jeremy Mackenzie, who had taken over command of the Queen's Own Highlanders on his return from Hong Kong. He commended the men of 2 Para for their fortitude and resilience in the most harrowing circumstances. It later emerged that Catholics across the Province feared a massacre in reprisal for the terrible deaths of so many soldiers at Warrenpoint. It was a tribute to the discipline and restraint of the Paras that no such reprisals occurred.

The most direct result of the massacre at Warrenpoint was the cessation of road movement between Ballykinler and South Armagh. More helicopter hours were made available, so that from then almost all troop movements were by air, though we sometimes used covert, unmarked vans. Even movements by air were not risk-free, however: on a number of occasions helicopters came under fire from small arms or even medium machine guns. A Wessex operating out of Crossmaglen came under fire from a heavy machine gun mounted on the back of a truck with armour plating. Unfortunately there was not enough room inside the compound at Forkhill for a helipad, so it was located outside the fence. This meant that helicopters on the ground were vulnerable to attack, but luckily the IRA never scored a hit on one.

During our tour the base at Forkhill was completely rebuilt with mortar-proof buildings, improved facilities and fortified defences. To protect the convoys bringing the building materials, we took part in large set-piece operations at battalion level. It required approximately a thousand soldiers to picket the whole route from Bessbrook to Forkhill, both close-in to the road itself and, crucially, on the high ground overlooking the road. The aim was to deny the IRA any point from which they could fire or plant or detonate a bomb. The pickets were maintained for three or four days while large convoys brought in building materials and then came out with the waste.

A complex of permanently manned observation towers on stilts was erected to provide surveillance over South Armagh. They were known in the Army as 'sangars', an Arabic word taken into British use. We put up one of the first, on high ground above Forkhill. These towers gave excellent surveillance over the TAOR, being equipped with, among other things, optics which could read a number plate a mile or so off. The IRA didn't like these at all, and attacked them from time to time, but without a lot of success. By definition they were not overlooked, and they were well defended with lots of barbed wire and security lights. The soldiers manning the towers were changed over at quiet times such as the small hours of the morning, always varying our procedures to avoid becoming predictable. The South Armagh towers have now been dismantled as part of the peace process.

Over the months that followed, 2 Para suffered further casualties. One of our soldiers was killed by a bomb blast while checking a culvert. On New Year's Eve 1979 there was a dreadful 'blue on blue', after one of our platoons had set up a speculative ambush on a border crossing. The platoon commander broke one of the golden rules: once the ambush is set and everybody's in position, you don't move until the ambush is formally lifted. For whatever reason, perhaps because he saw something suspicious and decided to take a look, he left the ambush, taking his signaller with him. On his return he walked straight into the trap that he himself had laid. As the lieutenant and his signaller approached the soldiers opened fire, killing both men. Then one of our sergeants died when he took a short cut through a gate where a bomb had been laid. With these deaths 2 Para gained the unenviable record for the most casualties sustained by any unit during a Northern Ireland tour.

Johnny Frost had commanded 2 Para at Arnhem; he was the figure immortalized by Anthony Hopkins in the film *A Bridge Too Far*. Of course, Frost was a living legend to us for what he'd done at Arnhem, holding the bridge for much longer than anyone had thought possible. The plan for Operation 'Market-Garden' had been for 6 Airborne Division to secure the bridge over the Rhine until relieved by heavy armour coming up the road from Eindhoven, but this failed to break through to Arnhem, and Frost's lightly armed force had fought a desperate battle against SS Panzer troops with much heavier firepower. Frost still took huge interest in the Battalion, and I'd met him several times. On Arnhem Day 1980 he came out to see us at Forkhill. Though almost seventy by this time, he was still spry, and of course he was intensely interested in all aspects of soldiering. I took him up to a bit of high ground above the railway line, a very good vantage point from which you could see much of the company area and across the border. This was rugged, Dartmoor-like country, and on the high ground we were quite secure. It was a privilege to spend some time in his company.

The end of 1980 marked the end of my two years with the Battalion. The military situation in Northern Ireland had reached stalemate, with each side developing tactics and counter-measures. There had been little political progress, but the very fact that terrorism had not prevailed was itself some kind of victory.

I left 2 Para at Christmas, even though they had another four or five months of their tour remaining. I was headed for the National Defence College at Latimer, near Aylesbury in Buckinghamshire, where I would undertake a six-month course with officers – all British – of similar age and rank from all three Services. The aim of the course was to provide selected officers with a broader and deeper understanding of defence on a joint-Service basis. This was a welcome change after eighteen months of full-on field soldiering.

But there would be a footnote to my second tour in Northern Ireland. On 4 July 1981 some 2,500 people attended the annual Airborne Forces Day Parade at Aldershot. There were marches, fly-pasts, and a parachute display by the Red Devils. The Colonel Commandant of the Regiment, General Sir Anthony Farrar-Hockley, presented awards. For my service as a company commander in Northern Ireland I was awarded the oak leaf symbol of a mention in dispatches 'in recognition of gallant and distinguished service'. It was a proud moment.

8

Commanding Officer

In June 1981, while still at the National Defence College, I was promoted to lieutenant colonel. I felt very gratified to have reached this rank at only thirty-seven, the earliest age at which you can do so.

The Army career structure dictates that officers from the rank of major upwards will alternate every two years or so between command and staff jobs. The concept is that you're getting a rounded person coming through at each level. Accordingly, my next posting was back to the Staff College as a member of the Directing Staff – a really plum job for a young lieutenant colonel. The DS consisted of, dare I say it, some of the sharpest of the younger officers of this rank, while the students were the cream of the generation of Army officers about five years younger, senior captains and young majors in their early thirties. It was stimulating to teach these bright young people in an invigorating environment. Having said that, I have to admit that I was frustrated to be in a staff job when the Falklands crisis blew up, early in 1982.

The events leading up to the Falklands War were in their own way as bizarre as those leading to the invasion of Anguilla. There is an atavistic Argentine belief that the Falkland Islands – which they call the 'Malvinas' – are theirs. The islanders, on the other hand, had for as long as anyone could remember been overwhelmingly in favour of remaining British. The Argentinian military junta headed up by General Galtieri had been making threatening noises towards the 'Malvinas' for some years, but it was not at all clear that this was any more than bluster. The Chiefs of Staff had anyway concluded some years before that the Islands were indefensible. The crisis began absurdly enough, with an Argentinian scrap-metal dealer landing illegally on the island of South Georgia just before Christmas, and escalated from then until the Argentinian invasion of the Falklands early in April. The Foreign Office and even the MOD were inclined to regard the whole thing as a *fait accompli* even before it happened, but the First Sea Lord, Admiral Sir Henry Leach, was made of sterner stuff. As soon as news of the invasion came through he went to the House of Commons to beard the Secretary of State for Defence, John Nott. It turned out that Nott was in a meeting with the Prime Minister at the time. When Mrs Thatcher learned that the First Sea Lord was waiting, she summoned him in to join them, whereupon he brushed aside the defeatist advice she'd been given by the Foreign Office and MOD bureaucrats. 'Prime Minister, we can do this,' he told her. Then and there she gave him the authority to start forming a Task Force to sail to the South Atlantic. Word has it that Nott went as white as a sheet on hearing her words. A few days later she announced in the House of Commons the British Government's determination to retake the Islands.

At the Staff College we were all totally absorbed by the developing situation. Of course everyone was behind the Government's decision 100 per cent. But the stakes were very high. I remember one of my more far-sighted colleagues saying to me, 'One government will fall, whatever happens. If Britain wins, Galtieri cannot survive. And if we lose, Thatcher will be out. Maybe both governments will fall.'

Then the question arose: who's going to go? We hadn't had a real war for more than a generation, and everyone wanted a taste of the action. Here was an opportunity to do what we'd all spent our lives training for. Within the Army, there was some rapid force generation, as everyone scrambled for a place aboard one of the many troop-ships, including the liners *Canberra* and *Queen Elizabeth II*. A force of approximately ten thousand soldiers was assembled very swiftly from a standing start, incorporating 3 Commando Brigade Royal Marines, with its three battalion equivalents, and two battalions of the Parachute Regiment, 2 and 3 Para. My previous battalion was now under the command of Lieutenant Colonel Herbert 'H' Jones, who had succeeded Colin Thomson after the latter's premature death from cancer the year before. Like Derek Wilford, 'H' had come in to command a parachute battalion from another regiment, in his case the Devon and Dorsets. Ian McLeod, the lieutenant colonel commanding 1 Para, flew from Belfast to London in order to lobby for his Battalion to form part of the Task Force – unsuccessfully, as it turned out – and his soldiers bombarded Downing Street with letters demanding the same.

It soon became clear that the military staff within the MOD would need extra bodies. Lieutenant General James 'Jimmy' Glover, Deputy Chief of Defence Staff (Intelligence), wanted a second military assistant (MA). He already had one MA, but the work was expanding at such a rate that he needed another, to concentrate solely on the Falklands campaign. So they cast around for someone suitable and alighted on me, probably thinking, 'The Staff College can spare him.' I'd known Jimmy Glover from my second tour in Northern Ireland, when he'd been Commander Land Forces there, deputy to the GOC. I knew him to be a demanding boss who didn't suffer fools gladly, but also to be highly intelligent with a good sense of humour. All in all, he was a good man to work for. Perhaps my Intelligence Corps background counted in my favour, plus the fact that I had learned something of the other two Services during my time at the National Defence College. I received a phone call out of the blue one day, telling me to get up to London as quickly as I could be released from the Staff College, to report to General Glover at the huge MOD main building on Whitehall. If I wasn't going to be part of the Task Force itself, at least I could be part of the planning. Within a day or two I was there.

An MA works directly for a general, of two-star rank or higher. He is usually a lieutenant colonel, though he can be a major. It's one of the sought-after jobs for an officer in his mid- to late thirties – usually, though not always, followed by the command of a battalion. The job of the MA is to process the work that goes through his general's office. A general will also have an ADC (aide-de-camp), who will handle all of the mundane but necessary tasks such as organizing his diary, his daily programme and his social activities, fixing transport, and so on; and he may well have a PA as well, who will be a staff sergeant or warrant officer. But it will be the MA who handles major policy issues: he will draft letters and papers after discussion with his general. It's a very personal relationship, and the chemistry has to be right for it to work. You are the general's right-hand man, and you share his confidences. It's a position of great influence, of course. The MA is always on the telephone: people will use him as a sounding board. 'How's the old bugger going to react to this?' they might ask, and he might say in response, 'I think this is the way the general sees it.' This sort of thing goes on all the time, and much of it doesn't reach the ears of the general, but occasionally the MA will come and tell him that so-and-so over at such-and-such is trying to find out what he's thinking about this or that. Or he might tell the general that he's had a worrying phone call, and that he suspects that all is not well for some reason or other. It's a very privileged position, and you learn a great deal, so it requires somebody who knows the importance of discretion.

The role of Defence Intelligence is to know as much as possible about the enemy, to understand what he is doing and what his intentions are. In the Falklands context, the job was to analyse the resources Argentina had at its disposal: what capabilities the enemy had on the Islands; what were his naval and air capabilities; and what was his ability to resupply. Of course, up until this point Defence Intelligence had been focused on the perceived threat from the Soviet Union and the Warsaw Pact; now we had been attacked from a completely unexpected direction. It's fair to say that we didn't know very much about the Argentinians' military resources at the start of the campaign. Fortunately, however, we were familiar with the capabilities of their most potent weapon, the air-launched Exocet missile, because the Royal Navy was equipped with the ship-launched version. Their Super Etendard fighter-bombers, which carried the Exocet, were French-manufactured, so we knew quite a bit about them as well.

My routine revolved around the daily meeting of the Chiefs of Staff at 09.00 or 09.30 hours, before which a great deal of work went on to ensure that they were in possession of all the latest information. I would be in for 05.00 every morning, as part of a small assessment group within the Defence Intelligence staff. We would see what had come in overnight, and pull together a briefing for General Glover at 08.00. Such long working hours, seven days a week, meant that commuting back to Camberley was not an option. Instead I cadged a bed off David Reece, an old friend of mine from my days in the Intelligence Corps, who was also working in the MOD as a lieutenant colonel and who lived in Clapham.

This daily Chiefs of Staff meeting was attended by the heads of the three Services – the First Sea Lord, the Chief of the

General Staff and the Chief of the Air Staff. It was chaired by the Chief of the Defence Staff (CDS). The Vice-Chief was also present. The Secretary of State would often be there as well, together with other senior MOD staff, including of course Jimmy Glover. Jimmy was very keen on visual aids, and he always had several prepared for each Chiefs of Staff meeting. Nowadays everybody uses PowerPoint, but back in those days you used 'vufoils' – sheets of clear plastic on a light tray, which would be projected on to a large screen. In the Chiefs of Staff's conference room, this projection was done from a cubby-hole on the other side of the screen. Maddeningly for the operator, this meant that the vufoils had to go on to the light machine upside down and back to front. Sometimes things called flips were used: overlays hinged to one edge of the cardboard frame of the vufoil, which could be flipped over the original image to build up the detail. Obviously the two images needed to match up; you kept the flips in position by taping them to the cardboard. All a bit of a fiddle.

It was my job to put the vufoils on to illustrate Jimmy Glover's briefing. Every morning I would be in the cubby-hole, waiting for the moment when Jimmy would give me the cue for a new display: 'Now, can we please have the map of East Falkland,' that sort of thing. I couldn't see him and he couldn't see or hear me, but I could hear what was being said through a pair of headphones. And of course, in order to respond when Jimmy wanted a new display, I had to listen in to all their discussions. This was a remarkable learning experience for a young lieutenant colonel, to be able to listen to the Chiefs as they discussed the progress of the war. What struck me most forcefully was the political dimension to any big military decision. In 1982 the political pressure to get a move on was intense, not least because the American Secretary of State Alexander Haig was still shuttling backwards and forwards between London and Buenos Aires, trying to broker a diplomatic deal.

It was the role of the Chiefs to define the strategic parameters; the actual operation was commanded from Fleet Headquarters at Northwood, in north-west London, and that's where the details were worked out. At least in theory, British military doctrine gives operational and tactical freedom of action to the in-theatre commanders. I say 'in theory', because the temptation to interfere from on high – to apply the so-called 'long-screwdriver' – can be difficult to resist, particularly for politicians. The Americans are much more 'top down', but we prefer to let the man on the spot get on with it.

However, the Chiefs of Staff were closely involved in the fate of the *General Belgrano*, the Argentinian cruiser that was eventually sunk by one of our torpedoes. This episode was especially fascinating to me, because the *Belgrano* was being tracked by HMS *Conqueror*, one of our nuclear-powered hunter-killer submarines, captained by Commander Christopher Wreford-Brown, whom I happened to know very well because we'd been students together at the National Defence College. The intelligence was that the only Argentinian aircraft carrier, the *Veinticinco de Mayo*, had sailed from its base halfway up Argentina, therefore north of the Falklands, and the *Belgrano* group of warships had set sail from the south. The obvious conclusion was that they were moving out in a pincer movement to attack the Task Force as it approached the Islands. The *Belgrano* was an old Second World War cruiser which the Argentinians had bought from the Americans, pretty outdated in many ways but nevertheless equipped with impressive firepower, capable of outgunning anything we had, while the *Veinticinco de Mayo* was assumed to be carrying Super Etendards armed with Exocet missiles. Merely by putting to sea, it considerably extended the range of the Argentinian aircraft on the mainland. This was a real issue, because the Falklands were at the limit of their range from their shore base, and as things turned out some aircraft had to ditch in the sea on the home run when they ran out of fuel.

After stalking the *Belgrano* for several days, Wreford-Brown received permission to attack. The effect of the *Belgrano*'s sinking was to bottle up the remainder of the Argentinian navy behind their 12-mile territorial waters line for the rest of the war for fear of being torpedoed, thus effectively removing the threat posed by the Argentinian surface navy. Later, some suggested that it had been wrong to send so many Argentinian sailors to their deaths when the *Belgrano* was sailing away from the Task Force. I've never understood this argument. If she had not been sunk at that point, and had re-emerged a week later to attack one of our aircraft carriers, that would have been an appalling outcome. The loss of life was very sad, but the *Belgrano* was an enemy warship, at sea, a perfectly legitimate military target. At the moment she was sunk she might well have been heading away from the Task Force, but a few minutes later she could have been heading back towards us: the question of her heading at the time of the attack was irrelevant.

Given the Royal Navy's command of the sea, the only practical means the Argentinians had of resupplying their garrison on the Falklands was by air. It was decided to deny the Argentinians this supply route by a bombing raid on the airfield at Port Stanley. One result of this was a very embarrassing moment for me.

The raid itself was an extraordinary feat of airmanship, given the huge distance between Port Stanley and the nearest available airfield at Ascension Island – over four thousand miles of featureless ocean. The operation involved two Vulcan bombers – one of which became unserviceable and had to return to Ascension – and fifteen Victor tankers, with seventeen air-to-air refuellings: the margin of error was minuscule. The point was not only to make holes in the runway, important though that was, but to demonstrate strategic reach: if we could hit Port Stanley, we could hit air bases on the Argentinian mainland, which would give the enemy something to think about. In those days, before the so-called 'smart bombs' which have GPS on the bomb itself, it wasn't easy to render a runway unusable by bombing; but the RAF pulled it off. The following morning the Chief of the Air Staff, who hadn't had a lot to say up until this point and who had been feeling a bit left out, was elated.

'Right,' said Jimmy Glover at his early morning briefing, 'I think we have some satellite photographs showing the damaged runway.'

My RAF colleague offered to produce the necessary visual aids in time for the 09.30 Chiefs' meeting.

At 09.29 all the Chiefs had assembled, but I still hadn't got the vufoil for the Port Stanley airport attack. I stood at the door of the projection room, somewhat concerned. I could hear Jimmy's forthcoming words in my head: 'If we can have the first vufoil now, please, Mike . . .'

Down the corridor came a sprinting wing commander. I saw with a sinking heart that there were several flips on the vufoil. As he handed it to me, all the flips fell off. I cursed, scooped them off the floor, dashed inside and put on the earphones just in time to hear Jimmy's dulcet tones: 'Now, Mike, if you could put on the base map, we'll build the picture up from there.'

I managed that all right, but then came the difficult part.

'Now, on the next flip you will see the bombing run and the distribution of the craters.'

Well, of course, this had to be upside down and back to front. I tried to get it right, but each time I did so it seemed to get worse and worse. I could hear the Chief of the Air Staff becoming irritable. 'No, no, it wasn't like that at all.' Everybody started to chip in with suggestions – 'Up a bit, no, down a bit' – while the Chief of Air Staff became crosser and crosser, because I'd ruined his big moment.

I apologized to Jimmy Glover afterwards. He gave a wry smile.

'Hmmm . . . Better not happen again, Mike, otherwise it's back to Camberley for you, my friend.'

He didn't mean it. At least, I don't think he did.

*

Goose Green was the most remarkable battle. I've now walked that bit of ground twice: the terrain is gently undulating grassland, with very little cover of any kind. Moreover, the sea on both sides of the isthmus restricts your room for manoeuvre. For infantry assaulting an enemy already dug in, this is about as difficult as it could possibly get. Nevertheless, 2 Para commenced their attack on prepared Argentinian positions shortly after 02.00 hours local time, and after more than a day's very hard fighting defeated, against the odds, a much larger number of defending Argentinians. As a Parachute Regiment officer and, moreover, as an officer who had not so long ago commanded a company in 2 Para, I was very proud of what they had achieved.

It was during the battle of Goose Green that my friend Lieutenant Colonel 'H' Jones, the commanding officer, was tragically killed at a critical moment. As in life, as in death: he was mortally wounded whilst leading from the front. The forensic analysis as to whether he should or should not have been so far forward is of course professionally absorbing; but it is entirely academic because H's total and passionate commitment to leading his soldiers made it impossible for him to be anywhere else. He was posthumously awarded the Victoria Cross. His second-in-command Major Chris Keeble took over and brought the battle to its stunningly successful conclusion. In the process he had there and then become a 'local' lieutenant colonel, just as Nick Ridley had done after David Blair was killed at Warrenpoint. This presented the Army with a dilemma. It was clear that 2 Para needed a new commanding officer. Chris Keeble had done everything that could be expected of a second-in-command under those desperate circumstances. But he had not yet been selected for command of a parachute battalion at the previous Command Board. The decision the Army had to take was whether to confirm Keeble as the new commanding officer, ignoring the fact that he had not yet been selected by the Command Board, or, hard though it might be for him, to put in someone else who had. This was discussed until late into the night by the then CGS and the Military Secretary. The Colonel Commandant of the Parachute Regiment also had his tribal say in the matter. These three Great Men had concluded that Chris Keeble should not be confirmed, and that an officer already selected for command should be sent out to relieve him. There were only two possible candidates: my close friend David Chaundler and myself.

Early the next morning David and I breakfasted together in the MOD's greasy-spoon café. We were pulling each other's legs, each making out that he would be the one to take over command of 2 Para. In fact there was never really any doubt about who would go. We'd already been given the nod that when the time came I'd be going to command 1 Para, and David would be going to 2 Para. He was H's designated successor: the only difference was that he would now be taking over much earlier than planned. As luck would have it, David had also been heavily involved in technical intelligence regarding the Argentinian Exocets.

David flew out to the Falklands three or four days later. The quickest way for him to get there was to parachute into the South Atlantic, as near as possible to one of the Task Force ships. They picked him up out of the water, and he assumed command shortly thereafter. Later, 2 Para fought their second major set-piece battle at Wireless Ridge (2 Para was the only battalion to fight two such battles). It wasn't easy to take over command of a battalion halfway through a campaign, and it was particularly difficult to have to say to Chris Keeble, 'Well done, Chris, but I'm in command now.'

Under the command of another good friend of mine, Lieutenant Colonel Hew Pike, 3 Para fought and won their fierce battle for Mount Longdon, one of the crucial final objectives leading to the capital, Port Stanley. Sergeant Ian McKay posthumously won the second VC of the campaign for his gallantry during this battle, and Hew was awarded the Distinguished Service Order for his leadership.

For me, missing out on the Falklands was frustrating, but I knew in my heart of hearts that there had been absolutely no reason to change what had already been decided.

I remember going out to RAF Brize Norton to meet the two Parachute Battalions when they came back from the war, a month or so after the Argentinian surrender on 15 June. It was a warm summer's day, and lots of people were there to greet them: the families, of course, but plenty of well-wishers too, including HRH the Prince of Wales in his capacity as Colonel in Chief. The two Battalions had taken a serious number of casualties, and the atmosphere was mixed: great pride in their military success, set against the sorrow for the forty soldiers who had not come home, and sympathy for their families.

Both 2 and 3 Para had come by sea from the Falklands to Ascension Island, and then flown on from Ascension by VC10. The aircraft landed and taxied to a halt in front of us. Steps were wheeled up. Then the doors opened, and the two commanding officers, David Chaundler and Hew Pike, appeared, pausing at the top of the steps. The crowd cheered their hearts out, with the Regimental Band playing 'Congratulations' as soldier after soldier came through the doors and down the steps. It had been only eighteen months since I'd left 2 Para, so of course it was a very poignant moment for me. I felt privileged to be able to congratulate Johnny Crosland, a superb fighting soldier who had been my successor as commander of B Company, and who would be awarded the Military Cross for his leadership in the Falklands. I was able to shake the hands of many of the soldiers with whom I had served.

The Falklands conflict had been proof of the competence, determination and resourcefulness of all three Services. The message was not lost on more formidable opponents than the

Argentinians. At home, the effect of the war was to prevent cuts that were already in the pipeline. The Secretary of State, John Nott, was forced to backtrack.

This was the end of my secondment to the MOD. I said goodbye to Jimmy Glover and returned to the Staff College in the high summer of 1982. In his personal report on me Jimmy Glover commented that 'provided that he can temper his ambition and retain a sense of humility and humanity, he should go far, both in command and on the staff'. According to him I still had both, but I needed to ensure that I didn't lose either in the future. Perhaps I was a bit pushy; you have to be, if you're going to get on.

My father died later that year, at the comparatively young age of sixty-seven. It was a cruel blow to us all, but of course particularly to my mother and my sister, Lynne. There was a void in all our lives. Though I was frustrated to have missed out on the Falklands, my presence in England did mean that I was able to be on hand during the long illness leading up to his death. It was fortunate indeed that I was at the Staff College at the time, so close to where my parents lived. At his funeral, with his coffin covered by the Union flag, I gave the tribute to his memory.

I still had another eighteen months at the Staff College, but as time went on I became increasingly impatient to move on to what is to a large extent the pinnacle of any officer's ambition – so much so, that some officers choose to leave the Army once they've done it: to command a battalion.

The commanding officer is lord of all he surveys. 'The Colonel' is like the captain of a ship. Like a ship, the battalion is a discrete entity, and like the captain, the colonel is solely responsible for its performance and personnel. Within the battalion he has almost unlimited responsibility. By the same token, if anything goes wrong, it's the CO's fault.

I had known for some time that I was destined for 1 Para. At that time the Battalion had a unique role. In 1983 it became the British component of the Allied Command Europe Mobile Force (Land): NATO's 'fire brigade', a lightly armed multinational force intended to deploy in times of tension to the flanks of Europe as a demonstration of Allied resolve. In particular, NATO planners envisaged attacks through Scandinavia in the far north and towards Turkey in the south-east. Norway was particularly vulnerable, both because of its common border with Russia, and because it was a large country but sparsely populated. The Norwegians were therefore especially reliant on NATO reinforcement, part of which would be supplied by 1 Para. An attack might take place at any time of the year, so we had to be prepared whatever the weather conditions; we had to be ready to live and fight in a Norwegian winter. The conditions can be very harsh indeed. One morning while we were conducting an exercise the temperature suddenly dropped from a mild -10 degrees Celsius to -30. One moment we were operating under a clear blue sky, the next we were enveloped by a howling blizzard. This happened within just a few minutes, forcing us to abandon the exercise: peacetime safety conditions dictate that you stop training when the temperature reaches this low level. In such conditions the margin of survival gets very tight, as one's mental and physical reactions slow right down.

The Battalion spent the months before I was due to take command in March 1984 on specialist Arctic training in the area inland from Bergen, around the Hardanger Icecap, in preparation for a big NATO exercise. I was due to take over command immediately afterwards. As the time drew nearer I began to feel uneasy about the fact that they would have done this training and I would not. It seemed to me that this wasn't an ideal position for a new commanding officer to be in. So I left the Staff College three months early and engineered a deal to do five weeks' basic Arctic warfare training near Lillehammer with the Royal Marines, who also had a reinforcement role to Norway. I was the most senior person on the course by quite a long way, but since we were all students, rank was immaterial. I was starting at the bottom again.

The aim of this basic Arctic training was to teach you how to survive in such extreme conditions: how to move on cross-country skis and snow shoes, pulling sledges (known in Norwegian as 'pulks'); how to live in the Arctic in the open, with all your kit on your back, if need be. I learned how to dig a snow hole, which will keep you comparatively warm whatever it's doing outside. Another of the training exercises is designed to prepare you for the shock of falling through ice into the freezing water below. You cut a hole in the ice on a frozen lake and then jump in with your kit on. You must climb out of the water and then strip off your wet clothes as quickly as possible, even if you're out in the open, because if you don't, your wet clothes dramatically increase the risk of fatal heat loss. It was therefore vital to keep a change of dry clothes in your rucksack.

It's actually safer and more pleasant in the Arctic if the temperature is below freezing. A thaw can be miserable, because everything starts to melt and you get wet – and then if the temperature drops again it can be dangerous, because your wet clothes will freeze.

Another risk comes when moving across deep powder snow: if you fall carrying a heavy pack, you will create a hole in the snow, and it is often very difficult to climb out again. You will probably lose one or both of your skis in the process, which makes it all the more difficult.

Map-reading in the Arctic is a problem, because the snow covers any recognizable features, altering their shape; you have to rely on reading the contours. Any flat bit of snow-covered ground is likely to be a lake. The Norwegians use an augur – a giant corkscrew – to check the thickness before venturing out on to the ice in vehicles.

Of course I came in for a bit of ribbing from my Army

colleagues for training with the Navy – all par for the course. Though the Marines might refer to me as a 'bloody pongo',* the Navy nickname for a soldier, in fact they were very welcoming and hospitable, and they taught me everything I needed to learn. After I had finished the course I still had a little time left before joining 1 Para, so I volunteered to be an umpire on the big NATO exercise inside the Arctic Circle, learning all the time. The purpose of the exercise was to practise how NATO would defend north Norway; our defence plan envisaged a Warsaw Pact attack either through Sweden, or, if the Russians were minded to observe Swedish neutrality, through the north Norwegian plateau of Finmark. Among those taking part in the exercise were a Canadian battalion, an Italian Alpini battalion and elements of the US Marine Corps, which also had a reinforcement role in the Arctic. It was interesting to be in a position to observe such a multinational exercise at close hand. While serving in Berlin I had become aware of how different armies can be: each has its own style and its own culture, reflecting its national culture. The exercise also provided a chance to learn more about operating in these Arctic conditions. In such extreme cold a lot of equipment needs particular care: helicopters, for example, need very rigorous de-icing drills, because ice on the rotor blades means loss of lift. By the end of my first winter I felt that I probably understood how to operate in this environment as well as any of the soldiers I was about to command. I was up to speed.

Naturally the Battalion was taking part in the exercise, and in fact my predecessor, Ian McLeod, handed over to me while we were still out there in Norway. It was an important moment, but there was nothing formal about it: just a handshake. We flew back to England a couple of days later.

The Battalion was based at Bulford, on the edge of Salisbury

* 'Anyone from the Army', according to the Royal Marines' website. The derivation of this term is apparently from the quip: 'Where the Army goes, the pong goes.'

Our wedding day, 4 May 1985: Sarah has her arm around my daughter Amanda, while my son Mark stands in front of me.

Jacko senior and Jacko junior. **Left**: *Mark's first parachute jump, with the Red Devils, summer 1989.* **Right**: *Mark's Sandhurst commissioning day, April 1995.*

Left: *As Commander of the 3rd Division, I had responsibility for organizing the British dimension of the events commemorating the fiftieth anniversary of D-Day. Towards the end of the day veterans paraded before HM the Queen on 'Gold' beach, where my father had led his squadron ashore half a century earlier. Unfortunately the programme ran late, and some of the veterans had difficulty with the incoming tide.*

Arctic training as commanding officer of 1 Para, mid-1980s. In this watercolour sketch for an oil painting by Peter Archer, I am the figure speaking on the radio, binoculars around my neck.

The 3rd Division contributed troops to the ill-fated United Nations Protection Force (UNPROFOR) trying to keep the peace in Bosnia. As their Divisional Commander I visited them in Goradze, wearing a UN beret. During this visit I encountered the Bosnian Serb General Ratko Mladic, later indicted for war crimes.

Things did not settle down immediately after Dayton. Here I visit the scene of a firefight on the 'confrontation line' between two of the rival factions soon after Dayton 'D-Day'. At the centre of the picture are the two Discoverys of my mobile HQ.

Left and main picture: *NATO's Implementation Force (IFOR) replaced the comparatively ineffective UNPROFOR after the Dayton Agreement. I commanded one of IFOR's three divisions in Bosnia. We had a lot of firepower at our disposal, as we demonstrated in this display to the local faction commanders.*

Bottom: *After a meeting of the Joint Implementation Committee (JIC), with the faction commanders in our sector. Some of these men had until very recently been fighting each other. On the left is Richard Dannatt, then commander of the 4th Armoured Brigade, who would eventually succeed me as Chief of the General Staff.*

Above: *Demonstration by relatives of Serb POWs at our Banja Luka HQ. Some of the placards are addressed to me personally.*

Right: *Al fresco lunch with General Dudakovic, one of the faction commanders, Bihac, spring 1996. Dudakovic is sitting opposite me, second from the right.*

NATO Secretary-General Javier Solana and Supreme Allied Commander, Europe, General George Joulwan visit our Banja Luka HQ. On the left is my Chief of Staff, Colonel Andrew Ritchie, and on the right is our artillery commander, Brigadier Freddie Viggers.

With my ADC, Captain Rory Gilbert, in a Lynx helicopter.

Left: *Major General Jackson lends a hand.*

Right: *In August 1996 I handed over command of the 3rd Division, and as usual there was a light-hearted ceremony to mark my departure. Here the Headquarters staff tow me in a knackered old car to a farewell lunch.*

With Prime Minister John Major in Banja Luka, early summer 1996. My son Tom (then aged six) commemorated the occasion in this picture.

Tuesday June 12th

This is my daddy in B

Bosnia with the prim

minister.

Tom had been looked after by Aida, a Bosnian au pair, whose parents Munir and Minka Pijailovic (right) were living in Sarajevo, then under siege by Bosnian Serb forces. We sent them food parcels, and in February 1995 I was able to meet them for the first time, during my visit to British forces serving with UNPROFOR. It was a moving occasion.

Plain. From Easter 1984 I lived in a large, comfortable 1930s house set aside for the CO called Stephen's Mount. Though by this time I was divorced, there was no question of my living in the officers' mess like the other single officers. Whether the CO is married or single, he will almost invariably occupy the house designated for the purpose, because his subordinates would find it awkward to have him around in the mess all the time. That said, the officers' mess was for me, as for all the officers, a form of social club, a place to wind down and to mix informally.

And so it is for the sergeants' mess. It is often said that a good sergeants' mess makes a good unit; it is as important as a good officers' mess, and many would argue even more important. Warrant officers (or NCOs) have their own parallel hierarchy, presided over by the regimental sergeant major just as the colonel presides over the commissioned officers. The RSM is always a formidable figure, one who commands enormous respect from everybody, soldiers and officers alike. It is not unknown for junior officers to receive a bollocking from the regimental sergeant major, and it would be foolhardy indeed to answer back. No officer would dream of calling on the sergeants' mess without prior invitation. From time to time I would be invited to the sergeants' mess on some kind of occasion, usually for dinner. At Christmas each mess entertains the other to dinner, and the two messes compete with each other on the playing field. Cliché it may be, but without doubt the sergeants' mess is the backbone of the British Army.

It was while CO of 1 Para that I somehow acquired the nickname 'the Prince of Darkness', though why I have little idea. That said, I am fond of the odd glass of whisky and a cigar in the evening, while putting the world to rights. Only occasionally did people find it a strain to keep up.

I first met Sarah at a dinner party in the summer of 1984. She had been working for some years as a picture researcher for a publisher in London. I thought that she was a breath of fresh air, sparky and fun, and we fell for each other immediately, though it took a while for her to agree to marry me. As the daughter of a career soldier, an officer in the Royal Engineers, she perhaps had an inkling of what she might be taking on. We married the following May, in the little Saxon church across the road from Bulford Manor, the house which would become our home fifteen years later. David Chaundler was my best man, and my son Mark – then aged twelve and about to start at Wellington College – his deputy; my daughter Amanda was the only bridesmaid. Sarah has been a wonderful wife to me, and a true friend and loving stepmother to the children. By their early teens, both Amanda and Mark were at boarding school, but we saw as much of them as we possibly could.

I took the Battalion to Norway for ten weeks' training in each of the following two winters. We would rent youth hostels and camp sites, and then go out into the country for exercises lasting about a week. It was challenging and demanding and sometimes very tough, but it was also very enjoyable and I have great memories of that time. There's something very satisfying about pushing yourself hard. As well as the Battalion itself, we had very good back-up: support and recce helicopters, artillery, engineers, communications, logistics – my own train set, you might say. Everything is slower in the snow, with vehicles skidding around, and you need special oils for your machinery to function properly. The Norwegians used the German Leopard tank, with an electric heater in the sump to get the oil warm enough to start the engine; in the Second World War, fires were lit under the sump to achieve the same effect. We also used over-snow vehicles: small trucks with rubber tracks to make them grip on snow- or ice-covered ground. In fact, one of the quickest ways to get about in the Arctic is on skis: we could travel between 15 and 20 miles overnight. As light infantry we would practise digging in, using blocks of compacted snow as cover. If you pack it hard enough it becomes as solid as concrete. To combat an armoured attack we carried anti-tank weapons and practised laying minefields.

One special memory that lingers in my mind is of a night move on skis. The conditions were perfect: dry, with not a breath of wind. The temperature was just at that point when you hear a squeak as you dig the point of the ski pole into the snow, about −6 degrees Celsius. There was a bright moon, and not a cloud in the sky. The snow reflected the moonlight, so that you could see for miles. And then the Northern Lights commenced, lighting up the sky with flashes of colour, an unforgettable and ethereal display. 'And they're paying me for this,' I thought happily.

The Allied Mobile Force (Land) was also responsible for defending NATO's southern flank, and we carried out a couple of exercises in Turkey, in midsummer, which provided a good contrast to our Arctic training. We exercised in Turkish Thrace, west of Istanbul, on a defensive line near the Bulgarian border, the idea being to simulate defence against a possible Warsaw Pact attack from the north. The countryside around there is rolling grassland, quite similar to Salisbury Plain, except of course that it was much hotter. South-east Turkey, down towards the Syrian border, was another deployment option for the Force.

In 1985 a new General Secretary of the Communist Party, Mikhail Gorbachev, had taken power in the Soviet Union, and had immediately initiated a reform process, epitomized by his concepts of *glasnost* ('openness') and *perestroika* ('restructuring'). I watched these developments with great interest, and indeed they were much discussed within NATO. While they seemed positive, the feeling was that we should not let our guard down.

One curious deployment was guard duty outside what was then the massive US Air Force base at Greenham Common, near Newbury in Berkshire. Since 1981 there had been a rather messy 'peace camp' of protestors living outside the base in a jumble of tents, tarpaulins and plastic sheeting, as part of a much wider campaign against the stationing of so-called 'intermediate' nuclear missiles in Europe. There was widespread unease that these new weapons – so-called 'cruise' missiles and Pershing II ballistic missiles – meant an end to the policy of 'Mutually Assured Destruction' which had restrained both sides since the 1950s; strategic thinkers began to discuss the possibility that the superpowers might fight a 'limited' nuclear war in Europe. There were large demonstrations against the introduction of these new missiles in many European capitals. The peace camp had been set up as part of this campaign, and had attracted special attention as it consisted exclusively of women. The protestors would regularly cut the perimeter wire and trespass on the base. The implied message was that women were resisting the male madness of war.

The Secretary of State for Defence, Michael Heseltine, was determined to face down the protests and to press ahead with the introduction of these missiles. For a while battalions were tasked in six-week rotation to go and guard the base against the threat posed by these ladies, and in due course 1 Para was given this onerous duty. There was something ludicrous about the deployment, giving rise to inevitable undignified stories, including the rumour that a soldier and one of the protestors had engaged in congress through the chain-link fence. I cannot comment on the veracity of this rumour.

In the summer of 1986 my two-and-a-half-year term as CO of 1 Para came to an end. 'Right, Colonel, that's it,' said my second-in-command: 'Time's up.' It's very much a matter of 'The King is dead; long live the King' when the moment comes. I was handing over to Lieutenant Colonel John Reith, whose career and mine would be increasingly intertwined as we moved up the Army ladder. As always when the CO leaves, there was a bit of light-hearted theatre to mark my departure: I was mounted on an armchair tied to the top of an over-snow vehicle, which was driven out of the barracks while the Battalion lined the route applauding. It was a poignant occasion for me, because this was the last time I would directly command troops on the ground, and my last experience of serving in the Regiment itself. From this time on I would continue to wear the red beret, but I would swap the regimental cap-badge for that of the General Staff. But it was time to leave the Battalion and move on.

On promotion to full colonel, I joined the Joint Services Defence College as the senior Army member of the Directing Staff. The new college was in effect Latimer Mark II. The MOD had closed Latimer in the mid-1980s as part of a cost-cutting exercise, but they wanted to keep the course going, as it was felt to be valuable to bring together mid-career officers from all three Services with a handful of civil servants. So they found some spare space at the Royal Naval College in Greenwich and established the Joint Services Defence College there as successor to the National Defence College. More recently, the Joint Services Defence College and the three single-Service staff colleges have all been merged into the Joint Service Command and Staff College, housed in a new building at Shrivenham, outside Swindon; combined with the old Military College of Science, it became the Defence Academy of the United Kingdom.

As my time with the Battalion had drawn towards its end I had looked at the list of available appointments and seen that this post was coming up. It looked attractive, so I had applied and the Board had decided to appoint me. I was pleased to get this job because I like teaching, and I enjoyed the cut and thrust of vigorous debate that went with it. I was succeeding my friend David Chaundler, who had been able to give me the inside story beforehand.

My boss for the first part of my time at Greenwich was Air Vice-Marshal Barry Newton, a strong believer in the joint Service approach and in the College itself. He was followed by

Rear-Admiral Guy Liardet, an erudite man with an irreverent sense of humour and great fun to work for. In one of my personal reports from this time he said of me: 'quite a character, tall, dark, dashing, with a lived-in face and a touch of flamboyance. I would expect to see a ruffianly component in the field.' What he meant by that I cannot imagine.

The old Royal Naval College building, once the home of naval pensioners and now the University of Greenwich, is magnificent. In particular, I had lunch most days and some splendid formal dinners in the Painted Hall, renowned as one of the finest dining halls in Europe. The ceiling, by Thornhill, depicts a series of allegorical themes celebrating Nelson's great victory at Trafalgar. It was, of course, where Nelson had lain in state prior to his funeral. Each year the Hall saw a splendid Trafalgar Dinner, with all present singing sea shanties. Thornhill's painted ceiling includes many naked or semi-clad ladies on view. Apparently there are 293 boobs up there – though I never counted them myself.

We weren't at all averse to living in London. Sarah had lived and worked there for years before we married. For the first six months we lived in an apartment in the College, over the residence occupied by Admiral Sir John Fieldhouse, Commander in Chief of the Fleet during the Falklands War, and now First Sea Lord. We then bought a house in Clapham, and for two years I commuted every day to Greenwich. It was a very happy time. But all the time I was thinking: what next? The next potential step was brigade command, but the competition was very fierce. There were then fourteen manoeuvre brigades – i.e. all-arms deployable brigades – and three Northern Ireland brigades in the British Army. About half of them changed hands each year, but there were five or six officers eligible for each available brigade command. By the promotion rules, my opportunity would come in 1988, my second full year at Greenwich – but it didn't happen. It was a blow.

Maybe I wasn't doing as well as I had thought. By this time I was forty-four. I knew perfectly well that if you don't get promoted to brigadier by your late forties, further progression is unlikely. Brigadier rank is the first rung on the ladder to the 'stars', a major general having two stars, a lieutenant general three and a full general four. Up to this point everything had gone reasonably smoothly for me. Perhaps I'd got as far up as I was going to go. Either I was going to have to settle for rather less than I'd hoped – or maybe this was the signal to move on.

I started looking around, trying to make up my mind whether to stay within the Army or to try something else. I went to see a few headhunters and careers advisory people, without identifying anything in particular that seemed right for me. It was at this point that Colonel Johnny Hall telephoned and suggested we meet for a chat. Though I've come to know him well since, I didn't really know him then, and I was intrigued to know what he had in mind. Johnny was serving under the Military Secretary, the two-star general responsible for appointments and promotions. As such he was in the best possible position to evaluate my prospects within the Army. I told him of my disappointment and that I was thinking about leaving.

Johnny didn't seem surprised. Perhaps he'd already had word that I was looking around. 'Mike,' he said, after a pause, 'I've had a good look at your book and I've done some thinking.' He was referring to the book of confidential reports, written on every officer by his superiors at the end of each year. Johnny reminded me that it was unusual – though not unheard-of – to be selected for brigade command at forty-five years of age. He had my complete attention.

'My strong advice to you,' he continued, 'is to give it one more year.'

9

Onward and Upward

When Johnny Hall had recommended that I should give it another year, he had also hinted that I had a good chance of being selected for the following year's Higher Command and Staff Course. This was a new three-month course at the Staff College for a dozen or so high-flying officers, mostly colonels, but with a few sailors and airmen as well. Although it had been held for the first time only the previous year, in 1988, it was already clear that selection for this course could put you in the fast lane.

The rationale of the course was to bring fresh thinking to the whole question of 'operational art', i.e. the level between tactics – how to attack that hill and take it – and strategy, which draws in political and other considerations. Operational art is the business of how to fight a campaign within a given theatre, how to sequence events and battles, in order to further the overall strategy.

The new course was the brainchild of Nigel Bagnall, CGS in the late 1980s and known to everybody as 'Ginge' because of his shock of red hair. General Bagnall, who had commanded 1st British Corps in Germany and afterwards had been Commander in Chief of the British Army of the Rhine, had thought long and hard about how to fight the battle against the Warsaw Pact, if it ever came to that, and he had come to the conclusion that our planning was unimaginative. Our assumptions were attritional, expecting both sides to sit there and slug it out. Bagnall had studied the German Army's campaign on the Russian Front during the Second World War, and he had been enormously impressed by their extraordinary ability to manoeuvre and regroup very quickly. Bagnall wanted the British Army at theatre level to think more in terms of manoeuvre, striking paralysing blows by removing the enemy's freedom of action, creating doubt in the enemy's mind, rather as the Israeli General Sharon had done so effectively during the 1973 Yom Kippur War. More generally, Bagnall hoped to get the Army's younger commanders thinking out of the box.

Johnny Hall was no false prophet. Not long after our discussion, I found my name on the list for the next Higher Command and Staff Course, starting in January 1989. It was at least a partial recovery. On the course with me in that second year were thirteen other colonels, one Royal Navy captain, one RAF group captain, plus one American, one Australian, one German and one Frenchman. It was three months of concentrated intellectual study and hard work, but enormously stimulating and rewarding. Everyone had to write a thesis: I chose the topic of 'out-of-area operations' – i.e. out of the NATO area – and argued that these might become more relevant in the future. The course involved lectures, syndicate discussions, private study, map exercises and the so-called 'staff ride', a sequence of battlefield tours that took us to sites in Normandy, Verdun and the Ardennes, among others. We were fortunate that our tour was conducted by Professor Richard Holmes. There was a lot one could learn from studying these past campaigns on the ground.

153

Though of course the tactics and technology were completely different, many of the principles remained the same.

As it happened, the Assistant Commandant of the Staff College then was Jeremy Mackenzie, now a brigadier, who had been second-in-command of the Queen's Own Highlanders at the time of Warrenpoint, and whom I had come to know quite well as a result. As you get nearer the top of the Army, the same names tend to crop up again and again. From being a huge, seemingly anonymous organization when you join, it becomes quite intimate as you reach the senior levels.

Having missed out in 1988, I was hoping to be selected for brigade command in 1989; of course, this was by no means certain, but I felt encouraged by that conversation with Johnny Hall. If I were to be selected, I would not take up the appointment until the end of the year, leaving a gap of almost nine months. So I decided to make the most of this opportunity. I applied for a Services Fellowship, under a similar arrangement to the one taken up by Frank Kitson almost twenty years before. This would give me the chance to undertake a study of a chosen area of defence in an academic environment.

Towards the end of the 1980s there was the sense that the old superpower stalemate that had governed strategic thinking since the Second World War might be opening up. Gorbachev had initiated a reform process inside the Soviet Union which was gathering its own momentum. An arms reduction process was taking place, with both sides scaling down their arsenals in a series of negotiated agreements. Meanwhile, the prospect of the Strategic Defense Initiative or SDI, Reagan's idea of a satellite-based defence system, was threatening the strategic balance. Suddenly, many of the assumptions that had governed our thinking for so long were in the melting-pot.

In the autumn of 1988 I had a number of discussions about what I might find interesting to study if I undertook one of these fellowships. Many of those I talked to argued that change was coming, and that the Army would have to adapt accordingly. I decided to look at the future of the British Army, in terms of size, organization and structure, should the Cold War become less cold. This topic would, incidentally, bring in my longstanding interest in the Soviet Union, with an opportunity to examine Gorbachev's changes. I submitted an outline for a thesis along these lines, and the powers that be gave it the thumbs-up.

Having decided to study the future of the British Army, the only question remaining was: where? Dr Gwyn Prins, a don at Emmanuel College, Cambridge, had been a frequent visiting lecturer at Greenwich, and I had come to know him quite well. He said he'd be delighted to act as my supervisor. As the idea of a few months at Cambridge also found favour with Mrs Jackson, I went up there to see if I could find a suitable college to take me on. Gwyn gave me lunch at Emmanuel, an obvious possibility. The experience was enough to make me realize that I might feel out of place among the undergraduates, who were much the same age as my own children. 'Gwyn,' I said, 'would you be very cross if I looked elsewhere?' The upshot was that I settled on Wolfson, the postgraduate college. There was a very varied collection of people studying there, not only from Britain but from abroad: members of the judiciary, senior policemen, journalists on scholarships, all sorts – company in which I would find kindred spirits.

I could have commuted to Cambridge from London, but both of us thought that this would be a wasted opportunity. Instead we rented a charming little two-up, two-down cottage in Eden Street, just off Parker's Piece, owned by a young don who was doing an exchange year at Berkeley, California. It was in a lovely part of Cambridge and very central. For us it was aptly named, a little paradise. We were beholden to nobody and it seemed like a golden interlude, time out of normal life. Sarah carried on with her freelance picture research, just as she had done before, taking the train to London when she needed to. Meanwhile we tried to make the most of our time in Cambridge. I set out to try to dine in every college: I didn't quite manage that, but I did dine in most of them.

It was a very happy time, an idyllic summer of bow ties, bicycles and boats . . . and a baby. Though we'd been married for four years, nothing had happened, so we'd investigated and established that there was a problem. By a happy coincidence it turned out that one of the pioneering fertility treatment clinics – Bourn Hall – was only just outside Cambridge. We thought, well, why not? And as luck would have it, it worked, first time. So that was another piece of serendipity. If I hadn't missed brigade command in 1988 I'd have missed both the Higher Command and Staff Course and the Services Fellowship, but, far more important, Sarah might never have become pregnant.

Earlier in the summer I had received the news I'd been hoping for: I had been selected for brigade command, starting in November. And it was to be Northern Ireland once again: 39 Brigade, based in Belfast, the same brigade that Frank Kitson had commanded during my first tour.

I had to choose my moment to tell Sarah that we would be going there, as I knew that her heart would sink at the news.

We were sitting on the river bank when I broke it to her. I had punted us up the Cam, and eventually we stopped for one of our many picnics. I moored up and we spread out a blanket in the grass to sit on. It was then that I told her. She was pleased for me, but I could tell straight away that it had given her much to think about. We would be living behind the wire, and that concerned her rather more than security issues. She worried that it would be too much like living in a goldfish bowl. I remember urging her to keep an open mind.

We went over to Northern Ireland to have a look around, staying with the chap I'd be taking over from, Brigadier Bryan Dutton, in the house that we'd be living in. Sarah also had an opportunity to talk to Bryan's wife Angela and some of the other Army wives, as well as some civilian friends of Angela's. She realized that you could make a life outside the wire if you chose to do so. For such a free spirit – and a pregnant one, at that – being independent and having her own life was important. She's that sort of person.

The idea was that I should finish my thesis before we left Cambridge. I had done all the necessary research, but we were having such a good time that I am afraid I neglected my writing, leaving it until the last moment like a typical student; so October 1989 was spent with my head down, writing furiously. I finished just before we left Cambridge and went back to London to pack up the house. It had been a close-run thing.

In the end I think it helped my thesis that I came from the Parachute Regiment, and as a result my career hadn't been focused on what was then seen as the main theatre in central Europe. At various points in the past, people had recommended that I should spend some time with 1st British Corps in north-west Germany, deemed to be the centre of gravity of the Army, where the crucial conflict would take place, if it ever came to that. In fact, of course, the British Army of the Rhine was about to lose its strategic significance, once the Cold War came to an end. So my being on the periphery, so to speak, actually proved an advantage.

I used the Staff College facilities to print and bind about fifty copies of my thesis. A lot of people knew of the work I'd been doing and asked me to send them a copy. Then it started being passed around. A second edition had to be printed. I occasionally go back to it and it still holds up reasonably well in principle. I concluded that a shift in UK defence policy and planning was required to take account of the increasing likelihood of conflict outside the NATO area, with the Army being restructured to provide a more balanced and flexible force capable of undertaking such operations. I highlighted the need to 'expect the unexpected', which now seems rather prescient. However, I must confess to a howler. One of a set of assumptions which I listed in the thesis was that change to the status of Berlin was 'unlikely in the time-frame of the next ten years'. In fact the ink was barely dry on the page before the Berlin Wall came down. Within the year, the city was once again capital of a reunified Germany.

The television pictures of the Wall being demolished by jubilant protestors made electrifying viewing. Gorbachev had made it clear that the Soviet Union would not interfere. The inevitable conclusion was that the Cold War was over. This was a seismic shift, which would require NATO to rethink the strategic assumptions on which planning had been predicated. Within a few years the threat which had dominated our thinking since the end of the Second World War had virtually evaporated. Germany would cease to be the front line, becoming instead a parking lot for forces to be used elsewhere.

It was time for the move to Northern Ireland. We sold the house in Clapham, actually managing to complete the sale on the very day we were due to leave London. We stopped in the Lake District and had two nights' stay in the much-feted Sharrow Bay Hotel before continuing up to Stranraer. There we caught the ferry across the Irish Sea to Larne, where we were met for the first time by our close protection team – a reminder, for Sarah in particular, that for the next two years or so security issues were going to be ever present. And so my new life as a brigade commander began.

This was a challenging assignment. The Brigade which I was coming in to run was big: varying in size, it usually consisted of about ten battalions, including two resident battalions and a number of Ulster Defence Regiment (UDR) battalions, so well over five thousand soldiers overall. It was based at Thiepval

Barracks in Lisburn, about 10 miles south of Belfast, a very big Army base which was also the home of Headquarters Northern Ireland. As Commander of 39 Infantry Brigade, I was one of three brigadiers reporting to Lieutenant General Sir John Waters, GOC in the Province. The other two brigades were based in Portadown and just outside Derry. As well as the Belfast area itself, I was responsible for the east of the Province, down to and including South Armagh. Halfway through the tour the Brigade shed quite a lot of this area in a complete boundary reorganization, done in order to harmonize the Army's areas of responsibility with those of the police. Ideally the two should work hand-in-hand at each level of command, but this had not been possible while there had been this mismatch, so the boundary change made complete sense.

In some ways not much had changed since my last tour in Northern Ireland. There was less mass rioting on the streets than there had been at the beginning of the Troubles, but the violence between the Protestant Loyalist and Catholic Republican communities was continuing, with appalling atrocities committed on both sides. There were also vicious feuds between factions within the terrorist groups, as the killers killed each other. The IRA had become technically much more proficient. They continued to target the Security Forces, within the Province and on the mainland, and also abroad, particularly British bases in Germany. A month before I left England they had killed eight members of a Royal Marine band in an explosion at a barracks in Kent. I had been in the Province only a few days when another terrorist incident provided a stark reminder of the risks. Mark and Amanda had flown out to join us for our first weekend in Lisburn – not least to choose their bedrooms and sort out their things. We were still unpacking when the phone rang: four soldiers from the Parachute Regiment had been killed by a roadside bomb, which had detonated as their Land Rover was driving past. This had happened by the racecourse outside Downpatrick in the southern part of County Down. 'I'm sorry,' I said to the family, 'but I've got to go.' Welcome back, Brigadier.

One reason why the IRA had taken its campaign to the mainland was that Security Force casualties in Northern Ireland had become routine: the death of another soldier, or of another policeman, no longer resonated with the British public as once it might have done. As if playing some kind of deadly poker game, they kept increasing the stakes in an attempt to force the Government to concede. Five years earlier they had bombed the Brighton hotel where many leading British politicians were staying during the Conservative Party Conference, almost killing Margaret Thatcher, the Prime Minister. In 1991, while I was still in Northern Ireland, they would launch a mortar attack on Downing Street, which, had it been more accurate, could have wiped out John Major's entire Cabinet.

The function of the 'Green Army' was the same as it had always been: so far as possible, to provide security, and maintain law and order in support of the police. Our aim was to stabilize the security situation and to contain the violence. One of the biggest challenges came during the Loyalists' summer marching season. These big set-piece marches were seen by the Nationalists as provocative triumphalism, and often sparked violent incidents. We did what we could to prevent the latter, essentially by flooding the areas with soldiers and policemen. We attempted to restrict the IRA's control of the Catholic areas by providing regular patrols, but it was next to impossible to prevent the intimidation that took place, enforced, for example, by the cruel practice of 'kneecapping' with electric drills. In a community too frightened to report such crimes to the legitimate authorities, the Army could only do so much to prevent hideous deeds taking place in the dark.

My job as Commander 39 Brigade did not involve me in manoeuvring troops on a day-to-day or hour-to-hour basis: that was for the battalion and company commanders. In Northern Ireland, as in any counter-insurgency campaign, each battalion has its own area, and within the battalion each company has its own patch. My job was to task, to coordinate, to encourage and to support the soldiers: to ensure that everybody knew what they were supposed to be doing, and that they had the resources they needed, including reinforcements if necessary. Each Friday morning at ten-thirty I held a meeting with my battalion commanders at Thiepval Barracks. The Brigade intelligence and operations staff would give a briefing, laying out the overall situation and the tactical picture; then each battalion commander would take a few minutes to summarize what had happened in the previous week. We would discuss future operations and logistical considerations. Sometimes there would be set-piece operations, for example during the marching season. Each Wednesday morning at ten I would gather with the other brigade commanders for a similar meeting at HQ Northern Ireland. I was glad that the selection board had given me a Northern Ireland brigade: it suited me perfectly, not least as I was able to draw on a good deal of experience, both urban and rural, in the range of areas for which 39 Brigade was responsible. I was a round peg in a round hole.

One of my responsibilities was to liaise with the other Security Forces and the wider community. I held a weekly meeting at the Knock Police HQ in East Belfast with my RUC opposite number, the Assistant Chief Constable for Belfast. In the first few years of the Troubles, when the RUC had been in such a bad way after the events of autumn 1969, the Army had taken the lead; but by 1989 we were long into the era of so-called 'police primacy'. Major decisions about how to prosecute counter-terrorism operations lay with the RUC; the Army played a supporting role. Nearly all our patrols – at least in the urban areas – were accompanied by a policeman. The police handled the Protestant paramilitaries, so we were not routinely required to patrol the strongly Loyalist Shankhill Road. I also used to hold meetings with local church leaders, who acted as spokesmen for their communities. I saw quite a bit of the Secretary of State, Peter Brooke, a patrician but wise and kind figure who lived in great style in Hillsborough Castle, a fine country house which in the old days had been the home of the Governor General. On 9 November 1990 Brooke made a speech in which he stated that Britain had no 'selfish strategic or economic interest' in Northern Ireland and would accept Irish unification if that was the wish of the people of the Province. Many regard this speech as paving the way for political progress after decades of stalemate.

Intelligence was handled by the intelligence branch at Headquarters Northern Ireland, and I had my own intelligence section in the Brigade. We were both consumers and collectors of intelligence: we received general intelligence about the IRA's thinking and tactics, with the occasional nugget of information that had a specific operational usefulness, and we fed back intelligence gathered on the ground to HQ Northern Ireland. A soldier on patrol with a sharp pair of eyes may spot something, or he may have a chance conversation on the street which might be important. The drill is that after every patrol the soldiers have a very thorough debriefing with their local intelligence section at company level. But the Brigade was not directly involved in the covert war against the IRA. Special Branch had the lead in this area, and details of their activities were restricted on the 'need to know' principle. Suffice it to say that detailed, specific intelligence would almost certainly be exploited by non-Green Army forces.

Though the IRA had taken their campaign to the mainland in an attempt to force a political settlement, there continued to be a succession of shootings and bombings in the Province, with my soldiers taking casualties. For the man on the ground it was a constant strain, testing his judgement and his patience to the limit: one wrong move and he could be dead. Equally, the consequence of a split-second decision could be desperate. If you put soldiers into a very tense and difficult situation in which they are under constant threat from the civilians around them, tragic mistakes are bound to happen. Rules of engagement are carefully drafted to ensure soldiers act lawfully, and in the end soldiers' actions will be judged under the law. However well soldiers are trained in the rules of engagement, they always face the risk of allegations that they have overstepped the mark and committed an offence. It's essential that the process of law continues, even if the judgments are very hard. Soldiers must be subject to the law like every other citizen: once you begin to depart from that principle, you are lost. My time as CGS was to see a number of such incidents stemming from the Iraq campaign.

Sarah's concerns about living in a goldfish bowl were quickly allayed. People were extraordinarily welcoming, and very soon we found ourselves part of a lively and generous circle of military and local friends. Though we lived behind the wire, we certainly weren't confined there. On the contrary, Sarah became involved in a charity called Women Caring for the Children of Northern Ireland, through Judy Lindsay, who had already become a firm friend; the purpose of the charity was to bring together families from both sides of the sectarian divide. This enabled Sarah to visit some of the hard-line areas in Belfast, such as the Ardoyne and the Divis Flats, to assess new projects. It was an opportunity for her to see what sectarianism meant for women and children at grass-roots level. We would often go out in the evening, though as a brigade commander I had to have close protection all the time. There was a team of four Royal Military Police and they would work in pairs, so there would always be two minders wherever we went. Off duty, we would use our own car and they would follow in a car equipped with security devices. I remember one evening attending a packed concert, marking the bicentenary of Mozart's death, at St Ann's Cathedral, not far from one of our regular haunts, the pretty little opera house which had already been bombed two or three times by the IRA. The concert was about to resume after the interval – the conductor had his baton raised ready to start – when a loud explosion rocked the cathedral. Few, if any, of the audience batted an eyelid. Only car-alarms triggered by the bomb interrupted an exceptional evening's performance.

I left immediately and went to find that the IRA had bombed the opera house again. The façade had been damaged, with rubble spilling on to the street. Police and soldiers were already on site. Once the concert had ended, Sarah joined me there. We were both saddened to see the damage to this lovely building where we had passed many enjoyable evenings. I am glad to say that it was once again rebuilt to its former splendour.

Commanders at brigade level and above benefit from having an NCO appointed to their personal staff to help with military administration in the house, which is used not only for official entertaining but also as an alternative office and, indeed, conference centre from time to time. It is in this role that Corporal Pete Mawby of the Parachute Regiment entered our lives. He had just rejoined the Army after finding life outside not to his liking. Pete is a stocky figure, and, like me, he is follicly challenged. Always cheerful, ever staunch, he would remain with us for most of the next eighteen years or so, until he retired from the Army as Colour Sergeant Mawby MBE.

Sarah was well into her pregnancy when we arrived in Northern Ireland. Though rather younger than me, she was comparatively senior to be having her first child. Medical advice was that she should have a series of tests at a precise time in her pregnancy – our first week in Northern Ireland – which could only be carried out at the Royal Victoria Hospital in West Belfast, a strongly Nationalist area. So Sarah became the subject of a major security operation: three armoured personnel carriers and an escort of sixteen policemen and soldiers escorted the new brigade commander's wife from Grosvenor Road police station to the hospital. I thought she would be horrified, but she was quite amused by the whole thing.

In due course our son Tom was born in the City Hospital, on the south side of the city. The obstetrician arranged, on security grounds, for Sarah to occupy an isolation ward, two nice big rooms all to herself. A day or two after Tom's birth, I found Sarah surrounded by girlfriends. It was a very obvious sign of how quickly she had found friends. Sarah has observed that it was a help to her for Tom to have been born so soon after we arrived in Northern Ireland, because people responded so immediately and warmly. They could see that she was looking for support, and they provided it.

On Friday 16 November 1990 I spent an hour or two with the Prime Minister. She'd flown over to Northern Ireland for the day, and spent the morning with the Secretary of State and other leading political figures. But in the afternoon, before leaving, she had decided to spend some time with the soldiers. That was typical of Mrs Thatcher. She liked soldiers and they liked her: she knew how to relate to them, and she liked to be photographed with them. Maggie was a popular figure with the Army. The boys liked her no-nonsense style and they admired her courage. And of course after the Falklands her reputation in military circles was sky-high.

I escorted her about that cold, wet November afternoon. We had met before, when she had come to South Armagh after the Warrenpoint massacre. But she wasn't there to see me; she had come to talk to the soldiers. She knew instinctively how to convey to them that sense of, 'Yes, I'm with you, I'm supporting you, whatever you're doing.' And they greatly appreciated it.

I was a little surprised that she hadn't cancelled her visit, because she was in the middle of a political crisis. In a sense this had been precipitated by the IRA, who had murdered her old confidant Ian Gow back in the summer, triggering a by-election in which the Conservative Party had suffered a crushing defeat. But that result was an expression of a deeper discontent with her Government, which by now had been in power for more than a decade. Sir Geoffrey Howe, her former deputy and the last survivor in Government of the close associates who had been with her throughout, had resigned a fortnight earlier. Three days before she came to Belfast he had made a damaging speech in the House of Commons, and the next day Michael Heseltine announced his intention of standing against her for the leadership of the Party. The election would be decided by the ballots of the Parliamentary Party, which were scheduled to continue until one candidate achieved a clear majority. The first of these ballots was due to take place on the following Tuesday, while Mrs Thatcher was attending a meeting of the Conference on Security and Co-operation in Europe (CSCE) in Paris. There had been indications that the vote would be very close, and it was by no means certain that she could hold off the challenge.

As it turned out, she did not. Two days later she would announce that she would not contest a second ballot, and a week later she resigned. But there were only two votes in it; had she gained those two votes she'd have won on the first ballot and been free to continue, to 'go on and on' as she had once put it. Many people believe that had she not gone to Paris but instead had remained in London to canvass more support, working the tea-rooms as the cry has it, she would have gained those extra two votes. Who knows what might then have happened? At the very least, she would have had more freedom to choose the time of her departure.

It seemed typical of her that despite all this pressure she carried on regardless, fulfilling her engagements with us and in Paris, scorning those who were trying to bring her down.

All this was in my mind as I accompanied Mrs Thatcher that November afternoon. We must have made an incongruous combination: I tall and lean, she much smaller, but indisputably the boss. It was getting dark at Thiepval Barracks when I walked with her along the concrete path towards the helipad. She was about to board a helicopter to fly to Aldergrove, the main Belfast airport, where she would take an RAF jet back to London, staying there only a day before flying on to Paris. It was wet and windy, and she was wearing a mackintosh and head-scarf, carrying her trademark handbag.

As we walked together I passed on the pleasantries appropriate to the end of such a visit. 'Well, Prime Minister, thank you very much, your visit has been much appreciated by the soldiers.'

We reached the pad where the helicopter was waiting, its rotors turning in the rain. I said goodbye, raising my voice to make myself heard. Then an impulse induced me to give voice to my thoughts:

'Prime Minister, are you sure you should be going to Paris at this time?'

She looked at me fiercely. 'Brigadier,' she said, in a tone that made it clear there should be no further discussion on the topic: 'You attend to your soldiering and I will attend to my politics.'

One of Mrs Thatcher's last acts as Prime Minister was to put pressure on the Americans to use force to expel the Iraqis from Kuwait, which they had invaded in August 1990. President George Bush Senior had been somewhat hesitant, but she had told him firmly that this was 'no time to go wobbly!' Early in 1991 the American-led Coalition launched Operation 'Desert Storm', which very quickly succeeded in driving the Iraqi Army out of Kuwait. I had been watching developments with a keen interest, of course. It was clear from the start that as a brigade commander in Northern Ireland I would not be involved. But though this was frustrating, I was very happy to be doing what I was doing. And although it must have been exciting to be there, and the Coalition troops won an overwhelming victory, it was all over very quickly – the one-hundred-hour war, as it has been described. No Parachute Regiment battalions were sent to the Gulf, though my old friend Rupert Smith served there, as the major general in command of the 1st (UK) Armoured Division. He had been a Para, and so had his Chief of Staff, Colonel John Reith, to whom I had handed command of 1 Para five years before.

In November 1990, during the planning for 'Desert Storm', the Assistant Chief of the General Staff circulated a selection of comments made by MOD civil servants in the previous year, questioning the need for a significant 'out-of-area' (i.e. outside Europe) capability. Events had already shown these comments to be short-sighted. 'It is hard to conceive any set of circum-stances where the UK would engage another country OOA . . . equipped with armour,' read one. 'It is difficult to see UK partic-ipation in a "larger Allied Force" in a conventional OOA conflict,' read another. A third was particularly scornful. 'Can one seriously imagine a British Prime Minister seeking the approval of the House of Commons for a military adventure . . . to embroil the UK in a Middle East war?' It would have been nice to think that those who had penned these comments felt embarrassed by them when only a few months later the UK went to war in the Middle East as a part of a coalition – but somehow I doubted it.

A few months after Operation 'Desert Storm' I was back in England, having a drink with my son Mark. He was still at Wellington, and I'd taken him out for the evening. We were chat-ting through his plans, because he was due to leave school that summer. Some years earlier, when he was only fourteen or fifteen, Mark had decided that he wanted to go into the Army, and had secured a place at Sandhurst with an Army scholarship.

At first he thought of joining a cavalry regiment, but a 48-hour visit to Aldershot had convinced him he should opt for the Paras. He certainly wasn't influenced by me: if anything, the opposite was true, because Mark was something of a long-haired rebel in those days. Subsequently he had applied for and obtained an Army bursary to fund him through university. Before that he planned to take a gap year, travelling with Amanda. They had it all worked out. They were going to St Moritz in December, where he would act as one of the 'tower boys' on the Cresta Run, while Amanda was going to be in charge of the Club shop. Then in February they would go travelling in Africa. What he hadn't fixed is what he'd be doing between leaving school and December.

'Look, Mark,' I said, 'here's a thought.' I'd done a bit of homework. I explained how he could join what was then the Ulster Defence Regiment on a wonderfully Irish basis of 'full-time, part-time'. That is, one could join the part-timers and work full-time, the advantage being that one had to give only twenty-eight days' notice to leave. 'The thing is, Mark,' I said, 'it means that you can come out to Northern Ireland as soon as you leave school, and you can serve as long as you like, gain some experience, save some money and then go off travelling.'

Mark's eyes lit up. 'Absolutely bloody marvellous, Dad,' he said. 'Great idea.'

As soon as he left school a few months later Mark came out to join us in Northern Ireland. He had passed his driving test, so I bought him an ancient pale blue Mini from a farmer just down the road from the barracks, and he had an extended teenage party travelling around with some of his Northern Irish friends. Then he joined the UDR, and at the end of his basic training I was very proud to be able to present him with an award as 'Champion Recruit' for his intake. From the late summer until about November, he served as a private soldier in the UDR. Mark was living with us at home in Lisburn, so it made sense for him to join the Lisburn-based UDR battalion. This was part of 39 Brigade, so theoretically he came under my command, though of course there were quite a few people in between.

The day came for his first early morning patrol, when he was due to report for duty at 05.00 hours. His UDR Centre was only a five-minute walk from our home. The night before I had tried to get him ready: 'Right, Mark, are you organized, have you got your kit ready, have you set your alarm clock?'

'Yes, Dad, all fixed, sorted.'

Knowing what teenagers are like about getting up, I set my own alarm for 04.30.

When I awoke the next morning I could hear some horrible music blaring from along the corridor. I found Mark still fast asleep. He had slept through his radio alarm – though how he could sleep with that racket blaring was a mystery. 'Come on,' I said, kicking him: 'You're going to be late.' Just then I heard the doorbell. I was wearing nothing but a towel around my waist, but of course I had to answer the door. It was a member of Mark's section, Lance Corporal Hagan, with two grinning soldiers in the background. 'Good morning, Sir,' he said, putting up a slightly exaggerated salute: 'Is that son of yours coming out to play?' It was bit cheeky, perhaps, but I was in no position to pull rank because my wretched son was late on parade – on his very first day!

Of course I was concerned about Mark, as any other father would be in the circumstances, but perhaps being in the firm myself made me a little less so, because I had a greater knowledge of the risks involved. The Army loses far more people to road traffic accidents, disease, heart attacks, and the kind of afflictions which might just as easily strike a civilian than it does to enemy action. It's a matter of perspective. Even in Northern Ireland, we weren't taking a lot of casualties at that point. We'd lost some people, and we'd had people wounded, but not in shocking quantities. So yes, of course, there was a fatherly concern, but I was also rather proud of him: proud that the boy had the bottle to do it. And the fact that Mark spent some time as a private soldier before he became an officer stood him in very good stead later. In my view that was a real feather in his cap.

I took a week's leave that winter, and we went out to St Moritz to join Mark and Amanda. Mark had been riding the Cresta Run. 'Come on, Dad,' he said. 'You've got to get down this; come on, if I can do it, you can do it.' He didn't leave me much choice! You lie flat on your chest on a special toboggan, with your face only six inches or so above the ice, and you must steer the toboggan precisely or you will come out of the run. Towards the finish, experts can reach a speed of 80 miles per hour. The main risk comes as you negotiate the 180-degree bend called 'Shuttlecock', round which the centrifugal forces are particularly powerful. If you do lose control and go over the edge, there's plenty of soft snow and straw to break your landing. The important thing is to hurl the toboggan away from you as you fly through the air, because otherwise you can be badly cut up by its razor-sharp runners. Coming out does qualify you to wear the Shuttlecock tie – and that very much includes me!

It's an addictive experience and I've been doing it off and on ever since. One year Mark and I entered the Cresta 'Fathers and Sons' event as a team. Sadly, this was a little too ambitious on my part, and we took the wooden spoon. For my last five years in the Army I was President of Army Winter Sports, which had the incidental bonus of a week in the Alps every year.

By this time I'd fulfilled my allotted two years as commander of 39 Brigade, but I stayed on another few months because my designated successor, Alistair Irwin, had been selected for the Higher Command and Staff Course. I was very happy to do so because I enjoyed the job so much. Around Easter 1992 we finally said farewell to Northern Ireland. We left with some sadness, because we had come to feel so much part of the place and made such good friends there. I was awarded the CBE, then customarily conferred on Northern Ireland brigade commanders.

We didn't know it then, but in fact an end to the Troubles in Northern Ireland was in sight. On the ground the security situation remained much as it was, but politically things were on the move. In December 1993, a 'Joint Declaration on Peace' (more commonly known as the Downing Street Declaration) was issued by the British and Irish governments. The following summer the IRA announced a ceasefire. In 1998, encouraged by President Clinton, the two governments and the political parties in Northern Ireland reached what became known as the 'Good Friday Agreement', renouncing violence and setting out a programme for political progress in the Province. The agreement was subsequently accepted by large majorities in referenda of the population on both sides of the border. I remember the cruel but accurate comment: 'The Prods have won but they're too stupid to understand it.'

For a long time the IRA had derived succour from the Irish political constituency within the United States. But the terrorist attacks on 11 September 2001 transformed American attitudes and meant that the IRA was no longer welcome in Washington. The IRA began decommissioning its weapons, a process said to have been concluded in 2005. In that same year the British and Irish governments issued another joint declaration. This contained a security annex laying out an end-state for the British Armed Forces within the Province. At the time of writing, the plan is for them to go non-operational at midnight on 31 July 2007. This would provide a considerable relief to our resources; for much of the previous forty years, there had been up to twenty thousand soldiers stationed in Northern Ireland, one-fifth of our total manpower. There were two important caveats to this decision: the police could call on military assistance to help contain widespread public disorder; and the Army would continue to provide technical assistance, in particular with EOD (explosive ordnance disposal). Going non-operational required a major planning effort. We were particularly concerned to retain the specialist capabilities, skills and equipment accumulated during the long struggle against the terrorist threat to the Province.

While still in Northern Ireland I was, of course, wondering what I should do next. In the normal course of events I would have been expected to do a staff job as a brigadier before being considered for promotion. As the end of my tour in Northern Ireland drew nearer I scanned what's known as the 'dream sheet', the list of upcoming jobs circulated by the personnel people at the MOD. One job caught my eye: Director of Public Relations (Army). I thought this looked particularly interesting. It would mean managing the interface between the Army and the media, spending a lot of time talking to the hacks, particularly of course the defence correspondents, largely off the record – 'Let me explain the thinking behind this' – and also negotiating with ministers as to when senior officers in prominent positions like the CGS or GOC Northern Ireland should give interviews.

Nowadays every senior officer undertakes media training. During any big exercise the commanders will be interviewed by professional journalists, and these interviews will be filmed and evaluated later. They will also be played back to the interviewees, the evaluators pointing out when they seemed evasive or shifty, drawing attention to body language and all those other unintended signals. Nevertheless, some officers remain uneasy with the media, and some even resent the press, concerned that they're going to get shafted. While I don't share these concerns, I accept that the media can be irritating. But they are an essential part of modern life, and soldiers need to adapt to this like everybody else. It is very important that senior military leaders understand how to work with the media, not least because they represent a significant additional dimension in any operational theatre.

So the job as DPR (Army) was right up my street. It was London-based, and both Sarah and I liked the idea of coming back to London for a while. I put in for the job, and was appointed. But then something rather unusual happened. I can only surmise, knowing what I do of the system, that somebody dropped out, or decided to leave the Army unexpectedly, so that the dominos started falling. A two-star appointment in the MOD, Director General of Organization and Territorial Army, suddenly became vacant. It appeared that the Army couldn't find an existing major general to do the job, so they said: Right, some lucky brigadier is going to get promoted. And that lucky brigadier was me.

It was a bitter-sweet feeling: I didn't get the job I would have relished, but I did get promotion after only one job at one-star level, which was very unusual in peacetime.

Almost as soon as this had been settled, everything changed again. There was yet another reorganization in the MOD, and the post to which I had been appointed disappeared. So then the Army offered me another two-star job within the Ministry, as Director General Personal Services. It was a job that covered an eclectic mixture of personnel functions in the Army: discipline and legal matters, welfare, pay and allowances, conditions of service and ceremonial, including Army bands. I reported to the Adjutant General, the Army Board member responsible for personnel matters. The Army Board, which has five members, is the Cabinet of the Army, chaired by the CGS.

We set ourselves up in London, renting a light and airy house in Putney belonging to an artist and his wife. Sarah resumed her freelance career, hiring an au pair to help look after Tom, who was now walking and causing mayhem in the way that active toddlers do. Working regular hours and wearing civilian clothes,

I commuted every day to an MOD outpost called Empress State Building, a stone's throw from Earls Court tube station. I did feel a bit of a military bureaucrat, but I told myself that these functions have to be fulfilled: somebody needs to set disciplinary policy; somebody needs to engage the Armed Forces Pay Review Body over pay and allowances. These functions are necessary to make the Army work well. And the directorate mattered to people. The welfare side was particularly important, including welfare arrangements for veterans, liaison with the various Armed Forces charitable bodies, and so on. It was a broad port-folio and an interesting one. The job also made me consider much more deeply social issues that I hadn't really focused on before, and in that sense it widened my horizons. And in the process one learned rather more about the byzantine workings of the Ministry of Defence.

At this time there were big changes happening in defence as a result of the end of the Cold War. The Government was anxious to cash in its so-called 'peace dividend'. There was much debate about the future shape and size of the Armed Forces – not a debate in which I was directly involved, but one I watched very carefully. A series of policy documents followed one after another: especially significant were *Options for Change* (1990) and *Front Line First* (1994). There were three particular economies in the personnel area which the MOD wanted to impose on us, and which I remember discussing with my boss, the then AG, David Ramsbotham (lately HM Inspector of Prisons), a man I admire a great deal. I remember a group of us sitting around David's table and saying, 'AG, we can't sign up to these.' They wanted to get rid of high-street recruiting offices, which have since had to be reinstituted. Then they wanted to abolish the junior entry, the scheme that allowed youngsters to join the Army at sixteen under somewhat different and more liberal terms of service. That had always been very successful. We pleaded with them not to jettison the scheme, but they went ahead and did it anyway, and to some extent we've had to re-introduce it subsequently. The third decision was to downsize the medical services very significantly, doing away with military hospitals, and so depending much more heavily on the National Health Service to treat military patients. This was truly a dreadful decision, and one that we have not been able to get rescinded, because the investment required is too great. But there remains a great deal of concern about the way wounded soldiers are cared for when they come back from the field. While I applaud the quality of clinical care, not all NHS staff really understand the psychology of the soldier. The psychological benefit of wounded soldiers being together in the same ward and being treated by military medical staff has been woefully underestimated.

I chaired the Board which considered written appeals on behalf of those who had been turned down for the Long Service and Good Conduct Medal. This was a 'soldier-only' award (on the Victorian basis that officers are assumed to be of good conduct), given for fifteen years' service and an unblemished conduct sheet. Many of the candidates were very great men indeed – regimental and company sergeant majors, for example. Our job was to hear appeals from those who had been turned down for the award on account of some unfortunate entry in their record. The morning of the Appeals Board was always one to look forward to in an otherwise humdrum routine. A typical charge would be for 'conduct to the prejudice of good order and military discipline contrary to Section 69 of the Army Act, in that he discharged a fire extinguisher at the guard commander' – or whatever. The appeals tended to follow familiar lines and often elicited wry smiles: 'I was a young soldier. I fell into bad company. This conduct was totally out of character . . .'

One policy in which I was deeply involved was the introduction of compulsory drug testing, to which everybody in the Army is now subject on a random basis, just as many are in sports and other professions. This measure was introduced in response to the growing drugs problem in society as a whole. We felt that we had to draw a line in the sand on this issue. Of course it's particularly important that soldiers should be drug-free because, for example, you don't want somebody on a 'high' when he's carrying a weapon. There were practical concerns: the cost of running the programme, and the fact that inevitably we would lose soldiers because some would be discharged after failing drug tests. But we felt it was something that we had to do. Random testing applies right throughout the Army, at every level. I have peed into a bottle several times myself. I call this 'leading from the front'.

There were a number of policy issues that arose as a result of the presence of women in the Army, especially of course the vexed issue of whether women should serve in the front line. The essential question is not one of ability or discrimination, but whether the presence of women in close-quarter battle is detrimental to operational effectiveness. The evidence suggests that it is. The issue came to a head in Geoff Hoon's time as Secretary of State for Defence; like so many others, I was much relieved when he accepted the unequivocal advice of the Chiefs of Staff that women should not serve in tanks, in the infantry, in submarines or in the RAF Regiment, the Air Force's own infantry force. There are also issues that arise when men and women are serving alongside each other, of privacy for example. Sexual relations can cause serious problems if the two people involved both live within the same tight little community, particularly if one or both are married. Human beings being what they are, and human nature being what it is, soldiers do have extra-marital affairs, but they can have very corrosive effects – particularly if you get an officer sleeping with a soldier's wife, or vice versa. (It is just as damaging when a woman in the Army sleeps with another female soldier's husband.) The problem is not one of morality per se, but rather of the effect of such conduct on the operational effectiveness of the unit.

The Armed Services were still intolerant of homosexuality in the early 1990s, and there was genuine concern about the effects of taking a more liberal approach. But change here did happen – and that concern proved groundless. Exactly the same rules now apply to homosexual behaviour as to heterosexual: sexual behaviour, whatever it may be, must not impinge on operational effectiveness, for example by undermining the chain of command.

Bullying was a concern throughout my time, but in the 1990s it did not seem to be the serious problem it became later. The subsequent deaths at the Deepcut recruit training centre have led some commentators to question whether there is a culture of bullying within the Army. I do not believe this to be true. While the death of any young person is a tragedy, such incidents must be considered in the context of the tens of thousands of young soldiers who have passed through recruit training, and the fact that, sadly, in any cross-section of the population there is bound to be a proportion of suicides. The Army does not tolerate bullying at any time, and if it is detected, the perpetrators can expect to be prosecuted.

The job as DG Personal Services involved quite a lot of travelling, visiting Army bases to address gatherings of officers and soldiers. My opening gambit would be to say, 'You probably don't know what I do, but let me explain. After bullets, bombs and bangs in Belfast, now it's everything else beginning with "b" – bands, belts, berets, badges, buttons, banners, bars (medals), bars (booze), burglary, bullying, barbiturates, bosoms, babies, bonking and buggery.'

That was always good for a cheap laugh, just to warm up the audience.

Some time during the summer of 1993 I had another of those father–son conversations with Mark. After the winter of 1991–2 in St Moritz, he and Amanda had spent the next six months or so in Africa together. I remember going to meet them at Heathrow off a flight from Nairobi the following summer. Two scruffy urchins came through the gate, still dusty from the African bush and bursting with stories of their adventures. That autumn Mark went off to Southampton University to read archaeology and anthropology, while Amanda found herself a job in an advertising agency in London and moved into a flat. A year later, Mark and I met for a drink.

'Dad, this studying is not me,' he said. 'I want to get soldiering.'

I understood how he felt, though I was a bit disappointed that he wasn't going to see his university course through to the end.

'Look, Mark,' I said to him, 'whatever you end up doing – whether you stay in the Army or leave in due course – it'll be useful to have a degree.' But Mark was adamant that he'd had enough of university. I sensed that he'd made his decision, and I didn't argue any further. The upshot was that he took up early the place at Sandhurst which would otherwise have been his after he had completed his university course. I remember meeting him there at the back of Old College on his first day, when he rolled up with his sister Amanda in his old soft-top Land Rover. It is almost a tradition that every cadet brings his own ironing-board. My great friend Hew Pike had insisted on carrying his son William's ironing-board two years before, so I did the same – despite the hideous floral cover.

As my two years in the MOD went by, I was thinking, as ever, about what might come next. What I really wanted was to command one of the so-called 'manoeuvre divisions', which is the job that any major general would give his eye teeth for. But there were only two possibilities, the 3rd Division in Britain or the 1st Division in Germany. One day I picked up the telephone to find the CGS on the line.

'I want you to go and command the 3rd Division,' he said. 'Is that OK with you?' It most certainly was.

It was a great thrill to be chosen to go and command the great 3rd Division, which has a long and distinguished history. Formed early in the nineteenth century by one of my great heroes, the Duke of Wellington, it had fought in the Peninsula and at Waterloo. During the bitter fighting of the First World War it had earned the nickname the 'Iron Division'. At the outset of the Second World War it had been commanded by Montgomery, and he had chosen the sign of three black triangles surrounding an inverted red triangle to represent the Division, composed as it was of three infantry brigades, each of three battalions. After being evacuated at Dunkirk, the Division had been the first British formation to return to France, landing at 'Sword' beach on D-Day. The divisional motto is 'Drive On', though typically the soldiers have adapted this to FIDO, short for 'Fuck It, Drive On'.

I left the MOD early in 1994, after saying my goodbyes to all the various aspects of the Army for which I'd been responsible. Brigadier Charles Bond and his staff at the Kneller Hall School of Army Music came up with this adaptation of Gilbert and Sullivan which is now framed and displayed on the wall of the loo at home (along with much other bog-ography, as Sarah calls it).

> He's been the ve-ry mod-el of a mod-ern Maj-or Ge-ne-ral,
> He came from bangs and bul-lets in the bogs sur-round-ing
> Cross-ma-glen,
> To con-cen-trate on bonk-ing, bands and bull-ies armed with just
> his pen,
> He's coped with drugs, a-llowing-an-ces and certain matters
> mu-si-cal,
> He's chaired the odd com-mit-tee on tend-en-cies be-hav-iou-ral,
> He's nailed some jell-ies to the wall but not been too pon-tif-i-cal,
> With style and guile he's done it all but now be-comes di-vis-ion-al,
> Thank God – he's been the mo-del of a mod-ern Ma-jor Gen-er-al.

I had managed to engineer a bit of extra leave before taking up my new command, and as this fell in the dreary winter months of February and March and I was about to turn fifty, Sarah and I decided to celebrate by taking a holiday in Zimbabwe. We took Tom, now almost four, and Amanda and Mark joined us for a fortnight. It was the most wonderful six weeks, and we fell in love with the country and its people. The recovery from the civil war that had ended only a dozen years before seemed miraculous. It was a happy, vibrant place – a far cry from the tragedy of Mugabe's Zimbabwe today.

While in Zimbabwe I was especially keen to see the marshalling yards of Bulawayo. There's a bit of me that will always be a small boy when it comes to trains. I have a deal with my eldest grandson Casper that when he gets his own model railway, grandpa may give him a hand. Like many of my generation I feel nostalgic for the age of steam, which ended in Britain while I was still young.

Anyone who knows anything at all about trains knows that the railways of Africa were the most extraordinary engineering achievements. I had done some reading in advance of flying out there, and I knew that if the golden age of the railways had in any sense entered your soul, you had to see these marshalling yards of Bulawayo. So we went there one morning – and there they were, these huge black machines, hissing and puffing and emitting steam from every orifice. We stood about twenty yards from one particular pair of vast back-to-back engines, with eight wheels either side, front and back. I took photographs while young Tom clutched Sarah's hand, a little overwhelmed by the heat and the noise. Suddenly the engine-driver, a middle-aged black man wearing overalls and a red and white polka-dot neckerchief, leaned out from the footplate and gave me a friendly wave. I waved back – and then he beckoned to me. I wasn't sure what he meant, and the din of the engine precluded conversation, so I pointed at my chest in a gesture of enquiry.

He beckoned harder, so I walked across until I was standing beside the engine and we could talk without shouting. Tom stayed behind with Sarah. I said hello to the driver, whose name was Moses. I suppose we were about the same vintage. We started chatting.

'What are you doing here?' he asked.

'I've come to see these machines,' I said. 'I think they're just amazing.'

'Humph. Well, they're very old-fashioned,' Moses replied loftily; 'I would prefer a diesel.'

And then he asked: 'Do you want to come up?'

'Do I want to do *what*?' I said, not quite believing my ears.

So up I climbed on to the footplate, and Moses and his fireman Aloysius showed me around his cab. Both were glistening with sweat: the heat of the boiler hit me as I climbed in.

'Maybe you would like to drive it?' Moses asked, sipping his tea out of a chipped enamel mug.

'You're not serious?' I said, but he nodded.

'Yes, I am. Steam's up, and we're ready to go.' He told me what to do: pull this, watch that, shove the other – and the mighty engine began to lumber forward, slowly at first. Aloysius shovelled coal into the boiler. I held up five fingers to indicate to Sarah that I would be back in as many minutes, and she nodded. Tom looked a little apprehensive as we moved off, but I smiled at him reassuringly from the footplate.

We steamed three or four miles down the track and then back again. It was pretty gentle stuff, never travelling at more than about twenty miles an hour at most, but I felt a sense of the massive strength of this great beast. At the end I thanked Moses and we shook hands, before I climbed down from the footplate and walked back to Sarah and a relieved Tom, still not quite believing what had happened.

10

A Modern Major General

Icame back to England after that relaxing holiday in Africa full of enthusiasm for the job that lay ahead. We packed up the house in Putney, which was a bit of a wrench, and drove down the A303 to begin our new life on Salisbury Plain. Our home for the next few years would be Clive House in Tidworth, a substantial pre-war villa in a leafy setting set aside for the divisional commander. My headquarters were nearby at Picton Barracks in Bulford, where 1 Para had been stationed, and where I had been living when I met Sarah, so the area had good memories for us both.

I took over the 3rd Division in April 1994 from my long-standing Parachute Regiment friend Hew Pike, one of Tom's godfathers. The Division was then about twenty thousand strong, consisting of three brigades: the 1st Mechanized Brigade, stationed in and around Salisbury Plain, mainly at Tidworth; the Airborne Brigade, 5 Airborne Brigade as it was then, in Aldershot, less than an hour's drive east; and the 19th Mechanized Brigade, then based at Colchester, on the far side of

London. With me in my Bulford HQ were my staff and the Division's signal regiment.

Very soon after I arrived, the Divisional HQ had the task of running the British dimension of the fiftieth anniversary of the D-Day landings in Normandy. With heads of state and other political leaders in attendance, there was no room for error. Nevertheless the stars of the show were the veterans, many of them by then in their seventies or even eighties. I had the privilege of meeting some of these old boys and spending some time in their company. This was a very moving occasion; there was a strong sense that this was the final such commemoration for many of them. I often thought of my father during that emotional day, wishing that he had lived long enough to share it with me. I felt proud that he had been one of these brave men.

The scheduled climax of the British celebrations was to be a parade on 'Gold' beach at Arromanches, to be reviewed by Her Majesty the Queen. Thousands of veterans were lined up on the beach waiting for her, the concrete hulks of the Mulberry harbour still protruding above the waves behind them. Several landing craft lay beached with their ramps down as they had been half a century earlier. The Queen's review of the veterans was programmed as the last event of the day, at 17.00 hours. Unfortunately the timing was very tight against the incoming tide, and earlier delays to the programme meant that the Queen arrived a few minutes late. I fear that the veterans on the far side of the hollow square got a bit damp – as no doubt many of them had fifty years before. After the Queen had reviewed the parade, the veterans marched past, singing wartime songs. On the beach, there was hardly a dry eye – and plenty of wet feet.

One of the veterans dropped stone-dead just after the Queen had passed him. After attempts to resuscitate him failed, he was stretchered off – to the applause of his old comrades. Later, one said to me, 'What a way to go: just been reviewed by the Queen, among your mates, straight to Valhalla.'

FORMER YUGOSLAVIA - Showing the Republics and the autonomous district of Kosovo and the autonomous province of Vojvodina.

AUSTRIA

HUNGARY

LJUBLJANA

SLOVENIA

ZAGREB

CROATIA

ROMANIA

Vojvodina

Novi Sad

BOSNIA
AND
HERZEGOVINA

BELGRADE

SARAJEVO

SERBIA

MONTENEGRO

Pristina

BULGARIA

Podgorica

Kosovo

Adriatic Sea

SKOPJE

ITALY

MACEDONIA

TIRANA

ALBANIA

Thessaloniki

GREECE

*Ionian
Sea*

ATHENS

	International border
	Republic border
	Autonomous district/province border
	Former Yugoslavia

0   100

miles

*

As the months passed my attention was increasingly focused on the deteriorating situation in Bosnia. Serbs, Croats and Bosnian Muslims (known as 'Bosniacs') had been fighting each other since 1992, when the former Yugoslav republics of Bosnia and Macedonia had declared their independence from Yugoslavia, following the successful secession of Slovenia and Croatia. Armies of these three ethnic factions – the first two aided by their 'parent' countries, Serbia and Croatia – were involved in a bloody struggle for control of territory. The Bosnian Serb army had occupied parts of Croatia: the Krajina (frontier) region in the west, and the area around Vukovar in the east, bordering Serbia itself. The consequent civilian suffering was causing increasing concern throughout Europe and in the wider world, particularly in America.

Yugoslavia had been created in 1918, as a union of south Slavs in territories formerly part of either the Austrian or the Ottoman empire. Though designated as a union of Serbs, Croats and Slovenians, Yugoslavia incorporated other national groups, including Bosnian and Kosovar Muslims, in an ethnic patchwork across the territories of the former empires. Initially a kingdom, it had become a Communist state after the Second World War, under the leadership of Josip Broz Tito, who had led the resistance to the Nazi occupation. Tito created what was in many ways an ideal multinational state, made up of semi-autonomous republics. Though Communist, Tito's Yugoslavia refused to join the Warsaw Pact, and maintained a neutral position during the Cold War. But after Tito's death in 1980 ethnic tensions increased, whipped up by nationalist politicians. The rise to power of Serbian President Slobodan Milosevic precipitated the break-up of Yugoslavia.

The disintegration of the Yugoslav state presented a challenge to national governments and international institutions. The Clinton administration in the United States was extremely reluc-

BOSNIA AND HERZEGOVINA 1996 (Post-Dayton)

CROATIA

Vojvodina

Prijedor

Bihac

Banja Luka

Republika Srpska

Tuzla

SERBIA

'The Anvil'

BOSNIA
AND
HERZEGOVINA

Srebrenica

Gorni Vakuf

SARAJEVO

Pale

Gorazde

Split

Mostar

Republika
Srpska

MONTENEGRO

Adriatic Sea

Inter-Entity Boundary line

0   50

miles

tant to become embroiled in the Balkans; and without American involvement, neither NATO nor the UN seemed capable of effective action. At the outset of the crisis the President of the Council of the European Union, Jacques Poos, then Foreign Minister of Luxembourg, had declared that 'the hour of Europe has dawned' – but in reality, the response of the European nations had been divided and ineffectual.

Bosnia and Herzegovina (to give it its full name) is a small country, approximately the same size as the Republic of Ireland, with a similar-sized population but a very different geography – varying from a high mountainous interior, which can be very cold indeed in winter, to a flat plain in the north and a very small length of coastline on the Adriatic Sea, where the climate remains temperate throughout the year. Its pepperpot ethnic distribution meant that there were isolated ethnic enclaves in many parts of the country.

Units of the 3rd Division were already deployed in Bosnia, serving with UNPROFOR, the United Nations Protection Force. Sadly, UNPROFOR had a very limited mandate, so although it was able to provide a certain amount of humanitarian aid, it was unable to provide real security for the civilian population. UNPROFOR was asked to police so-called 'safe areas', but this often led to the troops themselves being threatened. Sarajevo, the capital of Bosnia, was under siege from Bosnian Serbs, who regularly attacked anyone trying to negotiate the only route into the city, the road across Mount Igman, which became known as 'the most dangerous road in Europe'. The people of Sarajevo suffered severe shortages of food and other essential supplies, while being subject to regular sniper fire, as well as occasional shelling and mortar attack.

As a family we felt a personal connection with Bosnia, because for the past year or so a Bosnian Muslim girl had been living with us in London as an au pair, looking after young Tom. Aida's elderly parents lived in an apartment in the medieval part of Sarajevo, and she was naturally very anxious about their welfare. Day after day the television was showing images from Sarajevo of sniper victims, ruined buildings and hungry people trying to eke out a miserable existence. Sarah and I wanted to help Aida if possible, and we found a way to do this. I got in touch with an officer I knew fairly well, Andrew Cumming, a brigadier serving with UNPROFOR, and asked if it would be possible for him to convey a 'Red Cross parcel' to Aida's family. He agreed, and we assembled a large collection of basics, with a few goodies – birdseed for the budgerigar, lipstick for Aida's mother, chocolate, and some dollars, the universal currency of the black market. Aida was often exhausted with worry, and so she was relieved that something was being done to help her parents in this desperate situation. Andrew gave the parcel to a chap called Milos Stankovic, Yugoslav by birth but brought up in Scotland, and now a major in the Parachute Regiment serving with UNPROFOR in Sarajevo. As a fluent speaker of Serbo-Croat he was much in demand as a translator, and so he tended to go wherever the commanders went. He managed to get the parcel to Aida's parents; a month later I sent him another parcel, and so we went on. 'This is your own personal humanitarian mission,' I wrote to him.

We had been sending these parcels for almost two years before I took one to Bosnia myself. In February 1995 I flew out to Bosnia, partly to visit 3rd Division units serving with UNPROFOR, but also to see the place for myself. There already seemed a strong possibility that the Division might have to become more involved as the situation worsened. Milos gave me a whistle-stop tour of Sarajevo before taking me to see Aida's parents, Munir and Minka Pijailovic. It was a very emotional meeting, with tears and embraces all around. Their gratitude was almost overwhelming – without our help, they maintained, they would not have survived this long. The old lady put her arm around Milos: 'He is like a son to us,' she told me. There was something particularly poignant about this scene: in the midst of this ghastly war, while Serbs and Croats and Muslims were killing each other without compunction, here was an elderly Muslim lady embracing a young man of Serb origin. I handed over the parcel and some letters from Aida. I had also brought some photographs of Aida with young Tom, and we sat and looked through them together, with many sighs and exclamations from the elderly couple.

Milos and I returned to the Residency in Sarajevo, the headquarters of my old friend Rupert Smith, now a lieutenant general, who only weeks earlier had succeeded General Sir Michael Rose as Commander, UNPROFOR. Like Mike Rose, Rupert was frustrated to be operating with such a limited mandate. I was due to visit one of our battalions in Gorazde, a Muslim enclave deep in hilly Serb territory to the east of Sarajevo. The Serbs controlled all traffic in and out, by road or by air, and it seemed that they were refusing to give clearance for my helicopter flight into Gorazde. Milos, who acted as UNPROFOR's liaison officer with the Bosnian Serbs, telephoned their headquarters in Pale, a little skiing village on the east side of Sarajevo. He managed to obtain their agreement to my flight the following morning, the only stipulation being that the commander of the Bosnian Serb Army, General Ratko Mladic, wanted to meet me for lunch afterwards.

Mladic had not yet been indicted for war crimes, but he had already earned an ugly reputation as a brutal, boastful and manipulative thug – somebody to be very wary of. In August 1994 the American three-star general Wesley Clark, who had flown in for a quick fact-finding visit, had allowed himself to be manoeuvred into a PR disaster: he was photographed smiling alongside Mladic, having swapped hats in an apparent gesture of bonhomie. The photograph was widely published and caused Clark great embarrassment back at home, where two congressmen called for his dismissal. 'It's like clowning with

Hermann Goering,' one of them reportedly commented. I was a little apprehensive about our forthcoming encounter, though of course I knew that Mladic was a key player in the region and I was intrigued by the prospect of meeting him face-to-face.

The next morning snow was falling. We took off from Sarajevo Airport and after only ten minutes or so in the air landed again on the school football field at a mountain village called Sokolac. The Serbs insisted that, having crossed the line into Serb-held territory, you then had to land and be checked on your way in and then again on your way out. They would stop the UNPROFOR resupply convoys and search them from top to bottom. It reminded me of going in and out of Berlin. They wanted to ensure that we were not carrying any personnel who were not UN, or taking in weapons, ammunition or indeed rations to give to the Bosnian fighters. Everything UNPROFOR did had to be sanctioned by whichever faction controlled the ground. It was a humiliating sign of how weak the UN Force was.

I flew on to Gorazde, accompanied by Brigadier Robert Gordon, then commanding UN Sector South-West. It was useful to see the place for myself, and I hoped that the soldiers were encouraged by the fact that the Divisional Commander had made the effort to get to Gorazde and thank them. They were operating in very difficult circumstances, and it was impor-tant for them to receive some kind of acknowledgement. There was a lot of concern back home about what might happen to them if the UN effort collapsed. Though the terrain would have made it extremely difficult, there was none the less an extraction plan to go in, under NATO auspices if possible, create corridors to the isolated UN detachments and get them out – abandoning Bosnia to its fate.

On the way back we landed again at Sokolac to meet Mladic. Serb minders took us from the landing zone to an anonymous concrete building dating probably from the 1960s. This turned out to be a modest hotel, and there in the lobby, surrounded by his immediate staff and accompanied by a civilian interpreter, was Mladic – a squat, thick-set man in combat dress, with a ready grin and cold grey eyes. As he waved his hands in the air I noticed a gold ring on one finger, set with a large black stone. He greeted us effusively and led the party through into a dining room, where a dozen of us were seated around a simple wooden table. This was my first of many long and large Balkan lunches, often washed down with local wine and slivovic, a brandy made usually of plums and sometimes with pears. In this case, however, there was no alcohol: a plain meal of beans and a burger was served, which Mladic laughingly described as Serbian rations. Beaming and expansive, he presented himself as a simple soldier. He affected to be impressed that I had taken the trouble to come out here to see how my soldiers were doing.

I knew that Mladic was a cunning operator, and that I would have to keep my guard up in dealing with him, choosing my words with care. Robert Gordon did most of the talking. He had thoroughly briefed me beforehand on the issues that Mladic was likely to raise and how to handle them. The conversation centred on the logistic maintenance of the British battalion in Gorazde: what Mladic would be prepared to allow through and not allow through, and along which routes. Mladic's demeanour ranged from oiliness to bombast. His contempt for UNPROFOR was obvious. From his point of view, UNPROFOR was just an irritation, without the strength or the authority to impose itself in any meaningful way.

I was not sorry when the time came to leave. As a major general in the British Army, I found it irksome to have to come to a wretched place like this and to be harangued by such a despicable character as Ratko Mladic. But, as I was to experience time and again in the Balkans, it was essential to appear unemotional and to remain – at least outwardly – entirely objective.

*

I went back to Bosnia a month or two later and again visited the Pijailovic family in Sarajevo. The situation remained desperate, but the international community still seemed unwilling to risk more decisive action. In July 1995, however, an especially shocking massacre at Srebrenica outraged opinion all around the world, and proved to be the tipping point that at last drew in the United States. Until now NATO involvement had been limited to the sporadic enforcement of 'no-fly' zones – and without the commitment of NATO's lead nation the threat from NATO forces remained an empty one.

Srebrenica was another of those Muslim enclaves deep in Serb territory, very near the Serbian border. It too was a so-called 'safe area', protected by a Dutch battalion forming part of UNPROFOR. In the summer of 1995 Mladic's army, emboldened by the supine attitude of the Western powers, closed in on Srebrenica, determined to eradicate this Muslim enclave. The Dutch battalion, vastly outnumbered, let them pass after firing vainly into the air. The Dutch Government refused to allow NATO air strikes until all their troops were safely out of the area. The Serbs occupied the city, rounded up the Muslim men and massacred them, in the worst example of genocide in Europe since the Second World War. Reliable authorities estimate that at least seven thousand Muslim males were systematically murdered by the Serb forces. Many of those who fled Srebrenica on foot had a very long and difficult journey through the forests to the city of Tuzla, constantly harassed by Serb forces as they tried to escape. Of the ten to fifteen thousand who fled Srebrenica in a column of men, women and children, only three to four thousand are said to have reached their destination.

The massacre at Srebrenica concentrated Western minds. President Chirac of France was particularly active in calling for action. The Clinton Administration was at last stirred into

activity. The British Prime Minister, John Major, called an international crisis meeting in London at short notice, at which
Rupert Smith presented a very important paper entitled 'The
Fork in the Road'. He laid out the alternatives in stark terms.
One option was to get out. If you cannot, or will not do more
than you are prepared to do now, he said, you will achieve
nothing, and the sensible thing is to leave. If, on the other hand,
you want to secure an outcome that will last, then you must up
the ante. This meant securing a stronger mandate for
UNPROFOR at the very least. Thankfully, the London
Conference took the view that it would be ignominious for the
great powers of the Western world to withdraw from this small
European country, with relatively small numbers of antagonists.

It was agreed at the London Conference that NATO would
draw 'a line in the sand' around Gorazde, and that the decision
whether to use air power to protect the enclave would be made
within NATO, not by UNPROFOR or any UN body. These
terms of engagement were later broadened to include Sarajevo.
Rupert Smith also concentrated such artillery as UNPROFOR
possessed on Mount Igman, to assist NATO air power in
enforcing the decisions of the Conference – and, not least, to
deter further shelling by the Bosnian Serbs.

Meanwhile President Clinton's special representative in the
Balkans, Richard Holbrooke, was working hard to broker a
diplomatic deal leading to peace. He knew that it was not
enough to engage the parties on the ground; any lasting deal
would need the consent of their paymasters in Belgrade and
Zagreb, the rulers of Serbia and Croatia, Presidents Milosevic
and Tudjman. General Wesley Clark was appointed to
Holbrooke's team as military adviser. With the get-tough policy
that had emerged from the London Conference beginning to
bite, and a new Croat–Bosniac military alliance winning ground
from the Bosnian Serb army, it began to look as if the warring
parties would agree to some form of compromise. If this

happened, the plan was to deploy a NATO Force to replace UNPROFOR. NATO's Allied Rapid Reaction Corps (ARRC), commanded by British Lieutenant General Mike Walker, would form the ground force headquarters under NATO's Allied Forces Southern Europe HQ in Naples, with three so-called 'framework nations' heading up multinational divisions in different parts of the country: France, the United States and the UK. Should this scenario come about, the 3rd Division very much wanted to be part of the action. This was nothing to do with me personally. The British Army is by nature operationally hungry – particularly when there's a new challenge.

One evening in late June, Sarah and I were guests for dinner at Bulford Manor, the splendid old home of the Commander in Chief, Land Command, the second most senior officer in the Army and the one responsible for so-called 'force generation'. At one point during the meal our host, General John Wilsey, who had been GOC Northern Ireland for the latter half of my time commanding 39 Brigade, was called away from the table to take a telephone call. Afterwards he took me aside. 'Things are moving, Mike,' he said. 'You may have to go out to Bosnia very soon.' My first thought was of my daughter Amanda's wedding in a week's time. I was of course due to give her away. No sooner had I been presented with this dilemma than all the lights went out. It was only a fuse, but in my situation it seemed somehow appropriate. Fortunately, the apparent urgency went as quickly as it came.

Rupert Smith's appointment as Commander, UNPROFOR was only for one year and was due to finish at the end of 1995, when he would become GOC Northern Ireland. In the late summer I received a telephone call informing me that I had been selected as his successor. My reaction was somewhat mixed. On the one hand, this new appointment meant promotion to lieutenant general; on the other hand, it meant inheriting a position that both my predecessors had found immensely frustrating. I can remember thinking long and hard before deciding to accept. The new post would mean handing over the 3rd Division to my already nominated successor earlier than planned, and I began to make the necessary arrangements. On a practical level, I would have to find somewhere else for Sarah and Tom to live, because Clive House was tied to the post of GOC 3rd Division.

As Holbrooke's team engaged the factions in a whirlwind round of diplomacy, my own future was on hold. If an agreement was reached and the UK became one of the framework nations for the peacekeeping operation, this would mean putting a Corps Headquarters in the field, something we hadn't done since Suez. If, on the other hand, the parties failed to reach an agreement, my task as Commander, UNPROFOR might well be to oversee the Force's withdrawal from the region, which was bound to be messy and difficult.

All this was in the melting-pot when we took a late holiday in Singapore and Malaysia, tied in to an exercise being run by the Five Power Defence Agreement (FPDA) – UK, Singapore, Malaysia, Australia and New Zealand – the successor to the defunct South East Asia Treaty Organization (SEATO). Sarah, Tom and I stayed in an unpretentious but delightful beach guest-house on the east coast of Malaysia. It was a very simple place, with no landline telephones, and we were the only people there. On our second evening, the owner took a message from the British High Commission that Colonel Andrew Ritchie, my Chief of Staff at 3rd Division, needed to speak to me urgently. Our host kindly lent me his mobile telephone, warning me that reception was poor. To get a better signal, I walked on to the beach. 'Bosnia's looking more and more likely,' Andrew told me, 'but I think the Commander in Chief has his eye on 1 Div to do this. You might want to intercede now.'

The timing was not good. Here was I, sitting under a palm tree as a warm breeze blew in off the South China Sea, on the other side of the world from where the decisions were being taken. It was about nine in the evening local time, and I was dressed simply in a sarong. As I strolled up and down the sand in the moonlight, I managed to get hold of John Wilsey, and reminded him of all the planning for various Bosnian options we had done. 'Frankly, General, this makes 3 Div self-selecting,' I argued. I must have convinced him, because we heard no more after that about the possible involvement of the 1st Division.

Richard Holbrooke pressured all the parties involved in the Bosnian conflict to attend a conference at Dayton, Ohio – a US Air Force base chosen for its remoteness, which it was hoped would encourage the participants to hammer out an agreement. This was in mid-November, by which time I was once more in Bosnia. I had flown to Sarajevo via Zagreb, where I had met Kofi Annan, then Special Representative of the Secretary General (SRSG) for the Balkans. I stayed the night in Zagreb, in the rather upmarket hotel used by UN staff – contrasting sharply with the conditions in which UN soldiers were living in Bosnia. I found the ranks of smart white UN 4×4 vehicles in the hotel car park an uncomfortable sight; they seemed to be used only to commute between the hotel and the UN HQ by the airport.

When I reached Rupert Smith's HQ in Sarajevo the following day, I found he was away in Bihac for the night, which meant that I could borrow his bed – a good thing, because spare accommodation within UNPROFOR HQ was not easy to find. There were a lot of press hanging around, and much speculation about what was happening at Dayton. By midnight the general impression was that the Conference had failed. I went to bed in the early hours thinking: This is going to be where I sleep for the next year or so. It's a blue beret for Jackson, and three stars.

Rupert Smith returned the next day and we agreed a handover date in mid-December. Then I flew up to the UN Sector HQ at a small town called Gornji Vakuf, which had been on the front line between the Croats and the Bosniacs before they formed a federation to combat the Serbs. This Sector Headquarters was provided by the British 4th Armoured Brigade, commanded by Richard Dannatt – who, eleven years later, was to take over from me as CGS. In the late afternoon, just as it was getting dark, we were driving back from a visit to a British battalion when the radio in the vehicle burst into life, announcing that they'd settled at Dayton. I thought: Right – reference Plan A, cancel; insert Plan B. Back at Gornji Vakuf I watched the initialling ceremony on satellite television up in Richard's office.

So I finally knew where I was. I would not be the three-star commander of UNPROFOR, headquartered in Sarajevo; I would be the two-star commander of the new Multinational Division South-West – one of the three divisional commanders in the new NATO Force, known as IFOR (Implementation Force), remaining a major general and in command of the 3rd Division. I would deploy to Bosnia within a matter of weeks. HQ Multinational Division South West would be in Gornji Vakuf. Sarah and Tom could stay at Clive House. And this very room in which I was sitting would become my new office.

It had been a rollercoaster ride, not knowing what I was going to be doing right up until the last moment. But in the scheme of things my career was insignificant; the key thing was that, for the first time in five years, the outlook for Bosnia was hopeful.

I went out to Bosnia before Christmas, a few days before D-Day, 20 December 1995, the date when UNPROFOR handed over to IFOR. A couple of evenings earlier Sarah and I had thrown a party for the Headquarters staff, an event that became known as the Duchess of Richmond's Ball – although the comparison with Waterloo was more than a little far-fetched. In a short speech I urged the wives not to worry about their men: a forlorn hope, I suspect. In a symbolic gesture, the British soldiers who had formed part of UNPROFOR and were now coming under NATO command paraded formally to take off their light blue UN berets and put on their own British Army headgear. This was my first experience of commanding a multinational force: though more than half of the soldiers under my command were British, the Division also included Canadians, Czechs, Dutch and Malaysians. Of course, it would be unfair to expect the same capability from all national contingents. The Malaysians, for example, were hard pressed since they found – unsurprisingly – the Bosnian winters to be very harsh. And it is a curse of multinational operations that governments impose constraints on their national contingents, usually for domestic political reasons. Some may do this or that, some may not: the outcome is a complicated matrix of permitted actions for each nationality – and this is the bane of a multinational commander's life. Each national commander carries a so-called 'red card', allowing him to opt out of a specific operation if his national government finds it unpalatable.

Nevertheless, IFOR was a pretty formidable force of some sixty thousand soldiers. Though many of these, at least at the outset, were erstwhile members of UNPROFOR, they were now serving under NATO command with much tougher rules of engagement – and, moreover, with plenty of firepower at our disposal, including of course the threat of air strikes. UNPROFOR had possessed no heavy armour, and little enough artillery. We now shipped in tanks and self-propelled guns, which were brought up to our area on transporters in impressive convoys. My artillery commander, then Brigadier Freddie Viggers, moved quickly to open a live-firing range, and then organized a series of highly impressive live-firing displays for the faction leaders, as a clear demonstration of what they would face if they were unintelligent enough to take on IFOR. It was another way of getting over the message, 'We're serious, don't mess around.' They had nothing to compare with our firepower, of course.

During the Bosnian war the territory controlled by each of the warring factions had expanded and contracted depending on the success of their forces. Much of the fighting had concentrated around various 'pockets', where a population from one ethnic group – usually Bosnian – found itself isolated. At Dayton there had been a lot of horse-trading, with deals being done about control of this piece of territory or that. A so-called 'Clark Corridor' had been created to the Gorazde pocket, for example. Both the Serbs and the Croats had wanted to hive off as much territory as possible and join their parent states, leaving the poor Bosniacs in the middle with a tiny amount. But Dayton maintained the principle of a single Bosnian state, divided into two so-called 'entities' in a loose federal structure. One entity was the Croat–Bosniac Federation; the other, semi-autonomous entity became known as Republika Srpska, forming an extraordinary horseshoe shape around the east and north sides of the old Bosnian republic. Dayton laid down a boundary between the two entities, known as the 'Inter-Entity Boundary Line' (IEBL), which in many areas did not tally with the ceasefire lines on the ground. The Bosnian Serbs would try to treat the IEBL as an international boundary, though Dayton had insisted on the territorial integrity of Bosnia and the right of free movement within it.

Though the Force which I commanded was named the Multinational Division South-West (a hangover from the UN Sector South-West), we were in fact responsible for north-western Bosnia bordering Croatia, which curled round the country from the north right round to the south-west, cutting it off from the Adriatic Sea. In the early part of the war the Bosnian Serbs had dominated this part of Bosnia, though they had never eliminated the so-called 'Bihac pocket' in the north-west. Latterly a combined assault by Croats and Bosniacs had pushed the Bosnian Serbs back, nearly driving them out of the mountains on to the northern plain around their capital, Banja Luka.

In the freezing midwinter there were some heartrending scenes: lines of old vehicles, horses and carts, donkeys – anything to carry people who did not want to remain living in a place where in many cases their families had been for generations, once they could no longer rely on the protection of their own ethnic forces.

The boundaries agreed at Dayton were to be enshrined in detailed maps, but we hadn't received them by D+1, when I travelled up to Sarajevo for a meeting with Mike Walker and the other divisional commanders. In the airport car park I chanced upon an American full colonel with his driver and sidekick, who were asking the way to IFOR HQ. 'We have some urgent deliveries for them,' he explained.

'What have you got?' I asked.

It turned out that they had the newly printed Dayton maps.

'Aha,' I said, introducing myself. 'Perhaps I could have my slice now?' We transferred the maps directly from his vehicle into ours, and so – hallelujah! – we had our maps before anybody else.

The Dayton Agreement had been well thought through, with enough detail to make it all work, a tribute to the work of Richard Holbrooke and his team. Dayton laid out an end-state to which all the parties had agreed, with a clear mechanism for getting from start to finish. This clarity would prove invaluable in the weeks and months to follow. Dayton also stipulated strict timelines: what had to be done by D+30, D+60, D+90. For us, the Dayton Agreement became a kind of 'bible' to which I would refer whenever any kind of dispute arose. I carried a copy of Dayton with me everywhere. If there was any friction or altercation with any of the factions I just produced the document and pointed to the relevant clauses: 'This is what it says, this is what your leaders have signed up to.' That shut them up.

The military provisions of Dayton imposed three major obligations on the parties: a durable cessation of hostilities; support for IFOR; and security and arms control measures to promote a permanent reconciliation between the factions. These formal stipulations were amplified by a very detailed statement of procedures to be followed. The obligations thereby laid on the factions enabled IFOR to demand rigorous implementation of this or that provision – in the early days almost on a day-to-day basis.

Among many requirements, Dayton stipulated that the IEBL be marked on the ground, that no combatants from the opposing entity remain on the wrong side, and that weapons be centralized so that we could count them. Forces were not allowed to train without our permission. Those areas which were to be transferred from one entity to the other had to be vacated by D+45, and they would remain our responsibility until the forces of the other entity were permitted to enter at D+90, forty-five days later. In particular, there was a region shaped like an upturned anvil that had been occupied by the Croat–Bosniac alliance that was due to be handed back to the Serbs. This was a substantial area, as large as a medium-sized English county such as Leicestershire or Warwickshire. For the interim period between D+45 and D+90, we would be responsible for all the functions of government in the 'Anvil' – and in other areas where the IEBL did not tally with the ceasefire line – including security, policing, justice, civil administration and reconstruction. Many of the bridges had been destroyed, and the Royal Engineers enjoyed themselves putting in new ones. There is only one thing that engineers love more than building bridges, and that's blowing them up.

I had the Dayton Agreement and the accompanying IFOR statement of procedures translated into a set of orders which I gave to each of the factions, saying: Here, this is what you have to do and when. By D+30 forces would have to have withdrawn outside of what was called the 'Zone of Separation' (ZOS), 2 kilometres either side of the agreed ceasefire line. In the first few days, there were some exchanges of small-arms fire as each side took a last shot at the other, or – very occasionally – some bunch decided to have a go at us. But by and large the whole thing went more smoothly than we had dared hope. During these early days we were obliged to open fire on a number of occasions, but apart from one or two firefights on the cease-fire line, it was never very serious. Usually the trouble was sorted out at company commander level. But there were other risks. About a month after D-Day, a mine left over from the war detonated under one of our armoured vehicles, resulting in the deaths of a young officer and two of his soldiers.

The military annex to Dayton provided for a mechanism known as the Joint Military Commission, or Commissions: meetings between the faction commanders – both at national level, in Sarajevo, and locally, in each of the three areas. I called my first commission meeting on the morning of D+3, when I met for the first time the local big cheeses, so-called 'corps commanders' as they styled themselves, who were going to be part of my life for the next six months. There was no blueprint for these meetings, and to a large extent we were forced to make up the rules as we went along. The atmosphere was bound to be extremely tense, considering that these characters had only very recently been fighting each other.

The first meeting was held at a tented site astride the ceasefire line in the Vrbas valley, about halfway between Gornji Vakuf and Banja Luka and close to a big hydroelectric dam which by some miracle had kept functioning throughout the conflict. We assembled in a gloomily lit tent around four trestle tables arranged in a square. It was a cold day, with a bitter wind that kept the tent flapping throughout. With me were my Chief of Staff Andrew Ritchie and two or three others, including of course our interpreter. The Bosnian Serb side was led by General Momir Talic, commander of the 1st Krajina Corps: a short man with a deceptively easy-going, almost avuncular manner, who would later be indicted for war crimes by the International Criminal Tribunal for Yugoslavia (ICTY). His Croat opposite number was the bullet-headed Brigadier General

Zeljko Glasnovic, who spoke disarmingly perfect English and who, I later learned, had served as an NCO in the Canadian Army. The commander of the Bosniac forces in the Bihac pocket was another large man, General Atif Dudakovic, who regarded himself as a Balkan Rommel. Accompanying him was General Mehmed Aligic, a crude, sexist and bombastic individual. Aligic later attempted to bribe me over lunch, at which point I got up and walked out.

I was determined to stamp our authority on these individuals from the start, to show them that the days of the soggy UNPROFOR mandate were over. We were not going to permit them to intimidate us or to dictate the agenda. I decided that this first meeting should be on a strictly formal basis. Status was everything to such people. Instead of going out to greet them as they arrived in their convoys, I waited for them inside the tent. The faction commanders were compelled to surrender their weapons to British military police before entering. As each party arrived there were rather a lot of hard stares, but they all sat around the same square of tables. We had arranged that once all three parties were settled in the tent, armoured vehicles would drive past and then come back again several times over, to give the impression that we had far more of these than we in fact possessed. It was all part of the attempt to impress on them that we were in charge. The device worked almost too well, in that it was difficult to hear what was being said above the rumble of the passing vehicles.

I opened the meeting, speaking slowly and emphasizing my words. 'I'm not interested in the past,' I told them, 'and this is not a discussion forum. I'm here to tell you what your political leaders have agreed at Dayton and how we're going to implement this.'

I emphasized that this was a NATO operation, and whatever might have happened in the past, NATO did 'joined-up soldiering'. They weren't going to be able to play on differences between the different nationalities as they had done with UNPROFOR.

The reactions were difficult to discern, but I carried on, eyeballing each man in turn. 'Orders are orders, gentlemen,' I said in conclusion.

The Joint Military Commission went into formal session as often as necessary. In those early days it was once every ten days or so, but as things settled the intervals became longer. But of course I met each of the individual commanders regularly on a one-to-one basis, over many, many long, large and liquid Balkan lunches – all part of confidence-building, listening to their complaints, assessing whether these were legitimate and if so what we might do to help, trying to diminish their fears of being caught unawares by a resumption of hostilities.

While we had no hard evidence that any of these individuals had been involved in dark deeds, we inevitably had concerns. However, we had to do business with these people to make Dayton work.

In the latter days of the war, while soldiers from Croatia itself were heading up the Vrbas valley, Dudakovic had fought a critical battle at Sanski Most, only 25 miles or so west of Banja Luka. The planned pincer movement had been curtailed by Dayton. But pretty soon afterwards the erstwhile allies had fallen out. The Bosnian Croat forces were due to have withdrawn from Kulan Vakuf, a small village about 20 miles south of Bihac. In the days immediately before the deadline they seemed very reluctant to fulfil their obligation. The stocky Dudakovic responded in the typical Balkan way: thumping the table and shouting, 'This means war.' His forces began to move south towards the Croats, and we deployed to block them. We also put together a formal operation to evict the Croats if it came to that, and we manoeuvred in a very obvious way to show that we were serious. We were concerned, but I was confident that we could handle the situation, however the parties behaved.

Dudakovic's table-thumping was best understood as typical Balkan bombast, a piece of theatre rather than a real declaration of intent. The incident continued over several days, running up to the deadline. The Croats withdrew with only a few hours to spare.

I was lucky enough to have an excellent and highly intelligent interpreter, Elizabeth Soldo. The relationship with an interpreter is a very close one, because you spend a lot of time together, and it's crucial that it works well, because nuance is often everything when negotiating. Though a Bosnian Croat, Elizabeth accompanied me everywhere, even into Bosnian Serb territory, which obviously involved an extra element of risk for her personally. Not being able to communicate directly with those with whom one was dealing had some advantages, in that it gave one extra 'thinking time' in situations which often required careful consideration and in which a careless remark might easily have proved inflammatory.

Our final timeline would be D+120, when all forces were due to return to barracks and all heavy weapons had to be assembled in what were known as 'cantonment' areas, an expression straight out of British India. Once corralled, the weapons would be subject to IFOR inspection, to ensure that they remained so.

By D+30 the factions were required to release their prisoners of war, each to the other, and predictably they were all very worried that they might release the prisoners they held without getting their own people back from the other side. One large exchange was due to take place right on the confrontation line, on the main road between Banja Luka and Gornji Vakuf, in the valley of the River Vrbas. This was really an International Red Cross (ICRC) function, but we were providing security and for obvious reasons we tried to help. The prisoners were brought up to either side of the confrontation line in buses. Families were waiting there for them to be released: women in headscarves, elderly mothers, children, fathers and brothers. But then the officials from each side started to argue about how many prisoners were there, comparing the numbers on the buses with their lists of those missing. The ICRC did their absolute best to broker the deal, but in vain. Neither side could bring itself to trust the other. So the buses turned around and drove away again, the prisoners pressing their faces against the windows in the hope of glimpsing their loved ones, the families completely distraught.

I had an early warning of what we were up against on the morning of D-Day itself, 20 December 1995. That day 4 Brigade set up a deliberate operation to move into Serb-held territory. The main road north led down the valley of the River Vrbas through a spectacular gorge, before emerging on to the plain around Banja Luka, the biggest and most significant town in Republika Srpska. In the last days of the war, Croatian forces had launched a major offensive in this direction, pushing the Serbs back and threatening to advance down the Vrbas valley towards Banja Luka itself. As our soldiers were getting ready to move down the valley, I noticed three bodies lying in a field quite close to the road ahead. There was something strange about them. Looking through the binoculars I could see that they were soldiers: all three were face down, their trousers around their ankles. I asked one of the local interpreters what this meant. He explained that these were Serb soldiers who had been buggered before, during or after the moment of death – almost certainly by withdrawing Croat forces.

Liberal-minded people from civilized Western countries struggled to comprehend the savagery unleashed in the Balkans when Yugoslavia began to fissure. Such passionate loathing between different ethnic groups is outside the experience of most of us. In our largely secular Western world, religious fanaticism is anachronistic. These ethnic antagonisms seemed a throwback to earlier, more primitive periods in the distant past. In the Balkans, though, the past is the present – yet not, I fervently hope, the future. I learned not to be surprised when Bosnian Serbs referred to Muslims as 'Turks', for example, or when locals cited battles from past centuries as if they had occurred the day before. There is a sad parallel with the attitudes I had encountered in Northern Ireland, where the Protestants could provoke the Catholics to violence by celebrating battles that had taken place three hundred years earlier.

As time passed, we uncovered further grisly evidence of war crimes. The ICTY sent representatives to the area, to take forensic evidence and carry out exhumations. It was our job to protect them, because inevitably there were people around who did not want this evidence to come to light. I remember going up to Prijedor, a mining town about 25 miles north-west of Banja Luka, in the centre of the region where many of the worst atrocities had taken place. It was a very unpleasant feeling to be in an area where such terrible crimes had so recently been committed. The Chief of Police was himself a pretty distasteful character, very rude, very loud and bombastic – so much so, indeed, that he was told to quieten down by some of his own town worthies. This man was later indicted by the ICTY, thus becoming a 'Pifwic' (person indicted for war crimes). He and another man were the targets of the first Pifwic arrest operation, after I'd left Bosnia. He attempted to pull a gun and was killed by British Special Forces.

The two most notorious Pifwics were of course Ratko Mladic and the Bosnian Serb 'President', Radovan Karadzic. Later IFOR would be heavily criticized for not having arrested them in the early days of its mandate. Both men had gone into hiding after the indictments had been served, though we would receive the occasional report that one or other of them had been seen. But in the early months of IFOR's deployment the political situation remained delicate, with the NATO chain of command reluctant to do anything that might jeopardize the fragile peace that had so recently come into being. Both Mladic and Karadzic were believed to be hiding in the American-controlled area, and the Americans were very nervous about mounting operations that might put their soldiers at risk. IFOR originally stipulated that soldiers might arrest Pifwics 'in the normal course of their duties', but that no special operation would be mounted to arrest them for the time being. Given that these two indicted war criminals are still at large, I believe that IFOR should have been bolder when it had the greatest authority, immediately after the handover from the UN to NATO.

Two or three days after D-Day, I received an invitation via our Special Forces people from Rajko Kasagic, the so-called 'Prime Minister' of Republika Srpska, to go and meet him in Banja Luka, the following morning if possible. This seemed to me a remarkable opportunity. There was a tendency for the Bosnian Serbs to be regarded as denizens of the outer darkness. But we had already recognized that there was real political rivalry between the more moderate Bosnian Serb faction in Banja Luka and Karadzic's more extreme faction in Pale. It was clear which side should be encouraged. So I decided to go. I checked with the helicopter crew beforehand whether they were happy to take me, given that Serb territory was potentially hostile. They had no hesitation. We flew up the Vrbas valley and out on to the snow-covered plain, heading towards the city. The best place to land seemed to be the football stadium. Special Forces personnel met us there and drove us to their 'safe house' in the town. After a short briefing we then walked the short distance to Banja Luka town hall, an impressive early twentieth-century building in the local style, to be met by a crowd of local journalists. And that's where I met the Bosnian Serb Prime Minister, a man in his fifties who seemed a decent fellow with moderate views. We held a civilized private meeting, away from the press, accompanied by just a few aides and translators. It was the first bit of direct liaison with the Serb civil authorities that I had been able to achieve, and it was encouraging.

Before we'd even deployed to Bosnia, we'd done some careful thinking about where to site our HQ. The existing regional UNPROFOR Headquarters was sited in Gornji Vakuf, a small town with no airstrip. The result was that we had to slog by helicopter over the mountains from Gornji Vakuf to get to an airport capable of taking fixed-wing aircraft at Sarajevo or Split. Flying to and fro by helicopter was often difficult and sometimes, if the weather closed in, impossible. I frequently had to continue a journey by mountain road when the helicopter carrying me could not continue, and even then it was not always straightforward. I vividly remember flying back from Sarajevo on one occasion when the weather closed in. It was getting dark, and snow began to fall so heavily that visibility was reduced to zero. The helicopter pilot did his best, but it wasn't safe to continue. He put us down at Vitez, a British base, where we borrowed a couple of Land Rovers and continued on the unmetalled road over the mountains. It wasn't long before we were bogged down. Major General Jackson could be found outside in the cold and dark in the middle of nowhere, pushing with all his might to get the vehicle out of a snow drift.

As a rule we used a pair of Land Rover Discoverys, perhaps the ideal vehicle for the purpose. My capable driver Sergeant Jim Heron was an example of that modern phenomenon, the soldier married to the soldier: as circumstances extraordinarily had it, his wife was also deployed to Bosnia and was working in a base only a mile or two from our HQ in Gornji Vakuf. Not wanting to embarrass the Herons, I asked another soldier whether they were able to see each other from time to time. 'Indeed they are, Sir,' came the reply, 'and, before you ask, the romantic rendezvous is the back of your Discovery!'

The other two Divisional Headquarters were both in sizeable towns with airfields big enough to take fixed-wing aircraft, the French in Mostar and the Americans in Tuzla, but neither of these two, nor – once the IEBL was in place – the Force Headquarters in Sarajevo, was on the Serb side. The obvious place for us to site our HQ was therefore in Banja Luka. It was a political as well as a practical move that we were contemplating. Of course it was sensitive to site a NATO HQ on Serb-controlled territory, because NATO had bombed and shelled Serb forces; but if we could pull it off, this would inevitably diminish the influence of the hard-line Mladic/Karadzic faction in Pale. If Dayton was to work properly, the centre of gravity within Republika Srpska had to shift towards Banja Luka. Kasagic knew this, and was therefore very keen for us to come to his 'capital'. I handled the negotiations personally, because of their sensitivity. Eventually, after much looking, we found the Banja Luka Metal Factory, about 5 miles north of the city centre, which seemed ideal for our needs. It had an office block, a big industrial canteen, a huge hangar-like building where we could store equipment under cover, space outside to build a helipad, and a security fence. Under the Dayton Agreement IFOR had the right to requisition property without payment, but we felt that this was not the best way to win friends and influence people, so I negotiated a price. Something like half a million Deutschmarks (then about £150,000) was required to secure the deal. Then I spoke by satellite radio to the man with the money: my Civil Secretary, Simon Wren. Simon paid our bills, ran our locally employed workforce and answered the plethora of MPs' Questions forwarded by the MOD, managing it all with great aplomb. 'Simon,' I said, 'we've got the Metal Factory, can you get up here today with some cash?' From that moment on we were in business, with a headquarters in Republika Srpska – which is still in use today.

We decided to mark our arrival in Banja Luka by giving a reception, done in the best British Army style: Pimm's, canapés, a military band and a free-fall parachute display by the Red Devils. The British Ambassador came, the local politicians came, the military came: it certainly put us on the map in our new location.

Another tick in the box for the Metal Factory was that it was only twenty minutes' drive from Banja Luka airport. This had been closed for some years as a result of the war, but we hoped that it could be re-opened. I drove up to take a look at the place late one January afternoon, just as it was starting to get dark. The airport manager was amazed to see us, and even turned on the runway lights for our inspection. The airstrip was big enough to take RAF Hercules aircraft, and the RAF liaison officer inside my own headquarters, Squadron Leader Steve Smith, was tasked to get it up and running. A few weeks later there was another great extravaganza: the formal re-opening of Banja Luka Airport, known to us as Banja Luka International.

A succession of VIPs arrived in an almost daily flow. I remember in particular the then Prime Minister, John Major, changing out of his suit into casual clothes in one of the offices at the Metal Factory before coming out to see the soldiers.

I learned much from my experiences in Bosnia that was to prove invaluable later on in Kosovo. In particular, the experience of administering the 'Anvil' and other such areas, where for a limited period there would be no machinery of government or security, stood me in very good stead.

I use the analogy of a rope to describe peace support operations in a post-conflict situation. The provision of security is only one strand; the other strands are political progress, humanitarian aid, demobilization of the factions' armies, reconstruction and economic progress. Once the strands are woven together, the rope is stronger than the sum of its parts. It's essential to demonstrate that, for the vast majority of people, the future is going to be better than the past.

I spent a lot of time with the local media, giving interviews and doing phone-ins, spreading the message that IFOR was here to ensure that war didn't restart, and to help people rebuild their lives.

In fostering political progress we were lucky to have the assistance and support of Carl Bildt, who had succeeded Kofi Annan as SRSG. Carl is a Swede, a thoughtful, bespectacled character, a very experienced and impressive man and a great internationalist. Before coming to the Balkans as SRSG he had been Prime Minister of Sweden. I got to know him early on when he arrived unannounced at our Gornji Vakuf HQ after bad weather had curtailed his helicopter flight. We were in the middle of a farewell lunch for some of our staff officers and invited him to join us. A good discussion over lunch and a glass or two of wine followed, after which Sergeant Jim Heron drove him to Sarajevo. It was a good start to our working relationship, and we went on happily from there. Unlike us, Carl had virtually to beg, steal and borrow what he needed to do his job. He also had to contend with an attitude in IFOR's senior leadership which very largely shunned any civil dimension – which again I found difficult to understand. It was clear that not all shared my analogy of the strands of the rope. There was a lesson here which would prove invaluable in Kosovo a few years later.

For the Brits at least, the dual-track approach of military and civil measures was a given. There is a deep understanding in the British Army of how to run a post-conflict situation – or, to use an expression which, at least latterly, has been anathema to the Americans: how to nation-build. This understanding was shared by the Overseas Development Agency (ODA), then a sub-set of the Foreign Office, which had a positive, can-do approach and welcomed partnership with the military. Sadly, the ODA is no more. It has been replaced by the Department for International Development (DfID), which has a rather different culture – although to be fair the Department is constrained by the Act under which it was formed to 'the relief of poverty'.

We were lucky that the ODA sent out a consultant called

Gilbert Greenall to handle the civil reconstruction dimension. Gilbert is a man of many parts: doctor, pilot, landowner and a reconstructor of vast experience who has made a special study of post-conflict situations. He was probably worth a battalion or more in terms of the effect he achieved. His key point is that you've got to get a move on: the first hundred days is when you'll get it right or fail. If you can show the local population the prospect of a better future in that crucial early period, you have your best chance of winning them over.

We had a modest amount of money from the ODA for local development and rehabilitation projects: putting a roof back on the local school, for example, or reconnecting the water supply to a village. Gilbert Greenall instituted a very simple system, requiring the minimum of paperwork. The local commanding officer would identify a project and Gilbert would authorize it. Whenever possible we would get local workmen to do the work, so that we spent the money in a way that would benefit the local economy.

The 3rd Division's tour with IFOR finished at the end of June 1996, seven months after the Dayton Agreement. Afterwards I received many gratifying letters of congratulation on what we had achieved in Bosnia. Among those who wrote in such terms were the Prime Minister, John Major, and the Secretary of State, Michael Portillo. He was kind enough to mention my 'outstanding contribution to the civil effort'. According to him, we had shown 'a remarkable degree of sensitivity and even-handedness' and had 'established excellent relations with all three communities'. I also received several such letters from senior figures in the Army. I replied to one of these, a letter from the then CDS, Lord Inge, reflecting on the uncertainty in the months before my deployment, and telling him that I was pleased to have commanded a multinational force rather than UNPROFOR. 'I did not relish the prospect of keeping UNPROFOR on the road when just about every ploy had been tried,' I wrote. 'It may have cost me a bob or two. Far better to have commanded Multinational Division South-West under IFOR with its thoroughly positive objective.'

I was honoured to be appointed a Commander of the Most Honourable Order of the Bath in recognition of my services in Bosnia. Three years later I would receive a knighthood, the Knight Commander of the Bath – the so-called 'Deep End of the Bath'.

Already things were beginning to return to normal in Bosnia, and in the intervening eleven and a half years there has been no renewed outbreak of serious conflict. There is still an international force in Bosnia, now under EU rather than NATO auspices; Britain's contribution has been scaled right back to a handful of staff officers. Bosnia, which threatened to expose the impotence of Western governments, has so far proved a notable success.

And so the day came – D+189 – to hand over to HQ 1 (UK) Armoured Division under the command of Major General John Kiszeley. A little research showed that it was the first occasion on which one British Divisional HQ had relieved another in the field since the closing stages of the Second World War. John and I shook hands. I wished him luck and drove to the airport.

We had managed to arrange for a very smart BAe-146, a thirty-seater jet used mainly by the Royal Family and Government ministers, to take the command group home, flying from Banja Luka International directly to Boscombe Down. I thought we deserved it, since most of us had hardly seen our families for six months or more, other than a few days' break mid-tour. I did a round of farewells beforehand, when bottles of slivovic were pressed upon me at every turn. Many of these were consumed on the flight home, to the slight discomfiture of the cabin staff. It was a happy return.

11

Back to the Balkans

'I hope duties on Salisbury Plain do not seem too tame after Bosnia,' Carl Bildt wrote after I had left. In fact, my time with the 3rd Division was up: my original two-year appointment had already been extended by four months or so because of the Bosnia deployment. In August 1996, little more than a month after arriving back from the Balkans, I handed over to my successor, Major General Cedric Delves. As usual, there was a light-hearted ceremony to mark my departure. There is a picture of me in the 3rd Division's in-house magazine standing on the passenger seat of a camouflaged car, my upper half projecting through a hole in its roof, a glass of wine in my hand, watched by the amused staff. 'While Major General Jackson familiarises himself with the cupola of his new staff car,' the caption reads, 'his ADC, Captain Rory Gilbert, realises that the car has no brakes.' Afterwards volunteers towed the knackered vehicle to a farewell lunch.

I took a few weeks' leave after handing over, and we flew with Tom, then six years old, to Namibia for a holiday. Sarah and I both felt the need to get away from it all, and re-engage with each other after almost seven months' separation. All Service families know from experience that it is not always easy to settle back into family life after an operational tour – and that it's not going to happen overnight.

Then in September I began my next appointment, as Director General, Development and Doctrine, head of the Army's think tank at Upavon, on the north side of Salisbury Plain. We were busy revising our concept for peace support operations in the light of the NATO Bosnian experience, work which would prove useful to me later on in Kosovo. But I didn't have too long to think, because quite soon after taking up this post I received the welcome news that I would be succeeding Mike Walker as Commander of NATO's Allied Rapid Reaction Corps (ARRC), headquartered at Rheindahlen, near Düsseldorf. This entailed promotion to lieutenant general, the rank I would have assumed fourteen months earlier had I taken command of UNPROFOR towards the end of 1995.

And so we moved to Germany early in 1997. This was our seventh move in twelve years of marriage (by the time I left the Army in late 2006, the score was ten moves in twenty-one years, a rather better average).

One of the travel guides to Germany describes Rheindahlen as 'Little England', which says it all. Within this British Army base – the largest in Germany – there is in many ways a self-contained community, with all the facilities families need inside the wire. Foster House was one of the two generals' 'residences' set in woodland in the grounds of Wegburg Hospital, formerly one of the main military hospitals for British Forces Germany. A psychiatric unit remained, and we would occasionally see men in white coats walking patients in the hospital gardens. We were a short distance from the headquarters complex in Rheindahlen, and Tom would more often than not bike with Sarah through the woods to one of the three excellent British Forces primary schools on the main camp.

The ARRC had left Bosnia in November 1996, IFOR's role in Bosnia being taken over by a new NATO-led Force, SFOR, the Stabilization Force. A number of non-NATO countries contributed units to both IFOR and SFOR – including Russia. Thus Russian soldiers were serving under NATO command, only a few years after the ending of the Cold War. We had certainly come a long way in a short time. The Russians had a longstanding interest in Serbia, going back at least a century, and it was Russian support for Serbia that had started the dominoes falling in the summer of 1914. Since the West was trying to persuade Serbia to act responsibly as part of the international community, it seemed right to involve the Russians, with whom the Serbs had such well-established historical ties.

For the NATO nations, the gruesome civil war in the Balkans had been a searing experience, cruelly dashing the hopes raised by the ending of the Cold War. In 1992 a young American academic, Francis Fukuyama, had earnestly pronounced 'The End of History', prophesying the inexorable spread of Western liberal democracy throughout the world. Even those who judged this theory naïve had not predicted the eruption of primitive ethnic struggle within Europe itself. It rapidly became clear that the Cold War had contained ancient tensions, not destroyed them. Well might one Balkan specialist entitle his book *The Re-Birth of History*. Places that had seemed docile backwaters for almost a century were revealed as seething with ethnic hatred. For those trying to make sense of the post-Cold War world, it was back to the future.

The ARRC had emerged from the re-appraisals that followed the end of the Cold War. It was clear that NATO's structures had to change as a result to reflect the transformed situation. Much of the Alliance's organizational structure had been designed to fight the Warsaw Pact on the German plains, as part of the general defence plan for northern Europe. After this threat evaporated, there was a realization that NATO was going to need a more expeditionary capability, able to operate over long distances, and to this end the Rapid Reaction Corps had been created, devoid of any responsibility for territorial defence in Germany. It is in essence a Corps Headquarters of around four hundred permanent staff, a head to which a number of bodies can be attached. The ARRC Commander (COMARRC) does not command a substantial force on a permanent basis. But when the need arises, the contributing NATO nations will generate forces to come under his direct command, for the purposes of that specific deployment – as happened in Bosnia.

A parallel process of adjustment took place within the British Army, reflecting the shift in its focus from fighting a land war on the grand scale to mounting operations right across the spectrum of conflict, of greater or lesser intensity, from large-scale conventional warfare to modest humanitarian missions. Peace support operations seemed likely to form a priority for the future – an area in which the British Army was especially well qualified, for it had been pursuing what was essentially a peace support operation in Northern Ireland for the past quarter of a century. At the same time it was thought to be essential to maintain our full war-fighting skills at a high level. As with NATO as a whole, there was a shift of emphasis towards a more expeditionary capability, which implied a greater emphasis on joint operations with the other Services. These changes of role necessitated changes in attitudes, affecting every soldier from private to general. British soldiers were going to have to be yet more flexible and yet more resourceful in dealing with the more varied challenges of the future.

In peacetime, individual nations assign divisions to the ARRC for command and control training, but though we devised command post exercises to train their headquarters, we didn't get involved in field training, since they remained under their national commands. And so we had a constituency, with which we formed a close training relationship. My first year with the ARRC was spent working hard on getting our war-fighting skills back up to speed, following the Bosnia peace support operation. If and when the ARRC deployed on another operation, it would be up to each individual nation to decide under the particular circumstances what force contribution it would make, if any. Under Article 5 of the original North Atlantic Treaty, an attack on one member state is considered an attack upon all. This is the superglue of the Alliance. But since the end of the Cold War we've been in non-Article 5 territory, intervening outside the NATO area, and an individual nation can decide not to take part in one of these operations if it chooses – even if that nation's permanent representative (in effect, its ambassador to NATO) on the North Atlantic Council has agreed that NATO should take on this task.

When the ARRC HQ was formed in the mid-1990s, the UK volunteered to become the so-called 'framework nation', providing much of the funding and many of the staff, including the Commander. The first COMARRC had been Lieutenant General Jeremy Mackenzie, second-in-command of the Queen's Own Highlanders at the time of Warrenpoint and Deputy Commandant of the Staff College when I was on the Higher Command and Staff Course. He had been succeeded by Mike Walker, and I was the third COMARRC. The success of the ARRC concept has led to several other such HQs being formed within NATO; but in the late 1990s we were the only one of our kind.

HQ ARRC is supported by a small permanent force of specialist soldiers from the UK as framework nation: a signal brigade of two communications regiments, and one support battalion to handle all the admin and logistics, including tentage, vehicles, food, rations, fuel and so on. But on deployment the HQ is designed to command a very large force of corps dimensions (approximately fifty thousand soldiers). The ARRC insignia is a spearhead, signifying that the Corps' role is to be the leading element, the sharp point of the weapon. Its motto is 'Audentis Fortuna Iuvat', meaning 'Fortune Favours the Brave'.

The ARRC HQ is under operational command of the Supreme Allied Commander, Europe (SACEUR), and as COMARRC I therefore reported directly to him. The post of SACEUR is always filled by an American four-star general, reflecting the preponderance of American military might within NATO. He is so-called 'double-hatted', because he also holds the national post of Commander in Chief, US European Command (CINCEUR). When I took up my appointment these two jobs were held by General George Joulwan, whom I had come to know quite well while in Bosnia. He was a large, outgoing man, a soldier's soldier, and I found it easy to get on with him. Quite soon afterwards, in the summer of 1997, he came to the end of his term and was replaced by General Wesley 'Wes' Clark.

Wes Clark was something of a loner, a driven, intensely ambitious man with a piercing stare. Often described as 'tightly wound', he seemed to bring a disturbing zeal to his work. He had a reputation as a very political sort of general, antagonizing his military superiors by going over their heads when they did not give him what he wanted. He was not popular among many of his colleagues in the US Army, who knew him as the 'Perfumed Prince'. Like Bill Clinton he had adopted his stepfather's name, and like Bill Clinton he came from Little Rock, Arkansas. A Vietnam veteran, Wes Clark was a highly educated man – and, again like Bill Clinton, a former Rhodes Scholar. Shorter than average, wiry and youthful-looking in his midfifties, he was not a man who relaxed easily.

On Clark's first visit to the ARRC HQ at Rheindahlen, we briefed him on the lessons learned from the Bosnia deployment. When we put up a slide emphasizing the importance of impartiality and even-handedness, Clark reacted sharply. 'You cannot be impartial where the Serbs are concerned,' he declared. I was taken aback, because all our thinking was contrary to what he was saying. I had plenty of reasons to mistrust Serb leaders like Mladic, but I had also encountered Serbs who had behaved reasonably in very difficult circumstances. I had found that if you dealt in a straight manner with men like Kasagic, they reciprocated. Nor did I think the other sides without blemish: on the contrary, all my experience in the Balkans led me to believe that there was not much to choose between them. But even then, Clark seemed to see the Balkans in very black-and-white terms.

Clark remained deeply involved with developments in Bosnia, so much so that, as I learned afterwards, Jeremy Mackenzie – by now Deputy SACEUR (DSACEUR) – had felt the need to counsel him against interfering so closely and so often with the commanders on the ground. 'The boys are grumbling a bit,' Jeremy warned him. 'You really ought to leave them to it.'

In May 1998, we NATO commanders gathered at SHAPE for SACEUR's annual conference. During the conference Clark called a lunchtime meeting for his key subordinates. 'Things are beginning to hot up in Kosovo,' he told us. 'NATO may have to intervene.'

For years, informed observers had been warning of a potential bloodbath in Kosovo. This was where the break-up of Yugoslavia would reach its climax.

Kosovo is felt by Serbs to be the homeland of their nation. Many of their beautiful medieval Orthodox monasteries are located there. 'Wipe away Kosovo from the Serb mind and soul,' wrote the Yugoslav writer, politician and theorist Milovan Djilas, 'and we are no more.' In 1389 the Serbs had fought the Ottomans at the battle of Kosovo Polje, also known as the Field of the Blackbirds, suffering a heroic defeat that looms large in the national mythology: Serbs see themselves as Christians in the front line of the millennium-long struggle with Islam. Kosovo became, and for more than five hundred years remained, part of the Ottoman Empire, before being briefly reconquered by Serbia in the early twentieth century. At the end of the First World War, Kosovo became part of the new kingdom of Yugoslavia. Under Tito's post-war Communist rule, it then became a province of Serbia, one of the new republics within the federal system. Nevertheless Kosovo enjoyed a degree of autonomy, and ethnic tensions were kept in check.

Kosovo is small, less than half the area of Northern Ireland, though with a similar-sized population. It is strategically important, being a landlocked plain, almost surrounded by mountain ranges. High mountains ring Kosovo on its northern border with Montenegro, on its western border with Albania and on its southern border with Macedonia.* It is only on the eastern side, the Serbian side, that the ground is relatively open.

Like the Serbs, the Albanians also consider Kosovo important as the cradle of their own national movement. The proportion of the indigenous Kosovar population that is ethnically Albanian had been increasing steadily for many decades, and by the late 1990s had reached almost 90 per cent. Yet despite the demographic predominance of the Albanian Kosovars, most of the official positions were taken by Serbs, who dominated the security forces in particular. Kosovo was ruled as if it were a Serb colony. Ethnic Albanians in Kosovo speak a different language from the Serbs, a form of Albanian; and their religion is Islam, in contrast to the Christian Serbs.

After the death of Tito in 1980, Serb concern about the 'Albanianization' of Kosovo fuelled the rise of Serbian nationalism within Yugoslavia, and was skilfully exploited by Slobodan Milosevic in his rise to power. It was Serb nationalism that provided the pretext for the republics to start breaking away from federal Yugoslavia in the early 1990s. Thus it was said that

* The Former Yugoslav Republic of Macedonia, officially known by its initials FYROM, because of Greek objections to the use of the name Macedonia, which is also the name of the northern province of Greece. *Pace* Athens, Macedonia is used in this text out of convenience.

'the break-up of Yugoslavia began in Kosovo, and would end in Kosovo'. When he became President in 1989, Milosevic began the process of stripping Kosovo of the autonomy the province had enjoyed under the Yugoslav federal system. The result was to stimulate a movement for Kosovan independence. For some years in the 1990s, the Albanian Kosovars maintained their own parallel administrative structures under the benign leadership of Ibrahim Rugova, who advocated non-violent resistance to Serb rule. But not all were content with this approach, and in the mid-1990s the Kosovo Liberation Army (KLA, known also by its Albanian acronym, UCK) was formed and began a guerrilla campaign against the Serb security forces.

The KLA received support from Albania itself and from ethnic Albanians abroad, particularly in the United States, and by the summer of 1998 claimed to have thirty thousand men under arms. Clashes between the KLA and the Serb security forces intensified. A pattern began of KLA attacks and heavy-handed Serb reprisals, often involving civilian casualties. Ethnic Albanians fled the Serb security forces; by the autumn there were estimated to be several hundred thousand internal refugees living in the woods, and the prospect of a humanitarian disaster loomed. Richard Holbrooke warned Milosevic against repression in Kosovo and allowed himself to be photographed alongside KLA fighters, indicating American support for the KLA. On 23 September the UN adopted Security Council Resolution 1199 calling for a ceasefire and dialogue between the warring parties. It also called for a withdrawal of Serb security forces used for repression, particularly the Serb Army, the Vojska Jugoslavia (VJ), and the Serb special police (MUP).

Back in Rheindahlen, we tracked all these developments very closely. As the summer of 1998 turned to autumn, the odds began to shorten on an ARRC deployment to Kosovo. We carried out a series of increasingly complex planning exercises, from which emerged a clear concept of the ideal composition

and structure of a peace implementation force. At one stage in the autumn there was an absurd proposal for HQ ARRC alone to deploy to Kosovo, which would have left us exposed as potential hostages, just as UNPROFOR had been. Mercifully, this idea came and went almost overnight. We decided that, prior to entry into Kosovo, our in-theatre HQ should be sited near the Macedonian capital Skopje, only about 10 miles from the Kosovo border. Our line of communication would be from the Greek port of Thessaloniki, about 150 miles to the south, connected by a good, motorway-style road and a railway line. There were political difficulties, in that there was tension between Greece and Macedonia – not least over the name 'Macedonia' – but this seemed the only sensible supply route. The alternative through Albania, although shorter, was much less attractive, given that country's rudimentary infrastructure, inadequate ports and poor road network. There was also reason to think that the Albanian bridges could not support the weight of tanks and other armoured vehicles.

In October Holbrooke visited Milosevic, and came back with a deal. Faced with the threat of NATO air strikes, Milosevic offered concessions, and agreed to allow into Kosovo a two-thousand-strong force of unarmed observers, known as the Kosovo Verification Mission (KVM). Within NATO there was little faith that this deal would outlast the winter. We sent in a recce party, disguised as members of the KVM, who provided us with intelligence reports, both political and military.

In fact there was never a complete ceasefire, and towards the end of the year the fighting intensified. NATO deployed eighteen hundred troops to Kumanovo in northern Macedonia, ready to extract the KVM from Kosovo at short notice if they seemed threatened. There was already an American battalion in Macedonia, 'Task Force Able Sentry', stationed there some years before with a mission to deter Serbian aggression and, very unusually for US troops, serving under UN auspices.

In mid-January 1999, reports of a massacre of ethnic Albanians by the Serb security forces in the southern Kosovan village of Racak evoked memories of Srebrenica and prompted calls for NATO intervention. Talks between Serbs and Kosovar Albanians, organized by the so-called 'Contact Group' of France, Germany, Italy, Russia, the UK and the United States, took place at Rambouillet, near Paris. The proposed agreement provided for an independent military implementation force under NATO auspices to compel compliance. Four countries – Britain, Germany, France and Italy – decided to deploy battalion-sized forces to Macedonia on a nation-by-nation basis, in anticipation of a successful agreement which might then have to be implemented in very short order.

By then I had visited Macedonia several times. The plan was for the ARRC to integrate the various scattered forces there under a single unified NATO command known as KFOR (Kosovo Force). KFOR's outline mission at this stage would be to provide stability in Kosovo following a political settlement, to prevent any further outbreak of fighting, and to ensure the return of all refugees once the Serbs had withdrawn.

By early February we had narrowed down our choice of a headquarters site in the Skopje area to two: the Intercontinental Hotel, which would have been comfortable but was expensive and rather small for our requirements, and might have given out the wrong message; and the 1970s-style Gazela Shoe Factory on the outskirts of the city. This was largely disused, though a little shoe-making was still carried on at one end, even after we had taken over most of the building. Like the Metal Factory at Banja Luka, it had much of what we needed: an office block, a works canteen good for feeding large numbers, warehousing for storage under cover, hard standing outside for parking vehicles, an area where we could site a helipad, and a perimeter fence for security. I had no hesitation in opting for the Shoe Factory, though it meant that we would be living in what had been offices, working and sleeping on camp beds in the same rooms. My team occupied a suite of offices on the upper floor, which included a slightly shabby conference room big enough to accommodate a meeting of thirty people or more. It was all fairly spartan, but none the worse for that. I must admit that I did begin to wonder about my decision later on, when my Chief of Staff, Major General Andrew Ridgway, entered his office to find himself confronted by a large rat. But by then we were committed, and after all it wasn't the first rat we'd encountered on operations, some of whom had only two legs. By early March our Rear Headquarters was already in place, handling the logistics, liaising with the Macedonian government and attempting to corral the various national forces, although no formal command authority had been granted.

One thing still worrying me was the question of my new military assistant. In the middle of 1998, Miles Wade, the MA I had inherited from Mike Walker, had reached the end of his tour. I was given a list of three young lieutenant colonels from which to choose his replacement. None of them had what I was really looking for. I remember telephoning the Military Secretary and asking, 'Is there nobody else?' and his reply: 'I'm afraid not.' So I chose the best of them, as I thought, but with some misgivings.

Some months later, I realized that, for whatever reason, it wasn't working – and eventually, only about ten days before we were due to deploy to Macedonia, and with so much at stake, I told him so. I then telephoned the Military Secretary and said that I wanted the best man on his books by the next Monday morning. Faxes flew back and forth, and pretty soon I had a list with five names on it. Two of them I didn't know and there wasn't time to get to know them, but of the three I did know, one candidate stood out above the rest: James Everard, a scruffy cavalryman (for some, a contradiction in terms) who'd been Richard Dannatt's Brigade Chief of Staff in Bosnia. I'd got to know him very well out there, and I thought him an outstanding young officer: highly intelligent and well read, a lateral thinker, and great fun. So I rang him up. He had just finished a tour in Germany and started a new desk job back in the MOD.

We chatted inconsequentially for a bit, and then there was a pause.

'Very nice to hear from you, General Mike,' he said cheerfully, 'but why on earth are you ringing me up?'

'I'm in a pickle,' I explained. 'I've just had to part company with my previous MA. I'd like to offer you the job. If you're on, it would be great to have you. I think we're off to the Balkans imminently, maybe as soon as a week from now. I cannot promise you a great adventure, but it should be interesting. What do you think?'

'Great idea, General,' he replied. 'But there are one or two difficulties. We've just packed up the house in Germany. All our kit's on the road now, I've put down a thousand quid for young Archie's nursery school in London, and the dog's been in quarantine for four months.'

'OK, James, I get the picture.'

'No,' he said, 'you haven't got the whole picture. Caroline's having twins in August.'

'OK, James. Great to speak to you. Good luck with the new job.'

'Hang on a minute,' he interrupted. 'I'm not saying no, I'm just laying it out for you. Give me half an hour to square it with Caroline and I'll ring you back.'

He called back well within the half-hour. 'OK, General, you're on,' he said. 'But there are one or two things you could do for me.'

'Anything,' I replied, still not quite believing that he had said yes.

'First, get us a decent house in Rheindahlen.'

'Done.'

'Next, can you find Mr Pickford's van and stop it?' And we

did: we actually found it on the autobahn and said, do not go to Calais, turn left, drive to Rheindahlen. We got James his money back for the quarantine fees as well.

'Oh,' he added, 'one more thing.' What now? I thought. 'Can I be home for the twins' birth?'

'Of course,' I said, and that was that. A couple of days later he was at my side in Rheindahlen, and a week after that we were both in Skopje.

By mid-March 1999 the ARRC was established at the Gazela Shoe Factory, and was in the process of coordinating the various national contingents already deployed in Macedonia. At this stage there was still a hope that last-ditch efforts might salvage a diplomatic solution, even though the Serb negotiators at Rambouillet had refused to sign the agreement. Meanwhile, the Serbs in Kosovo began to step up the activity of their security forces. Richard Holbrooke flew to Belgrade in yet another unsuccessful attempt to persuade Milosevic to comply with the demands of the international community. He threatened that if Serbia did not comply, NATO would take military action. The crisis was seen as a test of Europe's ability to deal with problems 'in its own backyard'. For NATO, searching for a new role in its fiftieth anniversary year, this was both a challenge and an opportunity. For almost ten years commentators had been asking whether NATO's unity and resolve would persist after the ending of the Cold War. Here was an issue that could either show the way forward, or expose the weakness of the Alliance now that its original *raison d'être* was no more.

This was a test which threatened the stability of several west European governments, whose ruling parties were deeply divided on the issue. For all of them, the decision to take military action against Serbia was a tough one, but the unacceptable actions of Milosevic's security forces left them with no alternative. Grim stories of ethnic cleansing emerged from Kosovo in a steady stream. American politicians began to use the term 'genocide' to describe what was happening there.

Three former Warsaw Pact nations, the Czech Republic, Hungary and Poland, were in the process of joining NATO, and there was to be a ceremony at Rheindahlen on 19 March to mark their accession. Wes Clark had wanted me to remain 'on the scene' in Macedonia, but I felt that my presence was not absolutely essential at that moment and I wanted to get back home, not just for this important ceremony, but to brief the ARRC families at Rheindahlen on what was happening in the Balkans. It was very important on this occasion for them to hear what was going on from the Commander personally. There had been much uncertainty, much 'on the bus, off the bus', and it was right that they got as realistic a picture as possible from the horse's mouth. People who marry soldiers take on a lot, and the soldiers themselves are far happier when deployed if they know that their loved ones are being properly looked after and kept informed. Despite heavy snow, we managed to reach the community centre in Rheindahlen just in time for the briefing. This was the first of what became a regular monthly event, which our families much appreciated, and which helped to dispel misinformation from whatever source. It was an anxious time for the families, especially for the non-British wives – for many of whom this was their husbands' first operational deployment. I wasn't usually able to attend, of course; the briefings were given by whichever senior officer was available at the time.

The families' briefing was followed by a simple but symbolic ceremony at HQ to mark the accession of the three new NATO nations. But during the day we got the news that the KVM had been directed to withdraw from Kosovo the following day because of the deteriorating security situation. I had to get back to Skopje as soon as possible, in case the KVM withdrawal went wrong.

Captain Ed Sandry, my rock-solid ADC, moved heaven and

earth to get us an aircraft, and managed to wangle us a 'pocket rocket', an RAF HS-125 six-seater executive jet, which had us back in Skopje before midnight. I spent the following morning up at the border crossing-point greeting the withdrawing KVM observers, who arrived in a long stream of orange vehicles; they included some of our own recce party and some familiar Special Forces faces. The number two in the KVM was my old school-mate 'DZ', now Major General John Drewienkiewicz. It was great to see him, and of course we were relieved that everyone in the mission had got out safely. That night they had a celebration dinner in what was known as the 'Ally Pally', the Alexandra Palace Hotel in Skopje. Much red wine was drunk, and in the small hours of the morning I returned to the Shoe Factory feeling ready for whatever the next few days and weeks might bring.

The following day, 21 March, was my fifty-fifth birthday. Because of the sudden ending of the Rambouillet talks two days earlier and the need to get back to meet the KVM observers, we had not had time to collect much of our personal kit, so I decided to fly back to Rheindahlen again for one quick pit stop. By this time it was obvious that we would be going on to a war footing; NATO air strikes were due to commence imminently. We arrived back in Rheindahlen in the evening, and stayed for fourteen hours. I told Sarah that I was unlikely to be back for a while. She knew what that meant: she is a soldier's daughter. Ever practical, she asked me to remind her where all the family documents were kept, 'just to be on the safe side'. When the doorbell rang the next morning, I knew it would be Ed Sandry. I opened the door and told him I'd be with him in a minute. Sarah and I said our goodbyes. I picked up my beret, shouldered my rucksack, walked out to the car and slung it into the boot. Sarah had followed me out, and I gave her one last hug standing by the car. Then I climbed in and we drove away.

*

Two days later, on the evening of 24 March, NATO began air strikes. The bombing campaign dragged on for seventy-seven days, and during this period we in the ARRC were very much in the supporting role, almost spectators. In fact we were concerned about our vulnerability, being so close to the border. A quick attack towards Skopje by Serb units, particularly from Serbia proper down the Presevo valley, would have been a real problem. We were also within range of Serb artillery fire. As time passed and we were reinforced by air into Skopje and by regular convoys by road and rail from Thessaloniki, our fighting strength increased steadily, but at first we had only a few thousand troops to call on, scattered in different locations across northern Macedonia. SHAPE at last agreed to give HQ ARRC a degree of formal command over the various national troop contingents, now developing into five multinational brigades led respectively by France, Germany, Italy, the UK and the United States. As COMKFOR, my immediate superior officer was US Navy Admiral Jim Ellis, NATO's Commander in Chief for Southern Europe (CINC-SOUTH), who in turn reported directly to SACEUR. In practice, Wes Clark often bypassed Jim Ellis and dealt directly with me; this was very frustrating for both Jim and me. I got on very well with Jim, a sympathetic and understanding man who was always supportive. His staff and mine worked easily together – which wasn't always the case with the SHAPE staff.

There was also a concern about assassination attempts. On the day after the bombing commenced, Brigadier General Valentin, the French Brigade commander, was attacked with a Molotov cocktail. He escaped uninjured, though two British soldiers were not so lucky: they were hospitalized when their vehicles were stoned. I had a close protection team of two SAS soldiers, one very tall and one very short – unkindly nicknamed Pinky and Perky – who accompanied me everywhere I went for the next seven months or so. For getting about, we had two dedicated Lynx helicopters.

That same evening a mob attacked both the American Embassy and the Intercontinental Hotel in Skopje, where the KVM was staying. I learned that SACEUR in his national US role had ordered 'Task Force Able Sentry' to the rescue. I spoke to John Craddock, the US Brigade Commander, and advised him to make haste slowly. 'You do not want to become part of the problem,' I suggested. Luckily the Macedonian riot police arrived first and dispersed the mob, which moved off to disport themselves outside the British and German embassies. It seemed to me more than likely that this civil disorder had been orchestrated from Belgrade. The Macedonian Government was rattled, and called an emergency Cabinet meeting that night. Much of my time in the next few weeks would be spent calming them, reassuring them that we had the situation under control. I saw support to the Macedonian Government as fundamental to our operation.

Yet later that same evening we received a SITREP (situation report) from the American battalion that the Serbs had crossed the border. I was sceptical. It emerged that an American U-2 spy plane had mistaken French forces for invading Serbs. I was not at all happy about the confusion, and complained vigorously to Mike Short, the three-star US Air Force commander at the Air HQ of AFSOUTH (Allied Forces Southern Europe) in Vicenza, from which the air strikes were being coordinated. This was the kind of mistake that could have easily led to a 'blue on blue' disaster.

SACEUR was under a lot of pressure. I observed Clark each morning on the video conference (VTC) held twice daily among all the NATO centres involved in the Balkan operation. He seemed tired already, not helped by having to work Washington hours. This was a concern to us all. We knew that Wes was having trouble with his superiors at the Pentagon, many of whom saw little reason for America to become involved in Kosovo. President Clinton's administration had shown itself to be extremely reluctant to commit ground troops to overseas operations. The President declared that he 'had no intent' to use ground troops against the Serbs. But this seemed to make Wes all the more determined. At first he argued that the bombing would bring the Serbs to heel. 'I know Milosevic,' he would say time after time. It was a peculiarity of the Kosovo War that all the main protagonists had met beforehand.

My old friend Rupert Smith had by now succeeded Jeremy Mackenzie as Clark's deputy. He and I spoke at least once a day on the secure phone. Rupert was a moderating influence on Wes, as Jeremy had been before him. When the bombing started, Wes had wanted to come down to inspect personally the arrangements we had made for our defence should the Serbs come across the border. The implication was that we wouldn't know what to do, which didn't go down well with the Headquarters staff. In the end, Rupert persuaded SACEUR that he should come instead. Rupert knew perfectly well that we didn't need any guidance from him or anyone else. He arrived, had a briefing, had lunch with us and then went back to Belgium again without inspecting anything.

Clark's attitude to the Serbs convinced many that he was spoiling for an all-out war. He seemed dangerously stuck in a Cold War mentality of confrontation. At the end of March, he became very excited by reports that the Russians were planning to send warships from their Black Sea Fleet into the Mediterranean. On the morning VTC that day, he declared that they had to be stopped. Jim Ellis was clearly unhappy with this approach. 'What exactly do you want me to do?' he asked.

Clark told him to lean on the Turks to keep the Russians bottled up in the Black Sea by denying them access to their territorial waters.

'SACEUR, I can't do that,' Ellis replied. 'The Montreux Convention guarantees the right of free passage through the Bosphorus.' Clark went on to suggest that he should establish a maritime exclusion zone, rather as we had done in the Falklands. Fortunately nothing came of this.

I had more cause to question Clark's judgement a week or so later, when he asked CINCSOUTH to confirm that he had received a detailed map reference sent the day before. That the Supreme Commander should be personally passing such minutiae to another four-star officer was worrying.

A fortnight or so later, there was another extraordinary piece of rhetoric from Wes on the morning VTC. He gave the kind of gung-ho address the commander of a small unit might give immediately prior to battle, when the soldiers need to be fired up. It was totally inappropriate for a VTC with thirty or forty senior officers in a multinational force, watching in ten or so different locations.

'We are moving to total war,' he announced portentously. 'If there is a battle, it will be tough, very tough, hill to hill, house to house, street to street. It will be bayonets and close combat in guerrilla war. NATO soldiers must relearn the spirit of the bayonet.'

Listening to this stuff back at Skopje, we were all stunned. I glanced at my senior American staff officer, Brigadier General Mike Maples, and I could see that he was staring at the ground.

'Do you understand the spirit of the bayonet?' Clark asked. He addressed one of the German generals on the VTC. 'Klaus, do you understand the spirit of the bayonet?'

The general shifted uneasily. There was an embarrassing pause. 'Oh yes, SACEUR,' he replied eventually.

The next day Clark issued a statement. 'I wish to clarify any misunderstanding that may have arisen from what I said yesterday. All I meant was that the campaign would have administrative implications for NATO's staff vacation plans.'

Word began to get around regarding some of Wes's extraordinary behaviour. I remember a visit to Naples some time that spring, when Jim Ellis had called together a conference in his own Headquarters. At a supper party he gave that evening, I noticed a group of American three-stars in a huddle. 'Is this Americans only or can a Brit join in?' I asked jocularly.

'Of course,' one of them said. 'You'd better come in on this, because we're all having a beef about Wes.' It was alarming to encounter mutterings about Clark's judgement among his American subordinates – not from Ellis, but from those at three-star level and below.

All this took me back to a conversation I'd had in Sarajevo with the commander of SFOR, US Lieutenant General 'Monty' Meigs, not long before the Kosovo operation started. Monty and I had become quite good friends by this point. We were talking generally about the Balkans, and the likelihood of the ARRC being deployed to Kosovo, when Monty came out with an unexpected question. 'Have you thought about how you are going to handle Wes?'

The last of the Red Cross personnel to leave Kosovo painted a grim picture of a breakdown in law and order, with rape, executions and looting taking place on the streets of the capital, Pristina. One young woman broke down as she described finding the sole survivor of a burned-out village, a baby girl trying to feed from a bottle filled with her mother's blood. As the fighting worsened, the prospect of a humanitarian disaster loomed once more. Hundreds of thousands of displaced persons or those fearing for their safety were making their way west and south to the mountainous border regions, hoping to cross into Albania or Macedonia. Others were loaded on to trains by the Serb security forces and shunted to the border, where they were compelled to cross on foot, told to walk down the track because if they strayed off the road they risked walking into a minefield. At the height of the crisis, it was estimated that three-quarters of a million people, approximately one-third of the entire population, had fled Kosovo. The refugees came in waves, sometimes five thousand or more in a day, completely overwhelming the small number of personnel from the UN High Commission for Refugees on hand to provide them with food and shelter. Refugee assistance was not, of course, part of KFOR's mission as stated. But we had to take on the problem – in the first instance, on purely humanitarian grounds; secondly, because it was operationally essential in order to deny Milosevic his political goal, namely the fall of the Macedonian Government.

I was in constant contact with NATO HQ during this period, speaking several times a day to either Rupert Smith or Wes Clark. KFOR did most of the spadework, literally and metaphorically, of establishing the refugee camps, and we ran them until UNHCR and the various NGOs got their act together. We had a handover programme, camp by camp: some-body will take over water, somebody will take over food, somebody will take over medical aid; and then, when they were able to cope with the whole thing, we felt able to leave with a clear conscience. The lion's share of the administrative support for the refugee crisis was taken by the British 101 Logistic Brigade, under the inspired leadership of Brigadier Tim Cross. Some of the NGOs and professional relief people took a certain exception to the military being involved in the humanitarian effort. But this was a case of needs must.

NATO also assembled a force of about two thousand lightly armed soldiers in Albania to provide humanitarian aid to the refugees arriving there. Known as the Albania Force (AFOR), its HQ was formed by HQ Allied Command Europe (ACE) Mobile Force (Land), commanded by yet another member of the Airborne tribe, Major General John Reith, who back in 1986 had succeeded me as commanding officer of 1 Para, itself then part of ACE Mobile Force (Land). John was given the rank of lieutenant general for the duration of the operation.

The refugees had been only reluctantly allowed across the

border by the Macedonian authorities, who feared the effect of adding so many ethnic Albanians to their own significant Albanian minority. Like us, they recognized that this ethnic cleansing was a tactic of Milosevic's, intended to destabilize their Government. The huge numbers of refugees formed a substantial addition to Macedonia's Albanian population, already around 30 per cent of the total before their arrival. At the beginning of the refugee crisis over Easter, the Macedonians had denied the refugees entry, confining them to the no-man's-land between the two countries where they squatted on the ground, exhausted. Under pressure from international opinion, the Macedonian Government had relented and allowed the refugees in, but restricted them to camps only a short distance into the country. Though we could just about cope with the refugees during the warmer summer weather, it was obvious that if they were still there when the harsh Balkan winter arrived, many of them would die.

The refugee crisis was of intense interest to the world's media, attracting hundreds of journalists to Skopje. During this period we received innumerable visits from VIPs, many of whom were nothing more than a nuisance and some of whom appeared to be seeking photo-opportunities. I became irritated with the constant refrain, 'I'm here to help.' After hearing this for the umpteenth time, I handed one of the worthies a spade. 'Take this up to the camps,' I said, 'and start digging latrines.'

Clare Short, Secretary of State for International Development, arrived in Skopje on Easter Sunday. She successfully bullied the Macedonians into allowing the refugees to leave no-man's-land and to be dispersed into camps. Less helpfully, she tried to bully me too, breathing fire about the need to 'defeat Serb aggression' and accusing me of being 'weak-willed' in not wanting to march straight into Kosovo. I countered that we had no authority to do any such thing, and when she sniffed, I suggested that we withdraw to my office for a private chat. When we were alone I didn't mince my words. I explained to her the facts of life – that I had at that time approximately eight thousand soldiers under my command to oppose a Serb army more than twenty times that number; moreover, that we had only twenty or so tanks, a mere 380 fewer than the Serbs. 'I'm too old for a heroic but futile gesture,' I told her.

She calmed down after that. I offered her a whisky, and we parted on good terms. My staff, who had earlier heard raised voices coming from my office, were surprised to see her come out grinning.

In fact my planning team had been looking at the options for a forced entry into Kosovo if all other options failed. This had to be done very discreetly, as it was extremely politically sensitive. For one thing, NATO rules did not permit us to start formally planning a ground offensive without the prior authorization of the North Atlantic Council. For another, the Macedonian Government would not countenance their territory being used as a base for an invasion. A ground offensive was anyway a daunting prospect, given the formidable size of the Serb army and the challenging terrain. We reckoned we would need at least three corps of fifty thousand soldiers each. Even with those numbers, and complete command of the air, it would still be very difficult. Apart from anything else, there were only a few routes into Kosovo, all of which could easily be blocked. And there was little political support for a ground war. When Clark began to argue for an all-out ground offensive against the Serbs, he found himself cold-shouldered in Washington and denied access to the President. Immediately afterwards he gave a press conference in which he talked freely about the limitations of bombing and appeared to advocate a forced entry into Kosovo. His superiors in the Pentagon were livid. Clark received a call from General Hugh Shelton, Chairman of the US Joint Chiefs of Staff, who announced that the verbatim guidance he was about to give came directly from the Secretary of Defense,

Main picture and above left: *In the first half of 1999, almost one-third of the entire population fled Kosovo. A quarter of a million people were living in camps just inside Macedonia, run by the NATO Kosovo Force (KFOR) under my command. A humanitarian disaster loomed if the refugees were forced to remain in the mountain camps through a Balkan winter.* **Above right**: *The British Prime Minister Tony Blair visited us with the Chief of the Defence Staff General Sir Charles Guthrie. Blair was convinced of the need to stop Serbian President Slobodan Milosevic's ethnic cleansing, and took the lead in persuading the world community that military action was necessary.*

OPERATION JOINT GUARDIA

From 12 JUN (D Day) - 22 JUN 99 (D + 1

FEDERAL REPUBLIC OF YUGOSLAVIA

SERBIA

Novi Pazar

Zone I   E+6
Zone II   E+9
Zone III E+1 & 11
E Day - 09 JUN 99

MONTENEGRO

WITHDRAWAL STARTED 101300B J
TOTAL 47,000 VJ AND MUP FORC
WITHDRAWN BY 211200B JUN 9

SERBIA

KOSOVO

PRISTINA

Kosovska
Mitrovica

Zvecan

Vucitrn

Podujevo

Istok

MNB (N)

MNB (W)

Klina

Pec

Decane

MNB (W)
MNB (S)

IT

Kosovo
Polje

MNB (C)

Kosovska
Kamenica

4 UK ARMD BDE
18 JUN 99

RS RAPID REACTION BN
11 JUN 99

UCK Undertaking
Signed 21 JUN 99

Undertaking Talks
14 - 20 JUN 99

5 UK AB BDE
12 - 13 JUN 99

4 UK ARMD BDE
12 - 13 JUN 99

Gnjilane

GATE 5

Pasjane

Orahovac

Stimlje

Urosevac

Dakovica

Velika Krusa

Suva Reka

IT GARIBALDI BDE
12 - 14 JUN 99

Pozaranje

TF FALCON
18 JUN 99

FFB
13 JUN 99

ALBANIA

117,910 REFUGEES
RETURNED DURING PERIOD
13-22 JUNE 1999

Prizren

MNB (S)

MNB (E) Strpce

Kacanik

MTA Talks
06 - 09 JUN 99

Kumanov

Kükes

MTA Talks
05 JUN 99

Deneral Jankovic

TF FALCON
14 JUN 99

5 UK AB BDE
120500B JUN 99

4 UK ARMD BDE
12 JUN 99

5 UK AB BDE
120500B JUN 99

Tetovo

IT GARIBALDI BDE
12 JUN 99

12 GE PZ BDE
12 -14 JUN 99

TF FALCON
12 JUN 99

SKOPJE

Scale 1:450,000

10   0   10   20   30
Kilometres

83,371 REFUGEES
RETURNED DURING PERIOD
13-22 JUNE 1999

Katlanovo

FORMER YUGOSLAV REPUBLIC OF MACEDONIA

Produced by Engr (Geo),
19 September 1999 (K+90)

Operation 'Joint Guardian' provided for KFOR's entry into Kosovo and Serb withdrawal. Negotiation with the Serbs took over one hundred gruelling hours, with constant amendments to the draft agreement.

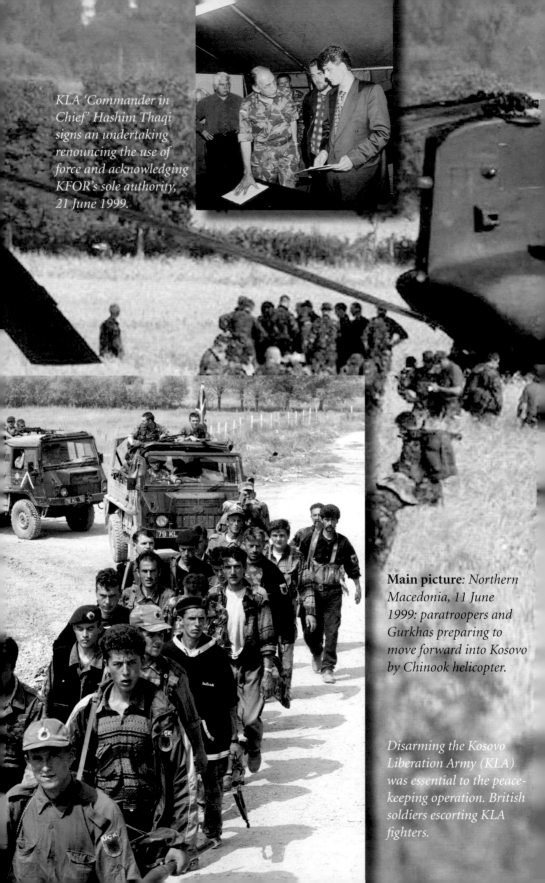

KLA 'Commander in Chief' Hashim Thaqi signs an undertaking renouncing the use of force and acknowledging KFOR's sole authority, 21 June 1999.

Main picture: *Northern Macedonia, 11 June 1999: paratroopers and Gurkhas preparing to move forward into Kosovo by Chinook helicopter.*

Disarming the Kosovo Liberation Army (KLA) was essential to the peace-keeping operation. British soldiers escorting KLA fighters.

A British soldier carries weapons surrendered by the KLA during the demilitarization process.

Shaking hands with KLA 'Field Commander' Agim Ceku on a visit to a weapons storage site. Ceku played a key role in the process of normalizing Kosovo and is now its Prime Minister.

As KFOR entered Kosovo, a column of Russian troops occupied Pristina Airport. Orders from my superior officer, NATO's Supreme Allied Commander, Europe, General Wesley 'Wes' Clark, could have led to a dangerous confrontation, but I was able to avert this and establish good relations with the Russian commander, General Viktor Zavarzin.

Left: *Russian armoured personnel carrier at Pristina Airport.*

Below: *with General Zavarzin at the airport, 26 June 1999.*

American President Bill Clinton, his wife Hillary and daughter Chelsea visit US troops in Skopje, Macedonia, 22 June 1999. I flew down from Pristina to meet them. Wes Clark stands at right.

US Secretary of State Madeleine Albright visits KFOR HQ, Pristina, 29 June 1999. With her is Bernard Kouchner, Special Representative of the Secretary General (SRSG) and head of UNMIK, the UN 'international civil presence' which ran Kosovo before a civil administration was in place. I jokingly called Bernard 'le roi'.

With Wes Clark and Prince Charles in Kosovo.

Negotiations on the transformation of the
KLA into a peacetime organization were
very difficult and continued until after the
KFOR-imposed deadline. We held regular
meetings in the 'Bat Cave' at KFOR HQ,
a huge room in a deserted film studio.
Artist in residence Nick Bashall (top right)
painted a moment in one of our sessions
when I confronted Ceku across the table
(above).

Right: In October 1999, after seven months
in the Balkans, I handed over command of
KFOR and returned with my immediate
staff to HQ ARRC's permanent base in
Rheindahlen, Germany. It was a great party.
With Caroline Everard, wife of my Military
Assistant (MA) James; Caroline had given
birth to twins while we were in Kosovo.

William Cohen. 'Get your fucking face off the TV,' he said. 'No more briefings, period.'

This was an extremely busy time for my team. We worked long hours, often late into the night. This suited my habits, though I occasionally compensated with an afternoon nap – known jocularly in the Factory as 'strategic thought'. This ability to cat-nap is something that you learn in the Army. There's always a lot of waiting around between intense periods of activity, and any soldier will have a kip if he's got nothing to do, whether he's sitting in the back of an aeroplane or waiting for orders to move off. Most nights I would telephone Sarah just before going to bed. This sometimes led to some incongruous conversations. I remember Sarah holding forth about car insurance at one particularly tense moment. But talking to her helped me to keep a sense of proportion.

There was a great deal to be done while we waited for the bombing campaign to force Milosevic to concede: not least the complex task of coordinating the disparate national forces into one effective fighting formation. We also steadily built up our strength as new units and supplies arrived by road, rail or air. I spent a lot of time in helicopters, on visits to the brigades dispersed across northern Macedonia. Then there was the need to keep our plans under constant review to take account of rapidly changing circumstances. The refugee relief effort complicated all of this, of course. Throughout I had to work hard to keep the Macedonians on side. There were also problems with the Greeks: over 90 per cent of the population there opposed the bombing campaign against another Orthodox country, and once the bombing began there was a succession of demonstrations and other difficulties. We relied on the Greek port of Thessaloniki for our line of communication, and from time to time I had to go down there – and once to Athens – for meetings with concerned Greek officials who were worried that public unrest would affect our logistics. Then there was the constant need to put out small fires. Early on, I had to deal with a panic about a Serb incursion when three American soldiers out on a patrol near the border reported that they had come under fire, and were subsequently captured by Serb forces. Wes Clark's version of this was that Serb special forces had kidnapped them from inside Macedonia. It turned out that they had strayed across the border before being detained by the Serbs. Later, a Norwegian captain driving up the wrong side of the road from Thessaloniki was involved in a head-on collision, killing the son of a Macedonian minister.

All the time we were operating in the spotlight of the world's media. I was very fortunate in having a quite excellent media operations staff. I gave press conferences when there was some new development, while trying to avoid the trap of giving them so regularly that one was merely providing a running commentary on the situation. I also gave occasional one-to-one interviews, and informal off-the-record briefings to the press, some of them to journalists from non-English-speaking countries – particularly Germany, Italy and Greece, to say nothing of Macedonia itself – aware that world opinion was a weapon in the struggle with Milosevic. My aim was always to be open and straight whenever possible. I have found that, by and large, journalists respond well to this. Weasel words and spin are generally counter-productive. I bridled when London tried to tell me what to say. 'If that's what you want, you're going to have to find someone else,' I told one of the more intrusive spin doctors.

In the process I came in for rather too much personal attention, including a *Sunday Telegraph* profile which caused much amusement at the Shoe Factory. 'He likes whisky and cigars ... prone to work all night ... keeps going in Churchillian style with an afternoon nap ... the pace is furious but his aides seem to adore him.' Why my staff seemed to think this so funny I couldn't imagine.

Early in May the Prime Minister, Tony Blair, visited

Macedonia to see the refugee situation for himself. He sent advisers ahead to arrange the details of his visit. They were obsessed with the media angle, of course. I enjoyed teasing them by saying that I intended to give him a public broadside. It was worth it just to see the look of horror on their faces. Blair arrived accompanied by a large party, including his wife Cherie, his chief press officer Alastair Campbell, and Anji Hunter, known as the gatekeeper, who ran his private office. I disliked the accompanying media circus, but the Prime Minister knew what he was about. He was relaxed and well briefed, and asked shrewd questions. Blair was leading the international community on this issue, and I felt that I was speaking not just to the British Prime Minister, but also to the political leader who would make the case internationally. Throughout the whole Kosovo crisis, the UK was the nation most on the front foot. Blair was arguing to the world that we couldn't let this appalling situation continue, that we must take action, however difficult or dangerous it might be. A few weeks before coming to Kosovo he had made an important speech in Chicago, outlining what he described as 'a new doctrine of international community', setting out criteria for intervention in the internal affairs of a sovereign state – in particular, the imperative of coming to the assistance of the oppressed.

Also with the prime ministerial party was the CDS, General Sir Charles (now Lord) Guthrie. I'd known Charles from the late 1970s, when he had commanded the Welsh Guards in Berlin and then in South Armagh, where my company had been under his command for a while. I had appreciated his guidance down the years, and it was good to see him, not least because I knew of his strong influence on the Prime Minister.

The most important part of the visit from my point of view was undoubtedly the hour and a half I spent in private with the PM and the CDS. It was a warm afternoon, and we sat under a camouflage net on one of our training areas, just hammering through where we were and what we might have to do, analysing the timelines for a decision on a ground invasion. At this point Blair had been in power two years and this was the first time that he had committed British forces to a strategic military operation, so of course he was on a serious learning curve. I stressed to him the urgency of prompt action: humanitarian disaster loomed if the refugees remained in the camps into the winter months.

The Prime Minister asked me to estimate the likely casualties if we had to fight our way into Kosovo. He wanted to know what the butcher's bill might be. I remember telling him that it was very difficult to say, but used the Falklands War as an analogy. In the worst case we might be talking about several hundred British deaths and well over a thousand wounded – to say nothing of the casualties which might be incurred by the other NATO nations.

This visit also provided an opportunity for the Prime Minister to speak to the soldiers and to thank them for what they were doing. After that, he and his wife visited the refugee camp at Stankovic, a few miles south of the Kosovo border. Both were visibly shocked by what they saw and moved by stories they were told of rape, murder and brutality. The refugees lionized him, and it was obvious that they saw him as a key to their future. The very fact that he'd bothered to go and see them was a statement that they were not being ignored. Blair made a powerful speech. 'This is not a battle for NATO,' he declared. 'This is not a battle for territory. This is a battle for humanity.' He demanded an end to Serb atrocities, so that the refugees could return to their homes. 'NATO will prevail. The butchers of Belgrade will be defeated.' The crowds cheered and chanted, 'Tony, Tony, Tony.'

By now, NATO's objectives had been simplified to sound-bites: Serbs out, NATO in, refugees back. NATO's strategy, as championed by Clark, had been to bomb the Serbs into backing down. But this was taking a long time to work. The bombing campaign continued for more than two months with little sign that Serbs were on the brink of capitulation. Overall, NATO aircraft flew more than thirty-eight thousand combat missions with surprisingly little effect on Serb military capability on the ground, as we discovered when we eventually occupied Kosovo. A few obvious buildings had been destroyed, but there were hardly any burned-out tank hulks to be seen. In part, this was because the Serbs had dispersed their formations and found clever ways to conceal their weaponry. In part too, this was because pilots were instructed not to fly lower than 20,000 feet for fear of being shot down. There was also, rightly, much sensitivity about 'collateral damage'. Pilots often found that their targets had been changed after they had taken off on a mission.

Inevitably, there were mistakes. Early in May, NATO aircraft attacked and largely destroyed a Kosovar refugee convoy, mistaking it for a convoy of Serb military vehicles and killing the very people it set out to protect. Then NATO in error bombed the Chinese Embassy in Belgrade, prompting a diplomatic uproar.

But there was a sense that the end-game might be in sight. Britain, ever on the front foot, decided to make the necessary arrangements to reinforce its existing contingent, then still largely based on 4 Armoured Brigade, commanded by Brigadier Bill Rollo. In the event, HQ 3 Division under Major General Richard Dannatt and 5 Airborne Brigade under Brigadier Adrian Freer deployed as reinforcements. Richard Dannatt took on the national role of Commander British Forces (COMBRITFOR) from Bill Rollo.

On 16 May Rupert Smith summarized the progress of the air campaign on the VTC by quoting from a little-known speech by Churchill. We were 'buggering on'. For the benefit of those watchers whose first language was not English, he explained what was meant by the term: 'an unnatural act . . . committed in a dark and unpleasant place . . . that produces nothing . . . but has a certain rhythm to it'. There was a lot of laughter in the Shoe Factory, but I could see on the monitor that some of the Americans were not amused. KBO ('Keep Buggering On') became our unofficial mission statement after this.

As it became more likely that we were headed for a showdown with the Serbs, I flew back to London for a private audience with Her Majesty the Queen at Buckingham Palace, with only the two of us present. This was unusual, but then it was an unusual situation. As ever, she was most perceptive and encouraging, and showed a very impressive grasp of the situation.

Late in May Viktor Chernomyrdin, President Yeltsin's special envoy to Serbia, issued a stark warning to the West. 'The world has never in this decade been so close to the brink of nuclear war. I appeal to NATO leaders to show the courage to suspend the air raids . . . it is impossible to talk with bombs falling.' Unless the bombing stopped soon, he warned, he would advise Russia's President to suspend Russian participation in the negotiating process, put an end to all military/technical agreements with the West, delay ratification of the SALT II arms reduction agreement and use Russia's veto to block any UN Security Council Resolution on Yugoslavia.

This was a chilling statement, but there was an element of bluster in it. The Russians felt protective towards their fellow Slavs and extremely sensitive about NATO's attack on a former Communist country – unauthorized by any UN Security Council Resolution. Nevertheless, they recognized the need to end the fighting in Kosovo. On behalf of the G8 group of industrialized nations, they put pressure on the Serbs to compromise.

On 2 June, Milosevic received Chernomyrdin and Finland's President Ahtisaari in Belgrade. Later that day we received a diplomatic telegram (DIPTEL) indicating that 'real progress towards some form of agreement may be genuinely possible'. I didn't get too excited, even when we heard a report that Milosevic had made an announcement to the effect that he would withdraw all military and paramilitary forces from Kosovo. We'd heard this sort of thing before. An annual conference of the ARRC's peacetime-assigned divisional commanders was scheduled to begin the next morning, and there seemed no convincing reason to postpone it. The conference had begun when the startling news came through that the Serb parliament had reluctantly approved the Kosovo plan presented by Ahtisaari and Chernomyrdin, which Milosevic had approved the day before. Suddenly it began to look as if there were some substance to Milosevic's concessions. Even today, it's still unclear why he backed down, but one can surmise some or all of the following: the bombing campaign, now including strategic targets in Serbia proper, rather than just tactical targets in Kosovo, was at last really hurting Milosevic and his coterie; NATO had not splintered under the political strains of going to war against his country; the threat of an eventual ground attack was known to him; Russia had made it clear that, in the last analysis, he would be on his own; on 27 May he had been indicted by the ICTY at The Hague for crimes against humanity in Kosovo. Less than three years later, Slobodan Milosevic would find himself in the dock.

Nobody knew what would happen next. Rupert Smith, chairing the VTC on the morning of 4 June, characteristically put it well: 'Give me two minutes to think about what I am going to say—' and then added sardonically, '—the first person to do so today.' The Russians were insisting on a suspension of the bombing, but NATO resisted this. The argument was that if we stopped bombing, politically we would never be able to start again, even if the Serbs didn't withdraw. The agreement provided for an international security force 'with substantial NATO participation under unified command and control'. This in turn implied a unified NATO chain of command, under the political direction of the North Atlantic Council. Talks were taking place in Moscow about the involvement of Russian forces, negotiated by the US Deputy Secretary of State, Strobe Talbott. Russia's opening position was that the Russian contingent would not be under NATO command, which would make life very difficult on the ground. Wes Clark was determined not to allow the Russians a sector of their own. If Russian troops occupied the northern part of Kosovo where most of the Serbs lived, it could result in *de facto* partition. In Bosnia, a Russian brigade had deployed as part of IFOR/SFOR within the American Sector. This was the model we were keen to adopt in Kosovo, but it was by no means certain that the Russians would go along with it.

Much debate followed about the wording of the so-called Military–Technical Agreement (MTA) that would determine the arrangements to be made between the withdrawing Serb security forces and the incoming KFOR. Such an MTA would provide for the replacement of one force by another. Within KFOR itself, we were naturally concerned that the MTA should not commit us to anything that we felt unhappy about doing. SHAPE was circulating a draft MTA but had not thought to copy it to us. At the daily NATO press conference on 4 June, the spokesman Jamie Shea announced that a meeting with the Serbs to finalize the details of the MTA would take place the following day, and that I would conduct it. This was the first any of us had heard of it. Imperturbable as ever, Andrew Ridgway made the necessary arrangements. Brigadier Jonathan Bailey, who in the last few days had joined us from Rheindahlen, was dispatched to the border to act as a liaison officer with the Serbs. He set up a meeting with Serb representatives for the following morning at the Café Europa, a small, run-down establishment similar to a British transport café 500 yards inside the Macedonian border. All day drafts of the MTA pinged backwards and forwards. At

01.20 hours on the morning of Saturday 5 June a 'final' MTA arrived – containing a number of errors. It looked as though I would be flying by the seat of my pants.

I spent an hour working through the text and finally got to bed at 02.30 hours. Half an hour later the telephone rang. It was the office of the Supreme Allied Commander. There was another draft of the MTA. It arrived at 04.00 hours. I sat up cross-checking the new version line by line with the previous version. It was mind-numbing, painstaking work, but it was vital to get it right. By 08.15 the next morning, after little enough sleep, I was waiting in our nearest base to the Café Europa, where apparently a hundred or more press were gathered. Jonathan Bailey phoned me and explained that the Serbs weren't prepared to cross the border, claiming that SACEUR had agreed to a meeting 500 yards on their side. I had had a hunch that the Serbs might be reluctant to come across, which was why I hadn't gone up to the café, not wanting to be seen waiting for them. It was an impasse, with neither wanting to give way. In the next few hours the phone rang hot. By 11.00 hours it seemed that I was faced with three choices: cancel, meet in no-man's-land, or go across the border myself. We looked at the possibility of erecting a tent right on the bridge that marked the border. Still undecided and getting impatient, at 11.45 I went up to the café; as luck would have it, very shortly afterwards the Serbs arrived. We could start.

The demeanour of the Serb delegation was resigned. They were obviously depressed. I was determined not to show any hint of triumphalism on our part, which would have been inappropriate and gratuitous. The atmosphere was workmanlike and professional. One sensed that the Serbs didn't really understand why we were there. 'You are an honourable officer, a general from Britain, a fine country, our allies in two world wars,' one of their officers said to me while we were chatting during a break. 'Of course we in the Serb army will treat you with honour. But

Albania is not a proper country. The Albanians are not a proper people. There is no requirement to treat them with honour.'

Occasionally while we were negotiating I reflected that if the talks broke down, I would be going into battle against the Serb generals on the other side of the table. The same thought must have occurred to them too.

On our side of the table I had my own small team: Mike Venables, an MOD civil servant who had been with us since deployment to Macedonia as my political adviser – inevitably nicknamed 'the Commissar'; US Air Force three-star general Robert H. Fogelsong, representing US national interests; Admiral Kaskeala, a Finn who had accompanied President Ahtisaari to Belgrade; and, of course, taking notes, James Everard (by now known to all as 'Ever-Ready').

The first thing we discovered was that the Serbian delegation had spent the night driving down from Belgrade and didn't have the latest version of the MTA. So we had to go through it again line by line, translating this time, of course. It was slow, ponderous work. The Serbs were insisting on a UN Security Council Resolution (UNSCR). It soon became clear that the delegation was not empowered to sign the MTA without consultation. At 18.00 hours the Serbs withdrew to consult with Belgrade. They announced that they needed further time and said they wouldn't be coming back that night. I was knackered and happy to agree. They also suggested that the next day's meeting should be up at Kumanovo in north-east Macedonia, where the French-led brigade was based. The advantage for them was that Kumanovo shared a border with Serbia proper rather than Kosovo, which was much more secure for them. They didn't like the idea of driving back into Kosovo each evening, with the KLA at large.

This was fine by me. Kumanovo was only a short helicopter ride away, and it was much easier for us to administer the talks within a KFOR base than a café. The next morning I woke up refreshed, to find that yet another version of the MTA had arrived. I flew up to Kumanovo and we reconvened in a tent at 09.23 hours. Then one of the Serb delegation announced that he could only discuss certain parts of the MTA and that everything else must be done through the Security Council. I insisted that the document must be considered as a whole. It was deadlock. At 09.37, after just fourteen minutes, the meeting broke up.

It was very difficult to negotiate when amended drafts of the MTA kept arriving in short order. I was aware that there was a lot of talking going on, but it seemed to me that all that should have been done before I was asked to start negotiating with the Serbs. What was happening here was, to some extent, a piece of theatre designed to keep the media happy while much of the game was played out elsewhere. To make matters worse, all sorts of hangers-on appeared, including the inevitable spin doctors from the Prime Minister's office who offered their unwanted views. I became quite cross. I phoned Clark and said to him that this was now a political, not a military matter. He told me to stick with it. A little later Charles Guthrie called to smooth things over.

Negotiations restarted. The Serbs proposed that the international security force be under UN auspices. After what had happened in Bosnia we could not accept this. After three hours of change and counter-change we found that we were back to where we had started. It was ridiculous. In another interesting twist, the Russian defence attaché from Belgrade arrived at Kumanovo later that afternoon; after some conversation with the Serb delegation, he seemed content to act merely as an observer.

An indication of the high level of interest in what was going on came in phone calls asking for a personal update from both Prince Charles and Tony Blair – among many others. Both the Prince and the Prime Minister offered me their encouragement and support.

By midnight on the second day we had reached another dead-lock. The Serbs wanted a text which was unacceptable to NATO and vice versa. At 01.15 hours I spoke to Wes back at SHAPE, not for the first time in the previous thirty-six hours. I told him that we had reached an impasse and that the Serbs wanted to leave. We had to get in first with the press if we didn't want to lose the initiative. Clark told me to wait while he sought clearance. The next thirty-five minutes were a farce: at one stage we had the Vice-President on one line, Strobe Talbott on another and Wes on the third. Eventually I'd had enough. I went back to tell the Serbs we couldn't make any progress for the time being. We arranged to keep our communication channels open. Afterwards I went outside to tell the press that the talks had stalled. It was about two o'clock in the morning, and all the hacks were waiting in a sort of grandstand. I made my statement and the Serbs made a short statement afterwards. Then it was back to the Shoe Factory for whisky and egg and chips at 03.10 hours.

Monday 7 June was a quiet day. I received welcome telephone calls from Wes, Rupert and others offering support for the way I had been conducting the negotiations. The media blamed the Serbs for failure to comply. Jonathan Bailey had a rendezvous with one of the Serbs at the border purely to keep the lines of communication open; the press mistook this for a resumption of the negotiations, encouraged by one of the spin doctors who wanted the impression given that progress was being made. General Fogelsong started muddying the waters by talking to the Serbs independently. It looked as though the Americans were negotiating separately, outside the NATO chain of command. I wasn't impressed. All that day and the next there was a great deal of confusion, with much talk of a new agreed text of the MTA which no one had seen. I was becoming very annoyed. At some point Anji Hunter arrived.

'I'm here to see what I can do to help,' she beamed.

In normal circumstances I would have been pleased to see her, but this time frustration got the better of me.

'We were fine until the spinners fucked it up,' I said furiously. She backed off.

By now we knew what we were trying to achieve. The aim was to choreograph several different events which all had to be sequenced: first, the text of a Security Council Resolution had to be approved by the G8; then the MTA had to be agreed and signed; then a verifiable withdrawal had to be agreed which would bring about an end to the bombing; then the Security Council Resolution had to be ratified – and only then would KFOR go into Kosovo. The MTA provided for phased Serb withdrawal from three designated zones of Kosovo, ending in complete withdrawal eleven days from signature. The concept was that we would enter the zones in phases as the Serb forces withdrew.

I flew back up to Kumanovo on the evening of 8 June, the fourth day. The Serbs arrived ten minutes after I did. But they still had a number of concerns. I had some sympathy with them. Once they withdrew their security forces, the Serb minority population in Kosovo would be unprotected. After all that had happened in Kosovo in the past year or so, one could well imagine that the Albanians might carry out reprisals on Serbs remaining there.

The Serbs weren't ready to sit down and discuss the document until 02.47 hours. We worked through the document until 05.34 hours, by which time it was light. Then the meeting broke up, with both sides seeking approval for changes negotiated to the text.

The next meeting was scheduled for midday. We were all weary. There was another text which needed to be painstakingly checked. I was constantly dragged to the telephone to speak to Wes. He couldn't or wouldn't leave it to me.

The meeting ended at 14.23 hours, without much progress. By

late afternoon the Serbs were talking about going back to Belgrade. At this stage we felt nothing but relief at the prospect of a decent meal and a proper night's kip. We were just climbing into the helicopters to go back to the Shoe Factory when Jonathan Bailey telephoned to say the Serbs wanted to reconvene immediately. At 17.25 hours they returned. They asked for some minor changes, which I approved. Then they indicated that they were content. 'I'm buying,' one of them announced. I suggested that they might like to delay signing until a minute past midnight, which would give them an extra day, but they said, no, we want to sign now. A helicopter arrived with a fresh supply of KFOR headed paper. We printed out clean copies. When everyone was happy, I penned my signature, and the Serbs added theirs. It was 21.07 on Wednesday 9 June 1999. We had been negotiating for more than a hundred hours.

12

An Airfield too Far

Our daily routine at KFOR HQ began with a morning update at 08.00 hours, when twenty-five to thirty members of the command team would gather in the conference room in the Shoe Factory. The morning update on Friday 11 June was good-humoured. We were all very tired, but there was a feeling that at last all the ducks were lined up. After much buggering about, we had a signed agreement with the Serbs for withdrawal of their forces. The bombing campaign had been suspended and we had the authority of UN Security Council Resolution 1244, passed the previous evening. We had agreed to a Serb request to postpone D-Day, provisionally agreed for Friday, to Saturday – they weren't ready, and we could use the extra twenty-four hours ourselves. H-Hour was now set for 05.00 hours the following day, Saturday 12 June. I planned to spend the day visiting each of the six brigades that would be moving into Kosovo at dawn the next morning, to answer any last-minute queries and to wish them all good luck. I didn't know then that all these plans were going to be overtaken by events.

The morning update was followed at 09.00 hours by the morning VTC, chaired by Wes Clark. On this occasion Jim Ellis, who was visiting KFOR, attended the VTC at the Shoe Factory.

Clark's anxiety about the Russians dominated that morning's VTC. Talks taking place in Moscow between the Russians and the Americans were not going well. There was still no agreement about the command and control or the deployment area of any Russian contingent to KFOR. SACEUR was particularly concerned by reports that a Russian column in Bosnia was on the move – despite vehement protestations to the contrary from SFOR in Sarajevo.

It was immediately obvious that other plans would have to be put on hold while we studied the implications of this news and acted accordingly.

At 10.34 we received confirmation from SHAPE that a Russian column of approximately thirty armoured vehicles carrying an estimated 250 soldiers had crossed the River Drina into Serbia, presumably headed for Kosovo. Moments later, images of the column on the move appeared on CNN. Interestingly, the Russian vehicles had 'KFOR' freshly painted on their sides. To some extent this was a conciliatory gesture, indicating that they were coming to take part in the peace-keeping mission as authorized by UN Security Council Resolution. We knew that the Russians were desperate to avoid the intervention in Kosovo being seen as a NATO operation in a former Communist country, one that had historically looked to Russia for protection and support.

SHAPE's assessment was that the Russians would try to secure the airfield at Pristina prior to the arrival of air-delivered troops from Russia. Pristina airfield was the only airport in Kosovo for both civilian and military aircraft. It looked as if the Russians might be trying to pre-empt us, establishing themselves on the ground prior to a possible partition of Kosovo. The Russians had initially wrong-footed the American negotiators by referring to the airfield by its local name, Slatina. The column was expected to reach Pristina by 15.00 hours. Clark phoned and gave me a warning order to secure the airfield before the Russians arrived.

I didn't like this idea one bit – and I could tell from his body language that Jim Ellis didn't either. This was only a warning order, to make a detailed plan and get preparatory moves under way, and it could not be executed without a confirmatory order. But if confirmed, it meant sending helicopter-borne troops into Serb-held territory where they could easily be isolated. We had already looked at a similar option – as part of KFOR's main force advance into Kosovo – a week or so before, at the instigation of the French, who were keen to have television pictures of French troops jumping out of helicopters. I had had a personal conversation over the telephone with the French Chief of Defence, who agreed with our own conclusion that it was too risky.

By going into Kosovo ahead of time we would be breaching our newly signed agreement with the Serbs, providing them with a pretext not to withdraw and perhaps to fight. They could say, well, bollocks to you; if you're tearing up the agreement now, then so will we, thank you very much. Though our bombing campaign had damaged the Serbs' capability, their armed forces remained formidable, with well over three hundred tanks in Kosovo alone. At the time KFOR was comparatively small, only about fifteen thousand men in six brigades – two of them British – with forty-odd tanks. The airfield was only 35 miles or so from the border, but intelligence had revealed that the bridges and tunnels on the road through the narrow Kacanic defile into Kosovo had been prepared for demolition. If any one of them were blocked or blown, we would have been in real difficulty. It would only take one bolshy Serb engineer and we'd have lost our overland route for quite a while. So even if we didn't have to fight our way in, it might be days or even weeks before we could relieve our soldiers at Pristina overland. Moreover, there would be a serious risk of a confrontation when the Russians arrived. The Russians had played a key part in persuading the Serbs to withdraw from Kosovo, and we needed their continued participation to make the agreement stick. We knew how raw Russian feelings were at the time, especially with the recent accession to NATO of three former Warsaw Pact nations. The situation might quickly escalate and become extremely dangerous.

Despite my misgivings, I instructed my staff to prepare a plan to secure the airport with at least one battalion of heliborne troops. I directed that the plan should be kept on very close hold, i.e. that only the bare minimum of people should be told about it. One person who had to be informed was COMBRITFOR Richard Dannatt, so that he could clear this with London. I then left with Jim Ellis for a pre-arranged meeting at Skopje airport with US Secretary of State Madeleine Albright, who was passing through. Perhaps she could tell us what the hell was going on.

As Commander of KFOR I was responsible for the welfare and safety of all the soldiers under my command. But at the back of my mind was another consideration. I knew that 5 (UK) Airborne Brigade would have to provide at least some of the force necessary to secure the airfield. Among those soldiers I would be ordering to Pristina airfield would be my son Mark, one of thirty or so of 5 Brigade's Pathfinder Platoon with an advance force reconnaissance role.

Madeleine Albright didn't seem to appreciate fully what was happening. In the VIP lounge at Skopje airport Jim Ellis persuaded her to call her opposite number at the Russian Foreign Ministry, Igor Ivanov, who assured her that there was nothing underhand in the Russian troop movements. But then perhaps he didn't know what the hell was going on either.

It was now 11.45. I received a call from my staff telling me that I was needed back at HQ. Their assessment was that a decision to launch the operation to secure the airfield needed to be taken by 14.00 hours at the latest, given the Russian convoy's estimated time of arrival (ETA) of 15.00 hours. Pristina airfield was not more than thirty minutes' flying time from northern Macedonia, where a battalion from 5 Airborne Brigade was based, so this left a maximum of half an hour for our soldiers to load up and take off, and then another half an hour to deploy to defensive positions when they arrived. I put the battalion – my old friends, 1 Para – on fifteen minutes' notice to move.

We had decided before I left the HQ that this had to be a multinational operation if at all possible, and while I had been away the French had offered to contribute a battalion and twenty-three Puma helicopters. That made the equivalent of two battalions – good news, but NATO's Combined Operations Air Centre in Vicenza had refused to provide close air support without a direct instruction from Jim Ellis. Their lack of enthusiasm was another reason for our waning confidence.

To say that I felt frustrated would be to understate the position. The helicopters might well attract Serb anti-aircraft fire on the way in. The Serbs had, after all, been firing at NATO aircraft until only a few days before. It was also unclear what the troops were supposed to do when they reached the airfield: were they supposed to block the runway to prevent the Russians from landing? If not – and worse still – were they to open fire on Russian soldiers as they deplaned? Or would the Russians initiate a firefight? To launch such an operation without close air support would be inviting disaster. We had not come to Kosovo to lose several hundred men on the first day. The pressure on me personally was intense – 'the stuff of heart attacks', as James Everard noted in his journal that evening.

The feeling among my staff was that Clark was shooting from the hip. I respected Clark's record and his overall aims, and of course I felt a duty to act loyally towards my superior in the chain of command, but my confidence in him was being severely tested. We had already been mucked about over the agreement with the Serbs, several times receiving fresh drafts of the agreement after the negotiation had already begun.

I arrived back at the Shoe Factory just as information was received from a Russian news agency that six aircraft had taken off from air bases near Moscow carrying a thousand airborne soldiers. It was alarming – but I wondered who had leaked this information, and why?

At 13.15 hours I received a written order from Clark 'to move and occupy Pristina Airfield'. But it contained a constraint. No move was to take place before Clark had approved a 'back-brief' of the operational plan.

To 'use the long screwdriver' was characteristic of Clark, and indeed of the US military in general. They were always reluctant to delegate, always interfering. In general I didn't much like this. To have your boss looking over your shoulder when you were already under such pressure was asking for trouble. But in this instance it gave me another chance to make the case against the operation.

Andrew Ridgway was down at the border liaising with the Serbs. Somewhat going through the motions, I got him to make a formal request for early entry into Pristina. The response was predictably negative. You could read this one of two ways. Maybe they were colluding with the Russians; or maybe they had perfectly understandable reasons for not wanting us there before the time agreed. I thought back to that Serb request to delay D-Day from the Friday to the Saturday: at the time, the request seemed to us to be nothing more than practicality; now, in the light of the Russian manoeuvre, it could be seen in a most conspiratorial light. The Serbs had MiG aircraft housed in bunkers at Pristina airfield, and you could see that they might not want us around when the MiGs emerged for take-off. After all, we had been bombing them until two days before. The control tower at the airfield and many of the surrounding buildings were badly damaged.

In the middle of scribbling notes of my own analysis of this extraordinary situation, at 13.30 I received an intelligence re-assessment of the Russians' progress. The new estimate was that the column would not reach Pristina until 18.00 hours. There seemed, moreover, to be no hard evidence that any military planes had left Russian airspace. These two pieces of information bought us a little more time. I telephoned Rupert Smith and ran through the logic behind my very grave reservations. He agreed that this was not a sensible operation. There was another potential problem with this order: the operation fell outside the terms of the UN Security Council Resolution, and so the commander of each national force was entitled to consult his superiors back home, and if the response was negative, he could decline to participate.

Sure enough, ten minutes later the French played their 'red card'. Paris had conducted a risk assessment and decided to pull out. Earlier we had also contacted the American Brigade. They offered six of their Apache attack helicopters to support the operation, but no ground troops. The view of my staff, including those Americans attached to KFOR HQ, was that Washington wanted the operation to take place but not at the risk of American lives. 1 Para – now lined up in a cornfield close to the border on fifteen minutes' notice to go – was on its own. This was not the way to do it. When all my staff had gone, leaving me alone with James in my office, I unbuttoned my rank badge and flung it on the table. 'I cannot do it; it makes no fucking sense.' James looked at me apprehensively. I knew that Richard Dannatt had been closely in touch with London. Almost certainly he was holding the British national red card in his pocket. But as KFOR commander I felt it would be a cop-out for me to rely on this. The planning staff agreed with my own analysis, but this was my call. Since my military judgement was so strongly against this operation I should be prepared to oppose it publicly, even if it meant putting my own career on the line.

Clark had called a video conference for 15.00 hours. This was obviously to be the decision point. I asked Richard Dannatt to attend. As we assembled in the conference room before the video camera, I was ready to resign. For the first time in my almost forty years in the army I had been given an order that I felt I could not in principle accept. In a few minutes' time my career could be over. But Clark had a surprise in store. 'We are not now going to execute this option,' he announced as the conference began. 'We will now wait to see if Yeltsin has lied to the President.' Clearly, there had been some communication between the two leaders. He had just begun to say that he wanted the plan to seize the airfield kept in readiness when the power went down and we lost the connection.

It seemed that I was not going to have to resign, at least not straight away. As I looked around it was obvious that I was not the only one in the room to feel relieved that the operation had been put on hold. By the time we had re-established the connection, Wes Clark was gone and Rupert Smith was in the chair. He took us through the arguments that had led to the stand-down of the operation. Apparently the decision had been founded on 'a balance of risk versus advantage'. Indeed; but my feeling was *that* sort of *key* judgement should be made before you put all these wheels in motion, not afterwards.

It was an interesting insight into Clark's thinking. He had perceived the Russian troop movements as a 'threat', and had drawn an analogy with the race to Berlin in 1945. It was the language of the Cold War.

We were back to Plan A, entry into Kosovo at first light the next morning. I was relieved that the operation to seize the airfield had been put on hold, but irritated that events had prevented me from making my planned final visits to all the brigades. But it was too late now. We just had to trust the mission.

After so much chopping and changing I felt I ought to at least fly up to 5 Airborne Brigade to explain why they had been mucked about all day. After all, they had been on fifteen minutes' notice to go, which is just about enough time to fire up the helicopter engines, get the boys on board and strapped in, carry out all the checks and lift off. The soldiers had been sitting for several hours by the helicopters in a cornfield under a hot sun, with all their equipment lined up on the ground beside them. One moment they were told they were flying into a potentially hostile situation and had psyched themselves up accordingly, the next moment they were back to the original peace support operation. In such circumstances a soldier can begin to lose faith in his superiors.

I flew up to the cornfield, where 1 Para had just received the order to stand down. There was the unforgettable sight of a dozen or so big twin-rotor Chinook helicopters stretched out in a long line ready for take-off, with rows of soldiers behind each aircraft sitting on their kit. I apologized to Adrian Freer, the Brigade Commander, a punchy character nicknamed 'Angry of Aldershot', at least in part because of his shock of ginger hair, and explained some of the background. Then I said, 'Right, I'm going to see my son,' and walked across to find Mark. He greeted me cheerily – 'Hello, Dad' – and we had a brief chat. He'd been in Macedonia almost a week, but this was the first time we'd seen each other. It was good to have him there. 'There's no way we'll be going to the airfield today,' I told him. The mood of the Pathfinder Platoon was mixed, a combination of frustration and disappointment. I lined up for a photograph with Mark and the Platoon before flying back to Skopje for the regular evening update at 18.00 hours. This was followed by the daily conference call at 19.00 hours, when the form was that I would speak by radio to all the brigade commanders and other senior staff, including Rear Support Command at Thessaloniki. The conference call that night was a fiasco. First we could not get hold of everybody, then the power collapsed again. After a day of so much tension I was not in a good mood. The difficulties with the conference were particularly worrying with H-Hour due next morning, but eventually the hard-pressed communicators got the net up and running again. It seemed the last straw when we heard that a large number of the refugees had broken out of their camp to celebrate the impending Serb withdrawal. The bloody idiots were blocking our route into Kosovo.

At 22.15 hours that night I received a personal message from Her Majesty the Queen, asking me to convey the following message to all the British servicemen and women under my command:

I have nothing but admiration for the way in which you have carried out your duties over recent weeks during this difficult time of preparation and improvisation in caring for the refugees. I have no doubt that much greater pressures now lie ahead as you prepare to move into Kosovo as part of KFOR with the eyes of the world on you. I am confident in your ability to rise to these challenges and I am proud of every one of you, as are your families and friends who watch and wait. My thoughts and prayers are with you all.

I replied as follows:

Your kind and gracious message has been most gratefully received by all British servicemen and women here in Macedonia. We plan to enter Kosovo tomorrow 12 June at first light. God save Your Majesty.

I got to bed about midnight and had just fallen asleep when the telephone rang. It was the Joint Operations Centre in Naples, informing us that H-Hour, scheduled for 05.00, was to be delayed twenty-four hours: 'Reason unknown'. None of us could believe that the operation could be postponed at such short notice, considering all that we had been through in the day that had just finished. The phone rang repeatedly in the next few hours, while an oddly dressed group of us gathered in the conference room. Mike Venables, my usually dapper political adviser, was wearing just a pair of trousers. James Everard, not known for his sartorial elegance at the best of times, had just a towel wrapped round his waist. Andrew Ridgway was the most appropriately clad in his dressing gown. I was wearing boxer shorts, a glass of whisky in one hand and a cigar in the other.

I tried to call Clark but I could not reach him. I managed to get hold of Jim Ellis, who was aware of the delay but knew nothing more. He promised to chase an answer down and called back fifteen minutes later. All he had been able to discover was that the delay was something to do with the need to integrate the Russians into the deployment plan. I was fairly irritated at this point. I told Jim in no uncertain terms that we would be into 'damage limitation like you have never seen before. If we carry on like this, the whole chain of command will be exhausted before we start.'

The logistical problems of delaying H-Hour at such short notice were bad enough. Six brigades from five different countries were ready to move across the border in a few hours' time from many different locations scattered across northern Macedonia. It was a complicated plan with plenty of opportunity for cock-ups. The plan had 5 (UK) Airborne Brigade securing the Kacanik defile, with 4 (UK) Armoured Brigade passing through and on to Pristina; at the same time the German Brigade would head for Prizren, in south-west Kosovo, through Albania; the French Brigade would move into south-east Kosovo over the mountains, before moving on to their final deployment area in the north; the Italian Brigade was to follow on through the Kacanik defile on their way to north-west Kosovo; and the US Brigade, with a complicated US Marine Corps/US Army handover, was to relieve the French in the south-east.

Perhaps even worse was the psychological effect of delay. Soldiers are used to being mucked about, but I was very reluctant to muck them about any further – particularly as I had a strong suspicion that the delay might be revoked. There was also the effect of further delay on international opinion and KFOR's credibility, and on the refugees – not to mention the Serbs. It had not been announced that we were due to go in that morning, but since the press conference on Thursday after the agreement was signed everyone had known that it was imminent.

After discussing the problem with my immediate staff in my office I thought: Bollocks, I'm not going to do this. I took the decision not to pass on the order to delay H-Hour – at least, not for the time being. Sky News and CNN were showing pictures of Russian troops in Pristina being welcomed by jubilant Serbs. There was much speculation from the pundits about the significance of what was happening. President Clinton was said to be 'stunned' by this development.

I called Rupert Smith at home. Rupert was a very old friend, pragmatic and highly operationally experienced, with an offbeat sense of humour, who understood the difficulties of multinational operations. His wife answered the phone rather sleepily. 'Suzie, it's Jacko,' I said. 'I'm really sorry, but I've got to talk to him.' Rupert came on the line. He hadn't even been aware of the delay. Oh, he said when I told him. I asked: 'Any bright ideas, Rupes?' He called back a few minutes later and I ran through the advantages and disadvantages of delaying H-Hour with him. We felt that the disadvantages overwhelmingly outweighed the advantages. I told Rupert, 'I'm going to have to have it out with Wes. I just cannot go on being buggered about like this – it's getting to the stage when I can't look my own people in the eye.'

At 02.29 hours Ivanov announced on television that the Russian troops should not have been deployed and would 'withdraw immediately'. But there was no evidence that they were doing so.

Jim Ellis called five minutes later. I took him through the

arguments against a delay. A land operation like this involved multiple small units carrying out different functions, all of which needed to be coordinated. 'It's not like a ship, Admiral,' I said. 'In a ship, the captain says to the bloke at the wheel, thirty degrees starboard, and everyone turns to starboard. With an army, particularly with a multinational army scattered over different assembly areas, it's a different matter altogether.'

Over the next hour or so I spoke to Jim several times. I knew that the CDS, Sir Charles Guthrie, and George Robertson, Secretary of State for Defence, were both putting pressure on the Americans to keep to the original H-Hour. It was clear that the mood was changing and that the decision to delay might be revoked. I informed Jim of our assessment that the last safe moment to put the operation back on was 04.00 hours. Of course, this was also the last safe moment to delay it, but I didn't go into that. Jim called at 03.46, fourteen minutes before our deadline. H-Hour was back on again at 05.00. We were back in business. Good call.

At 05.05 Sky TV showed the first Chinooks flying 5 Airborne Brigade forward across the border into Kosovo. We were all knackered. The whisky bottle was empty. Someone from SHAPE called to ask where we would be holding our press conference in Pristina. My ADC told him where to get off.

As the morning progressed, reports came in that the advance was going smoothly, though minefields and the very difficult terrain which they had to cross were delaying the French. We had expected to come under fire from scattered Serb units opposed to the order to pull back, but it seemed that there was very little resistance. I had to restrain 5 Airborne Brigade from confiscating weapons, which was not allowed by the terms of our agreement with the Serbs. Later in the day we received reports that Serb police and militia were coming under attack from the Kosovo Liberation Army. I tried to relay a message to the KLA leadership to get them to stop.

Not long after H-Hour we received a call from Jim Ellis's Chief of Staff, Lieutenant General Jack Nix, who commented that he was amazed we had managed to remount the operation at such short notice. He was much amused when James Everard told him that I had never passed on the order to cancel it.

I emerged from updating Clark at the morning video conference to find a Russian colonel in full dress uniform, peaked cap and all, waiting for me. I was introduced to Colonel Gromov, the local military attaché in Skopje. He handed me a letter from the Russian Ministry of Defence, informing me that 'the leading element of the Russian KFOR contingent' now controlled the airfield at Pristina. So Gromov had been told by his superiors in Moscow to come and see me. This bizarre performance was confirmation that the Russian column in Pristina wasn't just a rogue element of soldiers doing their own thing. They were part of 'the Russian KFOR contingent'. The other fact I noticed was that the letter was addressed to me by name as 'Commander, KFOR'. It seemed to me a significant acknowledgement. The Russians were saying that they were willing to be part of what we were doing. I had to fax the letter to both SHAPE and Jim Ellis's Naples HQ.

I've thought about this quite a bit since and my view is that the Russians were making a point by sending a column into Kosovo. They had been worsted in the Cold War, and there was considerable upset, even indignation, on the Russian side about NATO's expansion and the fact that the Alliance had undertaken military action against Serbia without a UN Security Council Resolution. The intervention was a reminder that the Russians were still players on the world stage, that they still needed to be treated with respect.

If Clark was thinking in these terms, he didn't show it. He wanted me to do all that we could to prevent the Russians from 'creating facts on the ground'. Over the secure telephone line he urged me to increase the tempo. He was planning to fly down to

Skopje himself early the next morning. I rejigged our plans, ordering 5 Airborne Brigade to push on towards the airport as quickly as possible. By mid-afternoon they had got there and Adrian Freer had established contact with the Russian commanding officer, who turned out to be a two-star general, a mark of the importance of this relatively small column in Russian eyes.

By 18.30 hours we had secured the 10-mile-long defile into Kosovo, and the leading British elements were closing on Pristina itself. The weather had turned filthy, with heavy clouds and a thunderstorm moving in, but the media people were very keen for me to fly in to give a short press conference at Pristina Airport that evening to mark KFOR's entry, and somewhat against my better judgement I said OK, I'll do it. It occurred to me that I could kill two birds with one stone: do the press conference and make contact with the Russians, to establish some kind of relationship, whatever might be happening at a higher level. We climbed into two Lynx helicopters and took off. This was the first time I had crossed the border, and it was quite a sight to look down and see columns of vehicles streaming north into Kosovo. As we came out of the defile we flew into driving rain and when we were about halfway to Pristina the pilot said that he would have to put down. He said that if we let the worst of the storm pass we would probably be all right to continue. The Lynx landed close to a filling station by the main road, where a bunch of British soldiers were having a brew. I walked over and joined them for a coffee before the weather eased and we took off again for the airfield.

The press conference was a bit of a washout, literally and metaphorically. Afterwards I introduced myself to one of the Russians and asked if I could see General Viktor Zavarzin. I was ushered into the back of his command vehicle. My first impression was of a burly man who seemed somewhat nervous. I greeted him in Russian, even though I had an interpreter with me. He was a bit frosty at first, and it was pretty hard going. Then the rain must have got into the electrics because the vehicle filled with acrid black smoke. We got out and stood in the rain, which was still bucketing down. I said to Zavarzin, 'Hey, listen, I used to get wet as a company commander, but generals don't need to get wet.' We found a dry place in what remained of the wrecked airport terminal. I had a flask of whisky in my map pocket and I dug it out and offered it to Zavarzin. Relations warmed up after that.

When I got back to the Shoe Factory I found that Clark had spoken personally to Andrew Ridgway. He seemed obsessed by the threat of Russian troops invading the Serb enclaves, particularly in the north, and establishing a *de facto* partition of Kosovo. To prevent this happening, he wanted the runway blocked by KFOR helicopters. My team failed to see the logic in this order. We already controlled the airspace, so the Russians would have to run the NATO gauntlet if they wanted to fly in fixed-wing aircraft. Putting helicopters down on the runway would simply confuse the situation, and provoke the Russians. Despite the team's reservations, Andrew had contacted the US Brigade, the only force with uncommitted helicopters available. Shortly afterwards the Americans called back: they were playing the red card! They declined to take part in the operation. Two hours later the Americans were on the phone again: they would do it after all. Obviously Clark had been talking to Washington. But by now the weather had deteriorated further. The American brigade commander felt that it was not possible to implement the order without serious risk. Andrew recommended that the operation be put on hold until Clark arrived in the morning and it was possible to 'clarify SACEUR's intent'. I agreed. I managed to get some sleep that night.

Clark arrived at 08.40 hours on Sunday and caught the end of the morning update. He still seemed obsessed by the Russians, and would not focus on anything else. Clark was convinced that they intended to reinforce their troops at the airport. We gave him our intelligence assessment, which was that the Russians had neither the capability nor the political will to confront the international community in this way. Again and again I stressed that confrontation was not the answer. Russian support had been crucial in delivering the deal with the Serbs. They were major players and must be treated as such. To alienate them would be counter-productive in both the short term and the long term. I argued for a more subtle approach, isolating the Russians as a prelude to obtaining their participation.

Either Wes wasn't listening, or he wasn't convinced. It seemed that he had discussed the situation by phone with the NATO Secretary General Javier Solana on the flight down to the Balkans, and they had agreed a common position. Clark ordered me to block the runway one way or another. I don't mind admitting that I was furious. We were all tired, frustrated with the stopping and starting, and fed up with being buggered about. After the morning update I indicated to Clark that I wanted a word with him in private, and led the way to my office, closing the door behind us.

'SACEUR, we cannot go on like this,' I said with some feeling: 'We need to move on. Let me sort it out with the Russians.'

But Clark was unmoved, and insisted that we should block the airfield.

'I won't do it! Sir, I just won't do it,' I said heatedly.

Clark seemed taken aback. 'Mike, let's talk about this,' he said.

Once again I ran through the reasons for my very grave reservations about implementing the order. We had established liaison with Russians on the ground. Blocking the runway would not help bring the Russians onside. They were dislocated anyway. Our troops were in position and had effectively isolated the Russians already. The airfield had no current operational value at this point. We controlled the airspace. Apart from anything else, the Russians could have flown reinforcements into Serbian airfields and then moved across the border into Kosovo by vehicle. As for us, we could continue to use Skopje. Pristina Airport just wasn't that important. Finally, the order fell outside the terms of the mandate.

I made it clear to Clark that I was fed up with taking orders from Washington, from people who seemed to have no appreciation of the problems on the ground.

'Mike, these aren't Washington's orders, they're coming from me.'

'By whose authority?'

'By my authority, as SACEUR.'

'You don't have that authority.'

'I do have that authority. I have the authority of the Secretary General behind me on this.'

'Sir, I'm not going to start World War Three for you.'

Again Clark stated what he wanted done.

I said to him, 'Sir, I'm a three-star general, you can't give me orders like this. I have my own judgement of the situation and I believe that this order is outside our mandate.'

'Mike, I'm a four-star general, and I can tell you these things.'

He insisted that he was giving me a direct order. I told him that I would have to talk to my superiors in London. He telephoned Charles Guthrie, and outlined the discussion that had just taken place. Guthrie asked to speak to me. I took the phone and moved away from Clark to speak to Guthrie in private. 'I cannot go on,' I told him, 'I'm going to have to resign.'

'For God's sake, Mike, don't do that,' Guthrie replied hastily. 'It would be a disaster.' He asked to speak to Clark again. 'Well, I must say, Wes,' he said, 'that I agree with Mike – and so does Hugh.'

Clark was visibly nonplussed. Hugh Shelton was his boss. He had gone out on a limb, and now he found that he had gone too far. I left the room so that he could call Shelton in Washington. I gathered later that Shelton told him that Washington did want the runways blocked, but not at the expense of a confrontation with the Russians – which seemed to me an outright contradiction in terms. When Clark said that I was resisting his orders, Shelton suggested that he had an 'authority problem'.

Clark called me back into the room. 'Mike, do you understand that as a NATO commander I'm giving you a legal order, and if you don't accept that order you'll have to resign your position and get out of the chain of command?'

'SACEUR, I do.'

'OK. I'm giving you an order to block the runways at Pristina airfield. I want it done. Is that clear?'

SACEUR was insistent, despite the risk of a confrontation with the Russians. I suggested that armoured vehicles would be better suited to blocking the runways than helicopters, in the almost certain knowledge that the UK would decline such a provocative move. Clark agreed that the vehicles would be preferable. I went out to pass the order for 4 Armoured Brigade to place a combat team on short notice to move to the airfield, knowing that it would be referred to Richard Dannatt for national approval. Meanwhile Clark called Shelton again. Apparently Shelton had been trying to reach Charles Guthrie, but had been told that he was in a meeting with the Prime Minister.

I returned to the room and reported to Clark that I had given the warning order. He tried to change the subject, but I wasn't prepared to leave it there. 'SACEUR, you're just testing me, aren't you? You don't really want me to do this, do you?' He denied any such motive. After a little more discussion I left again to check on what was happening. Andrew informed me that London had played the red card.

Clark seemed to feel somehow that this was my doing. On the contrary, I had deliberately not spoken to Richard Dannatt to avoid any accusation of collusion, as I felt very strongly that as a commander of a multinational force I should not act as a Brit per se, or favour any particular national contingent. And though Wes didn't seem to credit this, I also felt a soldier's loyalty to my chain of command. But I felt very strongly that it would be a mistake to confront the Russians, whichever nation's troops were on the spot.

Clark again phoned Shelton, and then tried to contact Guthrie, who was still unavailable. He didn't say anything to me, and I didn't say anything to him. There was nothing more to be said. After a short time Clark and his team left to return to SHAPE HQ in Belgium.

I telephoned Charles Guthrie, who had George Robertson with him, and my words were relayed to them both on the speakerphone. I told them what had happened. 'You may take the view I should go, Secretary of State, CDS,' I concluded. But both Guthrie and Robertson were very supportive of the line I had taken. Meanwhile the MOD had been in contact with Richard Dannatt as COMBRITFOR. He was authorized to deploy 4 Armoured Brigade to Pristina Airport and if necessary to isolate it, but not to block the runways. James Everard telephoned Wes Clark's MA to inform him of this. Clark's British MA (Lieutenant Colonel David Limb, also by chance a Parachute Regiment officer) assured James that he understood the problems, but he was less sure that SACEUR did.

Ten minutes later Clark's MA called again, anxious about a CNN report of tanks with Russian markings at the airfield. It sounded unlikely, and we soon established that the report referred to Serb Army tanks with Federal Republic of Yugoslavia (FRY) markings moving past the airfield as they withdrew. My view was that Clark's people needed to get a grip, and stop panicking in response to every unfounded rumour or ill-informed press report. The next ridiculous, poorly thought-out order I received would be the last, as I would refuse to implement it.

In fact, the crisis was over. We had avoided an unnecessary and potentially dangerous confrontation with the Russians. But my relationship with my superior officer, General Wesley Clark, had suffered. I had come to the brink of refusing a direct order, though in the event it had not quite come to that. And Clark himself had been damaged. Two months later it was announced that he would be replaced as Supreme Allied Commander earlier than expected. When Clark announced that he would be standing as a candidate for the Democratic Party's presidential nomination, Shelton said, in a public forum, that Clark being short-toured 'had to do with integrity and character issues', adding, 'Wes won't get my vote.' Despite my differences with him, I thought that this was a less than fair judgement. Wes Clark had not spared himself to achieve a successful outcome to the Kosovo campaign.

There was one last twist in the tale. At 01.00 hours the next morning, after I'd gone to bed, I received a call from Jim Ellis. Again it was the Russians. There had been a report that six aircraft had taken off from Moscow, headed for Pristina. This was the third such alarm. We were as sure as we could be that this scare contained no more substance than the previous two (and so it would turn out). I was exhausted, and I'm afraid that I replied rather sardonically to Ellis, a man I liked and respected: 'Admiral, if Russian planes are on their way I will go to Pristina and welcome them with open arms to KFOR.' Fatigue had made me facetious. 'If SACEUR wants to shoot them down with US aircraft, that's his business. Goodnight.'

13

Nation-Building

Operation 'Joint Guardian' proceeded according to plan. Within a few days units of KFOR had penetrated all parts of Kosovo. Whenever a KFOR vehicle drove through a village, children would run out waving and cheering. It was obvious that most of the inhabitants saw us as deliverers. The atmosphere was euphoric. People would applaud when they recognized me in the street, in Pristina and elsewhere. It was all rather embarrassing.

I flew around the brigades in the first few days, meeting the commanders and dealing with their immediate problems. From the air you could see plumes of smoke curling up from burning buildings: the Albanian Kosovars were indulging in the typical Balkan behaviour of burning the houses of the enemy. The Serbs fulfilled their obligations under the MTA, withdrawing their security forces on schedule and in good order, though some tanks had plunder strapped to their sides. Before long we began to discover grisly evidence of their activity: sites of mass graves scattered across the country. Jonathan Bailey was my liaison man at the Serb Army HQ in Pristina; he witnessed scenes of frantic activity, as files were hurled out of the windows into the courtyard below to be burned in the incinerator. On their last night they drank the place dry. Despite the difficult circumstances Jonathan forged a good relationship with the Serbs, and he continued to liaise with them after they'd left Kosovo. Once a week he would go over the border into Serbia proper, and they'd discuss issues arising over a Balkan lunch.

Many Serb officials – administrators, judges, prison warders, utility workers, teachers and doctors – had chosen to quit Kosovo when the security forces left, presenting KFOR with the task of filling the vacuum they left behind. The Serbs remaining in Kosovo were fearful – justifiably so – of revenge attacks by ethnic Albanians. Plenty of scores were settled in those first few days. Armed KLA units began to emerge from the woods and come down from the hills. There was widespread looting, burning of abandoned houses, grenade attacks, beatings and shootings. In the worst such incident, we found the bodies of fourteen Serb farmers lying in fields about 12 miles south of Pristina. It was one of our core tasks to try to retain as many Serbs as possible. If too many of the Serbs left, the Western ideal of ethnic balance would appear to be hollow. Their security was at the heart of this. The attitude of the Kosovo Serbs was a curious mixture of fear and defiance. On D+13 I attended a meeting of Serb teaching staff at the university after the murder of one of their professors: their anxiety was palpable, but when they spoke they alternated between arrogance and venom. They wanted my help, but they could not resist a litany of complaint and grievances. Bloody-mindedness is a defining Serb characteristic; appropriately enough, they have a word for it, *inat*. There were intelligence reports of a Serb plot to assassinate me, but I didn't take this seriously. If they had any sense, they would realize that we were there to protect them.

On 14 June, D+2, we had put our so-called Tactical

Headquarters (Tac HQ) – a group of core staff from the main headquarters – forward into Pristina. Somewhere between the airport and the city they found a half-built industrial building, and settled in there. I joined them the next day. We quickly realized that we needed to be closer to town, and less than a week later we moved main HQ up from Skopje to a new location, a film studio on a ridge overlooking the city. At night you could see many fires burning in the city below and in the surrounding countryside. The building was a modern office block which we referred to as the Film Factory, with a cavernous studio below which quickly became known as the Bat Cave. There was no accommodation, so to start with everybody was in tents. We set up a field kitchen, and every meal was al fresco. It was summer, the weather was warm and settled, and a copse of Mediterranean pine provided some welcome shade – and a place to relax and to entertain visitors, whether VIPs from abroad or local worthies. I and my immediate staff tended to eat later than the others, after the evening conference call. It was good to be back on fresh rations, after living for days in Tac HQ on field rations: a daily box of 'boil in the bag' food. I made a point of thanking the resourceful and enthusiastic Army chefs, who supplied us with excellent food whatever the local difficulties.

We built a large helipad about two or three hundred yards behind the building. There were also two smaller helicopter pads right in front – known, no doubt a bit optimistically, as the 'VIP LS' (landing site). Aircraft could be summoned from the main pad to be waiting there in the front, rotors whirling, ready for immediate take-off. In those early days my time was so precious that I needed to conserve every minute. Having a helicopter waiting at the front meant that I could dash straight out of the building, board and lift off immediately.

My six-man command group occupied the first floor of the office building, and here, just as at the Shoe Factory, we slept in our offices. At the far end was an 'executive' bathroom, which would have been an improvement on the field alternative had the shower been working. A Macedonian plumber arrived to mend it, but didn't bother to check that the waste pipe was connected to the outfall, with the inevitable consequences. I was first to use the shower. Jonathan Bailey had the misfortune to occupy the room below, and after a while my shower water began to drip through the ceiling on to his desk, causing much amusement to everyone except Jonathan and me.

This was a reminder – not that we needed one – that it was crucial to get the infrastructure working as soon as possible. If you don't get the water supply working pretty quickly, you start getting problems with hygiene and disease, and since many of the Serb doctors had left with their Army compatriots we couldn't afford to allow this to happen. But without electricity the pumps couldn't operate. Many of the Serb specialists who made everything work, the technicians and the engineers, had disappeared when the security forces withdrew. And without a working telephone exchange it would be more difficult for Kosovo to get itself back on its feet. So we set our Army signallers to sort out the telephone exchange, put Army medics into the hospitals and allotted Army engineers to reconstruction projects – just to keep as much as possible functioning until the UN civil administration was ready to shoulder the burden. I sent an engineer squadron up to the old lignite-fired power stations outside Pristina to see if there was anything they could do. The squadron commander used the satellite phone to speak to his uncle in the UK, who worked for the Central Electricity Generating Board. One can imagine the uncle's surprise on receiving a call from Kosovo. 'It's me – I need a bit of help!' And the uncle talked him through the process of how to run this less than state-of-the-art power station which used the dirtiest fuel of all. After that we had intermittent power. You could look out of the window at the power station on the skyline, and if you could see smoke belching out of one of the chimneys, you knew that the power was likely to be on. We had our own generator as a back-up, but of course that didn't pump the water, which came and went. Without regular water, living conditions rapidly become rather sordid. Later on the CEGB sent out two very capable engineers who soon had the power station running as well as – probably better than – it had ever done.

The Territorial Army railway gang came into their own, getting the train line south to Skopje up and running by D+14. I remember riding on the footplate for a while to celebrate its re-opening. Once the railway was working again it took a lot of traffic off the road. The line continued all the way down to the port of Thessaloniki, so from that moment on we could bring in supplies and vehicles by rail.

To me all this was basic stuff, which was why I was surprised by the failure to address infrastructure issues promptly in Iraq in 2003. It's not as though we haven't had enough experience to learn from. That hard-won experience should have impressed upon governments that if people's lives don't quickly improve, they rapidly become disenchanted. It's difficult enough to build a civil society in a country devastated by war; without the basics of life it's near impossible. Gilbert Greenall's rule of thumb of the first hundred days being crucial remains very pertinent. I go back to my analogy of a length of rope, made up of strands: a military strand, a security strand, a reconstruction strand, a humanitarian strand, a demobilization strand, a political strand, and an economic strand. The individual strands are easily cut, but once they are woven together, the rope is strong.

I think it was Donald Rumsfeld who said, 'We don't do nation-building.' To my mind, that kind of dismissal on principle is nonsensical – and operationally detrimental as well, because the overall success of the operation will depend upon reconstruction. In Iraq, the Americans had the naïve idea that the people would be so happy to be liberated that nothing else mattered; that once they had pushed over the statue of Saddam

Hussein, democracy would flourish overnight. It's a very ideo-logical approach, and one which is intellectually bankrupt. This difference in doctrine between us and the Americans would be a recurrent difficulty in the years ahead. Military force should never be used for its own sake, but always to achieve a political objective. The generic political objective of any intervention must be to bring about those circumstances in which the country becomes at peace with itself; at peace with its neighbours; with its boundaries unchanged; stable therefore; with a representative government accepted by at least a respectable majority of its citizens – and that doesn't necessarily mean a Western liberal democracy; and the prospect of a better future for all.

Early one morning, a few days after our entry into Kosovo, I was sitting outside Tac HQ on a camp stool talking to Andrew Ridgway and enjoying the sunshine when I heard somebody exclaim, 'What on earth—?' I looked up to see the most extraor-dinary sight: a group of figures in long black robes, striding towards us across the fields in a sort of arrowhead formation. As they approached, we saw that they were clergy of the Serbian Orthodox Church, led by the Patriarch himself, carrying a crozier.

I greeted him with great respect. The Patriarch of the Serbian Orthodox Church is not somebody to be treated lightly, and indeed he cut a very distinguished figure. We found some chairs and offered them some coffee. With the Patriarch was the Bishop of Kosovo, and among the retinue was a very tall young priest who spoke immaculate English and acted as translator. It turned out that he'd spent some time in America, and was an absolute IT wizard; at the Film Factory he soon acquired the nickname of 'Cyber-monk'.

The Patriarch told us that he had come to Kosovo to see for himself what was happening to his people. He told us tales of burning, rape and ethnic cleansing of Serb civilians, all the dreadful things that were being done to his long-suffering Serb parishioners by these terrible Albanians. He lamented the failure of KFOR to protect the Serb population. It was apparent to me that the Church was just about the only surviving institution from the former Serb regime, and the clergy the only surviving figures of authority: everyone else had fled to Serbia proper. So it was logical for the Bishop of Kosovo to represent the interests of the remaining Serbs. Subsequently he became one of two Serb members of the Transitional Council set up by the UN.

I laid out what KFOR was doing and the security that we intended to bring to *all* the people of Kosovo. We agreed to place a static guard on the main Serb Orthodox churches and monasteries, in case some Kosovar hothead decided to burn them down. We ended the meeting on good terms. The Patriarch left with a KFOR escort. Later he addressed a crowd in the court-yard of the fourteenth-century monastery at Gracanica, the seat of the Bishop of Kosovo. 'I call on you to be able and persevere to the end, because everything will pass. He who perseveres to the end will be saved.' That was very Serbian: we are down-trodden, but we will endure.

Afterwards the Bishop asked me to lunch two or three times, which was always a very splendid affair. We sat down with half a dozen or so of the clergy, the Bishop at the head of the table, being waited upon by nuns, in the medieval splendour of the monastery, drinking 'the best wine in Kosovo'.

On D+3 I had held another meeting with General Zavarzin. Any sense of threat was fast fading. The real obstacle to an agree-ment with the Russians was political, not military: they wanted a slice of the action. It rapidly became obvious that poor old Viktor Zavarzin had no real negotiating power. Everything had to be referred back to Moscow, because the situation was so political. I decided to play it long. I met Zavarzin regularly, without pushing for an immediate solution. Our relations became more cordial. Since the first time we met, when I had offered him that swig from my hip flask, he reciprocated with vodka on every occasion, no matter what the time of day. It was all very Russian. Soon after KFOR's entry, a chance meeting with his deputy revealed that his men were short of drinking water; so I arranged to have sent over to them all the spare bottled water we could find. They appreciated the gesture. Two or three days later I had another chat with Zavarzin.

'So, how's it going up at the airport?' I asked him.

'We are having problems with the KLA. They have snipers. We are vulnerable up here.'

I couldn't resist remarking, 'Well, Viktor, you did choose to go there.' He smiled.

'I'll tell you what we'll do,' I said. 'I will put some of my British soldiers around you in an outer security cordon. I don't think the KLA will give us any trouble. Would that help?' Indeed it would, was the reply. Then inspiration struck. 'Furthermore,' I went on, 'this force of British soldiers will be commanded by my own son.'

Zavarzin beamed, and advanced to give me a bear hug. The Russians are a very sentimental people.

The trouble with sending Mark and the Pathfinders to the airport was that it meant acting contrary to the philosophy of delegation that we in the British Army hold so dear. We have a guiding principle, whereby the senior commander tells the subordinate what he has to do, what objectives he has to achieve, what effect he is to bring about, what resources he has to do it – but not *how* he has to do it. That is always left to the subordinate commander. We call this 'mission command', and it's an essential part of the way we operate. What I had done went against everything I had been taught and believed in. Needs must, however, I thought to myself.

At the time 5 Airborne Brigade was established in a small market town about 6 miles south of the airport. I got on the radio to Adrian Freer.

'I've just had a meeting with Zavarzin,' I told him. 'He's feeling a bit insecure. Your task, Adrian, is to make the Russians feel loved and protected.'

Adrian said that he understood.

'Adrian, I'm now going to break the rules of mission command, because I am going to tell you how I want this done. I've told Zavarzin that Mark will be in command. So I want Mark and his merry men involved, whoever else you decide to use for whatever. Furthermore, find a bottle of whisky from somewhere, give it to Mark, and tell him to give it to General Zavarzin with his father's compliments.'

The bottle was a message to Zavarzin. He would appreciate that I had sent my own son to look after him. I am no psychologist, but I sensed that this would mean a lot. It seemed to work. Russian forces eventually deployed into the sectors headed by the French, German and Americans; they turned over responsibility for air traffic control and logistics at the airport to the British, while keeping the security function. The airport was soon functioning normally.

As I said, the Russians are a sentimental people.

The refugee crisis solved itself, melting away like spring snow in a thaw. When D-Day arrived, most of the people in the camps in Albania and Macedonia just got up and went home, many of them on foot. It was an amazing sight, these tens of thousands of people at any one time streaming back into Kosovo. It was extraordinary to think of hundreds of thousands of families repossessing their former homes, finding some of them burned out or occupied by squatters, picking up the threads of their former lives. There was one hell of a traffic jam on the road coming up from Macedonia, as our convoys of military and UN vehicles struggled to pass the slow-moving masses. But within a few days it was clear. The refugee problem was over.

The UNHCR had put together a complicated plan for the

return of the refugees, but as things turned out their help was not required. The people returned of their own accord. I remember talking to the regional head of UNHCR, a man called Denis McNamara, a New Zealander, not long after D-Day. 'The refugee problem is over,' I observed.

'Yes,' he conceded somewhat grudgingly, 'but they didn't follow *our plan*.'

Before KFOR moved into Kosovo, a negotiating mechanism had been set up with the KLA. Most of the talks took place in Albania, because that was their base. As AFOR Commander, John Reith had conducted the negotiations on NATO's behalf. We had hoped to have concluded an agreement before we went in, but that didn't happen. So we didn't have rules telling us how to deal with the KLA on entry, as we had in our dealings with the Serb armed forces. NATO had not forced the Serbs out in order to leave Kosovo in the hands of 'warlords' – though if KFOR was going to restrain the KLA, clashes were almost unavoidable. The issue became more and more pressing as each day passed. The Serb withdrawal resulted in a dangerous vacuum. Armed KLA fighters emerged, unrestricted by any Serb security presence. Many of them seemed to imagine that they were now free to lord it over the population. Despite our best efforts, different KFOR brigades took different national lines with the KLA. The British wanted the KLA fighters disarmed, which annoyed them no end. The Germans and the Dutch, on the other hand, were somewhat cosy with them – too cosy, in my opinion. These differences in attitude mirrored contrasting views of the KLA within NATO: some regarded them as not much better than terrorists, whereas others saw them as freedom fighters.

The concluding phase of NATO's negotiations with the KLA took place in their field headquarters in the hills, some 25 miles west of Pristina. John Reith continued to represent NATO, with the help of Jamie Rubin, Clinton's State Department spokesman and the husband of CNN's star reporter Christiane Amanpour, whom I had come to know well during my tours in the Balkans. Negotiations continued until D+8, the last day of the eleven given by the MTA for the Serbs to withdraw. Eventually the KLA agreed to sign an Undertaking, renouncing the use of force and acknowledging KFOR's sole authority under UNSCR 1244.

At 22.50 hours an RAF Chinook landed at our Tac HQ, bearing Reith, Rubin and the KLA leaders. The two most important were the self-styled 'Commander in Chief' Hashim Thaqi, a tall young man with wavy swept-back hair, and Agim Ceku, the Field Commander. We convened in a muddy tent, sitting on canvas chairs around a long trestle table. I was amused to note that Thaqi was wearing a patterned tie and a shiny suit, indicating his future political ambitions. Ceku, a big, heavy-jowled man, rather older than Thaqi, said little, but stared hard at me throughout; I realized after a while that he was trying to take my measure. Ceku's combat kit contrasted with Thaqi's civilian clothes. Before he joined the KLA, he had served with the Croats in Bosnia and the Krajina, and before that in the old Yugoslav army. It was strange to think that he'd been fighting a guerrilla campaign against the army in which he'd once served.

Jamie Rubin was a tall man with dark hair and a no-nonsense manner. He did most of the talking with Thaqi while I scrutinized the paper on the table in front of me. This was the KLA's 'Undertaking' to renounce the use of force and demilitarize. They'd been hedging about this for weeks, trying to avoid committing themselves while they extracted as much as they could from our side. The KLA leaders were insistent that their 'military contribution' should be recognized, and that they should enjoy 'special consideration in the administration and police force' – otherwise known as jobs for the boys. Even more contentious was their ambition for an army of Kosovo on the lines of the US National Guard. Western governments were nervous about being seen to reward 'terrorists'. I'd been under pressure not to give anything significant away. My instructions from NATO were that I could 'receive' the document, but not 'accept' it. Then someone pointed out that in Albanian the same word is used to mean both.

I took my specs off my nose and swung them in one hand as I explained our position. Thaqi nodded. We moved to the main tent, where others were waiting to witness the signing. Jamie handed Thaqi a pen. His hand shook as he signed.

'Right,' said Jamie. 'Now you get your reward.' He whipped out a satellite phone and called the President. After a few words of explanation he handed the phone to Thaqi, whose hand continued to shake as he spoke.

After Thaqi had finished his call, somebody poured out glasses of the local gut rot, and we drank a toast to Kosovo. This was an important moment in the transformation of the KLA into what would become a legitimate organization. The terms of the Undertaking committed the KLA to a timetable for their disbandment as a military force, commencing on its signature. Monday 21 June became 'K-Day' in our diaries, with a programme dating from then onwards. Within seven days (K+7) the KLA agreed to establish secure weapon sites, to be registered and verified by KFOR, to clear minefields and booby traps, to vacate any fighting positions, and to move to assembly areas as agreed with me as COMKFOR. Thereafter, only personnel authorized by COMKFOR would be allowed to bear arms outside these assembly areas: I restricted this concession to senior officers of the KLA with their close protection personnel (not exceeding three), carrying side arms only. By K+30 the retention of any rifles would be subject to my authorization, and all personnel not of local origin would be withdrawn. (The Americans were worried about *mujahedin*, as they had been in Bosnia.) And so on, up to K+90 (19 September), when KFOR would assume full control of the weapons storage sites. By then the KLA were to have completed their processes of demilitariz-ation and would cease wearing either military uniforms or KLA insignia.

In the weeks that followed, I flew around the country meeting KLA regional commanders and enduring a series of yet more elaborate Balkan lunches. It seemed to me important to make contact with the lower levels of the KLA as well as the leaders, to get everyone involved in the process of demilitarization. Meanwhile, I began to develop a good working relationship with Ceku. We had a Joint Implementation Committee (JIC) which met regularly to monitor the progress of demilitarization. At these meetings I would tell Ceku what he should do: we're not satisfied with this, you must do that. Periodically he would remind me of the 'special consideration' due to the KLA for their role in liberating the country. 'I'm still considering it, General Ceku,' I would say.

KLA members of the JIC carried a card entitling them to carry side arms. At the Film Factory we referred to these as the 'Get Out of Jail Free' cards.

The day after the Undertaking was signed, the President of the United States (POTUS) and the First Lady (FLOTUS) arrived in Skopje. They didn't come to Kosovo because of fears about security. I was asked to go down to the airport to meet the President. It was one of those events that the Americans love, but the British find embarrassing. A large group of American soldiers made their presence felt by whooping and cheering. Wes made a triumphal speech, referring to Milosevic personally: 'We won, he lost, and we won with the President behind us all the way. Mr President, I would like to thank you for your wonderful leadership, the guidance you have provided and I thank you for your support.' I imagine that Wes had his fingers crossed behind his back as he said these words. The President also made a short address, paying tribute both to KFOR and to me personally as the KFOR commander. Afterwards we had an exchange of pleasantries. This was before my clash with Wes had been made public. If the President had heard about it, he made no comment on the matter. Even in this very brief encounter, I was impressed by his ability to communicate. He seemed completely at his ease. I am not the first to make the observation that Bill Clinton is a very charismatic man.

My schedule was becoming alarmingly crowded. No two days were the same, but the programme for the next day, 23 June, gives an indication of how busy we were: morning update 08.00, DSACEUR telephone call 08.30, VTC 09.00, Ambassador Petritsch (EU envoy to Kosovo) 09.30, Ambassador Eiff (NATO Secretary General's Civil Representative in Macedonia) 10.15, General Zavarzin 11.00, the Bishop of Pristina and numerous clergy 14.30, British Foreign Secretary and foreign ministers of Italy, Germany and France 16.30, visit UN Headquarters for discussions with the SRSG and foreign secretaries 17.30, evening update 18.00, Minister Vujovic, Deputy Foreign Minister of Serbia (quite brave of him to come, but he did) 18.45, my conference call with the brigade commanders 19.00. Just another day at the office. All the time the telephone was ringing and messages were coming though on the radio. That's why it was so important to have a first-rate staff, who took as much off my shoulders as possible. I can't praise them highly enough for what they did at that time.

High-level visitors continued to arrive in quick succession. The following day it was Javier Solana and Wes Clark with their accompanying multitudes. They did a tour around Pristina, conducted with an air of triumphalism, many hurrahs and much glad-handing. The Albanian community, as if on cue, shouted 'NATO! NATO! Solana! Solana!' I found it embarrassing, frankly. It was as if they'd won an election.

At my meeting with General Zavarzin the previous day I had

explained the KLA Undertaking, and after that the conversation became more light-hearted. He expressed delight at having met Mark, and complimented me on having such a fine son. He thanked me too for the whisky. Then he shared with me some of the difficulties he had been having with Moscow. 'I am hacked off with the politicians,' he told me.

I raised the inevitable glass of vodka in his direction.

'You too, eh, Viktor?'

One person for whom I had a lot of time was the Brazilian SRSG Sergio de Mello, who was later to be killed by a suicide bomb attack in Iraq. Sergio and his small UN team were in Pristina almost as soon as KFOR were there; he immediately began building up UNMIK, the UN 'international civil presence' set up under UNSCR 1244 to work alongside the 'international security presence', which was of course KFOR. He was a great man, a true internationalist, and he saw the civil administration off to a flying start. But his appointment was only a temporary one, until a more permanent candidate was in place. Just before he left, on Friday 16 June, he instituted the Kosovo Transitional Council, which was an attempt to bring together leaders of the various factions in Kosovo under his chairmanship. UNMIK's role was to provide an interim administration until such time as it should be replaced by a locally elected government. At the time of writing, UNMIK is still the constitutional power in Kosovo, though proposals for a permanent settlement are moving forward.

Sergio was replaced by Bernard Kouchner, the founder of Médecins Sans Frontières, who'd been a government minister in France before and in 2007 was appointed French Foreign Minister. I made a point of going down to Pristina Airport to greet Bernard and to salute him, as a symbolic gesture as much as anything: it seemed to me important to show that in a civilized society the military should be subject to the civil authority.

After that I always made a point of deferring to Bernard on public occasions; in private I sometimes teasingly addressed him as 'le roi'. We worked hand-in-hand, meeting daily at 17.00 for as long as it took, sometimes half an hour, sometimes more.

There were no police; but also there was no system of justice, because the judiciary, prison warders and so on had all been Serbs, and almost all of them had chosen to leave. Under UNSCR 1244 KFOR had responsibility for maintaining a 'secure environment', so in effect we were the police – at least until the UN police had built up their strength. To stem the tide of killings you needed a system of justice. But it was very difficult. You'd catch an individual about to murder somebody, arrest him, and hold him. But what were you to do then? Sergio de Mello empanelled a number of judges, both Serbian and Kosovar Albanians. Initially the judges were given the power only to hold a prisoner on remand, but not actually to sentence him; that came later. There were no rules for this situation: Sergio and I had to make them up as we went along.

In the early days, when we were still feeling our way, a prisoner from one ethnic background was brought in front of a judge from another. The main witness was a British military police corporal. The corporal gave his evidence, and was alarmed to observe the judge frowning. 'I am not happy with this confession,' the judge announced.

The corporal assumed that he was being accused of mistreating the prisoner. 'I didn't lay a finger on him, Sir,' he hastened to assure the judge.

'No, no, corporal,' the judge said. 'You misunderstand me. This evidence is not good enough. Take him away and beat him harder.'

Tony Blair would be the first world leader to come to Kosovo after KFOR's entry. He was due to arrive at Pristina on the afternoon of 30 July. I was having lunch that day in the field kitchen behind the Film Factory when James Everard's mobile phone began to ring. It was in my pocket for some reason: I must have borrowed it and failed to give it back. James wasn't around, so I pulled it out of my pocket and answered it.

'Hello?' I said, and a female voice said 'Hello' back.

'Who is that?' I asked.

There was a pause and a deep sigh down the line, followed by, 'It's Caroline.'

'Ah,' I said, beginning to take in the situation. Another pause and another deep sigh. 'Caroline,' I said, 'are you, um . . . has it started?'

'Bloody right it has!'

I had promised James that he could be back for the birth of his twins, and I like to think that I am a man of my word. It turned out that there was an early evening Lufthansa flight from Thessaloniki direct into Düsseldorf, the nearest international airport to Rheindahlen. The timing couldn't have been better. So we put James in a helicopter and flew him down to Thessaloniki – but Sod's Law meant that the flight was an hour late. Caroline had to have the twins by Caesarean section. James didn't quite make it before she went under the anaesthetic, but he was the first thing she saw when she came round. If only the flight had been on time he'd have been with her before she went under, but there we are. I have a lovely photograph of Caroline with the twins and myself at the tremendous homecoming party we held at RAF Brüggen on our return from Kosovo.

On these deployments you live alongside each other and you share these extraordinary moments. It's much closer than a working relationship – it's more like an extended family.

Torrential rain and low cloud did not bode well for the Prime Minister's visit, but the weather cleared in time for his plane to land only thirty minutes behind schedule. After a walkabout on the streets of Pristina, Tony Blair met assorted but very much arranged groups, spoke to the press and posed for a number of photographs. The locals lionized him, because they knew what a key part he'd played in persuading other NATO countries to take military action in Kosovo. Then he and I had a one-on-one meeting, before being joined by Bernard Kouchner. My conversation with him showed that he had a real grasp of the political and security realities, of the need to lock the KLA into a democratic framework while retaining as much of the Serb population of Kosovo as possible. Afterwards he made time to go and talk to the soldiers.

It was good to see the Prime Minister taking a personal interest in our progress. Even though as COMKFOR I was commanding a multinational force, I was still a Brit, and I was proud of what we were achieving. Britain had played the lead role in KFOR and Tony Blair had played the lead role in mobilizing world opinion to intervene in Kosovo.

That evening Tony Blair and Alastair Campbell were our guests in the field kitchen behind the Film Factory. The atmosphere was much more relaxed than it had been during the Prime Minister's visit to Macedonia earlier in the year, when it seemed that we might be on the brink of a major war. It had been decided that the Prime Minister should not stay overnight in Pristina because of security concerns – in my view overplayed – but would fly down to Skopje and return the next day. His party decided that they wanted to depart somewhat earlier than expected. I sent word to get the helicopters up and running. A muddle ensued as to which of the two landing sites the PM's party was going to leave from: either the main one at the back, which was nearer the field kitchen, or the VIP site at the front. We were headed towards the main helipad at the back when we heard the aircraft taking off, and realized that they were expecting to pick up the Prime Minister's party at the front. By now it was dark, of course, and the ground was muddy after the heavy rain that had fallen earlier. Meanwhile, the Army Air

Corps captain who'd come to guide the Prime Minister to the aircraft had got lost somewhere. We had to stagger through the woods in the dark, slipping and sliding in the mud. The Prime Minister was very good about it, but I felt embarrassed by the cock-up.

There was much political activity among the Albanian Kosovar activists, both KLA and others, to the extent of attempting to establish a 'government', which contravened the terms of UNSCR 1244. With hindsight, one can see that the KLA Undertaking should have included a prohibition on political activity by its members. Early in August the self-styled 'Minister for Public Order' Rexhep Selimi, a KLA regional commander, was stopped at a military checkpoint and became very abusive when a soldier from the Royal Irish Regiment asked to see his weapon. On the return of his Smith & Wesson, Selimi ostentatiously reloaded it, retaining one bullet which he held up to show the soldier with the message 'This one is for you'. At this point he was promptly arrested and had his weapon and JIC card confiscated.

I was furious to hear that one of my soldiers had had to endure this kind of thuggish bullying. Thaqi asked to see me to discuss the matter. In the end he didn't turn up to the meeting, but sent three self-styled officials in his place, including the 'Deputy Prime Minister' and the 'Deputy Defence Minister'. They began to argue that as 'war heroes' they were not subject to the same law as other Kosovo citizens. I'd had enough of this. I gave them a little lecture about what the rule of law means in civilized countries. They started to challenge the soldier's account of what had happened – which riled me even more. When one of them stood up, I lifted the table off the ground and banged it down again. 'Sit down!' I shouted. That shut them up.

Immediately afterwards I had a private meeting with Ceku. I cut him off before he could start speaking. 'I don't like being lied to,' I snapped as I strode into the room. All this time there was a JIC meeting waiting to begin. When it finally started, more than an hour later than scheduled, I restated our position on the unacceptability of any KLA challenge to KFOR's authority. They could not remain an armed force if they wanted to be recognized by the international community.

More high-level visitors followed, including the American Secretary of State Madeleine Albright, and from Britain the Foreign Secretary Robin Cook and the Defence Secretary George Robertson. There was a routine for visitors, depending on their importance. I might meet them at the front door or arrange for somebody else to do that and bring them up; we would give them a full briefing on the situation; and then, depending on who they were, they might go and visit units on the ground. If they were politicians they'd go and see Bernard Kouchner. We strung the programme together and the boys took care of most of it.

Early in September, when the Adjutant General, the number three on the Army Board, was visiting us, I received the worrying news that my daughter Amanda had been taken into hospital for an emergency operation, after an ectopic pregnancy. Apparently she was out of danger and had been sent home. Sarah had rushed to be with her, but of course I wanted to get back to see her myself as soon as possible. My ADC put in several hours' work and no fewer than sixty-five telephone calls trying to get me home and back. The Adjutant General came up with a solution. He had come out in an HS-125, a small RAF executive jet, and was due to fly back the next day. He turned one of his party off the plane, and persuaded me that I must take the seat. We flew direct to RAF Lyneham, which handily was close to where Amanda and her family lived. She didn't know I was coming. We landed about eleven-thirty in the morning, and I reached the house at about midday. I quietly unlatched the front door and pushed it open to see Amanda's first child, young Casper, sitting in his high chair facing me, while she was shovelling goo down him. 'Hello, darling,' I said, my voice cracking a little as I spoke. Amanda looked round, amazed, and then tears filled her eyes. It was a very poignant moment.

I couldn't stay in England more than a few hours, because I was due back in Kosovo the next day for a visit by the Prince of Wales. Ed Sandry had arranged for an RAF Puma helicopter to pick me up from a field near Amanda's house in the small hours of the morning and fly me on to Mons, where the plan was to hitch a lift from Wes Clark, who was flying down to Skopje in his personal jet, before taking a helicopter ride up to Pristina. I 'appointed' Sarah as my helicopter marshaller: we brought the Puma in to land on the kale field across the lane in pitch darkness at 04.30 using a couple of torches. I was back in Kosovo before lunch, in time to greet Prince Charles.

The flight from Mons had given Wes and myself plenty of time to review the whole situation in Kosovo, particularly in the run-up to the K+90 deadline. Early in August, an account of my altercation with Wes had broken in the press, and I took the opportunity to assure him that I was not responsible for the leak. I am quite clear that nobody at my end was responsible for it.

Like Wes and me, the Prince of Wales was dressed in combat kit. The real purpose of his visit was to see some of the British soldiers serving in Kosovo. Since I had become Colonel Commandant – the tribal elder – of the Parachute Regiment in 1988 and would continue as such until 2004, I was to see a lot more of HRH Prince Charles in his capacity as Colonel in Chief. He is a very warm human being, much warmer than the press generally give him credit for. The soldiers enjoy meeting him, and are hugely appreciative of the trouble he takes to come and see them.

Wes made no secret of his belief that Milosevic had left behind in Kosovo some special police units in civilian clothes, with communications and weapons hidden, ready to foment trouble at a moment's notice. I didn't share this anxiety. I thought it very likely that the Serbs had left behind agents who would keep them informed of developments. But I was less convinced that there were still Serb fighting units in Kosovo.

As K+90 approached, our focus was increasingly on the transformation of the KLA into a legitimate organization. The pressure increased as the deadline drew nearer. The major issues of demilitarization had been agreed, but the emotional issues remained unresolved. The KLA had accepted that their weapons should be held in KFOR-controlled storage sites, but only reluctantly: for many of their members, possession of these was a virility symbol. 'They can go there and stroke them if they want,' I told Ceku. He smiled grimly.

Richard Holbrooke rightly commented that in this final negotiation we were caught on the horns of a dilemma: we had to persuade the KLA to change, but if we pushed them too hard they might go underground again. It would be a horrible irony if we found ourselves in the same position as the Serbs, fighting a counter-insurgency campaign against a national resistance movement. Inevitably there was going to have to be an element of compromise on both sides. Holbrooke told Thaqi that 'the degree of international support' for Kosovo depended on its commitment to democracy, and that democracy was the way to independence. Thaqi didn't seem to understand. It was not just the organization that had to change, but its leaders. I negotiated with Ceku, observing his difficult and often painful metamorphosis from a guerrilla commander into a national leader.

The KLA's insignia may have seemed a small point, but the symbolism was potent. The KLA had worn on their combat uniform the red and gold insignia of the double-headed

Albanian eagle. Such an emblem would have been unacceptable to the international community, suggesting as it did to many an aspiration for a Greater Albania, incorporating Kosovo. Moreover, it would have been intolerable to the sizeable Serb minority remaining in Kosovo. Ceku took the point intellectually, but he would have to sell any changes that he accepted to his military commanders, and it would be hard to overcome their emotional attachment to the double-headed eagle. This was the symbol under which they had fought; to abandon it would be insulting to the memory of those who had been killed. But I told Ceku that the eagle would have to go all the same. Even if I had agreed to it, NATO would have vetoed the proposal. At this, Ceku put his head in his hands and leaned forward on the table.

Ceku accepted that it was politically impossible for Kosovo to have its own army in the immediate future, and that the transformed and demilitarized KLA would have to be called something different. The name then being bandied around was the 'Kosovo Rescue and Protection Corps'. Ceku didn't like the word 'corps', which he felt was weak. His people came up with suggestion after suggestion, all of which needed to be carefully translated from the Albanian and then the nuances explored. We couldn't allow any name with a military connotation. They kept trying it on. He gave us a copy of a proposed new 'Kosovo Corps' ID card, which when translated read 'Kosovo Army Corps'.

As the eleventh hour arrived, the negotiations became extremely tense. Up until now we had been bouncing ideas around, but now the time had come to settle. Ceku was going through hell. His brain was telling him, 'I've got to play ball, for the long-term future of Kosovo, I've got to,' but his heart was working in the other direction. I kept saying to him, 'Don't be emotional,' 'You must comply with UNSCR 1244,' 'the world is watching' – banging on, repeating the same points again and again. We reached D+89. Thaqi turned nasty. 'Nobody plays games with the KLA,' he shouted at me. 'If you think you can issue directions to us, then you are mistaken and you will regret it.'

'I am too old to play games with anyone,' I replied wearily. 'If we don't get this right tomorrow, the KLA will cease to exist. There will be no successor organization, you will have no identity, you will be nothing. Anybody found with a weapon will be arrested. Your magic little JIC cards will be worthless.'

I was under a lot of pressure too. I received a cryptic message from Rupert Smith, saying that there was deep discomfort within NATO about some of the concessions I was making to the KLA. 'The ghost is not laid to rest,' he wrote.

The following day, Sunday 19 September, was K+90. The press were speculating that the talks had collapsed. We reached the evening. Thaqi sent a message that I should go downtown to meet him. 'Bollocks to that,' was the universal reaction up at the Film Factory. Eventually Thaqi was tracked down having supper in the Grand Hotel. He tried the same ploy, received the same answer, then agreed to come up to the KFOR HQ. He and his colleagues arrived at just after 22.00 hours, complaining about being kept waiting. Our meeting started at 22.15. It was clearly going to be a long night. Seventeen minutes before midnight we took a break.

Outside, my staff had set up a sweepstake on the time the pen would hit the paper. Jonathan Bailey had 06.00, Andrew Ridgway 05.50 hours. In the event nobody won. As the night wore on it was clear to me that we weren't near to closing the deal. At 06.10 hours I decided to stop the clock. I went outside to tell the press that we hadn't made it. In a statement, I reminded the KLA that the Undertaking had expired, and that officially they no longer existed as a legal organization. If there was no agreement by midnight on the following day, and their members continued to carry weapons or wear uniforms with the old KLA insignia, they would be deemed to be non-compliant and would face arrest.

I spoke to Wes Clark, who suggested that he should fly in to add weight to the negotiation. That seemed sensible to me. I finally got to bed at 06.30, and was up again at 10.00. Wes arrived at 14.00 hours, and the KLA delegation was with us forty-five minutes later. Wes was in his element, working the room confidently, telling stories about his experiences in Vietnam which had the KLA's zone commanders hanging on his every word. Afterwards he made a rousing, virulently anti-Serb speech that would have had our diplomats reeling if they could have heard what he was saying. It became clear that the differences between the two sides had narrowed. We resolved the issue of the insignia, agreeing on an outline of the shape of Kosovo itself. Off the top of her head, our new Canadian political adviser Wendy Gilmore came up with a wording on one of the remaining issues, access to weapons, which satisfied everybody. More names were bandied about. Would we be prepared to call the organization the Kosovo Guard? Silence.

'It sounds too military,' Ceku responded, and then everyone started laughing.

'Hey, that's meant to be my line,' joked Wes. And eventually we settled on the name Kosovo Protection Corps.

It was early evening on K+92, Tuesday 21 September, when we signed the agreement. We had got there at last.

Two days later there was a football match between a KFOR XI – including a young Russian soldier – and Pristina FC. Our team lost 4–0, but the crowd applauded both teams enthusiastically none the less. I returned to the Film Factory to find Ceku dressed as I had never seen him before, in smart civilian clothes.

Ceku is now Prime Minister of Kosovo. I have met him several times since, and when he came to England recently we had lunch together. He is proud of the fact that Kosovo still has a significant Serb population, and that one of his personal staff is a Serb. I saw him grow in stature, from 'freedom fighter' to statesman, renouncing violence and embracing democracy. It was a fine thing to watch.

Wes Clark was at his best in the negotiation with the KLA. When I saw him operating like that, I reflected on his outstanding qualities. It seemed tragic that his military career should be ending in bitter disappointment.

But only a few days later Wes began obsessing about the Serbs again. He was fixated on the possibility of a Serb re-invasion of Kosovo. Of course we'd considered that possibility, but it seemed to me extremely unlikely. For one thing, it wouldn't have made military sense to withdraw, to allow your enemy to occupy the ground, and then to have to fight your way back. I have no doubt that, having withdrawn, the next thing the Serb General Staff would have done was to examine the options should they be ordered to go back in. But that was very far from saying that it was a real possibility. Planning is one thing, execution is very much another. Even Milosevic would have known that NATO could not have allowed Kosovo to be retaken by the Serbs. However formidable the Serb Army, it would have been crushed by NATO's overwhelming strength. By September KFOR was fifty thousand strong, and of course we could call on a vast pool of potential reinforcements in an emergency.

'When the Serbs come over I am going to do everything I can to finish the fight,' Wes told me on the VTC from Mons. This time, he said, 'we will go the whole way' – presumably all the way to Belgrade. Clark talked a lot about Serbs coming back in. He said that we should 'welcome' a Serb attack. Can he really have wanted an all-out battle – a battle that would have meant thousands, maybe tens of thousands, of casualties?

I was not alone in thinking that this was barking mad.

*

HQ ARRC was due to go back to Germany in October, and though this could have been postponed, I knew that once we had implemented the KLA Undertaking, we had done what we set out to do – and more. The tempo had been non-stop for seven months, ever since we had deployed in March. We were tired, and it was beginning to show. A sluggishness was creeping in, a reluctance to do more than the minimum. It was time to go home.

In the last week the weather changed dramatically, and for the first time since our arrival in Kosovo we needed pullovers and jackets. I went on a round of farewell engagements. Even Thaqi was all sweetness and light. I gave Ceku a framed copy of the painting I had commissioned, showing us negotiating at a JIC meeting, him at one side of the table and me at the other. He absolutely loved it, and it seemed to seal the bond between us. It had been painted by Nick Bashall, who for a month had been an artist in residence with the Headquarters. Towering over most of us, Nick had cut a splendidly bohemian figure in his grotty, paint-stained shorts and bare feet.

Wes came down for the handover ceremony, at which I relinquished command of KFOR to a German four-star, General Dr Klaus Reinhardt. I reflected that this was almost certainly my last day of operational command in the field. The ceremony, which was presided over by Wes Clark, was a bit over-the-top for my taste, with a parade and a military band, followed by flowery speeches delivered from a lectern while the rest of us sat in a panel on a dais like the competitors in *University Challenge*. Andrew Ridgway described it as 'a press conference with music'. I was embarrassed when my own brief address was greeted with disproportionate cheering. Afterwards I went down to the big football stadium which we used as a helicopter landing site and flew to the airport, where the aircraft was waiting. There was still half an hour or so to kill before we left. General Yeftokovitch, the Russian commander who'd taken over when

Zavarzin had returned to Moscow, had gone to great efforts to provide us with a farewell drink, so we had a vodka or three. There were many handshakes and lots of 'Do zvidaniya' – farewell in Russian. Then, together with my immediate staff, I boarded the BAe-146 aircraft and we took off. I'd ensured that we were well stocked with fizz, which we cracked open as soon as possible. The stewards were unused to our high spirits, and disapproved when I declined an offer to close the sliding doors separating the VIP cabin from the 'steerage' passengers. The similar flight home from Bosnia three years earlier inevitably came to mind.

Many commentators had predicted genocide in Kosovo. Bad things had happened there, but we'd largely put a stop to them, and set Kosovo on a road to a better future. We reckoned that it had been a job well done.

Soon after my return from Kosovo, I attended a special dinner at No. 10 Downing Street to commemorate the Kosovo operation. Apparently Margaret Thatcher had hosted a similar occasion after the Falklands War. Wes Clark was among those attending, as was George Robertson, who had just succeeded Javier Solana as NATO Secretary General. It was a very select gathering: numbers were restricted to about sixty and very few wives were present, but I insisted that Sarah should come. I felt that she had played a vital role in keeping the home fires burning while I had been away.

On 2 December 1999 I went to Buckingham Palace to receive the Distinguished Service Order (DSO) from Her Majesty the Queen. This is the decoration which every officer, if given a choice, would probably most covet. It is a tri-Service medal, requiring a very strong element of leadership on operational service. In this respect it stands outside the hierarchy of medals awarded purely for gallantry. I received many gratifying messages congratulating me on the award, and on what we had achieved in Kosovo. Some came from soldiers, some from political and civilian leaders, and others from members of the public. I received a magnanimous letter from Wes Clark, which caused me to reflect once again on the character of that contradictory man.

More than five years later I would go to the Palace again to be invested as a Knight Grand Cross of the Order of the Bath (GCB) – jocularly known as the 'Very Deep End of the Bath'. At the same investiture, Private Johnson Beharry was presented with the Victoria Cross for his outstanding gallantry in twice rescuing comrades from an armoured vehicle during an ambush in Iraq, even though wounded. This was the first VC to be awarded since the Falklands; 'It's a long time since I've presented one of these,' the Queen remarked.

'I was overshadowed today by Private Beharry, and quite rightly so,' I commented to the press afterwards. 'It was an honour to stand alongside him.' I'd got to know Johnson Beharry beforehand and I knew him to be both modest and self-effacing, though obviously as brave as a lion. It was entirely appropriate that on that day he should be first of the hundred or so to be presented with an award by Her Majesty. He led, and I followed: the private soldier first, and the Head of the Army second.

*In Kabul, on a visit to
Afghanistan as Chief of
the General Staff.*

My elder son Mark with an unidentified colleague on active service in Sierra Leone. **Below:** *Mark later left the Army after a serious parachuting accident and has made a new career as an artist.*

Left: *Cadet Lance Corporal Jackson: my younger son Tom photographed with the Eton CCF, 2007.*

Below: *My daughter Amanda's wedding to Jason Gard, 21 October 2005. Standing in front of the picture are my grandchildren Jemima, Phoebe and Casper.*

Inspecting officer cadets at the Sandhurst Sovereign's Parade, 10 December 2004.

Right: *At the Palace after being presented with the DSO for my service in Kosovo, 2 December 1999.*

Above: *With Princes William and Harry at the Sovereign's Parade, 12 April 2006, Prince Harry's commissioning day.*

Below: *With Private Johnson Beharry VC, at Buckingham Palace, 27 April 2005.*

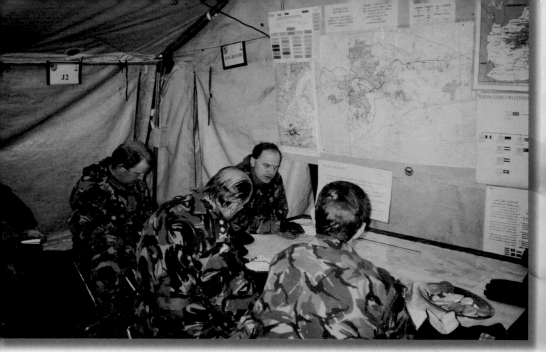

Above: *In the Kabul HQ of 16 Air Assault Brigade, early in 2002, during a visit in my capacity as Commander in Chief. In the middle of the picture is the Brigade Commander, Barney White-Spunner.*

Below: *In 7 Armoured Brigade HQ talking to Brigadier Graham Binns. His Brigade played a leading role in the Iraq operation.*

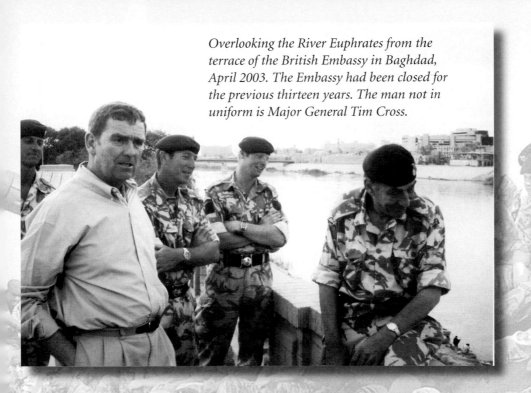

Overlooking the River Euphrates from the terrace of the British Embassy in Baghdad, April 2003. The Embassy had been closed for the previous thirteen years. The man not in uniform is Major General Tim Cross.

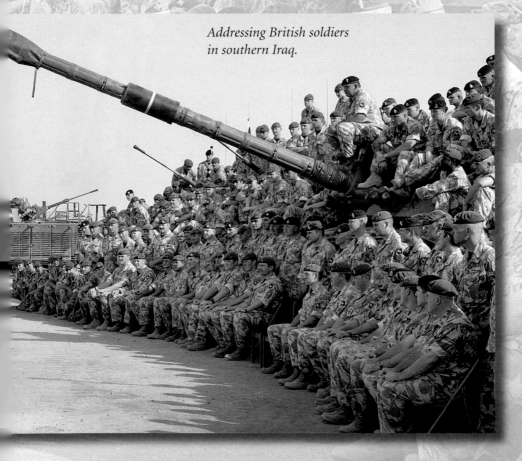

Addressing British soldiers in southern Iraq.

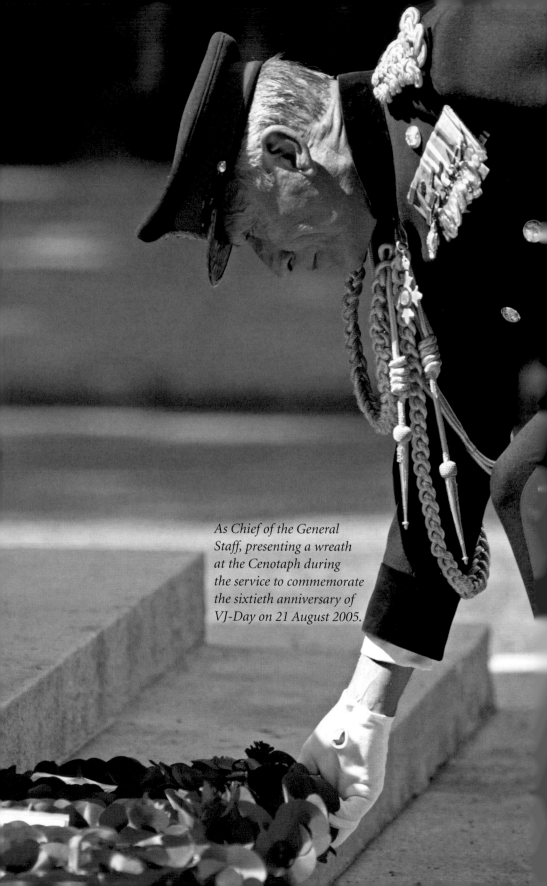

As Chief of the General Staff, presenting a wreath at the Cenotaph during the service to commemorate the sixtieth anniversary of VJ-Day on 21 August 2005.

14

High Command

While still in Kosovo I had learned what I'd be doing next. When my three-year tenure as COMARRC elapsed at the end of 1999 I would be succeeding Mike Walker – not for the first, or indeed the last, time – as Commander in Chief, Land Command (CinC Land), headquartered at Wilton, just outside Salisbury. This was the number two position in the Army, and entailed promotion to the rank of full general, four-star command. As Commander in Chief, I would automatically become a member of the Army Board, the formal institution that runs the Army. The promotion also meant that I would be a strong candidate to become CGS in due course.

The job came with a fine house, Bulford Manor, with four even gables and mullioned windows. It had plenty of bedrooms and a lovely drawing-room. Best of all, there was a glorious garden running down to the bank of the crystal-clear River Avon. We knew the house well, because it was close to Bulford Camp and opposite the church where Sarah and I were married. I had been dining at Bulford Manor in the summer of 1995 when the then Commander in Chief, John Wilsey, had warned me that I might have to go to Bosnia very soon.

I was of course delighted by the appointment, but I have to admit that the job took a bit of adjustment after the excitement of the previous year. Then I had been commanding a force in the field; this job was more sedentary and more managerial. By contrast with the intensity of what had gone immediately before, the work could be considered routine. It was, of course, important: the Commander in Chief has between two-thirds and three-quarters of all the Army's manpower under his command, and there's a very big budget to run, about £4.5 billion – not that you have much real control over it, as the MOD's overall spending pattern is largely in the hands of civil servants.

As Commander in Chief, your principal job is to run the Army on a day-to-day basis: to ensure that it's in good shape, that it's sufficiently trained and exercised, that it's structured properly and that it's ready to be deployed on operations. Of course, the future is very important – and that's where membership of the Army Board comes in. One of the most important aspects of the job is 'force generation', i.e. putting a force together to fulfil a particular task. I make the analogy with an orchestra: its make-up will vary, depending on the piece of music you want to play; similarly, the make-up of a force will vary depending on the requirements of the task. Just as for a piece of chamber music you might need only a string quartet, for example, so for a limited operation you might only need Special Forces. There are certain constants: in an orchestra you will always need violins, and in any operation you'll almost always need infantry. But other instruments are optional – percussion, for example – and some you use only rarely, like the organ (the Army equivalent might be artillery). Just as in an orchestra you don't always need every instrument, and for some pieces you may require more of one and less of another, so for a particular Army operation you may want to vary the proportions.

Of course, you also have to ensure that your musicians are competent, which is where the training cycle comes in. The analogy also holds good for the force commander and the conductor of the orchestra: both have to get the best from their teams.

During my time as Commander in Chief I restructured the command and control system. When I took up the post I had a three-star deputy and a dozen or so major generals reporting to me. I asked my Chief of Staff, Freddie Viggers, my erstwhile artillery commander in Bosnia, to look at how the command might be better organized. On his recommendation, I decided to split Land Command in two: on the one hand what we call the 'field army', i.e. the two manoeuvre divisions – the 3rd Division in Britain and the 1st Division in Germany – and the specialist brigades such as air defence, engineers, signals and logistics; and on the other the regional chain of command, including all of the TA. I was able, perhaps surprisingly, to cajole the MOD into authorizing another three-star post, so that a lieutenant general ran each of these two, both reporting to me. It was a much more efficient set-up.

In May 2000, soon after I took over Land Command, a desperate Sierra Leone Government requested British help. A group of tribal thugs calling themselves the RUF, the Revolutionary United Front, had virtually overrun the country and were getting very close to the capital, Freetown. One of the RUF's more gruesome activities was chopping off people's hands and legs.

There was a huge UN force in Sierra Leone of around 17,500 soldiers, the biggest UN deployment anywhere in the world at the time. But though there were some good units among them, the challenge once again showed the weakness of UN forces, with national governments deciding what their soldiers could and could not do. The result was a humiliating failure to deal with the rebels. Kofi Annan appealed for international action. Tony Blair's Government made the decision to deploy a national force to stop these brutes taking control of Freetown, which had to be done with great urgency as they had already reached its outskirts. A force of around six hundred soldiers, largely from 1 Para, was flown to Sierra Leone under the command of Brigadier David Richards. Most travelled aboard RAF Hercules aircraft, but a pair of Chinooks which had been conducting cold-weather training in Scotland flew all the way, with two crews 'hot-seating'. On landing, the first task of the battlegroup was to push out and secure the airport.

Captain Mark Jackson, then second-in-command of the Pathfinder Platoon, found himself part of the operation. After a journey to the British High Commission to deliver a mysterious briefcase, he then took part in the operation to evacuate EPs ('entitled persons'). With a patrol of four soldiers Mark cadged a helicopter ride across the estuary dividing the airport from the main part of the city. The situation in Freetown was very tense; as they arrived at the High Commission there was a firefight going on down the street. But the arrival of British soldiers effected a complete transformation, and the rebels withdrew. A while later rebels advanced on the airport in the hope of capturing a British soldier to use as a hostage. They were repelled after taking heavy losses in another firefight: the first and last time the rebels took on the British Army directly.

The British intervention in Sierra Leone was a huge success, preventing the fall of Freetown and stopping the insurrection in its tracks. Once again a small force of British soldiers, inserted rapidly at the *moment critique*, had succeeded where a much larger multinational force had failed. In 2002, elections were held in Sierra Leone for the first time in thirty years. Today the country is returning to normal, though there remains a small British presence of a hundred or so soldiers, acting as trainers for the Sierra Leone Army.

Another feature of my time as Commander in Chief was being called in to assist the civil authorities at home to help with a series of national emergencies. Within the Army these came to be known as the 'four Fs', the 'Fs' standing for flooding, the fuel-tanker drivers' strike, the firefighters' strike, and the crisis over foot-and-mouth disease. The first two were straightforward enough, but the firefighters' strike was a serious drain on our resources in the build-up to the second Gulf War. We had up to thirteen thousand soldiers on firefighting duties, which would be very difficult today, given the pressure on manpower arising from the current level of overseas deployments.

In principle, it could have been politically contentious to have the Army filling the gap – strike-breaking, to some – but in the case of the firefighters' strike, with lives potentially at risk, it was a no-brainer. Obviously most of our soldiers were not trained in the more esoteric firefighting skills, though the Navy and the Air Force do have a small number of very high-tech specialists. But a lot of firefighting is straightforward, and on the whole we didn't let people down. To have the necessary manpower trained in the basic skills and available right across the country was quite a logistical exercise. Some of our soldiers were camping out – in TA centres, for example. The famous – or infamous – old Green Goddesses trundled out of their depots. Now retired from service, these iconic vehicles had been procured for civil defence in the 1950s to put out fires after a Soviet nuclear attack on Britain. But though by now very ancient, they still did a good job. The soldiers quite enjoyed the firefighting, even if some might have been irritated to have to cover for people who were already paid a damn sight more than they were. There was always a chance that the boys might rescue a pretty girl from a blazing house . . .

The epidemic of foot-and-mouth disease in 2001 was a disaster for British agriculture. The Ministry of Agriculture, Fisheries and Food (MAFF) was struggling until we were called in to help. We put a logistics Brigade Headquarters into the Ministry to provide command and control, and used the regional chain of command to administer the crisis, treating it much like any other operation, using standard battle procedure, with command groups, morning updates and so on. MAFF were shown to be so hopelessly overwhelmed that soon afterwards they restructured and changed their name to the Department of Environment, Food and Rural Affairs (DEFRA). I flew up to Great Orton airfield in Cumbria with Geoff Hoon, the Secretary of State for Defence, to see for ourselves what was entailed in the slaughter and burial of thousands of animals in mass graves. The piles of corpses made a grisly sight, and the stench was appalling.

Among the soldiers, the 'four Fs' were inevitably known as the 'eight Fs': 'fookin' floods', 'fookin' fuel', 'fookin' fires', and 'fookin' foot and mouth'.

I was in the middle of a briefing in London in the late summer of 2000 when I received the news that Mark had been severely injured in a parachuting accident.

I left the briefing immediately, and within ten minutes or so had found out the details. Mark had gone out to north-east Spain for a week's holiday with a friend, Ed Paxton, who happened to be ADC to Rupert Smith. They had been free-fall parachuting, and Mark had misjudged the turn necessary to check his lateral speed (known in the sport as a 'low hook') just before he landed. He hit the ground too fast at the wrong angle, shattering a hip and fracturing his pelvis. From what I was told, it was clear that he was lucky to be alive.

Immediately after the necessary surgery, Mark was recuperating at the Haslar military hospital near Portsmouth when half a dozen or so wounded soldiers arrived from A Company, 3 Para. They'd been taking part in a spectacular rescue mission in Sierra Leone, to recover some British Army hostages taken by another bunch of lawless hoods called the West Side Boys. On the same ward as Mark, the wounded were in fine fettle, benefiting greatly from being together; here again was proof positive of the psychological advantage which wounded soldiers gain from being in a military environment, giving each other support and encouragement.

After his recovery, Mark started a junior staff course that summer, but abandoned it when 16 Air Assault Brigade undertook another short-notice deployment, this time a stabilization operation in Macedonia. This put him behind an ops-room desk. It was around this time that Mark decided against staying in the Army – with the permanent damage to his hip, transfer to another part of the Service would have been inevitable, and this had little attraction for him. More fundamentally, perhaps, he had always had a passion to be an artist and would probably have left the Army within the next decade to follow that course; now he would just go that bit sooner. Having identified the Charles H. Cecil Studios in Florence as where he wanted to study, he decided to stay with the Army for a year or two to save up the necessary money, and booked himself another tour to Sierra Leone for a year as an acting major.

I went back to the Balkans in June 2001. After consultation with the British Ambassador, I had arranged to pay a visit to Belgrade. This was my own initiative: it seemed to me an opportunity to extend a hand to the new, democratic Serbia, and perhaps to heal a few wounds. Slobodan Milosevic's regime had fallen the previous October, and at the end of March Milosevic himself had been arrested by the Serb authorities on charges of corruption and abuse of power, following an armed stand-off at his fortified villa. Back in 1999 he had been indicted by the ICTY to answer charges of crimes against humanity at The Hague, but despite strong international pressure the new Serbian government was resisting his extradition.

I flew into Pristina beforehand, and over lunch with Ceku I bet him a bottle of whisky that by the end of July Milosevic would be in The Hague. Afterwards I flew on to Belgrade. The effect of NATO air strikes could be seen as we came into land: broken bridges and bombed-out buildings. I was conscious that only two years before I had been one of the most public faces of the enemy that had caused this destruction. Nevertheless I was received with courteous formality by both politicians and the Serb High Command. In the course of the visit I had an amicable meeting with a member of the Serb delegation with whom I had negotiated the MTA just before KFOR's entry into Kosovo.

The Serbs made a point of telling me how they were dealing with the unrest in the Presevo valley, the area east of Kosovo where ethnic Albanians are in the majority. They described how they were handling the violence and outlined their rules of engagement. This was a message: they were telling me that they'd learned a lesson, that they weren't going to make the same mistakes as had been made in Kosovo.

The situation regarding Milosevic's extradition was developing rapidly, and at one stage during our visit it looked as though our seven-seater RAF aircraft might be retasked to fly him out to The Hague. As things turned out we flew out of Belgrade on 28 June, the anniversary of the assassination of Archduke Franz Ferdinand by Serb extremists in Sarajevo in 1914, the event that triggered the First World War. On the very same day Milosevic was transferred to UN custody in Bosnia, pending his extradition to The Hague. I have yet to claim my bottle from Ceku!

A year later I paid another visit to Belgrade, when again I was received courteously. In London I had come to know Crown Prince Alexander, heir to the throne of Yugoslavia, whose last crowned king had been deposed (with British support) in 1941. Since the fall of Milosevic the Prince had returned to Belgrade and installed himself back in one of the palaces built for the Yugoslav Royal Family, later commandeered by Tito to be his official residence, and later still occupied by Milosevic. The

Crown Prince asked me to go and see him there. He showed me around the ornately decorated palace, including the room used as a personal office by Tito and then by Milosevic – the very room where the latter had conceded to Ahtisaari and Chernomyrdin two years earlier.

In the second week of September 2001 I was in Canada, on a routine visit to watch one of our brigades in action at the Army's largest training area on the prairies of Alberta. It's a hell of a place, like a huge Salisbury Plain but thirty or forty times as big, so the Army can do almost anything it likes there, including plenty of live firing. On the morning of 11 September I came down to breakfast in the visitors' accommodation on the base camp to find my MA, Mark Carleton-Smith, and my ADC, Jez Rostron, glued to the television. 'There's mayhem in New York, General,' Mark said. It was 7.00 a.m. Alberta time, 9.00 a.m. New York time. Minutes afterwards we watched, horror-struck, as the second aircraft deliberately flew into the second tower – and then came the collapse of both towers. Just conceivably, the first aircraft hitting the Twin Towers might have been an appalling mistake, but now it became obvious that this was a coordinated terrorist attack of unprecedented scale – a conclusion reinforced when the third aircraft hit the Pentagon. Our immediate assumption was that this was the work of Islamic terrorists, almost certainly Al-Qaida. 'We've just witnessed the start of a new kind of war,' I commented to Mark and Jez, 'and now we're going out to see training for the old kind of war.' We flew out by helicopter to the exercise area. Knowing that the troops out on the prairie had little or no access to the media, I gathered the senior officers together and told them as much as I knew. I do remember saying to them, 'Life is not going to be the same after this.' Rather obvious, perhaps, but worth saying none the less. Like everybody else, I couldn't imme-diately see where this one was going, but I did make the comment that the attack would put an edge to their training. Other thoughts were in my mind: Was London next? Would it be a similar attack? Canary Wharf? The NatWest Tower? The Houses of Parliament? Buckingham Palace? And where were Sarah and the family? Were any of them in London?

I was in utterly the wrong place and needed to get back to the UK as soon as possible. It was hard to know what was happening back at home and how people had reacted. For some hours no telephone communication across the Atlantic was possible. After considerable difficulty I managed to get hold of my Chief of Staff back at Wilton, Freddie Viggers. Typically, he had already worked out what Land Command could provide if required. There was a sense of great uncertainty. While our intelligence services had been aware of a threat from Al-Qaida, an attack on this scale was totally unanticipated. Nobody knew if the attacks on the Pentagon and New York would be followed by attacks elsewhere. On both sides of the Atlantic, politicians were faced with the possibility of having to make a terrible decision: to order fighter aircraft to shoot down hijacked airliners filled with innocent passengers.

Though aircraft across North America were grounded for the next four or five days, I was able to take advantage of an opportunity to get back to England. Several days earlier there'd been a serious training accident on the range in which four or five soldiers had been wounded, and an RAF VC10 had arrived the day before to take them home. Since this was a casualty evacuation, the Canadians made an exception to allow this one aircraft to fly on humanitarian grounds, and we were able to cadge a lift on it. We took off at about 10.30 local time on 12 September. 'We are the only aircraft in Canadian airspace,' the captain told me.

Some hours later, as we were approaching the east coast of Canada, one of the crew came to tell me that the captain wanted a word.

'You know I said we were the only aircraft flying in Canadian airspace?' the captain asked, when I arrived in the cockpit.

'Yes,' I replied.

'Well, we're not any more. Down below us is a pair of F-16s.'

'Bloody hell,' I said. 'I hope they know who we are!'

We flew non-stop from Alberta to England, arriving back at RAF Brize Norton around 02.00 hours the next morning. Freddie's typically comprehensive written brief was waiting for me on landing. He'd answered all the questions in my mind, and so I felt able to spend what was left of the night at home. I was very relieved to be in Britain again. In Canada I was isolated from my HQ; back at Wilton I was in a position to deal with whatever force generation might be called for. Nobody knew then what the requirements might be. There still seemed the possibility of further attacks, including attacks on the UK itself. We were clear about our responsibility. In the event of a national emergency the lead service is the civil police, and it's for them to ask for military assistance, whether it be engineering assistance, specialist assistance in the event of a nuclear, biological or chemical attack, or just raw manpower. Soon after the attack on 11 September, intelligence was received of a possible terrorist threat to Heathrow Airport, and the police did request a military presence, which we provided, once ministerial approval had been granted.

The attacks of '9/11', as it became known, had come as a complete shock to the American body politic, and indeed to the world. Mainland America had been attacked for the first time in two centuries. Americans felt that they were 'at war'. Now they thought: These people have declared war on us, and therefore we will take the war to them. It was not immediately clear what this would mean for Britain and the British Army. We were, of course, ready to do whatever was asked of us in the event of an attack on British territory – but, more generally, there was a sense in the Army that overseas involvement was probably

315

inevitable. Where and when was still unknown. Pretty soon attention focused on Afghanistan, particularly the Afghan–Pakistani border area, the heartland of the Taliban which had provided a refuge for Al-Qaida. The Americans decided that they had to go into Afghanistan to deal with this threat. President Bush's immediate reaction was: 'You're either with us, or you're against us.' On 12 September George Robertson had demonstrated NATO's solidarity with the United States by invoking Article 5 of the founding treaty, for the first time in the organization's history. In essence, the Article says that an attack on one member is an attack on all, and its invocation was of enormous symbolic importance. At home, the Prime Minister pronounced his support for the United States, speaking – then, at least – for the country as a whole.

The first missile strikes on Afghanistan came less than a month after the 9/11 attacks. By 19 October the first US Special Forces had entered the country. The UK contributed to the air campaign and sent in a modest number of our own Special Forces, who as ever punched way above their weight. But most of the ground fighting was carried out by the Afghani Northern Alliance, an umbrella organization of *mujahedin* fighters who had been active in the resistance to the Soviet occupation in the 1980s. By 13 November Kabul was a free city. It was a neat solution to employ indigenous forces, assisted by the use of devastating air power, to get rid of the Taliban, rather than sending in a Western army. But this success had the effect of bolstering, rather than diminishing, the status of the warlords.

After the collapse of the Taliban, the UN convened a meeting in Bonn of the various factions to address the future of Afghanistan. There were three urgent priorities: the search for a new political order in the country, the desperate need for humanitarian supplies, and the hunt for Bin Laden and the remnants of Al-Qaida. The four Afghan factions signed a deal which promised a new future for the country. Shortly after

Bonn, a *loya jirga*, a traditional meeting of the clans, was held in Kabul and appointed a provisional government under President Karzai, pending elections. The Americans did not seem much interested in what would happen within Afghanistan after the Taliban had gone. While they were entirely right to prosecute the counter-terrorist campaign as vigorously as possible, their aversion to 'nation-building' was evident. But Tony Blair had made it clear that 'we will not walk away from Afghanistan as the outside world has done so many times before'.

The Bonn Conference provided for an International Security Assistance Force (ISAF) to support the embryo government in Afghanistan, to provide security and to train new Afghan security forces. Tony Blair volunteered Britain to lead ISAF first time around. This was essentially a political decision, though of course we were consulted on the operational factors. As Commander in Chief, I had to generate the necessary forces very quickly: as usual, we had to find a force commander and headquarters, and inevitably the finger finished up pointing at the 3rd Division, under its commander Major General John McColl. John, whom I knew to be a very able and humane officer, was to establish a remarkable personal rapport with President Karzai – so much so, that after the end of his tour in Kabul he became Tony Blair's personal envoy to Karzai.

I made my first visit to Afghanistan in January 2002, travelling with a small personal staff. It was very cold, with snow on the ground. This was a purely military visit: my purpose was to support John McColl, to receive briefings from local commanders and to see the situation on the ground for myself. There was still fighting going on in the south-east when I arrived, and the situation in Kabul had still not returned to normal: there was no mains electricity supply and aircraft were making only night-time landings at Kabul Airport. Once again I was able to snatch some time with Mark, who had deployed to Kabul before going on to Sierra Leone.

Introducing an international force into a country with its infrastructure in ruins, in the immediate aftermath of conflict, was a real challenge for the British Army, particularly as this had to be done during the winter. But this kind of challenge had become familiar to us in recent years after our experiences in Bosnia, Kosovo, Sierra Leone and elsewhere.

Under UNSCR 1386, ISAF's area of responsibility was restricted initially to the area around Kabul, which with hindsight was probably a mistake. In August 2003, NATO assumed command of ISAF – the first time the Alliance had operated outside Europe. ISAF gradually expanded its writ, but the critical area, the Tora Bora mountains adjoining Pakistan in the south-east, remained under a US-led Coalition command, with its emphasis on counter-terrorist combat operations. Now, this may sound a technical distinction, but to have two chains of command in the same country is to invite friction. It was not until the autumn of 2006 that a unified command structure under NATO was achieved.

Why was it so difficult to unify the chain of command? The Americans have always been wary about multinational forces, and perhaps understandably they regarded the ISAF with a jaundiced eye, because it was mainly, though not exclusively, composed of European troops and, as ever, hindered by various national caveats – they can't do this, they must do the other, they can't fly at night. These caveats are there because European governments are particularly nervous of the political effects of military risk-taking, not least when casualties are concerned. Britain has always been more sanguine in this regard. As for the US post-Vietnam aversion to body bags, 9/11 changed all that in a trice. The idea that somehow military operations can be risk-free is an absolute contradiction in terms. Unless a multinational force is prepared to accept a certain degree of risk it will never be able to fulfil its mission.

The American administration that had come to power in 2000

under President George W. Bush took a very different approach to foreign policy from its predecessors. Bush surrounded himself with neoconservative thinkers, who viewed the world in more aggressively ideological terms. Among these was his powerful Vice-President, Dick Cheney. The 'neocons' took the view that victory in the Cold War had demonstrated the superiority of American-style democracy, and that with American encouragement this model could spread across the world. Unlike the Clinton Administration, they were ready to intervene in other countries when they believed that American interests were at stake. Bush's Secretary of State, General Colin Powell, was an isolated figure among these ideologues. In a conversation with the British Foreign Secretary Jack Straw, Powell was quoted by the respected American journalist Sidney Blumenthal as having described the neocons within the Bush Administration as 'fucking crazies'. Powell was a professional soldier; his thinking had been formed by the chastening experience of Vietnam, and he was habitually cautious about risking American lives in overseas adventures. The Secretary of Defense, Donald Rumsfeld, and especially his deputy, Paul Wolfowitz, pursued radical neoconservative policies aimed at reshaping the world in the American image. While Powell was Secretary of State there was a running battle between the State Department and the Pentagon.

Rumsfeld proposed a new doctrine for the American military, seeking to increase force readiness and to decrease the amount of supply required to maintain forces by reducing the number of troops in theatre. A key component of what became known as the 'Rumsfeld Doctrine' was the use of light forces to seek out the enemy and call down air strikes. In contrast, Powell favoured the use of overwhelming force, with well-defined objectives and exit strategies. The apparent success of the Rumsfeld Doctrine in Afghanistan took little account of the major part played by the Northern Alliance. There was great tension between

Rumsfeld and his senior generals, particularly the Army Chief of Staff, Eric Shinseki, who had been fighting a rearguard action against Rumsfeld's desire to slim down the army. Rumsfeld felt that the American army was too cautious, too resistant to change and too unwilling to take risks. I believe events have shown him to be wrong.

In my view, Rumsfeld is one of those most responsible for the current situation in Iraq. He rejected the advice given to him by his generals, while at the same time he discarded the detailed plans for the post-conflict period prepared by the State Department.

Her Majesty Queen Elizabeth the Queen Mother died in March 2002, and I was privileged to take part in the cortège that followed her coffin from St James's Palace to Westminster Hall, where it would lie in state before her funeral. I took the part of the CGS immediately behind the Royal Family, since Mike Walker was acting as a pall-bearer, in his capacity as Colonel of the Royal Anglian Regiment.

My driver and I believed that we had allowed plenty of time to get to the Palace, but we had reckoned without the special measures put in place by the Metropolitan Police. In the event we arrived only just in time. I emerged from the car still a little bedraggled, my full ceremonial dress not yet complete. Greeting me was the awe-inspiring figure of the Garrison Sergeant Major, a very tall Guardsman called Mason and known inevitably as 'Perry'. He looked at his watch ostentatiously and sniffed. He sniffed again as I dragged on my frock coat and buckled my ceremonial sword.

'Very good to see you, Commander in Chief,' he said in a voice radiating disapproval. 'If you will move along smartly to the room on the left, you will find the other mourners, who have been here *for some time.*'

I felt duly put in my place. Only in the British Army could a four-star general be rebuked in such a way by a warrant officer.

*

Immediately after 9/11, President Bush announced that the war in Afghanistan was part of a broader battle against states sheltering terrorists. This caused a certain amount of discomfort in Britain, where public opinion didn't share that same sense of being 'at war'. Indeed, the phrase 'the global war on terrorism', much used by Washington, struck me as rather odd. Any use of military force must, by definition, be in pursuit of a political objective: this linkage is at the core of strategy. If we use the simple but powerful analytical tool of ends, ways and means, the end is the political objective; the means are the tools – diplomacy, sanctions, military force, etc.; and the ways are how you apply the tools to achieve the objective. Al-Qaida's end is not terrorism – that is their way of applying the means of violence; their end is the political one of achieving the ascendancy of Islamic fundamentalism.

So 'the global war on terrorism' equates to a war on a means, which makes little or no sense. Our objective – our end – must be the physical and intellectual defeat of Islamic fundamentalism as a threat to us. The means to this end certainly include the use of armed force, but also, very importantly, engagement in the battle of ideas. It is here, for me, that the US approach is inadequate: it focuses far too much on the single military means. Nation-building and diplomacy are fundamental to demonstrate the advantages of political and economic progress, both to nations as a whole and to individuals. Furthermore, it has to be understood that this 'war' is not conventional force-on-force war-fighting, in which the use of violence is maximized: in this 'war' the degree of violence has to be very carefully judged to avoid a detrimental effect overall.

In his State of the Union Address in January 2002, Bush identified three countries – Iraq, Iran and North Korea – as an 'Axis of Evil'. He accused these regimes of sponsoring terrorism and seeking to obtain weapons of mass destruction (WMD). As

2002 progressed, there was a sense that Washington's next priority would be Iraq. The Prime Minister's judgement was that Britain had to be alongside America – indeed, that the United Kingdom and the United States should always stand together, even if the cause is seen by some as muddled or misguided. Tony Blair believes passionately in the strategic importance of the Anglo-American alliance. There is no doubt in my mind that this belief, together with the 'doctrine of international community' he had set out in 1999, guided his decision to join the American-led Coalition against Iraq.

It has been suggested more recently that there should be an inquiry into why we went to war in Iraq. In February 2007 the Leader of the House, Jack Straw, indicated in the Commons that the Government would be open to an inquiry 'at the appropriate time', by which he seemed to mean once our troops were no longer involved on the ground. Speaking for myself, I would have no objection to such an inquiry. This seems to me a political rather than a military matter.

In Washington, a vigorous debate ensued about the number of troops required for the invasion of Iraq. Rumsfeld favoured using only a relatively small force of sixty thousand or so, on the model of Afghanistan – disregarding, or at least minimizing the contribution of the Northern Alliance in the defeat of the Taliban. The American military wanted four hundred thousand. The eventual number decided upon was a compromise between these two. From the earliest stage, British concerns focused not just on the war itself but also on what would happen afterwards – so-called 'Phase 4'. At issue was not so much the number of troops needed to topple the regime as the number needed to maintain the peace afterwards. Within meetings of the Chiefs of Staff, I voiced my concern that management of the post-conflict period was essential to the success of the operation. There was no divergence of view between the Chiefs on this issue, and the then CDS, Admiral Sir Mike Boyce, represented our concerns both to the Prime Minister and the Secretary of State – though it may not have helped that he didn't have an easy relationship with Geoff Hoon. In our discussions it became clear that the American State Department had done plenty of planning for Phase 4, and we placed our confidence in this.

By the autumn of 2002 it had become the received wisdom that Saddam Hussein's regime had and was continuing to develop WMD. This was not spin: every major intelligence agency on the planet was saying the same thing, including the Russians'. It was known that Saddam Hussein had used chemical weapons against the Kurds, and it seemed therefore entirely plausible to conclude that what Iraq sources were saying was accurate, i.e. that he was attempting to develop nuclear and biological weapons as well.

Since no evidence of WMD was found after the invasion of Iraq, some commentators have speculated that the scare about WMD was invented as a pretext for the invasion. I have no reason to give this any credence. We in the British Army were certainly not willing to discount the intelligence; to do so would have been extremely foolhardy. I know that our soldiers in northern Kuwait before the invasion were very concerned about WMD – particularly chemical weapons – being used against them. I myself visited the forces in the build-up to the invasion, and, like everyone else, I had to lug a respirator and chemical suit about with me. Our forces out there had to do a lot of training in respirators and protective clothing to rehearse their response to a chemical attack. You would not do this in the heat and dust of the desert unless you judged that a chemical attack was a serious possibility.

We know now that the intelligence was fool's gold. I can't pretend to know why this was. Intelligence-collecting in Saddam Hussein's Iraq was peculiarly difficult, and intelligence gathered there required cautious handling. I suspect there was only a very small number of high-ranking sources in Iraq. It's possible that these sources didn't have first-hand knowledge of what was happening, but had themselves been told that Iraq was developing WMD and believed it to be true. Perhaps the regime allowed this belief to circulate because it was thought to act as a deterrent to intervention. The obstructive Iraqi behaviour towards the UN weapons inspectors before the invasion reinforced the conclusion that they had something to hide. Of course, it's possible to draw the opposite conclusion: that the Iraqis hindered the inspectors to conceal the fact that they had no WMD – in other words, that they had been bluffing all along. That was a very high-risk game for the Iraqis to play, and as it turned out they lost.

Another possibility is that the sources knew that there was no WMD programme, but lied to their handlers to deter an attack. Much depends on what they perceived Western intentions to be. One could equally well argue that they lied to their handlers because they knew that intelligence of a WMD programme would provoke an attack and they wanted Saddam Hussein removed. Washington in particular was locked into a dialogue with some disgruntled and ambitious Iraqi expatriates, based both in America itself and in Jordan, no doubt working to an agenda which suited them. It's possible that they were telling their paymasters what their paymasters wanted to hear. These are recurring problems with intelligence.

The intelligence assessments produced by the Joint Intelligence Committee (JIC) are very measured documents indeed, and normally full of caveats. Every word is carefully considered. As Commander in Chief and later as CGS I used to receive such assessments on a regular basis, though in neither role did I sit on the committee myself. On 24 September 2002 the Government took an unprecedented decision to release a dossier, based 'in large part' on the work of the JIC, into the public domain. The wording of the dossier was less measured than was usual for JIC assessments. It concluded that Saddam

Hussein's regime possessed chemical and biological weapons, some of which 'are deployable within forty-five minutes of an order to use them'. This was taken by some commentators to mean that the UK could face a threat of attack at forty-five minutes' notice.

It was understood that the dossier was intended for public consumption. Nevertheless, its release caused a stir in military circles. We all knew that it was impossible for Iraq to threaten the UK mainland, even if the dossier left that impression open. Saddam's SCUD missiles could barely have reached our bases on Cyprus, and certainly no more distant target. We took the vague warning to mean that chemical warheads could be fitted to missiles in the field within forty-five minutes – though the public may have been left with a rather different impression.

I learned that I was to be the next CGS after an Army Board meeting in the MOD in the autumn of 2002. The Army Board meetings would last all morning, and then there would be an informal lunch in the office, after which members of the Board would drift away. At the end of one of these lunches Mike Walker asked me to stay behind, and afterwards he told me that he had been chosen as the next CDS once his time as CGS was up, early in 2003. I was to take over from him. For the third time in succession, I would be stepping into his shoes.

The choice of a new CGS is ultimately made by the Prime Minister and subject to approval by the Sovereign. In practice, the existing CGS puts forward a recommendation to the CDS and the Secretary of State after off-the-record discussions with a number of senior officials, including the Military Secretary. The recommendation is forwarded to No. 10 and finally to Buckingham Palace.

Of course I was delighted. To become head of the Service is a huge honour. To me personally, it meant staying in the Army for another few years. The alternative would have been retirement, because there was nowhere else for me to go – it was up or out at that point. I would take up the post of CGS fewer than seven weeks before my fifty-ninth birthday. I was already at least a couple of years or so older than the average CGS on appointment. Being somewhat older than the optimum age probably blew any chances I might have had of becoming CDS in due course – that and my discomfort with the MOD, which I found hard to conceal.

I knew that the job of CGS would be high-profile, especially as it was looking increasingly likely that we would be going into Iraq at some point. I discussed the matter with Sarah, and we thought that I should brief the whole family. Although Amanda and Mark now had their own lives, my taking this job would affect them none the less, as well as Tom. I told them my news over supper in the kitchen at Bulford. The first thing I wanted them to know was that I would be staying in the Army for another three years or so, and that we would be living in an official residence in London – in a small but charming apartment above the old stables of Kensington Palace, as luck had it. Any CGS inevitably becomes involved in difficult and sometimes unpopular decision-making, and there was no reason to suppose I would be exempt. I knew that taking the job meant that I would come in for a lot of criticism, often without being able to answer back. I have always held very strongly to the principle that soldiers should never become embroiled in politics: I would therefore have to defend decisions which were not mine, and to refrain from speaking out openly on issues about which I felt strongly. I would have to accept compromises even if I felt these were shabby ones. It was my constitutional duty not to express dissent in public for as long as I was in post. There was sure to be some sniping; it was important that, as a family, we would be able to take the rough with the smooth. I had a sense that it was not going to be an entirely easy ride. Though aware of the downside, the family was entirely supportive.

*

Before the invasion of Iraq there was much speculation about the legality of going to war without the backing of a specific UN Security Council Resolution authorizing military action. There was a bit of inconsistency about this. People forgot, or chose to forget, that the intervention in Kosovo, which had broad public support, was made without a UNSCR. It seems that it had been acceptable then, but wasn't acceptable when it came to Iraq. Cynics have pointed to Iraq's oil as a motive for going to war; I saw no evidence of this myself, and in any event it doesn't alter the principle. In the case of Kosovo, the legal argument used to circumvent the absence of a UNSCR was the emerging doctrine in international law that intervention on humanitarian grounds to prevent genocide or 'ethnic cleansing' may be adequate legal justification in itself. And indeed the fact that this had happened in Kosovo served as a kind of precedent. This is quite a controversial area: some accept the argument, some don't, but of course international law is a strange beast. It often doesn't have the precise clarity of domestic law, and often it applies to a particular country only if that country has signed up to a particular treaty or convention. In the case of Iraq, we were the junior partner in a coalition led by the United States, which doesn't acknowledge the authority of certain aspects of international law to the extent that the UK does. In particular, the Americans do not accept the authority of the International Criminal Court. The relevant legislation had been introduced into UK law in Charles Guthrie's time as CDS and he was on record as having been rather unhappy about it; but he had accepted an assurance given to him by the Government that it could not envisage circumstances in which a British soldier would find himself in front of the International Criminal Court. Now, an assurance given by a politician is one thing, but in law there was at least the theoretical – and worrying – possibility that a British soldier might find himself being tried by the ICC.

The same applied right up the chain of command, up to the very top.

Mike Boyce was CDS in the run-up to the Iraq War. He had been due to hand over to Mike Walker before the war started, but it was decided that it wouldn't be very sensible to change the Chief of the Defence Staff in the very early stages of the Iraq campaign, so he remained in post for a few months longer than originally intended. Tony Blair wanted a new UNSCR if possible, for internal political reasons as much as for anything else. It became clear that the Security Council were not going to back a so-called 'second' UNSCR (there had already been seventeen concerning Iraq); of the permanent members of the Security Council, the Russians would veto any Resolution authorizing military action, and the French might do the same.

The matter came to a head after I'd become CGS, in the immediate run-up to the war, but of course the debate had been running for some while before this. A lot of people had asked me in casual conversation, 'Are you sure you're OK on this one?' The Chiefs of Staff discussed the matter and collectively agreed that we needed to be sure of our ground. So Mike Boyce, on behalf of us all, sought the Attorney General's assurances on the legality of the planned military action. I remarked at the time that, having had some part to play in putting Slobodan Milosevic into a cell in The Hague, I had no wish to be his next-door neighbour. Notwithstanding the Attorney General's advice that the war was legal, I decided to do my own homework. I dug out what to me were the critical Security Council Resolutions (particularly 678, 687 and 1441) and went through them very carefully. By the end I had satisfied myself independently that military action against Iraq was legitimate under international law without a 'second' Resolution. There was much debate about whether or not UNSCR 1441 carried with it 'auto-maticity', i.e. whether nations were entitled to take military action if Saddam failed to comply with its provisions. But my own reading of the Resolutions is that the first Gulf War had ended in a ceasefire, and that if Saddam failed to do what he was obliged to do under UNSCR 687, the ceasefire no longer held. Indeed, it is entirely possible to regard the two Gulf Wars of 1990 and 2003 as being a single war, with the two ground actions separated by a long operational pause.

The political reasons for action against Saddam Hussein propounded at the time have proved to be flawed: Bush's position that Iraq was an Al-Qaida hotbed does not now withstand scrutiny; and Blair's reliance on WMD proved to be a chimera. It is something of a mystery to me why Blair did not extend the argument, as Bush did in mid-December, when he declared Iraq to be in material breach of various past UNSCRs. For a decade, Saddam Hussein had defied and obstructed the United Nations. Unenforced UNSCRs can only diminish and weaken the institution; he was a brutal tyrant who treated his own people with appalling cruelty, including gassing a Kurdish town; even if he did not possess WMD in 2003, it is likely that his intent was to obtain them.

I have given my own view as to the legality of the Coalition action, and certainly the Chiefs accepted the Attorney General's advice. In conversation with critics of the Iraq action, I have heard some seem to suggest that the British Armed Forces should have refused to take part. This is very dangerous ground. The Armed Forces of this country take their oath of allegiance to the Sovereign as Head of State, and they are constitutionally bound to follow the lawful directions of the duly elected Government of the day. It would be unthinkable for the Armed Forces not to do as they are directed – or, worse, to act without authorization. That is the road to anarchy.

The legal status of UK soldiers after the invasion was also an issue. I remember that the Army lawyers worked very hard on this, because military occupation was not an area of international law which had been used in the recent past (in the

Balkans, international forces had intervened with the agreement
– however reluctant – of the appropriate governments). During
the Iraq War itself, British soldiers were operating under the
international Law of Armed Conflict and, as ever, British military law. What happened once the war ended was more
complicated. International law defined the Coalition as 'occupying forces' under the Geneva Convention until a sovereign
Iraqi government was re-established. Once Iraq formally
regained its sovereignty under the interim government in the
summer of 2004, agreements were made which changed the
status of the Coalition forces from that of occupiers to that of a
military presence at the behest of the sovereign government,
which is perfectly valid in international law. So the period of
occupation lasted just over a year.

In the autumn of 2002, as options for military action against
Iraq were being explored within the MOD, the initial proposal
was that the British contribution should be based on naval and
air contingents, without any significant ground force. I never
quite got to the bottom of that. It was true that there was a
groundswell of anti-war opinion at home, though opinion polls
showed that public opinion was about two to one in favour of
military intervention in Iraq. I argued strongly that we would
never get traction with the Americans without ground troops. In
a coalition, as in a formal alliance, both political and military
risk must be shared.

  If you are going to commit a ground force to a major military
operation, whether on an independent national basis or as a
partner within a coalition, you need to do it on a scale which
gives you the confidence to say: Well, if it all goes wrong, we can
look after ourselves and we can fight our way out. In circumstances such as prevailed in Iraq, you needed a division to do
that. A brigade would not have been big enough.

  There were problems about deploying a sizeable ground force.

Not only were there some ten thousand soldiers still committed to firefighting in the UK because of the continuing firemen's strike; such a commitment would also be outside the MOD's 'Defence Planning Assumptions'. These assumptions define force structures and equipment stocks. In 2002 the assumptions provided for nothing more than what we call a 'small-scale' effort in desert conditions (small-scale being below a brigade, medium-scale being brigade level, and large-scale being the level of a division or more). The most charitable judgement is that this assumption lacked prescience. I am reminded of the definition of such an assumption produced by one of my fellow-officers: the genesis of a cock-up. So the MOD had based its procurement on equipping no more than a few thousand soldiers to operate in the desert. This is not something that you can change overnight. For example, you can't produce thirty thousand sets of desert combat kit in a few weeks; it just isn't possible.

There was a political element in this, too. The British Government wanted to demonstrate that the decision to invade was not a *fait accompli*, i.e. that Saddam Hussein would not be attacked if he cooperated fully with the weapons inspectors. Such political sensitivities delayed the necessary military preparations.

A further complication was that we had planned for the main British force to move south from Turkey into Kurdistan, which would have given greater autonomy to the British campaign, despite the very considerable logistic challenge of an overland line of communication six or seven hundred miles long from the nearest available port in the eastern Mediterranean. But by early January 2003 it had become clear that the Turks were highly unlikely to give the necessary permission for an invasion from Turkish soil, and the decision was made to switch to the south. So then the plan had to be rejigged at short notice, adding the complexity of having to mesh closely with the American entry plans, and increasing the pressure on time.

The switch to the south also required a re-appraisal of the ground force's size and shape. The outcome was the decision to adopt a full divisional structure comprising three brigades – a larger force than the northern option. This increase to full scale brought additional logistic pressure. The eventual British ground contribution would be approximately thirty thousand soldiers, around one-fifth of the total ground troops deployed. Time was not on our side. The logisticians went into overdrive. Personnel and materiel were moved to the Gulf much more quickly than in 1989–90. The build-up was helped by the fact that the UK had held an ambitious joint-Service exercise in Oman during the autumn of 2001, after which a lot of equipment was held in the Middle East rather than being returned to Britain.

Lack of proper equipment at the start of the war has become something of a *cause célèbre*. The main problem was that political decision-making had left too little time for the Defence Logistic Organization to equip every soldier with desert camouflage clothing and with the latest body armour. But in the judgement of the in-theatre commanders, this was not a showstopper. None of them said, 'We can't go in this time frame.' And too much emphasis on logistical difficulties was not the right message to send to the enemy just before the invasion. The alternative would have been to delay the operation until the autumn of 2003. But there were overwhelming counterarguments: it would have been a nightmare to have kept the Coalition forces in their assembly areas in the Gulf during the fierce summer heat – and Washington was simply not prepared to wait that long.

There was a mood of keen anticipation in the Army in late 2002. It's very much part of the job of the Commander in Chief to get around, visiting units in the barracks, visiting the Brigade Headquarters, seeing what's going on in field training exercises, talking to officers, talking to soldiers. In my last few months as Commander in Chief, during the build-up to the invasion of Iraq, I was lobbied wherever I went to favour the battalion I was visiting over others. This remarkable desire to get involved in operations gives the British Army the can-do character for which it is renowned.

I took over as CGS on 1 February 2003. By this time the invasion of Iraq was imminent. Many of our troops were already in their assembly areas in northern Kuwait, a flat landscape of greyish desert. I flew out to visit them in the second week of March, just a week before hostilities began. They were training hard and doing plenty of live firing. The weather was awful, with sandstorms making it unpleasant to venture outside. As the wind howled around our camps, sand found its way everywhere, into your clothes and into your equipment. I shared a tent with Major General Robin Brims, the UK Land Component Commander. While I was there I went off to find Mark, who was what we called 'watch-keeping', i.e. working in the ops room, taking the radio messages and all of that. We had about three-quarters of an hour together before I had to move on.

During this visit I had a memorable chat with a young private soldier from the Royal Regiment of Fusiliers, a northerner.

'How are you doing?' I asked him.

'Doing fine, Sir,' he replied. I asked him if he was getting the newspapers from home, and he told me that he was.

'Well, as you probably know then, there's a bit of a fuss going on about boots and bog rolls and whatnot,' I said. 'Are you all right for boots?' He told me that he was.

'Any worries, then?'

'Aye, Sir,' he said firmly. Wait for it, I thought. 'When are we going in, Sir? Fucking when?'

'I don't know,' I told him, stifling a grin. 'A week, ten days perhaps – you know, it's all down to the politicians.'

'Because what we need to do is get across that bloody border, kick that bugger's arse, get home and have a few bloody beers.'

As a succinct mission statement, I couldn't have matched it.

War began on 20 March. The Chiefs of Staff moved to meeting on a daily basis, as I had witnessed during the Falklands – only this time I wasn't a minion sitting in a cubby-hole manipulating the vufoils (now, of course, long out-of-date), but one of the Chiefs myself. At that point, I was the only soldier among the five Chiefs of Staff, because Admiral Mike Boyce was CDS, and his deputy, the Vice Chief, was Air Chief Marshal Tony Bagnall. These daily meetings were held in the morning in the splendidly appointed Old War Office building, which served as the MOD HQ while the main building was being refurbished. Meetings would begin with an intelligence and operations update, before moving on to discuss any special developments, logistics and 'force flow' – the coordinated movement of men and materiel. Day-to-day operational matters were overseen by the Permanent Joint Headquarters (PJHQ) in Northwood, which had permanent responsibility for all operations worldwide (except operations on the UK mainland). The Chief of Joint Operations (CJO) at the time was my old friend John Reith, now a lieutenant general, and he would participate in the Chiefs' meetings by video conference from Northwood.

During the war a dedicated Cabinet sub-committee met most mornings, attended by the Prime Minister, the Deputy Prime Minister John Prescott, the Foreign Secretary Jack Straw, the Attorney General Peter Goldsmith, the Defence Secretary Geoff Hoon, the International Development Secretary Clare Short and others. I attended in place of Mike Boyce on several occasions when he was busy elsewhere. This was my first experience of so-called 'sofa government'. I was included in the Prime Minister's discussion group, which would meet in his unprepossessing study beforehand. The room was furnished with a small desk and a couple of sofas, where I sometimes found myself perched on one of the arms. Informal agreement on the day's issues would be reached prior to rehearsing the discussions in Cabinet. Alastair Campbell was always present in the PM's study.

I was quite confident that the conventional war – what we in the Army call the 'manoeuvre war' – would be a resounding success, because this is what the US Army does best. My concerns centred on the aftermath of the inevitable fall of Saddam Hussein. One could see it was going to be very difficult: Iraq is a very much larger country than any other in which we had recently operated, and there was the constant problem of American aversion to nation-building. The difficulties were greatly exacerbated by the President's fateful misjudgement in transferring responsibility for the post-conflict period from the State Department to the Pentagon. All the planning carried out by the State Department went to waste. Rumsfeld and his fellow neocons paid little attention to the Phase 4 period; for them, it was an ideological article of faith that the Coalition forces would be accepted as a liberating army. Once you had decapitated Saddam Hussein's regime, a model democratic society would inevitably emerge.

As always in the British Armed Services, our inclination was to leave the tactical decisions to the commanders on the ground. There were plenty of Cassandras, both in the press and within the MOD itself, warning that the fighting in the Iraqi cities would be like Stalingrad, a grim struggle to the death in rubble-strewn streets. These ignoramuses didn't know what they were talking about. Graham Binns, the brigade commander responsible for taking Basra, bided his time, using probing attacks to test how the Iraqis would react. Graham had been my Chief of Staff in 39 Brigade, on my last Northern Ireland tour; I knew that 7 Armoured Brigade could not be in better hands. In close consultation with Robin Brims, his divisional commander, Graham fought a brilliant battle. He wore down the Iraqi defences on the periphery of Basra until – with exquisite timing – he was able to take the city in one fell swoop.

The Cassandras were always looking for something to go wrong. I well remember doing a press conference on the afternoon of the first Friday of the ground war, six days after the invasion began. In the morning meeting of the Chiefs of Staff, John Reith had given us an operational update on the VTC from Northwood. At that point the American spearhead had paused just short of the town of Karbala, where the only practical route north is through a narrow gap between the River Euphrates and a very large salt pan. They had advanced 300 miles or so in less than a week. And some of the press commented that the Americans were 'bogged down'!

'They've just advanced three hundred miles in contact with the enemy in a mere six days,' I told the press conference. 'Do you understand what an enormous military achievement that is?' After such a rapid advance the American soldiers needed to catch up on sleep, and stock up on fuel and ammunition. And of course they needed to regroup and replenish, to plan what they were going to do next, how they were going to advance through the Karbala gap and on to Baghdad. 'If you think that's being bogged down,' I went on, 'words fail me.'

Civilians might find it remarkable that the Iraqi Army, which had fought for many years against the Iranians in the 1980s, collapsed so quickly. But it was all a matter of manoeuvre, of paralysing your enemy by speed and by decisiveness. The Iraqis were completely outmanoeuvred and outfought, cut off from their lines of communication and logistics. I suspected, too, that many Iraqi soldiers had no wish to die for Saddam Hussein. I remember saying shortly before the war began: 'What we need is the mobile phone number of every Iraqi divisional commander. Our commanders on the ground should give each of them a ring twenty-four hours out and say something along the lines of, "Ahmed, my friend, you don't know me but I know about you.

You and I are going to meet: we can either meet with a hand-shake or we can meet over the dead bodies of your soldiers." ' I was pretty sure how they would have reacted to such an approach. Before the manoeuvre war began, I predicted that it would be finished in two weeks. In fact it took almost three. By the middle of April, that relatively straightforward bit was over.

Three weeks later I flew out to Iraq myself. Robin Brims had settled his Division down into its post-conflict areas of tactical responsibility. I was taken on several tours to see where the fighting had taken place, in particular to the large bridges outside Basra where the Iraqis had put up a stubborn resistance. My overall impression was that those who had taken part rightly felt a quiet sense of satisfaction for a job well done. The main purpose of my visit was to congratulate and thank the soldiers who had done so well – but I also wanted to get a feel for the place. Basra is a big city of low-rise buildings surrounded by flat desert. At that stage the insurgency had not begun, and the atmosphere seemed relaxed and good-natured. I remember walking through the souk in Basra and stopping to buy a carpet, haggling with the moneychanger in the traditional manner.

I listened to a lot of soldiers telling me their individual experiences. One of the most memorable accounts came from Lance Corporal of Horse Mick Flynn of the Blues and Royals, a redoubtable character who afterwards would be awarded the Conspicuous Gallantry Cross for his part in the Iraq War. Remarkably, he had also fought in the Falklands War as a very young soldier. Twenty years on, as a veteran vehicle commander in a squadron of the Household Cavalry in the armoured reconnaissance role, he was very much in the thick of the fighting. While 'turret down' behind a bund north of Basra he spotted several Iraqi T-55 tanks and called in airpower to destroy these. When the aircraft failed to find the tanks, Flynn made the decision to fire tracer rounds to indicate the targets. This would be visible from the air – but it meant moving forward to a 'hull down' position to allow the 30mm cannon to fire, thereby exposing the vehicle to retaliatory fire from the tanks. On being given the order to move, the young driver, fresh out of recruit training, hesitated. Flynn reached down from the turret and put his hand on the young man's shoulder. 'Steady, lad, steady,' he said comfortingly, before issuing the order again: 'Driver, advance!'

Three years later, in Afghanistan, Mick Flynn, now a Corporal of Horse, would be awarded the Military Cross for his exceptional courage and presence of mind during an ambush by the Taliban. His actions undoubtedly saved the lives of the crew of his Scimitar armoured vehicle, and contributed to saving the lives of the crew of another vehicle in his Troop.

Afterwards I flew up to Baghdad to talk to the Brits there. I stayed in the old British Embassy, a colonial-style building right on the banks of the River Euphrates, which had been evacuated after the invasion of Kuwait more than a dozen years earlier. Very soon after the end of hostilities, a platoon of Paras had deployed to Baghdad to secure the building at the request of the Foreign Office. The ambassador-designate arrived more or less the same time that I did, and the boys decided that this was reason enough to host a party that evening. Somehow they found cold beers and supplies for a barbecue. With the Union Jack flying above the Embassy, an eclectic mixture of guests arrived, Brits of all sorts materializing out of the darkness.

I found myself talking to the old caretaker, who showed me that the Royal coat-of-arms was once more up over the entrance to the building, and that framed photos of HM The Queen and HRH The Duke of Edinburgh had been re-hung on the Embassy walls.

'I have guarded these in the cellar all these years,' he said proudly. I made the appropriate noises of appreciation.

'One small thing,' he added. I looked at him quizzically.

'Thirteen years' back pay.'

When I got back to London I did raise the matter with Sir Michael Jay, Permanent Secretary at the Foreign Office. The records showed that the caretaker had continued to receive pay throughout those years when the Embassy was closed. I asked how the money had been sent. Apparently payments had been made through the Russian Embassy. I am pleased to say the caretaker was paid in full, and received an MBE as a further recognition of his efforts.

As CGS I was twice present at RAF Brize Norton to pay my respects when the bodies of those killed in combat were repatriated. Each was a sombre occasion. The relatives of the dead were present. This was essentially a private ceremony, but not a secret one, and one set of cameras was present on the basis that the film would be shared out among the broadcasters as required.

We gathered before the aircraft landed, and were seated on the edge of the apron outside the terminal building to watch the C-17 aircraft land and taxi into position, coming to a rest with the nose of the aircraft facing diagonally away from the mourners. Then the ramp was lowered. A bearer party of six soldiers in parade dress advanced and marched up the ramp to take the first coffin. As they came into view down the ramp carrying the coffin, a band began playing and everyone stood. We all saluted as the bearers marched past in slow time, carrying the coffin to the waiting hearse. This simple, but profoundly moving, ceremony was repeated for each coffin on board the aircraft.

The war was a quick fix, but predictably the peace hasn't proved so easy. The scale of the looting at the end of the manoeuvre war came as a surprise to everyone. It was perhaps the first indication that things were not as they should be. Our people on the ground found it very difficult to control, because the indigenous security forces were in disarray and there was no judicial system worth the name to deal with the looters. Since then, the insurgency and the appalling inter-ethnic violence have both made it extremely difficult to rebuild Iraqi society.

Going back to my analogy of the strands of the rope, in a post-conflict situation you need security and you need political authority. Once Saddam Hussein's regime collapsed, there was a complete vacuum at the top. It took a long time to establish a provisional government, and even today the Iraqi politicians continue wrangling while their country is torn by sectarian and tribal strife.

Reconstruction is another essential strand of the rope. Maybe it's apocryphal, but there is some substance in the Iraqi complaint that the Americans could put a man on the moon, but they couldn't fix the Iraqi power supply. Repair work to the infrastructure has proceeded at an agonizingly slow pace. Gilbert Greenall's maxim of the first hundred days being vital comes to mind here. It seems strange that the Washington planners didn't seem to have learned from our experiences in Kosovo and Bosnia. The waste of all our accumulated knowledge of how to manage post-conflict situations is a tragedy. We had a very good man inside the Coalition Provisional Authority, the body which ran Iraq after the collapse of Saddam Hussein's regime until an elected Iraqi government was ready to take over: Major General Tim Cross, who had run our logistics in Kosovo. The reports we received from Tim were alarming: 'This is a madhouse,' he was saying, 'the situation is terrible.' Tim had been with the Pentagon planners in Washington before the war and he had been saying then that they hadn't got their act together.

The first British envoy to Iraq, Sir Jeremy Greenstock, has recently commented in a BBC *Inside Story* television documentary that the Prime Minister took his 'eye off the ball' in the crucial first days and weeks after the liberation of Iraq.

In the days following the victory no one, it seems to me, was instructed to put the security of Iraq first, to put law and order on the streets first. There was no police force. There was no constituted army except the victorious invaders. And there was no American general that I could . . . establish who was given the accountable responsibility to make sure that the first duty of any government – and we were the government – was to keep law and order on the streets. There was a vacuum from the beginning in which looters, saboteurs, the criminals, the insurgents moved very quickly.

It is hard to argue with Sir Jeremy's conclusions, though in fairness to the Prime Minister one should acknowledge that, as the junior partner in a coalition, we were not in a position to call the shots. I have no doubt that Tony Blair has found this position frustrating at times. It should also be recognized that most of the Iraqi infrastructure was run down, and the utilities were creaking along after years of underinvestment, made worse by the sanctions imposed by the UN after the first Gulf War. The British Army may be able to get the odd power station working again, but it cannot build new ones. Such work requires highly skilled construction companies. I have to say once again that we found the DfID less than wholehearted about helping us in the reconstruction effort. Not for the first time, one had the impression that some of their people see soldiers as part of the problem rather than part of the solution. When the British Government has such a huge amount at stake, politically, economically and militarily, it does seem extraordinary that a key Government department should be dragging its heels.

It's very difficult to start rebuilding a country without proper security. I shared the view that the Washington-inspired decision to disband the Iraqi army was very short-sighted. I can remember stressing in a Chiefs of Staff meeting that we should not be doing this. We should have kept the Iraqi security services in being and put them under the command of the Coalition. I know that Mike Boyce shared this view and argued it with our political masters. To what extent the British Government communicated our concerns to the Americans I have no idea. For much too long the Coalition soldiers have had to carry out a policing function, which is very difficult indeed, especially as few of them speak the language. In the short run it is a case of needs must, but in the long run I don't think it's possible for a foreign army to provide security, or for a foreign police force to maintain law and order. At the end of the day, internal security must be a matter for the people who live there. It is a question of consent: with it, the intervention force can hold the ring while indigenous security forces are brought up to scratch; without it, the intervention forces can only be seen as repressive. And consent in Iraq has dwindled since Saddam Hussein's downfall.

I had a similar reaction to the decision – again made in Washington – to ban members of the former ruling Ba'ath Party from participating in the new government or holding other official posts. There is a precedent in the occupation of Germany after the Second World War, when it was accepted that at any time up to 1945, if you had been a schoolteacher and wanted to become a headmaster you'd probably have needed a Nazi Party membership card in your back pocket – but that didn't mean to say you were a Nazi, just that you wanted to get on. Interestingly enough, President Bush announced a reversal of this policy of 'de-Ba'athification' in October 2006. But by then much damage had been done.

Some people find it difficult to understand why, with all the resources at its disposal, the Coalition has been unable to suppress the insurgency. One answer is troop numbers. At the height of the Troubles in Northern Ireland, for example, we had twenty thousand or more soldiers in the Province to keep the peace, and even then we were unable to suppress terrorism altogether. Northern Ireland has only around 5 per cent of Iraq's population; a similar presence would thus equate to four hundred thousand soldiers, but the Coalition struggled to reach half that figure. Furthermore, in Northern Ireland the Army was working alongside a highly competent police force, which doesn't yet exist in Iraq. On the contrary, many of the Iraqi police are corrupt and making matters worse.

Since my first visit immediately after Saddam Hussein was deposed, I have made a number of subsequent visits to Iraq, and I have seen the Iraqi Army rebuilt from scratch. When I first visited the Iraqi Divisional HQ in Basra, it was still functioning on a very makeshift basis. I have watched the new Iraqi Army become gradually more capable, undertaking joint operations with British forces. I have also visited the Iraqi equivalent of Sandhurst just outside Baghdad, which under largely British guidance has grown from nothing into an impressive institution. Throughout, I had the sense of the Iraqi Army acquiring its own ethos of service to the nation – something which sadly cannot be said of the police force.

The insurgent tactic of suicide bombing has been particularly difficult for the Coalition forces. In Northern Ireland, we at least knew that the IRA would not initiate an attack unless they were very confident of their escape route. Defence against suicide bombers, however, requires almost instantaneous reaction, and therefore split-second decision-making. This is an enormous responsibility for the British soldier – and of course, the use of suicide bombers increases the risk that innocent civilians will be caught in the crossfire. Sooner or later it will be alleged that someone has overstepped the mark. There have been a minute number of cases in which British soldiers have been charged with murder – and no convictions – following allegations that they may have used excessive force. Other than in conventional war, the legal test is whether the amount of force used was 'reasonable'. It must be difficult for people who have not served in the military themselves to judge what is, or is not, 'reasonable' in confused and dangerous conditions (and this is one reason why a separate military justice system provides for courts martial made up of military personnel). I have the greatest sympathy with soldiers in such circumstances.

But I draw a clear line between alleged excessive force in the heat of the moment, and prisoner abuse in cold blood. Very sadly, a handful of British soldiers in Iraq have been found guilty of the latter; a few others have been tried and, thankfully, acquitted. Photographs of prisoner abuse irresponsibly published in the *Mirror* without proper verification turned out to be fakes, but shockingly similar events to those shown have actually taken place. I made it clear at the time that I deplored any such behaviour, not least because of its detrimental effect on operations. How can we expect to win the support of the Iraqi people if they believe that we are abusing their compatriots?

It has to be recognized that within an Army approximately a hundred thousand strong, there are bound to be a few who will take it out on prisoners if the opportunity arises to do so, particularly in a unit which has been taking casualties. We do our best to screen out such individuals, but inevitably some slip through the net. So abuses will occasionally happen – but they can never be tolerated. I am quite clear about this. During my time as CGS I came in for a certain amount of stick for not 'standing up for soldiers' accused of prisoner abuse. It beats me what people who say such things think should happen. Do they want cases of alleged prisoner abuse swept under the carpet? I am certain that any cover-up would do the Army great harm; we must adhere to the rule of law. The British public must be able to trust our soldiers at all times. In addition, once proceedings reach a certain stage, senior officers have to be mindful of the need to avoid making comments that could prejudice a fair trial.

I am appalled by the view that prosecutions of soldiers alleged to have abused prisoners in Iraq were politically driven. Such opinion is tantamount to saying that the Army

Prosecuting Authority dances to some political tune. Any prosecuting authority has difficult decisions to make, but those decisions are made on the evidence presented and emphatically not on the basis of personal whim, political direction or how the media may react. We are fortunate indeed in Britain to live under the rule of law, the bedrock of a civilized society. The absence of the rule of law, as one sees in far too many other countries, can only result, by definition, in lawlessness. I am saddened by criticism of decisions by an independent authority to prosecute which, of itself, is political in nature and fails to give proper weight to the due process of law. I think it's crucial that the head of the Army speaks unequivocally about such matters; he sets the standard. The mistreatment of prisoners tarnishes the fine reputation of the British Army, and constitutes a blatant breach of discipline; furthermore, it is an affront to the soldiers' pride in their profession. Ultimately it is detrimental to operations, because it creates suspicion and hostility in the minds of the civilian population. The Army cannot condone such behaviour.

I had operations overseas always very much in mind during my time as CGS, but these weren't my only concerns. I am always reluctant to use 'management speak', but it may help civilians to understand their different functions to think of the CGS as the Chairman and the Commander in Chief as the Managing Director of the British Army. It's the Commander in Chief's job to keep the Army machine ticking over; the CGS's job is at least as much about the future as it is about the present. His priority is to maintain the Army's ability to achieve operational success over the coming years.

For me, the biggest challenge of my time as CGS was without doubt getting the optimum future capability for the Army from the resources the Labour Government had seen fit to devote to increasingly hard-worked Armed Forces. The Government had already carried out a Strategic Defence Review soon after it came into power, the effect of which was to concentrate more resources on expeditionary forces. Fair enough; but it rapidly became clear that the programme of defence expenditure laid out for the future could not be met from the budget allocated. And so, besides dealing with Iraq, my first eighteen months as CGS were spent fighting the Army's corner in a cost-cutting exercise bizarrely entitled 'the medium-term work strands' – in effect, a mini defence review. The outcome was that the RAF had to shed about 10 per cent of its manpower and the Royal Navy lost some of its older ships. In the opinion of the MOD civil servants, the Army got away 'relatively lightly', losing some 1,500 soldiers from an establishment of about 104,000. In fact, we were in some ways ahead of the game: the Army staff in the MOD had already come to the conclusion that the balance of capabilities within the Army was out of kilter. Given finite resources, you have to make the best possible use of them, even if you have concluded that the resources allocated do not match the commitments you have been given. So what the Army staff did was to sit down and, on the basis of the Defence Planning Assumptions, try to work out what the best balance would be. The result was the 'Future Army Structure'. Some of this rebalancing was relatively uncontroversial. Field artillery, for example, was reduced because we decided we had too much of it, relative to the overall size of the Army. On the other hand, we actually increased the number of engineers, because experience told us that we would need more engineers for the kinds of operations we were likely to expect.

But the real rub was the future size and structure of the infantry. Under the Strategic Defence Review of the early 1990s, the Army had made the case for an infantry of fifty-five battalions, but that was deemed too many for the post-Cold-War budget and the figure of forty had emerged. Now the MOD was proposing an infantry of fewer than thirty battalions, based on the assumption that Northern Ireland would soon go non-operational. After a long attritional battle with the MOD Central Staff bean-counters, we got the figure up to thirty-six. At thirty-six, we ran out of specific arguments, and had to rely on the general justification of being prepared for the unexpected, of having resilience, of maintaining a reserve. Entirely sensible as this may seem, such justification cuts no ice in the MOD (or 'Head Office' as they like to call themselves) – or in the Treasury, which second-guesses the MOD in all such matters. None the less, given that so much infantry manpower had previously been allocated to Northern Ireland, these thirty-six battalions would in fact give us more general-purpose battalions available for use elsewhere. That said, the Army Board was faced with the agonizing decision of which four battalions were to be removed from the Order of Battle.

There was another, parallel, problem which was overdue for a definitive solution. The infantry was run on a system known as the 'Arms Plot', by which individual battalions were moved every few years – moved geographically and very often moved in role. The justification for this was that each battalion and every soldier needed variety, to maintain the interest of the job, to produce soldiers who were adaptable and versatile with a wide range of experience, and to even out geographical advantages and disadvantages. But the system had evolved largely in order to maintain the existing infantry regimental structure. Previous reductions in the infantry and previous decisions about its structure had produced a situation whereby approximately half the infantry were in single-battalion regiments. In such regiments there could obviously be no rotation between battalions. So the Arms Plot prevented battalions stagnating in one place for ever, while preserving regimental identity.

But the result of this system was that at any one time a significant number of battalions – up to 20 per cent of our infantry overall – were not available, because they were either changing their location, retraining, taking on new roles or generally in some form of 'baulk', as the cry has it. It was a high price to pay for the regimental system as it was then organized. To have battalions moving from one role to another was very inefficient and wasteful of expertise. For armoured infantry, for example, the perceived wisdom was that they didn't really master their job for about two years; and then after another four years they'd be moved to a different role. Given that the average length of service for a private soldier is about four and a half years, the loss of capability was impossible to justify. We were getting breadth at the expense of depth, an outcome which particularly concerned the other major combat arm, the Royal Armoured Corps. The Arms Plot also went against brigade coherence; each brigade had, on average, at least one battalion changing over each year.

Once or twice a year the Army Board would have an 'away-day', in which we would try to stand back and look at the way we did things. On 27 November 2003 the Board held an all-day session at the former Staff College at Camberley to concentrate on the infantry Arms Plot, comparing it with other models of how we might do things. We scored the options, just as a selection board scores individual candidates. The results made it quite clear that the Arms Plot could no longer be justified. It was so detrimental to operational effectiveness, and had so many inherent disadvantages built into it, that it would have to go. No one doubted the value of the regimental system to the British Army. But if all the infantry was organized in large regiments, you could move individuals between battalions when their career and personal circumstances suited, while still keeping them as members of the same tribe.

It was the obvious solution. Much of the rest of the Army had long been asking: 'Why should the infantry get this special deal?' Reform was long overdue. For many informed observers, the issue concerning this reorganization had been a question not of if but of when. But the loss of any cherished regimental names was bound to cause pain and grief, particularly to the Old and Bold. I myself felt considerable sadness at the prospect, and I knew that we would face a lot of opposition. But we had to grasp this nettle: staying as we were was not a realistic option for the future. If the British Army had never accepted the need for change, we'd still be in red coats and fighting in squares. I felt that it was the primary responsibility of the CGS to lead the Army Board in facing up to the Army's future.

I, along with my fellow Army Board members, thought that some historical research was needed. The structure of the British infantry has changed a number of times over the centuries. In the late nineteenth century, the then Secretary of State for War, Edward Cardwell, had decided to reform the system of the time by which all infantry battalions were numbered. He devised a structure whereby the infantry was put into regiments with county affiliations, each of two battalions, one battalion to be serving overseas and the other to be serving at home, with its own training depot. There was a predictable outcry from serving and retired alike, protesting that they didn't want to be part of these new-fangled regiments, they wanted to stay in their numbered battalions, the 49th, the 68th or whatever. *Plus ça change.* During the two world wars these county regiments expanded enormously, by twenty and more battalions each; but as the Army drastically reduced in size afterwards, the stage was reached where there were fewer battalions than counties, so that one started to get amalgamated regiments: the Devon and Dorsets, or the Ox and Bucks, for example.

With the end of conscription at the beginning of the 1960s, the then Army Board concluded that the only sensible way to produce a flexible infantry for the future was to put it on a 'large regiment basis', with three or four battalions in each regiment. But this, of course, implied the loss of many much-loved county names. The Army Board at the time funked the decision: it urged the infantry to adopt a large regimental system but did not make this compulsory. In broad terms, half the infantry accepted that urging and the other half didn't. The latter chose to remain as single-battalion regiments. The Army Board had promised that those who opted for this large regimental structure would be looked upon favourably if there were to be further reductions in the future – but when there was another reduction in the early 1990s as a result of the end of the Cold War, the Board of the time reneged on the undertaking given by its predecessors, removing the third battalions from the existing large regiments. A little later, the infantry of the Territorial Army was reduced in similar fashion. For reasons I have never fully understood, this reduction resulted in the invention of entirely new regiments in the TA; the TA infantry thereby lost their tribal links with their regular counterparts. I suspect this was done to avoid change in the regular infantry regimental structure. Whatever the reason, the outcome for the TA infantry was a complete mish-mash.

I remember saying on that fateful away-day, 'Are we all clear about the conclusion we've come to? The Arms Plot has run its course, but are we all clear about what the ramifications of that are? Because the current infantry structure cannot survive without the Arms Plot.' The Army Board was unanimous, even though some members were aware that they would face criticism and accusations of disloyalty from within their own regiments. Indeed, the Adjutant General, Sir Alistair Irwin, knew that one consequence of the decision would be that his own position as Colonel of the Black Watch – the tribal elder – would cease to exist. He was also Colonel Commandant of the Scottish Infantry as a whole. He deserves special credit for committing himself to a decision which would leave him particularly exposed.

As details of what we had decided emerged, people began saying to me, 'At long last somebody's got the balls to do it.' Others, of course, took a very different view. I had to face some pretty unpleasant comments, some addressed to me personally – as did Alistair. The accusation that we had destroyed the regimental system was nonsensical: the regimental system has changed again and again over time. What matters is that the regimental system adapts to changing circumstances and operational requirements.

At a subsequent Army Board meeting a couple of months later, we looked at how we would implement our decision, and came up with a set of principles and a direction to the infantry that those regiments which were not already on a large basis must now form regiments of two or more regular battalions. In fact, we thought that the optimum size for a regiment should be around four battalions, but that in some cases this might be too hard to achieve. We urged the infantry to give as much weight in their deliberations to the formation of what we called 'large-large' regiments of four or five battalions as to the formation of 'small-large' regiments of two or possibly three battalions. Some perceptively saw that large-large was the end-state that they would need to be in, and went for it straight away. To my surprise the Scots did that, forming themselves into the Royal Regiment of Scotland with five battalions. I had thought that a Highland/Lowland divide would prevail. In Yorkshire, for example, there were three single-battalion regiments which combined into the Yorkshire Regiment of three battalions. The Light Infantry and the Green Jackets were both regiments with two battalions each, which meant that they weren't obliged to change; but both regiments had a tradition of being unafraid of change and decided of themselves to combine anyway to form the Rifles, a name going right back to the Peninsular War. As part of this process we realigned the Territorial Army structure to put the TA battalions back in the new regimental structure, which is where they always should have been.

At the same time as all this was going on, we had to decide which four battalions were to go, as part of the reduction from forty to thirty-six. This was very difficult. We used a set of objective criteria: statistical data on recruitment and population figures in the recruiting area. The results showed which regiments were finding it most difficult to maintain their strength. Of the four lowest-scoring regiments, two were Scottish, which was no surprise because the Scots were trying to maintain a disproportionate number of battalions for their population. The figures suggested that two of the Scottish battalions should go, but we decided that for the Scots to lose two out of a total of only six would be seen as unfair, so our decision was for five. Then it was clear that one of the three in the north-west had to go, and that one in southern England would have to go too. Deciding which should be the fourth to go was very difficult, but Yorkshire was in the frame. But the sense of being singled out for the chop was softened by incorporation into the large regiment structure.

By the autumn of 2004 we were ready to announce all the final decisions. I knew that there were going to be ructions, with constituents writing in to their MPs and other pressures. I had sought political approval at the outset. I briefed Geoff Hoon, the Secretary of State for Defence, and told him that we could anticipate flak. He was very supportive about the whole thing. 'If that's what the Army has to do for the future,' he said, 'let's do it.'

The plan was for the announcements to be made after quite a long period of consultation. There was an understandable concern about the proposed changes, with the inevitable protests from the retired community, MPs, mayors et al. I received some angry letters. The outcry was loudest in Scotland, where it became overtly political when the Scottish Nationalist Party jumped on board, claiming that this was yet another example of the English 'screwing the Scots'. The 'Save our Scottish Regiments' campaign was run by a chap who had never even been in the Army. Some commentators suggested that this had been a political decision which the Army had been forced to carry out, with Jackson doing the Government's dirty work. They couldn't be more wrong, of course, because this was an Army Board decision. (An article in the *Spectator* attacking the proposed reforms spuriously linked them to a minor operation conducted on my eyelids the previous summer. In a riposte I explained that the surgery had been carried out for medical rather than cosmetic reasons: it had been a matter of 'vision not vanity'.)

Tony Blair was concerned about the political fuss, especially in Scotland. In particular, he had come under pressure from Scottish Labour MPs to save the Black Watch. There had been much speculation in the press that the Government would announce a U-turn. I was determined not to let this happen. Such a decision would make a mockery of our carefully considered plans. Shortly before the announcements, Geoff Hoon and I were summoned to see the Prime Minister at Downing Street. What he was looking for was a change to the plan which would turn down the political heat, particularly from north of the border. 'I need you to get me out of a hole,' he said.

'Prime Minister,' I replied, 'selection and maintenance of the aim is a fundamental principle of war.' The Secretary of State reiterated that we must stick to our guns. We ran through the logic with the PM. 'I know it's difficult,' I continued, 'but actually that's where we are and this is what we have to do.' Eventually the Prime Minister accepted what we were saying.

One of the ceremonial tasks of the CGS is to lay a wreath at the Cenotaph on Remembrance Day, along with the other Service Chiefs. It's the job of the CGS, who as an Army officer is deemed to know more about drill, to give the words of command to the other Chiefs. It's a tradition that many of the participants gather beforehand in one of the large rooms in the Foreign Office before going out on to Whitehall. Among those present are leaders of all the political parties. In 2004 I took the opportunity to speak to the SNP leader, Alex Salmond, about the Scottish regiments. 'I understand you're not happy with the changes,' I said, 'but they are for the overall good.'

'You're massacring our tradition,' he replied.

I told him that he was absolutely wrong, and explained the demographic problem underlying the difficulties the Scottish regiments were having with recruitment, as evidenced by the two hundred or more Commonwealth soldiers – mainly Fijians – who were serving in the Scottish infantry. 'The fact is that the Scots are over-represented in the British Army,' I told him; 'which is fine by me, provided that they can recruit enough soldiers.' Salmond seemed to be uncomfortable with this argument.

Just before the announcement of the new regimental structure, due to be made in December 2004, there was a last-minute twist to the story. The Director of Special Forces had taken stock that autumn, following three years of intense operational activity since 9/11; among other things, he had concluded that the Special Forces needed bolstering with additional manpower. To avoid Special Forces soldiers being employed on supporting tasks, and thus wasting their specialist skills and capabilities, they were having to find back-up from outside their own numbers; there were ad hoc arrangements to produce this back-up from elsewhere in the Armed Forces, but ad hoc arrangements are never very satisfactory. Here was a crystal-clear requirement for dedicated support to the Special Forces, with an equally clear recommendation that it should be based on a dedicated infantry battalion under command of the Director of Special Forces. This new role would raise the future number of battalions from thirty-six to thirty-seven.

So far, so obvious, one might conclude – as I did. But then comes MOD process: such a proposal is regarded as an 'enhancement', i.e. an improvement to capability, and the process requires all proposed 'enhancements' to be judged in competition, one against another, as part of the annual budget round. Fair enough, as a general principle. But in this case, circumstances had produced an out-of-process situation. It would have been ridiculous to have announced in December a reduction of four battalions, only to have announced in June that this 'enhancement' had been approved and only three battalions were to go. My recommendation that only three battalions be cut was accepted by Geoff Hoon, much to his credit – albeit at the eleventh hour, the night before he made his announcement in the House of Commons; his approval was given in the teeth of opposition from most senior MOD staff, some of whom seemed to think that their beloved process was more important than operational capability. Within the MOD, I made few friends and, I dare say, quite a few enemies over this – but it was the right solution.

Events throughout my time as CGS produced a sharply increased media focus on the Armed Services, and on the Army in particular. When I took over the job, the man who looked after media relations for the Army was the improbably named Director of Corporate Communications (Army), the new management-speak title for the post of Director of Public Relations (Army) – the post I might have gone to after commanding 39 Brigade in Belfast.

In this job you needed someone who was savvy, who knew the media personalities, who could explain the whys and wherefores. But this implied a degree of autonomy, which rested somewhat uneasily with the Labour Government's insistence on being 'on message'. By the summer of 2004 Geoff Hoon had become exasperated by what he perceived as a poor press. He took the view that the DPRs – and particularly the Army DPR – were briefing against the Government in general, and against him personally in particular. I do not believe there was any substance in this allegation, but it was his personal wish to abolish the

DPRs. The Chiefs of Staff were unanimously opposed to this proposal, and trooped in to see the Secretary of State en masse; but in vain. It was interesting to observe that the Permanent Secretary remained sitting on the fence. It was humiliating enough that the Chiefs had to seek ministerial approval for any contact with the media, but this was an outrageous move, explicable only in terms of a lack of confidence. I thought long and hard about resigning, but eventually concluded that, important though this issue was, there were bigger fish to fry.

Had there still been a DPR (Navy) in place in the spring of 2007, when fifteen Royal Navy personnel from HMS *Cornwall* were detained by the Iranians in the disputed waters of Shatt al-Arab, it seems likely to me that the media handling of the whole affair would have been rather better managed. Leaving aside the question of whether those personnel should have been patrolling there without full tactical precautions, the subsequent handling of the story was damaging to the reputation of the Navy, and to that of the Services as a whole. We pride ourselves on our fighting qualities, and I found it very unsavoury that the captured sailors allowed themselves to be paraded by their captors in the way that they did. However, this much was beyond the control of their superiors. But I thought it was appalling that they should have been greeted after their release as if they were returning heroes. In my view they should have been flown to an overseas base for a couple of days before being returned to their ship. And to crown it all, it was inept – to say nothing of unfair – to allow two of them to sell their stories to the media and to forbid the others from doing so.

Poor media handling was again evident in the coverage of the decision whether to allow Prince Harry to deploy to Iraq in the summer of 2007 with the rest of his squadron from the Blues and Royals. We had anticipated this problem during my time as CGS, and had carefully considered the methodology of reaching a decision about whether either of the two Royal Princes should serve on any particular deployment. Each situation is different, and has to be assessed separately. I discussed the matter with the boys' father the Prince of Wales, and their grandmother the Queen, and we laid out a set of principles. It was agreed then that there should be a certain amount of consultation, but that the final decision should rest with the CGS. When it came to it, this difficult decision-making process was played out in the press, to nobody's advantage. The Prince himself was rightly keen to go. Months of speculation followed the MOD's announcement in February that the Prince would be accompanying his regiment to Iraq. In mid-May, my successor Richard Dannatt announced that the Prince would not be deployed there. I believe that none of this need have been made public, and that if necessary a D-notice should have been issued to prevent its becoming so.

The MOD is an extraordinary place. It has two discrete roles. One is as a Department of State handling the policy issues, just as, for example, the Department of Education handles policy issues to do with education and schools. But it's also the supreme headquarters of the Armed Forces. These two functions are not, however, discrete in terms of personnel or, if you like, office space. There's a lot of intermingling here: uniforms and suits, side by side. Some servicemen 'go native', absorbing the culture of the MOD, but these are the exceptions. Half a century back, each of the Services had its own department and its own minister, with a Secretary of State for Defence above them all. But since then the bureaucrats have increasingly accumulated power in their own hands. There is a story, perhaps apocryphal but nevertheless symbolically true, of a senior MOD civil servant who remarked: 'The Ministry of Health is not full of doctors, the Ministry of Education is not full of teachers, the Ministry of Ag and Fish is not full of farmers and fishermen, so why on earth do they have all these bloody people in the Armed Forces in the MOD?' The same philosophy lay behind the decision to spend a quarter of a million pounds on specially commissioned abstract paintings as part of the refurbishment of the MOD. The Government art collection has many military paintings which would have been in keeping with the purpose and ethos of the Department and which would have been available at no cost; but civil servants preferred to spend on abstract art money which might otherwise have directly benefited soldiers and their families. It may seem a small point, but to me it was so indicative of the cultural divide in the MOD.

I didn't always find the MOD wholehearted about the interests of the soldiers. I was constantly battling the civil servants, and it was often very frustrating. I'd come back from a visit and say, 'We've got to do something about the state of those barracks,' but it was like trying to fight your way through cotton wool. A soldier's approach is very straightforward: this is the problem, all right, give me the tools and let's crack on. But bureaucrats are not like that at all. I remember the Army Board being told by the then Second Permanent Undersecretary that we must reduce our recruiting – then buoyant because we had taken on more soldiers that year than the budget had forecast – to meet the funding line. Quite absurd, but absolutely true. We all knew from hard-won experience that it would take years to recover from such a sharp application of the brakes.

Not many people realize, I suspect, that the Army Board has a statutory duty under the Army Act to investigate allegations by soldiers that they have been wronged, and in effect to ensure that they have been fairly treated. This is especially important in areas where soldiers cannot take a complaint to a civilian tribunal, for example an allegation of unfair dismissal, when the Army Board is the arbiter and protector of their rights. The Board takes this responsibility very seriously, and cases are considered in enormous detail. But I noticed a tendency for civil servants to want to limit the Board's power, especially in relation to the ability to grant compensation, and I fought a long battle with the MOD to retain as much of this as possible. As I stepped down, the issue was still rattling around the MOD, with lawyers arguing over the exact scope of the Board's powers. My determination to do what I saw as my legal duty and the 'right thing' in the face of those who cannot see beyond Government accounting rules did not endear me to the mandarins, who like the Chiefs to be more 'collegiate'.

The public doesn't realize that the Service Chiefs have no direct control over the way the money is spent. The single Services no longer have their own budgets, and much expenditure is centrally controlled. The MOD keeps us on a short rein. The Defence Planning Assumptions often seem to be given more importance than reality. That's why there wasn't enough of the right equipment in stock when the decision was made for a large-scale commitment in Iraq. It comes back to the contract with the soldier. If you will the end, you must will the means.

Decisions about arms purchases were made by the Defence Procurement Agency (now Defence Equipment and Support), whose record for acquiring the right equipment, at the right time and – crucially – at the originally contracted cost, is less than impressive. And housing, for example, is in the hands of the 'Defence Estates', as they are called, run by a chief executive. He gets a tick in his box for coming in on budget, and another one for not making waves within the MOD. Within the Ministry they use a lot of management jargon, talking about targets and indicators. One of these is the 'balanced scorecard', with a 'traffic lights system' of green, red and amber, according to whether you are doing well, badly or indifferently. Doing 'well' is not about ensuring that soldiers and their families have decent accommodation: it's about whether or not you've met your budget. You can get a 'green' even if some of the houses you're responsible for have green mould sprouting on the inside walls. This whole culture I found to be Kafka-esque.

I did not find the MOD a comfortable place to be. Its values were not mine.

In the previous few years I had gained two more grandchildren to add to my grandson Casper, born in 1997: two lovely girls, Jemima, born in 2001, and Phoebe, born a year later. Sadly, though, Amanda's marriage broke down. Sarah and I were therefore delighted when she married Jason Gard, an ex-Royal Green Jacket, at Chelsea Town Hall in October 2005. It was a wonderful family day, with all the children taking part. The following year they had a new baby brother, Charlie.

My youngest son Tom was by this time at Eton. In the same year he joined the CCF, a first indication that he would continue the family tradition of service in the Army. In the winter of the following year he would make the train journey to Westbury to undertake the admissions course before the Army Officer Selection Board. I am proud to say that he was accepted. When he finishes his university education Tom will be headed for Sandhurst, following his elder brother, his brother-in-law, his father and his grandfather into the Army. This was a few months after I stepped down as CGS, so nobody could claim that I had any hand in his being selected!

As CGS, one has the opportunity to make visits to one's opposite numbers abroad. And as it turned out, one of the earliest overseas visits I made was to Argentina. I was the first CGS to go there since the Falklands War. For the most part I was treated with great courtesy, though every briefing room I entered seemed to have a sodding great map on the wall with the unmistakable outlines of the Falkland Islands, captioned 'Las Islas Malvinas Argentinas'. The Argentinians' official position is that they do not in any sense cede their claim to sovereignty over the Falklands, though they accept that military force is not the way to achieve their objective. I had a couple of set-tos while I was there. I remember in particular an altercation when a somewhat worse-for-wear colonel came up to me after a dinner and started finger-poking. He began ranting about how they would throw us out of the Islands. 'It's very foolish what you're saying,' I told him at last, 'because if you try it again, we'll come down here again, and we'll do what we did to you last time – so best not do it, eh?'

Another early visit was to Russia, which was fascinating for me. The last time I had been there, in 1976, I had been one of the most junior members of the party; this time, I had the red-carpet treatment. It was amazing to reflect on how much had changed in the interim. In 1976 the main strategic function of the British Army had been to prepare to fight the Warsaw Pact, the alliance dominated by the Russians; now we were serving alongside them in the Balkans.

Whenever I could I tried to make use of my Russian, though it has become rusty over the years. The Russians seemed to be aware of my long-term interest in their country. They knew of me from Bosnia, where there had been a Russian deployment in the American Sector, and of course they were well aware of the Pristina Airport episode, which occasioned the odd jocular remark. I did ask after General Viktor Zavarzin, but unfortunately it turned out that he was in the Far East at the time. One of the highlights was a visit to Rostov-on-Don, the headquarters for the military district which includes Chechnya. I gather that this raised a few eyebrows among the American Embassy staff in Moscow, because their attaché had not been allowed to go there.

My visit took place in the early summer, during the short period of 'white nights' when it never gets dark in the north of the country. On the night of the summer equinox I strolled through St Petersburg at one o'clock in the morning, among thousands of other people out on the streets because it was still light. On this occasion, I was pleased not to be in uniform as I had been almost thirty years before; it was more than enough just to be one of the crowd.

I made many other interesting visits during my time as CGS. One of the most fascinating was to Vietnam; as far as I could tell, I was the first CGS to visit the country. This time Sarah came with me, and for her it was particularly exciting because she had vivid memories of living there in the late 1960s. Sarah's father had been the British defence attaché in Saigon during the Vietnam War, and she had gone out there to stay with her parents during her school holidays. After she left school she had lived in Saigon for a while, working as a stringer for *Newsweek*. This gave her a much-valued American press pass, and access to operational areas with American Huey helicopters to get her there.

Our visit started in Hanoi, which of course Sarah had never been to before, since it had been the enemy capital during the war. We were both captivated by the city, which retains its French influence even though half a century has passed since it was a French colony. Despite the heavy bombing it received from the USAF during the war, it remains a lovely landscape of lakes, shaded boulevards, parks and French colonial-style architecture.

These visits are always programmed from morning until night, so there are not often any surprises. But a few days after my arrival I received an unexpected invitation: General Giap wanted to see me.

Giap was a legendary figure, the victor at Dien Bien Phu, the battle which forced the French out in 1954. Until then the French had been fighting a counter-insurgency campaign against Vietnamese revolutionary forces known as the Viet Minh. Dien Bien Phu was a remote outpost up on the northern border of Vietnam, with a large garrison. The Viet Minh cut the road access and then besieged the French positions. They pounded the French with artillery which they had assembled from pieces carried through the jungle on the backs of pack animals. Eventually the French garrison surrendered, and more than eleven thousand of their soldiers were taken prisoner, of whom only three thousand or so ever saw France again. This was the first time the forces of a non-European independence movement had ever defeated a Western army in pitched battle. Later Giap had been the Commander in Chief of the North Vietnamese army, which had successfully defied American military might during the Vietnam War. After the Americans had withdrawn and the South Vietnamese had been defeated, Giap had fallen out of favour with the Communist authorities; but now in his tenth decade he was revered, a hero of the Vietnamese resistance.

The following morning I was taken to his home in Hanoi, quite a modest house with a small garden, but a shrine to his achievements with memorabilia everywhere. Giap himself was a diminutive old gentleman, physically frail but still bright as a button mentally. We had about half an hour together, talking mostly about the Indo-China war, but towards the end he asked me questions about the British Army. We were conversing in French, which he preferred to speaking through an interpreter. At the close he got up and put his arm through mine as we walked towards the door. 'It is interesting, isn't it,' he said, his eyes twinkling, 'that both of our countries have had some problems with the French, and that both of our countries appear to have resolved those problems satisfactorily?'

Sarah and I travelled south from Hanoi, calling at the old imperial capital of Hue before going on to Saigon. Once there, after a bit of jiggery-pokery with changed street names, we found the old residence of the British military attaché, now the headquarters of the All-Vietnam Engineering Union. This had been Sarah's family home almost forty years before. We hovered outside for a while, until I began a conversation in French with a young girl who invited us in. Inside it had changed somewhat. The old dining room was now a conference room adorned with a bust of Ho Chi Minh. The splendid mahogany staircase was still in place, though, and on the upper floor Sarah found the bedroom she had occupied as a teenager, and the balcony where she would go out and have a surreptitious smoke, watching the flares and red tracer bullets light up the night sky while the percussion of bombs dropped from B-52s rattled the stained-glass windows. For her it was extraordinary to be back in the same house so many years later, after all that had happened in between.

During my time as CGS I made several visits to Afghanistan. After Iraq, Afghanistan represents Britain's second largest operational commitment in recent years. It may in the long run prove to be strategically more important. The war in Iraq had to some extent taken eyes off the Afghan ball; without doubt, the initial intervention in Afghanistan had been a great success, but yet again events showed that it was not enough to remove a regime; you then had to rebuild the country. ISAF's initial deployment, to the immediate region of Kabul only, was able to give essential, although only local, support to the Karzai government. The flaw here was that this limited focus allowed the regional warlords to continue to put their own territorial interests and that of their regions ahead of the future of Afghanistan as a whole.

By the second half of 2005 it had become obvious that a much greater effort was required in Afghanistan – if for no other reason than that, though the Taliban had been defeated in 2001, they had not been completely destroyed. Despite heavy casualties, survivors had retreated to the Afghanistan/Pakistan border area, particularly to the Tribal Territories – Waziristan – just across the border in Pakistan. Eventually, it became more than clear that it was essential to bolster the Karzai government in establishing its writ throughout the country – not least, by taking on the now familiar role of helping to build up and train the indigenous Afghan security forces.

And so NATO developed a plan to take security responsibility throughout the country, region by region. In the early years of Karzai's government this was achieved by NATO establishing so-called Provincial Reconstruction Teams (PRTs) in the comparatively benign north and east of the country. The PRTs worked by influence. They were anything but manoeuvre or combat forces: rather, their mission was to support the expansion of the central government's remit, to help subordinate the regional warlords to Kabul, and to assist in local reconstruction and in the training of the Afghan security forces.

But the real challenge was NATO's further expansion to the south – into Helmand and Kandahar provinces – and eventually to the Pakistan border area in the east. In the autumn of 2005 the UK carried out an assessment of the situation in the south. It was clear that PRTs alone would not be nearly enough; given the Taliban influence in the region, combat forces would be required. The fundamental questions were: how big a force, with what capabilities? And could a sufficient force be generated, given our other commitments, notably Iraq? When we were working out the numbers there was an assumption that the commitment to Iraq would draw down more sharply than in fact it has done. In the event, the balance of judgement was for a relatively small force of around 3,500, based on a single infantry battalion, but with significant combat support – notably Harrier ground attack aircraft, artillery and, for the first time, the Apache attack helicopter.

There has been a lot of press comment about the supposed lack of equipment and support for the troops in Afghanistan. The Prime Minister was quoted as saying that the Army could have anything it needed – to which the cynical response was, 'Tell that to your next door neighbour.' For example, the RAF has found it difficult to meet the demands of current operations where transport aircraft and support helicopters are concerned. The RAF has an impressive programme for new fast-jet fighters, but their ageing VC10 and Tri-Star transport aircraft are unreliable and increasingly difficult to maintain.

My last visit to Afghanistan came in the early summer of 2006, just as the British effort in southern Afghanistan was ramping up. Our forces, serving under NATO command, took over security responsibility for the southern provinces of Kandahar and Helmand. Hard, but successful, fighting against the Taliban followed, including set-piece battles in which attacks by Taliban forces were repulsed after they had taken heavy casualties. 'We have not yet lost one tactical engagement,' commented our commander in the field, Brigadier Ed Butler, 'but we have yet to win at the operational level.' I was exasperated by some of the initial press reaction to our relatively few casualties, which seemed to conclude that any casualty meant mission failure. Here again was the absurd and naïve assumption that military operations against a determined enemy can be risk-free. The critics made much of the statement by John Reid, who succeeded Geoff Hoon as Secretary of State for Defence, that 'if we came here for three years to accomplish our mission and had not fired a shot at the end of it, we would be very happy indeed'. This was a hope, not a prediction; it was also sending a message to the people of southern Afghanistan that we were not, ourselves, choosing to prosecute an offensive mission. But Reid went on to say that 'it would be a complex and dangerous mission, because the terrorists will want to destroy the economy . . . and the government that we are helping to build up'. He also emphasized that 'if this didn't involve the necessity to use force, we wouldn't send soldiers'.

I have no doubt that we must continue to support the now democratically elected government of Afghanistan. To allow the Taliban to overthrow that government and once again to give succour to Al-Qaida would be strategic folly.

There is a sub-set of the British approach to Afghanistan: counter-narcotics. No doubt in the knowledge that the vast majority of heroin consumed in Britain originates in the poppy-fields of Afghanistan, the Prime Minister volunteered Britain to take the international lead on counter-narcotics. Well and good; but I would emphasize that the Foreign and Commonwealth Office, as the responsible Department, must understand that eradication is contrary – right now – to strategic success. In my view, we would be far better emulating the EU's set-aside policy.

My last reflection where Afghanistan is concerned has to do with the crucial position of Pakistan, a country of great contrasts: the gulf between the sophistication of Islamabad, for example, and the feudal Tribal Territories puts President Musharraf into a most difficult position. I have a vivid memory of flying by helicopter from Peshawar over barren mountain ranges to South Waziristan to visit the Pakistani Army division responsible for that area. The highly impressive divisional commander briefed me in some detail on the high intensity of fighting his soldiers had experienced as they carried out their mission to extend central government's writ to the region in which the Taliban and Al-Qaida had found refuge. Subsequently, President Musharraf has cut some sort of deal with the tribal leaders and largely withdrawn the Army. The wisdom of this remains to be seen . . .

On the morning of 7 July 2005 I was in London for a Defence Management Board meeting at the MOD. This is a meeting chaired by the Permanent Secretary and attended by all the Chiefs of Staff, various other civil servants, the Government's Chief Scientific Adviser and others, and normally starts around 10.00 a.m. I remember Sir Kevin Tebbit, then the Permanent Secretary, telling us that news was coming through of explosions in London: he wasn't quite sure what was going on, but we might have to adjourn the meeting.

As subsequently became clear, four bombs had exploded that morning in a coordinated terrorist attack, the worst bombing in London since the Second World War. In fact the meeting went ahead as planned. As a general principle it is a bad idea for senior officers to start interfering when systems are already in place to cope with the situation. The police had primacy in handling domestic terrorism, and the Armed Forces' role was to act in their support if so requested. Accordingly, we did supply a certain amount of specialist help to the police.

On 28 August 2006, I relinquished the post of CGS to my successor Richard Dannatt, and shortly afterwards retired from the Army. In fact, my last day in the office had been a month earlier, at the end of July, the date when most of Whitehall closes down and everyone goes on summer leave. There was no formal ceremony to mark my departure from the MOD, nor would I have wanted one. In the previous few weeks I had made a round of farewells. On that last Friday morning, I invited all the colonels and the brigadiers on the MOD Army Staff to join me in my office for a glass or two of champagne; and then all of us, down to the most junior of the military clerks, made our way to one of those boats moored off the Embankment that serve as floating pubs. Sarah, Mark, Tom and the house staff led by Colour Sergeant Mawby joined us there. We continued with a drink or three, and a bite to eat as well, until mid-afternoon, when people began to wander off for the weekend. It was a warm day, and the Thames glittered in the sunshine as the dwindling party chatted on deck. The moment came when I felt that we had said our goodbyes and that we should go home. It was time to move on.

15

Reflections

When I retired from the Army in 2006, I was within one month or so of forty-five years' service. I count myself fortunate indeed to have spent so long a time doing what I loved. It has been a wonderful career, so full of reward, variety and – above all – comradeship.

I have been lucky enough to have been on operations at every level of command from company to corps, apart from the battalion level, for some seven years in total. All these tours were some form or other of 'peace support operation'. To my regret – because it is the ultimate challenge for a soldier – I have not taken part in a conventional war. There were but two opportunities, and I missed them both: the Falklands, because the cards didn't play my way; and the First Gulf War, when I was otherwise engaged, as a brigade commander in Northern Ireland. *C'est la guerre* – or rather, in my case, it wasn't.

Soon after I retired I was asked to give the annual Richard Dimbleby Lecture, delivered at a Territorial Army Centre in central London on 6 December 2006 and broadcast live on BBC

TV. This offered me the opportunity to reflect on the changing role of the Army, and the challenges it is likely to face in the future. This chapter draws heavily on the text of that lecture, entitled 'The Defence of the Realm in the Twenty-First Century'.

My years in the Army have spanned three very different sets of strategic circumstances. The Cold War dominated the first half of my career, when the Army's focus was on defending north-west Europe against an invasion by the Warsaw Pact. This focus shifted abruptly after the fall of the Berlin Wall and the collapse of the Soviet empire at the end of the 1980s; and it shifted again after the dramatic events of 9/11.

While the importance of the Army's war-fighting capability remains paramount, training is now for war in general, not for *the* war against the Warsaw Pact. And it has become clear that the wars we may have to fight in the future will in all probability be at a strategic distance from the UK. We have fought two very short major wars since the end of the Cold War, both in the Middle East against Saddam Hussein. But the Army, in partic-ular, has spent the years conducting operations other than war – in Northern Ireland, the Balkans, Africa, Iraq and Afghanistan; and so the balance between war-fighting and the capability to conduct peace support operations – both in an expeditionary mode – has to be very carefully judged. The result has been a shift in emphasis from the 'heavier' end of our capability to the 'lighter', with the intention to improve our medium-weight forces by equipping them with a new family of armoured vehi-cles. This rebalancing has also put yet more emphasis on the helicopter as a major means of manoeuvre. These changes have been brought together under the 'Future Army Structure', with its modest shift of emphasis towards operations other than conventional war.

History may well judge that the so-called 'peace dividend' was too sharply taken in the euphoria and relief that followed the end of the Cold War. The effect of that momentous shift has proved to be rather like that of removing the lid of a pressure cooker, a lid screwed down by bilateral superpower rivalry. Once that lid was off, the pressures erupted – pressures of disputed boundaries, ethnic rivalry and regional conflict. The West in general, and NATO in particular, moved from its Cold War posture of strategic defence and groped its way towards a new policy of intervention on humanitarian grounds. Tony Blair's Government has taken a lead in this new role. Acting in some cases unilaterally and in others together with our NATO allies, we have chosen to deploy military power to contain the resulting conflicts – particularly in the Gulf, in the Balkans and in Africa. Operational tempo has increased markedly.

These events also highlighted the importance of international law. The United Nations – perhaps the most important fount of international law – is of course a major player on the world stage. But the UN has been criticized, particularly since the end of the Cold War, for failing to meet its founding ideals. I find this somewhat unfair. I would be more inclined to look critically at the behaviour of the member nation-states than at the institution itself. On a more general legal point, I am convinced from experience that the establishment and maintenance of the rule of law is the bedrock of both national and international stability – and that this principle applies in the national context to the Armed Forces of this country.

However, legality and legitimacy in international affairs are not necessarily the same concept. In an ideal world, what is legal is legitimate, and vice versa. But it doesn't always happen that way. The Iraq intervention was in my opinion legal but has perhaps ceased to be legitimate – in the eyes of certain beholders, at any rate. The Kosovo intervention was probably illegal, but has been largely deemed to be legitimate. The general principle holds that one shouldn't intervene in another sovereign state except in the most extreme circumstances. But if the

Kosovo action was legitimate, then it was because of an emerging doctrine which holds that the inviolability of the sovereign state should not legitimize genocide. There are circumstances in which rapid and determined intervention by a relatively small but well-equipped force can prevent large-scale slaughter. In such circumstances it seems that it is not only legitimate to intervene but that there is a strong moral case for doing so.

The history of intervention after the Cold War starts with the West's decision – under UN auspices, to be fair – to become involved in the Bosnian war. Thus was established a precedent of intervention. The received wisdom of the time was that of the three warring factions in Bosnia, it was the Muslim population who were at greatest risk of ethnic persecution; and of course, when it came to Kosovo in 1999, the West's intervention was almost entirely predicated on the protection of a Muslim population who were at risk. In the current difficult relations between the West and the Islamic world, it seems to me that this risking of Western blood and treasure on behalf of beleaguered Muslim populations has been somewhat, if not largely, forgotten. It is also worth noting that when NATO took military action over Kosovo without a UNSCR, that action was largely regarded as legitimate.

A second major change in strategic circumstances took place towards the close of my career, with the self-proclaimed declaration of war by Al-Qaida against the West and its values. The gauntlet was thrown down. Before 9/11, possession of terrain had much to do with the outcome of conflict, but we have now moved to a position in which terrain seems to be rather less important, and a battle of ideas has commenced.

Possession of terrain is a vital matter in war between states, in which opposing countries use military means to achieve their objectives, or in war within a state, when factions vie to rule that state. Wars between states are often described as 'symmetric' or 'force on force'. However, 9/11 – and, indeed, the Madrid bombings and the terrorist attacks on 7 July 2006 ('7/7') in this country – represent a very different sort of struggle, in which the battleground is people's attitudes, allegiances, values – their very identities. It seems to me that Clausewitz's famous dictum that 'war is nothing but a continuation of politics with the admixture of other means' holds good even in these different circumstances. This 'asymmetric' struggle is emphatically not one which can be solved by military means alone – far from it.

We are again confronted with terrorism on mainland Great Britain. The threat such terrorism poses should not be underestimated, even though we may find the ideology underlying it difficult to comprehend. At home, the Security Service and the police quite properly have the onerous responsibility of taking the lead in the counter-terrorist role, while the Armed Forces act in their support. Overseas, military intervention may be needed to counter the parallel threat of terrorist attack on British interests and personnel, say in the evacuation of non-combatant nationals, as in the case of Sierra Leone. Next, there can be rogue states which may be inclined to military adventurism in breach of international law, and we have seen examples of that in the recent past. Such adventurism, by definition, is likely to be gravely destabilizing. And in the face of instability, whether caused by ethnic conflict or by failed or failing states, the Armed Forces may well be required to respond. We should not ignore, also, the grim prospect of future conflict over access to sources of energy and water.

Defence of the Realm is difficult and complex in today's world. In particular, the terrorist threat, especially when the terrorist is willing to die in the course of his actions, is a grave challenge. This terrorism can originate in the UK itself, as we saw on 7/7, or abroad. We have to address both sources.

So how should the United Kingdom position and defend itself? Pulling up the drawbridge of a Fortress Britain is not a sensible strategy. The UK cannot isolate itself from the wider world. For us in Britain, the most fundamental strategic issue is how we position ourselves between the United States and Europe. While we are geographically much closer to the continent of Europe, politically we have often been closer to the United States. This has been a dilemma for many decades, one that requires careful strategic judgement, not merely tactical reaction. The judgement must be whether our own national strategic objectives are served by our American ally's proposed course of action, imperfect though it may be. A rational choice about any new deployment should not be decided by whether we like or dislike this or that President or, indeed, Prime Minister: such an *ad hominem* approach can serve only to distort our thinking. It is self-evident to me why we describe our relationship with America as special, by dint of common origin and therefore values and language, of history both before and after independence (and particularly the history of the last century), and of political, economic and military ties. But we are also part of the continent of Europe, and a member of the continent's polity, the European Union. I believe that we have to remain sitting on this fence; we should not come off it one way or the other, even if it is sometimes an uncomfortable place to perch. We are so closely involved strategically with both the United States and Europe that our strategy must embrace both. Our strategic ends may be much the same, ways and means may – almost certainly will – differ. I say ends may be much the same, because strategy must be directed towards a political goal. A war on terror is not a strategy *per se*, for terrorism is no more than a means of fighting; the strategy must address the politics behind that terrorism.

At the same time, we must be careful to guard our historic values, long and hard won: our freedoms, the supremacy of the rule of law. These attributes of our mature democracy are beyond price. But equally, we must accept that Western liberal democracy may not export itself that easily. And that means we should make an even greater effort to improve cultural under-standing, to appreciate how any given situation looks through the eyes of others, while still firmly supporting the principle of representative government.

At home, we should make greater efforts to ensure that a clear national identity and a multicultural approach can sit more comfortably together. But we must not delude ourselves; clarity of thought is essential. I am a great believer in live and let live, but not at the expense of my British way of life. The funda-mental political question here is what degree of tolerance the body politic should afford to those whose intolerance looks to destroy that body politic, and the rule of law which underpins it.

I served three tours of duty in Northern Ireland, and have witnessed the British Army's engagement in the Province almost from the start. For many of those years, violence there threat-ened the territorial integrity of the United Kingdom itself. Now we have the real prospect of a settlement. At the time of writing, it is planned that the British Armed Forces will go non-operational in Northern Ireland on 31 July 2007. If this happens, as I fervently hope it does, it will represent a remark-able achievement, notwithstanding the cost in blood and treasure: that of preventing unlawful violence from dictating political outcomes. With proper application, and perhaps a modicum of good luck, I believe that our commitment to the Balkans will also come to a successful conclusion. Note that the operation in Northern Ireland will have been thirty-eight years in duration, and at the time of writing Bosnia will have been fourteen, Kosovo seven. There is no quick fix.

We have then, of course, the major effort of our joint campaigns in both Iraq and Afghanistan. There is much noise about both, but the noise is as much about what is happening on a day-to-day basis as it is about the strategic issues. We must acknowledge that the success of the initial manoeuvre war was not followed by similar success in the immediate aftermath, to the detriment both of Iraq and of the Coalition forces. In particular, the disbandment of the Iraqi Army and the de-Ba'athification programme resulted in a worse security situation than probably would otherwise have prevailed. We are where we are, however, and the difficult question before Iraq and the Coalition is to decide on how best to secure the country's future. That future could still be bright, because Iraq has much going for it: a popularly elected government at long last, natural resources, a well-educated and energetic population. But that potentially bright future is threatened by brutal, and largely unforeseen, inter-sectarian strife. What is to be done?

It is strategically vital to all concerned that we get the right answer to this question. There has been growing pressure in both the United States and the United Kingdom for our forces to be withdrawn in relatively short order. As I said in a press interview while I was still CGS, the sooner our troops leave Iraq, the better for everybody – but we should not leave before it's right to do so. Our withdrawal from Iraq should not be defined by a date, but rather by conditions. To leave Iraq against the wishes of the sovereign Iraqi Government, and before the Iraqi security forces are fully able to deal with the current violence, would be both morally wrong and a fundamental strategic mistake. Great efforts are being made to bring on the Iraqi security forces: largely successful where the army is concerned, less so in respect of the police. Even when Coalition forces have handed over full responsibility for security across Iraq – and that process is well under way, province by province – there well may be an Iraqi request that we continue training assistance, as we do in many other countries. That said, the long-term solution to the Sunni/Shia violence must be political, not military.

It would be an equally flawed decision to stay in Iraq when no longer invited by the Iraqi Government to do so, with consent, patchy enough today, failing to hold. So we should not become mesmerized by dates: we must make the best judgement we can as to when the conditions are right to leave.

I also think it is worth emphasizing that while it may be that two-thirds of the British people now disapprove of our involvement in Iraq, in contrast to the two-thirds who approved three and a half years ago, such disapproval must not, of itself, dictate future strategy. The future will in all probability require a British Government to decide whether to intervene elsewhere in the world; such a decision must be taken on its merits, and not through the prism of the current campaign in Iraq. By the same token, lessons must be learned from the mistakes of the past. The tragedy of the planning for post-conflict Iraq is that we knew from our experiences in the Balkans what should have been done – but the message didn't get through to those taking the decisions.

In Afghanistan I see a long haul yet – and not only a military, but also a civilian, long haul. We must help Afghanistan to progress, we must support the sovereign and popularly elected government, and we must prevent the Taliban from once more taking control and providing Al-Qaida with a safe haven. That would indeed be a return to square one. Such a commitment means a preparedness to take casualties; the proposition of a casualty-free military campaign is a contradiction in terms. NATO is now very much the driving force in Afghanistan, and I would wish all contributing nations, NATO or otherwise, to pursue the common strategic goal – essential to us all, and particularly to Afghanistan itself – with a common vigour, accepting, if need be, the price to be paid. Faint-heartedness is not conducive to campaign success.

I emphasize again that the Defence of this Realm in the twenty-first century cannot be confined to our shores alone. I think it was Machiavelli who said that 'wars begin when you will, but they do not end when you please'. In principle, therefore, we must see these campaigns through to their proper conclusions. Not to do so would be a disaster. My coda is that a political settlement between Israel and the Palestinians is essential. The difficulties are immense, but I refuse to believe that they are insurmountable.

Over the last few years, both before and after 9/11, we have seen a pattern in the way campaigns have evolved: often an initial short, intense campaign which involves more or less conventional – 'symmetrical' – fighting is followed by long, sometimes very long, periods of peace support operations, nation-building, post-conflict operations, call them what you will. I cite here Bosnia, Kosovo, Macedonia (FYROM), Afghanistan and Iraq, to say nothing of Sierra Leone and East Timor – all involving British forces. We must maintain – enhance where possible – our capability in such asymmetric operations. This means preserving and improving our ability to put and to keep boots on the ground.

Experience of post-conflict situations has shown me time and again the importance of improving everyday life for the majority of the population as soon as possible. There is a sense that you must make a difference within a hundred days, or you may lose an opportunity. It gives me no pleasure to say that I fear this was not the case where Iraq was concerned.

This multifaceted approach requires the combined effort of the Government Departments involved, not just the Armed Forces. We have not yet got this as right as we should. Our ability to integrate the Departments of State in pursuit of strategic national objectives is hampered by a lack of sufficiently authoritative machinery in Whitehall.

My career in the British Army has provided plenty of reminders of that old adage, too easily forgotten: expect the unexpected. Two examples that spring to mind are the unpredicted attacks on the Falklands in 1982 and on Kuwait in 1990. The clear deduction to me is that we must retain our significant capability to fight conventional force-on-force manoeuvre wars, as well as the ultimate shield of our nuclear deterrent. We should indeed maintain our ability to create a terrible and terrifying uncertainty as to what we would or would not do *in extremis*. While terrorism is clearly today's dominant threat, it would be very imprudent to assume that we will never again be required to fight a conventional war. I strongly believe that we must retain the ability to fight and win such a war, if only as a form of national life insurance policy.

The defence budget, at some £32 billion, is just over 2 per cent of our gross national product, having been at the end of the Cold War double or more that figure. That is only 5.5 per cent of today's government spending. While 2 per cent of GNP is similar to France's spending on defence, it is higher than that of other European countries, reflecting the importance and significance of Britain's international role. Indeed, readers may question whether this is sufficient to represent the importance, the proportionate importance, of what the Armed Forces do for this country today, and what they may have to do in the future. But there we are; we have the defence budget we are allocated, and once that is defined, the question then for the Ministry of Defence is how most effectively to spend it. It is a complex and intellectually challenging exercise, leading to a set of assumptions which – at least in theory – define the military effects required, and so in turn the size and shape of the Armed Forces; for example, how much infantry, armour, logistics etc. should there be in the Army, how much anti-submarine warfare or amphibious capability in the Navy, how much fast jet or transport capability in the Air Force. Some may question whether we really need 232 Eurofighters, for example.

The difficulty, though, is that events have long since overtaken the formal MOD planning assumptions. There seems to be a considerable inertia in recognizing this and thereby adjusting those assumptions. The virtual world defined by those assumptions has been superseded by the real world. There is a mismatch between what we do and the resources we are given with which to do it.

How stretched is the Army? Although arithmetically the Army is on average more or less within its deployment guidelines, by definition the average includes those parts of the Army which are outside those guidelines. Some parts of the Army are well below the target of twenty-four months between operational tours. We could well be asking too much of our soldiers in terms of frequency of operational deployment over the long haul, to say nothing of the conditions of service under which they continue on this long haul. For example, some of our soldiers have undertaken three – or even more – tours in Iraq.

Decisions about the allocation of resources come down to a question of balance: balance between capabilities within the defence budget – how much of this, how much of that; balance between current operations and what may be required in the future – and not only current operations, but current training, which is the investment for our capability in the future; balance between people and technology – pay and accommodation, for example, against current and future equipment. This is not how it should be. We ought to be able to provide what is required for soldiers to be fully and properly equipped, thoroughly trained, decently paid and, together with their families, decently housed. They deserve nothing less. There are some difficulties here which explain, at least to some extent, why recruiting is the challenge it is.

On a different tack, have we got our procurement right? What of our ability, or is it our inability, to get the right equipment at the right time at the right cost? Large procurement cost overruns in the past have been rather meekly accepted to the detriment of spending on personnel and training. I acknowledge that the Defence Industrial Strategy, published in 2005, is designed to improve matters in this area.

The Army feels strongly that the greatest burden rests upon

its shoulders, not least when it comes to numbers deployed and casualties sustained. The facts speak for themselves. It is again a question of balance; taking away from Peter to pay Paul is a difficult and dangerous exercise and one that can be avoided by better provision for both.

The Ministry of Defence, is very much part of the equation. The role of the MOD is to translate the Government's political objectives into military capabilities and military operations; it is therefore both a Department of State and the supreme head-quarters of the Armed Forces. These two roles can be uneasy bedfellows, and that unease can be to the detriment of the Armed Forces. The Department of State appears to assume that commercial so-called 'best practice', with its proliferation of performance indicators and targets, can be applied to defence in general, and to the Armed Forces in particular; I don't agree. Who judges best practice? And this obsessive measurement is often against plans, not against real-world requirements. Fighting is demonstrably not a commercial activity. I am very clear about the only performance indicator which really matters to the Armed Forces, namely, the achievement of whatever objectives are set to us: that is, winning. Far too often, the MOD confuses activity with achievement.

There is far too much reverence for process. The purpose of process is to achieve an outcome, to achieve the mission; it is not the purpose of process to maintain process. As an example, I recently read of a senior MOD civil servant quoted as saying of an even more senior MOD civil servant that the latter was 'not just leading the workstream process, but driving it'. I hope he knew what he meant, because I'm not sure I do. This reverence for process matters, because process is an overhead; the more overheads can be reduced, the more capability we can obtain from a given defence budget.

I would also express my concern at the diminution, over years, decades even, of the position and authority of the single-Service

Chiefs of Staff. They are seen by the public, by those serving in the Forces themselves, and by the media, as responsible for all matters pertaining to their respective Services – but this is simply not the reality. As CGS, I did not hold the budget for the Army. Neither logistics nor procurement is any longer the direct responsibility of the Chiefs. In my view we have overcentralized, and this has diminished the ability of the Chiefs of Staff to take personal charge of the running of their Services and to determine, for example, personnel matters. While this is partly budget-driven, it is also partly policy-driven. There's an assumption that central is good, single-Service rather less good. Well, I don't agree. While the successive reforms to the top of the defence structure over the last half-century or so were largely right, I believe this process has now gone too far, to the detriment of the single Services themselves. Frankly, the Chiefs of Staff find themselves in rather the opposite position to that described in the old aphorism about the ladies of the night, who are deemed to have power without responsibility. The Chiefs bear a heavy responsibility, but without the power to match. It is time that real authority was restored to the Chiefs of Staff in order to match the responsibility which indubitably and rightly they carry.

Throughout my career, I have been taught, and I have striven to instil, the message that it is the soldiers themselves who will make the endeavour succeed. As implied by the Sandhurst motto 'Serve to Lead', one's loyalty must be from bottom up. Sadly, I did not find this fundamental proposition shared by the MOD as a whole. On the contrary, in my time working in the Ministry of Defence as Head of the Army, I felt that the culture of the Department put the welfare of members of the Armed Forces and their families too low in its priorities. But without those soldiers, sailors and airmen, ministers and indeed civil servants, generals, admirals and air marshals are nothing. While I acknowledge recent modest improvements in conditions of service, it remains true that not much over a thousand pounds a month for the private soldier on operations is hardly an impressive figure. And some of the accommodation we provide is still, frankly, shaming, and hemmed around by petty regulation.

I am concerned at a failure, even an unwillingness, to understand the fundamental ethos of soldiering. It is difficult to overestimate the importance of ethos: the can-do spirit; the us–us approach, rather than me–me; the conviction that we can hack it. At the heart of this ethos are perhaps some old-fashioned words: duty, honour, selflessness, discipline. These may not rest easily with some of today's values – but if they're not there, you will not have an Army, certainly not an Army capable of doing what it has to do. The soldiers' part of the contract with the nation which they serve and from which they very largely recruit is to take risks – if need be, to risk their lives. But this must be a two-way contract: the nation should honour its covenant with the soldier. Military operations exact costs in blood and treasure. It is our soldiers who pay the cost in blood; the nation must therefore pay the cost in treasure. Soldiers and their families must be properly valued – and when I talk of the soldier and his family, I am talking not only about the regular Army: I very much include the reserves, the Territorial Army, and the reserves in the other two Services. They too play their part, they too take risks, and the contract applies to them also.

The military is uniquely different from any other walk of life. Very few legislators and opinion-formers have served in the Armed Forces; they therefore find it difficult to accept this distinctness.

As CGS, I also became concerned at comment, presumably politically motivated, which seemed to imply that the Armed Services could pick and choose their tasks for themselves. This is dangerous ground. Let us be clear: the allegiance of the Armed Forces is to the Sovereign as Head of State, and it is their constitutional duty to follow the direction of the duly elected

Government of the day; the alternative is anarchy. The Government takes decisions on military as on other matters, and is answerable to the electorate for these. The media sometimes produce more heat than light on these issues, and we need to be just a little careful; the British Army must remain apolitical.

It is self-evident to me that we must defend what we have, and I hope cherish, against those enemies who would remove it. We would be foolish to take our good fortune for granted. I believe that the nation knows the value of what it has in our Armed Forces, who in turn are grateful indeed for that support. The Army is one of this country's greatest national assets; but to sustain that position – and, I hope, to improve it – the Army must have the right capabilities, the right structure, the right people, the right training, the right support and the right accommodation. In return, as the Army has proven so many times, it will provide the nation with operational success, wherever that may be, whenever that may be, however that may be.

We face an uncertain and unknowable future, and a variety of threats to our way of life. Attitudes, perceptions, even theologies, are now the dominant causes of conflict. How to defend this Realm in these complex and threatening times is the stuff not only of politics, but also of professional military judgement. The Armed Forces have a vital and irreplaceable part to play, in both war-fighting and peace support operations. Our opponents are very likely to be quick-thinking, agile and unconventional – and we have to match them. All of this requires an entirely dispassionate and objective strategic approach, not one seen only through today's political prism.

The Chiefs of Staff should have restored to them the power and authority to match their responsibilities in order that, above all, they may give their best effort and effect to the fighting capability of their Services, and to the well-being of those who produce it. My various points about the higher management and organization of defence are made with a view to getting more military effectiveness from the resources we are given. The Army's motto 'Be the Best' really says it all. The Defence of the Realm requires that when you will the ends – the political objectives which require the use of force – you must will the military means. And if you will the military means, you must also will the financial means.

Though the strategic environment which we inhabit has changed beyond recognition, the operational effectiveness and well-being of the British Army remains as crucial as it has always been. We neglect it at our peril.

Epilogue

In 2001, and again in 2004, I had the honour to represent Her Majesty The Queen on the Sovereign's Parade at Sandhurst, which allowed me an opportunity to look back over my long career in the Army. I proudly made my way up the King's Walk towards Old Building Square, where spectators sat in stands around the lines of cadets dressed in their immaculate Blues, much as I had been so many years before, while a band played a stirring march. Once I was in position on the dais, the Adjutant, mounted on his horse in front of me, gave the order: 'General Salute, Present Arms.' I walked along the lines to review the cadets, stopping every now and then to have a word with one. Then the cadets marched past, first in slow time and then in quick. Afterwards they stood at ease as I gave my address.

'You will all shortly be taking up your first commands,' I told them. 'Some of you will before long be in command of soldiers on operations. Do not underestimate the responsibility placed upon you and the judgement that will be required of you – but equally, relish the authority granted to you, and rise to the challenges ever present. Always lead by example, seize the initiative when you can, and never give in. Remember the values and standards of the British Army, founded as they are in the timeless virtues of integrity, honour, duty, loyalty and selflessness.

'We are nothing without our soldiers, who deserve the best leadership we can provide. In return, they will respect you, forgive you your inevitable mistakes, and follow you wherever you lead.

'Be true to yourselves. Honesty and integrity are absolutes, but you will need more. You will need the determination and the courage to see matters through, even when fainter hearts have already taken counsel of their fears. You will need to take hardship, danger, fatigue and – perhaps above all – uncertainty in your stride; and, vitally important, you will need an unfailing sense of humour. You will need the strength of will and confidence to take the right road when it is not an easy one. You will need to be resolute and undeterred by reverses or disappointments. In the British Army, we must come first, we must win; to come second is to lose. The Army has never been found wanting; its evident success has engendered the admiration of its friends and the awe of its foes.

'As, in all of this, you Serve to Lead, you will also realize – and, I hope, revel in – the rewards of soldiering: the sense of shared and unselfish endeavour, of achievement, of doing right, of collective and personal success. These rewards are beyond price.

'I envy you as you stand on the threshold of your commissions, since I am in the evening of my service and you are at the bright dawn. Grasp your opportunities with both hands, meet the challenges, enjoy your soldiering and, above all, make sure your soldiers enjoy it. I wish you all success and all good fortune.'

Picture Acknowledgements

Photographs not credited below have kindly been supplied by the author. The publishers have made every effort to contact copyright holders where known. Copyright holders who have not been credited are invited to get in touch with the publishers.

Section one
4/5: paratrooper comforts injured woman, 20 March 1972: Derek Brind/PA Archive/PA Photos

Section two
2/3: (main picture) sketch of Arctic training courtesy Peter Archer; veterans on parade, Arromanches, 6 June 1994: © Tim Graham/Corbis Sygma
4/5: tanks firing, Bosnia, 28 February 1996: Associated Press
8: Munir and Minka Pijailovic © Captain Milos Stankovic

Section three
1: refugee camp, Brazda, Macedonia, 6 April 1999: Associated

Press; Tony Blair talking to troops, Kosovo border, 3 May 1999: Reuters

2/3: signing of military technical agreement, Kumanovo airfield, Kosovo, 9 June 1999: Associated Press

4/5: (main photo) paratroopers put on stand down, Petrovac, 11 June 1999: © Reuters/Corbis; British paratroopers escort KLA: © Reuters/Corbis; Irish Guard carries KLA wapons, Pristina, 17 June 1999: Reuters/Corbis; MJ shakes hands with Agim Ceku, 20 July 1999: Associated Press

6/7: (background) a house burns in Serbian village: © Arben Celi/Reuters/Corbis; MJ and Colonel General Viktor Zavarzin, Pristina airport, 26 June 1999: Associated Press; Bernard Kouchner, Madeleine Albright and MJ, Pristina, 29 July 1999: Associated Press; the Clintons visit Kosovo, 22 June 1999: Boris Grdanosk/AP/PA Photos

Section four

1: MJ on a visit to Kabul to Defence Minister General Abdul Raheem Wardak, 27 June 2006: Heathcliff O'Malley/The Daily Telegraph

2/3: Mark Jackson: Julian Andrews/The Sunday Telegraph

4/5: MJ inspects Sandhurst cadets, 10 December 2004: Associated Press; MJ talks to Prince William and Prince Harry, Sandhurst, 12 April 2006: Lefteris Pitarakis/Associated Press; MJ receives DSO 2 December 1999: © Reuters/Corbis; MJ and Private Johnson Beharry VC, 27 April 2005: © Ian Jones

6/7: MJ with Brigadier Graham Binns at 7 Armoured Brigade planning meeting: Sergeant Wendy Summerell RLC/ MOD; MJ visits troops in southern Iraq, 16 May 2006: Corporal John Hawkes / MOD

8: MJ lays a wreath at the Cenotaph, Whitehall, 21 August 2005: Rex Features

Index